BY THE EDITORS OF CONSUMER GUIDE®
& JAY A. BROWN

RATING THE MOVIES

Manufactured in the United States of America
10 9 8 7 6 5 4 3 2

Library of Congress Catalog Card Number: 85-60390

ISBN: 0-88176-274-1

Film Research: Don Casciato, Calvin Green, Robert Edelstein, and Phyllis Brown. Acknowledgment: The Editors of Consumer Guide® wish to thank the Motion Picture Association of America for supplying MPAA ratings information.

Cover Design: Phyllis Ritthaler

The photographs in this book are courtesy of the following studios and organizations: Universal-International Pictures Corp.; Metro-Goldwyn-Mayer, Inc.; IFD/Romulus-Horizon; Warner Brothers, Inc.; Paramount Pictures Corp.; Universal City Studios; United Artists; Sheldrake Films, Ltd.; Columbia Pictures Industries, Inc.; 20th Century-Fox Film Corp.; Barclay's Mercantile Industrial Finance, Ltd.; Orion Pictures Co.; Merchant Trust Co.; RKO Radio Pictures, Inc.; Walt Disney Productions; Time-Life Productions; Master Mace, Ltd.; Avco Embassy Pictures; Lorimar Productions, Inc.; Filmways Pictures, Inc.; The Ladd Co.; Warner Bros.—Seven Arts, Inc.; Associated Film Distribution; ABC Pictures/Allied Artists; Eurasia Investments, Ltd.; Incorporated Television Co., Inc.; Gelderse Maatschappij N.V.; Simon Film Productions, Inc.; Titan Productions; Jalem/Warner; Dino De Laurentiis Corp.; American International Television, Inc.; Libra Films; Continental Distributing, Inc.; EMI Films, Ltd.; Vitagraph, Inc.; Brooksfilms Ltd.; Lucasfilm, Ltd.; Danjag, S.A.; Crown International Pictures; Associated R&R Films Pty., Ltd.; Spartan Film Partners, Ltd.; Rank/Cineguild; Newdon Co.; Henson Associates, Inc.; Wilderness/Filmhaus; Loew's, Inc.; National Screen Sevice Corp.; Motown Productions; Selznick International Pictures; The Saul Zdentz Production Co.; British Lion; EMI/Python Pictures; Hal Roach; American International Pictures; Zephyr Productions; Kudos Film Production, Ltd.; DC Comics, Inc.; Hemdale Leisure Corp. and Bind Films; Republic Pictures Corp.; Bing Crosby Productions; Lewis Milestone Productions; Palyc International B.V.; CBS, Inc.; MGM/UA; Buena Vista Productions; TriStar Films.

CONTENTS

An Introduction to Rating the Movies
Page 4

Alphabetical Movie Listings

Star Profiles

AN INTRODUCTION TO RATING THE MOVIES

The advent of cable TV and the introduction of the videocassette recorder has meant riches for movie lovers. Each week scores of films are shown on regular and cable television channels; thousands more are available on Beta and VHS videocassettes, so that you're not even restricted by television program schedules but can schedule your viewing as you please. What's more, movie viewing has never been so inexpensive. For the price of less than one movie ticket, you and your family or friends can rent a movie to watch on the VCR in your own home.

Sounds wonderful. And it is. But there's one drawback: How do you know which movies are really worth watching? Can you judge a film's worth by its publicity? Not necessarily. What about the movie critics' reviews or the reactions of your friends and colleagues? Critical reaction and word-of-mouth provide an important measure of guidance on well-known movies, but there are thousands of movies now available that you know little or nothing about—classics filmed before you were born, perhaps; or minor movies that never got the attention they deserved; or foreign movies that showed up briefly at an art house and disappeared before you caught up with them. That's why you need *Rating the Movies*. This comprehensive guide to over 2800 movies (new and old; great and not so great; forgotten, best forgotten, and never to be forgotten) is designed specifically to help you make the best use of your viewing time, and of the money you spend on building a movie library of videocassettes. This book is filled with facts and critical comments about motion pictures from the '30s to the '80s. You'll find just about every movie that's now being shown on network, cable, or pay TV. What's more, each film has

been marked as to its availability on videocassette. The symbol ⌾ indicates that you will be able to find this film in video stores. Not all films are available in all video stores.

Although the emphasis is on more recent movies—which are the ones most likely to appear on network or cable TV—there's extensive coverage of the movies that have made history since the first silent movie flickered across a screen. In fact, this new and revised edition of *Rating the Movies* owes a lot to reader input from earlier editions of the book...you reminded us of movies you felt should be included—among them some true classics—and we've put in as many as we had space for.

In the course of revising this book, our reviewers have also revised their opinions of a number of movies. It sometimes happens that a film that is received with wild enthusiasm when it first appears does not stand the test of time—watch it when the fuss has died down, and you wonder what the fuss was all about. Conversely, movies that receive little critical acclaim on first viewing improve, like wine, with age; repeated viewings reveal subtlety and depth that went unrecognized the first time around. So we consider it part of our responsibility to reflect these changes in viewer response to certain films.

THE STAR RATING SYSTEM

The key to *Rating the Movies* is CONSUMER GUIDE's® four-star rating system. The ratings have been assessed by experienced film historians who know and love movies. But even so, you're not

going to agree with every rating. Movie viewing is a subjective business, and one person's film of the year may put someone else to sleep in the first reel. What the star ratings will do, though, is give you a fair, carefully considered opinion on the overall quality (or lack of it) of a particular film.

This is how the star rating system works: The top four-star (★★★★) rating tells you that this film meets exceptionally high standards of performance, direction, and production. A four-star rating also indicates that the film is engrossing and enjoyable (using the term 'enjoyable' loosely, because some fine films can be emotionally demanding—perhaps satisfying would be a better word). Four stars also suggests, in most cases, that the film has something to say; it's not just empty entertainment. Three stars (★★★) indicate that a film is well worth watching and of generally high quality, but doesn't for one reason or another match up to our four-star criteria. A three-star movie is a good film. A two-star (★★) movie is a fair film; it's worth some interest but may suffer from a thin plot, poor characterization, or weak acting or direction. Don't expect a great movie. A one-star (★) rating indicates a movie that's unlikely to hold your interest or provide you with much satisfaction. Skip it unless you've got nothing better to do. If a film is awarded (**no stars**), we consider watching it a waste of time. Such a film may be in such poor taste that we don't want to recommend it to anyone. Or it might be a 'golden turkey'— a film so bad that it almost takes on a charm of its own.

AN INTRODUCTION TO RATING THE MOVIES

THE MOVIE REVIEWS

The format in which the movie reviews are presented has been designed to give you all the important facts about the film, along with critical comment to help you decide if the film is one that you will enjoy. A few notes on how the format works.

Title. Most movies only have one title. Once in a while, however, a film will have an alternate title, or will have been released in another country under a different name. Alternate titles are listed alphabetically and refer you to the title under which the review appears.

Year of release. The year that appears immediately after the title usually refers to the year in which the film was first released for public viewing. Occasionally another source will list a different year. This may occur, for instance, when a film has been kept off the market for a year or more, or when a foreign film is released in the United States after its release in the country of origin.

Review. Under the movie title appears a list of the film's leading actors; supporting actors may also be mentioned in the course of the review. The director is named either in the review or at the end of it. The review itself tells you what the film is about, and adds critical comment on performances,

direction, script, and production values. Foreign-language films with subtitles are noted—for example, "In French with English titles."

MPAA Rating. In the latter part of 1968 the Motion Picture Association of America (MPAA) introduced a rating system to enable people to judge what kind of audience a movie was meant for—and whether or not it was okay to take the kids to see it. The classification system now consists of five categories: "G" means "General Audiences"; people of any age may be admitted to see the film. "PG" indicates "Parental Guidance"; some material may not be suitable for children. "PG–13" is a new rating that strongly suggests parents give special guidance to children under 13. "R" indicates "Restricted"; a person under 17 requires accompanying parent or adult guardian. "X" indicates "no one under 17 admitted (age limit may vary in certain areas)."

Most films released since 1968 carry an MPAA rating, and some older re-releases may also be MPAA-rated. Some films released after 1968, including many foreign films, may not have been submitted to the MPAA. These films are designated by (No MPAA Rating); you should read the reviews carefully to determine their suitability. For instance, *Bolero*, which contains nudity and simulated sex, is unrated. Also, some films have been released in more than one version. For example, *Saturday Night Fever*, originally rated "R," was later released in a "PG" version to capture a younger audience.

Academy Awards. In most cases, the fact that a film or those who took part in making it won or received nominations for Academy Awards is a significant argument in favor of its value. Therefore we've included Academy Awards and nominations in major categories. Note that some descriptions of categories—such as music, cinematography, and writing—have changed slightly over the years.

Running Time. At the end of each review, we list the film's running time for the initial theatrical release. Keep in mind that most

films that appear on network television are edited—sometimes very heavily—to fit certain time slots. Finally, because most recent movies are in color, this fact is not noted after the running time; however, black-and-white movies are designated "b&w" immediately after the running time, and those few films that contain a few scenes in black and white or color are designated "b&w/color."

STAR PROFILES

Throughout *Rating the Movies* you will find profiles of some of the film industry's most popular stars. For example, you'll find interesting facts about such early film figures as Humphrey Bogart and Clark Gable, as well as about relative newcomers such as Sissy Spacek and Robert De Niro. An alphabetical list of the stars profiled appears on the Contents page.

A
- Abbott and Costello Meet Captain Kidd
- Abbott and Costello Meet Frankenstein
- Abe Lincoln in Illinois
- The Abominable Snowman
- Abraham Lincoln
- Absence of Malice
- The Absent-Minded Professor
- Accident

A

ABBOTT AND COSTELLO MEET CAPTAIN KIDD (1952)

 ★★

Bud Abbott
Lou Costello

Routine Abbott and Costello farce with the boys competing with the venerable pirate for buried treasure. Abbott and Costello are really not up to par here. Charles Laughton as Captain Kidd is on board having a high time in a role beneath his stature. **Director**—Charles Lamont.

70 minutes

ABBOTT AND COSTELLO MEET FRANKENSTEIN (1948)

 ★★★

Bud Abbott
Lou Costello

Abbott and Costello are at their funniest in this knockabout spoof of horror films. Costello's brain is slated for the monster. Dracula and the Wolf Man get in a few licks, too. It's a nice blend of laughs and scares, with Bela Lugosi and Lon Chaney, Jr. lending their talents to the merriment. **Director**—Charles T. Barton.

92 minutes b&w

ABE LINCOLN IN ILLINOIS (1940)

 ★★★

Raymond Massey
Ruth Gordon
Gene Lockhart

Massey *was* Abraham Lincoln for a generation of moviegoers, who probably would have recognized the actor as our great President sooner than they would've identified a likeness of Honest Abe himself. This reverential adaptation of Robert Sherwood's Pulitzer Prize-winning play seems a bit plodding today, but it's still earnest and literate, and the subject matter remains fascinating. The great James Wong Howe photographed this portrayal of Lincoln, the shopkeeper and suitor, lawyer and legislator—a trou-

bled idealist debating his way toward the White House. **Director**—John Cromwell.

110 minutes b&w

THE ABOMINABLE SNOWMAN (1957)

 ★★★

Peter Cushing
Forrest Tucker

Tucker and Cushing lead an expedition to high altitudes in this horror outing about the elusive and mysterious monster of the Himalayas. Effective scripting and acting help flesh out the characters. The suspense, however, lags somewhat. Maureen Connell and Richard Wattis co-star. **Director**—Val Guest.

85 minutes b&w

ABRAHAM LINCOLN (1930)

 ★★★

Walter Huston
Una Merkel
Henry B. Walthall

D. W. Griffith, the director who virtually "created" the feature film with his 1915 Civil War epic, *The Birth of a Nation*, returns to the Civil War era with this, his first sound film. It's a fine, artfully made motion picture, covering the life of the Great Emancipator from his youth and romance with Ann Rutledge to his Presidency and assassination in Ford's Theater. After two decades of feverish activity, Griffith's career was coming to a tragic end. He was able to make only one film after *Abraham Lincoln* during the remaining 18 years of his life. Huston turns in an effective, restrained performance. Stephen Vincent Benet wrote the script. *97 minutes b&w*

ABSENCE OF MALICE (1981)

 ★★★★

Sally Field
Paul Newman

A brisk, intelligent drama that takes a penetrating look at the ethics of journalism and the quest for truth and justice. Field stars as an over-eager newspaper reporter, who is duped into writing misleading and damaging stories about an investigation of a

Sally Field invades Paul Newman's privacy with the best of journalistic intentions in Absence of Malice.

mobster's son, who is played by Newman. In fact, the subject of her stories is guilty of nothing more than having unsavory relatives. Newman is magnificent as the innocent and outraged victim, and he extracts revenge in a clever climax. Sydney Pollack's direction is crisp and pointed. Superb supporting performances strengthen the production. (PG) **Academy Award Nominations**—Newman, best actor; Melinda Dillon, best supporting actress; Kurt Luedtke, best screenplay (written directly for the screen).

116 minutes

THE ABSENT-MINDED PROFESSOR (1961)

 ★★★

Fred MacMurray
Tommy Kirk
Keenan Wynn

Better-than-average Disney comedy about a scientist who invents flubber, a rubbery substance that overcomes gravity. First-rate special effects enhance the fun. MacMurray, in the title role, is in top form piloting his flubber-powered Model T through the skies. The story involves the pursuit of spies, led by Keenan Wynn, who want to steal the amazing material. Cast includes Nancy Olson and Ed Wynn. **Director**—Robert Stevenson. (G)

97 minutes b&w

ACCIDENT (1967)

★★★

Dirk Bogarde
Stanley Baker
Jacqueline Sassard

• Ace in the Hole
• Across the Pacific
• Across the Wide Missouri

• Adam's Rib
• The Adventures of Don Juan

• The Adventures of Marco Polo
• The Adventures of Mark Twain

A

The sometimes convoluted subtleties of Harold Pinter are often best dealt with on stage, but he is in good hands here with director Joseph Losey. Bogarde plays an Oxford professor who appears to be a happily married man—but is he really? He pines after an elusive Australian student who pines for someone else—but does she really? Needless to say, all the true drama is between the lines, and it's delicately, and often affectingly, drawn out by a fine cast that includes Delphine Seyrig, Alexander Knox, Vivien Merchant, and Michael York in his first major film role.   *105 minutes*

ACE IN THE HOLE (1951)
★★★★

Kirk Douglas
Jan Sterling

Powerful drama about a reporter, played by Douglas, who tries to promote his career by delaying the rescue of a man trapped in a cave. Splendid performances by Douglas and Sterling. Masterful direction adds to the hard-hitting impact. The film is unrelenting in its portrayal of cruelty and grim irony. **Director**—Billy Wilder. **Alternate Title**—*The Big Carnival*.
112 minutes b&w

ACROSS THE PACIFIC (1942)
★★★

Humphrey Bogart
Mary Astor
Sydney Greenstreet

Sydney Greenstreet weaves a web of intrigue in Across the Pacific.

Bogart, Greenstreet, and Astor are re-teamed for this sleek World War II spy caper. Bogey tracks down enemy agents in Panama, keeps a menacing Greenstreet at bay, and falls in love with Astor. The trio is as effective as they were in *The Maltese Falcon*. Cast includes Keye Luke and Richard Loo. **Director**—John Huston.
97 minutes b&w

ACROSS THE WIDE MISSOURI (1951)
★★

Clark Gable
Ricardo Montalban

Despite proficient acting by Gable and Montalban, this period western doesn't catch hold. Gable plays a stalwart fur trapper who marries an Indian girl. His talents are not fully realized. Cast includes John Hodiak, J. Carrol Naish, and Adolphe Menjou. **Director**—William Wellman.
78 minutes

ADAM'S RIB (1950)
 ★★★★

Spencer Tracy
Katharine Hepburn
Judy Holliday

Spencer Tracy and Katharine Hepburn are husband and wife in the comedy Adam's Rib.

A perfect teaming of Tracy and Hepburn, who play husband and wife—and attorneys on opposite sides of a murder trial. The rib-tickling comedy is expertly written and directed to bring out the special chemistry between the incomparable duo. Tom Ewell and David Wayne contribute their fine acting talents as well. **Director**—George Cukor. **Academy Award Nomination**—Ruth Gordon and Gar-

son Kanin, writing (story and screenplay).   *101 minutes b&w*

THE ADVENTURES OF DON JUAN (1948)
★★

Errol Flynn
Viveca Lindfors

Dashing Flynn romances Lindfors, who plays the Queen, and a number of maidens in this good-looking, tongue-in-cheek swashbuckler. This was one of the last of Flynn's lavish adventure films, and some self-mockery is evident. Cast includes Raymond Burr, Alan Hale, and Ann Rutherford. **Director**—Vincent Sherman.
110 minutes

THE ADVENTURES OF MARCO POLO (1938)
★★

Gary Cooper
Sigrid Gurie
Basil Rathbone

A slow journey that takes longer to get anywhere than did the multimillion dollar TV miniseries about Marco, produced more than four decades later. It's a light-hearted treatment, though you'd never know it, and Cooper looks anxious to escape on a horse. Samuel Goldwyn props up his historical romance with lush production values. **Director**—Archie Mayo.
100 minutes b&w

THE ADVENTURES OF MARK TWAIN (1944)
★★★

Fredric March
Alexis Smith

This is a straightforward biography of the renowned writer-humorist. March turns in a memorable performance in the title role. Smith plays Twain's wife. The film follows Twain's life from steamboat pilot to acclaimed literary figure. The effort, however, doesn't match such great film biographies as *Pasteur* or *Zola*. Cast includes John Carradine, Donald Crisp, and C. Aubrey Smith. **Director**—Irving Rapper.
130 minutes b&w

A

• The Adventures of Robin Hood
• Adventures of Sherlock Holmes
• Adventures of the Wilderness Family
• Advise and Consent
• Affair in Trinidad
• An Affair to Remember

THE ADVENTURES OF ROBIN HOOD (1938)

 ★★★★

Errol Flynn
Olivia de Havilland
Basil Rathbone
Claude Rains

Olivia de Havilland and Errol Flynn enjoy fighting oppression together in The Adventures of Robin Hood.

Excellent acting, brilliant photography, and an exciting story make this one of the finest adventure films of all time. After contemporary blood-and-guts action movies, the outlaw hero of Sherwood Forest, played by Flynn to swashbuckling perfection, seems downright wholesome. **Directors**—William Keighley and Michael Curtiz.　　　　*102 minutes*

ADVENTURES OF SHERLOCK HOLMES (1939)

 ★★★

Basil Rathbone
Nigel Bruce
Ida Lupino

A strong contender as the best of the 100-plus films that have been made about Sir Arthur Conan Doyle's ingenious sleuth of Baker Street. Here, archfiend Professor Moriarty (George Zucco), who has eluded Holmes for 11 years, plots the crime of the century. His target is the Tower of London's prize jewel, the Star of Delhi; his diversionary tactic is murder. The shocks and twists may all be pretty heady stuff for Watson (Bruce) and Lupino, as well as for us, but it's ultimately elementary for the man in the deerstalker cap. Fogbound Edwardian

England is atmospherically captured, and Rathbone pulls off a most amusing impersonation. From the play by William Gillette. **Director**—Alfred L. Werker.　　　　*85 minutes b&w*

ADVENTURES OF THE WILDERNESS FAMILY (1975)

 ★★★

Robert Logan
Susan Shaw

Children should enjoy this adventure of a latter-day Swiss Family Robinson who, fed up with the din and smog of Los Angeles, hightail it to the mountain wilderness and set up housekeeping. They build a log cabin, befriend orphaned bear cubs, and face a menacing grizzly and wolves. Lots of striking mountain scenery. **Director**—Stewart Raffill. (G)　　*101 minutes*

ADVISE AND CONSENT (1962)

 ★★★

Don Murray
Charles Laughton
Henry Fonda
Walter Pidgeon

Charles Laughton provides his wisdom to a reticent aide in Advise and Consent.

Fascinating screen adaptation of Allen Drury's novel of political maneuvering in Washington. Fine acting by a champagne cast heightens the drama surrounding the President's appointment of a controversial secretary of state. This was Laughton's last film. Other cast members include Gene Tierney, Franchot Tone, Lew Ayres, Burgess Meredith, and Peter Lawford. **Director**—Otto Preminger.

139 minutes b&w

AFFAIR IN TRINIDAD (1952)

★★

Rita Hayworth
Glenn Ford

Hayworth stands out in this sleek but routine tale of murder, espionage, and romance in the tropics. Hayworth, as a nightclub performer, seeks the murderer of her husband with the help of Ford, who plays her brother-in-law. Hayworth also does some notable dancing. Film is fun to watch on a double bill with *Gilda*, which also starred Hayworth and Ford. **Director**—Vincent Sherman.

98 minutes b&w

AN AFFAIR TO REMEMBER (1957)

★★★

Cary Grant
Deborah Kerr

Grant and Kerr star in this syrupy remake of *Love Affair*, which featured Charles Boyer and Irene Dunne. Grant, a debonair bachelor, romances former cafe singer Kerr aboard an ocean liner. The film begins as a comedy, turns into a tearjerker, and—of course—ends happily. Also includes Cathleen Nesbitt, Richard Denning, and Neva Patterson. **Director**—Leo McCarey.　　　　*119 minutes*

Cary Grant and Deborah Kerr have An Affair to Remember.

★ STAR PROFILE

• The African Queen   • After the Thin Man
• After the Fox   • Against All Flags
   • Against All Odds

A

THE AFRICAN QUEEN (1951)
 ★★★★

**Humphrey Bogart
Katharine Hepburn**

In The African Queen, *Katharine Hepburn and Humphrey Bogart find romance.*

Hepburn is a prim missionary and Bogart is a booze-soaked boat skipper. The odd couple find romance and danger on the Congo River during World War I. A triumph of acting and direction leads to a surprising achievement of wry comedy and adventure. Cast includes Theodore Bikel, Peter Bull, and Robert Morley. **Director**—John Huston. **Academy Award**—Bogart, best actor. **Nominations**—Huston, best director; Hepburn, best actress; James Agee and Huston, writing (screenplay).   *106 minutes*

AFTER THE FOX (1966)
 ★★

**Peter Sellers
Victor Mature
Britt Ekland**

A rather forgettable Sellers comedy about an ingenious criminal who becomes a movie director as a front to pull off a gold heist. Mature, however, steals some scenes as a pompous has-been actor. The movie never gets off the ground despite Neil Simon's satirical script. Cast includes Lilia Brazzi, Akim Tamiroff, and Martin Balsam. **Director**—Vittorio De Sica.
   103 minutes

AFTER THE THIN MAN (1936)
★★★

**William Powell
Myrna Loy
James Stewart**

A creditable sequel to Dashiell Hammett's *The Thin Man* and the first of several made between 1936 and 1947. Powell and Loy (joined by canine Asta) are back as Nick and Nora Charles, amateur detectives extraordinaire. This time it appears that a killer is circulating among Nora's blueblood San Francisco family. A young Stewart (this was only his second year in movies), Elissa Landi, Sam Levene, Joseph Calleia, and George Zucco add to the frothy and suspenseful fun. **Director**—W. S. Van Dyke. **Academy Award Nomination**—Frances Goodrich, Albert Hackett, writing (screenplay).
   113 minutes b&w

SISSY SPACEK

Sissy Spacek was born in Quitman, Texas, in 1950. She was christened Mary Elizabeth, but her older brothers called her Sissy and the name stuck.

At Quitman High, Spacek was a cheerleader, played drums in the band, and worked on the school paper. In rural Quitman, she was able to own a horse and became an outstanding rider. At that time, Spacek dreamed of a career as a singer-musician. She sang with a choral group and taught guitar for 50 cents an hour.

Her parents encouraged her professional aspirations and gave her permission to seek a career in New York City, where she first lived with her cousin, Rip Torn, and his wife, Geraldine Page. Spacek's visions of

AGAINST ALL FLAGS (1952)
★★

**Errol Flynn
Maureen O'Hara
Anthony Quinn**

Routine Flynn swashbuckler with Flynn as a dashing British officer challenging Caribbean pirate Quinn and romancing O'Hara. This is one of the last of Flynn's escapades, and he appears to wilt somewhat. With Mildred Natwick. **Director**—George Sherman.   *85 minutes*

AGAINST ALL ODDS (1984)
 ★★

**Jeff Bridges
Rachel Ward**

A thick, incoherent plot trips up this
(Continued)

musical stardom, however, didn't materialize. Instead, she earned a living as a model and attended acting classes under Lee Strasberg.

Spacek made her professional film debut in a small role in Prime Cut *(1972) with Lee Marvin and Gene Hackman. Next she was cast in* The Girls of Huntington House *(1973), a TV movie of the week.*

Spacek was hailed as the most talented young actress in years for her portrayal of a naive 15-year-old girl swept off her feet by a psychotic youth in Badlands *(1973). She was a guest star in two episodes of* The Waltons *television series, then won more honors for the television version of Tennessee Williams's* The Migrants *(1974) with Cloris Leachman. This was followed by the title role in the television movie* Katherine *(1975). Other feature film assignments include* Carrie *(1976),* Welcome to L.A. *(1976),* Raggedy Man *(1981), and* The River *(1984).*

She won an Academy Award for her moving portrayal of country singer Loretta Lynn in Coal Miner's Daughter *(1980). Her early musical training came in handy on this film in which she did her own singing and guitar-playing. She was also nominated for her role in* Missing *as the wife of a political prisoner.*

A
- Agatha
- The Agony and the Ecstasy
- Air Force
- Airplane!
- Airplane II: The Sequel
- Airport
- Airport '77

(Continued)

steamy melodrama about a football player (Bridges) sent to track down the runaway mistress (Ward) of a big-time bookie. The story ranges from a torrid love affair in Mexico, to corruption, murder, and double-crosses in Los Angeles. What worked brilliantly as a modestly produced '40s *film noir* (*Out of the Past*), now looks overblown. Not a good bet. James Woods and Jane Greer co-star. **Director**—Taylor Hackford. (R)   *125 minutes*

AGATHA (1979)

★★

Dustin Hoffman
Vanessa Redgrave

Mystery writer Agatha Christie disappeared for 11 days in 1926. This pointless film imagines what happened during her absence. Redgrave turns in a crisp portrayal of the famous author. Hoffman provides a measure of humor in his role as an American journalist who traces Mrs. Christie to a health spa. But there's nothing to arouse much interest in the affair. Perhaps the real Agatha Christie would have come up with an exciting story. **Director**—Michael Apted. (PG)   *98 minutes*

THE AGONY AND THE ECSTASY (1965)

★★

Charlton Heston
Rex Harrison

Handsome but plodding story of Michelangelo's troubles while painting the Sistine Chapel at the urging of Pope Julius II. There are also some tiresome biographical references to the great artist's life and career. Unfortunately, there's more agony than ecstacy. Heston plays Michelangelo. Harrison plays the pontiff. With Diane Cilento and Harry Andrews. **Director**—Carol Reed.
140 minutes

AIR FORCE (1943)

★★★

John Garfield
Gig Young
Arthur Kennedy

Effective and often exciting World War II bomber crew saga despite propaganda and flag-waving. Garfield, Young, and Kennedy are among the flyboys who fight the Japanese from Manila to the Coral Sea. Characterizations of the flyers are colorfully portrayed. Also stars Faye Emerson, Harry Carey, and Charles Drake. **Director**—Howard Hawks.
124 minutes b&w

AIRPLANE! (1980)

★★★★

Robert Hays
Julie Hagerty
Peter Graves
Lloyd Bridges

Air traffic controllers display the steely calm needed to guide runaway commercial airliners in Airplane!

Mel Brooks and Woody Allen have stiff competition from Jim Abrahams, David Zucker, and Jerry Zucker who wrote and directed this laugh-a-minute broadside spoof of airplane dramas. Their initial try was the unpolished comedy *The Kentucky Fried Movie*. But this time they unleashed a torrent of effective gags with style and finesse. So fasten your seat belts, observe the "no smoking" sign, and settle back for hilarity galore. (PG)
88 minutes

AIRPLANE II: THE SEQUEL (1982)

★★★

Robert Hays
Lloyd Bridges
William Shatner

This follow-up chapter, set in outer space, offers much of the good-natured charm and fun that enlivened the original spoof of disaster movies. Once again, we are on an ill-fated flight with an oddball assortment of passengers, crew, and ground controllers. The perky sight gags and wise-cracks are a bit too familiar, but they still deliver an abundance of laughs. Julie Hagerty and Peter Graves are also on board to help the stars cope with incipient calamity. **Director**—Ken Finkleman. (PG)   *85 minutes*

AIRPORT (1970)

★★★

Burt Lancaster
Dean Martin
Jean Seberg
Helen Hayes
Van Heflin

Slick, gripping melodrama based on Arthur Hailey's popular novel about a busy Midwest airport on a snowy night. Lancaster is the unflappable airport manager who keeps things in order during efforts to land a damaged plane safely. Hayes stands out as a habitual and unlikely stowaway. There are also entertaining performances from George Kennedy and Martin. The cast also includes Jacqueline Bisset, Maureen Stapleton, Lloyd Nolan, and Barry Nelson. **Director**—George Seaton. (G) **Academy Award**—Hayes, best supporting actress. **Nominations**—best picture; Ernest Laszlo, best cinematography; George Seaton, best screenplay (based on material from another medium).   *137 minutes*

AIRPORT '77 (1977)

★★

Jack Lemmon
Lee Grant
Brenda Vaccaro
George Kennedy
James Stewart

The *Airport* theme is thoroughly exhausted as demonstrated by this third and mediocre all-star disaster film inspired by the Arthur Hailey novel. This time it's a private 747 jumbo jet, outfitted like a flying Holiday Inn, that crashes somewhere in the Atlantic Ocean and sinks in 100 feet of water. All sorts of standard harrowing epi-

• The Alamo   • Alex and the Gypsy
• Al Capone   • Alfie
• Alexander Nevsky   • Algiers

A

sodes take place among the passengers and crew while waiting for the inevitable rescue by the U.S. Navy. Lemmon is out of place as the pilot. Darren McGavin, Olivia de Havilland, and Joseph Cotten also star. **Director**—Jerry Jameson. (PG)

113 minutes

THE ALAMO
(1960)
★★

John Wayne
Richard Widmark
Laurence Harvey
Richard Boone

Frankie Avalon plays Smitty in The Alamo.

John Wayne as Col. Davy Crockett leads the futile defense of the famous fort against the onslaught of the Mexican army. The drawn-out film is often sidetracked with cliché-strewn subplots, and it seems to take forever to reach the spectacular final attack, which is the only exciting part of the film. With Frankie Avalon, Patrick Wayne, and Linda Cristal. **Director**—John Wayne. *190 minutes*

AL CAPONE (1959)
★★★

Rod Steiger
Fay Spain
Martin Balsam

Steiger is ideally cast as the ruthless gangster chieftain in this better-than-average biography. Steiger's excellent energetic performance is enhanced by fine support from Spain and Balsam. The documentary account follows Capone's Prohibition days in Chicago up to his imprisonment for income tax evasion. Also with Murvyn Vye, Nehemiah Persoff, and James Gregory. **Director**—Richard Wilson.

105 minutes b&w

ALEXANDER NEVSKY (1938)
★★★★

Nikolai Cherkassov
Nikolai Okhlopkov

A masterpiece by director Sergei Eisenstein, this historical epic is one of the great Russian films of all time. The Soviets had found in Eisenstein an impassioned artist and film theorist whose works, which often posed the Russian masses as hero, were powerful both emotionally and as propaganda. Although he had fallen into disfavor with the government in the 1930s, he was summoned to serve his country when the Nazis loomed as a great threat in the years preceding World War II. In *Nevsky*, Eisenstein portrayed the 13th-century Russian prince who unified the nation to ward off Teutonic invaders. Features a breathtaking battle on the ice, Sergei Prokofiev's original operatic score, and superb photography by Edward Tisse. *112 minutes b&w*

ALEX AND THE GYPSY (1976)
★

Jack Lemmon
Geneviève Bujold

Lemmon looks tired and unappealing in this cynical and grubby film about the torturous relationship between a bailbondsman and a gypsy woman. Bujold, as the gypsy, isn't much help either. They scream a lot, fight a lot, and roam about the countryside. It's all a rather numbing experience. Also with James Woods. **Director**—John Korty. (R) *99 minutes*

ALFIE (1966)
★★★

Michael Caine
Vivien Merchant
Shelley Winters

Caine's career got a big boost for his

In Alfie, *Michael Caine plays a bachelor who seriously contemplates marriage by making close inspections of its participants.*

superb performance as a carefree womanizing Cockney. The film, based on Bill Naughton's play, also is noted for its frank treatment of sex. Winters and Merchant heighten the interest with no-nonsense performances as the objects of Alfie's affections. Alas, Alfie is shaken from his fancy-free lifestyle by a near-crisis. Also with Millicent Martin, Shirley Anne Field, and Denholm Elliot. **Director**—Lewis Gilbert. *114 minutes*

ALGIERS (1938)
★★★

Charles Boyer
Sigrid Gurie
Hedy Lamarr

Welcome to the Casbah—the twisting alleyways through which criminals and love affairs pass like fleeting shadows. This Hollywood amalgam of foreign intrigue and foreign players (French-born Boyer; Viennese Lamarr, making her American film debut; and Gurie, the Brooklyn-born, Norway-reared "Siren of the Fjords," launching in 1938 a stillborn career) was a surprisingly successful remake of the French sensation *Pepe Le Moko*, produced only one year earlier. The starring role of the amorous crook, who plays cat-and-mouse games with North African police solidified Boyer's career as a romantic star in much the same way it served Jean Gabin in the original version. Still eminently entertaining. **Director**—John Cromwell. **Academy Award Nominations**—

(Continued)

A
- Alias Jesse James
- Alias Nick Beal
- Alice Adams
- Alice Doesn't Live Here Any More
- Alice's Restaurant
- Alien
- All About Eve

(Continued)

Boyer, best actor; Gene Lockhart, best supporting actor; James Wong Howe, best cinematography.

95 minutes b&w

ALIAS JESSE JAMES (1959)
★★★

Bob Hope
Rhonda Fleming

Only Hope could sell an insurance policy to the notorious outlaw, and he claims a lot of laughs in the process. It's a funny vehicle for Hope as a lot of gags hit the mark. Fleming plays a pretty lass who does a singing number with Hope. There's an uproarious ending with cameos by many famous Hollywood cowboys. **Director**—Norman McLeod. *92 minutes*

ALIAS NICK BEAL (1949)
★★★

Ray Milland
Thomas Mitchell

An upstanding politician almost sells his soul to the devil in this on-target, latter-day version of Faust. Satisfying performances from sinister Milland as the devil's disciple promising money and power, and Mitchell as the vulnerable district attorney who nearly accepts the deal. Efficient direction helps to bring the fantasy into sharp focus. Other good performances by Audrey Trotter and George Macready. **Director**—John Farrow.

93 minutes b&w

ALICE ADAMS (1935)

★★★

Katharine Hepburn
Fred MacMurray
Fred Stone

Based on a lovely piece of Americana by Booth Tarkington, the film was a big hit for Hepburn, whose career was starting to founder, and a major step up in prestige for director George Stevens. A small-town adolescent, yearning to be accepted by her blueblood peers, pines over her family's lack of means and her father's lack of ambition. It's a successful blend of humor,

tears, and insight, best represented by the famous dinner scene, in which Alice invites her beau over, and everything seems to go wrong. Evelyn Venable, Charles Grapewin, Ann Shoemaker, Hedda Hopper, and Hattie McDaniel are among the fine supporting players. *99 minutes b&w*

ALICE DOESN'T LIVE HERE ANY MORE (1974)

★★★★

Ellen Burstyn
Alfred Lutter
Kris Kristofferson

Burstyn won an Oscar for her warm, funny, and energetic portrayal of a poor widow who learns to survive by her wits. She's broke, she has to care for her young son, and she wants to be a singer. Kristofferson also performs well as the new man in her life. The slice-of-life theme is somewhat of a cliché, but director Martin Scorsese adds vivid dimensions with a poignant reflection of contemporary America. With Jodie Foster. (PG) **Academy Award**—Burstyn, best actress. **Nominations**—Diane Ladd, best supporting actress; Robert Getchell, best original screenplay.

113 minutes

ALICE'S RESTAURANT (1969)

★★★

Arlo Guthrie
Pat Quinn

Folksinger Guthrie's popular song inspired this satirical melodrama about the freewheeling life-style of the

1960s. The theme is rather flimsy, but director Arthur Penn succeeds in wringing charm, energy, and comedy from the material. Guthrie, who does quite well in his film debut, is especially funny in a scene where he is briefly inducted into the U.S. Army. With James Broderick and Michael McClanathan. (PG) *111 minutes*

ALIEN (1979)

★★★

Tom Skerritt
Sigourney Weaver
John Hurt

The crew of a cargo-carrying spaceship, on a return voyage to earth, encounters a terrible monster. It's an effective horror film with impressive and scary special effects that should send you away with your knees knocking. But it's also familiar stuff, with elements of *Star Wars*, *The Exorcist*, and *Jaws* blended into the script, which dangles many loose ends. The small cast does a good job, especially Weaver, who performs much in the style of Jane Fonda. Also with Ian Holm, Harry Dean Stanton, and Yaphet Kotto. **Director**—Ridley Scott. (R) *124 minutes*

ALL ABOUT EVE (1950)

★★★★

Bette Davis
George Sanders
Anne Baxter

This biting backstage comedy-drama about a fading actress, played by Davis, brims generously with enter-

"Buckle your seatbelts; it's going to be a long night." Gary Merrill, Bette Davis, Celeste Holm, and Hugh Marlowe match wits at a dinner party in All About Eve.

• All Fall Down • All My Sons • All Quiet on the Western
• Alligator • All Night Long Front
 • All of Me • All That Heaven Allows
 • All That Jazz

A

tainment values: a witty screenplay, top performances by a marvelous cast, and no-nonsense direction. Davis gives a memorable bitchy performance as the aging Broadway star who is menaced by an overreaching younger actress played by Baxter. One of the best films ever made about the legitimate theater. **Director**—Joseph L. Mankiewicz. **Academy Awards**—best picture; Mankiewicz, best director and writing (screenplay); Sanders, best supporting actor. **Nominations**—Baxter, Davis, best actress; Celeste Holm, Thelma Ritter, best supporting actress. *138 minutes b&w*

ALL FALL DOWN (1962)
★★

**Warren Beatty
Brandon De Wilde
Angela Lansbury**

Warren Beatty has Eva Marie Saint thinking about younger men in All Fall Down.

A generally well-acted drama about a spirited young man, played by Beatty, who falls in love with an older woman—Eva Marie Saint—and then causes her death. Unfortunately, the screenplay is rather farfetched and isn't redeemed by several good performances. The cast includes Karl Malden. **Director**—John Frankenheimer. *110 minutes b&w*

ALLIGATOR (1980)
 ★★★

**Robert Forster
Robin Riker**

A baby pet alligator is flushed into a city sewer system and emerges 12 years later to devour some local citizens. At the outset, the film smacks of just another absurd horror picture, but

director Lewis Teague quickly lays on the style and excitement. There are polished special effects, a serviceable script, and capable performances from Forster and Riker. This reptile isn't a match for the shark in *Jaws*, but it does have plenty of bite. Also with Henry Silva, Jack Carter, and Dean Jagger in cameo roles. (R) *95 minutes*

ALL MY SONS (1948)
★★★

**Edward G. Robinson
Burt Lancaster**

This film version of Arthur Miller's play about family conflicts is generally compelling although it occasionally lacks conviction. A young man is shaken when he discovers that his wealthy father sold defective equipment to the military during World War II. Fine performances from Robinson, Lancaster, and Howard Duff. **Director**—Irving Reis. *94 minutes b&w*

ALL NIGHT LONG (1981)
★

**Barbra Streisand
Gene Hackman**

A futile attempt at contemporary comedy that awkwardly deals with the numbing side effects of corporate life. Superstar Streisand, as a seductive housewife, takes second billing. She is sadly miscast without a song or the verve to carry off a zany portrayal. Only Hackman, who plays a deflated chain store executive, breathes some life into this shallow and silly story. **Director**—Jean-Claude Tramont. (R) *100 minutes*

ALL OF ME (1984)
 ★★★

**Steve Martin
Lily Tomlin**

Martin and Tomlin are an engaging team in this wacky frolic that harks back to the screwball comedies of the '30s. Martin plays a frustrated lawyer whose body is inadvertently inhabited by the soul of an abrasive and wealthy spinster (Tomlin). This frustrating state of affairs leads to genuinely

funny shenanigans, although Martin's physical gags are occasionally awkward. The film is graced with delightful supporting players including Richard Libertini and Jason Bernard. **Director**—Carl Reiner. (PG)
93 minutes

ALL QUIET ON THE WESTERN FRONT (1930)
 ★★★★

**Lew Ayres
Louis Wolheim
Slim Summerville**

Despite dated moments, this powerful film about young German soldiers fighting in the trenches on the Western Front during World War I remains a classic. Director Lewis Milestone presents the pacifist novel of Erich Maria Remarque in a vivid and realistic manner. **Academy Awards**—best picture; Lewis Milestone, best director. **Nomination**—George Abbott, Maxwell Anderson, and Dell Andrews, writing (screenplay).
103 minutes b&w

ALL THAT HEAVEN ALLOWS (1955)
★★

**Jane Wyman
Rock Hudson**

Wyman and Hudson star in this slack and predictable soap opera about a widow who marries a younger man and is ostracized by her friends. Although the film reunites the stars of *Magnificent Obsession* and has a similar style, it doesn't work as well as the earlier film. Agnes Moorehead, Virginia Grey, and Conrad Nagel co-star. Heaven should allow more than this. **Director**—Douglas Sirk. *89 minutes*

ALL THAT JAZZ (1979)
 ★★★

**Roy Scheider
Jessica Lange
Ann Reinking**

Director Bob Fosse's autobiographical movie is the ultimate backstage musical drama—a masterpiece of dance,
(Continued)

A

- All the Brothers Were Valiant
- All the King's Men
- ...All the Marbles
- All the President's Men
- All the Right Moves
- All the Young Men

Ann Reinking sings and dances about her frustrating love life in All That Jazz.

(Continued)

ego, and soul. It's the story of a self-destructive Broadway director/choreographer—played by Scheider—his loves, obsessive work, and ultimate disintegration. Despite the adolescent shallowness of the central character, the overall production is completely absorbing. Fosse's breathtaking dance numbers are brilliantly staged, and Scheider's performance is outstanding. Leland Palmer, Cliff Gorman, and Ben Vereen co-star. (R) **Academy Award Nominations**—best picture; Fosse, best director; Scheider, best actor; Robert Alan Arthur and Fosse, best screenplay (written directly for the screen). *123 minutes*

ALL THE BROTHERS WERE VALIANT (1953)

★★

Stewart Granger
Robert Taylor

Granger and Taylor star in this soggy adventure, which is based on Ben Ames Williams's novel of sibling rivalry between two stubborn whaling sailors. Trouble ensues when one brother decides to shun blubber and hunt for treasure. There's lots of action, but the acting is below par. Ann Blyth co-stars as the wife of one brother, and she adds to the tension on board ship. **Director**—Richard Thorpe. *101 minutes*

ALL THE KING'S MEN (1949)

★★★★

Broderick Crawford
John Ireland
Mercedes McCambridge
Joanne Dru

A gripping, high-powered drama about political corruption in Louisiana, based on the career of Huey Long. The film is fleshed out with colorful detail and background. Most notable is the electrifying portrayal by Crawford as the honest small-town politician who is elected governor and is eventually overwhelmed by power. Commanding support from McCambridge, Ireland, and Dru. **Director**—Robert Rossen. **Academy Awards**—best picture; Crawford, best actor; McCambridge, best supporting actress. **Nominations**—Rossen, best director; Ireland, best supporting actor; Rossen, writing (screenplay). *109 minutes b&w*

...ALL THE MARBLES (1981)

 ★★★

Peter Falk

Director Robert Aldrich serves up pure and delectable Hollywood schmaltz with this rousing action-comedy about female wrestlers. Falk is excellent as the hustling manager of "The California Dolls," two young combatants, played by Vicki Frederick and Laurene Landon, who progress from tank-town matches to a championship bout in Reno's MGM Grand Hotel. The film offers good comic dialogue, appealing characterizations, a thrilling finale, and the "Dolls"—two gorgeous ladies who can act as well as wrestle. (R) *112 minutes*

ALL THE PRESIDENT'S MEN (1976)

 ★★★★

Robert Redford
Dustin Hoffman
Jason Robards, Jr.

The Watergate scandal comes into sharp focus and takes on a new dimension in this spellbinding film adaptation of Carl Bernstein's and Bob Woodward's best-selling book. It's a thriller from beginning to end and breathlessly entertaining. The exciting day-by-day account of how the two young *Washington Post* reporters conducted their investigation is portrayed in fast-paced, true-to-life documentary style through the screenplay of William Goldman. Acting by the entire cast is spectacular. Redford as Woodward and Hoffman as Bernstein perform with perfection. Robards gives what may be his finest performance as *Post* editor Ben Bradlee. Cast includes Hal Holbrook, Jack Warden, and Martin Balsam. Brilliantly directed by Alan J. Pakula. (PG) **Academy Awards**—Robards, best supporting actor; Goldman, best screenplay adaptation. **Nominations**—best picture; Pakula, best director; Jane Alexander, best supporting actress. *138 minutes*

ALL THE RIGHT MOVES (1983)

 ★★

Tom Cruise

Cruise stars as an ambitious high school football star who longs to escape life in an economically depressed mill town (à la *Flashdance*) by winning an athletic scholarship. The dank, depressing atmosphere of the dying community is realistically portrayed. Yet characters and their situations are not sufficiently compelling or convincing. A few wrong moves deflate the story's appeal. Also with Craig T. Nelson and Lea Thompson. **Director**—Michael Chapman. (R) *91 minutes*

ALL THE YOUNG MEN (1960)

★★

Alan Ladd
Sidney Poitier

Standard war yarn about a Marine unit in Korea that has to deal with internal tension as well as the enemy. Among the stereotypical situations is the problem of a black who is challenged because of his race when he takes command. Other clichés and platitudes abound. Also with Glenn Corbett, Ingemar Johansson, James Darren, and Mort Sahl. **Director**—Hall Bartlett. *87 minutes b&w*

• All Things Bright and
  Beautiful
• All This and Heaven Too

• All Through the Night
• An Almost Perfect Affair
• Alone in the Dark

• Along Came Jones
• Along the Great Divide
• Alpha Beta

A

ALL THINGS BRIGHT AND BEAUTIFUL
(1979)

★★★

**John Alderton
Lisa Harrow
Colin Blakely**

A gentle, mildly amusing family film based on the best-selling memoirs of Dr. James Herriott, the Yorkshire veterinarian. Alderton plays the young vet with likable charm; Harrow plays his wife. Alderton tends to a variety of animal illnesses and the anxieties of the animal owners. The story isn't very dramatic, except for a short graphic scene of the birth of a calf; but it should appeal to most. Blakely is fine as a cantankerous older veterinarian who takes Herriott as a partner. **Director**—Eric Till. (G)   *94 minutes*

ALL THIS AND HEAVEN TOO (1940)

★★★

**Charles Boyer
Bette Davis**

Boyer and Davis star in this somewhat stretched but well-made period melodrama, based on the Rachel Field novel, about a French nobleman who murders his wife after he falls in love with his children's governess. The elaborate story, set in the 19th century, is rather on the weepy side, but the acting has style and class. Barbara O'Neil, Virginia Weidler, and Jeffrey Lynn co-star. **Director**—Anatole Litvak.   *143 minutes b&w*

ALL THROUGH THE NIGHT (1942)

★★★

**Humphrey Bogart
Peter Lorre**

Bogart and Lorre team up in this entertaining spy caper set in New York City during World War II. Bogey's underworld gang helps the Feds nail some enemy agents. There are shades of wartime propaganda, but, it's good fun nevertheless with just the right touch of comedy. There's a young Jackie Gleason and Phil Silvers among

Bogey plays a gangster trying to do a good deed for his country by keeping Kaaren Verne and Conrad Veidt at bay in All Through the Night.

the cast. **Director**—Vincent Sherman.   *107 minutes b&w*

AN ALMOST PERFECT AFFAIR
(1979)

★★

**Keith Carradine
Monica Vitti**

The Cannes Film Festival is the backdrop to this satirical romance between a young American filmmaker, played by Carradine, and the wife of an Italian movie mogul, played by Vitti. Director Michael Ritchie handles the hoopla of the film festival with style and imagination, but the love story is essentially farfetched and rather uninteresting. There are some spirited performances, though, by the entire cast, which also includes Raf Vallone and Dick Anthony Williams. (PG)   *93 minutes*

ALONE IN THE DARK (1982)

★★

**Jack Palance
Donald Pleasence**

Under cover of a power blackout, homicidal maniacs break out of a mental hospital to terrorize the family of the institution's newly hired psychiatrist. The film is a cut above the typical horror schlock, and the suspense builds to an effective crescendo. Despite the fact that the story works well, the film is eventually undermined by excessive and ghastly bloodletting. Palance stars as the leading lunatic and Pleasence plays the head psychiatrist (who appears to be as crazy as his patients). **Director**—Jack Sholder. (R)   *92 minutes*

ALONG CAME JONES (1945)

★★★

**Gary Cooper
Loretta Young
Dan Duryea**

Cooper turned producer to let screenwriter Nunnally Johnson have fun with the star's straight-shooting image. The result is a sweet and winsome comedy/western about a Milquetoast who's mistaken for a wanted outlaw and grows to like the quaking respect he earns as a presumed bad guy. Along the way, he mixes it up with a trigger-happy cowgirl and the dreaded villain he's impersonating. Also with William Frawley and Melody Jones. **Director**—Stuart Heisler.   *90 minutes b&w*

ALONG THE GREAT DIVIDE
(1951)

★★

**Kirk Douglas
Virginia Mayo**

Lawman Douglas saves an innocent man from the noose and nabs the real criminal despite a desert storm in this soso western drama. The film has some spectacular scenery. John Agar, Ray Teal, and Walter Brennan round out the cast. **Director**—Raoul Walsh.   *88 minutes b&w*

ALPHA BETA (1976)

★★★

**Albert Finney
Rachel Roberts**

Moving and searing performances by
(Continued)

A
- Alphabet City
- Alphaville
- Altered States
- Always Leave Them Laughing
- Amadeus

(Continued)

Finney and Roberts in this filmed play about a failed English working-class marriage. The entire cast is from the original London stage company. The film is divided into three acts to dramatically emphasize the stages of the breakup and the accumulation of the agony. The experience may be too morose and exhausting for some, but an experience it is indeed. **Director**—Anthony Page. (No MPAA rating)
67 minutes

ALPHABET CITY (1984)
 ★★

Vincent Spano
Kate Vernon
Michael Winslow

Spano rises above the thin material of this crime melodrama. He's an up-and-

---

coming gangster operating amid the illicit drug community of New York City's Lower East Side. The film manages some artistic attempts at revealing the mean streets inner-city background, but the script is as shabby as the story's environment. **Director**—Amos Poe. (R)
98 minutes

ALPHAVILLE (1965)
★★★

Eddie Constantine
Anna Karina
Akim Tamiroff

The New Wave was still new and full of exciting promise, and the career of director Jean-Luc Godard, perhaps its foremost representative, was in high gear when he made this heady piece of existential science fiction. It's partly about a private eye who travels to a futurist

---

society where emotions are banned and who teaches the meaning of love to the daughter of a renegade scientist. It's also about moviemaking, contemporary society, and struggles between the brain and the heart. Constantine, an expatriate American popular in France as pulp-film detective Lemmy Caution, stars in that role and Karina, the former Mrs. Godard, plays the soulless, soulful-eyed heroine. *100 minutes b&w*

ALTERED STATES (1981)
 ★★

William Hurt
Blair Brown

Director Ken Russell's mind-blowing psychedelic monster movie begins with mystery and exhilaration and ends as mere preposterous mumbo jumbo. Hurt is cast as a young psychophysiologist who alters his consciousness to the point of changing himself temporarily into an apelike creature. Russell lays on dazzling visual displays to create an outrageous hallucinogenic effect. Then the film falls apart when it urges viewers to accept as reality what can only be taken as visionary. Also with Charles Haid. (R)
102 minutes

ALWAYS LEAVE THEM LAUGHING (1949)
★★

Milton Berle
Bert Lahr

Berle plays himself as a stand-up comedian on the rocky road to success. Berle, along with Lahr, hams it up delightfully for a few yuks, but the film falters somewhat when it dwells on sentimental stuff. At times, Lahr upstages the cocky Berle. You'll laugh—but not always. Virginia Mayo, Ruth Roman, and Alan Hale co-star. **Director**—Roy Del Ruth. *116 minutes b&w*

AMADEUS (1984)
★★★★

Tom Hulce
F. Murray Abraham

Opulent, magnificent adaptation of Peter Shaffer's play about Mozart as a vulgar, clownish musical prodigy

---

MERYL STREEP

Born in Bernardsville, New Jersey, in 1949, of a non-theatrical family, Meryl Streep has become a popular actress among playgoers and movie audiences. Growing up in a middle-class New Jersey suburb, she developed a promising coloratura voice and became a protégé of Estelle Liebling, the celebrated teacher of Beverly Sills. It was at Vassar College, however, that Streep discovered her true vocation.

At her first college audition, she won the lead in August Strindberg's Miss Julie *and caused an immediate stir with her performance. Streep went on to the Yale School of Drama.*

A summer with the O'Neill Playwrights Conference in Connecticut led to her debut in New York in Joseph Papp's Lincoln Center production of Trelawny of the Wells. *Her next performance, as the slovenly Flora in Tennessee Williams's* 27 Wagons Full of Cotton, *brought her the Outer Circle Critics' and*

Theater World awards—and a Tony nomination.

A season with the New York Shakespeare Festival led to such productions as the Broadway musical Happy End, Taming of the Shrew, *and the musical* Alice, *but it was Streep's Emmy-winning performance as a Catholic married to a Jew in the TV mini-series* Holocaust *that brought her to the notice of a larger audience.*

Streep made her screen debut in Julia *(1977), where she played Jane Fonda's society friend in a brief scene. Next came her performance as the steel-town girl friend in* The Deer Hunter *(1978), for which she received an Oscar nomination and the New York Film Critics Award. In* The Seduction of Joe Tynan *(1979), Streep played opposite Alan Alda as the tough-minded attorney having an affair with a married senator who is running for President. Next came her Academy Award-winning performance in* Kramer vs. Kramer *(1979), for which she also won a Golden Globe Award as best supporting actress. Streep was nominated for her dual role in* The French Lieutenant's Woman *(1981). She finally won a best actress Oscar for her role in* Sophie's Choice *(1982). She played the title role in* Silkwood *(1983), and starred opposite Robert De Niro in* Falling in Love *(1984).*

(Hulce) and the envy he aroused in the mediocre 18th-century composer, Antonio Salieri (Abraham). The stunning film shines in all departments: inspired acting, detailed period settings, Milos Forman's brilliant direction, and the soaring score of Mozart's great music. A grand celebration of genius. (PG)   *158 minutes*

AMARCORD (1974)

★★★★

**Magali Noel
Bruno Zanin**

Famed Italian director Federico Fellini takes a nostalgic stroll to the Italy of his youth. At times the movie may seem slow, but the beautiful photography and the poignant scenes of the life-styles in 1930s Italy as Fellini confronts Italian fascism make this worthwhile viewing. Solid acting performances reflect Fellini's directing skills. In Italian with English titles. **Academy Award**—best foreign-language film.   *127 minutes*

THE AMATEUR (1982)

★★★

**John Savage
Christopher Plummer
Marthe Keller**

John Savage steals CIA secrets in The Amateur, *a semi-thrilling spy story.*

The thick plot of this international spy thriller strains credibility, but it never loses its grip. Savage portrays a CIA code expert who seeks revenge on the terrorists who killed his girl friend. Excitement, intrigue, double crosses, and sinister encounters heighten the flavor of the exotic tale. Handsome

cinematography contributes to the film's professional flair. **Director**—Charles Jarrott. (R)   *111 minutes*

AMBUSH (1949)
★★

**Robert Taylor
John Hodiak
Arlene Dahl**

A routine western with the U.S. Cavalry led by an army scout looking for an Apache chief who has kidnapped a white woman. There's some rousing action, helped along by the talents of Taylor, Hodiak, and Dahl. **Director**—Sam Wood.   *89 minutes b&w*

AMERICAN DREAMER (1984)
★★

**JoBeth Williams
Tom Conti
Giancarlo Giannini**

Slightly bored American housewife (Williams) wins a trip to Paris in a mystery-writing contest. She soon finds herself embroiled in adventure and intrigue under similar circumstances to her fictional heroine. It begins like *Romancing the Stone*, but it becomes rather tame with the direction and script stumbling about. The thriller/farce bogs down in corny slapstick situations that sabotage the effervescent efforts of Williams. **Director**—Rick Rosenthal. (PG)   *104 minutes*

THE AMERICAN FRIEND (1977)

★★★★

**Dennis Hopper
Bruno Ganz
Lisa Kreuzer**

This stylish psychological thriller by German director Wim Wenders packs tension that's typical of an Alfred Hitchcock film. Hopper, in the title role, plays a rogue who persuades a man, who is convinced he's dying from a rare disease, to become a paid killer. There is high-level acting by a colorful cast. Also with Nicholas Ray. Action was filmed in Hamburg, Paris, and New York City. (No MPAA rating)   *127 minutes*

AMERICAN GIGOLO (1980)

★★

**Richard Gere
Lauren Hutton**

This melodrama about a high-class male prostitute is a film dressed up in fancy duds for a trip to the corner drugstore. The atmosphere is sleek and plush, but the story needs some zip. Gere in the title role is impressive as a hustler who takes a cynical, businesslike attitude toward the older women he services. However, we never know what really makes him tick. Director Paul Schrader, who wrote and directed *Hard Core*, continues to pursue his obsession with exposing moral degradation in this film. (R)   *117 minutes*

AMERICAN GRAFFITI (1973)

★★★★

**Richard Dreyfuss
Ronny Howard
Paul Le Mat**

In American Graffiti, *Cindy Williams worships Ron Howard from anear.*

A right-on portrait of American youth culture shown through the experiences of some high school seniors on the eve of leaving for college or military service in the early 1960s. There's very little plot, but this landmark film sparkles with nostalgic atmosphere and hilarious dialogue. The story involves a memorable night of chasing girls, racing cars, harassing the cops, and hanging out at the local drive-in restaurant. The production enhanced the career of director George Lucas. Cast also includes Cindy Williams, Charles Martin Smith, and Candy Clark. You also should spot Harrison

(Continued)

A
- American Hot Wax
- An American in Paris
- The Americanization of Emily
- American Pop
- An American Tragedy
- An American Werewolf in London
- Americathon

(Continued)
Ford and Suzanne Somers. (PG) **Academy Award Nominations**—best picture; Lucas, best director; Clark, best supporting actress; Lucas, Gloria Katz, and Willard Huyck, best story and screenplay (based on factual material or material not previously published). *110 minutes.*

AMERICAN HOT WAX (1978)
★★

Tim McIntire
Fran Drescher

Rock 'n' roll music of the 1950s pours forth at full volume in this nostalgic film that depicts the rise and fall of disc jockey Alan Freed. But the plot comes on at a whisper with no point of view and little insight into that period of youthful defiance. Fans of Chuck Berry, Jerry Lee Lewis, *et al*, may find this film of interest. Otherwise, it is an earache. Also with Jay Leno, Laraine Newman, and John Lehne. **Director**—Floyd Mutrux. (PG) *91 minutes*

AN AMERICAN IN PARIS (1951)
★★★★

Gene Kelly
Oscar Levant
Nina Foch

A vivacious, glittering musical blessed with the amazing choreography of Kelly and based on the music of George and Ira Gershwin. There's a simple romantic plot about an ex-GI, played by Kelly, who settles in Paris to

Gene Kelly dances with Leslie Caron in An American in Paris, *an Academy Award-winning musical.*

be an artist and falls for a *gamine*, played by Leslie Caron. But it's really the show-stopping dance and music sequences that make the film a fabulous hit. It's one of the best musicals of this golden era. **Director**—Vincente Minnelli. **Academy Awards**—best picture; Alan Jay Lerner, writing (story and screenplay). **Nomination**—Minnelli, best director. *113 minutes*

THE AMERICANIZATION OF EMILY (1964)
★★★

Julie Andrews
James Garner

Garner and Andrews star in this unusual black comedy about an American naval officer who procures luxuries for the top brass. Paddy Chayefsky's poignant screenplay, based on William Bradford Huie's novel, is effective in its antiwar point of view. Andrews is excellent as a British war widow who perceives the officer's cowardice but falls in love with him just the same. Includes Melvyn Douglas, James Coburn, and Joyce Grenfell. **Director**—Arthur Hiller. *117 minutes b&w*

AMERICAN POP (1981)
★★

Director-animator Ralph Bakshi (*Fritz the Cat; Heavy Traffic*) takes us down popular music's memory lane, from early burlesque to punk rock. This innovative cartoon feature is embellished with newsreel footage, still photographs, and rousing music spanning more than 80 years. Although Bakshi's style is fresh and vigorous, he tries to pack in too much historical detail, and his problem leads to awkwardness and confusion. The overall effect isn't too satisfying. (R) *95 minutes*

AN AMERICAN TRAGEDY (1931)
★★★

Phillips Holmes
Sylvia Sidney

Sergei Eisenstein was once in the run-

ning to direct this caustic work of Theodore Dreiser, but the job went to Josef von Sternberg, who was almost Eisenstein's polar opposite. A great filmmaker brings a great novelist to the screen, and despite the occasional aesthetic clashes, it's strong stuff. The story of a man torn between his poor girl friend and a wealthy beauty was remade in 1951 as *A Place in the Sun*. *95 minutes b&w*

AN AMERICAN WEREWOLF IN LONDON (1981)
★★★

David Naughton

David Naughton is forced into the distressing conclusion that he's An American Werewolf in London.

John Landis, who directed *Animal House*, applies his brand of comedy to the werewolf legend, and the result is a smoothly integrated mixture of humor and horror. Two American students touring England are attacked by a mysterious beast, and the survivor, Naughton, turns into a marauding werewolf at full moon. The grisly special effects are impressive, and the horror is very real, but the film is oddly touching and funny in a whistling-past-the-graveyard way. (R) *97 minutes*

AMERICATHON (1979)
★

Harvey Korman
John Ritter

It's 1998 and the United States is broke. Gasoline is so scarce that most people use bicycles to get around. The President is a clown who presides from the California White House. There's enough here for a minor sitcom, but the comedy never really builds mo-

• Amin—The Rise and Fall • The Amityville Horror • The Amorous Adventures
• Amityville 3–D   of Moll Flanders
• Amityville II: The   • The Amsterdam Kill
  Possession   • Amy

A

mentum. Korman stars as the host of a ridiculous telethon to raise money to save the country. With Fred Willard and Nancy Morgan. **Director**—Neil Israel. (PG)   *90 minutes*

AMIN—THE RISE AND FALL (1982)

 ★

Joseph Olita

The viciousness of the former Ugandan despot is exploited for all it's worth in this semidocumentary account, which was filmed in Kenya. The brutal Amin is shown eating human flesh, cutting up his wife's corpse, and preserving the heads of his enemies in the refrigerator, but the film sorely neglects to examine the reasons behind such barbarity. Olita, in the title role, is amazingly similar in appearance to the real Amin. Direction and acting, however, are merely marginal. **Director**—Sharad Patel. (R)   *101 minutes*

THE AMITYVILLE HORROR (1979)

 ★★

James Brolin
Margot Kidder

In The Amityville Horror, *Margot Kidder and James Brolin don't know that the property value of their new (and haunted) house is nil.*

This film would be just another haunted-house story were it not for plenty of effective hair-raising moments. Toilets ooze black goo, the front door is mysteriously ripped from its hinges, a rocking chair rocks with no one in it. Brolin and Kidder give adequate performances as the newlywed couple who finally flee this strange Long Island home where the previous family had been murdered. The screenplay is based on Jay Anson's

supposedly factual book. Cast includes Rod Steiger and Don Stroud. **Director**—Stuart Rosenberg. (R)
117 minutes

AMITYVILLE 3–D (1983)

 ★

Tony Roberts
Tess Harper

This trashy second rehash of the famed haunted-house tale has worn out the welcome mat. Now we have magazine reporter Tony Roberts setting up shop in the eerie dwelling by the shore. He initially pooh-poohs the existence of evil spirits until a few poorly conceived horror effects set him straight. The pacing is sluggish and the 3–D effect may have you reaching for the aspirin bottle. Candy Clark costars. **Director**—Richard Fleischer. (PG)   *93 minutes*

AMITYVILLE II: THE POSSESSION (1982)

 ★★

Burt Young
James Olson
Jack Magner

A patchy, somewhat tiresome reworking of the same haunted-house theme that was used in the original *Amityville Horror*. Yet another middle-class family encounters strange phenomena and evil spirits at work in the white frame Colonial dwelling at the water's edge. There are some effectively chilling moments, but the story does not hold up. The conclusion fails to satisfy. **Director**—Damiano Damiani. (R)
104 minutes

THE AMOROUS ADVENTURES OF MOLL FLANDERS (1965)

 ★★

Kim Novak
Richard Johnson
Angela Lansbury
George Sanders

This ambitious attempt to make a female version of *Tom Jones* doesn't quite make it. Novak, who fits awkwardly in the title role, is part of the

problem. She plays a servant girl who cavorts with rich men. There are some bawdy bedroom romps in 18th-century England, but nothing too exciting. Costumes and period settings are nice. The film is based on Daniel Defoe's novel. Cast includes Lilli Palmer, Leo McKern, and Vittorio De Sica. **Director**—Terence Young.
126 minutes

THE AMSTERDAM KILL (1978)

 ★★

Robert Mitchum
Bradford Dillman
Richard Egan

Robert Mitchum and George Cheung lay low in a greenhouse in The Amsterdam Kill.

Droopy-eyed Mitchum plays a narcotics agent who smashes an international drug-smuggling ring that operates in Hong Kong, Amsterdam, and London. Mitchum's performance is effective, but at times he seems too old to be slugging it out as the straight heavy. Robert Clouse directs this caper with a knack for fast-paced action. However, he overdoes the gunplay, and the body count climbs with each passing scene. Also with Leslie Nielsen and Keye Luke. (R)
90 minutes

AMY (1981)

 ★★★

Jenny Agutter
Barry Newman
Nanette Fabray

A sentimental, feel-good movie from the Disney studios about a woman who leaves her stuffy lawyer-husband to teach deaf children to speak. The title role is winningly portrayed by
(Continued)

A
- Anastasia
- Anatomy of a Murder
- Anchors Aweigh
- The Anderson Tapes
- ...And Justice for All
- And Now for Something Completely Different

(Continued)

Agutter. There's stalwart support from Newman and Fabray. But the film is most convincing because of the impressive performances of students from the California School for the Deaf. The format is rather old-fashioned, but it's executed with ample warmth and appeal. **Director**—Vincent McEveety. (G) *100 minutes*

ANASTASIA (1956)
★★★★

**Ingrid Bergman
Yul Brynner
Helen Hayes**

Ingrid Bergman is recruited to impersonate the late Russian czar's daughter in Anastasia.

A charming drama set in Paris in 1928, about an amnesiac young woman, played by Bergman, who is recruited by exiled Russians to impersonate the daughter of the late czar. Bergman's gracious and award-winning performance heightens the entertainment to grand style. Hayes, as the grand duchess, also makes a magnificent acting contribution as she strives to determine Bergman's credentials. Also with Akim Tamiroff and Martita Hunt. **Director**—Anatole Litvak. **Academy Award**—Bergman, best actress. *105 minutes*

ANATOMY OF A MURDER
(1959)
★★★★

**James Stewart
Ben Gazzara
Lee Remick**

A long but engrossing courtroom drama, adapted from Robert Traver's best-selling novel, about a small-town lawyer in Michigan who defends an Army officer accused of murdering a bartender. Stewart is superb as the crafty defense attorney, and George C. Scott makes his mark as the prosecutor. The explicit dialogue caused a stir when the film was released. Also stars Eve Arden and Arthur O'Connell. Duke Ellington wrote the musical score. **Director**—Otto Preminger. **Academy Award Nominations**—best picture; Stewart, best actor; O'Connell, Scott, best supporting actor; Wendell Mayes, best screenplay (based on material from another medium). *160 minutes b&w*

ANCHORS AWEIGH
(1945)
★★★

**Frank Sinatra
Gene Kelly
Kathryn Grayson**

A light and lively musical about two sailors on liberty in Los Angeles who befriend a small boy yearning to join the Navy. The cast, led by Kelly, Sinatra, and Grayson, perform energetically. The film is notable for Kelly's dance sequence with a cartoon mouse, and for the song, "I Fall in Love Too Easily." There's support from José Iturbi, Dean Stockwell, and Pamela Britton. **Director**—George Sidney. *140 minutes*

THE ANDERSON TAPES
(1972)
☿ ★★★

**Sean Connery
Martin Balsam
Dyan Cannon**

Stylish and lively crime drama about an ex-con's plan to stage a robbery at an apartment building, but the cops are on to the heist because of electronic surveillance. Connery is convincing as the thief, and the unusual climax is rather thrilling. However, a few plot holes mar the script. This was Christopher Walken's first film. Also stars Alan King and Ralph Meeker. **Director**—Sidney Lumet. (PG) *98 minutes*

. . . AND JUSTICE FOR ALL
(1979)
☿ ★★★

**Al Pacino
Jack Warden
John Forsythe**

Pacino stars as a scruffy, idealistic lawyer who tangles with a tyrannical judge played by Forsythe. The film smartly indicts the legal profession much in the same spirit that *Hospital* took on medicine. This is a fascinating and compelling movie, featuring unforgettable performances and Norman Jewison's well-paced direction. Pacino generates so much power and feeling in this role that he must be regarded as more than just a good actor. He's a superstar. Cast includes Lee Strasberg. (R) **Academy Award Nominations**—Pacino, best actor; Valerie Curtin and Barry Levinson, best screenplay (written directly for the screen). *120 minutes*

AND NOW FOR SOMETHING COMPLETELY DIFFERENT
(1972)
☿ ★★★

**John Cleese
Graham Chapman
Terry Gilliam
Eric Idle
Michael Palin
Terry Jones**

The zany stars of "Monty Python's Flying Circus," Britain's latter-day version of the Marx Brothers, present a series of riproaring, rib-tickling sketches (drawn from their television show). The production is somewhat uneven, but there's loads of sidesplitting comedy throughout. **Director**—Ian McNaughton. (PG) *89 minutes*

• Androcles and the Lion
• Android
• The Andromeda Strain

• And Then There Were None
• Andy Warhol's Bad
• Angel
• Angel and the Badman

 A

ANDROCLES AND THE LION
(1952)
★★

**Alan Young
Jean Simmons
Robert Newton
Victor Mature**

George Bernard Shaw's satiric fable set in the time of ancient Rome is marred by a lackluster production, although some good performances perk things up at times. The story concerns a Christian who removes a thorn from the paw of a lion. When the two meet later in the arena, the lion remembers the kindness and refuses to eat the man. Young plays the Christian. Cast includes Reginald Gardiner, Alan Mowbray, Maurice Evans, and Elsa Lanchester. **Director**—Chester Erskine. *98 minutes b&w*

ANDROID (1984)
 ★★★

**Klaus Kinski
Don Opper**

Tired of playing mad scientists, Klaus Kinski perfects a new type in Android: *the grumpy scientist.*

A charming, likable, low-budget science-fiction movie that features a robot with touching human characteristics. Max, the shy and sensitive robot, resides on a remote space station with obsessed scientist Kinski. Max wants to go to Earth to be his "own person," but unexpected events get in his way. Debuting director Aaron Lipstadt does the utmost with a limited budget and the film seems slated for sleeper and cult status. (R) *80 minutes*

THE ANDROMEDA STRAIN
(1971)
 ★★★

**Arthur Hill
David Wayne**

Scientists race the clock to decontaminate a remote village infected by a deadly virus from a downed satellite. The film, based on Michael Crichton's novel, is somewhat drawn out, but it packs plenty of suspense just the same. Also, there's some reference to man's injustice to man. Also with James Olson, Kate Reid, and Paula Kelly. **Director**—Robert Wise. (G) *137 minutes*

AND THEN THERE WERE NONE (1945)
 ★★★

**Walter Huston
Dame Judith Anderson
Barry Fitzgerald**

There have been several film versions based upon the Agatha Christie suspense novel about murder on a lonely island, but this one by director Reńe Clair is the best by far. Excellent performances enliven the tale as 10 people at a house party are murdered one by one. Because of Clair's able direction, the triteness of Christie's novel is kept to a minimum and the mystery and suspense remain strong up to the last slaying. *98 minutes b&w*

ANDY WARHOL'S BAD (1977)
(no stars)

**Carroll Baker
Perry King
Susan Tyrrell**

This is the revolting story of a suburban housewife who operates a small-scale murder-and-mayhem contracting business staffed by strange girls. There are numerous outrageous scenes of blood and gore, which probably will make you surrender your dinner. Much of the dialogue is boring. Some of the acting is fair; the rest is awful. "Bad" it certainly is. **Director**—Jed Johnson. (X) *105 minutes*

ANGEL (1984)
 ★

Donna Wilkes

Donna Wilkes is Angel, *a Los Angeles high school girl who lives a double life as a hooker.*

By day, she's an honor student at a swank Los Angeles prep school. At night, she's hustling tricks on Sunset Boulevard and hanging around with kooky characters. Also, she's dodging a mad-dog killer who slices up prostitutes like roast turkey. With all that, there's just enough time to knock off tomorrow's homework assignment. Donna Wilkes is in the title role of this sleazy outing, aided and abetted by Rory Calhoun and Cliff Gorman. Fledgling director Robert Vincent O'Neil shows his Roger Corman colors. (R) *93 minutes*

ANGEL AND THE BADMAN
(1947)
 ★★

**John Wayne
Gail Russell
Bruce Cabot**

Sooner or later, every matinee idol wants to do *Hamlet*, and every horse opera writer wants to do a morality play. Here, Wayne and writer/director James Edward Grant do penance for all the cowpokes and braves they've eagerly dispatched with sixguns. A wounded gunslinger is nursed back to health by Quaker Prudence Worth
(Continued)

A

- Angelo My Love
- Angel on My Shoulder
- Angels with Dirty Faces
- Animal Crackers
- Animal Farm
- Animal House
- Anna and the King of Siam

(Continued)

(Prudence Worth, get it?), who would have him see the folly of his ways. This was a change of pace even for the studio (Republic), and though it's actually genuine enough, it's also, alas, sleep-inducing. *100 minutes b&w*

ANGELO MY LOVE (1983)

 ★★

Angelo Evans

Actor Robert Duvall turns director for this unusual documentarylike fiction about New York gypsies. At the heart of the story is Evans, a bright-eyed urchin who gives an appealing performance as a pint-size, streetwise con artist. Other characters, played almost without exception by real gypsies, are well defined. Unfortunately, the movie drags and lacks cohesiveness. (No MPAA rating) *120 minutes*

ANGEL ON MY SHOULDER
(1946)

 ★★★

Paul Muni
Claude Rains
Anne Baxter

A light comedy-drama about a dead criminal who makes a deal with the devil for a new lease on life. He returns to Earth as a high-minded judge and turns the tables on Satan. The plot imitates *Here Comes Mr. Jordan*, but the film still maintains a lively entertainment level. Muni, Rains, and Baxter are excellent in starring roles. With Erskine Sanford and Hardie Albright. **Director**—Archie Mayo.

101 minutes b&w

ANGELS WITH DIRTY FACES
(1938)

 ★★★

James Cagney
Pat O'Brien
Humphrey Bogart

A top cast graces this drama about a New York hood, played by Cagney, who develops a conscience when a bunch of slum kids start looking on him as their idol. O'Brien gives a fine performance as the gangster's child-

James Cagney and Humphrey Bogart crack a safe in Angels with Dirty Faces.

hood friend who happens to be a priest. Bogart is notable as a criminal whose conscience remains unawakened. The Dead End Kids are effective as the impressionable youths. The film is a clever combination of brutality and moral comment. Also with Ann Sheridan and George Bancroft. **Director**—Michael Curtiz. *97 minutes b&w*

ANIMAL CRACKERS (1930)

 ★★★

The Marx Brothers
Margaret Dumont

The Marx Brothers' second film brings to the screen the delirious anarchy of their Broadway hit by Morrie Ryskind and George S. Kaufman. A valuable painting has disappeared from the home of the wealthy Mrs. Rittenhouse (Dumont), and who could be better qualified to find it than big-game

hunter Captain Spaulding. ("One morning I shot an elephant in my pajamas. How he got into my pajamas I'll never know.") Chico on piano, Harpo on harp, Groucho on overdrive, and Zeppo on cardboard mounting. Hooray for Captain Spaulding! **Director**—Victor Heerman.

98 minutes b&w

ANIMAL FARM (1955)

 ★★★

On-target animated cartoon faithfully based on George Orwell's political satire. The oppressed animals free themselves from their human masters and take over management of the farm only to find themselves governed by harsh restrictions. Some of the cartoon characters are pigs, but not the "Porky Pig" kind. **Director**—John Halas. *75 minutes*

ANIMAL HOUSE
See National Lampoon's Animal House

ANNA AND THE KING OF SIAM (1946)
★★★

Irene Dunne
Rex Harrison

Impressive period drama about an English governess who takes a job in

In Animal Crackers, *the globe-trotting Capt. Spaulding (Groucho) considers dropping ankle.*

- Anna Karenina
- Anne of the Thousand Days
- Annie
- Annie Get Your Gun
- Annie Hall
- Annie Oakley

A

the palace in Bangkok teaching the king's many children and wins the respect of the tyrannical king. Gracefully produced with heartwarming touches. Harrison and Dunne are impressive in the key roles. The story, however, is better known in the musical version, *The King and I*. Cast includes Linda Darnell, Gale Sondergaard, and Lee J. Cobb. **Director—** John Cromwell. *128 minutes b&w*

ANNA KARENINA (1935)
★★★

Greta Garbo
Fredric March
Basil Rathbone

A superb performance by Garbo compensates for the flaws in bringing to the screen Leo Tolstoy's great novel about the love affair of the wife of a Russian aristocrat and a dashing cavalry officer. Although Garbo shines brightest, there are also fine performances by March as Garbo's lover, Rathbone as her husband, and Freddie Bartholomew as her son. Also with Maureen O'Sullivan, May Robson, Reginald Denny, and Reginald Owen. **Director**—Clarence Brown.
95 minutes b&w

ANNE OF THE THOUSAND DAYS (1969)
★★★

Richard Burton
Geneviève Bujold

Burton gives one of his most impressive performances as Henry VIII in this somewhat inaccurate historical drama involving the king's controversial romance with Anne Boleyn, played by Bujold. It's a compelling account of a famous love affair that involved adultery. The film is based on the 1948 play by Maxwell Anderson. Lavish costumes and scenery enhance the production. With John Colicos, Irene Papas, and Anthony Quayle. **Director**—Charles Jarrott. (PG) **Academy Award Nominations**—best picture; Burton, best actor; Bujold, best actress; Quayle, best supporting actor; Richard Sokolove, best screenplay (based on material from another medium). *145 minutes*

ANNIE (1982)
★

Aileen Quinn

Aileen Quinn is greeted enthusiastically by Daddy Warbucks' staff in Annie.

What happens when you take 40 million dollars, an obnoxious little kid in a red wig, choreography that looks like ball bearings in a food processor, and a director who would rather be somewhere else, and put them all together? Well, you get *Annie*, as convoluted a mess of a musical as we've seen in a long time. A mildly entertaining Broadway musical is once again mugged on its way to the screen. Quinn tries too hard in the lead role— she might have been all right in a better film. The large supporting cast, including Albert Finney, Carol Burnett, and Ann Reinking, veer back and forth between overacting and looking out-to-lunch. **Director**—John Huston. (PG) *128 minutes*

ANNIE GET YOUR GUN (1950)
★★★

Betty Hutton
Howard Keel

Flashy film version of the Broadway hit musical about Annie Oakley, the celebrated female sharpshooter who toured with Wild West shows. Hutton and Keel belt out the lively Irving Berlin music with gusto. The direction is somewhat stilted, but the production is lavish. Edward Arnold, Keenan Wynn, Louis Calhern, and J. Carrol Naish lend support. Memorable songs include "Anything You Can Do" and "Doin' What Comes Naturally." **Director**—George Sidney. *107 minutes*

ANNIE HALL (1977)
★★★★

Woody Allen
Diane Keaton

Diane Keaton created a character so memorable in Annie Hall *that it has colored her other performances for the last eight years.*

Allen and Keaton glitter and shine in this hilarious and moving autobiographical film about their on-again, off-again romance. It's Allen's most personal film and one of his best. The familiar parade of Allen one-liners is there, but the film also is rich with emotion and introspection. He leans somewhat on Ingmar Bergman here, and this story could appropriately be named "Scenes from a Neurotic Love Affair." Cast includes Tony Roberts, Paul Simon, Shelley Duvall, Carol Kane, and Colleen Dewhurst. **Director**—Allen. (PG) **Academy Awards**— best picture; Allen, best director; Keaton, best actress; Allen and Marshall Brickman, best original screenplay. **Nomination**—Allen, best actor. *95 minutes*

ANNIE OAKLEY (1935)
★★

Barbara Stanwyck
Preston Foster
Melvyn Douglas

Fictionalized biography of the late 19th-century sharpshooter who toured with Buffalo Bill's Wild West Show and her peppery on-and-off romance with a fellow entertainer. Scrappy Stan-

A
- The Anniversary
- Another Man, Another Chance
- Another Man's Poison
- Another Country

- Another Time, Another Place (1958)
- Another Time, Another Place (1984)

- Any Number Can Play
- Any Wednesday
- Any Which Way You Can

(Continued)
wyck is in fine fettle, the film was one of the high points of her '30s career. But time hasn't been kind to this back-stage comedy/drama, much of which falls flat today. **Director**—George Stevens. *88 minutes b&w*

THE ANNIVERSARY (1968)
★★

**Bette Davis
Jack Hedley
James Cossins**

Davis, bitchy as ever and wearing an eye patch, stars as an overbearing mother who dominates her grown sons. She gathers her clan together on the anniversary of her husband's death. This black comedy-horror outing, based on the Bill MacIlwraith play, affords an opportunity to see Davis ham it up to the hilt. Otherwise, the film is routine. Also with Sheila Hancock and Elaine Taylor. **Director**—Roy Ward Baker. *95 minutes*

ANOTHER MAN, ANOTHER CHANCE (1977)
★★

**James Caan
Geneviève Bujold**

French director Claude Lelouch (*A Man and a Woman*) gives us his version of America's frontier days that looks like a western soap opera with a French accent. The complex plot concerns a veterinarian widower, played by Caan, who falls in love with a widowed photographer, played by Bujold, while both reside in a dusty frontier town. This film certainly isn't your typical western, but it cries out for some typical drama, action, and some dimensional characters. (PG) *128 minutes*

ANOTHER MAN'S POISON (1952)
★★

**Bette Davis
Anthony Steel
Gary Merrill**

A murky melodrama about a woman writer who poisons her husband and is subsequently blackmailed. Davis isn't up to par as the hysterical authoress in this low-budget film. The material is mediocre as well. Emlyn Williams, Barbara Murray, and Reginald Beckwith co-star. **Director**—Irving Rapper. *89 minutes b&w*

ANOTHER COUNTRY (1984)
 ★★★

**Rupert Everett
Colin Furth**

Revealing, well-acted melodrama that probes the confining atmosphere of an elite English boarding school. Based on Julian Mitchell's popular stage play, the story follows the experiences of several students who depart from the traditional expectations and become Russian spies. Everett is impressive as an ambitious upper-crust youth who engages in homosexual affairs and Marxist politics. Firth also is outstanding as a student with similar leanings. **Director**—Marek Kanievska. (PG) *90 minutes*

ANOTHER TIME, ANOTHER PLACE (1958)
★

**Lana Turner
Barry Sullivan**

Tearful soap-opera movie with Turner as an American newspaper woman during World War II who is involved in an affair with a British war correspondent. Turner goes to pieces when her love is killed. This film introduced Sean Connery as an actor worth watching. Also with Glynis Johns and Sidney James. **Director**—Lewis Allen. *98 minutes b&w*

ANOTHER TIME, ANOTHER PLACE (1984)
★★

Phyllis Logan

Dour, slow-moving melodrama about a bored Scottish woman who engages in a secret love affair with an Italian prisoner of war. The emotionally charged story, set in a small Scottish community during World War II, highlights the cultural differences and ten-sions between the local farmers and the captive soldiers. But a constant bleakness pervades the production and limits its impact. Logan gives an impressive portrayal as the farmer's wife who succumbs to passion. **Director**—Michael Radford. (R) *101 minutes*

ANY NUMBER CAN PLAY (1949)
★★★

**Clark Gable
Alexis Smith
Mary Astor**

Skillful acting by Gable, Smith, and Astor perk up this otherwise routine drama about a gambler beset with numerous problems. Gable, who plays a casino operator, is estranged from his family, but the situation turns around when health problems prompt his retirement. Also with Wendell Corey, Audrey Totter, Marjorie Rambeau, and Lewis Stone. **Director**—Mervyn Le Roy. *112 minutes b&w*

ANY WEDNESDAY (1966)
★★★

**Jane Fonda
Dean Jones
Jason Robards, Jr.**

A business executive, played by Robards, visits his mistress once a week, but tension develops when a company subordinate discovers the affair. This somewhat stretched out sex farce is based on the Broadway comedy. Fonda's spritely performance as the kept girl, however, helps maintain interest. Cast includes Rosemary Murphy and Ann Prentiss. **Director**—Robert Miller. *109 minutes*

ANY WHICH WAY YOU CAN (1980)
 ★★★

**Clint Eastwood
Sondra Locke**

This funny rollicking sequel to *Every Which Way But Loose* is better than the original. Eastwood once again teams up with Clyde the orangutan for more

• Anzio
• Apache
• The Apartment
• Apocalypse Now
• The Apprenticeship of
  Duddy Kravitz
• The April Fools

A

nonstop monkeyshines and two-fisted farcical mayhem. It's an undisguised comic-action vehicle for Eastwood, who has the good sense not to take himself too seriously. Locke again is pleasant as Eastwood's romantic interest. **Director**—Buddy Van Horn. (PG)   *115 minutes*

ANZIO (1968)
★

**Robert Mitchum
Peter Falk
Arthur Kennedy**

Trumped-up World War II drama about preparation for the 1944 invasion of the Italian peninsula. The flimsy film wastes the good cast seen struggling with their roles. Mitchum plays a war correspondent in on the action. Earl Holliman, Anthony Steel, and Robert Ryan also star. **Director**—Edward Dmytryk.   *117 minutes*

APACHE (1954)
 ★★

**Burt Lancaster
Jean Peters**

Lancaster stars as an angry Indian warrior who boldly crusades for justice for his tribe and then settles down. There are some good action scenes, but the unlikely story languishes in spots. Peters fills in the background as Lancaster's supportive squaw. John McIntire and Charles Bronson appear in supporting roles. **Director**—Robert Aldrich.   *91 minutes*

THE APARTMENT (1960)
★★★★

**Jack Lemmon
Shirley MacLaine**

Witty, bittersweet comedy-drama about a lonely, vulnerable young office worker, played by Lemmon, who lends his apartment to his superiors for their extramarital affairs. Lemmon and MacLaine turn in classic performances that are unforgettable. Billy Wilder's direction is on target with just the right blend of cynicism, pathos, and laughs. Fred MacMurray is superb as Lemmon's philandering boss.

Shirley MacLaine takes Jack Lemmon for a ride in the comedy-drama The Apartment.

Academy Awards—best picture; Wilder, best director; Wilder and I.A.L. Diamond, best story and screenplay (written directly for the screen). **Nominations**—Lemmon, best actor; MacLaine, best actress; Jack Kruschen, best supporting actor.

125 minutes b&w

APOCALYPSE NOW (1979)
★★★★

**Marlon Brando
Martin Sheen
Robert Duvall**

Francis Coppola's unforgettable masterpiece about the Vietnam War throbs with energy, horror, irony, and grandeur. It's a cinematic work of art; an involving adventure yarn, based on Joseph Conrad's *Heart of Darkness*. All the acting is first class, but Duvall stands out as a gung ho, pompous air-cavalry colonel who stages a brutal helicopter raid on a Viet Cong village. Top-billed Brando is finally seen in the last quarter of the film. He plays the shadowy Colonel Kurtz who has gone mad in the jungle and is slated for execution by an intelligence officer, played by Sheen. Also with Frederic Forrest, Albert Hall, and Sam Bottoms. (R) **Academy Award Nominations**—best picture; Coppola, best director; Duvall, best supporting actor; Coppola and John Milius, best screenplay (adapted from another medium).   *139 minutes*

THE APPRENTICESHIP OF DUDDY KRAVITZ (1974)
★★★

**Richard Dreyfuss
Micheline Lanctot
Jack Warden**

Poignant and amusing comedy-drama about a young Jewish man from Montreal trying to make it big in the world. Excellent scenes are brought to life from Mordecai Richler's bright screenplay adapted from his novel. Dreyfuss is superb as the ambitious teenager. Also with Randy Quaid, Denholm Elliott, and Joseph Wiseman. **Director**—Ted Kotcheff. (PG) **Academy Award Nomination**—Richler and Lionel Chetwynd, best screenplay (adapted from other material).

121 minutes

THE APRIL FOOLS (1969)
★★

**Jack Lemmon
Catherine Deneuve**

In The April Fools, *Jack Lemmon and Catherine Deneuve run away from their regimented lives and have an affair.*

Strained comedy-drama made as a star vehicle for Jack Lemmon, but it doesn't work too well. Lemmon is a restless business executive who runs off to Paris with the wife of his boss. All sorts of complications ensue, but everything is straightened out for the happy ending. Myrna Loy, Sally Kellerman, Charles Boyer, Jack Weston, Harvey Korman, and Peter Lawford are in supporting roles. **Director**—Stuart Rosenberg. (PG)   *95 minutes*

A
- April in Paris
- Arabesque
- Arabian Adventure
- Arch of Triumph
- The Aristocats
- Around the World in Eighty Days
- The Arrangement
- Arrowsmith

APRIL IN PARIS (1952)
★★

**Doris Day
Ray Bolger**

Claude Dauphin paints a verbal picture for Ray Bolger in April in Paris.

Lackluster, silly musical with a flimsy plot about a chorus girl, played by Day, who is mistakenly sent to Paris where she charms an awkward state department official. Songs and dances for Day and Bolger are all pretty much forgettable. The cast includes Claude Dauphin, Eve Miller, and George Givot. **Director**—David Butler.
100 minutes

ARABESQUE (1966)
★★

**Gregory Peck
Sophia Loren**

Peck and Loren star in this handsome spy thriller with a disappointing, empty plot. Peck plays a language professor who finds himself involved with espionage while on assignment for some Arabian oil men. Some amusing moments are lost amid the lavish settings. With Alan Badel, Kieron Moore, and Carl Duering. **Director**—Stanley Donen. *118 minutes*

ARABIAN ADVENTURE (1979)
★★★

**Christopher Lee
Milo O'Shea
Oliver Tobias
Puneet Sira**

Flying magic carpets, genies, assorted villains, and a clever orphan boy will keep the kiddies amused for an hour and a half. This colorful Ali Baba-like adventure offers continuous action and intriguing special effects. Lee plays an evil ruler, Tobias is a handsome prince, and Mickey Rooney is the custodian of a secret cave. **Director**—Kevin Connor. (G) *98 minutes*

ARCH OF TRIUMPH (1948)
★★

**Ingrid Bergman
Charles Boyer
Charles Laughton**

An ambitious melodrama with a first-class cast—Bergman, Boyer, Laughton—fails to catch hold despite expensive commitment from its producers. Boyer plays a refugee in Paris who has a tragic love affair with a troubled girl, played by Bergman. A depressing set of circumstances, indeed, and hardly a triumph. Louis Calhern is also in the cast. **Director**—Lewis Milestone. *120 minutes b&w*

THE ARISTOCATS (1970)
★★★

An inventive cartoon feature by the Walt Disney studios about a cat and her kittens who are abandoned in the country and then rescued by the other animals there. Fine characterizations enhanced by the voices of Eva Gabor, Phil Harris, and Sterling Holloway. The deft influence of Walt Disney is noticeably missing, yet it's still a nice lollypop for the kids. **Director**—Wolfgang Reitherman. (G) *78 minutes*

AROUND THE WORLD IN EIGHTY DAYS (1956)
★★★

**David Niven
Cantinflas
Shirley MacLaine
Robert Newton**

A splendid, charming film version of Jules Verne's magnificent travelogue with spectacular sketches from various parts of the world and scores of cameos from an all-star cast. Niven

Shirley MacLaine and David Niven have a brief encounter in Around the World in Eighty Days.

plays the British gentleman who, in 1872, honored a bet that he could circle the globe within 80 days. The lavish production works best on the large screen and unfortunately loses impact on television. **Director**—Michael Anderson. **Academy Awards**—best picture; James Poe, John Farrow, S. J. Perelman, writing (best screenplay—adapted). **Nomination**—Anderson, best director. *170 minutes*

THE ARRANGEMENT (1969)
★

**Kirk Douglas
Faye Dunaway
Deborah Kerr**

An unfocused melodrama about an advertising executive who becomes fed up with his job, bungles a suicide attempt, and then analyzes the meaning of his life. Elia Kazan, who directed from his own novel, provides rich detail about the stress of contemporary life, but the characters involved are colorless. Douglas, Dunaway, and Kerr are wasted. Also with Richard Boone and Hume Cronyn. (R) *127 minutes*

ARROWSMITH (1931)
★★★

**Ronald Colman
Helen Hayes
Myrna Loy**

Director John Ford has fashioned a moving film from the Sinclair Lewis novel about a medical researcher (Colman) who loses his wife and nearly strays from his calling when tempta-

26

tion comes his way. Sidney Howard provided the intelligent script. **Academy Award Nominations**—best picture: Howard, writing (adaptation); Ray June, cinematography.

108 minutes b&w

ARSENIC AND OLD LACE
(1942)
 ★★★

**Cary Grant
Josephine Hull
Jean Adair**

Amusing and charming film adaptation of the Broadway play about two old ladies who poison gentlemen visitors to their Brooklyn home and then bury them in the cellar. It's a lot of fun despite the concentration on corpses. Director Frank Capra pulls out all stops to induce energy and hilarity from the excellent cast, which also includes Raymond Massey, Peter Lorre, Edward Everett Horton, and James Gleason. *118 minutes b&w*

ARTHUR (1981)
 ★★★

**Dudley Moore
Liza Minnelli
John Gielgud**

In this lively, screwball comedy Moore has the title role as an often-inebriated, poor little rich man who falls in love with a waitress, played by Minnelli. Moore tosses off a succession of zingy, clever one-liners, but it's Gielgud as Arthur's snobbish valet and Jiminy Cricket conscience who provides the real comic chemistry. He steals scenes with undisguised relish. Minnelli is charming, but her role gives her little to work with. **Director**—Steve Gordon. (PG) **Academy Award**—Gielgud, best supporting actor. **Nominations**—Moore, best actor; Gordon, best screenplay (written directly for the screen). *100 minutes*

ARTISTS AND MODELS (1955)
★★

**Dean Martin
Jerry Lewis**

Martin and Lewis are up to their usual comic routines. Lewis has nightmares that inspire the grist for comic strips drawn by Martin. The film features gorgeous women, some musical numbers, and cornball gags. It tires after a while. Also with Shirley MacLaine, Dorothy Malone, Eddie Mayehoff, and Eva Gabor. **Director**—Frank Tashlin. *109 minutes b&w*

THE ASPHALT JUNGLE (1950)
★★★★

**Sterling Hayden
Sam Jaffe
Louis Calhern**

Compelling crime drama, astutely directed by John Huston, about a gang of criminals who try to commit the perfect crime. The film evolves as more of a character study than a mystery. Excellent, gritty performances by Hayden, Jaffe, and James Whitmore. Marilyn Monroe has a small part that she handles well. **Academy Award Nominations**—John Huston, best director; Ben Maddow and Huston, writing (screenplay). *112 minutes b&w*

ASSAULT ON A QUEEN
(1966)
★

**Frank Sinatra
Virna Lisi**

Some gangsters get their hands on a German submarine and set out to pirate a luxury liner. A rather unlikely crime caper that fails at many levels: Acting is stilted, special effects are unconvincing, and Rod Serling's screenplay falters. Also with Tony Franciosa, Richard Conte, and Alf Kjellin. **Director**—Jack Donohue. *106 minutes*

ATLANTIC CITY (1981)
 ★★★

**Burt Lancaster
Susan Sarandon
Kate Reid**

French director Louis Malle has come up with a real charmer in this unusual romantic melodrama. It's crowded with colorful people who pursue their private dreams against the backdrop of

Susan Sarandon hopes to break out of Atlantic City.

this resort city. The most engaging character is Lou, played by Lancaster, an elderly petty criminal who at last achieves a delightful moment of glory and thus regains his self-respect. Lancaster's gentle and touching portrayal is carried off with superb finesse. There are also polished performances from Sarandon, as a girl bent on a brighter future than she can look forward to in Atlantic City, and Reid as a widow mourning her girlhood from the safety of her bedroom. (R) **Academy Award Nominations**—best picture; Lancaster, best actor; Sarandon, best actress; Malle, best director; John Guare, best screenplay (written directly for the screen). *104 minutes*

ATTACK (1956)
★★★

**Jack Palance
Eddie Albert
Lee Marvin**

Gripping and intelligent drama about American soldiers involved in the Battle of the Bulge and led by a cowardly commander. The slick production is far above the routine war movie thanks to good acting, a finely tuned script, and impressive direction by Robert Aldrich. The theme touches on an antiwar element. Excellent performances from Palance, Albert, and Marvin. Also with Buddy Ebsen, Robert Strauss, and Richard Jaeckel. *107 minutes b&w*

A
- At War with the Army
- Audrey Rose
- Auntie Mame
- Author! Author!
- Autumn Sonata
- Avalanche Express
- Avanti

AT WAR WITH THE ARMY
(1950)

★★

Dean Martin
Jerry Lewis

Martin and Lewis demonstrate their comic chemistry together in this routine service comedy based loosely on a play by James Allardice. There are a few clever gags, but it's not all that funny. Martin and Lewis are song-and-dance men with girl trouble. Polly Bergen and Jimmie Dundee co-star. **Director**—Hal Walker.

93 minutes b&w

AUDREY ROSE
(1977)

★★

Marsha Mason
John Beck
Anthony Hopkins

Take a slice of *The Exorcist*, a measure of *The Omen*, a dash of *Rosemary's Baby*, and add plenty of water. The result is this tepid tale of an 11-year-old girl who is the reincarnation of another girl killed in a crash. The padded script contains a lot of mumbo jumbo about Indian mysticism and transmigration of souls. Mason, Beck, and Hopkins act their parts as if they have difficulty keeping a straight face. Also with Susan Swift, Norman Lloyd, and John Hillerman. **Director**—Robert Wise. (PG) *113 minutes*

AUNTIE MAME (1958)

★★★

Rosalind Russell
Forrest Tucker

Russell's tour-de-force portrayal of the eccentric aunt who takes a teenage boy under her wing graces this entertaining film rendition of Patrick Dennis's novel. Some priceless moments spark hilarity galore as Roz plays the colorful character to the hilt. Mame believes life is a bouquet, and she proves it. Peggy Cass is memorable for her "Miss Gooch" characterization. Coral Browne and Fred Clark also star. **Director**—Morton DaCosta. **Academy Award Nominations**—best picture;

In Auntie Mame, Rosalind Russell plays an eccentric who takes a teenage boy under her wing.

Russell, best actress; Cass, best supporting actress. *114 minutes*

AUTHOR! AUTHOR! (1982)

★★★

Al Pacino

Al Pacino and Tuesday Weld decide that Pacino should be the mommie for a while in Author! Author!

Pacino does an attractive portrayal of a struggling New York playwright who's gallantly trying to support five children from various marriages. This look at modern family life is not as compelling as that presented in *Kramer vs. Kramer*, which this film occasionally resembles. Bear with it, however, because this comedy-drama ends with a charming display of warmth and sympathy between Pacino and his kids—who survive in spite of their home life. Tuesday Weld and Dyan

Cannon are wasted in their brief roles. **Director**—Arthur Hiller. (PG) *110 minutes*

AUTUMN SONATA (1978)

★★★

Ingrid Bergman
Liv Ullmann

Ingmar Bergman directs Ingrid Bergman for the first time in this film about a mother and daughter love-hate relationship. Ingrid Bergman is a successful concert pianist, and Ullmann is her middle-aged daughter. They turn in dynamic and inspired performances. Ingmar is on familiar territory relentlessly exposing complex human relationships and emotions. In Swedish with English titles. (No MPAA rating) **Academy Award Nominations**—Ingrid Bergman, best actress; Ingmar Bergman, best original screenplay. *97 minutes*

AVALANCHE EXPRESS (1979)

★

Lee Marvin
Robert Shaw
Linda Evans

Shaw, Marvin, Joe Namath, and a few other familiar players fumble through this languid melodrama about Soviet and American agents aboard a train traveling through Europe. The action stumbles along with much banal dialogue and clumsy direction. About midway, an avalanche is set off in an attempt to eliminate a defected Russian, played by Shaw. From then on, the film continues to slide downhill. **Director**—Mark Robson. (PG)

88 minutes

AVANTI (1972)

★★★

Jack Lemmon
Juliet Mills

Lemmon stars in this black comedy about a wealthy young man who falls in love with the daughter of his father's mistress. The film is drawn out, yet plenty of wit and style in the script and classy acting by a good cast sustain interest. Director Billy Wilder isn't at

- The Awakening
- Away All Boats
- The Awful Truth
- The Babe Ruth Story
- Babes in Arms
- Babes in Toyland
- Baby Blue Marine
- Baby Doll

A·B

his top form, but his execution is satisfactory. Also with Clive Revill and Edward Andrews. (R)   *144 minutes*

THE AWAKENING (1980)

★★

**Charlton Heston
Stephanie Zimbalist**

Heston plays an archaeologist who invades the secret tomb of Egypt's Queen Kara and unleashes her nasty spirit on the world. The film, based on Bram Stoker's novel, starts off with intrigue and suspense as Heston uncovers the ancient crypt with its splendors. But with the mummy's curse on the loose, the atmosphere deteriorates to hokey horror fare with accentuated violence. Zimbalist does a fair job as Heston's daughter who is possessed by Kara's cruel spirit. **Director**—Mike Newell. (R)   *105 minutes*

AWAY ALL BOATS (1956)

★★

**Jeff Chandler
George Nader
Julie Adams**

Routine World War II action adventure with overwrought heroic displays dominating the film. Story revolves around a transport ship involved in the Pacific campaign. Chandler leads the troops into battle. There are supporting roles by Nader, Adams, Lex Barker, and Richard Boone. **Director**— Joseph Pevney.   *114 minutes*

THE AWFUL TRUTH (1937)

★★★

**Cary Grant
Irene Dunne
Ralph Bellamy**

Dunne, Grant, and Bellamy sparkle in this typical 1930s-style sophisticated comedy about a divorced couple who realize they still love each other. The script seems silly at times, but the actors are wise enough not to take themselves or the plot too seriously. Remade in 1953 as the musical "Let's Do It Again." **Director**—Leo McCarey. **Academy Award**—McCarey, best director. **Nominations**—best picture;

Dunne, best actress; Bellamy, best supporting actor; Vina Delmar, writing (screenplay).   *90 minutes b&w*

B

THE BABE RUTH STORY (1948)

★★

**William Bendix
Claire Trevor**

Bendix is convincing as the "Sultan of Swat," but an unpolished script hamstrings this film biography. Events are presented in an overly sentimental fashion. However, the Babe's image remains intact. Charles Bickford and William Frawley play supporting roles. **Director**—Roy Del Ruth.
    107 minutes b&w

BABES IN ARMS (1939)

★★★

**Mickey Rooney
Judy Garland**

If energy alone could make masterpieces, this MGM musical would blow off the roof. Rooney is the driving force, determined to stage a fund raiser with his pals to save their parents, ex-vaudeville stars, from bankruptcy. He sings and dances up a storm and impersonates Gable and FDR—all of which helped him become the most popular movie star of the year. You may or may not care for such an assault of irrepressibility, but it *is* vintage Rooney. It's also the first of the successful Rooney and Garland costarring vehicles and the first of the "Let's put on a show!" musical subgenres. Oddly, most of the songs from the original Rodgers and Hart show are gone (though "The Lady Is a Tramp" is spared), and Busby Berkeley's directing is at a low ebb.
    96 minutes b&w

BABES IN TOYLAND (1934)

★★★

**Stan Laurel
Oliver Hardy
Charlotte Henry**

A Christmas gift that's a year-round pleasure, especially for kids. Producer Hal Roach's rendition of the Victor Herbert operetta has Laurel and Hardy playing Stanley Dum and Oliver Dee, a toymaker's assistants. They misinterpret an order from Santa Claus and create a set of giant soldiers, who come in handy when the Bogeymen invade Toyland. Brooklyn-born Charlotte Henry, a popular child star of the early 1930s, and the star of the 1933 *Alice in Wonderland* plays Bo Peep. **Directors**—Gus Meins and Charles R. Rogers.   *73 minutes b&w*

BABY BLUE MARINE (1976)

★★

**Jan-Michael Vincent
Glynnis O'Connor**

Vincent plays a World War II bootcamp washout who pretends to be a Marine Ranger and is hailed as a hero in a small Colorado community. It's an overly sentimental story lacking significant impact to carry it through. There are warm and touching moments here and there, but the overall complexion is akin to a TV soap opera. Vincent and O'Connor, the girl who falls in love with him, are appealing and make the most of their parts. **Director**—John Hancock. (PG)
    90 minutes

BABY DOLL (1956)

★★★

**Karl Malden
Eli Wallach
Carroll Baker**

An engrossing screen adaptation of Tennessee Williams's moody comedy of depravity among poor people in the Deep South. Typical Williams plot is enhanced by incisive direction of Elia Kazan. Baker is impressive as the child-bride who is seduced by her husband's acquaintance. Wallach and Malden perform well in striking roles. Also with Mildred Dunnock and Rip Torn. **Academy Award Nominations**—Baker, best actress; Dunnock, best supporting actress; Williams, writing (best screenplay—adapted).
    116 minutes b&w

B

- Baby Face Nelson
- Baby, It's You
- Baby, The Rain Must Fall
- The Bachelor and the Bobbysoxer
- Bachelor in Paradise
- Bachelor Mother
- The Bachelor Party (1957)

BABY FACE NELSON (1957)
★★★

**Mickey Rooney
Cedric Hardwicke
Carolyn Jones**

Mickey Rooney and Leo Gordon show us what big guns they have in Baby Face Nelson.

Rooney's energetic and colorful performance in the title role graces this otherwise low-budget film about the notorious gangster of the Depression era. Lots of action involving bank heists, prison breaks, and shootings. Production looks good despite the skimpy budget. Also with Jack Elam, Chris Dark, Ted de Corsia, and Leo Gordon. **Director**—Don Siegel.
85 minutes b&w

BABY, IT'S YOU (1983)
★★★

**Rosanna Arquette
Vincent Spano**

An absorbing, highly charged, teenage romance by writer-director John (*Return of the Secaucus 7*) Sayles. The emotional story of star-crossed young lovers stumbles over occasional holes in the plot, yet the material is consistently compelling. Above all, the film works as a dazzling showcase for some hip performances by talented newcomers. Arquette displays much realism as the bright Jewish physician's daughter who is courted by the brash, Italian working-class youth, played by Spano. (R) *105 minutes*

BABY, THE RAIN MUST FALL (1964)
 ★★

**Steve McQueen
Lee Remick**

An ex-con returns home to his wife

Lee Remick tries to erase the memories that haunt Steve McQueen's sleep in Baby, The Rain Must Fall.

and daughter, tries to mend his ways but reverts to violence. His behavior leads to re-separation. McQueen and Remick give it a good shot but can't rescue the sentimental and pretentious material, which smacks of Tennessee Williams fare. The film is adapted from Horton Foote's play, *The Traveling Lady*. Cast includes Don Murray, Paul Fix, Josephine Hutchinson, and Ruth White. **Director**—Robert Mulligan. *100 minutes b&w*

THE BACHELOR AND THE BOBBYSOXER (1947)
 ★★★

**Cary Grant
Myrna Loy
Shirley Temple**

Ideal comedy vehicle for Grant, who plays a dashing playboy pursued by an impressionable teenager, played by Temple. Uncomplicated script paves the way for Grant's buoyant and breezy performance. It's a pleasant entertainment from every angle despite the triteness of the material. Also with Rudy Vallee, Ray Collins, and Harry Davenport. **Director**—Irving Reis. *95 minutes b&w*

BACHELOR IN PARADISE (1961)
★★

**Bob Hope
Lana Turner
Janis Paige**

Hope stars in this lightweight comedy about an unmarried columnist who settles in an upper-class community of married couples to write about its inhabitants. The film works only part of the time as romantic interludes inter-

rupt the comic flow. But there are sufficient moments to exploit Hope's talents. Turner is effective in a typical glamorous role. The supporting cast includes Agnes Moorehead, Paula Prentiss, and Jim Hutton. **Director**—Jack Arnold. *109 minutes*

BACHELOR MOTHER (1939)
 ★★★

**Ginger Rogers
David Niven
Charles Coburn**

David Niven and Ginger Rogers try to feed baby by the book in Bachelor Mother.

Heard the one about the woman who finds an abandoned baby, and everyone thinks it's really hers, and although she insists it isn't, she decides to adopt it anyway? This was familiar stuff even way back in '39, but it was freshly played and crisply written and directed. It turned out to be one of the surprise comedy hits of the year, firmly establishing its director Garson Kanin and reinvigorating Roger's faltering career. Niven plays the Good Samaritan son of Ginger's boss, whose innocent efforts to help out the new mama place him under plenty of suspicion. *81 minutes b&w*

THE BACHELOR PARTY (1957)
★★★

**Don Murray
E. G. Marshall
Jack Warden**

Paddy Chayefsky's TV play is expanded for the screen, and the result is an on-target social commentary graced by fine performances. A group of New York bookkeepers throw a party for a colleague prior to his wedding. The event emphasizes the emotional problems of the guests. The

• Bachelor Party (1984) • Back to Bataan
• Background to Danger • The Bad and the Beautiful
• Back Roads • Bad Boys
  • Bad Company

B

superb cast includes Carolyn Jones, Philip Abbott, and Patricia Smith. **Director**—Delbert Mann. **Academy Award Nomination**—Jones, best supporting actress. *93 minutes*

BACHELOR PARTY (1984)

  ★★

**Tom Hanks
Tawny Kitaen
Adrian Zmed**

Patchy, sophomoric comedy built around a wild party for a soon-to-be-married young man, played with moderate charm by Hanks. Aside from Hanks's likable presence, the film features an array of sleazy characters who instigate various vulgar sex escapades laced with the usual assortment of scatological jokes. There's a bit of high-minded philosophizing amidst the degenerate shenanigans: Will the recipient of this bash remain pure and faithful to his bride? **Director**—Neal Israel. *111 minutes*

BACKGROUND TO DANGER (1943)
★★★

**George Raft
Brenda Marshall
Sydney Greenstreet
Peter Lorre**

A thrilling World War II spy story with Raft in Turkey pursuing Nazi agents. Based on Eric Ambler's novel, *Uncommon Danger*, the film provides lots of intrigue and fast-moving action, including a hair-raising car chase. Greenstreet and Lorre stand out in supporting roles as two menacing characters. Also with Turhan Bey and Osa Massen. **Director**—Raoul Walsh. *80 minutes b&w*

BACK ROADS (1981)

  ★★

**Sally Field
Tommy Lee Jones**

Field stars as a likable hooker who falls in love with a drifter-boxer, played by Jones, as they hitchhike from Alabama to California. Both portray cheerful, gritty characters, but the pedestrian

screenplay quickly runs out of energy, and the film winds up on a dead-end street. It's difficult to perceive perky Field as a washed-up streetwalker. In one scene, she falls off a train smack into a mud puddle. (R) **Director**—Martin Ritt. *94 minutes*

BACK TO BATAAN (1945)

  ★★★

**John Wayne
Anthony Quinn**

John Wayne and Beulah Bondi don't relish the thought of going Back to Bataan.

Wayne plays a Marine colonel who leads guerrilla troops on the road to victory in the Philippines against the Japanese. It's a rather routine war adventure, but there is substantial action and excitement, especially for fans of the Duke. Wayne is at his macho best and is helped out nicely by Beulah Bondi, Richard Loo, and Leonard Strong. **Director**—Edward Dmytryk. *97 minutes b&w*

THE BAD AND THE BEAUTIFUL (1952)
★★★★

**Kirk Douglas
Walter Pidgeon
Lana Turner
Dick Powell**

A clever, slam-bang drama about ambitious Hollywood types, related as an inside story. Douglas is superb as a ruthless and ambitious producer who influences the lives and careers of people within his grasp. Other memorable performances from Gloria Grahame, who plays a Southern belle, and Tur-

ner, who plays an actress. There's electrifying entertainment throughout. Also with Barry Sullivan, Gilbert Roland, and Leo G. Carroll. **Director**—Vincente Minnelli. **Academy Awards**—Grahame, best supporting actress; Charles Schnee, writing (screenplay). **Nomination**—Douglas, best actor. *118 minutes b&w*

BAD BOYS (1983)

  ★★

Sean Penn

Sean Penn and Eric Gurry plot their escape from the correctional institution because they're Bad Boys.

Penn stands out with a convincing portrayal of a moody hard-boiled teenager who lands in a foul reform school where he has to fight for survival. Otherwise, this tense, atmospheric film is routine in narrative and fails to develop believable characters. Director Richard Rosenthal (*Halloween II*) employs various manipulative tactics which dwell too long on brutal confrontations. Eric Gurry steals scenes as Penn's crafty bunkmate. (R) *123 minutes*

BAD COMPANY (1972)
★★★

**Barry Brown
Jeff Bridges
John Savage**

David Newman and Robert Benton were the hot new writers on the Hollywood scene when their first film, *Bonnie and Clyde*, became a 1967 sensation. Five years later, the team showed the same sensitivity to youth-turned-criminal in *Bad Company*, which was Benton's first film as a director. It's a poignant account of alienated and

(Continued)

★ STAR PROFILE

B
- Bad Day at Black Rock
- Bad for Each Other
- Badlands
- Bad News Bears
- The Bad Seed

(Continued)

homeless kids robbing their way to the West during the Civil War. Told from the point of view of a well-raised draft dodger, it paints an affecting picture of how easily circumstances can lead the young and the unprotected into an irreversible life of crime. (PG)

93 minutes

BAD DAY AT BLACK ROCK
(1955)
★★★★

Spencer Tracy
Robert Ryan
Dean Jagger

Bully Ernest Borgnine hangs out with his only friend in Bad Day at Black Rock.

A crackling suspense drama about a one-arm stranger, played by Tracy, who encounters hostility in a small Western town, and then discovers the community has something to hide. Director John Sturges expertly builds tension to a smashing climax. There are fine performances from the cast, which also includes Walter Brennan, Ernest Borgnine, and Lee Marvin. **Academy Award Nominations**— Sturges, best director; Tracy, best actor; Millard Kaufman, writing (screenplay). *81 minutes*

BAD FOR EACH OTHER
(1954)
★

Charlton Heston
Lizabeth Scott

Heston plays a high-minded doctor who serves poor coal miners in a Pennsylvania town after a wealthy woman tries to persuade him to cater to the social set. It's mostly dreary soap-opera stuff with the players in awk-ward situations. The film borrows some from *The Citadel.* Dianne Foster and Marjorie Rambeau also star. **Director**—Irving Rapper.

83 minutes b&w

BADLANDS (1973)
★★★

Martin Sheen
Sissy Spacek

A dim-witted teenage girl and her somewhat older boyfriend cross the country murdering people along the way. This skillfully perceived drama, which eventually became a cult film, is based on the actual killing spree of Charles Starkweather and Carol Fugate in the 1950s. Sheen and Spacek are impressive in the lead roles. And it's a successful debut for director Terrence Malick, who also wrote the script. Warren Oates and Ramon Bieri are in supporting roles. (PG)

94 minutes

BAD NEWS BEARS (1976)
★★★

Walter Matthau
Tatum O'Neal

A rather carefree and touching comedy about a down-in-the-mouth Little League baseball team—The Bears— which is rescued by a cigar-chomping, beer-guzzling coach, played by Matthau. O'Neal, in her first film since *Paper Moon,* is the ace pitcher who helps save the day. Director Michael Ritchie (*Smile; The Candidate*) continues to dwell on his favorite social theme of competition and concocts the right mixture of warmth and emotion. Matthau is at his best, and the child actors are appealing. Although this film is about kids, it is aimed primarily at adults. *Bad News* is good news. Also with Vic Morrow and Joyce Van Patten. (PG) *102 minutes*

THE BAD SEED (1956)
★★★

Nancy Kelly
Patty McCormack

An intriguing story about an innocent-looking eight-year-old girl who

CHARLTON HESTON

Charlton Heston is perhaps best known as the idol of epics, portraying an athletic and strong-jawed hero in many classic Hollywood adventures.

Heston was born in 1924 in Evanston, Illinois. He studied drama at Northwestern University and worked at several Chicago radio stations before joining the U.S. Air Force.

After his discharge, Heston appeared on Broadway in Anthony and Cleopatra *and then starred in several classic roles in television specials.*

In 1950, he went to Hollywood and made his film debut in Dark City. *Soon he was portraying such historical figures as Moses, Michelangelo, and El Cid. For the title role in* Ben Hur *(1959), he won the Oscar as best actor.*

Some of Heston's movies include The Greatest Show on Earth *(1952),* The Private War of Major Benson *(1955),* The Ten Commandments *(1956),* The Wreck of the Mary Deare *(1959),* 55 Days at Peking *(1963),* The Greatest Story Ever Told *(1965),* The War Lord *(1965),* Khartoum *(1965),* Planet of the Apes *(1967),* Will Penny *(1968),* Julius Caesar *(1970),* Antony and Cleopatra *(1971),* The Three Musketeers *(1973),* Two Minute Warning *(1976), and* Gray Lady Down *(1978).*

maliciously murders various people, including some of her playmates. The film version faithfully recalls the stage play with Kelly repeating her role as the distraught mother. McCormack is convincing in the title role as the child who inherited evilness. Henry Jones

• Bad Timing/A Sensual   • Ball of Fire
Obsession   • Bambi
• La Balance   • Bananas
• The Balcony   • The Band Wagon

B

and Eileen Heckart are in supporting roles. **Director**—Mervyn Le Roy. **Academy Award Nominations**— Kelly, best actress; Heckart, best supporting actress; McCormack, best supporting actress. *129 minutes b&w*

BAD TIMING/A SENSUAL OBSESSION (1980)

Art Garfunkel
Theresa Russell
Harvey Keitel

Nicolas Roeg (*Don't Look Now*) directs this ponderous drama with a lush style and mystery. But this story of two Americans—played by Garfunkel and Russell—in Vienna who become sexually obsessed with one another is strangely distant and uninvolving. Garfunkel and Russell act as if they learned their lines only minutes before the beginning of each scene. Keitel is miscast as a police inspector. Also with Daniel Massey and Denholm Elliott. (No MPAA rating) *123 minutes*

LA BALANCE (1983)

Philippe Leotard
Nathalie Baye

Stylish, action-packed police thriller played out amid the back alley of the Paris underworld. A street-wise brigade of detectives painstakingly cultivates a network of informers to bring criminals to justice. The acting, pacing, and character development are accomplished with a skill that rivals the best of American gangster film. Leotard, Baye, and Richard Berry turn in credible performances. In French with English titles. **Director**— Bob Swain. (R) *102 minutes*

THE BALCONY (1963)

Shelley Winters
Peter Falk
Lee Grant

Intriguing low-budget screen adaptation of Jean Genet's complex play about a Paris brothel that offers a variety of services for its customers. A lot of vivid symbolism is brought to bear in this film, which deals with sex in an unusual fashion. Winters is nicely cast as the accommodating madam, Grant displays her fine talents as the madam's lesbian friend, and Falk fares well as the police chief. Also with Peter Brocco, Ruby Dee, and Leonard Nimoy. **Director**—Joseph Strick.
86 minutes

BALL OF FIRE (1941)
★★★★

Gary Cooper
Barbara Stanwyck

Cooper's brilliant comedy talent and Howard Hawks's skillful direction make this story of a burlesque dancer (Stanwyck) who seeks shelter with seven professors a delight. The comic situations are keyed to the contrast of the professor (Cooper), who is preparing a book about slang in the English language, and the dancer and her gangster friends, who use slang as their first and only language. Also with Dana Andrews, Dan Duryea, and Gene Krupa. *111 minutes b&w*

BAMBI (1942)
★★★★

This is one of Walt Disney's best cartoon features. It is the story of a fawn that grows to be a magnificent stag. The film, based on the book by Felix Salton, is sometimes overly sentimental, yet the forest animal characters are heartwarming and memorable. Thumper the rabbit is unforgettable. It's a remarkable achievement from a most skillful crew of animators.
72 minutes

BANANAS (1971)
 ★★★

Woody Allen
Louise Lasser

Allen plays a meek factory worker who runs off to South America where he leads a revolution and becomes a hero. It's a typical offering of Allen's humor and unusual comic ideas, with a generous dose of sight gags. Many jokes

In Bananas, *Sylvester Stallone has a bit part as a hood opposite Woody Allen.*

are hilarious, but a few miss the mark. Carlos Montalban and Howard Cosell have supporting parts, and Sylvester Stallone has a minor part as a gangster. **Director**—Allen. (PG) *82 minutes*

THE BAND WAGON (1953)
 ★★★★

Fred Astaire
Cyd Charisse
Jack Buchanan

Cyd Charisse and Fred Astaire raise aerobics to an art form in The Band Wagon.

Toe-tapping musical with the incomparable Astaire in splendid form. The standard simple plot, pegged on problems of producing a Broadway show, makes way for numerous delightful song-and-dance numbers, including "Shine on My Shoes," "Dancing in the Dark," "I Guess I'll Have to Change My Plan," and "Louisiana Hayride." Oscar Levant and Nanette Fabray are also in the cast. **Director**—Vincente Minnelli. *112 minutes*

B
- Bang the Drum Slowly
- The Bank Dick
- Bank Shot
- Barbarella
- Barbarosa
- Barbary Coast
- The Barefoot Contessa
- Barefoot in the Park

BANG THE DRUM SLOWLY
(1973)
 ★★★

Michael Moriarty
Robert De Niro

De Niro and Moriarty stand out in this film version of Mark Harris's novel about a baseball player stricken with leukemia who wants to play another season before he dies. The story is somewhat cliché-strewn, but doesn't become overly sentimental. A few comic moments are handled nicely. Also with Vincent Gardenia and Phil Foster. **Director**—John Hancock. (PG) **Academy Award Nomination**—Gardenia, best supporting actor.
98 minutes

THE BANK DICK (1940)
★★★★

W. C. Fields

W.C. Fields stops a bank robbery and then almost gets arrested for the job himself in The Bank Dick.

Yes indeed. The great Fields is at his funniest. As Egbert Sousé, a sort of nonentity, Fields foils a bank heist. As a reward he's hired as a bank guard. All sorts of hilarious high jinks take place. It's classic humor in the Fields tradition. And there's fine support from Franklin Pangborn, Shemp Howard, and Jack Norton. **Director**—Eddie Cline. *73 minutes b&w*

BANK SHOT
(1974)
★★

George C. Scott
Joanna Cassidy

Unusual comedy about a gang of thieves who pull off a bank robbery by actually stealing the whole building using house-moving gear. There are some funny moments, but the film doesn't deliver enough laughs. Scott stars as the gang leader, and he doesn't quite make it in this role. Sorrell Booke, Clifton James, and Robert Balaban co-star. **Director**—Gower Champion. (PG) *83 minutes*

BARBARELLA (1967)
 ★★

Jane Fonda
John Phillip Law

Fonda stars as an attractive 41st century astronaut in this French-Italian sci-fi based on comic strip fare. Razzle-dazzle special effects perk things up here and there, but the script is nonsense. There are supporting roles by Marcel Marceau, Anita Pallenberg, David Hemmings, and Ugo Tognazzi. **Director**—Roger Vadim. *98 minutes*

BARBAROSA (1982)
 ★★★

Gary Busey
Willie Nelson

Gary Busey and Willie Nelson arrive at a horse sale in Barbarosa.

Australian director Fred Schepisi (*The Chant of Jimmie Blacksmith*) makes his first American film—an intriguing, scrappy, and offbeat western. Even though the genre is somewhat dated, this romantic tale of a legendary desperado (Nelson) and his younger sidekick (Busey) offers a full dose of fresh charm. Nelson and Busey work well side by side. Schepisi has approached an old Hollywood theme from a new angle. (PG) *90 minutes*

BARBARY COAST (1935)
★★★

Edward G. Robinson
Miriam Hopkins
Joel McCrea

Sturdy, two-fisted drama that also has heart and complexity. In San Francisco gold rush days, a drifter (McCrea) and the town tryant (Robinson), who also runs the ever-packed gambling casino, clash over a dance hall queen (Hopkins). Stylishly written by Ben Hecht and Charles MacArthur, tightly directed by Howard Hawks, and evocatively performed by the stars and supporting players Walter Brennan, Brian Donlevy, Frank Craven, Harry Carey, and Donald Meek.
91 minutes b&w

THE BAREFOOT CONTESSA
(1954)
 ★★★

Humphrey Bogart
Ava Gardner
Edmond O'Brien

Bogart, Gardner, and O'Brien star in this handsome tale about the rise and fall of an actress. The film holds ample fascination, yet it is somewhat long-winded. The actors fare well with some clever dialogue. O'Brien stands out as a brassy press agent. **Director**—Joseph L. Mankiewicz. **Academy Award**—O'Brien, best supporting actor. **Nomination**—Mankiewicz, writing (story and screenplay).
128 minutes

BAREFOOT IN THE PARK
(1967)
 ★★★

Robert Redford
Jane Fonda

Neil Simon's Broadway comedy about some newlyweds coping with life in New York City holds up nicely on the screen with plenty of one-liners intact. Redford and Fonda are the charming couple who reside in a fourth-floor walk-up apartment. Mildred Natwick plays the bride's mother. Charles Boyer and Herb Edelman are also in the cast. **Director**—Gene Saks. **Academy**

• The Barkleys of Broadway
• The Barretts of Wimpole Street
• Barry Lyndon
• Basileus Quartet
• Bataan
• Bathing Beauty
• Battle Beyond the Stars

B

Award Nomination—Natwick, best supporting actress.   *109 minutes*

THE BARKLEYS OF BROADWAY (1949)
★★★

**Fred Astaire
Ginger Rogers**

The team of Ginger Rogers and Fred Astaire dance in The Barkleys of Broadway.

Astaire and Rogers star as a bickering song-and-dance couple who split and then make up. She wants to be a serious actress. Their dancing is delightful and some of the songs are memorable. Songs include "They Can't Take That Away From Me" and "You'd Be Hard to Replace." The script, however, is rather flat. Oscar Levant, Billie Burke, and Jacques François play supporting roles. **Director**—Charles Walters.
109 minutes

THE BARRETTS OF WIMPOLE STREET (1934)
★★★

**Norma Shearer
Fredric March
Charles Laughton**

This was the sort of prestige movie that many people believed at least partly exonerated Hollywood for its frequent tawdryness, in much the same way some credit PBS with reclaiming television from the wasteland. Adapted from a literate play about literary people (Elizabeth Barrett and Robert Browning), it is a drama about emotions—the poets' mutual love and Browning's attempt to free the invalid Barrett from her father's spiritual stranglehold. It was meticulously produced by MGM's boy wonder Irving Thalberg and intelligently directed by Sidney Franklin. By current standards, much of the film looks stodgy and predictable, but the stars still attract and its antique veneer still shines. **Academy Award Nominations**—best picture; Shearer, best actress.   *110 minutes b&w*

BARRY LYNDON (1975)
★★★

**Ryan O'Neal
Marisa Berenson
Patrick Magee**

Master director Stanley Kubrick turns to the 18th-century W. M. Thackeray novel for this ponderous costume drama about an Irish rogue who climbs to the top of English aristocratic society. It's an $11-million production—technically well made and beautifully photogaphed. But the energy is slowed to a creep, and emotion is sorely lacking. It's more like taking a stroll through a wax museum than watching a movie. Most moviegoers would probably walk out of this three-hour ordeal more dazed than entertained. O'Neal plays Lyndon, and Berenson plays the beautiful, sad, and wealthy countess he marries. Also with Hardy Kruger, Steven Berkoff, and Gay Hamilton. The production is set against the music of Bach, Handel, Schubert, Mozart, and Vivaldi. (PG) **Academy Award**—cinematography. **Nominations**—best picture; Kubrick, best director; Kubrick, best screenplay (adapted from another medium).
185 minutes

BASILEUS QUARTET (1983)
★★★

**Pierre Malet
Omero Antonutti**

A charming and intriguing little film about a string quartet composed of older musicians that acquires a young virtuoso. The witty screenplay presents a striking contrast between the youthful, charismatic musician and the older members burdened with their peculiar problems. The young man initially recharges the group's zeal but eventually leads them to a downfall. With Hector Alterio. In Italian and French with English titles. **Director**— Fabio Carpi. (No MPAA rating)   *118 minutes*

BATAAN (1943)
★★★

**Robert Taylor
George Murphy
Lloyd Nolan**

A rousing World War II drama about American soldiers who defend a bridge on a Pacific island against the Japanese. The film smacks somewhat of propaganda with cardboard characters, but combat action and suspense are handled nicely. Plot is reminiscent of *The Lost Patrol*. The excellent cast includes Desi Arnaz, Robert Walker, Thomas Mitchell, Lee Bowman, and Barry Nelson. **Director**—Tay Garnett.   *114 minutes b&w*

BATHING BEAUTY (1944)
★★

**Esther Williams
Red Skelton**

A foolish MGM musical comedy built around the aquatic talents of Williams, who plays a swimming instructor. Williams, however, is supported by an attractive cast that makes the most of some gags. Skelton, Basil Rathbone, Keenan Wynn, and Xavier Cugat lend their skills. **Director**—George Sidney.   *101 minutes*

BATTLE BEYOND THE STARS (1980)
★★★

**Richard Thomas
Robert Vaughn**

This intentional rip-off of *Star Wars* is actually superior to that film in some respects. Its sense of humor is less cute and more genuinely funny, for example, and it never takes itself seriously. The plot is taken from *Seven Samurai*: a peaceful planet threatened by invasion hires mercenaries to repel the bad
(Continued)

B
- Battle Circus
- Battle Cry
- Battleground
- Battle of Algiers
- Battle of the Bulge
- Battlestar Galactica
- Battle Stripes
- The Bawdy Adventures of Tom Jones

(Continued)
guys. The half sci-fi, half comic book adventure is replete with strange characters, including five clones wrapped in a beach towel, and the special effects are sometimes so cheap as to be hilarious (as with the spacecraft combat that seems lifted from a video arcade). Thomas and Vaughn star, with George Peppard, John Saxon, and Darleanne Fluegel obviously enjoying their supporting roles. **Director**—Jimmy T. Murakami. (PG)
104 minutes

BATTLE CIRCUS (1952)
★

Humphrey Bogart
June Allyson

Bogart is miscast as a doctor at an Army field hospital in Korea. A flimsy soap-opera script is slim inspiration for the cast. Allyson, who plays a nurse, is the love interest, but there's virtually no chemistry between her and Bogey. Keenan Wynn, Robert Keith, and William Campbell co-star. **Director**—Richard Brooks.
90 minutes b&w

BATTLE CRY (1954)
 ★★★

Van Heflin
Aldo Ray
Tab Hunter
Mona Freeman

Some good performances enhance this screen treatment of Leon Uris's World War II adventure of Marines on their way to war in the Pacific. Romantic subplots are woven in with some action scenes. Dorothy Malone is memorable as an older woman who falls for one of the young warriors. The cast also includes Raymond Massey, Nancy Olson, and James Whitmore. **Director**—Raoul Walsh. *148 minutes*

BATTLEGROUND (1949)
★★★★

Van Johnson
John Hodiak
Ricardo Montalban

This drama about a group of American infantrymen involved in the Battle of the Bulge is a cut above the routine World War II action film. Excellent characterizations, inspired acting, and a compelling script complement the exciting and suspenseful action sequences. Johnson, Hodiak, Montalban, and James Whitmore are fine in memorable roles. William Wellman's efficient direction hits the mark. **Academy Award**—Robert Pirosh, writing (story and screenplay). **Nomination**—Wellman, best director.
118 minutes b&w

BATTLE OF ALGIERS (1966)
★★★

Yacef Saadi
Jean Martin
Brahim Haggiag

Director Gilo Pontecorvo's semi-documentary style makes this depiction of Algeria's struggle for independence from France between 1954 and 1962 look like a succession of thrilling newsreels. Thousands of extras fill the streets of Algiers, with guerrillas confronting French paratroopers hiding out in the winding alleyways of the Casbah. In terse, taut, unsentimental vignettes, the film builds horror and compassion on both sides. It's very much a film of the '60s and has a punchy score by Ennio Morricone.
123 minutes b&w

BATTLE OF THE BULGE
(1965)
 ★★

Henry Fonda
Robert Shaw
Robert Ryan
Dana Andrews
George Montgomery

An overblown World War II action drama concerning the bloody and anxious confrontation with Nazi Panzers in the Ardennes, with Allied troops narrowly escaping defeat. Emphasis is on the action and the booming battle scenes. Script, acting, and character development take a back seat. The cast also includes Pier Angeli, Telly Savalas, Ty Hardin, Charles Bronson, and James MacArthur. **Director**—Ken Annakin. *167 minutes*

BATTLESTAR GALACTICA
(1979)
 ★★

Richard Hatch
Dirk Benedict
Lorne Greene

Disaster strikes—once again—in Battlestar Galactica.

This feature film is based on the short-lived TV sci-fi series that wasn't so hot to begin with. There's really not much improvement in this venture. Survivors of interplanetary warfare embark on a space journey to Earth to establish a new life there. Lavish special effects are notable, but the ragged story holds scant interest. The *Star Wars* format is mimicked right and left, but not its imagination and mysticism. Also with Ray Milland, Lew Ayres, Jane Seymour, and Laurette Spang. **Director**—Richard A. Colla. (PG) *125 minutes*

BATTLE STRIPES
See The Men

THE BAWDY ADVENTURES OF TOM JONES (1976)
★★★

Nicky Henson
Trevor Howard
Terry-Thomas

A British costume musical loosely based on Henry Fielding's novel. It's far removed in quality from the memorable *Tom Jones* film in 1963. Yet this current version is an inoffensive and pleasant romp. The standard "bawdy" antics are portrayed: low necklines, hiked skirts, leaps in and out of occupied beds. Cast also includes Arthur Lowe, Georgia Brown, and Joan Collins. Director Cliff Owen keeps the action going at a fast clip. (R)

94 minutes

BEACH PARTY (1963)
★★

**Frankie Avalon
Annette Funicello
Bob Cummings**

Who could have dreamed when *Beach Party* first surfed into neighborhood theaters two decades ago that it would one day be screened at the Museum of Modern Art? Art it's not, but it is interesting as a sociological phenomenon—a typical, modestly produced American International Pictures production that struck gold in the youth market and spawned sequels. Cummings plays an anthropology professor studying the sexual mores of California youth. Take a dip for the fun of it, though you may not want to stay in very long. Also with Dorothy Malone, Morey Amsterdam (if you can believe), and Harvey Lembeck. **Director**—William Asher. *101 minutes*

THE BEASTMASTER (1982)
 ★★

**Marc Singer
Tanya Roberts**

Hero Marc Singer fights and flexes his muscles simultaneously in The Beastmaster.

A lively but absurd fantasy adventure starring muscular Singer as a sort of medieval Tarzan who rescues a pretty slave girl (Roberts) from the clutches of barbarians. Singer pulls off countless heroic deeds with the help of his animal friends, which include two mischievous ferrets and an old tiger dyed black to look like a panther. Much silly dialogue accompanies the nonstop excitement. Rip Torn gets into the action as a sinister priest with a yen for sacrificing babies and virgins. **Director**—Don Coscarelli. (PG)

120 minutes

THE BEAST WITHIN (1982)
 ★

**Bibi Besch
Paul Clemens**

Paul Clemens tries to suppress an uncontrollable urge to kill in The Beast Within. *Okay, so he isn't trying very hard.*

This blood-drenched horror number faithfully delivers enough gore to delight fans of the genre. A newlywed woman (Besch) is raped by a mysterious creature, and 17 years later her teenage son (Clemens) turns into a vicious beast. Acting and direction are unexceptional, but some applause is due to the makeup people responsible for the amazing metamorphosis of a good-looking youth into a grotesque monster. **Director**—Philippe Mora. (R) *98 minutes*

BEATLEMANIA (1981)
 ★★

Since the Beatles disbanded, four look-and-sound-alikes have been perform-ing Beatles songs in live stage performances. And now, this production is on film along with news clips of protest marches, personalities, and trends of the 1960s. The imitators play the famous rock music with professionalism, but it's still far afield from the magic of the originals. Perhaps it would be more entertaining to recall film segments of the real Paul, John, George, and Ringo at the peak of their careers. **Director**—Joseph Manduke. (PG) *86 minutes*

BEAT STREET (1984)
 ★★

**Guy Davis
Robert Taylor**

The Beat Street *gang (star Rae Dawn Chong is in the center).*

Harry Belafonte co-produced and co-wrote the music for this celebration of three young New York ghetto friends who pursue recognition as break dancer, graffiti artist, and disco DJ. The film is largely an extended talent show, with some exhilarating dance numbers and appealing kids. With so little drama or characterization, however, it can't sustain much emotional involvement. Not enough joy spills off the screen. **Director**—Stan Lathan. (PG) *104 minutes*

BEAT THE DEVIL (1954)
★★

**Humphrey Bogart
Jennifer Jones
Gina Lollobrigida
Peter Lorre**

In the history of off-the-wall cinema,
(Continued)

B
- Beau Brummell
- Beau Geste
- Le Beau Mariage
- The Beautiful Blonde from Bashful Bend
- Beauty and the Beast
- Becket
- Bedazzled

(Continued)
Beat the Devil holds a very special place. It's an anarchic, tongue-in-cheek spoof of caper movies, scripted by Truman Capote and director John Huston, about a bunch of misfits scrambling after some uranium. But if you're not quickly won over, you may find its kookiness coy and cloying. The spirited cast also includes Robert Morley. *92 minutes b&w*

BEAU BRUMMELL (1954)
★★

Stewart Granger
Elizabeth Taylor
Peter Ustinov
Robert Morley

Granger plays a foppish and colorful Englishman who befriends the Prince of Wales, played by Ustinov. This historical production is lavish and exquisitely photographed, but the stilted story is hard to believe. Regardless, the cast—including Taylor, at the height of her beauty—does an admirable job in the costume epic. Morley plays George III. **Director**—Curtis Bernhardt. *111 minutes*

BEAU GESTE (1939)
★★★

Gary Cooper
Ray Milland
Robert Preston

No braver brothers ever defended God, country, and family than the three brothers Geste. Almost as venerable as The Three Musketeers, the Geste boys go on contending with desert varmints and Foreign Legion tyrant Sgt. Makoff (Brian Donlevy) in rerun after revival after replay. Old war-horses never die. Also with Susan Hayward, J. Carrol Naish, Albert Dekker, Broderick Crawford, and Donald O'Connor. **Director**—William Wellman. *120 minutes b&w*

LE BEAU MARIAGE (1982)
★★

Beatrice Romand
André Dussolier

Eric Rohmer presents a mildly amus-ing romantic comedy about a young art student (Romand) who chucks her liberated woman's life-style and embarks on a determined quest to marry "Mr. Right." Rohmer's observations of traditional values are interesting, but the film neglects any significant character development and often lapses into routine talkativeness. The sweet humor produces a few smiles, but some genuine laughter would be welcome. In French with English titles. (PG) *97 minutes*

THE BEAUTIFUL BLONDE FROM BASHFUL BEND (1949)
★★

Betty Grable
Cesar Romero

Preston Sturges made this tongue-in-cheek western about a tough saloon singer, played by Grable, who becomes a schoolteacher in a small town after she mistakenly shoots a sheriff. Nothing bashful about Grable, who seems right for the role, but Sturges doesn't execute the direction with a firm hand, and the film turns out to be rather silly. Hugh Herbert is funny as a doctor with eye problems. Rudy Vallee and Sterling Holloway are also in the cast. *77 minutes*

BEAUTY AND THE BEAST (1946)
 ★★★

Jean Marais
Josette Day
Marcel Andre

Beast loves Beauty but dares not go near her lest he frighten her in Jean Cocteau's version of Beauty and the Beast.

There's enchantment to spare in this adult retelling of the fairy tale about a hostage who is treated so kindly by her monstrous captor that she falls in love with him. The adult in this case is poet/painter/writer/filmmaker Jean Cocteau, who had a way with fanciful cinema. Exquisitely photographed at the Raray palace and park, the richness of it all may get too thick for some tastes, but it's certainly worth seeing. Georges Auric wrote the moody music, and the charismatic cast has the necessary panache. **Director**—Jean Cocteau. *90 minutes b&w*

BECKET (1964)
 ★★★

Richard Burton
Peter O'Toole
John Gielgud

Sumptuous medieval spectacle that's rich with historical drama about the Archbishop of Canterbury, Thomas à Becket, and his relationship with King Henry II. Burton and O'Toole are superb in the key roles and seem to thoroughly enjoy their acting assignments. Some of the energy, however, is drained away by a too-long and, at times, tedious script. The film is based rather faithfully on Jean Anouilh's stage play. Fine supporting performances are given by Gielgud, Donald Wolfit, and Pamela Brown. **Director**—Peter Glenville. **Academy Award**—Edward Anhalt, best screenplay (based on material from another medium); **Nominations**—best picture; Glenville, best director; Burton, best actor; O'Toole, best actor; Gielgud, best supporting actor. *149 minutes*

BEDAZZLED (1967)
 ★★★

Dudley Moore
Peter Cook
Raquel Welch

Moore and Cook wrote this pre-Monty Python comic madness in which Moore plays a modern-day Faust, a short, short-order cook who is granted seven sinful wishes by a modern-day Satan (Cook) in exchange for his soul. Some of these sinful escapades (as with Welch playing Lillian Lust) are

- The Bedford Incident
- Bedknobs and Broomsticks
- Bedlam
- Bedtime for Bonzo
- The Beguiled
- Behold a Pale Horse
- Being There

B

riotously disappointing; others are just disappointing. But the promise the two Britishers had shown on the New York stage a few years earlier was starting to be fulfilled on screen. **Director**—Stanley Donan.

107 minutes

THE BEDFORD INCIDENT
(1965)

 ★★★

Richard Widmark
Sidney Poitier

A suspenseful Cold War drama about a gungho skipper of an American destroyer, played by Widmark, who accidentally fires an atomic weapon while stalking a Soviet submarine in the North Atlantic. Widmark's portrayal of the obsessed naval officer is superb. There's excellent acting, too, from Poitier, who plays a reporter on board; James MacArthur; and Martin Balsam. Tension swirls on board ship in the manner of *The Caine Mutiny*. There's some reference to *Dr. Strangelove*. **Director**—James B. Harris.

102 minutes b&w

BEDKNOBS AND
BROOMSTICKS (1971)

 ★★

Angela Lansbury

Below-par Walt Disney musical about a good-natured witch, played by Lansbury, and some children who help the British war effort in the early 1940s. The film seems disorganized, despite the elaborate production. It's rather pale compared with the popular *Mary Poppins*, which it tries to imitate. Special effects and some of the cartoon sequences are handled well. It also stars David Tomlinson, Sam Jaffe, and Roddy McDowall. **Director**—Robert Stevenson. (G) **Academy Award**— Special visual effects. *117 minutes*

BEDLAM (1946)

 ★★★

Boris Karloff

Excellent atmospheric effects enhance this chilling Val Lewton horror story about the infamous London insane

Boris Karloff is about to receive a fate worse than death: sentencing to the asylum in Bedlam.

asylum that flourished in the 18th century. Anna Lee plays a sane woman who is confined in an effort to expose the miserable conditions. The venerable Karloff is the head of the institution. Also with Billy House, Richard Fraser, and Ian Wolfe. **Director**—Mark Robson. *79 minutes b&w*

BEDTIME FOR BONZO
(1951)

 ★★

Ronald Reagan

Nonsensical comedy with Ronald Reagan as a professor rearing a chimpanzee to prove that environment affects personality. The silly monkeyshines seem to have an appeal for grownups as well as kids. The film did well enough to spawn the sequel, *Bonzo Goes to College*. It should have some added interest since Reagan became President. Diana Lynn and Walter Slezak co-star. **Director**—Fredrick de Cordova. *83 minutes b&w*

THE BEGUILED (1971)

 ★★

Clint Eastwood
Geraldine Page
Elizabeth Hartman

Eastwood stars in this odd Civil War drama about a wounded Union soldier who is brought to a Confederate girls' school where he's to receive nursing care. Eastwood's presence sparks trouble among the sexually starved women. A strong finish with some brutal scenes along the way. Jo Ann Harris and Darleen Carr co-star. **Director**— Don Siegel. (R) *109 minutes*

BEHOLD A PALE HORSE
(1964)

 ★

Gregory Peck
Omar Sharif
Anthony Quinn

Behold a Pale Horse brings Anthony Quinn, Omar Sharif, and Gregory Peck together for a drama set in Spain.

Peck stars in this slow-paced drama about a Spanish renegade who goes into hiding and then returns to trap and kill a sadistic police chief. The film seems to have some class about it, but it eventually loses its way in a web of talky dialogue. Peck and others try their best but can't save the film. Behold a pale movie. **Director**—Fred Zinnemann. *121 minutes b&w*

BEING THERE (1979)

 ★★★

Peter Sellers
Shirley MacLaine
Melvyn Douglas

A droll comic fable about an innocent simpleton, played by Sellers, who is suddenly thrust into the world of

(Continued)

B

- Bell, Book and Candle
- The Bellboy
- The Belle of New York
- A Bell for Adano
- The Bell Jar
- Bells Are Ringing
- The Bells of St. Mary's

(Continued)

wealth and power politics. Sellers sets aside his familiar slapstick style, plays it rather straight-faced, and achieves a remarkably inspired funny performance. It's an insightful and intelligent adaptation of Jerzy Kosinski's novel. Hal Ashby's direction is to the point. But the film is too long, and finally overworks its wisdom-of-innocence theme. (PG) **Academy Award**—Douglas, best supporting actor. **Nomination**—Sellers, best actor.

130 minutes

BELL, BOOK AND CANDLE (1958)

 ★★

**James Stewart
Kim Novak
Jack Lemmon**

Screen version of John Van Druten's play ends up as a routine comedy with Novak miscast as a witch who falls in love with a book publisher, played by Stewart. However, the top cast manages to squeeze some engaging moments from the sentimental material. Ernie Kovacs, Hermione Gingold, and Elsa Lanchester contribute their fine talents. **Director**—Richard Quine.

103 minutes

THE BELLBOY (1960)

★★

Jerry Lewis

Typical Lewis shenanigans with the comedian causing a ruckus at a swank Miami Beach hotel. There's no plot to speak of; just a series of blackout sketches with the usual line of gags. Worthwhile for those who appreciate Lewis; otherwise, it's so much silliness. There are cameos from Milton Berle and Walter Winchell. Alex Gerry and Bob Clayton co-star. **Director**—Lewis.

72 minutes b&w

THE BELLE OF NEW YORK (1952)

★★

**Fred Astaire
Vera-Ellen**

Astaire dances on the ceiling, and that

Fred Astaire teams up with Vera-Ellen in The Belle of New York.

seems to be the high point in this so-so musical set in New York City during the Gay Nineties. The middling plot has Fred as a playboy who flips for a Salvation Army girl, played by Vera-Ellen. There are some comic moments along with the dancing. "Let a Little Love Come In" is included among the songs. Marjorie Main, Keenan Wynn, and Alice Pearce are also in the cast. **Director**—Charles Walters.

82 minutes

A BELL FOR ADANO (1945)

★★★

**John Hodiak
Gene Tierney**

Charming and moving film, based on the John Hersey novel, about American occupation soldiers who earn the respect of citizens in a small Italian town by replacing the local bell. Director Henry King creates a pleasant mood and presents warm characterizations. Hodiak is fine as the American officer in charge of the town. Tierney plays the local female attraction. William Bendix, Richard Conte, and Henry Morgan also star.

103 minutes b&w

THE BELL JAR (1979)

 ★★

**Marilyn Hassett
Julie Harris**

The film is based on the haunting

novel by Sylvia Plath, the extraordinary poet who committed suicide at 30. The screenplay faithfully follows the events of the book, but the movie fails to explore the mystery and the stress that led to the heroine's nervous breakdown. Drama and clarity are badly needed in place of the stifling flatness of Larry Peerce's direction. Anne Jackson, Barbara Barrie, and Robert Klein also star. (R)

107 minutes

BELLS ARE RINGING (1960)

 ★★★

**Judy Holliday
Dean Martin**

Dean Martin and Judy Holliday prove that they are better comedians than dancers in Bells Are Ringing.

Holliday is at her best in this adaptation of the Broadway musical. She plays an answering service operator who listens in on conversations and can't help getting emotionally involved with clients' problems. Martin portrays an anxious playwright who becomes the object of Holliday's affections. Songs by Jule Styne include "Just in Time" and "The Party's Over." Cast includes Fred Clark, Eddie Foy, Jr., and Jean Stapleton. This was Holliday's last film. **Director**—Vincente Minnelli.

126 minutes

THE BELLS OF ST. MARY'S (1945)

 ★★★

**Bing Crosby
Ingrid Bergman**

Crosby and Bergman star in this worthy follow-up to *Going My Way*. Bing is a priest at a Catholic school, and Ingrid is a nun there. The two launch a clever strategy to raise money for a school

• Beloved Infidel
• Beneath the Twelve Mile Reef

• Beneath the Valley of the Ultravixens
• Ben Hur

• Benji
• The Benny Goodman Story
• Berlin Alexanderplatz

B

addition. It's highly entertaining in a sentimental way, with the leads in top form. There's support from Henry Travers, William Gargan, and Ruth Donnelly. **Director**—Leo McCarey. **Academy Award Nominations**—best picture; McCarey, best director; Crosby, best actor; Bergman, best actress. *126 minutes b&w*

BELOVED INFIDEL (1959)
★★

Gregory Peck
Deborah Kerr

True story of F. Scott Fitzgerald's turbulent romance with Hollywood columnist Sheilah Graham lapses into soap-opera sentimentality. Peck is miscast as the famous novelist. Kerr fares better as Graham, who tries to cure Fitzgerald of alcoholism. The film mainly covers Fitzgerald's days in Hollywood in the late 1930s. It may satisfy someone looking for a good cry. Also with Eddie Albert and Philip Ober. **Director**—Henry King. *123 minutes*

BENEATH THE TWELVE MILE REEF (1953)
★★

Robert Wagner
Terry Moore

Wagner and Moore are involved with sponge divers off the Florida coast. The melodramatic plot offers a Romeo-and-Juliet romance and rivalries among the Greek businessmen who abide by their own set of rules. Spectacular scenery and breathtaking underwater photography upstage the acting; a menacing octopus harasses the divers. Gilbert Roland, Peter Graves, J. Carrol Naish, and Richard Boone co-star. **Director**—Robert D. Webb. *102 minutes*

BENEATH THE VALLEY OF THE ULTRAVIXENS (1979)
 ★★

Francesca Natividad
Ann Marie
Ken Kerr

Director Russ Meyer comes on strong once more with his particular brand of

satirical soft-core pornography. As with many of his other film ventures, the story is meager and the women are of mammoth proportions. This frantic farce involves sexual escapades in a small town. Meyer fans won't be let down. (No MPAA rating) *93 minutes*

BEN HUR (1959)
 ★★★

Charlton Heston
Haya Harareet
Jack Hawkins

The manger scene in Ben Hur; *the birth of Jesus profoundly affects Ben Hur's life.*

A spectacular and lavish rendition of Lew Wallace's historical novel about an aristocratic Jew, played by Heston, who is persecuted by the Romans and eventually follows Christ. Heston as Ben Hur is superb in the title role, and the film offers spectacular action sequences and magnificent cinematography. The tone, however, reverts to that of a good guy-bad guy western at times. A high point is the chariot race, with Ben Hur competing against a villain, played convincingly by Stephen Boyd. The outcome is predictable. Other cast members include Hugh Griffith, Martha Scott, and Sam Jaffe. **Directors**—William Wyler and Andrew Marton. **Academy Awards**—best picture; Wyler, best director; Heston, best actor; Griffith, best supporting actor; cinematography (color). **Academy Award Nomination**—Karl Tunberg, best screenplay (based on material from another medium). *217 minutes*

BENJI (1974)
 ★★

Higgins (the dog)
Peter Breck
Edgar Buchanan

Young children should enjoy this film

about a dog who saves two children from kidnappers and winds up as a member of their family. An improbable story but lovable animal characterization. Also with Terry Carter and Christopher Connelly. **Director**—Joe Camp. (G) *89 minutes*

THE BENNY GOODMAN STORY (1955)
★★

Steve Allen
Donna Reed

Allen portrays the famous clarinetist in this sentimental biography that's typical of Hollywood productions. The story traces Goodman's life from his upbringing in Chicago to celebrity status in the world of swing music. Allen is fairly convincing in the title role. And the film is enhanced significantly by the clarinet playing of the real Goodman and guest appearances by big band luminaries Gene Krupa and Harry James. Sammy Davis, Sr., and Martha Tilton lend support. **Director**—Valentine Davies.
117 minutes

BERLIN ALEXANDERPLATZ (1983)
 ★★★★

Gunter Lamprecht
Hanna Schygulla
Barbara Sukowa

Gunter Lamprecht and Barbara Sukowa in the German epic Berlin Alexanderplatz.

Monumental, ambitious film adaptation of Alfred Doblin's epic 1929 novel of post-World War I Berlin. Director Rainer Werner Fassbinder initially slated it as a television series. How-
(Continued)

 Movie is available in Beta and VHS videotape

B

- Best Boy
- Best Defense
- Best Friends
- The Best Little Whorehouse in Texas
- The Best Man
- The Best Things in Life Are Free
- The Best Years of Our Lives

(Continued)
ever, it is a genuine movie that takes more than 15 hours to view. Getting through it is as exhausting as climbing to the top of the Statue of Liberty, but probably more rewarding. The sweeping story centers on an ex-convict who wants to be decent, but whose efforts are sabotaged by his miserable, depressing environment. In German with English titles. (No rating)
15 hours 21 minutes

BEST BOY (1980)
★★★★

This is a documentary film about Philly Wohl, a 52-year-old mentally retarded man who progresses toward self-reliance. But don't be put off by the subject. It's a thrilling, uplifting, intelligent story about love, devotion, and the texture of family life. The style of director Ira Wohl—Philly's cousin—is direct and unembellished without being sentimental. Undoubtedly, this is one of the most extraordinary documentaries ever made. (No MPAA rating) **Academy Award**—Ira Wohl, feature documentary. *110 minutes*

BEST DEFENSE (1984)
 ★

Dudley Moore
Eddie Murphy

Moore and Murphy bruise their acting careers in this dreadful slapstick comedy that spoofs weapons contractors. The effort could use some droll humor and sophistication. Yet we only get a lot of noise and some corny jokes that lead to confusion. Moore is a bumbling engineer who designs a faulty gyro for tank guidance systems. Murphy plays an Army lieutenant who must use the unworkable hardware. **Director**—Willard Huyck. (R)
94 minutes

BEST FRIENDS (1982)
 ★★★

Burt Reynolds
Goldie Hawn

Reynolds and Hawn make a likable

In Best Friends, Burt Reynolds and Goldie Hawn find married life a little shaggy.

pair in this engaging romantic comedy. They are Hollywood screenwriters who finally marry after five years of living together. The low-keyed humor evolves when the couple visits their in-laws and their relationship starts feeling the strain. Savory moments of charm and honesty abound, but the story is rather thin. Jessica Tandy and Barnard Hughes co-star. **Director**—Norman Jewison. (PG)
116 minutes

THE BEST LITTLE WHOREHOUSE IN TEXAS (1982)
 ★★

Burt Reynolds
Dolly Parton

An aim-to-please film version of the hit Broadway musical about a legendary bordello known as The Chicken Ranch. Most of the song and dance numbers could use more bounce, but they do the job nevertheless. There are effective performances from Reynolds as the beleaguered sheriff and Parton as the golden-hearted madam. Charles Durning, playing the issue-dodging governor, stops the show with a sensational dance routine. Dom DeLuise and Jim Nabors also star. **Director**—Colin Higgins. **Academy Award Nomination**—Durning, best supporting actor. (R) *114 minutes*

THE BEST MAN (1964)
★★★★

Henry Fonda
Cliff Robertson
Lee Tracy

High drama on the campaign trail as two presidential aspirants vie for nomination and seek the blessing of

the dying ex-president. Rivals Fonda and Robertson are in top form in this engrossing film version of Gore Vidal's topical play, which gives a perceptive view of the political process. Tracy stands out as the dying former chief executive. Margaret Leighton, Edie Adams, Shelley Berman, Ann Sothern, Richard Arlen, and Mahalia Jackson are in supporting roles. **Director**—Franklin Schaffner. **Academy Award Nomination**—Tracy, best supporting actor. *102 minutes b&w*

THE BEST THINGS IN LIFE ARE FREE (1956)
★★

Ernest Borgnine
Gordon MacRae
Dan Dailey
Sheree North

The careers of songwriters DeSylva, Brown, and Henderson, who flourished in the 1920s, are the basis for this routine Hollywood musical. MacRae, Dailey, and Borgnine portray the Tin Pan Alley trio responsible for such hits as "Good News," "Sonny Boy," and "Birth of the Blues." As to be expected, there's not much plot but the music is enjoyable. Norman Brooks and Murvyn Vye are also in the cast. **Director**—Michael Curtiz. *103 minutes*

THE BEST YEARS OF OUR LIVES (1946)
★★★★

Fredric March
Myrna Loy
Teresa Wright
Dana Andrews

Myrna Loy, Fredric March, and Teresa Wright are three people torn by World War II in The Best Years of Our Lives.

STAR PROFILE

- Betrayal
- Betrayed
- The Betsy
- Between the Lines
- Beverly Hills Cop

B

A powerful, provocative film about three GIs who return from World War II to a small American town and face difficulties adjusting to civilian life. Filmmaking quality prevails throughout with superior acting, no-nonsense direction, and perfect pacing. There are many touching moments—some amusing, some sad—that capture the mood of post-World War II America. Harold Russell, Virginia Mayo, Cathy O'Donnell, Hoagy Carmichael, Gladys George, and Ray Collins also star. **Director**—William Wyler. **Academy Awards**—best picture; Wyler, best director; March, best actor; Russell, best supporting actor; Robert E. Sherwood, writing (screenplay).

172 minutes b&w

BETRAYAL (1983)
★★★

**Ben Kingsley
Jeremy Irons
Patricia Hodge**

This is Harold Pinter's film version of his intriguing play about infidelity. It's loaded with subtleties, revealing observations, and beautiful moments of acting. The absorbing tale, set in London, unfolds in reverse time to expose a trail of deceptions. Despite its poignancy, the production cannot fully overcome its stagy aspects. Kingsley is remarkable as the husband whose response to adultery is unique and ultimately effective. Irons and Hodge also are superb as the adulterous lovers. **Director**—David Jones. (R)

95 minutes

BETRAYED (1954)
★★

**Clark Gable
Victor Mature
Lana Turner**

Plodding and trumped-up spy yarn about a Dutch intelligence man who discovers that a trusted underground fighter is a turncoat. However, a top-notch cast occasionally spices up the melodramatics. Gable and Mature supply the macho images while Turner provides the glamour. Also with Louis Calhern, Wilfrid Hyde-White, and Ian Carmichael. **Director**—Gottfried Reinhardt.

108 minutes

THE BETSY (1978)
★★

**Laurence Olivier
Robert Duvall
Katharine Ross
Tommy Lee Jones**

This melodramatic saga of intrigue, sex, and power among the upper crust of the auto industry is like a '60 Cadillac—plush, but too much flash and too hard to handle. The classy cast, which also includes Jane Alexander and Lesley-Anne Down, turns out some neat performances. The unwieldy story line, based on the Harold Robbins novel, is a problem with too many twists and a lot of frivolous gloss. The dialogue is loaded with howlers. **Director**—Daniel Petrie. (R)

125 minutes

BETWEEN THE LINES (1977)
★

**John Heard
Jill Eikenberry**

Joan Micklin Silver, who did rather well directing *Hester Street*, disappoints with this shallow film about a successful underground Boston newspaper soon to be taken over by an establishment publisher. The story idea is interesting and inspired, but the loose script rambles with scant impact, and the characters seem lifeless. It's hard to believe these de-radicalized youths were once energetic and maverick journalists. Hopefully the earnest, fresh-faced young actors here may be destined for more important assignments and stardom. Also with Lewis Stadlen and Jeff Goldblum. (R)

101 minutes

BEVERLY HILLS COP (1984)
★★★

Eddie Murphy

Eddie Murphy, as a brash, street-wise, Detroit detective, shakes up posh Beverly Hills in his quest to find the killer of a friend. Murphy engagingly turns on his cool charm, pulls off numerous impersonations and teaches the local by-the-book cops some effective police tactics. The bloody ending is heavy-handed, but there are ample laughs and thrills for thorough enjoyment—Murphy style. **Director**—Martin Brest. (R) *105 minutes*

WARREN BEATTY

Born Warren Beaty in Richmond, Virginia, in 1937, Beatty first came to the attention of critics with his acclaimed Broadway debut in William Inge's play, A Loss of Roses.

His first film as an actor was Splendor in the Grass *(1961), directed by Elia Kazan. This was followed by José Quintero's* The Roman Spring of Mrs. Stone *(1961), John Frankenheimer's* All Fall Down *(1962), Robert Rossen's* Lilith *(1965), and Arthur Penn's* Mickey One *(1965). Penn also directed Beatty's production of* Bonnie and Clyde *(1967). This was followed by George Stevens's* The Only Game In Town *(1969), Robert Altman's* McCabe and Mrs. Miller *(1971), Richard Brooks's* $ *(1972), and Alan J. Pakula's* The Parallax View *(1974). Beatty also appeared in* Shampoo *(1975), which he produced and co-wrote with Robert Towne. After an appearance in Mike Nichols's* The Fortune *(1975), Beatty produced, co-wrote, co-directed, and starred in the box-office hit* Heaven Can Wait *(1978). He then produced, directed, wrote, and starred in* Reds *(1981).*

During his career, Beatty has received more than 10 Academy Award nominations, including two for best screenplay, three for best actor, two for directing, and three as the producer of the best picture.

He is the younger brother of actress Shirley MacLaine.

B
- Beyond a Reasonable Doubt
- Beyond Reasonable Doubt
- Beyond the Forest
- Beyond the Limit
- Beyond the Poseidon Adventure
- Beyond the Reef
- Beyond the Valley of the Dolls
- Bhowani Junction

BEYOND A REASONABLE DOUBT (1956)

★★★

Dana Andrews
Joan Fontaine
Sidney Blackmer

Dana Andrews and Barbara Nichols live it up in Beyond a Reasonable Doubt.

Just supposing someone wanted to prove the injustice of capital punishment. And supposing he had himself framed for a murder he didn't commit, to prove he could be wrongly condemned to death? That's the intriguing premise of *Beyond a Reasonable Doubt*, skillfully developed on screen by director Fritz Lang. The low budget shows and not every plot twist works, but this last film Lang made in America is still haunting.

80 minutes b&w

BEYOND REASONABLE DOUBT (1983)

 ★★

David Hemmings

From New Zealand, a somewhat rickety courtroom drama involving the complicated trial of a man accused of a double killing. Much of the plot, based on an actual murder case, centers on a gungho detective who goes overboard to solve the case. Acting and direction are mainly humdrum, although Hemmings often is impressive as the zealous police inspector. Also with John Hargreaves and Tony Barry. **Director**—John Laing. (No MPAA rating)
111 minutes

BEYOND THE FOREST (1949)

★

Bette Davis
Joseph Cotten

An absurd, hysterical murder mystery with Davis overacting and adding to the muddle of the screenplay. Davis, who plays the wife of a small-town doctor, has an affair with her wealthy neighbor, bungles a suicide attempt after murdering a witness, and then dies of a disease. The rest of the cast also is regrettably lost in the woods. Cotten plays the doctor; David Brian is the neighbor. Ruth Roman, Minor Watson, and Dona Drake also star. **Director**—King Vidor.

96 minutes b&w

BEYOND THE LIMIT (1983)

 ★

Richard Gere
Michael Caine

Much creative talent is wasted in this unfocused drama about Argentinean doctor Gere having an affair with an ex-prostitute (Elpidia Carrillo), who is the wife of British consul Caine. The rambling plot also has Gere searching for his long-lost father and mixed up with political rebels. The whole enterprise does no justice to Graham Greene's novel, "The Honorary Consul." Gere looks utterly puzzled throughout as the film tries to be torrid, but only manages to be horrid. **Director**—John Mackenzie. (R)
103 minutes

BEYOND THE POSEIDON ADVENTURE (1979)

★

Michael Caine
Sally Field
Telly Savalas
Peter Boyle

Irwin Allen takes us back to the overturned S.S. *Poseidon* for Chapter II of this disaster story. Here we find an all-star cast rummaging around the dark upside-down innards of the stricken ocean liner looking for loot, dodging bullets, and mumbling idiotic dialogue. Caine, Field, Savalas, and other

familiar performers have their acting reputations soaked to the skin. The audience may want to escape long before the players make it to the surface. Also with Jack Warden, Shirley Knight, Slim Pickens, Shirley Jones, and Karl Malden; what will they do? **Director**—Allen. (PG)   *122 minutes*

BEYOND THE REEF (1981)

★★

Dayton Káne
Maren Jensen

Raffaella DeLaurentiis (Dino's daughter) produced this innocent boy-and-his-shark movie using some of the scenic locations involved with *Hurricane*. Káne, the male star of *Hurricane*, plays a native lad who woos a beautiful native girl, played by Jensen, and raises a 16-foot tiger shark who knows enough to attack only the bad guys. The acting and script are limited, but the underwater photography is dazzling. **Director**—Frank C. Clark. (PG)   *91 minutes*

BEYOND THE VALLEY OF THE DOLLS (1970)

 ★

Dolly Read
Cynthia Myers
Marcia McBroom

Russ Meyer, the majordomo of soft-core pornography, serves up some exploitation fare with a bevy of young girls chosen more for their dimensions than their acting talents. The plot (from a script by film critic Roger Ebert) concerns an all-girl rock band trying to make it big in Hollywood. But this is merely incidental to the parade of bodies. You may find a laugh or two amid the frenzy. The film has no connection with Jacqueline Susann's novel. Also with Edy Williams. **Director**—Meyer. (X)   *109 minutes*

BHOWANI JUNCTION (1955)

★★★

Ava Gardner
Stewart Granger

A fairly faithful rendering of John Masters's novel about a beautiful Anglo-Indian girl involved in romance and

Stewart Granger—with clipboard—meets Ava Gardner in Bhowani Junction.

intrigue during the waning days of British rule in India. Gardner is convincing as the half-caste beauty who is torn between her love for an Englishman, played by Granger, and loyalty to her family. Impressive photography of the Pakistani locations enhance the drama. Bill Travers and Francis Matthews also star. **Director**—George Cukor.

110 minutes

THE BIG BRAWL (1980)
★★★

Jackie Chan

This martial-arts film is a step above the usual; it has a blend of humor, a decent script, and well-executed kung fu action. Chan, in his first American movie, plays the son of a Chicago restaurateur who subdues some local gangster bullies and then wins a free-for-all in Texas. The spunky and charming Chan trains hard for the big contest and finally wins the day in a flurry of kicks and chops against men three times his size. It's sort of the *Rocky* of chop-socky. **Director**—Robert Clouse. (R) *95 minutes*

THE BIG BUS (1976)

★

Joseph Bologna
Stockard Channing

This film is about a nuclear-powered bus that is a cross between a 747 jetliner and the Queen Elizabeth II. It's also a put-on of Hollywood disaster movies overstuffed with nonstop corny gags. A lot of frantic-looking passengers and crew members act silly as the bus makes its maiden

express trip from New York to Denver. Most of the audience may want to get off somewhere east of the Mississippi. Also with John Beck, Ned Beatty, José Ferrer, Larry Hagman, Sally Kellerman, Richard Mulligan, and Lynn Redgrave. **Director**—James Frawley. (PG) *85 minutes*

THE BIG CARNIVAL
See Ace in the Hole

THE BIG CHILL (1983)

★★

William Hurt
Kevin Kline
Glenn Close

Former college idealists of the '60s, now complacent and middle-class, gather to unload upon one another at the funeral of a comrade who has inexplicably committed suicide (maybe he knew what was coming). The ensemble acting by Hurt, Kline, Close, and the others is consistently admirable. Yet the hollow story merely goes in circles and ends nowhere. There's plenty of talk and self-pity but meager impact and insight. Tom Berenger and JoBeth Williams give support, and

JoBeth Williams, Kevin Kline, William Hurt, and Glenn Close are among the old college friends who meet for a weekend reunion in The Big Chill.

director/co-writer Lawrence Kasdan needs it. (R) **Academy Award Nominations**—best picture; Close, best supporting actress; Kasdan and Barbara Benedek, best original screenplay.
103 minutes

THE BIG CLOCK (1947)
★★★

Ray Milland
Charles Laughton

A ruthless pulp magazine publisher, played by Laughton, murders his mistress, and his top crime reporter, Milland, is assigned to solve the case. It's a suspenseful drama with ace talent. Laughton isn't quite up to par, while Milland is convincing as the writer with a sticky task on hand. Maureen O'Sullivan, Rita Johnson, and Elsa Lanchester round out the cast. **Director**—John Farrow. *95 minutes b&w*

THE BIG COUNTRY (1958)
★★★

Gregory Peck
Jean Simmons
Charlton Heston

Director William Wyler's overblown but entertaining spectacle western features a lively cast at top form. Peck plays a sailor who returns to settle down on the land and winds up in the middle of a bitter feud over water rights. Heston stands out as a mean-spirited cattle foreman, and Burl Ives is impeccably cast as a gruff patriarch of one of the feuding families. There are subtle references to the Cold War. Carroll Baker, Charles Bickford, and Chuck Connors have supporting roles. **Academy Award**—Ives, best supporting actor. *166 minutes*

THE BIG FIX (1978)
★★★

Richard Dreyfuss
Susan Anspach

Dreyfuss is perfectly cast as a small-time, contemporary gumshoe with a background in 1960s radical politics in this engaging comedy-thriller. The film takes an interesting and intelli-
(Continued)

B

- Bigger Than Life
- The Big Heat
- The Big Land
- Big Red
- The Big Red One
- The Big Shot
- The Big Sky

(Continued)

gent look at the tumultuous decade. The plot, unfortunately, is so complex you may need the services of a detective to figure it out. Dreyfuss's performance is more subdued than usual, and his unorthodox private-eye character is memorable. There's fine support from Anspach, Bonnie Bedelia, John Lithgow, and F. Murray Abraham. **Director**—Jeremy Paul Kagan. (PG) *108 minutes*

BIGGER THAN LIFE (1956)
★★★

**James Mason
Barbara Rush
Walter Matthau**

Another film that should be seen in a theatre in its original widescreen ratio (utilized so effectively by director Nicholas Ray). But even as is, this adaptation of the Berton Roueche *New Yorker* story about a man hooked on cortisone, still packs a wallop, and represents the first film effort to ponder the dark side of miracle drugs. Producer Mason sensitively portrays the tormented schoolteacher, whose overdoses lead to unpredictable and violent mood swings that threaten his family and himself. *95 minutes*

THE BIG HEAT (1953)
★★★

**Glenn Ford
Gloria Grahame
Lee Marvin**

Gloria Grahame raises Lee Marvin's temperature in The Big Heat.

Ex-cop seeks to avenge the murder of his wife by the mob. Ford gets fine acting support from Grahame, who plays the bad girl who decides to help fight the mob. Marvin as a sadistic killer adds to the harsh realism of the film, and when the movie was released some critics objected to the violent scene in which boiling coffee is hurled into Grahame's face. **Director**—Fritz Lang. *90 minutes b&w*

THE BIG LAND (1957)
★★

**Alan Ladd
Virginia Mayo
Edmond O'Brien**

Edmond O'Brien and Alan Ladd in The Big Land, *about building a rail link to Texas.*

Cattlemen and wheat farmers join to promote the building of a rail link to Texas. It's a somewhat ho-hum western with a few good production values. The cast, headed by Ladd, Mayo, and O'Brien, performs well enough despite the hackneyed material. The film is based on the novel *Buffalo Grass* by Frank Gruber. **Director**—Gordon Douglas. *92 minutes*

BIG RED (1962)
★★

**Walter Pidgeon
Gilles Payant**

Run-of-the-mill boy-and-dog story from the Disney studios that borrows somewhat from the "Lassie, Come Home" episodes. Payant is the lad who becomes attached to an Irish setter

owned by a wealthy man, played by Pidgeon. The dog eventually saves the boy from an attacking mountain lion. Nice diversion for the kids; nothing special for adults. The film was photographed in the magnificent outdoors of Quebec. **Director**—Norman Tokar. *89 minutes*

THE BIG RED ONE (1980)
★★

**Lee Marvin
Mark Hamill**

Samuel Fuller's intimate story of soldiers who fought with the First Infantry Division in World War II comes off as a glossed-over tour of famous battlefields. Marvin leads an infantry squad, which includes Hamill and Robert Carradine, from the North African deserts to Czechoslovakia. Part of the problem is the casting of Marvin, who looks like the oldest sergeant in the Army and hardly the type to lead young soldiers into battle. If you are expecting something on the order of *Battleground* or *Sands of Iwo Jima*, forget it. **Director**—Fuller. (PG) *113 minutes*

THE BIG SHOT (1942)
★★

**Humphrey Bogart
Irene Manning**

Bogart plays his familiar role as a hardened criminal who is framed for a robbery and then breaks out of the big house. Bogey's tough-guy character comes over well, but the routine plot is B-movie fare. Also with Susan Peters, Richard Travis, Donald Crisp, Arthur Kennedy, and Howard da Silva in supporting roles. **Director**—Lewis Seiler. *82 minutes b&w*

THE BIG SKY (1952)
★★★

**Kirk Douglas
Arthur Hunnicutt
Elizabeth Threatt**

Douglas is a Kentucky fur trapper who leads an expedition to establish a trading post on the Missouri River in 1830. All sorts of trouble ensues along the

- The Big Sleep (1946)
- The Big Sleep (1978)
- Big Wednesday
- Billy Budd
- Billy Jack
- Billy Liar

B

way as the party encounters Indians. The cast performs well, but the overloaded melodrama lapses after a while. The film is faithfully adapted from an historical novel by A. B. Guthrie, Jr. Dewey Martin and Buddy Baer also star. **Director**—Howard Hawks.

122 minutes b&w

THE BIG SLEEP (1946)
★★★★

Humphrey Bogart
Lauren Bacall

Humphrey Bogart and Lauren Bacall play games on the phone in The Big Sleep.

Bogart and Bacall make the sparks fly in this saucy private-eye drama based on Raymond Chandler's novel. The plot is complex, but Bogey and Baby make things click with crisp acting, spicy dialogue, and generous doses of suspense and excitement. Bogart is gumshoe Philip Marlowe, who's hired to keep tabs on the freewheeling daughter of a wealthy man. Before long, he's confronted with several mysterious murders. Lots of smoky atmosphere along the way. Also with Dorothy Malone, Martha Vickers, Regis Toomey, and Elisha Cook, Jr. **Director**—Howard Hawks.

114 minutes b&w

THE BIG SLEEP (1978)
★★

Robert Mitchum
Sarah Miles

This lukewarm remake of Raymond Chandler's classic gumshoe adventure, which originally starred Bogart and Bacall, is transplanted to contemporary London, where it loses its effective smoky atmosphere of Los Angeles in the '40s. This time Mitchum is private-eye Philip Marlowe, but he's no match for Bogart. Miles, who co-stars, is no Lauren Bacall either. The Bogey version of this caper remains the undisputed legend. Also stars Candy Clark, Richard Boone, James Stewart, John Mills, and Joan Collins. **Director**—Michael Winner. (R)

100 minutes

BIG WEDNESDAY (1978)
★

Jan-Michael Vincent
William Katt
Gary Busey

John Milius's ambitious tribute to surfing turned out all wet. The limp script follows the lives of three California surfing pals from 1962 to 1974. Vincent, Katt, and Busey—all capable performers—play the beach buddy roles with unusual stiffness. The tone throughout is one of muddled and uneventful seriousness. Also with Lee Purcell, Patti D'Arbanville, and Barbara Hale. **Director**—Milius. (PG)

120 minutes

BILLY BUDD (1962)
★★★

Peter Ustinov
Robert Ryan
Terence Stamp
Melvyn Douglas

Peter Ustinov portrays a sympathetic captain in Herman Melville's Billy Budd.

Ustinov directed and stars in this handsome film version of the Herman Melville classic allegory of good and evil, set in the 18th century. Young Billy goes to sea aboard a British man-of-war, where he kills a cruel officer and then faces execution for the deed. Ustinov stands out as a sympathetic captain, and Ryan is excellent as the evil master-at-arms. The screenplay, however, is somewhat dull. Also with Paul Rogers, David McCallum, and John Neville. **Academy Award Nomination**—Stamp, best supporting actor.

125 minutes b&w

BILLY JACK (1971)
★★★

Tom Laughlin
Delores Taylor

Tom Laughlin plays Billy Jack, a half-breed Indian who talks peace and busts jaws.

Laughlin plays the title role in this stylish and uplifting drama, which glorifies the counterculture of the '60s and '70s. He's effective as the half-breed Indian who fought in Vietnam and has returned to Arizona as a free-spirit champion of wildlife. Conflicts develop when local bigots interfere with his causes. Taylor, Laughlin's real-life wife, is excellent as principal of a "freedom school." Also with Bert Freed, Clark Howat, and Julie Webb. Laughlin directed under the pseudonym T. C. Frank. (PG) *113 minutes*

BILLY LIAR (1963)
★★

Tom Courtenay
Julie Christie

The fantasies of the middle-class British in the middle '60s. Tom Courtenay has some fun as an employee of a

(Continued)

B

- The Bingo Long Traveling All-Stars and Motor Kings
- Birdman of Alcatraz
- Bird of Paradise
- The Birds
- Birdy
- The Birth of the Blues

(Continued)

funeral parlor who daydreams himself into a more glamorous existence. The film's success extended the cinematic British invasion by advancing the careers of Courtenay, Christie, and director John Schlesinger. Both its exuberance and social commentary seem somewhat forced now; the Walter Mitty update has become dated.

96 minutes b&w

THE BINGO LONG TRAVELING ALL-STARS AND MOTOR KINGS (1976)

 ★★★

**Billy Dee Williams
James Earl Jones
Richard Pryor**

A high-spirited and highly entertaining comedy about a renegade black baseball team that barnstorms through mid-America in 1939, when black ballplayers were barred from the white-controlled leagues. The film also has its dramatic and touching moments. The almost-all-black cast is superb. It's headed by Williams and Jones, who play a pair of razzle-dazzle ballplayers. However, character development is weak in some cases. There is a clear portrayal of how the All-Stars must resort to clowning as a means of survival in those pre-Jackie Robinson days. **Director**—John Badham. (PG)

110 minutes

BIRDMAN OF ALCATRAZ (1962)

 ★★★★

**Burt Lancaster
Karl Malden
Thelma Ritter
Edmond O'Brien**

Lancaster is at his best in the title role of this engrossing biography of Robert Stroud, the celebrated convict who became a world authority on birds. Lancaster's measured delivery and John Frankenheimer's efficient direction perfectly illuminate Stroud's perplexing personality. The film also expertly explores the harshness and monotony of prison life. Malden stands out as the warden. Also with Telly Savalas, Betty Field, Neville Brand, and Hugh Marlowe. **Academy**

Burt Lancaster grows old in the Birdman of Alcatraz.

Award Nominations—Lancaster, best actor; Savalas, best supporting actor; Ritter, best supporting actress; Burnett Guffey, cinematography (black and white).

148 minutes b&w

BIRD OF PARADISE (1951)

★★

**Louis Jourdan
Jeff Chandler
Debra Paget**

A standard South Sea Island tale about a European man who marries a beautiful native girl. The wedding angers the gods, so a virgin (what else?) is sacrificed to quiet an exploding volcano. The film, a remake of a 1932 version, is a bit pompous in tone, yet the exotic and romantic atmosphere remains intact. Jourdan, Chandler, and Paget do an adequate job in the key roles. Also with Maurice Schwartz, Everett Sloane, and Jack Elam. **Director**—Delmar Daves.

100 minutes

THE BIRDS (1963)

 ★★★

**Rod Taylor
Tippi Hedren
Suzanne Pleshette
Jessica Tandy**

Director Alfred Hitchcock, the wizard of suspense, digs into his bag of tricks for this gripping thriller about a small California coastal town that comes

In The Birds, *Rod Taylor saves Veronica Cartwright from the infested house.*

under attack by thousands of birds. Taylor, Hedren, and Pleshette are adequate in the principal roles, but they fade into the background when upstaged by the onslaught of special effects and offbeat shock tactics devised by the master. The incidental plot is merely a vehicle. *119 minutes*

BIRDY (1984)

★★★★

**Matthew Modine
Nicholas Cage**

Sensitive, intriguing, film adaptation of William Wharton's offbeat psychological novel. It's played to perfection by Matthew Modine and Nicholas Cage as two working-class youths growing up in South Philadelphia. Modine, in the title role, skillfully portrays the eccentric teenager whose obsession with birds serves as an escape from his squalid environment. Cage also is impressive as Birdy's loyal friend. Cheers to director Alan Parker for his success with such challenging material. (R) *120 minutes*

THE BIRTH OF THE BLUES (1941)

★★★

**Bing Crosby
Brian Donlevy**

Crosby stars as a trumpet player who establishes a jazz band in New Orleans. The rather trivial plot is upheld by plenty of good jazz music, which makes the film worthwhile. Some of the classic tunes include "St. Louis Blues," "St. James Infirmary," and "Melancholy Baby." Bing gets support from Donlevy, Carolyn Lee, Eddie (Rochester) Anderson, Mary Martin, and jazz great Jack Teagarden. **Director**—Victor Schertzinger.

85 minutes b&w

THE BISHOP'S WIFE (1947)
 ★★★

Cary Grant
David Niven
Loretta Young

A warm, thoroughly diverting Christmas fantasy from Robert Nathan, author of *Portrait of Jennie*. Niven plays a bishop who's so obsessed with the building of a new cathedral that he neglects his wife (Young) and parish. He prays for guidance—and gets a debonair angel named Dudley (Grant), who tries to set everything straight. This best picture Oscar-nominee is richly photographed by the great Gregg Toland and winningly played by the three stars and a sparkling supporting cast, including Edmund Gwenn, Monty Woolley, James Gleason, and Elsa Lanchester. **Director**—Henry Koster. **Academy Award Nominations**—best picture; Koster, best director. *108 minutes b&w*

BITE THE BULLET (1975)
 ★★

Gene Hackman
Candice Bergen
James Coburn

Gene Hackman and Jan-Michael Vincent fight for the right to Bite the Bullet.

Who will win the 700-mile horse race through desert and other treacherous terrain of the Southwest? There's plenty of breathtaking scenery, but the story is loaded with platitudes and clichés. Also with Ben Johnson, Ian Bannen, Jan-Michael Vincent, and Paul Stewart. **Director**—Richard Brooks. (PG) *131 minutes*

BITTERSWEET LOVE (1977)
 ★★

Lana Turner
Robert Lansing
Celeste Holm
Robert Alda

An elegant-looking soapy tale of woe about a boy and girl who marry and later find out they're related. Scene after scene drips with emotion in dealing with the incestuous relationship, but the characters are too shallow to carry any dramatic charge. Turner, splendidly coiffed and dressed, is the girl's mother. Also stars Meredith Baxter Birney and Scott Hylands as the young anguished couple. **Director**—David Miller. (PG) *92 minutes*

BLACK AND WHITE IN COLOR (1977)
★★★★

Jean Carmet
Jacques Dufilho
Catherine Rouvel

A witty, intelligent satire attacking the arrogant human condition that leads to war. Droll and subtle performances by an excellent cast complement a moving screenplay about a bored group of Frenchmen in colonial West Africa, who fight a mini-war against a neighboring German garrison. The film was shot entirely in the Ivory Coast. In French with English titles. **Director**—Jean-Jacques Annaud. (PG) **Academy Award**—best foreign-language film (1976). *90 minutes*

BLACKBEARD'S GHOST (1967)
 ★★

Peter Ustinov
Dean Jones
Suzanne Pleshette

Ustinov stars in this slapstick Walt

ALEC GUINNESS

Sir Alec Guinness is a versatile stage actor who became a spectacular screen star. He performed Shakespeare on stage and starred as Disraeli, the Pope, Hitler, King Charles I, and Obi-Wan Kenobi in Star Wars (1977) in films. He also excelled in comedy, with superbly droll performances in such movies as The Lavender Hill Mob (1951) and The Captain's Paradise (1952).

Guinness was born in London in 1914. He started out as an advertising copywriter before studying acting. In the '30s, he was in various stage productions with the Old Vic; in 1941, he joined the British Navy, in which he served as an officer.

After World War II, Guinness began a serious film career. He soon became proficient in playing multiple roles in a single movie. In Kind Hearts and Coronets (1949), he amazed audiences by playing eight roles, but it was as a stiff-upper-lipped British officer in The Bridge on the River Kwai (1957) that he won an Oscar for best actor. In 1959, Queen Elizabeth II knighted Guinness for his outstanding work on the stage and in movies.

Some of his other memorable films include Great Expectations (1946), Oliver Twist (1948), The Mudlark (1950), The Man in the White Suit (1951), Our Man in Havana (1959), Lawrence of Arabia (1962), Doctor Zhivago (1966), The Comedians (1967), Brother Sun, Sister Moon (1973), and A Passage to India (1984).

Disney comedy, as the ghost of the infamous pirate who returns to prevent a hotel from being converted into a gambling casino. The film is rather overbearing, but the cast works hard *(Continued)*

 Movie is available in Beta and VHS videotape

B

- Blackbeard the Pirate
- The Black Bird
- The Blackboard Jungle
- The Black Cat
- The Black Hole
- The Black Marble
- Black Narcissus

(Continued)
to bring forth a few engaging moments. Elsa Lanchester and Richard Deacon co-star. **Director**—Robert Stevenson. *107 minutes*

BLACKBEARD THE PIRATE
(1952)
★★★

Robert Newton
Linda Darnell

Newton growls, scowls, and hams it up with glee as the 17th-century buccaneer out for more blood and treasure. Clichés abound, yet it's good fun all the way, with the spirited cast giving their all. Beautiful Darnell is aboard, all decked out in a satin gown, playing the captive of the rascally pirate. Keith Andes, William Bendix, Irene Ryan, and Richard Egan have supporting roles. **Director**—Raoul Walsh. *99 minutes*

THE BLACK BIRD (1975)
★

George Segal
Stephane Audran
Lee Patrick
Elisha Cook, Jr.

The Bogart classic of some 40 years ago, *The Maltese Falcon*, is back as a supposedly comic sequel. Segal plays Sam Spade, Jr., who's stuck with his father's private-eye business and involved in another struggle over the mysterious falcon statuette he finds stashed away in a file drawer. There are a few bright moments at the beginning, but the wobbly and narrow plot fails to develop. Characters are left milling about and aimlessly bumping into one another. Bogie, where are you? Also stars Lionel Stander, John Abbott, and Signe Hasso; includes Patrick and Cook, who were in the original film. **Director**—David Giler. (PG) *98 minutes*

THE BLACKBOARD JUNGLE
(1955)
★★★★

Glenn Ford
Anne Francis
Louis Calhern

Ford gives a credible and engaging performance as a young teacher who gets through to some tough kids in a New York City high school. The poignant film, adapted from Evan Hunter's novel, is an honest and straightforward portrayal of urban education. Sidney Poitier is outstanding as a rebellious student with repressed talent and sensitivity. Bill Haley and the Comets fill in the background with "Rock Around the Clock." The film is biting, penetrating entertainment, with top acting and direction. Also with Richard Kiley and Vic Morrow. **Director**—Richard Brooks. **Academy Award Nominations**—Brooks, writing (screenplay); Russell Harlan, cinematography (black and white). *101 minutes b&w*

THE BLACK CAT (1934)
★

Boris Karloff
Bela Lugosi

Boris Karloff plays a master of satanic arts in The Black Cat.

There is little to purr about in this horror movie, although fans of Karloff and Lugosi probably won't mind. Lugosi plays a doctor seeking revenge against devil-worshipping architect Karloff. The plot is fascinating, but the dialogue creaks, and even a castle blown to dust is tame by contemporary high-tech movie standards. Also with David Manners, Lucille Lund, Egon Brecher, and Jacqueline Wells. **Director**—Edgar G. Ulmer. *65 minutes b&w*

THE BLACK HOLE (1979)

★★

Maximilian Schell
Anthony Perkins
Robert Forster
Joseph Bottoms

The Disney studios joined Hollywood's space race with this $20 million job, which unashamedly rips off *Star Wars* and other sci-fi adventures. The comic-book plot has Schell as a mad scientist who commands a renegade spaceship on the edge of a mysterious black hole—the doorway to eternity. Two friendly robots, which resemble floating fireplugs, have the best lines and upstage the human characters. There's so little imagination here that it's hard to believe this is a Disney project. Also with Yvette Mimieux and Ernest Borgnine. **Director**—Gary Nelson. (PG) *97 minutes*

THE BLACK MARBLE (1980)
★★

Robert Foxworth
Paula Prentiss

Joseph Wambaugh (*The Onion Field*) is on his favorite subject again with this screenplay about police and crime, written from his own novel. It's a crude comic romance about two cops, played by Foxworth and Prentiss, who pursue a dognapper. There are some grisly details of animal mutilation and some offbeat humor that never goes over. A few moments of wit emerge, but it's a crime the way director Harold Becker finally drives the film into the ground. (PG) *113 minutes*

BLACK NARCISSUS (1946)
★★★★

Deborah Kerr
Flora Robson
Kathleen Byron

Kerr shines as a nun who deals with the tormenting problems of isolation and harsh climate in an effort to maintain a mission in the Himalayas. The film, based on Rumer Godden's novel, is exquisitely appointed and packs an emotional wallop. Sabu and Jean Simmons are excellent in supporting roles.

- Black Orpheus
- The Black Rose
- The Black Shield of Falworth
- The Black Stallion
- The Black Stallion Returns
- Black Sunday
- The Black Swan

B

Directors—Michael Powell and Emeric Pressburger. **Academy Award**—Jack Cardiff, cinematography (color). *100 minutes*

BLACK ORPHEUS (1959)

★★★

Marpessa Dawn
Breno Mello
Ademar da Silva

The myth of tragic lovers Orpheus and Eurydice is set against the pulsating background of Rio at Carnival time. The swirls of color, bright costumes and locales, and, most especially, the samba beat of Luis Bonfa and Antonio Carlos Jobim's music running throughout the film generate considerable excitement. In French with English subtitles. **Director**—Marcel Camus. **Academy Award**—best foreign language film. *98 minutes*

THE BLACK ROSE (1950)

★★

Tyrone Power
Cecile Aubry

Opulent but ponderous costume adventure, set in the 13th century, about an Englishman—played by Power—who travels to the Orient and triumphs over tyrannical rulers. Nothing new here, but there is some interesting action en route. Aubry, the French actress, co-stars in her first Hollywood film, which became her last when she failed the popularity test with American audiences. Orson Welles, Jack Hawkins, Michael Rennie, Herbert Lom, and Laurence Harvey have supporting roles. **Director**—Henry Hathaway. *120 minutes*

THE BLACK SHIELD OF FALWORTH (1954)

★★

Tony Curtis
Janet Leigh

Curtis and Leigh star in this medieval costume drama, which alternates from seriousness to adolescent humor. Curtis plays an English nobleman striving to achieve knighthood. He fends off numerous enemies with

swashbuckling swordsmanship; wait for him to say, "Yondah lies the castle of my fodda." Leigh, all decked out in sumptuous costumes, cheers from the sidelines. Elaborate period settings are impressive. Supporting cast includes David Farrar, Barbara Rush, and Herbert Marshall. **Director**—Rudolph Mate. *99 minutes*

THE BLACK STALLION (1979)

★★★★

Kelly Reno
Mickey Rooney

Boy meets horse, tames him, and races him in this splendidly photographed adventure fantasy that will please all age groups. Reno turns in a strong performance as the boy who develops a spiritual relationship with the wild Arabian stallion that saves his life in a shipwreck. Rooney is excellent as the trainer. But it's Cass-ole, a magnificent animal, who practically steals the film. Also with Teri Garr, Clarence Muse, and Hoyt Axton. **Director**—Carroll Ballard. (G) **Academy Award Nomination**—Rooney, best supporting actor. *103 minutes*

THE BLACK STALLION RETURNS (1983)

★★

Kelly Reno

This sequel to *The Black Stallion* is likely to please children, but not the adults who were charmed by the original film. There is plenty of action as Arab

Kelly Reno and Vincent Spano compete in the big race in The Black Stallion Returns.

tribesmen kidnap the powerful steed and bring him to the Sahara. Alec Ramsay (Reno) follows, and encounters intrigue, danger, and friendship—all of it quite predictable. Reno is consistently pleasing as the spunky young hero, and Vincent Spano and Woody Strode are fine in supporting roles. But the film lacks the unique imagery and vision that director Carroll Ballard gave to its predecessor. **Director**—Robert Dalva. (PG) *103 minutes*

BLACK SUNDAY (1977)

★★★

Robert Shaw
Bruce Dern
Marthe Keller

Meticulous direction and superb acting elevate an otherwise routine disaster film into a slick action adventure. Shaw, who skillfully plays a hardened Israeli government agent, races against time to thwart a Palestinian terrorist plot to drop a dart-spewing bomb from the Goodyear blimp onto 80,000 Super Bowl spectators. There's a powerful and extraordinary screen performance by Dern as the jangled and half-crazed blimp pilot who collaborates with the terrorists. Also with Fritz Weaver and Steven Keats. **Director**—John Frankenheimer. (R) *143 minutes*

THE BLACK SWAN (1942)

★★★

Tyrone Power
Maureen O'Hara

Rootin'-tootin' swashbuckler, with Power as a dashing pirate chasing some scruffy buccaneers at a fast clip through the Caribbean. The adventure has just the right amount of hokey humor to enhance the entertainment value without spoiling its spirit. O'Hara is charming as a damsel in need of rescuing from some villains, played convincingly by Anthony Quinn and George Sanders. The screenplay is based on the novel by Rafael Sabatini. Laird Cregar and Thomas Mitchell also star. **Director**—Henry King. **Academy Award**—Leon Shamroy, cinematography (color). *85 minutes*

 Movie is available in Beta and VHS videotape

B
- Black Tuesday
- Blade Runner
- Blame It on Rio
- Blazing Saddles
- The Blob
- Blonde Venus

BLACK TUESDAY (1954)
★★★

**Edward G. Robinson
Jean Parker
Peter Graves**

Robinson puts on his best scowl as a killer on the lam from the big house in this familiar but exciting gangster film. Graves is his accomplice. The duo try to elude the authorities by hiding out in an abandoned warehouse. Lots of tension and shoot-outs with the cops ensue. Parker is fine as a gun moll. Also with Milburn Stone, Warren Stevens, and Jack Kelly. **Director—**Hugo Fregonese.   *80 minutes b&w*

BLADE RUNNER (1982)
★★★

Harrison Ford

Space-age detective Harrison Ford pursues a villain in Blade Runner.

Ford stars as a hard-boiled, Philip Marlowe-style detective in a futuristic Los Angeles. His assignment is to track down sinister "replicants" (humanlike robots). The stylish, high-tech special effects are terrific. Photographic effects master Douglas Trumbull (*Close Encounters, Star Trek*) and his staff create a garish, chilling cityscape of sleaze and clutter. But, alas, the story is muddled and the film lacks dramatic momentum. Rutger Hauer and Sean Young also star. **Director—**Ridley Scott. (R)   *114 minutes*

BLAME IT ON RIO (1984)
★★

Michael Caine

Caine looks embarrassed most of the way through this contrived romantic comedy set against the backdrop of swinging, exotic Rio de Janeiro. He's seduced by his best friend's nubile teenage daughter (Michelle Johnson), who appears topless a lot. Attempts to keep this absurd love affair secret provoke a few laughs, but the crude story mainly comes off as offensive. Blame it on director and screenwriter Stanley Donen, who has done better and should know better. Joseph Bologna also stars. (R)   *109 minutes*

BLAZING SADDLES (1974)
★★★★

**Cleavon Little
Gene Wilder
Slim Pickens
Harvey Korman
Madeline Kahn**

Mel Brooks's howling comedy spoofs western movies and racial prejudice in a nonstop barrage of riotous skits and sight gags. Some of the comedy misfires, but there's still an onslaught of belly laughs, including a generous dose of scatological humor. Little is great as a black railroad worker who's elected sheriff of a western town. Brooks is hilarious in a brief role as a Yiddish-speaking Indian chief. Kahn is a riot in a Marlene Dietrich takeoff.

In the spoof Blazing Saddles, *Cleavon Little is elected sheriff of a troubled town.*

Korman, Wilder, and Pickens also pitch in with the lunacy. **Director—**Brooks. (R) **Academy Award Nomination**—Kahn, best supporting actress.   *93 minutes*

THE BLOB (1958)
★★

**Steve McQueen
Aneta Corseaut**

The Blob finds young Steve McQueen unprepared to deal with slime from outer space.

Slimy goo from outer space invades a small town, and a young McQueen comes to the rescue. This puffed-up sci-fi nonsense is primarily aimed at adolescent audiences. There are, however, a few scary scenes scattered here and there, and McQueen makes the most of the situation. Also with Olin Howlin and Earl Rowe. The film spawned a sequel called *Beware! The Blob,* also known as *Son of Blob.* **Director—**Irwin S. Yeaworth, Jr.

83 minutes

BLONDE VENUS (1932)
★★★

**Marlene Dietrich
Cary Grant
Herbert Marshall**

Passion is both the greatest curse and the greatest gift in the cinematic *tours-de-force* of director Joseph von Sternberg, and there's plenty of it here: mother love, illicit love, the love for a dying husband. Dietrich is the impassioned heroine; Marshall plays her scientist husband afflicted by radium poisoning; Grant is the wealthy playboy who has an affair with her; and Dickie Moore, the son she almost loses. The opening number, in which cafe singer Marlene makes her en-

• Blood Alley   • Bloodbrothers
• Blood and Sand   • Bloodline
• Blood Beach   • Blow Out
       • Blow-Up

B

trance in a gorilla suit (parts of which she seductively peels off) while singing "Hot Voodoo," is one of the director's most often-cited scenes.

97 minutes b&w

BLOOD ALLEY (1955)
★★

John Wayne
Lauren Bacall

Wayne and Bacall flee down a river from China to Hong Kong, with Chinese Communists hot on their tails. A routine anti-Red adventure, with Wayne as a bigger-than-life hero taking on the enemy single-handedly. The name cast and the slick production can't seem to overcome the threadbare script. Anita Ekberg is involved as a burlap-clad refugee. Also with Paul Fix, Joy Kim, Barry Kroger, and Mike Mazurki. **Director**—William Wellman. *115 minutes*

BLOOD AND SAND (1941)
★★

Tyrone Power
Linda Darnell
Rita Hayworth

If only for auld lang syne, this romantic chestnut is worth a look. Power stars as the ladykiller toreador whose meteoric success in the bullring leads him to prefer the attentions of society girl Hayworth over those of the sweetheart Darnell who's always loved him. Though Power lacks the animal magnetism Valentino brought to the 1922 silent film of the Ibanez scorcher, this version offers lush color. In fact, as directed by pictorialist Rouben Mamoulian, the film is practically a series of ravishing compositions, visually dynamic but dramatically inert. Cast includes Anthony Quinn, Nazimova, J. Carrol Naish, John Carradine, Laird Cregar, and Spanish guitarist Vicente Gomez.

123 minutes

BLOOD BEACH (1981)
 ★★

David Huffman
Mariana Hill
Burt Young

A mysterious creature lurks beneath a Los Angeles beach, and drags victims through the sand to its underground lair. Despite the title, there's little blood and gore in this low-budget horror film. Director Jeffrey Bloom manages to come up with a bit of suspense, thanks to a competent cast and a tight script that's a cousin to *Jaws*. However, there's only sparse action and vague contact with the subterranean monster. (R) *90 minutes*

BLOODBROTHERS (1978)
 ★★

Richard Gere
Paul Sorvino
Tony Lo Bianco

A high-pitched emotional story about an Italian-American family living in the Bronx. Gere plays a rebellious teenage son and nephew to construction-worker brothers who brawl, booze, and chase women. Good performances, but the characters are stereotypes, and the director goes overboard in exploiting emotions. **Director**—Robert Mulligan. (R) *116 minutes*

BLOODLINE (1979)
 ★★

Audrey Hepburn
Ben Gazzara
James Mason

In Bloodline, *Audrey Hepburn is a corporate mogul and Ben Gazzarra a murder suspect.*

Hepburn stars as the head of an international pharmaceutical empire in this tepid murder mystery, based on Sidney Sheldon's popular novel. Gazzara, Mason, Omar Sharif, and other well-known players appear as suspects in the murder of the company's patriarch. What little suspense there is quickly evaporates amid the complicated and ponderous plot. Hepburn looks rather weary much of the time, which seems to be in keeping with the pace of the film. Also with Michelle Phillips and Romy Schneider. **Director**—Terence Young. (R) *116 minutes*

BLOW OUT (1981)
 ★★★

John Travolta

John Travolta listens for a clue in Blow Out.

Director Brian De Palma fashions a stylish, electrifying drama about a movie sound man, played by Travolta, who stumbles upon a political assassination. The film bears some similarity to Antonioni's *Blow-Up*, and De Palma also cleverly weaves in subtle references to Chappaquiddick, Nelson Rockefeller's death, and Watergate plumbers. Travolta finally gets his teeth into an appealing, intelligent adult role, and sheds his hotshot teenage image. (R) *108 minutes*

BLOW-UP (1966)
 ★★★★

David Hemmings
Sarah Miles
Vanessa Redgrave

A fascinating and thought-provoking drama involving a London photog-
(Continued)

 Movie is available in Beta and VHS videotape

B
- The Blue Bird (1940)
- The Blue Bird (1976)
- Blue Collar
- The Blue Dahlia
- The Blue Lagoon (1949)
- The Blue Lagoon (1980)
- The Blue Max

(Continued)

rapher who believes he has witnessed a murder. Hemmings is effective as the baffled young man, and there is a stylish performance from Redgrave. The film brims with psychological twists and complex symbolism; much is accomplished with scant plot and undeveloped characters, in the trendy twilight world of London's fashion business. Jill Kennington and Verushka are also featured. **Director**—Michelangelo Antonioni. **Academy Award Nominations**—Antonioni, best director; Antonioni, Tonino Guerra, and Edward Bond, best story and screenplay (written directly for the screen). *110 minutes*

THE BLUE BIRD (1940)
★★

Shirley Temple
Spring Byington

Temple and Byington star in this classic fairy tale about two children who search for the bluebird of happiness, only to find true happiness at home. The film is based on Maurice Maeterlinck's fantasy, but the plot seems similar to *The Wizard of Oz*. The production is impressive, but it pales in contrast to the popular *Oz* film, which was released about the same time. Johnny Russell, Nigel Bruce, Gale Sondergaard, and Eddie Collins also star. **Director**—Walter Lang. *98 minutes*

THE BLUE BIRD (1976)
★

Elizabeth Taylor
Jane Fonda
Ava Gardner

Détente comes to the movies, but the result is a disappointment. The first major Soviet-American co-production, filmed in Leningrad, is the classic fable about two children who search for the bluebird of happiness; the audience will find the pigeon of boredom. Taylor, Fonda, Gardner, and Cicely Tyson appear briefly in cameo roles. The film is plagued with technical problems, dull dialogue, and lackluster sets. Also with Will Geer, Robert Morley, and Harry Andrews. Directed by George Cukor, who should have known better. (G) *99 minutes*

BLUE COLLAR (1978)
★★★

Richard Pryor
Harvey Keitel
Yaphet Kotto

Richard Pryor, and Yaphet Kotto take a break from the assembly line in Blue Collar.

Paul Schrader, who wrote the script for *Taxi Driver*, is so-so as director of this powerful and gritty film about frustrated automobile factory workers who are pushed around by their union and management. This fast-paced comedy-drama is awkward at times. Even so, Schrader scores with his colorful profile of believable contemporary characters. Pryor, Keitel, and Kotto are the heroes of the assembly line; they play their parts to the hilt. Also with Ed Begley, Jr. and Harry Bellaver. (R) *114 minutes*

THE BLUE DAHLIA (1946)
★★★

Alan Ladd
Veronica Lake
William Bendix

Ladd plays an ex-GI, home from the war, who discovers his wife has been unfaithful. After she's murdered, he becomes the prime suspect. The Raymond Chandler mystery packs excitement and suspense, with the cast turning in sharp performances. Also with Howard da Silva and Hugh Beaumont. **Director**—George Marshall. **Academy Award Nomination**—Chandler, writing (original screenplay). *99 minutes b&w*

THE BLUE LAGOON (1949)
★★

Jean Simmons
Donald Houston

A syrupy romantic adventure about a boy and a girl, stranded on a tropical island, who mature, fall in love, and then try to return to civilization. The lush island setting can't redeem the listless material, based on the novel by H. de Vere Stacpoole. There is a bit of suspense when the couple is threatened by smugglers. Also with Noel Purcell, Cyril Cusack, and James Hayter. **Director**—Frank Launder. *103 minutes*

THE BLUE LAGOON (1980)
★

Brooke Shields
Christopher Atkins

Emmeline, played by Shields, and Richard, played by Atkins, are two shipwrecked children on a tropical island who grow up to be lovers. Everything is picture-postcard pretty, including Brooke and Christopher. But excitement and drama are nowhere to be found. The story somewhat unrealistically and awkwardly emphasizes innocent sexual awakening. The 1949 version with Jean Simmons worked better as a Hollywood-style fantasy. Also with Leo McKern and William Daniels. **Director**—Randal Kleiser. (R) *102 minutes*

THE BLUE MAX (1966)
★★

George Peppard
James Mason
Ursula Andress

Spectacular photography of World War I aerial dogfights is the only worthwhile virtue of this tepid drama involving German military pilots. Peppard plays an ambitious German flyer who woos the wife of his commander; Mason portrays a stereotyped German officer; and Andress is Peppard's love interest. Performances are fair but not too convincing. Also with Jeremy Kemp and Karl Michael Vogler. **Director**—John Guillermin. *156 minutes*

• A Blueprint for Murder
• The Blues Brothers
• Blues in the Night
• Blue Skies

• Blue Skies Again
• Blue Thunder
• Blume in Love
• The Boat (Das Boot)

B

A BLUEPRINT FOR MURDER
(1953)

★★

Jean Peters
Joseph Cotten

Cotten plays a troubled man trying to prove that his sister-in-law, played by Peters, poisoned his brother and nephew. The rather familiar mystery plot twists and turns, with clues dangling left and right. Did Peters commit the perfect crime? If you're any good, you can figure it out before Cotten does. Gary Merrill, Catherine McLeod, and Jack Kruschen co-star. **Director**—Andrew Stone.

77 minutes b&w

THE BLUES BROTHERS (1980)
 ★★★

John Belushi
Dan Aykroyd

Belushi and Aykroyd star in this musical action comedy as improbable bandleaders who try to raise $5,000 for an orphanage and cause $50 million in property damage in the process. It's a rollicking smorgasbord of soul music, auto crashes, explosions, and crazy fun. But it's really the spirited musical numbers that glue this madcap mess together. Delightful cameo performances by James Brown, Aretha Franklin, Ray Charles, and Cab Calloway add to the froth and frolic. **Director**—John Landis. (R) *130 minutes*

BLUES IN THE NIGHT (1941)
★★★

Priscilla Lane
Richard Whorf
Lloyd Nolan

A pleasant score and a decent script go into this finely crafted musical drama about a jazz band that splits up, with the members suffering various problems. Music by Harold Arlen and Johnny Mercer includes "This Time the Dream's on Me." The earnest cast handles the smooth dialogue with conviction. Also with Jack Carson, Betty Field, and Elia Kazan. **Director**—Anatole Litvak.

88 minutes b&w

BLUE SKIES (1946)
★★★

Fred Astaire
Bing Crosby
Joan Caulfield

Crosby and Astaire star in this sunny musical loaded with Irving Berlin tunes. The threadbare, corny plot concerns a drawn-out rivalry for the attention of a girl. But that's incidental to the music and dancing. Bing sings the title song, and Fred dances to "Putting On the Ritz." What more do you need? Caulfield, Billy de Wolfe, and Olga San Juan are fine in supporting roles. **Director**—Stuart Heisler. *104 minutes*

BLUE SKIES AGAIN (1983)
 ★

Robyn Barto

Inept, silly, and predictable nonsense about a freckle-faced woman (Barto) who tries for a position on a major league baseball team. This half-baked female version of *The Jackie Robinson Story* is constructed on a preposterous plot line that lacks dramatic drive and believable characters. The cast, which also includes Harry Hamlin and Mimi Rogers, puts in minimal efforts. No hits, no runs, and lots of errors. **Director**—Richard Michaels. (PG)

96 minutes

BLUE THUNDER (1983)
 ★★★

Roy Scheider

Candy Clark plays the helicopter pilot's neglected girlfriend in Blue Thunder.

A super-duper, high-tech helicopter is the centerpiece of this fast-paced action yarn which plays out in the skies of Los Angeles. Scheider is effective as a maverick cop-pilot, who deals with an underhanded operation to subvert civil liberties. The plot has suspense, but it's too far off the wall to be plausible. The breathtaking aerial maneuvers, though, help suspend disbelief in the story line. Malcolm McDowell and the late Warren Oates co-star. **Director**—John Badham. (R) *110 minutes*

BLUME IN LOVE (1973)
 ★★★

George Segal
Susan Anspach
Kris Kristofferson

Writer-director Paul Mazursky takes on middle-class marriage and divorce in this droll comedy-drama about a lawyer, played by Segal, who longs for his ex-wife, played by Anspach, and wants to win her back. Segal and Anspach are both affecting as sympathetic characters. And the film is blessed with sparkling supporting acting—Shelley Winters as an older woman whose husband left her for a stewardess, and Kristofferson as Anspach's bedmate of the moment. Also with Marsha Mason. (R) *116 minutes*

THE BOAT (DAS BOOT) (1981)
 ★★★

Gripping, finely detailed German production about U-boat life during World War II. The superb atmospherics depict the hardships of sweaty, close-quarters existence and the ever-present consciousness of danger. In contrast to typical Hollywood war movies, the German submariners are portrayed here as real people rather than as cartoon characters. Jurgen Prochnow stands out as the sub's resolute skipper. Released in two versions: In German with English titles and with dubbed English. **Director**—Wolfgang Petersen. (R) **Academy Award Nominations**—Petersen, best director; Petersen, best screenplay (based on material from another medium); Jost Vacano, cinematography. *150 minutes*

B

- Boat People
- Bob & Carol & Ted & Alice
- Bobby Deerfield
- Bob Le Flambeur

- Body and Soul (1947)
- Body and Soul (1981)
- Body Double

BOAT PEOPLE (1983)
★★★

**Lam Chicheung
Cora Miao**

Ann Hui's blistering account of postwar life in Vietnam reveals appalling conditions under the Communist regime as witnessed by a Japanese photographer who is able to circumvent the official government views. Yet the film, shot in China, is somewhat propagandist in itself. Nevertheless, Hui's sensitive and affecting portrayal of the continuing Vietnamese tragedy is difficult to refute. In Chinese with English titles. **Director**—Ann Hui. (No MPAA rating) *106 minutes*

BOB & CAROL & TED & ALICE (1969)
 ★★★

**Natalie Wood
Robert Culp
Elliott Gould
Dyan Cannon**

An old-fashioned romantic comedy loaded with all sorts of trendy situations: wife-swapping, psychotherapy, pot smoking, and so on. A so-called modern couple envy what seems to be their friends' ideal marriage, and they almost end up swapping partners. Gould and Cannon are exceptional as Ted and Alice—the nervous experimenters. Wood and Culp are the chic Carol and Bob. The wacky screenplay and smart dialogue keep the situations moving along, but the ending is somewhat absurd. **Director**—Paul Mazursky. (R) **Academy Award Nominations**—Gould, best supporting actor; Cannon, best supporting actress; Mazursky and Larry Tucker, best story and screenplay (based on material not previously published or produced); Charles B. Lang, cinematography. *105 minutes*

BOBBY DEERFIELD (1977)
 ★

**Al Pacino
Marthe Keller**

Pacino, in his first romantic role, plays an emotionally drained race-car driver

Al Pacino is a racing driver and Marthe Keller is his ailing girlfriend in Bobby Deerfield.

who falls in love with a dying European beauty, played by Keller. Both are miscast in this flat-footed European version of *Love Story*. Alvin Sargent's superficial script has the two leads blabbing endlessly without generating any pathos. The beautiful Anny Duperey stands out as Bobby's enduring mistress of convenience. Also with Walter McGinn and Romolo Valli. **Director**—Sydney Pollack. (PG) *124 minutes*

BOB LE FLAMBEUR (1955)
 ★★★

Roger Duchesne

This is the late French director Jean-Pierre Melville's version of the familiar American gangster movie. The result is haunting and occasionally leans toward parody. Duchesne has some good moments in the title role, playing a middle-aged gambler and former bank robber who engineers one last glorious heist—the safe at a swank Paris casino. The murky black-and-white photography enhances the somber mood. Isabelle Corey co-stars. In French with English titles.
97 minutes b&w

BODY AND SOUL (1947)
 ★★★★

**John Garfield
Lilli Palmer**

Garfield stars as a young man from a poor family who becomes a top prizefighter by fair and foul means. It's a rough-and-tough drama that's perhaps a boxing film cliché. However, this study is compelling, exciting, and laced with impressive fight sequences.

Garfield is perfection as the determined slugger, and Palmer stands out as the female lead. There's support from Hazel Brooks, William Conrad, Anne Revere, and Canada Lee. **Director**—Robert Rossen. **Academy Award Nominations**—Garfield, best actor; Abraham Polonsky, writing (original screenplay). *104 minutes b&w*

BODY AND SOUL (1981)
 ★★

Leon Isaac Kennedy

Leon Isaac Kennedy stars as an earnest boxer who shelves a promising medical career in an effort to win big bucks by vying for the championship. This uninspired remake of the 1947 John Garfield classic lacks any sort of vitality and comes across in a rather undramatic way. Muhammad Ali is in the film as the aspiring champ's adviser, and he adds some levity merely playing himself. Jayne Kennedy and Peter Lawford also star. **Director**—George Bowers. (R) *109 minutes*

BODY DOUBLE (1984)
★★

**Craig Wasson
Gregg Henry
Melaine Griffith**

Deborah Shelton and Craig Wasson are shocked by the horrifying turn of events in Body Double.

• Body Heat
• The Body Snatcher
• Bolero
• Bombers B–52
• Bonjour Tristesse
• Bonnie and Clyde

B

Director Brian DePalma leans heavily on Hitchcock's *Rear Window* and *Vertigo* in this sleazy murder mystery that explores voyeurism and the world of porno movies. Wasson is an unemployed actor who watches a beautiful woman through a telescope and then becomes involved with her murder. DePalma creates some startling, suspenseful moments with his sophisticated camera work. But the ridiculous story makes no sense. (R)

110 minutes

BODY HEAT (1981)
★★★

William Hurt
Kathleen Turner

Lawrence Kasdan triumphantly debuts as director of this sultry movie, which smacks of such '40s films noirs as *Double Indemnity*. It drips with steamy atmospherics and lavishly dwells on passion and treachery. Hurt stars as an affable, second-rate lawyer who is lured into killing the well-heeled husband of a seductive woman, played by Turner. Again, Hurt demonstrates his fine acting ability. (R)
113 minutes

THE BODY SNATCHER (1945)
★★★

Henry Daniell
Boris Karloff
Bela Lugosi

Boris Karloff tells Bela Lugosi to work on his posture in The Body Snatcher.

A blood-chilling horror story about a doctor in 19th-century Scotland who experiments with bodies supplied by grave robbers. Lots of good creepy atmosphere in this Val Lewton thriller, with Karloff and Lugosi at their sinister best. The film is based on a familiar story by Robert Lewis Stevenson and is executed in an inventive manner. Edith Atwater and Russel Wade are also in the cast. **Director**—Robert Wise. *77 minutes b&w*

BOLERO (1984)
★

Bo Derek

A dreary, soft-core porn film made as a vehicle to display Derek's physical charms. And opportunities to see Bo in the buff are rather limited indeed. The audience must suffer through a silly plot, dumb dialogue, and bad acting while waiting for Bo's brief sex scenes with a sheik and a bullfighter. These trysts are played more for laughs than eroticism. George Kennedy and Andrea Occhipinti are in support roles. **Director**—John Derek. (No MPAA rating, contains nudity).
105 minutes

BOMBERS B-52 (1957)
★★

Karl Malden
Marsha Hunt
Efrem Zimbalist, Jr.
Natalie Wood

Routine romantic melodrama set against a military aircraft background. Zimbalist is a young pilot who wants to marry a fellow officer's daughter, played by Wood; Malden, as Wood's father, objects. The outcome is predictable. Spectacular shots of flying bombers are interspersed amid the domestic scenes. Also with Dean Jagger and Don Kelly. **Director**—Gordon Douglas. *106 minutes*

BONJOUR TRISTESSE (1957)
★★★

David Niven
Deborah Kerr
Jean Seberg

An elegant-looking film based on the

Françoise Sagan novel about a teenage girl who resents her philandering father's mistress. Tragedy results when the daughter tries to break up the romance. The film is set against the lavish background of the French Riviera. The script is a little melodramatic but entertaining nevertheless. Kerr is outstanding, with help from Niven and Seberg. Mylene Demongeot, Geoffrey Horne, Juliette Greco, and Martita Hunt are also in the cast. **Director**—Otto Preminger.
94 minutes

BONNIE AND CLYDE
(1967)
★★★★

Warren Beatty
Faye Dunaway
Michael J. Pollard

Warren Beatty and Faye Dunaway make outlawry seem glamorous as Bonnie and Clyde.

A vivid, penetrating, and stylish film biography of the notorious bank robbers who terrorized mid-America at the depth of the Great Depression. The exciting production seems to have a bit of everything—grim drama, comedy at the right moments, social commentary, and suspense. Stunning direction by Arthur Penn is complemented by the brilliant acting of Beatty and Dunaway in the title roles. The film was a huge box-office success and a pacesetter of modern gangster movies. Pollard, Gene Hackman, Estelle Parsons, Gene Wilder, and Denver Pyle are excellent in supporting roles. **Academy Awards**—Parsons, best supporting actress; Burnett Guffey, cinematography. **Nominations**—best picture; Penn, best director;
(Continued)

B
- Bon Voyage
- Boomerang
- Boom Town
- The Border
- Borderline
- Born Free
- Born Yesterday

(Continued)

Beatty, best actor; Dunaway, best actress; Hackman, best supporting actor; David Newman and Robert Benton, best story and screenplay (written directly for the screen).   *111 minutes*

BON VOYAGE (1962)
★★

Fred MacMurray
Jane Wyman

MacMurray plays a middle-class father who takes his family on vacation to Paris. Slow-paced, lightweight Disney fare about a family dealing with a variety of comic events. One of the misadventures is dad getting trapped in the Paris sewer system. It's an interesting tour of the French capital, however. Michael Callan, Tommy Kirk, and Deborah Walley are in the cast. **Director**—James Neilson.   *133 minutes*

BOOMERANG (1947)
★★★★

Dana Andrews
Jane Wyatt
Lee J. Cobb

A priest in a New England community is murdered, and a determined prosecuting attorney saves an innocent man from false conviction. The actual guilty person isn't apprehended although the audience knows who did it. This brilliant and fascinating drama is based on a true story and produced in semidocumentary form. First-class entertainment, with stylish direction and outstanding acting. Arthur Kennedy, Sam Levene, and Ed Begley also star. **Director**—Elia Kazan. **Academy Award Nomination**—Richard Murphy, writing (screenplay).   *88 minutes b&w*

BOOM TOWN (1940)
★★★

Clark Gable
Spencer Tracy
Claudette Colbert
Hedy Lamarr

A big-name cast livens up this action-packed drama of oil drillers who bring in black gold. Entertainment and ex-

Spencer Tracy, Hedy Lamarr, Frank Morgan, Claudette Colbert, & Clark Gable in Boom Town.

citement run high in a slick blending of romance, comedy, and suspense. Gable, Tracy, Colbert, and Lamarr top the cast. Frank Morgan, Chill Wills, and Lionel Atwill also lend a hand. **Director**—Jack Conway. **Academy Award Nomination**—Harold Rosson, cinematography (black and white).   *120 minutes b&w*

THE BORDER (1982)
 ★★★

Jack Nicholson

Nicholson brings considerable richness to his working-stiff characterization of a border patrol officer involved with corruption. The movie intelligently details the plight of illegal Mexican workers with sharp contrasts between their condition and the materialistic life-style of some Americans. Valerie Perrine and Harvey Keitel are excellent in supporting roles. Also with Warren Oates and Elpidia Carrillo. **Director**—Tony Richardson. (R)   *107 minutes*

BORDERLINE (1980)
 ★★

Charles Bronson

Bronson plays a border patrol officer on the trail of illegal aliens from Mexico. There's potential for some socially significant moviemaking. But alas, the film only halfheartedly examines the sorry plight of exploited Mexicans. Most of the time, the film is just another action vehicle, with Bronson seeking revenge for the killing of a fellow officer. Bronson does his usual credible job, but his inspiration seems merely borderline. **Director**—Gerrold Freedman. (R)   *97 minutes*

BORN FREE
(1966)
 ★★★

Virginia McKenna
Bill Travers
Geoffrey Keen

Pleasant family film based on Joy Adamson's best-selling book about the lioness Elsa, who was raised as a pet and then returned to the jungle. Photography of the animals, and especially of the lion's efforts to adapt to the wilds of Kenya, is impressive. Travers and McKenna star as the game warden and his wife who managed the retraining of Elsa. **Director**—James Hill. **Academy Award**—best song ("Born Free," John Barry and Don Black); Barry, best original score.   *95 minutes*

BORN YESTERDAY
(1950)
 ★★★★

Judy Holliday
Broderick Crawford
William Holden

Holliday is sensational in this screen adaptation of Garson Kanin's hit Broadway play on the *Pygmalion* theme. She plays a dumb blond (what else?), the girlfriend of a wealthy scrap dealer, played by Crawford. She starts out for education and sophistication and then falls in love with her tutor, played by Holden. The film brims with subtle humor and witty dialogue; the top cast turns in hilarious performances. Howard St. John also stars. **Director**—George Cukor. **Academy Award**—Holliday, best actress. **Nominations**—best picture; Cukor, best director; Albert Mannheimer, writing (screenplay).   *103 minutes b&w*

- The Bostonians
- The Boston Strangler
- Boulevard Nights
- Bound for Glory
- The Bounty
- A Boy and His Dog
- Boy, Did I Get a Wrong Number

B

THE BOSTONIANS (1984)
★★★★

Vanessa Redgrave

An exquisite film rendition of the Henry James psychological novel that explores the suffrage movement against the backdrop of 19th century Boston blue bloods. It's one of the finest period pieces to appear in some time, rich in detail, and capped with a glistening performance by Redgrave. She plays a passionate feminist caught up in a complex romantic web. Christopher Reeve, Madeleine Potter, Jessica Tandy, and Linda Hunt are part of the sterling silver supporting cast. **Director**—James Ivory. (No MPAA rating)   *120 minutes*

THE BOSTON STRANGLER (1968)
 ★★★

Tony Curtis
Henry Fonda

Curtis gives an effective performance as the maniac who murdered several women in Boston in the mid-60s. The semidocumentary film drags at times, but it remains a startling rendition of Gerold Frank's book about the brutal sex killings allegedly committed by Albert De Salvo, a deranged plumber. The compelling account follows the criminal's grisly deeds, his arrest, and his trial. George Kennedy and Sally Kellerman also star. **Director**—Richard Fleischer.   *118 minutes*

BOULEVARD NIGHTS (1979)
★★

Richard Yniguez
Marta Du Bois
Danny De La Paz

Mexican-American youths of East Los Angeles cruise the neon-lit streets and wage gang warfare. The film tries so hard to be the Chicano version of *West Side Story* or *Saturday Night Fever* that it loses sight of its characters. A cast of unknowns do only a fair acting job. Flash and gloss seem to be more important here than story development. **Director**—Michael Pressman. (R)   *102 minutes*

BOUND FOR GLORY (1976)
★★★

David Carradine
Ronny Cox

The great folksinger Woody Guthrie is played with slow and heartfelt perfection by Carradine. And director Hal Ashby carefully provides a stunning, detailed portrait of the Great Depression of the 1930s. The story follows Guthrie's separation from his poverty-stricken family, his experience with political activism among California's migrant laborers, and his initial radio career. The 2½ hour film doesn't build dramatically and rambles too often, yet Guthrie's social consciousness shines through. There's fine support from Melinda Dillon. Also with Gail Strickland, John Lehne, and Ji-Tu Cumbuka. (PG) **Academy Award**—Haskell Wexler, cinematography. **Nominations**—best picture; Robert Getchell, best screenplay adaptation.   *147 minutes*

THE BOUNTY (1984)
 ★★★

Anthony Hopkins
Mel Gibson

This lavish third film voyage of the classic high-seas adventure is perhaps closest to the truth of the 1787 mutiny

Mel Gibson updates the role of mutineer Fletcher Christian in The Bounty.

aboard the British naval ship. Lt. William Bligh, played with gripping intensity by Hopkins, is perceived as a multi-dimensional, somewhat heroic character. The retelling is as engrossing as ever, but the initial 1935 Charles Laughton-Clark Gable version is more enjoyable. **Director**—Roger Donaldson. (PG)   *132 minutes*

A BOY AND HIS DOG (1975)
 ★★

Don Johnson
Susanne Benton
Jason Robards, Jr.
Tiger (the dog)

Don Johnson finds the future fascinating in A Boy and His Dog.

A mixed breed of a film set in the 21st century when the Earth's surface has been reduced to a wasteland after World War IV. A young man and his talking dog, played by Tiger, prowl about looking for food and sex. The man, played smartly by Johnson, is lured into a weird subterranean city ruled by a dictatorship led by Robards. Director L. Q. Jones is still in the puppy stage with this one, which is at times stimulating and at times mildly revolting. From a Harlan Ellison novella. Also with Tim McIntire and Charles McGraw. (R)   *87 minutes*

BOY, DID I GET A WRONG NUMBER (1966)
★

Bob Hope
Elke Sommer
Phyllis Diller

Silly, unfunny Hope outing, with the comedian as a real estate agent who tries to call his wife and instead gets

(Continued)

 Movie is available in Beta and VHS videotape

B

- Boy on a Dolphin
- The Boys from Brazil
- The Boys in Company C
- The Boys in the Band
- Boys Town
- The Boy with Green Hair
- Brainstorm

(Continued)

hooked up with a movie star, played by Sommer. The dopey script generates little in the way of laughs, and the production is mostly an embarrassment for Hope and the rest of the cast. It's a wrong number, indeed. Also with Marjorie Lord and Cesare Danova. **Director**—George Marshall.

99 minutes

BOY ON A DOLPHIN (1957)
★★

Alan Ladd
Sophia Loren

Striking photography of the Greek islands, the sparkling sea, and the statuesque beauty of Loren are the main attractions of this otherwise routine adventure involving sunken treasure. Loren plays a Greek skin diver who uncovers a lost artifact. An archaeologist and an ambitious art collector join the recovery operations. Clifton Webb and Laurence Naismith are also in the cast. **Director**—Jean Negulesco.

113 minutes

THE BOYS FROM BRAZIL (1978)
 ★★

Gregory Peck
Laurence Olivier
James Mason

Peck and Olivier star in this weird drama that exploits the current inter-

Steve Guttenberg wishes that he had never met The Boys from Brazil.

est in cloning. In this case, the evil Dr. Josef Mengele, who conducted sadistic human experiments in Nazi death camps, is on the loose in South America with a scheme to produce 94 copies of Adolf Hitler. Mengele is played by Peck; Olivier plays a Jewish Nazi-hunter. There are moments of suspense here and there, but the shaky story, based on Ira Levin's best-selling novel, lapses into silliness. Also with Lilli Palmer, Uta Hagen, Denholm Elliott, and Steven Guttenberg. **Director**—Franklin Schaffner. (R) **Academy Award Nomination**—Olivier, best actor.

123 minutes

THE BOYS IN COMPANY C (1978)
 ★★

Stan Shaw
Andrew Stevens
James Canning

This drama about Marine warfare in Vietnam starts off on the right foot with an authentic account of bootcamp training. When the scene shifts to Southeast Asia, however, the story falls apart. The characters, played by an unfamiliar cast, are World War II stereotypes who mostly shout and screech at one another. The climax concerns an absurd soccer match that looks like a cheap rip-off of the football game from *M*A*S*H*. Lee Ermey, an ex-Marine drill instructor originally hired as a consultant, came up with the best acting job—playing his former real-life role. Also with Michael Lembeck and Craig Wasson. **Director**—Sidney J. Furie. (R) *127 minutes*

THE BOYS IN THE BAND (1970)
 ★★★

Frederick Combs
Leonard Frey
Cliff Gorman

This impressive film version of Mart Crowley's successful Broadway play about homosexuality is full of emotion, an honest exposure of feelings, and the right touch of humor. The rather confined production concerns a homosexual birthday party to which a heterosexual is inadvertently invited. Fine acting and efficient direction

keep the story moving right up to a stunning ending. Also with Laurence Luckinbill, Kenneth Nelson, and Reuben Greene. **Director**—William Friedkin. (R) *120 minutes*

BOYS TOWN (1938)
★★★

Spencer Tracy
Mickey Rooney
Henry Hull

"There's no such thing as a bad boy." So speaketh Father Flanagan (played here by Tracy), who is almost made to eat his words when tough punk Rooney is dumped into Flanagan's community for wayward boys outside Omaha. Art it's not, but it is pretty compelling sentimental drama, oozing with star chemistry (Tracy took an Oscar, and Rooney has a field day). Gene Reynolds and Tommy Noonan co-star. **Director**—Norman Taurog. **Academy Awards**—Tracy, best actor; Eleanore Griffin, Dore Schary, writing (original story). **Academy Award Nominations**—best picture; Taurog, best director; John Meehan, Schary, writing (screenplay).

90 minutes b&w

THE BOY WITH GREEN HAIR (1948)
 ★★★

Dean Stockwell
Pat O'Brien

A captivating drama with a social message opposing the senselessness of war. After an air raid takes the life of his parents, a boy's hair turns green. The boy, played by Stockwell, becomes an outcast, but he wins the sympathy of other war orphans. Fine acting overcomes some of the muddle in the plot. O'Brien stands out as a likable grandfather. Also with Robert Ryan and Barbara Hale. **Director**—Joseph Losey. *82 minutes*

BRAINSTORM (1983)
 ★★

Natalie Wood
Christopher Walken
Louise Fletcher

Wood's last film, completed hap-

• Brannigan
• The Bravados
• Bread and Chocolate

• Breaker! Breaker!
• Breaker Morant
• Breakfast at Tiffany's
• Breakheart Pass

B

Louise Fletcher, and Cliff Robertson look on as Natalie Wood becomes an experimental subject in Brainstorm.

hazardly after her death, concerns scientists who devise a spectacular headpiece that enables the transfer of thoughts, sensations, and emotions. The stars of this high-tech but confusing story are the blazing special effects from director Douglas Trumbull depicting the consequences of such brain wave sharing. Fletcher is outstanding as a workaholic researcher while Walken is convincing as her colleague. Wood, as Walken's wife, never had a chance to develop her role properly. (PG)   *106 minutes*

BRANNIGAN (1975)

★★

John Wayne
Richard Attenborough
Judy Geeson

Wayne stars as Brannigan, a Chicago cop who goes to London to retrieve a criminal. The plot is a bit overdrawn and familiar, but the London setting is a nice change of pace for Wayne. You can expect the regular round of slugfests and other macho action typical of the Duke, even though he seems old for this role. Attenborough does well as a Scotland Yard detective whose style is at odds with the American's. Also with Mel Ferrer, Ralph Meeker, and John Vernon. **Director**—Douglas Hickox. (PG)   *111 minutes*

THE BRAVADOS (1958)
★★

Gregory Peck
Joan Collins
Stephen Boyd

After four brutes rape and kill a man's

wife, the widower embarks on a manhunt to avenge the crime. Peck stars in this downtrodden western as the seeker of justice. But he becomes as despicable as the killers in his zeal for success. The production is handsome, but the execution of the story is uneven and plodding at times. Also with Albert Salmi, Henry Silva, and Lee Van Cleef. **Director**—Henry King.
98 minutes

BREAD AND CHOCOLATE
(1978)
★★★

Nino Manfredi

Italian director Franco Brusati's bittersweet satire takes a hard look at the plight of migrant workers. The story, told with pathos and humor, concerns a disorganized Italian waiter, played by Manfredi, who painfully tries to fit in among the stuffy and orderly Swiss. Our hero, at times, resembles Charlie Chaplin's woeful tramp. Brusati illustrates the agony of the outsider with force and intelligence. In Italian with English titles. (No MPAA rating)
108 minutes

BREAKER! BREAKER! (1977)

★

Chuck Norris

Martial arts whiz Norris stars in this shabby drama, which exploits the interest in heavy trucking, CB radio, and chop-socky action. The simple plot concerns the efforts of Norris, aided by some of his buddies, to rescue his kid brother from a remote town where sadistic citizens harass unsuspecting truckers. Cardboard acting and inept direction drag down the mediocre screenplay. Also with George Murdock and Terry O'Connor. **Director**—Don Hulette. (PG)   *86 minutes*

BREAKER MORANT
(1981)

★★★★

Edward Woodward
Jack Thompson
John Waters

This film from Australia is a stirring courtroom drama set during the Boer

War. Three officers tragically become scapegoats of a hypocritical British military. There are obvious parallels to Vietnam and references to the ambiguities of warfare ("We were only following orders."). The film shines with strongly developed characters. There's a powerhouse performance by Woodward in the title role, and Bruce Beresford's crisp direction is on target. Also with Charles Tingwell. (No MPAA rating) **Academy Award Nomination**— Jonathan Hardy, David Stevens, and Beresford, best screenplay (adapted from another medium).   *106 minutes*

BREAKFAST AT TIFFANY'S
(1961)

★★★★

Audrey Hepburn
George Peppard

A stylish and witty film version of Truman Capote's cosmopolitan story about a New York writer, played by Peppard, who has some kooky neighbors, including a daffy call girl. The lively production is graced with hilarious scenes, memorable performances, and colorful characterizations. There's a madcap party sequence that is unforgettable. Hepburn is charming and funny as the modish Holly Golightly. Henry Mancini wrote the score, which includes the award-winning "Moon River." Also with Patricia Neal, Martin Balsam, John McGiver, Buddy Ebsen, and Mickey Rooney. **Director**—Blake Edwards. **Academy Award**—Mancini, best song. **Nominations**—Hepburn, best actress; George Axelrod, best screenplay (based on material from another medium).   *115 minutes*

BREAKHEART PASS (1976)

★★★

Charles Bronson
Ben Johnson
Richard Crenna

The film is mainly set on an old wood-burning steam train chugging through picturesque mountain country. The ever-faithful Bronson is on board as a federal agent in disguise trying to track down a stolen arms shipment. The train is crawling with
(Continued)

B
- Breakin'
- Breakin' 2: Electric Boogaloo
- Breaking Away
- The Breaking Point
- Breathless
- Brewster McCloud
- Brewster's Millions

(Continued)

villains, corpses, and mystery. Shades of *Murder on the Orient Express*. Only in this case, the setting is the West in the 1870s. There's an intricate plot, but the film is a solidly entertaining whodunit packed with suspense and action. It's based on Alistair MacLean's book. Also with Jill Ireland, Charles Durning, and Archie Moore. **Director**— Tom Gries. (PG)   *95 minutes*

BREAKIN' (1984)
 ★★

Lucinda Dickey
Adolfo Quinones
Michael Chambers

Break dancing—lots of it—dominates this low-budget production filmed in the streets of Los Angeles. The faint plot serves primarily to introduce various dance sequences where some slick dudes show off their fancy footwork. Dickey heads the youthful cast as a waitress who wants to become a professional dancer. **Director**—Joel Silberg. (PG)   *90 minutes*

BREAKIN' 2: ELECTRIC BOOGALOO (1984)
★★

Lucinda Dickey
Adolfo Quinones
Michael Chambers

If you gotta dance, let it be break dancing. And the kids in this sequel dance up a storm. The simple plot, of course, is merely incidental to all the popping and spinning. The youngsters put on a fund-raising show to save their community club from the ravages of greedy developers. **Director**—Sam Firstenberg. (PG)   *94 minutes*

BREAKING AWAY (1979)
 ★★★★

Dennis Christopher
Dennis Quaid
Daniel Stern
Jackie Earle Haley

A simple, charming little comedy with a big heart and a gentle touch. It's about four working-class boys in Bloomington, Indiana, who challenge

Dennis Christopher plays an Indiana youth in Breaking Away.

the college stuffed shirts in a grueling bike race. The cast is unknown, but director Peter Yates obtains sparkling performances all around. Christopher is especially delightful as a first-class rider who idolizes Italian bike champs. The climactic yet predictable big race will leave you elated and cheering. Also with Barbara Barrie and Paul Dooley. **Academy Award**—Steve Tesich, best screenplay (written directly for the screen). **Nominations**— best picture; Yates, best director; Barrie, best supporting actress.
(PG) 100 minutes

THE BREAKING POINT
(1950)
★★

John Garfield
Patricia Neal

Garfield portrays a desperate charterboat skipper who falls in with criminals and transports some illicit cargo. The script, based on Ernest Hemingway's *To Have and Have Not*, is slightly tedious, but the film is partially salvaged by the superb performances of Garfield and Juano Hernandez, who plays Garfield's first mate. Also with Phyllis Thaxter and Wallace Ford. **Director**—Michael Curtiz.   *97 minutes*

BREATHLESS (1983)
 ★★

Richard Gere
Valerie Kaprisky

Richard Gere and Valerie Kaprisky in a rare clothed moment in Breathless.

An uneven remake of the 1960 Jean-Luc Godard classic, set against a contemporary, pop-culture Los Angeles backdrop. Gere stands out as the crazy, petty criminal hurrying toward his doom. Newcomer Kaprisky is the "nice girl" college student who falls in love with this desperate drifter. Her awkward acting lessens the impact of their peculiar romantic relationship. **Director**—Jim McBride. (R)
105 minutes

BREWSTER McCLOUD (1970)
 ★★★

Bud Cort
Sally Kellerman

This is a far-out, slapstick comedy as only director Robert Altman can create one. Brewster is an oddball character who wants to fly—with man-made wings—inside the Houston Astrodome. When he tries, he kills himself. Altman sets up many striking scenes—some of them are bizarre, some of them are funny, and some of them are funny and bizarre. Cort, in the title role, is effectively kooky. Also with Michael Murphy, William Windom, Shelley Duvall, and Stacy Keach. (R)   *105 minutes*

BREWSTER'S MILLIONS (1945)
★★

Dennis O'Keefe

A familiar comedy, adequately done,

- The Bribe
- The Bride Came C.O.D.
- Bride of Frankenstein
- The Bridge of San Luis Rey
- The Bridge on the River Kwai
- The Bridges at Toko-Ri
- A Bridge Too Far

B

about a young man, played by O'Keefe, who inherits a million dollars and knocks himself out trying to spend it in two months so he can inherit even more. Bright, fast-paced mirth with a fine cast helping out with the spending spree. It should happen to you. Also with Helen Walker, Eddie "Rochester" Anderson, and June Havoc. **Director**—Allan Dwan.

79 minutes b&w

THE BRIBE (1949)
★★

Robert Taylor
Ava Gardner

Taylor plays a G-man who pursues some criminals in Latin America and falls in love with sultry Gardner, the wife of one of the bad guys. Glossy, pretentious claptrap, which entertains on a rather low level. The usually competent players aren't at their best although the crooks are impressively menacing. Also with Charles Laughton, Vincent Price, and John Hodiak. **Director**—Robert Z. Leonard.

98 minutes b&w

THE BRIDE CAME C.O.D. (1941)
★★★

Bette Davis
James Cagney

Davis and Cagney star in this workable comedy in which the talent salvages a cornball script. Cagney is a charter pilot who must deliver runaway bride Davis, but the plane crashes. Guess who falls in love with whom? This is Davis's first comedy role. She's not bad, and she improved her skills in subsequent pictures. Supporting players include Harry Davenport, Jack Carson, and Stuart Erwin. **Director**—William Keighley.

92 minutes b&w

BRIDE OF FRANKENSTEIN (1935)
 ### ★★★★

Boris Karloff
Elsa Lanchester

Baron Frankenstein is coerced into reviving the monster and constructing

Elsa Lanchester created an unforgettable monster vogue as the Bride of Frankenstein.

a mate. This classic horror film, a sequel to *Frankenstein*, is better than the first film in many respects. It is expertly laced with wit, black comedy, pathos, and thrills galore. Karloff is back in his striking monster getup, and Lanchester is superb in dual roles; she plays the macabre mate of the monster and Mary Shelley. Also with Colin Clive, Valerie Hobson, and Ernest Thesiger. **Director**—James Whale.

80 minutes b&w

THE BRIDGE OF SAN LUIS REY (1944)
★★

Lynn Bari
Alla Nazimova
Louis Calhern

Painful, plodding film, based on Thornton Wilder's novel, about five people who are killed when a flimsy bridge in Peru collapses. A priest investigates the cause of the mishap and the reasons why the people were on the bridge at the moment of collapse. It's a hard pull for the cast and the director. The players also include Francis Lederer, Akim Tamiroff, and Donald Woods. **Director**—Rowland V. Lee.

85 minutes b&w

THE BRIDGE ON THE RIVER KWAI (1957)
 ### ★★★★

Alec Guinness
Jack Hawkins
William Holden
Sessue Hayakawa

A superb war drama distinguished by

magnificent acting and direction and an out-of-the-ordinary approach to its subject. Guinness stands out as a determined British commanding officer captured by the Japanese. He spurs his men to construct a railway bridge in Burma for their captors to maintain morale and demonstrate British engineering superiority; then he can't bear to see his own creation blown up by his own side. The film is blessed with gripping action, suspense, and a compelling script that bristles with ironies. The film is based on Pierre Boulle's novel. **Director**—David Lean. **Academy Awards**—best picture; Lean, best director; Guinness, best actor; Boulle, best screenplay (based on material from another medium); Jack Hildyard, cinematography. **Nomination**—Hayakawa, best supporting actor.

161 minutes

THE BRIDGES AT TOKO-RI (1954)
★★★

William Holden
Grace Kelly
Mickey Rooney

A powerful film about the adventures of a pilot during the Korean Conflict and the impact of the separation on his family. The action-packed thriller, based on James E. Michener's novel, is a cut above the usual war drama, with some impressive statements to make about fighting, comradeship, and family. Fine performances from Holden, Rooney, and Kelly. Also with Fredric March, Robert Strauss, and Charles McGraw. **Director**—Mark Robson.

104 minutes

A BRIDGE TOO FAR (1977)
 ### ★★

Dirk Bogarde
James Caan
Michael Caine
Sean Connery

It seems as if an entire regiment of movie notables appears in this $26-million epic based on Cornelius Ryan's best-seller about a disastrous Allied offensive during World War II. However, the Joseph E. Levine production is just another massive war movie mired in noise and confusion. Hardly

(Continued)

ROBERT DE NIRO

Robert De Niro was born in New York City's tough Lower East Side, in Little Italy, in 1945. As a child, he was extremely shy, but, at the age of 10, he played the role of the Cowardly Lion in a school production of The Wizard of Oz.

By 16, De Niro had dropped out of high school and had earned his first paycheck on a tour of high schools in the New England and New York area in Chekov's The Bear. He then spent 15 years learning his craft from such drama teachers as Stella Adler, Luther James, and Lee Strasberg.

De Niro made his motion picture debut in The Wedding Party (1969), directed by Brian De Palma. He co-starred with Shelley Winters in Bloody Mama (1970) for producer Roger Corman. In 1971, he made The Gang That Couldn't Shoot Straight, the film that first showed he was star material. He then received recognition for his performance as the dying ballplayer in Bang the Drum Slowly (1973). Also released that same year was Martin Scorsese's Mean Streets, a powerful film that won him the best supporting actor award of the New York Film Critics Circle.

Some of De Niro's other movies include The Godfather—Part II (1974), Taxi Driver (1976), The Deer Hunter (1978), Raging Bull (1980), True Confessions (1981), The King of Comedy (1983), Falling in Love (1984), in which he co-starred with Meryl Streep, and Once Upon a Time in America (1984). De Niro won an Academy Award for his portrayal of middleweight boxing champion Jake La Motta in Raging Bull.

Dirk Bogarde is the officer who orders his men to carry out a foolhardy mission in A Bridge Too Far.

(Continued)
any of the big American or British stars are on screen long enough to establish audience involvement. At an almost three-hour length, A Bridge Too Far is a movie too long. Also with Robert Redford, Elliott Gould, Laurence Olivier, and Ryan O'Neal. **Director**—Richard Attenborough. (PG)
175 minutes

BRIEF ENCOUNTER (1946)
 ★★★★

Celia Johnson
Trevor Howard

A touching and sensitive love story that works surprisingly well in light of its familiar theme. A housewife, played by Johnson, has an affair with a local doctor, played by Howard. It ends abruptly when he takes a job in another country. Outstanding craftsmanship in all quarters has produced a classic romantic drama, with memorable love scenes that are a pleasure to watch. Also with Stanley Holloway and Joyce Carey. The film is based on Noel Coward's play. **Director**—David Lean. **Academy Award Nominations**—Lean, best director; Johnson, best actress; Anthony Havelock-Allan, Lean, and Ronald Neame, writing (screenplay). 86 minutes b&w

---

BRIGADOON
(1954)
 ★★★

Gene Kelly
Cyd Charisse
Van Johnson

Gene Kelly and Van Johnson discover a magical Scottish village in Brigadoon.

Pleasant and charming film version of the Alan Jay Lerner and Frederick Loewe Broadway musical about two Americans—Kelly and Johnson—who discover a magical Scottish village that comes to life for a day every 100 years. Kelly and Charisse handle the dancing with grace and style, and the music is invigorating. The sets look artificial, but that doesn't distract much from the entertainment. Jimmy Thompson, Elaine Stewart, and Barry Jones have supporting roles. **Director**—Vincente Minnelli. 108 minutes

---

BRIMSTONE AND TREACLE
(1982)
 ★

Sting

Bizarre, unsavory psychological thriller starring Sting of the rock group Police. He convincingly portrays a sinister young drifter who cons his way into the home of a middle-class English couple and there molests their paralyzed daughter. The film is handsomely mounted and decently acted, but the weird scenario leaves a sour aftertaste. Forthright supporting work

• Bring Me the Head of Alfredo Garcia
• The Brink's Job
• Britannia Hospital
• Broadway
• Broadway Danny Rose
• Broken Arrow
• Broken Lance
• Bronco Billy

B

from Denholm Elliott and Joan Plowright as the perplexed husband and wife. **Director**—Richard Loncraine. (R)   *87 minutes*

BRING ME THE HEAD OF ALFREDO GARCIA (1974)
★

Warren Oates
Gig Young

A blood-and-gore drama about a Mexican seeking revenge on the person who seduced his daughter. Director Sam Peckinpah serves up his usual spread of violence garnished with plenty of gruesome details. However, the action is somewhat slow for this sort of outing. Isela Vega, Robert Webber, Emilio Fernandez, Helmut Dantine, and Kris Kristofferson are also in the cast. (R)   *112 minutes*

THE BRINK'S JOB (1978)
★★

Peter Falk
Peter Boyle

The $2.7-million Brink's stickup in Boston was called "the crime of the century," but in this flippant account the celebrated 1950 caper comes off as petty theft. William Friedkin, who gave us the exciting *French Connection*, directs here with scant energy or spirit. After sitting through this movie, you may feel that you've been robbed, too. Also with Allen Goorwitz, Warren Oates, and Gena Rowlands. (PG)   *103 minutes*

BRITANNIA HOSPITAL (1982)
 ★★

Leonard Rossiter
Graham Crowden
Malcolm McDowell

A boisterous, contemporary British satire that often takes itself too seriously. The farcical story centers on a modern hospital embroiled in a labor dispute. Various noisy incidents are loosely strung together and moments of bad taste surface when a doctor carries out bloody human transplant experiments. The film ends with shrill sermonizing. **Director**—Lindsay Anderson. (R)   *115 minutes*

BROADWAY (1942)
★★★

George Raft
Pat O'Brien

Raft takes us down memory lane to the Prohibition era when he danced in nightclubs. Gangsters, bootleggers, chorus girls, and speakeasies are the backdrops for this colorful drama, which involves a murder. Raft plays himself and does some dancing. O'Brien plays a cop, and Broderick Crawford is effective as a tough gangster. Also with S. Z. Sakall and Janet Blair. **Director**—William A. Seiter.
90 minutes b&w

BROADWAY DANNY ROSE (1984)
 ★★★★

Woody Allen
Mia Farrow
Nick Apollo Forte

Mia Farrow refuses to carry Woody Allen's luggage in Broadway Danny Rose.

Allen is again in comfortable comic shoes with this Runyonesque fable about a good-hearted, second-rate theatrical manager. He's the familiar schlemiel, spouting wry one-liners as he makes frantic efforts to revive the career of an over-the-hill singer, played with exceptional pizzazz by newcomer Forte. Mia Farrow is outstanding and almost unrecognizable as a bleached-blonde tootsie in dark glasses. Everything works: Woody's hilarious script and deft direction, Gordon Willis' dazzling cinematography—even Forte's self-composed lounge act. Watch for Milton Berle and a host of other old-time comedians playing themselves and having a ball. (PG)   *84 minutes*

BROKEN ARROW (1950)
★★★

James Stewart
Jeff Chandler
Debra Paget

A serious western drama, with Stewart as an Army scout sympathetic to the Indians and trying to promote peace and understanding between the redskins and the whites. The film is interesting because it doesn't present the Indians as cardboard characters; Chandler is impressive as Cochise, and Paget does well as Stewart's Indian wife. A few brisk action scenes perk up the straightaway narrative. Will Geer and Jay Silverheels co-star. **Director**—Delmer Daves. **Academy Award Nominations**—Chandler, best supporting actor; Michael Blankfort, writing (screenplay); Ernest Palmer, cinematography (color).   *92 minutes*

BROKEN LANCE (1954)
★★★

Spencer Tracy
Richard Widmark

Tracy is effective as the patriarch of a fading cattle empire who grapples with family conflicts. The taut western drama, remade from *House of Strangers*, also offers a fine performance by Widmark as the unlikable eldest son. Robert Wagner and Jean Peters manage the romantic interlude. Other fine supporting performances from Hugh O'Brien, E. G. Marshall, and Katy Jurado. **Director**—Edward Dmytryk. **Academy Award**—Philip Yordan, writing (motion picture story). **Nomination**—Jurado, best supporting actress.   *96 minutes*

BRONCO BILLY (1980)
 ★★★

Clint Eastwood
Sondra Locke

A sweet-natured, low-key comedy with Eastwood as star and owner of a rickety Wild West show. The predictable plot is strictly corn, but Eastwood has fashioned a warmhearted char-
(Continued)

B
- The Brood
- The Brother from Another Planet
- Brothers
- Brubaker
- Brute Force
- Buckaroo Banzai
- Buck Privates

(Continued)

acter, which keeps the film at a respectable comic level. Eastwood's "Billy" is a big kid, living in a fantasy world, who is sentimentally concerned about his likable ragtag troupe and his small-fry fans. Eastwood, who has played his Dirty Harry character to the hilt, is a charming "Mr. Clean." **Director**—Eastwood. (PG)

119 minutes

THE BROOD (1980)

 ★★

Oliver Reed
Samantha Eggar

An effective yet overly grotesque Canadian-made horror film, written and directed by David Cronenberg, who borrowed freely from such shockers as *Night of the Living Dead*. Eggar plays a mental patient under the care of a bizzare doctor, played by Reed. She gives birth to strange children, who murder a number of people, including her mother and father. Cronenberg builds adequate suspense, but there's plenty of plodding amid the gore. (R) *90 minutes*

THE BROTHER FROM ANOTHER PLANET (1984)

★★★

Joe Morton

Director John Sayles (*Return of the Secaucus Seven*) explores ghetto life through the eyes of an extraterrestrial in this low-budget comedy that works off and on—mostly on. Morton stars as an astonished black man from another planet who winds up in Harlem and becomes involved with various colorful characters. Sayle's peppy dialogue is salted with plenty of street lingo. Darryl Edwards and Steve James co-star. (No MPAA rating)

110 minutes

BROTHERS (1977)

★★★

Bernie Casey
Vonetta McGee

A dramatized semidocumentary, based on the love affair between black activist Angela Davis and George Jackson, one of the famed Soledad Brothers. The script is oversimplified and loaded in favor of the Jackson-Davis cause. Still, the film is an effective and jolting statement against racism, injustice, and the indignities of prison life. Casey in the Jackson role and McGee in the part of Davis display forceful and convincing characterizations. The film is a sober and refreshing departure from such black exploitation vehicles as *Superfly*. **Director**—Arthur Barron. (R) *104 minutes*

BRUBAKER (1980)

 ★★

Robert Redford
Yaphet Kotto
Murray Hamilton

Robert Redford stars as a harassed prison warden in Brubaker.

Redford stars as a reform-minded prison warden, who halts corruption and torture only to be dismissed by the political establishment. Redford starts out as a prisoner to secretly witness the brutality. But when he soon reveals his identity, the film loses impact; the grim drama ends and sentimental sermonizing begins. **Director**—Stuart Rosenberg. (R) **Academy Award Nomination**—screenplay (written directly for the screen); W. D. Richter (screenplay), Richter and Arthur Ross (story).

131 minutes

BRUTE FORCE (1947)

★★★★

Burt Lancaster
Charles Bickford

Exceptional big-house melodrama that lives up to its title with graphic detail of prison environment. Six desperate convicts plan to break out, getting revenge against a sadistic guard captain along the way. Tough, savage action leads up to a smashing climax. The fine cast also features Hume Cronyn, Ella Raines, Yvonne De Carlo, Ann Blyth, Howard Duff, and Sam Levene. **Director**—Jules Dassin.

96 minutes b&w

BUCKAROO BANZAI (1984)

 ★

Peter Weller
John Lithgow

Wacky, jumbled, sci-fi comedy with a confusing, off-the-wall plot that contains enough elements for 10 movies. Weller is in the title role as a neurosurgeon-rock singer-race car driver who battles aliens from Planet 10. Most of the cast doesn't act; they merely walk around in a daze. Only Lithgow, as a mad scientist, seems at all interesting. **Director**—W.D. Richter. (PG)

100 minutes

BUCK PRIVATES (1941)

★★

Bud Abbott
Lou Costello

Bud Abbott takes his orders without complaining in Buck Privates.

• Buck Privates Come Home
• Buck Rogers in the 25th Century
• Buddy Buddy
• The Buddy Holly Story
• The Buddy System
• Buffalo Bill and the Indians, or Sitting Bull's History Lesson

B

Abbott and Costello join the Army, and after an energetic romp of escapades, they accidentally become heroes. This is typical service comedy corn with some romantic subplots thrown in, but it works for Abbott and Costello. This was one of their first starring films, and their success won them promotions as the top sergeants of movie comedy. Lee Bowman, Alan Curtis, Jane Frazee, Nat Pendleton, and the Andrews Sisters round out the cast. **Director**—Arthur Lubin.

84 minutes b&w

BUCK PRIVATES COME HOME (1946)

 ★★

Bud Abbott
Lou Costello

Abbott and Costello muster out of the Army and care for a European war orphan. This is a rather flimsy slapstick comedy and certainly not at the level of *Buck Privates*. However, the film perks up considerably with a chase sequence at the finale. Beverly Simmons, Tom Brown, and Nat Pendleton co-star. **Director**—Charles T. Barton. *77 minutes b&w*

BUCK ROGERS IN THE 25TH CENTURY (1979)

 ★★

Gil Gerard
Pamela Hensley
Erin Gray

This is a film based on the sci-fi comic strip character, but there's more inspiration from *Star Wars*. You'll see space

Gil Gerard is Buck Rogers in the 25th Century.

hardware galore, a climactic shootout among rocket ships, and a pixie robot that's an obvious rip-off of R2-D2. The film looks dazzling most of the time thanks to the snappy direction of Daniel Haller. Small fry should be able to handle the simple good-guy/bad-guy plot and take delight in the wisecracks of Gerard, who plays the title role. (PG) *89 minutes*

BUDDY BUDDY (1981)

 ★

Jack Lemmon
Walter Matthau

In Buddy Buddy, *Klaus Kinski portrays the head doctor at a sex clinic.*

What a team: Billy Wilder directing Matthau and Lemmon in this farce about a hit man trying to bump off a stool pigeon while a suicidal schnook keeps interfering with the assassination plan. Matthau plays the hood, and Lemmon is the schnook—and what a disappointment. The comedy material is consistently off stride and only manages to generate a few smiles. It's all sadly trite and strained, not what anyone would expect from the folks responsible for hits like *The Fortune Cookie*. Paula Prentiss and Klaus Kinski co-star. (R) *96 minutes*

THE BUDDY HOLLY STORY (1978)

★★★★

Gary Busey
Don Stroud

A first-rate, realistic film biography of

the talented rockabilly composer-musician who introduced such '50s hits as "Peggy Sue" and "That'll Be the Day." Lanky, toothsome Busey, in the title role, lights up the screen with his energetic musical and dramatic performance. The story follows Holly's career beginning as a roller rink musician in Texas to his death at 22 in a plane crash. Best of all is the way the film captures the joy and enthusiasm of early rock 'n' roll and its effect on young people. **Director**—Steve Rash. (PG) **Academy Award Nomination**—Busey, best actor. *114 minutes*

THE BUDDY SYSTEM (1984)

 ★★

Richard Dreyfuss
Susan Sarandon

A sparse, boy-meets-girl romantic comedy with a few tender moments that surface occasionally amid the generally dry material. Dreyfuss is a sometime novelist-inventor who strikes up a rather shaky relationship with an insecure single mother played adroitly by Sarandon. The affair is eagerly engineered by the mother's precocious young son. After the couple maneuvers through various pat complications, true love predictably triumphs. **Director**—Glenn Jordon. (PG) *111 minutes*

BUFFALO BILL AND THE INDIANS, OR SITTING BULL'S HISTORY LESSON (1976)

 ★★★

Paul Newman
Joel Grey

Robert Altman's intelligent and penetrating study of the legendary showbiz hero of the late 1800s shows Buffalo Bill as an egotistical, inflated product of publicity. The film is also about genocide committed against the Indians. Newman gives a keen and often amusing performance in the title role. Frank Kaquitts plays an impressive, silent, and dignified Sitting Bull, who was signed to appear in Buffalo Bill's Wild West Show. There are some uneven and dreary moments, which lessen the film's impact. But it succeeds in its creativity and its reexamination of history. Also with Kevin McCarthy, Burt

(Continued)

B
• The Bugs Bunny/Road
    Runner Movie
• Bugs Bunny's 3rd Movie:
    1001 Rabbit Tales

• Bugsy Malone
• Bullitt
• Bundle of Joy

(Continued)
Lancaster, and Geraldine Chaplin. **Director**—Altman. (PG)   *120 minutes*

THE BUGS BUNNY/ ROAD RUNNER MOVIE (1979)
 ★★★

**Bugs Bunny
Road Runner
Daffy Duck
Wile E. Coyote
Porky Pig**

Now you can really indulge yourself in an hour and a half of nonstop fun with Bugs, Daffy, Wile E. Coyote, and other stars from the Warner Brothers cartoon stable. Animator Chuck Jones has compiled scenes from numerous cartoons and has included several complete short features. There's about 20 minutes of new animation with Bugs as narrator. It's a nostalgic, colorful parade of great animated comedy— that's what's up, Doc! (G)   *92 minutes*

BUGS BUNNY'S 3RD MOVIE: 1001 RABBIT TALES (1982)
 ★★★

Those colorful Warner Brothers cartoons are back with Bugs, Tweety Bird, Yosemite Sam, Daffy Duck, and other favorite characters up to their usual cute tricks. Essentially, it's the same stuff that shows up on Saturday morning TV, but it's more enjoyable here without the commercial interruptions. Many old sketches are recycled, and there's some new material. The versatile Mel Blanc provides most of the voice characterizations. **Directors**—Friz Freleng and Robert McKimson. (G)   *74 minutes*

RICHARD BURTON

Richard Burton, the brooding Welsh actor, was as competent on the stage as he was on the screen. He was known for his commanding presence and his fine speaking voice, but he was perhaps as well known for his tumultuous love affairs and two marriages to actress Elizabeth Taylor.

He was born Richard Jenkins in South Wales in 1925, the son of a coal miner. He took the name Burton from his schoolmaster, who was partly responsible for Burton receiving a scholarship to Oxford.

Burton made his stage debut in Druid's Rest, *in 1943. From 1944 to 1947, he served as a navigator in the Royal Air Force. After his discharge in 1948, he resumed his stage career and also starred in his first film,* The Last Days of Dolwyn. *By the mid-'50s, he was recognized as one of Britain's best young actors.*

In 1952, Burton came to Hollywood to star in My Cousin Rachel, *and then played in a series of costume dramas, such as* The Robe *(1953),* Prince of Players *(1954), and* Alexander the Great *(1956).*

During the filming of Cleopatra *(1962), his much publicized romance with Elizabeth Taylor, his co-star, began, and his reputation as a serious actor declined while his popularity as a movie idol rose. Burton still found opportunities to star in various legitimate productions including Shakespearean dramas.*

Burton starred in a variety of film roles during the late '60s and throughout the '70s, but many of the assignments made few demands on his acting talent. He received six Academy Award nominations, but never won an Oscar.

Some of Burton's other movies include Look Back in Anger *(1959),* The V.I.P.s *(1963),* Becket *(1964),* The Night of the Iguana *(1964),* Who's Afraid of Virginia Woolf? *(1966),* The Taming of the Shrew *(1967),* Anne of the Thousand Days *(1970),* Exorcist II *(1977), and* Equus *(1977). His last film was a remake of George Orwell's* 1984 *(1984), in which he had a supporting role.*

Burton died in August, 1984, in Geneva, Switzerland, at age 58.

BUGSY MALONE (1976)
 ★★★

**Scott Baio
Florrie Dugger
Jodie Foster**

An ingeniously conceived and lavish '20s gangster movie played entirely by kids whose average age is 12. Most of the youngsters perform rather well, dressed in pinstriped double-breasted suits and flapper outfits. The tommy guns splatter their victims with whipped cream. Veteran actress Foster (age 14) is outstanding as a brassy showgirl. The film is made with care and affection, yet it's top-heavy with old movie clichés, and momentum is lost toward the end. Also with John Cassisi and Martin Lev. **Director**— Alan Parker. (G)   *93 minutes*

BULLITT (1968)
 ★★★★

**Steve McQueen
Jacqueline Bisset
Robert Vaughn**

Stylish, stirring detective thriller with McQueen smartly cast as a San Francisco cop trying to put the lid on underworld activity. A key witness in McQueen's charge is killed, and he tracks down the murderers. The action-packed drama, graced by efficient direction, ends in a classic car chase that is well above the ordinary. The fine supporting cast includes Don Gordon, Robert Duvall, and Simon Oakland. **Director**—Peter Yates.
113 minutes

BUNDLE OF JOY (1956)
★★

**Debbie Reynolds
Eddie Fisher**

Reynolds and Fisher star in this thin and occasionally cute musical comedy remade from *Bachelor Mother*. Reynolds plays a department store clerk, who discovers an abandoned child; people suspect that her boyfriend, played by Fisher, is the father. Fisher sings some forgettable songs, and the cast milks a few laughs from the script. Also with Adolphe Menjou, Melville

Cooper, and Tommy Noonan. **Director**—Norman Taurog.   *98 minutes*

BURNT OFFERINGS (1976)

    ★★★

**Karen Black
Oliver Reed**

Skillful direction from Dan Curtis produces a lot of chills and tension in this thriller about a family who rents a creepy old mansion for the summer. There are solid performances, too, from Black, Reed, Lee Montgomery, and Bette Davis. Clichés are sprinkled throughout the plot, and the ending is predictable. But the eerie goings-on at that rambling murderous house and the mystery behind the locked door on the top floor will keep moviegoers on the edges of their seats. Also with Burgess Meredith and Eileen Heckart. (PG)   *115 minutes*

BUS STOP (1956)

    ★★★

**Marilyn Monroe
Don Murray**

Monroe displays competent acting talent as well as her familiar sex appeal in this comedy-drama about ordinary people. She plays a voluptuous cafe singer who entices a naive cowboy, played by Murray, while his friends urge him not to get involved. The film, based on William Inge's play, offers an entertaining mixture of sensitive drama and comic moments. Betty Field stands out as a waitress. Eileen Heckart, Arthur O'Connell, Hope Lange, and Hans Conreid co-star. **Director**—Joshua Logan. **Alternate Title**—*Wrong Kind of Girl*. **Academy Award Nomination**—Murray, best supporting actor.   *96 minutes*

BUSTIN' LOOSE (1981)

    ★★

**Richard Pryor
Cicely Tyson**

Pryor stars as a small-time thief who shepherds some rascally children to the West Coast in a rickety bus. Pryor fans will love some of his funny skits. His self-parodying style has great

charm, but as the script gains sentimentality, his talents are undermined; the tone becomes domesticated and even tacky. The kids are precocious (clones of *The Bad News Bears?*). Tyson is a social worker and the unlikely romantic interest of Pryor. **Director**—Oz Scott. (R)   *94 minutes*

BUTCH AND SUNDANCE: THE EARLY DAYS (1979)

★★

**William Katt
Tom Berenger**

A family portrait from Butch and Sundance: The Early Days.

This prequel to *Butch Cassidy and the Sundance Kid* explores how the two outlaws met and some of their preliminary escapades. Berenger and Katt are in the title roles, but there's no special chemistry between them as we witnessed with Paul Newman and Robert Redford in the original, which was made 10 years earlier. The prequel also lacks spirit and style, and the script is as hollow as a drainpipe. It seems their early days were dreary days. **Director**—Richard Lester. (PG)
    110 minutes

BUTCH CASSIDY AND THE SUNDANCE KID (1969)

    ★★★★

**Paul Newman
Robert Redford
Katharine Ross**

This humorous and cheerful western

offers a full complement of film excellence: superb direction, winning performances, effective comedy, and the memorable tune "Raindrops Keep Fallin' on My Head." Newman and Redford strike up perfect chemistry together as clownish outlaws with a sheriff's posse always one step behind. The appealing movie begins energetically and never flags. There is enthusiastic support from Ross, Strother Martin, Jeff Corey, and Cloris Leachman. **Director**—George Roy Hill. (PG) **Academy Awards**—William Goldman, best story and screenplay (based on material not previously published or produced); Conrad Hall, cinematography. **Nominations**—best picture; Hill, best director.   *110 minutes*

BUTTERFIELD 8 (1960)

★★

**Elizabeth Taylor
Laurence Harvey**

Elizabeth Taylor proves that she's no kid anymore in Butterfield 8.

The only thing going for this routine melodrama is a slick performance by Taylor as a high-priced call girl who longs to get out of the profession. The film, based on John O'Hara's novel, starts off awkwardly and never really picks up steam. Harvey is impressive as Taylor's Mr. Right. There's adequate support, too, from Dina Merrill, Mildred Dunnock, and Betty Field. **Director**—Daniel Mann. **Academy Award**—Taylor, best actress. **Nomination**—Joseph Ruttenberg and Charles Harten, cinematography (color).
    108 minutes

 Movie is available in Beta and VHS videotape

B·C

• Butterflies Are Free
• Bye Bye Birdie
• By Love Possessed
• By the Light of the Silvery Moon
• Cabaret
• Cabin in the Sky
• Cactus Flower

BUTTERFLIES ARE FREE (1972)

★★★

Goldie Hawn
Edward Albert

Goldie Hawn gives blind Edward Albert something interesting to feel in Butterflies Are Free.

Hawn stars in this lighthearted film as a flighty actress who falls in love with a blind young man next door. Then she has to deal with his overprotective mother. Based on Leonard Gershe's Broadway play, the film adaptation is somewhat confined, but good acting by the top cast overcomes the drawback. Hawn is perfectly cast, and Eileen Heckart is brilliant as the possessive mother. Albert plays the blind man. **Director**—Milton Katselas. **Academy Award**—Heckart, best supporting actress. **Nomination**—Charles B. Lang, cinematography.
109 minutes

BYE BYE BIRDIE (1963)
★★★

Janet Leigh
Dick Van Dyke
Ann-Margret

A teenage singing sensation gives his final TV show before leaving for military service. This frothy musical is based on the Broadway show and features some pleasant numbers, including "Put on a Happy Face." Van Dyke is good as a songwriter, and Paul Lynde and Maureen Stapleton are impressive as frantic parents. The film should have special appeal for younger audiences. Also with Bobby Rydell and Ed Sullivan. **Director**—George Sidney.
112 minutes

BY LOVE POSSESSED (1961)
★★

Lana Turner
Efrem Zimbalist, Jr.

A dour melodrama about a successful but lonely New England lawyer, played by Zimbalist, who has an affair with the restless wife of his partner. Turner plays the wife. The cast is presentable, but the soapy script is rather unmoving. This film is based loosely on a James Gould Cozzens novel. Jason Robards, Jr., Barbara Bel Geddes, George Hamilton, and Thomas Mitchell co-star. **Director**—John Sturges.
116 minutes

BY THE LIGHT OF THE SILVERY MOON (1953)
★★★

Doris Day
Gordon MacRae

A pleasant musical-comedy vehicle tailor-made for Day, who has lots of old-fashioned songs to sing. The film is set in a small American town just after World War I, and it involves family problems with a returning soldier. MacRae is a fine singing partner for Day. The screenplay, which is a sequel to *On Moonlight Bay*, is based on a Booth Tarkington story. Leon Ames, Rosemary DeCamp, and Mary Wickes co-star. **Director**—David Butler.
101 minutes

C

CABARET (1972)

★★★★

Liza Minnelli
Joel Grey
Michael York

Smashing, masterful musical with the showstopping performance of Minnelli as Sally Bowles, an American singer working in Berlin on the eve of World War II. The multitalented Minnelli proves to be a fantastic actress as

Liza Minnelli shows us where the best seat in the house is at the Cabaret.

well as a singer-dancer, and she's complemented nicely by Bob Fosse's stylish direction and choreography. The film loosely follows the Broadway musical, based on Christopher Isherwood's stories, but the script also relies on the plot of *I Am a Camera*. The political backdrop of Hitler's Germany is handled intelligently. Also with Helmut Griem, Fritz Wepper, and Marisa Berenson. (PG) **Academy Awards**—Bob Fosse, best director; Minnelli, best actress; Grey, best supporting actor; Geoffrey Unsworth, cinematography. **Nomination**—Jay Allen, best screenplay (based on material from another medium).
123 minutes

CABIN IN THE SKY (1943)
★★★

Eddie "Rochester" Anderson
Ethel Waters
Lena Horne

God and the Devil compete for the soul of a gambling man in this delightful musical, which features an all-black cast. The film doesn't quite live up to the play, but it's energetic and engrossing nevertheless. The superb cast also includes Cab Calloway and Louis Armstrong. With such giants of entertainment on board, it's watchable indeed. **Director**—Vincente Minnelli.
99 minutes b&w

CACTUS FLOWER (1969)

★★

Ingrid Bergman
Walter Matthau
Goldie Hawn

Despite the fine cast, this film version

• Caddie
• The Caddy
• Caddyshack
• La Cage aux Folles
• La Cage aux Folles II
• The Caine Mutiny

C

Nurse Ingrid Bergman tells off dentist Walter Matthau in Cactus Flower.

of the Broadway comedy doesn't hold up. Matthau plays a dentist in love with his nurse, who is played by Bergman. She drops her defensive attitude when she discovers he's sincere. Bergman is miscast for this sort of part, and the starchy dialogue is a noticeable drawback. But Hawn shines as the dentist's mistress, who is forsaken for the nurse. Also with Jack Weston, Vito Scotti, and Irene Hervey. **Director**—Gene Saks. (PG) **Academy Award**—Hawn, best supporting actress.

103 minutes

CADDIE (1981)
★★

Helen Morse

A well-intentioned but pedestrian Australian biographical film about a struggling single woman who supports two young children while working as a barmaid during the '20s and '30s. The sets are handsome and authentic-looking, but the story really goes nowhere. Morse stars as the resolute, independent lass who becomes involved in several on-again, off-again romances that are as interesting as the affairs in a soap opera that has gone on too long. **Director**—Donald Crombie. (No MPAA rating)

107 minutes

THE CADDY (1953)
★★

Dean Martin
Jerry Lewis

Martin and Lewis star in this film about golf. The production is organized in a series of vignettes, with Lewis as a golf enthusiast trying to build up Martin's game. This is certainly not the best the pair has to offer, but there are some good moments and Martin sings, "That's Amore." Donna Reed, Fred Clark, and Barbara Bates co-star. **Director**—Norman Taurog.

95 minutes b&w

CADDYSHACK (1980)
★

Chevy Chase
Ted Knight
Rodney Dangerfield
Bill Murray

There are silly high jinks on the golf links with Chase, Knight, Dangerfield, and Murray engaging in crude jokes that mostly misfire. There's only a ghost of a plot—something about a polite but poor caddy trying to wheedle help for a college scholarship from an influential club member. Generally, the film is a series of dopey throwaway vignettes that poke fun at the WASPy country club set. **Director**—Harold Ramis. (R)

98 minutes

LA CAGE AUX FOLLES (1979)
★★★★

Ugo Tognazzi
Michel Serrault

What do you do when you're in love with a beautiful, respectable girl, and your father is a homosexual who lives with a drag queen? Bring her folks over to meet your folks, of course. And that's when all the outrageous fun begins in this brilliant farce, which won France's version of the Oscar. Skilled performances and keen comic timing by Tognazzi and Serrault as the gay duo make this film a great comedy. In French with English titles. (R) **Director**—Edouard Molinaro. **Academy Award Nominations**—Molinaro, best director; Francis Veber, Molinaro, Marcello Danon, and Jean Poiret, best screenplay (adapted from another medium).

99 minutes

LA CAGE AUX FOLLES II (1981)
★★

Ugo Tognazzi
Michel Serrault

Serrault, as the temperamental drag queen, and Tognazzi, as his lover, return in this so-so sequel to the successful French comedy. This time, the duo is mixed up in a drab and predictable secret-agent melodrama with missing microfilm and several corpses. Serrault and Tognazzi generate some funny moments, but it's formula stuff without the relentlessly clever ingredients that made the first film a hit. In French with English titles. **Director**—Edouard Molinaro. (R)

100 minutes

THE CAINE MUTINY (1954)
★★★★

Humphrey Bogart
José Ferrer
Van Johnson

Humphrey Bogart is Queeg, the paranoid captain in The Caine Mutiny.

A powerful adaptation of Herman Wouk's gripping Pulitzer Prize novel of Navy officers who rebel against the neurotic captain of a destroyer escort during World War II. This absorbing film offers exciting action and first-class performances, which graphically portray the frustrations and character traits of the subjects. Bogart is especially memorable as the unhinged skipper. The film ends in a smashing court-martial climax with the resolution of justice under question. Also with Fred MacMurray, E. G. Marshall, Lee Marvin, and Tom Tully. **Director**—Edward Dmytryk. **Academy Award Nominations**—best picture; Bogart, best actor; Tully, best supporting actor;

(Continued)

C

- Cal
- Calamity Jane
- California Split
- California Suite
- Caligula
- Call Me Bwana
- Call Me Madam
- Call Me Mister

(Continued)
Stanley Roberts, writing (screenplay).
125 minutes

CAL (1984)
★★

John Lynch
Helen Mirren

Somber, tragic story of the numbing violence in Northern Ireland as seen through the experience of an unemployed Catholic youth. The performances are adequate, but events are slow moving and loosely connected. A depressing atmosphere pervades the film as if to illustrate the climate of endless terror. Lynch is in the title role, and Mirren is the older woman to whom he reaches out for love. **Director**—Pat O'Connor. (R)   *102 minutes*

CALAMITY JANE (1953)
★★★

Doris Day
Howard Keel

A pleasant, energetic musical that's just the right vehicle for Day, who stars in the title role. Doris plays the rough-and-ready frontier girl with plenty of vigor. She's tamed by Keel, who co-stars as Wild Bill Hickok. The film is a little on the order of *Annie Get Your Gun*. It has a pleasant score, including the Oscar-winning song, "Secret Love." Phil Carey, Allyn McLerie, Dick Wesson, and Paul Harvey lend support. **Director**—David Butler.   *101 minutes*

CALIFORNIA SPLIT (1974)
★★★

Elliott Gould
George Segal

Uneven but cheerful and entertaining comedy especially suited for those who like director Robert Altman's unique style. Gould and Segal are compulsive gamblers who become fast friends and go on a spree together. Altman manages to present these oddball characters in a way that's touching and amusing. Ann Prentiss and Gwen Welles are effective as a couple of amateur hookers. Also with Joseph Walsh and Bert Remsen. (R)
109 minutes

CALIFORNIA SUITE
(1978)
★★

Jane Fonda
Alan Alda
Maggie Smith
Michael Caine
Walter Matthau
Elaine May
Richard Pryor
Bill Cosby

Walter Matthau tries to think of a way out of his predicament with wife Elaine May and prostitute Denise Galik in California Suite.

A bevy of top film stars talk, talk, talk in this Neil Simon comedy, set in the Beverly Hills Hotel. This movie version of the Broadway stage production is changed from four separate playlets to a cohesive story, but the effect is a labored, ragged barrage of wisecracks. There's top-notch acting, but even the good performances wear thin from the tiresome dialogue, which sounds like incessant bickering after a while. **Director**—Herbert Ross. (PG) **Academy Award**—Smith, best supporting actress. **Nomination**—Simon, best screenplay adaptation.   *103 minutes*

CALIGULA (1980)
(no stars)

Malcolm McDowell
Peter O'Toole
John Gielgud

Penthouse magazine publisher Bob Guccione produced this vulgar $17-million porno spectacle set in first-century Rome. It's a lengthy smorgasbord of explicit sex, mixed with assorted horrors, such as disembowel-ment, castration, decapitation, and strangulation. Just watching this mess can be a real workout. **Director**—Giovanni Tinto. (No MPAA rating)
150 minutes

CALL ME BWANA (1962)
★★

Bob Hope
Anita Ekberg

Hope goes to Africa to find a lost space capsule and tries to elude foreign agents. Typical Hope farce with some effective jokes, but not quite enough to sustain the movie. Ekberg and Edie Adams are just lovely to look at. Lionel Jeffries, Percy Herbert, and Paul Carpenter are also in the cast. **Director**—Gordon Douglas.   *103 minutes*

CALL ME MADAM (1953)
★★★★

Ethel Merman
Donald O'Connor
George Sanders
Vera-Ellen

Merman belts out Irving Berlin songs with her typical gusto in this lively and colorful film version of the Broadway musical. She plays an energetic Washington party-giver ("the hostess with the mostess"), who is appointed U.S. Ambassador to Lichtenberg. Merman is supported by a splendid cast. Some of the political jokes, however, are out-of-date. Also with Billy de Wolfe, Helmut Dantine, and Walter Slezak. **Director**—Walter Lang.
117 minutes

CALL ME MISTER (1951)
★★

Betty Grable
Dan Dailey

Dailey, a GI stationed in Japan, goes AWOL to join his show-biz wife, played by Grable, who is dancing and singing with the USO. This version isn't as effective as the Broadway musical, but there are some good moments in the predictable screenplay. Danny Thomas, Dale Robertson, and Richard Boone have supporting parts. **Director**—Lloyd Bacon.   *95 minutes*

CALL NORTHSIDE 777 (1948)
★★★

**James Stewart
Lee J. Cobb
Helen Walker**

Stewart plays a determined Chicago reporter. He painstakingly uncovers evidence to free a man who was convicted of murder 11 years earlier. The compelling semidocumentary thriller, based on a true story, is executed with impressive atmosphere and excellent acting. Stewart's step-by-step assembly of the facts is handled with pacing that builds suspense toward a satisfying climax. Also with E. G. Marshall, Kazia Orzazewski, and Betty Garde. **Director**—Henry Hathaway. *111 minutes b&w*

CAMELOT (1967)
★★

**Richard Harris
Vanessa Redgrave**

An overblown, overstuffed version of the successful Lerner and Loewe Broadway musical that strains for style and charm, but never makes it. Harris and Redgrave star in the classic story of King Arthur and his gallant knights. The acting is fine, but no one really does justice to the memorable songs. And Joshua Logan's glossy direction lacks imagination. David Hemmings, Lionel Jeffries, and Franco Nero are also in the cast. **Academy Award Nomination**—Richard H. Kline, cinematography. *181 minutes*

CAMILLE (1936)
★★★

**Greta Garbo
Robert Taylor**

Garbo brings life and vitality to this screen version of Alexandre Dumas' novel about a dying prostitute who falls in love with an innocent young man, played by Taylor. Although Taylor is adequate, Garbo steals the show. Lionel Barrymore, Elizabeth Allen, and Laura Hope Crews also star. **Director**—George Cukor.
108 minutes b&w

CAN-CAN (1960)
★★

**Frank Sinatra
Shirley MacLaine**

This shallow version of the Cole Porter musical stars Sinatra as a 19th-century Parisian lawyer, who defends a nightclub entertainer, played by MacLaine, for performing an allegedly lewd dance. Sinatra doesn't seem to be with it, and MacLaine is miscast. Maurice Chevalier and Louis Jourdan add their charm, but it's not enough to prop up the sagging script. Some memorable songs are featured though, including "C'est Magnifique," "I Love Paris," and "Just One of Those Things." Also with Juliet Prowse and Leon Belasco. **Director**—Walter Lang.   *131 minutes*

THE CANDIDATE (1972)
★★★

**Robert Redford
Peter Boyle**

In The Candidate, *Peter Boyle is a campaign manager.*

Redford plays a liberal lawyer from California, who runs for senator and discovers there are more than issues and ideals at stake. He has a firm hand on the part and seems right at home in this probing and honest political satire that captures the flavor of the campaign trail. The film maintains its vibrant energy to the very end. Don Porter and Melvyn Douglas are effective in supporting roles. **Director**—Michael Ritchie. (PG) **Academy Award**—Jeremy Larner, best story and screenplay (based on factual material

or material not previously published).
110 minutes

CANDLESHOE (1977)
★★

**Jodie Foster
Helen Hayes
David Niven**

A charming sugarplum from Walt Disney. Foster is a streetwise orphan who poses as a lost heiress in the estate of Hayes to find a hidden family treasure. Niven plays the butler and three other characters with obvious relish. With such a first-rate cast and the winning Disney formula of comedy and suspense, it's fun and merriment all the way. Of course, there's a happy ending. Also with Leo McKern, Veronica Quilligan, and Ian Sharrock. **Director**—Norman Tokar. (G)
101 minutes

CANNERY ROW (1982)
★★

**Nick Nolte
Debra Winger**

Nick Nolte falls in love with Debra Winger (and even wears a necktie in Cannery Row.

Whimsical and set-bound adaptation of John Steinbeck's novellas about the characters living on Monterey's dilapidated waterfront. These stories are, perhaps, among the lesser of Steinbeck's works, and under the guidance of writer-director David Ward (*The Sting*) they evolve into a lesser movie. Nolte and Winger perform adequately as unlikely lovers (he's a marine biologist; she's a hooker), but they don't
(Continued)

C

- Cannonball
- The Cannonball Run
- Cannonball Run II
- Can She Bake a Cherry Pie?
- Can't Stop the Music
- Cape Fear
- Capone
- Capricorn One

(Continued)

have sufficient material at their command. (PG)　　　*120 minutes*

CANNONBALL (1976)

 ★

David Carradine
Bill McKinney

This is another car-wreck saga with special appeal to the crash crowd. This orgy of screeching tires and bashed fenders involves a race from Los Angeles to New York with $100,000 for the winner. Carradine and McKinney lead the convoy across the continent, leaving a wake of flaming wrecks. Directed by Paul Bartel, who seems to specialize in such hysteria. Also with Veronica Hamel, Judy Canova, and Gerrit Graham. (PG)　　*93 minutes*

THE CANNONBALL RUN
(1981)

 ★★

Burt Reynolds

Reynolds and many of his pals star in yet another reckless-driving movie on the order of *Smokey and the Bandit*. The story concerns a coast-to-coast car race that defies the country's speed laws. But this theme is so worn by now that the film runs out of steam long before the cars can cross the finish line. A steady stream of cornball gags accompany the crashes and breakdowns. The good breezy fun of the *Smokey* outings is sorely missing. **Director—** Hal Needham. (PG)　　*95 minutes*

CANNONBALL RUN II (1984)

 ★

Burt Reynolds

Reynolds and a huge cast of celebrities of the '50s and '60s embark on a familiar cross-country car chase that seems to wind up where it starts. The shopworn gags come off as tired and frazzled as the many cameo players who populate this silly sequel. Dean Martin, Sammy Davis, Jr., Frank Sinatra, Shirley MacLaine, Telly Savalas, etc., etc. tarnish their careers among the bent fenders. **Director—**Hal Needham. (PG)　　*108 minutes*

CAN SHE BAKE A CHERRY PIE?
(1983)

 ★★

Karen Black

Black chatters like a magpie, and sings some too, as a neurotic New Yorker seeking love in the big city. She finds her man (Michael Emil), whose orderly life-style seems to make up for her flightiness. This spontaneous comedy paints some amusing characters, but the plot lacks structure. **Director—**Henry Jaglom. (PG)

90 minutes

CAN'T STOP THE MUSIC
(1980)

 ★

Village People
Valerie Perrine
Bruce Jenner

Does anyone remember the Village People? Fortunately, they seem to have stopped whatever it was they were doing. But this gauche film never stops—it just keeps beating the viewer over the head with an ear-popping disco soundtrack, including such Village People hits as "YMCA." When the music does mercifully stop, there's a plot even sillier than those in the old MGM musicals. **Director—**Nancy Walker. (PG)　　*118 minutes*

CAPE FEAR (1962)

 ★★★

Gregory Peck
Robert Mitchum
Polly Bergen

A grim thriller with moderate suspense about an ex-convict who seeks revenge on the lawyer he believes responsible for his prison sentence. Mitchum plays the sadistic bad guy who threatens to rape the wife of lawyer Peck. The wife is played by Bergen. The performances are convincing. The film, based on a John D. MacDonald novel, is set in the bayous of the Deep South. Martin Balsam, Jack Kruschen, Lori Nelson, and Telly Savalas also star. **Director—**J. Lee Thompson.　　*106 minutes b&w*

CAPONE (1975)

 ★

Ben Gazzara
Susan Blakely

Ben Gazzara shows us that mob bosses were dapper dressers in Capone.

A film biography of Scarface Al, from his rise to power in Chicago to his imprisonment for tax evasion. There's lots of blood and gunfighting, laced with some Godfather treatment. It's a familiar and sometimes tedious gangster saga, but the action moves along efficiently. Also with Harry Guardino, John Cassavetes, Sylvester Stallone, and Frank Campanella. **Director—** Steve Carver. (R)　　*101 minutes*

CAPRICORN ONE (1978)

 ★★

Elliott Gould
James Brolin
Karen Black
Telly Savalas

James Brolin, O. J. Simpson, and Sam Waterston in Capricorn One.

NASA tries to pull off a fake landing on Mars in this action melodrama star-

• Captain Horatio Hornblower
• Captain Lightfoot
• The Captain's Paradise
• Caravans
• Carbon Copy
• Carefree
• Careful, He Might Hear You
• Carnal Knowledge

C

ring Gould and Brolin. The plot is far-fetched, and whenever the suspense and excitement start to build (which is often), the mood is broken by the wooden dialogue of director-writer Peter Hyams. One high point is a chase sequence with two helicopters and a crop-dusting plane piloted by Savalas, which seems reminiscent of a similar encounter in Hitchcock's *North By Northwest*. Also with Sam Waterston, Brenda Vaccaro, O.J. Simpson, and Hal Holbrook. (PG)   *124 minutes*

CAPTAIN HORATIO HORNBLOWER (1951)
★★★

**Gregory Peck
Virginia Mayo**

Peck plays Hornblower, the 19th-century English naval hero who out-maneuvers the Spanish and the French during the Napoleonic wars. Peck sweats and strains in this sprawling sea epic, but he manages to look valiant. The colorful film, based on the C. M. Forester novels, also features Robert Beatty, James Robertson Justice, and Denis O'Dea in supporting roles. **Director**—Raoul Walsh.
117 minutes

CAPTAIN LIGHTFOOT (1955)
★★

**Rock Hudson
Barbara Rush**

Hudson plays an Irish rebel adventurer in this handsome costume drama filmed in Ireland. The film is set in the time of the Irish rebellion in the 19th century. Rush is fine as the female lead, but Hudson looks like he would rather be cavorting with Doris Day. Also with Jeff Morrow, Kathleen Ryan, Finlay Currie, and Denis O'Dea. **Director**—Douglas Sirk.   *92 minutes*

THE CAPTAIN'S PARADISE (1953)

★★★

**Alec Guinness
Yvonne De Carlo
Celia Johnson**

A fine droll comedy starring Guinness

as a ferry boat skipper who has a wife at each end of his route. Guinness expertly fills the role with his usual measure of dry wit played rather straight-faced. De Carlo and Johnson are perfectly cast as the unsuspecting wives, who accommodate the contrasting aspects of the captain's personality. It's a great sophisticated romp. Bill Fraser and Charles Goldner also star. **Director**—Anthony Kimmins.
80 minutes b&w

CARAVANS (1978)
★★

**Anthony Quinn
Jennifer O'Neill**

This film, based on James Michener's tale of desert nomads, has the trappings of an epic: elegant photography, colorful native dances, and so on. But when the plot gets moving, it's evident there's scant drama and low credibility. The story deals with the search for an American woman, played by O'Neill, who is living with a desert tribe, led by Quinn. O'Neill, who constantly encounters sand storms and camels, looks as if she is ready to pose for *Vogue*. Incredible. Also with Michael Sarrazin, Christopher Lee, Joseph Cotten, and Barry Sullivan. **Director**—James Fargo. (PG)
123 minutes

CARBON COPY (1981)

★★

**George Segal
Susan Saint James**

George Segal in Carbon Copy, *a "black" comedy.*

Segal stars as a successful businessman who had an affair with a black woman long ago, and now his

black son comes knocking on his door. This silly comedy confronts racial prejudice in a rather absurd manner as Segal faces numerous problems because of the revelation. However, the cliché-strewn film ends on a happy note. Also with Jack Warden, Denzel Washington, and Paul Winfield. **Director**—Michael Schultz. (PG)
92 minutes

CAREFREE (1938)

★★★

**Fred Astaire
Ginger Rogers**

This frothy musical comedy about a psychiatrist who falls in love with his patient is one of the last teamings of Astaire and Rogers. The plot is limp and the dialogue fails to sparkle, but the dancing and the excellent Irving Berlin songs "Change Partners," and "I Used To Be Color Blind" make the production a joy. Astaire and Rogers are ably supported by Jack Carson and Ralph Bellamy. **Director**—Mark Sandrich.   *85 minutes b&w*

CAREFUL, HE MIGHT HEAR YOU (1984)
★★★

**Nicholas Gledhill
Wendy Hughes
Robyn Nevin
John Hargreaves**

An exceptionally moving psychological drama set in Australia in the Depression '30s. The story involves the emotional experience of a seven-year-old boy (Gledhill) who is used as a pawn by his rival aunts. Young Gledhill performs admirably and convincingly. Director Carl Schultz has a firm hold on the material and manages precise performances from a professional cast. (PG)   *116 minutes*

CARNAL KNOWLEDGE (1971)

★★★

**Jack Nicholson
Art Garfunkel
Candice Bergen
Ann-Margret**

Writer Jules Feiffer and director Mike
(Continued)

C
- Carny
- Carousel
- The Carpetbaggers
- Carrie
- Car Wash
- Casablanca

(Continued)
Nichols team up to explore the sexual attitudes and problems of the American male as seen through the experiences of two men from college to middle-age. Nicholson and Garfunkel do well as the main subjects in this uneven comedy-drama that strikes out in new directions. Ann-Margret deserves applause for her shining role as Nicholson's coquettish mistress. Also with Rita Moreno, Cynthia O'Neal, and Carol Kane. (R) **Academy Award Nomination**—Ann-Margret, best supporting actress.

97 minutes

CARNY (1980)

★★

**Jodie Foster
Gary Busey
Robbie Robertson**

Elisha Cook, Jr. hawks tosses in Carny.

A brassy, semidocumentary look at carnival life, with perceptive performances by Foster, Busey, and Robertson. Director Robert Kaylor captures the grimy atmosphere of carny life. Unfortunately, a feeble script fritters away the talents of the energetic cast. Busey is fascinating as a dunk-tank bozo, and Foster sheds some of her former innocence in her role as a bored teenager who joins the show. But the film bogs down in an unfocused romantic triangle and finally ends on an unsatisfying note. (R) *106 minutes*

CAROUSEL (1956)
★★★

**Gordon MacRae
Shirley Jones**

A handsome film musical based on Ferenc Molnár's play *Liliom*, with the memorable Rodgers and Hammerstein music pleasantly adapted. Mac-Rae plays a gruff carnival barker who wants a better way of life when he marries a modest girl, played by Jones. Tragedy, however, gets in the way of his ambition. MacRae and Jones sing beautifully, and the photography is stunning. Songs include "If I Loved You" and "You'll Never Walk Alone." Also with Cameron Mitchell, Robert Rounseville, and Gene Lockhart. **Director**—Henry King. *128 minutes*

THE CARPETBAGGERS (1964)
★★

**George Peppard
Carroll Baker
Alan Ladd**

A brash young man takes over an aircraft manufacturing business and then pyramids his fortune into other ventures, including moviemaking. This film version of the Harold Robbins novel, which parallels the career of Howard Hughes, is made in a garish fashion, but it's entertaining nevertheless. Peppard portrays the eccentric industrialist. This was Ladd's last film. Also with Martin Balsam, Bob Cummings, Elizabeth Ashley, Lew Ayres, and Archie Moore. **Director**—Edward Dmytryk. *150 minutes*

CARRIE (1976)

★

**Sissy Spacek
Piper Laurie**

Sissy Spacek doesn't like the prize awarded to the prom queen in Carrie.

An uneven horror tale about a weird teenage girl who is tormented by her high school classmates. She finally uses her power of telekinesis in revenge. Director Brian De Palma has tried to fashion a sort of *Death Wish* with overtones of Alfred Hitchcock-type suspense, but the scheme hardly works. The film is scary and taut for only a brief moment at the end; most of the time it's awkward and puzzling. Also with William Katt, John Travolta, and Amy Irving. (R) **Academy Award Nominations**—Spacek, best actress; Laurie, best supporting actress.

97 minutes

CAR WASH (1976)

★

**Richard Pryor
Irwin Corey
Franklyn Ajaye
George Carlin**

Zany characters jive, work in rhythm, and play jokes on one another in this noisy comedy about a day at a Los Angeles car wash. There's a certain formlessness to this lively pop film, much in the style of *American Graffiti*. But it's hardly in keeping with *Graffiti's* depth. Not much happens dramatically—two of the biggest gags involve a dog that relieves itself on the driveway and a boy who throws up all over his mother's car. The cast consists mostly of unknown players. Directed by Michael Schultz, who was responsible for *Cooley High*. (PG) *97 minutes*

CASABLANCA (1942)

★★★★

**Humphrey Bogart
Ingrid Bergman
Claude Rains
Paul Henreid**

Crackling intrigue, tingling romance, and a superb moody atmosphere make this taut melodrama one of the best World War II films. Bogart, in a memorable performance, is in top form as the owner of a Casablanca nightclub. He helps an old flame, played by Bergman, and her underground leader-husband, played by Henreid, escape the Nazis. This classic, witty thriller seems to earn more appreciation as time goes by. Also with Conrad Veidt, S. Z. Sakall, Peter Lorre, and Sydney Greenstreet. **Direc-**

• Casanova's Big Night   • Cat Ballou
• The Cassandra Crossing   • Catch-22
• Cass Timberlane   • The Catered Affair

C

Peter Lorre ponders Humphrey Bogart's next move in the wartime classic Casablanca.

tor—Michael Curtiz. **Academy Awards**—best picture; Curtiz, best director; Julius J. Epstein, Philip G. Epstein, and Howard Koch, writing (screenplay). **Nominations**— Bogart, best actor; Rains, best supporting actor; Arthur Edeson, cinematogaphy (black and white). *102 minutes b&w*

CASANOVA'S BIG NIGHT (1954)
★★

Bob Hope
Joan Fontaine

Hope plays a tailor's apprentice who masquerades as the great Italian lover and winds up in some intriguing comic situations. This film is the last of Hope's lavish costume farces, and it generally wastes his talents. However, just his presence is good for some laughs. The film plods haphazardly despite the supporting efforts of Basil Rathbone, Raymond Burr, and Audrey Dalton. **Director**—Norman McLeod. *86 minutes*

THE CASSANDRA CROSSING (1977)

★

Sophia Loren
Burt Lancaster
Richard Harris
Ava Gardner

This tedious film, directed by George Pan Cosmatos and produced by Carlo Ponti, is another all-star disaster epic filled with strained and hokey situations. It's mainly about 1,000 disease-exposed passengers trapped on board an express train heading for a rickety bridge somewhere in Poland. Loren, Harris, Lancaster, and others are hopelessly miscast. The cardboard script is loaded with dreary interpersonal problems. Half the train hurtles to destruction in a final special-effects gimmick. As for the deadly germs, they mutate to something like an annoying cold, which is similar to sitting through this movie. Also with Martin Sheen, O. J. Simpson, and John Philip Law. (PG) *127 minutes*

CASS TIMBERLANE (1947)

★★★

Spencer Tracy
Lana Turner

Tracy plays a judge in a midwestern community who marries a young working-class girl, played by Turner, and strives to keep up with her youthful ways. This nicely mounted drama, based on the Sinclair Lewis novel, offers Tracy an ideal, sympathetic role. Although the story is not among Lewis's best, it is played out well on the screen. The fine cast also includes Zachary Scott, Tom Drake, Mary Astor, and Albert Dekker. **Director**— George Sidney. *119 minutes b&w*

CAT BALLOU (1965)

★★★

Jane Fonda
Lee Marvin

Marvin is marvelous as a whiskey-soaked, over-the-hill gunslinger, who is hired to eliminate a vicious killer. He plays the role of the killer, too. This unusual western spoof features Fonda in the title role, as a young outlaw who employs the gunslinger. The smart screenplay contributes to the mirth and the direction is on the money. Michael Callan, Nat King Cole, Stubby Kaye, Dwayne Hickman, and Reginald Denny are in supporting roles. **Director**—Eliot Silverstein. **Academy Award**—Marvin, best actor. **Nomination**—Walter Newman and Frank R. Pierson, best screenplay (based on material from another medium). *96 minutes*

CATCH-22 (1970)

★★★★

Alan Arkin
Martin Balsam
Richard Benjamin
Art Garfunkel

This wry black comedy, based on Joseph Heller's popular novel, is one of the best antiwar films. The story concerns a medium-bomber group in the Mediterranean during World War II. One by one, officers are killed in various ways. Arkin leads the gallery of outsized characters by playing Yossarian, a desperate and logical flyer who strives to be classified insane so he can avoid going on bombing missions. Other fine performances are given by Jack Gilford, Buck Henry, Bob Newhart, Paula Prentiss, Anthony Perkins, Jon Voight, Martin Sheen, and Orson Welles. **Director**—Mike Nichols. (R) *122 minutes*

THE CATERED AFFAIR (1956)
★★★

Bette Davis
Ernest Borgnine
Debbie Reynolds
Rod Taylor

The Catered Affair *stars Ernest Borgnine as a Bronx taxi driver.*

The wife of a Bronx taxi driver wants her daughter to be married in style, but the planned affair is more than the family can afford. This intelligent comedy, which is adapted from Paddy Chayefsky's TV play, succeeds much in the style of *Marty*. Davis is excellent as the overreaching mother, and Reynolds is effective as the daughter. Borgnine plays Davis's husband. Barry *(Continued)*

C

- **The Cat from Outer Space**
- **Cat on a Hot Tin Roof**
- **Cat People (1942)**
- **Cat People (1982)**
- **Cattle Annie and Little Britches**
- **Caught in the Draft**
- **Caveman**

(Continued)

Fitzgerald and Dorothy Stickney also star. **Director**—Richard Brooks.

93 minutes b&w

THE CAT FROM OUTER SPACE (1978)

 ★★

**Ken Berry
Sandy Duncan
McLean Stevenson**

In The Cat From Outer Space, *Ken Berry and Sandy Duncan introduce spacecat Jake to Lucy Belle.*

Walt Disney Productions joins the space movie race with this film about a cat from another planet, who makes an emergency landing on Earth. The handsome feline—named Jake—encounters adventure and excitement as he attempts to return to the planet of the pussycats with the help of space scientists Berry and Duncan. The plot is predictable, but the special effects and fast pacing should delight the youngsters. Also with Harry Morgan, Roddy McDowall, and Ronnie Schell. **Director**—Norman Tokar. (G)

104 minutes

CAT ON A HOT TIN ROOF (1958)

 ★★★★

**Elizabeth Taylor
Paul Newman
Burl Ives**

This film version of Tennessee Williams's powerful play about a patriarchal Southern family is somewhat stage-bound, but is entertaining on many levels. Taylor is excellent as the wife of a frustrated young man, played by Newman, who's under the control of his dying father. Ives is convincing as "Big Daddy," the overwhelming plantation owner, and the rest of the cast turns in credible performances. Also with Jack Carson, Judith Anderson, and Madeleine Sherwood. **Director**—Richard Brooks. **Academy Award Nominations**—best picture; Brooks, best director; Newman, best actor; Taylor, best actress; Brooks and James Poe, best screenplay (based on material from another medium); William Daniels, cinematography (color). *108 minutes*

CAT PEOPLE (1942)

 ★★★

**Simone Simon
Kent Smith**

A man marries a beautiful woman who believes she can turn into a panther in this somewhat slow but well-plotted and engrossing horror film. The acting of Simon as the panthergirl and Smith as her lover is superior to most performances in such movies. This was the first of producer Val Lewton's horror films and was noteworthy at the time because the monster never appeared on screen. **Director**—Jacques Tourneur. *73 minutes b&w*

CAT PEOPLE (1982)

 ★★

Nastassja Kinski

John Heard hopes to snare Nastassja Kinski for his own in Cat People.

Director Paul Schrader revamps the 1942 horror classic with cold and flashy graphic effects that do small justice to the imaginative and haunting mood of the original. Kinski is captivating as the mysterious woman who turns into a vicious black leopard; Malcolm McDowell and John Heard also turn in strong performances. But the screenplay is thin and the style uneven. (R)

118 minutes

CATTLE ANNIE AND LITTLE BRITCHES (1981)

 ★★★

**Burt Lancaster
Rod Steiger
Amanda Plummer**

The western movie gets a comic kick in the pants with this lighthearted tale of two teenage girls who try to inject some spirit into the fading Doolin-Dalton gang. The cast is impeccable. Lancaster is magnificent as the aging outlaw boss. Steiger is brittle and eloquent as the U.S. marshal. And watch out for Plummer as Annie; this young actress, making her screen debut, gives class and dazzle to the spunky character. **Director**—Lamont Johnson. (PG) *95 minutes*

CAUGHT IN THE DRAFT (1941)

 ★★★

**Bob Hope
Dorothy Lamour**

One of Hope's better comedies. There are plenty of well-timed gags and nice support from a good cast. Bob is a movie star who resists joining the Army, but he accidentally enters the service at last. A sprightly, funny service comedy for its time. Effective performances, too, from Lynne Overman, Clarence Kolb, and Eddie Bracken. **Director**—David Butler.

82 minutes

CAVEMAN (1981)

 ★★

**Ringo Starr
Dennis Quaid**

A feeble spoof of our prehistoric ancestors, who defend themselves

Atouk (Ringo Starr) is leader of a group of misfit primitives in the comedy Caveman.

against dinosaurs and discover fire, the slingshot, love, and jealousy. The broad slapstick comedy is sort of a primitive version of Mel Brooks's *Silent Movie*, with some campy special effects tossed in. The tribesmen are cartoon characters who don't actually speak; they grunt bits of strange dialogue, which becomes tiresome before long. The Flintstones are funnier and more colorful. Also with Shelley Long, Jack Gilford, and John Matuszak. **Director**—Carl Gottlieb. (PG)

91 minutes

CHAIN LIGHTNING (1950)
★★

Humphrey Bogart
Eleanor Parker

Bogart plays a World War II flyer who adapts to the new and faster jet aircraft when the war ends. There are nice scenes of the jets in action, but Bogey can't keep a shallow script airborne. Also, he has more trouble trying to deal with Parker than he does with the new planes. Raymond Massey, Richard Whorf, and James Brown are also in the cast. **Director**—Stuart Heisler.

94 minutes b&w

THE CHALLENGE (1982)
 ★★

Scott Glenn

John Frankenheimer (*Birdman of Alcatraz*) directed this martial-arts actioner set in Japan. There's some

good acting and Frankenheimer invests the film with a touch of class, but eventually it winds up as just another chop-socky. Glenn stars as a young Californian who delivers an antique sword to a samurai warrior and soon becomes embroiled in a family feud. The adventure concludes in a vicious flurry of kung-fu excesses and bloody sword fighting. (R) *106 minutes*

THE CHAMP (1979)
★

Jon Voight
Faye Dunaway
Ricky Schroder

The tear-drenched Wallace Beery-Jackie Cooper tale of 1931 returns to the screen, with Voight as the has-been boxer and moppet Schroder as his adoring son. Along comes the boy's mother, played by Dunaway, after a seven-year absence to claim her child. What follows is such unrestrained pathos that any honest drama is drowned in its wake. Director Franco Zeffirelli doesn't spare a single gimmick to wrench tears from the viewer, but under the slick veneer is a distinct staleness. Also with Jack Warden, Arthur Hill, Strother Martin, Joan Blondell, and Elisha Cook, Jr. (PG)

121 minutes

CHAMPION (1949)
★★★★

Kirk Douglas
Arthur Kennedy
Lola Albright

A stylish, rousing fight film based on the Ring Lardner short story. Douglas is in the title role as a determined boxer, who bulldozes his way to the top, alienating friends and relatives along the way. He then dies as the result of a boxing match. Obviously, the story is a cliché by now, but it's nicely handled and acted with much energy. A good role for Douglas and effective backup from Kennedy, Albright, Marilyn Maxwell, and Ruth Roman. **Director**—Mark Robson. **Academy Award Nominations**—Douglas, best actor; Kennedy, best supporting actor; Carl Foreman, writing (screenplay); Frank Planer, cinematography (black and white).

99 minutes b&w

CHAMPIONS (1984)
★★★

John Hurt
Gregory Jones
Mike Dillon

This true story follows the career of English steeplechase jockey Bob Champion, played by Hurt, who overcame cancer and went on to win the Grand National. The well-worn theme (somewhat reminiscent of *Chariots of Fire*) unfolds with such cinematic and acting skill that it transcends a rather weak and clinical script. The grueling horse race finale is predictable but spirited nonetheless. **Director**—John Irvin. (PG) *115 minutes*

THE CHANGELING
(1980)
★★★

George C. Scott
Trish Van Devere
Melvyn Douglas

George C. Scott rents a haunted house in The Changeling.

A haunted Victorian mansion. Strange noises in the night. A piano plays by itself. An eerie seance. The dusty room in the attic. Déjà vu? Perhaps. But director Peter Medak adds stylish and chilling dimensions to this stock material that would frighten Dracula's mother. Scott, who rents the spooky old house, unravels a 70-year-old murder mystery with the help of a vengeful spirit. Scott and Douglas contribute strong performances to make this a relentlessly suspenseful story. Also with John Colicos and Jean Marsh. (R) *109 minutes*

C
- A Change of Seasons
- The Chant of Jimmie Blacksmith
- Chapter Two
- Charade
- The Charge of the Light Brigade
- Chariots of Fire

A CHANGE OF SEASONS
(1980)
 ★★

**Shirley MacLaine
Anthony Hopkins
Bo Derek**

Bo Derek decides she has too many clothes on in A Change of Seasons.

MacLaine, Hopkins, and Derek star in this complex comedy about the sexual revolution. When professor Anthony has an affair with fetching student Bo, wife Shirley fights back by having an affair with the young campus carpenter. The plot gets even more involved, and what's supposed to be satire becomes just silly and absurd. MacLaine turns in a fine performance; as for Bo, she's still only a sex symbol. Also with Michael Brandon and Mary Beth Hurt. **Director**—Richard Lang. (R)　　　　　　　*102 minutes*

THE CHANT OF JIMMIE BLACKSMITH (1980)
★★★

Tommy Lewis

This handsome, compelling Australian film explores racism through the experience of an earnest half-caste young man, who violently rebels after being exploited by white employers. The film bulges with excessive detail and plot. Nevertheless, director Fred Schepisi effectively hammers home a sense of helplessness and rage at the upshot of the encroachment of European culture on the Aborigines. Lewis is effective in the title role. (No MPAA rating)　　　　　　*122 minutes*

CHAPTER TWO (1979)
 ★★

**James Caan
Marsha Mason
Valerie Harper**

Neil Simon brings this semiautobiographical Broadway play to the screen. It's the story of a successful writer, played by Caan, who remarries shortly after his first wife's death, but guilt plagues his efforts to settle into an earnest romance. Simon's glib lines undercut the serious scenes. Caan is miscast, but Mason, as his second wife, grabs the full flavor of her role. As well she might, because she was the second Mrs. Simon. Also with Joseph Bologna. **Director**—Robert Moore. (PG) **Academy Award Nomination**—Mason, best actress.
124 minutes

CHARADE (1963)
 ★★★★

**Cary Grant
Audrey Hepburn**

Grant is suave as usual in this romantic comedy set in glittering Paris. Hepburn plays a widow whose late husband stashed away a fortune. Some bad guys want the money, and they believe Audrey knows where it's hidden. Along comes handsome Grant offering help and sympathy, but is he really on her side? It's lightweight fare patterned after Hitchcock's style, and it keeps moving along. The excellent supporting cast includes Walter Matthau, James Coburn, and George Kennedy. **Director**—Stanley Donen.
113 minutes

THE CHARGE OF THE LIGHT BRIGADE (1968)
 ★★

**Trevor Howard
John Gielgud
David Hemmings**

This handsome drama is well acted, but fails to come across. It's built on the events at the time of the 1854 battle at Balaclava, Turkey, during the Crimean War, when the British were defeated by the Russians. The film makes an antiwar statement and offers an impressive battle scene, but it stumbles into plot potholes too often. Richard Williams's special animated portions help a little. The cast includes Vanessa Redgrave and Jill Bennett. **Director**—Tony Richardson. (PG)
141 minutes

CHARIOTS OF FIRE (1981)
 ★★★★

**Ben Cross
Ian Charleson**

Olympic trainee Ben Cross is about to illegally pass in the left-hand lane in Chariots of Fire.

A handsome, well-made drama based on the true story of two English champion runners who compete in the 1924 Paris Olympics. Hugh Hudson, directing his first theatrical film, magnificently assembles a film that's full of finely detailed characterizations. His command of the atmosphere of the period is remarkable. Cross is genuinely compelling as running ace Harold Abrahams, who competes to compensate for religious bigotry. Charleson gives a lower-keyed but equally satisfying performance as Eric Liddell, who runs for the glory of God. It's an interesting exercise to examine the different circumstances that motivate these two athletes—or to contrast their dedication with the megabucks mentality that's often apparent on the contemporary sports scene. (PG) **Academy Awards**—best picture; Colin Welland, best screenplay (written directly for the screen). **Nominations**—Ian Holm, best supporting actor; Hudson, best director.
123 minutes

• Charley and the Angel
• Charley's Aunt
• Charlie Bubbles
• Charly

• The Cheap Detective
• Cheaper by the Dozen
• Cheech and Chong's Next Movie

C

CHARLEY AND THE ANGEL
(1974)
★★

**Fred MacMurray
Cloris Leachman
Harry Morgan**

Rather typical Walt Disney sentimental piece about a small-town merchant, played by MacMurray, who mellows his attitude toward his family when he finds out he only has a short time to live. Morgan plays the angel. There are some amusing moments and a predictably happy ending, but the expected Disney warmth seems trumped up. The plot partially follows the events of *On Borrowed Time*. Also with Kurt Russell, Kathleen Cody, and Vincent Van Patten. **Director**—Vincent McEveety. (G) *93 minutes*

CHARLEY'S AUNT (1941)
★★★

**Jack Benny
Kay Francis**

Benny hams it up with glee in this familiar Victorian farce about the Oxford student who impersonates a rich maiden aunt to help out a roommate. The comedy is strained at times, but it's a good opportunity to observe the great Benny do his stuff. Other cast members are also in top form, including James Ellison, Anne Baxter, Laird Cregar, and Edmund Gwenn. **Director**—Archie Mayo.
81 minutes b&w

CHARLIE BUBBLES (1968)
★★★

**Albert Finney
Billie Whitelaw
Liza Minnelli**

Finney directs and stars in this clever fantasy about a young man who suddenly becomes very wealthy, only to find boredom with the emptiness of an artificial environment. The film is sometimes slow and uneven, but it offers a fascinating character sketch and some effective scenes of the man inundated by pointless electronic gadgets. Minnelli turns in a good acting job as Finney's secretary. The ending is

sort of a letdown when Finney tries to return to his original life-style. Colin Blakely, Timothy Garland, and Alan Lake are also in the cast. (R)
91 minutes

CHARLY
(1968)
 ### ★★★

**Cliff Robertson
Claire Bloom
Lilia Skala**

Robertson's stellar performance dominates this tale of a mentally retarded baker who becomes a genius after submitting to a new surgical technique. It's based on Daniel Keyes's *Flowers for Algernon*. The screenplay, however, is overly sentimental and somewhat unconvincing—especially during a romantic interlude between Charly and an intelligent woman, played by Bloom, after the operation has taken effect. Also with Leon Janney and Dick Van Patten. **Director**—Ralph Nelson. **Academy Award**—Robertson, best actor. (PG) *106 minutes*

THE CHEAP DETECTIVE
(1978)
★★★

**Peter Falk
Ann-Margret
Sid Caesar
Louise Fletcher**

Writer Neil Simon fondly parodies a slew of Humphrey Bogart melodra-

Madeline Kahn adds some mystery to The Cheap Detective.

mas of the '40s, with wit, humor, and a good-natured elbow-poke to the ribs. The timing doesn't always work well and the plot tries to cover too much ground, but the Simon dialogue, loaded with stalwart one-liners, goes down easily. The blue-ribbon cast has a fine time carving up *The Maltese Falcon*, *Casablanca*, and *The Big Sleep*. Falk leads the pack with a priceless imitation of Bogart. Also with Nicol Williamson, Eileen Brennan, Stockard Channing, Dom DeLuise, James Coco, and many other stars. **Director**—Robert Moore. (PG) *92 minutes*

CHEAPER BY THE DOZEN
(1950)
★★★

**Clifton Webb
Myrna Loy**

Webb is perfectly cast as Frank Gilbreth, the patriarch who ran his large family with the same discipline and efficiency that he applied to motion and time study methods for industry. The lilting comedy, set in the '20s, is based on the popular book by two of the 12 Gilbreth children. This is definitely one of Webb's best performances, set in a somewhat corny but funny framework. Loy is exceptionally good, too, as the stalwart mother of the family. Other cast members include Jeanne Crain, Edgar Buchanan, Barbara Bates, and Mildred Natwick. **Director**—Walter Lang. *86 minutes*

CHEECH AND CHONG'S NEXT MOVIE (1980)
 ### ★

**Cheech Marin
Thomas Chong**

Another chapter in the silly misadventures of Cheech and Chong of counter-culture comedy fame. The scroungy, pot-smoking duo carry their inane antics to a welfare office, a massage parlor, the home of a wealthy family, and finally into space, all the while mumbling their repetitive and dopey dialogue. It's a sort of stoned version of a Marx Brothers comedy that wouldn't work even if they were acting sober. Unfortunately, this wasn't their last movie. **Director**—Chong. (R)
99 minutes

C

• Cheech and Chong's The
  Corsican Brothers
• Cheech and Chong's Nice
  Dreams

• Cheyenne Autumn
• The Cheyenne Social Club
• Chief Crazy Horse

• Children of the Corn
• The Children's Hour

CHEECH AND CHONG'S THE CORSICAN BROTHERS (1984)

 ★

**Cheech Marin
Thomas Chong**

The boys depart from their dreamy, freewheeling routine and portray brothers in France involved with chaotic events on the eve of the revolution. Big surprise—they lay off the pot. And big disappointment—the film is a dreary succession of crude comic routines, all so loosely connected it seems three movies are going on at once. One gag is tediously repeated: When one brother is hit, the other feels the pain. Roy Dotrice and Shelby Fiddis co-star. **Director**—Chong. (PG)
90 minutes

CHEECH AND CHONG'S NICE DREAMS (1981)

 ★★

**Cheech Marin
Thomas Chong**

A third round of spaced-out high jinks from "Los Guys," whose brand of humor seems to improve with age. This time the maestros of the marijuana set peddle their wares from an ice cream truck and engage in a variety of disjointed situations. The film is short on plot, and many skits are merely silly. But this outing is executed with the typical unflagging hazy humor that will surely appeal to the turned-on set. As Cheech might say, "Hey man, this is a groovy movie." **Director**—Chong. (R) *88 minutes*

CHEYENNE AUTUMN (1964)

 ★★★

**Richard Widmark
Carroll Baker
Karl Malden**

Director John Ford's sprawling epic western tells the harrowing story of starving Indians trekking from their barren Oklahoma reservation to their original home, 1,500 miles away in Wyoming. The Indians also have to fight the U.S. Cavalry, which wants them to stay put. The handsome production features fine acting by Wid-

Richard Widmark (center) plays a cavalry commander who must preside over the mistreatment of the Indians in Cheyenne Autumn.

mark, Baker, and Malden. Also with Dolores Del Rio, Ricardo Montalban, Gilbert Roland, Sal Mineo, and Victor Jory. There are nice cameos, too, from James Stewart and Edward G. Robinson. However, the historical drama seems rather ponderous after a while. **Academy Award Nomination**—William Clothier, cinematography (color).
160 minutes

THE CHEYENNE SOCIAL CLUB (1970)

 ★★

**James Stewart
Henry Fonda
Shirley Jones**

Stewart and Fonda running a brothel on the western frontier? That's good for some laughs, but there aren't enough of them in this comedy, which offers too many clichés and too much adolescent humor. A shoot-out at the end perks things up, but what we really need are some bawdy girls and some bawdy jokes that work. Jones plays the madam of the house. Also with Sue Anne Langdon, Robert Middleton, and Arch Johnson. **Director**—Gene Kelly. (PG) *102 minutes*

CHIEF CRAZY HORSE (1954)

 ★★

**Victor Mature
Suzan Ball
John Lund**

Mature is in the title role as the famous Indian chief who leads his braves at the Little Big Horn and defeats General Custer. The clichéd western, which is seen from the side of the Indians, involves the chief's dealings with an Army officer. Mature is convincing as the tough Indian warrior. Also with Keith Larsen and Ray Danton. **Director**—George Sherman.
86 minutes

CHILDREN OF THE CORN (1984)

 ★

**Peter Horton
Linda Hamilton**

Linda Hamilton wishes she'd never crossed the Children of the Corn.

In a small Nebraska town, children have slaughtered the adults and set up a sinister religious cult. Young physician Horton and his girlfriend Hamilton stumble into this terrifying community and encounter a variety of supernatural episodes. Based on Stephen King's short story, the film is trite, poorly acted, and filled with mumbo-jumbo dialogue. The thin, preposterous material unfolds at a slow pace. **Director**—Fritz Kiersch. (R) *93 minutes*

THE CHILDREN'S HOUR (1961)

 ★★★

**Audrey Hepburn
Shirley MacLaine**

MacLaine and Hepburn star in this touching drama about a malicious schoolgirl. She alleges that her teachers are lesbians, causing them

- China Doll
- The China Syndrome
- Chinatown
- Chitty Chitty Bang Bang
- The Choirboys
- The Chosen (1978)
- The Chosen (1982)

C

untold grief. The film, based on Lillian Hellman's play, was originally filmed as *These Three*. The explicit treatment of lesbianism was somewhat daring at the time of release, but the theme has lost impact. Yet the movie is compelling, and Hepburn and MacLaine are exceptional as the maligned teachers. There is good support from James Garner, Miriam Hopkins, and Fay Bainter. **Director—** William Wyler. **Academy Award Nominations**—Bainter, best supporting actress; Franz F. Planer, cinematography (black and white).

108 minutes b&w

CHINA DOLL (1958)

★

**Victor Mature
Li Li Hua
Bob Mathias**

Soggy, romantic story about a World War II pilot who accidentally buys a Chinese maid. They eventually get married, but are both killed in the war. Then their daughter comes to the United States. Mature and Hua star, but they cannot overcome the dull script. Ward Bond and Stuart Whitman are also in the cast. **Director—** Frank Borzage. *88 minutes b&w*

THE CHINA SYNDROME (1979)

 ★★★★

**Jane Fonda
Jack Lemmon
Michael Douglas**

The ubiquitous Wilford Brimley plays an assistant supervisor at a nuclear power plant in The China Syndrome.

A nuclear power plant goes on the fritz and touches off a dangerous confrontation. This dynamite thriller stars Fonda and Lemmon. Fonda gives a super performance as an ambitious "Brenda Starr" TV newswoman. Lemmon, meanwhile, performs convincingly as the plant engineer with a nagging conscience. Director James Bridges maintains relentless tension from the start right up to the hair-raising climax. It's classic entertainment that packs a wallop and makes a vivid social observation. Also with Scott Brady, James Hampton, Peter Donat, and Wilford Brimley. (PG) **Academy Award Nominations**— Lemmon, best actor; Fonda, best actress; Mike Gray, T. S. Cook, and James Bridges, best screenplay (written directly for the screen).

123 minutes

CHINATOWN (1974)

 ★★★★

**Jack Nicholson
Faye Dunaway
John Huston**

Compelling and suspenseful private-eye yarn filled with all sorts of goodies in the spirit of Hammett-Chandler mysteries. Nicholson is excellent as the Los Angeles gumshoe who becomes involved over his head in an intricate web of murder and political corruption concerning a fortune in land and water rights. He's led into this complex situation by the beautiful Dunaway as *femme fatale extraordinaire*. Director Roman Polanski handles the 1930s atmosphere with exceptional skill. Also with Perry Lopez. (R) **Academy Award**—Robert Towne, best original screenplay. **Nominations**—best picture; Polanski, best director; Nicholson, best actor; Dunaway, best actress; John A. Alonzo, cinematography.

131 minutes

CHITTY CHITTY BANG BANG (1968)

 ★★

**Dick Van Dyke
Sally Ann Howes**

Van Dyke and the rest of the cast mainly waste their time with this flimsy children's fantasy-musical

about an inventor who produces a flying car. Nothing seems to click, including the special effects and a score that features many forgettable songs. There are a few scenes for the kids to laugh at, but it's pretty tame stuff. The script is based on a book by Ian Fleming. Anna Quayle, Gert Frobe, Lionel Jeffries, Benny Hill, and James Robertson Justice also star. **Director**—Ken Hughes. (G) *145 minutes*

THE CHOIRBOYS (1977)

 ★

**Perry King
Don Stroud
James Woods**

A vulgar, cheap-looking, black comedy based on one of Joseph Wambaugh's best-selling novels about Los Angeles cops. The inept production is a series of rambling vignettes sprinkled with adolescent sex jokes and coarse cutups. The direction by Robert Aldrich is chaotic, and the acting is amateurish. Also with Charles Durning, Louis Gossett, Jr., and Tim McIntire.

119 minutes

THE CHOSEN (1978)

★

**Kirk Douglas
Agostina Belli**

Douglas plays an industrialist who gets all tangled up with the Antichrist and nuclear power plants. Even a nice fellow like Kirk can't rescue the confused plot that must have been cooked up by the Devil himself. Douglas, of course, goes on to save the world from nuclear destruction, but this film hardly saves his reputation as a respected actor. Simon Ward, Anthony Quayle, and Virginia McKenna are in supporting roles. **Director**—Alberto De Martino. (R) *105 minutes*

THE CHOSEN (1982)

★★★

**Rod Steiger
Maximillian Schell
Robby Benson**

Friendship between two young Jewish
(Continued)

C
- Christiane F
- Christine
- Christmas in Connecticut
- A Christmas Story
- Chu Chu and the Philly Flash
- C.H.U.D.

Robbie Benson plays a Hassidic Jew who breaks with the traditions of his father in The Chosen.

(Continued)

men is the subject of this film set in Brooklyn at the close of World War II. Their relationship, however, is affected by the divergent religious views of their strong-willed fathers. The story, adapted from Chaim Potok's novel, is moving and brilliantly captures the atmosphere of the period. The pacing, however, is rather slow. **Director**—Jeremy Paul Kagan. (PG)
108 minutes

CHRISTIANE F (1982)

★★

Natja Brunkhorst

This overwrought account of drug addiction among German teenagers is based on a true story and contains relentless graphic details of the wretched condition. There are so many sordid scenes of youngsters injecting themselves with heroin or vomiting amid filthy surroundings, that the semidocumentary film becomes merely sensational. Brunkhorst, in the title role, is convincing as the young girl with the golden arm who swiftly descends into a life of horror and degradation. **Director**—Ulrich Edel. (No MPAA rating) *124 minutes*

CHRISTINE (1983)

★★

Keith Gordon

A blood red '58 Plymouth Fury, restored in '78 by mild-mannered high school student Gordon, is an automobile possessed by demons. The born-again jalopy reveals a nasty disposition and even takes bloody revenge on the youth's tormenting schoolmates. The car is the star, and, although much of this occult vehicle remains pedestrian, director John Carpenter gets some extra mileage with his imaginative treatment. Also with Harry Dean Stanton and John Stockwell. (R) *110 minutes*

CHRISTMAS IN CONNECTICUT (1945)

★★★

Barbara Stanwyck
Dennis Morgan
Sydney Greenstreet

Stanwyck stars in this lightweight but delightful farce. She's a newspaper columnist who invites a war hero, played by Morgan, to her home for Christmas to impress her editor, played by Greenstreet. Since she has no family, she must assemble one for the occasion, and the excellent cast succeeds in making the most of this premise. A fine holiday film with many funny lines and a warm spirit. Also with Reginald Gardiner, S.Z. Sakall, and Robert Shayne. **Director**—Peter Godfrey.
110 minutes b&w

A CHRISTMAS STORY (1983)

★★

Melinda Dillon
Darren McGavin
Peter Billingsley

Peter Billingsley imagines how wonderful he will be if he gets his desired present of a Red Ryder air rifle in A Christmas Story.

This mushy holiday film based on humorist Jean Shepherd's book looks at family life in the early '40s. At the center of this silly candy cane account is 9-year-old Ralphie (Peter Billingsley) who longs for a genuine Red Ryder air rifle for Christmas. Director Bob Clark (*Porky's*) ably recreates the look of wartime Midwest America, but his idea of humor verges on the infantile. Still, there are some funny moments. Dillon and McGavin play the typically beleaguered parents. (PG)
98 minutes

CHU CHU AND THE PHILLY FLASH (1981)

★

Alan Arkin
Carol Burnett

Arkin and Burnett waste their talents and energy as two bedraggled characters in this plodding, no-laughs comedy set in San Francisco. Burnett plays a luckless entertainer, and Arkin is a derelict who was once a pro baseball player. They accidentally meet when they stumble onto some secret documents belonging to underworld characters. Arkin mopes through the movie wearing a raincoat so soiled that even Lieutenant Columbo would reject it. Burnett talks and yells a lot. **Director**—David Lowell Rich. (PG)
100 minutes

C.H.U.D. (1984)

★★

John Heard
Kim Greist
Christopher Curry

This low-budget horror tale has its moments of tension, but most often it chugs along in anticipation of a monster or two to prey on the next victim. The menacing creatures reside in New York City's underground passageways. They exist because some bad federal government guys dumped nuclear waste where they weren't supposed to. A photographer (Heard), his model/girlfriend (Greist), a courageous cop (Curry), and other public-spirited citizens help return the Big Apple to normalcy. **Director**—Douglas Cheek. (R) *88 minutes*

THE CINCINNATI KID (1965)
★★★

**Steve McQueen
Edward G. Robinson
Ann-Margret
Tuesday Weld**

McQueen does rather well in the title role, as a roving poker player who likes big games with big stakes. It's sort of *The Hustler* of card games. A big card game at the finale adds a dimension to the adventure. However, the romantic interludes don't fare as well. This film version of Richard Jessup's novel is set in the late '30s in New Orleans. There's nice support from the talented cast, which also includes Karl Malden, Joan Blondell, Rip Torn, Jack Weston, and Cab Calloway. **Director**—Norman Jewison. *113 minutes*

CINDERFELLA (1960)
★★

**Jerry Lewis
Ed Wynn
Judith Anderson**

Lewis puts his comic twist on the classic fairy tale, and the whole film turns into a pumpkin. The production is lavish, but Lewis's jokes are rather ordinary. There's lots of talk between gags, and the musical sequences are uninspired. There may be some enjoyment if you're a big Lewis fan; otherwise, there's not much to laugh at. Also with Anna Maria Alberghetti and Count Basie. **Director**—Frank Tashlin. *91 minutes*

CITIZEN KANE (1941)
 ★★★★

**Orson Welles
Joseph Cotten
Everett Sloane**

Welles's masterpiece is about a tyrannical newspaper publisher who built a vast empire. Every moment of the story, which parallels the career of William Randolph Hearst, is filled with intelligence, excitement, and pure entertainment. Welles co-wrote, directed, and starred in this magnificent production, which broke new ground in cinematic craftsmanship.

GENE HACKMAN

Gene Hackman, a character actor who became a star in the early '70s, was born in San Bernardino, California, in 1931. The son of a pressman who moved his family east to Danville, Illinois, Hackman joined the Marines at 16, and in four years served in China, Japan, Hawaii, and Okinawa. After his discharge, he enrolled at the University of Illinois and then attended the School of Radio Technique in New York. Returning to California, he decided to pursue an acting career and joined the Pasadena Playhouse.

Hackman began his professional career off-Broadway. He made his Broadway debut in Irwin Shaw's Children at Their Games, *for which he won a Clarence Derwent Award. His first Broadway hit was* Any Wednesday *in 1964, the year he made his film debut in Robert Rossen's* Lilith.

He was nominated for an Academy Award for his performance in Arthur Penn's Bonnie and Clyde *(1967), and again for Gilbert Cate's* I Never Sang for My Father *(1969). He won an Oscar as best actor for his work in William Friedkin's* The French Connection *(1971), and also appeared in John Frankenheimer's sequel,* The French Connection II *(1975).*

Hackman's many other films include The Poseidon Adventure *(1972),* Scarecrow *(1973), Francis Ford Coppola's* The Conversation *(1974), Mel Brooks's* Young Frankenstein *(1974), Arthur Penn's* Night Moves *(1975), Richard Brooks's* Bite the Bullet *(1975),* Superman *(1978) and* Superman II *(1981), All Night Long (1981), Warren Beatty's* Reds *(1981), Nicholas Roeg's* Eureka *(1982),* Under Fire *(1983),* Uncommon Valor *(1983), and* Misunderstood *(1984).*

Seeing it today is still a remarkable experience, and it surely will remain a gem among Hollywood's offerings. Also stars George Coulouris, Dorothy Comingore, Paul Stewart, and Agnes Moorehead. **Academy Award**—Herman J. Mankiewicz and Welles, writing (original screenplay). **Nominations**—best picture; Welles, best director; Welles, best actor; Gregg Toland, cinematography (black and white). *119 minutes b&w*

CITIZENS BAND
See Handle with Care

CITY HEAT (1984)
★★

**Burt Reynolds
Clint Eastwood**

Superstars Reynolds and Eastwood team up in this spoof of '30s private eye movies and their own reputations. Burt is a dapper but broke gumshoe and Clint is a stone-faced police lieutenant, both friends once but now bantering rivals. Unfortunately, a muddled plot and some excessive violence cool off the breeziness of this tongue-in-cheek affair. However, Burt and Clint work well together. Likable cast also includes Jane Alexander, Madeline Kahn, and Rip Torn. **Director**—Richard Benjamin. (PG) *94 minutes*

CITY OF WOMEN (1981)
★★★

**Marcello Mastroianni
Ettore Manni
Anna Prucnal**

Director Federico Fellini takes on women's lib as only Fellini can, with bombastic dream sequences that parade onward with exuberance and extravagance. Mastroianni is ideally cast as the maestro's alter ego, who stumbles on a feminist convention. Here, he's attacked as a spy and at last rescued by a macho man. Despite the usual Fellini flamboyance, the film is devoid of drama. However, serious Fellini fans may still rejoice. Also with Katren Gebelein and Donatella Damiani. (No MPAA rating) *140 minutes*

 Movie is available in Beta and VHS videotape

C
- Clash of the Titans
- Class
- The Class of Miss MacMichael
- Class of 1984
- Cleopatra
- Cloak and Dagger
- The Clock

CLASH OF THE TITANS (1981)

★★★

Harry Hamlin
Judi Bowker
Burgess Meredith

Greek mythology is the basis for this spirited, romantic adventure, featuring many glorious monsters created by special-effects wiz Ray Harryhausen. Square-jawed Hamlin plays Perseus, who engages in assorted daring feats to save his lady love, played by Bowker, from being sacrificed to the huge sea monster, the Kraken. Perseus gets around with the help of Pegasus, the flying horse. He valiantly battles a two-headed wolf, a giant vulture, and a woman whose stare can kill. **Director**—Desmond Davis. (PG)
120 minutes

CLASS (1983)

★

Jacqueline Bisset
Cliff Robertson
Rob Lowe

Jacqueline Bisset proves that she has Class *by cradle-robbing young Andrew McCarthy.*

A crudely made adolescent fantasy about a prep school boy who unwittingly has an affair with his roommate's mother, played by Bisset. This awkward takeoff of *The Graduate* is preposterous from start to finish. The entire cast strains with the garbled script and undeveloped characters. Robertson is wasted as the domineering, wealthy husband/father. It's hard to understand why director Lewis John Carlino, with *The Great Santini* under his belt, would bother with this second-class idea. (R)
98 minutes

THE CLASS OF MISS MACMICHAEL (1979)

★★

Glenda Jackson
Oliver Reed

Jackson, projecting her very proper British manner, plays a dedicated teacher who struggles with a roomful of unruly teenagers. It's her and the kids against the world and an authoritative principal, overplayed by Reed. This theme has been worn thin on the screen and on TV, and the situations are predictable. Jackson and most cast members do a serviceable job. Also with Michael Murphy and Rosalind Cash. **Director**—Silvio Narizzano. (R)
99 minutes

CLASS OF 1984 (1982)

★★

Roddy McDowall
Perry King

Another variation of *The Blackboard Jungle* theme with much violence woven into the fabric. The setting is an urban high school where a punk rock gang intimidates students and teachers at will. The story is engrossing for awhile, but the film finally deteriorates in an implausible, horror-filled climax. The acting is a mixed bag: McDowall does well as a cynical biology teacher, while King awkwardly portrays a mild-mannered music instructor who obtains brutal revenge. **Director**—Mark Lester. (R)
93 minutes

CLEOPATRA (1963)

★★

Elizabeth Taylor
Richard Burton
Rex Harrison

This historical drama was much heralded prior to its release, but turned out to be a horrendous disappointment. Despite its tremendous expense and length, there's perhaps less than an hour's worth of decent entertainment. Taylor, in the title role, is lovely to look at, but that's it. Harrison is good as Caesar, but Burton as

Cleopatra features Elizabeth Taylor in the title role.

Anthony turns in an uneven performance. Also with Pamela Brown, Roddy McDowall, Martin Landau, and Michael Hordern. **Director**—Joseph L. Mankiewicz. **Academy Award**—Leon Shamroy, cinematography (color). **Nomination**—Harrison, best actor.
243 minutes

CLOAK AND DAGGER (1984)

★★

Henry Thomas
Dabney Coleman

Uneasy mixture of Hardy Boys adventure, Hitchcock-style spy melodrama, and computer game fantasy. An 11-year-old tyke, played confidently by Thomas (*E.T.*), gets tangled up with a mysterious spy and murder caper. Only the adults don't believe him because his overactive imagination is stimulated by too much exposure to video games. This rather gimmicky plot is occasionally appealing, but the action turns unbelievable and unnecessarily brutal. **Director**—Richard Franklin. (PG)
101 minutes

THE CLOCK (1945)

★★★

Judy Garland
Robert Walker

Garland stars in this frothy romantic drama as a New York City secretary. She meets a soldier, played by Walker, and marries him before his 24-hour leave is up. During their whirlwind courtship, the lovebirds meet an assortment of pleasant characters. Garland is as charming as ever, but she doesn't sing. James Gleason, Lucille Gleason, Keenan Wynn, and Marshall Thompson are also in the cast. **Director**—Vincente Minnelli.

90 minutes b&w

A CLOCKWORK ORANGE
(1971)

★★★★

**Malcolm McDowell
Patrick Magee
Michael Bates**

Malcolm McDowell plays a dapper young juvenile delinquent in A Clockwork Orange.

Stanley Kubrick's perceptive dark satire about the future isn't as good as his *Dr. Strangelove*, but it hits the mark with plenty of impact. The film was adapted from Anthony Burgess's novel. The scene is 21st-century England, where gangs of young hoodlums run rampant, and ordinary citizens are afraid to venture far from their homes. A young murderer returns to society after being brainwashed by the authorities in a prison experiment and finds that the violent nature of society has increased. The film is generously laced with stark images and a chilling political message about the future. Also with Adrienne Corri, Aubrey Morris, and James Marcus. (R) **Academy Award Nominations**—best picture; Kubrick, best director; Kubrick, best screenplay (based on material from another medium).   *136 minutes*

CLOSE ENCOUNTERS OF THE THIRD KIND (1977)

★★★★

**Richard Dreyfuss
François Truffaut
Melinda Dillon**

Melinda Dillon and Cary Guffey reach and are touched by non-earthlings in Close Encounters of the Third Kind.

Steven Spielberg's $19-million epic about UFOs begins somewhat incoherently. The film lapses even more toward the middle. But wait. The final portion—when earthlings and extra-terrestrial beings rendezvous on a Wyoming mountain—suddenly flares to a dazzling climax. The special effects are stunning, and Spielberg's awesome imaginative effort comes into full focus. The faults are forgiven. It's sensational. Also with Teri Garr, Cary Guffey, and Bob Balaban. (PG) **Academy Award Nominations**— Spielberg, best director; Dillon, best supporting actress.   *135 minutes*

THE CLOWN (1953)

★★

**Red Skelton
Jane Greer**

Skelton has a rare dramatic role in this sentimental version of *The Champ*. He plays a has-been comic who is urged by his son to make a comeback. Skelton handles the part well, but he's better off working with comedy. There's adequate support from Tim Considine and Loring Smith. **Director**—Robert Z. Leonard.   *92 minutes b&w*

CLUNY BROWN (1946)

★★★

**Jennifer Jones
Charles Boyer**

This is a fine, pleasing romantic comedy, set in England just before World War II. Jones plays a plumber's niece who falls in love with a Czech refugee, played by Charles Boyer. The film works well as a spoof of the upper class, and it's helped by buoyant characterizations. Expertly directed by Ernst Lubitsch. Richard Haydn, Una O'Connor, and Peter Lawford give good support.   *100 minutes b&w*

COAL MINER'S DAUGHTER
(1980)

★★★★

**Sissy Spacek
Tommy Lee Jones**

In Coal Miner's Daughter, *Sissy Spacek plays Loretta Lynn, a girl who becomes a singing star.*

Spacek gives a stunning, virtuoso performance in the title role of this rags-to-riches biography of Loretta Lynn, the country singer superstar. First-rate support from Jones, as Lynn's everlovin' manager husband, also moves the film along, even when the screenplay seems to lose some energy. Director Michael Apted captures the authentic detail of Appalachia in a careful documentary style. It's a winning film, filled with plenty of heart, hope, and some surprisingly good singing from Spacek. Also with Beverly D'Angelo, Levon Helm, and Phyllis Boyens. (PG) **Academy Award**—Spacek, best actress. **Nominations**—best picture; Tom Rickman, best screenplay (adapted from another medium).   *124 minutes*

C

- Coast to Coast
- Cold Feet
- The Collector
- Coma
- The Comancheros
- Come Back, Little Sheba
- Come Back to the 5 & Dime Jimmy Dean, Jimmy Dean

COAST TO COAST (1980)

  ★★

Dyan Cannon
Robert Blake

Blake and Cannon barrel across the country in a huge trailer truck while various enemies intercept them along the way. This action-comedy is nothing more than another routine variation of such cat-and-mouse chase films as *Smokey and the Bandit.* Blake and Cannon, who seem to be imitating Burt Reynolds and Sally Field, ham it up with gusto. But it's a forgettable trip. Also with Quinn Redeker. **Director**—Joseph Sargent. (PG)

95 minutes

COLD FEET (1984)

  ★★

Griffin Dunne
Marissa Chibas
Blanche Baker

A slow-moving comedy about a man and a woman, previously stung by unhappy relationships, who now are cautiously trying to rekindle romance. The central characters are appealing enough, but the material tends to be overly talky and unfunny. Director-writer Bruce van-Dusen makes some sharp observations on contemporary life-styles. Too bad the film can't stand up for the full count. (PG) *96 minutes*

THE COLLECTOR (1965)

  ★★★

Terence Stamp
Samantha Eggar

An unusual story about a strange young man who collects butterflies and decides to add a beautiful art student, played by Eggar, to his collection. Stamp is convincing as the disturbed youth who kidnaps Eggar and keeps her in his basement. The suspense builds nicely under the fine direction of William Wyler. The chilling drama is based on John Fowles's popular novel. Maurice Dallimore and Mona Washbourne have supporting roles. **Academy Award Nominations**—Wyler, best director; Eggar, best actress; Stanley Mann and John

Terence Stamp tries to add Samantha Eggar to his collection in The Collector.

Kohn, best screenplay (based on material from another medium).

119 minutes

COMA (1978)

  ★★★

Geneviève Bujold
Michael Douglas

When the full moon rose in the sky and Count Dracula and the Wolf Man prowled about, it scared the daylights out of you. This horror story, which takes place in a Boston hospital, is scary enough, too, but the fun and satisfaction are absent. Bujold is a resident surgeon, who unravels a sinister plot to send healthy patients into irreversible comas and then steal their organs for transplants. The mystery unfolds amid the antiseptic glare of modern institutions with little style, imagination, or humor. Dr. Frankenstein, where are you? Also with Elizabeth Ashley, Rip Torn, and Richard Widmark. Michael Crichton directed this film, which is based on his novel. (PG) *113 minutes*

THE COMANCHEROS (1961)

★★★

John Wayne
Stuart Whitman

Wayne is right at home in this rough, tough western, as a Texas Ranger who is determined to rid the territory of a gang supplying guns and whiskey to the Indians. Whitman plays a gambler-prisoner forced to tag along with Wayne. The Duke gets involved with some lively gunplay, yet there's just the right amount of levity mixed in with the action. Big John and the rest of the cast seem to be having an enjoyable time with the material. Also with Lee Marvin, Bruce Cabot, Nehemiah Persoff, and Ina Balin. **Director**—Michael Curtiz. *107 minutes*

COME BACK, LITTLE SHEBA (1952)

★★★★

Shirley Booth
Burt Lancaster

Top-notch performances propel this emotionally charged drama about a slovenly housewife trying to cope with her alcoholic husband. The film, based on the William Inge play, is somewhat stagebound, but effective nevertheless. Booth is splendid as the wife, and Lancaster is superb as the husband. Terry Moore and Richard Jaeckel are fine in supporting roles. **Director**—Daniel Mann. **Academy Award**—Booth, best actress. **Nomination**—Moore, best supporting actress.

99 minutes b&w

COME BACK TO THE 5 & DIME JIMMY DEAN, JIMMY DEAN (1982)

★★

Sandy Dennis
Cher
Karen Black

Robert Altman's low-budget screen version of the failed Broadway play bogs down in its overbearing staginess. The confined setting is a seedy Texas dime store where a group of women are holding a 20-years-later reunion of their James Dean fan club. Superb ensemble acting captures the various kooky characters who here reveal their strange secrets and frailties. Yet those Altmanesque observations are often obscured by a confusing, overwritten script. (PG)

109 minutes

• Come Blow Your Horn
• The Comedians
• The Comedy of Terrors

• Come Fill the Cup
• Comes a Horseman
• Come to the Stable
• Comfort and Joy

C

COME BLOW YOUR HORN (1962)
★★★

Frank Sinatra
Tony Bill
Lee J. Cobb
Molly Picon

Sinatra plays a swinging bachelor with a stable of girls, who teaches his younger brother the ways of the world. The Neil Simon play is successfully transposed to the screen, with the funny characters and funny lines firmly intact. Ol' Blue Eyes is well cast as the bachelor, and Bill plays the awestruck kid brother with conviction. Cobb and Picon are good as anxious parents. Sinatra sings the title song. Jill St. John, Barbara Rush, and Dan Blocker have supporting roles. **Director**—Bud Yorkin. *112 minutes*

THE COMEDIANS (1967)
★★

Richard Burton
Elizabeth Taylor
Alec Guinness
Peter Ustinov

Richard Burton and Elizabeth Taylor aren't laughing in The Comedians, *a political drama.*

A champagne cast can't do much with this labored and awkward film version of Graham Greene's novel about politics and violence in Haiti under the rule of Papa Doc Duvalier. Burton and Taylor play odd characters involved with intrigue. The clumsy, cliché-heavy script seems to overwhelm the acting, and the direction lacks inspiration. Supporting players include Lillian Gish, Paul Ford, Roscoe Lee Browne, Raymond St. Jacques, James Earl Jones, and Cicely Tyson. **Director**—Peter Glenville. *160 minutes*

THE COMEDY OF TERRORS (1963)
★★

Vincent Price
Peter Lorre
Boris Karloff
Basil Rathbone

This spoof of the macabre features a quartet of horror-film greats. Although there are a few effective scenes, the film falls short of expectations. Price plays a sinister undertaker who schemes to increase his business by hastening the demise of prospective clients. They should have buried the script instead. Joe E. Brown and Joyce Jameson are also in the cast. **Director**—Jacques Tourneur. *88 minutes*

COME FILL THE CUP (1951)
★★★

James Cagney
Phyllis Thaxter

A solid performance by Cagney graces this melodrama. Cagney plays an ex-newspaperman trying to cure himself of alcoholism and get his life back together. He also tries to help the son of his boss, who has ties to gangsters. There's fine support from Gig Young, who plays the son—a tipsy playboy. Raymond Massey and James Gleason are also in the cast. **Director**—Gordon Douglas. *113 minutes b&w*

COMES A HORSEMAN (1978)
 ★★

Jane Fonda
James Caan
Jason Robards, Jr.

Young, struggling ranchers stand up to a cattle baron and oil industrialists. Sound familiar? It's a version of a theme for countless westerns of yesteryear, and they've used it again here with middling results. Only this time, they've blended in some sensitivity and added a dash of modern feminism. The film walks most of the time when it should gallop, despite the strong performances by the cast. Fonda plays a rancher, Caan is the rescuer, and Robards plays the cattle

Jane Fonda is embroiled in a land battle in Comes a Horseman.

baron. Also with George Grizzard, Richard Farnsworth, and Jim Davis. **Director**—Alan J. Pakula. (PG) **Academy Award Nomination**—Farnsworth, best supporting actor. *118 minutes*

COME TO THE STABLE (1949)
★★★

Loretta Young
Celeste Holm

Young and Holm star in this charming, heartwarming film about two French nuns who seek support to build a children's hospital in a New England town. The duo is perfectly suited for their parts, and they exude considerable grace and sweetness in this tasteful production. Henry Koster directs with simplicity and efficiency. Also with Hugh Marlowe, Elsa Lanchester, Mike Mazurki, and Regis Toomey. **Academy Award Nominations**—Young, best actress; Holm, Lanchester, best supporting actress; Clare Boothe Luce, writing (motion picture story); Joseph LaShelle, cinematography (black and white). *94 minutes b&w*

COMFORT AND JOY (1984)
 ★★

Bill Peterson

Scottish director Bill Forsyth (*Gregory's Girl*) offers a rather subdued, offbeat comedy that does not quite live up to
(Continued)

C

- Coming Home
- Command Decision
- Les Comperes
- The Competition
- Compulsion
- Conan the Barbarian
- Conan the Destroyer

(Continued) his earlier film projects. The frothy story centers on the career turning point of a Glasgow disk jockey (Peterson) who wants to break into news reporting. He's also trying to resolve the abrupt departure of his eccentric girl friend. Interesting characters could compensate for such loose plotting, but Forsyth does not come through in that category. (PG)

106 minutes

COMING HOME (1978)

★★

Jon Voight
Jane Fonda

Fonda apparently conceived this post-Vietnam melodrama, but where is the snap and spirit one would expect from a film associated with such a celebrated war protestor? The Vietnam experience seems more of a backdrop to the soapy and confusing love story about a Marine captain's wife, played by Fonda, who has an affair with a paraplegic Vietnam veteran, played by Voight. There are appealing performances by Fonda, Voight, and Bruce Dern in the major roles, but the ideas are foggy, and the film doesn't hit home. Also with Robert Carradine, Penelope Milford, and Robert Ginty. **Director**—Hal Ashby. (R) **Academy Awards**—Voight, best actor; Fonda, best actress; Nancy Dowd (story), Waldo Salt and Robert Jones (screenplay), best original screenplay. **Nominations**—best picture; Ashby, best director; Dern, best supporting actor; Milford, best supporting actress.

127 minutes

COMMAND DECISION (1948)
★★★

Clark Gable
Walter Pidgeon
Van Johnson

This gripping World War II drama focuses on the top brass who must make the distressing decisions that will send many men to their deaths. Gable is the general who huddles with his staff to discuss the strategy for bombing missions over Nazi Germany. This straightforward adaptation of William Haines's Broadway play also features Brian Donlevy, John Hodiak, Edward Arnold, and Charles Bickford. **Director**—Sam Wood.

112 minutes b&w

LES COMPERES (1984)
★★★

Gerard Depardieu
Pierre Richard

French writer-director Francis Veber *(La Cage aux Folles)* serves up a delicious, playful farce based on an odd couple routine. Depardieu is a tough, aggressive news reporter. Richard is a meek, depressive character. Both are duped into pursuing a teenager that each believes is his son. An array of screwball and sentimental situations ensue. In French with English titles. (No MPAA rating)

98 minutes

THE COMPETITION (1980)

★★

Richard Dreyfuss
Amy Irving

He (Dreyfuss) is a brilliant young classical pianist. She (Irving) is also a musical prodigy. They fall in love while vying for top honors in a piano competition. Beethoven and Prokofiev get a workout at the keyboards, but this overlong love story is drab and predictable. It's also bogged down with half-baked subplots that contribute to the film's awkwardness. Dreyfuss and Irving are convincing as dedicated musicians, but they don't seem to hit the right notes as young lovers. Also with Lee Remick and Sam Wanamaker. **Director**—Joel Oliansky. (PG)

129 minutes

COMPULSION (1959)
★★★

Dean Stockwell
Bradford Dillman

The infamous Leopold-Loeb murder case of the '20s is brought to the screen with solid performances and impressive direction. The plot mainly concerns the murder trial of the two brilliant but twisted Chicago students. The students, played by Stockwell and Dillman, are put on trial for killing a young boy for thrills. Orson Welles stands out in a cameo role as defense lawyer Clarence Darrow. And there are fine performances, too, from Diane Varsi, E. G. Marshall, and Martin Milner. **Director**—Richard Fleischer.

103 minutes b&w

CONAN THE BARBARIAN (1982)

★

Arnold Schwarzenegger
Sandahl Bergman
James Earl Jones

Arnold Schwarzenegger, Gerry Lopez, and Sandahl Bergman try to stop audiences from leaving early during Conan the Barbarian.

Even a true barbarian would wince at this dreary sword-and-sorcery saga based on the comic book hero. This witless film serves as nothing more than a showcase for the magnificent muscles of Schwarzenegger, who hulks about chopping off heads and flexing his biceps until he finally triumphs over the villainous, snake-worshipping Thulsa Doom (Jones). The minimal dialogue in the pointless screenplay comes off as incoherent mumbo jumbo. **Director**—John Milius. (R)

115 minutes

CONAN THE DESTROYER (1984)

★★

Arnold Schwarzenegger
Grace Jones
Wilt Chamberlain

Schwarzenegger, in the title role, mus-

- The Concorde—Airport '79
- The Concrete Jungle
- Condorman
- Conduct Unbecoming
- Coney Island
- Confidentially Yours
- A Connecticut Yankee in King Arthur's Court

C

Arnold Schwarzenegger gets ready to destroy something in Conan the Destroyer.

cles through another sword-and-sorcery, comic book adventure, flexing his biceps to the maximum and mumbling dialogue to the minimum. Some scenery is striking, but the sword-swinging action is as pedestrian as ever. This time, our hero must recover a magnificent stone and protect the virginity of a young princess. Arnold is always easy to spot among the assorted shaggy characters. He's the one without a shirt. **Director**—Richard Fleischer. (PG) *103 minutes*

THE CONCORDE—
AIRPORT '79 (1979)
★★

Alain Delon
Susan Blakely
Robert Wagner
Sylvia Kristel

The *Airport* saga continues. This time it's the supersonic Concorde jet, which encounters assorted hair-raising mishaps. The special effects are praiseworthy, but the plot, which mainly concerns an arms sale scandal, is rather déjà vu. The usual gallery of oddball characters is on board for the globe-trotting flight. The large cast also includes George Kennedy, Eddie Albert, Bibi Andersson, and Martha Raye. **Director**—David Lowell Rich. (PG) *113 minutes*

THE CONCRETE JUNGLE
(1982)
 ★

Tracy Bergman

Cheaply made, exploitative women's prison film shown with every imaginable cliché and poorly acted and written to boot. Sweet young thing Bergman lands in the slammer where she's constantly brutalized by fellow inmates and guards. Jill St. John looks awfully silly as the conspiring warden. It's a long, tough sentence for any moviegoer. **Director**—Tom DeSimone. (R) *99 minutes*

CONDORMAN (1981)
 ★★

Michael Crawford
Barbara Carrera

From the Walt Disney studios comes a flimsy parody of James Bond adventures, which features striking scenery from exotic locations and an adolescent, plodding script. Crawford plays a cartoonist who occasionally dresses up like the comic-book hero he has created. He's drawn into a CIA caper, in which he helps a beautiful Russian agent, played by Carrera, defect. Of course, he uses all the wonderful gadgets and schemes that he dreamed up for his comic strip. **Director**— Charles Jarrott. (PG) *90 minutes*

CONDUCT UNBECOMING
(1975)
★★★★

Michael York
Richard Attenborough
Trevor Howard

This magnificent British film, taken from the successful play by Barry England, smartly explodes myths about duty, valor, and honor in Victorian India. The suspenseful drama deals with the kangaroo trial of a young, aristocratic lieutenant, who is accused of attacking the widow of an officer. Excellent cinematography enhances the rich atmosphere. Also with Stacy Keach, Susannah York, Christopher Plummer, James Faulkner, and James Donald. **Director**—Michael Anderson. (PG) *107 minutes*

CONEY ISLAND (1943)
★★★

Betty Grable
Cesar Romero
George Montgomery

Grable struts and sings in this glossy, lighthearted period musical set at the turn of the century. She's a saloon songstress; Montgomery and Romero—two showmen—vie for her attention. Later remade by Grable as *Wabash Avenue*. Also with Phil Silvers and Matt Briggs. **Director**—Walter Lang. *96 minutes*

CONFIDENTIALLY YOURS
(1984)
 ★★★

Jean Louis Trintignant
Fanny Ardent

François Truffaut's romantic detective story, shot in black and white, is a homage to '40s *film noir* thrillers. Small-town businessman Trintignant is suspected of murdering his wife and her lover. Quick to the rescue is his beautiful girl Friday, played with exquisite charm and style by Ardant. The movie successfully straddles a fence between satire and seriousness. In French with English titles. **Director**—Truffaut. (PG) *111 minutes*

A CONNECTICUT YANKEE IN
KING ARTHUR'S COURT
(1949)
★★★

Bing Crosby
Rhonda Fleming
William Bendix

(Continued)

William Bendix and Bing Crosby in A Connecticut Yankee in King Arthur's Court.

C

- The Constant Nymph
- Continental Divide
- The Conversation
- Convicts Four
- Convoy
- Coogan's Bluff

(Continued)

Crosby is an engaging Sir Boss in this jazzed-up musical version of the classic Mark Twain comedy. Bing is a blacksmith, who's transported back in time to Camelot, where Merlin declares him a wizard. Bing sings some forgettable tunes, yet he handles the acting chores with aplomb. Also with Cedric Hardwicke and Murvyn Vye, who are fine in supporting roles. **Director—** Tay Garnett. *107 minutes*

THE CONSTANT NYMPH (1943)
★★★

Joan Fontaine
Charles Boyer

Fontaine is in top form as a young girl in love with a sophisticated musician, played smartly by Boyer. Top-notch performances by other cast members enhance this well-produced drama. Also with Alexis Smith, Brenda Marshall, Charles Coburn, Dame May Whitty, and Peter Lorre. **Director—** Edmund Goulding. **Academy Award Nomination**—Fontaine, best actress. *112 minutes b&w*

CONTINENTAL DIVIDE (1981)
★★

John Belushi
Blair Brown

John Belushi plays a muck-raking Chicago newspaper reporter in the romantic comedy Continental Divide.

Belushi plays a gruff Chicago newspaper columnist. Brown plays a brainy, reclusive ornithologist, working to save the bald eagle. They meet high in the Rocky Mountains. They argue. They fall in love. They part. They are in love again. This is a rather typical romantic comedy setup that Tracy and Hepburn handled so nicely so often. Belushi and Brown play interesting characters, but they're too diverse to be believable. The film strains to be witty, but much of it is for the birds. Also with Allen Goorwitz, Carlin Glynn, and Tony Ganios. **Director**—Michael Apted. (PG) *103 minutes*

THE CONVERSATION (1974)
★★★★

Gene Hackman
John Cazale
Frederick Forrest
Cindy Williams

Gene Hackman and Elizabeth MacRae share a dance in The Conversation.

Compelling, fresh mystery-drama about a determined wiretap expert, played by Hackman, who finally is bugged by his own conscience when he goes too far. Director Francis Ford Coppola, who also wrote the screenplay, hits home with this absorbing story in light of Watergate. The plot involves murder, but the theme also focuses on the loss of privacy and the erosion of democracy as new technologies are misused. Hackman digs into his role with straight-faced discipline. Also with Allen Garfield, Teri Garr, and Harrison Ford. (PG) **Academy Award Nominations**—best picture; Coppola, best original screenplay. *113 minutes*

CONVICTS FOUR (1962)
★★

Ben Gazzara
Vincent Price

An unusual film about a convict who is spared from execution and then becomes rehabilitated by developing skills as a painter. Gazzara plays the central character, based on the autobiography of John Resko. The production is a curious blend of drama, documentary, and character study, which begins with determination, but then trails off into uncertainty. Broderick Crawford and Rod Steiger appear briefly in cameo roles. Others in the cast include Stuart Whitman, Ray Walston, Jack Kruschen, and Sammy Davis, Jr. **Director**—Millard Kaufman. **Alternate Title**—*Reprieve*. *106 minutes b&w*

CONVOY (1978)
★★

Kris Kristofferson
Ali MacGraw
Ernest Borgnine

Scores of huge trailer trucks barrel across the screen to the tune of C. W. McCall's trucker ballad. Director Sam Peckinpah romanticizes the free-wheeling, cowboy image of these drivers and, as expected, pours on the violent action. Logic and good taste are often left stranded by the roadside. Also with Burt Young, Madge Sinclair, and Franklyn Ajaye. (PG) *110 minutes*

COOGAN'S BLUFF (1968)
★★★

Clint Eastwood
Lee J. Cobb
Susan Clark

Big, bad Eastwood plays an Arizona deputy sheriff who comes to New York City and tries to retrieve an escaped murderer, played by Don Stroud. After the thug slips away from him, Eastwood resorts to western-style methods, to the chagrin of the city cops, to recapture his man. Cobb plays a city detective. Lots of fast-paced action and good character contrasts

• Cooley High
• Cool Hand Luke
• Coonskin
• Copacabana
• Cornbread, Earl and Me
• Corvette Summer
• The Cotton Club

C

enliven the production. Also with Tisha Sterling, Betty Field, and Tom Tully. **Director**—Don Siegel. (PG)

100 minutes

COOLEY HIGH (1975)
★★★

**Glynn Turman
Lawrence-Hilton Jacobs
Garrett Morris**

The film is a bit like *American Graffiti*, but this time it's the story of black adolescents on Chicago's near North Side in 1964. Instead of cruising the main drag in flashy automobiles, they get together under elevated trains and hitch free rides on the backs of buses. Impressively written and directed, the film is blessed with the exceptional talents of Turman, Jacobs, and Morris. Also with Cynthia Davis, Corin Rogers, and Maurice Leon Havis. **Director**—Michael Schultz. (PG)

107 minutes

COOL HAND LUKE (1967)
 ★★★★

**Paul Newman
George Kennedy**

Paul Newman plays the title role in Cool Hand Luke; *George Kennedy is a chain-gang supervisor.*

Forthright, gripping drama about a chain-gang prisoner, played by Newman, who has a burning determination to maintain his individualism despite his compromising situation. Newman's portrayal is stunning, and he's backed to the hilt with an award-winning performance by Kennedy. There are some subtle references to Christ in this well-made production.

Also with Jo Van Fleet, J. D. Cannon, Lou Antonio, Robert Drivas, and Strother Martin. **Director**—Stuart Rosenberg. (PG) **Academy Award**—Kennedy, best supporting actor. **Nominations**—Newman, best actor; Don Pearce and Frank R. Pierson, best screenplay (based on material from another medium). *126 minutes*

COONSKIN (1975)
★

This movie is a blend of live action and animation from director Ralph Bakshi, who produced the X-rated feature cartoons *Heavy Traffic* and *Fritz the Cat*. Coonskin is about three black characters who leave the South for Harlem and try to take over the rackets. It's generally a dull story, filled with grotesque characters. The film has provoked denunciations from the Congress of Racial Equality and other black organizations for portraying blacks as stereotypes. The voices of Barry White, Scatman Crothers, and Charles Gordone are used. (R)

83 minutes

COPACABANA (1947)
 ★

**Groucho Marx
Carmen Miranda**

Not much doing in this uninspired musical-comedy involving nightclub performers. Things go awry when a girl with two different acts is needed for both parts at the same time. Even Marx in a key role can't save this one. Also with Steve Cochran and Andy Russell. **Director**—Alfred E. Green.

91 minutes b&w

CORNBREAD, EARL AND ME (1975)
★★★

**Moses Gunn
Bernie Casey
Rosalind Cash**

A sensitive story about a college-bound black basketball star, who is accidentally killed by the police. This urban tragedy and courtroom drama is a far cry from the typical black exploitation film. However, it's flawed by some uneven directing. Also with Madge Sinclair, Keith Wilkes, and Tierre Turner. **Director**—Joe Manduke. (PG) *95 minutes*

CORVETTE SUMMER (1978)
 ★★

**Mark Hamill
Annie Potts
Eugene Roche**

Mark Hamill and Annie Potts enjoy cars and each other in Corvette Summer.

Hamill of *Star Wars* fame plays a naïve high-school boy in love with a flashy car and an equally flashy would-be hooker, played by Potts. This unusual, breezy, and innocuous film is primarily aimed at teen audiences. Director Matthew Robbins keeps the action moving along, but the picture often stumbles over too much silliness. Also with Kim Milford and Richard McKenzie. (PG) *105 minutes*

THE COTTON CLUB (1984)
 ★★

**Richard Gere
Gregory Hines**

Lavish, slick blend of '30s gangster saga and Hollywood musical, desperately in search of a cohesive story. This uneven period piece revolves around the popular Harlem night club that featured famous black entertainers on stage but admitted only whites as patrons. A $47 million budget provides dazzling sets and lively dance numbers. The look is impressive, but plot and characters rarely come into focus. **Director**—Francis Coppola. (R)

121 minutes

COUNT DRACULA AND HIS VAMPIRE BRIDE
(1978)

★

**Chrisopher Lee
Peter Cushing**

Moviemakers won't let Count Dracula rest in peace as long as there are a few more dollars to be made. This version has the Count, played by veteran bloodsucker Lee, plotting to annihilate mankind with biological warfare. It's all familiar vampire doings, by now unexciting and silly. Cushing plays the good professor, who puts an end to the sinister scheme. **Director**—Alan Gibson. (R)   *87 minutes*

COUNTRY (1984)

★★★

**Jessica Lange
Sam Shepard**

An embattled Iowa farm family fights a faceless government bureaucracy to save their land. The powerful and poignant story emphasizes the courage, integrity, and grit of such rural Americans. And it carries a strong political message. Lange and Shepard provide believable and forceful performances as farmer and farm wife whose way of life is on the brink of bankruptcy. Also with Wilford Brimley and Matt Clark. **Director**—Richard Pearce. (PG)
108 minutes

THE COUNTRY GIRL
(1954)

★★★★

**Bing Crosby
Grace Kelly**

Fantastic performances by Crosby and Kelly enhance this absorbing drama about an alcoholic singer trying to make a comeback. When Bing, formerly feeling sorry for himself, is stimulated to get back on his feet, wife Grace demonstrates her support. The film, which is adapted from the play by Clifford Odets, features some songs by Ira Gershwin and Harold Arlen. Also with William Holden, Anthony Ross, and Gene Reynolds. **Director**—George Seaton. **Academy Awards**—Kelly, best actress; Seaton, writing (screenplay). **Nominations**—best picture; Seaton, best director; Crosby, best actor; John F. Warren, cinematography (black and white).
104 minutes b&w

COUNT YOUR BLESSINGS
(1959)

★★

**Deborah Kerr
Maurice Chevalier
Rossano Brazzi**

Unworkable comedy of manners about an English girl, played by Kerr, who marries a wealthy Frenchman, played by Brazzi, during World War II. The conflict separates them, and when they are united, their nine-year-old son learns his father is a philanderer. The plot limps along with occasional levity by the commentary of Chevalier. His charm, however, is only a slight blessing. Also with Mona Washbourne, Martin Stephens, Ronald Squire, and Tom Helmore. **Director**—Jean Negulesco.   *102 minutes*

HUMPHREY BOGART

Humphrey Bogart, in a long and distinguished acting career, established the image of the lonely, brooding, cynical antihero. He was born in 1899 in New York City, the son of a surgeon. Bogart attended Phillips Academy with the intention of studying medicine at Yale, but he was expelled because of disciplinary problems and joined the U.S. Navy, serving during World War I. While he was in the Navy, he received the injury to his lip that left him with his trademark lisp.

After his discharge, Bogart went to work in the theater, initially as an office boy and finally as a stage manager. In 1920, he tried acting with limited success; he played various minor stage roles. In 1930, he was offered a chance to star in a 10-minute short titled Broadway's Like That.

Bogart made his motion-picture debut in A Devil with Women *(1930), and during the early '30s he combined secondary film roles with acting assignments on Broadway. In 1935, he portrayed Duke Mantee, a gangster, in the Broadway production of* The Petrified Forest. *Warner Brothers bought the film rights, and Bogart demonstrated his acting ability by repeating his stage role in the movie, which became a hit.*

In the latter part of the '30s, Bogart starred in more than 25 films, primarily in gangster roles. Then in 1941 he established his legendary qualities with a smashing performance in High Sierra. *This was followed by his fabulous portrayal of private-eye Sam Spade in* The Maltese Falcon *(1941). Perhaps his best-remembered role was the cynical and mysterious Rick of* Casablanca *(1942). This film gave him a new image—the intriguing and sexy leading man.*

Casablanca, which won an Oscar for best picture, remains one of Hollywood's most enduring classics. Incidentally, the original actor scheduled to play the role of Rick was Ronald Reagan.

While making To Have and Have Not *(1943), he fell in love with and married his co-star Lauren Bacall, who became his fourth wife.*

In the '50s, Bogart displayed his acting skills in such movies as The African Queen *(1951) and* The Caine Mutiny *(1954). He received the Oscar as best actor for* The African Queen. *In 1957, soon after completing* The Harder They Fall, *he died.*

Some of Bogart's other movies include Marked Woman *(1937),* Dead End *(1937),* Angels with Dirty Faces *(1938),* The Roaring Twenties *(1939),* Across the Pacific *(1942),* Sahara *(1943),* The Big Sleep *(1946),* The Treasure of the Sierra Madre *(1947),* Key Largo *(1948),* The Enforcer *(1951),* Beat the Devil *(1954),* The Barefoot Contessa *(1954), and* The Left Hand of God *(1955).*

• Coup De Torchon
• The Court Jester

• The Court Martial of Billy Mitchell
• The Courtship of Eddie's Father

• Cousin, Cousine
• Cover Girl
• Cowboy

C

COUP DE TORCHON (1982)

★★

**Philippe Noiret
Isabelle Huppert
Stephane Audran**

Bertrand Tavernier's uneven account of French colonists in Africa just prior to World War II partly intrigues but mostly confuses. The strange, meandering story centers on a timid, sloppy village police chief (Noiret) who suddenly rebels by bumping off various unsavory citizens. Noiret's character is clearly colorful, but the haphazard progress of events rarely keeps him in proper focus. In French with English titles. (No MPAA rating) *128 minutes*

THE COURT JESTER (1955)

 ★★★★

**Danny Kaye
Glynis Johns
Basil Rathbone**

Kaye is a knockout in this superb, made-to-order comedy set in medieval times. The delightful romp, which spoofs costume movies, has Kaye posing as a jester to infiltrate a plot against the king. There are all sorts of effective comic situations, decorated with delightful tunes and well-staged action. The fine supporting cast includes Angela Lansbury, Mildred Natwick, Cecil Parker, Edward Ashley, and Robert Middleton. **Director**—Norman Panama and Melvin Frank.

101 minutes

THE COURT MARTIAL OF BILLY MITCHELL (1955)

★★★

**Gary Cooper
Rod Steiger
Ralph Bellamy**

Straightforward but slow-paced account of the prophetic American general who accused his superiors of being unprepared for invasion and was subsequently court-martialed. His warning came almost two decades prior to the sneak attack on Pearl Harbor. Cooper is convincing in the title role. The film concludes effectively in a stirring courtroom sequence. Also

Gary Cooper (right) handles the title role in The Court Martial of Billy Mitchell.

with Charles Bickford, Elizabeth Montgomery, Fred Clark, and Darren McGavin. **Director**—Otto Preminger. **Academy Award Nomination**— Milton Spirling and Emmett Lavery, writing (story and screenplay).

100 minutes

THE COURTSHIP OF EDDIE'S FATHER (1962)

★★★

**Glenn Ford
Ronnie Howard
Shirley Jones**

The Courtship of Eddie's Father *features young Ron Howard as Eddie and Glenn Ford as his father.*

A rather cute, teary-eyed comedy that is handled well for this sort of material. Ford plays the title role of a man who loses his wife. His young son plays cupid so the family can have a new mom. There's just the right measure of humor and sentimentality to maintain the film's charming aspects most of the way through. Other fine cast members include Stella Stevens and Dina Merrill. **Director**—Vincente Minnelli. *117 minutes*

COUSIN, COUSINE (1975)

 ★★★★

**Marie-Christine Barrault
Victor Lanoux**

This pleasant romantic comedy about French social mores, directed by Jean-Charles Tacchella, stops a step or two short of turning into a farce. Barrault and Lanoux turn in brilliant performances as cousins—by marriage—who first become friends and eventually fall in love. They finally have an affair when all their friends and relatives assume they are doing just that. Also with Marie-France Pisier, Guy Marchand, Ginette Garcin, and Sybil Maas. (No MPAA rating) **Academy Award Nominations**—Barrault, best actress; Tacchella and Daniele Thompson, best original screenplay.

95 minutes

COVER GIRL (1944)

★★★

**Rita Hayworth
Gene Kelly**

A lively, toe-tapping musical with the spectacular dancing of Kelly and the memorable music of Jerome Kern. Hayworth stars as a chorus girl, who breaks out of the chorus line to become a magazine cover model. That's it for the simple plot. The strength here is Kelly's solo numbers and a fine supporting role by Eve Arden as a wisecracking secretary. The score includes "Long Ago and Far Away." Also with Phil Silvers, Lee Bowman, Jinx Falkenburg, Otto Kruger, and Ed Brophy. **Director**—Charles Vidor.

107 minutes

COWBOY (1958)

★★★

**Jack Lemmon
Glenn Ford**

Generally pleasant western yarn, based on *On the Trail*, the autobiography of Frank Harris. It concerns a lad who becomes a cowboy and then discovers it's not the glamorous life he envisioned. Lemmon plays Harris, and Ford stars as his trail boss. Good

(Continued)

C
- The Cowboys
- Crackers
- The Creature from the Black Lagoon

- Creepshow
- Crime and Passion

- Crimes of Passion
- Criss Cross

(Continued)
western atmosphere out where the cattle roam. Also with Anna Kashfi, Brian Donlevy, Dick York, Richard Jaeckel, and King Donovan. **Director**—Delmer Daves. *92 minutes*

THE COWBOYS (1972)

 ★

John Wayne
Roscoe Lee Browne

Wayne stars in this drab and overly violent western, as a cattleman who is forced to recruit 11 schoolboys for his roundup after his regular drovers quit. The youngsters become killers to revenge the death of their boss. Big John isn't bad in a few scenes, but he has fared better with this genre. Also with Bruce Dern, Colleen Dewhurst, and Slim Pickens. (PG) **Director**—Mark Rydell. *128 minutes*

CRACKERS (1984)

 ★★

Donald Sutherland
Sean Penn

Sean Penn, Larry Riley, and Donald Sutherland are a trio of sloppy safe robbers in Crackers.

Fitfully amusing, half-baked caper comedy by director Louis Malle (*Atlantic City*). Sutherland plays an unemployed electrician who leads a group of misfits to burglarize a seedy San Francisco pawn shop. A few characters stand out, but Malle fails to sustain sufficient energy and the film concludes on an innocuous, stale note. Also stars Jack Warden. (PG) *92 minutes*

THE CREATURE FROM THE BLACK LAGOON (1954)
★★★

Richard Carlson
Julie Adams
Richard Denning

Surprisingly effective sci-fi thriller—originally a 3-D movie—about some explorers who discover a half-man/half-fish monster, which emerges from a lagoon adjacent to the Amazon River. This B-movie is rife with clichés and hokey horror gimmicks, but it delivers plenty of chills. It's sort of the cream of the crop of camp. Sequels include *Revenge of the Creature* and *The Creature Walks Among Us*. Also with Antonio Moreno, Nestor Paiva, and Ricou Browning. **Director**—Jack Arnold. (G) *79 minutes*

CREEPSHOW (1982)

 ★★

Hal Holbrook
Leslie Nielsen
E. G. Marshall

Director George Romero (*Night of the Living Dead*) and screenwriter Stephen King (*The Shining*) present a mixed bag of five horror vignettes. An intriguing moment surfaces occasionally, but for the most part the proceedings creep along, and there's an underlying tone of mild humor. Perhaps the best tale of the lot concerns a nasty patriarch, murdered by his relatives, who returns from a moldy grave to claim his piece of Father's Day cake. (R) *129 minutes*

CRIME AND PASSION (1976)
(no stars)

Omar Sharif
Karen Black
Joseph Bottoms

Director Ivan Passer, who is credited with sensitive and well-made films (*Law and Disorder; Born to Win*) is out of character with this disoriented mixture of sex and murder. It's also an embarrassment for Sharif and Black. Sharif plays an international financier, whose sexual appetite escalates when faced with fiscal disaster. Black plays his willing Girl Friday. This scenario somehow is supposed to be funny—it isn't. Also with Bernhard Wicki. (R) *92 minutes*

CRIMES OF PASSION (1984)

 ★

Kathleen Turner
Anthony Perkins

Anthony Perkins wants to reform Kathleen Turner's wicked ways; she wants to subdue him with lust. Both efforts are Crimes of Passion.

It looks like a sex exploitation film trying hard to be brutally incisive. It's merely awful. Turner plays a streetwalker who actually is a career woman. She's stalked by a minister (Perkins) who really is a lunatic. There is something here to repel everyone: sledge hammer obscenities and enough embarrassing moral posturing to put voyeurs to sleep. **Director**—Ken Russell. (R) *102 minutes*

CRISS CROSS (1948)
★★★

Burt Lancaster
Yvonne De Carlo
Dan Duryea

A brooding, suspenseful cops-and-robbers film about an armored-car guard who gets mixed up in a heist and is double-crossed by his ex-wife and friends. Lancaster does a commendable job, and Duryea plays a villain extraordinaire who is out to get Lancaster. Also with Stephen McNally, Richard Long, and Alan Napier. **Director**—Robert Siodmak.

87 minutes b&w

CRITIC'S CHOICE (1963)
★★

Bob Hope
Lucille Ball
Marilyn Maxwell

Hope plays a hard-nosed drama critic, whose wife, played by Ball, writes a play that he gives an unflattering review. This screen adaptation of Ira Levin's Broadway play can't be saved by such talented performers, so the film comes off as a lopsided and limp vehicle. Some of the supporting players have better moments than the leads. Also with Rip Torn, Jim Backus, and Marie Windsor. **Director**—Don Weis. *100 minutes*

CROMWELL (1970)
★★

Richard Harris
Alec Guinness
Robert Morley

A good-looking, but ponderous, historical drama at the time of Britain's 17th-century civil war and the rise to power of Oliver Cromwell, who became a revolutionary and then a dictator. The events include the execution of Charles I and some notable battle scenes. Harris handles the title role unconvincingly, while Guinness plays an acceptable King Charles. This subject may be tough to grasp in some school textbooks, but you don't expect the same treatment on the screen. Supporting players include Frank Finlay, Dorothy Tutin, and Patrick Magee. **Director**—Ken Hughes. (G)
140 minutes

CROSS CREEK (1983)
 ★★

Mary Steenburgen
Rip Torn
Alfre Woodard

The memoirs of author Marjorie Kinnan Rawlings (*The Yearling*) are set to film reflecting her remote life in the Florida backwoods. Director Martin Ritt successfully touches on the courage, sturdiness, and humanity of the area inhabitants. Yet the syrupy, sentimental story is in dire need of drama

and urgency. Steenburgen turns in a decent portrayal of the determined authoress. Torn, Woodard, and Dana Hill are effective in supporting roles. (PG) **Academy Award Nominations**— Torn, best supporting actor; Woodard, best supporting actress; Leonard Rosenman, best original score.
122 minutes

CROSSED SWORDS
See The Prince and the Pauper

CROSSFIRE (1947)
 ★★★★

Robert Young
Robert Mitchum
Robert Ryan

Robert Ryan warns Steve Brodie not to expose him in Crossfire.

A taut, exciting melodrama about an unhinged, bigoted soldier who murders a Jew in a New York City hotel and is pursued by the police. This landmark film is one of the first to deal so directly with racial prejudice. The film was shot mostly at night, and this technique contributes to its moody atmosphere. Fine performances are given by a top cast that also includes Gloria Grahame, Paul Kelly, Sam Levene, Jacqueline White, and Steve Brodie. **Director**—Edward Dmytryk. **Academy Award Nominations**—best picture; Dmytryk, best director; Ryan, best supporting actor; Grahame, best supporting actress; John Paxton, writing (screenplay). *86 minutes b&w*

CROSS OF IRON (1977)
 ★★

James Coburn
Maximilian Schell
James Mason

Sam Peckinpah's first World War II

movie is a puffed-up cliché about a small detachment of German soldiers fighting on the Russian front. Peckinpah, as can be expected, trowels on heavy doses of gore and violence— some of it in slow motion—while he skips lightly over plot, dialogue, and acting. There are dull and uneven performances from Coburn, Schell, and Mason. The film lasts two hours, which is more than enough time to inflict battle fatigue on any audience. Also with David Warner, Senta Berger, and Klaus Lowitsch. (R) *120 minutes*

THE CRUEL SEA
(1953)
 ★★★★

Jack Hawkins
Donald Sinden
Stanley Baker

A compelling screen adaptation of Nicholas Monsarrat's best-selling novel about the rigors aboard a British corvette in the North Atlantic during World War II. The taut drama depicts the dangers of encountering convoy-hunting Nazi subs as well as dealing with harsh weather. There are strong characterizations of the officers and men, too. Also with John Stratton, Denholm Elliott, John Warner, and Bruce Seton. **Director**—Charles Frend. **Academy Award Nomination**—Eric Ambler, writing (screenplay).
126 minutes b&w

CRUISING
(1980)
 ★★

Al Pacino
Paul Sorvino
Karen Allen

It's hard to tell what director William Friedkin (*The Exorcist*; *The French Connection*) is driving at in this grim tour of New York City's freaky leather bars. Pacino plays a young detective who infiltrates this bizarre fringe of the homosexual world to flush out a killer, and whose own sexual identity becomes blurred in the process. It's strong, disturbing, and ultimately confusing stuff, although Pacino is great (as usual) in the starring role. Also with Richard Cox and Don Scardino. (R) *106 minutes*

C

- Cry Terror
- Cry, The Beloved Country
- Cuba
- Cujo
- Cul-de-Sac
- The Curse of Frankenstein
- The Curse of the Pink Panther
- Cutter and Bone
- Cutter's Way

CRY TERROR (1958)
★★★

**James Mason
Rod Steiger
Inger Stevens**

Mason and Steiger are good in this taut drama about a tricky extortion scheme, which involves a kidnapping. Suspense is turned up full volume with Steiger as a crafty criminal who forces Mason, an electronics expert, to aid him with the caper. Stevens plays Mason's wife. New York City locations add to the tense atmosphere. Also with Angie Dickinson, Jack Klugman, Neville Brand, and Jack Kruschen. **Director**—Andrew Stone.

96 minutes b&w

CRY, THE BELOVED COUNTRY (1951)
★★★

**Canada Lee
Sidney Poitier**

Crisp drama and tense moments highlight this screen version of Alan Paton's novel about apartheid in South Africa. A black preacher travels to the city where he finds the black population living in dreadful poverty. This vivid account of the conditions separating the races is treated with candor and intelligence. The fine cast also includes Charles Carson, Charles McRae, and Joyce Carey. **Director**—Zoltan Korda. *96 minutes b&w*

CUBA (1979)
 ★★

**Sean Connery
Brooke Adams**

Cuba is about to succumb to Fidel Castro's revolution. The atmosphere is rich with vivid images of the corrupt and decaying Batista regime, but the movie is defeated by a weak script and numerous undefined characters. Connery plays a well-dressed British mercenary, who halfheartedly fights for Batista and pursues an old flame, played by Adams. Connery never earnestly swings into action—either on the battlefield or with the sultry

Sean Connery and Brooke Adams reignite an old flame in Cuba.

Adams, who portrays a wealthy Cuban beauty. Also with Chris Sarandon, Denholm Elliot, Jack Weston, and Hector Elizondo. **Director**—Richard Lester. (R) *121 minutes*

CUJO (1983)
 ★

**Dee Wallace
Daniel Hugh Kelly**

Manipulative, high-pitched horror yarn, based on Steven King's novel about a gentle St. Bernard who becomes rabid and viciously attacks humans. The uninspired plot involves a middle-class couple, and more than half the film dwells on their dull domestic problems. Finally, the snarling dog goes into action. He traps the mother and her child in their stalled car, and suspense picks up. But Cujo's whipped-cream makeup is more likely to leave you laughing than gasping. **Director**—Lewis Teague. (R)

97 minutes

CUL-DE-SAC (1966)
★★★

**Lionel Stander
Donald Pleasence
Jack MacGowran**

Roman Polanski's terse direction propels this black comedy, which is set on

a lonely island. Two fugitive gangsters hide out in a rambling castle and terrorize the inhabitants, a fey middle-aged man and his gorgeous wife. There are some bland moments, but the film works well overall. Also with Françoise Dorleac, William Franklyn, and Jacqueline Bisset.

111 minutes b&w

THE CURSE OF FRANKENSTEIN (1957)
★★

**Peter Cushing
Christopher Lee**

Another chapter in the tale of the famous monster, with Cushing and Lee in the key roles. This version lays on the gore, thus sacrificing some wit and stylish atmosphere. But there are a few effective scary moments of note. Yet the 1931 original and the sequels of that era remain the best. Also with Hazel Court, Robert Urquhart, and Valerie Gaunt. **Director**—Terence Fisher. *83 minutes*

THE CURSE OF THE PINK PANTHER (1983)
 ★★

**Ted Wass
Herbert Lom**

A Pink Panther film without the great Peter Sellers is cursed, indeed. Wass plays the world's worst detective, from New York City, recruited to find the long lost inspector Clouseau. Blake Edwards's direction and script offer funny situations. But Wass is no match for the legend. In fact, he's hardly a comic actor at all. As usual, Chief Inspector Dreyfus (Lom) gets his drubbing. Also with Robert Wagner and David Niven, looking tired in his final film role. (PG) *110 minutes*

CUTTER AND BONE
See Cutter's Way

CUTTER'S WAY (1981)
 ★

**Jeff Bridges
John Heard**

Bridges and Heard star in this peculiar

• Cyrano de Bergerac
• Daddy Long Legs
• Dakota

• The Dam Busters
• Damien—Omen II
• Damnation Alley
• Damn Yankees

C·D

murder mystery, which expends considerable energy and ends up nowhere. Bridges is Bone, a young freewheeling southern Californian, who is falsely accused of murdering a high school girl. Heard plays Cutter, a slightly loony Vietnam vet, who works up an absurd scheme to clear Bone. The entire screenplay and dialogue are absurd as well, and the film bogs down in utter confusion. Also with Lisa Eichorn, Ann Dusenberry, and Stephen Elliott. **Director**—Ivan Passer. (R)   *109 minutes*

CYRANO DE BERGERAC
(1950)
          ★★★★

José Ferrer
Mala Powers

An exceptional moving performance by Ferrer in the title role says it all, in this film version of Edmond Rostand's classic love story, which is set in the 17th century. Cyrano is the poet with the long nose who writes tender love letters to a beautiful lady for his friend. However, Cyrano genuinely loves the woman, too. Powers plays the Lady Roxanne. Ferrer requires little help to make this film worthwhile. Also with William Prince and Morris Carnovsky. **Director**—Michael Gordon. **Academy Award**—Ferrer, best actor.
112 minutes b&w

D

DADDY LONG LEGS (1955)
★★

Fred Astaire
Leslie Caron

The energetic dancing of Astaire and Caron top this romantic musical about a French orphan girl who is secretly supported by a rich playboy. Fred's the playboy, and Leslie's the waif. The production, however, is too long and somewhat awkward. The film, based on Jean Webster's popular novel, has sly references to the classic *Cinderella* story. Also with Fred Clark, Thelma Ritter, Terry Moore, and Larry Keating. **Director**—Jean Negulesco.
126 minutes

DAKOTA (1945)
          ★★

John Wayne
Vera Hruba Ralston

Typical western yarn with Wayne in the saddle and immersed in a territorial conflict involving a railroad line. The Duke handles the job with ease, and lovely Ralston, who plays a railway tycoon's daughter, is by his side. Other characters are played adequately by Walter Brennan, Ward Bond, and Ona Munson. **Director**—Joseph Kane.   *82 minutes b&w*

THE DAM BUSTERS (1954)
          ★★★★

Michael Redgrave
Richard Todd

Michael Redgrave and Richard Todd double-check their engineering in The Dam Busters. *Who ya gonna flood?*

Gripping, straightforward World War II account of the development of the RAF's skip-bombing technique, which was used to blow up the Ruhr dams in 1943 to cripple some vital German industries. An intense climate of suspense and danger builds as the British execute their plan step by step. Fine acting and impressive special effects enhance the production. Also with Ursula Jeans, Derek Farr, Patrick Ban, and Basil Sydney. **Director**—Michael Anderson.   *125 minutes b&w*

DAMIEN—OMEN II (1978)
          ★★

William Holden
Lee Grant

Damien, that little demon from *The*

Omen, is now 13 and living with his rich uncle in Chicago. After Damien is through this time, about a dozen victims are murdered in the most grisly fashion. The movie has a slick look; a good cast, led by Holden and Grant, is effective. Jonathan Scott-Taylor is Damien. But the film is burdened with much tedious dialogue interspersed with warmed-over mayhem. And the Devil apparently isn't finished making money for Hollywood. Also with Lew Ayres, Sylvia Sidney, and Robert Foxworth. **Director**—Don Taylor. (R)
107 minutes

DAMNATION ALLEY (1977)
★

Jan-Michael Vincent
George Peppard

Plodding and silly adventure about a tiny band of nuclear war survivors, who trek across the U.S. continent searching for signs of life. The acting is second-rate. Considerable emphasis is on special effects, which come off as half-baked and phony-looking. Also with Dominique Sanda and Paul Winfield. **Director**—Jack Smight. (PG)
91 minutes

DAMN YANKEES (1958)
          ★★★

Gwen Verdon
Tab Hunter

(Continued)

In Damn Yankees, *Gwen Verdon tempts Tab Hunter and sings "Whatever Lola Wants."*

D

• Daniel
• Danton
• Darby O'Gill and the Little
  People

• Darby's Rangers
• The Dark at the Top of the
  Stairs

• The Dark Mirror
• Dark Passage

(Continued)

This is a competent film version of the hit Broadway musical about a baseball fan who becomes a star player with the help of the Devil. Verdon tops the cast lineup as the temptress Lola, with lively dancing and singing. And she especially upstages Hunter, who plays the critical role of the spectacular athlete. Tab strikes out when it comes to the footwork and the songs, but Ray Walston is an amusing Devil. Famous songs include "(You Got to Have) Heart" and "Whatever Lola Wants." Also with Russ Brown and Shannon Bolin. **Directors**—George Abbott and Stanley Donen. *110 minutes*

DANIEL
(1983)

★★

**Timothy Hutton
Lindsay Crouse
Ed Asner**

Intense, often confusing, fictionalization about the agony-plagued children of Julius and Ethel Rosenberg, the American couple executed in 1953 for stealing atomic secrets. Director Sidney Lumet, working with a screen version of E. L. Doctorow's novel, never succeeds in bringing the harrowing events and emotions into proper focus. Apparently, Lumet is more interested in preaching than enlightening. Also with Mandy Patinkin, Ellen Barkin, and John Rubenstein. (R) *129 minutes*

DANTON
(1983)

★★★★

Gerard Depardieu

Danton (Gerard Depardieu) is held aloft by the cheering mob.

From Polish director Andrzej Wajda (*Man of Iron*), an engrossing historical account of the incipient despotism that followed in the wake of the French Revolution. Depardieu is outstanding in the title role as a patriot fighting vociferously for democratic ideals. Although the film is a period piece, it parallels modern Poland in that there are obvious similarities between Danton and Lech Walesa. In French with English titles. (No rating) *136 minutes*

DARBY O'GILL AND THE LITTLE PEOPLE (1959)

★★★

**Sean Connery
Albert Sharpe
Janet Munro**

A breezy Walt Disney fantasy based on an Irish folk tale. Darby, played by Sharpe, is a caretaker who tells tall tales and becomes involved with leprechauns. The Disney special effects are outstanding, and there's a lively script to keep the kids anchored to their seats. The fine cast also includes Jimmy O'Dea, and Jack MacGowran. **Director**—Robert Stevenson. (G) *90 minutes*

DARBY'S RANGERS (1957)

★★

**James Garner
Etchika Choureau
Jack Warden**

Garner plays Maj. William Darby, the heroic commander who led assaults in North Africa and Italy during World War II. The troops experience frontline action and romantic interludes. This rather uneven film has some adequate moments. Also with Edward Byrnes, Venetia Stevenson, and David Janssen. **Director**—William Wellman. *121 minutes b&w*

THE DARK AT THE TOP OF THE STAIRS (1960)

★★★

**Robert Preston
Dorothy McGuire**

William Inge's play about family life in

Robert Preston and Eve Arden in The Dark at the Top of the Stairs.

a small Oklahoma town in the '20s is expertly produced for the screen with much of the emotions unfettered. Preston stars as the father, and McGuire plays the wife with proper stateliness. However, Eve Arden, Angela Lansbury, and Shirley Knight stand out in supporting roles. **Director**—Delbert Mann. **Academy Award Nomination**—Knight, best supporting actress. *124 minutes*

THE DARK MIRROR (1946)

★★★

**Olivia de Havilland
Lew Ayres**

A taut, clever whodunit about identical twins, one of whom is a murderess. De Havilland is excellent playing the roles of the twins. Ayres plays a doctor who is faced with the challenge of identifying the killer. Lots of suspense in the offing. Also with Thomas Mitchell, Richard Long, Charles Evans, and Gary Owen. **Director**—Robert Siodmak. **Academy Award Nomination**—Vladimir Pozner, writing (original story). *85 minutes b&w*

DARK PASSAGE (1947)

★★★

**Humphrey Bogart
Lauren Bacall**

Bogart plays a man who escapes from the big house and then tries to prove he didn't kill his wife. He masks his identity with plastic surgery and hides out with Bacall. Not one of the best Bogey-Bacall films, but it entertains only because of the stars' professionalism and their magnetic appeal. The plot, however, is rather farfetched. There are good performances from

• Darling
• David and Bathsheba
• David and Lisa
• Dawn of the Dead
• Day of the Animals
• The Day of the Dolphin

D

Agnes Moorehead, Tom D'Andrea, Bruce Bennett, and Houseley Stevenson. **Director**—Delmer Daves.

106 minutes b&w

DARLING (1965)

★★★★

Julie Christie
Dirk Bogarde

A slick, stylish, and cynical drama about an ambitious London model who succeeds socially by having a series of affairs. Quite a perceptive and honest approach to contemporary morals, all graced with the brilliant performance of Christie, the efficient direction of John Schlesinger, and plenty of smart dialogue. Also with Laurence Harvey and Alex Scott. **Academy Awards**—Christie, best actress; Frederic Raphael, best story and screenplay (written directly for the screen). **Nominations**—best picture; Schlesinger, best director.

127 minutes b&w

DAVID AND BATHSHEBA
(1952)

★★

Gregory Peck
Susan Hayward

This is a rather routine Bible epic that's top-heavy with impressive sets and gorgeous costumes. However, someone neglected to work diligently on the script, so the film drags along without much excitement. Peck and Hayward,

Gregory Peck in the biblical epic David and Bathsheba.

who lead the cast, don't seem to have their hearts in the project. The familiar plot has to do with King David's love for the wife of one of his soldiers. His Majesty, played by Peck, conspires to have the man killed in battle. Hayward plays Bathsheba. Also with Raymond Massey, Jayne Meadows, and Francis X. Bushman. **Director**—Henry King.

116 minutes

DAVID AND LISA
(1962)
★★★★

Keir Dullea
Janet Margolin

Keir Dullea and Janet Margolin fall in love as David and Lisa.

An earnest and touching low-budget film that works beautifully because of its poignant script, efficient direction, and fine acting by a novice cast. The plot concerns two mentally ill teenagers at a private institution who share a bond of mutual understanding. Dullea and Margolin are exceptionally good as the troubled youngsters. Howard da Silva stands out as an understanding doctor. Neva Patterson, Clifton James, and Richard McMurray round out the cast. **Director**—Frank Perry. **Academy Award Nominations**—Perry, best director; Eleanor Perry, best screenplay (based on material from another medium).

94 minutes b&w

DAWN OF THE DEAD (1979)

★★

Gaylen Ross
Ken Foree

Director George Romero whips up the

The living try to protect a shopping mall from the Dawn of the Dead.

horror and gore again in this sequel to his 1968 *Night of the Living Dead*. This film, however, lacks the shock of its predecessor. But Romero outdoes himself with lavish grisly events, such as flesh being torn apart, severed heads, and spurting blood. An army of cannibalistic zombies invade a suburban shopping mall where our heroes slaughter them in an orgy of mayhem. The plot and acting are inconsequential; the emphasis is on blood and guts. Also with Scott Reiniger and David Emge. (No MPAA rating)

125 minutes

DAY OF THE ANIMALS (1977)

★★

Christopher George
Lynda Day George
Leslie Nielsen
Michael Ansara

Bears, wolves, large birds, and packs of dogs go crazy and attack a group of mountain hikers. The story is absurd, and the performances by the humans are routine at best. But there are some terrifying and convincing shots of the stalking critters. It's a movie about animals for animals; send your dog or cat to see this one. Also with Richard Jaeckel. **Director**—William Girdler. (PG)

98 minutes

THE DAY OF THE DOLPHIN
(1973)

★★

George C. Scott
Trish Van Devere

A so-so thriller about a marine biologist, played by Scott, who trains dol-
(Continued)

D

• The Day of the Jackal
• The Day of the Locust
• Days of Heaven
• Days of Wine and Roses
• The Day the World Ended
• D.C. Cab

(Continued)

phins to talk and becomes entangled in a plot to assassinate the President. Despite the big money and top talent involved, the film doesn't come off. There's a bit of comedy and suspense here and there, but the proceedings mostly suffer from the blahs. Also with Paul Sorvino, Fritz Weaver, John Korkes, and Edward Herrmann. **Director**—Mike Nichols. (PG)

104 minutes

THE DAY OF THE JACKAL (1973)

 ★★★

Edward Fox
Cyril Cusack

Frederick Forsyth's suspenseful novel about an OAS attempt to assassinate Charles de Gaulle is adapted for the screen with all the thrills neatly intact. Fox plays the role of the professional killer who is hired by some conspiring French generals for the dastardly deed. Tension mounts as the police step up their manhunt while the assassin prepares for his strike. Good supporting acting, excellent pacing, and impressive European locations add to the professional production. TV commercials, however, can ruin the pace. Michel Lonsdale, Eric Porter, Delphine Seyrig, and Alan Badel also star. **Director**—Fred Zinnemann. (PG)

142 minutes

THE DAY OF THE LOCUST (1975)

 ★★

Donald Sutherland
William Atherton
Karen Black

An overblown and alternately brilliant and disappointing movie based on Nathanael West's novel of Hollywood in the '30s. There are good performances by Burgess Meredith as an old vaudevillian and Billy Barty as a macho dwarf, but West's keen description of the wretchedness of dashed hopes on the fringes of Hollywood's dream factories is poorly interpreted. Also with Geraldine Page, Richard A. Dysart, and Bo Hopkins. **Director**—John Schlesinger. (R) **Academy Award Nominations**—Meredith, best sup-

porting actor; Conrad Hall, cinematography. *140 minutes*

DAYS OF HEAVEN (1978)

 ★★

Richard Gere
Brooke Adams

Linda Manz plays a wandering vagabond in Days of Heaven.

Writer-director Terrence Malick's spectacular art film is a technical achievement of exquisite photography and beautiful images. But alas, a skimpy plot, shallow characters, and a lack of drama lead to disappointment. The story, set in 1916, is about three poverty-stricken vagabonds, who become involved with a wealthy Texas wheat farmer. This production might have worked better in the days of silent movies. Also with Linda Manz, Sam Shepard, and Robert Wilke. (PG) **Academy Award**—Nestor Almendros, cinematography. *95 minutes*

DAYS OF WINE AND ROSES (1962)

 ★★★★

Jack Lemmon
Lee Remick

A brilliant, uncompromising drama about a public relations man, played by Lemmon, who becomes disillusioned with his work, turns to drink, and leads his wife down the alcoholic path. Remick plays the wife. Lemmon and Remick are at their acting best, and there's professional work from all quarters—direction, script, and supporting roles. The film is compelling from beginning to end, dwelling relentlessly on stark realism. Charles Bickford, Jack Klugman, Alan Hewitt, Tom Palmer, and Jack Albertson costar. **Director**—Blake Edwards. **Acad-**

emy **Award Nominations**—Lemmon, best actor; Remick, best actress.

117 minutes b&w

THE DAY THE WORLD ENDED (1956)

★

Richard Denning
Lori Nelson

Survivors of an atomic war discover a valley that is uncontaminated, but then start to fight among themselves. Denning, Nelson, Adele Jergens, and Mike Connors give adequate performances in this run-of-the-mill science fiction tale that makes the mistake of trying to be profound. An early and undistinguished effort by B-movie mogul and director Roger Corman.

80 minutes b&w

D.C. CAB (1983)

 ★

Mr. T
Gary Busey

Mr. T offers peace on earth, goodwill toward men in D.C. Cab.

The title refers to a broken-down, Washington, D.C. taxi company that consists of dilapidated cars and wacky drivers. For all the zaniness and rampant energy, this film's off-the-wall humor is merely stupid—on the level of *Animal House* and other exploitation comedies. The plot, what there is of it, starts late and the characters are all familiar and unfunny. The venerable Mr. T plays a glowering cabbie and Busey stars as an extroverted driver hung up on rock 'n' roll. **Director**—Joel Schumacher. (R) *104 minutes*

★ STAR PROFILE

• D–Day, The Sixth of June
• Deadline, USA
• The Deadly Affair
• Deadly Blessing
• Deadly Force

D

D-DAY, THE SIXTH OF JUNE (1956)
★★★

Robert Taylor
Richard Todd
Dana Wynter
Edmond O'Brien

Dana Wynter and Robert Taylor have a wartime romance in D–Day, The Sixth of June.

Two officers—one an American, the other British—fall in love with the same girl during the time of the World War II Normandy invasion. Taylor and Todd are the rivals; Wynter is the girl. The film is highlighted by impressive action scenes. The romantic plot is rather familiar, but it's executed with above-average flair. **Director**—Henry Koster.   *106 minutes*

DEADLINE, USA (1952)
★★★

Humphrey Bogart
Kim Hunter
Ethel Barrymore

Bogart stars in this terse drama as a courageous newspaper editor who promotes stories about an influential criminal and then must struggle to prevent his superiors from bending to intimidation. Bogey is enjoyable, and there are good dramatic scenes with him and Ethel Barrymore, who plays the publisher. Hunter plays Bogey's ex-wife. Some newspaper clichés here and there, but not enough to spoil the fun. Also with Ed Begley, Paul Stewart, Warren Stevens, Martin Gabel, and Jim Backus. **Director**— Richard Brooks.   *87 minutes b&w*

THE DEADLY AFFAIR (1967)
★★★

James Mason
Simone Signoret

A gripping whodunit, with Mason as a British agent investigating the apparent suicide of a colleague and uncovering a nest of spies. The film is nicely plotted, with suspense relentlessly building at an even pace. The story is based on the John Le Carre novel *Call for the Dead.* Mason is convincing, and he's backed up nicely with good acting by Signoret, Maximilian Schell, Lynn Redgrave, and Max Adrian. **Director**—Sidney Lumet.   *106 minutes*

DEADLY BLESSING (1981)

★

Ernest Borgnine

This is a strange horror story about some mysterious deaths among a religious sect called the Hittites. A farmer is run over by his own tractor, and others are murdered with knives, snakes, and spiders. It's not certain who does the killing in this illogical film, yet there are many suspects for the perpetrator, referred to as "the incubus" by the Hittites. Borgnine is interesting as the fanatical religious leader. **Director**—Wes Craven. (R)   *102 minutes*

DEADLY FORCE (1983)

★

Wings Hauser

Routine car chases and numerous gun fights fill a preposterous and predictable action melodrama that resembles countless TV police episodes. Hauser plays a one-time, tough Los Angeles cop who returns to his old territory to nab a madman killer. The task is, of course, extra difficult since he is persona non grata with most of his former associates. Lame acting by an unfamiliar cast adds to the many other draw-
(Continued)

JAMES CAGNEY

James Cagney, one of Hollywood's most famous stars of the '30s and '40s, was born in 1899. His father ran a saloon on New York's Lower East Side. At 14 he was an office boy at the New York Sun, at 17 a bellhop in the Friars Club, and in between, a bundle wrapper at Wanamaker's, a ticket-seller for the Hudson River Day Line, a waiter, and a page. His first serious brush with show business was in a vaudeville show called Every Sailor. *In 1920, he appeared in* Pitter Patter, *another musical, and managed to find time to court another member of the chorus, Frances Willard Vernon, whom he married in 1922.*

The year 1929 was a turning point for Cagney. After winning praise in George Kelly's Maggie the Magnificent, *he was hired for a role opposite Joan Blondell in* Penny Arcade, *which only lasted three weeks on Broadway, but finally got him to California.*

Cagney made his film debut in 1930 in Sinner's Holiday, *but made his first great impact on audiences and critics in* The Public Enemy *(1931), one of the first gangster films; he's remembered for smacking Mae Clark in the face with a grapefruit.*

Cagney quickly became a major star. Although primarily cast as a gangster, he also performed in comedies and musicals.

Some of Cagney's other memorable films include Lady Killers *(1933),* G-Men *(1935),* Angels with Dirty Faces *(1938),* The Roaring Twenties *(1939),* Yankee Doodle Dandy *(1942),* White Heat *(1949),* Mister Roberts *(1955),* Man of a Thousand Faces *(1957), and* One, Two, Three *(1961). He won an Oscar for his portrayal of George M. Cohan in* Yankee Doodle Dandy.

After a 20-year retirement, Cagney—at the age of 81—returned to the screen in Ragtime *(1981).*

D

- • Deadly Hero
- • Dead Men Don't Wear Plaid
- • Dead of Night
- • Dead Reckoning
- • The Dead Zone
- • Deal of the Century
- • Dear Maestro
- • Death Hunt

(Continued)

backs of this exercise in tedium. Also with Joyce Ingalls and Paul Shenar. **Director**—Paul Aaron. (R)

95 minutes

DEADLY HERO (1976)

 ★

**Don Murray
Diahn Williams
James Earl Jones**

Murray portrays a psychotic New York City cop, who kills a black mugger and shakedown artist. Williams plays a mugging victim; Jones is her attacker. Moments of suspense occasionally perk up the thin script, and the moody photography of the metropolitan jungle adds some color. But it still comes off as a rather commonplace melodrama. Also with Lilia Skala, George S. Irving, and Cochata Ferrell. **Director**—Ivan Nagy. (R)   *102 minutes*

DEAD MEN DON'T WEAR PLAID (1982)

 ★★★

**Steve Martin
Rachel Ward**

Steve Martin and Carl Reiner argue over who gets to reveal the plot of the movie in Dead Men Don't Wear Plaid.

A wonderful, witty parody of '40s detective movies, with gumshoe Martin cleverly interacting with actual clips from those marvelous classic melodramas. Carl Reiner wrote and directed this hilarious gem with affection and skill. The delightful gimmick sets Martin into the old scenes and involves him in conversations with such film greats as Humphrey Bogart, Alan Ladd, and Barbara Stanwyck. An engaging comic romp and irresistible fun, especially for movie buffs. (PG)

89 minutes b&w

DEAD OF NIGHT (1946)

 ★★★★

**Mervyn Johns
Roland Culver**

A superior bone-chilling thriller about a man who has strange dreams that appear to interconnect with the dreams of other people. The film is composed of five stories of the supernatural, which are blended well for the utmost in eerie atmosphere and suspenseful thrills. It's all topped off with fine acting. Also stars Michael Redgrave, Googie Withers, Antony Baird, Judy Kelly, and Sally Ann Howes. **Directors**—Alberto Cavalcanti, Basil Dearden, Robert Hamer, and Charles Crichton.   *104 minutes b&w*

DEAD RECKONING (1947)

★★★

**Humphrey Bogart
Lizabeth Scott**

Bogart plays a World War II veteran who investigates the murder of his friend, during a trip to Washington to receive a medal. Standard *film noir* fare, but it's enhanced by some good acting, especially Bogey's reliable performance as a tough character. Also with Morris Carnovsky, William Prince, and Wallace Ford. **Director**—John Cromwell.   *100 minutes b&w*

THE DEAD ZONE (1983)

 ★★★

**Christopher Walken
Martin Sheen**

Stephen King's suspenseful novel has been adapted into an intermittently engrossing and eerie film. Walken plays an auto accident victim who emerges from a five-year coma with the power of second sight. His dark visions—a child in a fire, a trigger-happy U.S. President—are numbing. Then he discovers he can use his clairvoyant powers to alter such catastrophies. Under David Cronenberg's subtle direction, the drama comes alive. Also with Brooke Adams and Colleen Dewhurst. (R)   *102 minutes*

DEAL OF THE CENTURY (1983)

 ★★

**Chevy Chase
Sigourney Weaver**

Chevy Chase hustles arms to third world nations in Deal of the Century.

The weapons industry is a juicy target for satirization, but director William Friedkin misses the mark in this uneven send-up. Chase stars as a sleazy arms salesman who peddles bazookas and machine guns to pip-squeak Third World dictators and revolutionaries. He finally graduates to high-tech military machinery while most of the gags fizzle out. Gregory Hines co-stars and delivers a few much-needed laughs. (PG)   *98 minutes*

DEAR MAESTRO (1984)

★★

**Michele Placido
Giuliana De Sio**

A small Italian town is the setting of this so-so comedy about some unexciting competition for the conductor's job of a new orchestra. The film is populated with oddball characters who talk too much and argue incessantly. Acting, though, is above par with Placido and De Sio at the head of the lively cast. In Italian with English titles. **Director**—Luciano Odorisio. (No MPAA rating)   *99 minutes*

DEATH HUNT (1981)

 ★★★

**Charles Bronson
Lee Marvin**

Granite-hard Bronson and grizzled, rawhide-tough Marvin are matched in

• Death of a Salesman   • Deathtrap
• Death on the Nile   • Death Weekend
• Death Ship   • Death Wish

D

this action-packed adventure filmed in northern Canada. Marvin is a whiskey-soaked Mountie on the brink of retirement, who reluctantly pursues a quiet trapper, played by Bronson, who is wrongly accused of murder. Both stars portray larger-than-life adversaries who gradually develop respect for one another. It's an old-fashioned story, set in the '30s amid perilous terrain, with heroes worth cheering. **Director**—Peter Hunt. (R)   *96 minutes*

DEATH OF A SALESMAN
(1951)
★★★★

Fredric March
Kevin McCarthy
Mildred Dunnock
Cameron Mitchell

Cameron Mitchell, Fredric March, and Kevin McCarthy in Death of a Salesman.

Arthur Miller's powerful and heartfelt drama is brought to the screen with all the emotion and pathos of the magnificent Broadway play. March has never been better than as the indelible Willy Loman, the over-the-hill traveling salesman who confronts the disappointment of his career and commits suicide. Flashbacks are cleverly used to bring out an extra dimension of this great American classic tragedy. Dunnock plays his wife; McCarthy and Mitchell play his sons. Also with Howard Smith, Royal Beal, and Jesse White. **Director**—Laslo Benedek. **Academy Award Nominations**—March, best actor; McCarthy, best supporting actor; Dunnock, best supporting actress; Frank Planer, cinematography (black and white).
112 minutes b&w

Peter Ustinov (third from left) plays Belgian sleuth Hercule Poirot in Death on the Nile.

DEATH ON THE NILE (1978)
 ★★★

Peter Ustinov
Bette Davis
David Niven
Mia Farrow
Angela Lansbury
George Kennedy
Maggie Smith

Celebrated Belgian sleuth Hercule Poirot, played by Ustinov, encounters suspects galore as he unravels a murder mystery on a Nile River cruise as only Dame Agatha Christie could tell it. A big first-rate cast, elegant settings, and lively acting add up to a charming, old-fashioned movie whodunit. Old pros Davis and Lansbury ham it up and steal a number of scenes on the way to an intriguing ending, where the droll Monsieur Poirot unmasks the killer of a beautiful heiress. Also with Jack Warden, Lois Chiles, and Olivia Hussey. **Director**—John Guillermin. (PG)   *140 minutes*

DEATH SHIP (1980)
★

George Kennedy

A ludicrous horror movie about a haunted ship, once used as a floating torture chamber by the Nazis, that prowls the Atlantic looking for victims. Despite numerous gruesome scenes—rotting corpses strapped to racks and so on—there's scant sense of suspense or thrills. It's just so much floating garbage. Kennedy, stalwart veteran of many disaster films, leads a shipwrecked cast. **Director**—Alvin Rakoff. (R)   *91 minutes*

DEATHTRAP (1982)
 ★★★

Michael Caine
Christopher Reeve
Dyan Cannon

Clever plot twists, plenty of smart dialogue, and superb acting overcome the staginess in this stylish film version of Ira Levin's Broadway mystery play. Caine is in best form as a has-been playwright with murder on his mind. And there are exceptional performances, too, from Reeve and Cannon. Direction and screenplay could have allowed for more humor. But there are enough surprises in this who'll-do-it thriller to maintain a buoyant level of enjoyment. **Director**—Sidney Lumet. (PG)   *116 minutes*

DEATH WEEKEND
See The House by the Lake

DEATH WISH (1974)
★★★

Charles Bronson
Hope Lange

In New York City, muggers brutally rape the wife and daughter of a placid businessman, who then launches a one-man vigilante crusade against nu-
(Continued)

D
- Death Wish II
- Deception
- The Deep
- Deep in the Heart
- The Deer Hunter
- The Defiant Ones

(Continued)

merous thugs he encounters on the streets. The script is farfetched. How could one man be confronted by so many attackers in such a short time? However, director Michael Winner pulls out the stops, and the film is watchable to the end. Bronson is at his best as the stone-faced citizen out for revenge. Also with Vincent Gardenia, Stuart Margolin, and Stephen Keats. (R) *94 minutes*

DEATH WISH II (1982)

★

**Charles Bronson
Jill Ireland**

Once more vigilante justice is dished out with unblinking determination in this retread of the 1974 melodrama that exploited self-righteous revenge. The setting, this time, is Los Angeles and the story is just as cynical and preposterous as before: stern-faced Bronson blazes away at the repulsive thugs who raped and killed his daughter and housekeeper, while the cops remain helpless and confused. **Director—**Michael Winner. (R) *89 minutes*

DECEPTION (1946)

★★★

**Bette Davis
Claude Rains**

Davis and Rains shine in this stylish but sloshy melodrama, set against the background of classical music. Rains is a wealthy pianist who loves Davis, but she weds her former boyfriend, played by Paul Henreid. That makes Claude jealous, indeed. Good acting all around, but Henreid is upstaged by the dynamic performances of Davis and Rains. Also with John Abbott and Benson Fong. **Director**—Irving Rapper. *112 minutes b&w*

THE DEEP (1977)

★★

**Robert Shaw
Jacqueline Bisset**

Peter (*Jaws*) Benchley wrote this underwater adventure, but if you're looking for *Son of Jaws*, forget it. Spec-

Jacqueline Bisset and Nick Nolte have discovered something in The Deep.

tacular underwater photography is the only virtue in this rather shallow production, which concerns a scramble for sunken treasure off the Bermuda coast. Most of the dialogue and acting is wooden. Peter Yates directed as if he was seasick most of the time. So-so acting jobs by Nick Nolte and Bisset; a realistic performance from Shaw. Also with Louis Gossett, Jr. and Eli Wallach. (PG) *123 minutes*

DEEP IN THE HEART (1984)

★

Karen Young

A pretty, young, and innocent school teacher (Young) is raped by a gun enthusiast. With revenge in her heart, she learns to handle a pistol and then proceeds to obtain some self-styled justice. This woman's version of *Death Wish* attempts some social commentary, but the movie remains shallow and sensationalistic all the way. Clayton Day and Suzie Humphreys also are in the cast, to no avail. **Director**—Tony Garnett. (R) *99 minutes*

THE DEER HUNTER (1978)

★★★★

**Robert De Niro
John Cazale
John Savage
Meryl Streep
Christopher Walken**

Director Michael Cimino's protracted film about the Vietnam experience is extraordinarily powerful and origi-

Returning vet Robert DeNiro is greeted by his pals in The Deer Hunter.

nal. Cimino uncorks a fascinating multitude of emotions and insights about war and violence. Essentially, the story deals with three young steelworkers from a small Pennsylvania town who are devastated by the horror of the war. Superb performances by De Niro, Walken, and Streep. Also with George Dzunda and Chuck Aspegren. (R) **Academy Awards**—best picture; Cimino, best director; Walken, best supporting actor. **Nominations**—De Niro, best actor; Streep, best supporting actress; Cimino, Louis Garfinkle, and Quinn K. Redeker (story) and Deric Washburn (story and screenplay), best original screenplay. *183 minutes*

THE DEFIANT ONES (1958)

★★★★

**Tony Curtis
Sidney Poitier**

An inspired racial drama, with Curtis and Poitier as escaped convicts who are chained together and attempt to flee a police dragnet. This is powerful stuff that deals squarely with hatred. There are some superbly powerful performances and well-paced action. Director Stanley Kramer outdoes himself with a great job. Theodore Bikel, Cara Williams, and Lon Chaney, Jr., turn in fine supporting performances. **Academy Award**—Nathan Douglas and Harold Jacob Smith, best story and screenplay (written directly for the screen). **Nominations**—best picture; Kramer, best director; Curtis, Poitier, best actor; Bikel, best supporting actor; Williams, best supporting actress. *97 minutes b&w*

• Deliverance
• Demetrius and the
  Gladiators

• Demon Seed
• The Desert Fox
• The Desert Rats
• The Desert Song

D

DELIVERANCE (1972)

★★★★

**Burt Reynolds
Jon Voight
Ned Beatty**

Four well-to-do young men embark on a canoe trip down a swift Georgia river, but their weekend outing turns into a nightmare when they're set upon by some sadistic mountain men. The engrossing film, adapted by James Dickey from his novel, offers lucid contrasts between the haves and have-nots, and it brims with suspense and terror. Superb direction and tight editing enhance the thrilling and terrifying adventure. Exceptionally good acting from Voight, Reynolds, Beatty, Ronny Cox, Billy McKinney, and Herbert Coward. **Director**—John Boorman. (R) **Academy Award Nominations**—best picture; Boorman, best director. *109 minutes*

DEMETRIUS AND THE GLADIATORS (1954)

★★

**Victor Mature
Susan Hayward
Michael Rennie**

Humdrum sequel to *The Robe*, with Mature hamming it up as a slave in possession of Christ's garment. Emperor Caligula, played by Jay Robinson, wants it. The hokey script dwells on heroics rather than religiousness. There is some worthwhile action in the arena with the gladiators battling away. The costumes and sets—probably left over from *The Robe*—are impressive. Also with Debra Paget, Anne Bancroft, Richard Egan, Ernest Borgnine, and Barry Jones. **Director**—Delmer Daves. *101 minutes*

DEMON SEED (1977)

★★★

**Julie Christie
Fritz Weaver**

Proteus IV is an ultra-sophisticated computer capable of philosophical decisions and creativity. It wants to perpetuate itself in the flesh by impregnating a human female. Just how this

Julie Christie has mechanical morning sickness in Demon Seed.

feat is accomplished evolves into a bizarre and intriguing science-fiction tale that's sort of a cross between *Rosemary's Baby* and *2001: A Space Odyssey*. Christie is excellent as the reluctant object of the electronic brain's affections. The story is preposterous, but it's smartly executed with effective direction by Donald Cammell, top-notch special effects, and a haunting climax. Also with Gerrit Graham, Berry Kroeger, and Lisa Lu. (R) *94 minutes*

THE DESERT FOX (1951)

★★★

**James Mason
Jessica Tandy
Cedric Hardwicke**

Mason is fantastic as German field Marshal Erwin Rommel in this film biography, which follows his defeat in North Africa and his disillusionment on his return to Nazi Germany. The

engrossing drama features some stunning desert location scenes. Mason followed up his Rommel role in *The Desert Rats*. Also with Luther Adler, Everett Sloane, Leo G. Carroll, George Macready, and Richard Boone. **Director**—Henry Hathaway. *88 minutes b&w*

THE DESERT RATS (1953)

★★★

**Richard Burton
James Mason**

A well-made follow-up to *The Desert Fox*, with Mason once again portraying German Field Marshal Erwin Rommel. This exciting war drama is seen from the Allied side, with Burton leading Australian troops against Nazi armor in the siege of Tobruk. There are impressive battle scenes, with Burton doing a fine acting job. There's good support, too, from Robert Newton as a soldier who was a professor in civilian life. Also with Robert Douglas, Torin Thatcher, and Chips Rafferty. **Director**—Robert Wise. **Academy Award Nomination**—Richard Murphy, writing (story and screenplay). *88 minutes b&w*

THE DESERT SONG (1953)

★★

**Gordon MacRae
Kathryn Grayson**

A third film version of Sigmund Romberg's endurable operetta with MacRae and Grayson acceptably singing and acting in the key roles. The score offers "The Riff Song" and "One
(Continued)

James Mason portrays German Field Marshal Erwin Rommel in The Desert Fox.

 Movie is available in Beta and VHS videotape

D
- Design for Living
- Desire Under the Elms
- The Desk Set
- The Desperate Hours
- Desperate Living
- Desperate Siege
- Destination Tokyo
- Destroyer

(Continued)

Alone." The setting is Africa, and MacRae plays the leader of the Riffs, who fight some evil tribesmen. Steve Cochran, Raymond Massey, and William Conrad are also in the cast. **Director**—Bruce Humberstone.

110 minutes

DESIGN FOR LIVING (1933)
★★

**Miriam Hopkins
Fredric March
Gary Cooper**

A ménage à trois about "three people who love each other very much" (Noel Coward's description of his play upon which the film is based). Ben Hecht's adaptation and screenplay unfortunately do not recapture the wit and style of the play. Hopkins is well cast, but March and Cooper as her live-in lovers, despite their physical charms, are no match for Alfred Lunt and Noel Coward who starred on Broadway. Ernst Lubitsch's touch as director adds the only real entertainment value.

88 minutes b&w

DESIRE UNDER THE ELMS (1958)
★★

**Sophia Loren
Anthony Perkins
Burl Ives**

Slow-paced and stagey screen version of Eugene O'Neill's play about conflicts of a New England farm family in the 19th century. Loren is out of her element as an elderly farmer's young wife who falls in love with her stepson. There are a few minor moments of visible drama, but most of the film is rather murky. Perkins plays the young stepson; Ives is the father. Frank Overton, Pernell Roberts, and Anne Seymour also star. **Director**—Delbert Mann.

111 minutes b&w

THE DESK SET (1957)
★★★

**Spencer Tracy
Katharine Hepburn**

Tracy and Hepburn head up this adult comedy, which is based on William Marchant's play. The chemistry is perfect, and the sparks fly. She runs a broadcast company's reference section. He's an efficiency expert who wants to improve the operation. They fight. They fall in love. Plenty of good dialogue and laughs along the way. Supporting roles are played by Joan Blondell, Gig Young, and Dina Merrill. **Director**—Walter Lang.

103 minutes

THE DESPERATE HOURS
(1955)
★★★

**Humphrey Bogart
Fredric March
Arthur Kennedy**

Three escaped convicts hide out in the home of a typical family and hold them hostage. A suspenseful battle of wits ensues, with Bogart as good as usual, playing one of the cons. Fine performances, too, from Martha Scott, Dewey Martin, and Gig Young. Based on the Joseph Hayes novel and play. **Director**—William Wyler.

112 minutes b&w

DESPERATE LIVING (1977)
(no stars)

A revolting, pointless episode by director John Waters, the sultan of bad taste, who is responsible for the similarly disgusting *Pink Flamingos*. The action includes sadism, emasculation, assorted murders, and vomiting. The film is obviously desperate, but it's certainly not for the living. (No MPAA rating)

90 minutes

DESPERATE SIEGE
See Rawhide

DESTINATION TOKYO (1943)
★★★

**Cary Grant
John Garfield
Alan Hale**

Taut, World War II action adventure, with Grant skippering a submarine that slips into Tokyo Bay. Good sus-

In Destination Tokyo, *Cary Grant is skipper of a U.S. submarine that slips into Tokyo Bay.*

pense as well as professional acting heighten this enjoyable wartime drama. There is fine interplay among the crew members as tension mounts. Garfield and Dane Clark come across as colorful submariners. Faye Emerson and John Forsythe are also in the cast. **Director**—Delmer Daves.

135 minutes b&w

DESTROYER (1943)
★★

**Edward G. Robinson
Glenn Ford**

Robinson plays an old salt who ships out on a destroyer and clashes with the younger sailors. A routine and pre-

Edward G. Robinson is an old Navy man who loves his country and hates his crew in Destroyer.

• Destry Rides Again
• The Detective
• Detective Story

• The Devil and Max Devlin
• The Devil and Miss Jones
• The Devil's Playground
• Diabolique

D

dictable flag-waving film with below-par production values. Ford is on board as a novice seaman with his own methods of doing things, but Robinson emerges as the real pro. Marguerite Chapman, Edgar Buchanan, and Leo Gorcey contribute support. **Director**—William A. Seiter.

99 minutes b&w

DESTRY RIDES AGAIN (1939)
★★★★

James Stewart
Marlene Dietrich
Brian Donlevy

Marlene Dietrich is an unforgettable floozy in Destry Rides Again.

A first-class classic western, loaded with such goodies as rousing action, suspense, satire, pathos, and even some fine musical numbers. Stewart is superb as a polite sheriff, who gets fed up with local rowdiness and corruption and decides to clean up the town. Dietrich is also great as a saloon dancer who sings "See What the Boys in the Back Room Will Have." This Hollywood gem spawned several imitators, but this version is still champ. Lively acting jobs, too, from Charles Winninger, Samuel S. Hinds, and Jack Carson. **Director**—George Marshall.

94 minutes b&w

THE DETECTIVE (1968)
 ★★★

Frank Sinatra
Lee Remick
Ralph Meeker

Sinatra makes the most of the sleazy material as he plays a tough New York City detective involved in the murder of a homosexual. The film is further helped along with smart dialogue and quick pacing. Remick does good work, and there is other able support from Jacqueline Bisset, Jack Klugman, Horace MacMahon, William Windom, Tony Musante, and Al Freeman. Based on Roderick Thorp's best-selling novel. **Director**—Gordon Douglas.

114 minutes

DETECTIVE STORY (1951)
★★★★

Kirk Douglas
Eleanor Parker
William Bendix

Douglas is excellent as a tough city detective whose sense of morality and honesty erodes after contact with criminals for so long. The setting is mostly a day in a New York City police precinct station. The film, adapted from Sidney Kingsley's fine Broadway play, retains much of its impact on the screen. Joseph Wiseman and Lee Grant are good as thieves, Bendix turns in a fine performance as a police sergeant, and Parker is magnificent as Douglas's neglected wife. Also with Cathy O'Donnell, George Macready, and Horace MacMahon. **Director**—William Wyler. **Academy Award Nominations**—Wyler, best director; Parker, best actress; Grant, best supporting actress; Philip Yordan and Robert Wyler, writing (screenplay).

103 minutes b&w

THE DEVIL AND MAX DEVLIN (1981)
 ★★

Elliott Gould
Bill Cosby

Gould plays Max Devlin, a grumpy Los Angeles landlord who escapes eternal damnation by conning three innocents into signing their souls over to Satan. Cosby plays the Devil. The plot is rather familiar (*Heaven Can Wait; Angel On My Shoulder*), and the ending is predictable. But this Disney production is executed with warmth and a decent amount of suspense. There are endearing performances, too—especially from Gould, who works like

the devil to secure the confidence of his young victims. **Director**—Steven Stern. (PG)

96 minutes

THE DEVIL AND MISS JONES (1941)
★★★

Jean Arthur
Charles Coburn

A delightful comedy filled with captivating moments and social awareness. Coburn is exceptionally effective as a department store owner who masquerades as a clerk in his own establishment to solve problems among his employees. The humor is rather old-fashioned, but it retains its impact. Robert Cummings, Spring Byington, S. Z. Sakall, and William Demarest also star. **Director**—Sam Wood. **Academy Award Nominations**—Coburn, best supporting actor; Norman Krasna, writing (original screenplay).

97 minutes b&w

THE DEVIL'S PLAYGROUND (1981)
★★

Simon Burke
Arthur Dignam
Nick Tate
Charles McCallum

This Australian film by director Fred Schepisi is filled with good intentions, but it isn't particularly moving. The somewhat autobiographical story, set in a Catholic seminary, involves the sexual awakening of a 13-year-old boy, played by Burke, who is studying for the priesthood. He's caught between temptations of the flesh and controls imposed by the brothers, who are also tormented by such restrictions. The performances are decent, with Dignam, Tate, and McCallum standing out. (No MPAA rating) *107 minutes*

DIABOLIQUE (1955)
 ★★★★

Simone Signoret
Charles Vanel

Signoret's masterful acting and Henri-Georges Clouzot's superb directing
(Continued)

D
- Dial M for Murder
- Diamond Head
- Diamond Horseshoe
- Diamond Jim
- Diamonds
- Diamonds Are Forever
- Diary of a Mad Housewife

(Continued)

turn this thriller into a film gem. Signoret portrays the mistress of a schoolmaster who gets involved in a murder plot that goes awry. The tension builds slowly and deliberately to a high pitch. Also with Vera Clouzot and Paul Meurisse. In French with English titles. *107 minutes b&w*

DIAL M FOR MURDER (1954)

★★★

Ray Milland
John Williams
Grace Kelly

Alfred Hitchcock adapted Frederick Knott's Broadway mystery drama for the screen with good results, but this isn't among Hitchcock's greatest efforts. A man (Milland) plots his wife's death to inherit money, but the scheme goes awry, and the police investigate. Kelly plays the wife; Williams is the police inspector. Also with Robert Cummings and Anthony Dawson. (PG) *105 minutes*

DIAMOND HEAD (1962)

★★

Charlton Heston
Yvette Mimieux

Heston stars as an overbearing Hawaiian plantation owner whose stubbornness makes things difficult for his family. The film, based on Peter Gilman's novel, comes off as a rather dazzling soap opera, with the cardboard characters involved in run-on conflicts. The tropical settings are easy on the eyes, but the script is predictable and labored. Supporting players also include France Nuyen, James Darren, Aline MacMahon, and Richard Loo. **Director**—Guy Green. *107 minutes*

DIAMOND HORSESHOE (1945)

★★★

Betty Grable
Dick Haymes

A lavish musical with some old pros doing their stuff in Billy Rose's famous night spot. The routine plot has Grable playing a nightclub singer who chucks fame and fortune to marry a struggling medical student, played by Haymes. "The More I See You" is among the musical numbers. William Gaxton, Phil Silvers, Beatrice Kay, Carmen Cavallaro, and Margaret Dumont also participate in the frolic. **Director**—George Seaton.

104 minutes

DIAMOND JIM (1935)

★★★

Edward Arnold
Jean Arthur
Binnie Barnes

Film biography of Diamond Jim Brady, the turn of the century millionaire with a grand appetite for food, money, and Lillian Russell. Brady's questionable business ethics reflect the Gay Nineties life-style in this light, period drama. Glittering costumes and sets and a strong performance by Arnold—in the title role of a likeable rogue—Arthur, Barnes, Cesar Romero, and Eric Blore add to the entertainment. Arnold made the role his own and seemed to literally and figuratively grow with it. **Director**—A. Edward Sutherland. *94 minutes b&w*

DIAMONDS (1976)

★

Robert Shaw

A weak, confused, illogical plot and a dumb ending tarnish any luster that Shaw brings to this joint Israeli-Swiss film. The story is about a London diamond merchant who plans to steal diamonds from an apparently supersecure safe in an Israeli diamond exchange. At literally the last moment, the would-be crook decides not to be a thief. Many fans of this sort of caper may wish they decided not to see this film. Also stars Barbara Seagull and Shelley Winters. **Director**—Menahem Golan. (PG) *101 minutes*

DIAMONDS ARE FOREVER (1971)

 ★★★

Sean Connery

Connery returns to the role of James Bond in the eighth of this popular series. Set in Las Vegas, the film boasts more gimmicks and stunts than its predecessors, often to the exclusion of the story line. But 007 fans will be happy to see their hero pitted once more against a villain bent on ruling the world, and we always know who'll win. Jill St. John, Bruce Cabot, Charles Gray, Lana Wood, and Bernard Lee are among the supporting cast who keep the entertainment value high. **Director**—Guy Hamilton. (GP) *119 minutes*

DIARY OF A MAD HOUSEWIFE (1970)

 ★★★★

Carrie Snodgress
Richard Benjamin

In Diary of a Mad Housewife, *Carrie Snodgress is maddened by Richard Benjamin.*

Thoroughly enjoyable satirical story of a husband-pecked and bored housewife who has an affair with an arrogant writer, played convincingly by Frank Langella. Snodgress gives an excellent performance as the wife. Smart dialogue, snappy direction, and fine performances are everywhere in this insightful look at a deteriorating contemporary marriage. Benjamin is also on target as the self-centered, overreaching husband whose law career founders. Lorraine Gullen and Frannie Michel contribute supporting work. **Director**—Frank Perry. (R) **Academy Award Nomination**—Snodgress, best actress. *95 minutes*

THE DIARY OF ANNE FRANK
(1959)

 ★★★★

**Millie Perkins
Joseph Schildkraut
Shelley Winters
Ed Wynn**

In The Diary of Anne Frank, *Millie Perkins and Richard Beymer pass the time.*

Moving and gripping account of a family of Dutch Jews who hide from the Nazis in a factory loft for two years. The film faithfully follows the Broadway play, based on the meticulous and touching diary of the young girl who eventually died in a Nazi concentration camp. Perkins, in the title role, looks a lot like the real Anne, but her performance isn't up to the role. But the film never falters, thanks to good direction and fine supporting acting. Also with Lou Jacobi, Richard Beymer, and Diane Baker. **Director**—George Stevens. **Academy Awards**—Winters, best supporting actress; William C. Mellor, cinematography (black and white). **Nominations**—best picture; Stevens, best director; Wynn, best supporting actor. *170 minutes b&w*

DIE LAUGHING (1980)

★

**Robby Benson
Charles Durning**

Benson co-wrote and stars in this dopey comedy-mystery, about a San Francisco cabdriver who wants to be a rock singer. The trivial plot involves the murder of a nuclear scientist and the pursuit of a spider monkey who knows the formula for an atomic weapon. Unfortunately, Benson is a poor singer. And that's no laughing matter, because the intent of the film is just the opposite. Linda Grosvenor, Elsa Lanchester, and Bud Cort are in supporting roles. **Director**—Jeff Werner. (PG) *108 minutes*

DILLINGER (1945)

★★★

**Lawrence Tierney
Edmond Lowe
Eduardo Ciannelli**

Tierney stars as John Dillinger, the infamous gangster and bank robber whose career ended abruptly in front of the Biograph Theater in Chicago, when he was gunned down by the police in 1934 after a well-documented manhunt. A sterling backup cast, including Elisha Cook, Jr., Marc Lawrence, and Anne Jeffries, turns in strong performances in this taut and well-paced thriller. Less violent than John Milius's 1973 version of *Dillinger* (though still a shocker in its time), this film says more with less and keeps our attention with its well-written script by Philip Yordan and tight direction by Max Nosseck. *89 minutes b&w*

DINER (1982)

★★★

**Kevin Bacon
Mickey Rourke
Ellen Barkin**

Screenwriter Barry Levinson debuts as director in this comedy. The action, set in the late '50s, converges on a local hangout eatery. The plot involves five male friends trying to cope with early adult life. Although the film is heavy going at times, it's an extraordinarily skilled portrayal of the period. The characters are so fully realized you can

Kevin Bacon, Mickey Rourke, Daniel Stern, and Paul Reiser chat it out in Diner.

even look into their futures—which don't appear too promising. There's laughter and high spirits throughout, sometimes tending to mask the comedy's darker side. This movie gains much of its impact fom the sharp, funny screenplay and the fine acting of several very talented new performers. (R) **Academy Award Nomination**—Levinson, best original screenplay. *110 minutes*

THE DIRTY DOZEN (1967)

★★★★

**Lee Marvin
Jim Brown
Ernest Borgnine
John Cassavetes
Robert Ryan
Charles Bronson**

Telly Savalas proves he belongs in The Dirty Dozen.

Slam-bang, overly violent World War II adventure with an intriguing angle on combat. Twelve convicts, most of them murderers, get out of prison in exchange for their services in an Army commando unit, where they're trained to kill on a different level. It's professionally done, with lots of tough, he-man action scenes. Director Robert Aldrich doesn't neglect character development, and he offers some insights into the personalities of these unusual recruits. Marvin and Cassavetes stand out among the cast, which also includes Donald Sutherland, George Kennedy, and Richard Jaeckel. **Academy Award Nomination**—Cassavetes, best supporting actor. *150 minutes*

D

- Dirty Harry
- The Disappearance
- A Dispatch from Reuters
- Disraeli
- Distance
- Distant Thunder
- Diva
- Divine Madness

DIRTY HARRY (1971)
★★★

Clint Eastwood
Harry Guardino

Clint Eastwood keeps law and order as Dirty Harry.

Eastwood stars as a San Francisco supercop who stops at nothing to bring in a crazy sniper who calls himself Scorpio. Eastwood is at his steely-eyed best, and whether or not you agree with the notions of vigilante justice put forth here, you have to admire the force with which they're presented. Director Don Siegel's lightning-fast pace makes this first Harry Callahan film superior to such sequels as *Magnum Force, The Enforcer,* and *Sudden Impact.* The cast also includes Reni Santoni, John Vernon, and Andy Robinson. (R) *103 minutes*

THE DISAPPEARANCE (1981)
★

Donald Sutherland
Christopher Plummer
John Hurt
David Hemmings

Some talented actors waste their skills in this meandering drama about a professional hit man whose wife suddenly disappears. Sutherland, who plays the paid killer, carries most of the burden, while Plummer, Hurt, and Hemmings have brief throwaway parts. The direction is uninspired, the plot is confusing, and the ending is annoyingly vague. **Director**—Stuart Cooper. (R) *88 minutes*

A DISPATCH FROM REUTERS (1940)
★★★

Edward G. Robinson
Edna Best
Eddie Albert

An interesting and informative film biography about the man who founded Europe's first news service. Robinson does a fine acting job as Reuter, and production details are first class. However, the film could use more drama. Also with Gene Lockhart, Otto Kruger, Nigel Bruce, and Albert Basserman. **Director**—William Dieterle. *90 minutes b&w*

DISRAELI (1929)
★★★

George Arliss
Joan Bennett
Anthony Lushell

Arliss steals this one as the brilliant British Prime Minister, wily statesman, and matchmaker who brought about the building of the Suez Canal. Arliss won an Oscar for his authoritative portrayal of the great man in this glamorized historical drama, after having played the same role in a silent version in 1921. His matchmaking centers on Bennett and Lushell in ingenue and junior roles. The script by Julian Josephson is well wrought and intelligently portrays the man of many facets in the title role. **Director**—Alfred E. Green. **Academy Award**—Arliss, best actor. **Nominations**—best picture; Josephson, writing. *89 minutes b&w*

DISTANCE (1976)
★★★

Paul Benjamin
Elija Pokkinen

A sensitive and admirable little film about a black sergeant at a Georgia Army post in the 1950s. The soldier is married to a white German girl, and their relationship is deteriorating. The screenplay, by Jay Castle, offers touching human characterizations and thoughtful issues. There's top-notch acting by Benjamin as the sergeant and Pokkinen, a Finnish actress, as his

---

wife. James Woods and Bibi Besch are excellent in other key roles. **Director**—Anthony Lover. (No MPAA rating) *93 minutes*

DISTANT THUNDER (1975)
★★★★

This vivid and powerful film by Indian director Satyajit Ray is about a famine that took the lives of five million people in 1943. The story, set in a remote Bengali village, focuses on the impact among the villagers as their rice supply is slowly depleted. The crisis prompts the social awakening of a pompous village Brahmin. Richly photographed, and exquisitely performed and directed. In Bengali with English titles. (No MPAA rating) *100 minutes b&w*

DIVA (1982)
★★★

Frédéric Andrei
Wilhelmenia Fernandez

French director Jean-Jacques Beineix is off to an impressive start with this remarkable, fast-moving mystery thriller set in Paris. The churning plot involves a young messenger who becomes the prey of sinister characters after he secretly tapes the performance of an opera soprano. Even though the story at times does not make much sense, the film's flamboyant energy and delicious imagery are always fascinating. In French with English titles. (R) *123 minutes*

DIVINE MADNESS (1980)
★★

Bette Midler

Midler belts out an assortment of musical numbers, struts about in wild costumes, and tells raunchy jokes in this concert film that intimately displays her extraordinary talents. The Divine Miss M demonstrates amazing energy and showmanship that should please her fans. But some of the songs are unappealing, and the pacing is often uneven. The result is a mixture of Midler's magical madness and many

- Divorce American Style
- Divorce Italian Style
- Doctor Detroit
- Doctor Dolittle
- Dr. Jeckyll and Mr. Hyde
- Doctor No

D

irritating lapses in her performance. **Director**—Michael Ritchie. (R)
94 minutes

DIVORCE AMERICAN STYLE
(1967)
★★★

**Dick Van Dyke
Debbie Reynolds**

Divorce American Style features Debbie Reynolds as Dick Van Dyke's better half.

The great talents of writer-producer Norman Lear and director Bud Yorkin combine for this stinging and stylish satire on suburban marriage and family problems. Van Dyke and Reynolds star as the upper-middle-class Los Angeles couple who are on the verge of splitting, but conclude they're in for more trouble if they divorce. This is a highly entertaining film with good performances all around. Others in the cast are Jason Robards, Jr., Jean Simmons, Van Johnson, Joe Flynn, Shelley Berman, Lee Grant, and Tom Bosley. **Academy Award Nomination**—Robert Kaufman and Lear, best story and screenplay (written directly for the screen). *109 minutes*

DIVORCE ITALIAN STYLE
(1962)
 ★★★★

Marcello Mastroianni

Excellent satirical comedy on modern Italian morals and life-styles. Mastroianni gives a fine performance as a Sicilian nobleman who, driven by archaic laws prohibiting divorce, manages to get rid of his wife by having her seduced and later eliminated by a jealous lover. With superb direction by Pietro Germi, this black comedy gem was the prototype for a series of lesser films that tried to imitate it but never captured its wit and sheer comic brilliance. **Academy Award**—Ennio de Concini, Alfredo Giannetti, Germi best story and screenplay (written directly for the screen). **Nominations**—Germi, best director; Mastroianni best actor. *104 minutes b&w*

DOCTOR DETROIT (1983)
 ★

**Dan Aykroyd
Howard Hesseman
Kate Murtagh**

Aykroyd hams it up here as a square college professor who masquerades as a big-time gangster. Such shifts in personality have been the subject of many a movie comedy, but Aykroyd pursues this well-worn theme on leaden feet. This is labored, sloppy filmmaking, heavy on confusion and short on good jokes. **Director**—Michael Pressman. (R) *89 minutes*

Dan Aykroyd, a real snappy dresser, stars in Doctor Detroit.

DOCTOR DOLITTLE (1967)
 ★★

**Rex Harrison
Anthony Newley
Samantha Eggar**

Overlong fantasy musical based on the novels of Hugh Lofting, about the magnificent veterinary doctor who can talk to animals. Some animals may get a kick out of this one, but for *Homo sapiens*, it's a charmless, plodding affair. The songs are forgettable; the acting is lackluster. Harrison is in the title role with support from Newley, Eggar, Richard Attenborough (rather good as Mr. Blossom), and Peter Bull. **Director**—Richard Fleischer. **Academy Award Nominations**—best picture; Robert Surtees, cinematography. *152 minutes*

DR. JEKYLL AND MR. HYDE
(1932)
★★★★

**Fredric March
Miriam Hopkins**

Of the several cinematic versions of this Robert Louis Stevenson classic, this one is most noted for its innovative use of makeup and camera tricks that highlight the transformation from good doctor to evil monster. March won an Oscar for his performance as the tormented scientist who discovers the formula that isolates and unlocks the evil in his soul. Hopkins performs beautifully as the temptress Ivy. The pace is exciting and the interpretation imaginative under the creative and skillful direction of Rouben Mamoulian. **Academy Award**—March, best actor. **Nomination**—Percy Heath, Samuel Hoffenstein, writing (adaptation). *82 minutes b&w*

DOCTOR NO (1962)
 ★★★★

**Sean Connery
Ursula Andress
Jack Lord**

This first in the popular James Bond superspy thriller series is one of the best. Connery plays British secret agent 007, who tries to save the world from a powerful fiend operating from a base in the West Indies. The film sparkles with fabulous tongue-in-cheek humor, snappy action, gorgeous girls, exotic hardware, and beautiful locales. After this success, Ian Fleming's indestructible hero just kept coming back to the screen for more adventures. Also with Joseph Wise-
(Continued)

D

- Dr. Strangelove: Or, How I
  Learned to Stop Worrying
  and Love the Bomb
- Doctor Zhivago
- Dodsworth
- Dog Day Afternoon

(Continued)

man, Bernard Lee, John Kitzmiller, Lois Maxwell, and Anthony Dawson. **Director**—Terence Young.

111 minutes

DR. STRANGELOVE: OR, HOW I LEARNED TO STOP WORRYING AND LOVE THE BOMB (1964)

 ★★★★

**Peter Sellers
George C. Scott
Peter Bull
Sterling Hayden**

Sterling Hayden lectures Peter Sellers on the importance of pure bodily fluids in Dr. Strangelove.

Director Stanley Kubrick's towering black comedy seems to become more poignant and pertinent as time marches on. The plot concerns a fanatical U.S. general who launches a nuclear attack on Russia. And when a bomber cannot be recalled, the U.S. sadly awaits devastating retaliation. Sellers, in the best acting job of his career, is magnificent in three memorable roles—the U.S. President, a British officer, and a creepy nuclear scientist. Other fabulous portrayals abound, with Hayden, Scott, Keenan Wynn, and Slim Pickens leading the way. Kubrick's perceptive view of our fragile security in the nuclear age is presented with biting humor and suspense. It's remarkable, classic movie-making. Also with James Earl Jones and Tracy Reed. **Academy Award Nominations**—best picture; Kubrick, best director; Sellers, best actor; Kubrick, Peter George, and Terry Southern, best screenplay (based on material from another medium). (PG)

93 minutes b&w

DOCTOR ZHIVAGO (1965)

★★★★

**Omar Sharif
Julie Christie
Rod Steiger
Alec Guinness**

Julie Christie comforts revolutionary Tom Courtenay after a brutal police attack in Doctor Zhivago.

An exquisite historical film with spectacular production detail based on Boris Pasternak's novel about Russia at the time of the Revolution. The movie seems overextended on various levels, yet it offers some engrossing moments and fine performances by a good cast. The plot concerns a Russian doctor who's forced into the army and longs for the woman he loves. The big-name cast also includes Tom Courtenay, Rita Tushingham, Ralph Richardson, and Geraldine Chaplin. **Director**—David Lean. (PG) **Academy Awards**—Robert Bolt, best screenplay (based on material from another medium); Freddie Young, cinematography (color). **Nominations**—best picture; Lean, best director; Courtenay, best supporting actor.

192 minutes

DODSWORTH (1936)

★★★★

**Walter Huston
Ruth Chatterton
Mary Astor
Maria Ouspenskaya**

A cinematic classic based on the Sinclair Lewis novel of a self-made American businessman and his wife whose lives are irrevocably altered when they confront European society's morals and values. The entire cast is superb with Huston in the title role and Chatterton as the frivolous wife who cannot face growing old gracefully. Brilliant performances are also turned in by Astor as the world-weary American divorcée who knows the real value of Dodsworth, and Ouspenskaya as a European dowager who puts Chatterton in her place. William Wyler's direction is intelligent and sensitive. **Academy Award Nominations**—best picture; Wyler, best director; Huston, best actor; Ouspenskaya, best supporting actress; Sidney Howard, writing (screenplay). *101 minutes b&w*

DOG DAY AFTERNOON (1975)

★★★★

**Al Pacino
John Cazale
Charles Durning**

In Dog Day Afternoon, John Cazale and Al Pacino try to rob a bank, but bungle the job.

A true story based on a bungled bank heist in Brooklyn on a hot summer day. It's a thrilling, energetic circus of a movie, packing comedy and tension. Brilliant acting by Pacino as the bisexual robber out to get money for a sex-change operation for his boyfriend, played by Chris Sarandon. There are other shining characterizations by a large supporting cast, which also includes Sully Boyar and James Broderick. **Director**—Sidney Lumet. (R) **Academy Award Nominations**—best picture; Lumet, best director; Pacino, best actor; Sarandon, best supporting actor; Frank Pierson, best original screenplay. *130 minutes*

STAR PROFILE

- The Dogs of War
- A Doll's House
- A Doll's House
- The Domino Principle
- Donovan's Reef
- Don's Party

D

MARLON BRANDO

Marlon Brando was born in 1924 in Omaha, Nebraska. His father was a salesman, and his mother was a local actress. He attended Shattuck Military Academy of Minnesota and was expelled. He then went on to the Dramatic Workshop in New York and made his debut in I Remember Mama on Broadway in 1944.

In 1947, Brando earned recognition as an actor with his astounding portrayal of the brutish Stanley Kowalski in A Streetcar Named Desire. His unique mumbling delivery ushered in the Method style of acting. Brando was also one of the first participants in Lee Strasberg's Actors' Studio.

In 1950, Brando made his screen debut as a paraplegic in The Men, and his film career soared in the early '50s with starring roles in the screen version of A Streetcar Named Desire (1951), Viva Zapata! (1952), and The Wild One (1953); he also played the young ex-fighter in On the Waterfront (1954), a part for which he won an Oscar.

Brando became known for his rebellious personality off the screen as well as in films. In the '60s, despite his charismatic appeal, his career faltered because of his involvement in many unappealing films. His astounding talent was resurrected with his magnificent portrayal of Don Corleone in The Godfather (1972), which earned him another Oscar, and again soon after with a portrait of middle-aged sexuality in Last Tango in Paris (1973).

Brando was married to actresses Anna Kashi and Movita. Other Brando movies include Guys and Dolls (1955), Mutiny on the Bounty (1962), The Chase (1966), The Missouri Breaks (1976), Superman (1978), and Apocalypse Now (1979).

THE DOGS OF WAR (1981)
 ★★

Christopher Walken
Colin Blakely
Tom Berenger

Steely-eyed, mysterious Jamie Shannon, played by Walken, runs a dial-a-mercenary service from his seedy New York City apartment. He and his pals are dispatched to overthrow an Idi Amin-type dictatorship. The final combat scenes are executed with stunning shoot-em-up flourish. The film, based on the Frederick Forsyth novel, never fully explores the psychology of soldiers of fortune. But director John Irvin, in his first feature movie, puts together a taut and intelligent action adventure, with smashing performances by Walken, Blakely, and Berenger. (R)   *102 minutes*

A DOLL'S HOUSE (1973)
 ★★★

Claire Bloom
Anthony Hopkins

Ibsen's 19th-century play about women's liberation is handled with efficient direction and good acting. Bloom and Hopkins do well in the key roles; Bloom is Nora, the mousey wife who declares her independence when her husband approaches death. Support-ing roles are performed by Ralph Richardson, Denholm Elliott, Anna Massey, and Edith Evans. (G)   *95 minutes*

A DOLL'S HOUSE (1973)
 ★★

Jane Fonda
Trevor Howard

Fonda takes a shot at playing Nora, the shy 19th-century housewife who strikes out for liberation from her overbearing husband. This should have been a piece of cake for Jane, but she handles the Ibsen character rather unevenly. Howard, however, does better as Dr. Rank. The movie's statement on behalf of women's liberation doesn't come over too clearly. Also stars David Warner and Edward Fox. **Director—**Joseph Losey. (G)   *103 minutes*

THE DOMINO PRINCIPLE (1977)
★

Gene Hackman
Candice Bergen
Richard Widmark

Hackman plays a convict who's sprung from prison by a powerful intelligence organization that wants his assistance in an assassination job. It's never explained in this incoherent and humdrum movie who the victim is, what the conspiracy is about, who is behind this nameless secret agency, or why we should even care. Also with Mickey Rooney, Edward Albert, and Eli Wallach. A bad mark for director Stanley Kramer, who is known for better film-making. (R)   *97 minutes*

DONOVAN'S REEF (1963)
★★★

John Wayne
Lee Marvin
Jack Warden

There's fun and frolic with this broad comedy about some war veterans who reside on a Pacific island. Their carefree life is interrupted when a daughter of one of the men pays them a visit. Everyone has a fine time with the bouncy comedy and spirited action. Also in the cast are Dorothy Lamour, Elizabeth Allen, Cesar Romero, and Mike Mazurki. **Director**—John Ford.   *108 minutes*

DON'S PARTY (1976)
 ★★

John Hargreaves
Jeanie Drynan

Australian director Bruce Beresford (Breaker Morant) tries his hand at comedy, but there's little here to laugh
(Continued)

D

- Don't Bother to Knock
- Don't Go Near the Water
- Don't Look Now
- Double Indemnity
- A Double Life
- The Double McGuffin

(Continued)

about. Various couples gather to toast an election victory and spend most of the evening arguing and fighting. The acting is first-class, but the sophisticated humor is rather vulgar and overwrought. Relentless verbal abuse drowns out the few funny scenes. Based on a play by David Williamson. (No MPAA rating)   91 minutes

DON'T BOTHER TO KNOCK
(1952)
★★

Marilyn Monroe
Richard Widmark

Monroe stars as an unhinged girl hired as a babysitter in a hotel, who threatens to kill the youngster in her care. A tough act for Monroe at the outset of her career. She's stuck with a shabby, absurd script. Veteran actor Widmark fares only slightly better, as a tough but nice guy who comes to the rescue. Anne Bancroft is on hand in a throw-away part. Jeanne Cagney, Donna Corcoran, Elisha Cook, Jr., Gloria Blondell, and Jim Backus also star. **Director**—Roy Baker.

76 minutes b&w

DON'T GO NEAR THE WATER
(1957)
★★

Glenn Ford
Fred Clark
Gia Scala

An adolescent service comedy about a World War II public relations operation on an exotic South Pacific island. The uneven farce offers moments of amusement with equal amounts of boredom. The film is based on William Brinkley's novel. Also with Anne Francis, Eva Gabor, Romney Brent, Mickey Shaughnessey, and Keenan Wynn. **Director**—Charles Walters.

107 minutes

DON'T LOOK NOW (1973)

★★★

Donald Sutherland
Julie Christie

Daphne du Maurier's suspense story is

Donald Sutherland examines a mosaic fragment intently in Don't Look Now.

handled with eerie style and a bit of artiness by director Nicolas Roeg, who filmed against the spooky winter background in Venice. A young British couple try to contact their young daughter, killed in an accident, through a medium. Their attempt only leads to further tragedy. Fine performances by Sutherland and Christie, with support from Hilary Mason, Clelia Matania, and Massimo Serrato. (R)   110 minutes

DOUBLE INDEMNITY (1944)

★★★★

Fred MacMurray
Barbara Stanwyck
Edward G. Robinson

Barbara Stanwyck and Fred MacMurray board a train in Double Indemnity.

This is one of the best *films noir* of the '40s. The Raymond Chandler script is based on the James M. Cain novel of conspiracy and murder. MacMurray plays an insurance salesman conned into killing the husband of a fetching beauty, played by Stanwyck to collect the insurance money. Director Billy Wilder coaxes dynamite performances from the entire cast, and the film effectively captures the seedy surroundings associated with the plot. Robinson also stands out as MacMurray's boss, who cracks the case. There's double suspense and triple excitement. Also with Tom Powers, Porter Hall, and Jean Heather. **Academy Award Nominations**—best picture; Wilder, best director; Stanwyck, best actress; John Seitz, cinematography (black and white).   107 minutes b&w

A DOUBLE LIFE (1947)

★★★★

Ronald Colman
Shelley Winters

Colman gives one of the best performances of his career, as a Shakespearean actor whose off stage life imitates his theater role. Colman, who is playing the role of Othello, kills a woman he believes to be Desdemona. The electrifying melodrama is laced with effective suspense and crackling dialogue. Fine support from Winters, Signe Hasso, Edmond O'Brien, and Millard Mitchell. **Director**—George Cukor. **Academy Award**—Colman, best actor. **Nominations**—Cukor, best director; Ruth Gordon and Garson Kanin, writing (original screenplay).   103 minutes b&w

THE DOUBLE McGUFFIN
(1979)

★★

Ernest Borgnine
George Kennedy
Elke Sommer

A band of teenagers foil an assassination plot in this comedy adventure by director Joe Camp, better known for his shaggy dog series starring Benji. The kids, mostly unknowns, do an exceptional job of keeping the film at a lively level of fun and mystery. The story is farfetched, but the pace is energetic, and Camp's execution is impressive. Borgnine, Kennedy, and Sommer help out as the adult heavies. Also with Rod Browning, Dion Pride, and Lisa Whelchel. (PG)   *89 minutes*

DRACULA (1931)
★★★★

**Bela Lugosi
David Manners
Helen Chandler**

This classic screen adaptation of Bram Stoker's haunting novel remains the granddaddy of horror films. Lugosi is fantastic as the Transylvanian vampire who travels to London looking for blood. The strange, misty atmosphere drives home the chills. Actually, the film is somewhat slow and uneven. Yet, for some uncanny reason, this version continues to cast its spell. Many sequels and imitations have gone in its wake. Also with Dwight Frye and Edward Van Sloan. **Director**—Tod Browning.   *84 minutes b&w*

DRACULA (1979)
★★★

**Frank Langella
Laurence Olivier
Donald Pleasence**

The evil count from Transylvania is on the prowl for more blood in this lavish, moody, and scary production starring Langella in the title role. At times, Langella is too sexy and sensual to be menacing. But there are enough howl-

Frank Langella is the latest Dracula.

ing wolves, squeaking bats, and murky graveyards to give a zombie the shivers. Olivier plays Dr. Van Helsing with conviction. It's an excellent rendition of the ageless fable, but the 1931 Bela Lugosi version is still top Drac. Also with Kate Nelligan, Trevor Eve, and Janine Duvitski. **Director**—John Badham. (R)   *109 minutes*

DRAGON SEED (1944)
★★

**Katharine Hepburn
Walter Huston**

This meandering film version of Pearl Buck's novel has good intentions but evolves in an artificial manner. Peasants in a Chinese village battle the Japanese invaders. However, there are some intense moments among all the flag-waving. Hepburn tops the cast, but she's not up to par here. Also with Turhan Bey, Agnes Moorehead, Akim Tamiroff, J. Carrol Naish, and Aline MacMahon. **Directors**—Jack Conway and Harold S. Bucquet. **Academy Award Nominations**—MacMahon, best supporting actress; Sidney Wagner, cinematography (black and white).   *144 minutes b&w*

DRAGONSLAYER (1981)
★★

Peter MacNicol

A Dark Ages fairy tale that's partly flawed with mediocre acting and a tedious script. Young MacNicol plays a sorcerer's apprentice who is called upon to slay a fearsome flying dragon; it seems that the citizens are fed up with appeasing the beast by sacrificing virgins. The super special effects are the real stars. When that huge, fire-breathing dragon goes into action, the story comes alive. But that's rather late in the film. **Director**—Matthew Robbins. (PG)   *108 minutes*

DREAMER (1979)
★★

**Tim Matheson
Susan Blakely
Jack Warden**

Remember Paul Newman shooting a

Tim Matheson and Susan Blakely are united in their love of bowling in Dreamer.

wicked game of pool in *The Hustler*? How about those boxing movies, like *Rocky*, where an unknown contender struggles to win the big fight? Well, here they've given this treatment to bowling, without much style or depth. There's some authentic detail about kegling and the Americana that surrounds it. Yet the story lacks real dramatic tension or credible moral conflict to give the characters stature. Also with Richard B. Shull, Barbara Stuart, and Pedro Gonzalez-Gonzalez. **Director**—Noel Nosseck. (PG)
          86 minutes

DREAMSCAPE (1984)
★★

**Dennis Quaid
Max Von Sydow
Christopher Plummer**

A patchy, sci-fi thriller that involves a research project whereby someone can manipulate another's dreams. Even the President of the United States participates in the experiment. As long as the script is slightly whimsical, the story remains entertaining. But the film eventually lapses into the artificial, taking in various unconvincing suspense gimmicks, a hokey romance, and a few car chases. **Director**—Joseph Ruben. (PG–13)   *98 minutes*

DRESSED TO KILL (1980)
★★

**Michael Caine
Angie Dickinson
Nancy Allen**

Director Brian De Palma liberally bor-
(Continued)

D

- The Dresser
- Drive-In
- The Driver
- The Drowning Pool
- Drum
- Drums Along the Mohawk
- The Duchess and the
  Dirtwater Fox

(Continued)

rows from Alfred Hitchcock's *Psycho* and other classics for this slick but shallow suspense movie about a transvestite who attacks women with a straight razor. De Palma sets up several impressive sequences and displays dazzling camera technique. But the characters are vague and uninteresting, despite decent performances by Caine, Dickinson, and Allen. The film offers much style but little substance. (R) *105 minutes*

THE DRESSER (1983)

★★★★

Albert Finney
Tom Courtenay

Finney and Courtenay pour out a torrent of eloquent acting skill in this magnificent film adaptation of the prize-winning play. Finney howls and roars as the temperamental veteran Shakespearean actor who musters his strength for yet another performance as England buckles under the Nazi blitz. And Courtenay is dead on target in the pivotal title role as the effeminate, mother-hen valet who prods the great man onto the stage. A double-barreled *tour de force*. Bravo, gentlemen. **Director**—Peter Yates. (PG) **Academy Award Nominations**—best picture; Finney, best actor; Courtenay, best actor; Ronald Harwood, best screenplay adaptation. *118 minutes*

DRIVE-IN (1976)

★★★

Lisa Lemole
Glen Morshower
Gary Cavagnaro

This easygoing, low-budget production focuses on youths at a drive-in theater in a rural Texas town. Much of the plot is composed of bits stolen from *American Graffiti* and *The Last Picture Show*, but the results are appealing. A bumbling stickup, a gang rumble, and troubled romance are confronted at the drive-in location. Meanwhile, the big screen features its own version of catastrophe in *Disaster '76*, which is a blend of *Jaws*, *The Towering Inferno*, and *The Poseidon Adventure*. A lot of fresh and unknown faces make up the lively cast. Also with Billy Milliken, Lee

Newsom, and Regan Kee. **Director**—Rod Amateau. (PG) *96 minutes*

THE DRIVER (1978)

★

Ryan O'Neal
Bruce Dern
Isabelle Adjani

This pretentious film glorifies the driver of a getaway car. It's filled with squealing tires, preposterous smash-'em-up car chase scenes, and dialogue so absurd that it's unintentionally funny. O'Neal is The Driver, Dern is The Detective who pursues him, and Adjani is The Player, a mysterious gambler who serves as an alibi for O'Neal. Their acting careers suffer as many dents as the wrecked cars. Also with Ronee Blakely, Matt Clark, and Felice Orlandi. **Director**—Walter Hill. (R) *90 minutes*

THE DROWNING POOL (1975)

★★

Paul Newman
Joanne Woodward
Tony Franciosa

Tony Franciosa tries to best Paul Newman, in The Drowning Pool.

Newman plays a second installment of his portrayal of Lew Harper, the 1950s-era private eye. It's a listless workout against the backdrop of some colorful surroundings of New Orleans and its bayou countryside. The talented cast, however, can't rescue the film. Also with Murray Hamilton, Melanie Griffith, and Richard Jaeckel. **Director**—Stuart Rosenberg. (PG) *108 minutes*

DRUM (1976)

(no stars)

Warren Oates
Ken Norton

This contemptible exploitation film about slavery in the antebellum South is a sequel to the financially successful *Mandingo*. Norton plays a slave on a Louisiana slave-breeding plantation. He's a fine athlete, but no actor. The plot is mostly concerned with titillation and encompasses beatings, castration, and homosexuality—all in bad taste. Also stars Yaphet Kotto and Pam Grier. Directed by Steve Carver and produced by Dino De Laurentiis, who removed his name from the credits. (R) *110 minutes*

DRUMS ALONG THE MOHAWK (1939)

★★★

Claudette Colbert
Henry Fonda
Edna May Oliver

Fine action drama of prerevolutionary colonists who fight to survive Indian attacks and the harshness of primitive farming conditions in upstate New York. A rich, warm story that mingles bravery and guts with love and humor, deftly handled in characteristic style by director John Ford. Colbert as the frightened wife who learns to cope and Fonda as her stern but loving husband are sympathetic and totally believable. Oliver is especially fine in a key support role. **Academy Award Nomination**—Oliver, best supporting actress. *103 minutes*

THE DUCHESS AND THE DIRTWATER FOX (1976)

★

George Segal
Goldie Hawn

A period western strung together with mostly corny gags that leads nowhere. Hawn plays a dance-hall hooker who teams up with Segal, a bumbling card shark. Segal is trying to escape from bank robbers whose $40,000 he has stolen. Hawn and Segal seem to work well together at times, but such mo-

• Duck Soup
• Duel in the Sun
• The Duellists
• Dumbo
• Dune
• The Eagle Has Landed
• The Earthling

D·E

Goldie Hawn and George Segal in The Duchess and the Dirtwater Fox.

ments are too few. This film seems as if it might have been better off as a 15-minute animated cartoon. Also with Conrad Janis, Thayer David, and Roy Jenson. **Director**—Melvin Frank. (PG)
103 minutes

DUCK SOUP (1933)
 ★★★★

The Marx Brothers
Margaret Dumont

A wild and seemingly bottomless offering of one-liners plus a famed mirror sequence put this comic romp in the Marx Brothers Hall of Fame. Groucho plays Rufus T. Firefly, the president of Freedonia, and ineptly wages war upon a scheming non-Marxist neighboring land. Instead of victory there are laughs and the antics of his brothers and eternal straight woman Dumont. Some critics find meaning and intentional satire in this farce, and they may be right, but viewers can certainly accept the silliness for the joy it is. Also with Edgar Kennedy. **Director**—Leo McCarey.
70 minutes b&w

DUEL IN THE SUN (1946)
★★★★

Jennifer Jones
Joseph Cotten
Gregory Peck
Lionel Barrymore
Lillian Gish

Big, sprawling epic western with the influence of writer-producer David O. Selznick very much in evidence. The plot centers on a half-breed Indian girl, played by Jones, who sparks

rivalry between two brothers—Cotten and Peck—when she comes to reside in the home of a powerful cattle rancher. The film boasts some great romantic scenes and rousing action—especially a bizarre gun battle in the finale. Barrymore and Gish are exceptional in supporting roles. Also with Walter Huston, Herbert Marshall, Charles Bickford, and Otto Kruger. Based on Niven Busch's novel. **Director**—King Vidor. **Academy Award Nominations**—Jones, best actress; Gish, best supporting actress.
138 minutes

THE DUELLISTS (1978)
 ★★

Keith Carradine
Harvey Keitel
Albert Finney

Screen adaptation of the Joseph Conrad short story about two Hussar officers, played by Carradine and Keitel, who fight a protracted series of duels during the Napoleonic wars. Director Ridley Scott has taken meticulous care in reconstructing the period. The lavish production abounds with elegant settings and breathtaking vistas. But the film comes up tragically short with a dull script and stiff dialogue. The principal characters seem rather awkward and unconvincing. Also with Edward Fox, Cristina Raines, and Robert Stephens. (PG)
101 minutes

DUMBO (1941)
 ★★★★

Memorable and touching Walt Disney cartoon feature, about the baby circus elephant with ears so big that he can use them as wings and fly. This project

Circus elephantlet Dumbo meets a new friend in Timothy Mouse.

represents the studio at the peak of its creative years. Unforgettable scenes include the crows' song and the drunken nightmare. Voices include Sterling Holloway, Edward Brophy, and Verna Felton. **Director**—Ben Sharpsteen.
64 minutes

DUNE (1984)
★★

Ponderous, overblown, and failed attempt to make sense of Frank Herbert's 1965 sci-fi epic. Director David Lynch packs in too many details and adorns the affair with outlandish, ornate sets. The film also sags under the weight of incomprehensible gobbledygook dialogue. The plot, for what it's worth, concerns a battle in the year 10191 for possession of a powerful, mind-blowing spice found on the title planet. Francesca Annis, José Ferrer, Linda Hunt, Kenneth McMillan, and Leonardo Cimino top the cast. (PG–13)
145 minutes

E

THE EAGLE HAS LANDED (1977)
 ★★★

Michael Caine
Donald Sutherland
Robert Duvall

Caine, Sutherland, and Duvall deliver first-rate performances in director John Sturges's film about a Nazi plot to kidnap Winston Churchill. There's a fair amount of suspense, drama, and battle action to overcome occasional plot potholes. The well-paced screenplay is based on Jack Higgins's novel. The photography is spectacular, especially the scenes on the beautiful Norfolk coast of England. Also with Jenny Agutter, Donald Pleasence, and Anthony Quayle. (PG)
123 minutes

THE EARTHLING (1981)
 ★

William Holden
Ricky Schroder

Schroder plays a recently orphaned
(Continued)

E
- Earthquake
- Easter Parade
- East of Eden
- East Side, West Side
- Easy Money
- Easy Rider

(Continued)

city boy who learns to survive in the Australian wilderness with the help of Holden, a cantankerous old man who returns to his birthplace to die. This muddled, cliché-strewn film pretends to be sentimental, but it can't fool anyone. However, there's no denying the appealing nature photography of the Australian bush country, with kangaroos and wallabies romping over the exquisitely beautiful landscape. Also with Jack Thompson and Olivia Hamnett. **Director**—Peter Collinson. (No MPAA rating) *97 minutes*

EARTHQUAKE (1975)

★★

Charlton Heston
Ava Gardner
Lorne Greene
Marjoe Gortner
George Kennedy

This disaster film has a dumb script and lackluster acting, but great visual and aural effects. There are disasters galore as a massive earthquake strikes Los Angeles. Also with Richard Roundtree, Geneviève Bujold, Lloyd Nolan, Walter Matthau, and Sensurround. **Director**—Mark Robson. (PG) *129 minutes*

EASTER PARADE
(1948)

★★★★

Judy Garland
Fred Astaire
Peter Lawford
Ann Miller

Fred Astaire and Judy Garland meet high society in Easter Parade.

MGM's golden age of musicals was at its peak with this delightfully entertaining film, brimming with Irving Berlin's fabulous songs. The trivial plot has Astaire avoiding dance partner Miller, while he latches on to new sensation Garland. Everyone is at perfection; sit back and enjoy. Also with Jules Munshin. **Director**—Charles Walters. *109 minutes*

EAST OF EDEN (1955)
★★★★

Raymond Massey
James Dean
Julie Harris

James Dean beseeches a father's love from Raymond Massey in East of Eden.

A splendid film version of John Steinbeck's novel, focusing on a teenager's torment over the lack of love from his father. Dean proves his superb acting ability in his starring debut as the rebellious adolescent. Jo Van Fleet is also magnificent as the boy's mother, who operates a brothel. Director Elia Kazan skillfully lays on the emotion and develops the characters to perfection. Also with Dick Davalos, Burl Ives, and Albert Dekker. **Academy Award**—Van Fleet, best supporting actress. **Nominations**—Kazan, best director; Dean, best actor; Paul Osborn, writing (screenplay). *115 minutes*

EAST SIDE, WEST SIDE (1949)
★★

James Mason
Barbara Stanwyck
Van Heflin
Ava Gardner

Slick soap opera, set among New York

City's upper crust. Mason and Stanwyck are a wealthy couple with marital problems involving Gardner and Heflin. There's some entertainment value thanks to the stylish treatment and a professional cast. But the story, based on Marcia Davenport's novel, is rather artificial. Also with Gale Sondergaard, Cyd Charisse, Nancy Davis, and William Conrad. **Director**—Mervyn Le Roy. *108 minutes b&w*

EASY MONEY (1983)
★

Rodney Dangerfield
Joe Pesci

Dangerfield waves his arms a lot, pops his eyes, and tosses out one-liners galore in this rather vulgar screwball comedy about a baby photographer. But where are the laughs? He plays a bumbling slob who must give up a variety of bad habits to inherit $10 million from his snooty mother-in-law. He and most of the cast overstrain with the flimsy comic material. Sorry, Rodney. Still no respect for you or this idiotic movie. Geraldine Fitzgerald costars, and Pesci is great, as always. **Director**—James Signorelli. (R) *95 minutes*

EASY RIDER
(1969)
★★★★

Peter Fonda
Dennis Hopper
Jack Nicholson

A trend-setting movie about two hippies who cross the Southwest on

Dennis Hopper and Karen Black get groovy in Easy Rider.

★ STAR PROFILE

• Eating Raoul • Eddie and the Cruisers
• Eat My Dust! • Edge of the City
• Edison, The Man

E

motorcycles and meet disaster at the hands of trigger-happy rednecks. This remarkable and unusual film seems to be a metaphor of the times with its casual statements on hatred and a society that for some is too structured and too organized. Hopper and Fonda are exceptionally good as the free-wheeling bikers. Nicholson is great as a tipsy small-town lawyer, who goes along for the ride. Also with Luana Onders, Robert Walker, and Karen Black. **Director**—Hopper. **Academy Award Nominations**—Nicholson, best supporting actor; Fonda, Hopper, and Terry Southern, best story and screenplay (based on material not previously published or produced). (R)

94 minutes

EATING RAOUL (1982)

★★★

Paul Bartel
Mary Woronov

Paul Bartel and Mary Woronov mug people in their kitchen in Eating Raoul.

A wry, fairly sophisticated black comedy by Bartel that satirizes swinging life-styles and middle-class values. Told in a matter-of-fact and amusing tone, the story concerns a prissy middle-aged couple who concoct an outrageous scheme to lure "sexual perverts" to their apartment and murder them for their money. The farce steers clear of slapstick. **Director**—Bartel. (R)

87 minutes

EAT MY DUST! (1976)
★★★

Ron Howard
Christopher Norris

Teenagers should enjoy this car-chase

LAURENCE OLIVIER

Sir Laurence Olivier, born in Dorking, England, in 1907, is acknowledged by many to be the preeminent actor of the age. He's also well known for his directing and producing credits. Olivier has received three Academy Awards and has been nominated 10 other times.

Olivier had appeared in movies for nine years before his first Oscar nomination in 1939 for his performance in Wuthering Heights, one of his most famous roles.

Olivier also received Oscar nominations for his performances in Rebecca (1940), Henry V (1946), Richard III (1956), The Entertainer (1960), Othello (1965), Sleuth (1972), Marathon Man (1976), and The Boys from Brazil (1978).

Olivier is also credited as the man who brought plays of Shakespeare to the screen and made them successful with movie audiences. In fact, in 1946 he received a special Academy Award for outstanding achievement as actor, producer, and director in bringing Henry V to the screen. In 1948, he won the Oscar for Hamlet, a film that he also produced and directed.

In 1970, Sir Laurence was granted a Life Peerage by Her Majesty Queen Elizabeth II of England, and Lord Olivier became the first actor to be so honored.

Some of his most recent movies include The Jazz Singer (1980) and Clash of the Titans (1981).

comedy starring Howard and Norris. The plot is simple. The teenage son of a small-town California sheriff swipes a stock car and takes a blonde for a joyride; the sheriff recruits a bumbling posse of cars to chase the madcap pair. The result is a demolition derby with no injuries. The wrecks and stunts are well done, and the photography is attractive. Also with Warren Kemmerling, Dave Madden, and Rance Howard. Directed and written by Charles Griffith. (PG)   *90 minutes*

EDDIE AND THE CRUISERS
(1983)

★★

Michael Paré

Rock 'n' roll nostalgia set in mystery is the theme of this uneven film that looks at an up-and-coming pop group of the mid-'60s. Paré portrays the young rocker who supposedly committed suicide at the height of his career. Or did Eddie purposefully go into hiding, bringing along some sensational unreleased tapes? There are compelling moments. Yet the story goes astray too often, lapsing into silliness and outright confusion. Tom Berenger and Ellen Barkin also star. **Director**—Martin Davidson. (PG)

94 minutes

EDGE OF THE CITY (1957)
★★★★

Sidney Poitier
John Cassavetes
Jack Warden

An exciting, gripping melodrama, filmed on the docks of New York City much in the style of *On the Waterfront*. Poitier and Cassavetes play longshoremen who confront a brutal and bigoted union boss, portrayed convincingly by Warden. The film, which has something significant to say about racial integration, is based on Robert Alan Aurther's TV play, *A Man Is Ten Feet Tall*. Also with Kathleen Maguire, Ruby Dee, and Robert Simon. **Director**—Martin Ritt.   *85 minutes b&w*

EDISON, THE MAN (1940)
★★★

Spencer Tracy
Rita Johnson

Straightforward and slightly sentimental film biography of America's most famous inventor, made as a sequel to *Young Tom Edison*. The script traces Edison's life from his obscure years in poverty to his emergence as
(Continued)

E
- Educating Rita
- Edward, My Son
- The Effect of Gamma Rays on Man-in-the-Moon Marigolds

- The Egg and I
- The Eiger Sanction
- 8½
- El Cid

(Continued) genious inventor of the lightbulb and the phonograph. Good casting of Tracy in the title role. There's earnest support from Charles Coburn, Gene Lockhart, and Lynne Overman. **Director**—Clarence Brown. **Academy Award Nomination**—Hugo Butler and Dore Schary, writing (original story). *107 minutes b&w*

EDUCATING RITA (1983)
★★★

**Michael Caine
Julie Walters**

Michael Caine is a professor of comparative alcohol in Educating Rita.

A predictable but fun latter-day version of Pygmalion with Caine and Walters in perfect form as teacher and student. He's a disillusioned, drunken professor whose life is turned around when—guess what?—he tutors plucky hairdresser Walters, who has an honest hunger for classic literature. The plot is threadbare and the direction somewhat stagey (the film started as a play). But this is an actor's picture, and it's a pleasure to watch Caine sink his teeth into a role, even when it's not nearly good enough for him. **Director**—Lewis Gilbert. (PG) **Academy Award Nominations**—Caine, best actor; Walters, best actress; Willy Russell, best screenplay adaptation.
110 minutes

EDWARD, MY SON (1948)
★★

**Spencer Tracy
Deborah Kerr**

An overbearing and somewhat artifi-

cial screen adaptation of a compelling play about a wealthy man's unbecoming conduct toward his son. Tracy, as the unscrupulous father, seems ill at ease in an unsuitable role. Kerr plays his distraught wife, and there is support from Ian Hunter, James Donald, Leueen McGrath, and Mervyn Johns. **Director**—George Cukor.
112 minutes b&w

THE EFFECT OF GAMMA RAYS ON MAN-IN-THE-MOON MARIGOLDS (1972)
★★★

Joanne Woodward

Fine adaptation of the Pulitzer Prize-winning play by Paul Zindel. Woodward deserves acting honors for her portrayal of the middle-aged, self-deluding loser who never loses hope that she and her daughters will achieve a measure of greatness. Director Paul Newman deftly handles the translation from stage to screen and brings a new dimension to the story. Nell Potts, Roberta Wallach, and Judith Lowry are all excellent in the supporting cast. (PG) *101 minutes*

THE EGG AND I (1947)
★★★

**Claudette Colbert
Fred MacMurray**

Colbert and MacMurray are effective in this warm comedy about a city couple who buy a chicken farm and struggle with numerous problems. The film is notable for introducing Marjorie Main and Percy Kilbride as Ma and Pa Kettle. The script is based on Betty McDonald's popular book. Also with Louise Allbritton, Richard Long, and Billy House. **Director**—Chester Erskine. *104 minutes b&w*

THE EIGER SANCTION (1975)
★★

**Clint Eastwood
George Kennedy**

Jonathan Hemlock, played by Eastwood, is hired to assassinate the killers of an American agent. Most of the year Hemlock teaches art, but on vaca-

tion he's a secret agent who works for a government organization. He uses the money he earns from his missions to buy works of art. Generally, it's a dreary film, with all the clichés of suspense thrillers thrown in. The film, based on one of Trevanian's popular novels, is set in the Swiss Alps; the Eiger is a Swiss peak. Some vitality and humor from the supporting cast, which includes Vonetta McGee, Jack Cassidy, and Heidi Bruhl. **Director**—Eastwood. (R) *128 minutes*

8½ (1963)
★★★

**Marcello Mastroianni
Claudia Cardinale
Anouk Aimee
Sandra Milo**

In this prime-time Fellini, a movie director (Mastroianni), spiritually paralyzed by a midlife crisis, loses himself in fantasy and reminiscences. His introspections spin around sexual, religious, and sociological themes in a free-form style that can be taken as cinematic poetry, self-analysis, or self-indulgence. From the moment the protagonist floats out of a traffic jam in the opening scene, 1960s cinema was opening out, for better or worse, to a more freewheeling, self-consciously stylized approach. Fellini's autobiographical *tour de force* was film number 8½ (counting each of three shorts as half a film) in his career. Nino Rota scored. *135 minutes b&w*

EL CID (1961)
★★★

**Charlton Heston
Sophia Loren
Raf Vallone**

Sprawling, opulent period epic with none other than Heston portraying the legendary hero who rid Spain of the Moors in the 11th century. The magnificent spectacle features an eyeful of flashy costumes, impressive settings, and big battle scenes. The script, however, doesn't live up to the visual splendor. The cast also includes Geraldine Page, Hurd Hatfield, Gary Raymond, Herbert Lom, and John Fraser. **Director**—Anthony Mann.
184 minutes

- El Dorado
- Electric Dreams
- The Electric Horseman
- The Elephant Man
- Elephant Walk
- Elmer Gantry
- Elvira Madigan
- Embryo

E

EL DORADO (1966)
★★★

John Wayne
Robert Mitchum

Big John straps on his shootin' irons and helps his friend, a drunken sheriff played by Mitchum, fight a crooked cattle baron. Director Howard Hawks whips together this funny, action-packed, old-fashioned western, based loosely on his *Rio Bravo*. Not the best of Hawks's features, but it's likable. James Caan, Charlene Holt, Michele Carey, and Ed Asner are also in the cast.
126 minutes

ELECTRIC DREAMS (1984)
★★

Lenny Von Dohlen
Virginia Madsen

A high-tech romantic comedy involving a young San Francisco architect and his almost-human computer, both competing for the affection of a young female concert cellist. The story aspires to be cute and hip, but it merely becomes silly and rather preposterous. For music fans, though, there are generous portions of classical and rock numbers woven in among the electronic gadgets and jargon. **Director**— Steve Barron. (PG)
96 minutes

THE ELECTRIC HORSEMAN (1979)
★★★

Robert Redford
Jane Fonda

Redford and Fonda generate the right chemistry together in this winning film that roasts conglomerates and consumer manipulation. Redford is a hard-drinking ex-rodeo star, who sells out to a giant company to promote breakfast cereal. Outraged at the abuse of a multimillion-dollar racehorse, he dramatically kidnaps the animal. Fonda, in a TV news reporter role similar to the one she played in *The China Syndrome*, pursues him through the picturesque Rocky Mountains. Also with Valerie Perrine, Willie Nelson, and John Saxon. **Director**— Sidney Pollack. (PG)
120 minutes

THE ELEPHANT MAN (1980)
★★★★

Anthony Hopkins
John Hurt
Anne Bancroft
John Gielgud

The story of John Merrick, the hideously deformed sideshow freak with the soul of an angel, is presented on film with dignity and compassion. Director David Lynch enhances the drama with a graceful dreamlike texture. But it's the magnificent performance of Hurt in a most difficult title role that really expresses the humanity and gentleness of this grotesque young man. Also with Wendy Hiller. (PG) **Academy Award Nominations**— best picture; Hurt, best actor; Lynch, best director; Christopher De Vore, Eric Bergren, and Lynch, best screenplay (adapted from another medium).
125 minutes b&w

ELEPHANT WALK (1954)
★★

Elizabeth Taylor
Peter Finch

Taylor stars as the new wife of a Ceylon tea plantation owner who has difficulty adjusting to her new environment. Liz looks beautiful, and there's an impressive elephant stampede finale; otherwise, the film is merely a puffed-up soap opera with a rather confused script. Finch plays the wealthy tea planter. Also with Dana Andrews and Abraham Sofaer. **Director**—William Dieterle.
103 minutes

ELMER GANTRY (1960)
★★★★

Burt Lancaster
Jean Simmons
Arthur Kennedy
Shirley Jones

Lancaster is fantastic as the hypocritical evangelist in this exciting and absorbing screen version of the Sinclair Lewis novel. The film brims with first-class performances by all involved. And there are some memorable scenes with Simmons as an ambitious lady preacher, Kennedy as a

Burt Lancaster portrays Elmer Gantry, a cynical evangelist.

sharp newspaper reporter, and Jones as Gantry's former girl friend turned prostitute. It's an intensive piece of work that grabs you early and won't let go. Also with Dean Jagger, Edward Andrews, and Patti Page. **Director**— Richard Brooks. **Academy Awards**— Lancaster, best actor; Jones, best supporting actress; Brooks, best screenplay (based on material from another medium). **Nomination**—best picture.
146 minutes

ELVIRA MADIGAN (1967)
★★★★

Pia Degermark
Thommy Berggren

A feast for the eyes and ears, this romantic tragedy is a triumph for writer, director, and editor Bo Widerberg. The film is based on a true story of a Swedish army officer and a circus performer who commit suicide rather than part from each other. The visual beauty in lush color and muted tones is a tribute to cinematographer Jorgen Persson, and the musical background put Mozart on the top ten record albums that year. The performances by Degermark and Berggren are adequate but take a back seat to the production.
89 minutes

EMBRYO (1976)
★

Rock Hudson
Diane Ladd

An absurd variation of the Frankenstein theme, with Hudson as a doctor
(Continued)

E
- The Emperor Waltz
- The Empire Strikes Back
- The Enchanted Cottage
- The End
- Endangered Species
- Endless Love
- Endless Summer

(Continued)

who injects a human fetus with a growth hormone. A little more than a week later, there's a full-grown, beautiful woman who can play chess. Of course, Rock falls in love with her, but then things turn sour as they did with Frankenstein's monster. The producers will just have to make a sequel: *Bridegroom of Embryo*, or something like that. Also with Barbara Carrera, Roddy McDowall, and Anne Schedeen. **Director**—Ralph Nelson. (PG)
104 minutes

THE EMPEROR WALTZ (1948)
★★

**Bing Crosby
Joan Fontaine**

Crosby stars as a phonograph salesman trying to get an order from Emperor Franz Joseph of Austria. This rather oddball operetta is pleasing in spots, but it carries scant impact. Also, director Billy Wilder is out of place with this sort of puffed-up material. The script is merely routine, and the music is forgettable. Others in the cast include Roland Culver and Richard Haydn.
106 minutes

THE EMPIRE STRIKES BACK
(1980)

 ★★★★

**Mark Hamill
Harrison Ford
Carrie Fisher
Billy Dee Williams**

Space-opera maestro George Lucas, creator of *Star Wars*, scores again with another lulu of a fantasy adventure in a galaxy far, far away. It's a worthy and sumptuous sequel, with action galore

Carrie Fisher and Harrison Ford discover something more fun than killing Imperial Storm Troopers in The Empire Strikes Back.

and imaginative special effects that are special indeed. Old friends are back—Luke Skywalker, Han Solo, Chewbacca, R2-D2, C-3PO—gallantly adventuring among the stars and planets. And there's a startling plot twist involving archvillain Darth Vader. Also with Alec Guinness, David Prowse, Frank Oz, and Anthony Daniels. **Director**—Irwin Kershner. (PG)
124 minutes

THE ENCHANTED COTTAGE
(1945)

 ★★★

**Dorothy McGuire
Robert Young**

An agreeable romantic fantasy that works well despite a syrupy and sentimental script. Young is a disfigured war veteran, and McGuire is a plain young girl. They discover beauty and love in each other. Is it really the enchantment of the New England cottage where they meet? Sensitive direction by John Cromwell pulls it off. Herbert Marshall, Mildred Natwick, Hillary Brooke, and Spring Byington also star.
91 minutes b&w

THE END (1978)

 ★★

**Burt Reynolds
Sally Field
Dom DeLuise**

How can a story about a man about to die be something to laugh about? Reynolds strains hard in this endeavor, but doesn't succeed. That lovable nut, DeLuise, steals many a scene. But mostly, the film is an embarrassing attempt at gallows humor. In this case, the end doesn't come soon enough. Also with Joanne Woodward, Kristy McNichol, Robby Benson, David Steinberg, Norman Fell, and Carl Reiner. **Director**—Reynolds. (R)
100 minutes

ENDANGERED SPECIES (1982)

 ★

**Robert Urich
Jobeth Williams**

Hyped-up melodrama about mysteri-

Robert Urich and Jobeth Williams solve the mystery of dying cattle in Endangered Species.

ous cattle mutilations investigated by a tough ex-cop from New York (Urich) and a spunky Colorado sheriff (Williams). The film, although nicely packaged, plays like supermarket tabloid journalism. Contrivances and clichés are mixed in with the suspense. Urich of TV fame makes an impressive theatrical film debut, but the character he portrays is hardly believable. **Director**—Alan Rudolph. (R)   *97 minutes*

ENDLESS LOVE (1981)

 ★

**Brooke Shields
Martin Hewitt**

This syrupy, soap-opera movie, based on Scott Spencer's sultry novel, stars Shields and Hewitt as obsessive, ill-fated teenage lovers. The screenplay, which begins with passionate puppy love, shifts midway to tragedy, embroiling the youngsters and their families in unbearable distress. Shields and Hewitt are impressively pretty, but there's hardly any acting talent between them. The erratic direction of Franco Zeffirelli merely emphasizes the film's puffed-up sentimentality. Endless nonsense. (R)
115 minutes

ENDLESS SUMMER (1966)

★★★

Two young surfers travel around the world in search of the perfect wave. The concept was unique, and it made an entertaining and visually attractive documentary. Bruce Brown as writer, director, and cinematographer did much to popularize the sport and simultaneously provide refreshing comments on almost all of the loca-

• End of the Game • Enigma
• The Enemy Below • The Entertainer
• The Enforcer (1951) • Enter the Dragon
• The Enforcer (1976) • The Entity

E

tions visited. You don't need to be a surfing fan to enjoy this gem.

95 minutes

END OF THE GAME (1976)
★

**Martin Ritt
Jon Voight
Robert Shaw
Jacqueline Bisset**

A confused plot and a lot of overacting dull the edge in this story of intrigue and murder. Ritt, better known as a director, plays a rumpled Swiss detective who pursues an acquaintance wanted for a murder committed 30 years ago. Along the way there's an excess of murky detail, more murder, and a surprise ending. **Director—** Maximillian Schell. (PG)   *106 minutes*

THE ENEMY BELOW (1957)
★★★

**Robert Mitchum
Curt Jurgens
Theodore Bikel**

An absorbing World War II action drama. An American destroyer and a German U-boat stalk one another in the South Atlantic. Interest is maintained throughout, thanks to gripping underwater action, notable photography, and impressive special effects. Lots of tense moments heighten the suspense. Also with David Hedison, Russell Collins, and Doug McClure. **Director—**Dick Powell.   *98 minutes*

THE ENFORCER (1951)
★★★

**Humphrey Bogart
Everett Sloane**

Bogart portrays a determined district attorney in this semidocumentary crime thriller, about the smashing of a gang of hired killers known as Murder, Inc. The suspenseful film is relentless in its attention to realism. Sharp dialogue and good pacing enhance the quality. Bogey is at his best, and he gets top support from Zero Mostel, Ted de Corsia, King Donovan, and Roy Roberts. **Director—**Bretaigne Windust.   *87 minutes b&w*

THE ENFORCER (1976)
 ★

**Clint Eastwood
Tyne Daly
Harry Guardino**

Eastwood, in this third Dirty Harry Callahan film, takes on a gang of San Francisco political terrorists. There's blood, gore, and howling sirens galore, as Harry, waving his .44 magnum, blows people's heads off. This time, his partner is a woman police officer, played by Daly. The witless plot comes off as a worn-out copy of the previous adventures of the self-righteous homicide cop. Also with Bradford Dillman, John Mitchum, and DeVeren Bookwalter. **Director—**James Fargo. (R)   *96 minutes*

ENIGMA (1983)
 ★★

**Martin Sheen
Sam Neill
Brigitte Fossey**

A rather routine Cold War spy caper swarming with red herrings and double crosses. Sheen is the good-guy secret agent who penetrates East Berlin security; his mission is to nab a mysterious code scrambler in hopes of intercepting assassination attempts on Soviet dissidents. The globe-hopping plot unwinds at such breakneck speed that characters and story line are lost amid the chaos. **Director—** Jeannot Szwarc. (PG)   *101 minutes*

THE ENTERTAINER (1960)
★★★★

Laurence Olivier

The magnificent Olivier is at his best in the role of a second-rate comedian with a bloated ego, in the twilight of his career. This screen version of John Osborne's play is obviously stagey, but Olivier's triumphant performance overcomes any obstacle. He brilliantly brings to bear the tragedy of this man with large expectations and little talent to achieve them. The atmosphere of a seedy seaside resort adds to the characterization. The fine supporting cast includes Roger Livesey, Alan

---

Bates, Joan Plowright, and Albert Finney. **Director—**Tony Richardson. **Academy Award Nomination—**Olivier, best actor.   *96 minutes b&w*

ENTER THE DRAGON (1973)
 ★★★

**Bruce Lee
John Saxon**

A surprisingly good martial-arts action film, with kung fu wiz Lee kicking up a storm. He's hired by British agents to infiltrate a remote fortress and smash a drug-smuggling operation. Forget about any logical script; it's the action that counts here. And this is a king-size portion of chop-socky. Also with Shih Kien, Jim Kelly, and Bob Wall. **Director—**Robert Clouse. (R)

99 minutes

THE ENTITY
(1983)
 ★

**Barbara Hershey
Ron Silver
George Coe**

Barbara Hershey has a visit from The Entity.

Hershey turns in a decent performance as a young woman possessed by an invisible spirit. But this documentarylike horror drama never builds momentum, mystery, or suspense. Predictably, psychiatrists and parapsychologists are called in to explain the phenomenon. Frank DeFelitta wrote the screenplay from his own novel, which supposedly is based on the actual case of a California woman. **Director—**Sidney Furie. (R)

116 minutes

E
- Entre Nous
- Equus
- Eraserhead
- The Errand Boy
- The Escape Artist
- Escape from Alcatraz
- Escape from Fort Bravo

ENTRE NOUS (1983)

★★★★

**Isabelle Huppert
Miou-Miou**

Diane Kurys's poignant and observant account of two women who become intimate friends and eventually shuck their dull marriages for newly found liberation. Set in the '50s in France, the film also deals sympathetically with the subtle pain and humiliation suffered by the abandoned husbands. The acting is superb, and the story builds to a startling climax. In French with English titles. **Director**—Kurys. (PG) **Academy Award Nomination**—best foreign-language film.

110 minutes

EQUUS (1977)
★★

**Richard Burton
Peter Firth**

Richard Burton is the doctor and Peter Firth is his troubled patient in Equus.

Peter Shaffer's prizewinning psychological play loses much of its emotional impact and imagination in the transfer from stage to screen. Director Sidney Lumet has perhaps injected too much realism into this story, about the relationship between a psychiatrist and a troubled stable boy who blinds six horses. The performances, however, are excellent all around. Burton plays the psychiatrist with steady fortitude; Firth brings depth and persuasiveness to his role as the boy. Also with Colin Blakely, Joan Plowright, and Harry Andrews. (R) **Academy Award Nominations**—Burton, best actor; Firth, best supporting actor. *138 minutes*

ERASERHEAD (1977)

★★★★

John Nance

David Lynch, who directed the award-winning *Elephant Man*, launched his career with this strange shocker that has found its way to the midnight movie theater circuit. The intentionally nightmarish story explores the relationship of man and monster, but image and atmosphere are the keys to this film. John Nance is in the title role as a weird character with a peculiar elongated head and hair that stands on end. His girl friend gives birth to a hideous, premature baby, but this film—six years in the making—is a fully developed classic. Also stars Charlotte Stewart and Allen Josephs. (No MPAA rating) *90 minutes b&w*

THE ERRAND BOY (1961)
★★

**Jerry Lewis
Brian Donlevy**

Typical Lewis silliness, with the comedian playing a bumbling paperhanger on the rampage in a Hollywood studio. There are sight gags galore—a few effective ones and many more that fall flat. Fans of Lewis, if there are any still around, may get a bang out of this. Sig Ruman, Fritz Feld, and Doodles Weaver are also involved with the nonsense. **Director**—Lewis.

92 minutes b&w

THE ESCAPE ARTIST (1982)
★★

**Griffin O'Neal
Raul Julia
Desi Arnaz**

Griffin O'Neal (son of Ryan, brother of Tatum) is fresh and appealing as a precocious teenage magician who takes on the adult world. But, alas, he's trapped in a fantasy film so muddled that interest is never sustained. The story, based on David Wagoner's novel, would seem to promise an intriguing movie, but the project is mishandled by director Caleb Deschanel, the talented cinematographer of *The Black Stallion*. (PG) *96 minutes*

ESCAPE FROM ALCATRAZ (1979)

★★★

**Clint Eastwood
Patrick McGoohan**

Clint Eastwood diligently tunnels for his Escape from Alcatraz.

Eastwood, looking mean and lean, stars in this tough and realistic prison film, which ranks with such classics as *White Heat* and *Brute Force*. Producer-director Don Siegel is in top form, creating tension and the grim mood of prison life. There's fine supporting work, too, especially from McGoohan as the cold-hearted warden. Richard Tuggle's efficient screenplay is based on the actual escape of three prisoners from "the Rock" in 1962. Also with Roberts Blossom and Jack Thibeau. (PG) *112 minutes*

ESCAPE FROM FORT BRAVO (1953)
★★★

**William Holden
Eleanor Parker
John Forsythe**

Better-than-average western yarn, with Holden as the commanding officer of a Union fort in Arizona during the Civil War. Some Confederates try to escape, but they're attacked by Indians who don't distinguish between adversaries of the North and the South. The climactic redskin ambush sequence is tense, indeed. Also with William Demarest and Polly Bergen. **Director**—John Sturges.

98 minutes

• Escape from New York
• E.T.—The Extra-Terrestrial
• The Europeans
• Every Man for Himself and God Against All
• Everything I Have Is Yours
• Everything You Always Wanted to Know About Sex (But Were Afraid to Ask)
• Every Which Way But Loose

E

ESCAPE FROM NEW YORK
(1981)
 ★★

**Kurt Russell
Ernest Borgnine**

Kurt Russell and Season Hubley are two outcasts who would like to Escape from New York.

It's 1997, and New York City is a walled-in, escape-proof prison, populated by thousands of criminals and loonies. John Carpenter (*Halloween; The Fog*) dreamed up this mindless melodrama, which features characters and action of exceptional viciousness and violence. In the midst of this ominous hellhole, the President's plane crash-lands, and a cunning criminal, played by Russell, masterminds the rescue in trade for his freedom. Also with Isaac Hayes. (R)   *99 minutes*

E.T.—THE EXTRA-TERRESTRIAL (1982)
★★★★

**Henry Thomas
Drew Barrymore
Robert MacNaughton
Dee Wallace**

Henry Thomas is about to become friends for life with an unusual playmate in E.T.

While most sci-fi pictures dwell on spectacular hardware, this extraordinary extra-terrestrial adventure by director Steven Spielberg concentrates on character, feelings, and friendship. It's a wonderful, magical story about an ungainly little space creature stranded on Earth who is befriended and protected by some California youngsters. Thomas never hits a false note as the ordinary boy who gets involved in an extraordinary friendship. But the real star is E.T., the loveable, frightened, and homesick alien creature. (PG) **Academy Awards—** John Williams, best original score; Carlo Rambaldi, Dennis Murren, and Kenneth F. Smith, best visual effects. **Nominations**—best picture; Spielberg, best director; Melissa Mathison, best screenplay (written directly for the screen); Allen Daviau, cinematography.   *115 minutes*

THE EUROPEANS (1979)
 ★★★

**Lee Remick
Robin Ellis**

Henry James's novel, which contrasts American and European cultures, is tastefully adapted to the screen as a literate comedy of manners. Remick and Ellis are the sophisticated Europeans—a brother and sister—who move in with their staid New England cousins. Remick is lovely and plays the Baroness Munster with grace. The New England autumn countryside is photographed in full glory, and the 1850 period is meticulously recreated. Also with Wesley Addy, Tim Choate, and Lisa Eichorn. **Director**—James Ivory. (No MPAA rating)   *90 minutes*

EVERY MAN FOR HIMSELF AND GOD AGAINST ALL
See The Mystery of Kasper Hauser

EVERYTHING I HAVE IS YOURS (1952)
★★

**Marge Champion
Gower Champion
Dennis O'Keefe**

Marge and Gower Champion star in

this routine musical that perks up only when the stars go through their dance routines. The uneventful plot has the dance team on the brink of Broadway success only to discover that Marge is pregnant. This sort of thing is well-outdated. Also with Eduard Franz. **Director**—Robert Z. Leonard.
92 minutes

EVERYTHING YOU ALWAYS WANTED TO KNOW ABOUT SEX (BUT WERE AFRAID TO ASK) (1972)
 ★★★

**Woody Allen
Lynn Redgrave
Anthony Quayle
John Carradine
Lou Jacobi**

Woody Allen helps John Carradine take aim in Everything You Always Wanted to Know About Sex (But Were Afraid to Ask).

Director Allen lampoons sex in a series of inventive comic sketches; some of them work, some fizzle. But those that succeed are a howl. Segments include a giant female breast, Gene Wilder as a doctor attracted to a sheep, Redgrave modeling a chastity belt, and a tour of the male body with Woody portraying a sperm. Others in the cast are Louise Lasser, Tony Randall, and Burt Reynolds. (R)   *87 minutes*

EVERY WHICH WAY BUT LOOSE (1978)
 ★

**Clint Eastwood
Sondra Locke**

Eastwood, seemingly tired of his *Dirty Harry* character, tries to latch on to
(Continued)

E
- The Evil of Frankenstein
- Evilspeak
- The Evil That Men Do
- Evil Under the Sun
- Excalibur
- Excuse My Dust
- Executive Suite

(Continued)

Burt Reynolds's good-ol'-boy routine in this dim-witted comedy. Eastwood earns money in pickup fistfights, travels with a cute orangutan, and is chased by mean cops and a gang of motorcycle toughs. The orangutan upstages the actors, which says it all about this film. Also with Geoffrey Lewis, Beverly D'Angelo, and Ruth Gordon. **Director**—James Fargo. (R)
119 minutes

THE EVIL OF FRANKENSTEIN (1964)
★★

Peter Cushing
Peter Woodthorpe

Another episode in the notorious monster series; this one lacks the style and impact of Boris Karloff's portrayals. Cushing plays Dr. Frankenstein, who returns to his laboratory where he finds the monster, played by Kiwi Kingston, frozen in ice. Terror ensues when the monster thaws out and rampages through the community. Also with Sandor Eles, Duncan Lamont, and Katy Wild. **Director**—Freddie Francis.
87 minutes

EVILSPEAK (1982)
Ⓐ (no stars)

Clint Howard

Pity poor Private Coopersmith (Howard). Just about everyone at the swank military academy he attends picks on him all the time. So, with the aid of a computer, the harassed cadet calls upon the power of Satan and murders his tormentors in a gruesome climactic bloodbath. The emphasis in this absurd and grisly shocker is mainly on the carnage. As for the acting, direction, and script, there's not much to speak about. **Director**—Eric Weston. (R)
89 minutes

THE EVIL THAT MEN DO (1984)
Ⓐ ★★

Charles Bronson
Joseph Maher

Bronson works his formula revenge routine in Central America against a vile assassin (Maher) and his henchmen. The unflappable Bronson is lured out of retirement after viewing video tapes of torture victims. He's soon at work eliminating the bad guys with an assortment of weapons and clever tactics. The film is heavy with scenes of brutality, blood, and mayhem. **Director**—J. Lee Thompson. (R)
89 minutes

EVIL UNDER THE SUN (1982)
Ⓐ ★★

Peter Ustinov
Maggie Smith
James Mason
Diana Rigg

Maggie Smith summons detective Peter Ustinov in the Agatha Christie mystery, Evil Under the Sun.

A nice-looking but rather dried-out film version of Agatha Christie's whodunit, set on a Mediterranean resort island. In typical droll fashion the indomitable Belgian sleuth, Hercule Poirot (Ustinov), points out the murderer during the inevitable drawing room showdown. But the events leading to the solution and the introduction of too many stuffy characters have all happened at too monotonous a pace to sustain interest. **Director**—Jack Hofsiss. (PG)
106 minutes

EXCALIBUR (1981)
Ⓐ ★★

Nigel Terry
Nicol Williamson

The Knights of the Round Table, dressed in full battle armor, clankety-clank through this good-looking but ponderous retelling of the Arthurian legend. King Arthur, Lancelot, Merlin, Guinevere, and other inhabitants of Camelot—played solemnly by an unfamiliar cast—plod through scenes of chivalry, adultery, grisly slaughter on the battlefield, sorcery, and finally a bit of Holy Grailing. The film smacks of a medieval version of *Star Wars*, without the razzle-dazzle. Also with Helen Mirren, Nicholas Clay, and Cherie Lunghi. **Director**—John Boorman. (R) **Academy Award Nomination**—Alex Thomson, cinematography.
140 minutes

EXCUSE MY DUST (1951)
★★

Red Skelton
Sally Forrest

Skelton stars as an automobile inventor in this mild and pleasant musical comedy. Red is in love with a livery stable owner's daughter, played by Forrest. The old man gets upset when Red unwraps a horseless carriage. Some funny moments, but it's light-weight stuff. MacDonald Carey and William Demarest provide support. **Director**—Roy Rowland.
82 minutes

EXECUTIVE SUITE (1954)
★★★

Fredric March
William Holden
June Allyson
Barbara Stanwyck
Walter Pidgeon

In Executive Suite, *Fredric March is a company vice-president who wants to become president.*

• Exodus
• The Exorcist
• Exorcist II: The Heretic
• Experience Preferred . . .
  But Not Essential
• Experiment in Terror
• Exposed

E

Effective screen treatment of Cameron Hawley's book about wheeling and dealing in the boardroom of a big company. When the president dies, the vice-presidents vie for control, and tension mounts. The story also explores some domestic matters, but the thrust is on corporate power. A big-name cast delivers the goods. Also with Shelley Winters, Paul Douglas, Louis Calhern, Dean Jagger, and Nina Foch. **Director**—Robert Wise. **Academy Award Nominations**—Foch, best supporting actress; George Folsey, cinematography (black and white).

104 minutes b&w

EXODUS (1960)

 ★★★

Paul Newman
Eva Marie Saint
Ralph Richardson
Peter Lawford
Lee J. Cobb
Sal Mineo

This sprawling epic, based on Leon Uris's chronicle about the formation of the state of Israel, offers some exciting moments with the struggling settlers. However, the direction is often heavy-handed, with some wooden performances distracting from the flow. A shorter version might have worked better; after three hours it ends on a tiresome note. Yet it's a well-intended historical film. The cast also includes John Derek, Hugh Griffith, David Opatoshu, and Martin Milner. **Director**—Otto Preminger. **Academy Award Nominations**—Mineo, best supporting actor; Sam Leavitt, cinematography (color). *213 minutes*

THE EXORCIST (1973)

 ★★★★

Ellen Burstyn
Max Von Sydow
Jason Miller
Linda Blair

A highly commercial and extremely effective fright film, based on William Peter Blatty's best-selling novel, about a young girl possessed by demons. Director William Friedkin goes to extremes to keep you on the edge of your seat from beginning to end. The film's compelling aspects are derived from

In The Exorcist, *Linda Blair and Ellen Burstyn find that it's tough to get some sleep when you're possessed by a demon.*

sensational tricks as well as chilling suspense; it's a humdinger of a horror experience. Blair is good as the bedeviled child, and Miller is memorable as the priest who attempts to rid her of the evil spirits. Also with Lee J. Cobb, Kitty Winn, and Jack MacGowran. **Academy Award**—Blatty, best screenplay (based on material from another medium). **Nominations**—best picture; Friedkin, best director; Burstyn, best actress; Miller, best supporting actor; Blair, best supporting actress; Owen Roizman, cinematography. (R) *121 minutes*

EXORCIST II:
THE HERETIC (1977)

 ★★

Richard Burton
Linda Blair
Louise Fletcher

This overstuffed sequel isn't up to the scary effectiveness of the original. It's just so much warmed-over, supernatural mumbo jumbo inspired by the initial story. The angelic-faced Blair is now four years older and still bothered by a demon. Burton plays a priest assigned to wrestle with it. He seems very busy chasing the devil to all parts of the globe, but actually there's not much happening. Also stars Max Von Sydow, Kitty Winn, James Earl Jones, and Ned Beatty. **Director**—John Boorman. (R) *120 minutes*

EXPERIENCE PREFERRED...
BUT NOT ESSENTIAL (1983)

 ★★★

Elizabeth Edmonds

Charming, warm, and typically Brit-

ish comedy bubbling with various odd-ball characters. The centerpiece of this breezy concoction is innocent student Edmonds, who takes a summer job as waitress in a seaside hotel where she attempts to acquire some romantic experience. Director Peter Duffell skillfully coaxes fine ensemble acting from the competent cast, which also includes Sue Wallace and Ron Bain. (PG) *80 minutes*

EXPERIMENT IN TERROR
(1962)

 ★★★

Glenn Ford
Lee Remick
Ross Martin

Ford and Remick head the cast of this gripping thriller, effectively mounted against the background of San Francisco. Ford is convincing as an FBI agent fast on the trail of a criminal who terrorizes a bank teller, played by Remick, and kidnaps her sister as part of a robbery scheme. Martin is the villain; Stefanie Powers plays the sister. Lots of meticulous detail and suspense are used effectively by director Blake Edwards. Also with Ned Glass and Roy Poole. *123 minutes b&w*

EXPOSED (1983)

 ★★

Nastassia Kinski
Rudolf Nureyev
Harvey Keitel

(Continued)

Rudolf Nureyev sultrily suggests that he and Nastassja Kinski get Exposed.

E·F

- Eye for an Eye
- Eye of the Devil
- Eye of the Needle
- Eyes of a Stranger
- Eyes of Laura Mars
- Eyewitness
- A Face in the Crowd
- The Facts of Life

(Continued)
Kinski stars as a farm girl, college student, waitress, pianist, and high-fashion model in this unfocused political thriller. She eventually becomes tangled in an international terrorist plot as the upshot of a fleeting romance with a screwball violinist (Nureyev). The Russian ballet wiz's graceless mangling of his dialogue is unintentionally funny. **Director—** James Toback. (R) *99 minutes*

EYE FOR AN EYE (1981)

 ★★

Chuck Norris

Martial-arts champ Norris takes on scores of bad guys packing guns and knives in his quest for revenge on the killers of his pals. But even as chop-socky films go, this one is uninspired and rather subdued. The routine plot features Norris as a San Francisco cop on the trail of murderous drug peddlers. He single-handedly faces a platoon of foes and is challenged by an Oriental thug twice his size, but the outcome is predictable. **Director—** Steve Carver. (R) *106 minutes*

EYE OF THE DEVIL (1967)

★

David Niven
Deborah Kerr

Some top actors waste their time and talents with this dreary thriller about spooky events in a French castle. Niven plays a nobleman who suddenly leaves Paris to visit his family's ancestral home. The atmosphere is more sullen than suspenseful. Not worth the strain on anyone's eyes. Others in the cast include Flora Robson, Donald Pleasence, David Hemmings, and Sharon Tate. **Director—**J. Lee Thompson. *92 minutes b&w*

EYE OF THE NEEDLE (1981)

 ★★★

Donald Sutherland
Kate Nelligan

This absorbing, suspenseful World War II spy thriller, based on Ken Follett's popular novel, combines a

Donald Sutherland and Kate Nelligan enjoy a seaside stroll in Eye of the Needle.

balanced working of romance and intrigue in war-torn England. Sutherland plays a master Nazi spy, who strives to smuggle out secrets of the impending Allied invasion of Europe. But he's thwarted in a breathtaking climax by beautiful Nelligan, who plays the wife of a crippled British pilot. Nelligan gives extraordinary warmth, intelligence, and excitement to her part. **Director—**Richard Marquand. (R) *111 minutes*

EYES OF A STRANGER (1981)

(no stars)

Lauren Tewes

A shabby horror film about a madman who rapes and murders young women, and sometimes carves up their boyfriends. The assembly-line brutality is tiresome and offensive. The story is loaded with trumped-up situations, clichés, and red herrings. Tewes of TV's *Love Boat* plays a Nancy Drew-type TV news hen who chases the killer. We've seen it all before. **Director—** Ken Wiederhorn. (R) *85 minutes*

EYES OF LAURA MARS (1978)

 ★★★

Faye Dunaway
Tommy Lee Jones

The world of chic fashion photography is the setting for this classy whodunit. There are suspects galore to keep the audience guessing right up to the moment of the clever ending. Dunaway, in the title role, puts it all together as the trendy photographer who has horrifying premonitions of murder. Director Irvin Kershner's even-handed direction, effective eerie backdrops,

and superb casting also contribute to this sharp-edged thriller. Also with Brad Dourif. (R) *103 minutes*

EYEWITNESS (1981)

 ★★

William Hurt
Sigourney Weaver

Director Peter Yates and writer Steve Tesich, conceivers of the hit *Breaking Away*, collaborate again with this romantic mystery. But this time, their effort is flawed by a farfetched plot that's loaded with red herrings. Yet there are charming performances by Hurt and Weaver. Hurt portrays a soft-spoken janitor who discovers a murder victim and woos the beautiful, sophisticated TV reporter covering the crime story; Weaver plays the reporter. Also with Christopher Plummer, James Woods, Irene Worth, and Steven Hill. (R) *102 minutes*

F

A FACE IN THE CROWD (1957)

★★★★

Andy Griffith
Lee Remick
Walter Matthau
Patricia Neal

Griffith is outstanding as a small-town yokel who becomes a celebrated TV wit after a manipulating reporter, played by Neal, discovers him and promotes his career. Budd Schulberg's script is on target in its perception of the entertainment business. Griffith's convincing performance and fine supporting work adds dimension to the fascinating melodrama. Also with Anthony Franciosa, Percy Waram, and Marshall Neilan. **Director—**Elia Kazan. *126 minutes b&w*

THE FACTS OF LIFE (1960)

★★★

Bob Hope
Lucille Ball

Hope and Ball team up in this romantic comedy; the result is lots of good laughs. The two comic pros play

• Fade to Black
• Fahrenheit 451
• Fail-Safe
• The Fallen Idol
• Falling in Love
• Falling in Love Again
• Fame

F

Bob Hope discovers The Facts of Life *in this romantic comedy.*

middle-aged suburbanites who have a brief extramarital fling. It's an effective poke at American middle-class values, done with finesse and only a small amount of slapstick. Hope and Ball are supported expertly by Ruth Hussey, Don Defore, Louis Nye, and Philip Ober. **Director**—Melvin Frank. **Academy Award Nominations**—Norman Panama and Frank, best story and screenplay (written directly for the screen); Charles B. Lang, Jr., cinematography (black and white).

103 minutes b&w

FADE TO BLACK (1980)
 ★★

Dennis Christopher

Christopher, the young biker in *Breaking Away*, plays a weird young man whose obsession with movies leads him to a spree of killings. He dresses up as Dracula, Hopalong Cassidy, and other movie immortals to carry out his revenge on various enemies. He most often imagines himself to be James Cagney playing Cody Jarrett in *White Heat*. But unlike such classics, this film is uneven, with mediocre acting. It's touted as a thriller but is more often silly than scary. **Director**—Vernon Zimmerman. (R)   *100 minutes*

FAHRENHEIT 451 (1966)
★★★★

Oscar Werner
Julie Christie

Sci-fi drama from the Ray Bradbury novel about a future civilization that bans the written word, burns all books, and punishes readers. A curiously touching and visually haunting masterpiece (lushly photographed by Nicolas Roeg) with an excellent musical score by Bernard Hermann. Werner and Christie are the lovers who attempt to preserve a part of history by memorizing whole novels. In a dual role, Christie also plays the stupid wife who collaborates with the authorities. A final scene of a recitation of David Copperfield in a snow-covered woods will linger in the viewer's mind for a long time. **Director**—François Truffaut.   *112 minutes*

FAIL-SAFE (1964)
 ★★★★

Henry Fonda
Walter Matthau
Dan O'Herlihy

An earnest and sober drama about the impending horrors and terrible decisions to be made after an American bomber is accidentally ordered to drop atomic bombs on Moscow. The theme is similar to the black comedy *Dr. Strangelove*, but here the point is made with gripping seriousness. First-rate performances all around. Also with Frank Overton, Fritz Weaver, Edward Binns, and Larry Hagman. **Director**—Sidney Lumet.   *111 minutes b&w*

THE FALLEN IDOL (1949)
 ★★★★

Ralph Richardson
Michele Morgan
Bobby Henrey

Graham Greene's short story is turned into a terse and stylish film that works on many levels. The plot involves a young ambassador's son who respects the family butler. When the servant's bitchy wife dies accidentally, the boy innocently focuses suspicion on his friend. The film offers an intelligent view of human emotions, with professional acting and efficient direction helping to make the point. The fine cast also includes Sonia Dresdel and Jack Hawkins. **Director**—Carol Reed. **Academy Award Nominations**—Reed, best director; Greene, writing (screenplay).   *94 minutes b&w*

FALLING IN LOVE (1984)
★★

Robert De Niro
Meryl Streep

Despite the powerhouse talent of De Niro and Streep, this thin, sudsy romance offers meager passion, drama, or star chemistry. They portray married suburbanites who strike up a love relationship on a commuter train and then agonize over continued temptations. The film, which bears resemblance to *Brief Encounter*, primarily serves as a showcase for the two superstars. **Director**—Ulu Grosbard. (PG-13)   *106 minutes*

FALLING IN LOVE AGAIN (1980)
★★

Elliott Gould
Susannah York
Kaye Ballard

Steven Paul—producer, writer, and director—completed this amateurish romantic comedy when he was 22. It's about a middle-aged Californian who grew up in the Bronx in the '40s and longingly returns there for a brief stroll down memory lane. Characters are warm and sympathetic, yet the corny screenplay is predictable. A noble first try for young Paul. Still, the outcome is unsatisfying. (PG)   *103 minutes*

FAME (1980)
★★★

Eddie Barth
Irene Cara
Gene Anthony Ray

An extraordinary film about students at New York's High School of the Performing Arts. Structured in semidocumentary vignettes, the film virtually overflows with joy, emotion, comedy, energy, and inspiration as it follows the budding performers from initial auditions to graduation. The cast is mostly young unknowns who display incredible talent. Director Alan Parker (*Midnight Express*) deserves credit for the film's amazing charm and zest.
(Continued)

(Continued)
(R) **Academy Award Nomination**—Christopher Gore, best screenplay (written directly for the screen).

133 minutes

FAMILY PLOT (1976)
 ★

**Karen Black
Bruce Dern**

Bruce Dern tries to puzzle out the Family Plot.

Director Alfred Hitchcock is still at it with this suspense-comedy about two pairs of con artists who get involved over a family fortune. It's the old master's 56th film. Unfortunately, it's out of character with his great features of yore. A complicated and shallow screenplay by Ernest Lehman fails to produce the expected degree of tension, although there are several moments of fun and interest. Also with Barbara Harris, William Devane, Cathleen Nesbitt, and Ed Lauter. (PG)

120 minutes

THE FAN (1981)
 ★★

**Lauren Bacall
James Garner**

Solid, brilliant acting by Bacall is the only high point of this routine suspense-thriller. As a Broadway star who is terrorized by an embittered fan, Bacall enlivens the part with the style and energy that marked her career opposite Humphrey Bogart. The story

Lauren Bacall signs an autograph for The Fan.

is a notch above the usual horror fare, but much appeal is frittered away by awkward handling of the psychotic young man whose adoration and rejection turns to murder. Garner is wasted in a secondary role. **Director**—Edward Bianchi. (R)   *95 minutes*

FANCY PANTS (1950)
★★★

**Bob Hope
Lucille Ball**

None other than Hope is all dressed up and posing as a butler to bring proper manners to a frontier town. With Ball on board, fun and laughs galore are

Lucille Ball and Bob Hope in Fancy Pants.

guaranteed in this remake of *Ruggles of Red Gap*. There are a few slow moments now and then, but the stars trod on in one of their better vehicles. Bruce Cabot, Eric Blore, and Jack Kirkwood help with supporting roles. **Director**—George Marshall.   *92 minutes*

FANNY (1961)
 ★★★

**Charles Boyer
Maurice Chevalier
Leslie Caron**

This standard version of three Marcel Pagnol films, about a girl in Marseilles involved with a sailor, is effectively carried along by the charm of a marvelous cast and beautiful photography. Boyer and Chevalier give colorful performances, and they are aided by the beautiful Caron. The songs from the Broadway musical version are used here only as background music. Also with Horst Buchholz, Georgette Anys, and Lionel Jeffries. **Director**—Joshua Logan. **Academy Award Nominations**—best picture; Boyer, best actor; Jack Cardiff, cinematography (color).   *133 minutes*

FANTASIA (1940)
★★★★

A rare, innovative animated feature

from Walt Disney that combines classical music with cartoons. The music of Bach, Tchaikovsky, Stravinsky, Beethoven, Moussorgsky, and other masters is presented under the direction of Leopold Stokowski and the Philadelphia Orchestra. The cartoon interpretations are especially inspiring. And this brilliant production serves as a wonderful introduction—especially for children—to the world of great classical music. **Supervisor**—Ben Sharpsteen. **Academy Awards**—special awards to Walt Disney, William Garity, John N. A. Hawkins, Leopold Stokowski, and RCA. (G)

135 minutes

FANTASTIC VOYAGE
(1966)
★★★

**Stephen Boyd
Raquel Welch
Edmond O'Brien
Donald Pleasence**

Here's a truly unusual science-fiction feature that's entertaining and informative. A scientist needs delicate brain surgery after an assassination attempt, so a medical team is shrunk to the size of bacteria and enters his bloodstream to perform the vital work. The photography, special effects, and animation are of the first order, and the action and suspense never let up. It's a fantastic trip, indeed. Also with Arthur Kennedy, Arthur O'Connell, and William Redfield. **Director**—Richard Fleischer.

100 minutes

THE FAR COUNTRY
(1955)
★★★

**James Stewart
Walter Brennan**

Cattleman Stewart, looking tall in the saddle and stoic, drives his herd to Alaska and finds trouble along the way. It's a solid adventure story, set handsomely against the Alaskan outback. Stewart is reliably effective, and there's an excellent supporting part by Brennan. Also with Ruth Roman, Jay C. Flippen, Corinne Calvet, and Harry Morgan. **Director**—Anthony Mann.

97 minutes

JACK LEMMON

Jack Lemmon, who was born in Boston in 1925, was educated at Harvard, where he was active in dramatics. After graduating in 1946, Lemmon served in the U.S. Navy as an officer aboard an aircraft carrier.

After military service, Lemmon worked in New York at odd jobs, such as a food checker in a restaurant, while waiting for a show-business opening. He finally got one as master of ceremonies at the Old Knick Music Hall, a converted movie house. Lemmon also worked in radio; he had running parts in several soap operas, including The Brighter Day *and*

Road to Life. *He soon found himself working steadily in television, and gave about 500 television performances, almost all of them live, on such shows as* Studio One, Robert Montgomery Presents, Suspense, *and* Playhouse 90.

In 1953, Lemmon made his Broadway debut in Room Service. *He started his screen career soon afterward in a pair of Judy Holliday movies,* It Should Happen to You *(1953) and* Phffft! *(1954). After making only five movies, Lemmon won an Academy Award, receiving an Oscar for best supporting actor for his portrayal of Ensign Pulver in John Ford's* Mr. Roberts *(1955). He won another Oscar, as best actor, for* Save the Tiger *(1973).*

Lemmon has also received six other nominations—all for best actor—during his career.

Some of Lemmon's other movies include Some Like It Hot *(1959),* The Apartment *(1960),* Irma La Douce *(1963),* The Great Race *(1965),* The Odd Couple *(1968),* The Entertainer *(1975),* The China Syndrome *(1979),* Tribute *(1980),* Buddy Buddy *(1981),* Missing *(1982), and* Mass Appeal *(1984).*

FAREWELL, MY LOVELY (1944)
★★★★

**Dick Powell
Claire Trevor**

Private eye Dick Powell searches for the color of Claire Trevor's eyes in Farewell, My Lovely.

A stylish, engrossing film based on Raymond Chandler's private-eye yarn. Powell is excellent as Philip Marlowe, the battered gumshoe, on the trail of a gangster's girl friend. And director Edward Dmytryk effectively brings out the rundown, moody atmosphere of a decaying big city. It's a remarkable *film noir* that sets the pace for more to come. Also with Anne Shirley, Mike Mazurki, and Otto Kruger. **Alternate Title**—*Murder, My Sweet.*

95 minutes b&w

FAREWELL, MY LOVELY (1975)
★★

**Robert Mitchum
Charlotte Rampling**

This remake of *Murder, My Sweet* portrays the efforts of detective Philip Marlowe, played by Mitchum, to find the lost love of an ex-con. The search involves a maze of multiple murders, blackmail, larceny, and prostitution. But the film, in an effort to link the

(Continued)

F

- A Farewell to Arms
- Far from the Madding Crowd
- The Farmer's Daughter
- Fast Break
- Fast Times at Ridgemont High
- Fat City

(Continued)
1940s with contemporary life-styles, spoils the hard-boiled character Chandler created so well, and thus deadens the spirit of the story. Rampling is an ersatz Lauren Bacall; Jack O'Halloran plays the ex-con. Also with John Ireland and Sylvia Miles. **Director**—Dick Richards. (R) **Academy Award Nomination**—Miles, best supporting actress. *97 minutes*

A FAREWELL TO ARMS (1932)
★★★

**Gary Cooper
Helen Hayes**

Frightened soldiers wait in terror for the bomb with their name on it in A Farewell to Arms.

Wounded American ambulance driver Cooper falls in love with nurse Hayes in a romantic adaptation of the Ernest Hemingway novel. Although the book was more vivid and realistic, the screen version is salvaged by Hayes's brilliant performance in one of her few film efforts. Under Frank Borzage's direction (and with cuts by the censors), the ill-fated love affair is a victim of the grim and brooding war scenes. Also with Adolphe Menjou. **Academy Award**—Charles Bryant Lang, Jr., best cinematography. **Nomination**—best picture. *78 minutes b&w*

FAR FROM THE MADDING CROWD (1967)
★★

**Julie Christie
Peter Finch
Alan Bates
Terence Stamp**

An overlong and somewhat plodding screen treatment of Thomas Hardy's

novel about a beautiful English farm girl who affects the lives of three men. Christie is out of step as the headstrong beauty, although Finch and Bates perform well as objects of her desire. However, the film boasts exceptional production values with exquisite photography and a stirring score. Also with Prunella Ransome. **Director**—John Schlesinger. (PG) *169 minutes*

THE FARMER'S DAUGHTER (1947)
★★★★

**Loretta Young
Joseph Cotten**

Joseph Cotten looks at Loretta Young and thinks about an old joke in The Farmer's Daughter.

A smartly made comedy-drama about a willful servant girl, played by Young, who runs for the congressional seat occupied by her boss. It's an effective treatment of the Cinderella theme, with a top cast providing excellent performances at every turn. Also with Ethel Barrymore, Charles Bickford, and Harry Davenport. **Director**—H. C. Potter. **Academy Award**—Young, best actress. **Nomination**—Bickford, best supporting actor.
97 minutes b&w

FAST BREAK (1979)
★★

Gabriel Kaplan

Kaplan of television's *Welcome Back, Kotter* series stars in his first feature film, which looks more like a TV sitcom. He plays a basketball coach at an

obscure Nevada college, who puts together a winning team comprised of misfits recruited from New York City streets. Kaplan's role isn't far removed from his familiar TV character. Sandor Stern's screenplay clips cheerfully along right up to the predictable ending. Also with Howard Sylvester and Mike Warren. **Director**—Jack Smight. (PG) *107 minutes*

FAST TIMES AT RIDGEMONT HIGH (1982)
★★

**Sean Penn
Jennifer Jason Leigh
Phoebe Cates**

Jennifer Jason Leigh and Phoebe Cates discuss the hunk update in Fast Times at Ridgemont High.

An untidy account of teenage life based on the observations of a young writer who posed as a high school student. Sex, drugs, rock'n'roll, and holding down their part-time jobs are foremost on the minds of these youngsters. The patchy film is warm and appealing in spots, but fails to be ultimately compelling. The production, however, introduces some fresh and likeable new performers. **Director**—Amy Heckerling. (R) *92 minutes*

FAT CITY (1972)
★★★

**Stacy Keach
Jeff Bridges
Susan Tyrell**

Keach brilliantly portrays an over-the-hill boxer trying to get back on his feet in this touching film adapted from Leonard Gardner's novel. The setting is a small California town, and the story incisively explores the frustrations and heartbreaks of poor people. Fine supporting work by Bridges and

Tyrell builds interest in the characters. John Huston's direction is on target, and it's among his best efforts. Also with Candy Clark and Nicholas Colasanto. (PG) **Academy Award Nomination**—Tyrell, best supporting actress. *96 minutes*

FATHER GOOSE (1964)

★★★

Cary Grant
Leslie Caron
Trevor Howard

This ordinary half-baked farce is salvaged mainly because of the special charms of Grant, who stars as a South Seas beach bum during World War II. Cary's part-time mission is to spot aircraft for the Australian navy, but then a beautiful French schoolteacher (Caron) and her pupils arrive, and the fun begins. **Director**—Ralph Nelson. **Academy Award**—S. H. Barnett (story), Peter Stone and Frank Tarloff (screenplay), best story and screenplay (written directly for the screen). *115 minutes*

FATHER OF THE BRIDE (1950)
★★★★

Spencer Tracy
Joan Bennett
Elizabeth Taylor

A fantastic middle-class comedy, graced with a champagne cast and a witty script. Tracy is in top form as the happy but frustrated father faced with organizing and financing his daughter's wedding. And the bride is none other than Taylor at her loveliest. Also

Spencer Tracy and Joan Bennett are among the stars in the lighthearted Father of the Bride.

with Don Taylor, Billie Burke, Leo G. Carroll, and Russ Tamblyn. **Director**—Vincente Minnelli. **Academy Award Nominations**—best picture; Tracy, best actor; Frances Goodrich and Albert Hackett, writing (screenplay). *93 minutes b&w*

FATSO (1980)
★

Dom DeLuise
Anne Bancroft

This flabby satire, about a fat man who struggles in vain to stop eating, may make you hungry, but there's not enough comic nourishment for honest entertainment. DeLuise is often funny and appealing as the overweight protagonist. Yet he cannot overcome the

Anne Bancroft cannot convince Dom DeLuise to stop eating in Fatso.

thin script by Bancroft, who debuts as writer and director. She fails to maintain the proper balance between humor and pathos. (PG) *94 minutes*

JOHN WAYNE

John Wayne's fabulous screen exploits and long film career began with his first leading role, in Raoul Walsh's The Big Trail (1930). From that time on, the rugged popular star invariably rang a happy tune at theater box offices around the world.

Known to his friends and fellow workers as Duke, Wayne was born Marion Michael Morrison in Winterset, Iowa, in 1907. His father's illness forced the family to move to California. After recovering his health, his father, a pharmacist, opened a drugstore in Glendale.

Wayne graduated from Glendale High School, where he was a football star and a talented debater. He received a scholarship to the University of Southern California, where he played on the championship football team.

His entry into motion pictures was completely unplanned. During summer vacations he worked as a property man at what was then the Fox Film Corporation. He became

acquainted with director John Ford, who was impressed with the young man and prodded him into taking a small role in Hangman's House (1928). After this minor debut, Wayne went back to props.

Director Raoul Walsh took Wayne out of the property department permanently by giving him his new name and entrusting him with the leading role in The Big Trail (1930). In the '30s, Wayne starred in about 100 westerns. In fact, he became the screen's first singing cowboy in a series of westerns, even though he couldn't carry a tune.

In 1939, Wayne's role of the Ringo Kid in Ford's Stagecoach finally let him achieve stardom.

During the next three decades, Wayne starred in numerous movies, including The Long Voyage Home (1940), Seven Sinners (1940), Red River (1948), She Wore a Yellow Ribbon (1949), Sands of Iwo Jima (1949), The Quiet Man (1952), The High and the Mighty (1954), The Searchers (1956), Rio Bravo (1959), The Alamo (1960), McLintock! (1963), In Harm's Way (1965), El Dorado (1967), and True Grit (1969), for which he finally received the Academy Award after appearing in hundreds of films.

Before his death in 1979, Wayne made another 10 films, including Rio Lobo (1970), The Cowboys (1972), Cahill (1973), Rooster Cogburn (1975), and The Shootist (1976).

F

- Fedora
- Fellini's Casanova
- Femmes Fatales
- Ffolkes
- F for Fake
- Fiddler on the Roof
- The Fiendish Plot of Dr. Fu Manchu
- The 5th Musketeer

FEDORA (1979)

William Holden
Marthe Keller

Director Billy Wilder's romantic melodrama is about a Garbo-like screen goddess, played by Keller, who retires at the height of her fame and beauty to live in seclusion on a remote Greek island with her "secret." The film is reminiscent of the director's 1950 success, *Sunset Boulevard*. Even Holden stars again to narrate the tragic tale in the same ironic tone. Wilder's satiric observations and comic touches can still be entertaining, but they've lost their bite over the years. Also with Hildegarde Knef, José Ferrer, Frances Sternhagen, Henry Fonda, and Michael York. (PG) *114 minutes*

FELLINI'S CASANOVA (1977)

Donald Sutherland
Tina Aumont
Cicely Browne

Director Federico Fellini's 2½-hour epic about the fabled 18th-century Venetian is a ponderous essay that reflects the director's own alienation from his subject. The film is strung together with repetitive and joyless scenes of a man who makes love like a robot. An eyepopping production design adds a measure of dazzle to this otherwise chilly spectacle. Sutherland, his face grotesquely rearranged, has the title role. Also with John Karlsen. (R) *158 minutes*

FEMMES FATALES (1977)

Jean-Pierre Marielle
Jean Rochefort

Clumsy and callous French satire about a gynecologist and a pimp who unsuccessfully try to escape from women. There are a few funny moments and interesting scenes before the film disintegrates. Bertrand Blier's direction is stiff, but the story is partially shored up by decent acting from Marielle and Rochefort in the lead roles. Marielle plays the doctor, and Rochefort plays the pimp. In French with English titles. (No MPAA rating) *81 minutes b&w*

FFOLKES (1980)

Roger Moore
James Mason
Anthony Perkins

Hijackers threaten to blow up a North Sea oil-drilling rig and a billion-dollar production platform. Moore, as an eccentric underwater commando, outsmarts the terrorists and saves the British empire from untold humiliation; he's delightful as an adventurer who loves cats and distrusts women. He undertakes his daring assignment with unblinking cockiness. Suspense is relentless as the hours tick off toward the impending disaster. Mason and Perkins are credible in supporting roles. Also with Michael Parks and Jeremy Clyde. **Director**—Andrew V. McLaglen. (PG) *99 minutes*

F FOR FAKE (1977)

Director Orson Welles conducts a playful and cynical tour of the world of fakery, forgery, and imposters in this semidocumentary that may itself be a put-on. Master of ceremonies Welles concentrates on the deceptions of literary forger Clifford Irving and art forger Elmyr de Hory. Welles suggests that the signature on a piece of art isn't as important as the work itself. The film is engrossing and clever. (No MPAA rating) *85 minutes*

FIDDLER ON THE ROOF (1971)

Topol
Norma Crane
Leonard Frey
Molly Picon

A worthy screen version of the long-running Broadway musical, with the rousing songs intact. Topol plays Tevye, the Jewish dairyman in the small Russian village who deals with family problems and the strain of persecution by the authorities. He's not quite as good as Zero Mostel, but he's convincing, and his "If I Were a Rich Man" song comes off quite well. Also with Paul Mann, Rosalind Harris, and Michele Marsh. The rooftop fiddling is by Isaac Stern. **Director**—Norman Jewison. (G) **Academy Award**—Oswald Morris, cinematography. **Nominations**—best picture; Jewison, best director; Frey, best supporting actor. *180 minutes*

THE FIENDISH PLOT OF DR. FU MANCHU (1980)

Peter Sellers

The last film starring the late great Sellers is a weak and disappointing attempt at comedy. It's obviously not the fault of the beloved comedian, who once more plays multiple roles with his usual versatile skill. *The Fiendish Plot* has a flat, no-laugh plot that concerns the efforts of master-criminal Dr. Fu Manchu to steal one of England's crown jewels. The direction and script aren't up to par for one of the movie industry's most prolific comic talents. **Director**—Piers Haggard. (PG) *100 minutes*

THE 5TH MUSKETEER (1979)

Beau Bridges
Sylvia Kristel
Ursula Andress

Ursula Andress tempts Beau Bridges in The 5th Musketeer.

Here's another remake of Alexandre Dumas's *The Man in the Iron Mask*. This lavish costume drama offers flashing swordplay and an international cast, but there's a lack of suspense, a lifeless

• Fighter Squadron • Fighting Mad • The Fighting 69th
• Fighting Back • The Fighting O'Flynn • Final Chapter—Walking
• The Fighting Kentuckian • The Fighting Seabees Tall

F

plot, and absurd dialogue. Beau Bridges doubles as Louis XIV and his twin brother, Philippe, who struggle for the crown of France. Andress, as Louis's mistress, is often in a state of semi-undress when decked out in low-cut dresses. The diverting title is an apparent attempt to benefit from Richard Lester's stylish Musketeer series. Also with Cornel Wilde, Ian McShane, Lloyd Bridges, Alan Hale, Jr., and José Ferrer. **Director**—Ken Annakin. (PG)
103 minutes

FIGHTER SQUADRON (1948)
★★

Edmond O'Brien
Robert Stack

Standard World War II action story with some good air combat sequences. O'Brien plays a gung ho pilot who takes unusual risks. The script is loaded with clichés. Also with John Rodney, Henry Hull, Walter Reed, and Rock Hudson (in his first film). **Director**—Raoul Walsh. *96 minutes*

FIGHTING BACK (1982)
 ★★

Tom Skerritt
Michael Sarrazin
Patti LuPone

Another look at vigilante justice that delves briefly into the social aspects of the situation but winds up being just as preposterous as *Death Wish*. The brisk story offers some thought-provoking ideas, but too much of the film is devoted to intense, violent confrontations. Skerritt stars as a hot-headed Philadelphia store owner who organizes a citizen's anticrime patrol after members of his family are brutalized by local thugs. **Director**—Lewis Teague. (R) *98 minutes*

THE FIGHTING KENTUCKIAN (1949)
 ★

John Wayne
Vera Ralston

A frontiersman battles bad guys planning to steal land from French settlers in Kentucky during the early 19th cen-

tury. In the process he courts a French general's daughter. A typical western vehicle for Wayne with plenty of action and little else. The story line is minimal and predictably banal. Also with Oliver Hardy in an unusual role without Laurel. **Director**—George Waggner. *100 minutes b&w*

FIGHTING MAD (1976)
★★★

Peter Fonda

Peter Fonda becomes Fighting Mad *when a strip-mining enterprise threatens his farm.*

The formula vengeance plot, which served *Death Wish* and *Walking Tall*, is effectively used in this action drama set in rural Arkansas. Fonda plays a young man who returns to the family ranch and wages a one-man battle against crooked strip-mining interests. The script is filled with holes large enough to drive a bulldozer through. But there's plenty of emotion and nonstop violent action to satisfy audiences who relish such fare. Also with Lynn Lowry, John Doucette, and Philip Carey. Written and directed by Jonathan Demme. (R) *90 minutes*

THE FIGHTING O'FLYNN (1949)
★★

Douglas Fairbanks, Jr.
Helena Carter

Fairbanks plays the title role with robust energy. He's a poor Irish swashbuckler who interferes with Napo-

leon's invasion scheme. But all in all, it's a low-level adventure, with the rest of the cast not up to Fairbanks's high spirits. The film is based on Justin McCarthy's novel. Also with Richard Greene, Patricia Medina, and Arthur Shields. **Director**—Arthur Pierson. *94 minutes b&w*

THE FIGHTING SEABEES (1944)
 ★★★

John Wayne
Susan Hayward
Dennis O'Keefe

Wayne is involved with the Navy's construction battalion, busy repairing installations and fighting the Japanese during World War II. There's plenty of action for Wayne fans, with a romantic subplot occasionally breaking the pace. The good cast also includes William Frawley, Duncan Renaldo, and Addison Richards. **Director**—Edward Ludwig. *100 minutes b&w*

THE FIGHTING 69TH (1940)
★★★

James Cagney
Pat O'Brien

A schmaltzy World War I film, with Cagney hamming it up as a tough Irish trooper who becomes a hero. The tale packs plenty of spirit, some rough-and-tumble comedy, ripsnorting battle scenes, and corny sentiment. It's pure Hollywood-style entertainment. Also with George Brent, Jeffrey Lynn, Alan Hale, and Dennis Morgan. **Director**—William Keighley. *90 minutes b&w*

FINAL CHAPTER—WALKING TALL (1977)
★★

Bo Svenson

Svenson continues with his impressive job as a heroic Tennessee sheriff in this third screen installment on the life of Buford Pusser. This chapter covers crusading sheriff Pusser's success in selling his life's story to a Hollywood producer and his efforts to wipe out a gambling joint owned by the
(Continued)

F

- **The Final Conflict**
- **The Final Countdown**
- **The Final Option**
- **Finders Keepers**
- **Fingers**
- **Finian's Rainbow**
- **Fire and Ice**

(Continued)
local crime boss. As usual, the violence is overdone, but the movie delivers for Pusser fans. Also with Margaret Blye, Forrest Tucker, and Lurene Tuttle. **Director**—Jack Starrett. (R)   *112 minutes*

THE FINAL CONFLICT (1981)
 ★★

Sam Neill

Sam Neill is the Antichrist (and a member of the National Security Council) in The Final Conflict.

Neill plays Damien, the Devil, in this third installment of the *Omen* series. This time, Damien is head of an international conglomerate; he attempts to track down Jesus Christ, who he believes has been reborn. There are the standard violent gore sequences and more of the preposterous horror plot that's rather shopworn by now. This film concludes the trilogy; apparently, Hollywood has decided to give the Devil a rest and the rest of us a break from such nonsense. **Director**— Graham Baker. (R)   *100 minutes*

THE FINAL COUNTDOWN (1980)
 ★★

Kirk Douglas
Martin Sheen
Katharine Ross
James Farentino

The USS *Nimitz*, the nuclear-powered aircraft carrier, is thrown back in time and confronts the fateful Japanese attack on Pearl Harbor. This plot idea generates rousing drama and excitement—for a few minutes. Not even the excellent cast can disguise the fact that this is a half-hour *Twilight Zone* plot posing as a feature film. The technical details are authentic, and Douglas is outstanding as the skipper of the *Nimitz*, but the enterprise as a whole sinks nonetheless. **Director**—Don Taylor. (PG)   *103 minutes*

THE FINAL OPTION (1983)
 ★★

Judy Davis

Gungho shoot-'em-up drama about British commandos who rescue American embassy officials from mad-bomber leftist terrorists. A political message, decrying radical elements of the peace movement, underlies this rickety film, which is short on credibility. The acting isn't any better than the trumped-up material. Davis is a machine-gun-toting terrorist and Lewis Collins is the suave military officer who infiltrates her group. **Director**—Ian Sharp. (R)   *125 minutes*

FINDERS KEEPERS (1984)
 ★★★

Michael O'Keefe
Beverly D'Angelo

This uneven, madcap farce about the pursuit of a stolen $5 million in cash begins sluggishly but builds a fair head of steam toward the end. Much action takes place aboard a transcontinental train headed for New York with an assortment of oddball characters staking claim to the loot. Some gags misfire, but more often they find their mark. O'Keefe plays an erstwhile roller skating team manager. D'Angelo is funny as the dizziest of blondes. **Director**—Richard Lester. (R)

92 minutes

FINGERS (1978)
 ★

Harvey Keitel
Jim Brown

Keitel dominates this strange and con-fusing melodrama, about an aspiring concert pianist who becomes caught up in gangland violence. Keitel is hardly up to the task and gives a performance that displays a lack of insight. The pointless screenplay by writer-director James Toback doesn't develop any characters worth caring about. Only the gritty New York City background elicits interest. Also with Tisa Farrow and Michael V. Gazzo. (R)   *91 minutes*

FINIAN'S RAINBOW (1968)
 ★★★

Fred Astaire
Petula Clark

Uneven and overdone film version of the Broadway musical, which combines social statements with Irish fantasy. The pacing and dialogue seem out of kilter, yet this colorful production still offers plenty of entertainment with the memorable music and the great talents of Astaire in a key role. Also with Tommy Steele, Keenan Wynn, Barbara Hancock, Al Freeman, Jr., and Don Francks. **Director**— Francis Ford Coppola.   *145 minutes*

FIRE AND ICE
(1983)
 ★★

A sword-and-sorcery animated feature, directed by Ralph Bakshi in the

Darkwolf in Fire and Ice, *an animated sword-and-sorcery epic.*

same style as his version of *Lord of the Rings*. The film dwells too much on violent, sinister situations, and is populated with stock heroes, villains, and fearsome monsters. A ho-hum struggle between good and evil characters takes place among glaciers, steamy swamps, and belching volcanoes. Fantasy artist Frank Frazetta contributes his skills to the production. (PG)   *81 minutes*

FIREFOX (1982)

★★★

**Clint Eastwood
Freddie Jones
David Huffman**

Clint Eastwood pilots a stolen Soviet super-jet in Firefox.

James Bond apparently went off on a working vacation so Hollywood called in stone-faced Eastwood for this high-flying spy adventure involving the abduction of a secret Russian super plane. Eastwood portrays a Vietnam veteran ace pilot who sneaks into the Soviet Union on this "mission impossible." There are some holes in the overlong screenplay, but Eastwood makes it work. And he gets plenty of help from the stunning special effects, which include a knockout aerial chase sequence. **Director**—Eastwood. (PG)   *136 minutes*

FIREPOWER (1979)

★

**Sophia Loren
James Coburn
O. J. Simpson**

Producer-director Michael Winner put

together this action-adventure with a heavy dose of explosions, fires, and shootings. All the hubbub seems to be about the tracking down of a Howard Hughes-type tycoon who is hiding out in the Caribbean. The violent episodes drown out the plot, and the film lapses into tiresome confusion. Also with Eli Wallach, Anthony Franciosa, and George Grizzard. (R)   *104 minutes*

FIRESTARTER (1984)

★★★

Drew Barrymore

The telekinesis theme perhaps has been overdone by Hollywood. But this version, based on a Stephen King novel, is deliciously campy and moves briskly with the proper mixture of suspense and special effects. Drew Barrymore (*E.T.*) is excellent as a charming 8-year-old who turns the bad guys into flaming shish kebab by thinking mean thoughts. David Keith, George C. Scott, Martin Sheen, Art Carney, and Louise Fletcher are delightful in supporting roles. **Director**—Mark Lester. (R)   *116 minutes*

FIRST BLOOD (1982)

★★

**Sylvester Stallone
Richard Crenna**

Sylvester Stallone is a one-man war machine in First Blood.

Stallone stars as a brooding, ex-Green Beret soldier provoked by hick-town

redneck police into fighting a grueling guerilla war. Plenty of shoot-'em-up macho action propels the film along. But the formula, one-man-against-the-world screenplay is hardly impressive or original. Stallone's physical presence dominates the proceedings, but he's given little opportunity to act. **Director**—Ted Kotcheff. (R)   *97 minutes*

FIRST BORN (1984)

★★★

**Teri Garr
Peter Weller
Christopher Collet**

A compelling domestic drama that features a teenage boy as a heroic, responsible person. Collet is the young son who rescues his divorced mother (Garr) from a disastrous relationship with her scoundrel boyfriend (Weller). Adult shortcomings are viewed through the eyes of the perceptive youngster who rises to the occasion with exceptional maturity and courage. Crisp direction and solid performances all around contribute to this first-class topical thriller. **Director**—Michael Apted. (PG–13)   *104 minutes*

THE FIRST DEADLY SIN (1980)
★

**Frank Sinatra
Faye Dunaway**

Frank Sinatra and Faye Dunaway make a cute couple in The First Deadly Sin.

Sinatra, ending a long pause from theatrical films, plays his familiar detective role in this dull and disappointing outing. Sinatra departs somewhat from his tough *Tony Rome*
(Continued)

 Movie is available in Beta and VHS videotape

F

- First Family
- First Monday in October
- The First Nudie Musical
- The Fish That Saved Pittsburgh
- F.I.S.T.
- Fitzcarraldo
- Five Card Stud

(Continued)

character to portray a mellow, close-to-retired cop—a role appropriate to his current age. Dunaway is wasted as Sinatra's dying wife. He entertains her by reading a children's book at her bedside, but she keeps falling asleep—so might the audience. **Director**—Brian Hutton. (R)   *112 minutes*

FIRST FAMILY (1981)
★★

**Bob Newhart
Gilda Radner
Harvey Korman**

What we need is some comic relief from politics, but this satire about an American Presidential administration doesn't fill the bill. Director Buck Henry's screenplay has a few hilarious moments, yet most of the gags fall flat, and some are in poor taste. Newhart plays the frustrated President, who cultivates diplomatic relations with a small African nation; Radner is his sex-starved daughter, and Korman is a flustered United Nations ambassador. All have had better opportunities to display their comic talents. (R)
104 minutes

FIRST MONDAY IN OCTOBER
(1981)
 ★★★

**Walter Matthau
Jill Clayburgh**

Walter Matthau is a wisecracking associate justice in First Monday in October.

Matthau and Clayburgh shine in this breezy comedy, based on the stage play, about the first woman appointed to the United States Supreme Court. Although Clayburgh is the center of attention as a conservative appointee from California, it's Matthau who steals the film as a wisecracking liberal associate justice, on the order of the late William O. Douglas. The two exchange funny and clever dialogue as they debate constitutional issues. **Director**—Ronald Neame. (R)
98 minutes

THE FIRST NUDIE MUSICAL
(1977)
 ★★

**Bruce Kimmel
Cindy Williams
Stephen Nathan**

This naughty double parody of porno movies and '30s musicals is often silly and amateurish, but it's loaded with eager young talent and hilarious musical numbers that make up for the deficiencies. It's a raunchy, sexual laugh-in. There's some nudity, but this doesn't detract from the gleeful appeal. Kimmel wrote the screenplay and music, co-directed, and has a leading part. Also with Diana Canova and Leslie Ackerman. (R)   *100 minutes*

THE FISH THAT SAVED PITTSBURGH
(1979)
★★

**Julius Irving
James Bond III
Stockard Channing
Jonathan Winters
Meadowlark Lemon**

A basketball team is on the skids, and it can only be saved by astrology. So, in this funny and imaginatively drawn spoof, the team is reorganized with a wacky bunch of players, all born under the astrological sign of Pisces (The Fish). Channing is the astrologer who draws their horoscopes and coaches them to a championship. Basketball greats Irving and Lemon turn in some fancy court work while Winters adds some humorous moments. **Director**—Gilbert Moses. (PG)
102 minutes

F.I.S.T.
(1978)
★★★

**Sylvester Stallone
Rod Steiger
Peter Boyle**

An ambitious, handsome melodrama, about a truckers' union, beginning in idealism and ending in corruption. Stallone is appealing as a two-fisted Jimmy Hoffa-like character, but the charm of his *Rocky* is missing. Director Norman Jewison's style evokes those early Warner Brothers social dramas. The entire cast is excellent. Also with Melinda Dillon, Tony Lo Bianco, and David Huffman. (PG)   *145 minutes*

FITZCARRALDO
(1982)
 ★★★

**Klaus Kinski
Claudia Cardinale**

From German director Werner Herzog comes this bold, imaginative comedy-drama about adventurers and entrepreneurs operating in the Amazon basin at the turn of the century. Kinski is magnificent in the title role as an eccentric and incorrigible dreamer who hatches a wild scheme to open a rubber plantation in a remote part of the jungle. Some impact is diminished by the film's extraordinary length and patchy construction, but its outrageousness and exquisite detail make up for the flaws. In German with English titles. (PG)   *157 minutes*

FIVE CARD STUD
(1968)
★

**Dean Martin
Robert Mitchum
Inger Stevens**

So-so western mystery with an unfortunate case of the blahs. Martin stars as a gambler in a poker game. One by one, the game's participants are killed. The predictable film also features Roddy McDowall, Katherine Justice, John Anderson, and Yaphet Kotto. They're all dealt bad hands by director Henry Hathaway.   *103 minutes*

• Five Days One Summer
• Five Easy Pieces
• Five Fingers
• Five Graves to Cairo
• Five Weeks in a Balloon
• The Fixer
• The Flame and the Arrow

F

FIVE DAYS ONE SUMMER
(1982)

 ★★

**Sean Connery
Betsy Brantley**

Majestic Swiss Alpine scenery in this elegant Fred Zinnemann film upstages a plodding romantic story. The plot, set in 1932, has Connery as a middle-aged Scottish doctor who romances his young niece (Brantley) while on a mountain-climbing holiday. Some suspense is generated on the icy slopes, but the bizarre love affair is uneventful, moody, and leaves the viewer rather cold. (PG)
108 minutes

FIVE EASY PIECES (1970)
★★★★

**Jack Nicholson
Karen Black
Susan Anspach**

Jack Nicholson runs into a bit of trouble in an oil field in Five Easy Pieces.

Nicholson is at his best in this inspired film that vividly observes middle-class values. He's a rather gifted musician from a wealthy, neurotic family, who drops out to work in oil fields and drift about the country. The story is some-what influenced by *Easy Rider*, but it has memorable moments that are most original. There are winning supporting parts all around, with Black, Anspach, and Helena Kallianiotes outstanding. Also with Lois Smith, Billy Green Bush, and Fannie Flagg. Bob Rafelson's direction packs a wallop. (R) **Academy Award Nominations**—best picture; Nicholson, best actor; Black, best supporting actress; Rafelson and Adrien Joyce, best story and screenplay (based on factual material or material not previously published).
98 minutes

FIVE FINGERS
(1952)
★★★★

**James Mason
Danielle Darrieux
Michael Rennie**

Mason stands out in this gripping espionage thriller set in Turkey during World War II. He plays a British diplomat's butler who peddles military information to the Germans. The compelling story is brought off in convincing semidocumentary style, and it's loaded with suspense. Based on the book *Operation Cicero*, a true story. Nice acting, too, from the supporting cast, which also includes Walter Hampden, Michael Pate, and Richard Loo. **Director**—Joseph L. Mankiewicz. **Academy Award Nominations**—Mankiewicz, best director; Michael Wilson, writing (screenplay). *108 minutes b&w*

FIVE GRAVES TO CAIRO
(1943)
★★★

**Erich Von Stroheim
Anne Baxter
Akim Tamiroff
Franchot Tone**

In this spy melodrama set in a Sahara Desert hotel during World War II, British spies try to destroy Rommel's supply dumps. The cast is generally excellent, with Von Stroheim doing a caricaturish Rommel interpretation, Baxter and Tamiroff as the hotelkeepers, and Tone as the hero. The team of Charles Brackett and director Billy Wilder on the screenplay comes through with an intelligent and intri-cately suspenseful script. Beautifully photographed by John Seitz.
96 minutes b&w

FIVE WEEKS IN A BALLOON
(1962)
★★

**Cedric Hardwicke
Peter Lorre
Red Buttons**

A pedestrian and strained comedy adventure, based on the Jules Verne story about a balloon expedition to claim territory in Africa in 1862. The comedy situations fall flat, and the script is rife with clichés. However, the film is kept aloft occasionally by the cast. Also with Fabian, Richard Hayden, and Billy Gilbert. **Director**—Irwin Allen.
101 minutes

THE FIXER (1968)
★★

**Alan Bates
Dirk Bogarde**

This screen adaptation of Bernard Malamud's prizewinning novel doesn't come into sharp focus. However, it does offer some entertainment thanks to the fine acting. Bates performs extraordinarily well as a poor handyman in csarist Russia, who is imprisoned and humiliated relentlessly on trumped-up charges. Bogarde plays a sympathetic defense attorney. Also with Georgia Brown and Hugh Griffith. **Director**—John Frankenheimer. *132 minutes*

THE FLAME AND THE ARROW
(1950)
★★★

**Burt Lancaster
Virginia Mayo**

A colorful costume drama set in medieval Italy. Lancaster performs with energy as a lusty rebel leading a campaign against evil forces. Lancaster, who goes all out with some of his best gymnastics, has the lovely Mayo by his side. Robert Douglas, Aline MacMahon, and Nick Cravat are also in the cast. **Director**—Jacques Tourneur.
88 minutes

FLAME OF THE BARBARY COAST (1945)

 ★★

Ann Dvorak
John Wayne

An adequate western comedy-drama set in San Francisco at the time of the 1906 earthquake. Wayne plays a gambling hall owner falling in love with a saloon singer, played by Dvorak. This film may be interesting for Wayne fans, but the low-key action doesn't exactly set the screen on fire. Also with Joseph Schildkraut. **Director**—Joseph Kane.   *91 minutes b&w*

THE FLAMINGO KID (1984)

 ★★★

Matt Dillon
Richard Crenna

Amusingly realistic coming-of-age comedy about a Brooklyn teenager (Matt Dillon) who is seduced by the easy living at a posh beach club. Working there as a cabana boy, he falls under the influence of a smooth-talking car dealer (Richard Crenna) who convinces him he would be better off selling Porsches than going to college. Ace TV director Garry Marshall scores well with comic charm and fine performances all around. (PG–13)
100 minutes

FLAMINGO ROAD (1949)

★★

Joan Crawford
Zachary Scott
Sydney Greenstreet

The screenplay is rather farfetched in this film version of Robert Wilder's novel about a carnival dancer involved with politicians in a small town. However, Crawford, as the tough entertainer, does rather well in this role, which suits her style. Greenstreet plays a crooked politician. Also with David Brian, Gertrude Michael, and Gladys George. **Director**—Michael Curtiz.   *94 minutes b&w*

FLASHDANCE (1983)

 ★★

Jennifer Beals
Belinda Baver
Michael Nouri

Beautiful Beals plays a welder by day and a trendy dancer by night (the actual dancing is done by Marine Jahan). The music and dancing, in a sort of high-tech rock'n'roll setting, are what really count here, but the film falls flat when it comes to script and characterization. Director Adrian Lyne (*Foxes*) aspired to make a youth movie akin to *Saturday Night Fever*, but *Flashdance* is merely a flash in the pan. (R) **Academy Award Nominations**—Don Petermen, best cinematography.   *96 minutes*

FLASH GORDON (1980)

 ★★

Sam Jones
Max Von Sydow
Melody Anderson

An overblown, overbudgeted extravaganza, based on those heroic space-opera serials of the '30s. For all the glitter and lavish special effects, this

SHIRLEY MacLAINE

Until she won an Oscar for Terms of Endearment *(1983), Shirley MacLaine had attained her greatest popularity as an actress in the '50s and '60s. MacLaine was born in 1934 in Richmond, Virginia, to Ira O. Beaty, a high-school principal, and his wife Kathlyn MacLean Beaty, a drama teacher and community theater actress. Shirley is the older sister of actor-director Warren Beatty. She began her professional career as a dancer and was in the chorus lines of* Kiss Me, Kate *and* Me and Juliet *and was understudying Carol Haney in* The Pajama Game *on Broadway when the star injured her ankle. In the best* 42nd Street *tradition, MacLaine took over, was spotted by Hollywood producer Hal B. Wallis, and she has been performing out front ever since.*

In 1955, MacLaine made her motion picture debut in Alfred Hitchcock's The Trouble With Harry, *and for the next 15 years averaged two pictures a year, among them* Around the World in 80 Days *(1956),* Hot Spell *(1957),* The Matchmaker *(1958),* Some Came Running *(1958),* The Sheepman *(1958),* Ask Any Girl *(1959),* Career *(1959),* Can-Can *(1959),* The Apartment *(1959),* My Geisha *(1962),* The Children's Hour *(1962),* Two for the Seesaw *(1963),* Irma La Douce *(1963),* What a Way to Go *(1964),* Gambit *(1966),* Sweet Charity *(1968), and* Desperate Characters *(1971).*

In the late '60s, MacLaine was actively involved in protests against U.S. involvement in Vietnam, and campaigned vigorously for George McGovern's presidential candidacy. At the 1968 and 1972 Democratic conventions, she was an outspoken delegate.

Beginning in 1972, MacLaine was off the screen for five years, but during that period she was hardly inactive. She joined the first women's delegation to China and produced and co-directed a documentary of her visit, The Other Half of the Sky, *which was nominated for an Academy Award and was telecast by the Public Broadcasting System. She also wrote three best-selling reminiscences,* Don't Fall Off the Mountain, You Can Get There From Here, *and* Out on a Limb.

Her years away from the screen also saw the emergence of MacLaine as the singing-and-dancing star of a one-woman show, touring nightclubs and theaters around the world.

In 1977, MacLaine returned to film acting with an acclaimed performance in The Turning Point. *Subsequently, she has starred with Peter Sellers in* Being There *(1979); with James Coburn, Susan Sarandon, and Stephen Collins in* Loving Couples *(1980); and in* A Change of Seasons *(1980).*

The year 1983 marked a comeback for MacLaine as she won her first Oscar for her starring role in Terms of Endearment.

• Flashpoint
• Fleshburn
• The Flight of the Eagle

• The Flight of the Phoenix
• The Flim Flam Man
• Flipper

F

puffed-up version isn't as much fun as the B-movie matinee cliffhangers. Platinum blond, pretty-boy Jones is in the title role; he has no screen presence. Only Von Sydow, as the menacing Emperor Ming, carries off his role with aplomb. Buster Crabbe, where are you? Also with Topol and Ornella Muti. **Director**—Mike Hodges. (PG)   *110 minutes*

A FLASH OF GREEN (1984)
★★★

**Ed Harris
Blair Brown
Richard Jordan**

Excellent performances by the entire cast and skillful direction mark this drama about conflicts between greedy land developers and conservationists in a small Florida community. Ed Harris stars as a local newspaper reporter, with a foot in both camps, who eventually strives to preserve the natural environment. The sultry atmosphere of the southern town is expertly delineated. **Director**—Victor Nuñez. (No MPAA rating)   *131 minutes*

FLASHPOINT (1984)
 ### ★★★

**Kris Kristofferson
Treat Williams**

Kristofferson and Williams play border-patrol officers who stumble on $800,000 in cash buried in the Texas desert some 20 years ago. Their startling discovery leads to mystery, conspiracy, murder, and relentless suspense that effectively builds notch by notch. The ending, though somewhat hokey, packs a wallop nevertheless. Kristofferson and Williams are believable as civil servants up against events beyond their comprehension. Kurtwood Smith and Rip Torn are good in supporting roles. **Director**—William Tannen. (R)   *93 minutes*

FLESHBURN (1984)
 ### ★★

**Steve Kanaly
Karen Carlson
Macon McCalman**

James Stewart and passengers seek a way to survive in The Flight of the Phoenix.

Four psychiatrists are kidnapped and stranded in the Arizona desert by a revengeful Vietnam veteran. This desperate situation is supposed to generate tension, but it's as gripping as trying to cope with mild sunburn. The three men and a woman encounter unbearable heat, a lack of food and water, personal injuries, dangerous animals, and a script that is as dry as the desert terrain. **Director**—George Gage. (R)   *90 minutes*

THE FLIGHT OF THE EAGLE (1983)
 ### ★★★

Max Von Sydow

Long yet intensely fascinating semi-documentary of a doomed three-man Swedish expedition bound for the North Pole. Director-cinematographer Jan Troell has captured magnificent vistas of the frozen wasteland, and some startling photos found in the cameras of the dead explorers also appear on screen. Von Sydow is capable as the brooding leader of the adventure. Goran Stangertz and Sverre Anker Ousdal play his comrades. In Swedish with English titles. (No MPAA rating)   *141 minutes*

THE FLIGHT OF THE PHOENIX (1965)
★★★★

**James Stewart
Richard Attenborough
Hardy Kruger
Peter Finch**

A plane carrying an oil-drilling crew

crash-lands in the Arabian desert, and the survivors use their wits and primitive skills to rebuild the plane and fly to safety. Tension mounts dramatically, and there are fine character studies of the desperate men. Stewart is right at home as the pilot, and there are other sterling performances by the cast, which also includes Dan Duryea, Ernest Borgnine, Ian Bannen, and George Kennedy. Director Robert Aldrich puts it all together in grand style. **Academy Award Nomination**—Bannen, best supporting actor.
                                    149 minutes

THE FLIM FLAM MAN (1967)
★★

**George C. Scott
Michael Sarrazin
Sue Lyon**

This lightweight comedy is improved some by the lively performance of Scott, who plays a rascally con man working small towns. Scott gives it his best shot, but the entertainment values flag after awhile. Sarrazin also does rather well as a young military deserter who joins Scott and learns that too much honesty gets in the way. Also with Harry Morgan, Jack Albertson, Alice Ghostley, and Albert Salmi. **Director**—Irvin Kershner.
                                    104 minutes

FLIPPER (1963)
★★

**Chuck Connors
Luke Halpin**

(Continued)

F

- • Flower Drum Song
- • Flying Down to Rio
- • Flying Leathernecks
- • Flying Tigers
- • FM
- • The Fog
- • Follow the Fleet

(Continued)
Routine animal adventure about a boy in Florida who rescues a wounded dolphin; they soon become great friends. Halpin is fine as the plucky lad. Nice fluff for the kids, but adults will probably find it tiresome. This film led to two sequels and a TV series. Also with Kathleen Maguire and Connie Scott. **Director**—James B. Clark.

87 minutes

FLOWER DRUM SONG (1961)
★★

Nancy Kwan
James Shigeta

James Shigeta watches Nancy Kwan in Flower Drum Song.

A mildly entertaining screen version of the Rodgers and Hammerstein Broadway musical about life and love in San Francisco's Chinatown. The staging is colorful, the choreography is adequate, and the songs are good, but nothing is memorable. And it goes on too long. Also with Juanita Hall, Benson Fong, Miyoshi Umeki, James Soo, and Sen Yung. **Director**—Henry Koster.

133 minutes

FLYING DOWN TO RIO (1933)
★★

Fred Astaire
Ginger Rogers
Gene Raymond

Rogers and Astaire get together for the first time in this musical about a beautiful woman who has to select between two men down in Rio. Without the dancing of the dazzling duo, this corny and flimsy movie would crash into the ocean. The ending, in which women dance on the wings of moving airplanes, is memorable. Also with Dolores del Rio and Franklin Pangborn. **Director**—Thornton Freeland.

89 minutes b&w

FLYING LEATHERNECKS
(1951)
★★

John Wayne
Robert Ryan

Wayne takes to the skies as a martinet Marine officer in World War II. There are some striking battle scenes against Japanese forces, but a poor script keeps most of the drama grounded. A standard macho performance by the Duke, with support from Ryan, Janis Carter, Don Taylor, and Jay C. Flippen. **Director**—Nicholas Ray. *102 minutes*

FLYING TIGERS (1942)
★★★

John Wayne
John Carroll

Wayne and company join the famous Flying Tiger squadron in China to fight the Japanese. Lots of good aerial combat scenes, with some time off for Wayne to romance an attractive nurse. The standard World War II clichés and heroics abound in this wartime movie, but it's exciting all the way. As usual, Big John is no pussycat. Also with Anna Lee, Paul Kelly, and Mae Clarke. **Director**—David Miller.

100 minutes b&w

FM (1978)
★★

Michael Brandon
Eileen Brennan
Alex Karras
Martin Mull

A silly youth film, about the tribulations of a fictitious popular rock radio station. The DJs and their loyal fans go on a rampage, all because the guys from the business office try to wring extra profits from the good vibes. The hollow plot doesn't hold up too well, but there's plenty of rock music—including some impressive numbers by Linda Ronstadt—to brighten things up now and then. Also with Cassie Yates and Norman Lloyd. **Director**—John A. Alonzo. (PG) *105 minutes*

THE FOG (1980)
★★

Adrienne Barbeau
Hal Holbrook
Janet Leigh
Jamie Lee Curtis

Janet Leigh returns to horror films after a twenty year absence in The Fog.

Director John Carpenter, who brought us the grisly and overbearing *Halloween*, strikes again with this traditional yet effective chiller. Carpenter is no Hitchcock, but he certainly is improving his ability to spin a scary tale. Leigh, Curtis, and Holbrook are residents of a seaside town in California, where a supernatural fog carries ashore ghosts from a century-old shipwreck to wreak revenge. Also with John Houseman. (R) *91 minutes*

FOLLOW THE FLEET (1936)
★★★

Fred Astaire
Ginger Rogers

Splendid Irving Berlin songs bring out the best in Astaire and Rogers. Astaire and Randolph Scott portray sailors

• Foolin' Around
• Footlight Parade
• Footloose
• Forbidden Planet
• Forced Vengeance
• Force of Evil
• Force 10 from Navarone

F

who romance sisters Rogers and Harriet Hilliard in this delightful musical. The songs include "Let's Face the Music and Dance," "Let Yourself Go," and "We Saw the Sea." Lucille Ball and Betty Grable also star. **Director**—Mark Sandrich.   *110 minutes b&w*

FOOLIN' AROUND (1980)

★★

Gary Busey
Annette O'Toole

Down-to-earth farm boy, played by Busey, courts and wins a well-heeled coed, played by O'Toole, after showing up the girl's snooty fiancé. The entire cast, which includes Cloris Leachman, Eddie Albert, and Tony Randall, performs with enthusiasm. But this predictable romantic plot has been exhaustively run through the Hollywood mill. It's yesterday's cold mashed potatoes. **Director**—Richard T. Heffron. (PG)   *103 minutes*

FOOTLIGHT PARADE (1933)

★★★

James Cagney
Joan Blondell
Ruby Keeler
Dick Powell

Busby Berkeley concocts a fantasy in Footlight Parade.

One of the best Warner Brothers/ Busby Berkeley musicals with an all-star cast. Cagney plays the producer of lavish Broadway shows trying to stage

a bigger and better one in the face of impossible odds and insurmountable problems. Naturally, the show goes on. Three of the best Berkeley numbers provide a truly spectacular finish: "Honeymoon Hotel," "By a Waterfall," and "Shanghai Lil." **Director**—Lloyd Bacon.   *104 minutes b&w*

FOOTLOOSE (1984)

★★★

Kevin Bacon
John Lithgow

Kevin Bacon gets ready to rock out in Footloose.

A toe-tapping, finger-snapping youth musical somewhat in the tradition of *Flashdance*, but gone country. In fact, it's a bit more brainy. Kevin Bacon stars as the new boy in town who has trouble adjusting to the stuffy community's law against school kids dancing. Surprisingly, the film is sympathetic to adults, especially a troubled fire-and-brimstone minister played by Lithgow whose daughter Bacon romances. And it boasts infectious music, exuberant dancing, and likable performances. **Director**—Herbert Ross. (PG)
107 minutes

FORBIDDEN PLANET (1956)

★★★★

Walter Pidgeon
Anne Francis
Leslie Nielsen

An excellent sci-fi adventure, stylishly executed with imagination and just the right touch of humor. The plot is loosely based on Shakespeare's *The Tempest*. A team of scientists visits a remote planet to make contact with previous explorers and finds a sinister

one-man empire in control. Pidgeon is the reclusive survivor of the pioneering explorers; Francis plays his daughter. You will notice effective use of Robby the Robot. Could this be the father of R2-D2? Excellent performances by Pidgeon, Francis, and Nielsen in the key roles. The cast also includes Warren Stevens, Jack Kelly, Richard Anderson, and Earl Holliman. **Director**—Fred McLeod Wilcox. (G)   *98 minutes*

FORCED VENGEANCE (1982)

★★

Chuck Norris

Karate ace Norris, who talks softly and wields a big kick, takes on some Hong Kong mobsters who are trying to muscle in on a small gambling casino. The stale and creaky plot is occasionally relieved by the martial arts action. Norris routinely puts away scores of bad guys who seemingly leap through the windows and pop out of the woodwork. The majestic Hong Kong cityscape contributes a modest amount of atmosphere. **Director**—James Fargo. (R)   *90 minutes*

FORCE OF EVIL (1948)

★★★

John Garfield
Thomas Gomez

A striking crime drama about the numbers racket, vividly filmed against the background of New York City. Garfield is excellent, portraying an involved man desperately trying to break away from crime. Expertly directed, with lots of sharp atmosphere and smart dialogue. Beatrice Pearson, Roy Roberts, and Marie Windsor also star. **Director**—Abraham Polonsky.
78 minutes b&w

FORCE 10 FROM NAVARONE (1978)

★★★

Robert Shaw
Harrison Ford

Familiar war adventure billed as a continuation—not a sequel—of *The Guns*
(Continued)

F
- Foreign Correspondent
- Forever Amber
- For Love of Ivy
- For Me and My Gal
- The Formula
- Fort Apache

Franco Nero plays a Yugoslavian officer in Force 10 from Navarone.

(Continued)

of Navarone. Lots of goodies for action fans: suspense, narrow escapes, spectacular destruction of a dam and a bridge, and other impressive special effects. Our heroes are a mixed bag of Allied commandos assigned to harass the Nazis in Yugoslavia. Shaw is good as an American major. Some appealing humor is occasionally offset by stretched credibility. Also with Edward Fox, Franco Nero, Barbara Bach, and Richard Kiel. **Director**—Guy Hamilton. (PG)   *118 minutes*

FOREIGN CORRESPONDENT
(1940)
★★★★

Joel McCrea
Laraine Day
Herbert Marshall

Alfred Hitchcock is at his best with this edge-of-your-seat tale of an American reporter in Europe, who's hot on the trail of spies. The master builds suspense to a glorious crescendo and spices the film nicely with effective atmospherics. Some of the memorable scenes include a murder attempt in Westminster Cathedral and a plane crash. McCrea is excellent in the title role, and there's fine supporting work from Day, Marshall, Albert Basserman, Edmund Gwenn, George Sanders, Robert Benchley, and Harry Davenport. **Academy Award Nominations**—best picture; Basserman, best supporting actor; Charles Bennett and Joan Harrison, writing (original screenplay); Rudolph Maté, cinematography (black and white).
120 minutes b&w

FOREVER AMBER (1947)
★★

Linda Darnell
Cornel Wilde
George Sanders

Kathleen Winsor's steamy novel about an ambitious woman in 17th-century England gets half-baked treatment on the screen. The production is handsome, but the script plods along, only to perk up for brief spells with some lively scenes. The players seem unenthusiastic most of the time. Darnell plays a girl trying to make good at the court of Charles II. Also with Richard Greene, Richard Haydn, Jessica Tandy, Robert Coote, and Leo G. Carroll. **Director**—Otto Preminger.   *138 minutes*

FOR LOVE OF IVY (1968)
★★

Sidney Poitier
Abby Lincoln

An ill-conceived, although well-intentioned, romance concerning a black maid and her bid to better her condition. When Ivy, played by Lincoln, decides to quit her job to go to secretarial school, the family pressures a congenial black man, played by Poitier, to be her boyfriend in hope of keeping her on the job. Also with Beau Bridges, Carroll O'Connor, Nan Martin, and Laurie Peters. **Director**—Daniel Mann.   *100 minutes*

FOR ME AND MY GAL
(1942)
★★★

Judy Garland
Gene Kelly
George Murphy

This is a marvelously entertaining old-fashioned musical with a star-studded cast. The routine plot, set prior to World War I, has two vaudeville hoofers trying to make the big time while grappling with romantic problems. Look for the great songs and dancing with Garland, Murphy, and Kelly, who is starring in his first film. Horace McNally, Keenan Wynn, and Ben Blue also grace the cast. **Director**—Busby Berkeley.   *104 minutes b&w*

THE FORMULA (1980)
★★

George C. Scott
Marlon Brando
Marthe Keller

The Formula is what Marlon Brando's selling in this story of international conspiracy.

Scott plays a police detective who pursues an intricate trail of clues and murders that leads to the inner sanctum of Big Oil and a secret formula for producing synthetic fuel. Scott's investigation also leads to a tense confrontation with an oil tycoon, played by Brando, who magnificently steals the few scenes in which he appears. But alas, Steve Shagan's cumbersome screenplay, adapted from his bestselling novel, is as complicated as the piping at an oil refinery. Also with Beatrice Straight, John Gielgud, and G. D. Spradin. **Director**—John G. Avildsen. (R)   *117 minutes*

FORT APACHE (1948)
★★★

Henry Fonda
John Wayne
Shirley Temple

A handsome and somewhat thoughtful epic western that plays out slowly with more attention to character than to action. Fonda excels as a gung ho Army colonel whose stubbornness irritates his troops and also prompts trouble with the Indians. Wayne plays a practical officer under Fonda's command. Moments of comedy appear occasionally. The cast also includes Ward Bond, Pedro Armendariz, John Agar, Anna Lee, and Victor McLaglen. **Director**—John Ford.   *127 minutes b&w*

• Fort Apache, The Bronx
• The Fortune
• The Fortune Cookie
• 48 Hrs.
• Forty Pounds of Trouble
• 42nd Street

F

FORT APACHE, THE BRONX (1981)

  ★★★

**Paul Newman
Edward Asner**

Paul Newman and Ed Asner discuss the hectic pace of life at Fort Apache, The Bronx.

A powerful, realistically portrayed drama involving an embattled police station house in one of New York's most poverty-stricken and crime-ridden neighborhoods. The film is more than a routine cops and bad guys story; it offers a moving and impressive view of the urban decay and the people intimately affected. Newman gives a first-rate performance as a veteran cop who struggles with his thankless assignments and his conscience. Also with Kathleen Beller and Rachel Ticotin. **Director**—Daniel Petrie. (R)
125 minutes

THE FORTUNE (1975)

★★★★

**Jack Nicholson
Warren Beatty
Stockard Channing**

A funny tale about two con men who covet the fortune of a dim-witted New York heiress. Inspired directing by Mike Nichols of slick, pencil-moustached Beatty; his seedy sidekick, Nicholson; and Channing, the lamebrained, filthy-rich heiress. The film is set in the '20s and mostly in southern California. Channing scores as a refreshing and accomplished comic actress. Also with Florence Stanley, Richard B. Shull, and John Fiedler. (PG)
88 minutes

THE FORTUNE COOKIE (1966)

★★★★

**Walter Matthau
Jack Lemmon**

This insightful Billy Wilder comedy effectively satirizes middle-class values and the pursuit of success. Lemmon is perfectly cast as a TV cameraman who's slightly injured during a football game. But it's Matthau who really ties the film together. He delivers a superb memorable performance as "Whiplash Willie," the shyster lawyer brother-in-law who schemes to collect outrageous personal-injury claims from the insurance company. Ron Rich, Cliff Osmond, Judi West, and Lurene Tuttle perform in supporting roles. **Academy Award**—Matthau, best supporting actor. **Nomination**—Wilder and I.A.L. Diamond, best story and screenplay (written directly for the screen).
125 minutes b&w

48 HRS. (1982)

 ★★

**Nick Nolte
Eddie Murphy**

Murphy of *Saturday Night Live* steals scene after scene as a wisecracking convict on a two-day furlough to help nab some San Francisco cop killers. He teams up with a sullen detective (Nolte) for some slam-bang violent action, which is laced with comic episodes. Murphy's film debut is impressive, indeed. He's cool and funny. The film falters when it dwells on cops-and-robbers excesses such as destructive car chases and brutal gun fights. **Director**—Walter Hill. (R)
96 minutes

FORTY POUNDS OF TROUBLE (1963)

★★

**Tony Curtis
Phil Silvers
Suzanne Pleshette**

Cutesy, sentimental romantic comedy, with Curtis as a casino manager who grudgingly looks after an abandoned six-year-old girl. Of course, complications follow. This obvious reworking of *Little Miss Marker* is routine at best, helped now and then by some decent acting and some spirited chases through Disneyland. Also with Larry Storch, Howard Morris, and Edward Andrews. **Director**—Norman Jewison.
106 minutes

42nd STREET (1933)

 ★★★

**Ginger Rogers
Ruby Keeler**

This zesty production is one of the few musicals that provide good music and dance numbers *and* a believable plot.
(Continued)

The chorus line rehearses in 42nd Street. *The girl in the black shorts is a young Ginger Rogers.*

F

- For Whom the Bell Tolls
- For Your Eyes Only
- Foul Play
- The Fountainhead
- Four Friends
- The Four Horsemen of the Apocalypse

(Continued)

Although some parts of the movie have aged, the Busby Berkeley musical numbers are still memorable and the splendid cast, including Rogers, Keeler, Warner Baxter, Bebe Daniels, and Ned Sparks, creates the authentic backstage atmosphere that makes the show so entertaining. Top songs include "Young and Healthy," "You're Getting to Be a Habit with Me," "Shuffle Off to Buffalo," and the title tune. Also with Dick Powell and Una Merkel. **Director**—Lloyd Bacon. **Academy Award Nomination**—best picture.

90 minutes b&w

FOR WHOM THE BELL TOLLS (1943)
★★★★

**Gary Cooper
Ingrid Bergman**

Ingrid Bergman and Gary Cooper meet in the midst of the Spanish Civil War in For Whom the Bell Tolls.

Ernest Hemingway's classic adventure of the Spanish Civil War is presented with high drama and mounting suspense. Cooper is at his best as an American mercenary who helps a band of peasants engaged in blowing up a bridge. Bergman is winning as the object of Cooper's affections. Effectively directed, with first-rate supporting performances by Katina Paxinou, Akim Tamiroff, Arturo de Cordova, and Joseph Calleia. **Director**—Sam Wood. **Academy Award**—Paxinou, best supporting actress. **Nominations**—best picture; Cooper, best actor; Bergman,

best actress; Tamiroff, best supporting actor; Ray Rennahan, cinematography (color). *170 minutes*

FOR YOUR EYES ONLY (1981)

★★

Roger Moore

Once again British secret agent James Bond, played by Moore, saves the world—this time outrunning and outfoxing his enemies on ski slopes, under water, and on the face of a vertical cliff. This 12th adventure in the popular series isn't the most exuberant; the villains aren't as terrifying as in past escapades, and the women aren't as sexy. But there are still plenty of hair-raising thrills with the usual lavish hardware and Bond suaveness. Good show, 007. Carry on. **Director**—John Glen. (PG) *127 minutes*

FOUL PLAY (1978)

★★

**Goldie Hawn
Chevy Chase**

Saucer-eyed Hawn is the best thing going for this action comedy, set in San Francisco. Her warm and mature performance as an innocent librarian caught up in a scheme to assassinate the Pope overshadows the entire movie. Chase plays a detective. The plot seems as if it was written by a computer; it steals from a half-dozen Hitchcock films and ends with an all too-familiar car chase episode. Also with Burgess Meredith, Dudley Moore, and Rachel Roberts. **Director**—Colin Higgins. (PG)

116 minutes

THE FOUNTAINHEAD (1949)

★★

**Gary Cooper
Patricia Neal
Raymond Massey**

An uneven screen adaptation of Ayn Rand's novel about an idealistic architect who bucks big business and makes sacrifices for the sake of principle. The script offers philosophical symbols that don't often register. Cooper plays the architect with some

credibility, but he seems ill at ease half the time. Also with Kent Smith and Robert Douglas. **Director**—King Vidor.

114 minutes b&w

FOUR FRIENDS (1981)

★★

**Craig Wasson
Jodi Thelen
Michael Huddleston
Jim Metzler**

Screenwriter Steven Tesich, who gave us the exhilarating *Breaking Away*, misses the mark with this grand tour of the turbulent '60s, as seen through the experiences of a young man from East Chicago, played by Wasson. Tesich's partly autobiographical story is intelligent and somewhat perceptive, but his jigsaw-puzzle script packs in too many underdeveloped and incoherent episodes; the pieces never come together, and many of the characters are out of focus. Also with Lois Smith and Reed Birney. **Director**—Arthur Penn. (R) *115 minutes*

THE FOUR HORSEMEN OF THE APOCALYPSE (1961)
★★

**Glenn Ford
Ingrid Thulin
Charles Boyer**

Glenn Ford can't seem to strike up a conversation on the set of The Four Horsemen of the Apocalypse.

Overblown and awkward updating of the 1921 silent film, which starred Rudolph Valentino. This version concerns an Argentine family's involvement in World War II, with members fighting on both sides. The script and the direction are no help to the actors, who approach their assignments with seemingly little enthusiasm. The cast also includes Paul Henreid, Lee J. Cobb, Paul Lukas, and Yvette Mimieux. **Director**—Vincente Minnelli.

153 minutes

THE FOUR MUSKETEERS
(1975)
  ★★★

**Michael York
Oliver Reed
Frank Finlay
Richard Chamberlain
Raquel Welch
Faye Dunaway
Charlton Heston**

Oliver Reed plays Athos in The Four Musketeers.

This sequel to *The Three Musketeers* has the same swashbuckling cast as the original. It is, however, lighter, funnier, and less burdensome than the first film. Both were filmed simultaneously. Also stars Christopher Lee, Simon Ward, and Geraldine Chaplin. **Director**—Richard Lester. (PG)

108 minutes

THE FOUR-POSTER (1952)
★★★

**Rex Harrison
Lilli Palmer**

Excellent performances by Harrison and Palmer liven up this comic story of a married couple's life, with scenes played about their bed. The script is pleasingly adapted from the successful Broadway play by Jan de Hartog. A

That old gang of theirs in The Four Seasons.

nice touch is using animated cartoons to connect the scenes. **Director**—Irving Reis. *103 minutes b&w*

THE FOUR SEASONS
(1981)
 ★★★

**Alan Alda
Carol Burnett
Sandy Dennis
Rita Moreno
Jack Weston**

Alda wrote, directed, and stars in this warm and friendly salute to the middle-aged and the middle-class. The low-key comedy involves three couples who vacation together at various locales. Alda overuses dialogue; the result is a rather stagey production. But a game cast injects ample humor and appeal in this good-natured slice of ordinary life. (PG) *107 minutes*

THE FOX AND THE HOUND
(1981)
 ★★

A new generation of Walt Disney animators made this $12-million cartoon about the deteriorating friendship of two animals. The film is full of obvious Disney playfulness and sentimentality. Yet the tone is often heavy-handed and overly serious, especially in dealing with a parable on race relations. Somehow, that special Disney magic hasn't been fully realized by the

new generation. Voices include those of Mickey Rooney, Kurt Russell, Pearl Bailey, and Jack Albertson. **Director**—Art Stevens. (G) *83 minutes*

FOXES (1980)
 ★★

**Sally Kellerman
Jodie Foster**

A moving and highly realistic story about the social and emotional problems of four teenage girls growing up in Los Angeles. Foster and Kellerman head a cast of mostly unknowns, but every performance is convincing. The film succeeds in depicting the adolescent world beset by the inadequacies of home and school. This portrait is the dark side of *American Graffiti*. **Director**—Adrian Lyne. (R) *106 minutes*

FRAMED (1975)
★★

Joe Don Baker

A professional gambler, played by Baker, is railroaded into prison and emerges, with fists swinging and guns blazing, in pursuit of the bad guys who framed him. Perhaps there's too much gore and violence for some—an ear shot off, a knife driven through a hand—but the film is adequately constructed and guaranteed to keep you awake. Also with Conny Van Dyke, Gabriel Dell, and John Marley. **Director**—Phil Karlson. (R)

106 minutes

F
- Frances
- Frankenstein
- Frankenstein Meets the Wolf Man
- Frankenstein '70
- Fraternity Row
- Freaky Friday

FRANCES (1982)

★★

**Jessica Lange
Sam Shepard
Kim Stanley**

*Jessica Lange poses for a publicity still in
Frances, a biography of Frances Farmer.*

Disturbing controversial film biography of '30s Hollywood golden girl Frances Farmer whose rebellious behavior led to her tragic confinement in various hell-hole mental institutions. The story is burdened with various ugly scenes, including shock treatments and a frontal lobotomy. Such depictions tend to disgust rather than convince, but Lange's spirited performance in the title role stands out from the bad taste. Stanley co-stars as the actress' ambitious mother. **Director—**Graeme Clifford. (R) **Academy Award Nominations**—Lange, best actress; Stanley, best supporting actress.
139 minutes

FRANKENSTEIN (1931)

★★★★

**Boris Karloff
Colin Clive
Mae Clarke**

*The creature sees something he likes in the
original Frankenstein.*

This is the granddaddy of horror films and still one of the most haunting and effective around. With somber mood and misty background, the film, based on Mary Shelley's fascinating novel, tells the tale of the determined scientist who recreates human life in the form of a monster assembled from corpses. Karloff is impressive as the mistreated monster who terrorizes the local community. And there are other fine performances by Clive, Clarke, and Edward Van Sloan. This film spawned a slew of sequels and launched its stars and director on their way to further fame. **Director—**James Whale.
71 minutes b&w

FRANKENSTEIN MEETS THE WOLF MAN (1943)
★★★

**Lon Chaney, Jr.
Ilona Massey
Bela Lugosi**

*In Frankenstein Meets the Wolf Man, Lon
Chaney, Jr. gets a cool reception from Bela
Lugosi*

The Wolf Man, alias Lawrence Talbot, takes a trip in hope of finding a cure to his moon madness, but all he finds is Frankenstein's monster on the loose. Chaney and Lugosi team up for the horror high jinks, and it's all done with stylish atmospherics. However, Lugosi isn't too convincing as the monster. Also with Patric Knowles, Maria Ouspenskaya, and Lionel Atwill. **Director—**Roy Neill.
73 minutes b&w

FRANKENSTEIN '70 (1958)
★

**Boris Karloff
Tom Duggan**

Almost all talk and few scares in this limp film, which doesn't do justice to the famous name. The silly plot has a TV crew, led by Duggan, using the gloomy Castle Frankenstein to make a horror feature, while the Baron is involved with his own monster work. Karloff is around, but he can't rescue the effort. Also with Jana Lund. **Director—**Howard Koch.
83 minutes b&w

FRATERNITY ROW (1977)
★★★

**Peter Fox
Gregory Harrison
Scott Newman**

The script for this sobering drama began as a student filmmaking project and evolved into an intelligent movie aimed at exposing the excesses and hypocrisy of college fraternity life. The film is set in the mid '50s at a small Eastern college. The young novice cast does rather well—especially Newman, as a sadistic frat brother, and Harrison, as an idealistic pledge who suffers under the hazing system. Also with Nancy Morgan and Robert Emhardt. There's sensitive direction from newcomer Thomas J. Tobin. (PG)
101 minutes

FREAKY FRIDAY (1977)

★★

**Barbara Harris
Jodie Foster**

*Barbara Harris and family go through
mayhem on Freaky Friday.*

Harris and Foster play a frustrated 35-year-old mother and a tomboy teenage daughter who mysteriously switch places for a day. This Disney family comedy is chock full of formula slap-

150

- The French Connection
- French Connection II
- The French Lieutenant's Woman
- French Postcards
- Frenzy
- Freud
- Friday the 13th
- Friday the 13th—Part II

F

stick and Freudian undertones. Harris and Foster turn on their talent and charm to salvage several scenes that would otherwise misfire because of the repetitive screenplay. As with most latter-day Disney fare, it's harmless fun with a few laughs here and there—if you stay alert to catch them. Also with John Astin, Patsy Kelly, Dick Van Patten, and Sorrell Booke. **Director**—Gary Nelson. (G)   *95 minutes*

THE FRENCH CONNECTION (1971)

 ★★★★

Gene Hackman
Roy Scheider

Slam-bang cops-and-smugglers film, filled with exciting action, mounting suspense, and colorful characterizations, and played to the hilt. The semi-documentary story is based on the experiences of New York City detectives who broke up a lucrative narcotics operation. Featured is one of the screen's most exciting and nerve-jangling chases, with a car pursuing a subway train. Hackman, Scheider, and Fernando Rey perform outstandingly. Also with Tony Lo Bianco and Marcel Bozzuffi. **Director**—William Friedkin. (R) **Academy Awards**—best picture; Friedkin, best director; Hackman, best actor; Ernest Tidyman, best screenplay (based on material from another medium). **Nominations**—Scheider, best supporting actor; Owen Roizman, cinematography.
104 minutes

FRENCH CONNECTION II (1975)

 ★★★

Gene Hackman
Fernando Rey

Hackman again plays detective Popeye Doyle, on leave from the New York City Police Department to battle the French police and the underworld. He takes Marseilles by storm, while on the trail of his old dope-dealing enemy. This sequel has its own distinct style and more concentration on mood and the supercharged character of Popeye. Also with Bernard Fresson and Jean-Pierre Castaldi. **Director**—John Frankenheimer. (R)   *104 minutes*

THE FRENCH LIEUTENANT'S WOMAN (1981)

 ★★★

Meryl Streep
Jeremy Irons

A handsomely mounted period drama, based on John Fowles's romantic Victorian novel. The novel uses asides to make its comments on society, the film uses a story-within-a-story structure, about a filmmaking company whose players duplicate their on-screen involvements when they're off the screen too. Streep, in the title role, plays as a young woman of doubtful reputation, and Irons is the wealthy Englishman who is fascinated by her. It's an intelligent, inventive production, yet at times it leans toward the pretentious. **Director**—Karel Reisz. (R) **Academy Award Nominations**—Streep, best actress; Harold Pinter, best screenplay (based on material from another medium).   *127 minutes*

FRENCH POSTCARDS (1979)

 ★★★

Miles Chapin
Blanche Baker

Gloria Katz and Willard Huyck, the screenwriters for *American Graffiti*, continue to come up with adolescent adventures in this sunny and likable tale of American students in Paris. The film gets a lot of its zing from the talents of some eager young newcomers; Chapin is especially pleasing as a shy American who gets an ego boost from a charming French girl, played by Valerie Quennessen. There are a few problems with plot and too many characters, but the film ends on a refreshing note. Also with David Marshall Grant and Marie-France Pisier. **Director**—Huyck. (PG)   *92 minutes*

FRENZY (1972)

 ★★★

Jon Finch
Alex McCowen
Barry Foster

Director Alfred Hitchcock does it again with this gripping tale about an innocent man tagged as the London

Strangler because of circumstantial evidence. The plot is déjà vu, but the maestro adds his unique touches and comes up with a good thriller. A cast of unknowns delivers the goods with style and just the right amount of savory black humor. Foster plays the strangler, and Finch plays the innocent man. Anthony Shaffer's taut screenplay is based on Arthur La Bern's novel *Goodby Piccadilly, Farewell Leicester Square*. Also with Vivien Merchant, Barbara Leigh-Hunt, and Anna Massey. (R)   *116 minutes*

FREUD (1962)

★★★

Montgomery Clift
Larry Parks
Susannah York

Straightforward, intelligent film biography of the founder of psychoanalysis. The story dwells on the treatment of a boy with a mother fixation and Freud's early efforts to find acceptance for his revolutionary methods. Clift gives a sensitive performance in the title role. Others in the cast include Eileen Herlie, David McCallum, and Susan Kohner. **Director**—John Huston.   *140 minutes b&w*

FRIDAY THE 13TH (1980)

 ★★

Betsy Palmer
Adrienne King
Harry Crosby

A diabolical murderer stalks a summer camp, dispatching several young counselors in bloody, bizarre fashion within a day's time. Director Sean Cunningham offers a few suspenseful moments, but most of the story is handled in a routine, unconvincing style. The young novice players act out their parts with appeal despite the wooden dialogue. (R)   *95 minutes*

FRIDAY THE 13TH—PART II (1981)

 ★

Amy Steel
John Furey
Adrienne King

(Continued)

 Movie is available in Beta and VHS videotape

★ STAR PROFILE

F
- Friday the 13th—Part III
- Friday the 13th—The Final Chapter
- Friendly Persuasion
- The Frisco Kid
- Fritz the Cat

CLARK GABLE

Clark Gable was affectionately known by his fans and in Hollywood as "The King," primarily because of his popularity as a rugged and attractive leading man for nearly 30 years.

He was born William Clark Gable in Cadiz, Ohio, in 1901, the son of an oil field worker. Gable left school at 14 and held a number of jobs, including tire factory worker and lumberjack, but his first love was acting.

Friend Lionel Barrymore arranged a screen test for Gable at MGM, which he failed. However, after Gable made an impressive film debut in The Painted Desert (1930), the studio changed its mind and signed him to a contract.

A series of successful films followed; in fact, he made eight movies in 1931 alone, but it was in 1934, when on loan to Columbia, that he scored a great triumph in Frank Capra's It Happened One Night, for which he received the Oscar as best actor.

Gable separated from his second wife, socialite Rhea Langham, in 1935 and married actress Carole Lombard in 1939, while he was in the midst of playing Rhett Butler in Gone With the Wind. In 1942, Lombard was killed in a plane crash, and shortly thereafter Gable joined the U.S. Army Air Force and flew several bombing missions over Germany during World War II.

After the war, Gable returned to Hollywood and made more films. Finally, in the '50s, age caught up with Gable and his popularity began to wane. In 1960, Gable died of a heart attack shortly after completing The Misfits, which also starred Marilyn Monroe.

Some of Gable's other films include Red Dust (1932), Mutiny on the Bounty (1935), San Francisco (1936), The Hucksters (1947), Command Decision (1948), Mogambo (1953), The Tall Men (1955), Soldier of Fortune (1955), Teacher's Pet (1958), Run Silent, Run Deep (1958), and It Started in Naples (1959).

(Continued)
This sequel to the commercially successful horror movie revisits the New Jersey summer camp for more grisly slaughter. There are a few romantic interludes among the young counselors; then it's time for assembly-line murder by a hooded killer with a mother fixation. He systematically dispatches his victims by garroting, an ax to the head, and other horrifying means aimed at increasing the shock effect. Will there be a Part III? Give us a break. **Director**—Steve Miner. (R)
87 minutes

FRIDAY THE 13TH—PART III (1982)

 (no stars)

Richard Brooker
Dana Kimmell

Unfortunately, there is a Part III, and here it is—an exceptionally vile horror-screamer that reworks the same plot as its predecessors. The terrible-tempered Jason (Brooker) again prowls Lake Crystal hacking, skewering, and slicing the teenagers with robot-like proficiency. Acting, direction, and logic are minimal while the blood and gore—filmed in 3-D—are overwhelming. One young girl (Kimmell) survives the slaughter, thus leaving the door open for Part IV. Have mercy. **Director**—Steve Miner. (R)
96 minutes

FRIDAY THE 13TH—THE FINAL CHAPTER (1984)

 (no stars)

Kimberly Beck
Corey Feldman

The vicious Jason is at work again, hacking, stabbing, and slicing dozens of victims in mechanical fashion. This blood-drenched film is no more than a rehash of the formula horror plot that served the previous outings. Only this time, the masked killer is stopped by a boy who wields a mean machete. And despite the title's final tone, the door is left ajar for another round of grisly mayhem. **Director**—Joseph Zito. (R)
91 minutes

FRIENDLY PERSUASION (1956)

 ★★★★

Gary Cooper
Dorothy McGuire
Anthony Perkins

A beautiful and sensitive story of a peace-loving Quaker family in Indiana whose lives are disrupted by the Civil War. Cooper and McGuire do well as the mother and father, but there's an especially winning performance by Perkins as their son. The outlook is perhaps a bit too sentimental, yet it's a fine piece of work. William Wyler's direction is on target. Also with Marjorie Main, Richard Eyer, and Robert Middleton. **Academy Award Nominations**—best picture; Wyler, best director; Perkins, best supporting actor.
139 minutes

THE FRISCO KID (1979)

 ★★

Gene Wilder
Harrison Ford

Wilder plays a befuddled Polish rabbi who sets off across the United States on horseback in 1850 to head a congregation in San Francisco. Wilder occasionally does well with this overdrawn ethnic joke, but the story is jagged and predictable, and fizzles just when we expect the gags to really sizzle. Part of the problem seems to be director Robert Aldrich, who's home on the range with action westerns, but not with this sort of comedy. Also with William Smith, Ramon Bieri, and Penny Peyser. (PG)
122 minutes

FRITZ THE CAT (1971)

★★★

Bitingly satirical animated feature that irreverently attacks the mores, standards, and styles of the '60s.

Writer/director/animator Ralph Bakshi spares no one in his vitriolic and witty near-masterpiece cartoon. Based on Robert Crumb's underground comic strip, it is probably the first cartoon to achieve an X rating. The overwhelmingly downbeat nature and violence may cause some viewers to wince, but the overall sophistication of its insights will please still more. (X)
78 minutes

FROM HERE TO ETERNITY
(1953)
★★★★

**Burt Lancaster
Deborah Kerr
Montgomery Clift
Frank Sinatra
Donna Reed**

First-rate, compelling drama about Army life in Hawaii on the eve of World War II. This screen version of James Jones's best-selling novel comes across with power and passion, thanks to sterling performances and taut direction. Clift, Lancaster, and Kerr head the cast, but the supporting performances of Sinatra and Reed highlight the film. Also with Ernest Borgnine, Philip Ober, and Mickey Shaughnessy. **Director**—Fred Zinnemann. **Academy Awards**—best picture; Zinnemann, best director; Sinatra, best supporting actor; Reed, best supporting actress; Daniel Taradash, writing (screenplay); Burnett Guffey, cinematography (black and white). **Nominations**—Clift, Lancaster, best actor; Kerr, best actress.
118 minutes b&w

FROM NOON TIL THREE
(1977)
★★★

**Charles Bronson
Jill Ireland**

Charles Bronson in From Noon Til Three.

Director Frank Gilroy's little comic western stars Bronson in an unconventional satirical role; he plays a two-bit bandit who holes up in a plush Victorian mansion belonging to an attractive and kooky widow, played by Ireland. The story is cheerful, mildly funny, and intelligent, although it takes a long time to make its point. Bronson's remarkable straight performance manages to be amusing. (PG)
100 minutes

FROM RUSSIA WITH LOVE
(1963)
 ★★★★

**Sean Connery
Robert Shaw**

More good rollicking spy adventures in this second James Bond film caper.

This time secret agent 007 is on the hit list of a Russian agent, played by Shaw, who also wants possession of a Russian coding machine. But don't worry. Our hero, played by Connery, takes care of the bad guys on a speeding train; he even deals with Lotte Lenya, who plays a vicious spy out for his scalp. It's all accomplished in high style and with tongue-in-cheek humor against exotic Istanbul and Venice backgrounds. Also with Pedro Armendariz, Daniela Bianchi, Bernard Lee, Eunice Gayson, and Lois Maxwell. **Director**—Terence Young. (PG)
118 minutes

FROM THE TERRACE (1960)
★★

**Paul Newman
Joanne Woodward
Myrna Loy**

Good-looking but leaden treatment of John O'Hara's novel, about family problems among the upper crust in Pennsylvania. Newman, Woodward, and Loy give adequate performances, but the film goes on too long, and the characters aren't developed with much interest. Also in the cast are Ina Balin, Leon Ames, George Grizzard, Patrick O'Neal, and Elizabeth Allen. **Director**—Mark Robson.
144 minutes

THE FRONT (1976)
 ★★★

**Woody Allen
Zero Mostel
Herschel Bernardi**

Here's a bold, entertaining, and moving comedy-drama about the entertainment industry's painful experience with the political witch hunts of the '50s. Allen is outstanding as a goggle-eyed schlemiel who fronts for blacklisted TV writers by submitting their scripts under his name. Many involved with this film—director Martin Ritt, screenwriter Walter Bernstein, and performers Mostel, Bernardi, Joshua Shelley, and Lloyd Gough—were themselves blacklisted. This uncompromising look at that tragic period is handled with intelligence, feeling, and humor. Also with
(Continued)

While Burt Lancaster listens, Frank Sinatra gives Montgomery Clift a piece of his mind in From Here to Eternity.

F
- The Front Page
- The Fugitive Kind
- The Fuller Brush Girl
- The Fuller Brush Man
- The Funhouse
- Funny Face
- Funny Girl

(Continued)
Michael Murphy and Remak Ramsay. (PG) **Academy Award Nomination**—Bernstein, best original screenplay.
94 minutes

THE FRONT PAGE (1931)

★★★★

**Pat O'Brien
Adolph Menjou**

Fast-paced, snappy drama from the stage play by Ben Hecht and Charles MacArthur, who also did the screenplay. O'Brien is the star reporter who wants to leave the hectic Chicago newspaper scene and marry. His editor, Menjou, talks him into covering one more story, a prison execution that misfires. The action is lively and rapid, with excellent direction from Lewis Milestone. Although an early talkie, this landmark film still stands out for its fast cutting techniques and cinematic style. Mary Brian as the fiancé O'Brien forgets, Edward Everett Horton, Frank McHugh, and George E. Stone all turn in good backup performances. **Academy Award Nominations**—best picture; Milestone, best director; Menjou, best actor.
101 minutes b&w

THE FUGITIVE KIND (1959)
★★

**Marlon Brando
Anna Magnani
Joanne Woodward**

This is a gloomy Tennessee Williams drama, based on his play *Orpheus Descending*. Brando stars as a footloose young man who becomes involved with women in a strange Southern town; Magnani and Woodward are the objects of his desires. Even with such heavyweights in the cast, the film never takes off. Victor Jory and Maureen Stapleton also star. **Director**—Sidney Lumet. *135 minutes b&w*

THE FULLER BRUSH GIRL
(1950)
★★

**Lucille Ball
Eddie Albert**

Lucille Ball tries to make a sale to the bridge club in The Fuller Brush Girl.

Ball stars in the title role, as an enthusiastic cosmetics saleslady who gets tangled up with murders and thieves. Typical slapstick stuff, with Lucy cutting up with delight. It's worthwhile if you love Lucy; otherwise, forget it. Supporting cast also includes Carl Benton Reid, Gale Robbins, Lee Patrick, Jeff Connell, and Jerome Cowan. **Director**—Lloyd Bacon.
85 minutes b&w

THE FULLER BRUSH MAN
(1948)
★★

**Red Skelton
Janet Blair**

Skelton dishes up the slapstick as an eager-beaver door-to-door salesman who becomes involved in murder. Predictable stuff, with some meandering, but it's well suited for Red. Lots of fun if you enjoy this sort of comedy. Don McGuire and Adele Jergens also co-star. **Director**—S. Sylvan Simon.
93 minutes b&w

THE FUNHOUSE (1981)

★★

**Elizabeth Berridge
Shawn Carson
Jeanne Auston**

Director Tobe Hooper, who established his horror-cult credentials with the frightful *Texas Chainsaw Massacre*, serves up another ration of gore, but this time there's too much nonsense mixed in with the terror. Four teenagers spend the night in an elaborate carnival funhouse where they are terrorized by a vile monster. Before the sun comes up, blood and dead bodies are strewn all over the place. Hooper puts his imagination and bizarre style into full force, but the film is deflated by amateurish performances. (R)
95 minutes

FUNNY FACE (1957)
★★★★

**Fred Astaire
Audrey Hepburn**

This is among the best of the Astaire musicals, with the dean of dancing turning in some fancy footwork to the beat of great Gershwin tunes. Fred plays a fashion photographer who meets a rather colorless bookstore clerk (Hepburn) and turns her into a glamorous fashion model. Sparkling Parisian locations enhance the stylish production. Kay Thompson, Michel Auclair, and Suzy Parker perform well in supporting roles. **Director**—Stanley Donen. *103 minutes*

FUNNY GIRL (1968)

★★★★

**Barbra Streisand
Omar Sharif
Walter Pidgeon**

Funny Girl features Barbra Streisand in the title role.

• Funny Lady
• A Funny Thing Happened
  on the Way to the Forum
• Fun with Dick and Jane

• Fury
• The Fury
• Gaby
• Gaily, Gaily

F·G

Streisand is perfectly cast as comedienne Fanny Brice in this glimmering musical. And she gives it her best shot, belting out a slew of show-stopping tunes with exceptional gusto. The Jule Styne-Bob Merrill score is first-rate; "Don't Rain On My Parade" and "People" are memorable. This was Streisand's film debut, and she proves that she's a powerhouse performer. The fine supporting cast also includes Kay Medford and Anne Francis. **Director**—William Wyler. (G) **Academy Award**—Barbra Streisand, best actress. **Academy Award Nominations**—best picture; Medford, best supporting actress; Harry Stradling, cinematography.   *155 minutes*

FUNNY LADY (1975)
★★

Barbra Streisand
James Caan
Omar Sharif
Ben Vereen

This sequel to *Funny Girl* involves the further adventures of Fanny Brice, again as depicted by Streisand. There are a few comic moments, and the film is occasionally shored up by the shining talents of the great Streisand. But when she stops singing, the picture limps along amid phony Hollywood-type romantic suffering and unconvincing characterizations. Also with Roddy McDowall and Larry Gates. **Director**—Herbert Ross (PG)
137 minutes

A FUNNY THING HAPPENED ON THE WAY TO THE FORUM (1966)
  ★★★

Zero Mostel
Phil Silvers

Mostel is fabulous in this musical comedy set in ancient Rome. Zero plays a scheming slave in the home of a wealthy family; he's trying hard to gain his freedom. Richard Lester directs with plenty of style and pep, and there's no shortage of good laughs. Most of the supporting roles are also performed excellently, with Silvers, Michael Crawford, Jack Gilford, Michael Horder, and Beatrix Lehmann in top form. The film is adapted from the Broadway production, with the score of Stephen Sondheim mostly intact.   *99 minutes*

FUN WITH DICK AND JANE (1977)
  ★★★

Jane Fonda
George Segal

Segal and Fonda are cheerful and intensely funny in this social comedy about a middle-class couple who turn to crime when the husband loses his job as an aerospace engineer. Both perform resourcefully and work hard to keep the laughter flowing in their perky slapstick routines. The story is as contemporary as the latest recession, and it pecks at some vulgar aspects of middle-class values. The supporting cast is excellent, especially Ed McMahon, who plays Segal's former employer. Also with Dick Gautier and Allan Miller. **Director**—Ted Kotcheff. (PG)   *95 minutes*

FURY (1936)
★★★

Spencer Tracy
Sylvia Sidney

Devastating social drama of small-town America where an innocent man is lynched by a crazed mob for a murder he didn't commit. Director Fritz Lang in his first American film vividly portrays the danger of mob rule and the ease with which the innocent can be corrupted. Tracy escapes the mob through a fluke but becomes a bitter, hardened man seeking revenge on his tormentors. Sidney is the girl he loses as his obsession grows. Excellent performances by Bruce Cabot, Walter Abel, and Walter Brennan. The second half of the film does not live up to the lynching, but this still remains forceful filmmaking. **Academy Award Nomination**—Norman Krasna, writing (original story).   *94 minutes b&w*

THE FURY (1978)
  ★

Kirk Douglas
John Cassavetes
Carrie Snodgress

Brian De Palma, who directed *Carrie*, uses the parapsychic gimmick again in this gruesome, blood-drenched chiller. The absurd and confusing script concerns a teenager with telekinesis power—the ability to move objects by will—who is kidnapped by a super-secret government agency. De Palma lays on plenty of slick action, but there isn't an ounce of logic in this story, and he only succeeds in insulting the intelligence of his audience. Douglas, Cassavetes, and Snodgress are on board to the detriment of their reputations. Also with Amy Irving and Charles Durning. (R)   *118 minutes*

G

GABY (1956)
★★

Leslie Caron
John Kerr

Caron and Kerr star in this tepid remake of *Waterloo Bridge*. It's the romantic story of a ballerina, played by Caron, who's in love with a soldier about to be sent into battle in World War II. Kerr plays the soldier. The film is rather too melodramatic and not as good as the original. Also with Cedric Hardwicke, Taina Elg, and Margalo Gillmore. **Director**—Curtis Bernhardt.   *97 minutes*

GAILY, GAILY (1969)
★★★

Beau Bridges
Melina Mercouri

A winning film biography about the early career of Ben Hecht, the colorful Chicago journalist. The film's script is somewhat uneven, but the early 1900s settings are impressive, and the production is executed with just the right amount of humor. Bridges gives an appealing performance of Hecht as a determined cub reporter. And he's assisted nicely by Mercouri, who plays the warmhearted madam of a Chicago bordello. Also with Brian Keith, George Kennedy, Hume Cronyn, Margot Kidder, Melodie Johnson, and Wilfrid Hyde-White. **Director**— Norman Jewison. (PG)   *117 minutes*

G
- Galaxina
- Galaxy of Terror
- Gallipoli
- Gambit
- Gandhi
- Gang War
- Garbo Talks
- The Garden of the Finzi-Continis

GALAXINA (1981)
★

Dorothy R. Stratten

Dorothy Stratten plays the alluring android Galaxina.

A flimsy, adolescent spoof of galactic films, with a surplus of silly dialogue and a critical shortage of laughs. The late Dorothy R. Stratten, a former *Playboy* Playmate, is in the title role, as a gorgeous robot who pilots a spacecraft. She can't act, and she isn't even as sexy as could be expected. Wooden performances and cardboard characters prevail amid the gleaming space hardware, and the action never even reaches orbit. **Director**—William Sachs. (R) *95 minutes*

GALAXY OF TERROR (1982)
★

Edward Albert
Erin Moran
Ray Walston

This thinly plotted sci-fi adventure is about astronauts who attempt to rescue a spaceship on a strange planet and are attacked by reptilelike monsters. The script, much on the order of *Alien*, is absurd, and the characters are strictly cardboard. In one sequence, a female astronaut is raped by a giant worm. How low can a movie scene go? **Director**—B. D. Clark. (R) *80 minutes*

GALLIPOLI (1981)
 ★★★

Mark Lee
Bill Kerr
Mel Gibson

Australian director Peter Weir fash-

ions a handsome and intimate historical film that deals intelligently with the exploitations of youthful zeal, ambition, and innocence. Lee and Gibson are convincing as two athletic young men who enlist in the Australian army and fight in the disastrous World War I battle of Gallipoli. Weir concentrates primarily on personal relationships, and the story unfortunately lacks drama and urgency. Nevertheless, his provocative statement is most memorable. Also with Bill Hunter and John Morris. (PG) *110 minutes*

GAMBIT (1966)
★★★

Michael Caine
Shirley MacLaine

A nifty crime caper, with Caine as a determined but rather inept thief out to steal a valuable statue from a wealthy man. He has the help of MacLaine, cast effectively as a mysterious Eurasian woman he hires to participate in the heist. The script is spotty, but it maintains an entertaining pace right to the end. Also with Herbert Lom, Roger C. Carmel, and John Abbott. **Director**—Ronald Neame. *109 minutes*

GANDHI (1982)
 ★★★★

Ben Kingsley

Ben Kingsley plays Gandhi, *spiritual leader and liberator of India.*

Richard Attenborough's magnificent, sweeping, inspirational biography of India's architect of nonviolent action who led his country to freedom from British oppression and occupation. At the center of this epic undertaking is Kingsley, the Anglo-Indian actor, as the saintly Mahatma (great soul). His towering portrayal is amazingly convincing and vivid. Although the film is more than three hours long, it never loses its power and passion. An unforgettable movie. Excellent support from Edward Fox, John Gielgud, and Rohini Hattangady. (PG) **Academy Awards**—best picture; Kingsley, best actor; Attenborough, best director; John Briley, best screenplay (written directly for the screen); Billy Williams and Ronnie Taylor, cinematography. *188 minutes*

GANG WAR
See Odd Man Out

GARBO TALKS (1984)
★★★

Anne Bancroft
Ron Silver

Bancroft is amusing as an eccentric woman stricken with cancer, whose last wish is to meet the great movie star Greta Garbo. Her son (Silver) tries to locate the reclusive screen legend. This warm, breezy comedy, though, is actually about New York City inhabitants and their effervescent spirit of urban life. Howard Da Silva, Dorothy Loudon, Harvey Fierstein, and Hermione Gingold are outstanding in their portrayals of colorful characters. **Director**—Sidney Lumet. (PG-13) *105 minutes*

THE GARDEN OF THE FINZI-CONTINIS (1971)
★★★★

Dominique Sanda
Helmut Berger

Beautifully photographed drama of a patrician Jewish family in fascist Italy in 1938. The well-bred Finzi-Continis live in their own naive dream world enclosed by a brick-walled garden, unaware and choosing to ignore the political changes going on around

- Gaslight
- Gator
- The Gauntlet
- The Gay Divorcee
- The Geisha Boy
- Geneviève
- Genghis Khan

G

them. Sanda is riveting as the daughter, and Berger is superb as her fragile brother. Vittorio De Sica's direction is masterly as he slowly tracks the family to its inevitable downfall. A harrowing portrayal of Jews being stripped of possessions, dignity, and freedom in a world whose physical beauty mocks its distorted spirit. In Italian with English titles. **Academy Award**—best foreign language film. **Nomination**—Ugo Pirro, Vittorio Bonicelli, best screenplay (based on material from another medium). (No MPAA rating)
95 minutes

GASLIGHT
(1944)
 ★★★

Charles Boyer
Ingrid Bergman

Dated but still entertaining drama about a man attempting to drive his wife mad. A top cast turns in stylish performances to bring out the chills. The screenplay is based on Patrick Hamilton's play. Also with Joseph Cotten, Dame May Whitty, and Angela Lansbury. **Director**—George Cukor. **Academy Award**—Bergman, best actress. **Nominations**—best picture; Boyer, best actor; Lansbury, best supporting actress; Joseph Ruttenberg, cinematography (black and white).
144 minutes b&w

GATOR (1976)
★★

Burt Reynolds
Jack Weston
Lauren Hutton

Reynolds is mischievous moonshiner Gator McClusky in this choppy follow-up to his lucrative *White Lightning* movie. This time, Gator is recruited to infiltrate the organization of a backwater county crime boss. Reynolds also is the director and handles the job in an uneven manner. There are moments of excitement and drama interlaced with unsophisticated humor, contrived action sequences, and lethargic romantic scenes. There are, however, interesting character portrayals by Weston, Hutton, and Jerry Reed. Also with Alice Ghostley, Mike Douglas, and Dub Taylor. (PG)
116 minutes

THE GAUNTLET (1978)
 ★★

Clint Eastwood
Sondra Locke

Eastwood is director and star of this caper about a hard-drinking detective who risks all to bring a Las Vegas hooker, played by Locke, to Phoenix to testify against the mob. Eastwood's character here is a departure from his familiar *Dirty Harry* routine. The film's action and violence are at par, with narrow escapes in assorted vehicles, including a motorcycle and an armored bus. The comic-book storyline is unbelievable. It's Eastwood's stylish mayhem that seems to count. Also with Pat Hingle, William Prince, and Bill McKinney. (R)
109 minutes

THE GAY DIVORCEE (1934)
★★★

Fred Astaire
Ginger Rogers
Betty Grable

Ginger Rogers and Fred Astaire enjoy post-marital bliss in The Gay Divorcee.

Astaire plays an infatuated dancer who mopes about until the woman he loves agrees to marry him. Despite the dated material, the star-studded cast, including Erik Rhodes, Edward Everett Horton, Eric Blore, and Alice Brady, is still fresh and contemporary. Top songs by Cole Porter include "Night and Day" and the Oscar-winning "Continental." **Director**—Mark

Sandrich. **Academy Award Nomination**—best picture. *107 minutes b&w*

THE GEISHA BOY (1958)
★★

Jerry Lewis

Lewis plays a bumbling magician traveling with a USO troupe in the Far East. Typical Lewis high jinks prevail, with a number of effective sight gags generating some laughs—but not enough to sustain interest. Lewis strains a little too much, and at times the film lapses into sentimentality. Also with Marie MacDonald, Sessue Hayakawa, Barton MacLane, and Suzanne Pleshette. **Director**—Frank Tashlin.
98 minutes

GENEVIÈVE (1954)
 ★★★★

Dinah Sheridan
John Gregson
Kay Kendall
Kenneth More

A warm British comedy done with exceptional skill and care. It involves a good-natured cross-country race between two couples, in vintage cars. Along the way, there are many charming and memorable moments, brilliantly executed by a delightful cast. Kendall stands out in some saucy comedy scenes. And there are other delicious performances from Sheridan, Gregson, More, Geoffrey Keen, Joyce Grenfell, Reginald Beckwith, and Arthur Wontner. **Director**—Henry Cornelius. **Academy Award Nomination**—William Rose, writing (story and screenplay). *86 minutes*

GENGHIS KHAN (1964)
★★

Omar Sharif
Stephen Boyd
Françoise Dorléac

A passable historical epic with some good action scenes, but hung up by a script loaded with nonsense. The plot follows the Chinese warrior's rise to power and his campaign of revenge against his old enemy Jamuga, who
(Continued)

G
- Genocide
- Gentleman Jim
- Gentleman's Agreement
- Gentlemen Prefer Blondes
- Georgy Girl
- Gestapo
- Get Crazy

(Continued)
murdered Genghis Khan's father. Moments of decent acting stand out among the routine. Cast also includes James Mason, Robert Morley, Telly Savalas, and Eli Wallach. **Director**—Henry Levin. *126 minutes*

GENOCIDE (1982)
★★★

A gripping, unforgettable documentary about the Nazis' war against the Jews. The horrors of Hitler's "final solution" are recounted through the skillful use of newsreel footage and still photographs. There are chilling reminders, too, about the rise of Nazi power and the policies of some countries, including the United States, of refusing entry to Jews seeking escape from the Holocaust. Orson Welles and Elizabeth Taylor narrate the film with authority and emotion. **Director**—Arnold Schwartzman. (No MPAA rating) *90 minutes*

GENTLEMAN JIM (1942)
★★★

**Errol Flynn
Alan Hale**

Errol Flynn (right) pummels an opponent as the famed prizefighter Gentleman Jim.

Flynn is in the title role of this pleasant film biography of famous 1890s boxer Jim Corbett. Flynn's portrayal offers just the right amount of dash and comedy in the role of this colorful hero, who fought when the sport was prohibited in some areas. Jack Carson, Alexis Smith, and Ward Bond are also among the co-stars. **Director**—Raoul Walsh. *104 minutes*

GENTLEMAN'S AGREEMENT
(1947)
★★★★

**Gregory Peck
Dorothy McGuire
John Garfield**

Fascinating and powerful story about a journalist, played by Peck who poses as a Jew and encounters much hatred. The film, based on Laura Hobson's intelligent novel, was rather startling at the time of its release, and it's still compelling. Fine acting all around, with Celeste Holm outstanding as a lonely fashion editor. Cast also includes Anne Revere, June Havoc, Albert Dekker, Jane Wyatt, and Dean Stockwell. **Director**—Elia Kazan. **Academy Awards**—best picture; Kazan, best director; Holm, best supporting actress. **Nominations**—Peck, best actor; McGuire, best actress; Moss Hart, writing (screenplay).
118 minutes b&w

GENTLEMEN PREFER BLONDES (1953)
★★★

**Jane Russell
Marilyn Monroe**

Marilyn Monroe proves that Gentlemen Prefer Blondes—*but they don't mind Jane Russell, either.*

Monroe and Russell are right at home in this agreeable musical-comedy, about a couple of Little Rock tootsies off to Paris to snag rich husbands. You can forget the dopey plot and keep your eyes on the girls, who sing songs like "Diamonds Are a Girl's Best Friend." Charles Coburn adds a touch of comedy to the splashy proceedings. Based on the Broadway musical of the '20s. Also with Tommy Noonan and George Winslow. **Director**—Howard Hawks. *91 minutes*

GEORGY GIRL (1966)
★★★★

**Lynn Redgrave
James Mason**

Redgrave is marvelous in the role of an awkward young girl who chucks her bizarre life-style and marries a wealthy widower old enough to be her father. Mason plays the widower. The charming comedy-drama examines contemporary attitudes and develops entertaining characterizations along the way. The entire cast performs splendidly, with an exceptional supporting role by Charlotte Rampling as Redgrave's freewheeling roommate. Alan Bates and Bill Owen also star. **Director**—Silvio Narizzano. **Academy Award Nominations**—Redgrave, best actress; Mason, best supporting actor; Ken Higgins, cinematography (black and white). *100 minutes b&w*

GESTAPO
See Night Train to Munich

GET CRAZY (1983)
★★

**Malcolm McDowell
Lori Eastside**

Director Allen Arkush, who gave us *Rock 'n' Roll High School*, sprinkles energetic high jinks and lively musical numbers throughout this mixed-bag send-up of a gala rock concert. Yet most gags fall flat and the proceedings are crowded with too many fleeting characters who become lost in the confusion. McDowell is convincing as a strutting rock superstar and Eastside puts on an impressive all-female punk rock act. Many of the other backstage

• Get Out Your
Handkerchiefs
• Getting Straight

• The Ghost and Mrs. Muir
• Ghostbusters
• Ghost Story
• Giant

G

portrayals are forgettable, but watch for Lou Reed. (R) *92 minutes*

GET OUT YOUR HANDKERCHIEFS (1978)

 ★★★★

**Gerard Depardieu
Patrick Dewaere
Carole Laure**

An exhilarating, audacious comedy by French director Bertrand Blier. Two bumbling pals can't understand why the beautiful wife of one of them is down in the dumps, but a precocious 13-year-old boy knows what the woman wants. Blier's observation of the feminine mystique has never been so funny. The subject of the film could have been offensive, but it's carried off with cool intelligence. Also with Michel Serreault and Eleonore Hirt. In French with English titles. (No MPAA rating) **Academy Award**—best foreign-language film. *109 minutes*

GETTING STRAIGHT (1970)

 ★★

**Elliott Gould
Candice Bergen**

A dated and only occasionally interesting comedy-drama about political radicalism of the '60s and '70s. Gould plays a veteran who returns to college as a student and is torn between idealism and the conventional attitude of the administration. An on-campus confrontation between the students and the cops comes off badly. Also with Jeff Corey, Max Julien, and Robert F. Lyons. **Director**—Richard Rush. (R) *125 minutes*

THE GHOST AND MRS. MUIR (1947)

★★★

**Gene Tierney
Rex Harrison**

Engaging and charming comedy about a widow, played by Tierney. She lives by the sea and strikes up a romance with the ghost of a sea captain, played by Harrison. It's a handsomely produced fantasy, with the proper measure of sentimentality included.

Also with George Sanders, Edna Best, Vanessa Brown, Robert Coote, Anna Lee, and Natalie Wood. **Director**—Joseph L. Mankiewicz.

104 minutes b&w

GHOSTBUSTERS (1984)

★★

**Bill Murray
Dan Aykroyd**

Elaborate slapstick satire starring *Saturday Night Live* alumni Murray and Aykroyd as fly-by-night parapsychologists who chase around New York City zapping demons. The loosely constructed film attempts to spoof *The Exorcist* and other horror fare. Although laughs are in short supply, there are plenty of tacky special effects that tend to upstage the comedy. Also with Sigourney Weaver and Harold Ramis. **Director**—Ivan Reitman. (PG) *105 minutes*

GHOST STORY (1981)

 ★

**John Houseman
Fred Astaire
Melvyn Douglas
Douglas Fairbanks, Jr.**

Four old men are haunted by a ghastly deed they committed 50 years ago, and a mysterious woman suddenly appears to seek revenge. The topic seems menacing, but the story quickly

bogs down with trite fright effects, unimpressive atmospherics, and other failed attempts to scare. The film resembles a fluffed-up version of cheap horror films like *Friday the 13th*. Houseman, Astaire, Douglas, and Fairbanks, as the elderly gentlemen, try to give the production some class, but they waste their talents. **Director**—John Irvin. (R) *110 minutes*

GIANT (1956)

★★★★

**Elizabeth Taylor
Rock Hudson
James Dean
Carroll Baker**

This sprawling epic, based on the novel by Edna Ferber, is about a Texas family involved in cattle ranching. The film is rendered with style and fine acting by a good cast. Hudson and Dean are excellent as men in love with the beautiful Taylor. Director George Stevens expertly develops a feeling for the period and the lives of the characters who achieved success from the land. There's fine supporting work, too, from Baker, Sal Mineo, Mercedes McCambridge, Chill Wills, Dennis Hopper, and Rod Taylor. This was Dean's last picture. (G) **Academy Award**—Stevens, best director. **Nominations**—best picture; Dean, Hudson, best actor; McCambridge, best supporting actress; Fred Guiol and Ivan Moffat, writing (best screenplay—adapted). *197 minutes*

Douglas Fairbanks, Jr., Fred Astaire, John Houseman, and Melvyn Douglas face up to a terrible secret in Ghost Story.

 Movie is available in Beta and VHS videotape

GIDGET (1959)
★★

**Sandra Dee
Cliff Robertson
James Darren**

Fluffy teenage comedy-adventure has Dee in the title role, making goo-goo eyes at a surfer, played by Darren; but mom and dad are skeptical of the romance. Robertson plays a beach bum. This original feature led to several *Gidget* sequels. Also with Doug McClure, Toby Baker, Arthur O'Connell, and Yvonne Craig. **Director**—Paul Wendkos. *95 minutes*

GIGI (1958)
★★★★

**Leslie Caron
Louis Jourdan
Maurice Chevalier**

In Gigi, Maurice Chevalier and Hermione Gingold look on as Louis Jourdan makes eyes at Leslie Caron as the young French girl.

Colorful and delightful Lerner and Loewe musical, graced with memorable songs and fine acting. Caron is ideal in the part of a young French girl who becomes a stunning woman and charms a handsome rake, played by Jourdan. The film, however, is best remembered for the performance of Chevalier as Gigi's guardian; he sings "Thank Heaven for Little Girls." The costumes and turn-of-the-century Paris settings are wonderful. Co-stars Hermione Gingold, Jacques Bergerac, Eva Gabor, and John Abbott. **Director**—Vincente Minnelli. (G) **Academy Awards**—best picture; Minnelli, best director; Alan Jay Lerner, best screenplay (based on material from another medium); Joseph Ruttenberg, cinematography (color). *116 minutes*

GILDA (1946)
★★★★

**Rita Hayworth
Glenn Ford
George Macready**

Rita Hayworth is the alluring Gilda.

A moody drama set in South America, with Ford as a gambling man emotionally involved with his boss's wife, played fetchingly by Hayworth. Macready plays Ford's boss. Rita is at her loveliest, and she performs the song "Put the Blame on Mame." Typical Hollywood atmospheric melodrama of the '40s era. Also with Steve Geray and Joseph Calleia. **Director**—Charles Vidor. *110 minutes b&w*

THE GIRL CAN'T HELP IT (1956)
★★

**Jayne Mansfield
Tom Ewell**

Mansfield stars in this routine comedy

Mobster Edmund O'Brien with his favorite moll, Jayne Mansfield, in The Girl Can't Help It.

as the girl friend of a mobster. She plays the role of a dumb blonde being promoted for stardom by press agent Ewell. There are many sight gags and some comic pokes at Jayne's famous figure. A number of rock 'n' roll stars, including Little Richard and Fats Domino, are featured. Also with Julie London and Ray Anthony. **Director**—Frank Tashlin. *97 minutes*

GIRL CRAZY (1943)
★★★

**Judy Garland
Mickey Rooney**

Garland and Rooney belt out some fabulous Gershwin numbers in this romantic musical. Rooney plays a rich young man from the East, sent off to a remote southwestern school to take his mind off girls, but Garland is there and the fun begins. Other fine talent includes Guy Kibbee, Gil Stratton, Rags Ragland, June Allyson, Nancy Walker, and Tommy Dorsey and his band. **Director**—Norman Taurog. *99 minutes b&w*

GIRL FRIENDS (1978)
★

**Melanie Mayron
Eli Wallach
Bob Balaban
Anita Skinner**

Producer-director Claudia Weill's first feature film is an amateurish and

160

• Give My Regards to Broad Street • Give My Regards to Broadway • Gizmo • The Glass Bottom Boat • The Glass Menagerie • The Glenn Miller Story • Gloria

G

overly emotional study of loneliness in the big city. This theme has been done many times before, and Weill doesn't add any new dimensions. Mayron stars as a young neurotic photographer, who is shaken when her roommate leaves to be married. Also with Viveca Lindfors. (No MPAA rating)

86 minutes

Band leader James Stewart (right) and his pilots make a fateful decision about the weather in *The Glenn Miller Story.*

GIVE MY REGARDS TO BROAD STREET (1984)

 ★★

Paul McCartney

A wealth of rock numbers enlivens this loosely structured romp starring McCartney of Beatles fame. The music alone is a treat for Beatles fans. Yet, the flimsy plot—something to do with Paul's search for a missing master recording tape—comes off as excess baggage. A few new songs are introduced along with some reworkings of old tunes. Ringo Starr, Barbara Bach, and Linda McCartney add their talents to the frolic. **Director**—Peter Webb. (PG) *108 minutes*

GIVE MY REGARDS TO BROADWAY (1948)

★★

Dan Dailey
Charles Winninger

Flimsy musical, about a veteran vaudeville hoofer, played by Winninger, trying to make a comeback even though this type of entertainment is on the wane. The creaky plot involves a lot of sentimentality about the love affairs of the vaudevillian's children. A few familiar songs are featured; otherwise it's a drag. Also included in the cast are Fay Bainter, Charles Ruggles, and Nancy Guild. **Director**—Lloyd Bacon. *89 minutes*

GIZMO (1980)

 ★★★

Hare-brained inventions have a field day in this zany and cheerful documentary, compiled by *Village Voice* columnist Howard Smith. Film clips show goggles with windshield wipers, an electric fork to turn spaghetti, rickety flying machines that go ker-plunk, a commuter airplane that ejects passengers at their destinations, and so on. Perhaps these loony schemes didn't bring fame and fortune to their inventors, but displayed here, they leave us with a laugh or two. (G)

77 minutes b&w/color

THE GLASS BOTTOM BOAT (1966)

★★

Doris Day
Rod Taylor
Arthur Godfrey

Routine foolishness, with Day as a widow who becomes involved with a spy ring. This flimsy farce bulges with unworkable slapstick and gags that fall flat. Godfrey is rather pleasant, as the captain of the title boat and Doris's father. Taylor plays a businessman and Doris's love interest. Paul Lynde, John McGiver, Edward Andrews, Eric Fleming, and Dom DeLuise co-star. **Director**—Frank Tashlin. *110 minutes*

THE GLASS MENAGERIE (1950)

★★★

Gertrude Lawrence
Jane Wyman
Kirk Douglas
Arthur Kennedy

Good film rendition of Tennessee Williams's thoughtful stage play. The drama is about a lonely crippled girl and her strained relationship with her mother, who lives a life of fantasy. There are many touching moments brought out by good acting from a top cast. Efficiently directed by Irving Rapper. *107 minutes b&w*

THE GLENN MILLER STORY (1954)

★★★

James Stewart
June Allyson

Sentimental and romantic film biography of the popular big-band leader of the '30s and '40s. Stewart is exceptionally convincing in the title role, and Allyson is fine as Miller's wife. However, it's Miller's fabulous music that really carries the film. Worthwhile, indeed, if you love the Miller sound; there's plenty of it here. Also with Harry Morgan, Frances Langford, Charles Drake, Louis Armstrong, and Gene Krupa. **Director**—Anthony Mann. (G) **Academy Award Nomination**—Valentine Davies and Oscar Brodney, writing (story and screenplay). *116 minutes*

GLORIA (1980)

 ★★

Gena Rowlands
Juan Adames

Gena Rowlands is a gun moll out to beat the mob in Gloria.

G

- The Go-Between
- The Goddess
- The Godfather
- The Godfather, Part II
- God Is My Co-Pilot
- God's Little Acre

(Continued)
Rowlands, in the title role, plays a tough-talking, quick-on-the-trigger ex-gun moll who is forced to protect an eight-year-old Puerto Rican boy marked for assassination by gangsters, even though she says she doesn't like the kid. Rowlands's performance is credible and appealing as the hard-bitten dame who suddenly discovers her mother instincts. But director John Cassavetes's threadbare screenplay is farfetched. And there's a lot of desperate chasing around New York City, which finally becomes tiresome. Also with Buck Henry and Julie Carmen. (PG) **Academy Award Nomination**—Rowlands, best actress. *123 minutes*

THE GO-BETWEEN (1970)
★★★

**Alan Bates
Julie Christie
Dominic Guard**

A beautiful and moody movie, set in turn-of-the-century England, involving a boy who passes love letters between an aristocratic woman and a farmer. Harold Pinter's screenplay is touching, and the production is mounted handsomely. Christie and Bates play the unlikely lovers with tenderness; Guard plays the boy. A most unusual and richly rewarding film. Cast also includes Michael Redgrave, Michael Gough, Margaret Leighton, and Edward Fox. **Director**—Joseph Losey. *116 minutes*

THE GODDESS (1958)
★★★★

**Kim Stanley
Lloyd Bridges**

Stanley is exceptionally appealing as a beauty from a small town seeking fame as a Hollywood sex symbol, but mostly finding heartache. Paddy Chayefsky's biting and intelligent script is partially based on the career of Marilyn Monroe. Parts of the film are slightly overwrought, but it's all held nicely together by Stanley's brilliant portrayal and other fine acting jobs. Also with Steven Hill and Betty Lou Holland. **Director**—John Cromwell. **Academy Award Nomination**—Chayefsky, best story and screenplay

(writing directly for the screen). *105 minutes b&w*

THE GODFATHER (1972)
★★★★

**Marlon Brando
Al Pacino
Robert Duvall
James Caan**

The Godfather, *Marlon Brando, confers with his son, Al Pacino, about the subtleties of racketeering.*

A brilliant and exciting epic crime drama, masterfully fashioned by director Francis Ford Coppola from Mario Puzo's best-selling novel. The engrossing plot follows the career of a Mafia leader and the struggle for power between his family and rival family organizations. Exceptional acting throughout. And the drama, suspense, and character development are of the highest order. The film is more than just a compelling gangster saga; it's also a fascinating study of the struggle for achievement and success in America. Memorable performances by Brando, Pacino, Duvall, Caan, Richard Castellano, and Diane Keaton. (R) **Academy Awards**—best picture; Brando, best actor; Puzo and Coppola, best screenplay (based on material from another medium). **Nominations**—Coppola, best director; Caan, Duvall, Pacino, best supporting actor. *175 minutes*

THE GODFATHER, PART II
(1974)
★★★★

**Al Pacino
Robert Duvall
Diane Keaton
Robert De Niro
John Cazale**

A worthy sequel to the first film. This continuation of the epic saga fills in the early life of family patriarch Don Corleone and then picks up the story after his death, with young Michael (Pacino) taking control and expanding the crime empire. Engrossing scenes and sensational acting abound. Pacino is excellent, and De Niro, somewhat underplaying his part, is outstanding as young Don Vito, establishing his family and power at the turn of the century. Duvall, Keaton, Cazale, Talia Shire, Lee Strasberg, and Michael Gazzo are terrific in supporting roles. **Director**—Francis Ford Coppola. (R) **Academy Awards**—best picture; Coppola, best director; De Niro, best supporting actor; Coppola and Mario Puzo, best screenplay (adapted from other material). **Nominations**—Pacino, best actor; Gazzo, Strasberg, best supporting actor; Shire, best supporting actress. *200 minutes*

GOD IS MY CO-PILOT (1945)
★★★

**Dennis Morgan
Dane Clark
Raymond Massey**

Better-than-average air-combat film, set in the Pacific during World War II. The plot involves fighting scenes with the Flying Tigers. There are some predictable moments among the good drama and action scenes. Also with Alan Hale, Andrea King, Donald Woods, John Ridgely, and Craig Stevens. **Director**—Robert Florey. *89 minutes b&w*

GOD'S LITTLE ACRE (1958)
★★

**Robert Ryan
Aldo Ray
Tina Louise
Buddy Hackett**

Watered-down screen version of Erskine Caldwell's novel, although some good acting and characterizations are featured. Ryan is effective as the patriarch of a family of poor Georgia farmers. He brings even more misery to the family in his desperate and unproductive search for gold on his land. Louise is fetching and convincing as a

• The Gods Must Be Crazy • Go for Broke
• Godspell • Going Berserk
• Godzilla vs. Megalon • Going in Style
• Going My Way

G

cheating wife. Also with Jack Lord, Fay Spain, and Vic Morrow. **Director**—Anthony Mann. (PG)

110 minutes b&w

THE GODS MUST BE CRAZY
(1984)
★★

Marius Weyers
Sandra Prinsloo

A wobbly farce, set in southern Africa, that contrasts the uncomplicated life of nomadic tribesmen with the frenzied existence of modern urban dwellers. The film is on solid ground as long as it concentrates on the affairs of the Bushmen in the Kalahari Desert. Enter "civilized" people, and the story turns to tiresome slapstick. **Director**—Jamie Uys. (PG) *109 minutes*

GODSPELL (1973)
★★

Victor Garber
David Haskell
Jerry Sroka

The life of Jesus, set as a rock musical in contemporary New York, is performed with much pep and enthusiasm, but fails to provoke interest in the story. A band of hippie disciples follows their leader to the beat of numerous musical numbers, composed splendidly by Stephen Schwartz. The young cast performs well with their dancing and singing, but the production runs out of steam before long. Also with Robin Lamont and Lynne Thigpen. **Director**—David Greene. (G) *102 minutes*

GODZILLA VS. MEGALON
(1976)
★★★

Katsuhiko Sasaki
Hiroyuki Kawase

This imaginative comic-book film from Japan has the good Tyrannosaurus Godzilla defending Tokyo from the ravages of similar prehistoric monsters. The film's story line is rather appealing, and the technical effects are superb. And, would you believe, the violence is low-keyed. Lots of fun

for the kiddies and even some adults. Also with Yutaka Hayashi and Robert Dunham. **Director**—Jun Fukuda. (G) *80 minutes*

GO FOR BROKE (1951)
★★★

Van Johnson
Lane Nakano
George Miki

Johnson plays the commander of Nisei troops—Americans of Japanese ancestry—fighting in Europe during World War II. Good action and interesting characterizations come off well in this unusual war movie. Also with Akira Fukunaga, Warner Anderson, and Gianna Canale. **Director**—Robert Pirosh. **Academy Award Nomination**—Pirosh, writing (story and screenplay). *93 minutes b&w*

GOING BERSERK (1983)
★

John Candy

Going Berserk features the better half of the Second City TV cast, Joe Flaherty, Eugene Levy, and John Candy.

Candy, Joe Flaherty, and Eugene Levy rib religious cults, politics, and fad exercise regimens. The corpulent Candy manages to put over a few gags as a limo driver who is convinced he must assassinate his future father-in-law. Yet most of the situations are merely blasé, not berserk. And director David Steinberg would be a lot funnier in front of the camera than behind it. Another tame comedy from

some highly talented SCTV graduates who don't seem to have reached their potential on film yet. (R) *85 minutes*

GOING IN STYLE
(1980)
★★

George Burns
Art Carney
Lee Strasberg

George Burns and Lee Strasberg are Going in Style.

Three senior citizens, frustrated with idleness and the limits of Social Security, plan and execute a bank robbery. Burns, Carney, and Strasberg play the aged robbers. The film comments on the problems of the aging, and the three old pros turn in appealing performances, but the story is predictable and unconvincing. Limp direction by newcomer Martin Brest makes the movie itself appear caught in the aging process—more drama and more comic energy are badly needed. Also with Charles Hallahan and Pamela Payton-Wright. (PG) *96 minutes*

GOING MY WAY (1944)
★★★★

Bing Crosby
Barry Fitzgerald

Crosby is perfectly cast in this sentimental comedy, as a young priest in a
(Continued)

G
- Goin' South
- Goldengirl
- The Golden Seal
- The Golden Voyage of Sinbad
- Goldfinger
- Gone With the Wind

Good Irish Catholic priest Bing Crosby checks in on his ailing monsignor Barry Fitzgerald in Going My Way.

(Continued)
New York slum parish. Fitzgerald also shines as the elderly pastor who is finally charmed by the personable newcomer. Bing, perhaps at the top of his film career, sings "Swinging On a Star" and "Too-ra-Loo-ra-Loo-ra." Many delightful scenes throughout. Good supporting work is provided by Rise Stevens, Frank McHugh, Gene Lockhart, James Brown, and Porter Hall. **Director**—Leo McCarey. **Academy Awards**—best picture; McCarey, best director; Crosby, best actor; Fitzgerald, best supporting actor; McCarey, writing (original story). **Nomination**—Lionel Lincoln, cinematography (black and white).

126 minutes b&w

GOIN' SOUTH (1978)
 ★★

Jack Nicholson
Mary Steenburgen

Thin, uneven comedy-western with Nicholson in the saddle as a scruffy outlaw who escapes the gallows by marrying a prim spinster, played by Steenburgen. Nicholson, who also directed, hams it up and essentially wastes his own remarkable talent on such hokey material. The film begins with promise, but never gets going. John Belushi, Christopher Lloyd, and Veronica Cartwright also star. (PG)
109 minutes

GOLDENGIRL (1979)
 ★★★

Susan Anton
Curt Jurgens
James Coburn

An intelligent, stylish melodrama about a statuesque young woman who is systematically groomed to be an Olympic track star. Tall, willowy Anton sparkles in the title role and contributes most to the movie's success. Coburn is especially good as a slick sports agent. Jurgens is fine, too, as Anton's adopted father, a doctor who once performed medical research under the Nazis. Also with Robert Culp, Leslie Caron, Harry Guardino, and Jessica Walter. **Director**—Joseph Sargent. (PG) *104 minutes*

THE GOLDEN SEAL (1983)
★★

Steve Railsback

Torquil Campbell hangs out with his buddy, The Golden Seal.

Slow-paced, sentimental boy-and-his-seal movie, set on a remote Aleutian island. Puppies or black stallions are not to be found in this outpost, so young Eric (Torquil Campbell) befriends a legendary golden seal that he protects from sinister adults who want it killed. Predictably, the youngster learns about nature and the realities of the adult world. The outdoor photog-raphy is striking, and the animals often upstage the human performers. **Director**—Frank Zuniga. (PG)
95 minutes

THE GOLDEN VOYAGE OF SINBAD (1973)
 ★★★

John Philip Law
Caroline Monroe

Lively reworking of the Sinbad story, with the adventurer dueling with a magician. The fantasy progresses in grand style, and it's beautifully enhanced by Ray Harryhausen's magnificent trick photography, which brings to life the figurehead of a ship and other inanimate objects. Also with Tom Baker, Douglas Wilmer, and John Garfield, Jr. **Director**—Gordon Hessler. (G) *105 minutes*

GOLDFINGER (1964)
 ★★★★

Sean Connery
Honor Blackman
Gert Frobe

Among the best of the James Bond adventures, with agent 007, played by Connery, stopping a sinister gold smuggler from plundering Fort Knox. Frobe plays the title role. The slick production brims with the expected spread of gadgetry, beautiful women, menacing villains, and lots of tongue-in-cheek humor. The indestructible Bond ties it up smartly in a spectacular climax. Harold (Oddjob) Sakata, Bernard Lee, Shirley Eaton, and Lois Maxwell join in the fun. **Director**—Guy Hamilton. (PG) *112 minutes*

GONE WITH THE WIND (1939)
 ★★★★

Clark Gable
Vivien Leigh
Olivia de Havilland
Leslie Howard

This stirring romantic spectacle is among the best and most memorable of all Hollywood productions. Based on Margaret Mitchell's compelling novel of the South during the Civil

Rhett Butler (Clark Gable) consoles widow Scarlett O'Hara (Vivien Leigh) in Gone With the Wind.

War, the epic tells the story of an aristocratic plantation family and its involvement with the war. Leigh is magnificent as Scarlett O'Hara, the spoiled beauty, and Gable is at his best as the dashing Rhett Butler. Many other sterling performances abound. Producer David O. Selznick went all out to provide the utmost in film entertainment. It's a tremendous movie that absolutely defies its title. It seems this masterpiece will be with us forever. Also with Thomas Mitchell, Barbara O'Neil, Hattie McDaniel, Butterfly McQueen, Victory Jory, and Ona Munson. **Director**—Victor Fleming. **Academy Awards**—best picture; Fleming, best director; Leigh, best actress; McDaniel, best supporting actress; Sidney Howard, writing (screenplay); Ernest Haller and Ray Rennahan, cinematography (color). **Nominations**—Gable, best actor; de Havilland, best supporting actress. (G)   *220 minutes*

GOODBYE AGAIN (1961)
★★

Ingrid Bergman
Anthony Perkins

Overwrought, weepy melodrama about a fortyish woman having an affair with a young law student. Bergman plays the woman; Perkins plays the student. This so-called woman's film, based on Françoise Sagan's novel, is nicely photographed against a Paris background, but it's typical, tearful, soap-opera stuff—a two-

hanky movie, perhaps. Supporting players include Yves Montand, Jessie Royce Landis, Diahann Carroll, and Jackie Lane. **Director**—Anatole Litvak.   *120 minutes b&w*

GOODBYE COLUMBUS (1969)
★★★

Richard Benjamin
Ali MacGraw

On-target screen version of Philip Roth's insightful look at a status-seeking Jewish family in suburban New York. The romantic drama centers on a young librarian from the Bronx who falls for a spoiled college girl from a *nouveau riche* family. Benjamin is superb in his film debut as the librarian, and MacGraw is excellent as the snobbish young woman with whom he becomes disillusioned. An opulent wedding sequence—for the girl's brother—is a gem. First-class sup-

porting performances from Jack Klugman, Nan Martin, Michael Meyers, and Lori Shelle. **Director**—Larry Peerce. (R)   *105 minutes*

THE GOODBYE GIRL (1977)
★★

Richard Dreyfuss
Marsha Mason
Quinn Cummings

Neil Simon's romantic comedy is a boy-meets-girl formula movie, about an over-the-hill dancer and a struggling actor who share a New York apartment. This latest wrinkle in the odd-couple theme is loaded with cornball wisecracks, a lot of whining, and verbal sparring. To no one's surprise, the boy, played by Dreyfuss, finally gets the girl, played by Mason. Who cares? **Director**—Herbert Ross. (PG) **Academy Award**—Dreyfuss, best actor. **Nominations**—best picture; Ma-
(Continued)

DUSTIN HOFFMAN

Dustin Hoffman was born in Los Angeles in 1937 and grew up in Hollywood, where his father was, at one time, a set dresser. Named after the screen cowboy Dustin Farnum (Dustin's brother is named after Ronald Colman), Hoffman didn't consider acting as a career until his college days when he enrolled in the Pasadena Playhouse.

Hoffman made his acting debut in a college production of Gertrude Stein's Yes Is for a Very Young Man; *he appeared on Broadway for the first time with a walk-on part in* A Cook for Mr. General. *He joined the Theater Company of Boston for one season before returning to New York to work as director Ulu Grosbard's assistant on* A View from the Bridge.

Off-Broadway, Hoffman appeared in Harry, Noon and Night; Journey of the Fifth Horse, *for which he won an Obie award; and* Eh?, *for which he was honored with the Drama Desk, Vernon Rice, and Theater World awards as well as an invitation from Mike Nichols to test for the film* The Graduate *(1967). Hoffman got the title role and his performance earned him unanimous critical acclaim and his first Academy Award nomination.*

Hoffman then returned to New York to co-star with Jon Voight in Midnight Cowboy *(1969) for director John Schlesinger; he was nominated for his second Oscar. Hoffman got his third Academy Award nomination for* Lenny *(1974).*

His other movies include John and Mary *(1969) opposite Mia Farrow,* Who Is Harry Kellerman and Why Is He Saying Those Terrible Things About Me? *(1971),* Sam Peckinpah's Straw Dogs *(1972),* All the President's Men *(1976),* Marathon Man *(1976), and* Kramer vs. Kramer *(1979), for which he finally won an Oscar as best actor. Hoffman's latest triumph was in* Tootsie *(1982), where he played an actor who poses as a woman in order to find work.*

G

- Goodbye Mr. Chips
- Good Guys Wear Black
- Good Neighbor Sam
- Good News
- The Good, the Bad, and the Ugly
- Gorky Park
- Go Tell the Spartans
- Go West

(Continued)

son, best actress; Cummings, best supporting actress; Simon, best original screenplay. *110 minutes*

GOODBYE MR. CHIPS (1939)
★★★★

Robert Donat
Greer Garson

Donat is perfectly cast in this story about an English schoolmaster, and the movie based upon the James Hilton novel is exquisite entertainment. Some critics feel the film has aged, but though it might be a bit slow moving the solid wholesomeness of the production prevails. Garson gives a skilled performance as the only person who gets the schoolmaster to overcome his shyness, and there is good support from Paul Henreid, Judith Furse, Austin Trevor, John Mills, and Terry Kilburn. **Director**—Sam Wood. **Academy Award**—Robert Donat, best actor. **Nominations**—best picture; Sam Wood, best director; Greer Garson, best actress; Eric Maschwitz, R.C. Sheriff, and Claudine West, writing (screenplay). *114 minutes b&w*

GOOD GUYS WEAR BLACK (1979)
 ★

Chuck Norris

A dull martial-arts adventure based on commando operations in Vietnam. Karate champ Norris handles most of the heavy action, but he really doesn't get warmed up until the film is more than half over. The scripting and character development are at low levels. Anne Archer, James Franciscus, Jim Backus, and Dana Andrews are also in the cast. **Director**—Ted Post. (PG) *96 minutes*

GOOD NEIGHBOR SAM (1964)
★★

Jack Lemmon

Lemmon stars in this drawn-out comedy, as an advertising man pretending to be the husband of a gorgeous divorcée living next door. Romy Schneider plays the divorcée. Good comic oppor-

tunities are frittered away by an unworkable script and gags that seem repetitious. Lemmon has some funny moments, but there's not enough substance to develop a satisfying film. Edward G. Robinson appears in a cameo role. Also with Senta Berger, Mike Connors, Edward Andrews, Dorothy Provine, Louis Nye, and Joyce Jameson. **Director**—David Swift. *130 minutes*

GOOD NEWS (1947)
★★★

June Allyson
Peter Lawford

A lively, toe-tapping college musical, based on the popular Broadway hit of the '30s, with a professional cast giving it their best shot. The minor plot concerns a football game intermingled with various campus romances. But the music is the thing, and there are plenty of snappy tunes, such as "Varsity Drag" and "The French Lesson." Allyson is fantastic belting out the numbers. Also with Patricia Marshall, Joan McCracken, and Mel Torme. **Director**—Charles Walters. *95 minutes*

THE GOOD, THE BAD, AND THE UGLY (1966)
 ★★★

Clint Eastwood

A brutal and violent but oddly compelling story about the search by three gunmen for stolen loot belonging to the Confederate government during the U.S. Civil War. This film became known as a spaghetti western because it was one of the first movies of its kind to be made in Italy. Eastwood appears in one of his first starring roles, with Eli Wallach and Lee Van Cleef turning in above-average performances. Director Sergio Leone's exaggerated dramatic style is just right for the material. *161 minutes*

GORKY PARK (1983)
 ★★★

William Hurt
Lee Marvin

William Hurt plays a world-weary

Joanna Pacula and William Hurt seek answers to what happened in Gorky Park.

Russian police detective trying to unravel a complex triple murder, while tangling with cynical American businessman Marvin. The film captures most of the intricate plot and characters of Martin Cruz Smith's best-seller, but little of the texture of Soviet daily life that made the book so fascinating. For all that, it's an effective thriller. It's set against the bleak, cold backdrop of a Moscow (actually Helsinki) winter. Brian Dennehy and Joanna Pacula co-star. **Director**—Michael Apted. (R) *128 minutes*

GO TELL THE SPARTANS (1978)
 ★★

Burt Lancaster

Lancaster plays an Army major who commands a detachment of military advisers, futilely defending an outpost in South Vietnam. Lancaster and the novice supporting cast make an earnest effort, but the story seems incompatible with post-war moods. Overall, the movie plods under the burden of heavy-handed symbolism and irony. Also with Craig Wasson, Marc Singer, Jonathan Goldsmith, and Joe Unger. **Director**—Ted Post. (R) *114 minutes*

GO WEST (1940)
 ★★

Marx Brothers

Groucho, Harpo, and Chico hit the trail and take on the western bad guys.

• The Graduate
• The Grand Illusion
• Grandview, U.S.A.

• The Grapes of Wrath
• The Grass Is Greener
• Gray Lady Down

G

Groucho, Harpo, and Chico Marx Go West.

A rather uneven comedy most of the way through until the smashing finale. Then it's the Marx Brothers in all their glory, as they take a moving train apart. It's certainly worth the trip. John Carroll, Diana Lewis, and Robert Barratt co-star. **Director**—Edward Buzzell.   *82 minutes b&w*

THE GRADUATE (1967)

 ★★★★

Anne Bancroft
Dustin Hoffman
Katharine Ross

A milestone masterpiece about a young college graduate who has an affair with the wife of his father's partner. Underneath it all, the story intelligently reveals the youth's intense feelings—that his success in college was primarily for the benefit of his wealthy, status-seeking parents—and he strives to establish his own set of values. The film entertains on many levels, with great moments of charm, humor, suspense, and drama. Hoffman nailed down a brilliant acting career, as the young graduate. Bancroft plays the seductive older woman; Ross plays her daughter, with whom Hoffman falls in love. Also with Murray Hamilton and William Daniels. Mike Nichols's direction is a triumph. (PG) **Academy Award**—Nichols, best director. **Nominations**—best picture; Hoffman, best actor;

Bancroft, best actress; Ross, best supporting actress; Calder Willingham and Buck Henry, best screenplay (based on material from another medium); Robert Surtees, cinematography.
105 minutes

THE GRAND ILLUSION (1937)

 ★★★★

Erich von Stroheim
Pierre Fresnay
Jean Gabin

Brilliant acting, an intelligent script, and superior direction create a masterpiece of filmmaking. The superb actors in this story of French prisoners during World War I and the German commandant who shapes their destiny include Fresnay, Dita Parlo, Gabin, and von Stroheim. The movie influenced a generation of filmmakers and appears on most lists of great motion pictures. In French with English titles. **Director**—Jean Renoir.
111 minutes b&w

GRANDVIEW, U.S.A. (1984)

 ★★

Jamie Lee Curtis
C. Thomas Howell

Innocuous piece of Americana, over-populated with uninteresting characters trying to sort out personal problems in a backwater Midwestern town. Curtis is a tomboyish woman who operates a demolition derby race track. Howell plays a high school senior who dreams of being a marine biologist. And Patrick Swayze portrays a frantic construction worker with a floozie wife who is fooling around with a dishwasher salesman (Troy Donahue). Call it "bland view of the U.S.A." **Director**—Randal Kleiser. (R)
98 minutes

THE GRAPES OF WRATH (1940)

 ★★★★

Henry Fonda
Jane Darwell
John Carradine

A magnificent film, based on John Steinbeck's moving account of poor Oklahoma farmers, moving from the

Henry Fonda drives his family out of the Dust Bowl to California in The Grapes of Wrath.

Dust Bowl to California during the Depression to reestablish their lives. Brilliant acting by a superb cast. The film, which brims with unforgettable moments of drama and poignant characterizations, reveals considerable compassion for poor, honest people struggling for dignity against seemingly insurmountable odds. Also with Charley Grapewin, Dorris Bowdon, and Russell Simpson. **Director**—John Ford. **Academy Awards**—Ford, best director; Darwell, best supporting actress. **Nominations**—best picture; Fonda, best actor; Nunnally Johnson, writing (screenplay).
128 minutes b&w

THE GRASS IS GREENER (1960)

★★★

Cary Grant
Deborah Kerr
Robert Mitchum

Stylish comedy of manners with an air of slow-paced staginess about it, yet it's enlivened by good performances. Grant and Kerr play a noble English couple. Their marriage is upset when an American millionaire, played by Mitchum, enters the picture. Based on a play by Hugh and Margaret Williams. Also with Jean Simmons and Moray Watson. **Director**—Stanley Donen.   *105 minutes*

GRAY LADY DOWN (1978)

★★

Charlton Heston
David Carradine
Stacy Keach

(Continued)

G
- Grease
- Grease 2
- Greased Lightning
- The Great Bank Hoax
- The Great Bank Robbery
- The Great Caruso
- The Great Dictator

(Continued)

What happens when an American nuclear sub is rammed by a freighter and sinks off the coast of Connecticut? The U.S. Navy, of course, comes to the official rescue with all sorts of wonderful gadgets, stiff upper lips, and disaster-movie clichés. Heston, who has seen better days riding chariots, plays the fearless sub skipper; Keach is one of his officers. Carradine plays a nonconformist officer and a designer of a diving craft who saves the day just before the sub's oxygen supply—and the audience's patience—wears out. Also with Ned Beatty and Ronny Cox. **Director**— David Greene. (PG)

111 minutes

GREASE (1978)

★★★★

John Travolta
Olivia Newton-John
Stockard Channing

A zesty dandy of a musical, based on the long-running Broadway hit show about a 1950s high school class. Travolta and Newton-John star as the sentimental teenage sweethearts. Both can really do their stuff in the way of dancing, singing, and acting. The excellent musical numbers are well-staged and come off with high spirits. The talented supporting cast does an impressive job. Channing, as the tough girl with a heart of gold, steals a few scenes. Also with Jeff Conaway, Didi Conn, Eve Arden, and Sid Caesar. **Director**—Randal Kleiser. (PG)

110 minutes

GREASE 2 (1982)

★★

Maxwell Caulfield
Michelle Pfeiffer

Aside from some buoyant song-and-dance numbers, this sequel to one of Hollywood's most successful musicals drags and sags. The trite script and foolish dialogue might have been conceived with less than half a mind, and newcomers Caulfield and Pfeiffer hardly fill the leather outfits of John Travolta and Olivia Newton-John. This time the story reverses the original roles, with Caulfield as the clean-cut student at Rydell High trying to

Maxwell Caulfield and Michelle Pfeiffer blow their cool in Grease 2.

win the attention of tough, foxy Pfeiffer. **Director**—Patricia Birch. (PG)

115 minutes

GREASED LIGHTNING (1977)

★★★

Richard Pryor
Beau Bridges

Pryor gives a cool and subtle performance in this action-filled biography of Wendell Scott, the first black stockcar racing champion. The zesty pace is captured nicely by director Michael Schultz. Bridges contributes effective support as a local driver who joins Scott's crew. The film might have been better with more emphasis on character; however, it's still good entertainment with a significant social message. Also with Pam Grier, Cleavon Little, and Vincent Gardenia. (PG)

94 minutes

THE GREAT BANK HOAX
(1979)

★

Richard Basehart
Burgess Meredith
Ned Beatty

Bumbling bank officers in a small town try to cover up an embezzlement by staging a robbery. It's supposed to be comedy, but you'll probably find more laughs in a life insurance policy. Basehart, Beatty, and Meredith play stereotyped characters who come close to the style of the Three Stooges. Such antics may have gone over in the early days of filmmaking; now, it's just so much silliness. Also with Paul Sand and Michael Murphy. **Director**— Joseph Jacoby. (PG)

89 minutes

THE GREAT BANK ROBBERY
(1969)

★★

Kim Novak
Zero Mostel
Clint Walker

This western spoof can't make it up the hill, even with the talents of Mostel, who plays a scheming bank robber in the town of Friendly. He also has to compete with other outlaws who have their eyes on the loot. There are a few agreeable moments here and there, but it's not so great. Also with Claude Akins, Akim Tamiroff, and Larry Storch. **Director**—Hy Averback. (PG)

98 minutes

THE GREAT CARUSO (1951)

★★★

Mario Lanza
Ann Blyth

Lanza plays the famous Italian tenor in this handsome film biography, embellished slightly with fiction. The production lacks sufficient drama, and the dialogue is somewhat stiff; yet the settings are colorful, and Lanza sings a wide variety of opera numbers. He's not as great as Caruso, but he does an adequate job. Also with Dorothy Kirsten, Jarmila Novotna, and Carl Benton Reid. **Director**—Richard Thorpe. (G)

109 minutes

THE GREAT DICTATOR (1940)

★★★

Charles Chaplin
Paulette Goddard
Jack Oakie

Effective spoof of Adolf Hitler with Chaplin in a dual role; he plays a Jewish barber and Adenoid Hynkel, the dictator of Tomania. Oakie is also outstanding as Benzino Napaloni, the ruler of the rival country of Bacteria. Chaplin's unique satire focuses on humanity by way of his familiar slapstick routine. Also with Reginald Gardiner, Henry Daniell, Billy Gilbert, and Maurice Moscovich. **Director**—Chaplin. **Academy Award Nominations**—best picture; Chaplin, best actor; Oakie, best supporting actor;

Charlie Chaplin bears a striking resemblance to a certain historical figure in The Great Dictator.

Chaplin, writing (original screenplay). (G) *129 minutes b&w*

THE GREAT ESCAPE (1963)

 ★★★★

James Garner
Steve McQueen
Richard Attenborough
James Donald
Charles Bronson

Steve McQueen acquires some new bonds to break in The Great Escape.

Slam-bang action adventure, about Allied prisoners attempting to bust out of a German POW camp during World War II. The film is based on a true story. A top cast keeps the excitement moving and building despite the film's length. There's an especially daring sequence with McQueen on a motorcycle, trying to reach freedom. Also with Donald Pleasence, James Coburn, and David McCallum. **Director**—John Sturges. (PG) *173 minutes*

THE GREATEST (1977)

 ★★★

Muhammad Ali
Ernest Borgnine
Robert Duvall

Boxing great Ali plays himself as no one else could in this charming movie biography, which recounts his career from Cassius Clay of Louisville to the bombastic world heavyweight champion of the '70s. Ali proves he can be a good actor; his performance matches that of the fine supporting cast. It's an old-fashioned upbeat movie, with Ali's colorful personality dominating scene after scene. There's a winning script by Ring Lardner, Jr., and excellent direction by Tom Gries. Also with John Marley, James Earl Jones, Roger E. Mosley, Ben Johnson, and Paul Winfield. (PG) *101 minutes*

THE GREATEST SHOW ON EARTH (1952)

★★★

Betty Hutton
Cornel Wilde
James Stewart
Charlton Heston

Director Cecil B. DeMille takes us to the circus and uncorks some thrilling excitement and drama in this slick, expensive production. The film brims with amusing cameos, especially Stewart dressed up as a clown. A train wreck climax is sort of a letdown. Also with Dorothy Lamour, Gloria Graham, Lyle Bettger, Henry Wilcoxon, Emmett Kelly, and John Ringling North. **Academy Awards**—best picture; Frederic M. Frank, Theodore St. John, and Frank Cavett, writing (motion picture story). **Nomination**—DeMille, best director. *153 minutes*

THE GREATEST STORY EVER TOLD (1965)

★★

Max Von Sydow
Dorothy McGuire
Claude Rains
José Ferrer
David McCallum
Charlton Heston

Overlong and unwieldy telling of the story of Christ. Von Sydow does an earnest job in the role of Jesus, but much of this plodding epic is taken up with many unworkable bit parts. For example, there's John Wayne as a Roman officer involved with the details of the Crucifixion. The elaborate settings look too perfect, too unreal—sort of like a series of Christmas cards. It's hardly the greatest picture ever made. Also with Sidney Poitier, Donald Pleasence, Roddy McDowall, Carroll Baker, Van Heflin, Shelley Winters, Ed Wynn, Telly Savalas, and Angela Lansbury. **Director**—George Stevens. (G) *225 minutes*

GREAT EXPECTATIONS (1946)

★★★★

John Mills
Bernard Miles
Finlay Currie
Martita Hunt
Valerie Hobson

A first-class screen adaptation of the beloved Charles Dickens classic. All the interesting characters, faithfully portrayed by a top cast, are brought brilliantly to life under the superb guidance of director David Lean. The film also boasts detailed settings and fine photography. There have been other attempts to film this story of the poor orphan boy who becomes a gentleman, thanks to the help of a mysterious escaped convict, but this version is tops. Superb performances are given by Mills, Hobson, Currie, Hunt, *(Continued)*

G
- The Great Gatsby
- The Great Imposter
- The Great Lie
- The Great McGinty
- The Great Muppet Caper
- The Great Race

A scene from Great Expectations, *a first-class screen adaptation of Charles Dickens's classic.*

(Continued)

Alec Guinness, and Jean Simmons. **Academy Award**—Guy Green, cinematography (black and white). **Nominations**—best picture; Lean, best director; Lean, Ronald Neame, and Anthony Havelock-Allan, writing (screenplay). *118 minutes*

THE GREAT GATSBY
(1974)
Ⓐ ★★

**Robert Redford
Mia Farrow
Karen Black**

Mia Farrow and Robert Redford in The Great Gatsby, *based on F. Scott Fitzgerald's novel.*

This third rendition of F. Scott Fitzgerald's novel of the Roaring Twenties is lavishly mounted, but the story and characters lack compelling interest. Redford, in the title role, is the hustling bootlegger who has everything except the woman he loves. He does an adequate job, but his performance is forgettable. Also with Scott Wilson, Bruce Dern, Sam Waterston, and Lois Chiles. **Director**—Jack Clayton. (PG) *146 minutes*

THE GREAT IMPOSTER
(1960)
★★★

**Tony Curtis
Raymond Massey
Karl Malden**

Curtis stars in the title role, as the incredible con artist, Ferdinand Waldo Demara, who successfully posed as a naval doctor, a prison warden, and a teacher. Curtis is right at home in this striking episodic tale, and the film maintains interest throughout. Also co-starring Edmund O'Brien, Arthur O'Connell, Gary Merrill, and Frank Gorshin. **Director**—Robert Mulligan. *112 minutes b&w*

THE GREAT LIE (1941)
★★★★

**Bette Davis
Mary Astor
George Brent**

This rather complex and talky soap-opera story is spruced up nicely, thanks to the supremely bitchy performances of Davis and Astor. Davis marries the man (Brent), who used to be married to Astor. Astor, meanwhile, is pregnant, and when Brent dies in a plane crash, Davis rears the child as her own. Soap fans should have fun sorting out this one. The film is set against a background of classical music. Lucile Watson, Hattie McDaniel, and Grant Mitchell also star. **Director**—Edmund Goulding. **Academy Award**—Astor, best supporting actress. *107 minutes b&w*

THE GREAT McGINTY
(1940)
★★★★

**Brian Donlevy
Akim Tamiroff**

Smashing debut for writer-director Preston Sturges, who fashioned this biting political satire. Donlevy plays a bum who gains political power and then lets it slip away. This inventive film gets its point across with unusual efficiency and a liberal amount of snappy dialogue; it starts with a bang and never lets up. Some good supporting players add to the fun. Also with Muriel Angelus, Louis Jean Heydt, and William Demarest. **Academy Award**—Sturges, writing (original screenplay).

83 minutes b&w

THE GREAT MUPPET CAPER
(1981)
Ⓐ ★★

Miss Piggy, Kermit the Frog, Fozzi Bear, and other adorable Muppet characters crack a London jewel heist in this cheerful musical-melodrama. The incomparable Miss Piggy steals scenes as the star of an Esther Williams water ballet and in a Busby Berkeley night-club production. The film is rather uncertain as to its intended audience; some of the humor is childish, but many gags are aimed at adults. The puppet characters perform with a live cast, including Charles Grodin and Diana Rigg. **Director**—Jim Henson. (G) *95 minutes*

THE GREAT RACE
(1965)
Ⓐ ★★

**Jack Lemmon
Tony Curtis
Peter Falk
Natalie Wood**

The first New York-to-Paris automobile race, set in the early 1900s, is the centerpiece of this comedy; it's uneven and strained, but it manages to offer a few funny moments. Some gimmicky slapstick is notable—a barroom brawl and a climactic pie-throwing melee. But after a while, it becomes tiresome. Lemmon plays Professor Fate, a dastardly villain; Curtis is the Great Leslie, a dashing hero in a white suit. Also with George Macready, Ross Martin, Vivian Vance, Keenan Wynn, and Larry Storch. **Director**—Blake Edwards. *150 minutes*

• The Great Santini
• The Great Scout and
　　Cathouse Thursday

• The Great Train Robbery
• The Great Waldo Pepper
• The Great White Hope

G

THE GREAT SANTINI (1980)

 ★★★

**Robert Duvall
Blythe Danner
Michael O'Keefe**

An affecting, modest movie about a gung ho Marine fighter pilot, who presides over his family with the same pile-driving authority he uses on his squadron. The setting is peacetime in the early '60s, and the focus is on family stress and a father-son conflict. Duvall plays the title role with a dynamic, overwhelming performance that makes this perplexing character totally believable and moving. O'Keefe plays his son. **Director**—Lewis John Carlino. (PG) **Academy Award Nominations**—Duvall, best actor; O'Keefe, best supporting actor. *115 minutes*

THE GREAT SCOUT AND CATHOUSE THURSDAY (1976)

 ★

**Lee Marvin
Oliver Reed
Kay Lenz**

Marvin stars as a legendary vagabond scout out to collect $60,000 from a wealthy ex-friend in Colorado about 1908. The slapstick western comedy tries to reach for the successful *Cat Ballou* brass ring, but falls flat on its face. The film is loaded down with hokey situation gags and a tedious plot. Marvin, however, does a fair enough job as the aging brawler. Also with Robert Culp, Elizabeth Ashley, and Strother Martin. **Director**—Don Taylor. (PG) *102 minutes*

THE GREAT TRAIN ROBBERY (1979)

 ★★★

**Sean Connery
Donald Sutherland
Lesley-Anne Down**

Connery plays the charming rascal who pulled off England's first recorded moving-train heist in 1855. Writer-director Michael Crichton, working from his own best-selling novel, serves up dazzling excitement and

Sean Connery perfects his timing for The Great Train Robbery.

spicy wit, wrapped in the elegant detail of early Victorian England. Sutherland is an amusing accomplice, along with Down, who radiates sex appeal and beauty to rival Marilyn Monroe. It's great movie entertainment, alive with classy action and spine-tingling suspense. Also with Alan Webb, Malcolm Terris, and Robert Lang. (PG) *111 minutes*

THE GREAT WALDO PEPPER (1975)

 ★★★

**Robert Redford
Bo Svenson
Bo Brundin
Susan Sarandon**

Robert Redford modestly acknowledges that he is The Great Waldo Pepper.

A former World War I pilot dreams of air combat against a German ace he never fought during the war. He realizes his dream at last when he gets a stunt-flying job in Hollywood and meets the German—also a stunt pilot. The flying sequences are impressive. Redford stars as the pilot. Also with Margot Kidder and Geoffrey Lewis. George Roy Hill directed and produced. (PG) *107 minutes*

THE GREAT WHITE HOPE (1970)

★★★★

**James Earl Jones
Jane Alexander**

James Earl Jones tries to shield his mama, Beah Richards, from the ridicule and scorn that he must face in The Great White Hope.

A high-voltage film biography of Jack Johnson, the black heavyweight boxing great who won the world title in 1908. Jones and Alexander repeat their Broadway roles on screen. The film is faithful to the play, and details much of the pain and humiliation Johnson suffered because of his affair with a white woman, played by Alexander. Jones is magnificent in the central role, nicely portraying this fascinating character. Lou Gilbert, Joel Fleullen, Chester Morris, Robert Webber, and Hal Holbrook star in supporting roles. **Director**—Martin Ritt. (PG) **Academy Award Nominations**—Jones, best actor; Alexander, best actress. *101 minutes*

THE GREEK TYCOON (1978)

★★

Anthony Quinn
Jacqueline Bisset

Anthony Quinn and Jacqueline Bisset pretend to be recent historical figures (hint, hint) in The Greek Tycoon.

This trashy film blatantly exploits the headlines and gossip columns about Jackie and Aristotle Onassis. The producers obviously spent a fortune on lush settings and fancy clothes, but apparently pinched pennies on a dull script. Quinn and Bisset plod through their roles as the world's most glamorous couple. The supporting cast, including Raf Vallone and Edward Albert, adds to the tedium. **Director—**J. Lee Thompson. (R) *106 minutes*

THE GREEN BERETS (1968)

★

John Wayne
David Janssen
Jim Hutton

This overblown and undernourished war movie, made at the height of the Vietnam war, is nothing more than flagwaving mumbo jumbo at its worst. Wayne plays a Special Forces colonel, with all his gung ho flourishes, leading troops against the enemy. It's a very shallow treatment of an extremely complex situation. Also with Aldo Ray, Raymond St. Jacques, Jack Soo, and Bruce Cabot. **Director—**Wayne. (No MPAA rating) *141 minutes*

GREEN DOLPHIN STREET (1947)

★★

Lana Turner
Richard Hart
Donna Reed

In Green Dolphin Street, *Lana Turner and Donna Reed are sisters who both love Richard Hart.*

Slick but humdrum period romantic drama set in New Zealand in the 19th century. Turner and Reed play sisters who want to marry the same man. The situation sets off all sorts of absurd complications. The tedium is relieved by a climactic earthquake. Also with Edmund Gwenn and Van Heflin. **Director—**Victor Saville.

141 minutes b&w

GREEN FOR DANGER (1946)

★★★★

Alastair Sim
Sally Gray
Trevor Howard

Smartly made whodunit that neatly mixes mystery and comedy in an English hospital during World War II. Sim is at his witty best as a determined detective who nails an operating-table murderer after some careful sleuthing. There's some effective humor at the right moments. The top cast also includes Rosamund John, Leo Genn, Megs Jenkins, and Judy Campbell. **Director—**Sidney Gilliat.

93 minutes b&w

GREEN MANSIONS (1959)

★★

Anthony Perkins
Audrey Hepburn
Lee J. Cobb

W. H. Hudson's intriguing romantic fantasy doesn't adapt comfortably to the screen. Perkins plays a young adventurer who enters a South American rain forest, where he encounters a mysterious nature girl and falls in love with her. Hepburn isn't up to the role

AL PACINO

Al Pacino was born in New York City in 1940. When his father, a mason, left the family, he was reared by his mother and grandparents. Pacino attended Manhattan's High School of Performing Arts and supported himself for several years with menial jobs. Finally, he was accepted in Herbert Berghof's acting school and later attended Lee Strasberg's Actors' Studio.

Pacino's training led to an impressive performance in The Indian Wants the Bronx, *an off-Broadway play for which he won an Obie Award. His first screen role was a small part in* Me Natalie *(1968), and then he gave a strong performance as a dope addict in* Panic in Needle Park *(1971).*

After only these two movies, he was selected to play the key role of Michael Corleone in Francis Ford Coppola's The Godfather *(1972), for which he was nominated for an Oscar as best supporting actor.*

In 1977, Pacino returned to the Broadway stage and won a Tony for the lead role in The Basic Training of Pavlo Hummel.

Pacino also starred in such films as Serpico *(1973),* The Godfather—Part II *(1974),* Dog Day Afternoon *(1975), . . . And Justice for All *(1979),* Cruising *(1980), and* Scarface *(1983).*

• Gregory's Girl   • Greystoke: The Legend of   • Guadalcanal Diary
• Gremlins   Tarzan, Lord of the Apes   • Guess Who's Coming to
• The Grey Fox   • The Group   Dinner?

 G

of Rima, a beautiful nymph dedicated to protecting the jungle wildlife. However, some effective scenes shine through. Also with Sessue Hayakawa and Henry Silva. **Director**—Mel Ferrer. *104 minutes*

GREGORY'S GIRL (1982)

★★★

Gordon John Sinclair
Dee Hepburn

From Scotland, a warm and engaging film about adolescent love. Gangling, cheerful Sinclair is just right for the part of the awkward high school youth who giddily falls for an athletic beauty (Hepburn). Although the pace is somewhat choppy, the well-observed story abounds with charm and the characters are engaging. The all-Scottish cast is exceptionally good, and young director Bill Forsyth displays an impressively deft style. (PG) *91 minutes*

GREMLINS (1984)
★★★

Zach Galligan
Phoebe Cates

Dad brings home an exotic Christmas gift, a cute, furry animal that suddenly multiplies into an army of repulsive creatures, and all hell breaks loose. Although they are nasty and vicious, the creatures carry out their mischievous work with appealing glee: they get drunk, foul up traffic signals, tear up a movie theater. Their disgraceful and wild antics produce a delicious mixture of comedy and horror. **Director**—Joe Dante. (PG) *105 minutes*

THE GREY FOX (1983)

★★★

Richard Farnsworth

"Train robbers are people, too," seems to be the theme of this offbeat western set in Canada. Former stuntman Farnsworth is impressive as the gentlemanly and grandfatherly bandit who can't resist holding up trains upon his release from a 30-year prison stretch. The film paints a rather sym-

Richard Farnsworth portrays an aging train robber in The Grey Fox.

pathetic and somewhat heroic picture of a man determined to remain a criminal. Photography of the Canadian Pacific Northwest is exquisite, as is the sound track by the Chieftains, a traditional Irish group. Also with Jackie Burroughs and Wayne Robson. **Director**—Philip Boros. (PG) *92 minutes*

GREYSTOKE: THE LEGEND OF TARZAN, LORD OF THE APES (1984)

★★★

Ralph Richardson
Andie McDowell
Christopher Lambert

This lavish production is closer to the original Edgar Rice Burroughs story than its B-movie predecessors. It's also surprisingly fresh and compelling. In 1886, the orphaned son of Scottish aristocrats is reared by apes in Africa and then brought to Europe. This moving film contrasts the exhilaration of jungle life with the suffocating constrictions of Edwardian "civilization." **Director**—Hugh Hudson. (PG) *129 minutes*

THE GROUP (1966)

★★★

Joanna Pettet
Candice Bergen
Jessica Walter
Joan Hackett

A decent adaptation of Mary McCarthy's novel that overcomes much of the

soap-opera aspects of the story. The plot follows the lives of eight women who were graduated from Vassar in 1933. An earnest effort is made to flesh out the characters. Fascinating performances from Pettet, Hackett, Walter, Shirley Knight, and Kathleen Widdoes. Also with Elizabeth Hartman, Larry Hagman, and Hal Holbrook. **Director**—Sidney Lumet. *150 minutes*

GUADALCANAL DIARY (1943)
★★★

Preston Foster
Lloyd Nolan
William Bendix

A top World War II action adventure, with the Marines slugging it out to capture a strategic base in the Pacific. It's a bit heavy on the heroics and flag-waving, but that's to be expected from this wartime film, based on Richard Tregaskis's book. The fine cast also includes Richard Conte, Anthony Quinn, and Richard Jaeckel. **Director**—Lewis Seiler. *93 minutes b&w*

GUESS WHO'S COMING TO DINNER ? (1967)
★★★

Spencer Tracy
Katharine Hepburn
Katharine Houghton
Sidney Poitier

A wealthy San Francisco white girl (Houghton) becomes engaged to a black man (Poitier), and announces their plans to her parents, who are considered very liberal-minded—or are they? The film is somewhat confined and overly cautious with its touchy subject. However, the picture succeeds primarily because of the adroit performances of Hepburn and Tracy as the perplexed elders. It's their last appearance together, and they present a sumptuous acting feast, indeed. Also with Cecil Kellaway, Beah Richards, and Roy E. Glenn, Sr. **Director**—Stanley Kramer. **Academy Awards**—Hepburn, best actress; William Rose, best story and screenplay (written directly for the screen). **Nominations**—best picture; Kramer, best director; Tracy, best actor; Kellaway, best supporting actor; Richards, best supporting actress. *112 minutes*

 Movie is available in Beta and VHS videotape

G
- The Gumball Rally
- Gunfight at the OK Corral
- The Gunfighter
- Gunga Din
- The Guns of Navarone
- Guyana: Cult of the Damned
- Guys and Dolls

THE GUMBALL RALLY (1976)

★

Michael Sarrazin
Normann Burten
Gary Busey

Kooky characters from every walk of life race their souped-up vehicles from New York to California in defiance of the 55-mile-an-hour speed limit. The skimpy plot and the adolescent comic situations quickly run out of gas while the autos noisily roar on, leaving a trail of contrived smash-ups. There's a limit to what can be done with scenes of passing cars, and after a while, the film becomes as tedious as a rush-hour traffic jam. **Director**—Chuck Bail. (PG) *107 minutes*

GUNFIGHT AT THE OK CORRAL (1957)

★★★

Burt Lancaster
Kirk Douglas

Doc Holliday (Douglas) and Wyatt Earp (Lancaster) team up to take on the Clanton gang. A slick, action-packed western that's a bit over-wrought, but delivers the goods with style and suspense. Fine perfor-mances by a first-class cast heighten the interest. Also with Rhonda Fleming, Jo Van Fleet, John Ireland, and Lee Van Cleef. **Director**—John Sturges. *122 minutes*

THE GUNFIGHTER (1950)

★★★

Gregory Peck
Helen Westcott

Peck is outstanding in this inventive western. He plays a gunfighter who would like to quit, but his past keeps catching up with him. The finely crafted screenplay is believable, and it's done with a lot more care than your average shoot-'em-up. Also with Karl Malden, Skip Homeier, Millard Mitch-ell, and Jean Parker. **Director**—Henry King. **Academy Award Nomination**—William Bowers and André de Toth, writing (motion picture story). *84 minutes b&w*

GUNGA DIN (1939)

★★★★

Cary Grant
Victor McLaglen
Douglas Fairbanks, Jr.
Sam Jaffe

Rudyard Kipling's memorable poem becomes a splendid action adventure with just the right amount of comic touches. Grant, Fairbanks, and Mc-Laglen are comrades-in-arms in India, fighting a native revolt. The film brims with sweeping battle scenes, swash-buckling derring-do, and a cheerful, fun-filled outlook. Director George Stevens coaxes great performances from the entire cast; Jaffe is particu-larly memorable as the smiling, loyal water boy. Also with Joan Fontaine, Robert Coote, and Edwardo Ciannelli. *117 minutes b&w*

THE GUNS OF NAVARONE (1961)

★★★★

Gregory Peck
David Niven
Stanley Baker
Anthony Quinn

A high-powered World War II action yarn, based on an Alistair MacLean novel, brought off nicely by a top cast. Allied commandos embark on a do-or-die mission to silence big German guns perched high on a cliff-top for-tress along the Aegean Sea. Suspense builds at a near-perfect pace, and it all leads to a ripsnorting, explosive climax. Also with Anthony Quayle, James Darren, Gia Scala, and James Robertson Justice. **Director**—J. Lee Thompson. **Academy Award Nomina-tions**—best picture; Thompson, best director; Carl Foreman, best screen-play (based on material from another medium). *159 minutes*

GUYANA: CULT OF THE DAMNED (1980)

(no stars)

Stuart Whitman
Gene Barry
John Ireland

The mass suicide at Jonestown in Guy-ana is exploited in this shabby and inept semidocumentary that was hast-ily put together in Mexico and Pana-ma. There's little effort to explain the reasons for the tragedy, or to probe the cult leader's personality. Scenes are narrated by the off-camera voice of someone described as a cult follower. Whitman plays Jim Johnson (the film's name for Jim Jones). Hollywood no-tables, such as Joseph Cotten and Yvonne De Carlo, show up in minor roles. **Director**—René Cardona, Jr. (R) *90 minutes*

GUYS AND DOLLS (1955)

★★★★

Frank Sinatra
Marlon Brando
Jean Simmons
Vivian Blaine

An entertaining musical-comedy, based on Damon Runyon's story about a gambler who takes a sucker bet that

The underground fighters prepare for their assault on The Guns of Navorone.

174

• Gypsy
• Hail the Conquering Hero
• Hair
• Halloween
• Halloween II
• Halloween III: Season of the Witch
• Halls of Montezuma

G·H

he can date a prudish Salvation Army girl, played by Simmons. Brando is miscast as the determined Romeo. However, the film succeeds marvelously because of saucy Runyonesque characters, played to the hilt by perfectly cast supporting actors. Sinatra is outstanding as the proprietor of "the oldest established, permanent floating crap game in New York." Also with Stubby Kaye, Sheldon Leonard, B. S. Pully, Robert Keith, and George E. Stone. **Director**—Joseph L. Mankiewicz.
149 minutes

GYPSY (1962)

★★

**Rosalind Russell
Natalie Wood**

Undernourished musical taken from the Broadway production about the career of Gypsy Rose Lee and her energetic stage mother. The main problem is Wood in the title role; she's an unlikely stripteaser, indeed. The Jule Styne-Stephen Sondheim score is appealing, but it sounded better on the stage. Russell is okay as the mother, but the part was made for Ethel Merman, who brought the character to life on Broadway. Also with Karl Malden and James Milhollin. **Director**—Mervyn Le Roy.
149 minutes

H

HAIL THE CONQUERING HERO (1944)
★★★★

**Eddie Bracken
Ella Raines
William Demarest**

Rip-roaring satire, starring Bracken as a military reject who is thought to be a war hero when he returns to his small-town home. This hearty comedy tickles the funnybone and offers some serious points to ponder as well. All hail writer-director Preston Sturges for a first-class job. There are effective supporting roles by Demarest, Raines, Franklin Pangborn, Raymond Walburn, and Alan Bridge. **Academy Award Nomination**—Sturges, writing (original screenplay).
101 minutes b&w

HAIR (1979)

★★★

**John Savage
Treat Williams
Beverly D'Angelo**

Director Milos Forman reworks the '60s "tribal love-rock musical" with effective screen results. The film is sometimes incoherent and slow-paced, but the big musical numbers burst forth with energy and euphoria. There are some impressive show-stoppers, such as a song-and-dance sequence when the flower children break up a high-society party. Also with Annie Golden, Dorsey Wright, and Don Dacus. (PG)   *121 minutes*

HALLOWEEN (1978)

★★★

**Donald Pleasence
Jamie Lee Curtis**

Nancy Loomis finds herself the object of psychopath's practical joke in Halloween.

A maniac escapes from a mental hospital to stalk and kill young women on Halloween night. The silly script offers minimal logic, but there are scares and suspense galore. Director John Carpenter builds the terrifying atmosphere with deft skill. The cast is mainly composed of novice actors. Curtis, daughter of Tony Curtis and Janet Leigh, is effective as an intended victim. Also with Nancy Loomis and P. J. Soles. (R)   *93 minutes*

HALLOWEEN II (1981)

★★

**Donald Pleasence
Jamie Lee Curtis**

More corpses pile up in this sequel, as a zombielike maniac prowls the corridors of a small hospital and performs gruesome unauthorized surgery on the staff. Plenty of inventive tricks heighten suspense and induce scares, but the film also drips with unnecessary gore and features a mechanical style of dispatching victims. Once again, scream-queen Curtis is pursued and terrorized, and narrowly escapes. Pleasence co-stars as a beleaguered psychiatrist. **Director**—Rick Rosenthal. (R)   *92 minutes*

HALLOWEEN III: SEASON OF THE WITCH (1982)

★

**Tom Atkins
Stacey Nelkin**

Tommy Lee Wallace directed this third chapter in the *Halloween* horror series begun by John Carpenter and associates. Instead of the familiar maniac in a mask on the loose, the central villain is a madman toymaker (Dan O'Herlihy) who makes wicked Halloween masks programmed to harm thousands of innocent children. The usual disgusting repertoire of gruesome effects is prominently featured. It's all pretty boring by now. (R)   *98 minutes*

HALLS OF MONTEZUMA (1950)
★★

**Richard Widmark
Jack Palance**

The Marines hit the beaches in the Pacific during World War II and defeat the enemy in a blaze of heroics. The film is recruiting-poster stuff, with lots of comic-book-type action and characterizations to match. It's all done to the beat of the Marine Corps Hymn. Widmark and Palance head the competent cast, which also includes Reginald Gardiner, Robert Wagner, Karl
(Continued)

H
- Hamlet
- Hammett
- The Hand
- Handle with Care
- Hangar 18
- Hang 'em High
- The Hanging Tree

(Continued)
Malden, Richard Boone, Skip Homeier, and Jack Webb. **Director—** Lewis Milestone. *113 minutes*

HAMLET (1948)
★★★★

Laurence Olivier
Eileen Herlie
Basil Sydney
Jean Simmons

Laurence Olivier is the Danish prince in Hamlet.

Even if you find Shakespeare heavy going, you'll probably appreciate this absorbing screen version of his magnificent play. Olivier stars as the melancholy Dane, and it's one of the greatest film performances of all time. Direction, also by Olivier, is on target, too; he presents the great drama with clarity and effective moody atmospherics. The Bard of Avon himself would be proud of this fine movie. Also with Felix Aylmer and Norman Wooland. **Academy Awards**—best picture; Olivier, best actor. **Nominations**—Olivier, best director; Simmons, best supporting actress.
153 minutes b&w

HAMMETT (1983)
★★

Frederic Forrest
German director Wim Wenders offers a fictitious account of hard-boiled detective writer Dashiell Hammett who alternates between his typewriter

and a search for a missing prostitute in San Francisco's Chinatown. The stylish production oozes '40s *film noir* atmosphere. Yet the story often turns suffocating with excessive twists and triple crosses that are hard to track. Apparently the focus got lost during Wenders's fight with producer Francis Ford Coppola over what direction the film should take. Peter Boyle co-stars. (PG) *94 minutes*

THE HAND (1981)
★★

Michael Caine
Psychological thriller about a cartoonist, played by Caine, whose severed hand becomes a symbol of uncontrolled rage and frustration. The disembodied hand, lost in an auto accident, follows Caine from location to location, perpetrating a chain of murderous events. The film is heavily laced with Freudian clichés, yet it's an impressive showcase for Caine's solid, unwavering performance. Oliver Stone wrote and directed. (R)
104 minutes

HANDLE WITH CARE (1977)
★

Paul Le Mat
Candy Clark
This slaphappy comedy revolves around the Citizens Band radio craze, and it borrows much of its style from *American Graffiti*. The film is cluttered with numerous plotlets, which give it a muddled tone. The script mainly involves the problems of a bigamous trucker and a lad who tries to enforce the regulations governing CB radio operation. Also with Ann Wedgeworth and Marcia Rodd. **Director—** Jonathan Demme. (PG) **Alternate Title**—*Citizens Band*. *98 minutes*

HANGAR 18 (1981)
★

Darren McGavin
Robert Vaughn
The U.S. Air Force captures a flying saucer and hides it from the public, thus causing assorted crises for gov-

ernment agencies and many lost lives. The main reason for such supersecrecy, according to this pretentious movie, is fear that the President—facing an election—would lose credibility if he revealed the spacecraft's existence. The not-so-special effects include scenes of the UFO, which look as if they were taken from close-ups at a five-and-dime toy department. It's a close encounter of the absurd kind. Also with Gary Collins. **Director—** James L. Conway. (PG) *93 minutes*

HANG 'EM HIGH (1968)
★★

Clint Eastwood
Inger Stevens
Ed Begley

In Hang 'em High, *Clint Eastwood forgets about revenge for a while and relaxes with Inger Stevens.*

Eastwood stars as a victim of a lynching party who survives the noose and then sets out for revenge on the nine men who tried to kill him. The film offers a double dose of brutality, much in the manner of a spaghetti western. The slick production moves along fairly well, with adequate performances throughout. Also with Pat Hingle, James MacArthur, Arlene Golonka, Bruce Dern, and Dennis Hopper. **Director**—Ted Post. (PG)
114 minutes

THE HANGING TREE (1959)
★★★

Gary Cooper
Maria Schell
A doctor who murdered his philander-

- Hanky Panky
- Hannah K.
- Hanover Street

- Hans Christian Andersen
- The Happiest Days of Your Life
- Happy Birthday, Gemini

H

ing wife tries to get his life back on track in a Montana frontier mining town. Cooper plays the doctor. Along the way, he helps a blind girl, played by Schell. It's an intelligent western drama, enhanced by fine photography and realistic background detail. Cooper is impressive in this serious portrayal. Also with George C. Scott, Karl Malden, and Ben Piazza. **Director**—Delmer Daves. *106 minutes.*

HANKY PANKY (1982)

★★

Gene Wilder
Gilda Radner

Gene Wilder admits to Gilda Radner who he's been having dirty thoughts about in Hanky Panky.

Wilder stars in this strained and muddled comedy-adventure as an unsuspecting architect caught up in a sinister plot to steal top military secrets. He's aided by Radner, who sadly wastes her talents in a throw-away romantic part that neglects her comic abilities. A few laughs surface here and there, but most of the film is taken up with repetitive and exhausting chase scenes. Richard Widmark co-stars in a typical heavy role. **Director**—Sidney Poitier. (PG) *110 minutes*

HANNAH K. (1983)

★★

Jill Clayburgh

Costa-Gavras directed this political drama with his usual radical slant but without his expected powerhouse punch. The half-baked film confronts the Israeli-Palestinian controversy and stars Jill Clayburgh in the title role. She's an American lawyer in Jeru-

salem who defends and then falls in love with an Arab who wants to reclaim his Left Bank homeland. The story, which seemingly sides with the Palestinians, trips up on soap-opera plotting. Also with Gabriel Byrne and Mohamed Bakri. (PG) *108 minutes*

HANOVER STREET (1979)

★

Harrison Ford
Lesley-Anne Down

An American bomber pilot has a secret love affair with a married British nurse amid the London blitz of 1943. Ford is the pilot; Down plays the nurse. More tears and war-film clichés fall than enemy bombs in this unbelievable turkey. Such excess sentimentality may have worked during the frantic World War II years, but now this sort of mush seems absurd. The acting doesn't help the limp screenplay by writer-director Peter Hyams. (PG) *105 minutes*

HANS CHRISTIAN ANDERSEN (1952)

★★★

Danny Kaye

Kaye is ideally suited to the title role in this appealing children's fantasy, about a poor shoemaker-storyteller who makes dancing slippers for a ballerina and then falls in love with her. The colorful production comes across with a thick coating of sugar, yet the

score is appealing. Danny sings such favorites as "Thumbelina" and "Ugly Duckling." Zizi Jeanmaire, Farley Granger, and John Qualen co-star. **Director**—Charles Vidor. *112 minutes*

THE HAPPIEST DAYS OF YOUR LIFE (1950)

★★★★

Alastair Sim
Margaret Rutherford
Joyce Grenfell

A cast of great British character players has a field day with this energetic comedy. There are fun and laughs galore when some schoolgirls are mistakenly quartered at a boy's boarding school. A first-rate, effective adaptation for the screen of John Dighton's popular postwar play. Also with Richard Wattis, Guy Middleton, Muriel Aked, and Edward Rigby. **Director**—Frank Launder. *81 minutes b&w*

HAPPY BIRTHDAY, GEMINI (1980)

★

Rita Moreno
Madeline Kahn

A shrill and, at times, offensive screen version of the award-winning Broadway comedy, *Gemini*. It's about a college student from a working-class Italian-American family, who faces a sexual identity crisis. The characters, *(Continued)*

Danny Kaye plays the title role in Hans Christian Andersen, a children's fantasy.

 Movie is available in Beta and VHS videotape

H
- The Happy Ending
- The Happy Hooker
- The Happy Hooker Goes to Washington
- The Happy Time
- Happy Times
- Hardbodies
- Hardcore
- A Hard Day's Night

(Continued)

which fit comfortably on stage, are blown out of proportion on the screen, with much overacting and screaming at one another. Kahn and Moreno are wasted in leading roles. Director Richard Benner guides the film with the grace of a drunken sailor. Also with Robert Viharo and Alan Rosenberg. (R) *112 minutes*

THE HAPPY ENDING (1969)
★★

**Jean Simmons
John Forsythe**

Simmons is convincing as a frustrated woman who chucks her marriage of 16 years to find a new life. This glossy production transcends its soap-opera mentality with an adequate number of interesting moments. The top cast also includes Shirley Jones, Lloyd Bridges, Teresa Wright, Dick Shawn, Nanette Fabray, Bobby Darin, and Tina Louise. **Director**—Richard Brooks. **Academy Award Nomination**—Simmons, best actress. *112 minutes*

THE HAPPY HOOKER (1975)

★★

**Lynn Redgrave
Jean-Pierre Aumont**

This story about Xaviera Hollander, distinguished by Lynn Redgrave's excellent characterization, is a comedy about greed and lust with some amusing behind-the-scenes looks at the kinky world of hookers. Also with Lovelady Powell and Nicholas Pryor. **Director**—Nicholas Sgarro. (R) *96 minutes*

THE HAPPY HOOKER GOES TO WASHINGTON (1977)

★

Joey Heatherton

This is a second shabby screen installment, loosely based on the life of Xaviera Hollander, the notorious madame. Heatherton, in the title role, is hardly convincing. While bit players in the film unblushingly shed their clothes, Joey stays modestly covered. The plot, involving sexual escapades in the nation's capital, is absurd and adolescent. George Hamilton and Phil Foster also star. **Director**—William Levey. (R) *89 minutes*

THE HAPPY TIME (1952)
★★★

**Charles Boyer
Louis Jourdan**

A nifty family situation comedy concerning the day-to-day lives of French Canadians in the 1920s. Boyer is appealing as the father of this oddball goup, involved in various comic interpersonal relationships. Jourdan plays an uncle. It's smartly directed by Richard Fleischer, with pleasant performances all around. Others in the cast include Bobby Driscoll, Linda Christian, and Marsha Hunt. *94 minutes b&w*

HAPPY TIMES
See The Inspector General

HARDBODIES (1984)

★

**Grant Cramer
Teal Roberts**

Teal Roberts, Grant Cramer, and Kathleen Kinmont rub their Hardbodies *together.*

Trite, silly beach party comedy that serves mainly as an excuse to display numerous barebreasted young women. The foolish story involves three middle-aged men experiencing second childhood. While frolicking at the shore, they hire a slick young Romeo to teach them the latest techniques of attracting girls. **Director**—Mark Griffiths. (R) *88 minutes*

HARDCORE (1979)

★★★

**George C. Scott
Peter Boyle**

A religious businessman from Grand Rapids, Michigan, searches for his teenage daughter who has fallen in with pornographic filmmakers. The businessman is played by Scott. Boyle plays a hardboiled detective who helps in the search. Writer-director Paul Schrader gives us a hard-hitting, vivid tour of the sleazy sex-for-sale underworld. He also presents a chilling contrast between complacent Middle American culture and the seamy big-city jungle. Boyle and Scott are convincing in this intelligent drama, which contains some heart-rending moments. Also with Season Hubley, Dick Sargent, and Leonard Gaines. (R) *108 minutes*

A HARD DAY'S NIGHT (1964)

★★★★

The Beatles

The Beatles run from their screaming fans in A Hard Day's Night.

The Beatles—George, Paul, John, and Ringo—star in this surprisingly sensational comedy, which revolves around their hectic schedule during a trip to London. The mop tops demonstrate that they can excel at clowning as well as singing, and the madcap affair comes off with enormous energy and good humor. There's also plenty of favorite Beatle songs. Wilfred Brambell and Victor Spinetti co-star. **Director**—Richard Lester. *85 minutes b&w*

• The Harder They Fall
• Hardly Working
• Hard Times
• Hard to Hold
• Harlan County, U.S.A.
• Harold and Maude
• Harper

H

THE HARDER THEY FALL (1956)
 ★★★

Humphrey Bogart
Rod Steiger

Humphrey Bogart checks out a young boxer in The Harder They Fall.

Bogart is reliably good as a press agent who blows the whistle on unethical dealings in the prizefight business. The searing drama, based on Budd Schulberg's novel, is sympathetic to athletes who are controlled by selfish managers. Steiger is also on board with a decent acting job. This is Bogey's last feature film. Also stars Jan Sterling, Mike Lane, and Max Baer. **Director**—Mark Robson.

109 minutes b&w

HARDLY WORKING (1981)
★★

Jerry Lewis

Lewis brings back his familiar repertoire of slapstick comedy in this story of a circus clown who loses his job and then bungles his way through a variety of other occupations. There are a few amusing episodes, but much of the humor is repetitious and merely desperate. Some of the gags are recycled from his earlier movies, and many of the new routines are uninspired. Scattered about are some serious moments that don't seem to fit in this confusing and uneven movie. **Director**—Lewis. (PG) *91 minutes*

HARD TIMES (1975)
 ★★★

Charles Bronson
James Coburn

It's 1936, the midst of the Depression.

The place: New Orleans. Bronson plays a moody, silent loner who earns a living—such as it is—by illegal bareknuckle prizefighting. It's a gripping and exciting action drama that's also frequently funny. Coburn does well as the shifty fight manager. Also with Jill Ireland and Strother Martin. A winning debut by director Walter Hill. (PG) *97 minutes*

HARD TO HOLD (1984)
 ★

Rick Springfield
Janet Eilber

Rick Springfield reaches deep within himself and attempts to portray a rock singer in Hard to Hold.

Only the rock music is at all worthwhile in this otherwise tedious vehicle custom-fitted for pop idol Springfield. The cliché-strewn soap-opera plot essentially explores a heartwrenching proposition: Can a self-indulgent rock superstar find happiness in the arms of a cultured teacher of retarded children? After a lot of silly dialogue and poor acting goes by, it's hard to care. **Director**—Larry Peerce. (PG) *93 minutes*

HARLAN COUNTY, U.S.A. (1976)
 ★★★★

This powerful, passionate documentary about a strike by coal miners has as much excitement going as any fictional drama. It's a pro-miner film that mainly revolves around a brutal confrontation in Brookside, Kentucky, in 1973. The film also illuminates a broader portrait of perilous mining conditions over the years and the corruption of some elements of organized labor and some managements. It's an impressive debut for Barbara Kopple who directed the project during a three-year period. (No MPAA rating) **Academy Award**—documentary feature. *103 minutes*

HAROLD AND MAUDE (1972)
 ★★★

Bud Cort
Ruth Gordon

A nutty black comedy that has evolved into a cult film. Cort plays a strange young man who often contemplates death. He pals around with an equally odd 79-year-old adventurous woman, hilariously portrayed by Gordon. The two fall in love; she shows him a picture of herself and it's a sunflower; she commits suicide but shows him how to live. Weird as it is, this campy outing is done with style, wit, and spirit, thanks to an inventive screenplay by Colin Higgins and Hal Ashby's perceptive direction. Also with Vivian Pickles, Cyril Cusack, Charles Tyner, and Ellen Geer. (PG) *92 minutes*

HARPER (1966)
 ★★★

Paul Newman
Lauren Bacall

A fast-paced detective yarn somewhat on the order of Bogart-type gumshoe capers of the '40s. It's based on John Ross MacDonald's novel *The Moving Target*. Director Jack Smight strains to capture the *film noir* flavor, but doesn't quite succeed; however, the fine cast carries it along in high style. Newman is Lew Harper, a private eye hired to track down the missing husband of a rich California woman, played by Bacall. He's a slick bird dog who gets himself into a variety of scrapes along the way. Other players include Julie Harris, Shelley Winters, Janet Leigh, Robert Wagner, and Arthur Hill. *121 minutes*

H

- Harper Valley PTA
- Harry & Son
- Harry and Tonto
- Harry and Walter Go to New York
- Harvey
- The Harvey Girls
- The Hasty Heart

HARPER VALLEY PTA (1979)
★★

**Barbara Eden
Ronny Cox
Nanette Fabray**

Inspired by the '60s pop tune of the same name, this flat comedy pokes fun at snootiness and hypocrisy. Eden plays the sexy mom in miniskirts who wreaks revenge on some stuffy PTA board members in Harper Valley, Ohio. Most of the gags don't work well. Also with Pat Paulsen, Susan Swift, Louis Nye, and John Fiedler. **Director**—Richard Bennett. (PG)
93 minutes

HARRY & SON (1984)
★

**Paul Newman
Robby Benson**

Son Robby Benson listens attentively to cranky father Paul Newman in Harry & Son.

Big disappointment from Newman who wrote, directed, and stars in this syrupy film. He plays a widowed construction worker trying to cope with Benson, badly miscast as his 21-year-old son, a would-be writer. The strained, unfocused story meanders among irritating situations without drawing any meaningful conclusions. Newman, as the callous father, mopes a lot and intermittently explodes at his sweet-tempered offspring, who works at menial jobs. Also with Ellen Barkin and Joanne Woodward. (PG)
118 minutes

HARRY AND TONTO (1974)
★★★

**Art Carney
Ellen Burstyn**

After being evicted, a New York senior citizen and his cat Tonto take a sentimental journey to Chicago, and a variety of funny and sad episodes occur along the way. Carney, in the title role, makes the character shine with affection and pathos. It's a lovely trip that never runs out of interesting events and scenery. There's good support from Burstyn, Chief Dan George, Geraldine Fitzgerald, and Larry Hagman. **Director**—Paul Mazursky. (PG) **Academy Award**—Carney, best actor. **Nomination**—Mazursky and John Greenfeld, best original screenplay.
115 minutes

HARRY AND WALTER GO TO NEW YORK (1976)
★

**James Caan
Elliott Gould**

Diane Keaton plays a schoolmarm in Harry and Walter Go to New York.

Caan and Gould play a couple of talentless vaudeville entertainers named Harry and Walter, who go to New York to organize the heist of a Massachusetts bank. What's supposed to be funny turns out pathetic and embarrassing; Caan and Gould scream, jump, pinch, and pull each other's ears, and strain their professional reputations. There's also clumsy direction by Mark Rydell. New York is in enough trouble; Harry and Walter should have stayed home. Also with Michael Caine, Diane Keaton, and Charles Durning. (PG)   *123 minutes*

HARVEY (1950)
★★★★

**James Stewart
Josephine Hull**

Mary Chase's touching play about a middle-aged tippler with an imaginary huge white rabbit as his companion comes to the screen with all the wonderful dialogue and memorable moments firmly in place. Stewart is wonderful as the gentle Elwood P. Dowd, under pressure by his relatives to enter a mental hospital. Hull also stands out as the perplexed sister who is constantly apologizing for Dowd's nutty behavior. The engrossing story wisely questions the true definition of insanity. There are other good performances from Victoria Horne, Peggy Dow, Cecil Kellaway, and Jesse White. **Director**—Henry Koster. **Academy Award**—Hull, best supporting actress. **Nomination**—Stewart, best actor.   *104 minutes b&w*

THE HARVEY GIRLS (1946)
★★★

**Judy Garland
Ray Bolger**

A delightful musical about young women who go west to be waitresses for a 19th-century restaurant chain operating in frontier communities. Much of the script is nonsense, but this drawback is more than redeemed by good performances and a memorable score. "Atchison, Topeka and the Santa Fe" is among the songs. Garland and Bolger head the fine cast, which also includes John Hodiak, Preston Foster, Angela Lansbury, and Marjorie Main. **Director**—George Sidney.
101 minutes

THE HASTY HEART (1949)
★★★

**Richard Todd
Patricia Neal**

Touching story about an overbearing Scottish soldier who's brought to an army hospital in Burma. The attitudes toward him drastically change when it's discovered that he will soon die. Todd is especially convincing as the young trooper. The film is based on John Patrick's play, which worked slightly better on the stage. Other cast members include Ronald Reagan and Orlando Martins. **Director**—Vincent Sherman. **Academy Award Nomination**—Todd, best actor.

104 minutes b&w

A HATFUL OF RAIN (1957)
★★★

**Eva Marie Saint
Don Murray**

A powerful story about a young man, played by Murray, who becomes addicted to drugs, and how his deteriorating condition affects his family and friends. Fine acting by a competent cast highlights this searing drama, which was one of the first to examine addiction with intelligence and understanding. Based on Michael V. Gazzo's Broadway play. Also with Anthony Franciosa, Lloyd Nolan, and Howard da Silva. **Director**—Fred Zinnemann.   *109 minutes b&w*

HAWAII (1966)
 ★★★

**Max Von Sydow
Julie Andrews
Richard Harris**

Jocelyn Lagarde gives it to Max Von Sydow in the epic film Hawaii.

Mammoth film epic based on portions of James Michener's ambitious historical novel, about the intrusion of western culture on native Hawaiians in the early 1800s. The narrative flow is handled in a choppy fashion, but the acting is adequate, and the production is presented with lavish care. Von Sydow stars in the key role of a young mis-

sionary who tries to impose his religious dogma on the islanders. Also with Jocelyn Lagarde, Carroll O'Connor, and Gene Hackman. **Director**—George Roy Hill. **Academy Award Nominations**—Jocelyn Lagarde, best supporting actress; Russell Harlan, cinematography (color).   *186 minutes*

THE HAWAIIANS (1970)
★★

**Charlton Heston
Tina Chen
Geraldine Chaplin**

This continuation of James Michener's chronicle brings the story up to the 1900s. However, this portion doesn't work too well, because the spectacular production takes in too many episodes in one bite. Heston stars as a businessman who comes to the islands and encounters a mixture of good fortune, disease, revolution, destruction, and anguish over morality. The huge cast also includes John Philip Law, Mako, Alec McCowen, and Ann Knight. **Director**—Tom Gries. (PG)   *132 minutes*

HAWMPS! (1976)
 ★

**James Hampton
Christopher Connelly
Slim Pickens**

Slapstick comedy of the Old West, when camels were briefly used in Texas to replace U.S. Cavalry horses. Adults will probably find the film tiresome, but there are plenty of laughs for the kids. There's a big saloon brawl, a comic shootout, and a camel vs. horse race. But it all drags on for nearly two hours, and even the youngsters will begin to nod at the end. Also with Jack Elam and Denver Pyle. Produced and directed by Joe Camp, who also presented *Benji*. (G)   *113 minutes*

HEAD OVER HEELS (1979)
★★

**John Heard
Mary Beth Hurt**

Joan Micklin Silver's adaptation of Ann Beattie's novel *Chilly Scenes of Win-*

ROBERT REDFORD

Robert Redford was born in 1937 in Santa Monica, California. As a child, he wanted to be an outlaw and an artist. Growing up near Hollywood where he could observe it at close quarters, he found it suspect and dropped out in Europe to "paint angry pictures."

Acting, however, tempted him, and he began acting in New York in 1959, going on to make a considerable splash in Neil Simon's Barefoot in the Park. *Redford made his film debut—a small part—in* War Hunt *(1961). Later, during casting for an off-beat western, Paul Newman told the studio "No Redford, no Newman."* Butch Cassidy and the Sundance Kid *(1969) justified his stand.*

Becoming fascinated with the Watergate affair when it was still a breaking news item, Redford was the moving spirit behind the film version of All the President's Men *(1976), helping to make it "the thinking man's Jaws."*

Redford's other major films include Inside Daisy Clover *(1965),* The Chase *(1966),* This Property Is Condemned *(1966),* Barefoot in the Park *(1967),* Tell Them Willie Boy Is Here *(1969),* Jeremiah Johnson *(1972),* The Candidate *(1972),* The Hot Rock *(1972),* The Way We Were *(1973),* The Sting *(1973),* A Bridge Too Far *(1977),* The Outlaw Trail *(1978),* The Electric Horseman *(1979),* and *The Natural (1984).*

In 1980, Redford received the Oscar as best director for Ordinary People.

ter is a rather uninteresting movie about some uninteresting people. Charles, played by Heard, is a bachelor

(Continued)

H

- Health
- The Hearse
- Heartaches
- Heart Beat
- Heartbeeps
- The Heartbreak Kid
- The Heart Is a Lonely Hunter

(Continued)
who has a dull job as a reports analyst. He falls in love with a librarian, played by Hurt, who is married to a dull husband. There's a lot of cutesy dialogue. He wins her. He loses her. He wins her back again. After a while, who cares? Also with Peter Riegert and Kenneth McMillan. (PG)   *97 minutes*

HEALTH (1979)
★★★

**Glenda Jackson
Carol Burnett
James Garner
Lauren Bacall
Dick Cavett**

Director Robert Altman uses a health food convention in Florida as an opportunity to satirize national politics in his highly individual style. The top-name cast has a field day with this rambling and shapeless material, and some splendid characterizations emerge. The film often appears flat and thin, but this is Altman doing his thing and many glorious moments shine through. (PG)   *102 minutes*

THE HEARSE (1980)
★★

**Trish Van Devere
Joseph Cotten**

Van Devere plays a daring divorcée who moves into an old house, and before long she's up to her neck with wicked ghosts from the past. Among the evil demons who pursue her is the chauffeur of the vehicle from the film's title. Cotten is effective as a grumpy lawyer who presents obstacles to Van Devere's taking legal possession of the house. The film offers enough frightening moments, but it's really just another routine twist to the haunted-house movie. Also with Perry Lang. **Director**—George Bowers. (PG)
95 minutes

HEARTACHES (1982)
★★

**Margot Kidder
Annie Potts**

Mushy, romantic comedy set in Toron-

to with two young women roommates trying to sort out their precarious love affairs. Kidder is believable as the brassy, free-spirited mattress factory worker who falls for the boss's suave nephew. She's slightly ahead of the material, which plays somewhat like a soap opera. Potts plays an insecure waif who's afraid to tell her adolescent husband that he is not the father of her expected baby. **Director**—Donald Shebib. (R)   *90 minutes*

HEART BEAT (1980)
★★

**Nick Nolte
Sissy Spacek
John Heard**

The '50s beat generation is explored rather timidly in this biographical film about novelist Jack Kerouac (*On the Road*) and his friends Neal and Carolyn Cassady. The story is engaging and stylish at times, as it delves into the nonconforming life-styles of the characters. But too often the loosely constructed movie wanders off the road and fritters away dramatic impact. Nolte, as the freewheeling Neal Cassady, turns in a sizzling performance that provides some much-needed energy. Spacek plays Carolyn, and Heard plays Kerouac. **Director**—John Byrum. (R)   *109 minutes*

HEARTBEEPS (1981)
★

**Andy Kaufman
Bernadette Peters**

Bernadette Peters and Andy Kaufman are androids in love in Heartbeeps.

A romantic comedy about robots that seems to have been written by a computer and could only be appreciated by someone with a mechanical brain. Kaufman and Peters play amorous robots who meet at a repair facility and venture into the wide world where they encounter similar creatures. One of them, called "Catskill," spouts Henny Youngman one-liners; another is "Crimebusters," which looks like a tank. There's enough mechanical corn generated here to overload anyone's memory bank. **Director**—Allan Arkush. (PG)   *88 minutes*

THE HEARTBREAK KID (1972)
★★★

**Charles Grodin
Cybill Shepherd
Jeannie Berlin**

Neil Simon's compelling screenplay, based on Bruce Jay Friedman's play, is alternately funny and sad—but either way, it cuts to the bone. Grodin plays a cocky young man on his honeymoon, who abruptly abandons his bride to pursue a seemingly more attractive girl. The situation is outrageous, but it's carried off with intelligence and played to the hilt for impact. Berlin is effective as the ditched newlywed, and Shepherd is fine as the new love interest. Eddie Albert and Audra Lindley have good supporting roles. **Director**—Elaine May. (PG) **Academy Award Nominations**—Albert, best supporting actor; Berlin, best supporting actress.   *106 minutes*

THE HEART IS A LONELY HUNTER (1968)
★★★

**Alan Arkin
Sondra Locke**

Arkin gives a moving performance as a kindhearted deaf-mute who resides in a small southern town. Based on the compelling novel by Carson McCullers, the film sensitively touches on isolation and cruelty. Locke plays a girl who befriends Arkin. It's all brought together nicely by a professional cast that also includes Stacy Keach, Cicely Tyson, and Laurinda Barrett. **Academy Award Nominations**—Arkin,

• Heartland
• Heart Like a Wheel
• Hearts of the West
• Heat and Dust
• Heaven Can Wait
• Heaven Knows, Mr. Allison

H

best actor; Locke, best supporting actress. *125 minutes*

HEARTLAND
(1981)

★★★

Conchata Ferrell
Rip Torn

The frontier family in Heartland.

Plucky spirit of American pioneer life is richly portrayed in this low-budget but handsomely made film chronicle set in 1910. The unpretentious story concerns a poor young widow, played by Ferrell, who signs on as housekeeper for a stoic Wyoming rancher, played by Torn, and eventually marries him. Megan Folsom plays Ferrell's daughter. All performances are remarkable, and the directing effort by Richard Pearce—his first—beautifully captures the challenges and hardships of frontier life without being overly sentimental. Also with Barry Primus and Lilia Skala. (PG) *93 minutes*

HEART LIKE A WHEEL (1983)
★★★

Beau Bridges
Bonnie Bedelia

An entertaining and winning film based on the life of Shirley ("Cha-Cha") Muldowney, a professional champion race car driver. Director Jonathan Kaplan brings this piece of Americana to life with vivid detail and excitement. The heart of this slight but realistic-looking production is Bonnie Bedelia's performance as the spunky woman racing ace who triumphs on the track but wrecks her family life. Excellent support from Leo Rossi and Hoyt Axton. (PG) *113 minutes*

HEARTS OF THE WEST
(1975)
★★★

Jeff Bridges
Alan Arkin
Andy Griffith

A warm, merry movie about an Iowa farm boy who goes to Hollywood in the '30s to become a cowboy actor and write western movies. Bridges plays the hero with style and charm, and there are other excellent performances by Arkin and Griffith. The film is artistically directed by Howard Zieff, who has a keen appreciation of moviemaking of that era. In all, it's a well-blended mixture of color, romance, suspense, nostalgia, and comedy. Also with Blythe Danner, Donald Pleasence, and Richard B. Schull. (PG) *102 minutes*

HEAT AND DUST (1983)
★★

Julie Christie
Greta Scacchi

Greta Scacchi plays a proper British lady whose affair shocks colonial India in Heat and Dust.

Drab, cluttered saga of mysterious India's effect on two English women separated by six decades. The film irritates as it oscillates from colonial India to the '80s, making it difficult to sort out characters and events. Christie handles the contemporary role with finesse, and Scacchi is equally competent as the young woman of the '20s. Lavishly photographed and brimming with details of India now and then, but without a meaningful story, who cares? **Director**—James Ivory. (R) *130 minutes*

HEAVEN CAN WAIT (1978)
★★★★

Warren Beatty
Julie Christie
Jack Warden
Dyan Cannon

Beatty's remake of the 1941 comedy-drama *Here Comes Mr. Jordan* is a cheerful gem of a movie, brimming with priceless moments and inspired dialogue. It's about an enthusiastic football quarterback who dies prematurely and returns to earth as a powerful industrialist. Beatty is sensational in the leading role and works harmoniously with the marvelous cast. Although the film is a retread, it's contemporary in most respects and shines with its own madcap personality; it satisfies. Also with Charles Grodin, James Mason, Buck Henry, and Vincent Gardenia. (PG) **Academy Award Nominations**—best picture; Beatty and Henry, best director; Beatty, best actor; Warden, best supporting actor; Cannon, best supporting actress; Elaine May and Beatty, best screenplay adaptation; William Fraker, cinematography. *100 minutes*

HEAVEN KNOWS, MR. ALLISON (1957)
★★★

Robert Mitchum
Deborah Kerr

Mitchum and Kerr perform well together in this mildly preposterous and predictable film. The story is set on a Pacific island during World War II. He's a gruff Marine corporal; she's a mild-mannered nun; together they conspire *(Continued)*

H
- Heaven's Gate
- Heavy Metal
- Hedda
- The Heiress
- Hellfighters
- Hell Night
- Hello, Dolly!

(Continued)
to outfox the Japanese. Doesn't this seem a little like *The African Queen*? John Huston directs with style and skill. *105 minutes*

HEAVEN'S GATE (1981)

 ★★

**Kris Kristofferson
Isabelle Huppert
Christopher Walken
John Hurt**

Michael Cimino's $40-million epic western about 1890 Johnson County, Wyoming, cattle wars is still muddled and overblown despite improvements from editing and voice-over narration. Kristofferson stars as a Harvard educated federal marshal, who sides with poor settlers marked for search and-destroy extermination by wealthy landowners. His role and others are ill-defined and mostly incoherent. It seems as if Cimino's theme of the corrupting influence of money and power has also corrupted the movie itself. (R) *219 minutes*

HEAVY METAL (1981)

★

A brash, crude, animated anthology, based on the grotesque fantasy magazine. The various segments deal with sword-and-sorcery, violence, sex, science fiction, drugs, and mysticism—all tied together with ear-blasting rock music. Those who like that sort of thing might enjoy it. The cartoon fantasies are bridged by a luminous green ball that represents evil. It's a heavy trip that begins with a bang and gradually runs out of energy. **Director**—Gerald Potterton. (R) *90 minutes*

HEDDA (1976)

 ★★

Glenda Jackson

The talented Jackson dominates this film version of Ibsen's *Hedda Gabler* with a steely and intelligent performance, playing the bored and impatient woman who wrecked the lives of the men who pursued her. It's a first-

class acting job, but the movie itself is stale and unmoving. Trevor Nunn directed and wrote the screenplay, based on the Royal Shakespeare production. The transferal from stage presentation to screen is strained. Also with Peter Eyre and Jennie Linden. (PG) *104 minutes*

THE HEIRESS (1949)

 ★★★★

**Olivia de Havilland
Montgomery Clift**

Olivia de Havilland is The Heiress.

De Havilland is brilliant as a plain, lonely, but rich spinster who is wooed by a sly, charming fortune-seeker, played by Clift. The smartly styled film, set in turn-of-the-century New York, is based on Henry James's play, *Washington Square*. All parts are played out nicely, with Ralph Richardson, Miriam Hopkins, Vanessa Brown, Mona Freeman, and Ray Collins in supporting roles. **Director**—William Wyler. **Academy Award**—de Havilland, best actress. **Nominations**—best picture; Wyler, best director; Richardson, best supporting actor; Leo Tover, cinematography (black and white). *115 minutes b&w*

HELLFIGHTERS (1969)

 ★★

**John Wayne
Jim Hutton
Katharine Ross**

This sophomoric action yarn about

rough-tough men who battle oil-well fires is upgraded a half-notch by the presence of Wayne. Big John leads his crew against the flames and finds time to deal with woman problems, too. Some action scenes have noticeable class. Also with Vera Miles, Bruce Cabot, and Barbara Stuart. **Director**—Andrew V. McLaglen. (G) *121 minutes*

HELL NIGHT (1981)

 ★

Linda Blair

This film is more teenage love-and-terror fare, cranked off the Hollywood horror assembly line with a minimum of inspiration and talent. Some fraternity pledges spend their initiation night at a haunted house where survivors of a family murder 12 years ago take their revenge on the youths. The usual head-choppings and other gory deaths go on until most of the kids are eliminated. Blair is the only familiar player, and she escapes the massacre. **Director**—Tom De Simone. (R) *101 minutes*

HELLO, DOLLY! (1969)

 ★★★

**Barbra Streisand
Walter Matthau
Michael Crawford**

Barbra Streisand conspires to match two couples in Hello, Dolly!

• Hells Angels Forever
• Hellzapoppin
• Hennessy

• Henry V
• Hercules
• Here Comes Mr. Jordan

H

Big, brassy musical, based on the Broadway success about a New York matchmaker in the early 1900s who ends up getting married herself. Streisand plays the title role in her usual powerhouse style, but she's obviously too young for the part. However, all is forgiven when she turns up the volume and belts out some enjoyable songs with exceptional gusto. Louis Armstrong is on board,too, adding immeasurably to the frolic. Armstrong and Streisand team up to sing the title song. The film is based on Thornton Wilder's play *The Matchmaker*. Other cast members include E. J. Peaker and Marianne McAndrew. **Director**—Gene Kelly. (G) **Academy Award Nominations**—best picture; Harry Stradling, cinematography.
129 minutes

HELLS ANGELS FOREVER (1983)
 ★★

The Hell's Angels
Bo Diddley
Willie Nelson

Hells Angels Forever is an official documentary of the rebellious motorcycle gang.

A murky-looking documentary that attempts to glorify and apologize for the notorious motorcycle gang. Much footage apparently was shot by the Angels themselves, and the scenes have a home-movie quality as well as a certain perverse fascination. We see the scruffy-looking bikers riding their motorcycles, partying on a boat, attending a wedding ceremony, discussing their peculiar free-wheeling philosophy, and engaging in fist fights. Also, there's much self-righteous comment about attempts by government agencies to destroy the organization. **Director**—Richard Chase. (R)
92 minutes

HELLZAPOPPIN (1941)
★★★

Ole Olsen
Chic Johnson

Olsen and Johnson present a screen version of their madcap Broadway burlesque show, and the results are pleasingly funny. The zany duo decides to make a movie, and they cook up their own plot as they progress. A few gags misfire, but most of them score high on the laugh meter. It's great fun if you enjoy the '40s-era brand of humor. The supporting cast also features Hugh Herbert, Martha Raye, and Mischa Auer. **Director**—H. C. Potter.
84 minutes b&w

HENNESSY (1975)
★★

Rod Steiger

A peace-loving Irishman, whose wife and child have been accidentally killed in a battle in Belfast, renounces his pacifism and seeks revenge on the Royal Family and the British Parliament. Steiger plays the title role. It's a slow-moving melodrama that exploits rather harmlessly one's emotions about assassination. There are several unbelievable situations, such as the ease with which Steiger assumes the identity of a member of Parliament he has kidnapped. There is some clever use of newsreel footage of the Royal Family in conjunction with the fictional story. Also with Lee Remick, Trevor Howard, and Richard Johnson. **Director**—Don Sharp. (PG)
103 minutes

HENRY V (1946)
 ★★★★

Laurence Olivier
Robert Newton

No one does Shakespeare like Olivier, and he triumphs here as both director and lead actor. The production is presented as an example of a play at the Globe Theatre in the early 1600s, and then it brilliantly evolves as a contemporary screen rendition. Olivier's acting is magnificent, and the film offers many glorious moments; the battle

scenes, splendidly photographed in color, are engrossing. It's a masterpiece of moviemaking. Also with Leslie Banks, Esmond Knight, Leo Genn, Renée Asherson, and Ralph Truman. **Director**—Olivier. **Academy Award Nominations**—best picture; Olivier, best actor.
137 minutes

HERCULES (1983)
 ★

Lou Ferrigno

Lou Ferrigno removes helmets the hard way in Hercules.

Hulking muscleman Ferrigno, grunting and flexing his bulbous biceps, is in the title role of this ridiculous epic adventure. Clad in skimpy gladiator skivvies to show off his overgrown physique, Ferrigno battles various villains and monsters in his quest to rescue a princess. The absurd screenplay makes a shambles of Greek mythology, and the film is rife with flashy effects more suited to sci-fi extravaganzas. Mirella D'Angelo and Sybil Danning co-star. **Director**—Lewis Coates. (PG)
98 minutes

HERE COMES MR. JORDAN (1941)
 ★★★★

Robert Montgomery
Evelyn Keyes

This is an inventive comedy-fantasy about a boxer who dies in a plane crash by mistake, and is sent to Earth to occupy someone else's body. Montgomery plays the prizefighter who dies before his time. The film's novel
(Continued)

Robert Montgomery and Edward Everett Horton in Here Comes Mr. Jordan.

(Continued)

twist about heaven and death works on many levels and sustains interest and comic vitality to the end; the theme has been reused in many subsequent movies. Also with Claude Rains, Rita Johnson, Edward Everett Horton, James Gleason, and Donald MacBride. **Director**—Alexander Hall. **Academy Award**—Harry Segall, writing (original story). **Nominations**—best picture; Hall, best director; Montgomery, best actor; Gleason, best supporting actor; Joseph Walker, cinematography (black and white).

93 minutes b&w

HERE COME THE WAVES (1944)
★★★

**Bing Crosby
Betty Hutton**

Bouncy World War II musical morale-builder, with Crosby in the Navy and romancing identical twin Waves. Hutton plays the twins. As expected, there's not much plot, but there are plenty of good songs. Bing sings "Accent-tchu-ate the Positive" and more. Sonny Tufts co-stars in his first singing role. Also with Ann Doran and Gwen Crawford. **Director**—Mark Sandrich. *98 minutes b&w*

A HERO AIN'T NOTHIN' BUT A SANDWICH (1978)
★

**Cicely Tyson
Paul Winfield
Larry B. Scott**

This frank family film, about a 13-year-old boy who grapples with a drug problem, is made in the tradition of such films as *Sounder* and *Lilies of the Field*. Tyson and Winfield give decent performances, but they're often upstaged by Scott, 16, as the intelligent but troubled youth. Scott knows how to turn on the charm and warmth at the correct moments. The movie, however, is preachy and pedantic. Also with Helen Martin and Glynn Turman. **Director**—Ralph Nelson. (PG)

105 minutes

HERO AT LARGE (1980)
★★

**John Ritter
Anne Archer**

Ritter of TV's *Three's Company* plays a struggling actor in New York City, who becomes an instant hero when he foils a robbery attempt. At the time, he was wearing a comic-book hero outfit for a movie promotion. Ritter is at his easygoing best, as the young man in the superhero suit who can save the world. But midway, the script runs out of steam, and what charm there is deteriorates into excessive sentimentality. Unfortunately, a good idea gets pushed too far. Archer plays the girl next door. Also with Kevin McCarthy. **Director**—Martin Davidson. (PG)

98 minutes

HEROES (1977)
★

**Henry Winkler
Sally Field**

Winkler and Field co-star in this erratic and poorly written story about the escapades of a troubled Vietnam veteran. Winkler, making his film debut, has trouble shaking off his television image of "The Fonz" and adapting to the big screen. Field, however, evokes energy and charm in her part as Winkler's companion. The film comes off as an exhausting commercial television drama, which doesn't work well. Also with Harrison Ford and Val Avery. **Director**—Jeremy Kagan. (PG)

113 minutes

HESTER STREET (1975)
 ★★★

**Steven Keats
Carol Kane**

Steven Keats is an immigrant who adjusts quickly to America in Hester Street.

Joan Micklin Silver wrote and directed this compassionate movie about Jewish immigrants struggling to adapt to the New World at the turn of the century. The story concerns a young immigrant, played by Keats, who is charmed with the ways of his new country. His wife, played by Kane, arrives later with their son and finds assimilation painful. The plot is familiar, but the performances are keen and extraordinary. Also with Mel Howard, Dorrie Kavanaugh, and Doris Roberts. Mostly in Yiddish with English titles. (PG) **Academy Award**

• Hide in Plain Sight
• The Hiding Place
• The High and the Mighty

• High Anxiety
• High-Ballin'
• High Barbaree
• High Noon

H

Nomination—Kane, best actress.
92 minutes b&w

HIDE IN PLAIN SIGHT (1980)

★★

James Caan
Jill Eikenberry

Caan directs and stars in this restrained drama about a divorced factory worker's frustrating efforts to locate his children, who are in hiding under the government's Witness Relocation Program, which is designed to protect witnesses from criminal retaliation. This is Caan's directorial debut, and he handles the assignment at a sluggish pace. The film, based on a true story, needs a shot of adrenalin. But the supporting cast is especially good, and Caan manages to depict ordinary people with authenticity. Also with Robert Viharo, Kenneth McMillan, and Danny Aiello. (PG)
91 minutes

THE HIDING PLACE (1975)

★

Julie Harris
Eileen Heckart
Arthur O'Connell

This film, elaborately produced by the Billy Graham Association, is based on a true account of a Dutch Christian family who led an underground operation in Holland to assist Jews during World War II. Here is a splendid opportunity to develop an exciting and moving movie; instead, the film plods along somewhat in the manner of an overlong sermon. The action hardly gets moving in situations that must have been suspenseful indeed. Also with Jeanette Clift and Robert Rietty. Filmed in the Netherlands and Great Britain. **Director**—James F. Collier. (PG)
145 minutes

THE HIGH
AND THE MIGHTY (1954)

★★★★

John Wayne
Robert Newton
Robert Stack

A gripping drama about a crippled airliner trying to reach safety during a long flight over the Pacific. The nervous passengers, contemplating a crash landing in the ocean, reveal their emotions. Wayne is effective as a co-pilot who keeps his cool. See *Airplane* for a terrific parody of this pioneer *Airport* film. Also with Doe Avedon, Claire Trevor, Laraine Day, Jan Sterling, Phil Harris, Sidney Blackmer, and David Brian. **Director**—William Wellman. **Academy Award Nominations**—Wellman, best director; Claire Trevor, Jan Sterling, best supporting actress.
147 minutes

HIGH ANXIETY (1978)

★★

Mel Brooks
Madeline Kahn
Cloris Leachman
Harvey Korman

Another parody from Brooks, who seems to be running out of ideas. This time he's very specific, and the films of Alfred Hitchcock are his target. Brooks seems convinced that merely making a visual reference to any well-known scene in a Hitchcock film constitutes a joke. Those who agree with him may find this romp funny. Those who prefer development or wit or original slapstick will again be disappointed, though Brooks's usual performing company tries hard. Brooks directed, produced, starred, and even wrote a song for this one. Dick Van Patten, Ron Carey, and Howard Morris co-star. (PG)
94 minutes

HIGH-BALLIN' (1978)

★★

Peter Fonda
Jerry Reed

Fonda and Reed are good guys who fight a gang of hijackers trying to put the squeeze on independent truckers. The action-adventure sends 18-wheelers careening through snowstorms in some daring chase scenes. The dialogue is rather pat, and the story line isn't original, but there's lots of flashy action along with some decent performances. Also with Helen Shaver and Chris Wiggins. Filmed in Canada. **Director**—Peter Carter. (PG)
100 minutes

HIGH BARBAREE (1947)

★★

Van Johnson
June Allyson

Two Navy pilots crash in the Pacific Ocean, and one reveals the story of his life while they wait for rescue. It's a rather flimsy story featuring a decent cast, and it can't sustain itself because of poor dialogue and a lack of inspired plotting. Also with Thomas Mitchell and Marilyn Maxwell. **Director**—Jack Conway.
91 minutes b&w

HIGH NOON (1952)

★★★★

Gary Cooper
Grace Kelly

Gary Cooper and Grace Kelly embrace in High Noon, *one of the period's best westerns.*

One of the best westerns of the period, with tight-lipped Cooper doing a sensational job as a determined lawman who bravely faces the bad guys alone when the town's citizens cop out. The production is well done, with suspense mounting in well-paced steps. It's high drama, indeed. Kelly is memorable as Coop's bride-to-be, and there's fine support from Thomas Mitchell, Lloyd Bridges, Otto Kruger, Lon Chaney, Katy Jurado, and Henry Morgan. **Director**—Fred Zinnemann. **Academy Award**—Cooper, best actor. **Nominations**—best picture; Zinnemann, best director; Carl Foreman, writing (screenplay). *85 minutes b&w*

H
- High Plains Drifter
- High Risk
- High Road to China
- High School Confidential!
- High Sierra
- High Society
- The Hindenburg

HIGH PLAINS DRIFTER (1973)

 ★★

Clint Eastwood
Verna Bloom

Eastwood is the director and star of this overly violent western. He plays a mysterious drifter who comes to a small town, terrorizes the people, and then stays on to shoot it out with some criminals just out of jail. The half-serious, semi-supernatural film comes off as a parody of Eastwood's own style. Also with Marianna Hill, Mitchell Ryan, Jack Ging, and Stefan Gierasch. (PG) *105 minutes*

HIGH RISK (1981)

 ★★★

James Brolin
Bruce Davison
Chick Vennera
Cleavon Little

A clever, lighthearted adventure about four "nice guys" who steal $5 million from a Colombian drug kingpin and then encounter unexpected obstacles during their escape. Writer-director Stewart Raffill offers an efficient script with a proper portion of humor amid the action. The film is nicely cast, with Brolin, Davison, Vennera, and Little as the unlikely heroes, and James Coburn, Ernest Borgnine, and Anthony Quinn in effective cameo roles. (R) *94 minutes*

HIGH ROAD TO CHINA (1983)

 ★★

Tom Selleck
Bess Armstrong
Jack Warden

Selleck, star of TV's *Magnum, P.I.* series, makes his movie star debut in this derring-do actioner set just after World War I. He manages to work up some charm and dazzle as a boozing daredevil pilot who escorts a beautiful heiress (Armstrong) on a dangerous mission to find her father in China. But the screenplay—a second cousin to *Raiders of the Lost Ark*—often takes the low road of strained credibility, which saps the appeal of the entire

Tom Selleck and Bess Armstrong are adventurers in High Road to China.

production. **Director**—Brian G. Hutton. (PG) *105 minutes*

HIGH SCHOOL CONFIDENTIAL! (1958)

 ★

Russ Tamblyn
Jan Sterling

A young undercover agent poses as a new student so that he can infiltrate a school dope-pushing gang. A passable idea is mishandled here, and in the end it is just a dumb youth exploitation film. The acting of Tamblyn, Sterling, John Drew Barrymore, and Mamie Van Doren fails to enrich the production. **Director**—Jack Arnold. *85 minutes b&w*

HIGH SIERRA (1941)

 ★★★

Humphrey Bogart
Ida Lupino

An interesting crime drama about a veteran gangster, played by Bogart, operating in the California mountain country. The film stays above water thanks to Bogey's fine performance as Mad Dog Earle, a ruthless killer who can muster some moments of kindness. Lupino is his moll. Also with

Joan Leslie, Alan Curtis, Arthur Kennedy, Henry Hull, and Henry Travers. **Director**—Raoul Walsh.
100 minutes b&w

HIGH SOCIETY (1956)

 ★★★

Bing Crosby
Grace Kelly
Frank Sinatra
Celeste Holm

High Society *features Grace Kelly and Bing Crosby—which is as high as they come.*

This musical version of *The Philadelphia Story* comes over well despite some heavy-going moments. Crosby stars as a man of means who tries to stop his ex-wife, played by Kelly, from remarrying. Sinatra and Holm play reporters who become involved in the affair. Cole Porter's score adds pleasure to the proceedings. Also stars Louis Armstrong, Louis Calhern, John Lund, and Sidney Blackmer. **Director**—Charles Walters. *107 minutes*

THE HINDENBURG (1976)

 ★★

George C. Scott
Anne Bancroft
Burgess Meredith

This is a disaster formula movie about the German dirigible that exploded while docking at Lakehurst, New Jersey, in 1937. The special effects are impressive, and for some this alone may prove worthwhile, but the script slowly blimps along, and the suspense is lighter than air. Scott stars as a Nazi security agent on board to identify a possible saboteur. Also with William Atherton, Roy Thinnes, Charles Durning, and Gig Young. **Director**—Robert Wise. (PG)   *125 minutes*

HIROSHIMA MON AMOUR
(1959)

   ★★★★

Emmanuele Riva
Eiji Okada

Alain Resnais catapulted into the front rank of the world's directors with this movie about the love story of French actress Riva and Japanese architect Okada. Resnais brilliantly contrasts the love affair against the grim and stark scenes of destruction caused by the bombing at Hiroshima. Excellent acting enhances the evocative mood created by Resnais. Also with Pierre Barband and Stella Dassas. In French with English titles.   *88 minutes b&w*

HIS GIRL FRIDAY (1940)

   ★★★★

Rosalind Russell
Cary Grant

Cliff Edwards teases Helen Mack about her escaped boyfriend in His Girl Friday.

A howlingly funny version of *The Front Page*, brought off at a fast clip and with a cast of pros giving it their all. Grant is great as a scheming editor. Russell is a riot as a prima donna reporter—in the Hildy Johnson role—tracking down a murder story. Lots of good live-wire supporting players add to the fun. Also with Ralph Bellamy, Gene Lockhart, Porter Hall, Ernest Truex, Clarence Kolb, Roscoe Karns, and Billy Gilbert. **Director**—Howard Hawks.
92 minutes b&w

BURT REYNOLDS

Born in Waycross, Georgia, in 1936, Burt Reynolds was reared in southern Florida, where his father was a police chief. He admits that he was a restless kid who at one point ran away from home and wound up in a South Carolina jail. The cell in which he spent a week now bears an engraved plaque that reads "Burt Reynolds Slept Here."

A high-school football star, Reynolds chose Florida State University over West Point because "the Academy didn't have any girls" and he was partial to FSU's football team. During his college grid career, he was named All-Florida and All-Conference halfback. He then enrolled at Palm Beach Junior College, where he credits the school's drama instructor with changing his life. A scholarship to New York's Hyde Park Playhouse led to his professional acting debut with Charlton Heston in a revival of Mister Roberts.

Moving to Los Angeles, Reynolds appeared in many television series, including Gunsmoke. *He also starred in three TV series—* Riverboat, Hawk, *and* Dan August.

Reynolds made his movie debut in Angel Baby *(1961), but it was his performance in* Deliverance *(1972) that made him a major star. His nude centerfold in* Cosmopolitan *magazine and the wry, self-deprecating humor he displayed on TV talk shows made him one of the most popular stars in the world. Some of his other movies include* The Longest Yard *(1974),* Hustle *(1976),* Gator *(1976),* Smokey and the Bandit *(1977),* Semi-Tough *(1977),* Hooper *(1978),* Starting Over *(1979),* Sharkey's Machine *(1981),* The Man Who Loved Women *(1983), and* City Heat *(1984), in which he starred opposite Clint Eastwood.*

HIS MAJESTY O'KEEFE (1953)

★★

Burt Lancaster

Lancaster swashbuckles around some islands in the South Seas helping the natives fend off pirates. Adequate action and a bit of romance make up the adventure film, but Lancaster doesn't reach his full potential here. Also with Joan Rice, André Morell, Benson Fong, Philip Ahn, and Grant Taylor. **Director**—Byron Haskin.
92 minutes

HISTORY OF THE WORLD—
PART I (1981)

   ★★

Mel Brooks
Dom DeLuise
Madeline Kahn
Harvey Korman

Funnyman Brooks rewrites history with comic pokes at the Roman Empire, the Spanish Inquisition, and the French Revolution. Brooks stars in various roles and generates a fair portion of belly laughs and inspired comic situations. However, many skits are undermined by excessive crudeness. The comedy is rather uneven, so Brooks earns only a "B" for his history report. **Director**—Brooks. (R)
92 minutes

HITLER (1961)

   ★★

Richard Basehart

Basehart stars in the title role as the bloodthirsty Nazi führer. The film traces Hitler's career from his early adult life to his defeat and suicide in his Berlin bunker. This film biography treads rather lightly on a subject that deserves more insight, and Basehart isn't all that convincing as the mad dictator. Others in the cast include
(Continued)

 Movie is available in Beta and VHS videotape

H
- Hobson's Choice
- Hold Back the Dawn
- Holiday Inn
- Hollywood Boulevard
- Hollywood Canteen
- The Hollywood Knights
- Hombre
- Home of the Brave

(Continued)
Mario Emo, Martin Kosleck, and John Banner. **Director**—Stuart Heisler.

107 minutes b&w

HOBSON'S CHOICE (1954)

 ★★★

**Charles Laughton
Brenda de Banzie
John Mills**

Laughton sparkles in this family comedy, based on a play by Harold Brighouse, as a strong-willed bootsmith in the 1890s who tries to control the lives of his daughters. It's a breezy and spirited film, played in the best style of British humor. All of the performances fall nicely into place. Also with Richard Wattis and Daphne Anderson. **Director**—David Lean.

107 minutes b&w

HOLD BACK THE DAWN (1941)

★★★

**Charles Boyer
Olivia de Havilland**

Boyer is in top form as a refugee from Nazi Germany who marries a schoolteacher in Mexico merely to gain entrance to the United States. De Havilland plays the teacher. It's a moving wartime melodrama, stylishly produced and heightened by fine acting and direction. The cast also includes Paulette Goddard, Victor Francen, Walter Abel, and Rosemary DeCamp. **Director**—Mitchell Leisen. **Academy Award Nominations**—best picture; de Havilland, best actress; Leo Tover, cinematography (black and white). *115 minutes b&w*

HOLIDAY INN (1942)

 ★★★★

**Bing Crosby
Fred Astaire**

Crosby sings and Astaire dances up a storm in this colorful musical. The routine romantic plot concerns competition between partners of a hotel—Crosby and Astaire—for the attention of a woman. However, the magnificent Irving Berlin score is the real cause for interest here, with Bing

Bing Crosby and Fred Astaire fight for the affections (and the dancing feet) of Virginia Dale in Holiday Inn.

crooning "White Christmas." Also with Walter Abel, Marjorie Reynolds, Virginia Dale, and Louise Beavers. **Director**—Mark Sandrich. **Academy Award Nomination**—Berlin, writing (original story). *101 minutes b&w*

HOLLYWOOD BOULEVARD (1977)

 ★

Candice Rialson

Here's a grade-B movie that's a spoof of grade-B movies. The result: just another shabby and silly grade-B movie from the Roger Corman factory. Rialson stars as an aspiring actress who breaks into low-budget films and becomes involved with a number of perilous situations, including some bizarre murders. Also with Mary Woronov and Rita George. **Directors**—Joe Dante and Allan Arkush. (R)

83 minutes

HOLLYWOOD CANTEEN (1944)

★★

**Joan Leslie
Robert Hutton
Dane Clark
Janis Paige**

A galaxy of Hollywood stars make guest appearances in this review of the entertainment community's supporting efforts during World War II. Some of the music is pleasant, but the story goes nowhere. It's about a soldier hankering for a date with a pretty girl. Other luminaries include Joan Crawford, Bette Davis, the Andrews Sisters,

Jack Benny, Eddie Cantor, Roy Rogers, Sidney Greenstreet, Peter Lorre, and Barbara Stanwyck. **Director**—Delmer Daves. *123 minutes b&w*

THE HOLLYWOOD KNIGHTS (1980)

★★

**Fran Drescher
Stuart Pankin
Tony Danza**

California teenagers pull off some outrageous monkeyshines on Halloween night in 1965 to protest the closing of their favorite drive-in restaurant. Most of the pranks are aimed at harassing authoritative adults. A few jokes go over, but much of the movie, which looks like a combination of *American Graffiti* and *Animal House*, is merely ill-conceived silliness. Also with Robert Wuhl and Michelle Pfeiffer. **Director**—Floyd Mutrux. (R) *91 minutes*

HOMBRE (1967)

 ★★★

**Paul Newman
Diane Cilento
Fredric March**

An engrossing western drama, starring Newman as a young white man brought up by Indians. The film picks up steam when Newman boards a stagecoach and helps the passengers in an encounter with outlaws. An intelligent script and interesting characterizations mix well with suspense and action. There's also a thread of moral considerations running through the production. Also with Richard Boone, Martin Balsam, Barbara Rush, and Cameron Mitchell. **Director**—Martin Ritt. *111 minutes*

HOME OF THE BRAVE (1949)

 ★★★

**Frank Lovejoy
Lloyd Bridges**

A compelling drama set during World War II, about a black soldier who suffers from the intolerance of his white fellow comrades-in-arms. The film had more impact at the time of its release, but it's still watchable. Based

• Homework   • Honky Tonk Freeway
• Hondo   • Honkytonk Man
• Honeysuckle Rose   • Hooper
• Hopscotch

H

on the play by Arthur Laurents. Also with James Edwards, Jeff Corey, and Steve Brodie. **Director**—Mark Robson. *86 minutes b&w*

HOMEWORK (1982)

 ★

Michael Morgan
Joan Collins

Hardly anything works in this silly, soft-core teen sex comedy. The half-baked story leads to an awkward affair involving an adolescent boy (Morgan) and his girl friend's mother (Collins). Along the way, the film meanders through numerous confused subplots. The few gags fizzle (most are in poor taste anyway), and the serious moments seem to have wound up in the wrong film. Various nude scenes are featured in an apparently desperate effort to keep the viewer's mind on the movie. **Director**—James Beshears. (R) *90 minutes*

HONDO (1953)

★★★

John Wayne
Geraldine Page

An out-of-the-ordinary western drama about a cavalry soldier who discovers a widow and her son living in an isolated part of Texas and stays to defend them against an Indian attack. Wayne plays the soldier, of course. Violence is toned down and warm characterizations are played up in this interesting story that takes on some of the aspects of *Shane*. Page is excellent in her role as the plucky widow. Ward Bond, James Arness, and Michael Pate also star. Originally a 3-D film. **Director**—John Farrow. **Academy Award Nomination**—Page, best supporting actress. *84 minutes*

HONEYSUCKLE ROSE (1980)

 ★★

Willie Nelson
Dyan Cannon
Amy Irving
Slim Pickens

Nelson picks a mean guitar and sings rousing country-western songs. He

Dyan Cannon takes a close look at what's underneath Willie Nelson's beard in Honeysuckle Rose.

does a lot of that rather well in this film, but when the music stops there's only a wisp of a plot—mostly borrowed from *Intermezzo*—about Nelson's infidelity while on the road. The scenario is a rather dull hillbilly soap opera. Cannon plays the long-suffering wife and sings country with style and gusto. **Director**—Jerry Schatzberg. (PG) *119 minutes*

HONKY TONK FREEWAY (1981)

 ★

Beau Bridges
William Devane

Director John Schlesinger (*Midnight Cowboy*) can't deliver the goods in this uneven, silly, and meandering comedy. The flimsy story mainly concerns efforts of citizens to secure a highway off-ramp at their small Florida town. Meanwhile, the film detours all over the country collecting some uninteresting people—and some animals—who finally converge on this community. Everyone has a few gags to play with, but most fall flat. (R) *107 minutes*

HONKYTONK MAN (1982)

 ★★

Clint Eastwood

Director-actor Eastwood shifts into low gear with this mildly appealing '30s tale of a hard-drinking country music singer. Eastwood, in the title role, has hopes of performing at the Grand Ole Opry. His 14-year-old nephew (played by Eastwood's son, Kyle) is along for some predictable rites-of-passage episodes. The story gradually peters out for lack of drama. (PG) *122 minutes*

HOOPER (1978)

 ★★

Burt Reynolds
Jan-Michael Vincent
Sally Field

Reynolds plays the greatest Hollywood stuntman of his time; he's being challenged by a younger man, played by Vincent. This movie-within-a-movie should please most fans of Reynolds, who plays his raucous, wiseguy character to the hilt. There's a variety of well-executed stunts—car crashes, a chariot race, and a helicopter jump. However, the pedestrian story takes the edge off the action, and many of the stunts have been performed in other films. By now, they look familiar and unexciting. Also with Brian Keith and John Marley. **Director**—Hal Needham. (PG) *100 minutes*

HOPSCOTCH (1980)

 ★★

Walter Matthau
Glenda Jackson

Glenda Jackson and Walter Matthau get the joke in Hopscotch.

Matthau stars as a disillusioned CIA agent who writes an embarrassing exposé about his bumbling colleagues and then leads them on a cat-and-mouse chase. The ever-appealing Matthau gives it his rumpled best, with Jackson adding a touch of class as his wily accomplice. The film can't seem to make up its mind whether it's a comedy or a drama. At times, the mood is straightforward, but then the movie lapses into silly slapstick. Also with Ned Beatty. **Director**—Ronald Neame. (R) *104 minutes*

H

- The Horn Blows at Midnight
- The Hospital
- Hot Dog... The Movie
- The Hotel New Hampshire
- Hotel Paradiso
- Hot Lead and Cold Feet
- Hot Stuff
- Houdini

THE HORN BLOWS AT MIDNIGHT (1945)

★★★

Jack Benny
Alexis Smith

Benny stars in this slapstick farce as an angel assigned to destroy Earth with blasts from Gabriel's horn. Benny took delight in panning this film, but it's a lot better than he made it out to be. The plot leans heavily on *Here Comes Mr. Jordan*. Also with Franklin Pangborn, Guy Kibbee, Dolores Moran, Reginald Gardiner, and Margaret Dumont. **Director**—Raoul Walsh.

78 minutes b&w

THE HOSPITAL (1971)

 ★★★

George C. Scott
Diana Rigg

A biting black comedy that firmly skewers incompetence and mismanagement within the medical profession as seen at a large city hospital. Paddy Chayefsky's award-winning screenplay digs into its subject with the force of a jackhammer, as a series of mishaps cause chaos and death. Scott is magnificent as a disillusioned chief doctor, and he gets plenty of professional support. Also with Barnard Hughes, Richard Dysart, and Nancy Marchand. **Director**—Arthur Hiller. (PG) **Academy Award**—Chayefsky, best story and screenplay (based on factual material or material not previously published). **Nomination**—Scott, best actor. *101 minutes*

HOT DOG...THE MOVIE (1984)

 ★★

Patrick Houser
Tracy Smith

This *Animal House* on skis features competition on California's Squaw Valley slopes by day and partying and sexual cavorting at night. Among the youthful high times are some splashing around in hot tubs, a wet T-shirt contest, and lots of booze consumption. The acrobatic skiing is quite spectacular. As for the dialogue, acting, character development, and infantile

Hot Dog...The Movie features Patrick Houser as a boisterous athlete.

humor, it's not so hot. **Director**—Peter Markle. (R) *96 minutes*

THE HOTEL NEW HAMPSHIRE (1984)

 ★

Nastassja Kinski
Jodie Foster
Beau Bridges
Rob Lowe

Rambling, offensive movie based on John Irving's best-seller about a weird family engaged in several hotel enterprises. The frantic plot involves various unsavory events, including gang rape, incest, terrorism, and suicide. This bizarre concoction attempts to be cute while making a desperate statement about survival. It's the audience that must worry about surviving. **Director**—Tony Richardson. (R)

110 minutes

HOTEL PARADISO (1966)

 ★★

Alec Guinness
Gina Lollobrigida

A capable cast flounders around in this uneven romantic farce, set in Paris at the turn of the century. The story concerns various love affairs and comic mix-ups at a seedy hotel. The production is handsomely mounted,

but the direction leaves much to be desired. Also with Robert Morley, Akim Tamiroff, and Peggy Mount. **Director**—Peter Glenville. *96 minutes*

HOT LEAD AND COLD FEET (1978)

★★

Jim Dale
Darren McGavin
Karen Valentine

This comedy western by the Disney studio plods along on its flat feet, trying to amuse the kids and adults; it generally fails in both categories. British comic Dale plays three characters, a cantankerous old land dealer and his two sons, who compete for their inheritance. Don Knotts and Jack Elam are on board with top billing, but actually they're assigned to cameo roles. **Director**—Robert Butler. (G) *90 minutes*

HOT STUFF (1979)

 ★★★

Dom DeLuise
Suzanne Pleshette
Jerry Reed

DeLuise directs and stars in this good-natured screwball comedy about some Miami cops who catch petty thieves through a fencing front. The script is silly and predictable, but DeLuise has assembled a fine cast of character actors to help him keep the fun and laughter perking from start to finish. It's the style of visual slapstick in which DeLuise excels, and he often steals the show. Pleshette and Reed do well as his partners in the undercover setup. Also with Luis Avalos and Ossie Davis. (PG) *87 minutes*

HOUDINI (1953)

★★★

Tony Curtis
Janet Leigh

Straight-down-the-middle film biography of the famous escape artist, with Curtis handling the title role with skill. The story, however, seems embellished some to underline the ro-

• The Hound of the
Baskervilles
• Houseboat

• The House by the Lake
• House Calls
• A House Is Not a Home

• House of Frankenstein
• House of Usher
• House of Wax

H

mantic aspects of Houdini's life. Interest is constantly maintained as Houdini gets involved with more and more difficult tricks. Leigh is good as the ever-faithful wife. Torin Thatcher and Sig Rumann also star. **Director—** George Marshall.   *106 minutes*

THE HOUND OF THE BASKERVILLES (1939)

★★★

Basil Rathbone
Nigel Bruce

Basil Rathbone plays Sherlock Holmes with a panache that no one can match in The Hound of the Baskervilles.

Rathbone, in his first appearance as Sherlock Holmes, solves the mystery of a weird dog that threatens the life of a man who has inherited an estate from his uncle. Rathbone, of course, gets solid acting support from Bruce as Dr. Watson. There is enough suspense to keep the average viewer—and Holmes—interested in this solid production. Also with Lionel Atwill, Wendy Barrie, Mary Gordon, and John Carradine. **Director—**Sidney Lanfield.   *80 minutes b&w*

HOUSEBOAT (1958)

★★★

Cary Grant
Sophia Loren

Grant and Loren make the sparks fly in this predictable but charming comedy. He's a widower residing in a houseboat with three children. She comes on board as a maid and provides some motherly love for the kids,

yet she's really a woman with social standing. Guess who falls in love with whom? Martha Hyer, Eduardo Ciannelli, and Harry Guardino perform very well in supporting roles. **Director—**Melville Shavelson. **Academy Award Nomination—**Jack Rose and Shavelson, best story and screenplay (written directly for the screen).
          110 minutes

THE HOUSE BY THE LAKE (1977)

★★

Brenda Vaccaro
Don Stroud

A grisly suspense drama about four sadistic punks who terrorize a playboy dentist and his girl friend at a remote hideaway in Ontario, Canada. This mindless exploitation of bloody violence depicts a rape and deaths by drowning, fire, slashed throat, and shotgun. The cast is convincing, especially Stroud as the leader of the hoodlums and Vaccaro as the rape victim who eventually gets revenge. But there's too much emphasis on wanton terror as a form of entertainment. Also with Chuck Shamata and Richard Ayres. Written and directed by William Fruet. **Alternate Title—***Death Weekend.* (R)   *89 minutes*

HOUSE CALLS (1978)

★★★

Walter Matthau
Glenda Jackson
Art Carney
Richard Benjamin

A lightweight romantic comedy that is firmly secured with the charm of Matthau and the steel demeanor of Jackson. Matthau is good as a middle-aged swinging surgeon—recently widowed—who falls for strong-minded Jackson—recently divorced. The uneven script has a moderate case of the clichés, but the one-liners and laughs roll along with ease. Carney gets some mileage out of his part as the senile chief of surgery. Also with Candice Azzara and Dick O'Neill. **Director—**Howard Zieff. (PG)
          98 minutes

A HOUSE IS NOT A HOME (1964)
★

Shelley Winters
Robert Taylor

This is a film biography of Polly Adler, New York's notorious madame. The shabby-looking production is brought off in a most dreary manner—no style and scant energy. Polly herself would surely be disappointed. Also with Broderick Crawford and Cesar Romero. **Director—**Russell Rouse.
          198 minutes b&w

HOUSE OF FRANKENSTEIN (1944)
★★★

Boris Karloff
John Carradine
Lon Chaney, Jr.

Universal Pictures once more rallies its monsters for sinister work. Karloff stars as an evil scientist and manager of a freak show who rejuvenates Frankenstein's creation and the Wolf Man and sets out to pay back those who crossed him. A regular cast of horror heavies gives it their best shot. Also with George Zucco, J. Carrol Naish, and Lionel Atwill. **Director—**Erle C. Kenton.   *71 minutes b&w*

HOUSE OF USHER (1960)
★★★

Vincent Price

Effective horror tale based on the classic Edgar Allen Poe chiller. Price heads the cast as a member of Usher, the family involved in various forms of madness and terror. Director Roger Corman puts it together with impressive style. Also with Myrna Fahey, Mark Damon, and Harry Ellerbe.
          79 minutes

HOUSE OF WAX (1953)

★★★

Vincent Price
Carolyn Jones

Adequate remake of *The Mystery of the*
(Continued)

H

- The House on 92nd Street
- The House Where Evil Dwells
- How Green Was My Valley
- The Howling
- How the West Was Won
- How to Beat the High Cost of Living

(Continued)

Wax Museum, with Price striking terror into the hearts of the innocent. He effectively plays the owner of a wax museum. After it's destroyed in a fire, he rebuilds his exhibit using dead bodies. The film was initially shot in 3-D, and many of the gimmicks have this process in mind. Also with Phyllis Kirk, Frank Lovejoy, Paul Picerni, and Charles Buchinski (Bronson). **Director**—André de Toth.   *88 minutes*

THE HOUSE ON 92nd STREET
(1945)
★★★★

**William Eythe
Lloyd Nolan
Signe Hasso**

The FBI searches for Nazi agents in The House on 92nd Street.

A fast-paced spy thriller set in New York City during World War II, with the FBI bearing down on Nazi agents seeking to steal atomic bomb secrets. This is a smartly styled production that effectively uses a combination of documentary technique and exciting drama. It set the trend for subsequent "realistic" films like *The Naked City*. Also with Gene Lockhart and Leo G. Carroll. **Director**—Henry Hathaway. **Academy Award**—Charles G. Booth, writing (original story).
88 minutes b&w

THE HOUSE WHERE EVIL DWELLS (1982)
★★

**Edward Albert
Susan George**

This is a standard haunted-house

Edward Albert is a switch hitter for swordplay in The House Where Evil Dwells.

story transplanted to Japan. An American family rents a home which was the site of murders committed over a century ago. Predictably, the ghosts of the victims are still hanging around to cause bloody mischief and reenact the initial tragedy. The Japanese scenery offers some picturesque and exotic atmosphere—an unusual twist for this sort of nonsense. **Director**—Kevin Connor. (R)   *88 minutes*

HOW GREEN WAS MY VALLEY
(1941)
★★★★

**Walter Pidgeon
Maureen O'Hara
Roddy McDowall
Donald Crisp**

Touching and heartwarming drama of life in a Welsh coal-mining town. Memorable and moving moments abound. Much effort was lavished on exquisite production detail, giving eloquent class to the film, which is based on Richard Llewellyn's novel. Cast also includes Barry Fitzgerald, Sara Allgood, and John Loder. **Director**—John Ford. **Academy Awards**—best picture; Ford, best director; Crisp, best supporting actor; Arthur Miller, cinematography (black and white). **Nominations**—Allgood, best supporting actress; Philip Dunne, writing (screenplay).   *118 minutes b&w*

THE HOWLING (1981)
 ★★★

Dee Wallace

A stylish and tongue-in-cheek horror film where practically the entire cast turns into yelping werewolves. Wallace plays an attractive TV reporter who goes to a secluded Esalen-like spa to unwind. Before long, she's face-to-face with monstrous werewolves who seem to pop out of the woodwork. The special effects by Rob Bottin are truly special—and terrifying. Director Joe Dante moves the film along with his flair for wildly skewed irony. (R)
102 minutes

HOW THE WEST WAS WON
(1963)
★★

**Debbie Reynolds
Carroll Baker
Lee J. Cobb
Henry Fonda**

Overlong, over-cast epic that follows the pioneering efforts of several generations of an adventurous farming family from New England across the continent. The trail is strewn with clichés and half-baked episodes. The production, however, is done lavishly, but such lavishness loses impact on TV screens. Cast also includes Karl Malden, Carolyn Jones, Gregory Peck, George Peppard, James Stewart, and John Wayne. Spencer Tracy narrates. **Directors**—Henry Hathaway, John Ford, and George Marshall. **Academy Award**—James R. Webb, best story and screenplay (written directly for the screen). **Nominations**—best picture; William H. Daniels, Milton Krasner, Charles Lang, Jr., and Joseph LaShelle, cinematography (color).
155 minutes

HOW TO BEAT THE HIGH COST OF LIVING
(1980)
 ★★

**Susan Saint James
Jessica Lange
Jane Curtin**

Three seemingly respectable young

- How to Marry a Millionaire
- How to Murder Your Wife
- How to Succeed in Business Without Really Trying
- The Hucksters
- Hud
- The Human Comedy

H

women burglarize a shopping mall because inflation has deflated their lifestyles. This listless comedy is a variation of *Fun With Dick and Jane*, but hardly as funny. Rising prices are no laughing matter, especially in this film. Saint James, Curtin, and Lange play the bungling, thieving threesome who pull off the caper. Also with Richard Benjamin and Eddie Albert. **Director**—Robert Scheerer. (PG)

110 minutes

Robert Morse in How To Succeed in Business Without Really Trying.

HOW TO MARRY A MILLIONAIRE (1953)

 ★★★

Lauren Bacall
Marilyn Monroe
Betty Grable
William Powell

Fun-filled comedy with Bacall, Monroe, and Grable perfectly cast as schemers out to trap wealthy men as husbands. The stars lend plenty of sparkle to the amicable proceedings, set in New York City, and there are plenty of lavish settings to heighten the frolic. It all leads to a happy ending, with the girls getting more than they intended. Also with Cameron Mitchell, David Wayne, and Rory Calhoun. **Director**—Jean Negulesco.

96 minutes

HOW TO MURDER YOUR WIFE (1965)

★★★★

Jack Lemmon
Virna Lisi
Terry-Thomas

Smart, sophisticated comedy with wry comic situations clicking off nicely at a fast pace. Lemmon is great as a bachelor comic-strip writer who wakes up one morning after a wild party to find himself unexpectedly married to beautiful Lisi. He thinks of ways to get rid of her. And when she vanishes, the police believe he murdered her. A top supporting cast contributes to the fun. Eddie Mayehoff plays a lawyer friend, and Terry-Thomas is a wisecracking butler. Sidney Blackmer and Claire Trevor also star. It's murderously funny. **Director**—Richard Quine.

118 minutes

HOW TO SUCCEED IN BUSINESS WITHOUT REALLY TRYING (1967)

★★★★

Robert Morse
Rudy Vallee
Michele Lee

Morse superbly repeats his Broadway role as an ambitious window washer who gets to be president of a large corporation through cunning rather than energy and talent. Many of the delights from the stage musical, based on Shepard Mead's book, are kept intact. Frank Loesser's songs are appealing, and the effective gags fall into place with perfection. A success, indeed. Also with Anthony Teague and Maureen Arthur. **Director**—David Swift.

119 minutes

THE HUCKSTERS (1947)

★★★

Clark Gable
Deborah Kerr
Ava Gardner

The advertising business is skewered in this impressive film drama based on Frederic Wakeman's insightful novel. Gable does well as an advertising executive who becomes frustrated by questionable methods of the profession; Sidney Greenstreet is nicely cast as a tyrannical soap company president. The story gets to the point and stays there. Also with Adolphe Menjou, Keenan Wynn, and Edward Arnold. **Director**—Jack Conway.

115 minutes b&w

HUD (1963)

 ★★★★

Paul Newman
Patricia Neal
Melvyn Douglas

Newman gives an excellent character portrayal as the irresponsible son of a hardworking Texas rancher. The powerful film takes a hard look at interpersonal family relationships and the deterioration of moral values. Neal stands out as the wise housekeeper who readily perceives the complex problems; Douglas is also fine as the harassed father. Martin Ritt's direction hits the mark. Also with Brandon de Wilde and John Ashley. **Academy Awards**—Neal, best actress; Douglas, best supporting actor; James Wong Howe, cinematography (black and white). **Nominations**—Martin Ritt, best director; Paul Newman, best actor; Irving Ravetch and Harriet Frank, best screenplay (based on material from another medium).

112 minutes b&w

THE HUMAN COMEDY (1943)

★★★

Mickey Rooney
Frank Morgan
James Craig

This screen adaptation of William Saroyan's novel is moving although it goes overboard at times with sentimentality. Touching characterizations are simply portrayed in this slice of life in small-town America during World

(Continued)

H
- The Human Factor (1975)
- The Human Factor (1980)
- Humanoids from the Deep
- Humoresque
- The Hunchback of Notre Dame
- The Hunger
- The Hunter

Mickey Rooney heads the cast of The Human Comedy.

(Continued)

War II. Rooney heads the cast of what seems to be a version of the *Andy Hardy* series. Also with Marsha Hunt, Fay Bainter, Van Johnson, and Donna Reed. **Director**—Clarence Brown. **Academy Award**—Saroyan, writing (original story). **Nominations**—best picture; Brown, best director; Rooney, best actor; Harry Stradling, cinematography (black and white).

117 minutes b&w

THE HUMAN FACTOR (1975)
★★

George Kennedy
John Mills

An American computer expert, working with NATO in Italy, stalks and kills a group of radicals who assassinated his family. It's a poor reworking of the vigilante angle of *Death Wish*. The film suffers from limp direction, unmoving performances, and a wobbly script. Kennedy's talent is wasted in the leading role. Co-stars Raf Vallone and Rita Tushingham. **Director**—Edward Dmytryk. (R) *96 minutes*

THE HUMAN FACTOR (1980)
★★★

Richard Attenborough
Derek Jacobi
Nicol Williamson

Espionage is, in all likelihood, a routine job carried out by drab civil servants. If such is the case, this Otto Preminger film of Graham Greene's topical novel is close to home. Williamson plays a mild-mannered double agent who leaks secrets to the Russians. The story is intelligent, and the cast of fine British actors is impressive. Also with Robert Morley, John Gielgud, and Ann Todd. (R) *115 minutes*

HUMANOIDS FROM THE DEEP (1980)
 ★★

Doug McClure
Vic Morrow

Amphibious beasts invade a fishing village, where they kill the men and rape the women. The monsters resemble relatives of *The Creature From the Black Lagoon*, and the silly plot is the formula stuff that served so many sci-fi films in the '50s. But because it's the '80s, the horror comes embellished with a fair amount of nudity. There's also an environmental angle about construction of a cannery that would spoil the coastline. **Director**—Barbara Peeters. (R) *80 minutes*

HUMORESQUE (1946)
★★★

Joan Crawford
John Garfield

Crawford stars as a wealthy patron of the arts who sponsors a promising violinist, played by Garfield. At times, the screenplay smacks of a soap opera, but exquisite settings and superb acting elevate the film to a higher level. A classical-music backdrop and some funny antics from Oscar Levant add to the quality. And there's a slam-bang tragic ending. Also with J. Carrol Naish, Craig Stevens, and Ruth Nelson. **Director**—Jean Negulesco.

125 minutes b&w

THE HUNCHBACK OF NOTRE DAME (1939)
 ★★★

Charles Laughton
Cedric Hardwicke
Maureen O'Hara
Edmond O'Brien

The Hunchback of Notre Dame stars Charles Laughton in the title role.

The classic Victor Hugo story receives superior screen treatment with impressive sets, costumes, and direction, aimed at recreating the mood of medieval Paris. And there's great acting to match, with Laughton as the deformed bell-ringer who rescues a gypsy girl from the clutches of a mob. It's a worthy remake of the silent version with Lon Chaney. Also with Thomas Mitchell and Harry Davenport. **Director**—William Dieterle.

117 minutes b&w

THE HUNGER (1983)
 ★★

Catherine Deneuve
David Bowie
Susan Sarandon
Ann Magnuson

A chic, flashy, latter-day vampire yarn with Deneuve and Bowie as Manhattan townhouse dwellers who haunt New Wave bars for victims. When Bowie begins to show his true age (200 years), Deneuve moves on to some lesbian lovemaking with Sarandon. All its kinky touches and glossy settings can't compensate for a script which is bloodless to the point of anemia. **Director**—Tony Scott. (R) *98 minutes*

THE HUNTER (1980)
 ★★

Steve McQueen
Eli Wallach

McQueen plays a modern-day bounty hunter who risks his neck tracking down bail-jumpers. It's a dirty job that only someone desperate for money would undertake, and McQueen sloshes through this film as if he's desperate for a paycheck. A jumbled script and too many undeveloped characters keep things at a low boil, but the story perks up during some spectacular chase scenes. However, there's not enough originality or style to prevent McQueen's star image from being tarnished. Also with Kathryn Harrold and Ben Johnson. **Director**—Buzz Kulik. (PG)　　*97 minutes*

HURRICANE (1979)

 ★★

**Jason Robards, Jr.
Mia Farrow
Max Von Sydow
Trevor Howard**

Dino De Laurentiis's $20-million romantic epic, filmed in Bora Bora, is boring, boring. The script is based on the engaging Nordhoff and Hall novel about ill-fated lovers. But here the story plods, characters are onedimensional, and the silly dialogue makes the actors appear foolish. The storm is impressive, but the rest is just tedious nonsense. Also with Dayton Ka'ne. **Director**—Jan Troell. (PG)

119 minutes

HURRY SUNDOWN
(1967)
★

**Jane Fonda
Michael Caine
Rex Ingram
Diahann Carroll**

Director Otto Preminger butchers this film drama, based on a best-selling novel by K. B. Gilden. Although the murky production boasts a superior cast and some lavish settings, it lapses into absurdity only a few minutes from the starting gate. The story concerns racial problems in a small Georgia community. In getting to the ending, this one doesn't hurry fast enough. Cast also includes Burgess Meredith, Faye Dunaway, Beah Richards, and George Kennedy.

142 minutes

HUSH...HUSH SWEET
CHARLOTTE (1965)
★★★

**Bette Davis
Olivia de Havilland
Joseph Cotten**

A stylish chiller about a lonely woman, played by Davis. She's set upon by her cousin and her boyfriend, who both want her property. The plot borrows liberally from *Whatever Happened to Baby Jane?*, but it's watchable to the end. The acting by a pro cast is reliably good, and Robert Aldrich's direction achieves the desired macabre effect. Also with Cecil Kellaway, Mary Astor, Victor Buono, and Agnes Moorehead.

133 minutes b&w

HUSTLE (1975)

 ★★

**Burt Reynolds
Catherine Deneuve**

An intriguing, fast-moving but disjointed cop movie about the investigation of the death of a young woman of middle-class origins. Reynolds plays a tough and suave detective who discovers that the dead woman has been exploited by a corrupt and powerful lawyer. The plot hopscotches confusingly from one situation to another; only at the end, and too late, does it all seem to make sense. Deneuve plays a high-class prostitute sentimentally attached to Reynolds. With Ben Johnson, Eddie Albert, Paul Winfield, Eileen Brennan, and Ernest Borgnine. **Director**—Robert Aldrich. (R)

120 minutes

THE HUSTLER (1961)

 ★★★★

**Paul Newman
Jackie Gleason
George C. Scott**

Newman gives a terrific character portrayal of a hustling pool shark whose game is spoiled when he meets the woman he loves, played by Piper Laurie. The film offers impressive atmosphere of the world of seedy pool halls, and there's effective suspense during the pool matches. Watch for

In The Hustler, *Paul Newman portrays a pool shark who meets a tough opponent.*

an unusual dramatic performance by Gleason as the venerable Minnesota Fats. Gleason plays it straight and subdued, and he's terrific. Good acting jobs, too, by Scott, Laurie, and Myron McCormick. **Director**—Robert Rossen. **Academy Award**—Eugene Shuftan, cinematography (black and white). **Nominations**—best picture; Robert Rossen, best director; Newman, best actor; Laurie, best actress; Gleason, Scott, best supporting actor; Sidney Carroll and Rossen, best screenplay (based on material from another medium).　　*135 minutes b&w*

I

I AM A CAMERA (1955)
★★★

**Julie Harris
Laurence Harvey**

Harris and Harvey play young adventurers in Berlin just prior to World War II. Harris is excellent as a freewheeling English girl; Harvey, as an English author who records events in the German capital, matches her performance. This romantic comedy is a fine, intelligent rendition of Christopher Isherwood's stories. The plot is also the basis for the Broadway musical and film *Cabaret*. Also with Shelley Winters, Ron Randell, and Patrick McGoohan. **Director**—Henry Cornelius.　　*98 minutes b&w*

I
- Ice Castles
- Iceman
- The Ice Pirates
- I Confess
- The Idolmaker
- I Dood It!
- ...If
- If It's Tuesday, This Must Be Belgium

ICE CASTLES (1979)

★★

**Lynn-Holly Johnson
Robby Benson**

A pretty girl from a small town in Iowa gets a crack at an Olympic skating medal, but is accidentally blinded on the brink of success. Yet she skates on with the encouragement of the boy she left behind. Johnson plays Alexis, the blinded skater; Benson is her sympathetic boyfriend. This schmaltzy story is aimed right at the tear ducts, so bring along a *big* handkerchief. The characters, however, are fuzzy, and the film seems to lose steam at crucial moments. The big attraction is newcomer Johnson; she does some good figure skating and impressive acting. Also with Colleen Dewhurst, Tom Skerritt, and Jennifer Warren. **Director**—Donald Wrye. (PG)

109 minutes

ICEMAN (1984)

★★★

**John Lone
Timothy Hutton**

Timothy Hutton is a scientist who befriends thawed out Neanderthal John Lone in Iceman.

Scientists bring back to life a Neanderthal man frozen in the Arctic wastes some 40,000 years ago. This unusual story is not merely another *Creature from the Black Lagoon* thriller but an exhilarating concept of a sympathetic and complex human grappling with a strange environment. Lone is convincing in the title role. Hutton stars as the anthropologist who tries to bridge the culture gap. **Director**—Fred Schepisi. (PG)

101 minutes

THE ICE PIRATES (1984)

★

**Robert Urich
Mary Crosby**

John Matuszak and Anjelica Huston wait to see how much their booty will buy in The Ice Pirates.

Jumbled, hyperactive sci-fi adventure that rips off *Star Wars* while appearing to be a backlash against that popular series. The madhouse events whiz by so fast it's hard to keep track of plot and characters—not that they matter much here. The story has something to do with hijacking spaceships that supply ice to a water-starved galaxy. Urich, Crosby, and a platoon of robots head the cast. **Director**—Stewart Raffill. (PG)

95 minutes

I CONFESS (1953)

★★★

**Montgomery Clift
Anne Baxter**

A murderer confesses his crime to a priest, played by Clift, who upholds the sanctity of the confessional even though he becomes a suspect in the murder. This Canadian-made mystery, directed by Alfred Hitchcock, isn't among his best, yet it's entertaining, mainly because of the moody atmosphere set against the background of Quebec. Clift's acting is adequate, and the story never gets out of control. Also with Brian Aherne, Karl Malden, and Dolly Haas.

94 minutes b&w

THE IDOLMAKER (1980)

★★★

**Ray Sharkey
Peter Gallagher
Paul Land**

An energetic and compelling drama about a hard-driving promoter of rock singers during the late '50s. Sharkey is superb in the title role as a sharp-eyed manager, whose dynamic behind-the-scenes manipulations create teeny-bopper idols on the order of Frankie Avalon and Fabian. The film presents the rock 'n' roll era in colorful detail. Gallagher and Land are fine as pop singers whose looks are more vital to stardom than their musical abilities. **Director**—Taylor Hackford. (PG)

119 minutes

I DOOD IT! (1943)
★★

**Red Skelton
Eleanor Powell**

In this rather sophomoric slapstick comedy, Skelton plays a tailor who romances a movie star, played by Powell. The film offers too much strained humor, but there are some memorable musical numbers, including "Take a Chance on Love." Red is known for better work. Also with John Hodiak, Lena Horne, and Jimmy Dorsey. **Director**—Vincente Minnelli.

102 minutes b&w

. . . IF (1969)

★★★★

**Malcolm McDowell
David Wood**

Searing, intelligent drama set in an English boarding school, where students rebel against harsh discipline. Director Lindsay Anderson cleverly portrays this school setting as an allegory for similar adult situations. A fine cast of pros and nonprofessional actors hammer home the powerful message with perfection. Also with Richard Warwick, Peter Jeffrey, Christine Noonan, and Robert Swann. (R)

111 minutes

IF IT'S TUESDAY, THIS MUST BE BELGIUM (1969)
★★★

**Suzanne Pleshette
Ian McShane
Mildred Natwick
Norman Fell**

• I'll Be Seeing You
• I'll Cry Tomorrow
• I Love You, Alice B. Toklas
• I'm All Right Jack

• I'm Dancing as Fast as I Can
• Imitation of Life
• Improper Channels

I

Fast-paced comedy about American vacationers on a whirlwind tour of seven European countries in 18 days. All sorts of hilarious adventures occur along the route, including some unexpected romantic situations. Apparently, this group didn't leave home without their sense of humor. Also with Murray Hamilton, Michael Constantine, Sandy Baron, Peggy Cass, and Marty Ingels. **Director**—Mel Stuart. (G)   *98 minutes*

I'LL BE SEEING YOU (1944)
★★

Ginger Rogers
Joseph Cotten

Rogers plays a convicted killer allowed to go home for the Christmas holidays. She meets and falls in love with a mentally ill soldier, played by Cotten. A good cast gets involved with some interesting scenes in this wartime romance, but the overripe sentimentality intervenes much too often. Also with Shirley Temple, Spring Byington, Tom Tully, and Chill Wills. **Director**—William Dieterle.

85 minutes b&w

I'LL CRY TOMORROW (1955)
★★★★

Susan Hayward
Richard Conte
Eddie Albert
Jo Van Fleet

Eddie Albert and Susan Hayward aren't crying yet in I'll Cry Tomorrow.

This is a powerful film biography of Lillian Roth, recounting her marital affairs and her bout with the bottle. Hayward's superb portrayal of the '30s stage and film star gives the produc-

tion an incisive sense of realism, and she gets excellent support from Van Fleet as Roth's despondent mother. Roth's husbands are played by Conte, Albert, and Don Taylor. **Director**—Daniel Mann. **Academy Award Nominations**—Hayward, best actress; Arthur Arling, cinematography (black and white).   *117 minutes b&w*

I LOVE YOU, ALICE B. TOKLAS (1968)
Ⓐ ★★★

Peter Sellers
Jo Van Fleet
Leigh Taylor-Young

What's this? Sellers as a hippie? Yes, indeed, and he's in top form as a Los Angeles lawyer with an overbearing mother, played by Van Fleet. Sellers decides to chuck it all to join the dropped-out generation. He then finds truth and happiness with his new lady-love, played by Taylor-Young. There are many excellent comic moments and even a subtle message in the film. Also with Joyce Van Patten, David Arkin, and Herb Edelman. **Director**—Hy Averback.

93 minutes

I'M ALL RIGHT JACK (1960)
Ⓐ ★★★★

Ian Carmichael
Peter Sellers
Terry-Thomas
Richard Attenborough

Spirited satire about the world of work, set in England in the '50s. The film touches on the questionable practices of both labor and management. The plot focuses on a youthful bumbler, played by Carmichael. He gets a factory job, provokes a strike, and is caught up in a controversy between the workers and the bosses. Sellers is memorable as an oafish labor official. Also with Dennis Price and Margaret Rutherford. **Director**—John Boulting.   *104 minutes b&w*

I'M DANCING AS FAST AS I CAN (1982)
Ⓐ ★★

Jill Clayburgh

Nicol Williamson comforts a drugged-out Jill Clayburgh in I'm Dancing as Fast as I Can.

This uneven film takes a serious look at Valium addiction much in the way alcohol and heroin have been studied in earlier movies. Clayburgh overplays the part of award-winning TV producer Barbara Gordon who becomes hooked on the tranquilizer and recovers after treatment in a mental hospital. Novice director Jack Hofsiss assembles the grim account in fits and starts, and the déjà vu screenplay never adequately explores the underlying causes of such dependency. (R)

117 minutes

IMITATION OF LIFE (1959)
★★

Lana Turner
Juanita Moore

Slick reworking of the Fannie Hurst tearjerker. Turner plays the beauty who becomes a successful actress only to find disappointment in her personal relationships; Moore is the black servant who shares her life with Turner. Moore's life is tragic because her daughter, played by Susan Kohner, passes for white. The racial aspect, however, gets shoved aside. The 1934 version, starring Claudette Colbert, worked better. Also with John Gavin, Sandra Dee, and Robert Alda. **Director**—Douglas Sirk. **Academy Award Nominations**—Moore, Kohner, best supporting actress.   *124 minutes*

IMPROPER CHANNELS (1981)
Ⓐ ★★

Alan Arkin
Mariette Hartley

Computers and bureaucracy are the
(Continued)

Ⓐ *Movie is available in Beta and VHS videotape*

I

- Impulse
- Inchon
- In Cold Blood
- The Incredible Sarah
- The Incredible Shrinking Man
- The Incredible Shrinking Woman

(Continued)

villains in this uneven, screwball comedy. Arkin and Hartley become tangled in red tape when their daughter accidentally bumps her head and an officious social worker charges child abuse. Arkin and Hartley handle their roles with moderate appeal, but the material never gives them the opportunity to sustain comic momentum. There are a few laughs along the way, but more are needed. **Director**—Eric Till. (PG)   *92 minutes*

IMPULSE (1984)

  ★★

Meg Tilly
Tim Matheson

Residents of a small town mysteriously begin acting irrational and hostile in this eerie thriller that eventually loses much credibility. A young woman (Tilly) and her physician boyfriend (Matheson) arrive on the scene and try to get at the source of such bizarre and dangerous behavior. While some sinister incidents arouse effective tension, the film ends in unsatisfying confusion. Hume Cronyn and John Karlen co-star. **Director**—Graham Baker. (R)   *91 minutes*

INCHON (1982)

★★

Laurence Olivier
Jacqueline Bisset
Ben Gazzara

Laurence Olivier and Richard Roundtree in the adventure, Inchon.

A big-budget, somewhat absurd epic telling of the landing at Inchon during the Korean War. The Reverend Sun Myung Moon is involved with the production, which may account for its flag-waving, quasi-religious flavor. The venerable General Douglas MacArthur is played, with an attitude of winking mockery, by none other than the great Olivier. Much attention is devoted to spectacular shoot-'em-up battle scenes which provide some diversion from the tired plot. **Director**—Terence Young. (PG)   *140 minutes*

IN COLD BLOOD (1967)

  ★★★★

Robert Blake
Scott Wilson

Robert Blake is one of two ex-cons in custody for killing a farm family in In Cold Blood.

First-class film rendition of Truman Capote's book about two young ex-convicts who brutally kill a Kansas farm family. The semidocumentary account digs deep into motives, characterizations, and the stark contrasts between the life-styles of the killers and the victims. The horrible murders, life on the run, capture, and execution are handled in taut step-by-step fashion for the maximum realistic effect. Blake and Wilson are excellent as the desperate killers. Also with John Forsythe, Paul Stewart, Gerald S. O'Loughlin, and Jeff Corey. **Director**—Richard Brooks. **Academy Award Nominations**—Brooks, best director; Brooks, best screenplay (based on material from another medium); Conrad Hall, cinematography.

134 minutes b&w

THE INCREDIBLE SARAH (1976)

★

Glenda Jackson

Jackson, who plays the remarkable and eccentric Sarah Bernhardt in this film, goes through some 40 costume changes and almost as many temper tantrums. Despite such lavishness and energy, this attempt at biography is no more than a series of humdrum vignettes, which fails to illuminate the legendary showmanship of the French actress. Also with Daniel Massey and Douglas Wilmer. **Director**—Richard Fleischer. (PG)   *106 minutes*

THE INCREDIBLE SHRINKING MAN (1957)

★★★

Grant Williams

A superior sci-fi thriller despite its modest budget. Williams plays a scientist exposed to a radioactive fog; he shrinks to a minute size, where he views the world from a new perspective. Inventive trick photography makes it all happen with exceptional interest and suspense. And there's even a decent script to heighten the proceedings. Incredible, indeed. Also stars Randy Stuart, April Kent, and Paul Langton. **Director**—Jack Arnold.

81 minutes b&w

THE INCREDIBLE SHRINKING WOMAN (1981)

  ★★

Lily Tomlin
Charles Grodin

Tomlin plays a modern housewife who shrinks to Barbie Doll proportions because of an intolerance to chemical additives in household products. Grodin is her bewildered husband. Tomlin is a first-rate comedienne, but her talents are subdued by a half-baked script that doesn't reach its potential as social satire on American consumerism. There are a few moments of inspired comedy; the rest is just so much dead air. Cast also includes Ned Beatty. **Director**—Joe Schumacher. (PG)

88 minutes

- Incubus
- Independence Day
- Indiana Jones and the Temple of Doom
- Indiscreet
- I Never Promised You a Rose Garden
- I Never Sang for My Father
- The Informer
- In God We Trust

I

INCUBUS (1982)

★★

John Cassavetes

A so-so supernatural horror film that emphasizes rape amid the violence inflicted by a mysterious demon. Several characters in the story suffer nightmares that are connected to brutal attacks on various women in a small Wisconsin community. This confused and uneven Canadian-made production is occasionally engrossing, but ultimately unsatisfying. Cassavetes heads the cast, which also includes Kerrie Keane and Erin Flannery. Director—John Hough. (R)   *92 minutes*

INDEPENDENCE DAY (1983)

★★

Kathleen Quinlan
David Keith
Dianne Wiest

Kathleen Quinlan picks up car mechanic David Keith in Independence Day.

Family crises in a small Southwestern town are fitfully dramatized in this predictable film. Quinlan tries hard as a young woman who longs to pursue a photography career in the big city. Meanwhile, she's romantically involved with a local auto mechanic (Keith) who wants to be the town's best drag racer. The picture's central theme is upstaged by a subplot involving Wiest as a battered wife. Director—Robert Mandel. (R)   *110 minutes*

INDIANA JONES AND THE TEMPLE OF DOOM (1984)

★★★★

Harrison Ford
Kate Capshaw

All stops are out in this second installment of the adventures of the two-fisted archaeologist. A relentless cavalcade of thrilling cliff-hangers will leave you exhausted as Ford deals with some nasty characters in India and rescues enslaved children. There's just the right dose of tongue-in-check humor, although some scenes are too intense for young children. Nevertheless, it's another humdinger from director Steven Spielberg. (PG)   *118 minutes*

INDISCREET (1958)

★★★

Cary Grant
Ingrid Bergman

Charming upper-crust comedy about a dashing American diplomat romancing a beautiful actress in London. Grant and Bergman are the perfect couple for this sort of ritzy, sophisticated production, enhanced with lush sets. The film is reliably based on Norman Krasna's play *Kind Sir*; Krasna also wrote the screenplay. Also with Phyllis Calvert, Cecil Parker, David Kossoff, and Megs Jenkins. Director—Stanley Donen.   *100 minutes*

I NEVER PROMISED YOU A ROSE GARDEN (1977)

★★

Bibi Andersson
Kathleen Quinlan

This sincere story, set in a psychiatric hospital, is about a young girl's fight against madness. The film is loaded with good intentions, but it's excessively grim and often confusing; don't expect another *One Flew Over the Cuckoo's Nest*. Yet there are impressive performances by Quinlan, as the disturbed girl, and Andersson, as her faithful psychiatrist. It's an exhausting movie, one more likely to be admired than enjoyed. Adapted from Joanne Green-berg's 1964 best-selling novel. Also with Reni Santoni, Susan Tyrell, and Signe Hasso. Director—Anthony Page. (R)   *96 minutes*

I NEVER SANG FOR MY FATHER (1970)

★★★

Melvyn Douglas
Gene Hackman

Douglas and Hackman are a fine acting duo in this moving film version of Robert Anderson's play. Hackman is a middle-aged man who tries to cope with his strong-willed father, played by Douglas. The old man is proud and sassy, even though he's in his 80's. There are intelligent and profound character studies all around. Co-stars Dorothy Stickney and Estelle Parsons. Director—Gilbert Cates. (PG) **Academy Award Nominations**—Douglas, best actor; Hackman, best supporting actor; Anderson, best screenplay (based on material from another medium).   *92 minutes*

THE INFORMER (1935)

★★★★

Victor McLaglen

A brilliant portrait of a traitor who is hounded by his own conscience. McLaglen is captivating as the IRA rogue who betrays his leader to collect a reward during the Irish rebellion. The direction of John Ford superbly sets the mood and tension down to the fog and grime of the Irish landscape, while Max Steiner's musical score creates the proper dramatic pace. Also with Preston Foster, Una O'Connor, Joseph Sawyer, Heather Angel, Margot Grahame, Donald Meek, and Wallace Ford. **Academy Awards**—John Ford, best director; McLaglen, best actor; Dudley Nichols, writing (screenplay). **Nomination**—best picture.   *91 minutes b&w*

IN GOD WE TRUST (1980)

★

Marty Feldman

Strained comedy with banjo-eyed
(Continued)

 Movie is available in Beta and VHS videotape

I

- Inherit the Wind
- The In-Laws
- The Inn of the Sixth Happiness
- In Praise of Older Women
- Inserts
- Inside Daisy Clover

In God We Trust features Marty Feldman as a monk who sees two sides to every question.

(Continued)
Feldman as a Trappist monk on the prowl for some fast cash to pay the monastery's debts. Out in the wicked world—Los Angeles—innocent Marty encounters a blustering television evangelist and a kindhearted prostitute. He also meets "God"—played by Richard Pryor—in the form of that big computer in the sky. What we don't meet are situations that make us laugh. **Director**—Feldman.

97 minutes

INHERIT THE WIND (1960)

★★★★

**Spencer Tracy
Fredric March**

Spencer Tracy is Clarence Darrow, and Gene Kelly is a reporter in Inherit the Wind.

A fascinating slice of American history is brought brilliantly to the screen as an adaptation of the Jerome Lawrence/ Robert E. Lee play, about the famous 1925 Scopes "monkey trial"

in Tennessee. Tracy and March are superb as Clarence Darrow and William Jennings Bryan, respectively. They argue the merits of Darwin's theory of evolution passionately. The sultry atmosphere of a small-town courtroom in midsummer adds to the realism. There is excellent supporting work by Dick York, Gene Kelly, Florence Eldridge, Elliott Reid, and Harry Morgan. **Director**—Stanley Kramer. **Academy Award Nominations**—Tracy, best actor; Nathan E. Douglas and Harold Jacob Smith, best screenplay (based on material from another medium); Ernest Laszlo, cinematography (black and white).

127 minutes b&w

THE IN-LAWS (1979)

★★★

**Peter Falk
Alan Arkin**

Falk and Arkin team up for laughs galore in this wacky and hilarious comedy about a New York dentist who unwittingly becomes involved with his future in-law who claims to be a CIA agent. Arkin plays the dentist; Falk plays the CIA man. Andrew Bergman, who collaborated with Mel Brooks in *Blazing Saddles*, has come up with a gem of a comic script; it falters occasionally, but at the right moments it escalates to provoke side-splitting laughter. Falk and Arkin make an effective and funny twosome. Also with Richard Libertini, Nancy Dussault, Penny Peyser, and Arlene Golonka. **Director**—Arthur Hiller. (PG)

103 minutes

THE INN OF THE SIXTH HAPPINESS (1958)

★★★

**Ingrid Bergman
Curt Jurgens
Robert Donat**

Engrossing drama set in China just prior to World War II. Bergman does a fine acting job as an English girl who becomes a brave missionary. She shepherds children through enemy lines and carries on a romance with Jurgens. Donat, in his last film, is notable in the role of a mandarin. An exciting happy ending wraps it up nicely.

Other performers are Athene Seyler, Ronald Squire, and Richard Wattis. **Director**—Mark Robson. **Academy Award Nomination**—Robson, best director.

158 minutes

IN PRAISE OF OLDER WOMEN (1979)

★

**Tom Berenger
Karen Black
Susan Strasberg
Alexandra Stewart**

An awkward soft-core porno film, set in Hungary and Canada, about a boy's sexual experiences with older women. Berenger, as the lad who strikes out with girls his own age, doesn't light any fires. Instead, he carries on with some married women played by Black, Strasberg, and Stewart, who appear semi-nude. Most of the sex scenes are embarrassing rather than erotic. Also with Helen Shaver and Marilyn Lightstone. **Director**—George Kaczender. (R)

108 minutes

INSERTS (1976)

★

**Richard Dreyfuss
Jessica Harper**

Despite its MPAA rating, this film is hardly pornographic, as might be expected; it's hardly a movie either. It's about making pornographic movies in the '30s. Dreyfuss stars as a has-been director who, in desperation, resorts to shooting porno flicks in his living room. The film never leaves this setting, and it drones on for almost two hours in sheer tedium. Harper plays a woman who tries to cure Dreyfuss's withdrawal from life. Also with Bob Hoskins and Veronica Cartwright. **Director**—John Byrum. (X) *117 minutes*

INSIDE DAISY CLOVER (1965)

★★

**Natalie Wood
Robert Redford**

Wood plays the title role in this half-baked story of a young movie star's hard-pressed Hollywood career in the '30s. Redford plays a troubled matinee

JACK NICHOLSON

Jack Nicholson appeared in some 15 movies before his performances in Dennis Hopper's Easy Rider (1969) and Bob Rafelson's Five Easy Pieces (1970) established him as an international film star.

Nicholson was born in Neptune, New Jersey, in 1937. He first came to Hollywood in 1958, and was at MGM from 1959 to 1968, where he became part of a group of talented and ambitious iconoclasts who were trying to expand commercial cinema. During that time, Nicholson appeared in Monte Hellman's The Shooting (1965) and Ride the Whirlwind (1965), which Nicholson co-scripted, as well as Hell's Angels on Wheels (1967) and Psych-Out (1968).

In 1969, Nicholson replaced Rip Torn as the dipsomaniacal southern lawyer in Easy Rider, and received an Academy Award nomination for his performance. He was also nominated for his work in Five Easy Pieces, and then appeared in Vincente Minnelli's On a Clear Day You Can See Forever (1970). He directed Drive, He Said (1970), appeared in Mike Nichol's Carnal Knowledge (1971) and Henry Jaglom's A Safe Place (1971), and then starred in Rafelson's The King of Marvin Gardens (1972). Nicholson also starred in Hal Ashby's The Last Detail (1974), for which he received another Oscar nomination.

Nicholson's other films include Chinatown *(1974), for which he was again nominated for an Oscar, and* One Flew Over the Cuckoo's Nest *(1976), for which he won the Academy Award as best actor. He appeared in Michelangelo Antonioni's* The Passenger *(1974); Ken Russell's* Tommy *(1975); Elia Kazan's* The Last Tycoon *(1976); Goin' South (1978), which he directed; Stanley Kubrick's* The Shining *(1980); Rafelson's remake of* The Postman Always Rings Twice *(1981); as Eugene O'Neill in* Reds *(1981); and most recently in* Terms of Endearment *(1983) for which he won an Academy Award as best supporting actor.*

idol. Many of the characters are wet cardboard—Wood included. Christopher Plummer, however, does well as a bombastic studio boss. A few moments shine through in this film, but not enough to be satisfying; the film is mostly style and little substance. Also with Ruth Gordon and Roddy McDowall. **Director**—Robert Mulligan. **Academy Award Nomination**—Gordon, best supporting actress.
128 minutes

INSIDE MOVES (1980)

 ★★

John Savage
David Morse

A sentimental drama about regulars at a neighborhood bar, where all are afflicted with some sort of physical ailment. Savage plays a cripple who helps his bartending buddy, played by Morse, obtain a knee operation that opens the door to a successful basketball career. The acting is fine, and the main characters are sort of Rocky Balboas of the handicapped. The plot, however, is rather corny and loosely constructed—a situation that detracts from the film's compassion for its characters. Also with Diana Scarwid and Amy Wright. **Director**—Richard Donner. (PG) **Academy Award Nomination**—Scarwid, best supporting actress.
113 minutes

THE INSPECTOR GENERAL (1949)

 ★★★

Danny Kaye

Top-of-the-line star vehicle for Kaye masquerading as an important official in 19th-century Russia. Kaye turns on the charm and the energy in this good-looking comedy of errors, tarnished only by a few plodding moments. Co-stars Walter Slezak, Barbara Bates, Elsa Lanchester, and Gene Lockhart. **Director**—Henry Koster. **Alternate Title**—Happy Times.
101 minutes

INTERIORS (1978)

 ★★★

Diane Keaton
Geraldine Page

Woody Allen's first serious drama as writer-director is surprisingly effective, considering its overall gloominess. The style reflects Woody's admiration for Ingmar Bergman, but the story is straight modern Americana, not unlike the plays of Arthur Miller. The plot involves a series of intense emotional crises in a wealthy New York family, whose members all strive for achievement and creativity but appear unhappy whether or not they get what they want. Excellent acting by Page, Keaton, Maureen Stapleton, E.G. Marshall, and Sam Waterston. (PG). **Academy Award Nominations**—Page, best actress; Stapleton, best supporting actress; Allen, best screenplay.
99 minutes

INTERMEZZO (1939)

 ★★★

Ingrid Bergman
Leslie Howard

Like any normal male, Leslie Howard can't resist having an affair with Ingrid Bergman in Intermezzo.

A well-done love story about a famous married violinist, played by Howard, who falls hopelessly in love with a young pianist, played by Bergman.
(Continued)

 Movie is available in Beta and VHS videotape

I

- International Velvet
- In the Heat of the Night
- Intruder in the Dust
- Invasion of the Body Snatchers (1956)
- Invasion of the Body Snatchers (1978)
- The Invisible Man

(Continued)

The movie gets right to the point and offers fine moments of charm and sentimentality. There's good acting all around, and Bergman is impressive in her English-speaking debut. Others in the cast include John Halliday, Edna Best, and Cecil Kellaway. **Director—** Gregory Ratoff. *69 minutes b&w*

INTERNATIONAL VELVET
(1978)
 ★★

Tatum O'Neal
Christopher Plummer
Nanette Newman

Tatum O'Neal and her horse win a race in International Velvet.

O'Neal stars in this warm and handsome sequel to *National Velvet*, the 1944 girl-meets-horse movie, which featured young Elizabeth Taylor. Velvet, now grown up and played in this film by Newman, resides in the picturesque English countryside. Along comes O'Neal, who plays her orphaned niece. Tatum takes a liking to a magnificent colt and wins a gold medal in the exciting Olympic equestrian competition. Plummer plays Newman's lover. Also with Anthony Hopkins and Dinsdale Landen. **Director—** Bryan Forbes. (PG) *127 minutes*

IN THE HEAT OF THE NIGHT
(1967)
 ★★★★

Sidney Poitier
Rod Steiger

Poitier plays a highly professional big-city homicide detective on a visit to a backwater Mississippi town. A murder is committed, and he joins forces with a bigoted police chief to solve the case. Steiger is exceptional as the pompous policeman who learns some professional crime-solving methods from the black cop. Director Norman Jewison brings out their personality clash with amazing skill, and the film, an insightful study of prejudices and lifestyles in the South, is wrapped up neatly by classy acting all around. Top supporting jobs from Lee Grant, Warren Oates, Quentin Dean, William Schallert, and Scott Wilson. **Academy Awards**—best picture; Steiger, best actor; Stirling Silliphant, best screenplay (based on material from another medium). **Nomination**—Jewison, best director. *110 minutes*

INTRUDER IN THE DUST
(1949)
 ★★★★

Juano Hernandez
Elizabeth Patterson
David Brian

A gripping drama, enhanced by indelible characterizations, about a black man who is wrongfully accused of murder. He's rescued from a lynch mob by a boy and an old woman who find the real killer. Hernandez is the accused black, and Brian and Patterson are his rescuers. The film, based on William Faulkner's novel, works as a fine mystery as well as straightforward social observation. There's top-notch acting with well-paced direction. Also with Claude Jarman, Jr., Porter Hall, and Will Geer. **Director**—Clarence Brown. *87 minutes b&w*

INVASION OF THE BODY SNATCHERS (1956)
 ★★★★

Kevin McCarthy
Dana Wynter

An amazingly good sci-fi thriller considering it's a low-budget film with a relatively unknown cast. A small American town is invaded by strange pods from space, and a sinister force takes over the bodies of the residents. The production progresses smartly with intelligence and mounting suspense. A classic of its time. Also with Larry Gates, King Donovan, Carolyn Jones, and Sam Peckinpah. **Director—** Don Siegel. *80 minutes b&w*

INVASION OF THE BODY SNATCHERS (1978)
 ★★★

Donald Sutherland
Brooke Adams

Donald Sutherland is horrified by the Invasion of the Body Snatchers.

The 1956 sci-fi classic gets a coat of gloss and some flashy new thrills in this remake by director Philip Kaufman. Aliens arrive on earth in the form of strange seed pods to replace humans, but this time the setting is San Francisco instead of a small town. Sutherland stands out as a beleaguered public health officer who tries to unscramble the mystery. The film slows down a bit about midway, but there are enough scary scenes to keep the chills flowing to the end. Kevin McCarthy, who played the Sutherland role in the original film, and Don Siegel, the director of the 1956 version, both appear in cameo roles. Also look for Robert Duvall in a bit part. Also with Jeff Goldblum, Veronica Cartwright, and Leonard Nimoy. (PG) *115 minutes*

THE INVISIBLE MAN (1933)
★★★

Claude Rains
Gloria Stuart

Rains became a star as the scientist who discovers how to make himself

• Invitation to a Gunfighter   • Iphigenia
• I Ought to Be in Pictures   • I Remember Mama
• The Ipcress File   • Irma La Douce

I

Claude Rains conveys a wide range of feelings without ever showing his face in The Invisible Man.

transparent. Excellent trick photography and a solid plot based on the H.G. Wells novel results in a superior sci-fi film, as Rains goes amok and vows to use his power to rule the world. E.E. Clive, Una O'Connor, Henry Travers, Dudley Digges, and William Harrigan perform admirably. James Whale (*Frankenstein*) provides suitably atmospheric direction.

80 minutes b&w

INVITATION TO A GUNFIGHTER (1964)
★★

Yul Brynner
George Segal

There's more talk than action in this tepid western drama about a community that recruits a gunman to do some dirty work. The characterizations come off rather pat despite the efforts of a decent cast. Also with Janice Rule, Brad Dexter, and Pat Hingle. **Director**—Richard Wilson. *92 minutes*

I OUGHT TO BE IN PICTURES (1982)
 ★★

Walter Matthau
Dinah Manoff
Ann-Margret

Matthau's delivery of cantankerous wisecracks adds some spice to this otherwise blasé film based on Neil Simon's Broadway play. Matthau plays a down-and-out Hollywood screen-writer who is reunited with his teen-age daughter (Manoff) after a 16-year separation. A lot of sarcastic sparring ensues, in typical Simon manner. But the relentless recriminations and sentimental gushings never develop beyond the banal. **Director**—Herbert Ross. (PG) *108 minutes*

THE IPCRESS FILE (1965)
★★★

Michael Caine
Nigel Green

Taut, relentlessly absorbing espionage caper, based on Len Deighton's novel, with Caine perfectly cast as Harry Palmer, a low-key secret agent who tracks a missing scientist behind the Iron Curtain and discovers one of his superiors is a spy. Sidney J. Furie's efficient direction upholds the tension throughout the film, and the script is plotted for maximum suspense. The film led to two sequels. Also stars Guy Doleman, Sue Lloyd, and Gordon Jackson. *92 minutes*

IPHIGENIA (1977)
 ★★★

Tatiana Papamoskou
Irene Papas

This Euripides drama transforms nicely to the screen, illuminating the power and passion of the classic Greek tragedy. It's the story of King Agamemnon, who is forced to sacrifice his daughter, Iphigenia, to appease the gods and assure favorable passage for his fleet to Troy. Fourteen-year-old Papamoskou is magnificent as the martyred daughter. Also with Costa Kazakos. Classy direction by Michael (*Zorba the Greek*) Cacoyannis. In Greek with English titles. (No MPAA rating) **Academy Award Nomination**—best foreign-language film. *127 minutes*

I REMEMBER MAMA (1948)
 ★★★★

Irene Dunne
Barbara Bel Geddes

A nice bit of sentimental nostalgia as a novelist remembers growing up with her stouthearted Norwegian family,

In I Remember Mama, *Barbara Bel Geddes recalls growing up in a warm and caring family.*

struggling to attain the American dream in San Francisco. Dunne is wonderful as the energetic mother whose devotion and fortitude keeps the family on an even keel; Bel Geddes plays the novelist. The film is filled with rich details of growing up wisely. Other good performances by Oscar Homolka, Edgar Bergen, Philip Dorn, Ellen Corby, and Cedric Hardwicke. **Director**—George Stevens. **Academy Award Nominations**—Dunne, best actress; Homolka, best supporting actor; Bel Geddes, Corby, best supporting actress; Nicholas Musuraca, cinematography (black and white). *134 minutes b&w*

IRMA LA DOUCE (1963)
 ★★★

Shirley MacLaine
Jack Lemmon

The delightful Broadway musical, without music, is done up for the screen with style and flavor. Writer-director Billy Wilder succeeds with this comic romp about a Paris cop, played by Lemmon, who falls in love with a prostitute, played by MacLaine. Lemmon is in top form, and he's matched by the spirited performance of MacLaine as the sweet, good-natured trollop. Nonstop fun, especially for adult audiences. Co-stars Lou Jacobi, Herschel Bernardi, Joan Shawlee, and Bruce Yarnell. **Academy Award Nominations**—MacLaine, best actress; Joseph LaShelle, cinematography (color). *146 minutes*

I
- Irreconcilable Differences
- Island in the Sky
- The Island of Dr. Moreau
- Islands in the Stream
- Is Paris Burning?
- It Came from Hollywood
- It Happened One Night

IRRECONCILABLE DIFFERENCES (1984)

★★

Ryan O'Neal
Shelley Long
Drew Barrymore

This satiric comedy opens with a cute 10-year-old girl (Barrymore) seeking a divorce from her neglectful, ever-bickering parents. But the clever scenario is merely a setup for the story of an ambitious Hollywood couple (O'Neal and Long) told mostly in flashbacks. He's a film director and she's a writer, both suffering from their own bloated egos brought about by quick success. This theme is worn thin and seems like déjà vu here. **Director**—Charles Shyer. (PG)   *112 minutes*

ISLAND IN THE SKY (1953)

★★★

John Wayne
Lloyd Nolan

Adequate adventure about the survival of a crew from a transport plane, forced to land in the frozen wastes of Greenland. The story is enhanced by impressive photography, and the action and suspense are elevated by the talents of Wayne. Also with Walter Abel, Allyn Joslyn, Andy Devine, and James Arness. **Director**—William Wellman.   *109 minutes b&w*

THE ISLAND OF DR. MOREAU (1977)

★★

Burt Lancaster
Michael York

In 1933, this adaptation of the H. G. Wells horror fantasy was called *The Island of Lost Souls*. Then, it starred Charles Laughton as a sinister scientist who tries to breed animals into humans and vice versa. This $6 million remake is a nice try with Lancaster in the title role, but alas, the strange critters aren't as creepy, and the atmosphere is hardly ghoulish. The horror movies just don't work the same as when Boris Karloff, Bela Lugosi, and their like were around. Also with Nigel Davenport and Barbara Carrera. **Director**—Don Taylor. (PG)   *104 minutes*

ISLANDS IN THE STREAM (1977)

★★

George C. Scott
David Hemmings
Claire Bloom

George C. Scott stars as a famous painter and sculptor in Islands in the Stream.

This introspective movie version of Ernest Hemingway's novel begins with feeling but peters out awkwardly. Scott plays the artist-hero—a self-exiled sculptor whose marriages have failed—with gruff macho spirit. But the film doesn't justify the Hemingway prose, and the story drifts and plods out of control. Also with Susan Tyrrell, Michael-James Wixted, and Gilbert Roland. **Director**—Franklin J. Schaffner. (PG)   *105 minutes*

IS PARIS BURNING? (1965)

★★

Leslie Caron
Gert Frobe
Charles Boyer
Yves Montand
Orson Welles

Meandering and overblown all-star epic account of the efforts to prevent the destruction of Paris by the retreating Germans in World War II. The story is put together as a succession of vignettes, and the film is loaded with half-baked cameos that only provoke annoyance and lead to dreariness. All in all, not so hot. Also with Alain Delon, Jean Pierre Cassel, Kirk Douglas, Glenn Ford, and Robert Stack. **Director**—René Clément.   *173 minutes b&w*

IT CAME FROM HOLLYWOOD (1983)

★★

A compilation of filmdom's schlocky moments with notable snippets from such potboilers as *Slime People* and *Attack of the Fifty Foot Woman*. Fans of outrageous B movies may find something to chuckle about, but the material is haphazardly assembled and this random cavalcade of the ridiculous finally becomes tiresome. Segments are introduced by Dan Aykroyd, Gilda Radner, Cheech and Chong, and John Candy. Their presence adds little to the proceedings. **Director**—Malcolm Leo. (PG)   *76 minutes*

IT HAPPENED ONE NIGHT (1934)

★★★★

Clark Gable
Claudette Colbert

In the screwball comedy It Happened One Night, *Clark Gable and Claudette Colbert fall in love.*

A spoiled little rich girl (Colbert) runs away from her daddy and sets off to marry her gigolo-boyfriend. She is accompanied on this crazy odyssey by

• It Happened One Summer
• It Happens Every Spring
• I, The Jury
• It's Alive!

• It's a Mad Mad Mad Mad World
• It's a Wonderful Life
• It's My Turn

I

a story-hungry reporter (Gable). She wants to use him, he wants to use her, and of course they fall in love. This delightful romance was a forerunner to all the great screwball comedies of the '30s and remains one of the best comedies of all time. Gable and Colbert make the ideal bickering couple: he points and she pouts. There is a sensuality between them that adds warmth to the witty dialogue and funny situations. A rare conjunction of talents. **Director**—Frank Capra. **Academy Awards**—best picture; Capra, best director; Gable, best actor; Colbert, best actress; Robert Riskin, writing (adaptation). *105 minutes*

IT HAPPENED ONE SUMMER
See State Fair

IT HAPPENS EVERY SPRING
(1949)
★★★

Ray Milland
Jean Peters

A chemistry professor, played by Milland, becomes an unlikely pitching ace after he discovers a formula that makes baseballs repel wood, including baseball bats. Milland handles the part with skill and coaxes plenty of chuckles and smiles from the buoyant material. It's as enjoyable as watching your favorite team win, with the pitcher hurling a no-hitter. Also stars Paul Douglas, Ed Begley, Ted de Corsia, and Ray Collins. **Director**—Lloyd Bacon. **Academy Award Nomination**—Shirley W. Smith and Valentine Davies, writing (motion picture story). *80 minutes b&w*

I, THE JURY (1982)
★★★

Armand Assante

Blazing nonstop action, laced with sex and violence, characterizes this reworking of Mickey Spillane's famous private eye adventure. The complex, supercharged plot includes new aspects such as CIA operatives, a sex clinic, mind control, and big-shot gangsters. Assante mostly overplays the hard-boiled gumshoe, Mike Hammer. **Director**—Robert T. Heffron. (R) *109 minutes*

IT'S ALIVE! (1977)
★

John Ryan
Sharon Farrell

Bad news on the phone: It's Alive!

This movie is some nonsense about a weird newborn baby with long fangs that goes on a killing spree, beginning with the doctors and nurses in the delivery room. The acting is awful, the dialogue silly. However, director-producer-writer Larry Cohen manages a few moments of suspense and a mild comment on the overuse of drugs. Also with Andrew Duggan and Guy Stockwell. (PG) *91 minutes*

IT'S A MAD MAD MAD MAD WORLD (1963)
★★★

Spencer Tracy
Jimmy Durante
Milton Berle
Sid Caesar
Ethel Merman

A full frontal assault on the funnybone, with virtually every Hollywood comedian getting in their licks. The 2½-hour romp is about a mad scramble to recover hidden loot from a robbery. Tracy plays a detective trying to recover the booty. All sorts of wild chases and slapstick antics abound. The large cast also includes Buddy Hackett, Mickey Rooney, Dick Shawn, Jack Benny, Jerry Lewis, Terry-Thomas, Phil Silvers, Edie Adams, Jonathan Winters, and many more. **Director**—Stanley Kramer. *162 minutes*

IT'S A WONDERFUL LIFE
(1946)
★★★★

James Stewart
Henry Travers
Donna Reed

James Stewart and Donna Reed quell a panic in It's a Wonderful Life.

This is perhaps Frank Capra's best film; it shows his uniquely warm and charming blend of humor. Stewart is superb as a small-town businessman who beats his brains out most of his life. When he decides to end it all because he thinks he's a failure, a guardian angel, played by Travers, comes to Earth to show him his accomplishments. Reed plays Stewart's wife. It is film sentimentality done to perfection and displayed with a silver lining; a Christmas favorite, and it's a wonderful movie. Also with Lionel Barrymore, Thomas Mitchell, Ward Bond, and Gloria Grahame. **Academy Award Nominations**—best picture; Capra, best director; Stewart, best actor. *129 minutes b&w*

IT'S MY TURN (1980)
★★

Jill Clayburgh
Michael Douglas
Charles Grodin

Clayburgh plays a successful math professor, trying to resolve her career and her love life in this vague comedy-
(Continued)

It's My Turn *features Jill Clayburgh as a math professor and Michael Douglas as her lover.*

(Continued)

drama. The performances are engaging, but Eleanor Bergstein's muddled screenplay keeps the film on the level of a soap opera. Finally, the movie just stops in its tracks, dangling all sorts of unanswered questions. Douglas and Grodin co-star as Clayburgh's lovers of the moment—one in New York, the other in Chicago. Also with Beverly Garland. **Director**—Claudia Weill. (PG)   *91 minutes*

IVANHOE (1952)
★★★

**Robert Taylor
Joan Fontaine
Elizabeth Taylor**

A splendid costume adventure, based on Sir Walter Scott's colorful tale of brave knights and fair damsels in medieval England. Robert Taylor plays the title role, galloping off on daring assignments and romancing beautiful Liz and lovely Joan. It's all done to a "T," with lavish sets and striking photography. The script, however, could have been a bit better. Also stars Emlyn Williams, George Sanders, Robert Douglas, and Sebastian Cabot. **Director**—Richard Thorpe. **Academy Award Nominations**—best picture; F. A. Young, cinematography (color).
106 minutes

I WALKED WITH A ZOMBIE
(1943)
★★★

**Frances Dee
Tom Conway
James Ellison**

I Walked With a Zombie *is an early film treatment of voodoo.*

A nurse visits a Caribbean island to take care of the zombielike wife of a planter and discovers skeletons and voodoo rituals lurking about. There is enough style and spooky atmosphere to keep the production interesting throughout in this early effort by director Jacques Tourneur. Dee as the nurse and Conway as the planter give the solid but unspectacular performances required in such movies. Also with James Bell and Theresa Harris.
69 minutes b&w

I WANNA HOLD
YOUR HAND
(1978)
★★

**Nancy Allen
Bobby DiCicco
Mark McClure**

Beatlemania breaks out in I Wanna Hold Your Hand.

A group of teenagers try to crash into the Beatles's New York hotel suite when the famous mop tops pay their first visit to America to appear on *The Ed Sullivan Show*. If you haven't been weaned away from *Archie* comics, you might find this adolescent slapstick comedy worthwhile. The film, set in 1964, is a series of silly routines and raucous chases, performed mainly by an unfamiliar young cast. First-time director Robert Zemeckis tries to copy the freewheeling spirit of *American Graffiti*, but he doesn't achieve that quality or style. (PG)   *104 minutes*

I WANT TO LIVE! (1958)
★★★★

**Susan Hayward
Simon Oakland**

Smashing crime drama, based on the case of Barbara Graham, who was executed in the gas chamber for murder amid debate over the severity of her punishment. Hayward gives a *tour-de-force* performance as the tough prostitute, and the production is neatly assembled for maximum impact by director Robert Wise. Especially compelling are the details of the execution. The film offers a moving plea for the abolition of capital punishment. Good supporting efforts by Oakland, Virginia Vincent, Theodore Bikel, and Philip Coolidge. **Academy Award**—Hayward, best actress; **Nominations**—Wise, best director; Nelson Gidding and Don Mankiewicz, best screenplay (based on material from another medium); Lionel Linden, cinematography (black and white).
120 minutes b&w

I WAS A MALE WAR BRIDE
(1949)
★★★

**Cary Grant
Ann Sheridan**

The title may sound absurd, but this energetic comedy really clicks. Grant plays a French army officer who gets all dressed up in women's clothing as part of a scheme to join Sheridan, his American WAC wife, on a return trip to the United States. Grant and Sheridan are hilarious, and they have a fine, funny script to work with. Also with

• I Was a Teenage
  Werewolf
• I Will, I Will...For Now
• I Wonder Who's Kissing Her
  Now
• Jabberwocky
• The Jackpot
• Jailhouse Rock
• Jane Eyre
• Jaws

I·J

Marion Marshall and Randy Stuart.
Director—Howard Hawks.

105 minutes b&w

I WAS A TEENAGE WEREWOLF
(1957)

 ★★★

Michael Landon
Whit Bissell

A low-budget monster movie that has unexpected style. A doctor uses a delinquent youth as a guinea pig for some experiments. Unfortunately, the young man, played by Landon, becomes a werewolf. It's an interesting mixture of horror and humor. And who can forget that crazy title? Also with Yvonne Leslie and Guy Williams. **Director**—Gene Fowler, Jr.

76 minutes b&w

I WILL, I WILL . . . FOR NOW
(1976)
(no stars)

Elliott Gould
Diane Keaton

Elliott Gould asks Victoria Principal if she's ever been to Dallas in I Will, I Will... For Now.

A stale and wretched sex farce right out of the Doris Day–Rock Hudson comedies of the '50s. Gould and Keaton play a rich, hip New York couple who get involved with a sex clinic, a contract marriage, and extramarital affairs. The film is full of adolescent gags that consistently fall flat. Norman Panama, who wrote and directed comedies back in the '40s, directed this one and helped with the writing. It's a poor job that just doesn't work today. He's obviously out of touch with current realities. Also with Paul Sorvino, Victoria Principal, and Robert Alda. (R)

96 minutes

I WONDER WHO'S KISSING HER NOW (1947)
★★★

Mark Stevens
June Haver

This film is a pleasant film biography of 1890s songwriter Joseph E. Howard. It works mainly because of its great music; the plot, embellished with some fiction, is merely routine. A talented cast, however, helps bring it along. Also stars Martha Stewart, Reginald Gardiner, Lenore Aubert, William Frawley, and Gene Nelson. **Director**—Lloyd Bacon. *104 minutes*

J

JABBERWOCKY (1977)
 ★★

Michael Palin
Max Wall

A shabby-looking medieval farce; a second cousin to *Monty Python and the Holy Grail*, but hardly achieving its quality. Occasionally, there are flashes of honest humor, which are quickly drowned in a confused outpouring of adolescent slapstick and bad taste. The wobbly script involves knights, a king, grubby peasants, a bumbling hero, and a vile monster—the Jabberwock. Also with Deborah Fallender, John Le Mesurier, and Annette Badland. Written and directed by Terry Gilliam. (No MPAA rating) *100 minutes*

THE JACKPOT (1950)
★★★

James Stewart
Barbara Hale

An ordinary guy wins a pile of money on a radio quiz show. After he attains notoriety, his life changes drastically. The film is a rather low-key comedy, adequately handled for a steady stream of amusing moments. Stewart excels as the winner who gets a fair share of headaches along with extra income. Others in the cast include James Gleason, Fred Clark, Alan Mowbray, and Natalie Wood. **Director**—Walter Lang. *85 minutes b&w*

JAILHOUSE ROCK (1957)
 ★★

Elvis Presley
Judy Tyler
Dean Jones

Hamlet it's not. But for Presley fans, this may be just the ticket anyway. Presley stars as a convict who learns about music in the slammer. He turns into a big-time record mogul when he gets out. The likeable Lieber and Stoller score includes the title song and "Treat Me Nice." Ingenue Judy Tyler died tragically after making her impressive screen debut in this film. **Director**—Richard Thorpe.

96 minutes b&w

JANE EYRE (1944)
★★★★

Joan Fontaine
Orson Welles

Charlotte Bronte's classic romantic story, set in Victorian times, is faithfully reproduced for the screen with the skillful use of brooding atmospherics. Fontaine heads the cast of this deliberately paced production about an unfortunate orphan girl who becomes a governess for a wealthy Englishman and gets involved with mystery and romance. Also with Margaret O'Brien, Henry Daniell, John Sutton, Agnes Moorehead, and Elizabeth Taylor. **Director**—Robert Stevenson. *96 minutes b&w*

JAWS (1975)
 ★★★★

Robert Shaw
Roy Scheider
Richard Dreyfuss

A man-eating shark comes to dine at a Long Island, New York, summer resort. The film has been designed to scare the hell out of you and may become a classic in the style of *King Kong* and *Frankenstein*. There's fine acting by Dreyfuss, Shaw, and, of course, the Great White Shark—a 25-foot mechanical marvel. Shaw plays an expert shark hunter, Dreyfuss is an ichthyologist, and Scheider is the area's po-
(Continued)

J
• Jaws 2
• Jaws 3–D
• The Jazz Singer
• J. D.'s Revenge
• Jekyll and Hyde...Together Again
• The Jerk
• Jesus Christ Superstar

Richard Dreyfuss, who plays an ichthyologist, cools off in shark-infested waters in Jaws.

(Continued)
lice chief. Clever directing by Steven Spielberg. Adapted from the novel by Peter Benchley. Also with Lorraine Gary, Murray Hamilton, and Carl Gottlieb. **Academy Award Nomination**—best picture. (PG) *124 minutes*

JAWS 2 (1978)

★★

**Roy Scheider
Lorraine Gary**

This sequel to the big moneymaking shark movie offers a moderate ration of excitement, when the huge mechanical man-eater swallows some skin divers or chomps on some sailboating teenagers. But this time it's all done without the imagination and slick style that director Steven Spielberg lavished on the original film. The plot, which is mostly a threadbare rehash of the initial *Jaws* theme, never quite builds to a satisfying climax. Scheider again plays the resort community's embattled police chief. Also with Murray Hamilton, Joseph Mascolo, and Jeffrey Kramer. **Director**—Jeannot Szwarc. (PG) *117 minutes*

JAWS 3-D (1983)

★★

**Dennis Quaid
Bess Armstrong
Lou Gossett, Jr.**

This third, and rather uneven, installment of the shark saga finds the giant white creating havoc at Florida's Sea World. There are some tense moments, but by now we're so familiar with the antisocial habits of the mammoth predator that its attacks on tourists and employees at the aquarium park are about as scary as feeding time at the zoo. The 3-D process is more of a distraction than an enhancement. **Director**—Joe Alves. (PG) *97 minutes*

THE JAZZ SINGER (1980)

★★

**Neil Diamond
Laurence Olivier
Lucie Arnaz**

Neil Diamond and Lucie Arnaz star in The Jazz Singer.

Pop singer Diamond stars as the cantor's son who pursues a show business career in this cliché-filled remake of the 1927 original melodrama that featured Al Jolson. Instead of singing "Mammy," Diamond belts out "Love on the Rocks" and other pop tunes; he's obviously a better singer than actor. But there are energetic performances from Olivier, as the heartbroken father, and from Arnaz, as the young woman who promotes Diamond's career. Also with Catlin Adams. **Director**—Richard Fleischer. (PG) *115 minutes*

J. D.'S REVENGE (1976)

★★

**Glynn Turman
Lou Gossett, Jr.**

Gore and violence dominate this black-themed thriller about a young law student possessed by the spirit of a slain hoodlum. Turman works hard in the lead role, and there's stylish support from Gossett as a revivalist minister. Professional direction from Arthur Marks and a tight script also help keep the film moving smartly, but much of the material is too far-out to be taken seriously. Also with Joan Pringle, David McKnight, and Carl Crudup. (R) *95 minutes*

JEKYLL AND HYDE ... TOGETHER AGAIN (1982)

★

**Mark Blankfield
Bess Armstrong**

Much energy is wasted in this tasteless send-up of the classic 19th-century science-fiction tale. In this contemporary version, Blankfield portrays the straitlaced surgeon-scientist who changes into a wild-eyed hippie and lusts after a hooker. Blankfield works up a sweat, but the gags leave us cold. One scene shows Robert Louis Stevenson, who wrote the original story, rolling in his grave; it's the only part of the film that rings true. **Director**—Jerry Belson. (R) *82 minutes*

THE JERK (1979)

★★

**Steve Martin
Bernadette Peters**

Wild and crazy Martin, in his first starring feature film, lives up to his title role; but he's a silly jerk, not so much a funny jerk. In this rather harmless story, Steve—the son of a poor, black sharecropper—leaves home at age 35 to take a series of odd jobs, becomes wealthy, and finally loses his fortune. If you're alert, you can catch a few good gags, but most of the humor is merely idiotic. Jerry Lewis did this sort of material with more energy and style. Also with Catlin Adams, Mabel King, and Richard Ward. **Director**—Carl Reiner. (R) *104 minutes*

JESUS CHRIST SUPERSTAR (1973)

★★

**Ted Neeley
Carl Anderson**

A rather uneven screen version of the Broadway rock opera, filmed on location in the Holy Land. The story of Christ is enacted to the beat of rock music and with some contemporary trappings. It's certainly an oddball way of presenting a portion of the Scriptures. The cast does a good job, and the music is invigorating, especially if you happen to like this style. Also with Yvonne Elliman and Barry Dennen. **Director**—Norman Jewison. (G)   *103 minutes*

JEZEBEL
(1938)
★★★★

**Bette Davis
Henry Fonda**

Davis is sensational in this excellent melodrama, as a southern belle with a knack for manipulating the men in her life. Fonda plays her fiancé. The film also abounds with other pluses, including a smart script, stylish direction, and superb photography. It packs plenty of dramatic power, and Davis gives it an extra shot of adrenalin. Other excellent performances from George Brent, Margaret Lindsay, Donald Crisp, Fay Bainter, Spring Byington, and Eddie Anderson. **Director**—William Wyler. **Academy Awards**—Davis, best actress; Bainter, best supporting actress. **Nominations**—best picture; Ernest Haller, cinematography.

104 minutes b&w

THE JIGSAW MAN
(1984)
★★

**Michael Caine
Laurence Olivier**

This complex spy thriller, which pits the Russian KGB against British Intelligence, keeps reaching new levels of confusion as the story progresses. Caine is a British agent who defected to the Soviets. He then returns to England where he's caught up in a web of intrigue. Olivier is consistently entertaining as the cranky British Secret Service Chief. Caine doesn't fare as well. It's a jigsaw puzzle movie that seems to take forever to piece together. **Director**—Terence Young. (PG)   *96 minutes*

JINXED (1982)
★★

**Bette Midler
Ken Wahl
Rip Torn**

The black cat discovers that Bette Midler is bad luck in Jinxed.

Midler's energetic talents are misused in this foolish, half-baked comedy-drama set in Nevada's gambling communities. She's a struggling lounge singer who conspires with a young blackjack dealer (Wahl) to murder her nasty gambler boyfriend (Torn). The Divine Miss M only gets a few cracks at some brassy musical numbers. Most of the time she's lost in uncomfortable dramatic situations in a story that vaguely resembles *Double Indemnity*. **Director**—Don Siegel. (R)

103 minutes

JOAN OF ARC (1948)
★★

**Ingrid Bergman
José Ferrer**

So-so treatment of the classic story based on Maxwell Anderson's play, with a general feeling of pretentiousness throughout the lavish production. Bergman stars as Joan, the French peasant girl who led military campaigns against British forces and was eventually burned as a heretic. Bergman and the rest of the cast seem to be suffering from a bout of tired

blood. Also with George Coulouris, Francis L. Sullivan, Gene Lockhart, Ward Bond, John Ireland, and J. Carrol Naish. **Director**—Victor Fleming. **Academy Award**—Joseph Valentine, William V. Skall, and Winton Hoch, cinematography (color). **Nominations**—Bergman, best actress; Ferrer, best supporting actor.   *145 minutes*

JOE (1970)
★★★★

**Peter Boyle
Dennis Patrick**

An uncanny, haunting film about a loudmouthed foundry worker and a well-heeled advertising executive who become unlikely friends and end up killing some hippies. Boyle gives a vivid performance as the raging, Archie Bunker-type reactionary, and Patrick is convincing as the smooth ad man. The compelling story makes a strong social statement about hatred and bigotry, and the message is hammered home by the similarities and the stark contrasts in the two characters. The film, which is humorous in some respects, ends on a sad note. Also stars Audrey Caire and Susan Sarandon. **Director**—John G. Avildsen. (R) **Academy Award Nomination**—Norman Wexler, best story and screenplay (based on factual material or material not previously published).

107 minutes

JOHNNY BELINDA (1948)
★★★

**Jane Wyman
Lew Ayres**

Wyman gives a magnificent performance as a deaf-mute who is raped; Ayres is effective as a doctor involved with the young girl. This film is highly dramatic and touching, with authentic-looking surroundings of the small fishing village. Wyman seems to say it all with her eyes. Also with Charles Bickford, Agnes Moorehead, Stephen McNally, and Jan Sterling. **Director**—Jean Negulesco. **Academy Award**—Wyman, best actress. **Nominations**—best picture; Negulesco, best director; Ayres, best actor; Bickford, best supporting actor; Moorehead, best sup-

(Continued)

J
• Johnny Dangerously
• A Joke of Destiny
• The Joker Is Wild
• The Jolson Story
• Jonah—Who Will Be 25 in the Year 2000
• Joseph Andrews
• Journey into Fear

Jane Wyman and Lew Ayres star in Johnny Belinda.

(Continued)

porting actress; Irmgard Von Cube and Allen Vincent, writing (screenplay); Ted McCord, cinematography (black and white). *103 minutes b&w*

JOHNNY DANGEROUSLY (1984)

★★

**Michael Keaton
Marilu Henner
Joe Piscopo**

Patchy spoof of '30s gangster movies with Michael Keaton in the title role doing a take off on James Cagney. Keaton keeps his head above water despite the uneven screenplay that bogs down too often with crude gags. The cliché-strewn plot has Johnny turning to crime to pay for his poor mother's various operations. He's finally brought to heel by his younger brother, a crusading district attorney. **Director**—Amy Heckerling. (PG–13) *90 minutes*

A JOKE OF DESTINY (1984)

★★

**Ugo Tognazzi
Piera Degli Esposti
Gastone Moschin**

Director Lina Wertmuller's satire on unmanageable technology and political hypocrisy is as clumsy as the inept bureaucrats it wants to lampoon. A chain of mishaps evolves when the Italian Minister of Interior becomes trapped in his electronically sophisticated, computer-controlled limousine. Unfortunately, the uninspired comedy stalls along with the disabled automobile. In Italian with English titles. (PG) *105 minutes*

THE JOKER IS WILD (1957)

★★★

**Frank Sinatra
Mitzi Gaynor**

Sinatra portrays nightclub singer Joe E. Lewis of the roaring '20s who had problems with gangsters. This atmospheric film biography is carried off with adequate energy, and it offers Ol' Blue Eyes an opportunity to belt out some favorite tunes, including "All the Way." Gaynor and Jeanne Crain are fine as objects of Sinatra's affections. Also with Eddie Albert, Beverly Garland, and Jackie Coogan. **Director**—Charles Vidor. *123 minutes b&w*

THE JOLSON STORY (1946)

★★★

**Larry Parks
William Demarest**

A highly successful film biography of the '20s superstar who might have been a cantor, but became one of the greatest singing entertainers of the century. Parks superbly portrays the great performer, with the real Jolson dubbing in his voice for a slew of popular songs, including "Swanee" and "April Showers." It's a first-class show on the subject of show business. Also with Evelyn Keyes, Ludwig Donath, Tamara Shayne, and Scotty Beckett. **Director**—Alfred Green. **Academy Award Nominations**—Parks, best actor; Demarest, best supporting actor; Joseph Walker, cinematography (color). *128 minutes*

JONAH—WHO WILL BE 25 IN THE YEAR 2000 (1976)

★★★

**Jean-Luc Bideau
Myriam Boyer**

A jaunty Swiss comedy about eight friends who were active in political disturbances of the late '60s and who still uphold utopian ideals. The film, rich with irony, is somewhat too talky. Set in Geneva, with a superb cast. Also with Jacques Denis, Rufus, and Miou-Miou. **Director**—Alain Tanner. In French with English titles. (No MPAA rating) *110 minutes*

JOSEPH ANDREWS (1978)

★

**Ann-Margret
Peter Firth**

Ann-Margret is a lustful noblewoman in Joseph Andrews.

Director Tony Richardson, who gave us the delightful *Tom Jones*, falls flat on his face with this similar 18th-century costume tale. It's about a young footman, played by Firth, who is the object of the lustful desires of Lady Booby, his employer; she's played by Ann-Margret. Firth's Andrews character is rather uninteresting. The film is mostly a noisy jumble of tasteless arguing and brawling. And, although the pace is upbeat, the overall tone is tedious. Also with Michael Hordern and Beryl Reid. (R) *103 minutes*

JOURNEY INTO FEAR (1942)

★★★★

**Joseph Cotten
Dolores del Rio**

This gripping spy caper, based on the Eric Ambler novel, is ablaze with atmospherics and embellishments as only Orson Welles could dream them up. The story concerns a cat-and-mouse situation during World War II, with an American munitions expert trying to escape from the clutches of enemy agents in Turkey. There are spine-tingling pursuits and tense confrontations, all expertly concocted for maximum shock. Also with Welles, Jack Moss, Agnes Moorehead, and Ruth Warrick. **Director**—Norman Foster and Welles. *71 minutes b&w*

JOURNEY TO THE CENTER OF THE EARTH (1959)
★★★

**James Mason
Arlene Dahl
Pat Boone**

James Mason and Pat Boone in Journey to the Center of the Earth.

Outlandish but enjoyable sci-fi nonsense, based on the Jules Verne fantasy about a Scottish professor and colleagues who enter an extinct volcano in Iceland and travel to the Earth's core. The special effects are the big thing here, with some good performances and a modest touch of humor. Also with Peter Ronson, Diane Baker, and Thayer David. **Director**—Henry Levin. *132 minutes*

JUDGMENT AT NUREMBERG (1961)
★★★

**Spencer Tracy
Marlene Dietrich
Burt Lancaster
Richard Widmark
Maximilian Schell**

A distinguished film treatment of the

Spencer Tracy and Marlene Dietrich discuss crime and punishment in Judgment at Nuremberg.

famous 1948 trial of Nazi bigwigs accused by the Allies of terrible crimes against humanity. It's intelligently done in semidocumentary style and graced with powerful performances. Primarily, the film confronts that nagging rationalization for such outrageous behavior: "We were only following orders." Schell is outstanding as a defense attorney, and Tracy is effective as the court's presiding judge. Also with Judy Garland, Montgomery Clift, William Shatner, Edward Binns, and Werner Klemperer. **Director**—Stanley Kramer. **Academy Awards**—Schell, best actor; Abby Mann, best screenplay (based on material from another medium). **Nominations**—best picture; Kramer, best director; Tracy, best actor; Clift, best supporting actor; Garland, best supporting actress; Ernest Laszlo, cinematography (black and white). *178 minutes b&w*

JULES AND JIM (1961)
★★★★

**Jeanne Moreau
Oskar Werner
Henri Serre**

François Truffaut's celebration of love and cinema is both playful and tragic, and consistently full of energy. It rode in on the crest of France's New Wave, and will probably remain the film with which star Moreau is most often linked. Two friends—a Frenchman and a German—fall for the same beguiling woman in pre-World War I Paris, and we follow their relationship into the postwar years. Georges Delerue wrote the haunting musical score. The basis for the American film

Willie & Phil. Also stars Marie Dubois. *104 minutes b&w*

JULIA (1977)
★★

**Jane Fonda
Vanessa Redgrave**

Vanessa Redgrave is Julia.

Fred Zinnemann (*High Noon*) directed this handsome but bland period film, based on Lillian Hellman's memoir of a friendship between two brilliant and strong-willed young women. Keen and subtle performances by Fonda, Redgrave, and the fine supporting cast are short-circuited by a lack of passion, drama, and suspense in the screenplay, but the film, set on the eve of World War II, still has some appeal. Also with Jason Robards, Maximilian Schell, and Hal Holbrook. **Academy Awards**—Robards, best supporting actor; Redgrave, best supporting actress. **Nominations**—best picture; Zinnemann, best director; Fonda, best actress. (PG) *118 minutes*

JULIUS CAESAR (1953)
★★★★

**John Gielgud
James Mason
Marlon Brando**

Excellent acting by a top cast and a sumptuous production do justice to Shakespeare's compelling tragedy about conspiracy and revenge in the

(Continued)

 Movie is available in Beta and VHS videotape

J·K

- Jumping Jacks
- The Jungle Book
- Just a Gigolo
- Just Tell Me What You Want
- Just the Way You Are
- Just You and Me, Kid
- The Karate Kid

Casca (Edmond O'Brien) strikes the first blow against Julius Caesar.

(Continued)
Roman Empire. Joseph L. Mankiewicz's direction captures the mood of this moment in history as imagined by the great bard. Mason, as Brutus, and Gielgud, as Cassius, stand out in key roles. Brando plays Marc Antony, and Louis Calhern is Julius Caesar. Also with Greer Garson, Deborah Kerr, Edmond O'Brien, and George Macready. **Academy Award Nominations**—best picture; Brando, best actor; Joseph Ruttenberg, cinematography (black and white).

121 minutes b&w

JUMPING JACKS (1952)
★★★

Dean Martin
Jerry Lewis

Martin and Lewis join the Army and sign up for paratrooper duty. Plenty of funny sight gags come along at a fast clip in predictable style, and the boys and the audience have a jolly time. However, the U.S. Airborne takes awhile to recover from the frolic. Co-stars Mona Freeman, Robert Strauss, and Don Defore. **Director**—Norman Taurog. *96 minutes*

THE JUNGLE BOOK (1942)
 ★★★

Sabu

This children's story by Rudyard Kipling is produced for the screen with lavish detail. Sabu stars as the lad who befriends animals in the Indian jungle and learns their ways. Also with Joseph Calleia, John Qualen, Frank Puglia, and Rosemary DeCamp. **Director**—Zoltan Korda. *109 minutes*

JUST A GIGOLO (1981)
★★

David Bowie
Kim Novak
Curt Jurgens
Marlene Dietrich

Bowie, Novak, Jurgens, and Dietrich star in this bizarre, baroque comedy set in post-World War I Germany. The story centers on Bowie as an aristocratic Prussian war vet who drifts in and out of menial jobs before becoming a gigolo. The performances are impressive, but the material is so uneven and loosely constructed that there's scant satisfaction from such notable talent. Dietrich, looking somewhat sad and uneasy, sing-talks the title song. **Director**—David Hemmings. (R) *105 minutes*

JUST TELL ME WHAT YOU WANT (1980)
 ★★

Ali MacGraw
Alan King

King is Max Herschel, a pushy tycoon who's as childish as he is shrewd in this mean-spirited romantic comedy. Despite all the trappings of elegance, King still comes off as a stand-up nightclub comedian. The meager plot involves an attempt by Max's mistress, played by MacGraw, to break away from his domination. Sidney Lumet directs with determined frenzy. There are a few funny moments, but all the shouting and bullying becomes tiresome. Also with Peter Weller, Myrna Loy, Dina Merrill, and Keenan Wynn. (R) *112 minutes*

JUST THE WAY YOU ARE (1984)
★★★

Kristy McNichol
Michael Ontkean
Robert Carradine

A witty, romantic comedy about a lame girl (McNichol) who overcomes her handicap and finds love. Director Edouard Molinaro (*La Cage Aux Folles*), in his first English language feature, avoids maudlin lingering and makes the most of clever dialogue and charming characters. McNichol's spunky charm and some impressive background scenery of the French Alps add to the film's appeal. (PG) *95 minutes*

JUST YOU AND ME, KID (1979)
★★

George Burns
Brooke Shields

George Burns fails to convince Brooke Shields that he's Errol Flynn in Just You and Me, Kid.

Lovable Burns plays a retired vaudeville performer who befriends a pretty 14-year-old orphan, played by Shields. As long as Burns does what comes naturally—ticking off one-liners and doing the old soft shoe—there's some appeal. Aside from that, it's a rather half-baked, lethargic comedy. Shields's stiff performance pales against the warm glow of the venerable old trouper. In this case, it's definitely age *before* beauty. Also with Lorraine Gary, Nicholas Coster, Burl Ives, and Ray Bolger. **Director**—Leonard Stern. (PG) *95 minutes*

K

THE KARATE KID (1984)
★★★

Ralph Macchio
Noriyuki Morita

Director John G. Avildsen (*Rocky*) ap-

- The Keep
- The Kentuckian
- Kentucky Fried Movie
- Key Largo
- Khartoum
- The Kidnapping of the President

K

plies his root-for-the-underdog formula to this teenage drama and comes up with heartwarming, satisfying fare. Macchio plays the scrawny lad who is tormented by bullies. Then, he learns the spiritual and physical disciplines of karate from an elderly master, played by Morita. The outcome is predictable and uplifting. The surrogate father-son relationship is a high point of the story with Morita the effective scene stealer. (PG)   *126 minutes*

THE KEEP (1983)

 ★

Scott Glenn

Alberta Watson earns her keep by keeping quiet about The Keep.

A rickety, pretentious horror film, overburdened with outlandish special effects. The gothic tale takes place during World War II in a mysterious Rumanian castle where German soldiers accidentally set loose a monster. The silly, trumped-up plot is utter confusion embellished with an ear-shattering sound track. And the dialogue is mere mumbo jumbo. Glenn, Ian McKellen, and Jurgen Prochnow (the U-boat skipper in *Das Boot*) stumble through this nonsense. **Director**—Michael Mann. (R)   *97 minutes*

THE KENTUCKIAN (1955)

 ★★★

Burt Lancaster

This is a frontier adventure set in the early 1800s with Lancaster, a Kentucky backwoodsman, braving the elements to establish a new home in Texas. The film offers some interesting moments of rugged action, romance,

and even a bit of humor. Some decent acting contributes to the interesting tale. Supporting players include Dianne Foster, Diana Lynn, Walter Matthau, Una Merkel, and John Carradine. **Director**—Lancaster.
        104 minutes

KENTUCKY FRIED MOVIE (1977)

 ★★

Evan Kim
Master Bong Soo Han

A mixed-bag of youth-oriented, satirical sketches on the order of *The Groove Tube* and *Tunnelvision*. The film, divided into 22 segments, takes on TV newscasts, martial-arts and porno movies, and commercials. Some of the skits are clever and funny, but frequent doses of bad taste spoil the fun. The project is the outgrowth of the Kentucky Fried Theater, a satirical group formed at the University of Wisconsin. There are cameos by Bill Bixby, Henry Gibson, Donald Sutherland, and George Lazanby. **Director**—John Landis. (R)   *90 minutes*

KEY LARGO (1948)

 ★★★★

Humphrey Bogart
Edward G. Robinson
Lauren Bacall
Claire Trevor

Humphrey Bogart and Claire Trevor in the gangster yarn Key Largo.

Tense, electrifying gangster yarn set in the Florida Keys, with Bogart and Robinson making the sparks fly as adversaries. Robinson plays a sinister criminal who holds a group of people captive at a remote hotel during a violent coastal storm; Trevor plays his moll. Bogey is an ex-GI who stands up to Robinson's intimidation. Director John Huston precisely captures the dramatic mood and coaxes excellent performances from the cast. Also with Lionel Barrymore and Thomas Gomez. **Academy Award**—Trevor, best supporting actress.   *101 minutes*

KHARTOUM (1966)

★★

Charlton Heston
Laurence Olivier

This slice of history, concerning England's involvement with the Arab nations in the late 19th century, is highlighted with some well-staged battle scenes, but it gets bogged down by too much dialogue. It stars Heston as General Charles "Chinese" Gordon, who meets his match against Arab warriors led by the Mahdi, played by Olivier. There's good acting by these two, but there's not enough depth to their characters. Also with Richard Johnson, Ralph Richardson, Hugh Williams, Nigel Green, and Johnny Sekka. **Director**—Basil Dearden. **Academy Award Nomination**—Robert Ardrey, best story and screenplay (written directly for the screen).
        134 minutes

THE KIDNAPPING OF THE PRESIDENT (1980)

 ★★

William Shatner
Hal Holbrook
Van Johnson
Ava Gardner

Terrorists abduct the President of the United States during a visit to Toronto and hold him captive in an explosive-filled armored car. This Canadian-made movie stirs up moderate suspense as authorities press their rescue plans. But the improbable plot is riddled with clichés and dumb dialogue that consistently spoils the atmo-
(Continued)

K
- The Killer Elite
- Killer Force
- The Killers
- The Killing Fields
- Killing Heat

BETTE DAVIS

Bette Davis, who was the queen of the movie box office in the late '30s and throughout most of the '40s, was born Ruth Elizabeth Davis in 1908 in Lowell, Massachusetts. In high school, her ambition was to be an actress, but her initial attempts to succeed in this profession were met with disappointment.

During 1930, she was turned down by MGM, but eventually she was granted some small parts at Universal. At Warner Brothers, her career began to improve as the result of hard work and her demands for better parts, but she continued to work in many films that were beneath her talents.

She began to be accepted as an actress of star quality in 1935 when she earned an Oscar for Dangerous, but she was later suspended by Warners for rejecting a role, and she went to England to star in some films there. The studio enforced its contract, but after the legal battles, Davis was offered better roles.

Her career prospered throughout the '40s and most of the '50s, as she primarily played the formidable and bitchy woman who cherished her independence.

In the late '50s, her career faltered, but she made an amazing comeback in the early '60s with effective portrayals in What Ever Happened to Baby Jane? (1962), and Hush...Hush, Sweet Charlotte (1964).

Davis won the American Film Institute's Life Achievement Award in 1977, the first woman to attain the honor.

Some of her memorable films include Of Human Bondage (1934); The Petrified Forest (1936); Jezebel (1938), for which she received an Oscar; The Little Foxes (1941); All About Eve (1950); and Death on the Nile (1978).

(Continued)

sphere. Shatner plays the man in charge of rescuing the President. Holbrook plays the President with conviction, and there are stylish performances from Johnson as the Vice President and Gardner as Holbrook's wife. **Director**—George Mendeluk. (R)
113 minutes

THE KILLER ELITE (1975)
 ★★

James Caan
Robert Duvall

A farfetched action drama about Japanese terrorists who try to kill an anti-Communist Chinese leader. There's a smorgasbord of violence involving the CIA, with guns, machine guns, karate, swords, and kung fu. It's somewhat similar to Three Days of the Condor—only the screenplay is thinner. It stars Caan and Duvall as a team of gun-toting operatives who eventually wind up on opposite sides. Also with Gig Young, Arthur Hill, and Bo Hopkins. **Director**—Sam Peckinpah. (PG)
122 minutes

KILLER FORCE (1976)
 ★★★

Peter Fonda
Telly Savalas

A fairly entertaining action drama about a bunch of desperados out to steal several million dollars worth of diamonds from a South American diamond syndicate. Fonda plays a double agent in the plan to rob the company. Savalas, menacing and coldhearted, is the company's security boss. The desert dunes bristle with security gadgets and armed patrols, which the diamond thieves must penetrate to reach the diamonds. The plot is hardly convincing, but the fast-paced action makes up for such drawbacks. Also with Hugh O'Brian, Christopher Lee, Maud Adams, and O. J. Simpson. **Director**—Val Guest. (R) *101 minutes*

THE KILLERS (1946)
★★★★

Burt Lancaster
Edmond O'Brien

A high-voltage crime drama, smartly directed, professionally acted, and partially based on an Ernest Hemingway short story. A prizefighter is killed in a small town, and an insurance investigator finds out why. The suspense is handled with skill. Also with Ava Gardner, Albert Dekker, Sam Levene, and William Conrad. **Director**—Robert Siodmak. **Academy Award Nominations**—Siodmak, best director; Anthony Veiller, writing (screenplay).
105 minutes b&w

THE KILLING FIELDS (1984)
★★★

Sam Waterston
Haing S. Ngor

Detailed, wrenching account of the fall and brutal devastation of Cambodia, based on New York Times correspondent Sydney Schanberg's magazine article. The story focuses on the friendship between Schanberg (Waterston) and his loyal Cambodian guide-translator Dith Pran (Ngor). Unfortunately, the narrative falters in illustrating this special, tormented relationship and the harrowing events of the war. Yet the film ultimately emerges as a gripping panorama of the Cambodian holocaust. **Director**—Roland Joffe. (R) *139 minutes*

KILLING HEAT (1984)
★★

Karen Black
John Thaw
John Kani

A 30-year-old city woman (Black) fails to adapt to farm life in southern Africa. She gradually lapses into hopeless depression, which leads to a tragic ending. This brooding, intense picture of rural Africa is based on Doris Lessing's novel, The Grass Is Singing. It's intelligent and well-meaning,

• The Killing of a Chinese Bookie
• The Killing of Angel Street
• Kim
• Kind Hearts and Coronets
• The King and I
• King Kong (1933)

K

yet too overwrought, uneven, and bleak to be entertaining. **Director**—Michael Raeburn. (No MPAA rating) *104 minutes*

THE KILLING OF A CHINESE BOOKIE (1976)
★

Ben Gazzara

John Cassavetes, who scored with *A Woman Under the Influence*, fizzles in directing this pointless tale about the sleazy world of nightclub entertainers. Cosmo Vitelli, played by Gazzara, is the owner of a Hollywood strip joint who pays off a gambling debt to the mob by bumping off a Chinese bookie. Gazzara's performance as the hit man is shallow, and the story fails to generate much interest. Also with Timothy Agoglia Carey and Seymour Cassel. (R) *136 minutes*

THE KILLING OF ANGEL STREET (1983)
★★

Liz Alexander
John Hargreaves
Alexander Archdale

Liz Alexander says she didn't do it when asked about The Killing of Angel Street.

This overblown melodrama comes from Australia. It's about citizens doggedly fighting the brutal land developers and corrupt government officials who want to force them from their neighborhood. The story, supposedly based on fact, is overdramatized and becomes finally unbelievable. **Director**—Donald Crombie. (No MPAA rating) *98 minutes*

KIM (1951)
★★★

Errol Flynn
Dean Stockwell

Kim set in India, features Laurette Luez and Errol Flynn.

Rudyard Kipling's tale of the English lad reared in 19th-century India among the Hindus is presented with energy and color. Stockwell plays the title role, as the young adventurer who becomes involved with intrigue and uprisings. Lots of lively action for the kids, and it's rather tolerable for the adults, too. Flynn co-stars, with assists from Paul Lukas, Robert Douglas, Thomas Gomez, and Cecil Kellaway. **Director**—Victor Saville. *112 minutes*

KIND HEARTS AND CORONETS (1949)
 ★★★★

Alec Guinness
Dennis Price

Dennis Price is the scheming young man in Kind Hearts and Coronets.

Guinness has a field day playing eight roles in this stylish black comedy set in Edwardian England. A scheming young man, played by Price, decides that the family fortune belongs to him, and he attempts to achieve his goal by knocking off the competing heirs. It's all done rather cleverly with a liberal amount of wit and irony. Also with Valerie Hobson, Joan Greenwood, and Miles Malleson. **Director**—Robert Hamer. *104 minutes b&w*

THE KING AND I (1956)
 ★★★

Deborah Kerr
Yul Brynner

A lavish musical, based on the Broadway production *Anna and the King of Siam*. Good acting and the Rodgers and Hammerstein music add up to pleasant entertainment; but the film doesn't achieve the high spirits of the stage version. Kerr does well as the perplexed young widow hired to teach the children of the stubborn Siamese monarch, played by Brynner. Brynner gives a powerful performance, and he's credible, indeed, as the mighty ruler with whom Kerr eventually falls in love. There are also some terrific songs, including "Hello Young Lovers" and "Getting To Know You." Also stars Rita Moreno, Martin Benson, Alan Mowbray, and Goeffrey Toone. **Director**—Walter Lang. **Academy Award**—Brynner, best actor. **Nominations**—best picture; Lang, best director; Kerr, best actress; Leon Shamroy, cinematography (color). *133 minutes*

KING KONG (1933)
 ★★★★

Robert Armstrong
Fay Wray

A thrill-packed monster movie that has achieved screen-classic status, thanks to the imaginative and skillful use of special effects and on-target direction. A giant ape is brought from the jungle to New York, where it escapes and causes havoc in the city; the memorable climax on the Empire State Building is a masterpiece. Wray stars as the beauty the beast finds irresistible. Also with Bruce Cabot and *(Continued)*

K
- King Kong (1976)
- The King of Comedy
- King of Hearts
- The King of Marvin Gardens
- King of the Gypsies
- King Solomon's Mines

(Continued)
Frank Reicher. **Directors**—Merian C. Cooper and Ernest Schoedsack.
100 minutes b&w

KING KONG (1976)

 ★★★

**Jeff Bridges
Jessica Lange**

Kong still reigns as king in this $24-million retread of the 1933 classic. The lavish Dino De Laurentiis production is substantially faithful in spirit and imagery to this enduring fantasy of beauty and the beast. In fact, the update contains noticeable improvements: superb special effects, richer characters, and a polished contemporary script. It's old-time movie magic that's intimate, amusing, sentimental, adventuresome, and marvelous fun all the way. Also with Charles Grodin and John Randolph. **Director**—John Guillermin. (PG)   *134 minutes*

THE KING OF COMEDY (1983)

★★★

**Robert De Niro
Jerry Lewis**

Robert De Niro laps up the applause in The King of Comedy.

There are lots of laughs in director Martin Scorsese's ironic and stimulating essay on America's obsession with celebrity, but this also is serious business. De Niro is fascinating as a brash stand-up comic who achieves national exposure by kidnapping a TV talk show host (Lewis). Lewis plays it straight and smart; he's terrific. There's much talk about the media-saturated climate that can breed a Manson or a Hinckley, and that's no joke. (PG)
108 minutes

Infantrymen surrender to lunatics in the whimsical King of Hearts.

KING OF HEARTS (1967)

★★★★

**Alan Bates
Geneviève Bujold**

A smashing, thought-provoking anti-war movie with a satirical punch that's unforgettable. Bates plays a Scottish soldier in World War I, sent on a mission to defuse a bomb in a French town. All the inhabitants have fled except the inmates of an insane asylum, and they turn out to be more rational than those engaged in fighting the war. Bujold is a dancer who's an asylum inmate. Directed and acted with exceptional style, the film has become a cult favorite. Co-stars Pierre Brasseur and Jean-Claude Brialy. In French with English titles. **Director**—Philippe De Broca.   *102 minutes*

THE KING OF MARVIN GARDENS (1972)

★★

**Jack Nicholson
Bruce Dern
Ellen Burstyn**

An out-of-kilter bittersweet comedy about two brothers, played by Nicholson and Dern, who long to achieve the American dream, but their ways and means aren't enough to reach the goal. Nicholson is excellent as a radio talk-show host, and Dern is impressive as a small-time operator with big ideas. Burstyn plays an aging beauty. But this overly talky film misses the mark. Director Bob Rafelson, whose earlier effort was *Five Easy Pieces*, isn't up to the level of that film here. Also with Julia Anne Robinson and Scatman Crothers. (R)   *104 minutes*

KING OF THE GYPSIES (1978)

 ★★

**Sterling Hayden
Eric Roberts
Shelley Winters**

This is a contemporary story of a feuding gypsy family, based on Peter Maas's book. There are some fascinating moments, but mostly the film is disorganized and unconvincing. There's an encouraging debut by Roberts as the young rebel who struggles to escape from the bizarre gypsy world, but Hayden, Winters, Judd Hirsch, and Susan Sarandon are miscast in stereotyped roles. Also with Annette O'Toole and Brooke Shields. It was a good opportunity for an exciting film, but writer-director Frank Pierson missed the mark. (R)   *112 minutes*

KING SOLOMON'S MINES (1950)

★★★★

**Stewart Granger
Deborah Kerr**

Ripsnorting adventure in darkest Africa, with Granger and Kerr heading an exploration team to find Kerr's missing husband and lost diamond mines. The impressive-looking production, based on H. Rider Haggard's novel, is nicely paced and leads to a magnificent climax, and there's adequate excitement and suspense along the way. Also with Richard Carlson, Hugo Haas, and Lowell Gilmore. **Director**—Compton Bennett. (PG) **Academy Award**—Robert Surtees, cinematography (color). **Nomination**—best picture. *102 minutes*

KING'S ROW (1942)

★★★★

**Ann Sheridan
Robert Cummings**

Ann Sheridan, Robert Cummings, and a bedridden Ronald Reagan in King's Row.

A penetrating look at a small American community at the turn of the century, with pettiness and anxieties laid bare. The story unfolds as an early-century *Peyton Place*, with much style and high drama. Superb characterizations abound, and there's plenty of fine acting throughout. Also with Ronald Reagan, Claude Rains, Charles Coburn, and Judith Anderson. **Director**—Sam Wood. **Academy Award Nominations**—Wood, best director; James Wong Howe, cinematography (black and white). *127 minutes b&w*

KISMET (1944)

★★★

**Ronald Colman
Marlene Dietrich**

Adequate telling of the Arabian Nights fable, with a good cast doing its utmost. The production, starring Colman and Dietrich, has a lot of polish,

Marlene Dietrich stars in Kismet, *based on the Arabian Nights tale.*

and there's a striking dance scene with Marlene all aglow in gold body paint. The proceedings could use a bit of levity, but it's worthwhile viewing nevertheless. Also with James Craig, Edward Arnold, Harry Davenport, and Florence Bates. **Director**—William Dieterle. *100 minutes*

KISMET (1955)

★★

**Howard Keel
Ann Blyth**

Disappointing film version, starring Keel and Blyth, of the hit musical stage production of romance and intrigue in Old Baghdad. Alexander Borodin's beautiful music comes over nicely, but the story is off stride. It's nice to listen to, but barely watchable. Also with Vic Damone, Monty Woolley, Dolores Gray, Sebastian Cabot, and Jack Elam. **Director**—Vincente Minnelli. *113 minutes*

KISS ME DEADLY (1955)

★★★★

**Ralph Meeker
Albert Dekker
Cloris Leachman**

It's a dark, grisly adaptation of a Mickey Spillane Mike Hammer mystery—and it may also be the ultimate *film noir*. Meeker stars as a harassed detective who rescues a damsel in distress,

only to find himself caught in a web of corruption and violence, spun by hoods on the trail of radioactive material. You can take it simply as a tight, compelling melodrama, or as a haunting, nightmarish vision of an amoral world rushing toward apocalypse. Either way it's strong stuff, expressively directed by Robert Aldrich. *105 minutes b&w*

KISS ME GOODBYE (1982)

★★

**Sally Field
James Caan
Jeff Bridges**

Jeff Bridges, Sally Field, and her dead husband James Caan in Kiss Me Goodbye.

Patchy, hollow romantic comedy loosely based on the Brazilian film, *Dona Flor and Her Two Husbands*. Field plays a young widow who's about to marry a stuffy Egyptologist (Bridges) when the ghost of her late husband (Caan) appears to stir up trouble. Some of the '30s-style comic complications come across, but the story is essentially so much hot air. The elegant production gets good supporting work from Claire Trevor as the huffy mother of the bride. **Director**—Robert Mulligan. (PG) *101 minutes*

KISS ME KATE (1953)

★★★

**Howard Keel
Kathryn Grayson**

A perky backstage musical taken from
(Continued)

(Continued)
the Broadway hit and filled with Cole Porter's delightful tunes. Keel and Grayson portray married thespians performing in Shakespeare's *Taming of the Shrew* adapted for music. It's decked out nicely with energetic dancing, a touch of comedy, and such great songs as "So In Love," "Wunderbar," and "Brush Up Your Shakespeare." Also among the cast are Ann Miller, Keenan Wynn, Bobby Van, James Whitmore, Tommy Rall, and Bob Fosse. **Director**—George Sidney.

109 minutes

KISS OF DEATH (1947)
★★★★

Victor Mature
Richard Widmark

Victor Mature doing time in the taut gangster thriller Kiss of Death.

Taut, moody gangster thriller played to the hilt for suspense. A thief rats on his pals, and then a ruthless hit man trails him to get revenge. There are outstanding performances by Mature and by Widmark, who is perfectly cast as the giggling, psychopathic killer. Remade as *The Fiend Who Walked the West*. Also with Brian Donlevy, Karl Malden, Mildred Dunnock, and Coleen Gray. **Director**—Henry Hathaway. **Academy Award Nominations**—Widmark, best supporting actor; Eleazar Lipsky, writing (original story). *98 minutes b&w*

KISS TOMORROW GOODBYE
(1950)
★★★

James Cagney
Barbara Payton

Barbara Payton and Helena Carter in Kiss Tomorrow Goodbye.

Cagney plays his typical gangster role in this violent drama that's watchable mainly because of the star's performance. The film, however, isn't up to the level of Cagney's *White Heat*. Here, the tough guy plays an escaped convict who marries and then embarks on some gun-blazing holdups. Also with Ward Bond, Luther Adler, Steve Brodie, and Helena Carter. **Director**—Gordon Douglas. *102 minutes b&w*

KITTY (1945)
★★★

Paulette Goddard
Ray Milland

Another version of the *Pygmalion* story. Set in 18th-century London, the film stars Goddard as a poor girl who be-

Paulette Goddard threatens a shopkeeper in Kitty.

comes a well-mannered woman with the help of an artist, played by Milland. The film is well made and there is excellent use of costumes and period detail. Goddard's performance is tops, and she's nicely assisted by Milland, Cecil Kellaway, Constance Collier, Reginald Owen, Patric Knowles, and Sara Allgood. **Director**—Mitchell Leisen.

103 minutes b&w

KITTY AND THE BAGMAN
(1983)
 ★★

Liddy Clark

From Australia, a slick, semicomic tale of brothels, booze, gambling, and corruption during the '20s. Clark portrays an unlikely rackets boss, yet cannot sustain the credibility of a rather difficult role. Period details are impressive but the chain of frantic events that make up the plot is not. The film is billed as homage to Warner Brothers gangster movies. The Warner folks are likely to cringe a bit. **Director**—Donald Crombie. (R) *95 minutes*

KITTY FOYLE (1940)
★★★★

Ginger Rogers

An above-average love story with a fine performance by Rogers as a working girl who has romantic problems. The film is expertly adapted from Christopher Morley's dramatic novel, and it features other good perfor-

• Klute
• Knightriders
• Knute Rockne—All American
• Kramer vs. Kramer
• Krull
• The Lacemaker

K·L

Ginger Rogers plays a hard-working secretary in Kitty Foyle.

mances from Dennis Morgan, Eduardo Ciannelli, Gladys Cooper, and James Craig. **Director**—Sam Wood. **Academy Award**—Rogers, best actress. **Nominations**—best picture; Wood, best director; Dalton Trumbo, writing (screenplay).

108 minutes b&w

KLUTE (1971)

 ★★★★

**Jane Fonda
Donald Sutherland**

Fonda gives a smashing performance as a sophisticated call girl in this gripping crime thriller. The story involves a small-town cop, played by Sutherland, who comes to New York City to locate a missing friend. During his investigation, he meets Fonda and falls in love with her. Fonda portrays her character expertly, with much credibility and colorful detail, and the film offers some insightful character studies. Also with Charles Cioffi, Roy Scheider, Jean Stapleton, and Rita Gam. **Director**—Alan J. Pakula. (R) **Academy Award**—Fonda, best actress. **Nomination**—Andy and Dave Lewis, best story and screenplay (based on factual material or material not previously published).

114 minutes

KNIGHTRIDERS (1981)

 ★★

**Ed Harris
Gary Lahti**

George Romero (*Night of the Living Dead*) applies the legend of King Arthur to modern-day knights who tour the country staging jousting contests on motorcycles. Harris and Lahti star in a cast of largely unknown actors. The performances are adequate, and the motorcycle stunts are well coordinated, yet there's meager dramatic impetus as these gasoline-propelled warriors pursue honor and glory atop their Harley-Davidsons. In fact, it's rather tame in contrast to Romero's former bloodletting horror excesses. Also with Tom Sauini and Amy Ingersoll. (R)   *145 minutes*

KNUTE ROCKNE—ALL AMERICAN (1940)

★★★

**Pat O'Brien
Gale Page**

This memorable film biography of the famous Notre Dame football coach is perhaps most intriguing since Ronald Reagan became President. O'Brien is very convincing as the determined coach, and Reagan is adequate as George Gipp, the team's star player. The story is rather predictable, with considerable emphasis on gridiron glory. The script contains the indelible locker room plea: "...win it for the Gipper!" Unfortunately, this scene is cut from TV prints due to legal problems. Also co-stars Donald Crisp and Albert Bassermann.   *98 minutes b&w*

KRAMER VS. KRAMER (1979)

 ★★★★

**Dustin Hoffman
Meryl Streep
Jane Alexander
Justin Henry**

A love story about the love of a father and son who really get to know each other when the wife and mother abruptly walks out on them. Hoffman plays the father, Henry is his son, and Streep is the woman trying to find herself; Alexander plays a concerned family friend. Ordinarily, such fare is grist for flimsy soap operas, but this film is blessed with insight, sensitivity, and intelligence; it also dissects a number of current social problems relentlessly. Hoffman, Streep, and six-year-old Henry are in rare form. Also with

Howard Duff and George Coe. **Director**—Robert Benton. (PG) **Academy Awards**—best picture; Benton, best director; Hoffman, best actor; Streep, best supporting actress; Benton, best screenplay (adapted from another medium). **Nominations**—Henry, best supporting actor; Alexander, best supporting actress; Nestor Almendros, cinematography.   *105 minutes*

KRULL (1983)

 ★★

**Ken Marshall
Lysette Anthony**

Lysette Anthony and Ken Marshall are a royal couple on a faraway world in Krull.

Visually striking yet overblown sword-and-sorcery fantasy that borrows brazenly and ineptly from similar sagas, from *King Arthur* to *Star Wars*. Marshall is a prince from a strange planet who fights his way through a predictably treacherous obstacle course to rescue his princess bride (Anthony) from The Beast. Despite the slick special effects and thundering sound track, the derring-do adventure seems stale and monotonous. **Director**—Peter Yates. (PG)   *126 minutes*

L

THE LACEMAKER (1977)

★★★

**Isabelle Huppert
Yves Beneyton**

(Continued)

L
- Lady Chatterley's Lover
- The Lady Eve
- Lady Hamilton
- Lady in a Cage
- Lady in Cement
- Lady in the Dark
- Lady Sings the Blues
- The Land That Time Forgot

(Continued)

Swiss director Claude Goretta's gentle and delicate film is about a tragic affair between mismatched lovers. Huppert dominates the film, with a warmly appealing performance as the sweet-natured beauty parlor assistant who is eventually dismissed by her lover, an intellectual student played by Beneyton. The material is familiar, but Goretta's masterful touch adds the extra sensitivity needed. In French with English titles. (No MPAA rating) *108 minutes*

LADY CHATTERLEY'S LOVER (1982)
 ★★

Sylvia Kristel

This is a disappointing screen adaptation of D. H. Lawrence's classic, smolderingly sexual story. Much of its eroticism is subdued, and the film turns the spotlight instead on the English nobility of the period and their lavish surroundings. Kristel brings minimal sensuality to the role of the frustrated noblewoman. Nicholas Clay co-stars as her gamekeeper lover, and Shane Briant is the war-wounded Lord Chatterley. **Director**—Just Jaecklin. (R) *101 minutes*

THE LADY EVE (1941)
★★★★

Barbara Stanwyck
Henry Fonda

Lively, witty, romantic farce, done in an engaging manner by director Preston Sturges for nonstop mirth. Stanwyck stars as a con artist who tries to pull a fast one on a seemingly gullible rich man, played by Fonda. The spoof progresses at a fast pace, and the laughs come at a gallop. Nice work by Stanwyck and Fonda, with expert support from Charles Coburn, Eugene Pallette, William Demarest, and Eric Blore. **Academy Award Nomination**—Monckton Hoffe, writing (original story). *97 minutes b&w*

LADY HAMILTON
See That Hamilton Woman

LADY IN A CAGE (1964)
 ★★

Olivia de Havilland

Overwrought suspense story about a rich woman trapped in an elevator by some young thugs who vandalize her apartment. There are some tense moments, but most of the film is pretentious and somewhat unsavory. De Havilland is wasted as the harassed and vulnerable widow. Supporting roles are played by James Caan, Ann Sothern, and Jeff Corey. **Director**—Walter Grauman. *97 minutes b&w*

LADY IN CEMENT (1968)
★★

Frank Sinatra
Raquel Welch

More adventures in the life of private-eye Tony Rome. This time the film is dressed up with an added portion of flashy sex and violence. Sinatra again plays the hip gumshoe, and he's on the trail of a killer after discovering a woman's corpse with its feet anchored in cement. There are predictable and plodding proceedings, bogged down with heavy-handed embellishments. Welch and Lainie Kazan add the glamour, with support from Richard Conte and Dan Blocker. **Director**—Gordon Douglas. (PG) *93 minutes*

LADY IN THE DARK (1944)
 ★★★

Ginger Rogers

Ginger Rogers is the Lady in the Dark; *Ray Milland is one of the men in her life.*

A lavish and colorful romantic comedy about a woman magazine editor who suffers mental anguish over the men in her life. Rogers, in the starring role, turns on the charm as the perplexed career girl. And there are ample comic moments for the entire cast, which also features Ray Milland, Warner Baxter, Jon Hall, Mischa Auer, and Barry Sullivan. Adapted from Moss Hart's Broadway musical, but lacking many of the songs. **Director**—Mitchell Leisen. *100 minutes*

LADY SINGS THE BLUES (1972)
 ★★★

Diana Ross
Billy Dee Williams

Diana Ross and Billy Dee Williams in Lady Sings the Blues, *a film about Billie Holiday.*

The tumultuous and tragic life of singing great Billie "Lady Day" Holiday is portrayed with amazing clarity and style by Ross, a singing sensation in her own right. This film biography seems light on facts and heavy on drama, but it's high-level entertainment nevertheless, thanks to Ross's grasp of the role. She belts out the tunes in convincing style, and her straight acting is impressive, too. Williams plays her husband. Also with Richard Pryor and Sid Melton. **Director**—Sidney J. Furie. (R) **Academy Award Nominations**—Ross, best actress; Terence McCloy, Chris Clark, and Suzanne de Passe, best story and screenplay (based on factual material or material not previously published). *144 minutes*

THE LAND THAT TIME FORGOT (1975)
 ★★

Doug McClure

The film, based on an Edgar Rice Bur-

• Lassie Come Home
• Lassiter
• The Last American Virgin
• The Last Angry Man

• The Last Detail
• The Last Embrace
• The Last Flight of Noah's Ark

L

roughs novel, is about German submariners and survivors of a British ship who discover a lost continent where prehistoric beasts roam. A trite and confusing script, but impressive special effects that may appeal to children more than adults. Also with John McEnery, Susan Penhaligon, and Keith Barron. **Director**—Kevin Connor. (PG)   *91 minutes*

LASSIE COME HOME (1943)
★★★★

**Roddy McDowall
Elizabeth Taylor
Donald Crisp**

Big tug at the heartstrings with this sentimental tale about a poor family that must sell its faithful collie, but the loyal dog makes a brave journey back to its familiar home. This is a family film of the highest order, and it spawned a lot of sequels and a TV series. The remarkable cast also includes Edmund Gwenn, Dame May Whitty, Elsa Lanchester, and, of course, Lassie. **Director**—Fred M. Wilcox. **Academy Award Nomination**—Leonard Smith, cinematography (color).   *88 minutes*

LASSITER (1984)
 ★★

**Tom Selleck
Jane Seymour
Lauren Hutton**

Selleck, in the title role, is suave and dressed to the nines as a slick jewel thief in London on the eve of World War II. His assignment: grab $10 million in diamonds from the Nazis before they use the fortune to buy weapons. While Selleck looks good, the film is merely predictable formula stuff that finally succumbs to its own lassitude. Co-stars Bob Hoskins. **Director**—Roger Young. (R)
100 minutes

THE LAST AMERICAN VIRGIN (1983)
 ★

**Lawrence Monoson
Diane Franklin
Steve Antin**

A typical, inane, adolescent exploitation film about the escapades of three high school boys in pursuit of sexual conquests. We get all the familiar situations: confrontations with frantic parents; stuffy teachers; awkward classmates; and lots of eager girls. There's even a locker room peephole scene on the order of *Porky's*. This mindless activity is carried on to the beat of a blaring sound track that features Blondie, The Cars, and The Police. **Director**—Boaz Davidson. (R)
90 minutes

THE LAST ANGRY MAN (1959)
★★★★

Paul Muni

Sensitive story, adapted from Gerald Green's book, about an elderly family doctor in a poor Brooklyn neighborhood, who is more concerned with the welfare of his impoverished patients than with making lots of money. The film makes a strong statement about commercialism within the professions, which obviously rings true about other corners of society. Muni, in his last screen role, is excellent as the idealistic physician. There's good support, too, from David Wayne, Betsy Palmer, and Luther Adler. **Director**—Daniel Mann. **Academy Award Nomination**—Muni, best actor.
100 minutes b&w

THE LAST DETAIL (1973)
 ★★★★

**Jack Nicholson
Otis Young
Randy Quaid**

A true-to-life, bittersweet comedy about justice without mercy in the Navy. Two senior petty officers—Nicholson and Young—escort a young sailor accused of petty theft on a two-day trip to the Portsmouth, New Hampshire, brig. En route, they take pity and treat him to a last fling before his imprisonment. Nicholson shines as the tough but sympathetic career man; Quaid is outstanding as the hapless sailor whose impending punishment doesn't fit the crime. And there are excellent character studies throughout. Also with Clifton James, Carol Kane, and Michael Marty. **Director**—

Jack Nicholson and Otis Young are a couple of lifers—career sailors—in The Last Detail.

Hal Ashby. (R) **Academy Award Nominations**—Nicholson, best actor; Quaid, best supporting actor; Robert Towne, best screenplay (based on material from another medium).
104 minutes

THE LAST EMBRACE (1979)
★★

**Roy Scheider
Janet Margolin**

Scheider plays a worried-looking government agent who believes someone is about to kill him. Margolin is a graduate student who mysteriously enters his life. Scheider and Margolin are excellent; they build suspense by virtue of their acting talents. But director Jonathan Demme's romantic thriller is meager, illogical, and often confusing. The movie winds up at the edge of Niagara Falls; by that time, the story seems all wet. Also with Sam Levene, John Glover, and Christopher Walken. (R)   *102 minutes*

THE LAST FLIGHT OF NOAH'S ARK (1980)
 ★★

**Elliott Gould
Geneviève Bujold
Ricky Schroder
Tammy Lauren**

Disney's takeoff on the well-known Bible story is a pat and predictable adventure film where kids once more get their way with adults. Gould and Bujold crash-land on a Pacific island in a lumbering B-29 full of animals and a couple of stowaway kids; the kids are Schroder and Lauren. They all finally
(Continued)

 Movie is available in Beta and VHS videotape   **223**

L

- The Last Hard Men
- The Last Hurrah
- The Last Married Couple in America
- The Last Metro
- Last of the Red Hot Lovers
- The Last Picture Show

(Continued)

escape by converting the plane into a ship, and they take the animals along at the youngsters' insistence. The animals should have stayed behind. Also with Vincent Gardenia. **Director—** Charles Jarrott. (G)   *97 minutes*

THE LAST HARD MEN (1976)
★★

**Charlton Heston
James Coburn**

Vengeance is the theme of this routine western, set in Arizona in the early 1900s. Coburn plays a half-breed Navajo who lures a retired lawman, played by Heston, to a slow and gruesome death. The plot gallops occasionally, but most often it moves at a slow walk. Coburn and Heston, however, are convincing as the hard-boiled adversaries. Some of the vivid brutality may be hard on the audience. Also with Barbara Hershey, Christopher Mitchum, and Michael Parks. **Director—** Andrew V. McLaglen. (R)   *98 minutes*

THE LAST HURRAH (1958)
★★★★

**Spencer Tracy
Jeffrey Hunter**

Donald Crisp in The Last Hurrah.

Entertaining account of big-city politics, with Tracy expertly portraying a mayor who holds power through shrewdness. Tracy is completely at ease in the role, and he receives top support from a veteran cast. Adapted from Edwin O'Connor's novel, inspired by the career of Boston May-

or James Curley. Also co-stars Pat O'Brien, Basil Rathbone, Edward Brophy, Donald Crisp, James Gleason, John Carradine, Jeffrey Hunter, Dianne Foster, and Wallace Ford. **Director**—John Ford.   *121 minutes b&w*

THE LAST MARRIED COUPLE IN AMERICA (1980)
      ★★

**George Segal
Natalie Wood**

George Segal and Natalie Wood wonder if they're not old-fashioned by staying married in The Last Married Couple in America.

Segal and Wood are Jeff and Mari of Los Angeles, who observe their friends' marriages breaking up and wonder if they're next. The predictable TV-sitcom screenplay is only mildly amusing as it examines the despair of the sexual revolution. The acting, however, is well above the material; Wood is especially good with her comic assignment. And there are some classy scenes with Richard Benjamin, Dom DeLuise, and Valerie Harper. **Director**—Gilbert Cates. (R)
103 minutes

THE LAST METRO (1981)
      ★★★★

Catherine Deneuve

Director François Truffaut (*The 400 Blows; Jules and Jim*) scores again with this affecting story of backstage theater life during the Nazi occupation of Paris. Beautiful Deneuve runs a small

Paris theater by proxy for her husband, a Jewish director who goes into hiding. He's played by Heinz Bennent. Gerard Depardieu is splendid as a rakish actor who turns out to be quite a patriot. A fine supporting cast adds to this charming slice-of-life drama of love and heroism. Also with Jean-Louis Richard, Jean Poiret, and Sabine Haudepin. In French with English titles. (No MPAA rating)   *130 minutes*

LAST OF THE RED HOT LOVERS (1972)
      ★★

Alan Arkin

So-so film version of Neil Simon's stage comedy about the owner of a seafood restaurant who attempts an extramarital fling with three women. Arkin, in the title role, manages to arouse a few smiles as the klutzy Don Juan, but there isn't enough comic energy to sustain the film. All in all, it's not so hot. Also with Paula Prentiss, Sally Kellerman, and Renée Taylor. **Director**—Gene Saks. (PG)
98 minutes

THE LAST PICTURE SHOW (1971)
★★★★

**Timothy Bottoms
Jeff Bridges
Cybill Shepherd
Ben Johnson**

A nostalgic look at life in a small Texas town in the early '50s, as seen through the experiences of some high-school students. There are fine, engrossing characterizations and exquisite atmospheric detail; the film is somewhat of a low-key *American Graffiti*. First-class performances by Bottoms, Bridges, Shepherd, Johnson, Cloris Leachman, and Ellen Burstyn. **Director**—Peter Bogdanovich. (R) **Academy Awards**—Johnson, best supporting actor; Leachman, best supporting actress. **Nominations**—best picture; Bogdanovich, best director; Bridges, best supporting actor; Burstyn, best supporting actress; Larry McMurtry and Bogdanovich, best screenplay (based on material from another medium); Robert Surtees, cinematography.
114 minutes b&w

• The Last Remake of Beau Geste • The Last Tycoon
• The Last Starfighter • The Last Unicorn
• Last Tango in Paris • The Last Waltz
• The Last Winter

L

THE LAST REMAKE OF BEAU GESTE (1977)
★★

**Marty Feldman
Ann-Margret
Michael York
Peter Ustinov**

Marty Feldman and Ann-Margret make a cute couple in The Last Remake of Beau Geste.

Pop-eyed Feldman strikes out on his own as star, director, and writer of this parody of Foreign Legion films, but he's left stranded in the desert. The uneven picture gallops about in fits and starts—at times funny, more often just strained silliness. Feldman borrows generously from his mentor, Mel Brooks, but his execution is heavy-handed and reckless. Some of the barren stretches are shored up by a first-rate cast that also includes Trevor Howard, James Earl Jones, Terry-Thomas, and Henry Gibson. (PG)
83 minutes

THE LAST STARFIGHTER (1984)
 ★★★

**Robert Preston
Lance Guest**

A delectable, intergalactic sugarplum about a bored teenager (Guest) who is visited by a fast-talking extraterrestrial (Preston). The alien decides the youth has just the right stuff to defend an embattled star league against rebel invaders. So he whisks the lad off to a distant planet to challenge evil forces. The film lacks the stylishness and budget of the genre's finest, but it's entertainingly tongue-in-cheek with good sci-fi creatures and effects, and Preston best of all. **Director**—Nick Castle. (PG)
100 minutes

LAST TANGO IN PARIS (1973)
 ★★★

**Marlon Brando
Maria Schneider**

Maria Schneider and Marlon Brando dance in the controversial Last Tango in Paris.

Controversial sex film about a middle-aged American widower and a young French girl who have a torrid love affair. Brando and Schneider play the couple in love. The patchy story is engrossing, but at times it's rather dull. Still, there are a few extraordinary scenes, and, in a most difficult role, Brando gives one of his best performances. Schneider also performs well. The uncut version depicts anal intercourse. The film co-stars Jean-Pierre Léaud. **Director**—Bernardo Bertolucci. (X) **Academy Award Nominations**—Bertolucci, best director; Brando, best actor.
129 minutes

THE LAST TYCOON (1976)
★★

**Robert De Niro
Tony Curtis
Robert Mitchum
Jack Nicholson**

Lethargy pervades this screen version of F. Scott Fitzgerald's unfinished novel about the flourishing Hollywood of the '30s. De Niro plays the film producer who's working himself to death. The all-star cast, including De Niro, Curtis, Mitchum, and Nicholson, is essentially wasted in muted roles. The production is a meandering and wistful story with no real climax. Harold Pinter wrote the screenplay.

Also with Ingrid Boulting, Donald Pleasence, Jeanne Moreau, and Ray Milland. **Director**—Elia Kazan. (PG)
125 minutes

THE LAST UNICORN (1982)
 ★★★

Children will adore this enchanting and magical animated feature. Adults will be charmed as well. Mia Farrow is the voice behind the title character, a lovely lady unicorn who strikes out on a dangerous journey to find her lost companions. The style is unusual, although the plot is sometimes reminiscent of events in *The Wizard of Oz*. Tammy Grimes, Angela Lansbury, and Alan Arkin supply some of the other voices. **Director**—Arthur Rankin, Jr. (G)
88 minutes

THE LAST WALTZ (1978)
★★★

**The Band
Bob Dylan
Neil Young**

Martin Scorsese directed this rock music documentary, focusing on the farewell concert by The Band in 1976 in San Francisco. Interviews with the group's members are interspersed among the musical numbers, which come on full blast in Dolby stereo. Dylan, Young, Joni Mitchell, Neil Diamond, Muddy Waters, and Eric Clapton join in with some rousing songs. Also with Van Morrison and Emmylou Harris. (PG)
117 minutes

THE LAST WINTER (1984)
★★

**Yona Elian
Kathleen Quinlan**

The 1973 Yom Kippur War is the backdrop for this awkward film concerning two women anxiously awaiting the return of their Israeli soldier husbands. The plot relies on a suspense gimmick where each woman identifies the same man, seen in a blurry newsreel of prisoners, as her spouse. Acting is ordinary and the emotional relationship between the women is unimpressive. **Director**—Riki Shelach. (R) *90 minutes*

L

- The Late George Apley
- The Late Show
- Laura
- The Lavender Hill Mob
- Lawman
- Lawrence of Arabia

THE LATE GEORGE APLEY
(1946)
★★★

**Ronald Colman
Peggy Cummins**

Mildy entertaining film based on John P. Marquand's satirical novel about an aristocratic Boston family. It's a sturdy, adequate family comedy, but without any particular snap. There are, however, some good performances by the cast, which also includes Edna Best, Vanessa Brown, Richard Haydn, and Charles Russell. **Director**—Joseph L. Mankiewicz. *98 minutes b&w*

THE LATE SHOW (1977)
★★★

**Art Carney
Lily Tomlin**

Art Carney and Lily Tomlin star in the comedy-mystery The Late Show.

Writer-director Robert Benton creates rich and unforgettable characters in this latter-day version of the '40s private-eye movie. Carney is sensational as an over-the-hill gumshoe who pursues the killer of an old colleague. He's matched by Tomlin's winning performance as his loony sidekick who dabbles in show biz, astrology, and Eastern religions. The top-heavy and complex plot is difficult to unravel, but it pays off in atmosphere rather than in detective-story thrills. Also with Bill Macy, Eugene Roche, Joanna Cassidy, John Considine, and Howard Duff. (PG) **Academy Award Nomination**—Benton, best original screenplay. *94 minutes*

LAURA
(1944)
★★★★

**Dana Andrews
Clifton Webb
Gene Tierney**

Gene Tierney gets Vincent Price excited in Laura.

A gripping murder mystery that's full of surprise, suspense, and atmosphere. A lovely girl, played by Tierney, is supposedly murdered, and a determined detective, played by Andrews, uncovers more than he expected. Webb is outstanding as a cynical columnist. It's a fascinating, classic whodunit with a mature outlook. Also with Judith Anderson, Vincent Price, Dorothy Adams, and Grant Mitchell. **Director**—Otto Preminger. **Academy Award**—Joseph LaShelle, cinematography (black and white). **Nominations**—Preminger, best director; Webb, best supporting actor. *85 minutes b&w*

THE LAVENDER HILL MOB
(1952)
★★★★

**Alec Guinness
Stanley Holloway**

A lively, droll comedy full of sharp wit and smart dialogue. Guinness triumphs as a mild-mannered bank clerk who engineers a clever scheme to steal a fortune in gold bullion from an armored car. The hilarity is relentless, and it ends with an effective, rollicking chase sequence. In this case, crime doesn't pay, but there's a big reward in the laughter. See if you can spot Audrey Hepburn. Also co-stars Sidney James, Alfie Bass, Marjorie Fielding, and John Gregson. **Director**—Charles Crichton. **Academy Award**—T.E.B. Clarke, writing (story and screenplay). **Nomination**—Guinness, best actor. *82 minutes b&w*

LAWMAN (1970)
★★★

**Burt Lancaster
Robert Ryan
Lee J. Cobb**

In Lawman, *Robert Ryan and Lee J. Cobb discuss a murder.*

A top cast helps this grim western story about a showdown between a marshal determined to arrest some lawbreakers and the local citizens who resist his efforts. Lancaster is good as the duty-bound lawman, and Cobb is convincing as the cattleman whose hired hands are involved with the killing of an old man. Also with Sheree North, Robert Duvall, Joseph Wiseman, Albert Salmi, John McGiver, and J. D. Cannon. **Director**—Michael Winner. (PG) *99 minutes*

LAWRENCE OF ARABIA (1962)
★★★★

**Peter O'Toole
Omar Sharif
Arthur Kennedy**

Grandiose epic about the exploits of enigmatic British adventurer T. E. Lawrence in the Middle East during World War I. The film features stunning photography, excellent performances, and an intelligent script;

★ STAR PROFILE

• Leadbelly
• Left Hand of God
• The Legacy

• The Legend of the Lone Ranger
• The Lemon Drop Kid

L

however, it offers little insight into Lawrence, a complex and mysterious character. O'Toole is outstanding in the title role, and there's impressive supporting work from Sharif, Kennedy, Claude Rains, Donald Wolfit, Anthony Quinn, Anthony Quayle, Alec Guinness, and José Ferrer. The spectacle, however, loses some of its impact on the small screen. **Director**—David Lean. **Academy Awards**—best picture; Lean, best director; Fred A. Young, cinematography (color). **Nominations**—O'Toole, best actor; Sharif, best supporting actor; Robert Bolt, best screenplay (based on material from another medium). *221 minutes*

LEADBELLY (1976)
★★★

Roger E. Mosley

An engaging biography of black bluesman Huddie "Leadbelly" Ledbetter who's known best for his songs "Goodnight Irene," "The Rock Island Line," and "The Midnight Special." Mosley plays the title role convincingly, although he occasionally seems too polished; the real Leadbelly spent much of his chaotic life serving time on prison chain gangs and singing in brothels. The film, however, is beautifully photographed and captures much of the old Deep South atmosphere. Gordon Parks directs with much feeling and dwells on Leadbelly's music, which is sung by HiTide Harris. Also with James E. Brodhead and John McDonald. (PG)
126 minutes

LEFT HAND OF GOD (1955)
 ★★

Humphrey Bogart
Gene Tierney
Lee J. Cobb

Bogart stars as an American pilot posing as a Catholic priest in China just after World War II. He gets involved with a renegade warlord, played by Cobb, who is immersed in conflict. The drama plods along, but it's watchable because of the top cast, which is much better than the material. Also co-stars E. G. Marshall, Agnes Moorehead, and Benson Fong. **Director**—Edward Dmytryk. *87 minutes*

CARY GRANT

Cary Grant was born Archibald Alexander Leach in 1904 in Bristol, England. He ran away from a poverty-stricken home at 13 to join an acrobatic troupe as a song-and-dance man. The troupe came to New York in 1920, and Grant stayed on to work as a lifeguard at Coney Island. In 1923, he returned to England to work in musical comedies, and he caught the attention of Arthur Hammerstein who brought him back to New York to appear in Golden Dawn, *a Broadway musical.*

Grant then went on to Hollywood and made his film debut in This Is the Night *(1932). After appearing in supporting roles, he established his reputation as a debonair leading man, usually in screwball comedies. For more than three decades, he was a leading box-office draw. Although he never won an Academy Award for a specific performance, Grant received a special Oscar in 1970.*

Grant has been married five times. His fourth wife, Dyan Cannon, bore him a daughter when he was past 60. In the mid '60s, he retired from movies and became an executive for a cosmetics company.

Grant's many films include She Done Him Wrong *(1933),* The Awful Truth *(1937),* Topper *(1937),* Bringing Up Baby *(1938),* Gunga Din *(1939),* My Favorite Wife *(1940),* His Girl Friday *(1940),* The Philadelphia Story *(1940),* Arsenic and Old Lace *(1944),* Notorious *(1946),* Mr. Blandings Builds His Dream House *(1948),* To Catch a Thief *(1955),* An Affair to Remember *(1957),* Indiscreet *(1958),* North by Northwest *(1959),* Charade *(1963), and his last movie,* Walk, Don't Run *(1966).*

THE LEGACY (1979)
★

Katharine Ross
Sam Elliott

Ross and Elliott are Los Angeles architects who travel to England to study a stately mansion inhabited by followers of Satan. In this dreary horror film, numerous gruesome deaths are offered to heighten the shock effect: a man is burned to a crisp, another has his throat brutally slashed, and someone else chokes to death. All this is sickening—not scary. The Devil's power is finally passed to Ross; let's hope she doesn't use it to make another movie like this. Also with John Standing, Ian Hogg, and Margaret Tyzack. **Director**—Richard Marquand. (R) *100 minutes*

THE LEGEND OF THE LONE RANGER (1981)
★

Klinton Spillsbury
Michael Horse

The legend is better off dormant if this bland version is the best that can be done with it. This straight-faced western tells the story of the well-known champion of justice—why he put on a mask and chose to fight crime. But the film is so out of kilter and so innocuous that some of the serious dialogue provokes unintentional laughter. Clean-cut Spillsbury plays the title role; Horse plays Tonto. Neither makes much impact. Who was that masked man? Who cares? Also with Jason Robards and Christopher Lloyd. **Director**—William A. Frakar. (PG) *98 minutes*

THE LEMON DROP KID (1951)
★★★

Bob Hope
Marilyn Maxwell

Lots of laughs and lots of sentiment in this well-made film, based on a Damon Runyon story. Hope plays a bookie who's in hock with the mob, and he must pay or face the consequences. Bob is right at home in this
(Continued)

L
• Lenny
• Let No Man Write My Epitaph
• Let's Do It Again
• Let's Scare Jessica to Death
• The Letter
• Letter from an Unknown Woman
• A Letter to Three Wives

(Continued) colorful vehicle set in New York City during the Christmas season. "Silver Bells" is the memorable song. Also with Lloyd Nolan, Jane Darwell, Andrea King, Fred Clark, and Jay C. Flippen. **Director**—Sidney Landfield.

91 minutes b&w

LENNY (1974)

 ★★★★

Dustin Hoffman
Valerie Perrine

Dustin Hoffman accompanies a battered Valerie Perrine in the biographical film Lenny.

Hoffman gives a powerhouse performance as the controversial nightclub performer Lenny Bruce, known best for his obscene monologues. The biographical film follows Lenny's rocky career, from his meager beginning to many run-ins with the law, and finally to his death from an overdose of drugs. Perrine is convincing as the faithful wife, stripper Honey Harlowe, who suffers along with her husband. Jan Miner, Stanley Beck, and Gary Morton also star. **Director**—Bob Fosse. (R) **Academy Award Nominations**—best picture; Fosse, best director; Hoffman, best actor; Perrine, best actress; Julian Barry, best screenplay (adapted from other material); Bruce Surtees, cinematography.

111 minutes b&w

LET NO MAN WRITE MY EPITAPH (1960)

★★

James Darren
Shelley Winters

A second-rate sequel to *Knock on Any*

Burl Ives and Shelley Winters in the slum-drama Let No Man Write My Epitaph.

Door that also focuses on the squalor of slum living. Darren stars as a poor youth with ambitions to be a classical pianist, but the harshness of his environment becomes an obstacle. Winters plays his drug-addicted mother. Some top players live up to their reputations in this film. Also with Burl Ives, Sal Mineo, Jean Seberg, Ricardo Montalban, and Ella Fitzgerald. **Director**—Philip Leacock.

106 minutes b&w

LET'S DO IT AGAIN (1975)

 ★★★

Sidney Poitier
Bill Cosby

Two lodge brothers—Poitier and Cosby—raise money for a new temple and raise lots of laughs, too, by fixing a prizefight and ripping off the mob. It's reminiscent of an Amos 'n' Andy comic adventure, only brought up to contemporary standards and tastes. Cosby is a howl, and Poitier makes an effective straight man. A fine supporting cast also includes Calvin Lockhart, Jimmie Walker, Ossie Davis, and Denise Nicholas. **Director**—Poitier. (PG)

112 minutes

LET'S SCARE JESSICA TO DEATH (1971)

 ★★

Zohra Lampert
Barton Heyman

Routine horror tale about a woman who recuperates from a nervous breakdown in an old country home where she hears strange sounds and sees creepy visions. There's enough here to generate a few screams, but there's nothing remarkable. Also with Kevin O'Connor and Mari-Claire Costello. **Director**—John Hancock. (PG)

89 minutes

THE LETTER (1940)

 ★★★★

Bette Davis
Herbert Marshall

Davis is outstanding as a woman who killed a man—apparently in self-defense—but a letter she wrote tells a different story. This Somerset Maugham story, set in Malaya, is well done and features some first-class performances; Davis is especially convincing. William Wyler's direction is on target. Also with James Stephenson, Sen Yung, Frieda Inescort, and Gale Sondergaard. **Academy Award Nominations**—best picture; Wyler, best director; Davis, best actress; Stephenson, best supporting actor; Gaetano Gaudio, cinematography (black and white).

95 minutes b&w

LETTER FROM AN UNKNOWN WOMAN (1948)

★★★★

Joan Fontaine
Louis Jourdan

A superior tearjerker about a woman who's madly in love with a suave, callow pianist, but he doesn't sincerely return her affection. Stunningly produced and set in Vienna, with the charm of the city much in evidence. Fontaine plays the woman, and Jourdan is the dashing musician. Also with Mady Christians, Art Smith, and Marcel Journet. **Director**—Max Ophuls.

89 minutes b&w

A LETTER TO THREE WIVES (1948)

★★★★

Jeanne Crain
Ann Sothern
Linda Darnell

Three women receive a letter from a mutual friend that says she has run

• Lianna
• Lies My Father Told Me

• The Life and Times of
  Grizzly Adams
• Life at the Top
• Lifeboat

L

Linda Darnell, Ann Sothern, and Jeanne Crain curse the postman in A Letter to Three Wives.

off with one of their husbands, but doesn't say which. The wives react by reexamining their marriages in a series of flashbacks. There are lots of ironic revelations, with expert direction and some fine acting from a good cast. Also with Kirk Douglas and Paul Douglas. A superior achievement from writer-director Joseph L. Mankiewicz. **Academy Awards**—Mankiewicz, best director; Mankiewicz, writing (screenplay). **Nomination**—best picture. *102 minutes b&w*

LIANNA (1983)

★★

Linda Griffiths
Jon De Vries

Writer-director John Sayles presents a flaccid tale of a young wife who falls in love with another woman when her marriage to an arrogant college professor collapses. At the beginning the film seems to promise some intelligent treatment of family emotions, but once attention turns to the lesbian encounters things gradually deteriorate into drab melodrama. Griffiths is only occasionally convincing in the title role. De Vries is somewhat better as the insecure husband. (R) *110 minutes*

LIES MY FATHER TOLD ME (1975)
★★★

Yossi Yadin
Len Birman
Jeffrey Lynas

A warm, colorful story about the close relationship between a six-year-old Jewish boy and his grandfather, a junk

man, in Montreal during the 1920s. The boy's father is an unsuccessful inventor who constantly seeks financial help from the bearded and deeply religious grandfather. There's sensitive direction by Jan Kada and appealing performances from Lynas, Birman, and Yadin. Also with Marilyn Lightstone. (PG) **Academy Award Nomination**—Ted Allen, best original screenplay. *102 minutes*

THE LIFE AND TIMES OF GRIZZLY ADAMS (1976)

★★

Dan Haggerty

The story of James Adams, a late-1800s trapper-mountaineer, who supposedly befriended lots of animals, including a big bear, while exiled in the wilderness. Disney-type sweetness and sentimentality abounds, but it's hardly a believable tale. The animals come off as polished actors, and a bearded Haggerty makes an impressive denizen of the forest. Filmed in Utah's Wasatch Mountains. Also with Don Shanks, Lisa Jones, and Marjorie Harper. **Director**—Richard Friedenberg. (G) *93 minutes*

LIFE AT THE TOP (1965)
★★

Laurence Harvey
Jean Simmons

This sequel to the well-made *Room at the Top* is routine and predictable at best, although there are a few worthwhile scenes. The story continues 10 years later, with Joe Lampton, played by Harvey, married to the daughter of

his boss. He's financially secure, but restless and unhappy, and involved in an affair. Harvey's performance is adequate, and he gets worthy support from Simmons as his unhappy wife. Also with Honor Blackman, Michael Craig, Margaret Johnston, Donald Wolfit, and Robert Morley. **Director**—Ted Kotcheff. *117 minutes b&w*

LIFEBOAT (1944)
★★★

Tallulah Bankhead
Walter Slezak

Hume Cronyn, Mary Anderson, and John Hodiak are among the survivors of a U-boat attack in Lifeboat.

Searing drama about survivors of a passenger ship, that was sunk by a German submarine during World War II. A group of passengers, including the commander of the attacking U-boat, are adrift together at sea and lay their emotions bare. Director Alfred Hitchcock handles the confined and stressful situation with amazing skill and extracts excellent performances from an interesting cast. Bankhead is outstanding as a pampered wealthy woman, and Slezak is convincing as the Nazi skipper. Also with Henry Hull, John Hodiak, Canada Lee, and William Bendix. **Academy Award Nominations**—Hitchcock, best director; John Steinbeck, writing (original story); Glen MacWilliams, cinematography (black and white). *96 minutes b&w*

L
- Lifeguard
- Life Is a Bed of Roses
- The Life of Brian
- Life with Father
- Li'l Abner
- Lilies of the Field
- Limelight
- The Lion in Winter

LIFEGUARD (1976)
★★

**Sam Elliott
Anne Archer
Kathleen Quinlan**

Lifeguards, unlike blondes, don't have more fun—at least when they're over the hill at age 32. This is a rather somber sociological study of one such aging southern California beach boy who exists as a perennial adolescent. Ron Koslow's lucid screenplay adroitly explores a series of personal conflicts, but without sufficient passion or energy. Elliott does well in the title role. Also with Stephen Young, Steve Burns, and Parker Stevenson. **Director**—Daniel Petrie. (PG)   *96 minutes*

LIFE IS A BED OF ROSES (1983)
★★

**Vittorio Gassman
Geraldine Chaplin**

Director Alain Resnais's fragile and elusive comedy shuffles back and forth from an exotic past to an absurd present with side trips to a fairy tale world of allegory. The shuffling takes place at a castle in the French countryside that is used as a pleasure palace (past) and a school of philosophy (present). The Resnais style is everywhere, but the comedy is thin when it should be witty. With Fanny Ardant. In French with English titles. (No rating)
111 minutes

THE LIFE OF BRIAN (1979)
 ★★★

**Graham Chapman
John Cleese
Terry Gilliam
Eric Idle
Terry Jones
Michael Palin**

Those rascals, England's Monty Python comic troupe, have really done it this time. They parody the story of Christ in this outrageous and hilarious comedy that stops at nothing in taking apart various biblical legends. Chapman plays Brian of Nazareth, a ne'er-do-well Judean, who is reluctantly chosen messiah. Many routines are masterpieces of satire and burlesque. **Director**—Jones. (R)   *93 minutes*

LIFE WITH FATHER (1947)
 ★★★★

**William Powell
Irene Dunne**

Charming and handsomely mounted screen version of the Broadway hit play about coming of age in turn-of-the-century New York under the influence of an eccentric patriarch. Powell is outstanding as the irascible head of the family, and Dunne does well as his long-suffering wife. The film is based on Clarence Day's book and the Lindsay and Crouse stage production. Others in the cast include Edmund Gwenn, Zasu Pitts, Elizabeth Taylor, Martin Milner, and Jimmy Lydon. **Director**—Michael Curtiz. **Academy Award Nominations**—Powell, best actor; Peverell Marley and William V. Skall, cinematography (color).
118 minutes

LI'L ABNER (1959)
★★★

**Leslie Parrish
Peter Palmer
Stubby Kaye**

Al Capp's wonderful cartoon characters come to life on the screen with plenty of energy and color, as taken from the Broadway musical. The comedy is strictly cornpone, but the music and dance numbers are done with extraordinary vigor. Palmer is believable in the title role, Parrish is fetching as Daisy Mae, and Kaye makes a good Marryin' Sam. Other denizens of Dogpatch include Howard St. John, Julie Newmar, Stella Stevens, Robert Strauss, and Billie Hayes. **Director**—Melvin Frank.   *113 minutes*

LILIES OF THE FIELD (1963)
★★★★

**Sidney Poitier
Lilia Skala**

Charming, sentimental drama starring Poitier as a jack-of-all-trades who helps a group of German nuns, led by Skala, build a chapel in New Mexico. The film is done on a small scale, but it offers a large portion of enjoyment, especially for Poitier's Oscar-winning performance. Ralph Nelson's direction is nicely paced. Also with Lisa Mann, Isa Crino, and Stanley Adams. **Academy Award**—Poitier, best actor. **Nominations**—best picture; Skala, best supporting actress; James Poe, best screenplay (based on material from another medium); Ernest Haller, cinematography (black and white).
94 minutes b&w

LIMELIGHT (1952)
 ★★★★

**Charles Chaplin
Claire Bloom**

Charles Chaplin keeps Claire Bloom from committing suicide in the poignant Limelight.

The wonderful skills of Chaplin are in full evidence in this touching love story set in London. Chaplin is charming and sentimental as a broken-down music-hall comedian who prevents the suicide of a ballerina, played by Bloom. There are many tender and compassionate scenes as only Chaplin could envision them. Bloom's brilliant performance is a fine compliment to the heartwarming production. Buster Keaton, Sydney Chaplin, and Nigel Bruce also star. **Director**—Charles Chaplin.   *144 minutes b&w*

THE LION IN WINTER (1968)
 ★★★★

**Katharine Hepburn
Peter O'Toole**

Fantastic acting by O'Toole and Hepburn adorns this splendid drama set in medieval England. O'Toole is a magnificent Henry II, and Hepburn is tremendous as Eleanor of Aquitaine. They are lovers who square off on

• A Lion Is in the Streets
• Lion of the Desert
• Lipstick
• Liquid Sky
• Lisztomania
• Little Big Man
• Little Caesar

L

Christmas Eve as the fate of the throne is debated. There are some dry moments, but many high-powered scenes dominate the film. Also with Jane Merrow, John Castle, and Anthony Hopkins. **Director**—Anthony Harvey. **Academy Awards**—Hepburn, best actress; James Goldman, best screenplay (based on material from another medium). **Nominations**—best picture; Harvey, best director; O'Toole, best actor. *134 minutes*

A LION IS IN THE STREETS
(1953)
★★★

James Cagney

Cagney gives a striking portrayal of a power-hungry politician with humble roots in this intense drama, which leans somewhat on *All the King's Men*. The plot goes astray now and then, but there's enough energy in the production to sustain interest. An expected climax has Cagney caught up in corruption, which brings on his decline; it's among Cagney's best roles. Also with Barbara Hale, Anne Francis, Warner Anderson, Jeanne Cagney, and Lon Chaney, Jr. **Director**—Raoul Walsh. *88 minutes*

LION OF THE DESERT (1981)
★★★

Anthony Quinn
Oliver Reed

Quinn plays a wise and majestic Bedouin warrior who wages a relentless and effective guerrilla campaign against the Italian occupiers of Libya from 1912 to 1931. Reportedly costing more than $30 million, the film is of epic proportions, with sweeping battle scenes of the determined Bedouins at times humiliating the well-equipped Fascist troops. A thread of propaganda runs through the spectacle, but this doesn't detract from its superb vigor and style. **Director**—Moustapha Akkad. (PG) *160 minutes*

LIPSTICK (1976)
 ★

Margaux Hemingway
Chris Sarandon

In *Lipstick*, *Margaux Hemingway comforts her younger sister Mariel.*

This disappointing film about rape is a bad debut for Margaux Hemingway. A beautiful photographer's model, played by Margaux, is raped by a shy music teacher. After the rapist goes free and attacks her younger sister, she arms herself with a rifle and seeks revenge. Mariel Hemingway, Margaux's 14-year-old sister, plays her sister in the film, and delivers a surprisingly impressive performance. Also with Anne Bancroft, Perry King, and Robin Gammell. **Director**—Lamont Johnson (R) *89 minutes*

LIQUID SKY (1983)
 ★★★

Anne Carlisle

An odd-ball, stylishly photographed sci-fi tragicomedy that should find a comfortable following on the midnight movie circuit. The somewhat absurd storyline concerns aliens who visit Manhattan in search of drugs. They murder by remote control while their victims are having sex and extract drugs from their bodies. Soviet emigré Slava Tsukerman directed this curiosity, which delves surrealistically into the new wave drug/rock scene. With Paula Sheppard. (R) *118 minutes*

LISZTOMANIA (1975)
 ★★

Roger Daltrey

Ken Russell wrote and directed this glittering and noisy movie, which portrays Franz Liszt and Richard Wagner as the pop stars of their time. At first, it's amusing, but quickly becomes overblown and garish. Daltrey, who starred in *Tommy*, plays Liszt. Ringo Starr portrays the Pope. Also with Sara Kestelman, Paul Nicholas, Fiona Lewis, and John Justin. (R) *105 minutes*

LITTLE BIG MAN (1970)
 ★★★★

Dustin Hoffman

Episodic western tale seen through the experiences of 121-year-old Jack Crabb, the sole survivor of Custer's last stand, who is played by Hoffman. The compelling film offers a grand tour of a portion of American history with liberal doses of satire and pathos. Perhaps this is a milestone film because it treated American Indians with genuine understanding. The complex story climaxes with Custer's defeat at the Little Big Horn. Also stars Martin Balsam, Faye Dunaway, Chief Dan George, and Richard Mulligan. Directed with extraordinary care by Arthur Penn. (PG) **Academy Award Nomination**—George, best supporting actor. *157 minutes*

LITTLE CAESAR (1930)
★★★★

Edward G. Robinson

(Continued)

Edward G. Robinson is the compelling gangster Little Caesar.

L
- Little Darlings
- The Little Drummer Girl
- The Little Foxes
- The Little Girl Who Lives Down the Lane
- Little Miss Marker
- A Little Night Music
- A Little Romance

(Continued)

More than 50 years later, this classic gangster movie is still fascinating. Robinson is magnificent as Enrico Bandello, the ruthless killer who takes over a gang of criminals and then is gunned down by the cops. The pace is fast, the story is exciting, and it even features a special style of sly humor. A young-looking Edward G. did such a convincing job with the role that he became identified with the character throughout his career. Also with Douglas Fairbanks, Jr., Glenda Farrell, William Collier, Jr., Stanley Fields, and Sidney Blackmer. **Director**—Mervyn Le Roy. **Academy Award Nomination**—Francis Faragoh and Robert N. Lee, writing (adaptation).

77 minutes b&w

LITTLE DARLINGS
(1980)

 ★

Kristy McNichol
Tatum O'Neal

How times have changed. Young Elizabeth Taylor's main concern in the '40s was whether National Velvet would win the crucial horse race. But in this shabby movie, teenagers McNichol and O'Neal race to see which one will be the first to lose her virginity. The youngsters are appealing, and they are certainly better than the simpleminded script. Despite the sexual titillation and exploitation, the ending is socially redeeming; yet the film leaves a bad aftertaste. Andy Hardy, where are you? Also with Kris Erickson and Armand Assante. **Director**—Ronald Maxwell. (R)   *92 minutes*

THE LITTLE DRUMMER GIRL
(1984)

 ★★

Diane Keaton

Overly complicated, implausible film adaptation of John Le Carre's best-selling spy yarn that is rather complex in the first place. Keaton, as an actress recruited by Israeli agents to trap a Palestinian terrorist, is lost in the convoluted shuffle. There's little room to develop sympathetic, fleshed-out characters in this lavish, overplotted story that marches out of step. Yorgo

Voyagis and Klaus Kinski co-star. **Director**—George Roy Hill.

130 minutes

THE LITTLE FOXES (1941)
★★★★

Bette Davis
Herbert Marshall
Teresa Wright

High drama with sharp characterizations about a Southern family involved in various nasty schemes. Davis is the formidable head of this clan of connivers, and she's at her bitchy best. The film is expertly adapted from Lillian Hellman's play. Other fine performances by Marshall, Wright, Dana Andrews, Dan Duryea, Charles Dingle, and Patricia Collinge. **Director**—William Wyler. **Academy Award Nominations**—best picture; Wyler, best director; Davis, best actress; Collinge, best supporting actress; Hellman, writing (screenplay).

116 minutes b&w

THE LITTLE GIRL WHO LIVES DOWN THE LANE (1977)

 ★★★

Jodie Foster
Martin Sheen
Alexis Smith

Foster comes across with a first-rate performance in this provocative thriller. She plays a composed and independent 13-year-old who dispatches a few nasty adults with aplomb. The script is flawed in part, but the suspense is good, and there's a moving love affair between Foster and Scott Jacoby, who supports her endeavors. Also with Mort Shuman. **Director**—Nicholas Gessner. (PG)   *94 minutes*

LITTLE MISS MARKER (1980)

 ★★★

Walter Matthau
Julie Andrews
Tony Curtis

Matthau is excellent as the grumpy gambler Sorrowful Jones, in this fourth version of Damon Runyon's sentimental tale. Originally, it starred Shirley Temple. In this film, new-

Julie Andrews, Walter Matthau, and little Sara Stimson in Little Miss Marker.

comer Sara Stimson plays the cute kid left in the care of Sorrowful as an IOU (or marker) for a gambling debt. Matthau's special style of sour, cynical humor saves the unlikely story. There's a great comic scene where "bought" jockeys knock themselves out restraining their mounts so a long shot can win. Andrews plays a once-wealthy socialite, and Curtis is a gangster. Also with Bob Newhart. **Director**—Walter Bernstein. (PG)   *112 minutes*

A LITTLE NIGHT MUSIC (1978)
★★

Elizabeth Taylor
Diana Rigg

This film version of the hit Broadway musical doesn't transfer successfully to the screen. The production looks elegant, but it's uneven, slow, and flat-footed. Even Taylor, somewhat plump and matronly, isn't that effective as the seductive Desiree Armfeldt. Stephen Sondheim's enchanting music and lyrics shine through and lift the spirits at times. Also with Len Cariou, Hermione Gingold, and Lesley-Anne Down. **Director**—Harold Prince. (PG)

124 minutes

A LITTLE ROMANCE (1979)

 ★★

Laurence Olivier
Arthur Hill
Sally Kellerman

• A Little Sex
• The Littlest Horse Thieves
• Live and Let Die
• Local Hero
• Logan's Run
• Lola
• Lolita

L

Director George Roy Hill's comedy of puppy love in Paris is too cute and often trite. Two teenagers, the son of a taxi driver and a rich American girl, run off to Venice to kiss under the Bridge of Sighs. The kids are played by Thelonious Bernard and Diane Lane. The couple is helped on the romantic escapade by a softhearted pickpocket, played by Olivier. The kids are winsome while the great Olivier, in a Maurice Chevalier role, hams it up shamelessly. Kellerman and Hill are wasted as Lane's concerned parents. Also with Broderick Crawford. (PG) **Academy Award Nomination**—Allan Burns, best screenplay (adapted from another medium). *108 minutes*

A LITTLE SEX (1982)
★★

Tim Matheson
Kate Capshaw

Matheson stars in this trite, meandering comedy about marital infidelity. There are a few amusing moments as Matheson chases just about every skirt in Manhattan, but the film is primarily talkative sit-com stuff with a predictable ending. The theme of the philanderer is familiar grist for the movie mill and by now it needs a little more originality than it's given here. **Director**—Bruce Paltrow. (R) *94 minutes*

THE LITTLEST HORSE THIEVES (1977)
★★★

Alastair Sim
Peter Barkworth

A trio of charming children come to the rescue of pit ponies slated for the glue factory when new machinery is introduced in a small English mining town. The pleasant Walt Disney adventure, set in picturesque Yorkshire, is rather bland, but the story relates well to children and their feelings toward animals. The film also makes a modest statement about the working conditions of miners. The children—Andrew Harrison, Benjie Bolgar, and Chloe Franks—handle their parts with sentimental appeal. Also with Maurice Colbourne and Susan Tebbs. **Director**—Charles Jarrott. (G) *104 minutes*

LIVE AND LET DIE (1973)
★★★

Roger Moore
Yaphet Kotto
Jane Seymour

Yaphet Kotto wonders if Roger Moore is comfortable in Live and Let Die.

Moore stars as superspy James Bond in this eighth agent 007 film, with the usual doses of tongue-in-cheek humor, wonderful gadgets, and sexy women. This time, our hero is after a formidable drug dealer, operating out of exotic Caribbean territory. It's pretty much the same sort of wild chases, narrow escapes, and so on, and pretty much the same amount of fun. Also with Clifton James, Bernard Lee, Lois Maxwell, David Hedison, and Geoffrey Holder. **Director**—Guy Hamilton. (PG) *121 minutes*

LOCAL HERO (1983)
★★★★

Peter Riegert
Burt Lancaster

Houston oil men want to buy up a picturesque Scottish fishing village to construct a refinery. Eager young company man Riegert is dispatched to make the deal. The townsfolk are only too eager to sell and pocket all those American dollars. A great setup for social commentary and two-way culture shock, and the movie treads this tricky path with total confidence, pointing up the idiosyncrasies of both sides with affection and accuracy. There's a wonderful performance from Lancaster as the oil company's head honcho. Bill Forsyth (*Gregory's Girl*) directed this wry, understated comedy with great attention to detail—the supporting cast is a delight. (PG) *110 minutes*

LOGAN'S RUN (1976)
★

Michael York
Richard Jordan
Jenny Agutter

A science-fiction adventure set in the 23rd century, when people reside in an elaborate, dome-enclosed city and aren't allowed to live past their 30th birthday. Those who try to avoid "renewal" and escape to the outside are chased and killed by special policemen. The elaborate production seems typical of many sci-fi films, with artificial sets that look as if they were borrowed from Disneyland. There is equally artificial action; York gives an unmoving performance as a turncoat policeman who does make it to the outside. Also with Roscoe Lee Browne, Farrah Fawcett-Majors, and Peter Ustinov. **Director**—Michael Anderson. (PG) *120 minutes*

LOLA (1982)
★★★

Barbara Sukowa

One of the last films of the late German director Rainer Werner Fassbinder examines moral corruption against the background of West Germany's amazing period of reconstruction in the '50s. The film is populated with intriguing characters, expertly realized by a fine cast. Sukowa plays Lola, a bewitching cabaret singer with powerful connections in business and politics. In German with English titles. (R) *114 minutes*

LOLITA (1962)
★★★

James Mason
Shelley Winters
Sue Lyon

This screen version of Vladimir Nabokov's sensational novel is watered down, but it's still effective. Mason performs well as the professor who's infatuated with a 14-year-old temptress, played by Lyon. To be near her, he marries her mother, played by Winters. The film offers notable moments
(Continued)

L

- The Loneliness of the Long Distance Runner
- Lonely Are the Brave
- The Lonely Guy
- The Lonely Lady
- Lone Wolf McQuade
- Long Day's Journey into Night

Peter Sellers and Shelley Winters make chitchat at a party in Lolita.

(Continued)

of satire and drama, and it's as bizarre as the book. First-class performances from Winters and Peter Sellers. Also with Marianne Stone and Diana Decker. **Director**—Stanley Kubrick. *152 minutes b&w*

THE LONELINESS OF THE LONG DISTANCE RUNNER
(1962)
★★★★

Tom Courtenay
Michael Redgrave

An exceptional story of a delinquent youth in a reform school who attains recognition by competing in track contests. Courtenay plays rebellious youth, and Redgrave plays the school headmaster. Magnificent direction by Tony Richardson and all-around excellent performances maintain interest from start to finish. The film, which is brilliantly photographed and exquisitely produced, ends with a rousing big race sequence. Also with James Bolam, Avis Bunnage, and Alec McCowen. *103 minutes b&w*

LONELY ARE THE BRAVE (1962)
★★★

Kirk Douglas

An unusual western about a middle-aged cowboy who gets himself thrown into jail to rescue a friend. The friend refuses to leave, so Douglas breaks out

and runs for Mexico; he escapes the posse that pursues him, but not the modern world. It's an excellent juxtaposition of old and new life-styles, with a strong, sardonic ending. Douglas is in top form as the fugitive cowhand. The supporting cast includes Walter Matthau, Gena Rowlands, Michael Kane, Carroll O'Connor, and George Kennedy. **Director**—David Miller. *107 minutes b&w*

THE LONELY GUY
(1984)
★★

Steve Martin
Charles Grodin

In The Lonely Guy, Steve Martin's best friend is his plant.

An uneven, schmaltzy comedy loosely constructed on Bruce Jay Friedman's "Lonely Guy's Book of Life." Martin stars in this thinly plotted tour of the single scene in New York City. He seems comfortable enough with the part and there are a few isolated moments of genuine hilarity. But the viewer most likely will come away lonely for consistent amusement. Judith Ivey co-stars. **Director**—Arthur Hiller. (R) *93 minutes*

THE LONELY LADY (1983)
★

Pia Zadora

One of Harold Robbins's minor novels

is adapted to the screen with minimal results. The predictable soap-opera story involves a young, energetic writer (Zadora) who struggles to success in Hollywood after marrying a famous screenwriter (Lloyd Bochner) who is old enough to be her father. Soft-porn queen Zadora stands out among the second-rate cast, and that really isn't saying much. **Director**—Peter Sasdy. (R) *92 minutes*

LONE WOLF McQUADE (1983)
★★

Chuck Norris
David Carradine

Chuck Norris welcomes his neighbors in Lone Wolf McQuade.

Remember the spaghetti western? Well, here's a taco western set near the U.S.-Mexican border. Martial arts champ Norris is in the title role as a no-nonsense Texas Ranger. Macho action explodes all over the screen, involving assorted weaponry and the usual quota of karate fights. There's abundant mayhem, beside which such details as the plot and the acting seem merely superfluous. **Director**—Steve Carver. (PG) *105 minutes*

LONG DAY'S JOURNEY INTO
NIGHT (1962)
★★★★

Ralph Richardson
Katharine Hepburn
Jason Robards, Jr.

Eugene O'Neill's brilliant autobio-

234

• The Longest Day   • The Long Gray Line
• The Longest Yard   • The Long Hot Summer
• The Long Good Friday   • Long John Silver

L

graphical play is transposed to the screen with considerable richness, and it's superbly highlighted with fine acting. The stagey but compelling production is about a Connecticut family in the early 1900s, beset with emotional problems. Hepburn is fantastic as a drug-addicted wife, and Richardson is outstanding as her overbearing actor-spouse. Robards repeats his fine stage performance as the alcoholic eldest son. Sidney Lumet directs the film with care, and the result is astonishing impact. Also with Dean Stockwell and Jeanne Barr. **Academy Award Nomination**—Hepburn, best actress.
136 minutes b&w

THE LONGEST DAY (1962)

 ★★★

John Wayne
Robert Mitchum
Henry Fonda
Robert Ryan
Rod Steiger

Sprawling, ambitious war saga about the Allied invasion in Normandy during World War II, starring an army of well-known actors. The film is impressive for its grand details of the various events of the D-Day landings, but the huge cast is spread around rather thinly, thereby thwarting proper characterizations. Yet the spectacular account offers relentless fascination. Also among the huge cast are Robert Wagner, Stuart Whitman, Steve Forrest, Richard Todd, Richard Burton, Sean Connery, and Peter Lawford. **Directors**—Andrew Marton, Ken Annakin, and Bernhard Wicki. **Academy Award**—Jean Bourgoin, Henri Persin, Walter Wottitz, cinematography (black and white). **Nomination**—best picture.
180 minutes b&w

THE LONGEST YARD (1975)

 ★★

Burt Reynolds
Eddie Albert

The movie is about life in prison, where the good guys are the cons and the bad guys are the guards. Reynolds plays a former professional football star who is sent to prison. Albert is the warden who sponsors a semi-pro team composed of the prison's guards. The

In The Longest Yard, *Burt Reynolds is a former pro football star who's sent to prison.*

cons put together a team, quarterbacked by Reynolds, and fight it out with the guards in a ferocious gridiron battle. Some fun, but hardly believable. Also with Ed Lanter, Michael Conrad, and James Hampton. **Director**—Robert Aldrich. (R) *123 minutes*

THE LONG GOOD FRIDAY (1982)

 ★★★

Bob Hoskins

A finely crafted British gangster movie in the tradition of those Hollywood underworld classics that made Edward G. Robinson and James Cagney famous. Hoskins is in rare form as a London crime bigwig struggling to keep his empire intact. At times the violence is overwhelming, and the British accents can be a problem for American viewers, but sharp acting and energetic direction overcome the drawbacks and the result is a powerful action story. **Director**—John MacKenzie. (R) *114 minutes*

THE LONG GRAY LINE (1955)

★★★

Tyrone Power
Maureen O'Hara

Warmhearted drama about the long career of an athletic trainer at West Point. Power stars as an Irish immigrant who came to the military academy under humble circumstances and stayed on as a trainer for many years. O'Hara plays his wife. Director John Ford contributes a special sentimental touch. Also with Donald

Tyrone Power and Maureen O'Hara in The Long Gray Line, *a warmhearted drama.*

Crisp, Ward Bond, Betsy Palmer, Robert Francis, Phil Carey, and Patrick Wayne.
138 minutes

THE LONG HOT SUMMER (1958)

★★★

Orson Welles
Paul Newman
Joanne Woodward

Moody, Deep South family drama expertly adapted from William Faulkner's short stories. Welles plays a strong-willed father with a determined daughter, played by Woodward. Sparks fly when Newman, a handyman, comes to town and wants to marry her. Director Martin Ritt lays on the atmosphere and brings out the characterizations, but the ending could have been better. The excellent cast also includes Anthony Franciosa, Lee Remick, and Angela Lansbury.
118 minutes

LONG JOHN SILVER (1953)

★★★

Robert Newton

Fairly entertaining continuation of the *Treasure Island* adventure, with Newton in the title role giving a hammy but
(Continued)

 Movie is available in Beta and VHS videotape

235

L
- The Long Riders
- Look Back in Anger
- Looker
- Looking for Mr. Goodbar
- Looking to Get Out

(Continued)

lusty portrayal of the gruff buccaneer. In this film, Long John Silver and young Jim Hawkins return to the mysterious island with new clues for another attempt to recover pirate's treasure. Filmed in Australia. Also stars Kit Taylor, Connie Gilchrist, Rod Taylor, and Grant Taylor. **Director**—Byron Haskin. *109 minutes*

THE LONG RIDERS (1980)

☮ ★★

James Keach
Stacy Keach
David Carradine
Keith Carradine
Robert Carradine
Dennis Quaid
Randy Quaid

This rehash of the Jesse James legend adds little to what Hollywood has already told about it. The James brothers, played by brothers James and Stacy Keach, are still portrayed as Robin Hood-type heros. But curiously, in this version, it's the other outlaws who ride with the James gang (the Miller boys, the Younger brothers) that seem more interesting. Allusions to the noble suffering of the post-Civil War homesteaders are supposed to provide social insight, but it's all rather vague. Also with Christopher and Nicholas Guest, Pamela Reed, and Amy Stryker. **Director**—Walter Hill. (R) *100 minutes*

LOOK BACK IN ANGER (1958)

☮ ★★★

Richard Burton
Claire Bloom
Mary Ure

Burton gives a powerful performance as a rebellious young man who displays anger at the government and at his marriage. This engrossing screen adaptation of John Osborne's stylish play features some smart dialogue and memorable scenes reflecting on the at- mosphere of contemporary British life. Also with Edith Evans, Gary Raymond, and Donald Pleasence. **Director**—Tony Richardson.

99 minutes b&w

LOOKER (1981)

☮ ★

Albert Finney
James Coburn
Susan Dey

This slick mystery-drama about computers, advertising, and murder begins with promise, but quickly deteriorates into farfetched nonsense. Finney stars as a Beverly Hills plastic surgeon who traces the murders of some of his women patients to a large corporation using strange advertising methods. Writer-director Michael Crichton tosses in numerous sci-fi gimmicks that are merely absurd and silly, and he never explains the reasons for the murders. (R) *94 minutes*

LOOKING FOR MR. GOODBAR (1977)

☮ ★★★

Diane Keaton
Richard Gere

Keaton gives an extraordinary, provocative performance in this powerful film version of Judith Rossner's best-selling novel. Keaton, as the girl who teaches deaf children by day and cruises singles bars at night, is sad, funny, vulnerable, sweet, and sexy. Writer-director Richard Brooks captures the sordidness and compassion throughout, as the film builds to its shattering climax. Great acting jobs, too, from Gere, Tuesday Weld, and Alan Feinstein. Also with William Atherton, Tom Berenger, Richard Kiley, and LeVar Burton. A devastating movie that will send you away with your mind churning. (R) **Academy Award Nominations**—Weld, best supporting actress; William A. Fraker, cinematography. *135 minutes*

LOOKING TO GET OUT (1982)

★★

Jon Voight
Burt Young

GARY COOPER

Gary Cooper was known to millions of moviegoers as a tall, silent man of action. He starred in romances, comedies, and adventure films, but perhaps he's best known for his work in westerns.

Cooper was born Frank J. Cooper in Helena, Montana, in 1901, the son of a state supreme court justice. He attended elementary school in England and later went to Wesleyan College in Montana and Grinnell College in Iowa.

After college, Cooper worked for a while as a guide at Yellowstone National Park and in 1924 went to California with the ambition of becoming a newspaper cartoonist. *However, he took jobs as a salesman for a photographer and as an advertising salesman for a theater.*

In 1925, Cooper met some Hollywood casting directors and was given minor cowboy parts in westerns. The following year he got a break when he was chosen at the last moment to replace the second lead in The Winning of Barbara Worth, *starring Ronald Colman. The film was a hit, and it led to bigger acting opportunities for Cooper.*

In 1942, Cooper won the Academy Award for the title role in Sergeant York. *He won the Oscar again in 1952 for* High Noon.

Cooper died in 1961 at the age of 60. Cooper's other films include Wings *(1927),* Lilac Time *(1928),* A Farewell to Arms *(1932),* City Streets *(1932),* The Lives of a Bengal Lancer *(1935),* Mr. Deeds Goes to Town *(1936),* The Plainsman *(1937),* Beau Geste *(1939),* Meet John Doe *(1941),* For Whom the Bell Tolls *(1943),* Vera Cruz *(1954),* The Court Martial of Billy Mitchell *(1955),* Friendly Persuasion *(1956),* Ten North Frederick *(1958), and* The Naked Edge *(1961).*

- The Looney Looney Looney Bugs Bunny Movie
- Lord Jim
- Lord of the Flies
- Lord of the Rings
- The Lords of Discipline
- The Lords of Flatbush
- Losin' It

L

Contrived, glossy, and sporadically funny buddy-buddy story about two small-time New York hustlers (Voight and Young) trying to make a big score in Las Vegas. Voight overstrains as the brash con artist who bamboozles his way into the posh MGM Grand Hotel as a big spender. Young goes to the other extreme and underplays the faithful sidekick. The film's energy lacks focus and eventually drains away. The filmmakers appear anxious to show off the glitter of MGM's entertainment palace. **Director**—Hal Ashby. (R)

104 minutes

THE LOONEY LOONEY LOONEY BUGS BUNNY MOVIE
(1981)

 ★★★

Animation maestro Friz Freleng presents a wonderful compilation of his best work, which represents some 50 years of cartooning. That "cwazy wabbit" and many of his sidekicks—Yosemite Sam, Daffy Duck, Porky Pig, and so on—are up to their usual high jinks, and the result is nonstop hilarity. About 20 minutes of new material is mixed in with the older stuff, for an enjoyable romp with these lovable and indelible characters. (G)   *80 minutes*

LORD JIM (1965)

 ★★★

Peter O'Toole

Peter O'Toole portrays Lord Jim.

Colorful screen version of Joseph Conrad's famous novel about the adventures of a British merchant seaman in the Far East during the late 1800s. The exotic tale, about a man's efforts to atone for an act of cowardice, is helped along with lavish location photography in the Orient and some decent acting. The film doesn't achieve the flavor and dramatic power of the book. Also with James Mason, Eli Wallach, Paul Lukas, Jack Hawkins, Daliah Lavi, Akim Tamiroff, and Curt Jurgens. **Director**—Richard Brooks.

154 minutes

LORD OF THE FLIES
(1963)

★★★★

James Aubrey
Tom Chapin

Unusual account of a group of English schoolboys stranded on a lonely island after a plane crash. Eventually, they revert to savagery. The compelling film, adapted from William Golding's allegorical novel, has many tense moments. The cast of youngsters also includes Hugh Edwards, Roger Elwin, and Tom Gaman. **Director**—Peter Brook.   *90 minutes b&w*

LORD OF THE RINGS (1978)

 ★★

Ralph Bakshi, an innovator of X-rated cartoons, applies his animating skills to the work of J.R.R. Tolkien. The two-hour film is technically impressive, but if you aren't skilled in the ways of Hobbits and Middle Earth, you'll most likely be overwhelmed by the flood of information. Bakshi only offers half a ring from the cult fantasy; the movie ends abruptly without reaching the conclusion of Tolkien's trilogy. The door is left open for a sequel to the saga. (PG)   *133 minutes*

THE LORDS OF DISCIPLINE
(1983)

 ★★★

David Keith
Robert Prosky
G. D. Spradlin

David Keith gets chastised in The Lords of Discipline.

A tense, compelling melodrama set in a Southern military academy, where a secret society of cadets resorts to torture in an attempt to rid the institution of its first black student. The film often overdoes its emphasis on brutality, but the story unfolds briskly in the spirit of a slick whodunit. Keith shines as a courageous senior cadet who exposes the school's phony code of honor. **Director**—Franc Roddam. (R)

103 minutes

THE LORDS OF FLATBUSH
(1974)

★★★

Martin Davidson
Perry King
Sylvester Stallone
Henry Winkler

A frisky comedy about tough high school youths in Brooklyn in the late 1950s. The film is perhaps best remembered for the budding talents of Stallone and Winkler, who play colorful members of a Flatbush gang. Set much in the style of *The Blackboard Jungle*, but hardly as serious. A few scenes are real standouts. Also with Paul Mace, Susan Blakely, and Renée Paris. **Director**—Stephen F. Verona. (PG)

88 minutes

LOSIN' IT (1983)

 ★

Tom Cruise
Jackie Earle Haley
Shelley Long

A mindless adolescent romp about four horny high school boys who visit
(Continued)

 Movie is available in Beta and VHS videotape

(Continued)

Tijuana with mischief in mind and include a visit to a bordello in their itinerary. The film seems bent on non-stop foolishness, and there's little effort to develop appealing characters. You don't have to strain to figure out what the lads are losing south of the border. As for the movie, it's pretty much a lost cause. **Director**—Curtis Hanson. (R)   *104 minutes*

LOST AND FOUND (1979)

★★

George Segal
Glenda Jackson

George Segal and Glenda Jackson compare casts in Lost and Found.

Jackson and Segal are reunited in this film for the first time since their successful 1973 film *A Touch of Class*. But in this lackluster romantic comedy, they lose their touch. Segal is a tweedy professor in a small-town university, and Jackson is his quarrelsome wife. Both strain at the slapstick routines, and the picture ends up a lost cause. Also with Maureen Stapleton, Hollis McLaven, and Paul Sorvino. **Director**—Melvin Frank. (PG)   *112 minutes*

LOST HONOR OF KATHARINA BLUM (1976)

★★★

Angela Winker
Dieter Laser

An emotional and compelling Ger-

Angela Winker shares an intimate moment with her lover in The Lost Honor of Katharina Blum.

man film, which focuses on the excesses of a modern democracy and views the world in terms of good and evil. A young and reserved waitress takes home a young man suspected of radical political activities. For several days, she's harassed and humiliated by the police and a ruthless reporter because of the brief association. There are realistic performances by Winker as Katharina the waitress and Laser as the unscrupulous newsman. Adapted from a novel by Nobel Prize-winner Heinrich Boll. Written and directed by Volker Schlondorff and his wife, Margarethe von Trotta. In German with English titles. (R)   *102 minutes*

LOST HORIZON (1973)

★

Peter Finch
Liv Ullmann

Foolhardy remake of the 1937 classic film based on James Hilton's romantic story of paradise found. The beginning adheres to the original movie's style about a small group of people who are kidnapped and find themselves in a strange but serene Tibetan mountain civilization. However, the film collapses into nonsense when Shangri-La is reached and some out-of-place song-and-dance numbers are injected. The rather good cast just can't pull it off. Also with Sally Kellerman, Bobby Van, George Kennedy, Michael York, Olivia Hussey, John Gielgud, and Charles Boyer. **Director**—Charles Jarrott. (G)   *143 minutes*

LOST IN A HAREM (1944)

★★★

Bud Abbott
Lou Costello

Energetic Abbott and Costello high jinks, with Bud and Lou as magicians on tour in the Middle East and involved with a cunning sultan and a beautiful harem girl, played by Marilyn Maxwell. This feature, with the usual doses of slapstick and sight gags, is among the best of their films. Douglass Dumbrille is good as the sultan. Also with John Conte and Jimmy Dorsey and his orchestra. **Director**—Charles Riesner.   *98 minutes b&w*

THE LOST WEEKEND (1945)

★★★★

Ray Milland
Jane Wyman

In The Lost Weekend, *Ray Milland is a struggling writer who becomes an alcoholic.*

Stark, powerful drama about a struggling writer, played by Milland, who becomes an alcoholic. Milland gives a striking performance, which effectively and sympathetically illuminates his desperate character. Billy Wilder's script and direction are relentless in providing the details of personal pain, dejection, and terror. Howard da Silva is exceptional in a supporting role as a bartender. There are other good performances, too, from Wyman, Philip Terry, Doris Dowling, and Frank Faylen. **Academy Awards**—best picture; Wilder, best director; Milland, best actor; Charles Brackett and Wilder, writing (screenplay). **Nomination**—John F. Seitz, cinematography (black and white).   *101 minutes b&w*

LOVE AND BULLETS (1979)
★

**Charles Bronson
Rod Steiger
Jill Ireland**

Bronson plays a craggy-faced cop on special assignment for the FBI in this limp and predictable adventure yarn. He flies off to Switzerland to retrieve a mobster's girl friend, played by Ireland, who hopefully will supply incriminating evidence. Steiger, of course, plays the gangster. Bronson and Ireland spend considerable time observing picturesque Swiss scenery, which is okay if you happen to like travelogues. But if you're looking for fast action and suspense, forget it. Also with Strother Martin, Bradford Dillman, and Henry Silva. **Director**—Stuart Rosenberg. (R)   *103 minutes*

LOVE AND DEATH (1975)
 ★★★

**Woody Allen
Diane Keaton**

Woody Allen survives a bloody duel in Love and Death.

Allen wrote, directed, and starred in this funny film of a militant coward in the land of *War and Peace.* He plays a Russian trying to avoid the draft during the Napoleonic War. Keaton plays his cousin Sonja, the girl he worships. Also with Georges Adel, Harold Gould, Frank Adu, and Alfred Lutter. (PG)   *82 minutes*

LOVE AND MONEY (1982)
★

**Ray Sharkey
Ornella Muti
Klaus Kinski**

Sharkey and Italian beauty Muti are lovers in this confused and spiritless romantic thriller. He plays an obscure bank teller who's assigned by a big-shot industrialist (Kinski) to deal with a South American political leader. The farfetched situation gains little in credibility from Sharkey's performance. He's miscast in this role, and he doesn't even score too well with the exotic-looking Muti, who plays the tycoon's wife. **Director**—James Toback. (R)   *90 minutes*

LOVE AT FIRST BITE (1979)
 ★★★

**George Hamilton
Susan Saint James**

Alas, Count Dracula is evicted from his Transylvania castle. So he goes to New York City, where he raids the blood bank and falls in love with a fashion model, played by Saint James. This B-movie romantic comedy, starring Hamilton as a funny and engaging vampire, works most of the time. There are enough clever gags and high spirits to even win a smile from Bela Lugosi. The excellent supporting cast, headed by Saint James, Richard Benjamin, Dick Shawn, Isabel Sanford, and Arte Johnson, hams it up with delight. **Director**—Stan Dragoti. (PG)   *96 minutes*

THE LOVE BUG (1968)
 ★★★

**Dean Jones
Michele Lee**

A fun-filled Disney romp about a Volkswagen Beetle automobile with a distinct personality and its own ideas of where it wants to go. This heart-warming family comedy is aimed at the kids, yet it offers a bit of unusual sophistication. The film contains ample slapstick and clever stunts, mostly set in the streets of San Francisco. Several *Love Bug* sequels fol-

lowed. Also with David Tomlinson, Buddy Hackett, and Joe Flynn. **Director**—Robert Stevenson. (G)   *107 minutes*

LOVE CHILD (1982)
 ★★★

**Amy Madigan
Beau Bridges
Mackenzie Phillips**

Amy Madigan plays a pregnant convict in Love Child.

Poignant, sympathetic women's prison film enhanced by a remarkable performance from Madigan in the central role. She gives a believable portrait of a young waif who becomes pregnant by a guard while she's in the prison and then has to fight for her right to keep the child. Prison life is shown with adequate realism, although the atmosphere here is rather mild in comparison with some conventional prison movies. **Director**—Larry Peerce. (R)   *96 minutes*

THE LOVED ONE (1965)
★★★

**Robert Morse
John Gielgud
Rod Steiger**

An effective satire, based on Evelyn Waugh's novel about the funeral industry in the United States, that consistently hits the target with a combination of style and offensiveness. Morse stars as a young Britisher who
(Continued)

L
- Love Is a Many-Splendored Thing
- Lovely to Look At
- Love Me or Leave Me
- Love Me Tender
- Lovers and Liars
- Lovers and Other Strangers

(Continued)

attends his uncle's funeral in Los Angeles and gets stuck with an outrageous bill for the burial services. The black comedy is handled in a grand manner by a large pro cast that also includes Liberace, Jonathan Winters, Robert Morley, Dana Andrews, and Milton Berle. **Director**—Tony Richardson. *116 minutes b&w*

LOVE IS A MANY-SPLENDORED THING (1955)

  ★★

Jennifer Jones
William Holden

William Holden and Jennifer Jones find that Love Is a Many-Splendored Thing.

A tear-drenched soap-opera romance about a Eurasian woman doctor who falls in love with an American correspondent in Hong Kong at the time of the Korean Conflict. Jones is the Eurasian, and Holden is the journalist. The plot is routine, but the film is fairly well acted and produced. The movie is based on the autobiographical book by Han Suyin. The popular theme song gave the film added recognition. Also with Torin Thatcher, Isobel Elsom, Murray Matheson, and Richard Loo. **Director**—Henry King. **Academy Award**—Sammy Fain and Paul Francis Webster, best song ("Love Is a Many-Splendored Thing"). **Nominations**—best picture; Jones, best actress; Leon Shamroy, cinematography (color). *102 minutes*

LOVELY TO LOOK AT (1952)

★★

Howard Keel
Kathryn Grayson

A tepid remake of the musical *Roberta*,

set against the background of Paris fashion houses. The storyline is flimsy, but the great Jerome Kern songs, like "Smoke Gets In Your Eyes," and the lavish settings contribute some entertainment value. Grayson and Keel handle the singing with adequacy, and Marge and Gower Champion display their dancing talents. Ann Miller and Red Skelton round out the cast. **Director**—Mervyn Le Roy. *102 minutes*

LOVE ME OR LEAVE ME (1955)

 ★★★

Doris Day
James Cagney

James Cagney orders Doris Day to Love Me or Leave Me.

On-the-mark show-biz film biography about '20s singer Ruth Etting. Day, in the lead role, shows her talent to best advantage. Cagney, however, steals many a scene as her gangster boyfriend who propels her career, but also contributes to her drinking problem. Doris belts out some fine songs of the period, including "Ten Cents a Dance" and the title tune. Also with Cameron Mitchell, Robert Keith, Tom Tully, and Richard Gaines. **Director**—Charles Vidor. **Academy Award**—Daniel Fuchs, writing (motion picture story). **Nomination**—Cagney, best actor. *122 minutes*

LOVE ME TENDER (1956)

 ★★

Elvis Presley
Debra Paget
Richard Egan

There's only one reason to see this film: it's Elvis Presley's screen debut. If that's of no interest to you, forget this one. Otherwise, however ordi-

nary this vehicle is, it has an irresistible fascination. Made at the peak of Elvis's career, this post-Civil War western centers on a troubled Texas family. An ex-soldier finds that his younger brother, thinking him dead, has married the ex-soldier's sweetheart. And as if that weren't enough to stir up some explosive sibling rivalry, there's a quarrel over newfound wealth. Elvis sings (though not enough) and sometimes acts. **Director**—Robert D. Webb. *89 minutes b&w*

LOVERS AND LIARS (1981)

★

Goldie Hawn
Giancarlo Giannini

Hawn teams up with Italy's popular Giannini for this mixed-bag comedy, but the film turns out half-baked. She's on vacation in Rome, and he's the liar who's married and looking for a fast fling. They're off to Pisa for a few days of romance, but it's an ill match from the start. A shabby script and awkward direction hamper Goldie's attempts at her familiar dizzy humor; she should have vacationed in the Bahamas. **Director**—Mario Monicelli. (R) *96 minutes*

LOVERS AND OTHER STRANGERS (1970)

 ★★★★

Gig Young
Anne Jackson

A rib-tickling, sophisticated comedy about two young people who decide to marry and their families who get hilariously wound up in the wedding plans. Bonnie Bedelia and Michael Brandon play the engaged couple. The witty farce abounds in priceless funny scenes, with many good players having a field day with some good lines. Young is memorable as the stalwart father of the bride; Jackson plays a castoff mistress, and Richard Castellano is good as the father of the bridegroom. Also with Beatrice Arthur, Robert Dishy, Harry Guardino, Cloris Leachman, Anne Meara, and Marion Hailey. **Director**—Cy Howard. (PG) **Academy Award Nominations**—Castellano, best supporting actor; Renée Taylor, Joseph Bologna, and David Zelag

• Lovesick   • Love with the Proper
• Love Story   Stranger
• Love Streams   • Loving Couples
              • The L-Shaped Room

L

Anne Meara and Harry Guardino in the comedy Lovers and Other Strangers.

Goodman, best screenplay (based on material from another medium).

104 minutes

LOVESICK (1983)
★★

**Dudley Moore
Elizabeth McGovern**

Dudley Moore looks up to Elizabeth McGovern in Lovesick.

A watered-down romantic comedy starring Moore as a prominent New York shrink who commits the ultimate no-no—he falls in love with his beautiful patient (McGovern). Writer-director Marshall Brickman's subdued humor pokes at the psychiatric profession, but the satire soon becomes tiresome. Moore is okay, and McGovern projects innocent charm, but the stars are given little workable material to get to grips with. Alec Guinness and John Huston have supporting roles. (PG)

96 minutes

LOVE STORY (1970)
★★

**Ali MacGraw
Ryan O'Neal**

Effective film treatment of Erich Segal's sad tale of two college students. They fall in love and marry, and just when things are looking up, she dies. MacGraw and O'Neal play the star-crossed lovers. Ordinarily, this cliché-strewn film would be just another piece of sentimental Hollywood fluff. But the movie is made with above-average care and offers some good acting along with the flood of tears. Ray Milland and John Marley have supporting roles. **Director**—Arthur Hiller. (PG) **Academy Award Nominations**—best picture; Hiller, best director; O'Neal, best actor; MacGraw, best actress; Marley, best supporting actor; Segal, best story and screenplay (based on factual material or material not previously published).

100 minutes

LOVE STREAMS (1984)
★★

**John Cassavetes
Gena Rowlands**

Cassavetes and Rowlands marshal their magnificent acting talents and imaginative skills in portraying eccentric, neurotic persons desperately seeking love and dignity. The film bursts with emotion and poignant character studies. But, alas, this intense psychodrama drags on too long and some scenes seem to repeat other events in the movie. Cassavetes is an unstable, hard-drinking, skirt-chasing writer. Rowlands is just as quirky as his sister with multiple hangups. **Director**—Cassavetes. (PG-13)

141 minutes

LOVE WITH THE PROPER STRANGER (1963)
★★★

**Steve McQueen
Natalie Wood**

Finely tuned romantic comedy-drama about an easygoing musician, played by McQueen, who falls in love with a store clerk, played by Wood. A combination of classy acting and impressive New York East Side setting makes this film above the ordinary. Edie Adams is good in a supporting role, and there are also excellent assists from Tom Bosley and Herschel Bernardi. **Director**—Robert Mulligan. **Academy Award Nominations**—Wood, best actress; Arnold Schulman, best story and screenplay (written directly for the screen); Milton Krasner, cinematography (black and white).

100 minutes b&w

LOVING COUPLES (1980)
★★

**Shirley MacLaine
James Coburn**

Sally Kellerman wonders whose bed she's in now in Loving Couples.

An overly cute and predictable romantic comedy with MacLaine and Coburn as husband and wife doctors, who take a brief fling at mate-swapping. This theme had appeal in the '60s when Doris Day made bedroom eyes at Rock Hudson. But in regard to current moral standards, such escapades seem rather uneventful. Craggy-faced Coburn flashes a lot of teeth, while MacLaine strains to appear 10 years younger than she is. The film offers a few mild chuckles; the rest is just banal conversation. **Director**—Jack Smight. (PG) *97 minutes*

THE L-SHAPED ROOM (1963)
★★★★

Leslie Caron

Top adult romantic drama with Caron

(Continued)

L·M

- Lucky Lady
- Luna
- Lust for Life
- MacArthur
- The Mackintosh Man
- The Macomber Affair

(Continued)

in an outstanding role as a poor and pregnant French girl, living in a sleazy London rooming house. There, she encounters all sorts of interesting characters, including a determined young writer who offers her love and hope. Caron is perfectly cast, and she's backed up with superb supporting performances by Tom Bell, Brock Peters, Cicely Courtneidge, Avid Bunnage, and Emlyn Williams. Writer-director Bryan Forbes gets it all together with style. **Academy Award Nomination**—Caron, best actress.

125 minutes b&w

LUCKY LADY (1975)

★

Liza Minnelli
Gene Hackman
Burt Reynolds

The film cost about $13 million. The script is by Willard Huyck and Gloria Katz, who helped write *American Graffiti*. And it stars such heavies as Minnelli, Hackman, and Reynolds. With all that, this action comedy still turns out as a ridiculous, incoherent, and tasteless mess that's hardly funny. The stars are miscast together, and all seem to strain too hard. The three play small-time bootleggers who battle rival mobsters and the U.S. Coast Guard while transporting booze from Mexico to California. Also with Michael Hordern and Geoffrey Lewis. **Director**—Stanley Donen. (PG)

118 minutes

LUNA (1979)
★★

Jill Clayburgh
Matthew Barry

Matthew Barry thinks naughty thoughts about his mother in Luna.

Clayburgh is miscast as an American opera star, a widow, who lives in Rome with her disturbed and drug-addicted teenage son, played by Barry. As she tries to console him and relieve his addiction, they develop a morbidly erotic relationship that involves a good deal of emotional and physical mayhem. Director Bernardo Bertolucci, who made *Last Tango in Paris*, directs with eloquence, but this long melodrama is unbelievable and absurd. Also with Veronica Lazar, Renato Salvatori, and Fred Gwynne. (R)

137 minutes

LUST FOR LIFE (1956)
★★★

Kirk Douglas
Anthony Quinn

Vivid and colorful screen treatment of Irving Stone's biography about the stormy life of famous artist Vincent Van Gogh. Douglas provides an absorbing portrayal of the master, who encountered much anguish along with his great artistic talent. Quinn excells as Van Gogh's close friend and mentor, artist Paul Gauguin. Many superb Van Gogh masterpieces are displayed. Also stars James Donald, Pamela Brown, Everett Sloane, and Lionel Jeffries. **Director**—Vincente Minnelli. **Academy Award**—Quinn, best supporting actor. **Nominations**—Douglas, best actor; Normin Corwin, writing (best screenplay—adapted).

122 minutes

M

MacARTHUR (1977)

★★★

Gregory Peck
Ed Flanders

Don't expect the snap and spirit of *Patton* here, but this biographical feature is an earnest and interesting account of the egocentric general's career from the beginning of World War II to his dismissal during the Korean Conflict. Peck's portrayal of the Great Commander is imposing and hauntingly convincing. Most of the supporting characters seem lost in the background, but Flanders sparkles as Pres-

Gregory Peck plays the title role in the biographical film MacArthur.

ident Harry S Truman. A straight-forward directing job by Joseph Sargent. Also with Dan O'Herlihy, Sandy Kenyon, Dick O'Neill, and Art Fleming. (PG)

144 minutes

THE MACKINTOSH MAN (1973)

★★

Paul Newman
James Mason

Busy, fast-paced spy caper about a British agent, played by Newman, who is assigned to expose a Communist infiltrator. The film offers ample excitement with the usual chases and narrow escapes, but the cold-war plot is déjà vu by now. The performances, however, are generally good, and the production is fairly well done. Mason stars as the double agent, and other supporting roles are played by Dominique Sanda, Nigel Patrick, Harry Andrews, and Ian Bannen. Filmed in England, Ireland, and Malta. **Director**—John Huston. (PG) *98 minutes*

THE MACOMBER AFFAIR (1947)
★★★

Gregory Peck
Joan Bennett
Robert Preston

Taut, well-made safari adventure based on an Ernest Hemingway story, about the relationships among a husband, his wife, and their guide on a big-game hunting expedition. Peck turns in a superb performance as the guide, and there are fine acting jobs as well from Preston and Bennett as the couple with marital difficulties. An intelligent script contributes to the impact. Also stars Reginald Denny and Carl Harbord. **Director**—Zoltan Korda.   *89 minutes b&w*

MADAME CURIE (1943)
★★★

Greer Garson
Walter Pidgeon

A lofty, well-made film biography about the woman scientist who discovered radium. Rather slow-paced at times, but this intelligent production offers ample historical information and proceeds with showing the discovery of this vital element in an entertaining manner. Garson and Pidgeon shine as the Curies. There's notable

support from Henry Travers, Albert Baserman, Robert Walker, C. Aubrey Smith, and Dame May Whitty. **Director**—Mervyn LeRoy. **Academy Award Nominations**—best picture; Pidgeon, best actor; Garson, best actress; Joseph Ruttenberg, cinematography (black and white).   *124 minutes b&w*

MADAME ROSA (1978)
★★

Simone Signoret

Signoret plays an aging former prostitute with a big heart who cares for the children of streetwalkers. She summons a vivid characterization of a weary, proud woman grasping at the last threads of life. But aside from the dominant presence of Signoret, this overlong French drama is all downhill, with a muddled plot and excess sentimentality. Also with Claude Dauphin, Samy Ben Youb, and Gabriel Jabbour. **Director**—Mose Mizrahi. In French with English titles. (No MPAA rating) **Academy Award**—best foreign language film (1977).   *105 minutes*

MAD DOG
(1976)

★★

Dennis Hopper

Hopper stars in the title role of "Mad Dog" Daniel Morgan, a 19th-century Australian outlaw who terrorized the kangaroo territory and antagonized colonial officials. The film is rife with gore and brutality, such as a man choking to death on his own blood after his throat is slit. It depicts the so-called civilized people who hunt down the pitiful and mentally disturbed Morgan as no more moral than their quarry. Directed and written by Philippe Mora, whose efforts at social commentary fall flat. (R)   *102 minutes*

MADIGAN
(1968)
★★★

Richard Widmark
Henry Fonda

A tough-talking, action-packed police yarn realistically set in New York City. Widmark is nicely cast as a determined detective who brings in his man at all costs. Other excellent characterizations are featured, especially Fonda as a hard-nosed police commissioner and Harry Guardino as Widmark's partner. The film offers some clear details of the workings of a big-city police department. Also stars James Whitmore, Inger Stevens, Michael Dunn, and Susan Clark. **Director**—Don Siegel.   *100 minutes*

MADMAN (1983)

★

Alexis Dubin
Tony Fish

Here's a routine horror outing, overflowing with clichés and with the requisite ration of blood and gore to exploit the fancy of devotees. Made to formula and on the cheap, the flimsy shocker has an ax-wielding lunatic lumbering through the woods to prey on campers and counselors. Bodies pile up in assembly-line fashion while credibility disintegrates. **Director**—Joe Giannone. (R)   *88 minutes*

SPENCER TRACY

Spencer Tracy, born in Milwaukee, Wisconsin, in 1900, attended a Jesuit prep school with ambitions of becoming a priest, but interrupted his studies to join the Navy during World War I.

After the war, Tracy went to Northwestern Military Academy and Ripon College in Wisconsin, where he decided to make acting his profession. He also attended the American Academy of Dramatic Arts in New York City. After graduation, he supported himself by working as a janitor and bellhop while seeking

theater work. Finally, after some success on Broadway in the 1920s, director John Ford chose him for a major role in Up the River *(1930), a gangster film. Quickly he became one of Hollywood's top actors, winning Oscars for* Captains Courageous *(1937) and* Boys Town *(1938).*

Tracy married actress Louise Treadwell in 1923, but it was well known that Katharine Hepburn, his co-star in many films, was his true love. Tracy never divorced his wife although they lived apart for many years.

Tracy and Hepburn co-starred in his last film, Guess Who's Coming to Dinner *in 1967. Tracy died soon after finishing the film.*

Tracy's other major films include The Power and the Glory *(1933),* San Francisco *(1936),* Stanley and Livingstone *(1939),* Edison, the Man *(1940),* Tortilla Flat *(1942),* Cass Timberlane *(1947),* Adam's Rib *(1949),* Father of the Bride *(1950),* Pat and Mike *(1953),* The Old Man and the Sea *(1958),* The Last Hurrah *(1958),* Inherit the Wind *(1960), and* Judgment at Nuremberg *(1961).*

 Movie is available in Beta and VHS videotape

M
- Mad Max
- The Madwoman of Chaillot
- Magic
- The Magic Flute

- The Magic of Lassie
- The Magnificent Ambersons
- The Magnificent Seven

MAD MAX (1980)

★★★

Mel Gibson

Out of an apocalyptic, post-World War III Australian outback roars one of the most violent and action-packed cycle dramas you're ever likely to see. Details of this futuristic vision are sketchy as the film focuses in on the ravaging hordes of degenerates that drive the few remaining cars and burn up the last gallons of gasoline. Good cop Max (Gibson) tries to keep the peace à la Dirty Harry until he goes on a rampage and *really* fights dirty. The film is intense but engaging, and certainly doesn't lack for excitement. Watch out for the poor dubbing. **Director**—George Miller. (R)   *90 minutes*

THE MADWOMAN OF CHAILLOT (1969)
★★

Katharine Hepburn

Katharine Hepburn in The Madwoman of Chaillot.

Much money and talent are squandered on this foolhardy effort to film Jean Giradoux's small-scale play about an oddball Parisian woman and her kooky friends who want to do good. The opulent treatment just doesn't fit the material, and the all-star spectacle quickly lapses into tedium. Hepburn is wasted in the title role, and some other talented actors are equally at sea. However, there are a few minor patches of brightness. Also stars Yul Brynner, Danny Kaye, Edith Evans, Charles Boyer, Claude Dauphin, Paul Henreid, and Richard Chamberlain. **Director**—Bryan Forbes. (G)
132 minutes

MAGIC (1978)

★★

Anthony Hopkins
Ann-Margret
Burgess Meredith

Magic is the story of a dummy named Fats and his struggles to break free of Anthony Hopkins.

William Goldman's horror-suspense tale of a ventriloquist controlled by his dummy is reminiscent of the classic 1946 British chiller *Dead of Night*. This screen version of the popular novel, however, never lives up to its expectations, despite high-powered performances by Hopkins, as the ventriloquist, and Meredith. Ann-Margret plays an old sweetheart of Hopkins's. Director Richard Attenborough comes up with a few interludes of eerie suspense, but he doesn't have the magic touch to maintain tension to the end. Also with Ed Lauter and Jerry Houser. (R)   *106 minutes*

THE MAGIC FLUTE (1975)

★★★★

Ulrik Gold
Josef Kostlinger

Filming an opera is difficult indeed. But the magic of Swedish director Ingmar Bergman has pervaded *The Magic Flute*, the Mozart opera, and the result is a sparkling, funny, and intelligent movie. The film was initially made for Swedish TV at a modest cost of $650,000. Yet superb casting, quality camera work, exceptional sound reproduction, and Bergman's extraordinary directional ability have wrought a triumphant cinema experience. In Swedish with English titles. (G)   *134 minutes*

THE MAGIC OF LASSIE (1978)
★

James Stewart
Mickey Rooney
Alice Faye

A contrived, sugary dog episode that flagrantly manipulates children's emotions. This lackluster effort has none of the imagination or style of the popular 1943 *Lassie Come Home* film, which starred young Elizabeth Taylor. In this bland movie, Lassie, actually a descendant of the original movie collie, runs through a series of tragic adventures leading up to the eventual happy ending. It's not magic; it's more of a cheap trick. Also with Pernell Roberts and Mike Mazurki. **Director**—Don Chaffey. (G)   *100 minutes*

THE MAGNIFICENT AMBERSONS (1942)

★★★★

Joseph Cotten
Dolores Costello
Agnes Moorehead
Tim Holt

Excellent adaptation of the Booth Tarkington novel, directed by Orson Welles at the peak of his creative prowess. The rich period drama concerns the decline of a wealthy family and the emotional relationship between the mother and the youngest son. It's a fascinating cinema treat, fast-paced and very much in control of its material; it's magnificent indeed. Good performances are given by Cotten, Costello, Moorehead, Holt, Anne Baxter, and Ray Collins. **Academy Award Nominations**—best picture; Moorehead, best supporting actress; Stanley Cortez, cinematography (black and white).   *88 minutes b&w*

THE MAGNIFICENT SEVEN (1960)

★★★

Yul Brynner
Steve McQueen

A supercharged western that closely follows the theme of the Japanese film *The Seven Samurai*. A Mexican village is harassed by bandits, led by a greedy

Eli Wallach, and the people hire seven American gunslingers to protect them. There's plenty of shoot-'em-up activity by a good cast especially suited for such parts. Also with Robert Vaughn, James Coburn, Charles Bronson, and Horst Buchholz. **Director**—John Sturges. *126 minutes*

MAGNUM FORCE (1973)

 ★★

Clint Eastwood
Hal Holbrook

More unrestrained gunfire in this diluted sequel to *Dirty Harry*. Tight-lipped Eastwood again stars as Harry Callahan, the invincible homicide cop, but this time he's after some colleagues, led by Holbrook, who do most of the killing as self-appointed executioners of underworld thugs. It has the usual amount of violence and brutality, but with less style than the first film. Also with Mitchell Ryan, David Soul, and Felton Perry. **Director**—Ted Post. (R) *124 minutes*

MAHOGANY (1975)

 ★★

Diana Ross
Billy Dee Williams
Anthony Perkins

The incomparable Ross is stunning as a poor Chicago secretary turned inter-

In Mahogany, *Diana Ross portrays an international model and fashion designer.*

national model and fashion designer, but a silly and shoddy script wastes such talent. Perkins plays a homosexual photographer responsible for her success in the fashion world. Directed by Motown mogul, Berry Gordy. Also with Jean-Pierre Aumont, Nina Foch, and Beah Richards. (PG) *110 minutes*

MAIN EVENT (1979)

 ★★★

Barbra Streisand
Ryan O'Neal

Barbra Streisand takes aim at her critics in Main Event.

Streisand plays a wealthy perfume manufacturer who becomes the victim of embezzlement. She loses everything except her tax-shelter contract with reluctant prizefighter O'Neal. The screwball romance runs a delightful course of riotous comedy. Director Howard Zieff and script writer Gail Parent keep the film as witty as it is zany. Also with Paul Sand, Patti D'Arbanville, and Whitman Mayo. (PG) *112 minutes*

MAKING LOVE (1982)

 ★★

Michael Ontkean
Kate Jackson
Harry Hamlin

A slick soap opera about a young doctor, happily married to a beautiful woman for eight years, who discovers that he is gay. Director Arthur Hiller applies a liberal top coat of sentimentality, reminiscent of his *Love Story*.

Michael Ontkean and Kate Jackson star in the gay love story, Making Love.

The homosexual theme is handled gingerly but with sympathy. All the same, the story comes off as syrupy and trite, and the happy ending fails to touch the heart. (R) *111 minutes*

MAKING THE GRADE (1984)

 ★

Judd Nelson
Gordon Jump
Jonna Lee

We'll give this silly teen comedy a D minus for déjà vu gags that fall flat and amateurish direction by Dorian Walker. The clash-of-cultures theme involves a stuck-up rich kid who hires a desperate city lad to earn his diploma at a snobby prep school. An unknown ensemble cast makes the most of the limited screenplay and struggles through a string of colorless preppie jokes. (R) *105 minutes*

MALIBU BEACH (1978)

 ★★

Kim Lankford
James Daughton

Formula youth at-the-beach movie reminiscent of those beach-blanket movies of the late '50s. The empty-headed plot, aimed at young audiences, is a series of episodes concerning casual sex, pot-smoking, car-racing, and fistfights. Some nudity enters in with the help of a dog trained to snatch the tops of girls' bathing suits. Lankford and Daughton head the cast of unknowns having fun in the sun. **Director**—Robert J. Rosenthal. (R) *93 minutes*

M

- The Maltese Falcon
- A Man, a Woman and a Bank
- A Man Called Horse
- The Manchurian Candidate
- Mandy
- A Man for All Seasons

Humphrey Bogart, Peter Lorre, Mary Astor, and Sydney Greenstreet all lust after The Maltese Falcon.

THE MALTESE FALCON (1941)

 ★★★★

**Humphrey Bogart
Mary Astor
Sydney Greenstreet**

This is the king of the crime capers, smartly executed by director John Huston with zip, punch, and even a bit of sentiment. Bogart is sensational as private-eye Sam Spade, hot on the trail of a mysterious statuette in this remake of a 1931 film. And he's backed to the hilt with memorable supporting parts from his client Astor, Greenstreet as the Fat Man, Peter Lorre as Joel Cairo, and gunsel Elisha Cook, Jr. Also with Barton MacLane, Lee Patrick, and Gladys George. See it twice, three times—it never seems to lose its fascination. Based on the novel by Dashiell Hammett. **Academy Award Nominations**—best picture; Greenstreet, best supporting actor; Huston, writing (screenplay).

101 minutes b&w

A MAN, A WOMAN AND A BANK (1979)

 ★

**Donald Sutherland
Brooke Adams
Paul Mazursky**

Sutherland and Mazursky play clever con men whose plans to rob a Vancouver bank include invading the sophisticated security system during construction stages of the bank building. This drawn-out caper seems to have everyone running in place. There are so many unexciting complications and dull romantic interludes along the way, one wishes the crooks would get on with the job, which isn't that exciting when they finally pull it off. Also with Allen Magicovsky. **Director**—Noel Black. (PG)   *100 minutes*

A MAN CALLED HORSE (1970)

★★

Richard Harris

An unusual story about American Indians, which strives to capture the authenticity of their culture and rituals, but mostly comes across with excessive harshness and gore. Harris portrays a polished Englishman who is captured by the Sioux in 1825 in the Dakotas; after some brutal torture, he's converted and accepted by the tribe and becomes a leader. Also with Judith Anderson, Jean Gascon, Manu Tupou, and Corinna Tsopei. It spawned a sequel, *The Return of a Man Called Horse.* **Director**—Elliot Silverstein. (PG)   *114 minutes*

THE MANCHURIAN CANDIDATE (1962)

★★★★

**Frank Sinatra
Janet Leigh
Laurence Harvey**

An intelligent and brilliantly conceived spy thriller about a Korean war veteran, played by Sinatra, who's brainwashed by the Communists. Turned into a zombie, he returns to the United States and attempts to assassinate a liberal politician, played by Harvey. The film, based on Richard Condon's novel, is both eerie and satirical, and it's well done in all departments. The film was shot in Korea and in the United States. Also in the excellent cast are Angela Lansbury, Henry Silva, and James Gregory. **Director**—John Frankenheimer. **Academy Award Nomination**—Lansbury, best supporting actress.   *126 minutes b&w*

MANDY (1952)

★★★

**Jack Hawkins
Terence Morgan**

An engrossing drama about a young girl who is deaf and mute, struggling to make the most of her life. The semi-documentary film is handled with much sympathy and played professionally by a good cast that also includes Phyllis Calvert and Godfrey Tearle. Little Mandy Miller is excellent in the title role. Based on the novel *This Day Is Ours* by Hilda Lewis. **Director**—Alexander Mackendrick. **Alternate Title**—*The Crash of Silence.*

93 minutes b&w

A MAN FOR ALL SEASONS (1966)

 ★★★★

**Paul Scofield
Wendy Hiller
Robert Shaw**

Impeccable screen version of Robert Bolt's intelligent play about the falling out between Sir Thomas More and King Henry VIII. Scofield plays More, Hiller is Alice More, and Shaw is the monarch. Period detail is brought out with splendor by director Fred Zinnemann, but the film truly soars because of the intense attention to character development. Scofield, as the exceptional religious leader, provides a superbly rich portrayal, and he's backed all the way with great support from Hiller, Shaw, Orson Welles, Leo McKern, Susannah York, and Vanessa

• Man Friday
• The Man from Laramie
• The Man from Snowy River
• The Mango Tree

• Manhattan
• The Man in the Gray Flannel Suit
• The Man in the White Suit

M

Redgrave. **Academy Awards**—best picture; Zinnemann, best director; Scofield, best actor; Robert Bolt, best screenplay (based on material from another medium); Ted Moore, cinematography (color). **Nominations**— Shaw, best supporting actor; Hiller, best supporting actress. *120 minutes*

MAN FRIDAY (1976)
★

Peter O'Toole
Richard Roundtree

The Robinson Crusoe adventure classic is reworked into a chaotic blend of drama and whimsy with a modern twist. This version has Crusoe, played by O'Toole, as a Bible-banging white supremist, and his manservant Friday, played by Roundtree, as a black revolutionary. The idea quickly turns to tedium, the acting is disappointing, and stuck in the inane dialogue are several song-and-dance numbers. Also with Peter Cellier and Christopher Cabot. **Director**—Jack Gold. (PG) *115 minutes*

THE MAN FROM LARAMIE (1955)
★★★

James Stewart

Stewart is excellent as a stalwart cattleman who relentlessly pursues the killers of his brother. The gripping western combines moments of brutal action with some interesting characterizations. The supporting cast is good, too, with Arthur Kennedy, Donald Crisp, Cathy O'Donnell, Alex Nicol, Wallace Ford, and Jack Elam. **Director**—Anthony Mann. *104 minutes*

THE MAN FROM SNOWY RIVER (1983)
 ★★★

Tom Burlinson
Kirk Douglas

A sweeping, handsome Australian western with a delightfully old-fashioned script. Against lush, panoramic vistas and heart-pounding scenes of thundering wild horses, a bright-eyed

Sigrid Thornton is beguiled by Tom Burlinson, The Man from Snowy River.

lad (Burlinson) wins his spurs as a man and woos the refined daughter of a wealthy rancher. Douglas stands out with a remarkable dual performance as the rancher and the grizzled miner who is the rancher's brother. **Director**—George Miller. (PG) *105 minutes*

THE MANGO TREE (1983)
 ★★

Christopher Pate
Geraldine Fitzgerald

This loosely constructed Australian film, set during World War I, centers on the rites of passage of a high school student (Pate). Director Kevin Dobson fails to establish continuity, and the confused story unfolds haphazardly. The handsome production, however, splendidly captures the atmosphere of the period. There's a standout performance by veteran actress Fitzgerald as the boy's wise and feisty grandmother. (No MPAA rating)

93 minutes

MANHATTAN (1979)
 ★★★★

Woody Allen
Diane Keaton

Director-actor Allen returns to the satiric style of *Annie Hall* with greater success in his portraits of sophisticated New Yorkers and their foibles, fancies, loves, and frustrations. Not only do he and Keaton once again reveal their special brilliance for hilarious comedy, but Woody has developed

a much deeper and more serious romantic spirit. His witty observations stir feelings while drawing laughter. A truly touching comic valentine to the Big Apple. Also with Michael Murphy, Mariel Hemingway, Meryl Streep, and Anne Byrne. (R) **Academy Award Nominations**—Hemingway, best supporting actress; Allen and Marshall Brickman, best screenplay (written directly for the screen). *96 minutes b&w*

THE MAN IN THE GRAY FLANNEL SUIT (1956)
★★★

Gregory Peck
Fredric March

First-class rendering of Sloan Wilson's poignant novel about a New York public relations executive caught in the dilemma of succeeding in his high-pressure job or maintaining his integrity. It's all very slick and melodramatic, but the story moves briskly and maintains consistent interest. Peck is right at home in the title role as the button-down Madison Avenue type. Also with Jennifer Jones, Ann Harding, Arthur O'Connell, Henry Daniell, Lee J. Cobb, Keenan Wynn, and Gene Lockhart. **Director**—Nunnally Johnson. *153 minutes*

THE MAN IN THE WHITE SUIT (1952)
 ★★★★

Alec Guinness
Joan Greenwood
Cecil Parker

A nonstop comedy with Guinness and a top supporting cast generating an avalanche of fun and humor. Guinness is in great form as a scientist who invents an amazing textile that apparently won't wear out and actually repels dirt. Britain's textile industry is thrown into turmoil, and clothing makers scramble to get their hands on the astonishing material. A fantastic combination of wit and rollicking high spirits. Also with Vida Hope, Michael Gough, and Ernest Thesiger. **Director**—Alexander Mackendrick. **Academy Award Nomination**—Roger MacDougall, John Dighton, and Mackendrick, writing (screenplay). *81 minutes b&w*

M
- The Man of a Thousand Faces
- Man of Iron
- Man of La Mancha
- The Man on the Eiffel Tower
- Manpower
- The Man Who Came to Dinner
- The Man Who Fell to Earth

THE MAN OF A THOUSAND FACES (1957)
★★★★

James Cagney
Dorothy Malone

An engaging film biography of silent-screen great Lon Chaney, who devised many intriguing characters with his amazing makeup skills. In *The Hunchback of Notre Dame*, Chaney wore some 40 pounds of makeup. The plot follows Chaney's screen career and private life. There's impressive detail and atmosphere from this period of film-making, yet interest is sidetracked at times because of numerous subplots. Cagney, in the title role, gives another of his fantastic performances; Malone plays Chaney's first wife. Also with Jane Greer, Marjorie Rambeau, and Jim Backus. **Director**—Joseph Pevney. **Academy Award Nomination**—Ralph Wheelright, R. Right Campbell, Ivan Goff, and Ben Roberts, best story and screenplay (written directly for the screen). *122 minutes b&w*

MAN OF IRON (1981)
★★★

Jerzy Radziwilowicz
Krystyna Janda

Fact and fiction are excitingly interwoven in this fresh account of recent history—the workers' rebellion in Poland and the rise of the Solidarity labor movement. Polish director Andrzej Wajda made this film as a sequel to his *Man of Marble*. This continuation involves political activities during the shipyard strike in Gdansk and a worker's love affair with a woman filmmaker. Even Solidarity leader Lech Walesa and other union notables have theatrical parts and appear in newsreel inserts. In Polish with English titles. (No MPAA rating) *140 minutes*

MAN OF LA MANCHA (1972)
 ★

Peter O'Toole
Sophia Loren

The classic Cervantes fable of Don Quixote, produced with extraordinary power and beauty on the stage, is incomprehensible on the screen. The brilliant musical numbers come across with dreariness, and the entire endeavor plods lamely along. The settings are impressive, but it's an essentially disappointing experience. Also with James Coco, Harry Andress, and John Castle. **Director**—Arthur Hiller. (PG) *140 minutes*

THE MAN ON THE EIFFEL TOWER (1949)
★★★

Charles Laughton
Burgess Meredith

An intense and intriguing crime drama, impressively set against the backdrop of Paris. Police Inspector Maigret and a mad killer relentlessly match wits and nerves until the mystery is solved in a tense climax. The production, based on a Simenon novel, is enhanced by excellent acting. Also with Franchot Tone, Robert Hutton, Jean Wallace, and Wilfrid Hyde-White. **Director**—Meredith. *97 minutes*

MANPOWER (1941)
★★★

Edward G. Robinson
George Raft
Marlene Dietrich

Powerful, action-packed adventure about the men who work on high-voltage power lines. Robinson and Raft, two such workers, argue over nightclub hostess Dietrich. The upshot is a gripping man-to-man fistfight on a powerline tower during a stormy night; the sparks fly in all directions. Also with Alan Hale, Frank McHugh, Eve Arden, Barton MacLane, and Ward Bond. **Director**—Raoul Walsh. *103 minutes b&w*

THE MAN WHO CAME TO DINNER (1941)
 ★★★★

Monty Woolley
Bette Davis

Woolley is riotously funny in this side-splitting comedy, as a bombastic celebrity who's injured while on tour and

Monty Woolley in The Man Who Came to Dinner.

must stay with a local family to recuperate. He drives his hosts up the wall with his wacky antics and with the assorted oddball characters who come to visit him. Despite its stagey setting, the activity moves quickly and generates an avalanche of laughter. Davis is wasted, but there are good caricatures from Jimmy Durante, Reginald Gardiner, and Ann Sheridan. Also with Billie Burke, Richard Travis, and Grant Mitchell. **Director**—William Keighley. *112 minutes b&w*

THE MAN WHO FELL TO EARTH (1976)
 ★★★★

David Bowie

David Bowie gets strapped in tight so he won't become The Man Who Fell to Earth.

Nicolas Roeg's riveting and fascinating sci-fi tale is about an extraterrestrial traveller who comes to Earth to find water for his dying planet. He organizes a vast scientific conglomerate, à la Howard Hughes, and becomes entangled in lots of earthly corruption. Rock star Bowie plays the visitor from outer space with credibility. Rip Torn, Buck Henry, and Candy Clark also deliver

• The Man Who Loved Cat Dancing
• The Man Who Loved Women (1977)
• The Man Who Loved Women (1983)
• The Man Who Shot Liberty Valance
• The Man Who Wasn't There
• The Man Who Would Be King

M

appealing performances. The film says much about life on Earth through the eyes of a man from another world. (R)   *125 minutes*

THE MAN WHO LOVED CAT DANCING (1973)

 ★

Sarah Miles
Burt Reynolds
Lee J. Cobb

A sluggish western adventure about a restless wife who is kidnapped by train robbers and falls in love with one of the outlaws. Miles is the unhappy wife, and Reynolds plays the main desperado. Cobb leads a posse after the bandits. A rather impressive cast can't make much of this movie based on the novel by Marilyn Dunham. And it gave Reynolds a double hernia for doing his own stunts. Also with Jack Warden, George Hamilton, Bo Hopkins, and Jay Silverheels. **Director**—Richard C. Sarafian. (PG)
114 minutes

THE MAN WHO LOVED WOMEN (1977)

 ★★★★

Charles Denner
Leslie Caron

Director François Truffaut's charming tale of a Frenchman who is obsessed by women is witty and sophisticated. The appealing cast is headed by Denner, whose gentle manner makes the title character shine with a mixture of comic delight and innocence. The film is fun to watch for its clever variations on a familiar theme. Also stars Brigitte Fossey and Nelly Borgeaud. In French with English titles. (No MPAA rating)
119 minutes

THE MAN WHO LOVED WOMEN (1983)

 ★★★

Burt Reynolds
Julie Andrews

Macho Reynolds is convincing as an appealing lothario who is more helpless than heartless in his pursuit of the opposite sex. The film is part sensitive

A psychiatrist tries to cure Burt Reynolds of his romantic obsessions in The Man Who Loved Women.

psychological drama, part slapstick farce, though it is not as compelling as its star. Director Blake Edwards's reworking of the 1977 François Truffaut comedy is frequently charming and, at times, surprisingly effective in its serious moments. On target supporting performances by Andrews (as the psychiatrist who cares for him), Kim Basinger, and Marilu Henner. (R)
118 minutes

THE MAN WHO SHOT LIBERTY VALANCE (1962)

 ★★★

James Stewart
John Wayne
Vera Miles

A young man, played by Stewart, takes the bows for killing a notorious outlaw. But did the tenderfoot really fire that fatal shot? Fairly entertaining John Ford western with a good cast doing their utmost, although the story is unnecessarily strung out. Wayne is firmly in the saddle again, competing with Stewart over Miles. And Lee Marvin plays the villain again. Others in the cast include Edmond O'Brien, Andy Devine, and Jeanette Nolan.
122 minutes b&w

THE MAN WHO WASN'T THERE (1983)

 ★

Steve Guttenberg

Guttenberg stars in this uneven and

farfetched 3–D comedy as a Washington bureaucrat caught up in an international plot to steal invisibility potions. The well-worn, gimmicky plot involves much chasing around, with Russian and American agents and some gangsters all trying to recover the amazing formula. The 3–D in this case stands for "Dumb, Dumb, Dumb." Lisa Langlois and Jeffery Tambor appear in supporting roles. **Director**—Bruce Malmuth. (R)
111 minutes

THE MAN WHO WOULD BE KING (1975)

 ★★★★

Sean Connery
Michael Caine
Christopher Plummer

Sean Connery gets a group massage in The Man Who Would Be King.

Connery and Caine play two soldiers-turned-con men who set themselves up as rulers of Kafiristan, a remote and primitive country, so they can loot the royal treasury. The film, based on Rudyard Kipling's romantic short story, succeeds as an exotically charming old-fashioned adventure tale, laced with comradeship and courage. The duo's scheme falls apart when Danny Dravot, played by Connery, becomes attached to his responsibilities as god-king. Plummer gives a remarkable but brief performance as Kipling. Also with Saeed Jaffrey and Jack May. **Director**—John Huston.
(Continued)

M

- The Man with the Golden Arm
- The Man with Two Brains
- Man, Woman and Child
- Marathon Man
- March or Die
- Marianne and Juliane

(Continued)
(PG) **Academy Award Nomination—**Huston and Gladys Hill, best screenplay (adapted from another medium).
127 minutes

THE MAN WITH THE GOLDEN ARM (1955)

 ★★★

Frank Sinatra
Kim Novak

Frank Sinatra and Kim Novak disillusion one another in The Man with the Golden Arm.

Sinatra is surprisingly good in this stark drama, based on a Nelson Algren novel, as a drug addict who painfully kicks the habit. The film was sensational at the time of its release, and it retains much of its power. Otto Preminger's direction, however, is slow-paced and even-handed. Elmer Bernstein's jazzy score heightens the mood. Also with Eleanor Parker, Darren McGavin, Arnold Stang, and Robert Strauss. **Academy Award Nomination—**Sinatra, best actor.
119 minutes

THE MAN WITH TWO BRAINS (1983)

 ★★★

Steve Martin
Kathleen Turner
David Warner

Martin is a wacky brain surgeon with wife problems in this brisk comedy. The film is skillfully directed by Carl Reiner, and Martin's wry humor works to the utmost advantage of the witty and inspired script. Turner handles her role of the alluring but difficult wife with surprising finesse, and there are times when her own brand of

Steve Martin tackles the subject of brains head on (er, off) in The Man with Two Brains.

scene-stealing hilarity makes the proceedings doubly funny. (R)
90 minutes

MAN, WOMAN AND CHILD (1983)

 ★★

Martin Sheen
Blythe Danner

Martin Sheen has to deal with an unknown son in Man, Woman and Child.

Dewy-eyed mush from the tear-stained pages of Erich (Love Story) Segal. The schmaltzy script tells of a comfortably married California college professor who is suddenly confronted by his ten-year-old illegitimate son. This turn of events creates predictable family anxiety—and torrents of sentimentality. Despite the artificiality of the material, Sheen and Danner manage to come up with skillful and watchable performances as teacher and wife. **Director—**Dick Richards. (PG) *99 minutes*

MARATHON MAN (1976)

 ★★★

Dustin Hoffman
Laurence Olivier

Director John Schlesinger's super-charged thriller is about a Columbia University graduate student who, for reasons he cannot understand, is pursued and tormented by a surviving Nazi war criminal. Hoffman is the student, and Olivier is the long-dormant Nazi who is also a former dentist. The film is paradoxical. At times, it generates tension that is nearly unbearable, and there are moments of intense excitement. It's crammed with brutal killings, bone-chilling torture, and triple crosses. Yet it's all wrapped in a murky and confusing plot that hardly makes much sense. Hoffman, Olivier, and the rest of the cast are in fine form. The screenplay was written by William Goldman from his own novel. Also with Marthe Keller, Roy Scheider, and William Devane. (R) **Academy Award Nomination—**Olivier, best supporting actor. *125 minutes*

MARCH OR DIE (1977)

 ★★

Gene Hackman
Catherine Deneuve
Terence Hill

Stiff, listless French Foreign Legion adventure that's high on beautiful location photography, but short on acting. Hackman, Deneuve, and other cast members mope about the desert as if they are suffering from sunstroke. Hill is lively, but acts silly. The story, which concerns an expedition to steal Arab treasure buried in the Sahara, is complicated and pedestrian. Also with Max Von Sydow and Ian Holm. **Director—**Dick Richards. (PG)
104 minutes

MARIANNE AND JULIANE (1982)

 ★★

Jutta Lampe
Barbara Sukowa

Margarethe von Trotta, the West German writer-director, presents a grim,

• Marjorie Morningstar
• The Mark of Zorro
• Marlowe
• The Marriage of Maria Braun
• The Marrying Kind
• Marty

M

overwrought account of the quarrelsome relationship between two sisters caught up in the political turmoil of the '60s and '70s. The film touches on the girls' strict upbringing, but too much of the story is devoted to incessant arguing—much of it when Juliane (Lampe), a magazine writer, visits terrorist Marianne (Sukowa) in prison. Heavy going most of the way. In German with English titles. (No MPAA rating)   *106 minutes*

MARJORIE MORNINGSTAR (1958)
★★

**Natalie Wood
Gene Kelly**

A young Jewish girl with stars in her eyes strives to make it to the big time in New York City, but winds up as an ordinary housewife. This screen adaptation of Herman Wouk's popular novel never takes off, although a few scenes are moving. Wood seems ill at ease in the title role and so do most of the supporting players. Also with Claire Trevor, Everett Sloane, Ed Wynn, Martin Milner, Carolyn Jones, and Martin Balsam. **Director**—Irving Rapper.   *123 minutes*

THE MARK OF ZORRO (1940)
   ★★★★

**Tyrone Power
Basil Rathbone**

Eugene Pallette plays a plump friar in The Mark of Zorro.

A ripsnorting swashbuckling adventure starring Power as Diego de Vega,

an aristocrat who dons a mask and routs the bad guys in California in the early 1800s. Well-staged and executed with much energy, the film offers some of the best dueling scenes around. It's great fun for boys of all ages. Power is as dashing as ever, and the excellent cast also includes Linda Darnell, J. Edward Bromberg, Eugene Pallette, and Montagu Love. **Director**—Rouben Mamoulian.
                          94 minutes b&w

MARLOWE (1969)
★★★

**James Garner
Rita Moreno**

Garner tries his hand at playing Philip Marlowe, the Raymond Chandler private-eye character, and the results are fairly good. A girl loses track of her brother so she hires Marlowe to find him. Moreno plays a stripper. The thriller, based on Chandler's *The Little Sister*, moves along at a brisk pace and displays some of the squalid atmosphere associated with such capers. But don't expect this adventure to match the Humphrey Bogart versions. Garner gets first-class assistance from Gayle Hunnicutt, Sharon Farrell, Carroll O'Connor, and Bruce Lee. **Director**—Paul Bogart. (PG)   *95 minutes*

THE MARRIAGE OF MARIA BRAUN (1980)
★★★

**Hanna Schygulla
Klaus Lowitsch**

Sultry and beautiful Schygulla plays the title role in this film about survival in postwar Germany. As Maria, she achieves success through shrewdness and energy as Germany emerges into a period of miraculous prosperity. Rainer Werner Fassbinder directs in his usual straightforward style. Also with Ivan Desny and Gottried John. In German with English titles. (No MPAA rating)   *120 minutes*

THE MARRYING KIND (1952)
★★★

**Judy Holliday
Aldo Ray**

Aldo Ray and Judy Holliday find that they are The Marrying Kind.

An intelligent tragicomedy played with style and sensitivity by Holliday and Ray, a couple with marital problems who straighten things out after analyzing their lives. Holliday does a fine job with the serious moments as well as the comic opportunities. Madge Kennedy and Mickey Shaughnessy also star. **Director**—George Cukor.   *93 minutes b&w*

MARTY (1955)
   ★★★★

**Ernest Borgnine
Betsy Blair**

This is one of the most compassionate and touching films about the lives and problems of ordinary people ever produced. Borgnine is perfectly cast as the lonely middle-aged butcher resigned to an unmarried life, who finally falls in love with a girl in similar circumstances; Blair plays the lonely girl. Paddy Chayefsky's script was initially written as a TV play, and it gains further impact and importance as a feature film. It's a movie masterpiece, filled with subtleties, irony, and truth. Borgnine's performance is magnificent, and there's excellent support from Blair, Esther Minciotti, Joe Mantell, and Jerry Paris. **Director**—Delbert Mann. **Academy Awards**—best picture; Mann, best director; Borgnine, best actor; Chayefsky, writing (screenplay). **Nominations**—Mantell, best supporting actor; Blair, best supporting actress; Joseph LaShelle, cinematography (black and white).
                          91 minutes b&w

M

• Mary Poppins
• M*A*S*H
• The Mask of Dimitrios

• Mass Appeal
• A Matter of Time
• Mausoleum

MARY POPPINS (1964)

★★★★

Julie Andrews
Dick Van Dyke

Dick Van Dyke and Julie Andrews in the Walt Disney fantasy Mary Poppins.

This delightful fantasy from Disney is about two English children minded by a strict but wonderful nanny who has magical powers and takes them on exciting adventures. Andrews, in her film debut, is splendid in the title role, and the film proceeds with charm and energy. It's great entertainment for the kids, and adults won't find it boring or trite. There's also a serious message involved: Kids need love and attention, not just wealthy surroundings, to truly make them happy. Also with David Tomlinson, Glynis Johns, Ed Wynn, Elsa Lanchester, and Arthur Treacher. **Director**—Robert Stevenson. **Academy Award**—Andrews, best actress. **Nominations**—best picture; Stevenson, best director; Bill Walsh and Don DaGradi, best screenplay (based on material from another medium); Edward Colman, cinematography (color). *139 minutes*

M*A*S*H (1970)

★★★★

Donald Sutherland
Elliott Gould
Sally Kellerman

Director Robert Altman scores big with this smart black comedy about doctors at a Mobile Army Surgical Hospital (MASH) in Korea who relieve the boredom, tension, and horror of their situation by pulling pranks and defying authority. A trend-setting film and a most unusual farce, splendidly acted by Sutherland, Gould, and Kellerman in the key roles. The extraordinary screenplay by Ring Lardner, Jr., touches all the bases, and it's hilarious from start to finish. A great film that spawned an excellent TV show. Also stars Tom Skerritt, Robert Duvall, John Schuck, Jo Ann Pflug, and Gary Burghof. (PG) **Academy Award**—Lardner, best screenplay (based on material from another medium). **Nominations**—best picture; Altman, best director; Kellerman, best supporting actress. *116 minutes*

THE MASK OF DIMITRIOS (1944)

★★★

Peter Lorre
Sydney Greenstreet
Zachary Scott

Sydney Greenstreet is a gangster who gives his gat a go at a gumshoe in The Mask of Dimitrios.

Lorre and Greenstreet are right at home in this stylish tale of intrigue, based on an Eric Ambler novel. Lorre is a Dutch writer in the Middle East, seeking out a clever criminal, played by Scott. Plenty of good smoky atmosphere enhances the story and the characters. Also with Faye Emerson, Victor Francen, Steven Geray, and Florence Bates. **Director**—Jean Negulesco. *113 minutes b&w*

MASS APPEAL (1984)

★★★★

Jack Lemmon
Zeljko Ivanek
Charles Durning

Winning screen adaptation of Bill C. Davis's stage comedy of conflicting consciences in the Catholic church. Jack Lemmon is superb as the popular, complacent priest assigned to tone down an idealistic young seminary student (Ivanek) who challenges conventional morality. The film succeeds brilliantly on its witty, bantering dialogue between the two protagonists. Appealing, indeed. **Director**—Glenn Jordan. (PG) *99 minutes*

A MATTER OF TIME (1976)

★★

Liza Minnelli
Ingrid Bergman
Charles Boyer

Vincente Minnelli directs daughter Liza in this Cinderella story of a chambermaid who's transformed into a glamorous movie star. The film, set in Rome in 1949, is rich in lush scenery and glittery costumes, but the plot is tacky, and the dialogue is awkward. Bergman co-stars as an eccentric, down-and-out contessa who inspires the young peasant girl. Minnelli and Bergman perform spectacularly, but they're much too good for such mediocre material. Also with Tina Aumont and Spiros Andros. (PG) *99 minutes*

MAUSOLEUM (1983)

(no stars)

Bobbie Bresee
Marjoe Gortner
Norman Burton

Routine, exploitative gore fest with Bresee as a rich young woman, possessed by demons, who embarks on a killing spree. The absurd, hackneyed story has Bresee constantly changing from beauty to snarling beast to carry out various acts of destruction. Amateurish acting and uninspired direction are only two of the film's problems. **Director**—Michael Dugan. (R) *96 minutes*

• Max Dugan Returns • McLintock!
• McCabe & Mrs. Miller • Mean Streets
• The McKenzie Break • Meatballs
• Meatballs Part II

M

MAX DUGAN RETURNS (1983)

 ★★

**Jason Robards, Jr.
Marsha Mason**

Marsha Mason lets Jason Robards, Jr. know that nobody missed him in Max Dugan Returns.

Mason is a spunky, widowed schoolteacher living on the brink of poverty in Venice, California. Along comes her long lost, ex-con father (Robards) with a suitcase full of cash which he lavishes on the forlorn household. The script is from Neil Simon, who seems to have lost his comic touch here. The movie manages a few smiles, a chuckle or two here and there—but it's mostly stale stuff. Return to sender. **Director**—Herbert Ross. (PG) *98 minutes*

McCABE & MRS. MILLER (1971)

 ★★★

**Warren Beatty
Julie Christie**

Director Robert Altman shows off his resourceful ability in this turn-of-the-century western, about a gambler who established a bordello in a remote Northwest community. Beatty's performance, as the gambler-braggart, is exceptionally moving and displays just the right amount of pathos and droll humor. He's matched all the way by Christie as his rather exceptional manager of operations. Based on the novel *McCabe* by Edmund Naughton. Supporting roles by René Auberjonois, Hugh Millais, Shelley Duvall, John Schuck, and Keith Carradine. (R) **Academy Award Nomination**—Christie, best actress. *120 minutes*

THE McKENZIE BREAK (1970)

★★★

**Brian Keith
Helmut Griem**

An intelligent and intense action drama about German prisoners during World War I who plot an escape from a POW camp in Scotland. There are convincing performances by Keith as an Irish prison commander and Griem as the leader of the prisoners. Suspense builds to a rousing climax. Also stars Ian Hendry, Jack Watson, and Patrick O'Connell. **Director**—Lamont Johnson. (PG) *106 minutes*

McLINTOCK! (1963)

★★★

**John Wayne
Maureen O'Hara**

Big John demonstrates his ability as a laugh-getter in this wild and wooly western comedy. The Duke plays a formidable cattle baron who knows how to run his business and the community, but has trouble controlling his wife. Lots of high spirits and raucous slapstick maintain steady interest in this farce that parodies Shakespeare's *The Taming of the Shrew*. O'Hara is effective as Wayne's difficult wife, and there are other good performances by Yvonne de Carlo, Patrick Wayne, Stefanie Powers, Chill Wills, and Bruce Cabot. **Director**—Andrew V. McLaglen. *127 minutes*

MEAN STREETS (1973)

 ★★★★

**Harvey Keitel
Robert De Niro**

A compelling and sharply detailed story about life in New York City's Little Italy, as seen through the experiences of a group of small-time hoods. Director Martin Scorsese captures the atmosphere of the area and expertly brings out the sense of competitiveness and family life of the inhabitants. Scorsese made a name for himself with this moody and brutal portrait. Also with David Proval, Amy Robinson, Cesare Danova, and Richard Romanus. (R) *110 minutes*

MEATBALLS (1979)

 ★

**Bill Murray
Harvey Atkin
Kate Lynch**

Bill Murray counsels a young loner on how to be just like him in Meatballs.

This silly farce about life at summer camp is a concoction of *Animal House* crossbred with *M*A*S*H* and aimed at the under-16-year-old set. A lack of fresh comic invention will make anyone with an iota of sophisticated taste restless. What's left is predictable and infantile nonsense that might tickle the funnybones of kids just old enough to go to the movies by themselves. Also with Kristine DeBell, Russ Banham, and Sarah Torgov. **Director**—Ivan Reitman. (PG) *92 minutes*

MEATBALLS PART II (1984)

 ★

**Paul Reubens
Archie Hahn**

This desperate, flabby sequel to the 1979 summer camp comedy goes out of control quickly and only gets worse as the ridiculous events progress. The tired, uninspired plot primarily involves competition between some good-guy adolescent campers and the vicious inhabitants of a nearby military camp. After suffering a deadly flurry of lame sex jokes, gay jokes, wimp jokes, and terrible acting, who could care? **Director**—Ken Wiederhorn. (PG) *87 minutes*

M
- Medium Cool
- Meet Me in St. Louis
- Megaforce
- Melvin and Howard
- The Memory of Justice
- The Men

MEDIUM COOL (1969)

★★★

Robert Forster

A remarkable and revealing semi-documentary film about the effects of television on our life-styles and our perceptions of violence in contemporary society. Director Haskell Wexler sets his story in the arena of conflicts at the 1968 Democratic National Convention in Chicago, where he focuses on a TV news cameraman who mechanically goes about his duties in the midst of emotional events. Executed with style and intelligence and wrapped up with a thoughtful ending. Forster plays the detached cameraman; he's supported by Verna Bloom, Peter Bonerz, and Marianna Hill. (R)   *110 minutes*

MEET ME IN ST. LOUIS (1944)

★★★★

Judy Garland
Margaret O'Brien

Margaret O'Brien and Judy Garland put on a show for the rest of the family in Meet Me in St. Louis.

A bright, charming musical in Hollywood's best tradition, about a family in St. Louis at the time of the 1903 World's Fair. Garland tops the cast, and she has a wonderful time with the sentimental songs, including "The Boy Next Door" and "Trolley Song." Leon Ames and Mary Astor are her parents; O'Brien is Judy's sister. It's all exceptionally romantic, nostalgic, and heartwarming. There's also fine support from June Lockhart, Harry Davenport, and Marjorie Main. **Director**—Vincente Minnelli. **Academy Award Nomination**—George Folsey, cinematography (color). *113 minutes*

MEGAFORCE (1982)

★

Barry Bostwick
Michael Beck
Persis Khambatta

High-tech, military hardware dominates this action adventure about elite soldiers defending a small nation from invasion. An array of super-lasers, computer-guided rockets, and flying motorcycles zap the bad guys. This looks as though they made a movie out of an arcade video game. As for the dialogue, it's strictly gibberish. The cast performs woodenly against a background of smoke and noise. **Director**—Hal Needham. (PG)   *93 minutes*

MELVIN AND HOWARD (1980)

★★★★

Paul Le Mat
Jason Robards, Jr.
Mary Steenburgen

Paul Le Mat strikes up an improbable friendship with Jason Robards, Jr. in Melvin and Howard.

A charming and often hilarious social satire taken from the much-publicized account of Melvin Dummar, the service station attendant who claims to be a beneficiary in Howard Hughes's will. Le Mat plays Melvin with a likable freshness that colorfully illuminates this good-hearted character who is eluded by the American dream. Supporting players Robards, who plays Hughes, and Steenburgen contribute energy and a sense of reality to this stylish comedy. **Director**—Jonathan Demme. (R) **Academy Awards**—Steenburgen, best supporting actress; Bo Goldman, best screenplay (written directly for the screen). *95 minutes*

THE MEMORY OF JUSTICE (1976)

★★★★

An extraordinary documentary epic by director Marcel Ophuls, re-examining the principles of justice established at the 1946 Nuremberg Trials. This extremely long, intense film classic hammers the emotions with such questions as: Has one nation the right to judge another? How does Nuremberg justice apply to U.S. military actions in Vietnam, or to the conduct of French soldiers in Algeria? The production is mainly composed of old newsreel footage and filmed interviews of more than 40 persons. The experience is exhilarating. This is monumental filmmaking. (PG)
278 minutes

THE MEN (1950)

★★★★

Marlon Brando
Teresa Wright

Brando debuts in this absorbing drama as a wounded war veteran struggling to overcome his disability, and his performance is impressive indeed. The entire production is excellent; there's fine acting and direction all around. The film is a realistic and penetrating treatment of a sensitive subject. Also with Everett Sloane, Jack Webb, and Howard St. John. **Director**—Fred Zinnemann. **Alternate Title**—*Battle Stripe*. **Academy Award Nomination**—Carl Foreman, writing (story and screenplay). *85 minutes b&w*

STAR PROFILE

• Men of the Fighting Lady
• Merrill's Marauders
• Merry Christmas, Mr. Lawrence
• Message from Space
• Metalstorm

M

MEN OF THE FIGHTING LADY (1954)
★★★

Van Johnson
Walter Pidgeon

Above-average saga of action aboard a U.S. aircraft carrier during the Korean Conflict. The characters are rather wooden, but the film moves briskly, with a semidocumentary flavor enhanced effectively by actual combat scenes worked in with the theatrics. Also with Keenan Wynn, Frank Lovejoy, Dewey Martin, Robert Horton, and Louis Calhern. **Director**—Andrew Marton.   *80 minutes*

MERRILL'S MARAUDERS (1962)
★★★

Jeff Chandler
Ty Hardin

Rough, tough combat adventure with battle-hardened U.S. Army troops winning the hard way against enemy forces in Burma during World War II. Typical heroic stuff, with the emphasis on the limits of hardship under life-or-death conditions. Decently acted by Chandler—his final film—and supporting players, including Hardin, Andrew Duggan, Peter Brown, Will Hutchins, and Claude Akins. **Director**—Samuel Fuller.   *98 minutes*

MERRY CHRISTMAS, MR. LAWRENCE (1983)
 ★★

David Bowie

David Bowie is a British inmate and Ryuichi Sakamoto an officer at a Japanese prisoner of war camp in Merry Christmas, Mr. Lawrence.

ELIZABETH TAYLOR

Elizabeth Taylor is perhaps as well known for her off-screen romances, marriages, and divorces as she is for her acting talent and beauty. She was born in 1932, in London, of American parents who returned to the United States in 1939 and settled in Los Angeles.

Enchantingly beautiful at age 10, Taylor made her screen debut in 1942 in There's One Born Every Minute. *The following year, she signed on with MGM, where she made a number of films as a child star and then continued on through the '60s in numerous dramatic roles.*

Her personal life was tumultuous almost from the start. She married hotel heir Nick Hilton at the age of 17 and divorced him a few months later.

In 1952, actor Michael Wilding became her second husband. They parted in 1957, and she then married film producer Michael Todd.

Taylor's relationship with Todd was probably the most significant in her life. Todd, however, died in the crash of his private plane in 1958.

A year later, Taylor married singer Eddie Fisher, only to divorce him in 1964, when she fell in love with Richard Burton during the filming of Cleopatra.

Her relationship with Burton was the subject of considerable publicity throughout the '60s and '70s. After a divorce, remarriage, and a second divorce from Burton, she married U.S. Senator John Warner. This seventh marriage failed in 1981, when the couple separated.

Taylor won her first Oscar as best actress for Butterfield 8 (1960), and she won her second Academy Award for Who's Afraid of Virginia Woolf? (1966).

Among her other notable movies are Lassie Come Home (1943), National Velvet (1944), Life with Father (1947), Father of the Bride (1950), A Place in the Sun (1951), Rhapsody (1954), Giant (1956), Cat on a Hot Tin Roof (1958), The Taming of the Shrew (1967), and A Little Night Music (1978).

Rock star Bowie's meticulous performance as a New Zealand officer confined to a Japanese prisoner-of-war camp is consistently intriguing. The film, however, is uneven and often unnecessarily harsh and gory. It tries to explore the differences and similarities of Western and Oriental cultures; a sort of intellectual version of *Bridge on the River Kwai*. But it pulls in too many directions at once and fails to achieve coherence. Tom Conti and Ryuichi Sakamoto also star, and Sakamoto's soundtrack music is impressive. **Director**—Nagisa Oshima. (R)   *120 minutes*

MESSAGE FROM SPACE (1978)
★★

Vic Morrow
Sonny Chiba

Squadrons of spaceships rocket among the planets. Heroes and villains duel with laser-beam swords. There's even a cute little robot. The message, obviously, is from *Star Wars*, and this imitation was made in Japan. The special effects have lots of zip, but the acting and plotting come through as warmed-over sukiyaki. Morrow, in a brief role, is the only familiar face in the crowd of unknown players, which includes many Japanese. **Director**—Kinji Fukasaku. (PG)   *105 minutes*

METALSTORM (1983)
 ★

A slow-paced, mangy-looking sci-fi adventure, shot in pointless 3–D and overloaded with nonsense about evil forces at work in the universe. The patchwork plot is lifted from *Star Wars*
(Continued)

 Movie is available in Beta and VHS videotape

M

- Meteor
- Metropolis
- Micki & Maude
- Middle Age Crazy
- Middle of the Night
- The Middle of the World
- Midnight Cowboy

Metalstorm—the Destruction of Jared-Syn is the long title of a movie short on plot, featuring Jeffrey Byron as an adventurer in space.

(Continued)
and Road Warrior. Jeffrey Byron heads the undistinguished cast as a heroic space ranger assigned to rescue a damsel and put an end to a villain. Also with Tim Thomerson and Kelly Preston. **Director**—Charles Band. (PG)   84 minutes

---

METEOR (1979)

 ★★

**Sean Connery
Natalie Wood
Karl Malden**

This is one more disaster epic for fans who can't get enough of devastation by earthquakes, tidal waves, and so on. This time it's a gigantic meteor speeding toward earth, and the Americans and Russians combine nuclear technology to stop it. Connery, Wood, and other notables put in time at the movie factory to portray cardboard characters. Some of the special effects are interesting, such as Manhattan's destruction. Henry Fonda plays the President again. Also with Brian Keith, Martin Landau, Trevor Howard, and Richard Dysart. **Director**—Ronald Neame. (PG)   103 minutes

---

METROPOLIS (1926)

 ★★★★

Brigitte Helms

Fritz Lang directed this visually impressive classic of silent German cinema. The film is a brooding vision of life in the year 2000, and its real star is the awesome set of the futuristic city (said to have been based on Lang's interpretation of the New York City skyline) and the expressively architectural compositions. The story (written by Lang's wife, Thea von Harbou) involves a female automaton who incites the dronelike workers—who live beneath the elite's elegant metropolis—to revolt against their employers. The imagery (37,000 extras moving through the geometric landscapes) is compelling. And its expression of a dehumanized society is still affecting.   120 minutes b&w

---

MICKI & MAUDE (1984)

 ★★★

**Dudley Moore
Ann Reinking
Amy Irving**

Oh, the mess Dudley Moore has on his hands: He plays a frustrated TV reporter with two wives (Reinking and Irving) who are both pregnant at the same time. This farcical setup leads to a maternity ward full of belly laughs as frantic Dudley attends to both women simultaneously while trying to maintain his secret. It's an ideal vehicle for Moore's likable charm. Director Blake Edwards delivers the goods from a clever script. (PG–13)   115 minutes

---

MIDDLE AGE CRAZY (1980)

★★

**Bruce Dern
Ann-Margret**

Bruce Dern and Ann-Margret are Middle Age Crazy, but they seem to like it.

Dern stars as a successful architect with a beautiful wife, played by Ann-Margret, who confronts a mid-life crisis. Dern gives the part ample warmth and appeal, but the tedious script is bogged down with clichés and sentimentality. The upshot is a disappointing film. This social problem has been explored time and again, and here the subject is overworked. The theme seems beset by its own mid-life crisis. **Director**—John Trent. (R)
89 minutes

MIDDLE OF THE NIGHT (1959)

★★★

**Fredric March
Kim Novak**

Satisfactory film rendition of Paddy Chayefsky's teleplay about a middle-aged widower in love with a much younger girl. March is convincing as the world-wise businessman seeking a new experience, but Novak isn't that persuasive as the youthful object of his affections. This isn't among the best of Chayefsky's efforts, but the story is moving nevertheless. Glenda Farrell, Jan Norris, Lee Grant, and Martin Balsam are adequate in supporting roles. **Director**—Delbert Mann.
118 minutes b&w

THE MIDDLE OF THE WORLD (1975)

★★★

**Olimpia Carlisi
Philippe Leotard**

An innovative film about a young actress from Italy with a deep sense of self-esteem. Carlisi portrays the sensitive heroine who refuses to accommodate a Swiss engineer, played by Leotard, who runs as a candidate for Parliament. It's simplistically funny at times and erotic with a complex intellectual underlay. Also with Juliet Berto. **Director**—Alain Tanner. In French with English titles. (No MPAA rating)   115 minutes b&w

---

MIDNIGHT COWBOY (1969)

 ★★★★

**Jon Voight
Dustin Hoffman**

Outstanding atmospheric drama about a naïve young man from Texas

• Midnight Express
• A Midsummer Night's Sex
   Comedy

• Midway
• Mighty Joe Young
• Mike's Murder

M

who comes to New York City to make it as a gigolo. He ends up being hustled, and he discovers it's just as dreary and lonesome in the big city as it was in the hick town he came from. The stark chain of events is played out against the squalid backdrop of New York's decaying 42nd Street area, and the film offers some memorable character studies of desperate souls. Voight is triumphant in the title role, and his excellent performance is matched beautifully by Hoffman as Ratso Rizzo, his disheveled friend. Sylvia Miles, John McGiver, and Brenda Vaccaro also star. **Director**—John Schlesinger. (R) **Academy Awards**—best picture; Schlesinger, best director; Waldo Salt, best screenplay (based on material from another medium). **Nominations**—Hoffman, Voight, best actor. *113 minutes*

MIDNIGHT EXPRESS (1978)

 ★★★★

**Brad Davis
John Hurt
Randy Quaid**

Brad Davis plays an American youth trapped in the hell of a Turkish prison in Midnight Express.

Realistic, gut-wrenching portrayal of brutality, degradation, and frustration suffered by a young American in a Turkish prison. The film is based on the true story of Billy Hayes, who was arrested in 1970 in Istanbul for trying to smuggle two kilos of hashish. Newcomer Davis, playing Billy, gives a remarkable performance; at times he resembles the late James Dean. Director Alan Parker expertly crafts the harrowing moods and sordid scenes of this latter-day version of Dante's *Inferno*. Also with Irene Miracle and Bo Hopkins. (R) **Academy Award**—Oliver Stone, best screenplay adaptation. **Nomination**—best picture; Parker, best director; Hurt, best supporting actor. *121 minutes*

A MIDSUMMER NIGHT'S SEX COMEDY (1982)

 ★★

**Woody Allen
Mia Farrow
José Ferrer**

Mary Steenburgen straps Woody Allen into his chair in A Midsummer Night's Sex Comedy.

In this picturesque but empty production, Allen presides over a romantic roundelay among three couples at a turn-of-the-century country home. Allen gets off a few wisecracks, but the film bogs down in ceaseless chatter about sexual problems. Once more, Allen seems to be rehashing someone else's movie; there are obvious references to Ingmar Bergman's *Smiles of a Summer Night*. Give us a break, Woody, and do your own thing. **Director**—Allen. (PG) *88 minutes*

MIDWAY (1976)

 ★

**Charlton Heston
Henry Fonda
Glenn Ford
James Coburn
Hal Holbrook**

Officers spring into action in Midway.

The sea-air Battle of Midway was a turning point in the Pacific during World War II, but this plodding and cliché-strewn film version is hardly a turning point in war movies. The lame script covers well-worn territory, and it's all wrapped in the Sensurround gimmick, which is more of an earache than an emotional effect. Veteran actors, including Robert Mitchum and Cliff Robertson, appear briefly to deliver a few stiff lines. Fonda has a somewhat larger part as Admiral Nimitz. (PG) *132 minutes*

MIGHTY JOE YOUNG (1949)

 ★★★

**Terry Moore
Ben Johnson**

A fairly competent retread of the King Kong fable, but not as stylish as the 1933 movie. A promoter brings back a gorilla from the African jungles and uses it in a nightclub routine. The animal breaks away and terrorizes the city. Just standard monkey business, with good special effects; Moore is in the Fay Wray role. Also with Robert Armstrong and Frank McHugh. **Director**—Ernest B. Schoedsack. *94 minutes b&w*

MIKE'S MURDER (1984)

 ★★

Debra Winger

Low-key melodrama set against Los Angeles', cocaine underworld. Winger stars as a lonely bank teller who falls in love with a charming tennis player (Mark Keyloun). When he is killed because of his drug connections, she

(Continued)

Mark Keyloun and Debra Winger have a brief but memorable affair in Mike's Murder.

(Continued)

attempts to unravel the mystery and eventually uncovers his dismal background. The slick film plays up atmosphere, but the characters are mostly uninteresting and the pace is slow—possibly the result of writer-producer-director James Bridges biting off more than he could chew. Also with Paul Winfield and Darrell Larson. (R)
109 minutes

MILDRED PIERCE (1945)
Ⓐ ★★★

Joan Crawford

Ann Blyth and Joan Crawford are mother and daughter in Mildred Pierce.

First-class, glossy soap opera starring Crawford busily succeeding and suffering as a restaurateur, harassed mother, and lover. The mother-daughter relationship stands out, with Ann Blyth in top form as Crawford's unthankful offspring. There's also lots of romantic entanglement. Competent supporting roles by Jack Carson, Zachary Scott, Eve Arden, and Bruce Bennett. **Director**—Michael Curtiz.

Academy Award—Crawford, best actress. **Nominations**—best picture; Arden, Blyth, best supporting actress; Ronald MacDougall, writing (screenplay); Ernest Haller, cinematography (black and white). *113 minutes b&w*

THE MIRACLE OF MORGAN'S CREEK (1944)
★★★★

**Betty Hutton
Eddie Bracken**

Eddie Bracken and Betty Hutton wonder who did what to create The Miracle of Morgan's Creek.

A tip-top comic extravaganza by director Preston Sturges, about the misadventures of a girl made pregnant by a soldier at a party. But which soldier? This subject would have no problem today, but Hollywood faced persnickety censors in the '40s, and Sturges's treatment saved the film. It's an effective and fantastic assault on the funnybone dressed up smartly with good performances. Hutton is excellent as the hapless mother-to-be. William Demarest, Diana Lynn, and Brian Donlevy also star. **Academy Award Nomination**—Sturges, writing (original screenplay). *99 minutes b&w*

THE MIRACLE ON 34TH STREET (1947)
Ⓐ ★★★★

**Edmund Gwenn
Maureen O'Hara
John Payne**

An amazingly cheerful, heartwarming, and uplifting fable, about an elderly gentleman, hired as a department store Santa Claus, who claims to be the real St. Nick. It's a clever and charming blend of humor and pathos with a holiday message for young and old. This film seems as endurable as Christmas itself. Gwenn is delightful as "Kris Kringle." O'Hara, Payne, Natalie Wood, and Gene Lockhart are in fine supporting roles. **Director**—George Seaton. **Academy Awards**—Gwenn, best supporting actor; Valentine Davies, writing (original story); George Seaton, writing (screenplay). **Nomination**—best picture.
94 minutes b&w

THE MIRACLE WORKER (1962)
Ⓐ ★★★★

**Anne Bancroft
Patty Duke**

An absorbing account of the early life of Helen Keller and her amazing struggle to overcome the multiple handicaps of being blind, deaf, and mute. The story is as much about her determined teacher, and the role is played brilliantly by Bancroft. Duke is excellent, too, as the young Keller who finally learns to communicate. A few of the scenes are exceptionally moving. Also with Victor Jory, Inga Swenson, Andrew Prine, and Beah Richards. **Director**—Arthur Penn. **Academy Awards**—Bancroft, best actress; Duke, best supporting actress. **Nominations**—Penn, best director; William Gibson, best screenplay (based on material from another medium).
107 minutes b&w

MIRAGE (1965)
★★★

**Gregory Peck
Diane Baker
Walter Matthau**

Expertly conceived thriller, presented much in the Hitchcock style, about a man with amnesia who becomes tangled in a murder mystery. Peck plays the amnesiac, Baker is a mysterious girl, and Matthau is a rumpled private detective. The suspense is effectively paced and developed, and the film is enhanced with striking photography of New York City locations. Peck does a fine acting job in the key role, and there's an interesting performance from Matthau. Also with Walter Abel,

• The Mirror Crack'd
• The Misfits
• Miss Grant Takes
   Richmond

• Missing
• Missing in Action
• The Missionary
• The Missouri Breaks

M

Kevin McCarthy, Jack Weston, Leif Erickson, and George Kennedy. **Director**—Edward Dmytryk.

109 minutes b&w

THE MIRROR CRACK'D (1980)

 ★★★

Angela Lansbury
Edward Fox

Angela Lansbury plays sleuthstress Miss Jane Marple in Agatha Christie's The Mirror Crack'd.

Stylish, tart Agatha Christie whodunit with an all-star cast, about murders on the set of an American movie being made in England. Elizabeth Taylor and Kim Novak, in their best roles in years, are delightful as rival fading movie stars. Lansbury is a convincing Miss Jane Marple who figures out who poisoned the drink at the cocktail party. Also with Rock Hudson, Tony Curtis, and Geraldine Chaplin. **Director**—Guy Hamilton. (PG)

105 minutes

THE MISFITS (1961)

 ★★★

Clark Gable
Marilyn Monroe
Montgomery Clift

Arthur Miller's pensive story about latter-day cowboys is alternately compelling and sullen. Monroe plays a confused divorcée involved with some western adventurers concerned with rounding up wild horses in the desert. Gable and Clift play the men in her life. The script only trots along, but some of the horse-chasing moves with energy. Monroe and Gable died shortly after the film's release. Also with Eli Wallach, Thelma Ritter, and Kevin McCarthy. **Director**—John Huston. *124 minutes b&w*

MISS GRANT TAKES RICHMOND (1949)

★★

Lucille Ball
William Holden

Ball plays a birdbrained secretary who helps put the lid on a bookie operation. Typical slapstick shenanigans, enjoyable if you love Lucy. Holden is an effective co-star. Also with Janis Carter, James Gleason, and Frank McHugh. **Director**—Lloyd Bacon.

83 minutes b&w

MISSING (1982)

 ★★★

Jack Lemmon
Sissy Spacek

Sissy Spacek and Jack Lemmon are looking for a political prisoner in Missing.

A powerful, compelling political melodrama masterfully directed by CostaGavras (Z) and played to perfection by Lemmon and Spacek. The slam-bang plot has Lemmon as an American businessman involved in a frustrating search for his missing son who's been caught up in a South American coup. The father is jolted out of his complacency when he runs into a wall of double-talk and red tape from American embassy and local government officials. In all respects this is a superior film. (PG) **Academy Award**—CostaGavras and Donald Stewart, best screenplay (based on material from another medium). **Nominations**—best picture; Lemmon, best actor; Spacek, best actress.

122 minutes

MISSING IN ACTION (1984)

 ★★

Chuck Norris

Plenty of shoot-'em-up action, reminiscent of a John Wayne western, propels this simpleminded adventure about the rescue of a few American war prisoners from Vietnam. Norris stars as a one-man army who blasts away with machine guns, grenades, and explosives against scores of Vietnamese soldiers. They obligingly bite the dust without showing much blood or gore. In typical B-movie fashion, the Americans are portrayed as brave and virtuous while the enemy is composed of cardboard villains. **Director**—Joseph Zito. (R) *94 minutes*

THE MISSIONARY (1982)

 ★★

Michael Palin
Maggie Smith
Trevor Howard

Palin of the Monty Python comedy troupe stars in this meandering satire on Edwardian morality. He's a missionary preacher assigned to rescue London's "fallen women," but he can't resist taking a very nonclerical interest in his charges in the process. The British production is exquisitely appointed, well acted, and quietly amusing a lot of the time. But it's a pretty thin story underneath all the surface charm. **Director**—Richard Loncraine. (R) *90 minutes*

THE MISSOURI BREAKS (1976)

 ★★★

Marlon Brando
Jack Nicholson

Superstars Brando and Nicholson deliver delightful and dazzling performances in Arthur Penn's 1880 period western set in the majestic Montana hills. Brando plays an eccentric and sadistic hired gun commissioned by a wealthy cattle baron to wipe out a gang of horse thieves headed by Nicholson. But without these two magnificent talents, the film would be just another average horse

(Continued)

M
- Mr. Blandings Builds His Dream House
- Mister Cory
- Mr. Lucky
- Mr. Mike's Mondo Video
- Mr. Mom
- Mr. Peabody and the Mermaid
- Mister Roberts

Marlon Brando fights rustlers in The Missouri Breaks.

(Continued)

opera. Screenwriter Thomas McGuane merely set the clock back on the plot that served his earlier film, *Rancho Deluxe*, and jazzed it up some with late 20th-century philosophizing. Newcomer Kathleen Lloyd demonstrates extraordinary potential in the role of the cattleman's liberated daughter, who falls in love with the likable Nicholson. Also with Randy Quaid and Frederic Forrest. **Director—Arthur Penn. (PG)** *126 minutes*

MR. BLANDINGS BUILDS HIS DREAM HOUSE (1948)

 ★★★★

Cary Grant
Myrna Loy
Melvyn Douglas

A rib-tickling middlebrow comedy about a New York advertising executive who decides to build a house in the suburbs and discovers the project is no piece of cake. There are loads of clever and funny moments in this slick production with the stars at their hilarious best. Grant is perfectly cast as the exasperated homeowner. Also with Reginald Denny, Louis Beavers, and Jason Robards, Jr. **Director—H. C. Potter.** *84 minutes b&w*

MISTER CORY (1957)

★★★

Tony Curtis
Martha Hyer

Engaging, fast-paced account of a young man from a poor background who's taken in by high-society people and becomes wealthy. The smooth, no-frills script maintains consistent

interest. Curtis is much at ease in the title role, which seems tailor-made for his style. Also with Charles Bickford and Kathryn Grant. **Director—Blake Edwards.** *92 minutes*

MR. LUCKY (1943)

 ★★★

Cary Grant
Laraine Day

Grant is effectively charming and amusing as a gambling-ship owner who concocts a dubious scheme to raise cash. But love intervenes, and he goes straight. A smooth blend of comedy and drama, handled skillfully by a professional cast, which also includes Charles Bickford, Gladys Cooper, and Alan Carney. **Director—H. C. Potter.** *98 minutes b&w*

MR. MIKE'S MONDO VIDEO (1979)

(no stars)

Director-producer Michael O'Donoghue apparently slapped this mess together for NBC, and then it was rejected as being inappropriate for television. The film seems to be a parody of the various *Mondo* movies of many years ago. Most of the gags flop, and many of the sketches are in bad taste or are merely absurd. For example, there's a piece about a swimming school for cats, and there's a clip of the late Sid Vicious wailing "My Way." (R) *60 minutes*

MR. MOM (1983)

★★★

Michael Keaton
Teri Garr

Dad (Keaton) loses his job at the recession-plagued auto factory. He stays home to mind the kids while Mom (Garr) goes to work and becomes a successful ad agency executive. This role reversal bit has been done to death, especially on TV. Yet the performances are spirited and help the story move at a lively gait until the mushy conclusion. John Hughes, who wrote *National Lampoon's Vacation*, did the

Teri Garr and Michael Keaton reverse roles with comic consequences in Mr. Mom.

script. If nothing else, the film establishes Keaton as one of the best comic actors around. Martin Mull co-stars. **Director—Stan Dragoti. (PG)** *91 minutes*

MR. PEABODY AND THE MERMAID (1948)

★★

William Powell
Ann Blyth

Mildly amusing whimsy about a middle-aged man who discovers a beautiful mermaid and takes a fresh look at his life. A few scenes work, but just as many are silly in this fantasy. Powell is suited for the title role. Also with Irene Hervey, Andrea King, and Clinton Sundberg. **Director—Irving Pichel.** *89 minutes b&w*

MISTER ROBERTS (1955)

★★★★

Henry Fonda
James Cagney
William Powell
Jack Lemmon

Boredom and pettiness are the targets of this winning comedy set aboard a supply ship in the Pacific during World War II. Fonda is great in the title role as a restless but likable Navy officer just itching to be transferred to a fighting

• Mr. Smith Goes to
Washington
• Mrs. Miniver
• Mrs. Soffel

• Mitchell
• Misunderstood
• Ms. 45
• Moby Dick

M

ship. And there's rampant scene-stealing by Lemmon as a bumbling Ensign Pulver and Cagney as the neurotic skipper of the cargo vessel. Powell is the ship's doctor. A superb blend of hilarity and sentiment, based on the Broadway play by Joshua Logan and author Thomas Heggen. Also with Ward Bond, Betsy Palmer, and Phil Carey. **Directors**—John Ford and Mervyn Le Roy. **Academy Award**—Lemmon, best supporting actor. **Nomination**—best picture.   *123 minutes*

MR. SMITH GOES TO WASHINGTON (1939)

★★★★

James Stewart
Claude Rains
Jean Arthur

This is among the best of director Frank Capra's comedy-dramas. Stewart gives a stirring performance as a forthright freshman senator who encounters corruption in the nation's capital. It's a rather inspiring portrait of how elected officials ought to behave. The production is first-class in every department, and there are other brilliant performances from Rains, Arthur, Harry Carey, Thomas Mitchell, Edward Arnold, Guy Kibbee, and Beulah Bondi. **Academy Award**—Lewis R. Foster, writing (original story). **Nominations**—best picture; Capra, best director; Stewart, best actor; Carey, Rains, best supporting actor; Sidney Buchman, writing (screenplay).   *130 minutes b&w*

MRS. MINIVER (1942)

★★★★

Greer Garson
Walter Pidgeon

A highly moving account of courageous British villagers struggling to cope with the hardships and dangers of World War II. The film is rather melodramatic, but it's extremely well made, and it served as an effective wartime morale booster. Fine performances throughout. Also with Teresa Wright, Henry Travers, Richard Ney, and Dame May Whitty. **Director**—William Wyler. **Academy Awards**—best picture; Wyler, best director; Garson, best actress; Wright, best supporting ac-

tress; George Froeschel, James Hilton, Claudine West, and Arthur Wimperis, writing (screenplay); Joseph Ruttenberg, cinematography (black and white). **Nominations**—Pidgeon, best actor; Travers, best supporting actor; Whitty, best supporting actress.
     134 minutes b&w

MRS. SOFFEL (1984)

★★

Diane Keaton
Mel Gibson
Matthew Modine

This potentially exciting tale is stripped of its dramatic impact and emerges flat and subdued. Keaton adequately portrays the title character, a proper prison warden's wife who falls in love with a condemned murderer and helps him escape. But good performances cannot overcome the plodding way the events unfold. Based on a true story set in 1901. **Director**—Gillian Armstrong (PG–13)
     110 minutes

MISUNDERSTOOD (1984)

★★

Gene Hackman

Drab, two-hanky weepy starring Hackman as a shipping tycoon residing in Tunisia. Mom recently died and Gene can't seem to fulfill the emotional needs of his two precocious young sons. The tykes are engagingly played by Henry (*E.T.*) Thomas and Huckleberry (*Terms of Endearment*) Fox. Their interrelationship is the only interesting aspect of this otherwise contrived and sappy story, which is difficult to understand. **Director**—Jerry Schutzberg. (PG)   *91 minutes*

MITCHELL (1975)

★

Joe Don Baker

The film is about an honest Los Angeles detective on the trail of a big-time narcotics operation. There's plenty of violence and chasing around in automobiles within a dreary script, which lacks character development. Baker, who did well in *Walking Tall*, is

miscast in the title role. Also with Martin Balsam, John Saxon, Linda Evans, and Merlin Olsen. **Director**—Andrew V. McLaglen. (R)   *96 minutes*

MS. 45 (1981)

(no stars)

Zoe Tamerlis

Gory, absurd movie, about an attractive young mute girl who embarks on a revengeful killing spree after being raped twice in one day. In one particular grisly sequence, she kills the second rapist, cuts the body into small pieces, and stows the parts in her refrigerator. Despite such horrendous scenes, Tamerlis displays impressive talent in the title role, and Abel Ferrara directs with noticeable style and pacing. Perhaps next time they'll find decent outlets for their skills. (R)
     90 minutes

MOBY DICK (1956)

★★★

Gregory Peck
Richard Basehart

Gregory Peck searches for the great white in Moby Dick.

Herman Melville's classic tale of a ship captain fiercely struggling to land a great white whale is impressively produced for the screen, but the pace is somewhat patchy. Peck is ill at ease as Captain Ahab, the obsessed skipper, but there are some good moments here and there nevertheless. Basehart, Friedrich Ledebur, Leo Genn, Harry Andrews, and Orson Welles appear in supporting roles. **Director**—John Huston.   *116 minutes*

M

- Modern Problems
- Modern Romance
- Modern Times
- Mogambo
- Mohammad, Messenger of God
- The Molly Maguires
- Moment by Moment

MODERN PROBLEMS (1981)

 ★

Chevy Chase

A creaky clunker of a comedy with Chase playing a young blade who accidentally acquires telekinetic powers, which he uses to win back his former girl friend. The production is beset with problems—stale jokes, sloppy direction, shabby performances, and an unbearable script. Chevy mopes about with an amazing lack of energy and comic skill; the film is an unmitigated fiasco. Also stars Patti D'Arbanville, Mary Kay Place, Nell Carter, and Dabney Coleman. **Director**—Ken Shapiro. (PG)   *92 minutes*

MODERN ROMANCE (1981)

 ★

Albert Brooks
Kathryn Harrold

Brooks, co-writer, director, and star, displays his limited talent in this tedious, low-key comedy about an on-again, off-again love affair. The lackadaisical script doesn't develop into anything significant. As a slice of life, it's cut rather thin. Brooks, who seems infatuated with his own performance, is on screen most of the time, engaged in slightly comic and irritating monologues. Beautiful Harrold plays the object of his confused affections. Also with Bruno Kirby. (R)   *93 minutes*

MODERN TIMES (1936)

 ★★★★

Charlie Chaplin
Paulette Goddard
Chester Conklin

Chaplin wrote, directed, starred in, and scored this comedy for all seasons. It was his last silent film (there's music, effects, and limited speech), made nine years into the sound era, and the last incarnation of the little tramp. His pantomimic art had reached its peak, and an age of innocence was ending forever. The film is a wonderful satire of the perils of modern life. Charlie plays a factory worker who goes berserk, tries his hand at a variety of jobs, and befriends a home-less young woman—played by his wife Goddard—who steals his heart. The humor is witty and wise, slapstick and visual. At times it's disarmingly romantic. There's something here for almost everyone to enjoy through several viewings.   *87 minutes b&w*

MOGAMBO
(1953)

 ★★★

Clark Gable
Ava Gardner
Grace Kelly

In Mogambo, *Ava Gardner hunts big romantic game in Africa.*

Romantic, adventuresome, darkest-Africa/white-hunter saga with plenty of colorful performances. Gable is tops as the pursuer of big game who becomes involved with two alluring women—Gardner and Kelly. A gorilla hunt highlights the jungle action. The film is a remake of *Red Dust*, with Gable repeating his role. Also with Donald Sinden, Laurence Naismith, and Philip Stainton. **Director**—John Ford. **Academy Award Nominations**—Gardner, best actress; Kelly, best supporting actress.   *116 minutes*

MOHAMMAD, MESSENGER OF GOD
(1977)

★

Anthony Quinn
Irene Papas

This well-intentioned attempt to detail the last 20 years of the Moslem proph-et's life is uninspiring, mechanical, and innocuous. The sprawling epic, produced and directed by Moustapha Akkad, who appears to have studied at the Cecil B. DeMille school of religion, drones on for three hours. Yet it takes only 15 minutes to get the message. Quinn, in the key role, portrays Mohammad's uncle, who fights for the right of the prophet to practice his religion. Mohammad never appears on screen, in accordance with Islam. Also with Michael Ansara, Johnny Sekka, and Michael Forest. (PG)   *180 minutes*

THE MOLLY MAGUIRES (1970)
★★

Richard Harris
Sean Connery

Partly engrossing account of a secret society of Pennsylvania coal miners in the 1870s using extreme measures to improve working conditions. A private detective infiltrates the group and reports on their violent activities. The serious, well-made film is based on true events. However, the story ends with a sense of vagueness. Connery is convincing as a leader of the society, and Harris performs well as the undercover Pinkerton man. Also stars Samantha Eggar, Frank Finlay, Anthony Zerbe, and Art Lund. **Director**—Martin Ritt. (PG)   *123 minutes*

MOMENT BY MOMENT (1978)
★

Lily Tomlin
John Travolta

Lily Tomlin and John Travolta have an affair in Moment By Moment.

• Mommie Dearest
• Monkey Business
• Mon Oncle D'Amerique

• Monsignor
• Montenegro
• Monty Python and the Holy Grail

M

Tedious claptrap about a well-heeled middle-aged woman who has an affair with a young drifter. Tomlin and Travolta are the odd couple. Here we have two of Hollywood's brightest stars, but they don't click together. The main trouble seems to be with the humdrum script by writer-director Jane Wagner, who has worked with Tomlin for some time. With all the dumb dialogue, drippy clichés, and contrived situations, the film seems to drag on hour by hour. Also with Andra Akers and Bert Kramer. (R)

102 minutes

MOMMIE DEAREST (1981)

 ★

Faye Dunaway
Diana Scarwid

Faye Dunaway portrays actress Joan Crawford in Mommie Dearest.

Dunaway plays screen idol Joan Crawford in this tacky version of the tacky book by Crawford's adopted daughter, Christina. Her characterization is lifelike, but the script is not. The dialogue is so bad that Dunaway's portrayal of the hard-driving, ambitious, insecure, and occasionally raving mad movie queen is totally wasted. Mara Hobel plays Christina as a suffering child, and Scarwid plays her as an insufferable adult. Also with Steve Forrest and Henry Da Silva. **Director**—Frank Perry. (PG)　　　*129 minutes*

MONKEY BUSINESS (1952)
★★★

Cary Grant
Ginger Rogers

A lot of good talent got together for

this madcap comedy about a scientist who discovers an amazing elixir that restores youth. Grant plays the researcher, and Rogers plays his wife. A certain amount of corn is involved, but there's plenty to laugh about, with Cary performing at top speed. Charles Coburn plays Grant's boss, and Marilyn Monroe is a secretary. **Director**—Howard Hawks.　　*97 minutes b&w*

MON ONCLE D'AMERIQUE (1981)
★★

Gerard Depardieu
Nicole Garcia

When Roger-Pierre runs away to live with his girlfriend, Nicole Garcia, in Mon Oncle D'Amerique, *the scene is as clinically observed as if they were laboratory rats.*

Alain Resnais's dull comedy is a complex examination of human behavior. The film follows the lives of three ambitious but mixed-up characters. Resnais treats his subject with coyness, charm, and intelligence; but the various case histories aren't clearly connected, and this situation becomes an annoying distraction. Also with Roger-Pierre. In French with English titles. (No MPAA rating) **Academy Award Nomination**—Jean Gruault, best screenplay (written directly for the screen).　　　*125 minutes*

MONSIGNOR (1982)
 ★

Christopher Reeve
Geneviève Bujold

Cumbersome, lethargic, and ludicrous melodrama about corruption among the Catholic church's hierarchy. Reeve delivers a wooden portrayal of a cynical, ambitious priest with Mafia connections, who ends up controlling

Geneviève Bujold plays a nun in Monsignor.

the Vatican's finances. The awkward screenplay and dreary dialogue lead to much confusion and tedium. Such trespasses are unforgivable. **Director**—Frank Perry. (R)　　*122 minutes*

MONTENEGRO (1981)
 ★★

Susan Anspach

Yugoslav director Dusan Makavejev presents a loosely constructed comedy that can be recognized for its intelligence, but fails to come across as worthwhile entertainment. The film, set in Sweden, centers on Anspach, the restless and rather loony American wife of a wealthy Swedish industrialist. She's kidnapped, almost willingly, by some freewheeling immigrants and held at a sleazy nightclub where she experiences a spiritual awakening. Makavejev makes an interesting social statement, but it's conveyed in a hodgepodge manner. Also stars Erland Josephson and Per Oscarsson. (No MPAA rating)

95 minutes

MONTY PYTHON AND THE HOLY GRAIL (1975)
 ★★★★

Graham Chapman
John Cleese
Terry Gilliam
Eric Idle
Michael Palin

A cheerful, comic reworking of the legend of King Arthur and the search for the Holy Grail. The quest leaves Camelot in a shambles of laughter. It's

(Continued)

M

- Monty Python Live at the Hollywood Bowl
- Monty Python's The Meaning of Life
- Moon in the Gutter
- The Moon Is Blue
- Moonlighting
- Moon Over Miami
- Moonraker

Graham Chapman plays King Arthur in Monty Python and the Holy Grail.

(Continued)

written and acted by the brilliant Monty Python troupe, who were first made famous on British TV. Plenty of laughs, chuckles, sight gags, sick jokes, and wit in this loony satire. **Directors**—Terry Gilliam and Terry Jones. (PG)   90 minutes

MONTY PYTHON LIVE AT THE HOLLYWOOD BOWL (1982)

     ★★★

This filmed performance of the noted English comedy group is an extension of their famous TV shows, adapted for the stage and with a few new bits. A couple of skits miss the mark but most are hilarious, and the material seems as fresh as ever—especially with a live audience enjoying it immensely. Among the acts: a soccer match between famous philosophers, and a game show starring Marx, Lenin, Che Guevara, and Mao Tse Tung. **Director**—Terry Hughes. (R)   77 minutes

MONTY PYTHON'S THE MEANING OF LIFE (1983)

★★★

Britain's bad boys of outrageous satire serve up a mixed grill of sketches that touch on such subjects as birth, sex, religion, death, war, and middle-class life-styles. Much of the film is out of control and offensive, yet moments of inspired hilarity shine through. One unforgettable, repulsive scene shows a bloated patron of a posh French restaurant alternately ordering gourmet entrees and vomiting. With Graham Chapman, John Cleese, Terry Gilliam, Eric Idle, Terry Jones, and Michael Palin. **Director**—Terry Jones. (R)   103 minutes

MOON IN THE GUTTER (1983)

★

**Gerard Depardieu
Nastassja Kinski**

French director Jean-Jacques Beineix, who fared well with *Diva*, falls on his face with this second effort, a suffocating and pretentious film based on the novel by David Goodis. Depardieu plays a lumbering stevedore on the prowl for the rapist of his sister. In the process, he latches on to sultry, wealthy Kinski. Both stars come off poorly as Beineix overindulges the production with murky, listless atmospherics. There is a good deal of unintentional humor. In the gutter, indeed. In French with English titles. (R)   126 minutes

THE MOON IS BLUE (1953)

★★

**Maggie McNamara
David Niven
William Holden**

This sex comedy raised eyebrows at the time of release because of the use of such then-shocking words as "virgin" and "mistress." Now the film is rather mild stuff, indeed, with most of the gags straining to evoke a smile or two. The story involves the escapades of an attractive lass, played by McNamara, who stirs the passions of several gentlemen. Also with Tom Tully and Dawn Adams. **Director**—Otto Preminger. **Academy Award Nomination**—McNamara, best actress.
96 minutes b&w

MOONLIGHTING (1982)

★★★

Jeremy Irons

Polish filmmaker Jerzy Skolimowski makes a weighty statement about his country's political situation. This moody film is set in England, and the subtle story involves the plight of four

Moonlighting features Jeremy Irons as a Polish worker in London during the imposition of martial law.

Polish workers who are temporarily in London to restore a townhouse for a mysterious "boss." Their English-speaking foreman (Irons) desperately maneuvers to hide from his men the news of the military takeover back home. (PG)   97 minutes

MOON OVER MIAMI (1941)

★★★

**Don Ameche
Betty Grable
Carole Landis**

A pleasant musical, graced by a likable cast and based on the familiar theme of gorgeous girls on the prowl for rich husbands. Grable, Landis, and Charlotte Greenwood are the fortune hunters who find romance and more in this colorful film. Musical numbers include the title song and "You Started Something." Also with Jack Haley and Robert Cummings. **Director**—Walter Lang.   92 minutes

MOONRAKER (1979)

★★★

**Roger Moore
Lois Chiles
Richard Kiel**

Ageless, tireless James Bond saves the world from a cunning aerospace tycoon in this fantastic superspy thriller. It's the 11th film feature for Agent 007, played here by Moore, and the formula

Roger Moore is James Bond in Moonraker.

still works wonders. It's an irresistible entertainment feast, complete with spectacular sets, breathtaking stunts, secret-agent gadgets, and gorgeous women. Chiles is stunning as Bond's romantic interest, and Kiel reappears as the towering steeltoothed "Jaws." Also with Michael Lonsdale, Corinne Clery, Bernard Lee, and Lois Maxwell. **Director**—Lewis Gilbert. (PG)

126 minutes

MORE AMERICAN GRAFFITI
(1979)

Candy Clark
Bo Hopkins
Ron Howard
Cindy Williams
Paul Le Mat

Ron Howard grows up to be a subversive radical in More American Graffiti.

This clumsy sequel to the popular 1973 hit follows the lives of the characters through the turmoil of the mid '60s. The story is jumbled into four disjointed vignettes that range from the battlefields of Vietnam to the antiwar movement at home. Most of the original cast is back, and they're certainly appealing. But writer-director B.W.L. Norton overreaches, and he hasn't maintained the innocence and warmth that marked the original George Lucas version. Also with Charles Martin Smith and Mackenzie Phillips. (PG)   *111 minutes*

THE MORE THE MERRIER
(1943)

Jean Arthur
Joel McCrea
Charles Coburn

There's no shortage of effective comic situations in this funny tale of a girl who shares a small apartment with two men in Washington during a housing shortage during World War II. Arthur, McCrea, and Coburn keep the laughter and romance sailing along, with plenty of sparkling dialogue and excellent acting. It's thoroughly charming and exceptionally bright. Also with Richard Gaines and Bruce Bennett. **Director**—George Stevens. **Academy Award**—Coburn, best supporting actor. **Nominations**—best picture; Stevens, best director; Arthur, best actress; Frank Ross and Robert Russell, writing (original story); Richard Flournoy, Lewis R. Foster, Frank Ross, and Robert Russell, writing (screenplay).   *104 minutes b&w*

THE MORTAL STORM (1940)
★★★★

James Stewart
Margaret Sullavan
Frank Morgan
Robert Young

This was Hollywood's first major film to strike out against Nazism; but far more than potent propaganda, it has endured as searing drama. Morgan was never better than as the German professor who stands up against the Nazis in 1933, and is carted off to a concentration camp. His stepsons (Young is one) become Nazis, while his daughter (Sullavan) tries to flee Germany with her boyfriend, played by Stewart. The entire cast gives wrenching performances, under the guidance of one of MGM's greatest directors, Frank Borzage. Also starring Robert Stack, Bonita Granville, and Maria Ouspenskaya.

99 minutes b&w

MORTUARY (1984)
★

Mary McDonough
David Wallace

Routine, uneven, stab-'em-slab-'em horror story built around young lovers and a psychotic mortician. The usual red herrings and gory murders abound. For the morbidly minded there are graphic details of embalmers at work. Students of human nature may appreciate the psychological revelations about the unbalanced undertaker who attempts to embalm one of his victims while she is alive. Lovers of film may wish that director Howard Avedis had met the same fate. (R)

91 minutes

MOSCOW ON THE HUDSON
(1984)

 ★★★

Robin Williams
Maria Conchita Alonso
Cleavant Derricks

(Continued)

Robin Williams plays a Russian defector who loves all things American, including his brother in Moscow on the Hudson.

M
- Motel Hell
- Mother, Jugs & Speed
- Mother Wore Tights
- Moulin Rouge

(Continued)

Director Paul Mazursky's gentle comedy intelligently explores the differences between Russian and American cultures. Although the plot is somewhat patchy, the observations are appealing. In a remarkably restrained performance, Williams is delightful as a Russian circus musician who abruptly defects to America. His bewildered immigrant characterization offers fresh insights into the great American melting pot. (R)

115 minutes

MOTEL HELL (1980)
(no stars)

Rory Calhoun

Kindly farmer Vincent, played by Calhoun, is also a motel keeper who runs a smoked-meat business on the side. His secret ingredient is human flesh blended in with the pork. A few laughs and a dash of suspense are mixed with

the blood and gore, but there's not an iota of logic in this absurd horror film that aims for cult status. "Don't worry. I have a cast-iron stomach," chirps Nina Axelrod, as she innocently tours Vincent's meat preparation building. That's a warning for the audience, too! Also with Nancy Parsons. **Director—**Kevin Connor. (R)   *106 minutes*

MOTHER, JUGS & SPEED
(1976)
★★★

Bill Cosby
Raquel Welch
Harvey Keitel

Cosby, Welch, and Keitel star in a fast-paced black comedy about Los Angeles ambulance drivers. It's *M*A*S*H* in civilian clothes. There are some outrageous moments, but it does entertain with a contrasting blend of farce and serious drama. Welch, in a strong role as a fetching switchboard operator,

complements her physical attractiveness with a competent performance. Cosby, Keitel, and the rest of the cast give their best. Director Peter *(Bullitt)* Yates lays on the freewheeling spirit. Also with Allen Garfield and Larry Hagman. (PG)   *95 minutes*

MOTHER WORE TIGHTS
(1947)
★★★

Betty Grable
Dan Dailey

Excellent showcase for the talents of Grable and Dailey as a vaudeville couple involved with their colorful career and raising a family. The production is colorful, and the film moves along smartly with charming song-and-dance numbers. Based on the book by Miriam Young. Also with Mona Freeman, Connie Marshall, Vanessa Brown, and Veda Ann Borg. **Director**—Walter Lang. **Academy Award Nomination**—Harry Jackson, cinematography (color).   *107 minutes*

MOULIN ROUGE (1952)
★★★★

José Ferrer
Zsa Zsa Gabor

Colette Marchand and José Ferrer in Moulin Rouge, *a biography of Henri Toulouse-Lautrec.*

Brilliant film biography of French painter Henri Toulouse-Lautrec, who suffered from a tragic deformity. The dramatic and colorful account details the famous artist's sad outlook on the world and its despairing effect on his love affairs. Director John Huston presents a striking view of 19th-century Montmartre and its many flavorful characters. A magnificent can-can sequence is a real showstopper. Also with Suzanne Fion, Katherine

JANE FONDA

Born in New York City in 1937, Jane Fonda spent her early years in California. She made a hesitant acting debut with her father, Henry Fonda, in a summer stock production of The Country Girl *and appeared briefly with him in* The Male Animal *in Cape Cod. But her main interests were painting and languages, so, after studying at Vassar, Fonda left to study painting at l'École de Chauvinière in Paris.*

Fonda returned to New York, and took up modeling; she appeared on the cover of Vogue *magazine twice. Then, in 1958, a meeting with Lee Strasberg led to studies at his Actors' Studio and to a sudden passion for acting.*

Fonda made her formal stage debut

in The Moon Is Blue. *This led to her Broadway bow in 1960 in* There Was a Little Girl. *In the same year, she made her film debut in* Tall Story.

During her so-called "coltish ingenue" days, Fonda made a dozen more pictures including A Walk on the Wild Side *(1961),* The Chapman Report *(1962),* La Ronde *(1964), and* Cat Ballou *(1965), a western that changed the genre and established her as a superb comedienne.*

After her husband, French director Roger Vadim, launched her as a sex-tigress in Barbarella *(1968), Fonda returned to California and made her dramatic film breakthrough as the embittered marathon dancer in* They Shoot Horses, Don't They? *(1969). For* Klute *(1971), her next film, she won her first Oscar. She won her second Academy Award for* Coming Home *(1978).*

Fonda has also starred in Steelyard Blues *(1972),* A Doll's House *(1973),* The China Syndrome *(1979),* The Electric Horseman *(1979),* 9 to 5 *(1981), and with her father in* On Golden Pond *(1982), a film that earned her an Oscar nomination as best supporting actress.*

• Mountain Family Robinson
• The Mountain Men
• Mourning Becomes Electra
• The Mouse That Roared
• Move Over, Darling
• Movie, Movie
• The Muppet Movie

M

Kath, Colette Marchand, Eric Pohlman, and Christopher Lee. **Academy Award Nominations**—best picture; Huston, best director; Ferrer, best actor; Marchand, best supporting actress. *119 minutes*

MOUNTAIN FAMILY ROBINSON (1981)

 ★★

Robert Logan
Heather Rattray
Ham Larsen

This is the third film about the sentimental adventures of the rosy-cheeked family of four who escape traffic-snarled Los Angeles to reside in a mountain log cabin. But even in this wilderness paradise, they can't avoid government bureaucracy. A cranky forest ranger tries to evict them because they're on a government-controlled mining-claim area. Once again, the forest animals and the spectacular scenery upstage the human cast. **Director**—John Cotter. (G) *100 minutes*

THE MOUNTAIN MEN (1980)

 ★★

Charlton Heston
Brian Keith

Heston and Keith are grizzled Davy Crockett types who trap beavers and fight Indians in this routine outdoor adventure. Heston falls in love with a beautiful Indian girl, played by Victoria Racimo. She's also claimed by an Indian chief, and this conflict leads to some spectacular hand-to-hand combat. The film offers picturesque Wyoming settings and some snappy action scenes. But it's still familiar fare. **Director**—Richard Lang. (R) *102 minutes*

MOURNING BECOMES ELECTRA (1947)

★★

Michael Redgrave
Rosalind Russell

A good cast is bogged down in this heavy drama about tragedy striking a New England family during the Civil War. A wife murders her husband, and the children plot revenge. This film is based on the play by Eugene O'Neill. Also with Kirk Douglas, Katina Paxinou, and Raymond Massey. **Director**—Dudley Nichols. **Academy Award Nominations**—Redgrave, best actor; Russell, best actress.
170 minutes b&w

THE MOUSE THAT ROARED (1959)

 ★★★

Peter Sellers
Jean Seberg

In The Mouse That Roared, *Peter Sellers has a novel scheme for getting foreign aid.*

A snappy topical satire about the Duchy of Grand Fenwick, a small bankrupt country that seeks to solve its financial problems by declaring war on the United States with the intention of losing the conflict and then receiving aid through the Marshall Plan. Sellers has a grand time playing three roles, including that of the Grand Duchess. There are many delightful moments that hit home. **Director**—Jack Arnold. *85 minutes*

MOVE OVER, DARLING (1963)
★★★

Doris Day
James Garner
Polly Bergen

Day, Garner, and Bergen have a fine time with this patchy remake of *My Favorite Wife*, although the original with Cary Grant and Irene Dunne was much better. A wife, presumed dead in a plane crash, returns home after five years and finds her husband on the threshold of remarrying. Some hilarious moments still work here, thanks to good jobs by the top cast. Also with Thelma Ritter, Chuck Conners, and Fred Clark. **Director**—Michael Gordon. *103 minutes*

MOVIE, MOVIE (1978)

 ★★★

George C. Scott
Trish Van Devere
Eli Wallach
Red Buttons
Barbara Harris
Art Carney

An affectionate, funny, and clever parody of '30s movies. The program, of course, is a double feature: first an up-from-the-slums boxing drama and then a corny backstage musical. Scott, Buttons, and Wallach have a great time twisting all those old movie clichés. Newcomers Harry Hamlin, Barry Bostwick, and Ann Reinking exude extraordinary youthful zeal. The film occasionally falls flat, but all in all it's a pleasant trip down Hollywood's memory lane. **Director**—Stanley Donen. (PG) *107 minutes color/b&w*

THE MUPPET MOVIE (1979)

 ★★★

The Muppets

Kermit the Frog strums his way to Hollywood in The Muppet Movie.

Jim Henson's lovable puppet characters star with style in their first feature film—an updated version of *The Wizard of Oz*. It's a bright, cheerful dandy of
(Continued)

M
- The Muppets Take Manhattan
- Murder by Death
- Murder by Decree
- Murderer's Row
- Murder, My Sweet
- Murder on the Orient Express

(Continued)

a musical comedy that will please children and adults. Kermit the Frog, who plans to become a star, sets off for Tinsel Town with Miss Piggy, the Great Gonzo, and other Muppeteers. Along the way they briefly encounter Mel Brooks, Steve Martin, Bob Hope, and other Hollywood notables. **Director**—James Frawley. (G)   *94 minutes*

THE MUPPETS TAKE MANHATTAN (1984)

★★★

The Muppets

This third feature with Jim Henson's colorful puppet brigade spoofs old-time Hollywood musicals. Kermit the Frog makes a gallant effort to launch a song-and-dance extravaganza on The Great White Way with plenty of the-show-must-go-on spirit. And the divine Miss Piggy has wedding bells on her mind as she pursues the frog of her dreams. Snappy musical numbers and lively comedy routines will delight the kids and adults alike. Also with Juliana Donald and Lonny Price. **Director**—Frank Oz. (G)   *93 minutes.*

MURDER BY DEATH (1976)

★★

Peter Falk
Alec Guinness
Peter Sellers
Truman Capote
David Niven

An all-star cast and stylish acting shore up Neil Simon's lightweight comedy spoof of detective fiction. Falk, Niven, Sellers, James Coco, and Elsa Lanchester play five famous fictional detectives invited to a spooky old mansion for dinner and a murder to be committed. The performances are superb, but the script makes little sense, and there aren't enough amusing lines to keep it moving briskly. Capote debuts as the host of honor—an eccentric amateur criminologist who believes he can outsmart the world's greatest sleuths. He's better off with his typewriter and the late-night talk shows. Also with Maggie Smith, Eileen Brennan, and Nancy Walker. **Director**—Robert Moore. (PG)

94 minutes

MURDER BY DECREE (1979)

★★

Christopher Plummer
James Mason

Plummer plays the intrepid Sherlock Holmes, and Mason is a delightful Dr. Watson. They attempt to solve the savage Jack the Ripper murders. The production design of 19th-century London is handsomely staged, with swirling fog, flickering gaslights, and rumbling carriages; but the plot is hardly elementary, my dear fellow—it's too complicated and unsuspenseful. This is the 134th movie to feature the famous English gumshoe; Holmes made his screen debut in a 1903 one-reeler. Also with Donald Sutherland, Geneviève Bujold, David Hemmings, John Gielgud, and Susan Clark. **Director**—Bob Clark. (PG)   *121 minutes*

MURDERER'S ROW (1966)

★★

Dean Martin
Ann-Margret

Flimsy continuation of novelist Donald Hamilton's Matt Helm character, with Martin again playing the super-spy role as a spoof. This time, Helm is after a sinister international operator, played by Karl Malden, who has kidnapped a scientist. Ann-Margret is the scientist's daughter. Martin handles his part rather badly, and the sluggish material has little to offer. Set against the background of the Riviera. Also with Camilla Sparv, James Gregory, and Beverly Adams. **Director**—Henry Levin.   *108 minutes*

MURDER, MY SWEET
See Farewell, My Lovely (1944)

MURDER ON THE ORIENT EXPRESS (1974)

★★★

Albert Finney
Ingrid Bergman
Lauren Bacall
Wendy Hiller
Sean Connery
Vanessa Redgrave

Lavish treatment of Agatha Christie's suspenseful whodunit, set in the 1930s aboard a train bound for Calais from Istanbul. On board is Belgian sleuth Hercule Poirot, played by Finney, who solves the murder of a passenger done in when the train hits a snowdrift. Many colorful characters are on board as suspects. There are many plodding moments along with the thrills, but mystery fans should have a good time all the same. Also among the all-star cast are Martin Balsam, Richard Widmark, Jacqueline Bisset, Rachel Roberts, John Gielgud, and Anthony Perkins. **Director**—Sidney Lumet. (PG) **Academy Award**—Bergman, best supporting actress. **Nominations**—Finney, best actor; Paul Dehn, best screenplay (adapted from other material); Geoffrey Unsworth, cinematography.   *131 minutes*

There's a valuable clue in the hankie in Agatha Christie's Murder on the Orient Express.

• Murders in the Rue Morgue
• The Music Man
• Mutiny on the Bounty (1935)
• Mutiny on the Bounty (1962)
• My Bodyguard
• My Brilliant Career
• My Darling Clementine

M

MURDERS IN THE RUE MORGUE
(1971)
★★

**Jason Robards, Jr.
Herbert Lom
Christine Kaufman**

So-so film version of Edgar Allen Poe's classic chiller, set in a Paris theater. The actors in a murder mystery become the real-life victims, and the police investigate. Lots of gory details. Also with Lilli Palmer, Adolfo Celi, and Michael Dunn. **Director**—Gordon Hessler. (PG)   *86 minutes*

THE MUSIC MAN
(1962)
★★★★

**Robert Preston
Shirley Jones**

A buoyant, thoroughly enjoyable romantic musical based on Meredith Wilson's hit Broadway production. Preston is fantastic as the city-slicker salesman who cons the citizens of a small Iowa town into organizing a high school band so he can sell them musical instruments. Jones also stands out as Marian the librarian, Preston's romantic interest. The film boasts colorful turn-of-the-century period detail and a strong statement about narrow-mindedness. Many of the musical numbers are real showstoppers; they include " 'Til There Was You" and "76 Trombones." There's outstanding support from Hermione Gingold, Paul Ford, and Buddy Hackett. **Director**—Morton Da Costa. **Academy Award Nomination**—best picture.   *151 minutes*

MUTINY ON THE BOUNTY
(1935)
 ★★★★

**Charles Laughton
Clark Gable**

A classic movie adventure, indeed, based on Nordhoff and Hall's moving account of hardships aboard an 18th-century British man-of-war. Laughton is unforgettable as the heartless Captain Bligh, whose sadistic treatment of the crew provokes mutiny. The entire production is expertly handled, and its entertainment value is indelible. Gable also excels as first mate Fletcher Christian, and there are other good acting jobs from Franchot Tone, Herbert Mundin, Eddie Quillan, Dudley Digges, and Donald Crisp. **Director**—Frank Lloyd. **Academy Award**—best picture. **Nominations**—Lloyd, best director; Gable, Laughton, Tone, best actor; Jules Furthman, Talbot Jennings, and Carey Wilson, writing (screenplay).   *135 minutes b&w*

MUTINY ON THE BOUNTY
(1962)
 ★★★

**Trevor Howard
Marlon Brando**

Opulent, somewhat overblown remake of the 1935 film, competently done but not as effective despite the lavish production effort. Howard plays Captain Bligh, and Brando is Fletcher Christian; they're adequate, but not as good as Charles Laughton and Clark Gable in the earlier film. Brando's British accent also throws the movie slightly off course. Also stars Richard Harris, Hugh Griffith, Tarita, Richard Haydn, Percy Herbert, and Noel Purcell. **Director**—Lewis Milestone. **Academy Award Nominations**—best picture; Robert L. Surtees, cinematography (color).

185 minutes

MY BODYGUARD
(1980)
 ★★★

**Chris Makepeace
Adam Baldwin
Ruth Gordon**

A sensitive comedy-drama about high school students that depicts adolescent problems with realism and sympathy. Makepeace stars as a frail rich kid who is relentlessly harassed by bullies at school. He enlists a mysterious and strong classmate to protect him, and this relationship sparks a friendship that adds warmth and intelligence to the story. Tony Bill, making his directorial debut, brings out the best in the cast of young people. (PG)   *99 minutes*

MY BRILLIANT CAREER (1980)
★★★

**Judy Davis
Sam Neill
Wendy Hughes**

This Australian film is a remarkable and spirited movie; it tells of the struggle of an impoverished and proud farm girl to become a writer. The movie is based on a 1901 semiautobiographical novel by Miles Franklin, who wrote convincingly on women's liberation when she was 16 years old. The story lapses at times, but the film is, nevertheless, skillfully directed by Gillian Armstrong. It features an energetic performance by Davis in the lead role. Let's hope we see more of her amazing talent. (No MPAA rating)
98 minutes

MY DARLING CLEMENTINE
(1946)
★★★★

**Henry Fonda
Victor Mature
Walter Brennan**

Ward Bond and Victor Mature prepare for the shoot-out at the OK corral in My Darling Clementine.

Among the best of director John Ford's westerns, all about Wyatt Earp, Doc Holliday, and the rest of that crowd; their activities in Tombstone, Arizona; and the famous shoot-out at the OK corral. Scene after scene is done with expert skill, and the acting is among the best for this sort of low-key production. Fonda shines as Earp, and Mature is credible as Holliday. Also with Linda Darnell, Cathy Downs, Tim Holt, Ward Bond, Alan Mowbray, and John Ireland.   *98 minutes b&w*

M
- My Fair Lady
- My Favorite Blonde
- My Favorite Brunette
- My Favorite Wife
- My Favorite Year
- My Friend Flicka
- My Friend Irma
- My Little Chickadee
- My Man Godfrey

MY FAIR LADY (1964)

★★★★

**Rex Harrison
Audrey Hepburn
Stanley Holloway**

Exuberant and highly entertaining screen version of the Broadway smash musical, based on George Bernard Shaw's *Pygmalion*. Harrison is delightful as Professor Henry Higgins, who sets out to make a lady of Eliza Doolittle, a cockney flower-seller, played by Hepburn. He succeeds, of course, and then falls in love with her. The Lerner and Loewe music is firmly intact and provides much charm. Scenery, photography, and costumes are enchanting, and most of the acting is tops. Also with Wilfrid Hyde-White, Theodore Bikel, and Gladys Cooper. **Director**—George Cukor. **Academy Awards**—best picture; Cukor, best director; Harrison, best actor; Harry Stradling, cinematography (color). **Nominations**—Holloway, best supporting actor; Cooper, best supporting actress; Alan Jay Lerner, best screenplay (based on material from another medium). *175 minutes*

MY FAVORITE BLONDE (1942)
★★★

**Bob Hope
Madeleine Carroll**

Top-notch Hope comedy caper. Bob plays a second-rate vaudeville performer who reluctantly gets mixed up in a spy adventure with beautiful British agent Carroll. The film is well put together, and the result is a laugh a minute. Also in the cast are Gale Sondergaard, George Zucco, and Victor Varconi. **Director**—Sidney Lanfield. *78 minutes b&w*

MY FAVORITE BRUNETTE
(1947)

★★★

**Bob Hope
Dorothy Lamour**

Laughs galore with Hope as a photographer masquerading as a private eye to help Lamour while he's being pursued by mobsters. Peter Lorre and Lon Chaney, Jr., are in the cast for a dash of realism in this romp, which parodies *Farewell, My Lovely*. Also with John Hoyt, Charles Dingle, and Reginald Denny. **Director**—Elliott Nugent. *87 minutes b&w*

MY FAVORITE WIFE (1940)

★★★★

**Cary Grant
Irene Dunne**

Irene Dunne is one of Cary Grant's wives in the comedy My Favorite Wife.

Grant and Dunne have this clever comedy well in hand, and the result is a barrel of laughs. Dunne is an explorer, presumed lost in a shipwreck, who returns after five years to find her husband (Grant) remarried. It's a familiar situation, but the good talent gives it an expert and effective workout. Also with Gail Patrick, Randolph Scott, and Ann Shoemaker. **Director**—Garson Kanin. **Academy Award Nomination**—Leo McCarey, Bella Spewack, and Samuel Spewack, writing (original story).
88 minutes b&w

MY FAVORITE YEAR (1982)

★★★

**Peter O'Toole
Mark Linn-Baker
Jessica Harper**

Television's Golden Age is fondly remembered in this backstage story of a comedy program modeled after *Your Show of Shows*. The wobbly satire concerns frantic efforts to get O'Toole a faded, drunken Errol Flynn-like actor to perform live on the show. O'Toole's sleek, larger-than-life performance is the best thing going for this movie, but the screenplay is hectic and overdone. **Director**—Richard Benjamin.

(PG) **Academy Award Nomination**—O'Toole, best actor. *92 minutes*

MY FRIEND FLICKA (1943)
★★★

**Roddy McDowall
Preston Foster**

Engaging and sentimental story about a boy who befriends a maverick horse. An expertly crafted animal film enhanced with magnificent scenery. McDowall does well as the winsome lad. Rita Johnson, James Bell, and Jeff Corey are also in the cast. A sequel, *Green Grass of Wyoming*, was made in 1945 with most of the same cast. **Director**—Harold Schuster. *89 minutes*

MY FRIEND IRMA (1949)
★★

**Marie Wilson
John Lund**

Wilson stars in the title role as a dumb blonde who becomes involved with a new singing sensation discovered at a refreshment stand. Comic-book-style humor abounds in this wacky comedy, based loosely on the radio series. Dean Martin and Jerry Lewis got their start in films in this movie. **Director**—George Marshall. *103 minutes b&w*

MY LITTLE CHICKADEE (1940)

★★★

**Mae West
W.C. Fields**

Memorable pairing of West and Fields in this western comedy. Just watching the great Fields and the voluptuous West batting the corny dialogue back and forth is supreme joy. The plot and other characters are completely irrelevant and treated as such by these two comic giants. Joseph Calleia, Dick Foran, Margaret Hamilton, and Donald Meek also star. **Director**—Edward Cline. *83 minutes b&w*

MY MAN GODFREY (1936)

★★★★

**William Powell
Carole Lombard**

- My Six Convicts
- The Mystery of Kasper Hauser
- Mystery Street
- The Naked and the Dead
- The Naked City
- Nashville
- Nasty Habits

M·N

Screwball comedy—the fast, zany style of screen humor of the '30s—was at its zenith in this film, as were its two deliciously droll stars. Lombard plays the wealthy daughter of a well-to-do family, unscathed by the Depression. She wins a scavenger hunt during a party by coming back with a "forgotten man," unemployed and homeless, played by Powell. After she takes him into her home as the family butler, she makes some surprising discoveries about him—and herself. The sterling cast also includes Eugene Pallette, Alice Brady, Gail Patrick, Mischa Auer, Grady Sutton, Franklin Pangborn, Jean Dixon, and Alan Mowbray. Gregory La Cava, who also worked with W.C. Fields, directed. **Academy Award Nominations**—La Cava, best director; Powell, best actor; Lombard, best actress; Auer, best supporting actor; Brady, best supporting actress; Eric Hatch, writing (screenplay). *90 minutes b&w*

MY SIX CONVICTS (1952)
★★★

**John Beal
Millard Mitchell
Gilbert Roland**

An inventive comedy that takes place in a prison where a group of inmates strive to make the most out of a tough situation. They're helped by a sympathetic psychologist. The film is presented in semidocumentary fashion and offers some engagingly funny moments. Also stars Marshall Thompson and Regis Toomey. **Director**—Hugo Fregonese. *104 minutes b&w*

THE MYSTERY OF KASPER HAUSER (1975)
 ★★

Bruno S.

A provocative film by director Werner Herzog about a mute 15-year-old boy who mysteriously appears in the Nuremberg main square in 1828, with apparently no prior contact with civilization. His educational development and innocence clash with his new environment. It's artistically portrayed, but it may be too ponderous for some. Stars Bruno S., believed to be an actual schizophrenic, as Hauser. Also with

Walter Landengast and Brigitte Mira. In German with English titles. (No MPAA rating) *110 minutes b&w*

MYSTERY STREET (1950)
★★★

**Ricardo Montalban
Sally Forrest**

Taut, well-made police caper set in Boston and accomplished with an authentic atmosphere. Detectives, with the help of pathologists, track down a killer by obtaining clues from the victim's body. Professional performances from Montalban, Forrest, Elsa Lanchester, Marshall Thompson, and Jan Sterling. **Director**—John Sturges. **Academy Award Nomination**—Leonard Spigelgass, writing (motion picture story). *93 minutes b&w*

N

THE NAKED AND THE DEAD (1958)
 ★★

**Aldo Ray
Cliff Robertson**

This is a disappointing treatment of Norman Mailer's novel about a platoon of U.S. soldiers in combat in the Pacific during World War II. The story also touches on the tension between officers and the troops. There's a certain ordinariness about the production; there's second-rate direction, a so-so screenplay, and mediocre acting. Also with Raymond Massey, William Campbell, and Richard Jaeckel. **Director**—Raoul Walsh. *131 minutes*

THE NAKED CITY (1948)
★★★★

**Barry Fitzgerald
Don Taylor
Howard Duff**

A captivating police drama—one of eight million stories in the naked city—filmed with realism in the streets of New York City. A girl is found brutally murdered, and cops launch a manhunt to find the killer. The documentary thriller offers con-

siderable detail on police work and authentic scenes of city life. The good cast also includes Dorothy Hart, Ted de Corsia, and Adelaide Klein. **Director**—Jules Dassin. **Academy Award**—William Daniels, cinematography (black and white); Marvin Wald, writing (motion picture story). *96 minutes b&w*

NASHVILLE (1975)
 ★★★★

**Ronee Blakley
Lily Tomlin**

Henry Gibson and Michael Murphy are just two of the many characters in Nashville.

Nashville's country-and-western music scene is the setting for this panoramic reflection of America's joys, frustration, and complacency. Robert Altman, who directs the film with style, presents this mosaic of life as seen through more than 20 characters at a Nashville political rally. It's a masterful and free-flowing film with memorable performances and a shocking ending. Cast includes Karen Black, Keith Carradine, Geraldine Chaplin, Michael Murphy, Barbara Harris, Shelley Duvall, and Ned Beatty. (R) **Academy Award Nominations**—best picture; Altman, best director; Blakley, Tomlin, best supporting actress. *159 minutes*

NASTY HABITS (1977)
★★

**Glenda Jackson
Melina Mercouri
Geraldine Page
Sandy Dennis**

This feeble lampoon of Nixon and the
(Continued)

N
- Nate and Hayes
- National Lampoon's Animal House
- National Lampoon's Class Reunion
- National Lampoon's Vacation
- National Velvet
- The Natural

(Continued) Watergate mess takes place in an imaginary Philadelphia convent, with some of the ambitious nuns engaging in assorted dirty tricks to win an election. It's a good comedy idea, but it could have been better executed. The vaguely written and choppy script lacks comic punch and generates only a few minor laughs. An aristocratic Glenda Jackson is the equivalent of Nixon, and a bespectacled Dennis plays a John Dean sort with blissful wit. **Director**—Michael Lindsay-Hogg. (PG)   *96 minutes*

NATE AND HAYES (1983)
  ★★

Tommy Lee Jones
Michael O'Keefe

This hyperactive buccaneer adventure, set in the 1880s, offers a grand array of sword and musket fights, boarding-party skirmishes, and narrow escapes. Yet most of the characters are rather pat and the action is déjà vu. Jones stars as a grinning "good" pirate who teams up with young preacher O'Keefe to rescue the latter's fiancée (Jenny Seagrove) from the clutches of a marauding scoundrel. Errol Flynn did it much better. **Director**—Ferdinand Fairfax. (PG)   *100 minutes*

NATIONAL LAMPOON'S ANIMAL HOUSE (1978)
  ★★

John Belushi
Tim Matheson
John Vernon
Verna Bloom

James Widdoes and Tim Matheson cram for their mid-term in alcoholic consumption in National Lampoon's Animal House.

A raunchy, uneven comedy of frat-house silliness set in a small college in 1962. The film follows the bawdy style of the famed humor magazine, but the parody is soft-pedaled. Too many gags fall flat. The youthful players, led by Belushi, make an earnest effort, but they are thwarted by the unpolished material. However, there are enough glimpses of potential talent in all aspects of the film. Cast includes Thomas Hulce, Cesare Danova, and Donald Sutherland. **Director**—John Landis. (R)   *109 minutes*

NATIONAL LAMPOON'S CLASS REUNION (1982)
 ★

Gerrit Graham
Shelley Smith

National Lampoon's Class Reunion proves that sometimes it's better not to know whatever happened to that old gang of yours.

Crude, vulgar comedy that's a feeble spoof on horror films. The frantic shenanigans are set at a high school reunion attended by assorted crazies and one vengeful madman who murders some of his classmates. A rather large cast is spread thin throughout the film, and everyone seems to be struggling with flimsy, witless material that is more annoying than amusing. **Director**—Michael Miller. (R)   *85 minutes*

NATIONAL LAMPOON'S VACATION (1983)
 ★★★

Chevy Chase
Christie Brinkley

Chase for once strikes the proper note as a square, middle-class father who takes his family on a cross-country trip to a Disney-like fun park called Wally World. The breezy comedy is worth a laugh every 100 miles as dad, mom, and kids get lost in the desert, encounter dead-beat relatives, and survive various tourist traps. Ordinary situations are made quite funny thanks to good direction by Harold Ramis and a clever screenplay by John Hughes. (R)   *100 minutes*

NATIONAL VELVET (1945)
  ★★★

Mickey Rooney
Elizabeth Taylor

In National Velvet, *Elizabeth Taylor trains her horse for the Grand National race.*

A captivating family drama about a plucky youngster who trains a horse to win the Grand National race. Enid Bagnold's novel is adapted for the screen with much of the heart-tugging sentiment in place. The film is most notable for the presence of Taylor as the young rider. Also with Anne Revere, Donald Crisp, Angela Lansbury, and Reginald Owen. **Director**—Clarence Brown. (G) **Academy Award**—Revere, best supporting actress. **Nominations**—Brown, best director; Leonard Smith, cinematography (color).   *125 minutes*

THE NATURAL (1984)
 ★★★

Robert Redford
Robert Duvall
Glenn Close
Wilford Brimley

Redford slugs at least a double in the

• Natural Enemies   • Network   • Never Give an Inch
• Neighbors   • Never Cry Wolf   • Never Give a Sucker an
• The Nesting   • The Neverending Story   Even Break

N

title role as an aging baseball superstar of the '30s. This arty, low-keyed film adaptation of Bernard Malamud's novel contains the necessary stuff of myth and failed legend. Although the story occasionally turns overly sentimental, it still adequately relates the trials of an all-American wonder-boy confronting the cynicism of big-league sports. **Director**—Barry Levinson. (PG)

134 minutes

NATURAL ENEMIES (1979)
★

Hal Holbrook
Louise Fletcher

Holbrook plays a successful magazine publisher who contemplates killing his wife, his children, and himself. Gloom and anguish relentlessly pervade this strange film. Almost every character is a grouch who rattles off lengthy lists of complaints, ranging from the national debt to potholes in the streets. Fletcher is the beautiful but depressed wife who checks in and out of psychiatric hospitals. Also with Peter Armstrong, José Ferrer, and Viveca Lindfors. **Director**—Jeff Kanew. (R)

100 minutes

NEIGHBORS (1981)
 ★

John Belushi
Kathryn Walker
Cathy Moriarty
Dan Aykroyd

A weird couple moves next door to a peaceful suburbanite couple, played by Belushi and Walker, and sets out to drive Belushi up the wall with their peculiar antics. This fairly good comic idea soon turns sour and eventually falls apart at the seams. Many of the boisterous gags are tasteless and crude; they fizzle as rapidly as they're presented. Aykroyd and Moriarty overstrain as the strange new neighbors, and director John G. Avildsen is at sea with the absurd material. (R)

95 minutes

THE NESTING (1982)
★★

Robin Groves

Groves stars as a novelist suffering from writer's block (and other disorders) in this lackluster, haunted-house horror drama. It appears the novelist's strange new residence used to be a brothel where the whores were butchered by local brutes. And now the ghosts of the dead women are astir and out for revenge. The evil proceedings are hardly engrossing, but at least they lead to a cure for writer's block. Gloria Grahame has a cameo as a ghostly madam. **Director**—Armand Weston. (R)

102 minutes

NETWORK (1976)
 ★★★★

Faye Dunaway
William Holden
Peter Finch

Peter Finch parodies Jerry Falwell in Network.

Television gets a working over in this provocative and outrageous satire about a network news department that will do anything to grab an audience. Paddy Chayefsky's original script is brilliant and audacious. There are excellent performances by Holden as a scrupulous news division chief, Dunaway as a cunning and predatory programming executive, and Finch as an anchorman who goes mad. The rest of the cast is also outstanding. Also with Robert Duvall, Beatrice Straight, Wesley Addy, and Ned Beatty. Sidney Lumet's superb direction helps to hammer the message home. (R) **Academy Awards**—Finch, best actor; Dunaway, best actress; Straight, best supporting actress; Chayefsky, best original screenplay. **Nominations**—best picture; Lumet, best director; Holden, best actor; Beatty, best supporting actor; Owen Roizman, cinematography.

120 minutes

NEVER CRY WOLF (1983)
 ★★★

Charles Martin Smith

An exhilarating and visually spectacular wilderness film that examines the behavior of Arctic wolves. The screen adaptation of Farley Mowat's best-selling book traces the adventure of a young biologist (Smith) assigned to determine if wolves are responsible for the decline in the caribou herd. His discovery leads to a realistic appreciation of the often maligned wolves. Much of the humor and feel of Mowat's book is left intact, though true depth is missing. The real stars are the wolves, the eloquent photography of Hiro Narita, and the direction by Carroll Ballard who succeeds here as well as he did in *The Black Stallion*. (PG)

105 minutes

THE NEVERENDING STORY
(1984)
 ★★

Noah Hathaway
Barret Oliver

Lavish, technically striking children's fantasy that quickly bogs down in complex philosophizing. The meandering screenplay follows the quest of a youthful warrior bent on saving a mythical land (Fantasia) from destruction by a strange force (The Nothing). During his mission, he encounters various strange and unappealing creatures who either help or interfere with his progress. Most kids are apt to be confused by such heavy-handed whimsy. **Director**—Wolfgang Petersen. (PG)   *94 minutes*

NEVER GIVE AN INCH
See Sometimes a Great Notion

NEVER GIVE A SUCKER AN EVEN BREAK (1941)
 ★★★★

W. C. Fields

The great Fields is the whole show in this wacky mishmash of a farce; it has virtually no plot, but plenty of hilari-

(Continued)

N
• Never on Sunday
• Never Say Never Again
• The New Centurions
• Newsfront
• New York Confidential
• New York, New York

(Continued)

ous scenes. Fields, three sheets to the wind, falls out of an airplane and lands in a strange country, where he meets an attractive girl who's never met a man. Much fun and frolic ensues, and it ends with an inventive chase sequence. Co-stars Margaret Dumont, Gloria Jean, Leon Errol, Franklin Pangborn, and Ann Miller. **Director**—Edward Cline.

70 minutes b&w

NEVER ON SUNDAY (1960)
★★★★

Melina Mercouri
Jules Dassin

Mercouri stands out in a memorable performance as a world-wise prostitute who resists being reformed by a stuffy tourist visiting Greece. Dassin, who directed, plays Homer, the frustrated tourist. The film is charmingly rendered, with the magnificent Melina shining all the way, and the title song helps set the mood. Also with Georges Foundas and Titos Vandis. **Academy Award Nominations**—Dassin, best director; Mercouri, best actress; Dassin, best story and screenplay (written directly for the screen).

91 minutes b&w

NEVER SAY NEVER AGAIN (1983)
 ★★★

Sean Connery

Sean Connery is in Bondage again as 007 in Never Say Never Again, *happily trapped in the arms of Fatima Blush (Barbara Carrera).*

After a 12-year hiatus, Connery is back in the familiar role of super spy James Bond. The excitement and intrigue are as rich as ever, and the film doesn't hesitate to poke fun at the already ridiculous Bond image. Agent 007 is now a rejuvenated middle-ager and still smartly debonaire. He's pitted against a sinister villain (Klaus Maria Brandauer) who is blackmailing the world with stolen nuclear-tipped cruise missiles. A new array of glitzy gadgets, tongue-in-cheek humor, and gorgeous dames are in ample supply to keep moviegoers happily in Bondage once again. **Director**—Irvin Kershner. (PG) *137 minutes*

THE NEW CENTURIONS (1972)
 ★★★

George C. Scott
Stacy Keach

An unusual and insightful police drama, focusing on the personal and psychological pressures of being a cop. Scott contributes considerable dignity to the proceedings as the cynical veteran officer who shows his rookie partner the ropes; Keach plays the rookie cop. Competently based on Joseph Wambaugh's novel about men on the Los Angeles police force. Top performances all around. Also with Jane Alexander, Rosalind Cash, and Scott Wilson. **Director**—Richard Fleischer. (R) *103 minutes*

NEWSFRONT (1979)
 ★★★

Bill Hunter
Chris Haywood

An intriguing Australian film that vividly portrays the theatrical newsreel business during its waning years, just prior to the advent of television. This isn't a documentary, but actual clips of newsreel stories are woven into the fictional story, which romanticizes the personal lives of the characters behind the cameras. An excellent cast, headed by Hunter and Haywood, delivers polished portrayals of those almost-forgotten journalists. Also with Wendy Hughes, Gerard Kennedy, and Angela Punch. **Director**—Phillip Noyce. (No MPAA rating)

110 minutes color/b&w

NEW YORK CONFIDENTIAL (1955)
 ★★

Broderick Crawford
Anne Bancroft

Rather undramatic yet authentic-looking account of organized crime in New York. A local syndicate boss is bumped off by one of his own henchmen. A good cast, headed by Crawford and Bancroft, heightens the otherwise routine proceedings, which depict racketeers as shrewd businessmen. Also with Richard Conte. **Director**—Russell Rouse. *87 minutes b&w*

NEW YORK, NEW YORK (1977)
★★★

Liza Minnelli
Robert De Niro

Robert De Niro won't take no for an answer from Liza Minnelli in New York, New York.

Director Martin Scorsese's big-band-era backstage romance is a downbeat musical, but a very fine one nonetheless. De Niro gives an outstanding performance as a nasty but talented jazz saxophonist who falls for band singer Minnelli, and eventually has a falling out with her. The intentional contrast between the happy swing music and this sordid emotional situation is poignant and powerful, Scorsese recaptures the feel of the great Hollywood musicals of the '40s and '50s (such as those by Minnelli's father Vincente) in order to tell the kind of story seldom told in such vehicles. Also with Lionel Stander, Mary Kay Place, and Barry Primus. The video release restores some worthy footage left out originally. (PG)

137 minutes

- The Next Man
- Next Stop, Greenwich Village
- Niagara
- Nickelodeon
- Night and Day
- A Night at the Opera
- Night Games
- The Night Has a Thousand Eyes

N

THE NEXT MAN (1976)
★

Sean Connery
Cornelia Sharpe

Connery, who earned fame and fortune as James Bond, returns to the world of intrigue and adventure in this dull and confusing movie about power politics in the Middle East. He plays a Saudi Arabian diplomat who provokes violence when he tries to promote peace with Israel. Sharpe co-stars as a spy who falls in love with the noble Arab, and her performance is awful; the rest of the cast is a mixed bag. Also with Albert Paulsen and Adolfo Celi. Richard C. Sarafian directs the film as if it were a travelogue with occasional murders. (R)   *108 minutes*

NEXT STOP, GREENWICH VILLAGE (1976)
★★★

Lenny Baker
Shelley Winters

Director Paul Mazursky's warm and touching autobiographical film is about an aspiring young comedian's life in the Village in the 1950s. Lanky newcomer Baker, playing the awkward-looking Larry Lapinsky, heads an outstanding cast, which lends credibility and humanity to the story. Winters is convincing as an overbearing Jewish mother. The film is full of clear and nostalgic memories of this period. Also with Ellen Greene, Lou Jacobi, Christopher Walken, and Mike Kellin. (R)   *109 minutes*

NIAGARA (1952)
 ★★★

Joseph Cotten
Jean Peters
Marilyn Monroe

Monroe plays Monroe to the hilt in this suspenseful tale about a faithless wife who schemes to kill her husband while on their honeymoon. Monroe is the bride, and Cotten plays the husband. Monroe is at her wiggling best, and the magnificent backdrop of Niagara Falls enhances the scenic interest. The Hitchcock-style plot packs a punch, although it leans toward the melodramatic at times. The cast also includes Don Wilson and Casey Adams. **Director**—Henry Hathaway.   *89 minutes*

NICKELODEON (1976)
★★★

Ryan O'Neal
Burt Reynolds
Tatum O'Neal

This movie is director Peter Bogdanovich's affectionate and entertaining tribute to the early pioneers of filmmaking. An excellent cast portrays the rollicking slapstick and madcap adventures of Hollywood before World War I, when America was charmed with its new plaything, the moving picture. It's uneven in places, but it's rich in feeling and educational as well. Also with Brian Keith, Stella Stevens, and John Ritter. (PG)   *121 minutes*

NIGHT AND DAY (1946)
★★★

Cary Grant
Alexis Smith
Mary Martin

The life of songwriter Cole Porter receives a Hollywood fictional treatment, and the events are presented in a creaky fashion. Yet Porter's wonderful music stands out, and an excellent cast puts on a worthy show. Grant is effective as the popular composer, and he sings "You're the Top." Another pleasant moment comes when Martin belts out "My Heart Belongs To Daddy." Also with Monty Woolley, Jane Wyman, Eve Arden, and Dorothy Malone. **Director**—Michael Curtiz.   *132 minutes*

A NIGHT AT THE OPERA (1935)
 ★★★★

Marx Brothers

A Marx Brothers comedy classic, with Groucho, Chico, and Harpo destroying and finally saving an opera production. The trio does many wacky deeds with the help of an effective musical score that perks up the hilarity to fever pitch. The magnificent

Groucho nails the manicurist in A Night at the Opera.

lunacy is side-splitting and opera-splitting as well. Also with Margaret Dumont, Kitty Carlisle, Allan Jones, and Sig Rumann. **Director**—Sam Wood.   *96 minutes b&w*

NIGHT GAMES (1980)
 ★

Cindy Pickett

French director Roger Vadim, who helped launch the careers of Brigitte Bardot and Jane Fonda, introduces Pickett in the role of a Beverly Hills woman who is haunted by sexual fantasies. The screenplay is so absurd that some of the most serious scenes generate laughter. Pickett displays meager acting talent. It's a silly, forgettable film, and Pickett will probably be forgotten as well. (R)   *100 minutes*

THE NIGHT HAS A THOUSAND EYES (1948)
★★

Edward G. Robinson

Robinson stars as a vaudeville mentalist who discovers he actually has the ability to predict the future. The patchy drama is intriguing at times, but there are many dull moments. However, Edward G. is as watchable as ever. Co-stars Gail Russell, John Lund, Virginia Bruce, and William Demarest. **Director**—John Farrow.   *80 minutes b&w*

N
- Nighthawks
- A Night in Casablanca
- A Night in Heaven
- Nightmare Alley
- A Nightmare on Elm Street

NIGHTHAWKS (1981)

★★★

**Sylvester Stallone
Billy Dee Williams
Rutger Hauer**

Sylvester Stallone and Billy Dee Williams stop someone from sneaking onto the train in Nighthawks.

Stallone steps out of his Rocky role to play a tough New York City cop who, along with Williams, tracks down a diabolical international terrorist. This standard police story is uneven in spots, but it delivers excitement at a fast-paced clip. Stallone's cop is an enraged character, but he remains a hero with a conscience, and he eventually triumphs over evil. Dutch actor Hauer is quite impressive as the cold-blooded fiend who is brought to bay in a heart-pounding surprise finale. Also with Persis Khambatta. **Director**—Bruce Malmuth. (R)   *99 minutes*

A NIGHT IN CASABLANCA
(1946)
★★

Marx Brothers

Groucho, Chico, and Harpo check into a Casablanca hotel where they smoke out some Nazi spies. Not the best of the Marx Brothers, but there's enough sustained lunacy to please devotees. This film was perhaps the last big one for the zany trio. Co-stars Sig Rumann, Lisette Verea, Charles Drake, and Lois Collier. **Director**—Archie Mayo.   *85 minutes b&w*

A NIGHT IN HEAVEN (1983)
★

**Lesley Ann Warren
Christopher Atkins**

Sleazy, dreary tale of square high school teacher (Warren) who has a brief affair with one of her students (Atkins) after she discovers him moonlighting as a male stripper. Events progress with the pace of a rush-hour traffic jam, and this ridiculous mess seems an embarrassment for all involved. Warren, the talented dizzy moll in *Victor/Victoria*, is tragically wasted and, it's hard to believe John Avildsen (*Rocky*) directed such drivel. (R)   *83 minutes*

NIGHTMARE ALLEY (1947)
★★★

Tyrone Power

Power skillfully portrays a carnival barker who succeeds for a while as a con man until his luck runs out. This is an odd, moody, and captivating drama, filled with strange intriguing characters; it's rather well done in all departments. Based on the novel by William Lindsay Gresham. Also with Colleen Gray, Joan Blondell, Helen Walker, Mike Mazurki, and Taylor Holmes. **Director**—Edmund Goulding.   *111 minutes b&w*

A NIGHTMARE ON ELM STREET (1984)
★

**Heather Langen Kamp
Ronee Blakely
John Saxon**

Grisly, blood-splattered mayhem is the centerpiece of this trashy teenage slasher film. A somewhat clever plot twist has various young people sharing similar hideous nightmares that are hard to distinguish from reality. Yet this premise is not developed to full potential. Acting talent is minimal—a typical expectation of such fare. (R) **Director**—Wex Craven.   *91 minutes*

GREGORY PECK

Gregory Peck was born in La Jolla, California, in 1916, and began acting while attending the University of California at Berkeley. He then moved to New York, where he appeared with the Neighborhood Playhouse for two years before making his Broadway debut in Emlyn Williams's Morning Star in 1942.

During the next two years, while Peck spent most of his time playing a double role in the play The Willow and I, he received some movie offers. Finally, he accepted one from scriptwriter Casey Robinson to co-star as a Russian guerrilla in Days of Glory *(1943).*

Peck's first screen appearance resulted in instant recognition, and soon 20th Century-Fox cast him as the gentle Scottish missionary in The Keys of the Kingdom *(1944), a role that brought him an Academy Award nomination. He then starred in* The Valley of Decision *(1944) opposite Greer Garson. Both this film and his next,* Spellbound *(1945), were among the top money-makers of the year, and* Duel in the Sun *(1946) and* The Yearling *(1946) were equally big hits the following year.*

He also starred in Gentleman's Agreement *(1947),* Twelve O'Clock High *(1949),* The Gunfighter *(1950),* The Man in the Grey Flannel Suit *(1956), and* The Big Country *(1958).*

In 1963, Peck finally received an Oscar as best actor for his performance as the liberal country lawyer in To Kill a Mockingbird. *Since then, Peck has made many films, including* Arabesque *(1966),* Marooned *(1969),* The Omen *(1976),* MacArthur *(1977), and* The Boys from Brazil *(1978).*

• Nightmares
• Night of the Comet
• The Night of the Hunter
• The Night of the Iguana
• Night of the Juggler
• Night of the Living Dead
• The Night of the Shooting Stars
• Night Passage

N

NIGHTMARES (1983)

★

Lance Henrikson

Cristina Raines doesn't like what she sees in Nightmares.

Four moderately tense horror tales make up this *Twilight Zone* rip-off that was initially slated for television and appears best suited for that medium. A segment about a disillusioned priest menaced by a strange, devilish pickup truck is quite compelling. Otherwise, the episodes are dreary and poorly acted. The film hardly lives up to its title. With Cristina Raines and Emilio Estevez. **Director**—Joseph Sargent. (PG)   *99 minutes*

NIGHT OF THE COMET (1984)

★★★

Catherine Mary Stewart
Kelli Maroney

Effective tongue-in-cheek humor and some remarkable performances elevate this doomsday, B-movie, sci-fi fantasy. A deadly comet devastates the Southern California population. Two young sisters (Stewart and Maroney) survive the deadly rays. Now they must deal with carnivorous zombies and evil scientists who want their life-giving blood. Writer-director Thom Eberhardt has the proper comic touch for such low-budget fare. (PG–13)   *100 minutes*

THE NIGHT OF THE HUNTER (1955)

★★★★

Robert Mitchum
Shelley Winters

A sinister, brooding tale about a reli-gious zealot, played by Mitchum, relentlessly pursuing hidden money after he murders his wife. The film is ingeniously constructed and crackles with suspense and unexpected shocks. This was Charles Laughton's only film as director, and he handles the job expertly. Also with Lillian Gish, James Gleason, Evelyn Varden, and Peter Graves.   *93 minutes b&w*

THE NIGHT OF THE IGUANA (1964)

★★★

Richard Burton
Deborah Kerr
Ava Gardner

Intense, moody, and often amusing tale of a defrocked clergyman, played by Burton, struggling to reestablish his life in Mexico. There he becomes intimately involved with various women, including Kerr, a spinster, and Gardner, the sultry owner of a run-down tourist hotel. The screenplay faithfully adheres to Tennessee Williams's play and offers a vivid account of some interesting characters. There are competent performances, too, from Sue Lyon, Grayson Hall, and Cyril Delevanti. **Director**—John Huston. **Academy Award Nominations**—Hall, best supporting actress; Gabriel Figueroa, cinematography (black and white).
125 minutes b&w

NIGHT OF THE JUGGLER (1980)

★★

James Brolin

A nonstop chase thriller, with Brolin playing an ex-cop who relentlessly pursues his daughter's kidnapper through the crowded streets of New York City. The film has plenty of frantic action; apparently, dozens of cars were smashed up to achieve the breathless chase scenes. But the thin screenplay has credibility problems, and characters aren't developed in sufficient detail. Cliff Gorman, Richard Castellano, and Julie Carmen also star. **Director**—Robert Butler. (R)
100 minutes

NIGHT OF THE LIVING DEAD (1968)

★★★

Judith O'Dea
Russell Streiner

Plotwise, the title says it all. Ghouls rise up from the cemetery to terrorize and sup on the unfortunate souls who cross their path. Not a pretty picture. But it is stylish and tingling in its low-budget, graphic way, and it's the film that put director George A. Romero (*Creepshow*) on the map. Curtly dismissed by many critics on its initial release, it went on to become one of the most popular independently made films of all time, and was to the '60s what John Carpenter's original *Halloween* was to the '70s. Shot in Pittsburgh, where Romero has made all of his movies, and co-starring Duane Jones. (R)   *96 minutes*

THE NIGHT OF THE SHOOTING STARS (1983)

★★★★

Omero Antonutti
Margarita Lozano

The Taviani brothers (Paolo and Vittorio) detail various crises among Tuscan villagers during the final days of World War II. Townsfolk are caught between the desperate, retreating Germans and the advancing Americans. The film recalls harrowing moments of courage, pathos, and tragedy. In Italian with English titles. (R)
66 minutes

NIGHT PASSAGE (1957)

★★★

James Stewart
Audie Murphy

A competently made western about a railroad man in charge of a train payroll that an outlaw gang wants to steal. Further complications arise when it's learned that the railroad worker and the gang leader are brothers. Stewart plays the railroad man, and Murphy is the bandit leader. Sufficient action and excitement follow, and the film ends with a tense gunfight.
(Continued)

 Movie is available in Beta and VHS videotape

N
- Night Shift
- The Night the Lights Went Out in Georgia
- The Night They Raided Minsky's
- A Night to Remember (1942)
- A Night to Remember (1958)
- Night Train to Munich
- Nightwing

Also with Dan Duryea, Brandon de Wilde, and Dianne Foster. **Director—** James Nielson.
90 minutes

NIGHT SHIFT (1982)
★★★

Henry Winkler
Michael Keaton
Shelley Long

Henry Winkler and Shelley Long sleep in the bathtub in Night Shift.

Winkler plays a timid night attendant at the city morgue, which becomes the hub of a call girl operation. He handles this offbeat, sentimental comedy with aplomb. The plot is a bit far-fetched and the film stumbles at times, but there are generous portions of charm, breezy dialogue, and some fresh comic situations. **Director—** Ron Howard. (R) *105 minutes*

THE NIGHT THE LIGHTS WENT OUT IN GEORGIA (1981)
★★

Dennis Quaid
Kristy McNichol
Mark Hamill

A listless story about the misadventures of a skirt-chasing country-western singer and his precocious teenage sister, who serves as his manager. The couple is played by Quaid and McNichol. While traveling to Nashville, the two are sidetracked at a hick town, where Quaid runs afoul of the law and falls for a local beauty. The script, padded with much idle chatter, resembles a few TV episodes strung together. Mark Hamill of *Star Wars* fame is hopelessly waxen as a friendly

state trooper. **Director—** Ronald F. Maxwell. (PG) *120 minutes*

THE NIGHT THEY RAIDED MINSKY'S (1968)
★★★

Jason Robards, Jr.
Britt Ekland
Elliott Gould

A colorful and captivating behind-the-scenes look at burlesque of yesteryear. The story revolves around the experiences of a shy country girl, played by Ekland, who comes to the big city and gets a job as a stripper in a burlesque show. She gets involved with Robards, a burlesque comic. The background detail is what really stands out, with nostalgic moments showing baggy-pants comics and the squalid atmosphere of the theater. Also with Norman Wisdom, Forrest Tucker, Joseph Wiseman, Bert Lahr, and Harry Andrew. **Director—** William Friedkin. (PG) *99 minutes*

A NIGHT TO REMEMBER (1942)
★★★

Loretta Young
Brian Aherne

Aherne and Young play mystery writers living in Greenwich Village. After they discover a body in their apartment, the two set out to find the murderer. It's a clever and buoyant whodunit, with amusing moments and plenty of sparkling dialogue. Top performances bolster the production. Also with Jeff Donnell, William Wright, Sidney Toler, Gale Sondergaard, Donald MacBride, and Lee Patrick. **Director—** Richard Wallace.
91 minutes b&w

A NIGHT TO REMEMBER (1958)
★★★★

Kenneth More
Honor Blackman
David McCallum

An inspired semidocumentary about the sinking of the luxury liner *Titanic* in the North Atlantic in 1912. The account, based on Walter Lord's book, features much striking detail and

scores of cameo roles to describe the heroism and drama of that fateful night when the vessel struck an iceberg. Expert direction and superb performances combine for an admirable movie. Also with Michael Goodliffe, George Rose, Anthony Bushell, Jill Dixon, Alec McCowen, and Laurence Naismith. **Director—** Roy Baker.
123 minutes b&w

NIGHT TRAIN TO MUNICH (1940)
★★★★

Rex Harrison
Margaret Lockwood

Night Train to Munich, *a suspense film, features Rex Harrison and Margaret Lockwood.*

Intrigue and comedy are cleverly blended in this excellent suspense film about the efforts of British agents to keep a secret formula from the clutches of the Nazis. Skillful use of meticulous detail enhances this movie, which is made much like an Alfred Hitchcock thriller. Also with Paul Henreid, Basil Radford, and Naunton Wayne. **Director—** Carol Reed. **Alternate Titles—** *Gestapo; Night Train.* **Academy Award Nomination—** Gordon Wellesley, writing (original screenplay). *93 minutes b&w*

NIGHTWING (1979)
★★

Nick Mancuso
David Warner
Kathryn Harrold

Thousands of plague-infested vampire bats invade an Indian reservation in yet another Hollywood version of Mother Nature on the rampage. It's supposed to scare the daylights out of you, but nothing doing: Up close, the bats reveal big teeth, but there's little bite in the predictable screenplay, and the special effects are unimaginative. Also with Stephen Macht, Strother Martin, and George Clutesi. **Director**—Arthur Hiller. (PG)   *105 minutes*

NIJINSKY (1980)
★★

**Alan Bates
George de la Pena**

Alan Bates plays Diaghilev, friend to Nijinsky.

Director Herbert Ross (*The Turning Point*) tries another movie with a ballet theme, and this time it's based on the career of the legendary Vaslav Nijinsky, the great Russian dancer who ultimately descended into madness. The opulent but lethargic film basically dwells on Nijinsky's homosexual relationships. There really isn't enough dancing to satisfy ballet fans, and de la Pena, who plays the title role, never strikes any sparks as an actor or a great dancer. Bates plays impresario Sergei Diaghilev. Also with Leslie Browne. (R)   *129 minutes*

1900 (1977)
★★

**Burt Lancaster
Robert De Niro**

Director Bernardo Bertolucci's monumental chronicle of Italy's peasant-landowner struggle begins with grace and grandeur, but eventually withdraws into a bloated Marxist tract. A fine cast, including De Niro, Lancaster, Sterling Hayden, Donald Sutherland, and Dominique Sanda, creates moments of feeling. However, much of

the acting and script are uninspired. The film contains some frontal nudity and disturbing violence. (R)
243 minutes

1941 (1979)

★★

**Dan Aykroyd
John Belushi
Ned Beatty
Treat Williams**

Steven Spielberg (*Jaws; Close Encounters of the Third Kind*) tries his hand at comedy and comes up with a film that's generous with style, but miserly with comic inspiration. This overblown, adolescent farce concerns a Japanese invasion of California on the heels of the Pearl Harbor attack. There's hysteria, brawling, silliness, destruction of buildings and vehicles, lots of noise, and minimal humor and wit. Belushi, Aykroyd, Williams, and Beatty are essentially wasted. Also with Robert Stack, Tim Matheson, Christopher Lee, and Toshiro Mifune. **Academy Award Nomination**—William A. Fraker, cinematography. (PG)
118 minutes

1984 (1955)
★★★

**Michael Redgrave
Edmond O'Brien
Jan Sterling**

A provocative screen version of George Orwell's prophetic tale of a sinister world, where people have limited freedom and live under the watchful eye of "Big Brother." O'Brien and Sterling play lovers who try to rebel. The film, like the novel, is convoluted and not completely satisfying, but there are many thoughtful points to ponder in this absorbing drama. Also with David Kossoff, Mervyn Johns, and Donald Pleasence. **Director**—Michael Anderson.   *91 minutes b&w*

1984 (1984)
★★★

**John Hurt
Richard Burton**

This second movie version of George

Orwell's powerful novel captures the bleakness and monotony of his nightmarish vision of a totalitarian state. Hurt is convincing as the pitiful government drone who challenges the authority of Big Brother. And Richard Burton, in his final performance, stands out as the ruthless inner-party torturer. Though well-produced (with an appropriately washed-out blue/gray look), the film is a relentless downer and difficult to watch. **Director**—Michael Radford. (R)
117 minutes

9 TO 5 (1980)

★★

**Jane Fonda
Lily Tomlin
Dolly Parton**

Jane Fonda works from 9 to 5 in the comedy of the same name.

Fonda, Tomlin, and Parton are secretaries who engineer an office revolt and wage war on their chauvinistic boss. With such a cast lineup and such a subject, the film should have been a ripsnorting comedy, but alas, its potential is only partially realized. The half-baked screenplay erratically hops from farce to satire to drumbeating about the feminist movement. The leading ladies put in their 35-hour work week, but it's not worth anybody's overtime. Also with Dabney Coleman, Sterling Hayden, Henry Jones, and Marian Mercer. **Director**—Colin Higgins. (PG)   *110 minutes*

92 IN THE SHADE (1976)
★★★

Peter Fonda

Thomas McGuane, who wrote *Rancho*
(Continued)

N
- Ninotchka
- No Man Is an Island
- None But the Lonely Heart
- No Nukes
- Norma Rae
- The Norseman
- El Norte

(Continued)

DeLuxe, wrote and directed this cool film, and it has a genuine fascination. He again drives home his favorite theme of youth and the pursuit of false values. Fonda delivers a stylish performance; he plays a restless, spoiled, rich young man who breaks into the charter-fishing business in Key West. Warren Oates, Burgess Meredith, and Elizabeth Ashley play their parts with remarkable clarity. Also with Margot Kidder, Harry Dean Stanton, and Sylvia Miles. (R)   *93 minutes*

NINOTCHKA (1939)
★★★★

Greta Garbo
Melvyn Douglas

This is one of the brightest screen comedies Hollywood ever turned out, and represents the very best of two veteran comedy men—director Ernst Lubitsch and screenwriter Billy Wilder. An austere Russian agent, played by Garbo, is sent by the Soviet government to Paris to sell a former duchess's jewels. There she meets debonair playboy Douglas, who woos her desperately. Though at first she's all hard-edged ideology, before Paris and her suitor are done with her she's in love and doubting her own dogma. The sparkling script celebrates love and spontaneity superbly. The cast also includes Sig Rumann and Bela Lugosi. **Academy Award Nominations**—best picture; Garbo, best actress; Melchior Lengyel, writing (original story); Charles Brackett, Walter Reisch, and Billy Wilder, writing (screenplay).
110 minutes b&w

NO MAN IS AN ISLAND (1962)
★★

Jeffrey Hunter

A Navy radioman, played by Hunter, is left behind on Guam after the Japanese attack, and fights the enemy as a guerrilla. This rather routine war adventure, based on a true story, is a bit adolescent in nature, but Hunter handles the acting well. The patchy production, however, isn't above the usual. Nicely photographed in the Philippines. Supporting roles by Marshall Thompson, Barbara Perez, and Ronald Remy. **Directors**—John Monks, Jr., and Richard Goldstone.
114 minutes

NONE BUT THE LONELY HEART (1944)
★★★

Cary Grant
Ethel Barrymore

An excellent drama that strikes the proper mood and profits from some good acting. Grant stars as a young cockney roamer seeking self-satisfaction as World War II approaches; he's astonishingly good in this straight dramatic part. And there's top support from Barrymore, who plays his dying mother. An excellent script contributes to the film's quality. Also with June Duprez, Barry Fitzgerald, Jane Wyatt, George Coulouris, and Dan Duryea. **Director**—Clifford Odets. **Academy Award**—Barrymore, best supporting actress. **Nomination**—Grant, best actor.   *113 minutes b&w*

NO NUKES (1980)
★★

Jane Fonda
Ralph Nader

An earsplitting concert movie, based on a series of Madison Square Garden performances by well-known rock stars protesting the use of nuclear power. Scattered among the musical segments are some brief antinuclear documentary films and backstage conversations in which performers comment about the dangers of nuclear misuse; even Nader and Fonda pop in for a few remarks. The appeal is primarily for rock fans. Bruce Springsteen; the Doobie Brothers; Crosby, Stills & Nash; and others belt out the pounding musical numbers. **Directors**—Julian Schlossberg, Danny Goldberg, and Anthony Potenza. (PG)
103 minutes

NORMA RAE (1979)
★★★★

Sally Field
Ron Leibman

Field stars in the title role of this refreshing, gritty, and intelligent film about textile factory workers in a Southern mill town. Under the superb direction of Martin Ritt, Field portrays a valiant young woman struggling with work, love, and family. And what a spirited performance it is. There are fine acting jobs by Leibman, as a union organizer, and Beau Bridges, as Norma Rae's husband. Also with Pat Hingle and Barbara Baxley. (PG) **Academy Award**—Field, best actress. **Nominations**—best picture; Irving Ravetch and Harriet Frank, best screenplay (adapted from another medium).   *113 minutes*

THE NORSEMAN (1978)
★

Lee Majors

Majors, TV's *Six Million Dollar Man,* makes his film debut in what looks like a $600 B-movie. The story recounts the adventures of a band of Vikings that landed on North American shores about the 11th century. Majors and his buddies, all decked out like so many tin woodsmen of Oz, slosh around the Florida Everglades and fight the Injuns. Cornel Wilde and Mel Ferrer help out with the acting, which is mostly mediocre. Also with Jack Elam and Chris Connelly. **Director**—Charles B. Pierce. (PG)   *90 minutes*

EL NORTE (1984)
★★★★

David Villalpando
Zaide Silvia Gutierrez

A remarkable, touching account of two young Guatemalan Indians (brother and sister) who make a torturous journey from their strife-torn country to the promised land of Los Angeles. Director Gregory Nava brings forth much sympathy for these complex and moving characters played with amazing skill by Villalpando and Gutierrez. And the semi-documentary style offers a vivid contrast between the two cultures. In Spanish with English titles. (R)
139 minutes

• The North Avenue
Irregulars
• North by Northwest

• North Dallas Forty
• Northwest Mounted Police
• Northwest Passage
• No Small Affair

N

THE NORTH AVENUE IRREGULARS (1979)
★★★

Edward Herrmann
Barbara Harris
Susan Clark
Karen Valentine

An eager-beaver minister and a posse of daffy housewives mop up local racketeers in this zany and frisky Walt Disney comedy. The plot is mostly Disney formula, but there are plenty of good characterizations and clever gags to keep mom and dad in stitches along with the kids. Herrmann makes a likable and amusing preacher, but the biggest scorer on the laugh meter is Harris, who pursues the crooks in a station wagon bulging with pets and youngsters. Also with Michael Constantine, Cloris Leachman, and Patsy Kelly. **Director**—Bruce Bilson. (G)
99 minutes

NORTH BY NORTHWEST (1959)
 ★★★★

Cary Grant
Eva Marie Saint
James Mason

A lulu of a comedy-thriller from director Alfred Hitchcock, the master himself, who serves up a delightful smorgasbord of favorite tongue-in-cheek tricks. Suave Grant plays a businessman who's pursued by foreign agents; they believe he's a spy. The excitement never slackens, and some scenes are unforgettable—especially Grant being menaced in a corn field by a crop-dusting plane. First-class support from Saint, Mason, Leo G. Carroll, Martin Landau, and Jessie Royce Landis. (PG) **Academy Award Nomination**—Ernest Lehman, best story and screenplay (written directly for the screen). *136 minutes*

NORTH DALLAS FORTY (1979)
★★★★

Nick Nolte
Mac Davis

This is a hard-hitting, realistic look at the win-at-all-cost business of pro football. Nolte gives a powerful performance as an over-the-hill wide receiver who rebels against any notion of team spirit. Lots of fine acting support from G. D. Spradlin as a goading head coach and Davis and Bo Svenson as spirited teammates. It's a rough-and-tumble comedy that also effectively displays its anger and soul. Also with Charles Durning, Dayle Haddon, and Steve Forrest. **Director**—Ted Kotcheff. (R) *119 minutes*

NORTHWEST MOUNTED POLICE (1940)
★★

Gary Cooper
Paulette Goddard

Madeleine Carroll finds it easy to look glamorous in the wilderness in Cecil B. DeMille's Northwest Mounted Police.

A lavish action-adventure in the director's best style, yet the story is unmoving and rather forgettable. The plot involves the efforts of a Texas Ranger, played by Cooper, to locate a criminal hiding out in Canada. Goddard is a half-breed. The colorful outdoor scenes are obviously set-bound. Also with Preston Foster, Robert Preston, Lynne Overman, Madeleine Carroll, George Bancroft, and Akim Tamiroff. **Director**—Cecil B. DeMille. **Academy Award Nomination**—Victor Milner and W. Howard Greene, cinematography (color). *125 minutes*

NORTHWEST PASSAGE (1940)
★★★★

Spencer Tracy
Robert Young
Walter Brennan

Tracy is outstanding as frontier captain Robert Rogers of the Queen's Rangers in this rousing historical saga about adventurers seeking a route to the sea and braving hardships and Indian attacks along the way. Young and Brennan play two recruits under Tracy's command. The film is well made, with a sense of reality about it. Lots of excitement and suspense—especially likable for the kids. Also with Ruth Hussey, Nat Pendleton, and Donald MacBride. **Director**—King Vidor. **Academy Award Nomination**—Sidney Wagner and William V. Skall, cinematography (color). *126 minutes*

NO SMALL AFFAIR (1984)
 ★★

Jon Cryer
Demi Moore

Demi Moore and Jon Cryer zoom into each other's hearts in No Small Affair.

A labored, romantic comedy about a square 16-year-old boy (Cryer) who is obsessed with a 22-year-old rock singer (Moore). The predictable film is only intermittently funny and it never reaches its intended comic tempo. Cryer is occasionally charming as the awkward adolescent. The attractive Moore's performance is merely adequate. As a rites-of-passage film, it's no big deal. **Director**—Jerry Schatzberg. (R) *102 minutes*

N
- Not as a Stranger
- Nothing Personal
- Nothing Sacred
- No Time for Sergeants
- Notorious
- No Way to Treat a Lady
- Now, Voyager

NOT AS A STRANGER (1955)
★★★★

Robert Mitchum
Olivia de Havilland

Competent screen version of Morton Thompson's best-selling novel about a young physician who struggles with his career and his marriage. The story is part soap opera, but there are enough strong details about medical school and hospitals to offset such drawbacks. Mitchum does a credible job in the key part as a poor but bright medical student who becomes a country doctor. De Havilland is his wife, who supports him through medical school. Also with Broderick Crawford, Frank Sinatra, Charles Bickford, and Gloria Grahame. **Director**—Stanley Kramer. *125 minutes b&w*

NOTHING PERSONAL (1980)
 ★

Donald Sutherland
Suzanne Somers

Donald Sutherland and Suzanne Somers in Nothing Personal, *a romantic comedy.*

A hopelessly romantic comedy that introduces Somers in her first major film feature. She plays a sexy lawyer who helps Sutherland, a professor, save baby seals from destruction. Somers is rather stiff in this acting assignment, and Sutherland looks as if he would rather be somewhere else than involved with such tedium. Direction, scripting, and editing are ragged and uninspired. Also with Dabney Coleman. **Director**—George Bloomfield. (PG) *96 minutes*

NOTHING SACRED (1937)
 ★★★★

Carole Lombard
Fredric March

Ben Hecht, a one-time newspaperman, gave us two of the movies' greatest newspaper comedies. *The Front Page* (remade as *His Girl Friday*) was the first, and this the second. Dazzling comedienne Lombard stars as a young woman who's said to have only six weeks to live as a result of radium poisoning. She's exploited by a small newspaper with big ambitions, which drums up publicity by sending her to New York and turning her final days on Earth into a royal gala—only to find that the diagnosis was wrong. The pace is brisk, the dialogue cutting, the early Technicolor rich, the score by Oscar Levant delectable. With Walter Connolly, Charles Winninger, Sig Rumann, Hedda Hopper, and Hattie McDaniel. **Director**—William Wellman. *77 minutes b&w*

NO TIME FOR SERGEANTS (1958)
★★★★

Andy Griffith

Griffith successfully repeats his Broadway role as the Georgia farm boy who joins the Army and cheerfully drives his superiors up the wall. It's obviously Griffith's best screen performance, and his hilarious antics are worth at least a laugh a minute. The supporting cast sparkles, too. Also with William Fawcett, Murray Hamilton, Myron McCormick, Nick Adams, and Don Knotts. **Director**—Mervyn Le Roy. *111 minutes b&w*

NOTORIOUS (1946)
 ★★★★

Cary Grant
Ingrid Bergman
Claude Rains

Another gem from director Alfred Hitchcock's collection of thrillers, smoothly played. The setting is Rio de Janiero at the height of World War II. Bergman is involved in an espionage scheme to marry a Nazi spy, played by

Claude Rains is charmed by lovely spy Ingrid Bergman in Notorious.

Rains, in the hope of helping an American agent, played by Grant. The atmosphere is heavily charged with romance, tingling suspense, and high drama. Also with Louis Calhern, Leopoldine Konstantin, and Reinhold Schunzel. **Academy Award Nominations**—Rains, best supporting actor; Ben Hecht, writing (original screenplay). *101 minutes b&w*

NO WAY TO TREAT A LADY (1968)
 ★★★

Rod Steiger
George Segal

A smart mixture of mystery, suspense, and black farce, with Steiger doing a fabulous job as a psychotic killer of women. He traps his victims by the clever use of disguise. Segal is also outstanding as a detective tracking down the elusive mass murderer. Steiger shows off his acting skills by playing seven roles. The production is uneven in spots, but it succeeds overall. Also stars Lee Remick, Eileen Heckart, Murray Hamilton, and Michael Dunn. **Director**—Jack Smight. *108 minutes*

NOW, VOYAGER (1942)
 ★★★

Bette Davis
Claude Rains
Paul Henreid

A star-studded soap opera that works to perfection because of the extraordinary skills of the performers; they seem to revel in the suffering of their emotional situations. Davis is out-

Bette Davis has to choose between white tie or black in Now, Voyager.

standing as a lonely spinster who's helped by a psychiatrist, played by Rains. Then she becomes involved in a tragic romance with Henreid. Slickly produced for the utmost in sentimental, yet effective, drama. Other supporting roles by Gladys Cooper, Ilka Chase, Bonita Granville, John Loder, and Franklin Pangborn. **Director**—Irving Rapper. **Academy Award Nominations**—Davis, best actress; Cooper, best supporting actress.

117 minutes b&w

THE NUDE BOMB (1980)
★

Don Adams
Sylvia Kristel

Aha! It's the old "let's-make-a-feature-movie-out-of-a-popular-TV-show" trick. Adams, as bumbling secret agent 86, saves the world from the sinister KAOS organization which attempts to render mankind naked with clothes-destroying missiles. Adams is good enough to wring a few laughs from the plodding material based on the '60s *Get Smart* TV series. But would you believe this shtick was better on the tube? The biting satire, engaging dialogue, and such supporting-cast stalwarts as Barbara Feldon and Ed Platt are sorely missing. **Director**—Clive Donner. (PG) *94 minutes*

THE NUN'S STORY (1959)
★★★★

Audrey Hepburn
Peter Finch

An exceptionally appealing story about a young nun played by Hepburn, who serves under harsh conditions in the Belgian Congo and then quits the convent for an ordinary existence. The film, an intelligent rendition of Kathryn C. Hulme's book, is presented in a straightforward manner with outstanding performances. Finch plays a physician, and Colleen Dewhurst is exceptional as a suicidal patient; Hepburn is convincing as the dedicated nun. Also with Edith Evans, Peggy Ashcroft, Dean Jagger, Mildred Dunnock, and Beatrice Straight. **Director**—Fred Zinnemann. **Academy Award Nominations**—best picture; Zinnemann, best director; Hepburn, best actress; Robert Anderson, best screenplay (based on material from another medium); Franz Planer, cinematography (color).

151 minutes

Peter Finch and Audrey Hepburn give excellent performances in The Nun's Story.

NUNZIO
(1978)
★★★

David Proval

Proval is convincing in his stalwart portrayal of a retarded Brooklyn grocery boy who's the object of ridicule, but at last becomes the neighborhood hero. The sentimental story has elements of *Rocky* and *Marty*, and is an earnest and endearing film that touches the heart despite too much reliance on melodramatics and emotional clichés. Also with James Andronica, Morgana King, Tovah Feldshuh, and Vincent Russo. **Director**—Paul Williams (R) *87 minutes*

THE NUTTY PROFESSOR
(1963)
★★★★

Jerry Lewis
Stella Stevens

The best of Lewis's comedies, with a strong psychological message in its Dr. Jekyll and Mr. Hyde theme. Jerry portrays an awkward and shy professor who accidentally discovers a chemical potion that changes him into a brash, self-assured swinger. His handling of the two extreme personalities makes the picture most interesting and funny. Also with Howard Morris and Kathleen Freeman. **Director**—Lewis. *107 minutes*

O

OBJECTIVE—BURMA (1945)
★★★

Errol Flynn
William Prince

A lively World War II adventure with Flynn leading American paratroopers against a Japanese radar station in Burma. It's somewhat drawn out, but there's plenty of exciting action and vivid combat scenes. Also with James Brown, George Tobias, Henry Hull, and Warner Anderson. **Director**—Raoul Walsh. **Academy Award Nomination**—Alvah Bessie, writing (original story). *142 minutes b&w*

Movie is available in Beta and VHS videotape

O
- Obsession
- The Octagon
- Octopussy
- The Odd Couple
- Odd Man Out
- The Odessa File

OBSESSION (1976)
★★

Cliff Robertson
Geneviève Bujold

In Obsession, *Cliff Robertson and Geneviève Bujold star in a romantic suspense drama.*

Director Brian De Palma's psychological mystery owes much to *Vertigo* in story and style, but it lacks the clarity and crispness of the Alfred Hitchcock classic. Screenwriter Paul Schrader leaves loose ends dangling everywhere. Yet there is adequate suspense and ample atmosphere in this story of a young New Orleans businessman who agonizes over the kidnapping and then the deaths of his wife and daughter. Vivid performances by Robertson and Bujold, and a powerful score by Bernard Herrmann. Also with John Lithgow, Sylvia Kuumba Williams, and Wanda Blackman. (PG)
98 minutes

THE OCTAGON (1980)
★★

Chuck Norris

Kung fu whiz Norris comes out of retirement to put down a cult of international terrorists. Chop-socky fans won't be disappointed by the flashy finale when Norris dispatches a small army of bad guys in a blaze of martial-arts action. But for most of the movie, the audience will have to suffer through a complicated plot and boring dialogue that's akin to the Chinese water torture. This action exploitation film would have worked better with more chop-chop and less talk-talk. **Director**—Eric Karson. (R)
103 minutes

OCTOPUSSY (1983)
★★★

Roger Moore

Roger Moore over enthusiastically tries to light a cigarette in Octopussy.

This 13th James Bond superspy adventure finds our dashing, tireless hero grappling yet again with treacherous villains, incredible gadgets, hair-raising escape schemes, and plenty of gorgeous women. Debonaire Moore (in his sixth Bond film) handles the part with aplomb. His intrigues take place in sumptuous locations from Berlin to India. And once more the world is saved, this time from a madman Russian general who tries to explode a nuclear bomb. **Director**—John Glen. (PG)
130 minutes

THE ODD COUPLE (1968)
★★★★

Jack Lemmon
Walter Matthau

The excellent pairing of Lemmon and Matthau in this Neil Simon comedy adds up to loads of laughter. The two play recently divorced characters—one meticulous and the other messy—who become roommates and quickly drive each other up the wall because of their contrasting habits. Simon's screenplay, developed from his Broadway play, offers plenty of reliable comic material for the duo to chew on. Also with John Fiedler, Herb Edelman, Monica Evans, and Carole Shelley. **Director**—Gene Saks. (G) **Academy Award Nomination**—Simon, best screenplay (based on material from another medium). *105 minutes*

ODD MAN OUT (1946)
★★★★

James Mason
Robert Newton

Searing drama about a wounded Irish rebel and his desperate struggle to avoid capture following a daring holdup in Belfast. The amazingly suspenseful story is assembled with expert skill and vivid detail; an unforgettable man-on-the-run movie. Excellent performances by Mason, Newton, Kathleen Ryan, and Dan O'Herlihy. **Director**—Carol Reed. **Alternate title**—*Gang War.*
115 minutes b&w

THE ODESSA FILE (1974)
★★

Jon Voight
Maria Schell
Maximilian Schell

Jon Voight is quite determined to find The Odessa File.

Voight does a convincing job portraying an eager German journalist who tracks down a Nazi war criminal. The screenplay is heavy-going and cumbersome, and the film eventually bogs down, although a few scenes stand out. It's a so-so screen adaptation of Frederick Forsyth's suspenseful novel. Maximilian Schell's portrayal of the sinister SS officer is interesting. Also with Mary Tamm, Derek Jacobi, and Noel Willman. **Director**—Ronald Neame. (PG)
129 minutes

• Ode to Billy Joe
• An Officer and a Gentleman
• Of Human Bondage
• Of Mice and Men
• Of Unknown Origin
• Oh, God!
• Oh God! Book II

O

D. I. Lou Gossett, Jr., tells trainee Richard Gere he's all wet in An Officer and a Gentleman.

ODE TO BILLY JOE (1976)

 ★★

Robby Benson
Glynis O'Connor

Bobbie Gentry's successful 1967 ballad has been transposed to a dreamy and romantic film drama. This story of puppy love and tragedy in Mississippi in 1953 fumbles and plods under the direction of Max Baer; there are just too many contradictions. Only a first-rate performance by O'Connor as a 15-year-old Juliet keeps the film above water. There are some appealing glimpses of Southern family life. Benson stars in the title role. Also with Joan Hotchkiss, Sandy McPeak, and James Best. (PG)   *108 minutes*

AN OFFICER AND A GENTLEMAN (1982)

 ★★★

Richard Gere
Debra Winger
Lou Gossett, Jr.

A captivating love story about a young man (Gere) with a burning desire to be a Navy jet pilot, and a local girl (Winger) who yearns to escape the drudgery of her job in a paper mill. The engaging production is a fine example of old-fashioned Hollywood filmmaking, with believable characters and rich, romantic sentimentality. Gere and Winger make the most of their meaty roles, while Gossett shines as a brass-hearted drill instructor. **Director**—Taylor Hackford. (R) **Academy Award**—Gossett, best supporting

actor. **Nominations**—Winger, best actress; Jack Nitzsche, best original score; Douglas Day Stewart, best original screenplay.   *126 minutes*

OF HUMAN BONDAGE (1964)

★★

Laurence Harvey
Kim Novak

Harvey and Novak are unfortunately miscast in this third film version of the classic Somerset Maugham story of a doctor's tragic affair with a waitress. The overall production is a disappointment and doesn't do justice to Maugham's novel. The 1934 version, with Bette Davis and Leslie Howard, was better. Co-stars Nanette Newman, Roger Livesey, and Robert Morley. **Director**— Ken Hughes.
          105 minutes b&w

OF MICE AND MEN (1939)

 ★★★★

Burgess Meredith
Lon Chaney, Jr.

Masterful filming of John Steinbeck's tragic tale of a migrant worker who protects his mentally retarded yet physically strong friend. Persuasively told and presented with much sensitivity. Chaney is excellent as Lenny, the feebleminded young man, and Meredith is outstanding as the dedicated friend. Also with Betty Field, Charles Bickford, and Noah Beery, Jr. **Director**—Lewis Milestone. **Academy Award Nomination**—best picture.
          107 minutes b&w

OF UNKNOWN ORIGIN (1983)

 ★★★

Peter Weller

Young executive Weller battles a super-rat that makes a shambles of his posh Manhattan townhouse. This unusual, intelligent horror tale has a taut pace and is craftily directed. The movie playfully educates the audience in the history, biology, and sociology of rats. Worthwhile thoughts on ambition, competition, and what gets lost in the drive to the top. Jennifer Dale and Shannon Tweed co-star. **Director**—George Cosmatos. (R)   *85 minutes*

OH, GOD! (1977)

 ★★★

George Burns
John Denver

A schmaltzy, entertaining, middle-brow comedy about a supermarket manager who is chosen by God to be a latter-day Moses. Denver, exuding his apple-pie good nature, debuts as the astonished storekeeper and does justice to the part. Burns plays the Almighty, and—well—he's George Burns. Carl Reiner's direction has the proper control. Also with Teri Garr, Paul Sorvino, George Furth, and Ralph Bellamy. (PG) **Academy Award Nomination**—Larry Gelbart, best screenplay adaptation.   *104 minutes*

OH GOD! BOOK II (1980)

 ★★

George Burns
Suzanne Pleshette
David Birney
Louanne

Burns returns as the Almighty in this movie sequel, spreading his gospel via one-liners. John Denver, who clicked smartly with Burns in the first film, is replaced by Louanne—a cute kid—to help deliver God's message. Although she and some of her playmates exude innocent charm, the script is stale, and most of the gags are rather familiar. Pleshette and Birney star as Louanne's estranged parents, who finally reconcile, thank God. **Director**—Gilbert Cates. (PG)   *94 minutes*

O

- Oh God! You Devil
- Oh Heavenly Dog
- Oh! What a Lovely War
- Oklahoma!
- Oklahoma Crude
- Old Boyfriends
- The Old Man and the Sea

OH, GOD! YOU DEVIL (1984)

 ★★★

George Burns

George Burns, America's senior citizen laureate, proves effective as a sly Devil in this schmaltzy but clever comedy, the third in the *Oh, God!* series. George's Devil assumes the role of a theatrical agent who transforms a so-so songwriter (Ted Wass) into a rock superstar. The screenplay gets somewhat complex at times, but the effervescent George, even at 88, keeps the material at a buoyant level. **Director—**Paul Bogart. (PG)   *96 minutes*

OH HEAVENLY DOG (1980)

 ★

Chevy Chase
Jane Seymour

Benji, the cute pooch and delight of children, tracks down a killer in London in his third feature film. But this time, director Joe Camp aims at an older audience by throwing in some sexual innuendoes and a bit of mild profanity. The flea-bitten plot, which leans on *Heaven Can Wait*, casts Chase as a gumshoe; Benji is his reincarnation. The result is scenes like Benji—with the mind of Chevy—jumping with glee into the bubble bath of an attractive magazine writer, played by Seymour. (PG)   *103 minutes*

OH! WHAT A LOVELY WAR (1969)

 ★★★

Laurence Olivier
John Gielgud
Ralph Richardson

Uneven yet inspired antiwar movie, set to music and presented as vignettes of events in World War I. Many of the musical sketches are impressive, but there are many slow moments as well. The satire of man's fascination with war has sufficient bite. The large all-star cast of British players also includes Jack Hawkins, John Mills, Kenneth More, Susannah York, Dirk Bogarde, and Vanessa Redgrave. **Director—**Richard Attenborough. (G)   *144 minutes*

Gloria Grahame and Eddie Albert get a lesson in sparking in Oklahoma!

OKLAHOMA! (1955)

 ★★★

Gordon MacRae
Shirley Jones
Rod Steiger

Appealing family entertainment in the form of Rodgers and Hammerstein's fanciful musical about the love affair between a cowboy and a country girl. The memorable hit songs that captivated Broadway come across on the screen with gusto, and the colorful sets help maintain the pleasant mood. MacRae and Jones are ideally cast in the key roles, and they do justice to such numbers as "Oh, What a Beautiful Morning" and "People Will Say We're In Love." Also with Gloria Grahame, Charlotte Greenwood, James Whitmore, and Eddie Albert. **Director—**Fred Zinnemann.   *143 minutes*

OKLAHOMA CRUDE (1973)

★★★

Faye Dunaway
George C. Scott

This typical story about independent small-time operators up against big, impersonal business interests is quite entertaining. Dunaway portrays a gritty, hard-driving oil well owner in the early 1900s, desperately trying to hang on to her claim in the face of ruthless pressure from a giant petroleum company. Faye is impressive, and she gets good support from Scott, a drifter who comes to her aid. Jack Palance is convincing as the sinister company representative trying to drive Faye off her land. Also with John Mills and Woodrow Parfrey. **Director—**Stanley Kramer. (PG)   *108 minutes*

OLD BOYFRIENDS (1979)

 ★★

Talia Shire

Joan Tewkesbury, who wrote Robert Altman's *Nashville*, tries her hand at directing this ambitious film and achieves only middling results. It's about a young woman, played by Shire, who tracks down old boyfriends in an effort to get her head together. Some appealing moments—especially Buck Henry as a private eye with a roving eye for his beautiful secretary. But most of the story is unclear because of a weak and wobbly script. Richard Jordan, Keith Carradine, John Belushi, and John Houseman also star. (R)   *103 minutes*

THE OLD MAN AND THE SEA (1958)

 ★★★

Spencer Tracy

Tracy, who gives this Ernest Hemingway tale his best, plays the aging fisherman braving rough seas in hope of catching a big fish. This one-character adventure isn't readily adaptable to the screen, but all hands try hard to sustain interest. Tracy's performance is really the main reason for seeing the film. Felipe Pazos and Harry Bellaver also star. **Director**—John Sturges. **Academy Award Nominations**—Tracy, best actor; James Wong Howe, cinematography (color).   *89 minutes*

OLD YELLER (1957)

 ★★★

Dorothy McGuire
Fess Parker
Tommy Kirk

Tommy Kirk and Old Yeller are greeted by Beverly Washburn and a young yeller.

Typical sentimental boy-and-his-dog movie from Walt Disney. Kirk plays a Texas farm boy in the mid-1800s who befriends a stalwart mongrel hound, and they become involved in numerous adventures. It's based on Fred Gipson's novel. Excellent family fare and almost a classic by now. McGuire and Parker play the hearty parents. Also with Kevin Corcoran and Chuck Connors. **Director**—Robert Stevenson. (G)   *83 minutes*

OLIVER! (1968)

★★★★

Ron Moody
Oliver Reed
Mark Lester

A first-class musical based on Dickens's *Oliver Twist* and expertly adapted from the Broadway hit. The colorful production abounds with atmospheric setting, invigorating choreography, and memorable tunes by Lionel

Jack Wild (Oliver) and Mark Lester in the successful musical Oliver!

Bart. Child-star Lester is exceptionally good in the title role, as the young orphan who becomes involved with a group of thieves led by the unsavory Fagin, played by Moody. Songs include "Consider Yourself" and "As Long as He Needs Me." Top supporting work by Reed, Shani Wallis, and Jack Wild. **Director**—Carol Reed. (G) **Academy Awards**—best picture; Reed, best director. **Nominations**—Wild, best supporting actor; Vernon Harris, best screenplay (based on material from another medium); Oswald Morris, cinematography.
146 minutes

OLIVER'S STORY (1978)

★

Ryan O'Neal
Candice Bergen

Oliver, played by O'Neal, is numbed by the death of his young wife, and takes out his frustration by numbing the audience in this sequel to Erich Segal's *Love Story*. Oliver is now approaching middle age. He meets a rich girl, played by Bergen, but the romance soon falls apart. The movie is rather gloomy and far from the romantic mood of the first film. Also with Nicola Pagett, Edward Binns, and Ray Milland. **Director**—John Korty. (PG)
92 minutes

OLIVER TWIST (1948)

 ★★★★

Alec Guinness
Robert Newton
Francis L. Sullivan
Kay Walsh

This straight version of Charles Dickens's classic story is expertly done in all departments. Guinness perfectly portrays Fagin, the scoundrel who recruits the innocent orphan Oliver into a life of street crime. David Lean's direction is consistently on target, and he keeps the story moving along without a hitch. Excellent supporting performances all around. Also with John Howard Davies, Anthony Newley, Henry Stephenson, and Diana Dors.
116 minutes b&w

THE OMEN (1976)

 ★★

Gregory Peck
Lee Remick

Peck and Remick unwittingly rear the son of Satan in this brutal and blood-obsessed horror film. The diabolical plot is implausible, but there are plenty of gory scare tactics to maintain tension and interest throughout. The entire effort, it seems, isn't to offer a meaningful story, but to bring on the shock effects—creepy graveyards, mysterious hangings, attacks by mad dogs, howling baboons. The cast performs well, and Richard Donner's direction is slick. Also with David Warner, Billie Whitelaw, and Leo McKern. (PG)   *111 minutes*

ON A CLEAR DAY YOU CAN SEE FOREVER (1970)

★★★

Barbra Streisand
Yves Montand

Streisand is outstanding in this vibrant musical; she plays a young woman who relives the past after undergoing hypnotic sessions from a psychiatrist, played by Montand. The production isn't as invigorating as the Broadway show yet there are numerous good moments and outstanding

(Continued)

O
- Once in Paris
- Once Is Not Enough
- Once More, With Feeling
- Once Upon a Time in America
- Once Upon a Time in America
- The One and Only
- One-Eyed Jacks

Yves Montand and Barbra Streisand in On a Clear Day You Can See Forever.

settings that maintain consistent interest. The music by Alan Jay Lerner and Burton Lane is pretty much intact; memorable songs include "He Wasn't You" and "Come Back to Me." Vincente Minnelli's direction is among his best. There's fine support from Bob Newhart, Jack Nicholson, Larry Blyden, and Simon Oakland. (G)
129 minutes

ONCE IN PARIS (1978)
  ★★

**Wayne Rogers
Gayle Hunnicutt
Jack Lenoir**

Wayne Rogers and Gayle Hunnicutt find themselves in an either oar situation in Once in Paris.

A good-natured but sluggish little movie about an American screenwriter (Rogers) who goes to Paris on a short assignment. He becomes involved with a colorful French chauffeur (Lenoir) and an attractive English woman (Hunnicutt). Rogers, Hunnicutt, and Lenoir turn on the charm, but this romantic outing never really gets into high gear. Also with Clement Harari, Tanya Lopert, and Doris Roberts. Frank D. Gilroy wrote, directed, and produced. (No MPAA rating)
100 minutes

ONCE IS NOT ENOUGH (1975)
★

**Kirk Douglas
Alexis Smith**

Based on Jacqueline Susann's sexual, psychological best-seller, about the Hollywood, New York, and Spain jet set. The performances are mediocre; the screenplay is ludicrous and boring. Also with David Janssen, Deborah Raffin, George Hamilton, Melina Mercouri, and Brenda Vaccaro. **Director**—Guy Green. (R) **Academy Award Nomination**—Vaccaro, best supporting actress.
121 minutes

ONCE MORE, WITH FEELING (1960)
★★★

**Yul Brynner
Kay Kendall**

Brynner and Kendall battle one another as husband and wife in this scrappy upper-crust comedy of marital blitz. Brynner is commanding as a tyrannical symphony orchestra conductor who seems to have more control with his musicians than he does with his gorgeous wife, who wants out of the marriage. Kendall handles her part with skill and charm. Also with Geoffrey Toone, Maxwell Shaw, and Mervyn Johns. **Director**—Stanley Donen.
92 minutes

ONCE UPON A TIME IN AMERICA (1984)
  ★★

**Robert De Niro
James Woods
Elizabeth McGovern**

Director Sergio Leone's sprawling film tapestry of American gangsters spans some 50 years and unfolds in incoherent fits and starts. The story, which has ambitions of being a Jewish "Godfather," is overly contemplative and punctuated with moments of brutality. Yet the production, with its exquisite period details, is sumptuously photographed. An excellent cast is set adrift amid the fuzzy material. (R)
135 minutes

ONCE UPON A TIME IN AMERICA (1984)
  ★★★★

**Robert De Niro
James Woods
Elizabeth McGovern**

Restored, full-length version of Leone's epic (see above) almost seems like a completely different film. It reinstates the film's grandeur and fleshes out the story to true epic proportions. Don't pass judgement on this film until you've seen the long version. (R)
227 minutes

THE ONE AND ONLY (1978)
 ★★★★

**Henry Winkler
Kim Darby**

Henry Winkler plays a professional wrestler in The One and Only.

Winkler is hilarious as a brassy show-off who fails to make it as a Broadway actor, but makes it big in the carnival world of professional wrestling. The story line of this fine film, directed by Carl Reiner, has a sweet upbeat flavor and a satisfying happy ending. Darby as Winkler's enduring wife, Herve Villechaize as a lascivious midget wrestler, and Gene Saks as a cynical promoter add warm and funny moments. Also with William Daniels and Polly Holiday. (PG)
98 minutes

ONE-EYED JACKS (1961)
  ★★★

**Marlon Brando
Karl Malden**

Brando directed and stars in this

• One Flew Over the Cuckoo's Nest
• One Foot in Heaven
• One from the Heart
• One on One
• One Touch of Venus
• One-Trick Pony

O

Jack Nicholson is overjoyed by an imaginary home run in One Flew Over the Cuckoo's Nest.

tough western as an outlaw determined to settle a score with a buddy who was responsible for his imprisonment. Good character study and vivid detail, but Brando goes overboard with his acting and with the length of the film. Malden is convincing as the bandit's erstwhile friend turned sheriff. Also with Katy Jurado, Pina Pellicier, Slim Pickens, Ben Johnson, and Elisha Cook, Jr. **Academy Award Nomination**—Charles Lang, Jr., cinematography (color). *141 minutes*

ONE FLEW OVER THE CUCKOO'S NEST (1975)

 ★★★★

Jack Nicholson
Louise Fletcher

Ken Kesey's 1962 novel of rebellious insane asylum patients is faithfully reproduced in director Milos Forman's stylish and moving film. Nicholson was practically born to play the role of fast-talking R. P. McMurphy, the free-spirited fighter of the system. He's supported by excellent performances from Fletcher—a nurse—William Redfield, and Will Sampson. Dale Wasserman's off-Broadway version of this comedy-melodrama was popular among the young, mainly because of its anti-establishment theme. Also with Brad Dourif and Christopher Lloyd. (R) **Academy Awards**—best picture; Nicholson, best actor; Fletcher, best actress; Forman, best director. **Nominations**—Dourif, best supporting actor; Laurence Hauben and Bo

Goldman, best screenplay (adapted from another medium); Haskell Wexler and Bill Butler, cinematography (color). *129 minutes*

ONE FOOT IN HEAVEN (1941)

★★★★

Fredric March
Martha Scott

A moving and charming story of a small-town minister and his wife trying to cope with fast-changing attitudes in America. Solid acting by March as the clergyman carries the film along despite an uncohesive plot. Scott is also good as his ever-faithful wife. A warmhearted, well-handled movie. Co-stars Beulah Bondi, Gene Lockhart, Elizabeth Fraser, and Harry Davenport. **Director**—Irving Rapper. **Academy Award Nomination**—best picture. *108 minutes b&w*

ONE FROM THE HEART (1982)

 ★★

Teri Garr
Frederic Forrest
Nastassja Kinski
Raul Julia

Lavish dreamlike sets and dazzling effects practically swallow up both the story and the characters in this ambitious and misguided romantic musical by Francis Ford Coppola. The simplistic plot, set in Las Vegas, is right out

of '40s and '50s Hollywood musicals: Boy (Forrest) loses girl (Garr) and wins her back. Vincente Minnelli, Judy Garland, Fred Astaire, and their like extracted extraordinary joy and romance from such productions. Coppola, regretfully, doesn't have the heart for it. (R) *101 minutes*

ONE ON ONE (1977)

★★★

Robby Benson
Annette O'Toole

An engaging little movie about big time college basketball, following the upbeat style of *Rocky*. Benson, who co-wrote the script with Jerry Segal, is fine as a naive, small-town basketball player who bucks a sadistic coach and finally triumphs on the college courts. The story is a strong statement against the overcommercialized world of college athletics. Effective performances, too, from G. D. Spradlin as the coach and O'Toole as Benson's romantic interest. Also with Gail Strickland and Melanie Griffith. **Director**—Lamont Johnson. (PG) *98 minutes*

ONE TOUCH OF VENUS (1948)

★★★

Ava Gardner
Robert Walker

Pleasant and inventive romantic comedy about a statue of Venus that comes to life in a swank department store and becomes the love interest of a young employee. Gardner is exceptional as the beautiful Venus with arms, and she sings "Speak Low" with passion. Walker plays the employee. Based on the Broadway play by S. J. Perelman. Also stars Eve Arden, Dick Haymes, Olga San Juan, and Tom Conway. **Director**—William A. Seiter.

82 minutes b&w

ONE-TRICK PONY (1980)

★★

Paul Simon
Blair Brown

Simon, one of the singing sensations of the '60s, wrote and stars in this personal story of a popular musician be-

(Continued)

Movie is available in Beta and VHS videotape

O • One, Two, Three
• On Golden Pond
• On Her Majesty's Secret
  Service

• The Onion Field

(Continued)

set by fading career and family problems. Simon is front and center throughout, and his music and lyrics continually accompany the film. In fact, the music is often more appealing than the laidback dialogue or the colorless plot. Simon provides detailed glimpses of the music industry, but he doesn't allow for very much excitement. Also with Rip Torn. **Director—** Robert M. Young. (R)   *98 minutes*

ONE, TWO, THREE (1961)

★★★★

James Cagney

Smart, fast-paced Billy Wilder comedy set in West Berlin during the cold war. Cagney churns up a lot of laughs as a Coca-Cola executive trying to sell his product to the communists. The invigorating plot offers nonstop satire heavily laced with clever one-liners. Andre Previn's music adds to the sophisticated mood. Also stars Horst Buchholz, Arlene Francis, Pamela Tiffin, Red Buttons, and Lilo Pulver. **Academy Award Nomination**—Daniel L. Fapp, cinematography (black and white).

115 minutes b&w

ON GOLDEN POND (1981)

 ### ★★★

Henry Fonda
Katharine Hepburn
Jane Fonda

The drawing power of this sentimental drama is mainly due to the magnificent casting of Henry Fonda and Hepburn as an elderly couple trying to enjoy what may be their last summer together. Inevitably, family conflicts occur to complicate the issue. The atmosphere (despite the gorgeous scenery) is stagy, and the plot sketchy. All the same, Henry invests the story with pathos and humor. As the crotchety professor, forced at last to recognize his own areas of vulnerability, he's as good as he's ever been. Jane Fonda is outstanding as the resentful daughter. **Director**—Mark Rydell. (PG) **Academy Awards**—Henry Fonda, best actor; Hepburn, best actress; Ernest Thompson, best screenplay (based on material from another medium).

AUDREY HEPBURN

Born in 1929 in Brussels of Irish-Dutch parents, Audrey Hepburn lived in the Netherlands during World War II and later moved to London to study dance at the Rambert Ballet School. She made her stage debut in 1948, as a ballerina in the musical High Button Shoes, and later danced in Sauce Tartare. After some initial film roles in Britain, France, and Holland, Hepburn was chosen to play the starring role in Gigi, which Anita Loos had converted into a Broadway hit play. Then William Wyler saw an earlier screen test Hepburn had made for Paramount and demanded her for the princess in Roman Holiday (1953), opposite Gregory Peck; her performance brought her an Academy Award.

Although Hepburn had appeared in many earlier movies, Roman Holiday really began her striking screen career, including such early successes as Billy Wilder's Sabrina (1954), King Vidor's War and Peace (1956), Stanley Donen's Funny Face (1957), and Wilder's Love in the Afternoon (1957). On Broadway, she also starred in Ondine, for which she won the Drama Critics' Award. Her co-star was Mel Ferrer, whom she married at the end of the play's run.

In 1957, Hepburn appeared in Mayerling with Ferrer and Raymond Massey. One of her best portrayals was in Fred Zinnemann's The Nun's Story (1959). Other films from the early 1960s were The Unforgiven (1960), Breakfast at Tiffany's (1961), The Children's Hour (1962), Charade (1963), and Paris When It Sizzles (1964).

Hepburn was then chosen over Julie Andrews, who played Eliza on Broadway, for the expensive film version of My Fair Lady (1964). She then co-starred with Peter O'Toole in How To Steal a Million (1966), with Albert Finney in Two for the Road (1966), and in the thriller Wait Until Dark (1967). Lately, she has appeared in Robin and Marian (1976) and Bloodline (1979).

Hepburn's marriage to Ferrer ended in 1968, and, a year later, she married Andrea Dotti, an Italian psychiatrist.

Nominations—best picture; Jane Fonda, best supporting actress; Rydell, best director; Filly Williams, cinematogaphy.   *109 minutes*

ON HER MAJESTY'S SECRET SERVICE (1969)

 ### ★★

George Lazenby
Diana Rigg
Telly Savalas

Lazenby substitutes for Sean Connery in this sixth James Bond adventure, and he's marginally competent. But don't despair; this movie is liberally salted with loads of exciting action, tongue-in-cheek humor, and gorgeous women to keep you comfortably in Bondage. As expected, Ian Fleming's hero saves mankind, this time from

scoundrels threatening to unleash a deadly virus. Agent 007 travels to breathtaking Switzerland for his assignment and encounters the bad guys, led by Savalas, on the snowy slopes, with thrilling chases on skis. Rigg plays a Spanish contessa. Also with Ilse Steppat, Gabriele Ferzetti, Bernard Lee, and Lois Maxwell. **Director**—Peter Hunt. (PG)

140 minutes

THE ONION FIELD (1979)

 ### ★★★

John Savage
James Woods

This true story, about the abduction of two policeman and the murder of one of them by a couple of hoods, is based on a book by Joseph Wambaugh, who

• Only Two Can Play   • On the Beach
• Only When I Laugh   • On the Double
• On Moonlight Bay   • On the Right Track
• On the Town

O

also wrote the screenplay. Decent acting and authentic atmosphere are the major virtues of a potentially absorbing portrayal of social, psychological, and moral development. Also with Franklyn Seales, Ronny Cox, Ted Danson, and Diane Hull. **Director**—Harold Becker. (R)   *122 minutes*

ONLY TWO CAN PLAY (1962)
★★★★

Peter Sellers
Mai Zetterling

Sellers is at his comic best in this lively adult comedy featuring several outstanding scenes. Sellers portrays an assistant librarian in a Welsh town, supposedly devoted to his wife. But he attempts an extramarital fling with a wealthy woman, and his bumbling efforts at lovemaking lead to many laughs. Zetterling is a riot as the desirable society woman. Also with Virginia Maskell, Richard Attenborough, Raymond Huntley, and Kenneth Griffith. **Director**—Sidney Gilliat.
106 minutes b&w

ONLY WHEN I LAUGH (1981)
★★

Marsha Mason
Kristy McNichol

Kristy McNichol practices laughing for Only When I Laugh.

Neil Simon reworks his play *The Gingerbread Lady* as a screen comedy-drama; it's about a reformed alcoholic Broadway actress trying to reestablish her career and improve her relationship with her teenage daughter. Mason plays the actress, and McNichol is her daughter. Mason is excellent, but despite some moments of bittersweet comedy she's working

with soap-opera material. This show-biz story lacks Simon's usual humor. James Coco and Joan Hackett do well in supporting roles. **Director**—Glenn Jordan. (R) **Academy Award Nominations**—Mason, best actress; Coco, best supporting actor; Hackett, best supporting actress.   *120 minutes*

ON MOONLIGHT BAY (1951)
★★★

Doris Day
Gordon MacRae

A syrupy musical, competently made and ideally suited for the wholesome talents of Day and MacRae, who play sweethearts in Indiana. The nostalgic story, based on Booth Tarkington's novel, is set just before World War I. It's a lighthearted family tale, mixing drama, music, and comedy. Also stars Leon Ames, Rosemary De Camp, and Billy Gray. **Director**—Roy Del Ruth.
95 minutes

ON THE BEACH (1959)
★★★

Gregory Peck
Ava Gardner
Fred Astaire
Anthony Perkins

Intelligent, thought-provoking account of survivors of a nuclear attack awaiting their fate in Australia. The film is enhanced by top performances from Peck and Gardner, and convincing supporting roles by Astaire and Perkins. It's a grim subject, yet it presents a searing comment on atomic warfare and what could be the end of the world. Based faithfully on the novel by Nevil Shute. Also with Donna Anderson, John Tate, and Lola Brooks. **Director**—Stanley Kramer.
134 minutes b&w

ON THE DOUBLE (1961)
★★

Danny Kaye

Rather typical vehicle for Kaye, who plays a private impersonating a high-ranking British officer during World War II because of their resemblance to each other. The dowdy script limits

some of Kaye's comedic opportunities, but he has a good time with several funny scenes. Others in the cast are Dana Wynter, Wilfrid Hyde-White, Margaret Rutherford, Diana Dors, and Jesse White. **Director**—Melville Shavelson.   *92 minutes*

ON THE RIGHT TRACK (1981)
★★

Gary Coleman

TV child-star Coleman makes his film debut in this innocuous comedy about a shoeshine boy whose home is a locker in Chicago's Union Station. Coleman is predictably adorable as a pint-sized con man who can predict the outcome of horse races. The script is adequately pleasing with its required romantic interludes, but this sort of stuff is familiar enough in countless TV sitcoms. Also with Michael Lembeck, Lisa Eilbacher, and Maureen Stapleton. **Director**—Lee Philips. (PG)   *97 minutes*

ON THE TOWN (1949)
★★★★

Gene Kelly
Frank Sinatra
Jules Munshin

Betty Garrett, Frank Sinatra, Ann Miller, Jules Munshin, Vera-Ellen, and Gene Kelly in the toe-tapping musical On the Town.

Energetic, toe-tapping musical that's among the best of its kind. Three sailors—Kelly, Sinatra, and Munshin—make the most of their 24-hour liberty
(Continued)

O
- On the Waterfront
- On the Yard
- Operation Petticoat
- Operation Thunderbolt
- Orchestra Rehearsal
- Orchestra Wives

(Continued)

in New York City. Kelly and Sinatra head the exuberant cast, dancing and singing all over town, with lively choreography designed by Kelly and tuneful songs from the hit Broadway show by Leonard Bernstein, Betty Comden, and Adolph Green. Effective moments of comedy enhance the proceedings. Excellent supporting work by Munshin, Vera-Ellen, Betty Garrett, Ann Miller, and Alice Pearce. **Directors**—Kelly and Stanley Donen.

98 minutes

ON THE WATERFRONT (1954)

★★★★

Marlon Brando
Eva Marie Saint
Lee J. Cobb

Marlon Brando finds out that they play pretty rough down On the Waterfront.

Stark, powerful drama about corruption and despair among New York City longshoremen, brilliantly conceived and capped with a terrific performance by Brando. His portrayal of the young stevedore who bravely exposes the criminals who control the waterfront union is among the best of his distinguished career. Saint plays the girl he loves, and Cobb is Brando's waterfront boss. The pacing, the brooding atmosphere, and the intelligent dialogue are all consistently good. Excellent supporting performances by Rod Steiger, Karl Malden, Pat Henning, and Leif Erickson. **Director**—Elia Kazan. **Academy Awards**—best picture; Kazan, best director; Brando, best actor; Saint, best supporting actress; Budd Schulberg, writing (story and screenplay); Boris Kaufman, cinematography (black and white). **Nominations**—Cobb, Malden, Steiger, best supporting actor.

108 minutes b&w

ON THE YARD (1979)

★★

John Heard
Thomas Waites
Mike Kellin

Thomas Waites prepares for prison brutality in On the Yard.

Day-to-day prison life is rather routine and so is this film, directed by Raphael D. Silver. It's about a power struggle among inmates. Convict Heard makes a mistake when he runs afoul of inmate chieftain Waites. Silver avoids the usual clichés of familiar big-house movies, but he also neglects drama and emotion. It needs a little bit of Cagney, a dash of Bogart—or something. It's nicely acted, though, by Waites, Heard, and Kellin. The screenplay is based on a novel by Malcolm Braly, a former San Quentin inmate. Also with Joe Grifasi, Richard Bright, and Lane Smith. (R) *102 minutes*

OPERATION PETTICOAT (1959)

★★★

Cary Grant
Tony Curtis

A better-than-average comedy made even better by the charming talent of Grant as skipper of a submarine in the South Pacific during World War II desperately trying to reactivate his damaged boat. Plenty of hilarious misadventures take place, and things really perk up when a group of nurses come aboard. Curtis shines as an officer with many outrageous schemes for getting the sub seaworthy. Also stars Joan O'Brien, Dina Merrill, Gene Evans, Richard Sargent, and Arthur O'Connell. **Director**—Blake Edwards. **Academy Award Nominations**—Paul King and Joseph Stone (story), Stanley Shapiro and Maurice Richlin (screen-

play), best story and screenplay (written directly for the screen).

124 minutes

OPERATION THUNDERBOLT (1978)

★★

Klaus Kinski
Assaf Dayan
Yehoram Gaon

This Israeli-made film retells the events of the lightning commando raid on Entebbe, when 104 hijacked passengers were rescued. There are occasional moments of suspense—especially the daring action sequences at the Ugandan airport. But mostly, the film smacks of official government propaganda. The characters are uninteresting cardboard stereotypes. Perhaps the real-life episode that dominated the headlines that July day in 1976 is too thrilling to rehash for the screen. Also with Gila Almagor and Shai K. Ophir. **Director**—Menahem Golan. (No MPAA rating)

125 minutes

ORCHESTRA REHEARSAL (1979)
★★

Balduin Baas
Clara Colosimo
Elisabeth Labi

Italian movie maestro Federico Fellini uses a rebellious symphony orchestra as a metaphor for the decline of Western civilization. The musicians revolt against their conductor and quarrel with one another until the conductor restores order by turning into a ranting dictator. Clever moments, but rather tiresome overall. Fellini's parable is a somewhat simplistic and unconvincing description of a complex subject. In Italian with English titles. (No MPAA rating) *70 minutes*

ORCHESTRA WIVES (1942)
★★★

Glenn Miller
Ann Rutherford
George Montgomery

Miller and his orchestra take the spotlight in this backstage story about

• Ordinary People
• Oscar Wilde
• The Osterman Weekend

• Othello
• The Other Side of Midnight
• The Other Side of the Mountain

O

the private lives of the musicians and their spouses. The plot sustains adequate interest, but it's the wonderful swing music that keeps the film at a buoyant level. Miller and company belt out "I've Got a Gal in Kalamazoo," "Serenade in Blue," and more. Also with Lynn Bari, Jackie Gleason, Cesar Romero, and Carole Landis. **Director**—Archie Mayo.

97 minutes b&w

ORDINARY PEOPLE (1980)

★★★★

Donald Sutherland
Mary Tyler Moore
Timothy Hutton

Donald Sutherland and Mary Tyler Moore are two troubled parents in Ordinary People.

Redford, first time out as director, fashions a moving, intelligent, but somber film about family conflict as seen through the eyes of a troubled teenage boy. Based on Judith Guest's best-selling novel, this powerful movie examines human behavior with extraordinary sensitivity. Moore, Sutherland, and Hutton are excellent as members of an ordinary affluent family who have difficulty expressing love. Also with Judd Hirsch. (R) **Academy Awards**—best picture; Hutton, best supporting actor; Redford, best director; Alvin Sargent, best screenplay (adapted from another medium). **Nominations**—Hirsch, best supporting actor; Moore, best actress. *123 minutes*

OSCAR WILDE (1959)

★★★

Robert Morley

Adequate biography of the talented 19th-century playwright who was im-

prisoned on charges of being a sexual deviate. Morley, in the title role, repeats his stage portrayal and does a convincing job of conveying the complex personality. A similar account, *The Trials of Oscar Wilde*, was filmed about the same time, but this version is better. Also stars Ralph Richardson and John Neville. **Director**—Gregory Ratoff. *96 minutes b&w*

THE OSTERMAN WEEKEND (1983)

★★

Rutger Hauer
Burt Lancaster
John Hurt

Robert Ludlum's jumbled spy novel becomes even more confusing on screen under the stylish but unsure direction of Sam Peckinpah. Dutch actor Hauer is a TV newscaster who conspires with the CIA to set up some of his friends believed to be Russian spies. The farfetched plot eventually goes out of control with an outrageous killing spree that makes use of hunting bows, laser rays, explosions, and guns. And at the end we're still not sure who did what to whom—or why. (R) *102 minutes*

Rutger Hauer jealously guards the midnight snacks in his refrigerator from Dennis Hopper and Chris Sarandon in The Osterman Weekend.

OTHELLO (1965)

★★★

Laurence Olivier

Magnificent screen version of Shakespeare's classic, with Olivier doing what comes naturally in repeating his brilliant stage portrayal. This production perhaps isn't as effective as other filmings of Shakespeare's dramas, but the performances are unexcelled. A

worthwhile experience all the way in this virtually complete rendering of the great story of the Moor of Venice. Excellent supporting work from Frank Finlay, Joyce Redman, Maggie Smith, and Derek Jacobi. **Director**—Stuart Burge. **Academy Award Nominations**—Olivier, best actor; Finlay, best supporting actor; Redman, Smith, best supporting actress. *166 minutes*

THE OTHER SIDE OF MIDNIGHT (1977)

★★

Marie-France Pisier
John Beck

Marie France Pisier doesn't want to talk to Raf Vallone in The Other Side of Midnight.

This slick adaptation of Sidney Sheldon's best-selling novel is a complex soap opera dripping with just about every movie cliché. Pisier plays a poor French girl who finally becomes wealthy and famous and tries to get revenge on a dashing American cad, played by Beck, who abandoned her after a brief wartime romance. The corny plot spans some eight years and jumps between Europe and the United States. The title may have something to do with the film's length. Also with Susan Sarandon and Raf Vallone. **Director**—Charles Jarrott. (R) *165 minutes*

THE OTHER SIDE OF THE MOUNTAIN (1975)

★★

Marilyn Hassett
Beau Bridges

Hassett and Bridges star in this so-so tearjerker about Jill Kinmont, a prom-
(Continued)

 Movie is available in Beta and VHS videotape

O

- The Other Side of the Mountain Part 2
- Our Hearts Were Young and Gay
- Our Man in Havana
- Our Town
- Outland
- The Outlaw
- Outlaw Blues

(Continued)

ising young skier who was critically injured in 1956 while competing for the U.S. Olympic team. There are a few genuinely touching moments, but most of it is formula moviemaking, leaning on the *Love Story* theme. Bring plenty of handkerchiefs. Also with Belinda Montgomery, Nan Martin, and William Bryant. **Director**—Larry Peerce. (PG)   *101 minutes*

THE OTHER SIDE OF THE MOUNTAIN PART 2 (1978)
★★

**Marilyn Hassett
Timothy Bottoms**

Part I told the tragic and true story of skier Jill Kinmont, who was crippled as the result of a downhill accident. Hassett is effective again as Jill in the second installment of this formula weepie, which has our heroine in love with a truck driver, played by Bottoms. The script, however, begs for interesting story angles. Director Larry Peerce manages to wring plenty of tears from moviegoers in the mood for a good cry. Also with Nan Martin, Belinda Montgomery, Gretchen Corbett, and William Bryant. (PG)   *100 minutes*

OUR HEARTS WERE YOUNG AND GAY (1944)
★★★

**Gail Russell
Diana Lynn**

An appealing piece of adolescent froth about two young women—Russell and Lynn—who, in 1923, travel to Paris where they have some romantic adventures. Not very deep, but a pleasant and scrubbed minor comedy, based on the book by Cornelia Otis Skinner. Also with Charles Ruggles, Dorothy Gish, Beulah Bondi, and James Brown. **Director**—Lewis Allen.   *81 minutes b&w*

OUR MAN IN HAVANA (1960)
★★★★

**Alec Guinness
Noel Coward**

Guinness stars as the owner of a

vacuum cleaner shop in pre-Castro Cuba. He's recruited by British intelligence agent Coward to spy for England. The blend of satire and drama works well, and the steamy setting of tropical Havana provides a good atmospheric mood. The script is based on Graham Greene's novel—not too faithfully, but it works well nonetheless. Ernie Kovacs is good as a skeptical Cuban police chief. Adequate performances, too, from Burl Ives, Maureen O'Hara, Ralph Richardson, and Jo Morrow. **Director**—Carol Reed.   *107 minutes b&w*

OUR TOWN
(1940)
 ★★★★

**Frank Craven
William Holden
Martha Scott**

Thornton Wilder's classic story of life and love in a small New England community at the turn of the century is brought to the screen with its earnest, heartfelt attributes finely displayed. An excellent production in all departments, with outstanding performances by a top cast. Also with Thomas Mitchell, Beulah Bondi, Guy Kibbee, and Fay Bainter. **Director**—Sam Wood. **Academy Award Nominations**—best picture; Scott, best actress.   *90 minutes b&w*

OUTLAND
(1981)
 ★★★

**Sean Connery
Peter Boyle**

Connery plays a federal marshal with principle and determination; he tries to crack a drug-smuggling ring at a remote mining camp on Jupiter's third moon. Boyle is the manager of the mine colony. This rousing and stunning space opera is a close cousin to *High Noon* with a dash of James Bond thrown in. The drama and suspense are enchanced magnificently by some great special effects and sci-fi settings that detail the bleak, synthetic outerspace environment and the rigors of working there. Also with Frances Sternhagen. **Director**—Peter Hyams. (R)   *109 minutes*

THE OUTLAW (1943)
 ★★★

**Jack Beutel
Jane Russell**

Jane Russell and Jack Beutel are sweethearts in The Outlaw.

The main attraction in this tongue-in-cheek western seems to be the bosom of a young Russell, who frequently bulges forth in a low-cut blouse. But all this hoopla aside, the episodes involving Billy the Kid and Doc Holliday pack some punch, and there are decent performances by gunslingers Beutel and Walter Huston, who scrap over a half-breed beauty, played by Russell. Also with Thomas Mitchell and Joe Sawyer. **Director**—Howard Hughes.   *126 minutes b&w*

OUTLAW BLUES (1977)
★★★

Peter Fonda

Fonda plays an ex-con who tries some picking and singing in this country musical-adventure; he does both rather well. The lighthearted plot moves along smartly, generating ample laughs and smiles; even a few standard chase scenes are appealing. Most of the performances and Richard Heffron's direction are easy going, making this not-too-serious but energetic film palatable fare for country-western fans. Also stars Susan Saint James, John Crawford, and James Callahan. (PG)   *100 minutes*

• The Outlaw Josey Wales • Outrageous!
• Out of the Past • The Outsiders
• The-Out-of-Towners • Over the Brooklyn Bridge
• Over the Edge

O

THE OUTLAW JOSEY WALES
(1976)

 ★★★

Clint Eastwood

There's a new corpse just about every other minute in this post-Civil War drama about vengeance. Despite the excess violence, there's an intriguing and grimly suspenseful story supported by professional performances. Eastwood plays the lean, cool, tobacco-chewing Josey Wales, who embarks on a long trail of revenge and self-preservation after marauding Union soldiers kill his wife and son. Eastwood is also the director, and he capably handles the action scenes in a no-nonsense manner. Chief Dan George, Sondra Locke, Bill McKinney, and John Vernon also star. (PG)

135 minutes

OUT OF THE PAST (1947)

 ★★★★

**Robert Mitchum
Kirk Douglas
Jane Greer**

Robert Mitchum is forced to relive old memories in Out of the Past.

This tough, crackling melodrama hits the heights of *film noir*. Mitchum plays the owner of a California gas station and a former private eye, who's hired by hood Douglas to track down the sullen young woman (Greer) who's run out on him. When the hunter finds his prey he also falls in love with her, and gets mixed up in murder and treachery. It's hard to keep up with all the double crosses, but the dialogue is punchy, Jacques Tourneur's direction is expressive in a way that's rarely seen

any more, and the entire cast is dead on target. With Rhonda Fleming and Steve Brodie. The basis of the 1984 *Against All Odds.*   *97 minutes b&w*

THE OUT-OF-TOWNERS (1970)

 ★★★

**Jack Lemmon
Sandy Dennis**

New York City is seen as a nightmare of mishaps in this spry Neil Simon comedy about an executive who comes to the Big Apple for a job interview. The comedy is rather patchy, but there are some fine moments, with Lemmon, as the uptight visitor from Ohio, involved in some hair-raising episodes. Dennis plays his wife. Also with Sandy Baron, Anne Meara, Billy Dee Wiliams, and Carlos Montalban. **Director**—Arthur Hiller. (G)

98 minutes

OUTRAGEOUS! (1977)

 ★★★

**Craig Russell
Hollis McLaren**

Likable, energetic, but somewhat flawed Canadian film about an odd-couple relationship between a female impersonator and a beautiful schizophrenic girl. There's a winning, touching performance by McLaren as the troubled young woman. Some of the highlights, though, are the witty impersonations of famous women entertainers by Russell, who plays the transvestite. The film is more offbeat than it is outrageous. Written and directed by Richard Benner. (R)

100 minutes

THE OUTSIDERS (1983)

 ★★

**C. Thomas Howell
Matt Dillon
Ralph Macchio
Diane Lane**

Director Francis Ford Coppola mishandles this film adaptation of S. E. Hinton's novel about rival teenage gangs in Oklahoma during the '60s. The production drips with sentimental slush about poor kids ("greasers")

Matt Dillon, C. Thomas Howell, and Ralph Macchio are greasers in The Outsiders.

who are tormented by rich youths. The relatively simple story is puffed up to the point where it becomes pretentious and confusing. Coppola's reputation suffers. (PG)   *91 minutes*

OVER THE BROOKLYN BRIDGE (1984)

 ★★

**Sid Caesar
Margaux Hemingway
Elliott Gould**

Wobbly romantic comedy built around a clash-of-cultures theme that parallels *Abie's Irish Rose.* Gould plays a Brooklyn luncheonette owner with a dilemma: Shall he marry within the Jewish faith under pressure or remain loyal to his Irish girlfriend Hemingway, whom he truly loves? The film is top-heavy with ethnic jokes and Yiddish expressions. But it's a pleasure to see Caesar in a funny and dramatic role as the rich patriarch uncle. **Director**—Menahem Golan. (R)   *108 minutes*

OVER THE EDGE (1982)

 ★★

**Michael Kramer
Pamela Ludwig
Matt Dillon**

This vivid account of rebellious middle-class youths holds some fascina-
(Continued)

O·P

- The Owl and the Pussycat
- The Ox-Bow Incident
- Oxford Blues
- Paint Your Wagon
- The Pajama Game
- The Paleface
- Pal Joey

(Continued)
tion, but it is routinely acted. The kids in the movie turn to vandalism and drugs because of the boring sterility of their environment and the benign neglect of their well-fixed parents. Their situations may be secure, but life offers little challenge. At times, the film seems as undramatic as the youths' banal existence. **Director—** Jonathan Kaplan. (PG)   *95 minutes*

THE OWL AND THE PUSSYCAT (1970)

 ★★★

Barbra Streisand
George Segal

Streisand and Segal work well together and cook up some funny situations in this risqué comedy. She's a dopey prostitute, and he's a stuffy bookstore clerk. They become roommates when she's ousted from her apartment. This odd-couple theme is déjà vu, but there are enough fresh antics to uphold interest. Funky dialogue and bawdy situations abound. Also with Robert Klein, Roz Kelly, and Allen Garfield. **Director—**Herbert Ross. (R)   *96 minutes*

THE OX-BOW INCIDENT (1943)

★★★★

Henry Fonda
Dana Andrews

Henry Fonda holds the rope as a mob deals with accused murderers in The Ox-Bow Incident.

Powerful, realistically told western about a mob that lynches three men for murder despite the pleas of others who cry out for reason and justice. Fonda plays a cowboy with a conscience. The film is a strong statement against mob justice, expertly done. Also with Anthony Quinn, Henry Morgan, Mary Beth Hughes, William Blythe, and Jane Darwell. **Director—** William Wellman. **Academy Award Nomination—**best picture.
75 minutes b&w

OXFORD BLUES (1984)

★★

Rob Lowe

A 1980s treatment of Robert Taylor's 1938 film, *A Yank At Oxford.* Now we find Lowe as a wise guy from Nevada who finagles his way into the prestigious British university. Here he pursues an aristocratic woman student, joins the crew team, and adopts a flippant attitude toward his courses. Such events are hardly believable. Lowe's performance is constantly upstaged by various English character actors. Ally Sheedy, Julian Sands, and Amanda Pays co-star. **Director—**Robert Boris. (PG–13)   *96 minutes*

P

PAINT YOUR WAGON (1969)

 ★★

Lee Marvin
Clint Eastwood
Jean Seberg

Lavish but humdrum screen version of the Lerner and Loewe Broadway musical about a couple of gold rush prospectors in the 1800s married to the same woman. Marvin and Eastwood are the prospectors, and Seberg is their wife. The dancing is minimal, and some of the songs are forgettable; but there are a few bright moments in the long production. This wagon, unfortunately, is overloaded. "They Call the Wind Mariah" is among the songs. Also with Harve Presnell and Ray Walston. **Director—**Joshua Logan. (PG)   *166 minutes*

THE PAJAMA GAME (1957)

★★★

Doris Day
John Raitt

A labor-management dispute in a pajama factory is the theme of this lively movie musical, nicely adapted from the Broadway production. Day, well cast as the head of the grievance committee, winds up in love with the factory manager, played by Raitt. The film hums along, with some good songs, like "Hey There, You With the Stars in Your Eyes," and a good deal of effective humor. The main point of the labor dispute is a 7½¢ pay raise, but they all deserve more than that for such a good job of acting, singing, and dancing. Also with Eddie Foy, Jr., Carol Haney, Reta Shaw, and Bob Fosse. **Directors—**George Abbott and Stanley Donen.   *101 minutes*

THE PALEFACE (1948)

★★★

Bob Hope
Jane Russell

Highly entertaining spoof of western films, with Hope cast as a bumbling frontier dentist who helps pistol-packing Calamity Jane, played by Russell, take on some bad guys. There's nothing pale about the gags; they come across with plenty of zing. The Oscar-winning song "Buttons and Bows" is featured. Also stars Robert Armstrong, Iris Adrian, Robert Watson, and Jack Searle. This production led to a sequel, *Son of Paleface,* and a remake, *The Shakiest Gun in the West.* **Director—**Norman Z. McLeod.
91 minutes

PAL JOEY (1957)

★★★

Frank Sinatra
Rita Hayworth
Kim Novak

Sinatra is right at home in this slick musical as a nightclub operator who vacillates between being a heel and a good guy. There are plenty of good Rodgers and Hart tunes for Frank to sing, including "My Funny Valentine" and "The Lady Is a Tramp." And there are adequate romantic opportunities, with Hayworth and Novak vying for Sinatra's attention. The film isn't quite as vibrant as the Broadway production, but it's good fun all the same. **Director**—George Sidney.

109 minutes

THE PALM BEACH STORY
(1942)

★★★★

**Claudette Colbert
Joel McCrea
Rudy Vallee
Mary Astor**

A smart screwball comedy, abounding with delightful zaniness, touching moments, and colorful characters. Colbert plays the ambitious wife of an engineer; she runs off to the posh Florida city where she engages in a romance with a snobby millionaire, played by Vallee. McCrea plays Colbert's husband, and Astor is Vallee's sister. An inventive, well-made production offering hilarity galore. Also with William Demarest, Sig Arno, and Jack Norton. **Director**—Preston Sturges. *88 minutes b&w*

THE PANIC IN NEEDLE PARK
(1971)

★★★

**Al Pacino
Kitty Winn**

Hard-hitting account of a small-time thief and his girl friend who become involved with heroin and hit the skids. Pacino is the thief, and Winn is his hooked mistress. The squalid atmosphere of Manhattan's upper West Side ghetto is skillfully portrayed, and the production is made even more vivid by Pacino's astounding debut film performance. The movie is sort of an echo of *Days of Wine and Roses*. Also with Adam Vint and Richard Bright. **Director**—Jerry Schatzberg. (PG) *110 minutes*

PANIC IN THE STREETS (1950)

★★★★

**Richard Widmark
Jack Palance**

Tense story of efforts to locate a gangster who's carrying the plague. Suspense mounts effectively in this semi-documentary film, set with considerable realism on the docks of New Orleans. Widmark and Palance have first-class support from Zero Mostel, Paul Douglas, and Barbara Bel Geddes. **Director**—Elia Kazan. **Academy Award**—Edna and Edward Anhalt, writing (motion picture story).

96 minutes b&w

THE PAPER CHASE (1973)

 ★★★

**Timothy Bottoms
Lindsay Wagner
John Houseman**

Timothy Bottoms studies hard for his law degree in The Paper Chase.

A captivating and intense story of the agony and frustration of a graduate student trying to make it through Harvard Law School. His problems are compounded when he falls in love with the divorced daughter of a demanding and cynical law professor. Bottoms is the student, and Wagner is the woman. Most of the performances are outstanding, and there are some realistic moments of classroom tension and humiliation. Houseman is exceptionally convincing as the tyrannical law professor. Well-done supporting roles by Wagner and James Naughton. Also with Graham Beckel and Edward Herrmann. **Director**—James Bridges. (PG) **Academy Award**—Houseman, best supporting actor; James Bridges, best screenplay (based on material from another medium). *111 minutes*

PAPER MOON (1973)

 ★★★★

**Ryan O'Neal
Tatum O'Neal**

Tatum O'Neal and dad Ryan are naturals as an oddball father-and-daughter team in Paper Moon.

An appealing offbeat comedy set in mid-America in the '30s. The story works to perfection, thanks in part to the nifty pairing of Ryan O'Neal and his real-life daughter, Tatum, as a couple of Bible-selling con artists. The precocious and beguiling Tatum steals many a scene, and the film shines with much glossy sentimentality. Based on the novel *Addie Pray* by Joe David Brown. Co-stars Madeline Kahn, John Hillerman, and P. J. Johnson. **Director**—Peter Bogdanovich. (PG) **Academy Award**—Tatum O'Neal, best supporting actress. **Nominations**—Kahn, best supporting actress; Alvin Sargent, best screenplay (based on material from another medium).

103 minutes b&w

PAPER TIGER
(1976)

★★

David Niven

Niven stars as a kindly English schoolmaster who daydreams of becoming a hero. He finally gets his chance when he and his pupil, the son of the Japanese Ambassador, are kidnapped by terrorists. Ando plays the pupil, and Toshiro Mifune plays his distraught father. The story, awash in sentiment, may have emotional appeal for some. The direction by Ken Annakin lacks style. (PG) *99 minutes*

P

- • Papillon
- • Paradise
- • Paradise Alley
- • The Parallax View
- • The Parent Trap
- • Paris, Texas
- • Partners
- • The Passage

PAPILLON (1973)
★★★

Steve McQueen
Dustin Hoffman

A tense, gut-wrenching tale of horrible conditions at the infamous Devil's Island prison colony, and of the daring escape of a man who claims he was falsely convicted of murder. McQueen plays the title role. There are lots of graphic scenes depicting the brutality of prison life—filthy living conditions, sadistic guards, and homosexuality among the inmates. They make the yearning for escape extremely compelling, and you'll be cheering for success. Based on the book by Henri "Papillon" Charrière. Also with Victor Jory, Don Gordon, Anthony Zerbe, and Robert Deman. **Director**—Franklin J. Schaffner. (R) *150 minutes*

PARADISE (1982)
 ★

Phoebe Cates
Willie Aames

Willie Aames and Phoebe Cates (and two chimps) go joy-riding on a camel in Paradise.

If *The Blue Lagoon* only flirted with teenage sex, then this trashy look-alike gets right down to business, with innocence and loincloths tossed aside in quick succession. The story is set in the Middle East in 1823. Bright-eyed Cates and Aames play adolescent lovers on the run after their parents' murder. The youngsters find brief shelter at a sunny oasis where they learn about lovemaking from the chimpanzees. Direction and acting appear as if they came from the monkeys, too. **Director**—Stuart Gillard. (R)
100 minutes

PARADISE ALLEY (1978)
★★★

Sylvester Stallone

Stallone, who triumphed with *Rocky*, has another winner with this uplifting, powerful film about three brothers who fight their way out of New York's Hell's Kitchen shortly after World War II. Stallone who stars as one of the brothers, debuts as director; he skillfully draws winning performances from many promising new actors. The film is brimful of warm characters and the smoky atmosphere of New York City in the '40s. Also with Armand Assante and Lee Canalito. (PG) *109 minutes*

THE PARALLAX VIEW (1974)
 ★★★

Warren Beatty
Paula Prentiss

Beatty stars as a determined reporter who relentlessly investigates the intrigue surrounding the assassination of a U.S. Senator. The gripping political thriller is executed with much style and skill by director Alan Pakula, who keeps the suspense pot boiling to the end. Many subtle references to the Kennedys. Also with William Daniels, Hume Cronyn, and Walter McGinn. (R) *102 minutes*

THE PARENT TRAP (1961)
 ★★★

Hayley Mills
Maureen O'Hara
Brian Keith

Mildy amusing and often-clever adolescent romp from the Walt Disney studio, about twins who try to repair the broken marriage of their parents, played by O'Hara and Keith. Mills is likable in the roles of twin sisters who meet at a summer camp and discover they have the same mother and father. There are many bright scenes, but there's also some awkward slapstick. Also with Charles Ruggles, Leo G. Carroll, Una Merkel, and Joanna Barnes. **Director**—David Swift.
124 minutes

PARIS, TEXAS (1984)
★★★

Harry Dean Stanton
Dean Stockwell
Nastassja Kinski

Somber, somewhat poetic drama of a man who is reunited with his family after a mysterious four-year absence. German director Wim Wenders invests much tenderness and humanism in this gentle story of ordinary people who fail to communicate their emotions. The climactic reuniting of the estranged family is captivating indeed, but some of the film is heavy going. Rich, convincing performances from Stanton, Stockwell, and Kinski. (R) *145 minutes*

PARTNERS (1982)
 ★★

Ryan O'Neal
John Hurt

French screenwriter Francis Veber (*La Cage aux Folles*) dishes up this unusual comedy about a homosexual cop and a straight cop who team up to solve murders in San Francisco's gay world. There are some funny and touching moments, to be sure, but the script offers caricatures of homosexuals rather than fully-understood characters. O'Neal is effective as the macho straight detective. But it is Hurt's delicate performance as the mousy homosexual cop which carries the film. **Director**—John Burrows. (R)
98 minutes

THE PASSAGE (1979)
★

Anthony Quinn
James Mason
Malcolm McDowell

Pedestrian direction, trite dialogue, and an excess of violence permeate this World War II action movie. Mason plays an American scientist trying to escape from a German SS officer, played by McDowell. Mason acts as if he has a stomachache, and McDowell resembles a grotesque cartoon character. Quinn plays a Basque shepherd who guides the professor and his fam-

• A Passage to India • A Patch of Blue
• La Passante • Paternity
• Pat and Mike • Paths of Glory
• Patton

P

The Passage *features Anthony Quinn and James Mason.*

ily through the Pyrenees; he kills the enemy with emotionless abandon and does his familiar *paisan* folk dance. Also with Patricia Neal and Christopher Lee. **Director**—J. Lee Thompson. (R)   *99 minutes*

A PASSAGE TO INDIA (1984)
★★★

**Judy Davis
Victor Banerjee
Dame Peggy Ashcroft
James Fox
Alec Guinness**

David Lean's eloquently crafted film adaptation of E. M. Forster's classic novel focuses on the clash of cultures in British-ruled India during the '20s. Judy Davis plays a young English woman, essentially critical of British policy, who accuses an Indian doctor (Victor Banerjee) of raping her. The smugness of the British colonists is vividly illustrated in a tense courtroom drama. All characters are expertly portrayed by a top cast. (PG)   *160 minutes*

LA PASSANTE (1983)

★★

Romy Schneider

Schneider handles two roles well in this complex melodrama that interweaves the present with the Nazi occupation of Europe. She is the faithful wife of a wealthy Jewish activist who realizes revenge by killing a for-

mer Nazi collaborator. And in flashback scenes she is the wife of an anti-Nazi publisher in Germany. The story is difficult to follow and hardly compelling. Michael Piccoli also stars. In French with English titles. **Director**—Jacques Rouffio. (No MPAA rating)   *106 minutes*

PAT AND MIKE (1952)
★★★

**Spencer Tracy
Katharine Hepburn**

Katharine Hepburn has a leg up on Spencer Tracy in Pat and Mike.

The delightful teaming of Tracy and Hepburn transcends any minor drawbacks in this frothy comedy about the world of professional sports. Kate plays a champion athlete, and Spence latches on as her manager; the partnership leads to romance. Sporting greats appear in cameo roles. Also with Aldo Ray, Jim Backus, and Sammy White. **Director**—George Cukor. **Academy Award Nomination**—Ruth Gordon and Garson Kanin, writing (story and screenplay).
    95 minutes b&w

A PATCH OF BLUE (1965)
★★★

**Sidney Poitier
Elizabeth Hartman**

A touching story about a poor blind girl who falls in love with a kindhearted black and is unaware of his color. Hartman is the girl, and Poitier is the man. The film is a little too sentimental, but fine acting all around maintains interest. Shelley Winters is outstanding as the girl's mean-spirited mother. Also with Wallace Ford, Ivan Dixon, and John Qualen. **Director**—

Guy Green. **Academy Award**—Winters, best supporting actress. **Nominations**—Hartman, best actress; Robert Burks, cinematography (black and white).   *105 minutes b&w*

PATERNITY (1981)

★★

**Burt Reynolds
Beverly D'Angelo**

Reynolds stars in this essentially flat romantic comedy as a slightly sappy man-about-town looking for a woman to have his baby without the bother of marriage. The girl for the deal is a needy musician, played by D'Angelo. Now guess who's really in love and doesn't realize it? It's predictable and sentimental stuff unevenly directed by stand-up comedian David Steinberg with many contrived skits and one-liners and only a few truly funny situations. Reynolds's charm isn't enough to carry the film to full satisfaction. (PG)   *94 minutes*

PATHS OF GLORY (1957)

★★★★

**Kirk Douglas
Adolphe Menjou**

A striking, powerful tale about incompetence in the French army's high command during World War I. Douglas is great as an officer who treats his troops with dignity; Menjou is among those in the high command. The sordid conditions in the trenches are vividly detailed. Director Stanley Kubrick brings out the best in a top cast; it's superb moviemaking. Also with George Macready, Wayne Morris, and Ralph Meeker.   *86 minutes b&w*

PATTON (1970)

★★★★

**George C. Scott
Karl Malden**

Expertly crafted screen biography of Gen. George S. Patton, the brilliant and quick-tempered Army commander who led American forces in Europe and North Africa during World War II. Scott, in the title role, is cast as the
(Continued)

P

- Pauline at the Beach
- The Pawnbroker
- Peking Express
- Penitentiary
- Penitentiary II
- Pennies from Heaven

George C. Scott portrays Gen. George S. Patton in Patton.

(Continued)
bombastic general, and he gives the performance of his career in this magnificent, bigger-than-life portrayal. Malden is also outstanding in the role of Gen. Omar Bradley, displaying an impressive contrast as the tactful military strategist. Many of the battle scenes are realistically staged. Also with Michael Bates, Stephen Young, Michael Strong, and Fran Latimore. **Director**—Franklin Schaffner. (PG) **Academy Awards**—best picture; Schaffner, best director; Scott, best actor (award declined); Frances Ford Coppola and Edmund H. North, best story and screenplay (based on factual material or material not previously published). **Nomination**—Fred Koenekamp, cinematography. *170 minutes*

PAULINE AT THE BEACH (1983)
★★

Amanda Langlet

Director Eric Rohmer's playful comedy involves brief love affairs among six persons of various ages vacationing on the Normandy coast. While there are flashes of wit, the characters engage in incessant, tiresome chatter. At the center of this complex mating game is budding teenager Langlet whose innocent summer romance is in contrast with the childish behavior of the adults. Also with Arielle Dombasle. In French with English titles.
94 minutes

THE PAWNBROKER (1965)
 ★★★★

Rod Steiger

Steiger is memorable in the title role of this compelling melodrama about a Harlem hock shop owner haunted by the lingering memories of his experiences in a Nazi concentration camp. Steiger keeps the complex character in perfect control, and the result is an honest study of a distrustful man who struggles to regain faith in mankind. Sidney Lumet's direction is nicely paced. Fine supporting work from Brock Peters, Geraldine Fitzgerald, Jaime Sanchez, and Thelma Oliver.
114 minutes b&w

PEKING EXPRESS (1951)
★★

Joseph Cotten
Corinne Calvet

Unimpressive rehash of *Shanghai Express* with various characters aboard a train traveling through Red China. Cotten stars as a doctor who becomes involved with an intriguing lady played by Calvet. It's a routine romantic adventure at best. Also with Edmund Gwenn, Marvin Miller, and Benson Fong. **Director**—William Dieterle.
90 minutes b&w

PENITENTIARY (1980)
 ★★

Leon Isaac Kennedy

A rough, tough prison drama, reminiscent of the black exploitation films of years ago. Kennedy is a young convict who avoids sexual abuse in prison by becoming a competent boxer. There's plenty of raw street language and a lot of brutal encounters among the inmates, but not much credibility about prison life. Also with Thommy Pollard, Hazel Spears, and Badja Djola. **Director**—Jamaa Fanaka. (R)
99 minutes

PENITENTIARY II
(1982)
 (no stars)

Leon Isaac Kennedy
Ernie Hudson
Glynn Turman

Leon Isaac Kennedy has a rematch with Donovan Womack in Penitentiary II.

Kennedy returns for more violent confrontations in and out of the ring in this shabby and preposterous sequel. This exploitative low-budget movie initially finds our young hero out of prison and supposedly through with boxing. Soon, however, an escaped convict is after him and he winds up fighting the champ back at the penitentiary. The brutality is nonstop; just watching this bloody mess is cruel and unusual punishment. **Director**—Jamaa Fanaka. (R) *103 minutes*

PENNIES FROM HEAVEN (1981)
 ★★

Steve Martin
Bernadette Peters

This movie is a strange mix of comedy and drama set to music. It's a feeble attempt to contrast upbeat Hollywood musicals with the grim realities of the period. Martin stars as a sheet-music peddler who lives the lyrics of his songs in his fantasies, even though his life is filled with doom and gloom. Many of the lavish musical numbers are inspired, but the film suffers too often from an awkward script and unconvincing dialogue. Martin, Peters, Christopher Walken, and Jessica Harper display amazing skill in the song and dance routines. **Director**—Herbert Ross. (R) **Academy Award Nomination**—Dennis Potter, best

• The People That Time Forgot
• Peppermint Soda
• A Perfect Couple
• Performance
• The Perils of Pauline
• Personal Best
• Pete Kelly's Blues

P

screenplay (based on material from another medium). *107 minutes*

THE PEOPLE THAT TIME FORGOT (1977)

 ★

Patrick Wayne
Doug McClure

In 1919, a band of hardy adventurers go on a mission to rescue McClure, marooned several years earlier, in the midst of prehistoric monsters and unfriendly natives on an imaginary Antarctic island. This comic-book movie, based on an Edgar Rice Burroughs fantasy, is a sequel to *The Land That Time Forgot*. The limited script and direction lack imagination, and the prehistoric trappings are as artificial as the acting. All in all, it's a film you're bound to forget quickly. Also with Dana Gillespie, Sarah Douglas, and Thorley Walters. **Director**—Kevin Connor. (PG) *90 minutes*

PEPPERMINT SODA (1979)

★★★

Elenore Klarwein
Odile Michel

French director Diane Kurys made this understated yet effective film about the traumas of adolescence as seen through the eyes of two teenage sisters, played by Klarwein and Michel. It's a sensitive chronicle that hits home because of a concentration on vivid and engaging details. Klarwein stands out as the younger sister, encountering the familiar crises of growing up. Also with Anouk Ferjac. In French with English titles. (PG) *97 minutes*

A PERFECT COUPLE (1979)

★★★

Paul Dooley
Marta Heflin

There's something uncanny and intelligent in this film from director Robert Altman, about a man and a woman from contrasting backgrounds who meet via a computer dating service. The story occasionally lapses, but there are so many warm and funny moments that the experience is unforgettable. Dooley and Heflin are convincing as the unlikely lovers. It's not the best of Altman, but it's rousing social parody from an extraordinary filmmaker. Also with Henry Gibson, Belita Moreno, and Titos Vandis. (PG) *110 minutes*

PERFORMANCE (1970)

 ★★★

Mick Jagger
James Fox
Anita Pallenberg

Mick Jagger helps the ultra-conservative James Fox to wig out in Performance.

A vicious gangster fleeing from the mob (Fox) holes up in the basement apartment of a townhouse owned by a former rock star turned recluse (Jagger, of course). A complex relationship develops between landlord and tenant, and between both men and the two women also living in the English residence. If nothing else, the film is a flashy, Pinteresque drama of intertwined lives with plenty of mordant humor and visual virtuosity, although its sheer bizarreness and sadomasochism can ultimately be alienating. Jagger sings "Memo from Turner." **Director**—Nicolas Roeg. (X) *105 minutes*

THE PERILS OF PAULINE (1947)

 ★★★

Betty Hutton
John Lund

The screen escapades of silent-film star Pearl White are fondly remembered in this energetic musical comedy, nicely adorned with Frank Loesser tunes. Hutton plunges into the title role with gusto as the frantic heroine who becomes involved in cliff-hanging predicaments. Lots of colorful slapstick scenes hark back to the days of Hollywood silents; but too much sentimentality finally creeps into the film. Others in the cast include Billy De Wolfe, William Demarest, and Constance Collier. **Director**—George Marshall. *96 minutes*

PERSONAL BEST (1982)

 ★★★

Mariel Hemingway
Patrice Donnelly
Scott Glenn

Patrice Donnelly, Jodi Anderson, and Mariel Hemingway are athletes happy to have done their Personal Best.

Two female athletes (Hemingway and Donnelly) train hard for the Olympics and fall in love. The film avoids any lurid melodramatics of the lesbian relationship in favor of a close-up look at the intensity of athletes in training. Unlike most sports films, *Personal Best* shows how matches are really won in the training, in the endless hours of running, exercising, and sweating. The performances are extremely good at conveying the amount of dedication and concentration required of world-class athletes. The film is engrossing and authentic, but tends to drag on a little too long. **Director**—Robert Towne. (R) *124 minutes*

PETE KELLY'S BLUES (1955)

★★

Jack Webb
Edmond O'Brien
Janet Leigh

The jazz world of the '20s is recreated
(Continued)

Trumpeter Jack Webb looks on as Peggy Lee tells off Edmond O'Brien in the jazzy world of Pete Kelly's Blues.

(Continued)
in this unmoving film. But it's improperly handled by Webb, who directs and plays the lead. The music is really of interest here, and that department is filled nicely with the talents of Peggy Lee and Ella Fitzgerald. Lee has a rare dramatic role, and she displays some extraordinary acting skills. Also with Andy Devine, Lee Marvin, and Martin Milner. **Academy Award Nomination**—Lee, best supporting actress.

95 minutes

PETE 'N' TILLIE (1972)
★★

Walter Matthau
Carol Burnett

Walter Matthau tells Carol Burnett he'll respect her in the morning in Pete'n'Tillie.

Matthau and Burnett are nicely paired as middle-aged oddball characters who marry. The film begins as wry comedy and then lapses into sentimental soap opera when the couple's son dies. The stars make the most of some absorbing moments, but there's not too much going on in between. It's merely an adequate time-passer. Also with Geraldine Page, René Auberjonois, Barry Nelson, and Henry Jones. **Director**—Martin Ritt. (PG) **Academy Award Nominations**—Page, best supporting actress; Julius J. Epstein, best screenplay (based on material from another medium).

100 minutes

PETER PAN (1952)
★★★

Lively and colorful animated story from the Walt Disney studio, about the amazing boy who takes a trio of English children on an adventure to a magical land. They have a number of adventures involving Captain Hook, Tiger Lily, and Tinker Bell. Disney's fantastic skills are obviously in evidence. It's an exhilarating fantasy, based on Sir J. M. Barrie's book, for the small fry—and for adults, too. (G) **Directors**—Wilfred Jackson, Clyde Geronomi, and Hamilton Luske.

76 minutes

PETE'S DRAGON (1977)
★★★

Helen Reddy
Jim Dale
Mickey Rooney
Red Buttons

What child could resist a jolly, cuddly green dragon—especially one with a potbelly and tiny pink wings? Elliot, the cartoon dragon in this Walt Disney romantic fantasy, is especially appealing as the companion and protector of Pete, a runaway orphan played by Sean Marshall. The music is bright, the action is vigorous, and the performances by the veteran cast are pleasant. The Disney folks, famous for this kind of children's treat, have done it again. Also with Shelley Winters and Jane Kean. **Director**—Don Chaffey. (G)

134 minutes

THE PETRIFIED FOREST (1936)
★★★

Humphrey Bogart
Leslie Howard
Bette Davis

Humphrey Bogart got his first major screen part, recreating his Broadway role of vicious gangster Duke Mantee, in this screen adaptation of the Robert E. Sherwood play. Fleeing from the law, Mantee and his gang hold a small group of people hostage at a desert cafe. Among those trapped at the Black Mesa Bar B-Q are a dreamy-eyed intellectual, played by Howard, and the waitress he falls for, played by Davis. Although it's a bit dusty after some 50 years, the film still has plenty of tension, and the three luminous stars play off each other impressively. **Director**—Archie Mayo.

83 minutes b&w

PEYTON PLACE (1957)
★★★★

Lana Turner
Arthur Kennedy
Hope Lange

What could have been standard soap opera is handled with style and impressive dramatic skill. Grace Metalious's sensational novel about scandalous activity in a small New Hampshire community is expertly adapted, with talented performances and top production. Turner heads the fine cast of Peyton Place residents, which also includes Diane Varsi, Lee Philips, Lloyd Nolan, Russ Tamblyn, Terry Moore, and Betty Field. The film is an engrossing account of plain folks doing what is unexpected of them.

• Phantasm
• The Phantom of the Opera
• Phantom of the Rue Morgue
• Phar Lap

• Phffft!
• The Philadelphia
  Experiment
• The Philadelphia Story

P

Director—Mark Robson. **Academy Award Nominations**—best picture; Robson, best director; Turner, best actress; Kennedy, best supporting actor; Lange, Varsi, best supporting actress; John Michael Hayes, best screenplay (based on material from another medium); William Mellor, cinematography (color). *157 minutes*

PHANTASM (1979)

 ★

Michael Baldwin
Bill Thornbury

Cheap scare tactics and overblown gore dominate this shabby horror story about strange happenings in a suburban mortuary. The illogical plot lacks imagination or honest suspense. The most grisly scenes are unimpressive; the blood—both red and yellow—looks like spilled nail polish. Director-writer Don Coscarelli seems to be reaching for spookiness and sinister characters, but he merely serves up a lot of confusion. Also with Reggie Bannister, Kathy Lester, and Angus Scrimm. (R) *87 minutes*

THE PHANTOM OF THE OPERA (1943)
★★★

Claude Rains
Nelson Eddy
Susanna Foster

A worthy remake of the impressive 1925 silent melodrama that starred Lon Chaney. There are some colorful scenes in this well-produced rendition, with Rains in the title role as the mad and disfigured composer who hides in the sewers under the Paris Opera House and plots revenge. Many moments are devoted to Eddy and Foster singing. Also stars Edgar Barrier, Leo Carrillo, and Hume Cronyn. **Director**—Arthur Lubin. **Academy Award**—Hal Mohr and W. Howard Greene, cinematography (color). *92 minutes*

PHANTOM OF THE RUE MORGUE (1954)
★

Karl Malden

Silly moustaches abound in Phantom of the Rue Morgue.

A rather limp rehash of the Edgar Allan Poe chiller "Murders in the Rue Morgue," which isn't scary at all. The setting is Paris, where a mad killer of pretty girls is on the loose. Malden gives a hammy and lackluster performance in a key role, and other characters do as well. Claude Dauphin, Patricia Medina, Steve Forrest, and Merv Griffin are also in the cast. Originally a 3-D film. **Director**—Roy Del Ruth. *84 minutes*

PHAR LAP (1984)

 ★★★

Tom Burlinson
Ron Liebman
Martin Vaughan

Typical horse-racing saga that follows in the hoof steps of similar outings, such as *National Velvet* and *The Story of Seabiscuit*. This true story traces the career of the scrawny colt from New Zealand who became Australia's legendary race track champion during the Depression era and then died mysteriously in California. Ample root-for-the-underdog elements and taut accounts of behind-the-scenes manipulation place this sports biography in the money. **Director**—Simon Wincer. (PG) *107 minutes*

PHFFFT! (1954)
★★★

Jack Lemmon
Judy Holliday

Lemmon and Holliday sparkle in this buoyant adult comedy, as a couple who separate and then discover that they were happier married. The situation is somewhat shopworn, but Lemmon and Holliday pull it off with style. Also with Kim Novak, Jack Carson, Donald Randolph, and Luella Gear. **Director**—Mark Robson. *91 minutes b&w*

THE PHILADELPHIA EXPERIMENT (1984)

 ★★

Michael Paré
Bobby DiCicco

Two sailors engaged in an experiment in 1943 to make a warship impervious to radar find themselves transported to the year 1984. This time-warp, sci-fi fantasy begins with some promise, but it eventually deteriorates to a predictable and unimpressive chain of events. Acting throughout is rather flat, and most of the high-tech special effects seem artificial. Yet the film is filled with ideas that could have been profitably developed under inspired talent. **Director**—Steward Raffill. (PG) *102 minutes*

THE PHILADELPHIA STORY (1940)

 ★★★★

Katharine Hepburn
Cary Grant
James Stewart

James Stewart, Katharine Hepburn, John Howard, and Mary Nash in The Philadelphia Story.

A top cast, expert direction, and a smooth script combine to make this wise and witty romantic comedy, set among the upper crust of Philadelphia, worth viewing. The story, based on Philip Barry's play, involves a
(Continued)

P
- Pickup on South Street
- Picnic
- Picnic at Hanging Rock
- The Picture of Dorian Gray
- A Piece of the Action
- Pillow Talk

(Continued)

wealthy woman, played by Hepburn, who longs for the simple life as she's about to be married for the second time. Grant plays her ex-husband, and Stewart is a reporter who falls in love with her. All three shine in the choice roles. Also stars Ruth Hussey, Roland Young, John Howard, John Halliday, and Mary Nash. **Director**—George Cukor. **Academy Awards**—Stewart, best actor; Donald Ogden Stewart, writing (screenplay). **Nominations**—best picture; Cukor, best director; Hepburn, best actress; Hussey, best supporting actress. *112 minutes b&w*

PICKUP ON SOUTH STREET
(1953)
★★★

Richard Widmark
Jean Peters

Thelma Ritter makes mincemeat out of a flatfoot in Pickup on South Street.

A well-crafted spy thriller about a pickpocket who steals a woman's wallet containing secret information; this small crime leads to his involvement with communist agents. Widmark is the light-fingered thief in this tough melodrama, which combines fast action and some violence. Excellent performances by a capable cast, which also includes Thelma Ritter and Richard Kiley. **Director**—Samuel Fuller. **Academy Award Nomination**—Ritter, best supporting actress.
80 minutes b&w

PICNIC (1955)
★★★★

William Holden
Kim Novak
Rosalind Russell

A memorable movie about a drifter, played by Holden, who comes to a Kansas farming community and has a profound impact on the local residents. This smart psychological drama, based on William Inge's play, combines wit and romance in a way that goes far beyond stereotyped characters in small-town America. It's well-acted throughout by a cast that also includes Susan Strasberg, Arthur O'Connell, Cliff Robertson, Betty Field, Verna Felton, and Nick Adams. **Director**—Joshua Logan. **Academy Award Nominations**—best picture; Logan, best director; O'Connell, best supporting actor. *113 minutes*

PICNIC AT HANGING ROCK
(1975)
★★★

Rachel Roberts
Dominic Guard

One of the breakthrough Australian films of the '70s, directed by the highly original Peter Weir. Three schoolgirls and their teacher go off to the geological formation known as Hanging Rock for an innocent Valentine's Day outing in 1900. Only one of the group ever returns—and she has no recollection of what happened. The film is more style than substance, and the mystery isn't resolved. But the style is engrossing, the eerie atmosphere hard to resist. (PG) *110 minutes*

THE PICTURE OF DORIAN GRAY (1945)
★★★★

George Sanders
Hurd Hatfield

A clever and elegant Oscar Wilde tale about a man who remains forever young-looking while his portrait reveals his true age and evil nature. A stylish and sophisticated twist to the Jekyll and Hyde story, all well acted and effectively mounted. Hatfield is

Dorian. The cast also includes Angela Lansbury, Peter Lawford, and Donna Reed. **Director**—Albert Lewin. **Academy Award**—Harry Stradling, cinematography (black and white). **Nomination**—Lansbury, best supporting actress. *110 minutes b&w*

A PIECE OF THE ACTION
(1977)
★★

Sidney Poitier
Bill Cosby

Poitier and Cosby team up again in this comedy-adventure. The two play likable and successful con men who are blackmailed into helping delinquent youths. The social comment seems too long, the comedy is too shallow, and the pacing is out of step. Also stars James Earl Jones, Denise Nicholas, and Hope Clark. **Director**—Poitier. (PG) *135 minutes*

PILLOW TALK (1959)
★★★

Doris Day
Rock Hudson
Tony Randall

Tony Randall tries to come between Doris Day and Rock Hudson in Pillow Talk.

Hudson and Day are perfectly matched in this fluffy romantic comedy as two people who can't stand each other, but fall in love on a telephone party line. Randall interferes with their romance. The lightweight story is handled with skill and style, and witty dialogue keeps the fun moving along. Doris is typically virginal, and Rock handles his part rather skillfully. Their successful pairing here led to similar movies. Also with

Thelma Ritter, Nick Adams, Julia Meade, and Lee Patrick. **Director**—Michael Gordon. **Academy Award**—Russell Rouse, Clarence Greene (story); Stanley Shapiro and Maurice Richlin (screenplay), best story and screenplay (written directly for the screen). **Nominations**—Day, best actress; Ritter, best supporting actress.
105 minutes

PINK FLOYD: THE WALL (1982)
 ★

Bob Geldof

From director Alan Parker (*Fame*) comes this bizarre, mind-blowing film based on the popular rock album. There's minimal dialogue; the teenage rantings about alienation and deterioration are conveyed in a flood of astounding surreal imagery and overpowering rock music. The production is bold and tantalizing, certainly, but it is hard to follow and can hardly be described as entertaining. Geldof stars as the crazy, burned-out rock performer. (R)   *99 minutes*

THE PINK PANTHER (1964)
 ★★★★

David Niven
Peter Sellers

The incomparable Sellers is a riot as bumbling French Inspector Jacques Clouseau, who pursues a jewel thief in the Swiss Alps and, in the process, drives everyone around him up the wall. Niven plays the sophisticated thief, and Capucine is the inspector's wife. The film is a masterpiece of clever sight gags, pratfalls, and characterization. Smartly directed by Blake Edwards, who went on to do several more *Panther* movies with Sellers. You'll be tickled pink. Also with Claudia Cardinale and Robert Wagner.
113 minutes

THE PINK PANTHER STRIKES AGAIN (1976)
 ★★★

Peter Sellers
Herbert Lom

French Inspector Jacques Clouseau,

JUDY GARLAND

The fabulous career of Judy Garland was marked by exuberance and brilliance as well as disasters, nervous breakdowns, and various failed marriages. Judy was born Frances Gumm, the daughter of vaudeville parents, in Grand Rapids, Minnesota, in 1922. She made her stage debut at the age of three with her sisters as The Gumm Sisters singing act. When she was nine, the stage name was changed to Garland, and the act eventually broke up when one of the sisters married.

At 13, Garland was hired by MGM, where she gained success as a teenage star, often opposite Mickey Rooney. Her career soared when she captivated audiences with her portrayal of Dorothy in The Wizard of Oz (1939), a role initially slated for Shirley Temple, and one which

won Garland a special Oscar.

In 1941, Garland married musician David Rose, but divorced him a few years later. In 1944, Judy starred in Meet Me in St. Louis, and a year later married Vincente Minnelli, the film's director.

Some of Garland's best movies were made during her association with Minnelli, including The Clock (1945), Ziegfeld Follies (1945), and The Pirate (1947).

Garland made a comeback with personal performances in London and New York and an excellent screen performance in A Star Is Born (1954).

In the late '50s, her career faltered again, and she was plagued with breakdowns, lawsuits, and chronic marital problems with Sid Luft, her third husband, whom she divorced in 1965.

After a brief marriage to actor Mark Herron, Garland went to London and married Mickey Deans, a nightclub manager, and starred in a disastrous cabaret act. In 1969, she died from an accidental drug overdose.

Some of Garland's other movies include Babes in Arms (1939), Strike Up the Band (1940), Babes on Broadway (1942), For Me and My Gal (1942), The Harvey Girls (1946), Easter Parade (1948), Judgment at Nuremberg (1960), and I Could Go On Singing (1963).

played with faithful perfection by Sellers, bumbles through a fourth chapter of comic misadventures. This time the zany Clouseau has driven his former superior—ex-Chief Inspector Dreyfus, played by Lom—insane. Lom then gains control of a doomsday device. The thin plot has many slow stretches, but the humor is solidly present as several honest belly laughs and lots of smiles. Also with Colin Blakely, Leonard Rossiter, Burt Kwouk, and Lesley-Anne Down. **Director**—Blake Edwards. (PG)
103 minutes

PINKY (1949)
★★★

Jeanne Crain

Powerful drama about a light-skinned black girl, played by Crain, who

passes for white and encounters assorted problems. The subject, which was rather daring at the time of the film's release, seems dated now. But the story still packs a punch, and it's quite well done. Top performances from a good cast, which also includes Ethel Barrymore, Ethel Waters, William Lundigan, and Nina Mae McKinney. **Director**—Elia Kazan. **Academy Award Nominations**—Crain, best actress; Barrymore, Waters, best supporting actress.   *102 minutes b&w*

PINOCCHIO (1940)
★★★★

This children's classic from Walt Disney is certainly among the studio's great achievements. A poor lonely
(Continued)

P

- Piranha
- The Pirate
- The Pirate Movie
- The Pirates of Penzance
- The Pit and the Pendulum
- Pixote

(Continued)

woodcutter builds a puppet, which comes to life only to fall in with bad company. When the puppet mends its ways, it becomes a real boy. The animation is colorful and lively, and the story brims with energy and charming characters; the fascination never ends. **Supervisors**—Ben Sharpsteen and Hamilton Luske. (G) **Academy Awards**—Leigh Harlin and Ned Washington, best song ("When You Wish Upon a Star"); Harlin, Paul J. Smith, and Washington, original score.

77 minutes

PIRANHA (1978)
★

**Bradford Dillman
Heather Menzies**

Swimmers have fun before schools of toothy critters show up in Piranha.

Schools of deadly piranha are no match for one shark as another movie tries to cash in on the success of *Jaws*. In this movie, we find the toothy little critters escaping from a military experimental station into a nearby lake, where they put the bite on summer campers and school kids taking refreshing dips. The acting is routine, and the familiar scare tactics are hardly convincing. Also with Kevin McCarthy, Keenan Wynn, Dick Miller, and Barbara Steele. **Director**—Joe Dante. (R) *92 minutes*

THE PIRATE (1948)
★★★★

**Gene Kelly
Judy Garland
Walter Slezak**

MGM's golden age of musicals produced no more exhilarating treat than this colorful, tongue-in-cheek spectacular. The charismatic stars are terrific together—Garland as a young woman in the West Indies with a richly romantic imagination, Kelly as the flamboyant traveling player, who pretends to be notorious Caribbean pirate Macoco to steal Judy away from the old windbag who intends to marry her. Top musical director Vincente Minnelli stages it all with tremendous panache, and Kelly does some of his most acrobatic dancing, abetted by the Nicholas Brothers. The tuneful Cole Porter score includes "Be A Clown" and "Love of My Life." *102 minutes*

THE PIRATE MOVIE
(1982)
★

**Kristy McNichol
Christopher Atkins**

McNichol and Atkins bumble and stumble through this foolish musical fantasy loosely based on Gilbert and Sullivan's operetta, *The Pirates of Penzance*. The adolescent story, about a plain girl (McNichol) who dreams she is the love object of a young buccaneer (Atkins), bogs down in silly comic situations and half-baked song and dance numbers. Veteran director Ken Annakin (*The Longest Day*) fails to sustain a coherent comic mood. An apology is owed to Gilbert and Sullivan. (PG) *99 minutes*

THE PIRATES OF PENZANCE
(1983)
★★★

**Kevin Kline
Linda Ronstadt
George Rose
Angela Lansbury**

This latter-day film version of the classic Gilbert and Sullivan operetta comes off with adequate charm, color, and good cheer. The stage production had more zip, but plenty of rousing musical numbers and lively dance routines are offered here. Most of the Broadway cast is on board: Kline swashbuckles as the Pirate King, and Ronstadt sings with gusto as the delightful Mabel. Rose makes the grade

Lovers Linda Ronstadt and Rex Smith give the operetta The Pirates of Penzance *its lightness.*

as the Major-General. **Director**—Edward Pressman. (G) *112 minutes*

THE PIT AND THE PENDULUM
★★★

Vincent Price

Price is at his sinister best in this creepy horror tale, loosely based on the Edgar Allan Poe story. The setting is just after the Spanish Inquisition, and the film is well stocked with all sorts of spooky goodies to make your skin crawl—musty torture chambers, misty castles, thunder and lightning, entombed bodies, and so on. The first half drags some, but then Price gets going and swings a mean pendulum. Also with Barbara Steele and John Kerr. **Director**—Roger Corman.

80 minutes

PIXOTE (1982)
★★

**Fernando Ramos da Silva
Marília Pera**

This Brazilian film is a grim account of poor Sao Paulo children who graduate from a squalid juvenile institution to a life of serious crime. Ten-year-old da Silva is convincing in the title role. He plays an innocent-looking lad who engages in purse snatching, dope

• A Place in the Sun • Players
• Places in the Heart • Play It Again, Sam
• Planet of the Apes • Play Misty for Me
• Plaza Suite

P

dealing, and finally murder; it's sort of a latter-day version of *Oliver Twist*, realistically told, but heavy going. Pera plays a prostitute who befriends da Silva. Also with Jorge Juliao and Gilberto Moura. In Portuguese with English titles. **Director**—Hector Babenco. (R)   *115 minutes*

A PLACE IN THE SUN (1951)
★★★

Montgomery Clift
Elizabeth Taylor

A striking sociological/psychological film based on Theodore Dreiser's novel *An American Tragedy*. Clift is outstanding as a blue-collar worker who shuns a poor working girl for the love of a wealthy girl, played by Taylor. The dramatically brilliant film emphasizes the contrasts between the wealthy and the lower classes. Also stars Shelley Winters, Raymond Burr, Ann Revere, Keefe Brasselle, and Fred Clark. **Director**—George Stevens. **Academy Awards**—Stevens, best director; Michael Wilson and Harry Brown, writing, (screenplay); William Mellor, cinematography (black and white). **Nominations**—best picture; Clift, best actor; Winters, best actress.
122 minutes b&w

PLACES IN THE HEART (1984)
★★★★

Sally Field

A tender, loving movie about a young widow in Depression-era Texas, struggling to support her two children and hold on to her heavily mortgaged home. Writer-director Robert Benton, reaching into his childhood memories, fashions a beguiling heart-tugger, full of truth, tears, chuckles, and suspense. Field, in the lead role, teaches a powerful lesson in the value of perseverance. Also with Danny Glover, John Malkovich, Lindsay Crouse, and Ed Harris. (PG)   *110 minutes*

PLANET OF THE APES (1968)
★★★

Charlton Heston
Roddy McDowall
Kim Hunter

Innovative and thought-provoking science-fiction thriller about astronauts who land on an Earth-like planet where the apes have taken over and humans are subservient to them. The script, based on Pierre Boulle's novel *Monkey Planet*, is consistently engrossing. Special applause for the guys who did the magnificent ape makeup. Also with Maurice Evans, James Whitmore, James Daly, and Linda Harrison. A slew of sequels and a TV series followed. **Director**—Franklin Schaffner. (G)   *119 minutes*

PLAYERS (1979)
★

Ali MacGraw
Dean-Paul Martin

The world of professional tennis is the backdrop to this tedious film, that's continually marred by a love story so embarrassingly trite it gets unintentional giggles at every other line. Martin is convincing as the young man with tennis in his blood, but MacGraw looks rather shopworn as a rich older woman torn between a rich older man, played by Maximilian Schell, and our hero. Also with Pancho Gonzalez and Steve Guttenberg. **Director**—Anthony Harvey. (PG)   *120 minutes*

Dean-Paul Martin and Ali MacGraw in Players, *a film set in the world of pro tennis.*

PLAY IT AGAIN, SAM (1972)
★★★

Woody Allen
Diane Keaton

Allen mines some lively humor from the Bogart legend. He's an avid film fan who wants to revitalize his love life after his wife, played by Susan Anspach, abandons him. Keaton plays the wife of Woody's best friend. Woody uses the Bogey and Bergman encounters from *Casablanca* to best advantage, and there's plenty of Allen's skill at work to delight his fans. Also with Tony Roberts and Jerry Lacy. **Director**—Herbert Ross. (PG)   *86 minutes*

PLAY MISTY FOR ME (1971)
★★★

Clint Eastwood
Jessica Walter

Clint Eastwood tells Jessica Walter that he doesn't do requests in Play Misty for Me.

An effective psychological shocker about a radio disc jockey, played by Eastwood, whose involvement with one of his female listeners leads to murder. This is Eastwood's first effort as director, and he does an impressive job of maintaining suspense and heightened drama. Walter also does a fine job as the unhinged woman who repeatedly asks him to *Play Misty for Me*. Also with Donna Mills and John Larch. (R)   *102 minutes*

PLAZA SUITE (1971)
★★★

Walter Matthau
Maureen Stapleton
Barbara Harris
Lee Grant

This Neil Simon comedy is among the best of the playwright's efforts to be adapted for the screen. The film is composed of three vignettes about dif-
(Continued)

P
- Please Don't Eat the Daisies
- Pocketful of Miracles
- Police Academy
- Poltergeist
- Polyester
- Pony Express
- The Pope of Greenwich Village

(Continued)

ferent people who stay at a particular room in the posh New York hotel. Matthau is in all three segments in three different roles, and he scores in each situation. He's helped nicely with the talents of Stapleton, Harris, and Grant. Lots of laughs and lots of good scenes, all expertly Simonized. **Director**—Arthur Hiller. (PG)   *115 minutes*

PLEASE DON'T EAT THE DAISIES (1960)
★★★

**Doris Day
David Niven**

In Please Don't Eat the Daisies, *David Niven and Doris Day play a country couple.*

Buoyant situation comedy, based on Jean Kerr's play, about a drama critic who faces numerous problems with his job and his family when they move to the country. Cleverly executed with bright performances by the entire cast, which also includes Janis Paige, Spring Byington, Richard Haydn, and Patsy Kelly. Doris sings the title song. **Director**—Charles Walters.

111 minutes

POCKETFUL OF MIRACLES (1961)
★★★

**Bette Davis
Glenn Ford**

Director Frank Capra retreads his 1933 *Lady for a Day* as a slicker production for the wide screen. This version of the Damon Runyon tale isn't as bright as the earlier one, but it retains much of its charm and sentimentality. Davis plays the apple-seller who, with the help of gangsters, poses as a rich lady to impress her visiting daughter. There are some bumpy moments, but there are plenty of good scenes as well. A talented cast handles the Runyonesque character parts competently. Also with Hope Lange, Arthur O'Connell, Peter Falk, Jack Elam, Sheldon Leonard, Thomas Mitchell, and—in her first film—Ann-Margret. **Academy Award Nomination**—Falk, best supporting actor.   *136 minutes*

POLICE ACADEMY (1984)
   ★★

**Steve Guttenberg
George Gaynes
Kim Cattrall**

The police department lowers its academy entrance requirements, setting the stage for some *Animal House* antics among the new misfit recruits. The uneven, adolescent romp, which primarily pokes fun at authority figures, offers a few effective comic moments. But the bulk of the material is rather crude and commonplace. Guttenburg heads the cast as a young recruit who tries hard to get expelled but constantly bounces back. **Director**—Hugh Wilson. (R)   *101 minutes*

POLTERGEIST (1982)
   ★★★

**Jobeth Williams
Craig T. Nelson**

A visually spectacular, contemporary haunted-house movie, produced by Steven Spielberg. Jolting, supernatural happenings occur when evil spirits take over a suburban California home. The hair-raising special effects are amazing, but the silly story is just so much excess baggage. This horror film could have been a classic if more effort had been made to develop some logic in the story. **Director**—Tobe Hooper. (PG) **Academy Award Nomination**—Richard Edlund, Michael Wood, and Bruce Nicholson, best visual effects.

115 minutes

POLYESTER (1981)
★★

**Divine
Tab Hunter**

A charming young mental defective from Polyester.

Writer-director John Waters (*Pink Flamingos*) made this fractured, soap-opera burlesque about the middle class, which is somewhat tamer than his previous outrageous fare. Divine—actually a transvestite—plays an overweight housewife who cares for a family of degenerates, and the strain is driving her insane. At last she's rescued by debonair Hunter, the man of her dreams. There's a steady stream of tacky humor, but the campy farce soon begins to wear, and the garishness becomes annoying. (R)
86 minutes

PONY EXPRESS (1953)
★★★

**Charlton Heston
Forrest Tucker**

Better-than-average western story, set in the 1860s, about the introduction of express mail service via a relay system of riders on horseback. The legendary Buffalo Bill Cody and Wild Bill Hickok take a hand in establishing the mail service routes in this film. Adequate action scenes and some decent acting enhance the production. Also with Rhonda Fleming and Jan Sterling. **Director**—Jerry Hopper.   *101 minutes*

THE POPE OF GREENWICH VILLAGE (1984)
   ★★★

**Mickey Rourke
Eric Roberts**

This spicy tale of two small-time

- Popeye
- Popi
- Porgy and Bess
- Pork Chop Hill
- Porky's
- Porky's II: The Next Day
- Portnoy's Complaint

P

New York City hustlers falls somewhere between Martin Scorsese's *Mean Streets* and *The Bowery Boys*. Rourke and Roberts are the young hoods who burglarize a safe containing mob money and find themselves in big trouble with Mafia types and the cops. Crude dialogue and strained situations abound, but rich characterizations and high-voltage acting sustain the film. Geraldine Page and Bert Young co-star. **Director**—Stuart Rosenberg. (R)   *122 minutes*

POPEYE (1980)

★★★

Robin Williams
Shelley Duvall

Director Robert Altman based this strange musical on the lesser-known Popeye of the comic strip, and not the simpler character made famous in the animated cartoons. The result is a somewhat dark and atmospheric yet quite entertaining film. Williams is perfect in the title role, decked out with huge forearms and muttering asides like W.C. Fields. Duvall is equally right as Olive Oyl, his sweetheart, and the songs by pop star Harry Nilsson are charming. Children expecting lots of action may be disappointed until the very end when Popeye finally downs some spinach, but adults should find the style and characters interesting throughout. Also with Paul L. Smith, Paul Dooley, and Wesley Ivan Hurt. (PG)   *114 minutes*

POPI (1969)
★★★★

Alan Arkin

A heartwarming and moving story about the struggles of a Puerto Rican widower in Spanish Harlem trying to secure a better life for his young sons. Arkin is extremely convincing in the title role, as a determined man who works at multiple jobs and confronts the problems of ghetto life. The charming screenplay features an appropriate mixture of comedy and sentimentality. It's well done in all departments. Rita Moreno, Miguel Alejandro, and Ruben Figueroa perform in supporting roles. **Director**—Arthur Hiller. (G)
115 minutes

PORGY AND BESS (1959)
★★★

Sidney Poitier
Dorothy Dandridge

George Gershwin's moving romantic opera could have been adapted for the screen with more skill, but the memorable music shines through with brilliance and keeps the film afloat. Poitier plays the crippled denizen of Catfish Row who falls in love with a beautiful but vulnerable girl, played by Dandridge. Sammy Davis, Jr. stands out in the role of Sportin' Life. The unforgettable songs include "Summertime" and "It Ain't Necessarily So." Pearl Bailey, Brock Peters, and Diahann Carroll are in supporting roles. **Director**—Otto Preminger. **Academy Award Nomination**—Leon Shamroy, cinematography (color).
138 minutes

PORK CHOP HILL (1959)
★★★

Gregory Peck
Harry Guardino

Gregory Peck is an officer in Korea facing tough decisions in Pork Chop Hill.

The film is among the best war movies based on the Korean Conflict. Lots of gripping, rugged moments, as American troops try to gain a foothold on a strategic position as negotiators seek a truce at Panmunjom. There are plenty of authentic-looking fighting scenes embellished with rugged dialogue. Peck leads the fine cast, which also includes Rip Torn, George Peppard, George Shibata, and Woody Strode. **Director**—Lewis Milestone.
97 minutes b&w

PORKY'S
(1982)

★

Dan Monahan
Scott Colomby
Kaki Hunter

A mind-boggling cavalcade of corny sex jokes and foolish pranks make up this adolescent comedy about students at a Florida high school in the '50s. The raunchy teenage romp features a relatively unknown but likable cast, but their good-natured energy is undermined by mindless and meandering material. The title refers to a local bordello. **Director**—Bob Clark. (R)
99 minutes

PORKY'S II: THE NEXT DAY
(1983)

★

Dan Monahan
Wyatt Knight

More adolescent high jinks from the raunchy gang at sun-drenched Angel Beach High School. Again, the students are involved with sex jokes, toilet jokes, and complex pranks directed at themselves and various adults. The teenagers, as usual, control every situation, while the adults are portrayed as buffoons. This time, the kids purportedly address social issues, but the film's prime concern is with hyped-up silliness. **Director**—Bob Clark. (R)
103 minutes

PORTNOY'S COMPLAINT
(1972)

★

Richard Benjamin

Director Ernest Lehman mangles Philip Roth's sensational novel about a young Jewish man overwhelmed with hangups. Benjamin plays the role of the neurotic Portnoy. Most of the performances are undermined by poor handling of the production and an absurd screenplay. The satirical spirit of the novel is left on the shelf. Portnoy isn't the only one who should complain. Also with Karen Black, Lee Grant, Jack Somack, and Jill Clayburgh. (R)   *101 minutes*

P

- Portrait of Jennie
- The Poseidon Adventure
- Posse
- Possessed
- The Postman Always Rings Twice (1946)
- The Postman Always Rings Twice (1981)
- Pressure Point
- Pretty Baby

PORTRAIT OF JENNIE (1948)
★★★★

Jennifer Jones
Joseph Cotten

Cotten stars as a poor artist who comes in contact with an unusual young woman, played by Jones. She becomes the subject of his paintings, they fall in love, and he wonders if she's the ghost of someone who died long ago. An unusual, haunting tale, obviously preposterous, but smoothly executed with style and intrigue; the acting is tops. It's a superb example of Hollywood fantasy in the best tradition. Also with Ethel Barrymore, David Wayne, and Lillian Gish. **Director**—William Dieterle. **Academy Award Nomination**—Joseph August, cinematography (black and white).

86 minutes b&w

THE POSEIDON ADVENTURE (1972)
 ★★★

Gene Hackman
Ernest Borgnine
Shelley Winters
Red Buttons

Typical Hollywood disaster extravaganza about trapped passengers in a capsized luxury liner who gallantly struggle to escape a watery tomb. A somewhat absurd script and numerous flimsy characters are displayed, but the film has some heroic moments that offer sufficient thrills. Special effects seem to be the most entertaining attraction. It's escapist fare, indeed. Also with Carol Lynley, Leslie Nielson, Arthur O'Connell, Roddy McDowall, and Stella Stevens. **Director**—Ronald Neame. (PG) **Academy Award Nominations**— Winters, best supporting actress; Harold E. Stine, cinematography. *117 minutes*

POSSE (1975)
★★★

Kirk Douglas
Bruce Dern

An ambitious Texas marshal, played by Douglas, stakes his campaign for the U.S. Senate on the capture of a notorious outlaw, played by Dern, who's been robbing trains. A provocative and clever script and excellent performances by Douglas and Dern. Also with Bo Hopkins, James Stacy, and Luke Askey. **Director**—Douglas. (R) *94 minutes*

POSSESSED (1947)
★★★

Joan Crawford
Raymond Massey
Van Heflin

Crawford pours on the melodramatics in this highly charged romantic story about an unhinged woman involved in several love affairs. Massey and Heflin are two men in her life. The script is rather heavy going, but Crawford handles the material with unusual flair. An excellent piece of work for Crawford fans. Also with Geraldine Brooks. **Director**—Curtis Bernhardt. **Academy Award Nomination**—Crawford, best actress.

108 minutes b&w

THE POSTMAN ALWAYS RINGS TWICE (1946)
★★★★

Lana Turner
John Garfield

Lana Turner makes John Garfield hear bells in The Postman Always Rings Twice.

Stylish, moody drama about a young woman who conspires with her lover to kill her husband. Turner and Garfield, who play the lovers, are perfectly matched in this efficient rendition of the James M. Cain novel. There are plenty of gripping and seductive scenes as the murderers execute what they believe to be the perfect crime. Also with Cecil Kellaway, Hume Cronyn, Leon Ames, and Audrey Totter. **Director**—Tay Garnett.

113 minutes b&w

THE POSTMAN ALWAYS RINGS TWICE (1981)
 ★★★

Jack Nicholson
Jessica Lange

The second Hollywood version of James M. Cain's 1941 novel of passion, greed, and murder stars Nicholson and Lange as the brooding, adulterous lovers. The film is well acted and beautifully photographed, with explicit detail of the Depression era. Nicholson is at his best as the obsessive drifter who comes upon a dingy diner and lusts after the owner's wife. But keep your eye on the beautiful Lange as the sultry wife with murder on her mind; she makes the sparks fly. Also with John Colicos, Michael Lerner, and Angelica Huston. **Director**—Bob Rafelson. (R) *122 minutes*

PRESSURE POINT (1962)
★★★

Sidney Poitier
Bobby Darin

Captivating high drama about a black prison psychiatrist, played by Poitier, struggling to deal with a violent inmate who's an American Nazi. The unusual story is quite engrossing, and it efficiently conveys the tense feelings surrounding a touchy subject. Darin is surprisingly good as the hate-filled prisoner, and Poitier's professional and cool demeanor offers an effective contrast. Supporting roles by Peter Falk and Carl Benton Reid. **Director**—Hubert Cornfield. *120 minutes b&w*

PRETTY BABY (1978)
 ★★

Brooke Shields
Keith Carradine

French director Louis Malle's first American film is about a 12-year-old prostitute, played by Shields, in New Orleans's legendary tenderloin district

• Pride and Prejudice
• The Pride of St. Louis
• Pride of the Marines

• The Pride of the Yankees
• Priest of Love
• The Prime of Miss Jean Brodie

P

of the early 1900s. Carradine plays her photographer husband. The settings are pretty and lush, but the movie is tedious and shallow and filled with hopelessly undefined characters. Too bad, because this intriguing subject could have been developed with drama and compassion. The title role is played with subtleness by 12-year-old Shields. Also with Susan Sarandon, Francis Faye, and Antonio Fargas. (R)   109 minutes

PRIDE AND PREJUDICE (1940)

★★★★

Laurence Olivier
Greer Garson

Delectable comedy of manners set in 19th-century England, about five sisters who want to get married. The film, based faithfully on the Jane Austen novel, sparkles with wit and strikes the right mood of the period. Best of all, it features a splendid cast with everyone handling their parts with perfection. Also with Edmund Gwenn, Mary Boland, Melville Cooper, Edna May Oliver, Ann Rutherford, and Maureen O'Sullivan. **Director**—Robert Z. Leonard.
116 minutes b&w

THE PRIDE OF ST. LOUIS
(1952)
★★

Dan Dailey
Joanne Dru

Standard film biography of baseball great Dizzy Dean, with Dailey in the role of the extraordinary pitcher who later became a baseball announcer. The production has its limits, but all involved seem to make an earnest effort. Also with Richard Haydn, Richard Crenna, and Hugh Sanders. **Director**—Harmon Jones. **Academy Award Nomination**—Guy Trosper, writing (motion picture story).
93 minutes b&w

PRIDE OF THE MARINES
(1945)
★★★

John Garfield
Eleanor Parker
Dave Clark

Sentimental yet thoughtful account of a Marine who was blinded while fighting the Japanese during World War II. Garfield is convincing as brave fighting man Al Schmid, who struggles to adjust to his disability. Clark plays his buddy. An excellent production enhanced by fine performances. Also with John Ridgely, Rosemary De Camp, and Tom D'Andrea. **Director**—Delmer Daves. **Academy Award Nomination**—Albert Maltz, writing (screenplay).
119 minutes b&w

THE PRIDE OF THE YANKEES
(1942)

★★★★

Gary Cooper
Teresa Wright

An exceptional film biography of Yankee baseball star Lou Gehrig. Cooper is just right in the role of the sports hero who died of ALS at the peak of his astounding career; Wright plays Gehrig's wife. The sentimentality is predictable, yet it's handled with taste. The film ends with Gehrig's emotional farewell in Yankee Stadium. Also with Babe Ruth, Walter Brennan, and Dan Duryea. **Director**—Sam Wood. **Academy Award Nominations**—best picture; Cooper, best actor; Wright, best actress; Paul Gallico, writing (original story); Herman J. Mankiewicz and Joe Swerling, writing (screenplay); Rudolph Maté, cinematography (black and white).   127 minutes b&w

PRIEST OF LOVE (1981)
★★

Ian McKellen
Janet Suzman

A rather hollow film biography of controversial writer D. H. Lawrence, the author of *Lady Chatterley's Lover* and other much-censored novels. The story meanders from country to country as Lawrence, played adequately by McKellen, raves against the authorities and deals with a fatal case of tuberculosis. Most important, perhaps, is the role of his wife Frieda, played by Suzman, who was his inspiration and his protector. In any case, Lawrence's writings are far more engrossing than this story of his life. Also with Ava Gardner, Penelope Keith, Jorge River, and Sir John Gielgud. **Director**—Christopher Miles. (R)   125 minutes

THE PRIME OF MISS JEAN BRODIE (1969)
★★★

Maggie Smith

Smith turns in an extraordinary *tour de force* performance as an eccentric schoolteacher at a swank Edinburgh girls' school during the 1930s. She invests much energy and skill in this unusual character, who finally reaches her downfall. Based on the novel by
(Continued)

Robert Stephens and Maggie Smith shock a pupil in The Prime of Miss Jean Brodie.

P
- The Prince and the Pauper
- The Prince and the Showgirl
- Prince of the City
- The Princess and the Pirate
- The Prisoner of Zenda
- Private Benjamin
- The Private Files of J. Edgar Hoover

(Continued)

Muriel Spark. Also stars Robert Stephens, Pamela Franklin, and Celia Johnson. **Director**—Ronald Neame. (PG) **Academy Award**—Smith, best actress. *116 minutes*

THE PRINCE AND THE PAUPER (1978)

 ★★★

Mark Lester
Oliver Reed
Raquel Welch
Ernest Borgnine
George C. Scott
Rex Harrison
Charlton Heston

George C. Scott is king of the beggars in the adventure The Prince and the Pauper.

A likable, robust, costume adventure, based on Mark Twain's classic *The Prince and the Pauper*. An impressive cast enlivens the handsome saga about a ragged street urchin who trades identities with young Prince Edward of England. There's lots of derring-do and swashbuckling action to delight the kids and accompanying adults. **Director**—Richard Fleischer. (PG) *113 minutes*

THE PRINCE AND THE SHOWGIRL (1957)

 ★★★

Laurence Olivier
Marilyn Monroe

Plush-looking period comedy with Olivier and Monroe perfectly matched in contrasting roles. He plays a European aristocrat, and she's an American showgirl. The setting is the 1911 coronation of George V in London. They meet, and together they find love and understanding. The film's pace is a little slow and stiff, but the performances are delightful. The movie, based on Terence Rattigan's play *The Sleeping Prince*, co-stars Sybil Thorndike, Richard Wattis, and Jeremy Spencer. **Director**—Olivier. *117 minutes*

PRINCE OF THE CITY (1981)

 ★★★

Treat Williams

Director Sidney Lumet's supercharged drama about a New York City undercover detective investigating corruption. The film evokes mixed emotions. The story is powerful and fascinating in its treatment of such issues as conscience, loyalty, and human emotions; yet it's overlong and painfully complex. Williams stands out as the double-agent cop who exposes his colleagues, and there are good supporting performances from Jerry Orbach, Richard Foronjy, and Don Billett. (R) **Academy Award Nomination**—Jay Presson Allen and Lumet, best screenplay (based on material from another medium). *167 minutes*

THE PRINCESS AND THE PIRATE (1944)

★★★

Bob Hope
Virginia Mayo

In this film, Hope and Mayo try to elude a sinister pirate, played by Victor McLaglen. Walter Slezak plays a potentate. There's loads of wacky fun in this costume comedy to delight Hope fans. Other supporting roles are played by Walter Brennan, Marc Lawrence, and Hugo Maas. **Director**—David Butler. *94 minutes*

THE PRISONER OF ZENDA (1979)

 ★★

Peter Sellers

Sellers plays multiple roles in this remake of the masquerade story about the king of Ruritania. Sellers reliably delivers some pleasing comedy and milks the listless material for more laughs than it's worth. But the film receives minimal help from director Richard Quine, who lacks the zip and flair to keep things humming along. Also with Lynne Frederick, Lionel Jeffries, Elke Sommer, and Gregory Sierra. (PG) *108 minutes*

PRIVATE BENJAMIN (1980)

 ★★★

Goldie Hawn
Eileen Brennan

Hawn plays a pampered young woman who gets away from it all by joining the Army, where she wages comic warfare on the brass hats. Brennan plays her superior officer. The serviceable script is somewhat reminiscent of those "this is the Army" type comedies that were popular in the '40s and '50s. Goldie, as the Army's most unlikely soldier, updates this routine with her perky charm and comic style, and keeps the gags marching along at double time. After this, she deserves a promotion to corporal. **Director**—Howard Zieff. (R) **Academy Award Nominations**—Hawn, best actress; Brennan, best supporting actress; Nancy Meyers, Charles Shyer, and Harvey Miller, best screenplay (written directly for the screen). *110 minutes*

THE PRIVATE FILES OF J. EDGAR HOOVER (1980)

★★

Broderick Crawford

Director-writer Larry Cohen deglorifies the late top cop in this rather undramatic B-movie, which covers events from the killing of Dillinger to Watergate. Crawford plays the famous G-man with enough credibility, but the historical details are handled in a pedestrian style that produces few revelations about Hoover and his law-enforcement empire. Also with Dan Dailey, José Ferrer, Rip Torn, Raymond St. Jacques, and Ronee Blakley. (PG) *112 minutes*

• Private Lessons
• The Private Life of Henry VIII
• Private School
• Privates on Parade
• Private's Progress
• The Private War of Major Benson
• The Prize

P

PRIVATE LESSONS (1981)
★★

**Eric Brown
Sylvia Kristel**

Sylvia Kristel shows Eric Brown the proper way to watch a movie in Private Lessons.

This is a dubious comedy about a shy 15-year-old boy who's seduced by the family's attractive housekeeper. Brown is the boy, and Kristel is the seducer. The low-budget film is done with obvious eagerness, and it primarily exploits soft-core sex with frequent nude scenes. The portrayal of an adolescent involved with an older woman adds a provocative dimension to the mostly awkward proceedings. Howard Hesseman and Ed Begley, Jr., also star. **Director**—Alan Myerson. (R)
87 minutes

THE PRIVATE LIFE OF HENRY VIII (1933)
★★★★

**Charles Laughton
Elsa Lanchester**

Charles Laughton receives royal pampering in The Private Life of Henry VIII.

Classic movie about England's eccentric and much-married king. Laughton is sheer delight as the 16th-century ruler who beheaded two wives and acquired four others, and he captures the spirit of the part in fine style. Lanchester plays Anne of Cleves. Other rousing performances from Robert Donat, Miles Mander, Merle Oberon, and Binnie Barnes help make this historical film a gem. **Director**—Alexander Korda.
97 minutes b&w

PRIVATE SCHOOL (1983)
★

**Phoebe Cates
Betsy Russel
Martin Mull
Ray Walston**

Matthew Modine and Phoebe Cates get low marks in Private School.

A sleazy, threadbare, adolescent romp set in private high schools where the students are primarily concerned with sexual escapades. A dead-panned Sylvia Kristel appears briefly as a sex education teacher. Other members of the no-talent cast are caught up in similar foolishness. This sort of teenage exploitation fare typically shows the kids in control while the adults come off second best. **Director**—Noel Black. (R)
90 minutes

PRIVATES ON PARADE (1984)
★★★

**John Cleese
Denis Quilley
Michael Elphick**

Wacky, witty English farce about the exploits of an Army entertainment troupe operating near Singapore just after World War II. Based on Peter Nichols's stage play, the uproarious film features sidesplitting song and dance numbers, clever dialogue, and excellent performances by a top cast of character actors. Cleese, of Monty Python fame, is droll and funny as the stuffy major in charge of this zany outfit. **Director**—Michael Blakemore. (R)
96 minutes

PRIVATE'S PROGRESS (1956)
★★★

**Ian Carmichael
Terry-Thomas**

Delightful parody of the British army, with plenty of good gags and lively scenes. An awkward young man is called to serve his country and everything goes haywire. This British version of *No Time for Sergeants* and *Private Hargrove* works effectively, thanks to a good script and a top cast of British character actors. Also with Richard Attenborough, Dennis Price, Peter Jones, William Hartnett, and Ian Bannen. **Director**—John Boulting.
97 minutes b&w

THE PRIVATE WAR OF MAJOR BENSON (1955)
★★

**Charlton Heston
Julie Adams**

Heston stars as a tough Army officer who mellows a bit after taking charge, of a military academy run by nuns. Heston handles the humor and the romantic stuff with ease. Adams plays the love interest in this rather syrupy comedy with some funny scenes, but mostly the film is farfetched and too sentimental. Also stars Tim Hovey, Sal Mineo, William Demarest, and Tim Considine. **Director**—Jerry Hopper. **Academy Award Nomination**—Joe Connelly and Bob Mosher, writing (motion picture story). *100 minutes*

THE PRIZE (1963)
★★★

**Paul Newman
Elke Sommer
Edward G. Robinson**

Slick, sleek spy thriller set against

(Continued)

(Continued)
the backdrop of the Nobel Prize awards in Stockholm. An American writer, played by Newman, finds himself involved in a plot to abduct a famous scientist, played by Robinson. Sommer plays Robinson's daughter. The film, based on the Irving Wallace novel, takes on the style of a Hitchcock suspense movie and works with precision. The excellent cast also includes Diane Baker, Kevin McCarthy, and Leo G. Carroll. **Director—** Mark Robson.   *135 minutes*

THE PRODUCERS (1968)

★★★

Zero Mostel
Gene Wilder

This film is an audacious mixture of hilarity, brilliance, and bad taste; it's about a Broadway producer who cooks up a wild scheme to raise money from investors by staging a flop musical. He sells much more than 100 percent of the show, but the plan backfires when the production becomes a hit. The script is patchy, but there are some inventive wild moments that keep the satire firmly afloat. The best portions involve the play, entitled *Springtime for Hitler.* Mostel is funny as the hustling theater producer; Wilder plays Mostel's meek accountant. Good support, too, from Kenneth Mars, Dick Shawn, Renée Taylor, and Estelle Winwood. **Director**—Mel Brooks. **Academy Award**—Brooks, best story and screenplay (written directly for the

screen). **Nomination**—Wilder, best supporting actor.   *98 minutes*

THE PROFESSIONALS
(1966)

★★★★

Burt Lancaster
Lee Marvin

The Professionals features Burt Lancaster and Lee Marvin, as mercenaries.

Rousing, spicy western adventure about a band of mercenaries sent to Mexico to rescue the wife of a wealthy rancher from the clutches of a vile bandit. Ralph Bellamy plays the rancher, and Claudia Cardinale is his abducted wife. Lancaster and Marvin lead the band of mercenaries, and Jack Palance is the chief villain. The expedition across the border pits rugged men against rugged men, and the film bristles with excitement and well-mounted suspense. A first-rate cast goes all out to provide gripping action. Also with Robert Ryan and Woody Strode. **Director**—Richard

Brooks. **Academy Award Nominations**—Brooks, best director; Brooks, best screenplay (based on material from another medium); Conrad Hall, cinematography (color).   *123 minutes*

PROMISES IN THE DARK
(1979)

★★

Marsha Mason

The right-to-die issue is taken up in this gloomy movie about a bright-eyed 17-year-old girl, played by Kathleen Beller, who has terminal cancer. It's a difficult subject for a film, which could succeed if handled with sensitivity and pathos. But here, the story is a bland hype of tragic circumstances. The uninspired acting of Mason as the girl's gallant doctor doesn't help matters. Also with Ned Beatty, Susan Clark, Michael Brandon, and Paul Clemens. **Director**—Jerome Hellman. (PG)
115 minutes

PROM NIGHT (1980)
★★

Jamie Lee Curtis
Leslie Nielsen

Scream queen Curtis and Nielsen star in this film in which a masked killer seeks revenge on teenagers attending a high school prom. This Canadian-made melodrama smacks of such chillers as *Carrie* and *Halloween.* The murder scenes are gruesome, but they always seem to stop short of producing the shock effects expected of this sort of movie. Director Paul Lynch set up a few tense moments, but most of the film is merely marking time while waiting for the killer to get into the act. Also with Eddie Benton. (R)
91 minutes

PROPHECY (1979)
★★

Talia Shire
Robert Foxworth

Shire and Foxworth star in this silly minor-league monster movie that pretends to be spectacular. The villain is mercury poisoning from industrial pollution. Animals, including hu-

Zero Mostel shows Gene Wilder that you're never too old to be a dirty lecher in The Producers.

mans, are turned into horrible mutants that attack campers and forest rangers in the Maine woods. Director John Frankenheimer serves up plenty of gore and a lot of monster movie clichés. Also with Armand Assante, Richard Dysart, and Victoria Racimo. (PG)   *100 minutes*

PROTOCOL (1984)
★★

Goldie Hawn

This tailor-made Goldie Hawn vehicle gets off to a promising start and then falters at the halfway mark. Goldie plays a cocktail waitress in Washington who inadvertently becomes entangled in the swirl of government diplomacy and Middle Eastern politics. The contrived script is based on Goldie's *Private Benjamin* formula. It gets out of control when it turns to some "Miss Smith Goes to Washington" philosophizing. **Director**—Herbert Ross. (PG)   *96 minutes*

PROVIDENCE (1977)
 ★

**Dirk Bogarde
John Gielgud
Ellen Burstyn**

French director Alain Resnais (*Last Year at Marienbad; Hiroshima, Mon Amour*) makes his first film in English with unfortunate results. The puzzling comedy, starring Bogarde, Gielgud, and Burstyn, is difficult to unravel. It's set inside the mind of a dying 78-year-old writer who drunkenly constructs a last novel about his family members. Most of the performances are feeble by way of miscasting or inadequate effort. The audience must work hard to fathom this film, which is actually a lot of fuss about nothing. Also with David Warner and Elaine Stritch. (PG)   *104 minutes*

PSYCHIC KILLER
(1976)
★★

**Jim Hutton
Julie Adams
Paul Burke**

This is an often-repulsive suspense shocker about a madman who seeks revenge on various people through parapsychology—a butcher is put through his own meat grinder; a nurse is scalded to death in a shower. It takes a friendly psychiatrist to finally figure out who has committed the string of gruesome murders. The film, which moves along energetically, liberally imitates Hitchcock's *Psycho* but hardly touches its depth. Also with Aldo Ray, Neville Brand, and Whit Bissell. **Director**—Raymond Danton. (PG)   *90 minutes*

PSYCHO (1960)
 ★★★★

**Anthony Perkins
Vera Miles
John Gavin
Janet Leigh**

Janet Leigh never finishes her shower in Psycho.

This classic horror story, based on the novel by Robert Bloch, is smartly served up by the great director Alfred Hitchcock, who goes right for the jugular and never lets go. Perkins plays the weird manager of a remote motel who isn't too accommodating to some of his guests; after a young woman and a private investigator hired to find her are killed, Perkins goes to great lengths to protect his mother. Watch out for that legendary shower scene—and mom. Also with John McIntire, Martin Balsam, and Simon Oakland. (PG) **Academy Award Nominations**—Hitchcock, best director; Leigh, best supporting actress; John L. Russell, cinematography (black and white).   *109 minutes b&w*

PSYCHO II (1983)
 ★★★

**Anthony Perkins
Vera Miles
Meg Tilly**

Anthony Perkins is back and looking for trouble in Psycho II.

This follow-up to the classic 1960 chiller is a workable spoof and a welcome homage to the master of suspense. Perkins once again portrays the frantic Norman Bates, now released from an insane asylum, back at the shabby motel and Victorian mansion seen in the original *Psycho*, and up to his twitching eyebrows in murder and mystery. The inside jokes fall precisely into place, and there are ample shocks and eerie surprises. Hitchcock would be flattered. **Director**—Richard Franklin. (R)   *115 minutes*

PT 109 (1963)
 ★★

Cliff Robertson

Mildly interesting account of the wartime exploits of John F. Kennedy, who skippered a PT boat in the Pacific during World War II as a Navy lieutenant. The famous personality makes the story somewhat intriguing, but the film is long and routinely done. Robertson does well in the role of Kennedy. Also with Ty Hardin, Robert Blake, and James Gregory. **Director**—Leslie H. Martinson.   *140 minutes*

P

- Puberty Blues
- The Public Enemy
- Pumping Iron
- The Pumpkin Eater
- Purple Haze
- Purple Hearts
- Purple Rain

PUBERTY BLUES (1983)
★★★

Nell Schofield
Jad Capelja

Australian director Bruce Beresford (*Breaker Morant*) scores with this poignant, sometimes humorous examination of adolescence. Set in a Sydney suburb, the film focuses on two high school girls (Schofield and Capelja) who fret about popularity, fall in with some callous surfer boys, experiment with sex and drugs, and finally wise up. This subject has been thoroughly explored before, but Beresford offers a fresh and satisfying approach. (R)
87 minutes

THE PUBLIC ENEMY (1931)
 ★★★★

James Cagney

James Cagney blazed his way to stardom as a ruthless gangster in The Public Enemy.

Powerful, stunning gangster film starring Cagney, who starts out as a small-time hood and graduates to the big leagues of gangsterdom. Cagney puts on quite a show as an Irish gangster, nails down his acting career, and establishes his reputation as a tough character in this film. The nerve-jangling story features some impressive and vivid scenes, including the notorious scene when Jimmy mashes a grapefruit into the face of Mae Clarke. Co-stars Edward Woods, Jean Harlow, Joan Blondell, and Donald Cook. **Director**—William Wellman. **Academy Award Nomination**—John Bright and Kubec Glasmon, writing (original story).
90 minutes b&w

PUMPING IRON (1977)
 ★★★

Arnold Schwarzenegger

This intelligent and lively documentary, all about the subculture of body-building, is based on the popular book by Charles Gaines and George Butler. It stars Schwarzenegger, that charming and spectacular champion of muscle-men who calls himself a sculptor of his own body. There's a good deal of suspense about who will win the titles of Mr. Universe and Mr. Olympia. The film makes it clear that the object of all the strenuous and painful weightlifting isn't strength, but appearance. Stylishly directed by Butler and Robert Fiore. (PG)
85 minutes

THE PUMPKIN EATER (1964)
★★★

Anne Bancroft
Peter Finch

Solid acting by a fine cast enhances this soapy story about a thrice-married woman having husband trouble. Bancroft gives a superb performance as the bewildered and rather unstable mother of eight who finds yet another marriage falling apart. Finch is her unfaithful husband. The film is executed with considerable sensitivity and perception, and some of the scenes are memorable, indeed. Also with James Mason, Cedric Hardwicke, Maggie Smith, and Eric Porter. **Director**—Jack Clayton. **Academy Award Nomination**—Bancroft, best actress.
110 minutes b&w

PURPLE HAZE (1983)
★★

Peter Nelson

Rambling, backward look at the volatile late '60s through the experiences of an alienated college dropout played by Nelson. The off-kilter story leans heavily on characters and situations from J.D. Salinger's *Catcher in the Rye.* (The central character is even named Caulfield.) Nothing new or interesting takes place and the film more or less lives up to its "hazy" title. Chuck

McQuary and Bernard Baldan co-star. **Director**—David Burton Morris. (R)
97 minutes

PURPLE HEARTS (1984)
 ★

Ken Wahl
Cheryl Ladd

Cheryl Ladd and Ken Wahl experience the love, the pain, the joys and the sorrow of the Vietnam War in Purple Hearts.

A drippy medical soap opera plopped in the middle of the Vietnam War, which makes it all the more ludicrous. Wahl's a heroic surgeon, gallantly tending battle casualties. Ladd's the stalwart front-line nurse. They intermittently leave the horrors of combat behind for some heavy romantic interludes. Anyone who can sit through such mush deserves a medal. **Director**—Sidney Furie. (R)   *116 minutes*

PURPLE RAIN (1984)
 ★★

Prince

Funk rocker Prince sparkles when he's belting out the numerous songs in this semi-autobiographical, musical melodrama. Otherwise, the backstage story is rather stiff, mean-spirited, and awkward. Various details of the young singer's tumultuous home life and a love affair with a beautiful vocalist (Apollonia Kotero) are highlighted. Yet Prince's music always takes center stage with such hits as "When Doves Cry," "Darling Nikki," and the title song. (R)   *111 minutes*

THE PURSUIT OF D. B. COOPER (1981)

★★★

**Treat Williams
Robert Duvall**

A spirited bit of tongue-in-cheek fiction based on the daredevil skyjacker who jumped from a 727 jet with $200,000 ransom and was never found. Williams is sensational as the slippery extortionist who leads an insurance company detective, played by Duvall, and other pursuers on a merry chase. Duvall is also in top form in this lightweight high adventure. The film owes much of its success to some slick energetic stunts. Also with Kathryn Harrold, Ed Flanders, R. G. Armstrong, and Paul Gleason. **Director**—Robert Spottiswoode. (PG)

100 minutes

Q

Q (1982)

★★★

**Michael Moriarty
David Carradine
Candy Clark**

Q is the kind of movie that *should* have been awful: It was directed by Larry Cohen, best known for *It's Alive!*; it has cheap, even ludicrous special effects; and it has a zany plot about a giant flying lizard that lives atop the Chrysler Building in New York City and eats rooftop sunbathers. Yet, somehow all the absurdity is played tongue-in-cheek and is bolstered by some first-rate acting. Moriarty plays an ex-junkie who discovers the lizard and employs it to eat his enemies. He brings a pathos to his part that is quite unexpected, and unnerving. (R)

93 minutes

QUADROPHENIA (1979)

★★★

Phil Daniels

This poignant British feature, with Daniels in the leading role, throbs with the music of The Who, but this isn't a rock concert film; it's an enter-

Mods and Rockers clash in Quadrophenia, *a story set in mid-1960s England.*

taining drama that effectively illuminates the frustrations and conflicts of British youth in the '60s. These are the disaffected young men and women who sought identity by joining such groups as the Mods or the Rockers. An excellent cast, which also includes Mark Wingett, Philip Davis, and Leslie Ash. **Director**—Franc Roddam. (R)

115 minutes

QUEST FOR FIRE (1982)

★★★★

**Everett McGill
Ron Perlman
Rae Dawn Chong**

Ron Perlman is a cavemen in Quest for Fire.

Much imagination and intelligence are present in this remarkable adventure of primitive people who inhabited the Earth 80,000 years ago. This is no Fred Flintstone caveman burlesque. It's an authentic-looking drama about man's struggle for survival and his acquisition of knowledge. The cast communicates by means of body language and grunts. A fascinating movie about early human life. **Director**—Jean-Jacques Annaud. (R)

97 minutes

THE QUIET AMERICAN (1958)

★★

**Michael Redgrave
Audie Murphy**

A diluted film version of Graham Greene's complex novel about an American who goes to Vietnam with vague plans for ending the fighting. Murphy is only partially effective in the title role, but the film offers some notable performances by the rest of the cast. Redgrave plays the journalist who's deceived into betraying Murphy to the communists. Also with Claude Dauphin, Bruce Cabot, Giorgia Moll, and Richard Loo. **Director**—Joseph L. Mankiewicz. *122 minutes b&w*

THE QUIET MAN (1952)

★★★★

**John Wayne
Maureen O'Hara**

Highly entertaining story about an ex-prizefighter who settles down in his native Ireland and woos a willful Irish lass. The film brims with energy and carries just the right amount of good-natured humor. The excellent production features sparkling scenes of the Irish countryside. Wayne does a good job in the title role, and O'Hara is perfect as the woman he tames. There are other outstanding performances from Barry Fitzgerald, Victor McLaglen, and Ward Bond. Also with Mildred Natwick, Francis Ford, and Arthur Shields. **Director**—John Ford. **Academy Awards**—Ford, best director; Winton C. Hoch and Archie Stout, cinematography (color). **Nominations**—best picture; McLaglen, best supporting actor; Frank S. Nugent, writing (screenplay). *129 minutes*

Q·R

- Quintet
- Quo Vadis
- Race for Your Life, Charlie Brown
- Race with the Devil
- Rachel, Rachel
- Racing with the Moon
- A Rage to Live
- Raggedy Ann and Andy

QUINTET (1979)

★

Paul Newman

Director Robert Altman's 13th film is his fantasy of apocalypse. In a bleak, ice-crusted city, survivors play a deadly backgammonlike game where the winners murder the losers. It's a tedious movie about a relentlessly gloomy world. Newman heads the international cast, which also includes Vittorio Gassman, Fernando Rey, Bibi Andersson, and Nina Van Pallandt. They all seem bored and frozen to the bone. Even Altman devotees may have a hard time sitting through this one. (R)   *110 minutes*

QUO VADIS (1951)

★★★

**Robert Taylor
Deborah Kerr
Peter Ustinov**

Lavish extravaganza about the plight of Christians under the heavy hand of Roman Emperor Nero. Rome burns, the lions eat some Christians, and Taylor plays a Roman soldier who romances Kerr. There's really too much to digest in this long movie, and boredom will eventually set in. But there are moments of impressive acting, and some spectacular scenes are outstanding. Also with Leo Genn, Patricia Laffan, Finlay Currie, and Buddy Baer. **Director**—Mervyn Le Roy. **Academy Award Nominations**—best picture; Genn, Ustinov, best supporting actor; Robert Surtees and William V. Skall, cinematography (color).   *171 minutes*

R

RACE FOR YOUR LIFE, CHARLIE BROWN (1977)

 ★★

The mere appearance of the lovable Peanuts gang should delight the kids, but this third animated screen feature of the famous comic strip is showing some wear. This time Charlie Brown and his pals are packed off to summer camp, where they give their neuroses the usual workout. The plot rambles, and the animation seems flat. Charles M. Schulz wrote the screenplay. **Director**—Bill Melendez. (G)   *75 minutes*

RACE WITH THE DEVIL (1975)

★

**Peter Fonda
Warren Oates**

An adolescent, lamebrained horror film about four vacationers who are chased by a group of devil worshippers after stumbling upon a ritual killing in Texas. Fonda, Oates, Loretta Swit, and Lara Parker are the vacationers. Also with R. G. Armstrong. **Director**—Jack Starrett. (PG)
89 minutes

RACHEL, RACHEL (1968)

★★★★

**Joanne Woodward
Estelle Parsons**

Joanne Woodward portrays a lonely schoolteacher in Rachel, Rachel.

Woodward is splendid as a schoolteacher in this deeply moving portrait of a middle-aged spinster facing a midlife crisis. She's lonely, frustrated, and trapped in a small New England town. Parsons plays one of her colleagues. Under Paul Newman's direction, the film is a realistic slice of life and doesn't turn into a soap opera. Also with James Olson, Kate Harrington, Geraldine Fitzgerald, Donald Moffat, and Bernard Barrow. **Academy Award Nominations**—best picture; Woodward, best actress; Parsons, best supporting actress; Stewart Stern, best screenplay (based on material from another medium).   *101 minutes*

RACING WITH THE MOON (1984)

 ★★★

**Sean Penn
Elizabeth McGovern**

Sweet, sensitive, nostalgic romance that looks at the transition to adulthood among some youths in a small California town during World War II. Director Richard Benjamin expertly captures the flavor of the period. And the young, talented cast turns in some impressive performances. Penn and McGovern are exceptionally appealing as lovers faced with dramatic changes in their lives because of the war. Nicholas Cage co-stars. (PG)
110 minutes

A RAGE TO LIVE (1965)

★

**Suzanne Pleshette
Bradford Dillman
Ben Gazzara**

This screen version of John O'Hara's popular novel about a woman of easy virtue has been marred by heavy-handed Hollywood treatment. The film lacks the irony and characterization that make most of O'Hara's work famous. Pleshette does as well as can be expected as the near-nymphomaniac who discovers she needs more in life than just a husband. Also with James Gregory, Peter Graves, Bethel Leslie, and Ruth White. **Director**—Walter Grauman.   *101 minutes b&w*

RAGGEDY ANN AND ANDY (1977)

 ★★

This animated cartoon, based on the famous Johnny Gruelle children's stories, is a technical achievement of sorts—but alas, the $4-million project fails to deliver enough satisfying entertainment for youngsters or adults. It's about two rag dolls who encounter a variety of unappealing creatures that screech and gurgle in a monotonous and ill-humored fashion. Songs by Joe Raposo of *Sesame Street* fame all seem to sound the same; they lack the lighthearted charm of the pleasant Disney cartoon features of years ago. **Director**—Richard Williams. (G)   *85 minutes*

RAGGEDY MAN (1981)
★★

**Sissy Spacek
Eric Roberts**

Spacek is convincing as a lonely divorcée with two sons in a small Texas town in the mid '40s. She has a brief affair with a sailor, played by Roberts. The screenplay starts with such good intentions, as a charming, sensitive love story. But unfortunately, events turn sour as the sailor abruptly leaves, and Sissy is at the mercy of two redneck brutes. Finally the film emerges as merely another violent melodrama with an unsatisfying resolution. Also with Sam Shepard and R. G. Armstrong. **Director**—Jack Fisk. (PG)   *94 minutes*

RAGING BULL (1980)
★★★★

**Robert De Niro
Cathy Moriarty
Joe Pesci**

Robert De Niro plays a boxer who loves the pain in Raging Bull.

Director Martin Scorsese's hard-hitting, high-voltage characterization of middleweight champ Jake La Motta is a brilliant study of brutality and torment in and out of the ring. De Niro, in the title role, stunningly portrays the Bronx Bull with grim, unsentimental reality. There's credible support from newcomers Pesci and Moriarty. The brief, supercharged boxing scenes are perhaps the best ever filmed. Superb direction and dazzling acting—a triumph for all involved. Also with Frank Vincent and Nicholas Colasanto. (R) **Academy Award**—De Niro, best actor. **Nominations**—best picture; Scorsese, best director; Pesci, best supporting actor; Moriarty, best supporting actress.   *119 minutes b&w*

RAGTIME (1981)
★★★

**Brad Dourif
Howard E. Rollins, Jr.
James Cagney**

Mandy Patinkin in a fuzzy beard in Ragtime.

Exquisite period detail, impeccable photography, and impressive acting by a large, first-rate cast characterize this screen adaptation of E. L. Doctorow's multifaceted novel about America at the turn of the century. Despite these advantages, the movie is seriously hampered by the complications of the plot. The movie's running time isn't long enough to figure out the convoluted story, and much of the film's punch and style is lost in the confusion. Old pro Cagney plays a crusty police commissioner, and newcomer Rollins makes an impressive first appearance as a young black piano player who takes extreme measures to soothe his wounded pride. Also with Moses Gunn, Elizabeth McGovern, Kenneth McMillan, James Olson, Mandy Patinkin, and Mary Steenburgen. **Director**—Milos Forman. (PG) **Academy Award Nominations**—Rollins, best supporting actor; McGovern, best supporting actress; Michael Weller, best screenplay (based on material from another medium); Miroslav Ondricek, cinematography.   *156 minutes*

RAIDERS OF THE LOST ARK (1981)
★★★★

**Harrison Ford
Karen Allen**

George (*Star Wars*) Lucas and Steven (*Jaws*) Spielberg joined talents to make this riproaring, thrill-a-minute adventure. Ford plays Indiana Jones, a stubborn, rough-and-ready archaeologist who races the Nazis to find a lost ark supposedly containing remnants of the Ten Commandments. Allen is the leading lady who helps him in this undertaking. The exotic, action-packed film harks back to those derring-do serials of the '30s and '40s, but this version is blessed with magnificent technical sophistication. It's the ultimate in escapist entertainment. Also with Paul Freeman, Ronald Lacey, John Rhys-Davies, and Denholm Elliott. **Director**—Spielberg. (PG) **Academy Award Nominations**—best picture; Spielberg, best director; Douglas Slocombe, cinematography.   *115 minutes*

THE RAINMAKER (1956)
★★★

**Katharine Hepburn
Burt Lancaster**

Richard Nash's hit play about Starbuck, a phony rainmaker who's more successful at seducing a confirmed spinster, is too talky and doesn't make a good movie. But Hepburn performs well as the spinster in a Kansas town. She's romanced by the visiting con man, played by Lancaster, who overacts in the title role. Also with Wendell Corey, Lloyd Bridges, Earl Holliman, and Wallace Ford. **Director**—Joseph Anthony. **Academy Award Nomination**—Hepburn, best actress.   *121 minutes*

RAINTREE COUNTY (1958)
★★★

Montgomery Clift
Elizabeth Taylor

Taylor and Clift, with the help of an excellent supporting cast, keep this rambling Civil War story from becoming a dud. Taylor portrays a woman who stops at nothing to get what she wants. But when she gets her man, happiness still eludes her, and the war eventually tears her world apart. Clift plays her romantic interest. Also with Eva Marie Saint, Nigel Patrick, Lee Marvin, Rod Taylor, and Agnes Moore-head. **Director**—Edward Dmytryk. **Academy Award Nomination**—Taylor, best actress. *166 minutes*

RAISE THE TITANIC (1980)
★

Jason Robards, Jr.
Richard Jordan
Anne Archer

There are some striking visual effects to simulate the resurrection of the famous ocean liner from the deep, but the script, acting, and direction should be relegated to Davy Jones's locker. This bloated film wastes con-

Jason Robards, Jr. proves how easy it is to Raise the Titanic.

siderable time with cardboard characters talking themselves into a stupor, and there's not much else in the screenplay to pep up the pace. The basic plot concerns the urgent recovery of a mysterious ore on board the vessel so the Russians can't grab it. **Director**—Jerry Jameson. (PG) *112 minutes*

A RAISIN IN THE SUN (1961)
★★★★

Sidney Poitier
Ruby Dee
Claudia McNeil

Sidney Poitier in A Raisin in the Sun, *a tale of a black family in a Chicago ghetto.*

This is one of the first commercial films that makes an honest attempt to deal with the black experience in a realistic and sensitive manner. This tale of a black family in Chicago, attempting to leave the ghetto to live in an all-white neighborhood, is enhanced by the fine acting of Poitier, Dee, and McNeil. The movie doesn't differ much from Lorraine Hansberry's Broadway play; the dialogue still bristles, and the story makes a sharp impact. Also with Diana Sands, Ivan

JAMES STEWART

James Stewart, who was born in 1908, left his hometown of Indiana, Pennsylvania, for the first time to enroll at Mercersburg Academy to get ready for his college choice, Princeton. As a Princeton freshman, he elected to major in electrical engineering, but later switched to architecture. He might have succeeded in either one had it not been for his love of acting.

Stewart graduated from Princeton with a degree in architecture, but promptly forgot it and joined a theatrical stock company led by Joshua Logan. When one of the company's efforts made it to New York, Stewart went with it and made his professional debut in Goodbye Again. *He also appeared in a series of New York plays before he won the role of Sergeant O'Hara in* Yellow Jack, *a part which put his name up in lights on Broadway for the first time. Soon afterward, Stewart signed a film contract and made his film debut in* The Murder Man *(1935).*

Within a few years, he had a string of movie hits—Made for Each Other (1938); It's a Wonderful World *(1939);* Mr. Smith Goes to Washington *(1939), his first Oscar nomination;* Destry Rides Again *(1939);* The Shop Around the Corner *(1939); and* The Mortal Storm *(1940). He then won the Academy Award as best actor for* The Philadelphia Story *(1940).*

Stewart was among the first top screen stars to enter military service in World War II. He became a private in the Army Air Force before the attack on Pearl Harbor. Nine months later, because of his previous flying experience and education, Stewart was commissioned as a lieutenant. He served in the Air Force until 1945, when he was discharged from active duty with the rank of colonel. In 1959, he was promoted to brigadier general.

After the war, Stewart appeared in a number of successful movies. They include It's a Wonderful Life *(1946), for which he was nominated for an Oscar;* Call Northside 777 *(1947);* Rope *(1948), his first film for Alfred Hitchcock;* Winchester 73 *(1950);* Broken Arrow *(1950);* Harvey *(1950), which earned him his fourth Oscar nomination;* Rear Window *(1954);* The Man from Laramie *(1955);* Anatomy of a Murder *(1959), which got him his fifth Oscar nomination; and* Shenandoah *(1965).*

In recent years, Stewart has appeared in The Shootist *(1976) with John Wayne,* The Big Sleep *(1978), and* The Magic of Lassie *(1978).*

- Rally 'round the Flag, Boys!
- Ramrod
- Rancho Deluxe
- Random Harvest
- Ransom
- Rashomon
- The Rat Race
- The Raven

R

Dixon, John Fielder, and Lou Gossett, Jr. **Director**—Daniel Petrie.

128 minutes b&w

RALLY 'ROUND THE FLAG, BOYS! (1958)

★★

Paul Newman
Joanne Woodward

Hollywood mishandles this film version of Max Shulman's witty novel, about Putnam's Landing, a small community upset over a proposed missile base. Newman and Woodward, a couple who get involved in the controversy, lack the comic acting touch needed to salvage this comedy, and they fail to bring the humor and charm of the book onto the screen. Jack Carson, Joan Collins, and Tuesday Weld also star. **Director**—Leo McCarey.

106 minutes

RAMROD (1947)
★★

Veronica Lake
Joel McCrea
Charles Ruggles

Lake plays a ruthless ranch owner in this western story about a territorial dispute. She hires a rough and vicious foreman to assist her in a confrontation with her father, played by Ruggles. There are several deaths and a stampede before the issues are resolved. Also with Preston Foster and Lloyd Bridges. **Director**—André de Toth. *94 minutes b&w*

RANCHO DELUXE (1975)

★★★

Jeff Bridges
Sam Waterston

A kinky comedy of the tamed West, where modern buckaroos ride around in pickup trucks and fat-cat ranchers roam the range via helicopters. Bridges and Waterston star as aimless latter-day cattle rustlers, whose antics include sawing up steers with a chainsaw and holding a prize bull for ransom in a motel room. Screenwriter Thomas McGuane cleverly injects some off-beat dialogue, and director

Frank Perry emphasizes the freewheeling spirit against the backdrop of wasted lives. Also with Elizabeth Ashley, Charlene Dallas, Clifton James, and Slim Pickens. (R)

93 minutes

RANDOM HARVEST (1942)

★★★

Ronald Colman
Greer Garson

Greer Garson and Philip Dorn in Random Harvest, *about a man who forgets the woman he loves.*

Colman and Garson shine in this romance about an amnesia sufferer who forgets the woman he loves. Colman plays a shell-shocked army officer who escapes from an asylum. Garson dutifully becomes his secretary as she attempts to rekindle the relationship he can't recall. Eventually, another shock years later restores Colman's memory, and this Hollywood-style romance ends on a happy note. The superior acting of this splendid duo prevents an unbelievable plot, based on a James Hilton novel, from becoming mush. Also with Susan Peters, Philip Dorn, Reginald Owen, Edmund Gwenn, and Margaret Wycherly. **Director**—Mervyn Le Roy. **Academy Award Nominations**—best picture; Colman, best supporting actor; Peters, best supporting actress; George Froeschel, Claudine West, and Arthur Wimperis, writing (screenplay).

126 minutes b&w

RANSOM (1955)

★★

Glenn Ford

Ford gives an uneven performance as an industrialist who debates whether to pay the ransom when his son is

kidnapped. The story has been done better before and since, but there's enough suspense to keep the film interesting. Ford gets competent support from Donna Reed, Leslie Nielsen, and Robert Keith. **Director**—Alex Segal. *104 minutes b&w*

RASHOMON (1951)

★★★★

Toshiro Mifune

The film that brought director Akira Kurosawa international recognition created a sensation at the Venice Film Festival and won the Oscar as best foreign film. It's a *tour de force*—built entirely around one incident. In medieval Japan, a merchant and his wife are attacked in the woods by a bandit. The merchant is killed, the wife raped. The incident is seen through the eyes of each of the protagonists—the three participants, and a woodcutter who witnessed the event. With unusually vivid imagery and sound track, the film probes into what motivates human behavior at its deepest level. In Japanese with English titles. **Academy Award**—best foreign-language film.

83 minutes

THE RAT RACE (1960)
★★

Tony Curtis
Debbie Reynolds

Curtis is a young jazz musician and Reynolds is a dancer in this comedy-drama based on the Garson Kanin play. The story of show business people trying to make it in New York City has been told many times before, but the scenery of New York is pleasant, and some of the dialogue is top-notch. In addition, Jack Oakie, Kay Medford, and Don Rickles deliver interesting characterizations of typical New Yorkers. **Director**—Robert Mulligan.

105 minutes

THE RAVEN (1963)

★★

Vincent Price
Peter Lorre
Boris Karloff

Boris Karloff considers suing his plastic surgeon, Bela Lugosi, in The Raven.

(Continued)

Price, Lorre, Karloff, and Jack Nicholson prevent this horror film from becoming a horrible bore. A climactic sorcerers' duel, in which two 15th-century conjurers battle each other in a deadly duel of magic, is the best part of the film. Alas, that part takes a long time to reach, and the earlier segments of the movie are less interesting. Also with Hazel Court. **Director**—Roger Corman. *86 minutes*

RAWHIDE (1950)

 ★★

Tyrone Power
Susan Hayward

A gang of four desperate outlaws terrorize Power and Hayward at a remote stagecoach stop in this suspenseful but slow-moving western. The shoot-out at the end highlights this film. Hugh Marlowe, Jack Elam, Dean Jagger, George Tobias, Edgar Buchanan, and Jeff Corey also star. **Director**—Henry Hathaway. **Alternate Title**—*Desperate Siege.* *86 minutes b&w*

THE RAZOR'S EDGE (1946)

 ★★★

Tyrone Power
Gene Tierney

Long and glossy version of W. Somerset Maugham's famous philosophical novel about a wealthy young man's search for faith. It becomes a rambling and tedious film, but some fine acting salvages this overly long movie. Power portrays the hero seeking goodness in life; Tierney is a social climber who rejects Power; Anne Baxter plays an alcoholic; Herbert Marshall plays the author; and Elsa Lanchester sparkles in a small role as a social secretary. Clifton Webb and John Payne also star. **Director**—Edmund Goulding. **Academy Award**—Baxter, best supporting actress. **Nominations**—best picture; Webb, best supporting actor.

146 minutes b&w

THE RAZOR'S EDGE (1984)

 ★★

Bill Murray
Theresa Russell
Catherine Hicks

Glossy, patchwork-quilt remake of the 1946 classic, based on W. Somerset Maugham's novel, which starred Tyrone Power. Funnyman Bill Murray is now in the central role of the disillusioned World War I veteran who wanders through Europe and Asia seeking escape and inner peace. Murray tries his utmost to handle the serious drama, but his portrayal comes off as strained and awkward. The film itself is languid and too long. Also with Theresa Russell and Catherine Hicks. **Director**—John Byrum. (PG–13) *130 minutes*

REAL LIFE (1979)

 ★

Albert Brooks
Charles Grodin

Writer-director Brooks tries to parody the Public Broadcasting System TV series about the day-to-day events of a typical American family, but the film is an embarrassment to all involved. Brooks—who also stars—jabbers incoherently, acts silly, and fires off corny jokes that fall flat. Some of it is just bad taste—such as an attempt to film the wife's visit to her gynecologist. Also with Frances Lee McCain, J. A. Preston, and Matthew Tobin. (PG)

99 minutes

REAR WINDOW (1954)

 ★★★★

James Stewart
Grace Kelly

Director Alfred Hitchcock combines sophisticated comedy with superlative suspense scenes in this movie about a news photographer confined to his wheelchair who witnesses a murder. Stewart plays the photographer, and Kelly is charming as a society girl friend. The tension builds and becomes almost excruciating toward the end of the film as Hitchcock works his magic. Raymond Burr, Judith Evelyn, Wendell Corey, and Thelma Ritter perform well in supporting roles. **Academy Award Nominations**—Hitchcock, best director; John Michael Hayes, writing (screenplay); Robert Burks, cinematography (color).

112 minutes

Grace Kelly and James Stewart star in Alfred Hitchcock's Rear Window.

- Rebecca
- Rebel Without a Cause
- Reckless
- The Red Badge of Courage
- Red Ball Express
- Red Dawn
- Red River

R

REBECCA (1940)

★★★★

**Laurence Olivier
Joan Fontaine
George Sanders
Judith Anderson**

Director Alfred Hitchcock adapted this award-winning story from Daphne du Maurier's novel about a naïve woman who marries a brooding British nobleman and finds that she must live in the shadow of Rebecca—his beautiful first wife. Hitchcock deftly combines romance, comedy, suspense, and mystery, with sets in Monte Carlo and Cornwall. Fontaine, Anderson, and Olivier perform superbly and receive excellent support from Sanders, Nigel Bruce, Gladys Cooper, Florence Bates, and Reginald Denny. Also with C. Aubrey Smith and Leo G. Carroll. **Academy Awards**—best picture; George Barnes, cinematography (black and white). **Nominations**—Hitchcock, best director; Olivier, best actor; Fontaine, best actress; Anderson, best supporting actress; Robert E. Sherwood and Joan Harrison, writing (screenplay).
130 minutes b&w

REBEL WITHOUT A CAUSE (1955)

★★★

**James Dean
Natalie Wood**

Nick Adams taunts newcomer James Dean into a fight in Rebel Without a Cause.

Dean became a symbol to the nation after his role as a troubled teenager in this film. He plays a young man in conflict with the middle-class values of his parents, who finally finds some meaning in life when he befriends Wood and Sal Mineo, who perform well in supporting roles. But his friendship with the pair is shattered in an exciting and tragic end. Jim Backus, Ann Doran, Dennis Hopper, and Nick Adams also star. **Director**—Nicholas Ray. **Academy Award Nominations**—Mineo, best supporting actor; Wood, best supporting actress; Ray, writing (motion picture story). *111 minutes*

RECKLESS (1984)

★★

**Daryl Hannah
Aidan Quinn**

Just another smoldering youth film that rips off just about every other smoldering youth film from *Rebel Without a Cause* to *All the Right Moves*. Quinn seems to make all the wrong moves as the moody, motorcycle-riding high school senior who woos moody, blonde, pampered Hannah. Quinn knocks himself out copying the mannerisms of James Dean, Marlon Brando, and Sylvester Stallone. It's been seen before. Ho hum. **Director**—James Foley. (R) *90 minutes*

THE RED BADGE OF COURAGE (1951)

★★★★

Audie Murphy

Stephen Crane's classic Civil War novel becomes one of the greatest war films under the brilliant writing and direction of John Huston. Murphy, Bill Mauldin, and John Dierkes give natural performances that further brighten this realistic drama of combat as seen through the eyes of a young recruit. Before the young soldier becomes a brave soldier, he experiences fear, and the viewer gets a hint of the hell of war. Also with Douglas Dick, Royal Dano, Andy Devine, and Arthur Hunnicutt. *69 minutes b&w*

RED BALL EXPRESS (1952)

★★

Jeff Chandler

Chandler plays the gruff but human leader of an Army truck division—known as the Red Ball Express—that ferries war supplies from the beaches of Normandy to the outskirts of Paris during World War II. Sidney Poitier, Alex Nicol, Hugh O'Brien, Jack Kelly, and Jack Warden blend well in this conventional war story that has its share of action and adventure. **Director**—Budd Boetticher.
83 minutes b&w

RED DAWN (1984)

★

**Patrick Swayze
C. Thomas Howell**

Preposterous, gung ho war movie imagining the United States has been invaded by Russian and Cuban troops. A band of all-American teenagers hightails it to the mountains to launch guerrilla counterattacks. It's the Pepsi generation versus the Commies. Some of this nonsense may be considered tongue-in-cheek, but too much of it is badly written and overflowing with clichés. **Director**—John Milius. (PG) *114 minutes*

RED RIVER (1948)

★★★★

**John Wayne
Montgomery Clift**

Montgomery Clift forgets all about poking cattle when he sees Joanne Dru in Red River.

Wayne and Clift star in this classic western story of a cattle baron and the dynasty he builds. Clift rebels against his foster father, played by Wayne, and the empire Wayne has developed. Joanne Dru, Walter Brennan, Colleen Gray, John Ireland, and Noah Berry, Jr., are also in top form in supporting roles. Besides the excellent acting and top-flight action-packed story, the *(Continued)*

R
- Reds
- The Red Shoes
- Reflections in a Golden Eye
- The Reincarnation of Peter Proud
- The Reluctant Debutante
- The Reluctant Dragon
- The Remarkable Mr. Pennypacker
- Remember the Night

(Continued)

movie, under the direction of Howard Hawks, is beautifully filmed. **Academy Award Nomination**—Borden Chase, writing (motion picture story).

133 minutes b&w

REDS (1981)

 ★★★

**Warren Beatty
Diane Keaton**

A brilliant and passionate slice of history. Beatty is splendid playing radical journalist John Reed, who chronicled the Russian Revolution. The epic adventure also presents the stormy love affair between Reed and writer Louise Bryant who is played exquisitely by Keaton. Although this remarkable story deals heavily in radical politics, it's surprisingly lucid and invigorating. A triumph for Beatty, who also produced, wrote, and directed. He gets superb support from Jack Nicholson and Maureen Stapleton. Also with Edward Hermann, Jerzy Kosinski, Paul Sorvino, and Gene Hackman. (PG) **Academy Awards**—Stapleton, best supporting actress; Beatty, best director; Vittorio Storaro, cinematography. **Nominations**—best picture; Beatty, best actor; Keaton, best actress; Nicholson, best supportiing actor; Beatty and Trevor Griffiths, best screenplay (written directly for the screen).

200 minutes

THE RED SHOES (1948)

 ★★★★

**Anton Walbrook
Moira Shearer
Marius Goring**

This sensitive and beautiful movie about a ballerina who gives up her romance with a composer to dedicate her life to ballet is enriched by superb dancing. The production, which stars Walbrook, Shearer, and Goring, offers an intimate and realistic slice-of-life view of the ballerina's world backstage. Also with Robert Helpmann, Albert Bassermann, Frederick Ashton, and Leonide Massine. **Director**—Michael Powell. **Academy Award Nominations**—best picture; Emeric Pressburger, writing (motion picture story).

136 minutes

REFLECTIONS IN A GOLDEN EYE (1967)

 ★

**Marlon Brando
Elizabeth Taylor**

A star-studded cast, which includes Brando, Taylor, Brian Keith, and Julie Harris, fails to salvage this cinema clunker about a homosexual Army officer stationed in Georgia. Most of the characters are insane, or at least eccentric, in this debased film version of Carson McCullers's perceptive novel. Some of the acting, however, is excellent. Brando, despite the faults of his Method acting, still conveys, in a moving way, the anguish of a homosexual Army officer. Robert Forster is the object of his affection, and Taylor plays Brando's wife. John Huston provides stylish direction, but fortunately his reputation has been secured by his other cinema efforts.

108 minutes

THE REINCARNATION OF PETER PROUD (1975)

★★★

**Michael Sarrazin
Jennifer O'Neill
Margot Kidder**

A California college professor, played by Sarrazin, believes he led an earlier life that ended in violence. He searches for his past in a suburban Massachusetts town and finds more than he bargained for. A suspenseful and moody drama, but there's no solid solution to the mystery. Good performances by Sarrazin, O'Neill, and Kidder. Also with Cornelia Sharpe and Paul Hecht. **Director**—J. Lee Thompson. (R)

104 minutes

THE RELUCTANT DEBUTANTE (1958)

★★

**Rex Harrison
Kay Kendall**

Harrison and Kendall brighten this ho hum British drawing-room comedy about an unorthodox British couple who choose to permit their daughter, educated in America, to make her society debut in England. Sandra Dee

plays the daughter. Despite such a lean plot, there are some pleasant moments that make the movie mildly enjoyable. Also with John Saxon, Peter Myers, and Angela Lansbury. **Director**—Vincente Minnelli.

96 minutes

THE RELUCTANT DRAGON (1941)

★★

Robert Benchley

This studio tour of the fantastic and magical universe of Walt Disney gives young and old moviegoers an excellent chance to see how cartoons of the '30s and '40s were made. During this Disney studio tour, the enjoyable mixture of short subjects presented include *Baby Weems*, *How To Ride a Horse*, and the title story. The pleasant experience is enriched by the presence of Benchley, who's better known for his humorous essays. **Director**—Alfred Werker.

72 minutes

THE REMARKABLE MR. PENNYPACKER (1959)

★

Clifton Webb

Can a movie about bigamy be funny? Webb makes a valiant effort to be humorous in this story about a businessman who leads two lives and raises two families with a total of 17 children, but he doesn't succeed. Dorothy McGuire, Charles Coburn, Ray Stricklyn, Jill St. John, Ron Ely, and David Nelson also appear in this effort at sophisticated comedy, but fail to brighten it. **Director**—Henry Levin.

87 minutes

REMEMBER THE NIGHT (1940)

★★★

**Barbara Stanwyck
Fred MacMurray**

MacMurray and Stanwyck shine in this delightful and sentimental story of an assistant district attorney who takes a shoplifter home with him when court recesses for the Christmas holidays. MacMurray plays the attorney who falls in love with Stanwyck,

• Renaldo and Clara
• Repo Man
• Report to the Commissioner
• Reprieve

• Repulsion
• Requiem for a Heavyweight
• The Rescuers
• Resurrection

R

the shoplifter. Under Mitchell Leisen's direction, the film is typical of the special blend of comedy, romance, and drama that some of the finer films of this era achieved. Beulah Bondi, Elizabeth Patterson, Sterling Holloway, Paul Guilfoyle, and Willard Robertson do their share in supporting roles.

94 minutes b&w

RENALDO AND CLARA (1978)

★

Bob Dylan

Only some Dylan devotees may find this film of interest; others will be frustrated by the nearly four-hour-long mishmash of musical interludes and an incoherent script. The movie mainly concerns a 1975 concert tour by Dylan, Joan Baez, and friends. Dylan was the writer, director, and musical supervisor. (R) *232 minutes*

REPO MAN (1984)

 ★★★

Harry Dean Stanton
Emilio Estevez

Emilio Estevez finds that he can steal cars legally as a Repo Man.

Bizarre mishmash of a farce that features punk rockers, CIA agents, strange scientists, and other oddball characters all chasing a used car with alien creatures in the trunk. The title refers to one particular weirdo, a sleazy repossessor of automobiles, played intensely by Stanton. The story is rife with off-the-wall material that produces laughs in spite of itself. The film seems destined for the cult, midnight-movie circuit. **Director**—Alex Cox. *92 minutes*

REPORT TO THE COMMISSIONER (1975)

★★

Michael Moriarty
Yaphet Kotto
Susan Blakely

A hippie undercover cop, played by Moriarty, is destroyed by his inept and aloof police department supervisors. Blakely plays an undercover cop. The film is more exploitation of the *French Connection* and *Serpico* themes, but the suspense hardly gets off the ground, and the plot bogs down in unlikely complications. Also with Hector Elizondo, Tony King, and Michael McGuire. **Director**—Milton Katselas. (PG) *112 minutes*

REPRIEVE
See Convicts Four

REPULSION (1965)

 ★★★

Catherine Deneuve
Ian Hendry
Yvonne Furnaux

Catherine Deneuve goes crazy in Repulsion.

Director Roman Polanski let his macabre imagination run wild, and the result is this nightmarish portrayal of young London beautician Deneuve's descent into madness. Isolating herself from the outside world, the beautiful, sexually repressed young woman murders those who try to reach out to her. With images of menacing arms bursting through walls, it's a grisly, often surrealistic visualization of a disturbed mind, and one that might have done Luis Buñuel proud. The film isn't

as deep as Hitchcock can be but, shock for shock, it's impressive.

105 minutes b&w

REQUIEM FOR A HEAVYWEIGHT (1962)

 ★★★★

Anthony Quinn
Jackie Gleason
Mickey Rooney
Julie Harris

Quinn, Gleason, Rooney, and Harris contribute excellent performances in this tough, hard-hitting drama of a prizefighter in the twilight of his career. Quinn plays the washed-up boxer, Rooney is a pathetic friend, and Harris is a social worker. The movie, based on Rod Serling's play, has realistic and harsh fight scenes, which blend well with the superior acting. Also with Nancy Cushman, Madame Spivy, and Stan Adams. **Director**—Ralph Nelson. *87 minutes b&w*

THE RESCUERS (1977)

★★★

Imagination, expert craftsmanship, loving care, and plenty of expense have gone into this 22nd full-length animated feature by the Walt Disney studio. It's a lively and charming adventure about two brave mice who set out to rescue a kidnapped girl. The voices of Eva Gabor, Bob Newhart, Jim (Fibber McGee) Jordan, and Geraldine Page add delightful dimensions to the cartoon subjects. The Disney wizards have created magic again. **Directors**—Wolfgang Reitherman, John Lounsbery, and Art Stevens. (G) *76 minutes*

RESURRECTION (1980)

 ★★

Ellen Burstyn

Burstyn dominates this unusual and uneven film with a glowing virtuoso performance. She plays an ordinary woman who discovers that after a serious accident, she can heal people with the laying on of hands. The flimsy story, however, never connects dra-
(Continued)

R

- Retreat, Hell!
- Return from Witch Mountain
- The Return of a Man Called Horse
- The Return of Frank James
- Return of the Jedi
- The Return of the Pink Panther

(Continued)

matically or emotionally; the treatment is neither an exposé of hokum nor a plug for divine faith. It is, more or less, a beautifully acted fable with vague perceptions of psychic healing. As for Burstyn's acting, she walks on water. Also with Eva Le Gallienne. **Director**—Daniel Petrie. (PG) **Academy Award Nominations**—Burstyn, best actress; Le Gallienne, best supporting actress. *103 minutes*

RETREAT, HELL! (1952)
★

Frank Lovejoy
Richard Carlson

Action scenes and a few tense moments enliven this run-of-the-mill war story of a Marine unit fighting in Korea. Lovejoy and Carlson, in starring roles, provide the rough-and-tough characterization that's required in such movies. Also with Anita Louise and Russ Tamblyn. **Director**—Joseph H. Lewis. *95 minutes b&w*

RETURN FROM WITCH MOUNTAIN (1978)
★★★

Bette Davis
Christopher Lee
Kim Richards
Ike Eisenmann

Richards and Eisenmann, two appealing kids from outer space, return in this Walt Disney-made sequel to *Escape from Witch Mountain* with their extraordinary powers. Lee and Davis play a pair of meanies who try to exploit the moppets for power and profit, but the two youngsters have dazzling Disney special effects on their side. The children will be enthralled; for adults, it's déjà vu. Also with Denver Pyle and Dick Bakalyan. **Director**—John Hough. (G) *95 minutes*

THE RETURN OF A MAN CALLED HORSE (1976)
 ★★

Richard Harris

Harris stars in this mystical sequel to

Enrique Lucero and Richard Harris in The Return of a Man Called Horse.

A Man Called Horse, in which he played the leading role. This time, he portrays an English nobleman who returns to South Dakota to rescue the Yellow Hand Sioux, his adopted tribe, from annihilation. Harris participates in yet another gruesome purification ritual in which his chest is pierced by small bones and then stretched; it's not for the squeamish. The film is mostly placid, but it's highlighted here and there with short periods of action. Also with Gale Sondergaard, Geoffrey Lewis, Bill Lucking, and Jorge Luke. **Director**—Irvin Kershner. (PG) *129 minutes*

THE RETURN OF FRANK JAMES (1940)
★★★

Henry Fonda
Gene Tierney

Fonda plays Frank James, attempting to avenge brother Jesse's death, in this colorful and excellently photographed tale. The action is balanced by more characterization and humor than is found in most westerns of this era. Tierney makes her film debut in this sequel to *Jesse James*. Jackie Cooper, John Carradine, Henry Hull, J. Edward Bromberg, and Donald Meek also star. **Director**—Fritz Lang. *92 minutes*

RETURN OF THE JEDI (1983)
★★★

Mark Hamill
Harrison Ford
Carrie Fisher

George Lucas's third chapter in the *Star Wars* saga offers the expected array of colorful, spectacular effects

Harrison Ford and Mark Hamill are brought before Jabba the Hutt in Return of the Jedi.

and novel space creatures—including some we haven't met before. The elaborate space opera also answers a lot of questions about Luke Skywalker's relationships with Darth Vader and Princess Leia. But, alas, the honeymoon is over for this sci-fi extravaganza. It suffers from anticlimactic sequelitis. **Director**—Richard Marquand. (PG) *133 minutes*

THE RETURN OF THE PINK PANTHER (1975)
 ★★★

Peter Sellers
Christopher Plummer
Herbert Lom

Inspector Clouseau (Peter Sellers) defends himself in Return of the Pink Panther.

Funnyman Sellers once again plays the accident-prone Inspector Jacques Clouseau—hot on the trail of the fabled Pink Panther diamond, the national treasure of the State of Lugash, after it's stolen once more. Lom plays the Chief Inspector. It's slapstick carried to the most reckless degree, as the bumbling Clouseau drives those around him up the wall and gets him-

• The Return of the Vampire • Return to Peyton Place • Revenge of the Nerds
• Return to Macon County • Reuben, Reuben • Revenge of the Ninja
• The Revenge of • Revenge of the Pink
Frankenstein Panther

R

self into outrageous comic entanglements. Also with Catherine Schell, Bert Kwouk, Peter Arne, and Grégoire Aslan. **Director**—Blake Edwards. (PG) *113 minutes*

THE RETURN OF THE VAMPIRE (1943)
★★

Bela Lugosi

Lugosi returns in this spinoff of his previously successful performance as Dracula. One version of this monster would have been enough, and it seems unpatriotic to have Dracula reappear during the London Blitz. Despite these faults, this is an expertly plotted horror film with a fantastic final scene. Lugosi gives an excellent performance. Also with Nina Foch, Frieda Inescort, and Miles Mander. **Director**—Lew Landers. *69 minutes b&w*

RETURN TO MACON COUNTY (1975)
 ★★

Nick Nolte
Don Johnson
Robin Mattson

In this sequel to *Macon County Line*, two young racing-car sports—Nolte and Johnson—head for California in a bright-yellow stock car, bent on becoming drag-racing champs. Along the way they latch on to a young girl—Mattson—who wants to be a movie star. The dull plot leans on the *American Graffiti* and *Bonnie and Clyde* themes, but it's merely another '50s nostalgia piece. Also with Robert Viharo and Eugene Daniels. Written and directed by Richard Compton. (PG) *90 minutes*

RETURN TO PEYTON PLACE (1961)
★

Jeff Chandler
Carol Lynley
Eleanor Parker
Mary Astor

This early 1960s version of a TV soap opera will appeal to the fans of such things. Parker, Astor, and Lynley per-

form competently, but the rest of the cast, including Chandler, Robert Sterling, Luciana Paluzzi, Brett Halsey, and Tuesday Weld, seem to be underachievers in this trite story. The action centers on the fallout after Allison Mackenzie, played by Lynley, writes a book about her notorious hometown and falls in love with her publisher. **Director**—José Ferrer. *122 minutes*

REUBEN, REUBEN (1983)
 ★★

Tom Conti

Conti is believable as a boozing, baggy-pants, Scottish poet who makes a career of seducing middle-aged women of the garden club variety. There are enough witty lines, too, thanks to a screenplay by Julius Epstein (*Casablanca*). But this one-man, one-note satire eventually goes astray when the slothful poet overindulges in self-pity and impregnates a beautiful girl (Kelly McGillis) half his age. **Director**—Robert Ellis Miller. (R) **Academy Award Nominations**—Conti, best actor; Jules J. Epstein, best screenplay adaptation. *100 minutes*

THE REVENGE OF FRANKENSTEIN (1958)
★★

Peter Cushing

In this well-made and well-acted sequel to *The Curse of Frankenstein*, Baron Von Frankenstein makes a new creation with the brain of a homicidal dwarf. Cushing is excellent as Dr. Frankenstein, and he gets able support from Michael Gwynn, Oscar Quitak, Lloyd Pack, Francis Matthews, Lionel Jeffries, John Welsh, and Eunice Gayson. The movie isn't without a message—especially in light of the advances in gene-splicing. **Director**—Terence Fisher. *89 minutes*

REVENGE OF THE NERDS (1984)
 ★★

Robert Carradine
Bernie Casey

The nerds get their day in the sun in

this affable, yet predictable and uninspired adolescent comedy. They are the ungainly, unattractive, but everresourceful, misfit college freshmen. Along with a sorority of sister outcasts, they fight for their dignity and better housing against the bullying jocks and their female counterparts who dominate the school. The appealing young cast often compensates for the crude gags. They turn at least one sequence—the obligatory party scene—into a genuine charmer. **Director**—Jeff Kanew. (R) *87 minutes*

REVENGE OF THE NINJA (1983)
 ★★

Sho Kosugi

Masked warriors get down (according to traditional customs) in Revenge of the Ninja.

A clean-cut Japanese artist-warrior (Kosugi) comes to America where he's soon embroiled in an illegal drug operation and face-to-face with old enemies. Our slightly built hero dispatches an assortment of brutes with kung fu maneuvers and various weapons including swords, daggers, darts, chains, clubs, claws, and axes. Excessive blood and gore are evident. The black belt crowd may get a kick out of this martial arts adventure. Others may merely wince. **Director**—Sam Firstenberg. (R) *90 minutes*

REVENGE OF THE PINK PANTHER (1978)
 ★★★

Peter Sellers
Dyan Cannon

Sellers as the bumbling French Inspector Jacques Clouseau is as durable a
(Continued)

R
- The Revolt of Mamie Stover
- Rhapsody
- Rhapsody in Blue
- Rhinestone
- Rich and Famous
- Richard Pryor Here and Now

Peter Sellers disguised as a herring fisherman in Revenge of the Pink Panther.

(Continued)

laugh-maker as W. C. Fields and Jack Benny. In this fifth *Pink Panther* film, the "world's greatest detective" breaks up the French Connection drug ring while the audience breaks up with laughter. Sellers is helped by Cannon, who's hilarious as the discarded mistress of the drug ring's boss. Robert Walker plays the drug kingpin. The film should tickle you pink. **Director**—Blake Edwards. (PG)   *99 minutes*

THE REVOLT OF MAMIE STOVER (1956)

★

Jane Russell

Russell plays a woman who's forced to leave town and goes to Hawaii. As a saloon singer in the islands during World War II, she becomes wealthy. Jane does well in several enjoyable scenes, but can't overcome the weak plot, based on William Bradford Huie's novel. She's at her best when she sings "Keep Your Eyes on the Hands." Russell is joined by Agnes Moorehead and Richard Egan. **Director**—Raoul Walsh.   *93 minutes*

RHAPSODY (1954)
★

Elizabeth Taylor
Vittorio Gassman
John Ericson

Taylor enlivens this romantic film about a three-cornered love story in which she can't decide between Gassman, a violinist, and Ericson, a pianist. Taylor's wardrobe resembles a fashion show for stylish 1954 clothing.

Vittorio Gassman attempts to put Elizabeth Taylor into a Rhapsody.

The musical interludes are pleasing, but the movie still fails. Louis Calhern, Michael Chekhov, Barbara Bates, Celia Lovsky, and Richard Hageman also appear in supporting roles. **Director**—Charles Vidor.   *116 minutes*

RHAPSODY IN BLUE (1945)

★★★

Robert Alda
Joan Leslie

Alexis Smith and Robert Alda in Rhapsody in Blue, *a biography of George Gershwin.*

This biography of George Gershwin, starring Alda and Leslie, captures the great composer's enthusiasm for his work and reveals some of the conflicts he faced, but as a biography it's thin and shallow. Fortunately, the movie is sprinkled with Gershwin's wonderful music. The cast also includes Alexis Smith, Charles Coburn, Julie Bishop, Albert Bassermann, Oscar Levant, Herbert Rudley, Al Jolson, Paul Whiteman, and Hazel Scott. **Director**—Irving Rapper.   *139 minutes b&w*

RHINESTONE (1984)

★

Sylvester Stallone
Dolly Parton

Corny, trumped-up comedy with Stallone as a gruff New York cab driver trying to be a country singer under the guidance of Parton. Stallone merely looks foolish attempting the down-home songs. Only Dolly manages a few good scenes with her perky charm and genuine singing ability. Dolly bets she can turn Sly into a successful rhinestone cowboy. Whatever the outcome, the audience loses. **Director**—Bob Clark. (PG)   *111 minutes*

RICH AND FAMOUS (1981)

★

Jacqueline Bisset
Candice Bergen

Jacqueline Bisset and Candice Bergen wish they were Rich and Famous.

Bisset and Bergen play friends from their Smith College days, who carry on a love-hate relationship over the years as they pursue separate literary careers. Veteran Director George Cukor fashioned this so-called woman's film, which looks slick enough, but gradually deteriorates into a hysterical soap opera. Gerald Ayres's rather irritating screenplay is loosely based on the 1943 film *Old Acquaintance*, which starred Bette Davis and Miriam Hopkins. (R)   *117 minutes*

RICHARD PRYOR HERE AND NOW (1983)

★★★

Richard Pryor

Richard Pryor delivers his latest stand-up routines on sex, drugs, and racism in Richard Pryor Here and Now.

Pryor presents a cavalcade of sharp, satirical observations in his relentlessly shocking and street-wise style. His usual raucous monologue, peppered with expletives, embraces a wide range of subjects, from sex, drugs, racism, poverty, and politics, back to sex and drugs. Pryor's energetic and unique physical humor is often better than his punchlines. This third Pryor concert movie was filmed in New Orleans' French Quarter, with Pryor directing himself. (R)

94 minutes

RICHARD PRYOR LIVE ON THE SUNSET STRIP (1982)
 ★★

Richard Pryor

The energetic comedian rambles on for some 80 minutes in this outrageous monologue. Lacing his speech heavily with obscenities, he lashes out at a number of targets. Mostly, however, the subject is sex. Pryor, filmed in performance at the Hollywood Palladium, is a gifted performer, and there are splendid moments of wit and hilarity. But the patter goes on too long, and the viewer runs out of endurance well before Pryor runs out of words. **Director**—Joe Layton. (R)   *82 minutes*

RICHARD III (1956)
★★★★

Laurence Olivier

Olivier, one of the greatest actors of the century, turns in a magnificent performance as both actor and director in this Shakespeare play about Richard Crookback, the evil king. The world's greatest playwright is difficult to transform to the screen, but Olivier has made the adaptation brilliantly in this story of Richard's seizure of the throne, his devious dealings in court, and his conquests on the battlefield. Superb performances are also delivered by Claire Bloom, Ralph Richardson, Cedric Hardwicke, John Gielgud, and Clive Morton. **Academy Award Nomination**—Olivier, best actor.

161 minutes

RICH KIDS (1979)
★★★

Trini Alvarado
Jeremy Levy

This is a warm, witty, and touching comedy about a disturbing and often sad situation—the effect of divorce on children. Alvarado and Levy are remarkable as bright New York adolescents who form a puppy-love relationship as shelter from their parents' messed-up marriages. Robert M. Young directs with style from an appealing script by Judith Ross. The adult roles are handled by rather unfamiliar players, who all perform splendidly. Also with John Lithgow, Kathryn Walker, and Terry Kiser. (PG)

101 minutes

THE RIDDLE OF THE SANDS (1984)
 ★★

Michael York

A stiff-upper-lip spy adventure about two stuffy British men (York and Simon MacCorkindale) who foil a German scheme to invade England. This rather drab melodrama, set at the turn of the century, has nothing to do with camel caravans or desert outposts.

(Continued)

INGRID BERGMAN

Known for her beauty, charm, energy, and superb acting ability, Ingrid Bergman was a popular screen actress and leading lady in American and Swedish films. Born in 1915 in Stockholm, Sweden, she was orphaned at an early age and was reared by relatives. After graduation from high school, she studied at the Royal Dramatic Theater School in Stockholm and became a major Swedish screen star by the mid '30s.

Producer David O. Selznick brought her to Hollywood in 1939 to star in an American version of Intermezzo, *and she was well on her way to becoming a popular film and stage actress in America.*

Bergman's career gained impetus with remarkable performances in Casablanca *(1943),* For Whom the Bell Tolls *(1943),* Gaslight *(1944),* Notorious *(1946), and* Joan of Arc *(1948). She received an Oscar as best actress for* Gaslight. *In 1949, her popularity nose-dived after she left her dentist husband for director Roberto Rossellini. Public indignation over the affair prevented her appearance in American films for some seven years, but all was forgiven when she starred in* Anastasia, *filmed in London in 1956, for which she won another Oscar as best actress.*

Her marriage to Rossellini was dissolved in 1958, and she married Swedish producer Lars Schmidt and moved to Europe. From time to time, she continued to make films, and she won an Oscar as best supporting actress for her role in Murder on the Orient Express *(1974).*

Some of Bergman's other major films include Spellbound *(1945),* Saratoga Trunk *(1945),* The Bells of St. Mary's *(1945),* Indiscreet *(1958),* Cactus Flower *(1969), A* Matter of Time *(1976), and* Autumn Sonata *(1978). Ingrid Bergman died in 1981.*

R
- Ride a Wild Pony
- Ride the High Country
- Ride, Vaquero
- Riffraff
- The Right Stuff
- Rio Bravo
- Rio Grande
- Rio Lobo

(Continued)

The predictable action unfolds unconvincingly, taking place mostly at sea. Settings tend to be lavish, and the main riddle here is why so much money and effort were expended to prop up a weak script. **Director**—Tony Maylam. (No MPAA rating) *98 minutes*

RIDE A WILD PONY
(1976)
★★

**Robert Bettles
Eva Griffith**

A poor boy and a wealthy handicapped girl struggle over the ownership of a pony in this middling melodrama from the Walt Disney organization. Youngsters Bettles and Griffith perform adequately in the pre-World War II Australian setting, but a sluggish plot fails to develop the needed suspense. Also with Michael Craig, John Meillon, and Graham Rouse. **Director**—Don Chaffey. (G) *91 minutes*

RIDE THE HIGH COUNTRY
(1962)
★★★★

**Joel McCrea
Randolph Scott**

Sam Peckinpah artfully directed this classic western about two aging lawmen—Scott and McCrea—who are reunited after 20 years to deliver a gold shipment but meet trouble along the way. Peckinpah, who has since become obsessed with violence, directed this fine yarn with sensitivity and subtlety. Scott and McCrea are excellent in their last performances as western heroes. The movie was shot on location at the beautiful Inyo National Forest in California. Also with Edgar Buchanan, Mariette Hartley, James Drury, and Warren Oates.
94 minutes

RIDE, VAQUERO (1953)
★★

**Robert Taylor
Ava Gardner**

Sultry Gardner throws off enough sparks to make this western tale

mildly interesting. The story, set on the Mexican border after the Civil War, is about a beautiful woman who causes the downfall of notorious outlaws. Also with Anthony Quinn and Howard Keel. **Director**—John Farrow. *90 minutes*

RIFFRAFF (1947)
★★★

Pat O'Brien

O'Brien defeats the bad guys in this well-done, fast-paced melodrama about shady characters attempting to take over oil fields in Panama. Besides some excellent scenes, there are above-average performances by O'Brien, Walter Slezak, Anne Jeffreys, Jason Robards, Percy Kilbride, and Jerome Cowan. **Director**—Ted Tetzlaff.
80 minutes b&w

THE RIGHT STUFF (1983)
 ★★★

**Sam Shepard
Ed Harris
Scott Glenn**

Director-writer Philip Kaufman's overblown, overlong, and overstuffed, yet highly entertaining and exhilarating docu-drama about the evolvement of America's space program. Based on Tom Wolfe's book, the high-flying film offers an intimate look at the much publicized astronauts and the less-known test pilots who orbited the earth and broke the sound barrier. Most prominently portrayed are Chuck Yeager (Shepard), Alan Shepard (Glenn) and John Glenn (Harris), with Shepard turning in his best performance ever. (PG) **Academy Award Nominations**—best picture; Shepard, best supporting actor; Caleb Deschanel, best cinematography.
192 minutes

RIO BRAVO (1959)
 ★★★

**John Wayne
Dean Martin
Ricky Nelson**

Famed director Howard Hawks is in top form for this story about a sheriff

In Rio Bravo, John Wayne is a lawman trying to keep a killer in jail.

trying to prevent the bad guys from helping a killer escape the town jail. Hawks has assembled a fine cast that includes Wayne, as the sheriff, Martin, as the town drunk, and Nelson, as the young cowhand ready to prove his manhood. Angie Dickinson is the love interest. Although the movie is long and, at first, seems to inch along, it's worthwhile to hang in there. Also with Walter Brennan, Ward Bond, Claude Akins, and Bob Steele.
141 minutes

RIO GRANDE (1950)
 ★★★

**John Wayne
Maureen O'Hara**

Wayne is excellent as a tough cavalry commander on the Mexican border in the 1880s, conducting a vain campaign against Indians on the warpath. John Ford's classic directorial touch is aided by beautiful scenery, some good action scenes, and lots of human interest. The film is helped by the fine cast, which also includes Ben Johnson, Harry Carey, Jr., Chill Wills, J. Carrol Naish, and Victor McLaglen.
105 minutes b&w

RIO LOBO (1970)
 ★

**John Wayne
Jennifer O'Neill**

The usually surefire western guaran-

- Risky Business
- The Ritz
- The River
- The River Niger
- River of No Return
- The River's Edge
- Road Games

R

tee of Wayne and director Howard Hawks falls short in this rambling Civil War-era story. Wayne plays a Union colonel who recovers a gold shipment after it's stolen. The train robbery scenes at the beginning of the film are exciting, but after that the movie bogs down and becomes a slow-moving bore. O'Neill is beautiful, but a below-par actress here. The performances of Jorge Rivero, Jack Elam, and Chris Mitchum are average at best. (G)   *114 minutes*

RISKY BUSINESS (1983)

★★

**Tom Cruise
Rebecca DeMornay**

Young hookers with high school pimp Tom Cruise in Risky Business.

A muddled social satire about an upper-middle-class youth played by Cruise who turns his swank, suburban home into a temporary brothel while his parents are on vacation. Debuting director-writer Paul Brickman manages some insights into youthful rebellion. But this film is far from *The Graduate*. There are too many missed opportunities, too many events that don't ring true, and the whole premise is more than a little distasteful. Also with Curtis Armstrong. (R)
98 minutes

THE RITZ (1976)

★★★

**Jack Weston
Rita Moreno**

Moreno steals the show in this rip-roaring film version of the brassy Broadway comedy about high jinks in a homosexual bathhouse. She was in

Jerry Stiller, Rita Moreno, and Jack Weston are among the stars in The Ritz.

the stage production, and she delivers the same energetic and madcap portrayal of Googie Gomez the fiery Puerto Rican singer yearning for discovery by a gay Broadway producer. Weston plays a man fleeing from his brother-in-law. Richard Lester's direction is uneven and jumpy, but the fun and hilarity burst forth just the same. Also with Jerry Stiller, Kaye Ballard, Bessie Love, Treat Williams, and George Couloris. (R)   *91 minutes*

THE RIVER (1984)

★★

**Mel Gibson
Sissy Spacek
Scott Glenn**

Mel Gibson and Sissy Spacek are a farm couple in Tennessee, stalwartly struggling with crops, bank debts, and especially the menacing nearby river. Their lives and hardships are portrayed realistically. Yet the sentimental, uneven plot doesn't develop so much as accumulate hard luck experiences. The actors turn in good performances, with Spacek faring especially well. Mark Rydell's directing is strenuous and too slick. (PG–13)
122 minutes

THE RIVER NIGER (1976)

★★

**James Earl Jones
Cicely Tyson**

The moving, award-winning Broadway play by Joseph A. Walker loses its punch on the screen. Much of the fault is uneven direction by Krishna Shah

and a lot of unnecessary dialogue. The story is about a black family's struggle to survive in contemporary America. Jones stars as a house painter who writes poetry. Also with Glynn Turman, Lou Gossett, Jr., and Roger E. Mosley. (R)   *105 minutes*

RIVER OF NO RETURN (1954)

★★

**Robert Mitchum
Marilyn Monroe**

The chemistry of Monroe and Mitchum under the direction of Otto Preminger and with some excellent location photography is stronger than the weak plot in which these two actors must function. Monroe, a saloon singer, and Mitchum, a widower, search for the gambler who deserted her along with Mitchum's 10-year-old son. The action takes place during the California gold rush. Tommy Rettig, Rory Calhoun, and Murvyn Vye also star.   *91 minutes*

THE RIVER'S EDGE (1956)

★★★

**Ray Milland
Anthony Quinn
Deborah Paget**

Milland delivers an excellent portrayal as a fugitive bank robber who menaces his old girl friend, Paget, and threatens her husband, Quinn, in his attempt to escape over the mountains into Mexico with his fortune. Also with Byron Foulger. **Director—Allan Dwan.**   *87 minutes*

ROAD GAMES (1981)

★★★

**Stacy Keach
Jamie Lee Curtis**

Keach plays a poetry-quoting truck driver in this Australian road-chase thriller. The cops suspect Keach of being a latter-day Jack the Ripper, so he must clear himself by nabbing the real killer. He encounters a number of strange characters, among them Curtis as a damsel-in-distress whom he strives to rescue. The film is effectively
(Continued)

 Movie is available in Beta and VHS videotape

331

R

- Roadie
- Road to Morocco
- Road to Singapore
- Road to Zanzibar
- The Road Warrior
- The Roaring Twenties
- The Robe

(Continued)
crafted somewhat in the Hitchcock style. **Director**—Richard Franklin. (PG) *100 minutes*

ROADIE (1980)

★★★

Meat Loaf

An energetic, madcap parody of the rock 'n' roll scene, which stars popular rock star Meat Loaf in an effective nonsinging role. The screwball story features a number of hilarious slapstick escapades, and it zips along like a comic strip full of inventive chaos. There's a lot of nonstop, earsplitting rock music from a half-dozen performers, including Blondie and Alice Cooper. Also with Art Carney, Hank Williams, Jr., and Roy Orbison. **Director**—Alan Rudolph. (PG)

106 minutes

ROAD TO MOROCCO (1942)

★★★

Bob Hope
Bing Crosby
Dorothy Lamour

Bing gets ready to sock it to Bob in Road to Morocco, *one of their great comedies.*

One of the best of the Hope and Crosby Road films. In this one, Bing sells Bob into slavery in exotic Morocco. Lamour is present for romantic high jinks, and Monte Blue, Yvonne de Carlo, Anthony Quinn, and Dona Drake join in the silliness. A

few good songs, including "Moonlight Becomes You," and a talking camel add to the entertainment value of this fun-filled movie. **Director**—David Butler. **Academy Award Nomination**—Frank Butler and Don Hartman, writing (original screenplay).

83 minutes b&w

ROAD TO SINGAPORE (1940)

★★★

Bob Hope
Bing Crosby
Dorothy Lamour

Hope and Crosby are rich playboys who swear off women, but then they meet a Singapore maiden, played by Lamour, and quarrel over her. As long as you don't take the flimsy plot too seriously, this first of the duo's *Road* films is enjoyable. Also with Charles Coburn, Judith Barrett, Anthony Quinn, and Jerry Colonna. **Director**—Victor Schertzinger. *84 minutes b&w*

ROAD TO ZANZIBAR (1941)

★★★

Bob Hope
Bing Crosby
Dorothy Lamour

Anything goes in this satire of jungle pictures. Hope and Crosby play carnival hustlers on a safari in Africa. They are joined again by Lamour, and the trio searches for a diamond mine. The cast also includes Una Merkel, Eric Blore, Luis Alberni, and Douglass Dumbrille. **Director**—Victor Schertzinger. *92 minutes b&w*

THE ROAD WARRIOR (1982)

 ★★★★

Mel Gibson

Essentially, this Australian feature is B movie, comic book fare, but it is accomplished with exceptional imagination and slam-bang energy. In this post-World War III story, a handful of scrubby survivors fight over dwindling gasoline supplies. Gibson stars as a loner who helps some good guys

make a mad dash for safety. The high-powered climax is carried off with such dazzling skill that it outshines some of the key action scenes in *Raiders of the Lost Ark*. **Director**—George Miller. *94 minutes*

THE ROARING TWENTIES (1939)

 ★★★★

James Cagney
Humphrey Bogart

James Cagney plays an ambitious hoodlum in The Roaring Twenties.

After World War I, Army pals Cagney, Bogart, and Jeffrey Lynn run into each other again. But now, Cagney is a gangster. This film version of the Mark Hellinger story, about a World War I veteran who becomes involved in crime during Prohibition, has a familiar plot, but Cagney is fantastic as the New York bootlegger who finds success in the underworld before dying in a gang war. Also with Priscilla Lane, Gladys George, and Frank McHugh. **Director**—Raoul Walsh.

106 minutes b&w

THE ROBE (1953)

 ★★★

Richard Burton
Jean Simmons
Michael Rennie
Victor Mature

This Bible epic features Burton as Gallio, a Roman tribune put in charge of the execution of Jesus Christ. Burton later converts to Christianity when he

332

• Roberta
• Robin and Marian
• Robin and the Seven Hoods

• Rock 'n' Roll High School
• Rocky
• Rocky II

R

dons Christ's robe. Burton is joined by a large cast, which also includes Richard Boone, Dawn Addams, and Dean Jagger. The movie, the first film made in the Cinemascope process, is impressively produced, but the plot is mediocre. **Director**—Henry Koster. **Academy Award Nominations**—best picture; Burton, best actor; Leon Shamroy, cinematography (color).

135 minutes

ROBERTA (1935)
★★★

**Irene Dunne
Randolph Scott
Fred Astaire
Ginger Rogers**

Astaire and Rogers were still getting second billing at this point in their meteoric career, but they're the major reason for seeing the film. An All-American grid star travels to Paris to contend with the very chic shop he's inherited from his late aunt. There's entertainment throughout, but when the hoofers go at it there are fireworks. Top Jerome Kern songs include "Smoke Gets in Your Eyes," "Lovely To Look At," and "I Won't Dance." **Director**—William A. Seiter.

105 minutes b&w

ROBIN AND MARIAN (1976)

★★

**Sean Connery
Audrey Hepburn
Robert Shaw**

The legend of Robin Hood is revised in this film. A middle-aged and battle-scarred Robin, played by Connery, returns to Sherwood Forest after fighting in the Crusades for 20 years. He looks up his old girl friend, Maid Marian, played by Hepburn, now an abbess. The Sheriff of Nottingham—Shaw—still controls the neighborhood. Robin takes him on, but appears to be suffering from a bad back and tired blood. The acting and photography are impressive, but screenwriter James Goldman has turned the colorful myth of Robin Hood and his merry men into a state of confusion. Also with Richard Harris, Nicol Williamson, and Ian Holm. **Director**—Richard Lester. (PG) *112 minutes*

ROBIN AND THE SEVEN HOODS (1964)
★★★

**Frank Sinatra
Dean Martin
Bing Crosby
Sammy Davis, Jr.
Peter Falk**

Sinatra, Martin, Crosby, Davis, and Falk star in this musical spoof set during Prohibition in Chicago. Sinatra and his friends—known as the Rat Pack by gossip columnists—seem to enjoy themselves and are well suited to their roles of small-time hoodlums who work as Chicago-style Robin Hoods; they steal from the rich and give to the poor. "My Kind of Town" and "Style" highlight the music. The cast also includes Barbara Rush, Edward G. Robinson, Victor Buono, Jack La Rue, and Hans Conreid. **Director**—Gordon Douglas. *123 minutes*

ROCK 'N' ROLL HIGH SCHOOL (1979)

★★

**P. J. Soles
Vincent Van Patten
Clint Howard**

Silliness and exuberance are the mainstays of this youth fantasy, which seems to be inspired by such movies as *Grease* and *Animal House*. The kids engage in assorted escapades and provoke the displeasure of the school's stern principal; all this is carried out against a booming sound track of rock music. The young, unknown players go through their paces with plenty of gusto and minimal professional style. Also with The Ramones, Paul Bartel, and Alix Elias. **Director**—Allan Arkush. (PG) *93 minutes*

ROCKY (1976)

★★★★

**Sylvester Stallone
Talia Shire**

This gritty Cinderella story of a luckless Philadelphia boxer who gets a chance at the world heavyweight championship is uplifting to the human spirit. Stallone, who wrote the

Sylvester Stallone trains for his big chance in Rocky.

film script, plays the prizefighter with feeling and power. Nice work, too, from the rest of the cast, especially Shire as the boxer's shy girl friend. The schmaltzy plot owes much to *Marty* and *On the Waterfront*, yet the cliché takes on new life with energy and atmosphere. Also with Burt Young, Carl Weathers, Burgess Meredith, and Thayer David. Crisply directed by John G. Avildsen. (PG) **Academy Awards**—best picture; Avildsen, best director. **Nominations**—Stallone, best actor; Shire, best actress; Meredith, Young, best supporting actor; Stallone, best original screenplay.

119 minutes

ROCKY II (1979)

★★★★

**Sylvester Stallone
Talia Shire**

Sequels seldom live up to the original, but this second chapter in the life of underdog boxer Rocky Balboa is an exception, indeed. The plot drags in spots, but that fantastic uplifting spirit is there again as Rocky, played by Stallone, prepares for the big bout with Apollo Creed, played by Carl Weathers. The same top-notch supporting cast is back in fine form. It all leads to an exciting and realistic fight finale that will have you cheering with gusto. Also with Burgess Meredith and Burt Young. **Director**—Stallone. (PG) *119 minutes*

R
- Rocky III
- Rogues of Sherwood Forest
- Rollerball
- Rollercoaster
- Rolling Thunder
- Rollover
- Romancing the Stone

ROCKY III (1982)

★★★★

**Sylvester Stallone
Carl Weathers
Mr. T**

Sylvester Stallone lands a left on the jaw of Mr. T in Rocky III.

This third chapter about the loveable boxer still packs plenty of punch, and the humor is still endearing. Writer-director-star Stallone continues the schmaltzy formula plot with Rocky struggling hard to keep his title when faced by a snarling challenger. This time, former opponent Weathers has an important role as the champ's trainer and inspiration. And there's that fantastic fight scene at the end. The Italian Stallion is still someone to cheer about. (PG)   *99 minutes*

ROGUES OF SHERWOOD FOREST (1950)
★★

John Derek

This time, the son of Robin Hood, played by Derek, helps the barons force the signing of the Magna Carta. The film's theme is tiresome and familiar, but the production is well done, and the sets and costumes are splendid. The competent cast also includes Diana Lynn, George Macready, Alan Hale, and Billy House. **Director—** Gordon Douglas.   *80 minutes*

ROLLERBALL (1975)

(no stars)

James Caan

This sci-fi film, based on William Har-

rison's story, concerns a new sport that combines hockey, Roller Derby, motorcycle racing, and gladiatorial combat. Supposedly, it works off aggressions and keeps billions of people glued to their TV sets because other forms of violence have been outlawed. The planet has come under the control of the "major corporate conglomerates," but one man—Caan—attempts to regain individual freedom in this brave new world. The script drags the film down with an air of imitation Stanley Kubrick. Also with John Houseman, Ralph Richardson, Maud Adams, and Moses Gunn. **Director—** Norman Jewison. (R)   *128 minutes*

ROLLERCOASTER (1977)

★★★

**George Segal
Richard Widmark
Timothy Bottoms**

Thrill seekers ride the Rebel Yell at King's Dominion in Rollercoaster.

There's plenty of suspense, ample excitement, and just the right touch of humor in this straightforward drama. It's about a clever mad bomber, played by Bottoms, who sabotages rollercoasters to blackmail amusement park owners. Segal is amusing and relaxed as a safety inspector who pursues the wily terrorist from coast to coast. The plot is uncluttered, and the violence isn't excessive. Widmark, Bottoms, and Henry Fonda contribute their talents. Also with Harry Guardino and Susan Strasberg. **Director—**James Goldstone. (PG)   *119 minutes*

ROLLING THUNDER (1977)

★★★

William Devane

A finely crafted film about a Vietnam veteran, played by Devane, who hunts down the killers of his wife and son. Scriptwriter Paul Schrader, who wrote *Taxi Driver*, uses his familiar explosive and complicated character again. The acting is excellent, and there's a convincing portrayal of small-town middle America. There's a considerable amount of blood and gore, which may be too heavy for some. Also with Tommy Lee Jones, Linda Haynes, James Best, and Dabney Coleman. **Director—**John Flynn. (R)

99 minutes

ROLLOVER (1981)

★★

**Jane Fonda
Kris Kristofferson**

Fonda and Kristofferson star in this meandering message movie about the vulnerability of the world monetary system. The romantic thriller, set against the backdrop of banking and multinational corporations, is overburdened with technical economic jargon. Fonda, dressed to the nines, plays a widow who takes over a petrochemical company after her husband's murder and tries to save the business from financial ruin. The film and Fonda look elegant, but the bottom line is confusion. Also stars Hume Cronyn, Josef Sommer, and Bob Gunton. **Director—**Alan J. Pakula. (R)

118 minutes

ROMANCING THE STONE (1984)
★★★★

**Kathleen Turner
Michael Douglas**

Slam-bang romantic adventure with all sorts of goodies: a steamy love affair, cliff-hanging suspense, twinkling humor, colorful scoundrels, and a mad dash for buried treasure. Turner is on target as a lonely pulp-fiction writer suddenly thrust into her own hair-raising escapade when her sister is kidnapped in Columbia. In the jungle, she teams up with an American

- Roman Holiday
- Romanoff and Juliet
- Romantic Comedy
- The Romantic Englishwoman
- Romeo and Juliet
- Room at the Top

R

wildlife enterpreneur, played by Douglas, for some rousing excitement. **Director**—Robert Zemeckis. (PG)
101 minutes

ROMAN HOLIDAY (1953)
★★★★

Gregory Peck
Audrey Hepburn

Peck and Hepburn are delightful in this story of a lonely princess who runs away from her official duties, meets a newspaperman, and falls in love with him. Hepburn is the princess, and Peck is the reporter. This captivating comedy—filmed in Rome—has enough drama under director William Wyler's skillful hand to make it a memorable film from start to finish. It also stars Eddie Albert, Hartley Power, and Harcourt Williams. **Academy Awards**—Hepburn, best actress; Ian McLellan Hunter, writing (motion picture story). **Nominations**—best picture; Wyler, best director; Albert, best supporting actor; Hunter and John Dighton, writing (screenplay); Frank Planer and Henry Alekan, cinematography (black and white).
118 minutes b&w

ROMANOFF AND JULIET (1961)
★★★

Peter Ustinov
Sandra Dee
John Gavin

Ustinov is a triple-threat—he wrote, directed, and acted—in this satire, set in Concordia, a mythical land, where the daughter of the U.S. ambassador falls in love with the Russian ambassador's son. Dee and Gavin are the loving couple. Some of the comic-strip action falls flat, and at times, it seems Ustinov took too much upon himself; but his wit and the inspired premise make this movie worthwhile. Ustinov gets solid supporting help from Dee, Gavin, Akim Tamiroff, Tamara Shayne, and Peter Jones. *103 minutes*

ROMANTIC COMEDY (1983)
★★

Dudley Moore
Mary Steenburgen

Mary Steenburgen and Dudley Moore laugh their way into a relationship in Romantic Comedy.

Moore and Steenburgen, highly respected for their acting in previous romantic comedies, can't save this charmless production. They star as a successful playwriting team whose long-standing collaboration keeps threatening to blossom into a hot romance. Naturally, assorted boring problems continually interfere. Moore and Steenburgen try hard, but Bernard Slade's adaptation of his own play doesn't spark any fireworks. Director Arthur Hiller can do better than this. With Ron Leibman and Frances Sternhagen. (PG) *103 minutes*

THE ROMANTIC ENGLISHWOMAN (1975)
★★

Glenda Jackson
Michael Caine

Joseph Losey directed this sophisticated yet complicated love story about a successful paperback novelist whose money and intense love fail to fulfill his wife, who runs away with a gigolo poet. Jackson plays the would-be liberated housewife; Caine is her novelist-husband. There's lavish scenery and some witty dialogue, but the confusing love-triangle plot and poor casting override the assets. Also with Helmut Berger, Marcus Richardson, and Kate Nelligan. (R) *115 minutes*

ROMEO AND JULIET (1968)
★★★

Leonard Whiting
Olivia Hussey

Director Franco Zeffirelli has a flair for bringing dazzling élan to classic theater and opera pieces, without unduly

Milo O'Shea is a monk quite fond of young Romeo, Leonard Whiting, in Romeo and Juliet.

altering the original text. For this lush, breathlessly paced and acted production, he cast two youngsters—Whiting and Hussey—for the lead roles, and they do a very fine job as Shakespeare's star-crossed lovers of Verona. They look sensational (as does the entire production), and they're often quite moving. The film has an exciting, contemporary feel to it, with an outstanding score by Nino Rota. Also with Michael York, Milo O'Shea, John McEnery, and Robert Stephens. (PG) **Academy Award**—Pasquale De Santis, best cinematography. **Nominations**—best picture; Zeffirelli, best director. *152 minutes*

ROOM AT THE TOP (1959)
★★★★

Laurence Harvey
Simone Signoret

(Continued)

Laurence Harvey jilts his real love to marry the boss's daughter in Room at the Top.

(Continued)

Despite Harvey's wooden performance, this drama is a vivid and realistic look at British industrial life. He plays an egotistical, selfish clerk in a factory who jilts the woman who loves him to marry the daughter of the factory owner. Signoret plays Harvey's jilted mistress. Heather Sears, Donald Wolfit, Raymond Huntley, Donald Houston, Mary Peach, and Hermione Baddeley also star in this skillful screen adaptation of John Braine's novel. **Director**—Jack Clayton. **Academy Awards**—Signoret, best actress; Neil Paterson, best screenplay (based on material from another medium). **Nominations**—best picture; Clayton, best director; Harvey, best actor; Baddeley, best supporting actress.

117 minutes b&w

ROOSTER COGBURN (1975)
 ★★

John Wayne
Katharine Hepburn

Wayne—a one-eyed, booze-guzzling U.S. marshal—is on the trail of outlaws. Hepburn—the pastor's daughter—is at his side. The movie is a patchwork affair taken from *True Grit* and *The African Queen*. Watching such filmdom institutions as Wayne and Hepburn acting together may be entertaining for some, but the movie itself is nothing to get excited about. Also with Anthony Zerbe, Richard Jordan, John McIntyre, and Strother Martin. **Director**—Stuart Millar. (PG)
107 minutes

Katharine Hepburn and John Wayne team up to make the golden age of Hollywood seem like a long time ago in Rooster Cogburn.

ROPE (1948)
 ★★★

James Stewart

Director Alfred Hitchcock is less than masterful in this film about two young men who kill a college friend as part of a thrill-seeking experiment. As the movie unfolds, the men ghoulishly reveal clues to the crime. The below-par effort was obviously inspired by the Loeb-Leopold murder case. It was also Hitchcock's first color film, and he unsuccessfully experimented with 10-minute takes in an effort to perfect the flow of the movie. Although he didn't perfect anything, the movie has its virtues. The performances of Stewart, John Dall, Farley Granger, Cedric Hardwicke, Joan Chandler, and Douglas Dick are above average.

80 minutes

THE ROSE (1979)
 ★★

Bette Midler
Alan Bates
Frederic Forrest

Midler, in her screen debut, plays a rock 'n' roll queen who self-destructs on alcohol, drugs, and the stresses of stardom. Forrest is good as the lover who wants her to quit. The screenplay is obviously based on the career of the late Janis Joplin. The film's hysterical, hair-pulling pitch helps compensate for a shallow script—everything to be said comes in the first 10 minutes. If

Bette Midler is The Rose, *a rock star.*

anything saves the film, it's Bette belting out the songs with all-out gusto. Also with Harry Dean Stanton, Barry Primus, and David Keith. **Director**—Mark Rydell. (R) **Academy Award Nominations**—Midler, best actress; Forrest, best supporting actor.

125 minutes

ROSELAND (1977)
 ★★

Lou Jacobi
Teresa Wright

This study of loneliness, set in New York City's famous Roseland dance hall, is divided into three interlocking vignettes and has a made-for-TV quality. There's pathos here, but it barely transcends the soft script. First-rate performances carry the film—especially a touching segment with Jacobi and Wright. Also with Christopher Walken, Helen Gallagher, Geraldine Chaplin, and Lilia Skala. **Director**—James Ivory. (No MPAA rating)

103 minutes

ROSEMARY'S BABY (1968)
 ★★★★

Mia Farrow
John Cassavetes

An excellent cast combined with the provocative idea of witchcraft yields a top-notch thriller under director Roman Polanski's deft handling. Farrow and her overly ambitious husband, played by Cassavetes, naïvely

- The Rose Tattoo
- Rough Cut
- The Rounders
- Royal Flash
- Royal Wedding
- Ruby Gentry

R

Mia Farrow happily applies herself to her weird new house in Rosemary's Baby.

become involved with diabolical neighbors—Ruth Gordon and Sidney Blackmer—resulting in devilish consequences. The top-flight cast also includes Ralph Bellamy, Patsy Kelly, Maurice Evans, Charles Grodin, and Elisha Cook, Jr. Based on the novel by Ira Levin. **Academy Award**—Gordon, best supporting actress. **Nomination**—Polanski, best screenplay (based on material from another medium). *117 minutes*

THE ROSE TATTOO (1955)
★★★★

Anna Magnani
Burt Lancaster

Anna Magnani portrays a troubled widow who finds love again in The Rose Tattoo.

Magnani gives a robust and earthy performance as a troubled widow who finds love again when she meets a rough-and-tumble truck driver, played by Lancaster. At times she seems larger than life and appears to be too powerful for the screen. This movie version of the Tennessee Williams play is ably directed by Daniel Mann and well photographed, with excellent supporting efforts from Virginia Grey, Jo Van Fleet, Ben Cooper, and Marisa Pavan. Williams's productions often have too many eccentrics, but this time there are more real people, and this addition makes it a better film. **Academy Awards**—Magnani, best actress; James Wong Howe, cinematography (black and white). **Nominations**—best picture; Pavan, best supporting actress.
117 minutes b&w

ROUGH CUT (1980)
 ★★

Burt Reynolds
Lesley-Anne Down

Reynolds plays the smooth-talking American jewel thief who stages a diamond heist in Europe and seduces the beautiful woman sent to lure him into the crime. Down plays the alluring woman. Reynolds displays his reliable charm, but he's saddled with a hopeless script and wooden dialogue that merely mark time for most of the film. The story springs to action in the final quarter, but it's too late—interest has flagged by that time. Also with David Niven, Patrick Magee, and Timothy West. **Director**—Don Siegel. (PG) *112 minutes*

THE ROUNDERS (1965)
★★

Henry Fonda
Glenn Ford

Fonda and Ford are congenial modern cowboys in this comedy. The two are foiled by a stubborn horse that refuses to be trained. The horse gives them plenty of trouble and supplies many of the gags. Although the story is insubstantial and never seems to get going, this film, written and directed by Burt Kennedy, is pleasant fare for the entire family. Also with Sue Anne Langdon, Edgar Buchanan, Chill Wills, and Denver Pyle. *85 minutes*

ROYAL FLASH (1975)
★★

Malcolm McDowell

This film about the misadventures of Captain Harry Paget Flashman is a spoof at Victorian England, but it comes off as low-grade slapstick. Leading man McDowell tries hard, but director Richard Lester has exploited this swashbuckling theme before in *The Three Musketeers* and *The Four Musketeers*. The outcome this time is overkill; it's more of a flush. With Alan Bates, Britt Ekland, Oliver Reed, and Florinda Bolkan. (PG) *98 minutes*

ROYAL WEDDING (1951)
 ★★

Fred Astaire
Jane Powell

Astaire's brilliant dancing and Powell's delightful singing overcome a pedestrian plot in which he and Powell—who plays his sister—perform in London at the time of Queen Elizabeth II's marriage to Prince Philip. Alan Jay Lerner, of *My Fair Lady* fame, and Burton Lane wrote the songs. True to form in such films, brother and sister each eventually find true love. Watch for Fred to dance on the ceiling. Sarah Churchill, Peter Lawford, and Keenan Wynn also star. **Director**—Stanley Donen. *93 minutes*

RUBY GENTRY (1952)
★★★

Jennifer Jones
Charlton Heston
Karl Malden

Jones was never better than as the sultry Carolina woman from the wrong side of the tracks. When the blueblood she loves (Heston) won't have her, she marries the town's Croesus (Malden), and avenges herself against those who have spurned her. Passion has seldom been more vividly incarnated on the screen, especially as depicted by director King Vidor. The title song became a popular tune of the era.
82 minutes b&w

R
- Rumble Fish
- Runaway
- The Runner Stumbles
- Running
- Run Silent, Run Deep
- The Russians Are Coming, The Russians Are Coming!

RUMBLE FISH (1983)

★★★

Matt Dillon
Mickey Rourke

One of the finest and most overlooked films in Francis Coppola's brilliant career. He calls it his "art film for kids," but this downbeat, surreal story is probably too wrenching for most kids. Adapted from S. E. Hinton's novel, the plot is pure Greek tragedy concerning the disillusionment of street-punk Dillon and the inevitable fall of the older brother he idolizes (played with grace and feeling by Rourke). Unique, jarring style is in evidence everywhere, from Coppola's dreamlike direction to the percussive sound-track by Police drummer Stewart Copeland. Tom Waits and Diane Lane are superb in their supporting roles. (R)   *94 minutes*

RUNAWAY (1984)

★★

Tom Selleck

Robots with sabotaged innards go on the rampage and kill people. Tom Selleck plays the high-tech police detective who has the task of stopping the mechanical murders. It's a clever idea that unfolds with a noticeable lack of style and energy. Unfortunately, the human characters seem as mechanical as the robots. Gene Simmons (of the pop group Kiss) and Cynthia Rhodes also star. **Director**—Michael Crichton. (PG–13)   *99 minutes*

THE RUNNER STUMBLES (1979)

★★

Dick Van Dyke
Kathleen Quinlan

Director Stanley Kramer, known for tackling touchy subjects, presents this film about a priest's romantic interest in a young vivacious nun. Van Dyke plays the distraught priest with self-consciousness; Quinlan plays the perky nun. But celibacy is perhaps a bit too touchy even for Kramer, who seems overly cautious about treating the issue with depth or passion. The movie merely drifts along, and the story never comes into focus. Also with Maureen Stapleton, Ray Bolger, Tammy Grimes, and Beau Bridges. (PG)   *99 minutes*

RUNNING (1979)

★★

Michael Douglas
Susan Anspach

Douglas plays a chronic loser who seeks redemption by competing for the United States Olympic running team. This is yet another athletic situation film that tries to parallel *Rocky*, but can't match the spirit of the Italian Stallion. Douglas is far above the meager material, which merely runs its course with minimal suspense and drama; Anspach is wasted as Douglas's ex-wife. Also with Larry Dane and Eugene Levy. **Director**—Steven Hilliard Stern. (PG)   *103 minutes*

RUN SILENT, RUN DEEP (1958)

★★★

Clark Gable
Burt Lancaster

Gable, as the commander of a U.S. submarine, and Lancaster, as his lieutenant, provide competent, realistic portrayals in this suspenseful World War II drama. Besides the larger conflict with the Japanese Navy in Tokyo Bay, there's feuding between the two naval officers. There are also excellent sea-fighting sequences—an improvement over most submarine movies. Also with Jack Warden, Brad Dexter, Nick Cravat, Joe Maross, and Don Rickles. **Director**—Robert Wise.

93 minutes b&w

THE RUSSIANS ARE COMING, THE RUSSIANS ARE COMING! (1966)

★★

Carl Reiner
Eva Marie Saint
Alan Arkin

There are enough star performers in this cold-war farce about the forced landing of a Russian submarine off the shore of Nantucket to keep the plot from sinking into oblivion. Arkin, Reiner, and Jonathan Winters provide excellent comic acting, and are helped by the competent performances of Saint, John Philip Law, Paul Ford, Tessie O'Shea, Brian Keith, Theodore Bikel, and Ben Blue. If you don't expect too much and are willing to laugh at the Russians, this is a mildly enjoyable movie. The perceptive viewer will also notice that the movie was not photographed off Nantucket and that the scenes are those of northern California. **Director**—Norman Jewison. **Academy Award Nominations**—best picture; Arkin, best actor; William Rose, best screenplay (based on material from another medium).

126 minutes

Clark Gable and Jack Warden in Run Silent, Run Deep, *a realistic war movie.*

• Ryan's Daughter
• Sabrina
• The Sad Sack
• Safari
• Sahara
• Sailor Beware
• The Sailor Who Fell from Grace with the Sea

R·S

RYAN'S DAUGHTER (1970)
★★★

Sarah Miles
Robert Mitchum
Chris Jones

The beautiful Irish scenery, superbly photographed, makes this simple love story seem more majestic than it really is. The story, about a schoolteacher's wife who falls in love with a British officer in 1916, in Ireland, is too long and fails to attain the greatness sought by director David Lean. His filmmaking technique is excellent, however, and the acting is above average. Miles plays the romantic adulteress, Mitchum is the moody schoolteacher, and Jones plays the soldier. John Mills, Trevor Howard, and Leo McKern also star. (R) **Academy Awards**—Mills, best supporting actor; Freddie Young, cinematography. **Nomination**—Miles, best actress. *206 minutes*

S

SABRINA (1954)
★★★

Humphrey Bogart
William Holden
Audrey Hepburn

Hepburn is exquisitely delightful in this excellent comedy about a chauffeur's daughter. She's romanced by Bogart, who plays a middle-aged tycoon, and by Holden, who's a playboy. There are many enjoyable scenes in this well-staged comedy, although Hepburn, Bogart, and Holden have been shown to better advantage in other films. Also appearing are Joan Vohs and Marcel Dalio. **Director**—Billy Wilder. **Academy Award Nominations** —Wilder, best director; Hepburn, best actress; Wilder, Samuel Taylor, and Ernest Lehman, writing (screenplay); Charles Lang, Jr., cinematography (black and white). *113 minutes b&w*

THE SAD SACK (1957)
★★

Jerry Lewis

The French believe that Lewis is a comic genius; Americans know better—far too often he's just plain silly. In this uneven comic effort, inspired by the George Baker comic strip, Lewis plays a woebegone soldier who gets involved with spies and Arabian intrigues. Aside from Peter Lorre, who appears as an Arab in the latter part of the film, the rest of the cast is either 4F or below average. Also with David Wayne, Phyllis Kirk, and Joe Mantell. **Director**—George Marshall.
98 minutes b&w

SAFARI (1956)
★★

Victor Mature
Janet Leigh

Mature gives an above-average performance in this suspenseful and actionpacked adventure film. He plays the brave white hunter who heads a safari that encounters the vengeful Mau Maus. The savages kill Mature's boss, which works out because Mature has fallen in love with Leigh, the wife of his boss; widows don't spend too much time grieving in such films. Also with Roland Culver, John Justin, Earl Cameron, Liam Redmond, and Orland Martins. **Director**—Terence Young. *91 minutes*

SAHARA (1943)
★★★

Humphrey Bogart

Humphrey Bogart heads an Allied tank unit stranded in the Sahara.

Bogart stars in this action-packed war story, with fine supporting performances by J. Carrol Naish and Rex Ingram. Bogey heads a British-American tank unit stranded in the Sahara Desert; they not only manage to survive, but outwit the Nazis. Other strong characterizations in this realistic drama are provided by Bruce Bennett, Lloyd Bridges, Dan Duryea, and Kurt Kreuger. **Director**—Zoltan Korda. **Academy Award Nominations**—Naish, best supporting actor; Rudolph Maté, cinematography (black and white). *97 minutes b&w*

SAILOR BEWARE (1952)
★★

Dean Martin
Jerry Lewis

Kids will probably find the adventures of Martin and Lewis in the U.S. Navy hilarious; adults will find them less amusing. This is one of the funnier movies the two made before going their separate ways. As unlikely as it sounds, in this film Lewis gets a reputation as a suave man among the ladies. The boxing and Army induction scenes are the highlights in this comedy, which also includes Robert Strauss, Leif Erickson, Marion Marshall, and Corinne Calvet. **Director**—Hal Walker. *103 minutes b&w*

THE SAILOR WHO FELL FROM GRACE WITH THE SEA (1976)
★

Sarah Miles
Kris Kristofferson

Miles and Kristofferson star in this film adaptation of an erotic novel by the Japanese writer Yukio Mishima. The setting is disastrously transplanted from Yokohama to Dartmouth, England, and Mishima's chilling story, which is reminiscent of *Lord of the Flies*, becomes merely grotesque as a movie. It's about a sailor who gives up the sea for domestic tranquility—an affair with a widow—and is gruesomely killed by a band of teenage boys, who determine he has violated the "perfect order of things." Miles is the widow and Kristofferson is the sailor. Also with Jonathan Kahn,

(Continued)

Movie is available in Beta and VHS videotape

S
- St. Ives
- Saint Jack
- Saint Joan
- The St. Valentine's Day Massacre
- Salome
- Same Time, Next Year
- Sam Marlow, Private Eye
- Samson and Delilah

(Continued)

Margo Cunningham, and Earl Rhodes. **Director**—Lewis John Carlino. (R)   *104 minutes*

ST. IVES (1976)
★★★

Charles Bronson

Bronson the unflappable plays an ex-crime reporter who suddenly finds himself involved as a go-between for an eccentric millionaire seeking the return of his stolen and incriminating journals. It's a change of pace for Bronson, who lays low on the violence. This witty and action-filled film manages to entertain despite an excessively complicated plot that finally unravels toward the end. It's reminiscent of those Bogart capers of the '40s and '50s. Also with John Houseman, Jacqueline Bisset, Maximilian Schell, and Elisha Cook, Jr. **Director**—J. Lee Thompson. (PG)   *93 minutes*

SAINT JACK (1979)

★★

Ben Gazzara
Denholm Elliott

Director Peter Bogdanovich's low-key melodrama is set in Singapore in the early '70s. It's rife with atmosphere, but the weak story never develops momentum. Jack Flowers, played by Gazzara, is a pimp with a heart of gold and a sense of honor, who's determined to run the best brothel in town. There are masterful performances by Gazzara and Elliott, who plays a woebegone Englishman; their acting seems to tower over the sparse material. Also with James Villiers and Rodney Bewes. (R)   *112 minutes*

SAINT JOAN (1957)
★★

Jean Seberg

Although novelist Graham Greene wrote the screenplay for this George Bernard Shaw play, most of the high-quality actors are wasted, and the brilliant play is a clunker on the screen. Seberg is especially miscast as the Maid of Orleans. John Gielgud, however, is excellent, and Anton Walbrook, Richard Todd, Harry Andrews, Richard Widmark, and Felix Aylmer are worth watching. **Director**—Otto Preminger.   *110 minutes b&w*

THE ST. VALENTINE'S DAY MASSACRE (1967)
★

Jason Robards, Jr.
George Segal

As gangsters, Robards and Segal fail to measure up to the acting standards of James Cagney and Edward G. Robinson. Robards plays the role of Al Capone. When the famous massacre finally occurs in this uneven story, about Chicago racketeers of the 1920s, only diehard fans of this kind of adventure film will care. The performances of Ralph Meeker, Jean Hale, Bruce Dern, Clint Ritchie, and Reed Hadley help prevent this from being a total disappointment. **Director**—Roger Corman.   *99 minutes*

SALOME (1953)
★

Rita Hayworth

Rita Hayworth dances through her role as Salome.

Even a superior actor like Charles Laughton looks below-average in this tedious biblical drama about a dancer, played by Hayworth, who offers to sacrifice her own life to save John the Baptist. Others who get mangled in the unwieldly script include Stewart Granger, Judith Anderson, Cedric Hardwicke, Basil Sydney, Arnold Moss, and Rex Reason. Even the dance of the seven veils is scant justification for viewing this movie. **Director**—William Dieterle.   *103 minutes*

SAME TIME, NEXT YEAR (1978)

★★

Ellen Burstyn
Alan Alda

This movie version of Bernard Slade's two-character Broadway hit looks somewhat stagebound, but this is a minor drawback—the warmth, humor, and appeal of the original play remain intact on the screen. Burstyn—repeating her stage role—and Alda give engaging performances as adulterers who meet for one weekend a year for 26 years. The finely crafted screenplay is rich with touching characterizations and intriguing surprises. **Director**—Robert Mulligan. (PG) **Academy Award Nominations**—Burstyn, best actress; Slade, best screenplay adaptation.   *117 minutes*

SAM MARLOW, PRIVATE EYE (1980)
★★

Robert Sacchi

A mystery comedy spoofing Humphrey Bogart and private-eye films of the '40s. Sacchi plays a man who undergoes plastic surgery so he resembles Bogart. He then becomes involved in a caper on the order of *The Maltese Falcon*. Sacchi does a convincing Bogey imitation, and there's a delightful takeoff by Misty Rowe as the dumb blonde secretary. But the film has problems with a complex script, which turns serious too often to sustain parody. Also with Michelle Phillips and Franco Nero. **Director**—Robert Day. (PG)   *111 minutes*

SAMSON AND DELILAH (1949)

★★

Hedy Lamarr
Victor Mature

• The Sand Pebbles   • The San Francisco Story
• The Sandpiper   • Sante Fe Trail
• Sands of Iwo Jima   • Saratoga Trunk
                      • Sasquatch

S

Fans of epic films produced on a grand scale should enjoy this biblical story about Samson, whose strength is sapped after devious Delilah cuts his curls. Mature and Lamarr play the title roles. Despite the epic theme, grand photography, and spectacular special effects—including the destruction of the temple and Samson's fight with a lion—the movie often drags and, at times, even seems silly. The cast also includes Angela Lansbury, George Sanders, Fay Holden, Russ Tamblyn, and Olive Deering. **Director**—Cecil B. DeMille. **Academy Award Nomination**—George Barnes, cinematography (color). *128 minutes*

THE SAND PEBBLES (1966)

★★★★

Steve McQueen
Richard Crenna

McQueen is superb as a sailor aboard a river gunboat who quarrels with his superiors and tries to warn them of the potential diplomatic pitfalls in dealing with Chinese warlords. Crenna plays the captain of the vessel. The well-paced movie, based on Richard McKenna's best-selling novel, is set on the Yangtze River during the 1920s. There are many inspired scenes, filled with suspense and excitement. Also with Candice Bergen, Richard Attenborough, Marayat Andriane, Mako, Simon Oakland, and Larry Gates. **Director**—Robert Wise. **Academy Award Nominations**—best picture; McQueen, best actor; Mako, best supporting actor; Joseph MacDonald, cinematography (color). *193 minutes*

THE SANDPIPER (1965)

★

Elizabeth Taylor
Richard Burton
Eva Marie Saint

Hollywood concocted this superficial tale to capitalize on the real-life romance of Taylor and Burton. The lovely scenery of the Big Sur and the exquisite beach scenes have more redeeming quality than the trite plot, which involves Taylor, playing a liberated artist with an illegitimate son, and Burton, who's an errant minister. Saint plays Burton's

Richard Burton and Robert Webber discuss their wives as Eva Marie Saint looks on in The Sandpiper.

wife. Also with Charles Bronson, Robert Webber, and Torin Thatcher. **Director**—Vincente Minnelli. *116 minutes*

SANDS OF IWO JIMA (1949)

★★★

John Wayne
John Agar

Wayne shines as a tough and capable Marine sergeant who must train young recruits and turn them into disciplined combat troops during World War II. Although some of the characterizations in this terse drama are obvious two-dimensional portraits and standard war-picture fare, the battle scenes are among the best ever filmed. The cast also includes Forrest Tucker, Arthur Franz, Adele Mara, Richard Jaeckel, and Julie Bishop. **Director**—Allan Dwan. **Academy Award Nominations**—Wayne, best actor; Harry Brown, writing (motion picture story). *109 minutes b&w*

THE SAN FRANCISCO STORY (1952)
★★

Joel McCrea
Yvonne De Carlo

McCrea and De Carlo star in this well-paced action film set in California during the gold rush era. The story focuses on the efforts of a miner and a newspaper editor in ridding San Francisco of vice and sweeping out the city's criminals. Sidney Blackmer and Florence Bates also star. **Director**—Robert Parrish. *90 minutes b&w*

SANTA FE TRAIL (1940)

★★

Errol Flynn
Olivia de Havilland
Raymond Massey

Flynn and de Havilland top the cast of this formula western, but the weak plot, indecisive direction, and slow pace spoil a potentially good tale. Flynn plays cavalry officer Jeb Stuart, and the action focuses on his efforts to capture John Brown, played by Massey. The supporting cast also includes Alan Hale, Gene Reynolds, Van Heflin, Henry O'Neill, and, oh yes—Ronald Reagan. **Director**—Michael Curtiz. *93 minutes b&w*

SARATOGA TRUNK (1946)

★★

Ingrid Bergman
Gary Cooper

This curious vehicle mounted for star performers is mishandled from beginning to end, and never seems to get unstuck from its mediocre plot. The movie is based on the novel by Pulitzer Prize-winning author Edna Ferber. Bergman plays a notorious woman who returns to New Orleans. She falls in love with Cooper, who portrays a handsome cowboy involved in a squabble among railroad owners. Supporting actors include Florence Bates, Flora Robson, and John Warburton. **Director**—Sam Wood. **Academy Award Nomination**—Robson, best supporting actress. *135 minutes b&w*

SASQUATCH (1978)
★

George Lauris

Seven men go tramping around the wilds of British Columbia to find the legendary Bigfoot. The semidocumentary film merely suggests that such a creature exists, and most moviegoers won't be impressed. Some of the sequences dwell on the scenic beauty and natural wildlife of the area. At least this part is credible. Also with Steve Boergadine and Jim Bradford. **Director**—Ed Ragozzino. (G) *102 minutes*

S

- Saturday Night and Sunday Morning
- Saturday Night Fever
- Saturn 3
- Savage Streets
- Save the Tiger
- Sayonara

SATURDAY NIGHT AND SUNDAY MORNING (1960)

★★★★

**Albert Finney
Rachel Roberts
Shirley Anne Field**

Finney rose to stardom in this stark rendition of working-class life-styles in an English industrial community. Finney plays an impish, devious nonconformist who's unhappy as a factory worker. He also has an affair with a married woman, until he eventually settles for a more conventional existence. Roberts, as the married woman, and Field, as Finney's girl friend, give solid supporting efforts in this finely crafted drama. Other supporting actors include Hylda Baker, Bryan Pringle, and Norman Rossington. **Director**—Karel Reisz. *89 minutes b&w*

SATURDAY NIGHT FEVER (1977)

 ★★★

John Travolta

John Travolta strikes his famous pose in Saturday Night Fever.

Travolta stars as a young disco stud in this energetic film about tough dead-end Brooklyn teenagers. He brings credibility to the role, and he stops the show several times with some impressive dancing; it's a stunning film debut. The pulsing music of the Bee Gees adds to the mood. The erratic script is loaded with clichés, yet it conveys a convincing statement about some aspects of our youth culture. Also with Karen Lynn Gorney, Barry Miller, Joseph Cali, Paul Pape, and Donna Pescow. **Director**—John Badham. (R) **Academy Award Nomination**—Travolta, best actor.

119 minutes

SATURN 3 (1980)

 ★

**Kirk Douglas
Farrah Fawcett**

Two research scientists—Douglas and Fawcett—are busy growing food in outer space when along comes a bad spaceman, played by Harvey Keitel, who spoils their fun in this far-out Garden of Eden. That's the extent of the flimsy plot in this rather unappealing movie, which suffers from the blahs from beginning to end. The outer-space setting is peculiarly vast and gaudy and, at times, seems out of place in contrast to the routine action. Also with Douglas Lambert. **Director**—Stanley Donen. (R) *88 minutes*

SAVAGE STREETS (1984)

★★

**Linda Blair
John Vernon
Robert Dryer**

High school gang members do battle on the streets of Los Angeles. Blair tops the untalented cast as a girl gang leader who seeks revenge for the rape of her mute younger sister. The film goes overboard to exploit violence and tough-talking, vulgar dialogue. **Director**—Danny Steinmann. (R) *93 minutes*

SAVE THE TIGER (1973)

★★★

**Jack Lemmon
Jack Gilford**

This honest effort—by Hollywood standards—to examine contemporary ethics in the United States is interesting, but less than satisfying as a course in ethics or as a film. Lemmon is excellent as a troubled businessman at the breaking point because of financial difficulties; it makes him decide to torch his warehouse so he can collect the insurance money. Gilford plays his partner. Lemmon's performance is ably supported by Gilford, Laurie Heineman, Thayer David, and Norman Burton. **Director**—John G. Avildsen. (PG) **Academy Award**—Lemmon, best actor. **Nominations**—Gilford, best supporting actor; Steve Shagan, best story and screenplay (based on factual material or material not previously published).

100 minutes

SAYONARA (1957)

★★★

**Marlon Brando
Miyoshi Umeki
Red Buttons
Miiko Taka**

Marlon Brando and Miikio Taka have an oriental affair in Sayonara.

This is another case in which the acting genius of Brando makes an average movie worthwhile. He plays an Air Force pilot who falls in love with Taka, who plays a Japanese entertainer, after the Korean Conflict. In this movie based on the James Michener novel, Brando gets quality support from Umeki and Buttons. The movie is also enhanced by Irving Berlin's theme song. Without Brando, this production would be a travel feature about life in the Far East. Also with Ricardo Montalban, James Garner, Patricia Owens, Kent Smith, and Martha Scott. **Director**—Joshua Logan. **Academy Awards**—Buttons, best supporting actor; Umeki, best supporting actress. **Nominations**—best picture; Logan, best director; Brando, best actor; Paul Osborn, best screenplay (based on material from another medium); Ellsworth Fredericks, cinematography. *147 minutes*

SCANDALOUS (1984)

★

**John Gielgud
Robert Hays
Jim Dale**

Robert Hays plays a television reporter involved in a murder mystery in Scandalous.

It begins promisingly—as a perky spy spoof. It falls apart rapidly—as it turns into a scandalously muddled murder mystery. Hays plays a TV journalist suspected of killing his wife. He tangles with London con artists Gielgud and Pamela Stephenson, and with giddy Scotland Yard inspector Dale. If the opportunity to see Sir John in punk regalia doesn't seem worth the effort, skip it. It's probably the best of the film's handful of bright moments. **Director**—Rob Cohen. (PG)

94 minutes

SCANNERS (1981)

★★

**Jennifer O'Neill
Patrick McGoohan**

A sci-fi horror film with some grisly shock effects and a routine, cliché-filled script, which is only moderately suspenseful. Scanners are seemingly normal people with telepathic superpowers who can physically manipulate and even kill other humans. In one gory scene, a man's head literally explodes. McGoohan plays a pompous scientist, and lovely O'Neill is cast as a "good guy" scanner. But the real stars are the makeup artists responsible for some mind-blowing scenes. **Director**—David Cronenberg. (R)

103 minutes

SCARAMOUCHE (1952)
★★★

**Stewart Granger
Eleanor Parker
Janet Leigh**

The near-perfect casting of Granger as a swashbuckler determined to avenge the death of his brother sets the tone and pace of this exciting adventure story based on Rafael Sabatini's novel set in 18th-century France. Granger is ably joined by two beauties—Parker and Leigh—who vie for his love. Mel Ferrer, Nina Foch, Henry Wilcoxon, Robert Coote, and Lewis Stone also star. **Director**—George Sidney.

115 minutes

SCARED STIFF (1953)
★★

**Dean Martin
Jerry Lewis**

In this comedy, Martin, a singer, and Lewis, his busboy sidekick, land on a mysterious island after fleeing from the police. Once settled, they get involved with Carmen Miranda. The combination of escape, escapades, romance, and a spooky castle spawns enough laughs to please fans of this zany duo. Also with Lizabeth Scott, George Dolenz, Dorothy Malone, Jack Lambert, and William Ching. This is a remake of *The Ghost Breakers* with Bob Hope. **Director**—George Marshall.

108 minutes b&w

SCARFACE (1932)

★★★★

**Paul Muni
Ann Dvorak
George Raft**

One of the first of the great gangster films, this remains one of the greatest. Muni is in top form as Roaring Twenties Chicago mobster Tony Camonte, killing his way to become king of the underworld—a role said to have been modeled after Al Capone. The compelling, hard-edged script is by Ben Hecht, the fierce direction by Howard Hawks. It's the film that forever linked Raft to his malignantly cool coin-tossing gesture. Also with Boris

The first version of Scarface *has Paul Muni in the tough-guy title role.*

Karloff. Reworked in the 1983 version starring Al Pacino.   *99 minutes b&w*

SCARFACE (1983)

★★★

Al Pacino

Al Pacino plays a big man with a funny accent in Scarface.

Savage, lavish gangster epic that follows in the footsteps of Howard Hawks's 1932 crime saga. But instead of Chicago and booze, it's now Miami and cocaine. Pacino acts up a storm as the spunky Cuban refugee who machine guns his way to czar of a lucrative drug empire. The story is a bloody, sometimes comical study in greed with Pacino's character eventually wallowing in excess until his demise. Steven Bauer and Michelle Pfeiffer stand out in supporting roles. **Director**—Brian De Palma. (R)

170 minutes

S

• Scavenger Hunt
• School for Scoundrels
• Scorpio
• Scotland Yard
• Screwballs
• Scrooge (1951)
• Scrooge (1970)
• The Sea Chase

SCAVENGER HUNT (1980)

(no stars)

Richard Benjamin
James Coco
Tony Randall
Cloris Leachman

Ruth Gordon is glad she found a Willie Aames in Scavenger Hunt.

A noisy and absurd comedy that features a large cast of familiar names in brief and embarrassing roles. Benjamin, Leachman, Coco, Randall, and others greedily scramble for strange objects, after Vincent Price, who plays an eccentric game manufacturer, wills $200 million to the winner of a scavenger hunt. The callous humor delights in degrading people with physical impairments. Also with Scatman Crothers, Ruth Gordon, Roddy McDowall, and Cleavon Little. Director Michael Schultz seems to have gone to the limit of bad taste. (PG)

117 minutes

SCHOOL FOR SCOUNDRELS (1960)

★★★

Ian Carmichael
Alastair Sim
Terry-Thomas

Capable performers headed by Carmichael, Sim, and Terry-Thomas make this a school worth attending. The film is based on Stephen Potter's books. In this movie, the training school teaches one-upmanship so that graduates can always come out on top in the game of life. Janette Scott, Dennis Price, Peter Jones, John Le Mesurier, and Edward Chapman also star in this amusing

and enjoyable romp at a unique school. **Director**—Robert Hamer.

94 minutes b&w

SCORPIO (1972)

 ★★

Burt Lancaster
Alain Delon
Paul Scofield

The top-level cast in this unbelievably complicated spy thriller has an international flavor, but the viewer is left in the cold trying to figure out what's happening at times. Lancaster is just right as the serious, intense CIA agent ticketed for extinction by fellow-agent Scorpio, played by French actor Delon. British actor Scofield plays a Russian agent. Also with John Colicos, Gayle Hunnicutt, and J. D. Cannon. **Director**—Michael Winner. (R)

114 minutes

SCOTLAND YARD (1941)

 ★

Nancy Kelly
Edmund Gwenn

If the viewer doesn't permit the almost unbelievable plot of this spy story to bother him, then this melodrama is mildly interesting. The tale concerns the kidnapping of a London banker by the Nazis during World War II, and their use of his double to trick the Allies into turning funds over to their evil cause. The competent cast also includes Henry Wilcoxon, Norman Varden, Melville Cooper, and Gilbert Emery. **Director**—Norman Foster.

68 minutes b&w

SCREWBALLS (1983)

(no stars)

Peter Keleghan
Lynda Speciale

This anemic, adolescent comedy is a desperate rip-off of *Porky's*. Like its not-so-illustrious forebear, it features a generous array of dumb sex jokes and horny sight gags. The setting is a dubious high school where the major concern of some eager male students is to seduce a prudish girl named Purity. The chain of foolish events is crudely

directed and awkwardly acted. **Director**—Rafal Zielinski. (R) *80 minutes*

SCROOGE (1951)

★★★★

Alastair Sim

This classic Charles Dickens tale, about a Victorian miser who meets the ghost of Christmas and then reforms his ways, gets expert handling in this British film. Sim plays the title role. The superb cast also includes Mervyn Johns, Kathleen Harrison, Jack Warner, Michael Hordern, George Cole, Miles Malleson, and Hermione Baddeley. Director Desmond Hurst has taken the superior cast and directed them with just the right emphasis so the film never seems superficial.

86 minutes b&w

SCROOGE (1970)

 ★

Albert Finney

Perhaps some future film historian will be able to figure out why anyone would want to make a musical out of Dickens's classic story. At times, partly due to the skills of Finney and competent supporting actors, this version seems almost bearable, but then the characters burst into song, and the spirit of tolerance dissipates. Also with Michael Medwin, Alec Guinness, Kay Walsh, David Collings, Laurence Naismith, Edith Evans, and Kenneth More. **Director**—Ronald Neame. (G)

113 minutes

THE SEA CHASE (1955)

★★

John Wayne
Lana Turner

Wayne is competent as the German captain of a fugitive freighter trying to reach the fatherland from Australia, but it seems downright un-American to have him toiling for the other side in this World War II adventure. Other aspects of the melodrama are standard and not as farfetched, including Turner as the romantic interest in Wayne's life. The assorted crew of supporting actors includes David Farrar, Tab

Hunter, Dick Davalos, Lyle Bettger, and James Arness. **Director**—John Farrow. *117 minutes*

THE SEA GYPSIES (1978)
★★★

Robert Logan
Heather Rattray
Mikki Jamison-Olsen

Beautiful scenery, effective acting, and a lively plot enhance this engaging family adventure film. It's about a man, his two daughters, and a photographer, who are marooned on the Alaskan coast and learn to survive among the wild bear, moose, caribou, and sea lions. The story is predictable, but there's lots of excitement to delight the youngsters and involve the adults. Also with Shannon Saylor. **Director**—Stewart Raffill. (G) *101 minutes*

THE SEA HAWK (1940)
 ### ★★★

Errol Flynn
Claude Rains
Flora Robson

Swashed and buckled, Errol Flynn leads his rag-tag crew in The Sea Hawk.

Avast, ye swabs!—When Warner Brothers launches a big-budget pirate picture with Flynn its all-time king of the swashbucklers, you can be sure it's a winner. Flynn stars as a privateer rooting out treacherous Spaniards on the high seas and in the court of Her Majesty Queen Elizabeth I. There's

KATHARINE HEPBURN

Katharine Hepburn's long and distinguished film career has earned her 13 Academy Award nominations and four Oscars. Despite her remarkable talent, however, she was once regarded as an outsider by the Hollywood establishment and for a while had a reputation as box-office poison.

Hepburn was born in Hartford, Connecticut, in 1907, one of six children of an upper-class family. She began acting while at Bryn Mawr College.

Shortly after graduation, she made her professional stage debut in Baltimore. She then left for Broadway, where she gained a reputation for temperamental and independent behavior; she was often fired by the director or producer before a play opened.

Her first film, A Bill of Divorcement (1932), was an immediate success and this led to a succession of film roles. Her third movie, Morning Glory (1933), brought her first Academy Award. In

the late '30s, she co-starred with Cary Grant in some of her finest movies.

Hepburn was turned down for the part of Scarlett O'Hara in Gone With the Wind, so she returned to Broadway to play the lead in The Philadelphia Story, for which she obtained the film rights. The story was later brought to MGM for a movie. This 1940 film, which also starred Cary Grant and James Stewart, became a box-office success. In 1942, Hepburn made The Woman of the Year, her first film with Spencer Tracy. This experience led to their legendary 27-year romance and eight more films together, including State of the Union (1948), Adam's Rib (1949), and Pat and Mike (1952). Their last film together was Guess Who's Coming to Dinner? (1967). She won her second Oscar for her performance, and Tracy died shortly after the film was released.

Hepburn starred with John Wayne in Rooster Cogburn (1975) and acted in the TV version of The Corn Is Green (1979). She was splendid opposite Henry Fonda in the sentimental film On Golden Pond (1981), for which she received her latest Oscar nomination.

Other notable films include Bringing Up Baby (1938), The African Queen (1951), Long Day's Journey into Night (1962), and The Lion in Winter (1968), the movie that earned her a third Academy Award.

plenty of colorful action in this adaptation of the novel by Rafael Sabatini. Juicy performances by Henry Daniell, Donald Crisp, Brenda Marshall, Alan Hale, and Gilbert Roland. **Director**—Michael Curtiz. *127 minutes b&w*

SEARCH AND DESTROY (1981)
 ### ★

Perry King

An ill-conceived, grim drama about a Vietnamese soldier who comes to the United States seeking revenge on some Americans who abandoned him in the South Vietnam jungles. The far-fetched script has the disgruntled soldier and a veteran GI, played by King,

shooting it out on the streets of Niagara Falls. Some picturesque views of the falls are the only interesting aspects of this otherwise desperate movie. Tisa Farrow and George Kennedy co-star. **Director**—William Fruet. (PG) *93 minutes*

THE SEARCHERS (1956)
 ### ★★★★

John Wayne
Jeffrey Hunter
Natalie Wood

Wayne and Hunter search for a girl, played by Wood, who was kidnapped by Indians. This attractive western, *(Continued)*

S
- The Sea Wolf
- The Sea Wolves
- Second Hand Hearts
- The Secret Life of an American Wife
- The Secret Life of Walter Mitty
- The Secret of Nimh

John Wayne and neighbors mourn the victim of Indians in The Searchers.

(Continued)

set after the Civil War, is buoyed by excellent photography, beautiful scenery, and John Ford's direction. The acting of Wayne, Hunter, and Wood, and solid supporting performances by Vera Miles, Antonio Moreno, Ward Bond, John Qualen, and Henry Brandon also help the film. *119 minutes*

THE SEA WOLF (1941)
★★★

Edward G. Robinson

A great cast keeps this fast-paced adventure at sea afloat. This movie version of Jack London's novel about a sadistic sea captain is overly involved with what makes the captain, played by Robinson, tick. The story deals with how the captain brutally treats the survivors he has rescued from a ferry boat collision in San Francisco Bay. Among the survivors and the rest of the cast are such excellent supporting actors as Alexander Knox, Ida Lupino, John Garfield, Gene Lockhart, Barry Fitzgerald, Howard da Silva, and David Bruce. **Director**—Michael Curtiz. *90 minutes b&w*

THE SEA WOLVES (1981)
 ★★★

Roger Moore
Gregory Peck
David Niven
Trevor Howard

Potbellied, polo-playing, British businessmen form a commando team and destroy a secret Nazi radio transmitter somewhere in the Indian Ocean. This daring charge of the geriatric brigade is a likable World War II adventure with plenty of stiff-upper-lip atmosphere. Stars of yesteryear—Peck, Niven, Howard—keep the suspense and action moving, but the film really belongs to Moore who, as a British officer, contributes a proper amount of dash and romance. **Director**—Andrew V. McLaglen. (PG) *120 minutes*

SECOND HAND HEARTS (1981)
★

Robert Blake
Barbara Harris

Blake and Harris star as a couple of lost souls on their way to California, trying to make the most of a rickety marriage. The performances are exceptionally bad, but it's only in keeping with the dialogue, which wavers from silly to absurd. The two travel in a beat-up station wagon, run out of gas, lose their way, and suffer mechanical breakdowns. Clutter and confusion are everywhere. **Director**—Hal Ashby. (PG) *98 minutes*

THE SECRET LIFE OF AN AMERICAN WIFE (1968)
★

Walter Matthau
Anne Jackson

Jackson portrays a bored suburban housewife who decides to seduce a movie star sex idol in this insipid and unsatisfying comedy, which has a message lurking somewhere on suburban life-styles of the 1960s. Matthau plays the cinema sex idol. Both stars have done much better work in other films and seem miscast in this production. Patrick O'Neal, Edy Williams, Richard Bull, and Paul Napier appear in supporting roles. **Director**—George Axelrod. *92 minutes*

THE SECRET LIFE OF WALTER MITTY (1947)
★★★★

Danny Kaye

Kaye is charming in this entertaining story about a man who lives in a fantasy world where he leads an exciting life. In the real world, he's mild-mannered and cowardly. Viewers expecting a faithful film version of James Thurber's story will be disappointed, but excellent songs—including Kaye's rendition of his famed "Anatole of Paris"—and enjoyable comedy sequences make this a movie the whole family will enjoy. Also with Virginia Mayo, Boris Karloff, Reginald Denny, Florence Bates, Ann Rutherford, and Fay Bainter. **Director**—Norman Z. McLeod.

110 minutes

THE SECRET OF NIMH (1982)
 ★★★

A group of former Disney animators have revived the original, classic cartoon technique in this handsome fantasy. For those who still like to wish upon a star, here's the story of a poor widowed mouse caught in the path of man's progress and struggling to save her family. More than 1.5 million individual drawings are put together to convey the fast-paced action. The film is a dazzling display of mirth, charm, and color—and it has its times of terror, too. If Papa Walt could see it, he'd certainly applaud. Dom DeLuise and John Carradine are two of the voices behind the characters. **Director**—Don Bluth. (G) *82 minutes*

• The Secret of Santa Vittoria
• The Seduction
• The Seduction of Joe Tynan
• See Here, Private Hargrove
• Seems Like Old Times
• The Sellout
• Semi-Tough

S

THE SECRET OF SANTA VITTORIA (1969)
★★★

Anthony Quinn
Anna Magnani

Anthony Quinn tries to keep Hardy Kruger from discovering The Secret of Santa Vittoria.

The entertaining tale takes place in an Italian village during the last months of World War II and depicts the efforts of the villagers in saving their precious hoard—one million bottles of wine—from German soldiers during the occupation. The story, based on Robert Crichton's novel, is interesting at times, but the film is too long and needlessly meanders. The stars, Quinn and Magnani, are adequate, and Hardy Kruger is excellent as a German officer. Also with Virna Lisi, Sergio Franchi, and Renato Rascel. **Director**—Stanley Kramer. (PG)
140 minutes

THE SEDUCTION (1982)
 ### (no stars)

Morgan Fairchild
Andrew Stevens

This amateurishly made turkey stars Fairchild of TV fame. She plays a glamorous news reporter who's pursued by a Peeping-Tom photographer, played by Stevens. Fairchild displays plenty of flesh, but her "Barbie Doll" beauty is as plastic as her acting. Writer-director David Schmoeller's idea of suspense is cheap fright tactics embellished with purring telephone conversations. It's a trite, aimless effort, which hardly lives up to its title. Michael Sarrazin and Vince Edwards also star. (R)
104 minutes

THE SEDUCTION OF JOE TYNAN (1979)
 ### ★★

Alan Alda
Barbara Harris
Meryl Streep

Alda is in the title role, playing a liberal, charming New York senator ambitiously pursuing his career and struggling with his domestic life. Harris plays the senator's attractive wife, and Streep is a Southern labor lawyer who has an affair with the senator. Alda, Harris, and Streep deliver some remarkable performances, but the flat yet literate script, written by Alda, fails to offer badly needed excitement and drama. Also with Rip Torn, Charles Kimbrough, and Melvyn Douglas. **Director**—Jerry Schatzberg. (R)
107 minutes

SEE HERE, PRIVATE HARGROVE (1944)
★★★

Robert Walker
Donna Reed
Keenan Wynn

If you've served in the military, you should appreciate the humor in this story about a raw recruit going through his paces in the U.S. Army. Walker, Reed, and Wynn star in this film adaptation of Marion Hargrove's best-selling novel. Also with Robert Benchley, Bob Crosby, Chill Wills, Ray Collins, and Grant Mitchell. **Director**—Wesley Ruggles.
102 minutes b&w

SEEMS LIKE OLD TIMES (1980)
 ### ★★

Goldie Hawn
Chevy Chase
Charles Grodin

Hawn plays an affluent liberal lawyer with a soft spot for stray dogs, her down-and-out clients, and her ex-husband, played by Chase, who's on the lam after two criminals force him to help them rob a bank. Grodin plays her current husband, a district attorney. Hawn, making the most of this broad comedy, is as bright-eyed and zany as ever, and she works well with Chase. But Neil Simon's uneven screenplay never catches hold; the familiar one-liners are mostly uninspired, and the laughs come at infrequent intervals. **Director**—Jay Sandrich. (PG)
102 minutes

THE SELLOUT (1951)
★★

Walter Pidgeon
John Hodiak
Audrey Totter

Pidgeon, Hodiak, and Totter star in this melodrama about political corruption. Pidgeon portrays a small-town crusading newspaper editor at odds with corrupt police and city officials. Thomas Gomez, who plays a sheriff on the take, is joined in supporting roles by Karl Malden, Cameron Mitchell, Everett Sloane, and Paula Raymond. **Director**—Gerald Mayer.
82 minutes b&w

SEMI-TOUGH (1977)
 ### ★★★

Burt Reynolds
Kris Kristofferson
Jill Clayburgh

Semi-Tough features Burt Reynolds as a football star and Jill Clayburgh as the bride.

A lively, wacky, romantic satire that demolishes professional football and self-improvement fads. Reynolds, Kristofferson, and Clayburgh work well together as a platonic *ménage-à-trois*. Director Michael Ritchie (*Smile; Bad News Bears*) is at home with this material, which tosses barbs at various hypocrisies. Walter Bernstein's script contains a lot of locker-room language. Also with Robert Preston, Bert Convy, and Lotte Lenya. (R)
108 minutes

S
- The Sender
- The Sentinel
- Separate Tables
- September Affair
- September 30, 1955
- Sgt. Pepper's Lonely Hearts Club Band
- Sergeants Three

THE SENDER (1982)

 ★★

**Kathryn Harrold
Zeljko Ivanek
Shirley Knight**

Zeljko Ivanek has extraordinary powers in The Sender.

Eerie, convoluted, sometimes outrageous horror film that plays the mental telepathy theme to the hilt. Harrold stars as an attractive psychiatrist involved with a strange, suicidal, amnesiac patient (Ivanek). Soon she's sharing the young man's hallucinations and nightmares. There are enough spooky gimmicks to keep you absorbed, but much of the action is basically absurd. **Director**—Roger Christian. (R)   *92 minutes*

THE SENTINEL (1977)

★★★

**Christina Raines
Ava Gardner
Chris Sarandon
Burgess Meredith**

There's enough creepy goings-on in this bone-chilling horror film to give you nightmares for weeks. It's about an innocent and attractive fashion model, played by Raines, who rents a room in an old Brooklyn brownstone building that's actually a gateway to Hell. Director Michael Winner assembles a horrifying assortment of grotesque characters and nerve-jangling effects—mysteriously swaying chandeliers, strange footsteps in the night.

And there's a final scene so gruesome that you may lose your appetite, so view it after dinner. Effective performances from Raines, Meredith, and Sarandon. Also with Sylvia Miles, José Ferrer, Arthur Kennedy, and John Carradine. (R)   *93 minutes*

SEPARATE TABLES (1958)

 ★★★★

**Burt Lancaster
Rita Hayworth
David Niven
Deborah Kerr**

Brilliant acting and excellent direction smooth the transition of Terence Rattigan's play from the stage to the screen. Under Delbert Mann's direction, the characterizations are sensitive, and the emotional conflicts are deftly portrayed in this story about the guests at a British seaside resort. Among the stars are Kerr, who plays a spinster; Niven, a troubled ex-colonel; and Wendy Hiller, the owner of the resort and Lancaster's mistress. Hayworth is surprisingly good as Lancaster's ex-wife who begs him for another chance. Also with Gladys Cooper, Cathleen Nesbitt, Felix Aylmer, Rod Taylor, May Hallat, and Audrey Dalton. **Academy Awards**—Niven, best actor; Hiller, best supporting actress; **Nominations**—best picture; Kerr, best actress; Rattigan and John Gay, best screenplay (based on material from another medium); Charles Lang, Jr., cinematography (black and white).

98 minutes b&w

SEPTEMBER AFFAIR (1950)

★★

**Joseph Cotten
Joan Fontaine**

Cotten and Fontaine star in this romantic melodrama. It's about two lovers married to other people who suddenly have a chance to start life anew together when they discover they are erroneously reported as missing in an airplane crash. The treatment is standard and competent considering the farfetched plot. Françoise Rosay, Jessica Tandy, Robert Arthur, and Jimmy Lydon appear in supporting roles. **Director**—William Dieterle.   *104 minutes b&w*

SEPTEMBER 30, 1955 (1978)

★

Richard Thomas

The title, in case you're wondering, has to do with the day actor James Dean died in a car crash. This tedious '50s youth film tells how Arkansas college student Jimmy J. goes bananas over the news of Dean's death. It's rather difficult to identify with such a peculiar and naïve adolescent character. Thomas, who played John-Boy on TV's *The Waltons*, gives an unconvincing and bland performance as Jimmy J. And James Bridges directs with an eye on *American Graffiti*; he doesn't come close. Also with Susan Tyrell, Deborah Benson, and Lisa Blount. (PG)

101 minutes

SGT. PEPPER'S LONELY HEARTS CLUB BAND (1978)

 ★

**Peter Frampton
The Bee Gees**

This loosely constructed film is based on the music of the Beatles—more than 25 songs are featured—and stars Peter Frampton, the Bee Gees, and dozens of other rock performers. A few scenes are outstanding, but the outcome is a garish mishmash. The silly plot—what there is of it— is merely a vehicle for introducing the musical numbers. Most of the musicians aren't particularly good actors. Also with George Burns, Frankie Howard, Donald Pleasence, and Steve Martin. **Director**—Michael Schultz. (PG)   *111 minutes*

SERGEANTS THREE (1962)

★★

**Frank Sinatra
Dean Martin
Peter Lawford
Sammy Davis, Jr.
Joey Bishop**

Sinatra and some of his cronies— Martin, Davis, Lawford, and Bishop— star in this adventure yarn that resembles a western parody of *Gunga Din*. In this movie, Davis turns heroic in Gunga Din fashion. The story is set

- Sergeant York
- Serial
- The Serpent's Egg
- Serpico
- Seven Beauties
- Seven Brides for Seven Brothers

S

just after the Civil War, when three cavalry sergeants—Sinatra, Martin, and Lawford—with the assistance of Davis, dispose of hostile Indians. There's more than enough spirited action and fun for fans of this quintet, but the plot is trite, and much of the story is boring. Ruta Lee and Henry Silva also appear. **Director**—John Sturges. *112 minutes*

SERGEANT YORK (1941)
★★★★

Gary Cooper

In Sergeant York, *Gary Cooper portrays a pacifist who's drafted in World War I.*

Cooper is perfectly cast as the backwoods farm boy—a pacifist—drafted into the Army who becomes the greatest U.S. hero of World War I. Under Howard Hawks's intelligent direction, the portrait of York is sensitive and compassionate, yet Hawks keeps the film moving along nicely without making it just another action-packed war movie. Besides Cooper, the excellent cast includes Joan Leslie, Walter Brennan, George Tobias, David Bruce, Ward Bond, Margaret Wycherly, and Dickie Moore. **Academy Award**—Cooper, best actor. **Nominations**—best picture; Hawks, best director; Brennan, best supporting actor; Wycherly, best supporting actress; Harry Chandlee, Abem Finkel, John Huston, and Howard Koch, writing (original screenplay); Sol Polito, cinematography (black and white).
134 minutes b&w

SERIAL (1980)
★★

Martin Mull
Tuesday Weld

Mull and Weld star as a me-generation couple in this silly satire of trendy lifestyles in affluent Marin County, California. The rapid-fire dialogue seems as if it were gleaned from *Psychology Today* magazine. The soap-opera screenplay delves into hot tubs, open-marriages, cult religions, consciousness-raising, and organic foods. There are some amusing moments amid the smorgasbord of pop jargon, but a lot of it is just dead air. Also with Sally Kellerman, Bill Macy, Peter Bonerz, Christopher Lee, and Tom Smothers. **Director**—Bill Persky. (R) *91 minutes*

THE SERPENT'S EGG (1978)
★★

Liv Ullmann
David Carradine

This film is set in Berlin during the early '20s, when poverty, fear, and despair haunted the populace on the eve of Hitler's rise to power. In this English-language film, director Ingmar Bergman captures the grim and depressing mood in his usual intelligent fashion, but the point of the story is unclear. Bergman, who wrote the screenplay, leaves unanswered questions dangling everywhere. Carradine plays an out-of-work American circus performer floundering among the demoralized Germans, and Ullmann is a cabaret performer—both roles lack depth. Also with Gert Frobe, Glynn Turman, and James Whitmore. (R)
120 minutes

SERPICO (1973)
★★★

Al Pacino

Pacino is brilliant as Frank Serpico, a dedicated New York City cop, who's appalled by police corruption and decides to expose the sleazy practices. The story, based on a book by Peter Maas, is about the problems and adventures of this honest nonconformist, but there's enough hard-hitting action

for fans of cops-and-robbers movies. On-location filming gives the production a realistic tone under the excellent direction of Sidney Lumet. Also with John Randolph, Jack Kehoe, Biff McGuire, Barbara Eda-Young, Cornelia Sharpe, and Tony Roberts. (R) **Academy Award Nominations**—Pacino, best actor; Waldo Salt and Norman Wexler, best screenplay (based on material from another medium).
130 minutes

SEVEN BEAUTIES (1976)
★★★★

Giancarlo Giannini
Shirley Stoler

Director Lina Wertmuller's fifth movie is a masterpiece; it's rich with irony, paradox, and humor, and deals with the fundamental theme of survival. Giannini, in one of his best performances, plays a small-time hood from Naples, nicknamed "Seven Beauties," who deserts the Italian army and is sent to a concentration camp by the Germans. To survive, he desperately attempts to seduce the camp's hefty and ferocious female commandant, played effectively by Stoler. The movie is Wertmuller's best effort to date, as she reaffirms her political and philosophical beliefs. Also with Fernando Rey, Elena Fiore, and Enzo Vitale. In Italian with English titles. (R) **Academy Award Nominations**—best foreign-language film; Wertmuller, best director; Giannini, best actor; Wertmuller, best original screenplay.
115 minutes

SEVEN BRIDES FOR SEVEN BROTHERS (1954)
★★★★

Howard Keel
Jane Powell

Powell and Keel star in this delightful western musical. After Keel decides to marry Powell, his six rowdy brothers resolve to find wives for themselves. There are comic antics, skillful dance numbers, and pleasant musical selections, all focusing on the manner in which the brothers get their brides. The fun in this robust film is topped by the barn-raising scenes. Stanley
(Continued)

Howard Keel and Jane Powell catch up on their reading in Seven Brides for Seven Brothers.

(Continued)

Donen's direction is excellent, but Michael Kidd's choreography makes the movie something special. The production, inspired by a Stephen Vincent Benét story, also stars Jeff Richards, Russ Tamblyn, and Jacques d'Amboise. **Academy Award Nominations**—best picture; Albert Hackett, Frances Goodrich, and Dorothy Kingsley, writing (screenplay); George Folsey, cinematography (color).

104 minutes

SEVEN DAYS IN MAY (1964)
 ★★★

**Kirk Douglas
Burt Lancaster
Fredric March**

Kirk Douglas and Ava Gardner decide to keep drinking for Seven Days in May.

This tense and exciting political drama about a plot by the military to overthrow the United States government is enhanced by a fine cast, solid direc-tion, and a first-rate script. Lancaster and Douglas play military leaders, and March is outstanding as the President who must confront the plotters. Rod Serling wrote the taut, intelligent screenplay, which, under John Frankenheimer's direction, moves right along to a suspenseful climax. Also with Ava Gardner, John Houseman, Edmond O'Brien, George Macready, and Martin Balsam. **Academy Award Nomination**—O'Brien, best supporting actor. *120 minutes b&w*

THE SEVEN LITTLE FOYS
(1955)
★★★

Bob Hope

Hope stars in this spirited musical biography of vaudevillian Eddie Foy and his family of performers. Hope is surprisingly skilled in his role, displaying admirable footwork and even some acting talent. He's aided by above-average production numbers and James Cagney's guest appearance as George M. Cohan. Milly Vitale, George Tobias, Herbert Heyes, and Angela Clark also star. **Director**—Melville Shavelson. **Academy Award Nomination**—Shavelson and Jack Rose, writing (story and screenplay). *95 minutes*

THE SEVEN-PERCENT
SOLUTION (1976)
 ★★

**Nicol Williamson
Alan Arkin
Robert Duvall**

Nicholas Meyer wrote the screenplay for this film, based on his own bestseller about the imaginary collaboration between Sherlock Holmes and Sigmund Freud on a criminal investigation. A star-studded cast adds class, but a confusing and colorless storyline detracts from the production. Williamson plays Holmes, Arkin is Dr. Freud, and Duvall is Dr. Watson. But alas, the spirit and intrigue associated with stories of the master sleuth are nowhere to be found. Someone owes an apology to Sir Arthur Conan Doyle. Also with Vanessa Redgrave, Laurence Olivier, Joel Grey, and Samantha Eggar. **Director**—Herbert Ross. (PG)

Sherlock Holmes (Nicol Williamson) is tempted with The Seven-Percent Solution *by Dr. Watson (Robert Duvall) and Dr. Sigmund Freud (Alan Arkin).*

Academy Award Nomination—Meyer, best screenplay adaptation.

113 minutes

THE SEVEN SAMURAI (1954)
 ★★★★

Toshiro Mifune

This epic action film, also known as *The Magnificent Seven* (also the title of Hollywood's western remake), is one of the most striking of them all, both violent and poetic, beautifully directed by Akira Kurosawa. In 16th-century Japan, a lethal gang of 40 bandits threatens to wreak havoc on a farming village. The menaced citizens go out and hire themselves seven professional soldiers—the samurai—who agree to ward off the invaders. The film has been duly celebrated by fans and critics around the world for its humor, heroism, and humanity. In Japanese with English titles.

208 minutes b&w

1776 (1972)
 ★★★

**William Daniels
Howard Da Silva**

Peter Stone's Pulitzer Prize-winning musical about the heroes involved in America's struggle for independence is competently adapted to the screen. The film is entertaining; fortunately, it doesn't seem like a dry history lesson, although a few awkward moments mar the movie. Almost all of the original Broadway cast members appear, with Daniels as John Adams and Da Silva as Ben Franklin. Donald Madden, David Ford, Ron Holgate, Virginia Vestoff, Blythe Danner, and Ken

• The Seventh Seal
• The Seventh Veil
• The Seven Year Itch

• Sex and the Single Girl
• Shadow of a Doubt
• Shaft
• The Shaggy D.A.

S

Howard star in supporting roles. **Director**—Peter H. Hunt. (G) **Academy Award Nomination**—Harry Stradling, Jr., cinematography.

141 minutes

THE SEVENTH SEAL (1957)
★★★★

Max Von Sydow
Gunnar Bjornstrand
Bibi Andersson

Ingmar Bergman's haunting allegorical drama is a one-of-a-kind masterpiece. As plague sweeps across 14th-century Sweden, black-robed Death comes to claim a knight who's just returned from the Crusades. The knight challenges the Grim Reaper to a game of chess, which leads to a contemplation of life's meaning. It's heavy going, and sometimes elusive, but full of striking images, and a seminal work in the director's career. In Swedish with English titles. *95 minutes b&w*

THE SEVENTH VEIL (1946)
★★★

James Mason
Ann Todd

Mason and Todd star in this modern romantic drama about a woman who leaves her family to become a concert pianist. She's romantically torn among her psychiatrist, her guardian, and two other men. Mason plays the role of her guardian. At times, this excellent movie borders on soap opera, but it's technically well done and tastefully produced in light of the subject matter. The performances of Mason and Todd are masterful. Also with Herbert Lom, Yvonne Owen, Manning Whiley, David Horne, Albert Lieven, and Hugh McDermott. **Director**—Compton Bennett. **Academy Award**—Muriel and Sydney Box, writing (original screenplay). *94 minutes b&w*

THE SEVEN YEAR ITCH (1955)
 ★★★★

Tom Ewell
Marilyn Monroe

Ewell and Monroe are a delightful combination in this comedy about a

Marilyn Monroe pays homage to The Lady in Red *with this scene from* The Seven Year Itch.

married man who becomes infatuated with a model. She moves into his apartment building while his wife is away on a long summer vacation. Monroe plays the sexy model; Ewell is the married man. He has a fine comic touch, which energizes the film just when it seems ready to falter. Robert Strauss, Marguerite Chapman, Evelyn Keyes, Sonny Tufts, Victor Moore, Carolyn Jones, and Oscar Homolka appear in supporting roles. **Director**—Billy Wilder. *105 minutes*

SEX AND THE SINGLE GIRL (1964)
★★

Natalie Wood
Tony Curtis
Lauren Bacall
Henry Fonda

This splashy comedy has major stars, but it's never as witty or funny as it intends to be and never realizes its potential. Curtis is a writer for a smut magazine, who woos Wood, a psychologist. Everyone is supposed to be surprised when we learn what makes her tick. Bacall and Fonda play an embattled married couple. Otto Kruger, Mel Ferrer, Edward Everett Horton, and Fran Jeffries also appear in this sexcapade based on the successful

book by Helen Gurley Brown. **Director**—Richard Quine. *114 minutes*

SHADOW OF A DOUBT (1943)
★★★★

Joseph Cotten
Teresa Wright

Director Alfred Hitchcock is in top form in this story about a psychopathic killer known as the Merry Widow murderer. The killer, played by Cotten, visits relatives in a small California town, in a desperate effort to escape the police. Wright is a niece who suspects her uncle is the murderer. The memorable suspense yarn about a killer on the run is contrasted with noble values and virtues of small-town America. Cotten is marvelous as the glib and devious killer, posing as a congenial relative. He gets excellent support from Wright, Hume Cronyn, Henry Travers, Wallace Ford, Patricia Collinge, and MacDonald Carey. The script was well written by Thornton Wilder, Sally Benson, and Alma Reville. **Academy Award Nomination**—Gordon McDonell, writing (original story). *108 minutes b&w*

SHAFT (1971)
Ⓐ ★★★

Richard Roundtree

Roundtree plays John Shaft, a tough but cool black private eye, in this action-packed thriller; it seemed more relevant in the 1970s when civil rights and equal opportunity were very intense issues. It remains an interesting action movie, although there are heavy doses of sex and violence. Gwenn Mitchell, Moses Gunn, Charles Cioffi, and Christopher St. John appear in supporting roles. The film inspired some sequels—*Shaft's Big Score* and *Shaft in Africa*. **Director**—Gordon Parks. (R) *100 minutes*

THE SHAGGY D.A. (1977)
★

Dean Jones

The Walt Disney studio trots out their faithful pooch in this sequel to their successful 1959 moneymaker *The*
(Continued)

S

- The Shaggy Dog
- Shake Hands with the Devil
- Shall We Dance
- Shampoo
- Shamus
- Shane

(Continued)

Shaggy Dog. Jones plays a man who is miraculously transformed into the canine while running for district attorney against a corrupt incumbent. All the familiar slapstick tricks—pie-throwing, auto chases, shoot-outs, and so on—are there en masse; such stuff is boring by now. Suzanne Pleshette, Tim Conway, Keenan Wynn, and Jo Ann Worley also star. **Director**—Robert Stevenson. (G)

91 minutes

THE SHAGGY DOG (1959)

  ★★

Fred MacMurray

This enjoyable Walt Disney fantasy about a boy who changes into a shaggy Old English sheepdog by means of a magical device is pleasant film fare for the kids. The switch from boy to dog is made so some thugs can be caught and brought to justice. There are enough funny moments, despite the sluggish script, to keep parents and kids amused. The cast also includes Jean Hagen, Annette Funicello, Jack Albertson, Tim Considine, Alexander Scourby, and Tommy Kirk. **Director**—Charles Barton.   *101 minutes b&w*

SHAKE HANDS WITH THE DEVIL (1959)

★★★

James Cagney

Cagney gives a solid performance in this action-packed drama about Ireland during the rebellion of the 1920s. Cagney, who plays a rebel leader, gets excellent supporting help from Don Murray, Dana Wynter, Glynis Johns, Michael Redgrave, Richard Harris, Noel Purcell, Cyril Cusack, and Sybil Thorndike. Despite the fine acting and vivid on-location photography, the weak script detracts from the film's effectiveness. **Director**—Michael Anderson.   *110 minutes b&w*

SHALL WE DANCE (1937)

  ★★★

Fred Astaire
Ginger Rogers
Edward Everett Horton

Astaire plays a Russian in ballet shoes, and Rogers co-stars as a ballroom dancer. They meet on a boat to America, and a web of intrigue leads them to pretend to be husband and wife, and to dance up a storm—on board, in Central Park, on roller skates. The film features George and Ira Gershwin's only score for Fred and Ginger, with such wonderful songs as "They Can't Take That Away From Me," "Let's Call The Whole Thing Off," "They All Laughed," and "Slap That Bass." Bright, breezy fun. **Director**—Mark Sandrich.

116 minutes b&w

SHAMPOO (1975)

  ★★★

Warren Beatty
Julie Christie

Julie Christie and Warren Beatty star in the witty and funny Shampoo.

Beatty plays a hedonistic Beverly Hills hairdresser whose clients like to get into his bed as well as under his drier. It's witty, funny, and sometimes disturbing cynical mayhem, set against the backdrop of Nixon's 1968 election victory. Also with Lee Grant, Goldie Hawn, Jack Warden, Tony Bill, and Carrie Fisher. **Director**—Hal Ashby. (R) **Academy Award**—Grant, best supporting actress. **Nominations**—Warden, best supporting actor; Robert Towne and Beatty, best original screenplay.   *110 minutes*

SHAMUS (1972)

  ★★

Burt Reynolds
Dyan Cannon

Reynolds stars in this simple-minded, confusing, and violent remake of a "typical" 1940s private-eye film. Reynolds is hired to recover stolen jewels and find a killer. In the process, he performs numerous heroic feats and tries to recover from a number of beatings. Cannon plays one of his girl friends. John Ryan, Joe Santos. Giorgio Tozzi, and Ron Weyland are also in the cast, but everyone is overshadowed by Reynolds. **Director**—Buzz Kulik. (PG)   *98 minutes*

SHANE (1953)

★★★★

Alan Ladd
Jean Arthur
Van Heflin

Farmers bury their dead in Shane.

This story about a mysterious ex-gunfighter who helps a family of homesteaders is one of the finest westerns ever made. Under the skilled direction of George Stevens, the film unfolds slowly with just the proper amount of dramatic tension. Ladd is the stranger, and Heflin, Arthur, and Brandon De Wilde are members of the homesteading family he aids. The excellent story and cast are enhanced by superb, prize-winning photography. Also with Jack Palance, Ben Johnson, Edgar Buchanan, and Elisha Cook, Jr. **Academy Award**—Loyal Griggs, cinematography (color). **Nominations**—best picture; Stevens, best director; De Wilde, Palance, best supporting actor; A. B. Guthrie, Jr., writing (screenplay).   *118 minutes*

• Sharky's Machine   • Sheena   • Sherlock Holmes' Smarter
• She   • Shenandoah   Brother
                     • The Sheriff of Fractured   • She Wore a Yellow Ribbon
                       Jaw   • Shine on Harvest Moon

S

SHARKY'S MACHINE (1981)

 ★★★

Burt Reynolds

Reynolds is director and star of this gripping, action-packed police thriller, and he handles the assignments with extraordinary flair and energy. He plays a wily undercover cop, who cracks a high-flying prostitution and drug operation while encountering an overwhelming amount of blood, gore, and brutality in the process. In fact, Sharky bears a likeness to Clint Eastwood's *Dirty Harry* character, but Reynolds accomplishes the feat with more style and glamour. Also with Vittorio Gassman, Brian Keith, Charles Durning, Earl Holliman, Bernie Casey, Henry Silva, and Rachel Ward. (R)
122 minutes

SHE (1965)

★★

Ursula Andress
John Richardson

Andress and Richardson spark enough energy in this story about the search for the Flame of Eternal Life to please fans of African adventure films. Andress plays Ayesha, the queen who never grows old. Richardson leads the quest for the Flame. The production, based on the H. Rider Haggard novel, takes itself too seriously, however, and would have been more effective as a fantasy. Peter Cushing, Christopher Lee, Bernard Cribbins, Rosenda Monteros, and André Morell appear in supporting roles. **Director**—Robert Day. *105 minutes*

SHEENA (1984)

 ★★

Tanya Roberts
Ted Wass

Campy, comic book trifle that features scantily clad Roberts in the title role as the female answer to Tarzan. The story, set in Africa, is filled with two-dimensional characters and corny melodramatic events. These include a military coup, a romance with a TV reporter (Wass), and the expected communication with the jungle ani-

mals. The production is taken far too seriously—a situation that provokes unexpected laughter. **Director**—John Guillermin. (PG) *117 minutes*

SHENANDOAH (1965)

 ★★★

James Stewart

James Stewart is the head of a Virginia family in Shenandoah.

Stewart portrays the head of a Virginia household disrupted by the Civil War in this well-acted and competently directed western. The film is loaded with crisis upon crisis and, at times, borders on a western soap opera. But the fine performance of Stewart and quality supporting efforts of Rosemary Forsyth, Doug McClure, Katharine Ross, George Kennedy, Patrick Wayne, Glenn Corbett, and Philip Alford keep the production on track. **Director**—Andrew V. McLaglen. *105 minutes*

THE SHERIFF OF FRACTURED JAW (1959)

★

Kenneth More
Jayne Mansfield

This British comedy western is about an English gunsmith who becomes the sheriff of a troubled town. More makes a solid effort as the gunsmith-turned-lawman, and Mansfield, who plays a saloon hostess, is pleasing to look at, but the film falls flat. Also with Robert Morley, Eynon Evans, Bruce

Cabot, William Campbell, David Horne, Henry Hull, and Ronald Squire. **Director**—Raoul Walsh.
103 minutes

SHERLOCK HOLMES' SMARTER BROTHER (1975)

★★

Gene Wilder

Maybe this title should have been *Sherlock Holmes' Silly Brother*. Wilder, who apprenticed at the Mel Brooks comedy school, wrote, directed, and stars in this spoof about the famous fictional sleuth. However, the film isn't the clever, zany romp expected from a member of the Brooks family. It is, rather, adolescent foolishness with only a smattering of true comic situations. Marty Feldman, Madeline Kahn, and Dom DeLuise—all of the Brooks company—are on board for this slapstick workout, which is merely elementary. (PG) *91 minutes*

SHE WORE A YELLOW RIBBON (1949)

★★★

John Wayne

Wayne is excellent as a rugged cavalry officer about to retire. But before he can leave the range for a retirement home, he faces a last encounter with some rampaging Indians. The film has all of director John Ford's vintage ingredients: quality acting, beautiful photography, and a good story. Joanne Dru, John Agar, Ben Johnson, Harry Carey, Jr., Mildred Natwick, Arthur Shields, Victor McLaglen, and George O'Brien also star. **Academy Award**— Winton Hock, cinematography (color). *103 minutes*

SHINE ON HARVEST MOON (1944)

★★

Ann Sheridan
Dennis Morgan

Some enjoyable tunes make this lightweight musical about the lives of vaudevillians Nora Bayes and Jack Norworth worthwhile. Sheridan and
(Continued)

(Continued)

Morgan play the two entertainers. If you want to learn the real story about these famous entertainers, you won't find it in this film. But the performances of Sheridan and Morgan are pleasant enough, and they receive competent support from S. Z. Sakall, Marie Wilson, the Step Brothers, Robert Shayne, Jack Carson, and Irene Manning. **Director**—David Butler.

112 minutes b&w/color

THE SHINING
(1980)

Ⓐ ★★★

Jack Nicholson
Shelley Duvall

Director Stanley Kubrick's haunted-hotel film, based on Stephen King's best-selling novel, is a fascinating

PETER O'TOOLE

Peter O'Toole was born in 1932, in Connemara, County Galway, Ireland, and spent his childhood in Kerry, Dublin, Gainsborough, and, finally, Leeds. Following two years of National Service in the Royal Navy, he won a scholarship to the Royal Academy of Dramatic Art.

O'Toole's first professional engagement was with the Bristol Old Vic Company, and during the 3½ years that followed, he played 73 different roles. O'Toole made his West End (the London equivalent of Broadway) debut in the musical Oh, My Papa, and later toured England in The Holiday, in which the young Welsh actress Sian Phillips played the part of his sister. They married and had two children.

In 1959, O'Toole was named "Actor of the Year" for his performance as Charlie Bamforth in

thriller about horror, rage, and frustration. Yet as sumptuous and spellbinding as it is, many horror scenes wind up in puzzling dead ends; Kubrick seems to be trying too hard to be diabolical. Nicholson gives a smashing performance as a congenial father who is gradually transformed into a snarling demon bent on killing his family with an ax. Duvall plays his wife, and Danny Lloyd is his son. Also with Scatman Crothers and Anne Francis. (R) *146 minutes*

SHINING STAR
(1977)

★

Harvey Keitel

A thin, awkward exposé of grubby and corrupt business practices in the pop music scene. Keitel is convincing

the West End play The Long, the Short and the Tall; while appearing in this play, he made his film debut with a small part in Kidnapped. O'Toole was then signed by Jules Buck for the role of a young Scots Guards lieutenant in The Day They Robbed the Bank of England (1960).

O'Toole then starred at the Stratford-on-Avon Memorial Theatre, playing three roles—Shylock in The Merchant of Venice, Petruchio in The Taming of the Shrew, and Thersites in Troilus and Cressida. In 1960, he was asked to play the title role in Lawrence of Arabia (1962), a film that won awards around the world and made O'Toole an international star. Although he has yet to win an Oscar, he has been nominated more than half a dozen times.

O'Toole's list of film credits also includes Becket (1964), Lord Jim (1965), What's New, Pussycat? (1965), How to Steal a Million (1966), The Lion in Winter (1968), Goodbye, Mr. Chips (1969), Murphy's War (1970), Under Milk Wood (1971), The Ruling Class (1971), Rosebud (1975), and The Stunt Man (1980). O'Toole made a spectacular comeback in My Favorite Year (1982), where he played a drunken matinee idol.

as an influential but frustrated record producer. However, there's not enough going on to overcome Sig Shore's choppy direction; the monotone music by the rock group Earth, Wind, and Fire; and lackluster performances by the rest of the cast. The screenplay is by newspaper columnist Robert Lipsyte. Also with Ed Nelson, Cynthia Bostick, Bert Parks, and Jimmy Boyd. (PG) *100 minutes*

SHIP OF FOOLS (1965)
★★★

Vivien Leigh
Simone Signoret
Oskar Werner
Heinz Ruhmann

Director Stanley Kramer tries hard to be faithful to the best-selling novel by Katherine Anne Porter, but far too often he fails to do the book justice. Fortunately, the superior performances of Leigh, Signoret, Werner, and Ruhmann keep the ship from sinking. The movie is about a voyage in 1933 from Vera Cruz to Bremerhaven and the eccentricities of its various passengers. Leigh plays a divorcée, and Signoret and Werner are lovers. Also with Michael Dunn, Lee Marvin, José Ferrer, Elizabeth Ashley, Lilia Skala, José Greco, George Segal, and Karen Verne. **Academy Award**—Ernest Laszlo, cinematography (black and white). **Nominations**—best picture; Werner, best actor; Signoret, best actress; Dunn, best supporting actor; Abby Mann, best screenplay (based on material from another medium).

150 minutes b&w

SHOCK TREATMENT (1982)
Ⓐ ★

Cliff DeYoung
Richard O'Brien

This film is a failed effort to capture the magic of *The Rocky Horror Picture Show* by the same folks who conceived the earlier cult classic. This musical follow-up tries to lampoon TV game shows and soap operas; the result is a dull, witless, and confusing production, which isn't worth viewing. The attempt at camp is all too obvious and strained. **Director**—Jim Sharman. (PG) *94 minutes*

• The Shoes of the Fisherman
• Shogun Assassin
• Shoot
• The Shootist
• Shoot the Moon
• Short Eyes
• A Shot in the Dark

S

THE SHOES OF THE FISHERMAN (1968)
★★

**Anthony Quinn
David Janssen
Laurence Olivier**

A fine cast can't salvage this confusing, boring, and long saga of a Russian cardinal who becomes the Pope. Quinn plays the Pontiff, Janssen is a journalist, and Olivier is the Russian premier. The story is supposedly based on Morris L. West's best-selling novel; but the book was a thoughtful and sensitive effort to explore complex life and death issues; the movie is superficial and fails to be of interest to either Christians or non-Christians. Also with Vittorio de Sica, Clive Revill, Paul Rogers, Barbara Jefford, and Leo McKern. **Director**—Michael Anderson.
157 minutes

SHOGUN ASSASSIN (1980)
 ★

Tomisaburo Wakayama

This is an exceedingly gory film set in medieval Japan. A samurai warrior, played by Wakayama, has been exiled, so he's forced to wander around the countryside, pushing his small son in a cart. Every few minutes it seems, they're attacked by bands of Ninja. Heads, hands, and feet are whacked off with abandon and blood gushes freely—all to the tune of disco music. The samurai manages to leave plenty of bodies in his wake, while his son tries to keep an accurate body count. It appears that at least two Japanese films were spliced together and redubbed to create *Shogun Assassin*. The dialogue is ridiculous, and the acting is second-rate; but the result is a grisly parody of such movies that's often hilarious. **Director**—Robert Houston. (R)
86 minutes

SHOOT (1977)
★

**Cliff Robertson
Ernest Borgnine**

Robertson and Borgnine star in this farfetched movie about two groups of weekend hunters who engage in a military-type shoot-out. The film is supposed to be a statement favoring gun control, but it's too simplistic and unbelievable to be taken seriously. The performances are dreary, and the direction is lackluster. *Shoot* is way off target. Also with Larry Reynolds, Henry Silva, and James Blendick. **Director**—Harvey Hart. (R) *98 minutes*

THE SHOOTIST
(1976)
 ★★

**John Wayne
Lauren Bacall
James Stewart**

Ron Howard sets out to meet The Shootist.

A moving, last film performance by Wayne as an aging frontier gunfighter who's dying of cancer. He wants to die in peace, but his reputation won't let him. He meets death his own way in a *High Noon* shoot-out with local adversaries. Bacall plays the owner of a rooming house, and Stewart is a doctor friend of Wayne's. The film, which might have been one of the Duke's greatest, is unfortunately bogged down with too much useless dialogue and a lot of pompous philosophizing. There's no significant action until the end, and it's rather pat. Also with Ron Howard, Richard Boone, Hugh O'Brien, Harry Morgan, John Carradine, and Scatman Crothers. **Director**—Don Siegel. (PG) *99 minutes*

SHOOT THE MOON (1982)
 ★★★

**Albert Finney
Diane Keaton**

An honest drama about the breakup of a 15-year marriage and the devastating effect on family members. Finney and Keaton are exceptionally good as the estranged couple, and many scenes are moving, indeed. Director Alan Parker (*Fame*) relentlessly lingers on the pain but does arrive at some telling revelations about what keeps people together and what drives them apart. Also with Karen Allen and Peter Weller. (R) *124 minutes*

SHORT EYES (1977)
 ★★★

**Bruce Davison
José Perez
Joe Carberry**

Davison, Perez, and Carberry star in this tough-talking, semidocumentary based on Miguel Pinero's award-winning play about prison life. It has a rawboned sort of entertaining quality that steers clear of the usual prison movie sentimentality. The cast—a mixture of ex-cons, street people, and professional actors—performs well. Filmed entirely in The Tombs, New York City's Men's House of Detention. Also with Don Blakely and Nathan George. **Director**—Robert M. Young. (R) *104 minutes*

A SHOT IN THE DARK (1964)
 ★★★

**Peter Sellers
Elke Sommer
George Sanders**

Sellers is at his best in this comic adventure as he once again plays the inept French police inspector Jacques Clouseau. Sommer, a refreshing partner in this comic romp through Paris, is a murder suspect in a crime at the home of Sanders. Pacing is a main ingredient in such a film, and under the direction of Blake Edwards, everything flows so perfectly you don't have time to question some of the more pre-
(Continued)

 Movie is available in Beta and VHS videotape

S

- The Shout
- Shout at the Devil
- Show Boat
- Silence of the North
- The Silencers
- Silent Movie
- The Silent Partner

(Continued)

posterous sequences. The scene at a nudist colony is hilarious. Also with Herbert Lom, Tracy Reed, and Graham Stark.   *101 minutes*

THE SHOUT (1979)

   ★★

**Alan Bates
Susannah York
John Hurt**

An eerie and thoroughly muddled movie about a strange madman who can kill someone with a loud yell. Bates delivers a keen performance as a mental patient who acquired his terrifying knack from Australian Aborigines. Hurt plays a composer, and York is his wife. The film's material is unfathomable, and the sound track, as if to emphasize the point of the film, is turned up extra loud. Also with Tim Curry and Robert Stephens. **Director**—Jerzy Skolimowski. (R)
          87 minutes

SHOUT AT THE DEVIL (1976)

★★★

**Lee Marvin
Roger Moore**

Action fans should like this old-fashioned African adventure; there are sea battles, run-ins with hungry crocodiles, narrow escapes, aerial derring-do, and hand-to-hand combat. It's based on a novel by Wilbur Smith. Marvin plays a gin-soaked ivory poacher who feuds with the local German commissioner on the eve of World War I. And there's Moore as Marvin's very British partner. The film is perhaps too long, and the plot sags in places; otherwise, it's acceptable escapist entertainment. Also with Barbara Parkins, René Kolldehoff, Karl Michael Vogler, Ian Holm, and George Coulouris. **Director**—Peter Hunt. (PG)   *126 minutes*

SHOW BOAT (1951)

   ★★★

**Kathryn Grayson
Howard Keel**

Some excellent Jerome Kern songs and energetic dancing make this a worthwhile film for muscial fans. The movie, based on Edna Ferber's novel about life on the Mississippi River in the 1900s, is enriched by the performances of Grayson, Keel, and Joe E. Brown. Marge and Gower Champion, Ava Gardner, William Warfield, Agnes Moorehead, and Robert Sterling appear in supporting roles. Songs include "My Bill," "Can't Help Loving That Man," and "Old Man River." **Director**—George Sidney. **Academy Award Nomination**—Charles Rosher, cinematography (color).   *108 minutes*

SILENCE OF THE NORTH (1982)

   ★★

Ellen Burstyn

Ellen Burstyn and Tom Skerritt float upstream to the Silence of the North.

Burstyn portrays a plucky young woman who survives harrowing experiences and brutal conditions in the northern Canadian territory in the early 1900s. The story, based on the life of Olive Fredrickson, is presented as an undramatic series of episodes. The film seems to work best as a travelogue, with breath-taking wilderness scenery upstaging everything else. Co-stars Tom Skerritt and Gordon Pinsent. **Director**—Allan Winton King. (PG)   *94 minutes*

THE SILENCERS (1966)

★★

**Dean Martin
Stella Stevens**

Martin plays secret agent Matt Helm in this effort to capitalize on the success of James Bond films. But this movie lacks all of the charm of the Bond productions. Stevens, however, perks up the movie slightly. There are other sexual attractions and action scenes galore, but most of the footage falls flat. Nevertheless, there were several sequels. Arthur O'Connell, Cyd Charisse, Robert Webber, James Gregory, Victor Buono, and Daliah Lavi appear in supporting roles. **Director**—Phil Karlson.   *103 minutes*

SILENT MOVIE (1976)

★★★

**Mel Brooks
Marty Feldman
Dom DeLuise**

Comedy king Brooks proves that silence is golden by taking a chance and making an actual silent movie. The result is a procession of hilarious sight gags (what else?), somewhat on the order of The Marx Brothers and The Three Stooges. The film also conveys warmth as well as humor, but don't expect the outrageous side-splitting antics of Brooks's *Blazing Saddles*. In the movie, Brooks plays a director named Mel Funn who tries to save a film studio from a takeover by a New York-based conglomerate. DeLuise and Feldman are his lunatic sidekicks. Splendid cameo appearances by Paul Newman, Burt Reynolds, and Liza Minnelli, and an uproarious nightclub tango routine with Anne Bancroft and the three leads. With English titles. (PG)   *86 minutes*

THE SILENT PARTNER (1979)

   ★★★

**Elliott Gould
Christopher Plummer**

A drab bank teller and a vicious, psychotic bank robber engage in a battle of wits in this nifty suspense film from Canada. Gould is the teller, and Plummer is the robber. The story moves briskly along with intriguing twists and turns while cleverly depicting the monotonous lives of the central characters. Performances throughout are superior; Gould is especially convincing as a man constantly teetering on the brink of disaster or victory. Also with Susannah York, Celina Lopez, Michael Kirby, and John Candy. **Director**—Daryl Duke. (R)   *103 minutes*

SILENT RAGE (1982)

★

Chuck Norris

Chuck Norris comforts Toni Kalem when one of her genetic experiments starts killing people in Silent Rage.

Karate champ Norris plays a Texas sheriff in pursuit of a mad killer whom genetic engineering has made virtually indestructible. There's an interesting sci-fi angle here, but it's handled awkwardly in this slow-paced story. Norris kicks and chops with his usual proficiency, and finally dumps the psychopath down a well. But is the vicious murderer really dead? This could be the stuff of which sequels are made. **Director**—Michael Miller. (R) *105 minutes*

SILENT RUNNING (1971)

★★★

Bruce Dern

A fairly well-made sci-fi adventure about a 21st-century space station crew trying to keep the last of Earth's vegetation from being destroyed. Dern is outstanding as the head of the space scientists aboard the verdant space ark, and there's a nice touch from two charming robots. The big star of this movie is the magnificent special effects handled skillfully by director Douglas Trumbull who contributed so much to *2001: A Space Odyssey.* Also with Cliff Potts, Ron Rifkin, and Jesse Vint. (PG) *90 minutes*

SILENT SCREAM (1980)

★

Yvonne De Carlo
Cameron Mitchell

A maniac murders some college students who move into a spooky old house. This is a predictable, cheaply made fright film that grows more ludicrous by the minute. The shabby-looking production stars De Carlo and Mitchell in rather unappealing roles. This formula haunted-house number has been done to death, yet haunted houses continue to haunt Hollywood. Also stars Rebecca Balding and Barbara Steele. **Director**—Denny Harris. (R) *86 minutes*

SILK STOCKINGS (1957)

★★★

Fred Astaire
Cyd Charisse

Astaire and Charisse star in this musical version of the famous *Ninotchka,* which starred Greta Garbo. Charisse plays a Russian agent trying to bring a Russian composer living in Paris back to Moscow. Astaire is a dapper Hollywood producer who sidetracks Charisse from her mission. The Garbo film was better, but the personable team of Astaire and Charisse and the Cole Porter music make this a highly acceptable substitute. Janis Paige, Peter Lorre, George Tobias, Jules Munshin, and Joseph Buloff also star. **Director**—Rouben Mamoulian. *116 minutes*

SILKWOOD (1983)

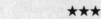

★★★

Meryl Streep
Cher
Kurt Russell

Often compelling biographical account of the spunky Oklahoma plutonium plant worker who died mysteriously in an auto crash as she was about to expose nuclear safety violations. Streep gives a brilliant, true-to-life portrayal in the title role, and the film examines the plight of many workers who toil under dangerous conditions. Yet many complex circumstances are not adequately resolved. **Director**—

Mike Nichols. (R) **Academy Award Nominations**—Streep, best actress; Cher, best supporting actress; Nichols, best director; Nora Ephron and Alice Arlen, best original screenplay.
131 minutes

SILVER BEARS (1978)

★

Michael Caine
Martin Balsam

A crude, cynical comedy adapted from Paul Erdman's best-selling 1974 novel about the world silver market. Caine is sent on a mission to Switzerland to buy a bank for syndicate head Balsam. A talented group of performers is wasted straining to produce laughs that never come. Ivan Passer directed this disaster, which also stars Cybill Shepherd, Louis Jourdan, and Tom Smothers. (PG) *113 minutes*

SILVER STREAK (1976)

★

Gene Wilder
Richard Pryor

Richard Pryor and Gene Wilder have a little trouble staying on their train in Silver Streak.

An exasperating and witless comedy-adventure set mostly aboard a Los Angeles-to-Chicago train. Wilder plays an editor who becomes involved in a murder. There's really nothing much to laugh about until Pryor comes along about an hour into the film. He teams up with Wilder for a few hilarious scenes, but these moments quickly cut to a heavy-handed tangle of action and a phony train crash special effect. Colin Higgins's tacky screenplay just keeps getting sidetracked, and director Arthur Hiller is little help at the throttle. Also with Jill Clayburgh, Pat-

(Continued)

 Movie is available in Beta and VHS videotape

S
- Simon
- Sinbad and the Eye of the Tiger
- Sinbad the Sailor
- Since You Went Away
- Singin' in the Rain
- Sink the Bismarck!
- Sirocco

(Continued)

rick McGoohan, Ned Beatty, Ray Walston, and Scatman Crothers. (PG)

113 minutes

SIMON (1980)

★★

Alan Arkin

Writer-director Marshall Brickman, who collaborated with Woody Allen on several hit films, solos with this droll half-baked comedy. It's about some zany think-tank geniuses who, out of boredom, brainwash a psychology professor into believing he's an alien from outer space. The professor is played by Arkin, who relentlessly hams it up. The Brickman script needles some absurdities of contemporary civilization, but after awhile, the needle becomes dull. Allen may be able to go it alone, but Brickman seems to need Allen's magic. Also with Madeline Kahn, Austin Pendleton, Fred Gwynne, William Finley, and Judy Graubart. (PG)

97 minutes

SINBAD AND THE EYE OF THE TIGER (1977)

★★★

Patrick Wayne
Jane Seymour

Dazzling special effects are the mainstay of this third Arabian Nights film adventure aimed at preteen audiences. Sinbad, played by Wayne, and Princess Farah, played by Seymour, go on a dangerous journey to rescue her brother who has been changed into a baboon. They battle supernatural creatures and prehistoric monsters along the way, so parents may find it a bit silly. Also with Taryn Power and Margaret Whiting. **Director**—Sam Wanamaker. (G) *113 minutes*

SINBAD THE SAILOR (1947)

★★★

Douglas Fairbanks, Jr.
Maureen O'Hara

With Fairbanks as the swashbuckling hero, this high-seas adventure is great fun for fans of seafaring thrillers. Fairbanks has just the right touch for this kind of film fare, as he seeks the lost treasure of Alexander. The movie also has a lovely princess, played by O'Hara, which, of course, is another necessary ingredient in such stories. Walter Slezak, Jane Greer, Anthony Quinn, Sheldon Leonard, George Tobias, and Mike Mazurki appear in supporting roles. **Director**—Richard Wallace. *117 minutes*

SINCE YOU WENT AWAY (1944)

★★★

Claudette Colbert
Joseph Cotten
Jennifer Jones
Shirley Temple

Jennifer Jones talks with the military men in Since You Went Away.

This star-studded tearjerker deals with how a typical family copes with the tragedies of World War II as well as its daily ordeals. Colbert, Cotten, Jones, and Temple are used to good advantage; Colbert is especially radiant in this well-made movie. It's so refreshing to see such an unabashedly pro-American film, that its faults and excess flag-waving are easily forgiven. Also with Lionel Barrymore, Guy Madison, Agnes Moorehead, Monty Woolley, Robert Walker, Hattie McDaniel, Albert Basserman, Keenan Wynn, and Craig Stevens. **Director**—John Cromwell. **Academy Award Nominations**—best picture; Colbert, best actress; Woolley, best supporting actor; Jones, best supporting actress; Stanley Cortez and Lee Garmes, cinematography (black and white).

172 minutes b&w

SINGIN' IN THE RAIN (1952)

★★★★

Gene Kelly
Donald O'Connor
Debbie Reynolds
Jean Hagen

Kelly, O'Connor, Reynolds, and Hagen sparkle in this marvelous musical spoof about Hollywood during the period when talkies first replaced silent films. Among the hit songs are "Make 'em Laugh," "My Lucky Star," "Broadway Melody," "Good Morning," and the title tune. Rita Moreno, Cyd Charisse, Douglas Fowley, and Millard Mitchell also star in what many critics consider the greatest Hollywood musical of all time. **Directors**—Kelly and Stanley Donen. **Academy Award Nomination**—Hagen, best supporting actress.

102 minutes

SINK THE BISMARCK! (1960)

★★★

Kenneth More
Dana Wynter

Exciting sea battles and good acting make this semidocumentary about the British hunt for the famed German battleship during World War II worthwhile viewing. Besides the search and eventual sinking of the German man-of-war, the personal dramas of the British sailors heighten the film's realism. More and Wynter star, with Karel Stepanek, Geoffrey Keen, Esmond Knight, Michael Hordern, Maurice Denham, Laurence Naismith, and Carl Mohner in supporting roles. **Director**—Lewis Gilbert.

97 minutes b&w

SIROCCO (1951)

★★

Humphrey Bogart
Marta Toren
Lee J. Cobb

Bogart manages to make this melodrama about gunrunning in the 1920s mildly interesting. Toren and Cobb also give artful performances, but the slow-moving story, set in Damascus, lacks firepower. Zero Mostel also makes an appearance in a supporting role, but he doesn't make any difference to the outcome. Also with Gerald Mohr, Onslow Stevens, and Everett Sloane. *Casablanca* it ain't. **Director**—Curtis Bernhardt. *98 minutes b&w*

SITTING PRETTY (1948)
★★★

Clifton Webb
Robert Young
Maureen O'Hara

Clifton Webb is an effective but stern babysitter in the comedy Sitting Pretty.

Webb is delightful in this comedy. He plays Mr. Belvedere, an eccentric genius who works as a babysitter for Young and O'Hara. When he writes a successful novel about his experiences, he throws gossipy neighbors into a tizzy. Webb became famous in this role, and two other Mr. Belvedere films followed. Also with Richard Haydn, Larry Olsen, Louise Allbritton, Ed Begley, and Randy Stuart. **Director**—Walter Lang. **Academy Award Nomination**—Webb, best actor.
84 minutes b&w

SIX BRIDGES TO CROSS (1955)
★★

Tony Curtis

Apparently inspired by the Boston Brink's robbery, this well-made film depicts the life and hard times of a Boston gangster in the 1930s. Curtis is at his best as the hoodlum who gets involved with crime and can't abide by the law no matter how hard he tries to go straight. He finally masterminds a robbery involving more than 2½ million dollars. George Nader, Sal Mineo,

Jan Merlin, Julie Adams, and Jay C. Flippen appear in supporting roles. **Director**—Joseph Pevney.
96 minutes b&w

SIX PACK (1982)
 ★★

Kenny Rogers
Diane Lane
Erin Gray

Country singer Rogers is moderately pleasing in this well-intentioned piece of fluff. He's a racing car driver trying to make a comeback with the help of six orphans. Rogers turns on his charm, but he's really not that impressive as an actor, and this is a shallow story. One of his hit songs on the sound track helps the production somewhat. The kids are cute, and the story ends on a happy note. **Director**—Daniel Petrie. (PG) *110 minutes*

SIXTEEN CANDLES (1984)
 ★★

Molly Ringwald
Anthony Michael Hall
Michael Shoeffling

Molly Ringwald gets her birthday wish in beau ideal hunk *Michael Schoeffling in* Sixteen Candles.

Oh, the agony of being 16 years old: Her sister's marriage upstages her birthday, the school dreamboat won't pay any attention, and a freshman "geek" tries to seduce her. This frantic, lowbrow teenage comedy, starring Ringwald in the pivotal role, is a mixture of hip, corny dialogue and bad-taste humor. Characters are mostly familiar, but interesting at times. **Director**—John Hughes. (PG)
95 minutes

SIX WEEKS (1982)
 ★

Mary Tyler Moore
Dudley Moore
Katherine Healy

Dreary, syrupy tearjerker with a plot so contrived as to defy belief. A cosmetic tycoon (Mary Tyler Moore) and her precocious daughter (Healy), who has leukemia, strike up a sentimental friendship with a California politician (Dudley Moore). Soon these unlikely chums are off to New York City, where the 12-year-old heroine skates at Rockefeller Center, assumes the lead in *The Nutcracker* ballet, and dies on the subway all (gasp) in a single weekend. Preposterous nonsense, and manipulative as well. **Director**—Tony Bill. (PG) *107 minutes*

SKIRTS AHOY! (1952)
★

Esther Williams
Vivian Blaine
Joan Evans

Williams, Blaine, and Evans star in this typical 1950s musical. Although they perform with energy and vitality, they're sunk by the silly plot's triteness. The trio joins the Navy as Waves and find romance with Dean Miller, Barry Sullivan, and Keefe Brasselle—a switch of the usual procedure in such films. Even the music of Billy Eckstine and the DeMarco Sisters fails to keep this production afloat. Also with Debbie Reynolds and Bobby Van. **Director**—Sidney Lanfield.
105 minutes

SKY RIDERS (1976)
★★★

James Coburn
Susannah York
Robert Culp

Daredevil hang-gliding stunts jazz up this well-photographed action drama filmed in Greece. The familiar and unbelievable plot, however, hardly gets off the ground. A wife and two children of a wealthy industrialist,
(Continued)

S
- The Slap
- Slap Shot
- Slaughterhouse Five
- Slaughter on Tenth Avenue
- Slayground
- Sleepaway Camp
- Sleeper

(Continued)
played by Culp, are kidnapped by political terrorists and are held at a remote mountain fortress. The wife's ex-husband, played by Coburn, tracks down the hideaway and hires a group of hang-gliding commandos for the thrilling rescue. Douglas Hickox does a fair job of directing. Bob and Chris Wills and their hang-glider team fly away with the movie. Also with Charles Aznavour, Werner Pochath, and Harry Andrews. (PG)

93 minutes

THE SLAP
(1976)

★

Isabelle Adjani
Lino Ventura
Annie Girardot

A French comedy of sorts, featuring such big-name stars as Adjani, Ventura, and Girardot. But the story is lightweight fare; it resembles a 1960s TV sitcom. The plodding film is about a conflict between a 51-year-old professor and his rebellious 18-year-old daughter who contemplates moving in with her boyfriend. Limp direction by Claude Pinoteau. In French with English titles. (No MPAA rating)

98 minutes

SLAP SHOT
(1977)

 ★★★

Paul Newman

An exhilarating and freewheeling comedy that probes the violence of professional ice hockey. Newman stars as a broken-down player-coach of a fourth-rate minor-league team, which suddenly becomes popular by playing dirty. The zestful screenplay by Nancy Dowd presents some lively and believable characters, although several soap-opera-like subplots get in the way. The film is well salted with locker-room humor and plenty of expletives. Newman handles his part well, and the lesser roles are all excellent. Also with Michael Ontkean, Lindsay Crouse, Melinda Dillon, Jennifer Warren, and Strother Martin. Directed with gusto by George Roy Hill. (R)

122 minutes

SLAUGHTERHOUSE FIVE
(1972)

 ★★★

Michael Sacks
Ron Leibman
Sharon Gans

Michael Sacks and Valerie Perrine honeymoon on the planet Tralfamadore in Slaughterhouse Five.

The very bizarre—almost mystical—antiwar novel by Kurt Vonnegut, Jr., is difficult to transfer to the screen. But there are still many good moments in this complex film about a New York optometrist who has fantasies about a strange futuristic planet and nightmares about Nazi prisoner-of-war camps. Many of the images are brilliant, but the movie is hard to follow at times, even for those who read the book. Sacks, Leibman, and Gans star, with Eugene Roche, Valerie Perrine, John Dehner, and Sorrell Booke in supporting roles. **Director**—George Roy Hill. (R)

104 minutes

SLAUGHTER ON TENTH AVENUE (1957)

★★★

Richard Egan
Jan Sterling
Dan Duryea
Walter Matthau

Another drama about murder and corruption on the New York City waterfront. Egan, Sterling, Duryea, and Matthau star in this well-constructed production about an assistant district attorney struggling to convict gangsters who control the waterfront. The movie *On the Waterfront* was better, but this is a respectable movie in the genre. The fine cast also includes Julie Adams, Charles McGraw, Sam Levene, and Harry Bellaver. **Director**—Arnold Laven.

103 minutes b&w

SLAYGROUND (1984)

★

Peter Coyote

In Slayground, *Peter Coyote gets a bad deal.*

Drab, poorly made crime melodrama that overindulges in mayhem. Coyote plays a gangster who is blamed for killing a child during a holdup. The child's wealthy father hires a hit man to avenge the death. This unappealing scenario leads to a cavalcade of shootings and a resulting pile of corpses, not to mention yawns of the viewer. Mel Smith and Billie Whitelaw have supporting roles. **Director**—Terry Bedford. (R)

89 minutes

SLEEPAWAY CAMP (1983)
(no stars)

Felissa Rose
Jonathan Tierston

Exceptionally vile, cheaply made teen horror film that is awful in every department. The well-worn plot formula of grisly murders takes place among summer campers and progresses toward an unsatisfying climax. Acting is dreadful, direction is haphazard, and the dialogue is just so much babble. Rose and Tierston lead the no-talent cast. **Director**—Robert Hiltzik. (R)

84 minutes

SLEEPER (1973)

 ★★★★

Woody Allen
Diane Keaton

Allen is in top form as writer, actor,

- The Sleeping Beauty
- Sleeping Dogs
- Sleuth
- Slither
- Slow Dancing in the Big City
- The Slumber Party Massacre
- Small Change

S

and director in this story. It's about a health food store owner who's frozen after an operation and awakens 200 years later in 2173 to find himself in a weird police state. Keaton is charming as his love interest of the future. There are good sight gags and enough one-liners to keep the story rolling at a brisk pace. John Beck, Mary Gregory, Don Keefer, and John McLiam are competent in supporting roles, and the Preservation Hall Jazz Band gives the enterprise an extra lift. (PG)

88 minutes

THE SLEEPING BEAUTY
(1958)

★★★

This classic fairy tale gets conscientious and sensitive handling from the gang at Walt Disney. By and large, they have followed the original story faithfully and with great detail. Kids will enjoy this cartoon feature, and parents might also find themselves watching it with more than routine interest. **Director**—Clyde Geronomi.

75 minutes

SLEEPING DOGS (1977)

★★★

Sam Neill
Warren Oates

An intriguing New Zealand-made political thriller that packs plenty of lively action and suspense. Neill stars as a man unwittingly caught between revolutionaries and a repressive government. He's hounded by the military and the chase scenes work up to a spectacular climax. The story ends on a routine note, but the pace is well maintained up to that point. Neill fares well as a frantic man-on-the-run; Oates turns in an impressive performance as an American officer who's in league with the military regime. **Director**—Roger Donaldson. (No MPAA rating)

107 minutes

SLEUTH (1972)

Ⓐ ★★★

Laurence Olivier
Michael Caine

Director Joseph L. Mankiewicz brings Anthony Shaffer's *tour-de-force* Broadway thriller to the stage, with smashing success. Mystery writer Olivier invites his wife's lover (Caine) to his English country house—ostensibly to propose an unusual scheme that would benefit both of them. But what's his real purpose? And what is his rival really thinking? Stay on your toes—just when you think you know what's happening, the rug's pulled out from under you. The stars have a ball with the cunning, twisting script. (PG) **Academy Award Nominations**—Mankiewicz, best director; Caine and Olivier, best actor.

138 minutes

SLITHER (1972)

★★★

James Caan
Sally Kellerman
Peter Boyle
Louise Lasser

James Caan and Peter Boyle eyeball one another in Slither.

Caan, Kellerman, Boyle, and Lasser star in this zany romp about a search—by means of trailers and campers—for a hidden cache of money in California. At times the movie appears shrill, and it isn't always easy to tolerate the glib blend of violence and comedy. However, the film is engaging and well made. Allen Garfield and Richard B. Shull appear in supporting roles. **Director**—Howard Zieff. (PG)

96 minutes

SLOW DANCING IN THE BIG CITY (1978)

★★

Paul Sorvino
Anne Ditchburn

A cliché-strewn boy-meets-girl story set in New York City. It's directed by John G. Avildsen who brought us *Rocky.* Again, Avildsen goes all out for sentimentality and the uplifting spirit, but the approach is so overdone the film lapses into triteness. Sorvino is excellent as a gruff newspaper columnist who falls for a struggling but ailing young ballerina, played by Ditchburn. It's sort of *Rocky* in leotards. Also with Nicolas Coster, Anita Dangler, and Hector Jaime Mercado. (PG)

101 minutes

THE SLUMBER PARTY MASSACRE (1982)

(no stars)

Michele Michaels
Robin Stille

A pair of women filmmakers—director Amy Jones and screenwriter Rita Mae Brown—cooked up this horror cheapie. It's the same old garbage: The standard maniac is running loose, this time doing his bloody deeds with a power drill. Scores of scantily-clad coeds and a few adolescent boys get slaughtered. It's all very mechanical. (R)

78 minutes

SMALL CHANGE (1976)

Ⓐ ★★★★

Eva Truffaut
Geory Desmouceaux
Philippe Goldman
Tania Torrens

French children who star in François Truffaut's entertaining film Small Change.

Director François Truffaut's 15th feature film is an endearing and entertaining celebration of childhood. The film consists of a series of vignettes

(Continued)

S
- A Small Circle of Friends
- Small Town Girl
- A Small Town in Texas
- Smash Palace
- Smile
- Smithereens
- Smokey and the Bandit

(Continued)

about a group of French children in a small village who manage to survive in an adult world with or without love. Truffaut lovingly treats his children as human beings—not as gimmicks for entertainment or exploitation. *Small Change* is for everyone, except perhaps those who don't like children. Also with Jean-François Stevenin, Claudio Deluca, and Frank Deluca. In French with English titles. (PG)   *104 minutes*

A SMALL CIRCLE OF FRIENDS
(1980)

★★

**Brad Davis
Karen Allen
Jameson Parker**

A glossed-over look at student life in the late '60s, when Vietnam war protests, drugs, and the sexual revolution made news. The story follows the college careers of three students, played enthusiastically by Davis, Allen, and Parker. But Rob Cohen directs at such a frantic pace that the story loses its perspective and burns out in the final segments. It seems as if the principals in this venture were too close to this period to effectively reflect on the times. (R)   *113 minutes*

SMALL TOWN GIRL
(1953)

★★

**Jane Powell
Farley Granger
Ann Miller
Bobby Van**

Powell, Granger, Miller, and Van star in this pleasant musical about a small-town girl. In this case, Powell falls in love with Granger, a handsome playboy who gets arrested in her Connecticut hometown for speeding. This musical version of a 1936 film lacks the dynamic pace and tempo of the better musicals, but it's still enjoyable. Miller almost steals the show with "I've Gotta Hear That Beat," staged by Busby Berkeley. S. Z. Sakall, Billie Burke, Robert Keith, Nat King Cole, and Fay Wray also appear. **Director—**Leslie Kardos.   *93 minutes*

A SMALL TOWN IN TEXAS
(1976)

    ★★

**Timothy Bottoms
Susan George
Bo Hopkins**

A young man comes home after serving time in prison on a pot rap and seeks revenge on the sheriff who busted him. It's pretty much B-picture melodrama, with plot sections stolen from *The Last Picture Show* and *Dirty Mary, Crazy Larry*. There's plenty of car-chase action and stunt crashes apparently aimed at the youth audience. Hopkins performs rather well as the mean sheriff, and he upstages Timothy Bottoms who plays the lead. George helps Bottoms against the cops. **Director—**Jack Starrett. (PG)   *95 minutes*

SMASH PALACE (1982)

    ★★★★

**Bruno Lawrence
Anna Jemison**

From New Zealand, a pretty straightforward story of a marital breakup distinguished by fine acting from the protagonists. A frantic auto mechanic (Lawrence) kidnaps his young daughter after his wife (Jemison) walks out on him. Director Roger Donaldson pursues the various emotional confrontations with restraint up to a conclusion that appears, for a moment, to have concluded nothing. An interesting movie. The background convincingly conveys the bleakness that prompted Jemison to walk out on her spouse. (No MPAA rating)   *90 minutes*

SMILE (1975)

    ★★★

**Barbara Feldon
Bruce Dern**

This satirical film, directed by Michael Ritchie, dissects the callousness and competitiveness of beauty contests, while also taking a hard look at small-town life in America. The somewhat documentary story, starring Feldon and Dern, is alternately amusing and tragic. Dern plays the pageant's sponsor—a used-car salesman—and Feldon is the woman who shepherds the contestants. Also with Michael Kidd, Geoffrey Lewis, Nicholas Pryor, Colleen Camp, and Melanie Griffith. (PG)   *113 minutes*

SMITHEREENS (1982)

    ★★

**Susan Berman
Richard Hell
Brad Rinn**

Young Susan Berman gets an early start toward becoming a bag lady in Smithereens.

Susan Seidelman directs her first feature film, an interestingly different character study of an eccentric, footloose teenage girl (Berman) trying to establish contact in New York's world of punk rock. A fair amount of energy has gone into this low-budget production, but the story, like the heroine's life, is haphazard and appears to go nowhere. (No MPAA rating)   *90 minutes*

SMOKEY AND THE BANDIT
(1977)

    ★★

**Burt Reynolds
Sally Field
Jackie Gleason
Jerry Reed**

Fast cars and an 18-wheel trailer truck are the stars of this comedy about a couple of good ol' boys who try to bootleg 400 cases of beer from Georgia

• Smokey and the Bandit II
• Smokey and the Bandit III
• The Smurfs and the Magic Flute

• The Snake Pit
• The Snows of Kilimanjaro
• Snow White and the Seven Dwarfs

S

to Texas under the noses of the cops. The film evolves into a drawn-out car chase, punctuated with predictable crash stunts and laced with CB jargon. Grinning Reynolds and singing Reed are so-so as the happy-go-lucky bootleggers. Gleason overacts as the frustrated Texas sheriff in hot pursuit. Field, a damsel in distress, gives the only commendable performance. Also with Mike Henry, Paul Williams, and Pat McCormick. **Director**—Hal Needham. (PG)   *96 minutes*

SMOKEY AND THE BANDIT II (1980)

 ★★★

Burt Reynolds
Sally Field
Jackie Gleason
Dom DeLuise

Once again the frustrated Sheriff Buford T. Justice, played by Gleason, is in long, hot pursuit of the Bandit (Reynolds), the Frog (Field), and their pals, who are transporting a pregnant elephant to Dallas to earn $400,000. Reynolds and company have spiced up their act to make this mindless, cartoonlike comedy more entertaining than the 1977 *Smokey* film. There are plenty of laughs and plenty of spectacular stunts, and the cast carries on in good-natured harmony. It's adolescent humor at best, but it works. Also with Paul Williams. **Director**—Hal Needham. (PG)   *95 minutes*

SMOKEY AND THE BANDIT III (1983)

 ★

Jackie Gleason

Jackie Gleason proves just how bad a great actor can be in Smokey and the Bandit III.

Burt Reynolds and Sally Field have nothing to do with this diluted continuation of the good ol' boy formula road movie. Only Gleason, as Sheriff Buford T. Justice, is left to carry on with the nonstop car chasing and smashups involving a race between Florida and Texas to deliver a large plastic fish. The characters and corny jokes wore thin long ago. Jerry Reed and Paul Williams are in supporting roles. **Director**—Dick Lowry. (PG)   *88 minutes*

THE SMURFS AND THE MAGIC FLUTE (1983)

 ★★

Utterly forgettable children's animated adventure, initially produced in Europe and awkwardly reworked with an English sound track for American audiences. The lackluster story, set in the Middle Ages, centers on a young musician's efforts to recover a magical flute from a villain. The bland band of Smurfs, who bear a vague resemblance to The Seven Dwarfs, don't become involved until about midway through the film. **Director**—John Rust. (G)   *80 minutes*

THE SNAKE PIT (1948)

★★★★

Olivia de Havilland

Olivia de Havilland and Mark Stevens in The Snake Pit, *about life in a mental hospital.*

This drama about life in a crowded mental hospital is a fine example of what Hollywood can do to improve society when it latches onto a worthwhile cause and makes a plea. In this case, there's a pitch for improved care of the mentally ill. De Havilland is excellent as a woman trying to over-

come mental illness and who has horrifying experiences in a mental institution. Leo Genn, Mark Stevens, Celeste Holm, Lee Patrick, Natalie Schaefer, Glenn Langan, Beulah Bondi, and Leif Erickson give good performances in supporting roles. **Director**—Anatole Litvak. **Academy Award Nominations**—best picture; Litvak, best director; de Havilland, best actress; Frank Partos and Millen Brand, writing (screenplay).
          108 minutes b&w

THE SNOWS OF KILIMANJARO (1952)

★★

Gregory Peck
Susan Hayward
Ava Gardner

Hollywood gives the star treatment to this Ernest Hemingway short story about a wounded white hunter contemplating his life as he awaits death. Unfortunately, most of the performers are less than stirring, although Peck is competent as the wounded man. Hayward and Gardner are less than satisfactory, and a weak film script doesn't help them overcome their limitations. Also with Leo G. Carroll, Marcel Dalio, Torin Thatcher, and Hildegard Neff. **Director**—Henry King. **Academy Award Nomination**—Leon Shamroy, cinematography (color).   *117 minutes*

SNOW WHITE AND THE SEVEN DWARFS (1937)

★★★★

The witch offers Snow White a poisoned apple in Snow White and the Seven Dwarfs.

This classic cartoon—Disney's first full-length feature—is as fresh and delightful now as when it was made. Besides the excellence of the produc-

(Continued)

S

- • S.O.B.
- • So Dear to My Heart
- • Sodom and Gomorrah
- • So Fine
- • The Soldier
- • Soldier in the Rain
- • Soldier of Fortune
- • A Soldier's Story

(Continued)
tion, the superb filming, and wonderful songs, there's the first-rate dramatic tension of Ms. White and her little friends confronting villains. Eight Disney writers worked on the Brothers Grimm fairy tale, with Larry Morey and Frank Churchill writing the songs. *82 minutes*

S.O.B. (1981)

★★

Julie Andrews
Richard Mulligan

Director Blake Edwards (*The Pink Panther* series; *10*) fries the Hollywood establishment in a cauldron of bitter comedy that often backfires and peters out midway. The hysterical broadside comes off mostly as an inside joke. Mulligan plays a producer who makes a $30-million flop musical, which he salvages by turning it into a soft-core porn extravaganza. Squeaky-clean Andrews, the star of the movie-within-the-movie, goes topless to salvage the project. The event is a cheap shot. (R) *121 minutes*

SO DEAR TO MY HEART (1948)

★★

Burl Ives
Beulah Bondi

Adults will find this Walt Disney story about a boy's determination to tame a black sheep and enter it in the competition at the state fair too nostalgic and sentimental, but it should appeal to most young children. The film, which includes some animated sequences, manages to capture the mood and charm of an American farm in the early 1900s. The cast also includes Harry Carey, Bobby Driscoll, and Luana Patten. **Director**—Harold Schuster. *84 minutes*

SODOM AND GOMORRAH (1962)

★

Stewart Granger
Stanley Baker
Pier Angeli
Anouk Aimée

This made-in-Italy biblical extravaganza about the Helamite plot to take over the wicked cities of Sodom and Gomorrah stars Granger, Baker, Angeli, and Aimée. Fortunately, the acting has merit, because the overly long story becomes boring despite the vice and gore. Such violence, however, doesn't pass for action. Part of the problem in this production is caused by the inability of the French and Italian producers to work well together. Also with Rossana Podesta. **Director**—Robert Aldrich. *154 minutes*

SO FINE (1981)

★★

Ryan O'Neal
Jack Warden

O'Neal seems out of place in this uneven comedy involving New York City's garment industry. He plays a tweedy college professor who improves his father's faltering clothing business by accidentally introducing designer jeans with see-through bottoms. The improbable story wavers between sophisticated humor and slapstick, with too few laughs coming across. Only Warden registers well, as the unrefined, huffing and puffing dress factory owner. Mariangela Melato and Richard Kiel also star. **Director**—Andrew Bergman. (R) *89 minutes*

THE SOLDIER (1982)

★★

Ken Wahl
Alberta Watson
Jeremiah Sullivan

Stone-faced Wahl stars as a romantic superhero who saves humanity from an international terrorist plot aimed at destroying half the world's oil supply. The lavish, breathless production is styled on the order of a James Bond adventure, but it pales in the comparison. A humorless, globe-hopping plot bogs down in unnecessary complications and grisly killings. Acting is no more than so-so, and for action the film relies mainly on hokey stunts and effects. **Director**—James Glickenhaus. (R) *96 minutes*

SOLDIER IN THE RAIN (1963)

★★

Steve McQueen
Jackie Gleason

McQueen and Gleason star in this tragi-comedy about the friendship between two Army sergeants. As expected, Gleason brings humor and mirth to the film, but his attempts at meaningful drama falter; he never seems to accomplish much on a serious level. However, there are enough comic moments to make the film worthwhile—especially for Gleason or McQueen fans. Tuesday Weld, Tom Poston, John Hubbard, Tony Bill, and Ed Nelson also star. **Director**—Ralph Nelson. *87 minutes b&w*

SOLDIER OF FORTUNE (1955)

★★

Clark Gable
Susan Hayward

Gable and Hayward are slightly better than average in this adventure film set in Hong Kong. Gable, a smuggler, is hired to find Hayward's photographer husband, played by Gene Barry, who's missing in Red China. The plot and script are slightly less than adequate, although the excellent photography and adventure sequences should make viewing worthwhile if you're a Gable fan. Also with Anna Sten, Michael Rennie, Leo Gordon, Russell Collins, Tom Tully, and Alex D'Arcy. **Director**—Edward Dmytryk. *96 minutes*

A SOLDIER'S STORY (1984)

★★★★

Howard Rollins, Jr.
Adolph Caesar

Tense drama and mystery occupy this superb film adaptation of Charles Fuller's prize-winning play about internal conflicts among black soliders. Set at an Army base in Louisiana during World War II, the literate and intriguing plot follows the murder investigation of a tyrannical black sergeant. Yet the story explores, in a deeper sense, the pain and outrage inflicted by racial prejudice. Powerhouse ensemble acting. **Director**—Norman Jewison. (PG) *102 minutes*

• The Solid Gold Cadillac
• Solomon and Sheba
• So Long at the Fair
• Somebody Killed Her Husband
• Somebody Up There Likes Me
• Some Came Running
• Some Kind of Hero

S

THE SOLID GOLD CADILLAC
(1956)
★★★

**Judy Holliday
Paul Douglas**

Paul Douglas and Judy Holliday in the comedy The Solid Gold Cadillac.

The comic genius of Holliday merges expertly with the brilliant acting skills of Douglas in this enjoyable comedy. She plays a minor stock-holder in a big company who tries to fire a corrupt board of directors. The movie is based on the play of George S. Kaufman and Howard Teichman, with the screen version written by Abe Burrows. John Williams, Fred Clark, Neva Patterson, Ray Collins, and Arthur O'Connell also star; George Burns narrates. Originally, the final scene was in color. **Director**—Richard Quine.
99 minutes b&w/color

SOLOMON AND SHEBA (1959)
★★

**Yul Brynner
Gina Lollobrigida**

This well-filmed biblical spectacle, photographed in Spain, takes a light-hearted try at telling what happened when David's older son plotted revenge after learning that David had named a younger brother heir. Mostly, this is just a splashy action film, with Lollobrigida as the alluring Queen of Sheba and Brynner as King Solomon. The large cast includes George Sanders, David Farrar, Marisa Pavan, Harry Andrews, and Alejandro Rey. **Director**—King Vidor. *139 minutes*

SO LONG AT THE FAIR (1950)
★★★

**Jean Simmons
Dirk Bogarde**

Simmons and Bogarde star in this mystery, set during the 1889 Paris Exposition. It's about a woman searching for her brother, who has mysteriously vanished during their visit to the exposition without a trace. The theme of torment and terror of vainly seeking help to find a missing person has been done better by Alfred Hitchcock and others, but this rendition is well made and worth viewing. David Tomlinson, Marcel Poncin, Cathleen Nesbitt, Felix Aylmer, André Morell, and Honor Blackman star in supporting roles. **Director**—Terence Fisher.
86 minutes b&w

SOMEBODY KILLED HER HUSBAND (1978)
★★

**Farrah Fawcett-Majors
Jeff Bridges**

Fawcett-Majors proves her worth as an adroit screen actress in this glossy mystery-comedy set in New York City. Farrah and friend, played by Bridges, set out to solve the murder of her estranged husband. But director Lamont Johnson fails to keep the tension working, and the film peters out in the final frames. Farrah's winning performance and her famous smile survive the rough treatment. Also with John Wood, Tammy Grimes, Patricia Elliott, and John Glover. (PG)
97 minutes

SOMEBODY UP THERE LIKES ME (1956)
★★★

**Paul Newman
Pier Angeli**

Boxer Rocky Graziano rose from the slums of New York City and reform school to become the middleweight boxing champion of the world. Newman does an excellent job of portraying Rocky in this film biography, and Angeli is splendid as his wife. Joseph

Paul Newman portrays Rocky Graziano in Somebody Up There Likes Me.

Buloff plays an earthy, streetwise philosopher. Eileen Heckart is Rocky's mom, and Everett Sloane is a fight promoter. The production is well done, although at times there's an excess of sentiment and violence. Sal Mineo, Robert Loggia, and Steve McQueen appear in supporting roles. **Director**—Robert Wise. **Academy Award**—Joseph Ruttenberg, cinematography (black and white).
112 minutes b&w

SOME CAME RUNNING (1958)
★★

**Frank Sinatra
Dean Martin
Shirley MacLaine**

Some viewers will be disappointed by the hatchet job that was done on the novel by James Jones. This melancholy story about a moody writer trying to adjust to his small hometown in the South after returning from the Army after World War II becomes an aimless melodrama on screen. However, excellent performances by Sinatra, MacLaine, and Martha Hyer make the movie worthwhile. Dean Martin, Nancy Gates, Leora Dana, and Arthur Kennedy appear in supporting roles. **Director**—Vincente Minnelli. **Academy Award Nominations**—MacLaine, best actress; Kennedy, best supporting actor; Hyer, best supporting actress.
127 minutes

SOME KIND OF HERO (1982)

★★

**Richard Pryor
Margot Kidder
Ray Sharkey**

(Continued)

(Continued)

Pryor's versatile and engaging performance is the only respectable asset that this otherwise second-rate movie can lay claim to. Pryor plays a Vietnam veteran who returns home to face a barrage of personal problems. At times, the film comes off as serious drama, then it abruptly switches to comedy, and this baffling vacillation destroys both the movie's impact and its credibility. Pryor's extraordinary talent deserves better material than this. **Director**—Michael Pressman. (R)
97 minutes

SOME LIKE IT HOT (1959)
 ★★★★

Jack Lemmon
Tony Curtis
Marilyn Monroe

In Some Like It Hot, *Marilyn Monroe and Tony Curtis stare into the bubble-bath to see what might pop up.*

Lemmon, Curtis, and Monroe form a fine comic trio in this free-flowing comedy about two unemployed musicians—Lemmon and Curtis—on the run from mobsters after they witness a gangland slaying. Disguised as women, they join an all-girl orchestra. At times, the laughs seem to gush forth in this uninhibited farce—and one of Hollywood's funniest movies ever. The trio gets fine supporting performances from George Raft, Joe E. Brown, Joan Shawlee, Pat O'Brien, Nehemiah Persoff, and George E. Stone. For extra measure, Monroe sings "Running Wild," and wide-mouthed Brown delivers the film's classic closing line. **Director**—Billy Wilder. **Academy Award Nominations**—Wilder, best director; Lemmon, best actor; Wilder and I.A.L. Diamond, best screenplay (based on material from another medium); Charles Lang, Jr., cinematography (black and white).
122 minutes b&w

SOMETHING SHORT OF PARADISE (1979)
★★

Susan Sarandon
David Steinberg

This contemporary romantic comedy is about an on-again, off-again affair between a klutzy art house proprietor and a magazine writer. Sarandon is the writer, and Steinberg is the proprietor. The movie often appears to parallel the Woody Allen/Diane Keaton style of film with a few variations: Steinberg is less of a sad sack than Allen, while Sarandon is less zany than Keaton. There are some funny moments, although the humor is generally low-key. Marilyn Sokol is excellent as a cunning member of the singles jungle. Also with Robert Hitt, Jean-Pierre Aumont, and Joe Grifasi. **Director**—David Helpern, Jr. (PG)
91 minutes

SOMETHING WICKED THIS WAY COMES (1983)
 ★★

Vidal Peterson
Shawn Carson
Jason Robards, Jr.

With such a title, you sort of expect a lot from this Disney-produced horror movie, which is based on the Ray Bradbury tale. But an uncomfortable and listless atmosphere envelops this period fantasy about a sinister carnival that causes havoc in a small midwestern town. Peterson and Carson do reasonably well with their roles as adventuresome boys, but Robards is under par as the meek librarian who gathers his courage to save them from their fate. **Director**—Jack Clayton. (PG)
94 minutes

SOMETIMES A GREAT NOTION (1971)
 ★★★

Paul Newman
Henry Fonda
Michael Sarrazin
Richard Jaeckel

Newman directed and stars in this beautifully filmed story about a log-

Paul Newman directs and stars in Sometimes a Great Notion.

ging family in Oregon. The members of the family believe in individuality so they defy a local strike by staying on the job. The father is played by Fonda, and Newman, Sarrazin, and Jaeckel are his sons. The movie isn't particularly faithful to Ken Kessey's novel nor even to its own good intentions, but the acting is excellent. The star-studded cast also includes Lee Remick, Cliff Potts, and Linda Lawson. (PG) **Alternate Title**—*Never Give an Inch.* **Academy Award Nomination**—Jaeckel, best supporting actor.
114 minutes

SOMEWHERE IN TIME (1980)
★

Christopher Reeve
Jane Seymour

A schmaltzy, sentimental love story with Reeve as a young playwright who crosses the time barrier to find his true love, played by Seymour. After falling in love with an old photograph, Reeve wills himself back in time to meet the woman. This sort of mystical romance was done well in the '40s. Remember *Portrait of Jennie*? But Reeve is no Joseph Cotten, and this silly film misfires for lack of inspiration and imagination. Seymour looks beautiful, but she's all surface and bogged down with trite dialogue. Also with Teresa Wright. **Director**—Jeannot Szwarc. (PG)
103 minutes

• A Song is Born
• The Song of Bernadette
• Song of Norway
• Song of the South
• The Song Remains the Same
• Son of Dracula
• Son of Frankenstein

S

A SONG IS BORN (1948)

★★

Danny Kaye
Virginia Mayo

Kaye and Mayo get great support from jazz greats Benny Goodman, Charlie Barnet, Louis Armstrong, Lionel Hampton, and Tommy Dorsey, but the weak script sinks the whole show in this musical remake of *Ball of Fire*, a comedy starring Gary Cooper. Hugh Herbert, Jr., Edward Bromberg, Mary Field, Steve Cochran, Felix Bressart, and Mel Powell appear in supporting roles. **Director**—Howard Hawks. *113 minutes*

THE SONG OF BERNADETTE (1943)

★★★★

Jennifer Jones

In Song of Bernadette, *Jennifer Jones plays the role of a pious French girl.*

Jones became a star after her portrayal of Bernadette, a pious French girl who has a vision of the Virgin Mary at Lourdes, a site that became a shrine. Although the movie is long and the handling of a sensitive religious subject is at times heavy-handed, the film's virtues outweigh its faults. Also with Vincent Price, William Eythe, Charles Bickford, Lee J. Cobb, Sig Rumann, Gladys Cooper, and Anne Revere. **Director**—Henry King. **Academy Awards**—Jones, best actress; Arthur Miller, cinematography (black and white). **Nominations**—best

picture; King, best director; Bickford, best supporting actor; Cooper, Revere, best supporting actress; George Seaton, writing (screenplay).
156 minutes b&w

SONG OF NORWAY (1970)

 ★

Florence Henderson
Toralv Maurstad

This biographical mishmash about the life of Edvard Grieg is pleasant to watch—especially with its splendid landscapes. However, it's poorly made and almost totally lacking in substance; the music is also substandard. The cast also includes Edward G. Robinson, Harry Secombe, Oscar Homolka, Robert Morley, Christina Schollin, and Frank Porretta, but none is able to salvage this dud. **Director**—Andrew L. Stone. (G) *141 minutes*

SONG OF THE SOUTH (1947)

★★★

Ruth Warrick
Bobby Driscoll

This charming children's story about Uncle Remus and Brer Rabbit is interspersed with cartoon segments. Most adults find only the cartoons charming and the rest of the Disney enterprise weak. But many kids will probably enjoy the whole show, as small boys on a southern plantation listen to Uncle Remus, an old black servant, tell Brer Rabbit stories. The cast also includes James Baskett, Lucile Watson, Hattie McDaniel, and Luana Patten. **Director**—Harve Foster. *94 minutes*

THE SONG REMAINS THE SAME (1976)

(no stars)

This long, ear-shattering feature covers the Led Zeppelin's 1973 Madison Square Garden appearance. Going to this movie is supposed to be the equivalent of attending such a concert by the British rock group, but it doesn't work. Gone is the sense of physical presence and the ability of an audience to communicate excitement to the performers. What's left is an unbearable

sound assault, which may leave you with a headache. **Directors**—Peter Clifton and Joe Massot. (PG)
136 minutes

SON OF DRACULA (1943)

★★

Lon Chaney, Jr.
Louise Albritton

The Son of Dracula, *Lon Chaney, Jr., says thanks but no thanks to the offer of a crucifix.*

The cast in this horror film has all the standard operatives for such tales—Albritton, Chaney, Frank Craven, J. Edward Bromberg, Evelyn Ankers, Samuel S. Hinds, and Robert Paige. If horror fare is your pleasure, then this story of Count Alucard—Dracula spelled backward—who visits a southern plantation and terrorizes much of the neighborhood might even be enjoyable. **Director**—Robert Siodmak.
80 minutes b&w

SON OF FRANKENSTEIN (1939)

★★★

Basil Rathbone
Boris Karloff
Bela Lugosi
Lionel Atwill

Classic horror film characters, including Rathbone, Karloff, Lugosi, Atwill, and Edgar Norton, make this a top-rated entry of the genre. There are numerous tense, spine-tingling moments as the son of Frankenstein tries to capture an old monster created by his father. The production is well staged, although at times there's

(Continued)

S

• Son of Paleface
• Sons and Lovers
• The Sons of Katie Elder

• Sophie's Choice
• So Proudly We Hail
• Sorcerer

In Son of Frankenstein, *Basil Rathbone shows Boris Karloff the ropes.*

(Continued)

too much dialogue. Lawrence Grant, Donnie Dunagan, Josephine Hutchinson, and Emma Dunn appear in supporting roles. **Director**—Rowland V. Lee. *99 minutes b&w*

SON OF PALEFACE (1952)
★★★

**Bob Hope
Roy Rogers
Jane Russell**

Hope stars in this wacky comedy about a bumbling fellow who goes West to collect his inheritance. Some of the bids at humor are a bit strained and pale, but there's enough fun to make viewing worthwhile. Shapely Russell is a pleasant addition and inspiration for Hope. Rogers and his famous horse Trigger also make an appearance. Bill Williams, Harry Von Zell, Douglass Dumbrille, and Lloyd Corrigan appear in supporting roles. **Director**—Frank Tashlin. *95 minutes*

SONS AND LOVERS (1960)
★★★★

**Dean Stockwell
Trevor Howard
Wendy Hiller**

D. H. Lawrence's autobiographical novel about a sensitive youth pushed by his mother to make a life for himself away from the Nottingham coal mines is faithfully brought to the screen by director Jack Cardiff; it's also well adapted by the screenplay of Gavin Lambert and T.E.B. Clarke. Stockwell plays the youth, Hiller is his mother. The movie is enhanced by the star performances of Howard as the boy's

gruff father and Mary Ure as the woman in the life of the would-be artist. The photography does an excellent job of conveying the mood probably intended by Lawrence. Heather Sears, Donald Pleasence, Ernest Thesiger, and William Lucas also star. **Academy Award**—Freddie Francis, cinematography (black and white). **Nominations**—best picture; Cardiff, best director; Howard, best actor; Ure, best supporting actress; Lambert, best screenplay (based on material from another medium). *103 minutes b&w*

THE SONS OF KATIE ELDER (1965)
★★

**John Wayne
Dean Martin
Michael Anderson, Jr.
Earl Holliman**

Wayne, Martin, Anderson, and Holliman—the sons of frontier woman Katie Elder—set out to avenge their mother's death, but town thugs and other villains give them trouble. Much of the action is predictable, but the stars make the film worthwhile and entertaining for western fans. George Kennedy, Martha Hyer, James Gregory, Paul Fix, and Jeremy Slate appear in supporting roles. **Director**—Henry Hathaway. *112 minutes*

SOPHIE'S CHOICE (1982)
★★★

**Meryl Streep
Kevin Kline
Peter MacNicol**

Kevin Kline, Meryl Streep, and Peter MacNicol enjoy an outing at Coney Island in Sophie's Choice.

An unforgettable performance by Streep in the title role dominates this film adaptation of William Styron's haunting novel. She plays a guilt-ridden survivor of a Nazi concentration camp, and her subtle mannerisms and Polish-accented English contribute to a heart-wrenching portrait of a tragic heroine. The lengthy film often lapses into staginess, but the many powerful moments compensate for the slow passages. **Director**—Alan J. Pakula. (R) **Academy Award**—Streep, best actress. **Nominations**—Pakula, best screenplay (based on material from another medium); Nestor Almendros, cinematography. *157 minutes*

SO PROUDLY WE HAIL (1943)
★★

**Claudette Colbert
Paulette Goddard
Veronica Lake**

This patriotic film about Army nurses serving bravely on Bataan during World War II is conscientiously done and makes a valiant bid to give another view of the hell of war. It seems dated now and too melodramatic, but the performances of Colbert, Goddard, and Lake were well received at the time the movie was released. The cast also includes George Reeves, Barbara Britton, Walter Abel, Sonny Tufts, and John Litel. **Director**—Mark Sandrich. **Academy Award Nominations**—Goddard, best supporting actress; Allan Scott, writing (original screenplay); Charles Lang, cinematography (black and white). *125 minutes b&w*

SORCERER (1977)
★★★

Roy Scheider

Director William Friedkin has done a masterful job at building suspense and capturing the gritty details of despair in this intense thriller, which is a remake of H. G. Clouzot's *The Wages of Fear*. The film is about four desperate men, stuck in a squalid South American country, who drive two truckloads of nitroglycerin on bumpy roads through 200 miles of steaming jungle. Scheider stands out as one of the antiheroes; it's a role Humphrey Bogart would have found to his liking. (PG)   *122 minutes*

SORROWFUL JONES
(1949)
★★

**Bob Hope
Lucille Ball**

Hope and Ball star in this overly sentimental Damon Runyon comedy about a bookie, deeply involved with mobsters, who unofficially adopts an orphan. Hope, of course, plays the title role of the bookie. There are some pleasant moments and occasional laughs, but the earlier film, *Little Miss Marker* with Shirley Temple, was superior. Also with William Demarest, Thomas Gomez, Houseley Stevenson, Bruce Cabot, Mary Jane Saunders, and Tom Pedi. **Director**—Sidney Lanfield.   *88 minutes b&w*

SORRY, WRONG NUMBER
(1948)
 ★★★

**Barbara Stanwyck
Burt Lancaster**

Barbara Stanwyck reaches the wrong party in Sorry, Wrong Number.

This tense thriller, with Stanwyck as a bedridden neurotic who overhears a plot to murder her, tries a bit too hard to be a classic instead of just a good film. But at times, Stanwyck's performance is near perfection, and Lancaster, who plays her murderous husband, helps to make the production an effective suspense movie. Wendell Corey, Ed Begley, Leif Erickson, William Conrad, Harold Vermilyea, and Ann Richards also star. **Director**—

DIANE KEATON

Born in Los Angeles, in 1949, Diane Keaton was raised in nearby Santa Ana, where she attended grammar and high schools. Even as a teenager, she was interested in acting and appeared in a number of high school productions.

Keaton majored in drama at Santa Ana College, where she began her theatrical career by playing a wide variety of roles in productions ranging from contemporary musicals to Shakespeare. Her summers were spent performing in stock company productions of such plays as The Importance of Being Earnest; Little Mary Sunshine; Oklahoma!; Kiss Me, Kate; The Sound of Music; Bye, Bye Birdie; and Oh! What a Lovely War.

She moved to New York City, where she studied at the Neighborhood Playhouse and in 1968 made her first professional stage appearance, replacing Lynn Kellogg in the Broadway production of Hair.

Keaton's next Broadway assignment was co-starring with Woody Allen in his hit play Play It Again, Sam; in 1970, she made her motion-picture debut in Lovers and Other Strangers.

Since then, Keaton's film credits have included the role of Al Pacino's wife in The Godfather (1972) and The Godfather—Part II (1974), the recreation of her stage performance in the movie version of Play It Again, Sam (1972), and five other motion pictures with Woody Allen—Sleeper (1974), Love and Death (1975), Annie Hall (1977), Interiors (1978), and Manhattan (1979). For her performance in Annie Hall, she won the Oscar as best actress. After Annie Hall, Keaton played Theresa Dunn, the lead in Richard Brooks's film version of Judith Rossner's best-selling novel, Looking for Mr. Goodbar (1977).

Keaton also appeared in two 1976 comedies, I Will, I Will . . . For Now and Walter and Harry Go to New York. In the same year, she returned to the New York stage in Israel Horovitz's off-beat comedy, The Primary English Class. Her most recent films are Reds (1981), which won her another Oscar nomination, Shoot the Moon (1982), The Little Drummer Girl (1984), and Mrs. Soffel (1984).

Anatole Litvak. **Academy Award Nomination**—Stanwyck, best actress.   *89 minutes b&w*

THE SOUND AND THE FURY
(1959)
★★

**Yul Brynner
Joanne Woodward**

There's too much misspent fury and not enough sound filmmaking in this strange production based on William Faulkner's novel. Hollywood tries to convey the decadence of the South in this story of a young lady seeking independence from her strict family, but they end up showing a misconception of the Faulkner novel. Brynner, Woodward, Margaret Leighton, Stuart

Whitman, Ethel Waters, Jack Warden, and Françoise Rosay are good enough to create some fine moments amid the rubble. **Director**—Martin Ritt.   *117 minutes*

SOUNDER (1972)
 ★★★★

**Paul Winfield
Cicely Tyson**

Brilliant performances by Winfield and Tyson help to make this story about a family of sharecroppers in Louisiana during the Depression one of the finest movies about blacks ever filmed in this country. The excellent direction of Martin Ritt and splendid supporting performances by Kevin
(Continued)

 Movie is available in Beta and VHS videotape

S
- Sounder, Part 2
- The Sound of Music
- Soup for One
- Southern Comfort
- South Pacific
- Spacehunter: Adventures in the Forbidden Zone

(Continued)

Hooks, Carmen Mathews, James Best, and Taj Mahal make the experiences of the family devastatingly real and compelling. Although this is a realistic view of problems faced by blacks, it's still a warm and compassionate movie for the whole family. (G) **Academy Award Nominations**—best picture; Winfield, best actor; Tyson, best actress; Lonne Elder III, best screenplay (based on material from another medium).

105 minutes

SOUNDER, PART 2 (1976)
★★

**Harold Sylvester
Ebony Wright**

This sequel about the struggles of poor black sharecroppers in Louisiana during the '30s isn't in the same league with the popular and moving 1972 film. This episode has the Morgan family involved with building a schoolhouse for the neighborhood. The idea is embarrassingly drowned in sentimentality and gloominess, and the film has nothing to do with the family's battered hound dog Sounder, who remains merely in the background. Also with Darryl Young, Annazette Chase, and Taj Mahal. **Director**—William Graham. (G)

98 minutes

THE SOUND OF MUSIC (1965)
 ★★★★

Julie Andrews

Andrews sings and acts and radiates with such vitality that her performance overshadows some of the sugary excesses in this film and one even forgets that the movie is too long. The beautiful scenery and excellent music also make this film worthwhile. The movie is based on the life of the Von Trapp family. Andrews plays Maria Von Trapp, who escapes the Nazis in Austria with her children to Switzerland. Other stars in this Rodgers and Hammerstein musical include Peggy Wood, Christopher Plummer, Richard Haydn, Anna Lee, Eleanor Parker, and Marni Nixon. **Director**—Robert Wise. **Academy Awards**—best picture; Wise, best director. **Nominations**—Andrews,

Julie Andrews portrays Maria Von Trapp in the musical The Sound of Music.

best actress; Wood, best supporting actress; Ted McCord, cinematography (color).

172 minutes

SOUP FOR ONE (1982)
 ★★

**Saul Rubinek
Marcia Strassman
Gerrit Graham**

Saul Rubinek falls in love with questionairess Marcia Strassman in Soup for One.

There's a certain similarity to Woody Allen's comedies in this attempted satire on the singles scene, written and directed by novice filmmaker Jonathan Kaufer, but it's way below Allen's class. The film perks up occasionally with some clever scenes, but Kaufer cannot sustain the necessary degree of wit. The amateurish acting matches the material, which is generally inept and pretentious. Rubinek stars as the desperate young man pursuing the girl of his dreams (Strassman). (R)

84 minutes

SOUTHERN COMFORT (1981)
 ★★

**Keith Carradine
Powers Boothe**

Nine weekend warriors in the National Guard become lost in the Louisiana bayous and wind up in a mini-war with local Cajun hunters. The uneven story is unconvincing, mean-spirited, and unnecessarily violent. The pretentious plot apes *Deliverance*, but this film hardly delivers any worthwhile entertainment. Carradine and Boothe have key roles as the only intelligent soldiers in the military unit. **Director**—Walter Hill. (R) *101 minutes*

SOUTH PACIFIC (1958)
 ★★

**Mitzi Gaynor
Rossano Brazzi**

This musical version about life in the South Pacific during World War II and the love story of an American Navy nurse and a middle-aged French planter lacks the superstars needed to make it a production with clout. The location photography is beautiful, and the Rodgers and Hammerstein music is delightful; numbers include "Some Enchanted Evening," "Younger Than Springtime," "There Is Nothing Like a Dame," "Bali Ha'i," and "You've Got To Be Taught." Gaynor is pleasant but not dynamic enough as the nurse, and Brazzi is lackluster as the planter. Other performers in this long musical are France Nuyen, John Kerr, Ray Walston, and Juanita Hall. **Director**—Joshua Logan. **Academy Award Nomination**—Leon Shamroy, cinematography (color). *170 minutes*

SPACEHUNTER: ADVENTURES IN THE FORBIDDEN ZONE (1983)
 ★

**Peter Strauss
Molly Ringwald
Ernie Hudson**

This grubby-looking space-honor saga, shot in 3-D, features Strauss as a man-about-planets on a mission to rescue three damsels. Strauss pursues his ob-

• The Spanish Main
• Sparkle
• Spartacus
• A Special Day
• Special Delivery
• Special Section
• Spellbound

S

jective at the wheel of a futuristic junk-mobile, and much lavish technical work has been expended to create a background in 21st century junkyard chic. The script of this noisy production is strictly third-rate. **Director—** Lamont Johnson. (PG)   *90 minutes*

THE SPANISH MAIN (1945)

   ★★★

**Paul Henreid
Maureen O'Hara
Walter Slezak**

In this pirate movie a swashbuckling adventurer (Henreid) confronts the bad guy (Slezak) and eventually wins the hand of the beautiful maiden (O'Hara). There's plenty of fun and adventure for fans of this genre, and the actors give the story the right emphasis. Supporting actors include Jack LaRue, Victor Kilian, Binnie Barnes, Barton MacLane, Fritz Leiber, Nancy Gates, Mike Mazurki, and J. M. Kerrigan. **Director—**Frank Borzage. **Academy Award Nomination—**George Barnes, cinematography (color).

101 minutes

SPARKLE (1976)

   ★★

**Lonette McKee
Irene Cara
Philip M. Thomas**

A familiar melodrama about three Harlem sisters who become pop singers in the '50s. Aside from scattered bright moments, the story and acting are routine and shallow, following well-worn paths of violence, drug addiction, and family crisis. The music of Curtis Mayfield helps out at times, and there are some well-composed scenes of murky nightclubs. Also with Dwan Smith, Mary Alice, Tony King, and Dorian Harewood. **Director—**Sam O'Steen. (PG)   *100 minutes*

SPARTACUS (1960)

   ★★★

**Kirk Douglas
Laurence Olivier
Peter Ustinov**

Between the gaudy scenes and the trite moments, there are some thoughtful sequences and excellent characterizations in this long and, at times, thrilling historical epic about slaves in revolt in ancient Rome. Douglas, Olivier, and Ustinov are superb in major parts; Kirk plays the title role. The script by Dalton Trumbo is another plus. The large cast also includes Charles Laughton, John Gavin, Nina Foch, Jean Simmons, Tony Curtis, Woody Strode, Herbert Lom, and John Ireland. **Director—**Stanley Kubrick. **Academy Awards—**Ustinov, best actor; Russell Metty, cinematography (color).   *196 minutes*

A SPECIAL DAY (1977)

   ★★

**Sophia Loren
Marcello Mastroianni**

Loren plays a bedraggled Italian housewife who finds a brief moment of passion with an intellectual homosexual neighbor, played by Mastroianni. As always, the two stars work well together. But the syrupy, two-character drama is as shabby and trite as the downtrodden apartment setting, which it never leaves. This brief encounter—Italian style—takes place in 1938 on a day when all Rome turned out to rally for Hitler. Also with John Vernon, Nicole Magny, and Françoise Berd. **Director—**Ettore Scola. In Italian with English titles. (No MPAA rating) **Academy Award Nominations—** best foreign-language film; Mastroianni, best actor.   *106 minutes*

SPECIAL DELIVERY (1977)

   ★★

**Bo Svenson
Cybill Shepherd**

Shepherd, looking like a scrubbed campus queen, plays a divorcée who cuts herself in on a bank heist pulled off by an ex-Marine, played by Svenson. The comic melodrama maintains a degree of suspense as other bystanders try to horn in on the loot. It's a better-than-average B-movie, with some interesting performances and a touch of good humor. The adventure ends with a screeching car chase that's rather overused in such films. Also with Tom Atkins, Vic Tayback, Michael

Gwynne, and Sorrell Booke. **Director—**Paul Wendkos. (PG)   *99 minutes*

SPECIAL SECTION (1975)

   ★★

**Louis Seigner
Michel Lonsdale**

A political drama about the Vichy government in France, which set up special courts (special sections) to try and sentence Frenchmen to appease the Nazis. The film is directed by Costa-Gavras, the maker of *Z* and *State of Siege*. But *Special Section* lacks the drive and emotional impact of his previous works. Characters come and go rather mechanically, and the cast consists mostly of unfamiliar actors. The story is based on an actual event—the killing of a German officer by young Marxists in a Paris subway. Also with Ivo Garrani, Bruno Cremer, Pierre Dux, and Henri Serre. In French with English titles. (PG)   *110 minutes*

SPELLBOUND
(1945)

   ★★★

**Ingrid Bergman
Gregory Peck**

In Spellbound, *Ingrid Bergman hides a patient from the law.*

Bergman portrays a psychiatrist who hides a patient accused of murder from the police until she's able to solve his emotional problems in this less-than-perfect Alfred Hitchcock suspense film. There are many fascinating aspects to this psychological mystery, including fine acting and Salvador Dali dream sequences, but the plot is occasionally farfetched and too tricky to be believable. Michael Chek-

(Continued)

 Movie is available in Beta and VHS videotape

S
- Spencer's Mountain
- Sphinx
- The Spiral Staircase
- The Spirit of St. Louis
- Splash
- Splendor in the Grass
- Split Image

(Continued)

hov, Rhonda Fleming, Leo G. Carroll, Steve Geray, Wallace Ford, and Norman Lloyd also star. **Academy Award Nominations**—best picture; Hitchcock, best director; Chekhov, best supporting actor; George Barnes, cinematography (black and white).

111 minutes b&w

SPENCER'S MOUNTAIN (1963)
★★

Henry Fonda
Maureen O'Hara
James MacArthur
Wally Cox

Fonda, O'Hara, MacArthur, and Cox are saddled with an inferior script in this soap opera about a Wyoming landowner who keeps promising to build another house for his family of nine. Despite its faults, this sentimental entry, set in the '30s, evolved into the TV series *The Waltons*. Also with Donald Crisp, Mimsy Farmer, and Lilian Bronson. **Director**—Delmer Daves.

121 minutes

SPHINX (1981)
 ★

Lesley-Anne Down
Frank Langella

Egyptologist Erica Baron, played by Down, goes to the land of the pharaohs, where she witnesses a murder, dodges bullets, fends off a rape attack, gets thrown into a dungeon, and—get this—falls through the floor of a men's room into a tomb filled with ancient treasures. She's out of breath by the second reel, and so is the audience. Langella, playing an Egyptian diplomat, pops up now and then; it's his worst film performance. Franklin Schaffner lamely directed this idiotic gibberish. *Sphinx* stinks. (PG)

119 minutes

THE SPIRAL STAIRCASE
(1946)
 ★★★★

Dorothy McGuire

There isn't a wasted action or word in this taut and well-directed suspense film about a killer who terrorizes deformed girls. McGuire is brilliant as the mute servant girl in an eerie house trying to avoid the killer's evil clutches. At times, it seems—with the vivid and dreary New England setting—that Alfred Hitchcock's hand is present, but the credit goes to director Robert Siodmak for this masterful mystery. George Brent, Kent Smith, James Bell, Sara Allgood, Gordon Oliver, Ethel Barrymore, and Rhonda Fleming appear in supporting roles. **Academy Award Nomination**—Barrymore, best supporting actress.

83 minutes b&w

THE SPIRIT OF ST. LOUIS
(1957)
 ★★

James Stewart

James Stewart flies solo across the Atlantic in The Spirit of St. Louis.

Stewart is fine as Charles Lindbergh and makes a spirited effort to create a passable movie, but there are too many trite and dull scenes. The production seems long because there are many scenes that show Lindy flying solo, especially on his 3,600-mile, 33½-hour New York-to-Paris flight in 1927, and it isn't possible to have much interesting action in such situations. Marc Connelly, Patricia Smith, and Murray Hamilton are competent in supporting roles. **Director**—Billy Wilder.

135 minutes

SPLASH (1984)
 ★★★

Daryl Hannah
John Candy
Tom Hanks

A familiar man-meets-mermaid romantic comedy that delivers big portions of clever satire though it is often too sentimental and obvious. Tom Hanks plays a lonely New York bachelor who falls in love with winsome mermaid Hannah. In the big city, she must cope with sophisticated living and ambitious scientists who seek to exploit her. Ron Howard's sure direction wrings the most out of some very funny visual and verbal gags, and Candy, as usual, is a delight. (PG)

111 minutes

SPLENDOR IN THE GRASS
(1961)
 ★★

Natalie Wood
Warren Beatty

Elia Kazan skillfully directed this William Inge story about two young people falling in love. Kazan has captured the feel of a small Kansas town in the 1920s superbly, but the characterizations and story ring false at times. Beatty—in his film debut—and Wood are splendid as the young lovers. Also with Pat Hingle, Audrey Christie, Sean Garrison, Phyllis Diller, Sandy Dennis, Zohra Lampert, and Barbara Loden. **Academy Award**—Inge, best story and screenplay (written directly for the screen). **Nomination**—Wood, best actress.

124 minutes

SPLIT IMAGE (1982)
 ★★

Michael O'Keefe
James Woods

Elizabeth Ashley and Brian Dennehy, as Michael O'Keefe's parents, suffer in Split Image.

• Spring Break
• Springfield Rifle
• The Spy Who Came in from the Cold

• The Spy Who Loved Me
• Squeeze Play
• Stagecoach (1939)
• Stagecoach (1966)

S

A bright, clean-cut college student (O'Keefe) gets caught up in a religious cult and his distraught parents hire a deprogrammer to break the spell. The film, directed by Ted Kotcheff, is well-meaning and offers some engrossing moments of suspense and drama. However, all the loose ends that are left dangling weaken the story's effectiveness. (R)   *111 minutes*

SPRING BREAK (1983)

★

**David Knell
Perry Lang
Paul Land**

A noisy, mindless, adolescent comedy about college students living it up in Fort Lauderdale during spring recess. Typical high jinks include beer guzzling, girl chasing, and a wet T-shirt contest. These escapades seldom raise any laughs and the performances by the unfamiliar cast are forgettable. Sean (*Friday the 13th*) Cunningham directed this nonsense half-heartedly. (R)   *95 minutes*

SPRINGFIELD RIFLE (1952)

★★

Gary Cooper

Cooper gives a conventional performance in this standard Civil War-era western. He plays an ex-Union officer who joins the Confederates as a spy to find a traitor who is stealing government rifles. Also with Phyllis Thaxter, Guinn Williams, Paul Kelly, David Brian, and Lon Chaney, Jr. **Director**—André de Toth.   *93 minutes*

THE SPY WHO CAME IN FROM THE COLD (1965)

★★★

**Richard Burton
Claire Bloom
Oskar Werner**

The mood, tempo, and tension are adequately conveyed in this film based on the best-selling John Le Carré spy novel, but the plot becomes needlessly tangled and complex. Burton is well-cast as the bitter agent who goes undercover in a bid to infiltrate the communists. Bloom and Werner are in top form, and the skilled photography of Oswald Morris contributes the vivid realism needed for this kind of story. At the time of release, James Bond movies were much in vogue and glorified the spying in a superficial manner; this movie put the grisly trade of espionage into its proper perspective. Rupert Davies, Peter Van Eyck, Sam Wanamaker, Cyril Cusack, Beatrix Ichmann, Bernard Lee, and George Voskovec appear in supporting roles. **Director**—Martin Ritt. **Academy Award Nomination**—Burton, best actor.   *112 minutes b&w*

THE SPY WHO LOVED ME (1977)

★★★

**Roger Moore
Curt Jurgens**

British superspy James Bond is back for his 10th action-packed screen adventure, and this one is lavish and sleek, indeed. Debonair Moore is enjoyable as agent 007, who has one hour to overcome Karl Stromberg, a villain deluxe, who wants to rule the world by gaining control of the seas. Jurgens is the heavy in this thriller. As usual, the special gadgets are fascinating, the locales are exotically stunning, and the women are fetching. Also with Barbara Bach, Richard Kiel, Caroline Munro, and Bernard Lee. Classy direction by Lewis Gilbert. (PG)   *125 minutes*

SQUEEZE PLAY (1981)

★★

**Jim Harris
Jenni Hetrick**

The guys are forever playing softball, so the gals fight back by forming their own team, in this goofy but lively low-level comedy. There are plenty of harmless pranks, slapstick happenings, and sexual shenanigans, which manage to provoke a few laughs. The players—mostly unknowns—frolic through their routines with ample energy. It all ends with a predictable softball game between the sexes. **Director**—Samuel Well. (R)   *92 minutes*

STAGECOACH (1939)

★★★★

**John Wayne
Claire Trevor
Thomas Mitchell
George Bancroft**

John Wayne and Claire Trevor are the young leads in the classic western Stagecoach.

This classic by director John Ford about the relationship among passengers on a stagecoach under the stress of an Indian attack is a model for all subsequent serious westerns. The brilliant acting of Wayne, Trevor, Mitchell, Bancroft, Berton Churchill, John Carradine, and Donald Meek is enhanced by the splendid photography of Bert Glennon. This production shows that westerns can be serious with well-written scripts, yet still have lots of action. Andy Devine, Louise Platt, Tim Holt, and Chris-Pin Martin also star. **Academy Award**—Mitchell, best supporting actor. **Nominations**—best picture; Ford, best director; Glennon, cinematography (black and white).   *99 minutes b&w*

STAGECOACH (1966)

★★

**Ann-Margret
Alex Cord
Bing Crosby
Van Heflin**

This remake might more appropriately
(Continued)

(Continued)

be called *Son of Stagecoach* or *Stagecoach Returns*. Although there's still plenty of action and some vivid scenery, it's at best half as good as the 1939 John Ford classic. This time around, Cord has the John Wayne role. Cord, Ann-Margret, Crosby, Heflin, and Red Buttons do a conscientious job, but the characterizations are much weaker than those in the earlier film. Also with Slim Pickens, Robert Cummings, Michael Connors, Stefanie Powers, and Keenan Wynn. **Director**—Gordon Douglas.

114 minutes

STAIRWAY TO HEAVEN (1946)
★★★

**David Niven
Kim Hunter
Raymond Massey**

Michael Powell and Emeric Pressburger, who gave us *The Red Shoes*, among other stylish screen entertainments, wrote and directed this lovely British fantasy. Pilot Niven bails out over the English Channel during World War II. He should be dead, but isn't—and he finds himself before a heavenly court, arguing that he was wrongly chosen to die. The film is colorful and charming, with animated performances by the entire cast, including Roger Livesey, Robert Coote, and Richard Attenborough.

104 minutes

STALAG 17 (1953)
 ### ★★★★

**William Holden
Don Taylor
Otto Preminger**

This is one of the most popular and well-liked American movies of all time. The story of U.S. prisoners in a Nazi POW camp has all the necessary ingredients for a quality viewing experience—good acting, fine plot, tension, a message, good guys and villains, expert characterization, a well-written script, a mixture of humor and drama, and action. Holden heads the list of stars, but Taylor, Preminger, Robert Strauss, Sig Rumann, and Harvey Lembeck are almost as good. If you find the viewing tame, maybe it means you've seen this film too often.

P.O.W.s check out the contraband goodies in Stalag 17.

Director—Billy Wilder. **Academy Award**—Holden, best actor. **Nominations**—Wilder, best director; Strauss, best supporting actor.

120 minutes b&w

THE STAR CHAMBER (1983)
 ### ★★

**Michael Douglas
Hal Holbrook**

Some California judges, frustrated with loopholes in the legal system, resort to vigilante justice to dispose of some vile criminals. This thinking man's version of *Death Wish* begins with promise, but it soon turns pretentious and preposterous, like most of director Peter Hyams' films. Douglas stars as one of the justices who wrestles with his conscience. Yet he seems far too young for the part. Sharon Gless and Yaphet Kotto perform well in supporting roles. (R)   *109 minutes*

STARDUST (1975)
★★

**David Essex
Adam Faith**

Essex and Faith star in this story about a young, working-class British rock star who finally makes it to the big time and becomes a victim of his own success. The story seems to accurately parallel the world of Richie Havens or Janis Joplin—a dazzling display of money, screaming groupies, unscrupulous promoters, internal squabbles, and finally death from a drug overdose. Yet, instead of probing deeply, the movie skips from one situation to another, and it's as commercial as rock itself. Also, it's difficult to understand much of the cockney dialect. Also with Larry Hagman and Dave Edmunds. **Director**—Michael Apted. (R)

97 minutes

STARDUST MEMORIES (1980)
 ### ★★★

**Woody Allen
Charlotte Rampling**

Woody Allen finds himself on the wrong track, metaphysically speaking, in Stardust Memories.

This overcrowded and jumbled film is Allen's version of Fellini's *8½*. Allen plays a harassed celebrity filmmaker who discovers there's meager satisfaction in such adoration. The movie is filled with numerous harried crowd

- Star 80
- A Star Is Born (1954)
- A Star Is Born (1977)
- Starman
- Stars and Stripes Forever
- Starship Invasions
- Star Spangled Rhythm

S

scenes, which produce a desperate and overheated tone, although Woody's caustic wit does occasionally shine through. Also with Jessica Harper and Marie-Christine Barrault. (PG)

89 minutes b&w

STAR 80 (1983)

 ★★★

Mariel Hemingway
Eric Roberts

Star 80 features Mariel Hemingway and Eric Roberts in a film treatment of model Dorothy Stratten's tragic life and death.

Compelling and uncompromising film about the rise and horrid murder of centerfold model Dorothy Stratten. Hemingway is all sweetness and innocence as the exploited pinup doll. But the story's focal point is her sleazy manager-husband, Paul Snider (Roberts). He turns a shotgun on Dorothy and then on himself after he is left in the dust of her rocketing career. Roberts's *tour de force* performance underscores the rage and frustration of this unsavory character. Director Bob Fosse successfully duplicates the documentary style he introduced in *Lenny*. (R)

102 minutes

A STAR IS BORN (1954)

 ★★★

Judy Garland
James Mason

This musical version of the 1937 David O. Selznick movie is still good entertainment, but it loses some of its dramatic force in the shift to music. Garland is in top form and makes the movie as good as it is, as she belts out such songs as "Born in a Trunk" and "The Man That Got Away." Mason's performance is just a notch below Judy's. Videotape version includes restored footage. Also with Charles Bickford, Jack Carson, Tommy Noon-

an, Lucy Marlow, and Amanda Blake. **Director**—George Cukor. **Academy Award Nominations**—Mason, best actor; Garland, best actress.

154 minutes

A STAR IS BORN (1977)

 ★★

Barbra Streisand
Kris Kristofferson

Streisand dominates this third rehash of the show-biz soap opera so much that it comes off as her own ego trip. In this rock version about an unknown singer's rise to fame, Streisand is billed as the star, executive producer, co-songwriter, and wardrobe consultant; it's obvious she usurped the direction from Frank Pierson, and she had a hand in the editing. The result is a lukewarm movie hardly the caliber of the 1954 Judy Garland-James Mason production. Kristofferson has a major part, but he too is unnecessarily upstaged. Also with Gary Busey, Paul Mazursky, and Oliver Clark. (R)

140 minutes

STARMAN (1984)

★★

Jeff Bridges
Karen Allen

Jeff Bridges plays the title role of this sci-fi romantic adventure as an alien who comes to earth. He assumes the human form of a dead house painter and falls in love with his widow (Karen Allen). The story takes on many aspects of *Close Encounters* and *E.T.* Yet, it mainly plays as a routine car chase film with scores of cops and federal officials trying to nab the alien before he can rendezvous with a spaceship. **Director**—John Carpenter. (PG)

112 minutes

STARS AND STRIPES FOREVER (1952)

★★

Clifton Webb

Webb does a fine job as march king John Philip Sousa, a musician who wanted to write ballads, but eventually found success as a bandmaster

Clifton Webb (left) receives a commendation as bandleader John Philip Sousa in Stars and Stripes Forever.

and writer of rousing marches. Some of the march music gets a bit tedious and jarring after a while, but the band plays on, and its music is expertly spliced into the plot. Debra Paget, Robert Wagner, Lester Matthews, Finlay Currie, and Ruth Hussey appear in supporting roles. **Director**—Henry Koster.

89 minutes

STARSHIP INVASIONS (1978)

★

Robert Vaughn
Christopher Lee

This low-budget film from Canada is bent on capitalizing on the success of science-fiction hits. However, this junky film has neither the charm of those old Flash Gordon episodes nor the special-effects razzle-dazzle of blockbusters like *Star Wars*. The plot is old hat, and the shoddy sets are unimpressive. Vaughn plays one of the good guys. Lee plays the villainous alien. Also with Helen Shaver. **Director**—Ed Hunt. (PG)

89 minutes

STAR SPANGLED RHYTHM (1942)

★★★

Bing Crosby
Betty Hutton
Victor Moore
Walter Abel

This is the kind of movie that must be

(Continued)

S
- Starting Over
- Star Trek—The Motion Picture
- Star Trek II: The Wrath of Khan
- Star Trek III: The Search for Spock
- Star Wars
- State Fair

(Continued)

taken on its own terms. If you expect a plot or any degree of meaningful characterization, you'll be disappointed. However, if you accept the fact that it's a star-studded variety show, you'll find a great deal of enjoyment in this World War II song-and-dance fest. Tunes include "Time To Hit the Road to Dreamland" and "That Old Black Magic." Some of those within this galaxy of stars are Preston Sturges, Eddie Bracken, Bob Hope, Paulette Goddard, Veronica Lake, Dorothy Lamour, Ray Milland, William Bendix, Arthur Treacher, Rochester, Alan Ladd, and Susan Hayward. **Director**—George Marshall.

99 minutes b&w

STARTING OVER (1979)

★★★★

**Burt Reynolds
Jill Clayburgh
Candice Bergen**

In Starting Over, *Jill Clayburgh and Burt Reynolds begin a romance.*

Reynolds casts aside his good ol' boy macho routine for a superb sympathetic role in this thoroughly enjoyable romantic comedy, which views the man's side of divorce. There's a witty script, crisp direction by Alan J. Pakula of *Klute* fame, and a richness of satire. Other first-rate performances are turned in by Clayburgh and Bergen. Clayburgh plays a nursery school teacher who establishes a romance with our hero. Bergen is the ex-wife. Also with Charles Durning, Frances Sternhagen, Paul Sorvino, Mary Kay Place, and Austin Pendleton. **Academy Award Nominations**—Clayburgh, best actress; Bergen, best supporting actress. (R) *106 minutes*

STAR TREK—THE MOTION PICTURE (1979)

★★

**William Shatner
Leonard Nimoy**

The producers lavished millions of dollars on hardware and special effects for this epic, based on the popular television series. But they seemed to have run out of funds when it came to character and script development. The spaceship U.S.S. *Enterprise* is back in action with Captain Kirk (Shatner), Mr. Spock (Nimoy), and other familiar crew members combatting a menacing force in space. The super gadgetry blasts away while the story—reminiscent of an old TV episode—plods. Strictly for Trekkies. Also with Stephen Collins, Persis Khambatta, DeForest Kelley, George Takei, and Nichelle Nichols. **Director**—Robert Wise. (G) *132 minutes*

STAR TREK II: THE WRATH OF KHAN (1982)

★★★

**William Shatner
Leonard Nimoy
Ricardo Montalban**

Here it is, Trek fans—a sequel that's even better than the initial big-budget space adventure. This time, the affecting story superbly captures the spirit of the popular TV sci-fi series. Admiral Kirk (Shatner), Mr. Spock (Nimoy), and the familiar crew aboard the Starship *Enterprise* are gallantly protecting the frontiers of space from the evil ambitions of Khan, played impressively by Montalban. The elaborate special effects are delightful indeed. **Director**—Nicholas Meyer. (PG)

113 minutes

STAR TREK III: THE SEARCH FOR SPOCK (1984)

★★★

**William Shatner
Christopher Lloyd
Leonard Nimoy**

Everyone's favorite Vulcan, Mr. Spock, isn't quite dead after all. And the Starship *Enterprise* is spared an ignomini-

ous forced retirement in order to go after him. In this third installment, the search for the intriguing half-human takes the *Enterprise* crew to a planet on the verge of self-destruction. With Shatner (and all the regulars), Lloyd, and Nimoy (both acting and directing), it's manna for Trekkies. Beam us up. (PG) *108 minutes*

STAR WARS (1977)

★★★★

**Mark Hamill
Harrison Ford
Alec Guinness
Carrie Fisher**

Mark Hamill repairs a runaway android in Star Wars.

A magnificent intergalactic adventure for the kid in everyone. The movie is part *Flash Gordon*, part *Wizard of Oz*. Dazzling special effects, a booming sound track, and a simple good-guys bad-guys plot bring back old-time fun. A marvelous achievement for writer-director George Lucas. R2-D2 and C-3PO, a pair of robots, steal the show. Also with Anthony Daniels, Kenny Baker, Peter Cushing, and David Prowse. (PG) **Academy Award Nominations**—best picture; Lucas, best director; Guinness, best supporting actor; Lucas, best original screenplay.

121 minutes

STATE FAIR (1945)

★★★

**Charles Winninger
Jeanne Crain
Dana Andrews**

The fine songs of Rodgers and Hammerstein flourish in this entertaining musical about a family's experiences at the Iowa State fair. The script and plot lack substance, but that's not very important in this kind of musical show. Tunes include "Grand Night for Singing" and "It Might As Well Be Spring." Fay Bainter, Frank McHugh, Vivian Blaine, Donald Meek, and Dick Haymes also star. **Director**—Walter Lang. **Alternate Title**—*It Happened One Summer*. *100 minutes*

STATE OF THE UNION (1948)
 ★★★★

Spencer Tracy
Katharine Hepburn

Tracy and Hepburn click in this political comedy about a man who runs for President and has problems with his wife. Tracy and Hepburn are the couple. Angela Lansbury plays a millionairess who bankrolls the campaign, and Van Johnson is appealing as the campaign manager. This film version of the Howard Lindsay-Russel Crouse play is expertly directed by Frank Capra. It has the rare quality of being intelligent and enlightening about political campaigns while being entertaining. Lewis Stone, Howard Smith, Charles Dingle, Raymond Walburn, and Adolphe Menjou appear in supporting roles. *124 minutes b&w*

STAY AS YOU ARE (1980)
 ★★

Marcello Mastroianni
Nastassja Kinski

Mastroianni is smitten by a coquettish beauty, played by Kinski, who's young enough to be his daughter. In fact, she is his daughter! This dilemma of incest is the centerpiece of this comedy-romance, which gives Mastroianni ample opportunity to display his talent and charm. But it really goes no further than this. The comedy is strained and mired in sentimentality. **Director**—Alberto Lattuada. In Italian with English titles. (No MPAA rating) *118 minutes*

STAY HUNGRY (1976)
 ★★

Jeff Bridges
Sally Field

Essentially this is a story about a wealthy young man of the New South who becomes involved with the freaky world of body builders by investing in a gym. The rich heir is played by Bridges, who, as usual, does a fine job. Field helps out with a professional performance. Muscle-man Arnold Schwarzenegger plays a muscle man. The film is a mulligan stew of plots, subplots, characters, and themes that become tangled up to the point of utter confusion. Bob Rafelson's ramshackle direction lacks appeal and impact. Also with Joe Santo, Scatman Crothers, Roger Mosley, and R. G. Armstrong. (PG) *103 minutes*

STAYING ALIVE (1983)
 ★★

John Travolta
Cynthia Rhodes
Finola Hughes

Cynthia Rhodes and John Travolta watch a dance number in Staying Alive.

Despite the potential powerhouse combination of Sylvester Stallone directing Travolta, this sequel to the popular *Saturday Night Fever* is an inferior product. Our young dancing hero, Tony Manero (Travolta), has left Brooklyn and now wants to make it big on Broadway. Songs by the Bee Gees and Stallone's brother Frank are forgettable, and the contrived dance numbers irritate more often than they excite. And given this limping script, the audience may have difficulty staying awake. (PG) *96 minutes*

STEEL (1980)
 ★★★

Lee Majors
Jennifer O'Neill

High drama on the high-rise building, as tough, gritty steelworkers rush to complete a skyscraper before the bank forecloses. The uncomplicated script is reminiscent of those '30s formula melodramas from Warner Brothers. Majors, O'Neill, Art Carney, and George Kennedy turn in good performances, along with several supporting players who portray the redoubtable construction men. The film is innocent, predictable, and hokey—but some fun nevertheless. **Director**—Steven Carver. (PG) *99 minutes*

THE STEEL TRAP (1952)
★★★

Joseph Cotten
Teresa Wright

Cotten is ideally cast as a banker manager who steals a half-million dollars from his bank on Friday, but decides to return it by Monday because his conscience troubles him. This twist on the common crime caper is pleasant viewing and well done, with plenty of suspense and an element of doubt until the conclusion. Also stars Jonathan Hale and Walter Sande. **Director**—Andrew L. Stone. *85 minutes b&w*

STEELYARD BLUES (1973)
★★

Donald Sutherland
Jane Fonda
Peter Boyle

With three stars like Sutherland, Fonda, and Boyle in the same film, you might expect more than what is produced here. Still, despite the trio's failure to deliver as expected in this anti-establishment yarn, there are some funny moments as they try a bizarre plan to get an abandoned airplane working again. John Savage, Garry Goodrow, and Howard Hesseman appear in supporting roles. **Director**—Alan Myerson. (PG) **Alternate Title**—*The Final Crash*. *92 minutes*

S

- The Stepford Wives
- The Sterile Cuckoo
- Stevie
- Still of the Night
- Still Smokin'
- The Sting

THE STEPFORD WIVES (1975)
★★★

Katharine Ross
Paula Prentiss

Men who feel threatened by the women's liberation movement may take mild delight in this suspense film about suburban Connecticut housewives who are always pleasant; they're never shrill or overly strident. Women may want to watch to see the vile deeds of men who oppose equality of the sexes. Some viewers will say that the wives in Stepford become docile because they read mediocre Connecticut newspapers too often, but the answer—based upon Ira Levin's best-selling novel—is a bit more complex than that. Toward the end of the film, the story weakens, but the performances of Ross, Prentiss, and Tina Louise sustain the movie. Peter Masterson, Nanette Newman, and Patrick O'Neal appear in supporting roles. **Director**—Bryan Forbes. (PG)
110 minutes

THE STERILE CUCKOO (1969)
★★★★

Liza Minnelli
Wendell Burton

Liza Minnelli and Wendell Burton have a fragile first affair in The Sterile Cuckoo.

Minnelli steals the show in this story about Pookie Adams, a neurotic college student who plays at love and then finds it on campus with Burton. It's fortunate that Minnelli is so fine in this portrayal, because the script and plot are sometimes trite and cumbersome. But the movie is a sensitive look at young love. Also with Tim McIntire, Austin Green, and Sandra Faison. **Director**—Alan J. Pakula. (PG) **Academy Award Nomination**—Minnelli, best actress.
107 minutes

STEVIE (1981)
★★★

Glenda Jackson

Jackson, in the title role, delivers a spellbinding performance straight from the heart in this screen adaptation of Hugh Whitemore's play about the late British poet, Stevie Smith. The film is rather stage-bound, but the extraordinary acting and characterizations more than make up for such drawbacks. Jackson's acute portrayal of the gentle woman's life is enhanced with expert reading of her verses. Mona Washbourne is remarkable as Stevie's stalwart spinster aunt. Also with Trevor Howard and Alec McCowen. **Director**—Robert Enders. (No MPAA rating)
102 minutes

STILL OF THE NIGHT (1982)
★★

Roy Scheider
Meryl Streep
Jessica Tandy
Joseph Summer

A sleek psychological thriller, cast in the Hitchcock mold, about a pensive New York shrink (Scheider) who falls in love with the fidgety blonde (Streep) who's suspected of murdering one of his patients. Director Robert Benton (*Kramer vs. Kramer*) unfolds some tingling, intelligent scenes and the suspense builds nicely. The electricity between the two leads, however, is strictly low-voltage, and the conclusion is a letdown. (PG)
91 minutes

STILL SMOKIN' (1983)
★

Cheech Marin
Thomas Chong

Those maharajahs of marijuana, Cheech and Chong, frolic about Amsterdam pursuing various fantasies, usually involving sex and drugs. Some sketches generate modest chuckles, but the construction of the film is loose and lazy, and the boys seem drained of their usual energy. And their "hey, man" dialogue has begun to pall. **Director**—Chong. (R)
91 minutes

THE STING (1973)
★★★★

Paul Newman
Robert Redford
Robert Shaw

Robert Redford and Paul Newman pull off a complicated con in The Sting.

This story of two small-time Chicago con men who avenge the death of a friend by tricking, or stinging, a big-time mobster sparkles with vibrant action. Newman and Redford play the con men, and Shaw is the subject of the sting. The plot is complex, but that doesn't really spoil the overall enjoyment of the film. More important, the key scenes at the end, when the swindle of the mobster takes place, are easily comprehensible. Eileen Brennan, Ray Walston, Harold Gould, and Charles Durning also star. Scott Joplin's ragtime music is another plus. **Director**—George Roy Hill. (PG) **Academy Awards**—best picture; Hill, best director; David S. Ward, best story and screenplay (based on factual material or material not previously published). **Nominations**—Redford, best actor; Robert Surtees, cinematography.
129 minutes

THE STING II (1983)

★★

Jackie Gleason
Mac Davis
Teri Garr
Karl Malden
Oliver Reed

Teri Garr and Jackie Gleason leer across the dance floor in The Sting II.

Gleason and Davis take over the Newman and Redford roles in this lukewarm follow-up to the popular, bouncy film about cons and their own brand of artistry. This time the scam, which is not much different from the original, unfolds at a painfully slow pace despite all the twists and turns of the plot. This *Sting* packs only a mild punch; there's not even much of the charm which made the original work so well. **Director**—Jeremy Kagan. (PG)
103 minutes

STIR CRAZY (1980)

★

Gene Wilder
Richard Pryor

Wilder and Pryor mug and bumble through this lamebrained comedy about two buddies who land in the slammer because they're mistaken for bank robbers. Practically all the gags fizzle, and many comic setups run into dead ends. Part of the problem seems to be Bruce J. Friedman's uninspired script. Wilder and Pryor strain under this witless material, as they try to outmaneuver prison officials and fellow inmates, but they merely look silly, and the audience gets a bum rap. Also with Georg Stanford Brown. **Director**—Sidney Poitier. (R)   *111 minutes*

THE STONE BOY (1984)

★★

Jason Presson
Robert Duvall

Dour, harrowing account of a rural family's grief over the accidental shooting death of a teenage son by his younger brother. Twelve-year old Presson is impressive as the lad who bottles up his emotions following the tragedy. Yet the film unfolds at a strained, slow pace with characterizations that are far too studied and repressed to be effective. Frederic Forrest and Glenn Close also star. **Director**—Chris Cain. (PG)
93 minutes

THE STORK CLUB (1945)

★★

Betty Hutton
Barry Fitzgerald

A very ordinary story about a poor nightclub hat-check girl, played by Hutton. She meets Fitzgerald, a wealthy man, but she thinks he's broke. The lightweight comedy is saved by above-average acting. Hutton sings "Doctor, Lawyer, Indian Chief." Also with Mary Young, Bill Goodwin, Don Defore, Andy Russell, Iris Adrian, Robert Benchley, and Mikhail Rasumny. Ironically, the Stork Club in New York City has closed down, but the film survives. **Director**—Hal Walker.   *98 minutes b&w*

STORMY WEATHER (1943)

★★★

Bill Robinson
Lena Horne

Many musicals have silly plots, and this all-black talent show based on the life of Bill Robinson is no exception. But the delightful performers far overshadow the triteness in this movie. The stars also include Fats Waller, Ada Brown, Eddie Anderson, Flournoy Miller, Dooley Wilson, Cab Calloway, and Katherine Dunham. Horne sings the title song, and Waller does "Ain't Misbehavin'." **Director**—Andrew L. Stone.   *77 minutes b&w*

STORY OF ADELE H (1976)

★★★★

Isabelle Adjani

Director François Truffaut has created a passionate and intelligent movie about a woman obsessed with love itself. It's the true story of the youngest daughter of French writer Victor Hugo. When she's rejected by a young British officer, her love becomes more intense and devastating. Adjani plays the lead role with impact and grace, and the film is beautifully photographed. Also with Bruce Robinson, Sylvia Marriott, Joseph Blatchley, and Reubin Dorey. In French with English titles. (PG) **Academy Award Nomination**—Adjani, best actress.
97 minutes

STORY OF GI JOE (1945)

★★★

Burgess Meredith
Robert Mitchum

Meredith gives a stirring performance as Ernie Pyle, the famed war correspondent, in this drama set during the Italian campaign of World War II. Pyle earned a reputation as a friend of the typical infantry soldier and lived with them in the foxholes and on the front lines. The movie offers thoughtful characterization and the usual combat action seen in such films. Mitchum stars as a soldier, with Freddie Steele, Wally Cassell, Jimmy Lloyd, and Jack Reilly in supporting roles. **Director**—William Wellman.   *108 minutes b&w*

THE STORY OF O (1975)

(no stars)

Corinne Clery

A sadomasochism story based on Pauline Reage's classic novel. This is really just another trashy soft-core movie. "O" is passed from man to man for numerous sexual torments and humiliations, including whippings and a branding; much of the action is heard and not seen. The monotony of this film is likely to induce as much suffering on the audience as "O" supposedly faces from her lashings. Clery
(Continued)

S
- The Story of Seabiscuit
- The Story of Will Rogers
- Straight Time
- Strange Behavior
- Strange Brew
- Strange Cargo
- The Strange Door
- Strange Invaders

(Continued)
plays the title role. **Director**—Just Jaeckin. In French with English titles. (X) *97 minutes*

THE STORY OF SEABISCUIT (1949)
★★

Shirley Temple
Barry Fitzgerald

Fitzgerald is very believable as a crusty trainer of racehorses, but this movie about the famous racehorse runs out of the money. This below-average racing picture does star Temple and has several excellently photographed racing scenes, but even they aren't enough to make it a winner. Donald McBride, Lon McCallister, Pierre Watkin, and Rosemary DeCamp appear in supporting roles. **Director**—David Butler. *98 minutes*

THE STORY OF WILL ROGERS (1950)
★★

Will Rogers, Jr.
Jane Wyman

Rogers gives a faithful and conscientious portrait of his folk-philosopher father, one of the nation's best-loved public figures, who was killed in a 1935 plane crash. Unfortunately, the movie's pace is too slow, and it's a tall order for the son to follow in his father's footsteps, even in a film. Will, Jr. does a good job, but he doesn't have his father's charm and wit. Wyman plays Will's wife. Also with James Gleason, Eddie Cantor, Mary Wickes, and Carl Benton Reid. **Director**—Michael Curtiz. *109 minutes*

STRAIGHT TIME (1978)
 ★★★

Dustin Hoffman

Hoffman portrays Max Dumbo, an ex-con who's his own worst enemy and is following a course of self-destruction. Hoffman's performance is stylish and cleanly executed; genuine interest in the character develops with clarity. The film is based on a novel by ex-convict Edward Bunker. Harry Dean

Stanton, M. Emmet Walsh, and Gary Busey are excellent in supporting roles. Also with Theresa Russell and Rita Taggart. **Director**—Ulu Grosbard (R) *114 minutes*

STRANGE BEHAVIOR (1981)
 ★★

Michael Murphy
Louise Fletcher
Fiona Lewis

A slightly addled, offbeat horror drama about a series of teenage murders in a small Midwestern college town. The film, which smacks of a '50s-style thriller, offers some impressive special effects and a bit of campy horror, but the plot often goes awry, and the usual predictable gruesome killings are much in evidence. Michael Laughlin debuts as director in this film, and he shows promise of better work to come. (R) *99 minutes*

STRANGE BREW (1983)
 ★

Dave Thomas
Rick Moranis
Max Von Sydow

It's hard to believe that two guys so talented could make such a stupid, witless movie. SCTV's Thomas and Moranis are to beer as Cheech & Chong are to pot. The boys from north of the border have tossed off an inconsequential, slapstick comedy involving the takeover of a brewery by madman Von Sydow who wants to control the world with spiked beer. After a lot of beer-guzzling and chasing around, the film fizzles out with hardly a decent laugh. Von Sydow seems especially out of place amid the sophomoric humor. **Directors**—Thomas and Moranis. (PG) *90 minutes*

STRANGE CARGO (1940)
★★

Clark Gable
Joan Crawford

If you take this film too seriously, you'll find it strange, indeed. But as an adventure or as a chance to see Gable and Crawford in action, it's worth-

Clark Gable romances Joan Crawford in Frank Borzage's Strange Cargo.

while viewing. The story is about a group of convicts who escape from Devil's Island. They are forced to choose between good in the form of Ian Hunter or evil in the form of Paul Lukas. Peter Lorre, J. Edward Bromberg, Eduardo Ciannelli, and Albert Dekker also brighten the cast of characters. **Director**—Frank Borzage. *105 minutes b&w*

THE STRANGE DOOR (1951)
★

Charles Laughton
Boris Karloff

Laughton and Karloff star in this horror story. Laughton plays a deranged tyrant who traps a nobleman in a castle. The movie is based on the Robert Louis Stevenson chiller, but instead of chills, there's unintentional comedy as Karloff and Laughton overact in a futile bid to salvage this horrid horror film. Also with Alan Napier, Sally Forrest, Michael Pate, and Richard Stapley. **Director**—Joseph Pevney. *81 minutes b&w*

STRANGE INVADERS (1983)
 ★★★

Paul LeMat

Monsters-from-outer-space movies of the '50s are spoofed in a deadpan manner. This droll satire stars LeMat as a New York professor who wants to

Diana Scarwid seems unaware of the two aliens flanking her and Kenneth Tobey in Strange Invaders.

rescue his daughter from creepy aliens who landed in a small Illinois town 25 years ago. Even though it's 1983, the creatures still adopt the styles and manners of the Eisenhower era. The film seems to be mostly style with little substance, but it draws laughter as it manages to recreate the sci-fi films of the '50s. Louise Fletcher, Nancy Allen, and Wallace Shawn co-star. **Director—** Michael Laughlin. (PG)   *93 minutes*

THE STRANGER (1946)

 ★★★

Edward G. Robinson
Orson Welles
Loretta Young

Robinson is well cast as a government agent with a keen mind who's tracking down a Nazi, played by Welles. The trail ends in a small Connecticut town, where the Nazi poses as a respectable professor. Young plays the woman in the life of the Nazi—unaware of his real convictions. The skilled direction of Welles and the vivid photography sweeten this melodrama, which seems slightly dated now. Richard Long and Philip Merivale also star. **Academy Award Nomination**—Victor Trivas, writing (original story).

95 minutes b&w

THE STRANGER (1967)
★★★

Marcello Mastroianni

Mastroianni is superb as the antihero estranged from society in this film version of Albert Camus's existential tale *L'Étranger*. Although the French author and existentialism were more popular at the time of the filming, the story under Luchino Visconti's direction is still meaningful and relevant to our times. Also with Anna Karina, Bernard Blier, Bruno Cremer, and Georges Wilson.   *105 minutes*

A STRANGER IS WATCHING
(1982)

 ★★

Rip Torn
Kate Mulgrew

Director Sean Cunningham, best known for his low-budget *Friday the 13th* bloodbath, tones down the gore in this shocker, but it's still a routine movie at best. The complex plot involves a brutal criminal who holds a child and a woman TV reporter hostage in the murky bowels of Grand Central Station. Torn is convincing as the nasty kidnapper, but other cast members perform rather woodenly. Mulgrew plays the reporter. Also with James Naughton and Shawn Von Schreiber. (R)   *92 minutes*

STRANGERS KISS (1984)

 ★★

Victoria Tennant
Blaine Novak
Peter Coyote

An off-beat, edgy love story wrapped in a movie-within-a-movie quandary. It covers terrain similar to Stanley Kubrick's *Killer's Kiss*. Set in Hollywood of the '50s, the pretentious story involves young movie stars whose off-screen romance parallels their roles before the cameras. The brisk performances often are ahead of the peculiar material. **Director**—Matthew Chapman. (R)   *93 minutes*

STRANGERS ON A TRAIN
(1951)

 ★★★★

Farley Granger
Robert Walker

This super Alfred Hitchcock suspense film is based on the outrageous premise that two strangers who meet on a train can agree to swap murders to make it difficult for the authorities to catch each killer. In a world in which most strangers barely grunt hello to one another, it's a testimonial to Hitchcock's genius that he not only makes this film work, but that it's believable and extremely suspenseful. Another reason for the success of the movie is Walker's brilliant acting, as the psychotic who promptly acts on his part of the murder deal. Granger plays a tennis star who's reluctant to uphold his end of the murderous bargain; he's also convincing. Superb script by Raymond Chandler. Also with Ruth Roman, Marion Lorne, Laura Elliott, Leo G. Carroll, and Howard St. John. **Academy Award Nomination**—Robert Burks, cinematography (black and white).   *101 minutes b&w*

Farley Granger and Robert Walker make an unusual pact in Strangers on a Train.

S
- Stranger Than Paradise
- Strategic Air Command
- The Strawberry Blonde
- The Strawberry Statement
- Straw Dogs
- Streamers
- A Streetcar Named Desire
- Street People

STRANGER THAN PARADISE (1984)

★★★

Despite its meager budget, this quirky, droll comedy has a luxurious charm all its own. Innovative filmmaker Jim Jarmusch weaves a gritty, original story about the American scene as viewed by two Hungarians who drift from New York to Cleveland to Florida. The film shines because of strong emphasis on well-defined characters and intriguing performances by John Lurie, Eszter Balint, and Richard Edson. (R)
90 minutes

STRATEGIC AIR COMMAND (1955)

★★

**James Stewart
June Allyson
Frank Lovejoy**

Stewart, Allyson, and Lovejoy are vibrant and wholesome in this story about a baseball star who interrupts his career to return to the U.S. Air Force and the Strategic Air Command. Stewart plays the baseball player, and Allyson plays his wife. Hollywood doesn't make such unabashed pro-American movies anymore, but it's still nice to see them occasionally. This movie is ordinary at best; the flying sequences and patriotism are all that make the movie worth viewing. Also with Jay C. Flippen, Alex Nicol, Barry Sullivan, and Bruce Bennett. **Director**—Anthony Mann. **Academy Award Nomination**—Beirne Lay, Jr., writing (motion picture story). *114 minutes*

THE STRAWBERRY BLONDE (1941)

★★★

**James Cagney
Olivia de Havilland
Rita Hayworth**

Cagney is at his best in this 1890s love story about a Brooklyn dentist. Hayworth and de Havilland are competent as the women in his life, but without Cagney this comedy enterprise would be worthless. **Director**—Raoul Walsh. *97 minutes b&w*

THE STRAWBERRY STATEMENT (1970)

★★

**Bruce Davison
Kim Darby**

Students occupy a college campus building in this film adaptation of James Simon Kunen's novel, but after that the movie limps along with nothing better to do than offer watered-down radical philosophy from the late '60s. Some of the intellectual posturings seem dated, but the performances of Darby and Davison are still vivid reminders of that historical and hysterical period. Murray MacLeod, Bud Cort, Jeannie Berlin, James Kunen, and Bob Balaban are also in the cast. **Director**—Stuart Hagman. (R) *109 minutes*

STRAW DOGS (1971)

 ★★

**Dustin Hoffman
Susan George**

Senseless violence reigns in this tasteless film in which director Sam Peckinpah pushes his gruesome themes to their outer limits. Hoffman plays a pacifist American professor living in England who's provoked into violence by the men of a remote Cornish village. George plays his wife, and her rape by villagers is the trigger to the violent excess. Despite its faults, the movie is well conceived and deftly executed; Hoffman and George give good performances. Also with T. P. McKenna, Colin Welland, Peter Vaughan, and David Warner. (R) *118 minutes*

STREAMERS (1983)

 ★★★

Matthew Modine

Riveting film version of David Rabe's stage play about friction among Army misfits awaiting assignment to Vietnam. Director Robert Altman coaxes powerful ensemble acting from an unknown yet talented cast. The film provides a close-cropped portrait of charged hostility in a claustrophobic barracks setting that reaches a violent

Streamers, a drama about the effects of the Vietnam war, features Matthew Modine, Guy Boyd, and David Alan Grier.

and breathtaking conclusion. Michael Wright and Mitchell Lichtenstein also star. (No MPAA rating) *118 minutes*

A STREETCAR NAMED DESIRE (1951)

★★★★

**Marlon Brando
Vivien Leigh**

Brando is masterful in this Tennessee Williams story about a brute who's in conflict with his wife's neurotic sister, played by Leigh. The story often creaks, as Williams attempts to contrast the new cultural values (Brando) with the decaying values of the Old South (Leigh), but the acting is among the best in American cinema history. The on-location New Orleans photography of Harry Stradling blends vividly with the mood created by the actors. Kim Hunter and Karl Malden star in supporting roles. **Director**—Elia Kazan. **Academy Awards**—Leigh, best actress; Malden, best supporting actor; Hunter, best supporting actress. **Nominations**—best picture; Kazan, best director; Brando, best actor; Williams, writing (screenplay); Harry Stradling, cinematography (black and white). *122 minutes b&w*

STREET PEOPLE (1976)

★★

**Roger Moore
Stacy Keach**

Moore and Keach perform with gusto in this action-filled Mafia story about narcotics smuggling. The confusing plot, which is mostly warmed-over and reworked portions of *The Godfather*, fails to develop characters properly. There's an amusing car-smash se-

• Streets of Fire
• Streets of Laredo
• Strike Up the Band

• Stripes
• Stroker Ace
• Student Bodies
• The Student Prince

S

quence, which adds some comic relief to the mystery of who smuggled $3 million worth of narcotics into San Francisco inside a crucifix imported from Sicily. Also with Fausto Tozzi, Ivo Garrani, and Ettore Manni. **Director**—Maurice Lucidi. (R)   *92 minutes*

STREETS OF FIRE (1984)

★★

Michael Paré
Amy Madigan
Diane Lane

Michael Paré and Diane Lane method-act their way into rock'n'roll heaven in Streets of Fire.

It's all style and ear-splitting music in this clanging, banging youth film described as rock 'n' roll fable. A young outsider (Paré) and friends battle motorcycle thugs over the abduction of a female rock singer. The atmosphere is dark urban decay, embellished with tough-talking dialogue. Such nonstop ruckus is enough to give you a first-class headache. It's a three aspirin movie. **Director**—Walter Hill. (PG)   *94 minutes*

STREETS OF LAREDO (1949)

★★★

William Holden
MacDonald Carey
William Bendix

Holden, Carey, and Bendix star in this nicely plotted western. Two ex-outlaws who become law-abiding citizens and join the Texas Rangers confront an old friend who has remained an outlaw. Mona Freeman appears in a supporting role. **Director**—Leslie Fenton.   *92 minutes*

STRIKE UP THE BAND (1940)

★★★

Judy Garland
Mickey Rooney

Garland and Rooney energize what would otherwise be a dated and trite musical. Even with this talented duo, the production still seems slightly out of step. Rooney leads a high school band competing in Paul Whiteman's nationwide radio contest, and Garland shines when she sings "Our Love Affair," "Nell of New Rochelle," and "Do the Conga." William Tracy, Larry Nunn, and June Preisser are also in this well-plotted venture by director Busby Berkeley.   *120 minutes b&w*

STRIPES (1981)

★★

Bill Murray

P.J. Soles arrests an obviously repentent Bill Murray in Stripes.

Murray stars in this typical Army comedy, which pits reluctant privates against sergeants and officers. The film is composed of inconsistent episodes strung together with Murray's wise-guy humor. After bungling their way through basic training, Murray and his fellow misfits hightail it to Europe, where they inadvertently create havoc in Czechoslovakia. As far as lampooning the military, Goldie Hawn did it better in *Private Benjamin*, and Beetle Bailey does it better in the comics. **Director**—Ivan Reitman. (R)   *106 minutes*

STROKER ACE (1983)

★

Burt Reynolds
Loni Anderson

Good ol' boy Reynolds sleepwalks through this dreary comedy that mixes stock car racing with fast-food retailing. When Burt isn't zooming around the track, he's chasing bright-eyed Anderson, a public relations worker for a fried-chicken king (Ned Beatty). Burt even dresses up in an oversized chicken outfit, but the desperate gag merely lays an egg. **Director**—Hal Needham. (PG)   *96 minutes*

STUDENT BODIES (1981)

★

Kristen Riter
Matthew Goldsby
Richard Brando

Writer-director Mickey Rose attempts to parody those heavy-breathing teenage horror films like *Friday the 13th*, but he doesn't earn a passing grade. Rose, who collaborated with Woody Allen on many successes, just can't muster enough good gags to sustain comic momentum here. The silly high jinks in this attempt involve a high school class where numerous young people are murdered as they are about to engage in sex. Much strained humor is substituted for the usual graphic violence and gore. (R)   *86 minutes*

THE STUDENT PRINCE
(1954)

★★

Edmund Purdom
Ann Blyth

The music of Sigmund Romberg and the singing of Mario Lanza brighten this otherwise dull operetta about a young prince who falls in love with a beautiful barmaid in old Heidelberg. Purdom plays the prince, and Blyth is the barmaid. The voice of Lanza is dubbed on the sound track because he became too fat to play the leading role. Also with John Williams, Evelyn Varden, Louis Calhern, Betta St. John, Edmund Gwenn, and S. Z. Sakall. **Director**—Richard Thorpe.   *107 minutes*

S
- The Stunt Man
- The Subject Was Roses
- Sudden Impact
- Suddenly Last Summer
- The Sugarland Express
- Sullivan's Travels

THE STUNT MAN (1980)

 ★★★

Peter O'Toole
Steve Railsback

Peter O'Toole prepares Steve Railsback to perform a daredevil stunt in The Stunt Man.

A rowdy, off-beat movie-within-a-movie about a fugitive, played by Railsback, who stumbles on a movie in the making and becomes a stunt man. The busy script is cluttered with riddles and tricky illusions, but such drawbacks are often overcome by the film's amazing energy and subtle humor. O'Toole, playing the omnipotent and fey director, gives a virtuoso comic performance—his best in years. The film offers plenty of hair-raising stunts. Also with Barbara Hershey. **Director**—Richard Rush. (R) **Academy Award Nominations**—Rush, best director; O'Toole, best actor; Rush, best screenplay (adapted from another medium). *129 minutes*

THE SUBJECT WAS ROSES (1968)

★★★

Patricia Neal
Jack Albertson
Martin Sheen

Frank D. Gilroy's Pulitzer Prize-winning play is weakened when it is transferred to the big screen, but the story of a young World War II veteran trying to cope with his quarreling parents is still vivid and compelling. Neal and Albertson play Sheen's parents. Neal's appearance was her first movie after a near-fatal stroke. Elaine Williams, Don Saxon, and Grant Gordon star in supporting roles. **Director**—Ulu Grosbard. (G) **Academy Award**—Albertson, best supporting actor. **Nomination**—Neal, best actress.

107 minutes

SUDDEN IMPACT (1983)

 ★★

Clint Eastwood
Sondra Locke

Eastwood blasts away at scores of thugs in this fourth "Dirty Harry" Callahan chapter that predictably takes an eye-for-an-eye approach toward crime control. The tightly wound plot is occasionally intriguing. The independent-minded San Francisco detective pursues a female killer (Locke) with personality traits similar to his own. Yet the violence-saturated film ultimately settles for crude exploitation by way of its high body count. **Director**—Eastwood. (R)

117 minutes

SUDDENLY LAST SUMMER (1959)

 ★★★

Katharine Hepburn
Elizabeth Taylor
Montgomery Clift

Montgomery Clift and Katharine Hepburn look on intently as Elizabeth Taylor shifts through whatever marbles she can find for the answer to what happened Suddenly Last Summer.

The great acting of Hepburn and Clift salvage this mediocre Tennessee Williams play and make Gore Vidal's incompetent film script even seem coherent at times. Future film historians will probably wonder if the screenwriter, or anyone else involved in the production, knew what it was about. Clift plays a neurosurgeon thrust into the position of acting as a psychiatrist so he can determine what caused Hepburn's niece, played by Taylor, to have a nervous breakdown. Also with Gary Raymond, Albert Dekker, and Mercedes McCambridge. **Director**—Joseph L. Mankiewicz. **Academy Award Nominations**—Hepburn, Taylor, best actress. *114 minutes b&w*

THE SUGARLAND EXPRESS (1974)

 ★★★

Goldie Hawn
William Atherton

Goldie Hawn becomes a fugitive for her kids in the taut thriller The Sugarland Express.

Hawn and Atherton star in this overly involved comic adventure of fugitive parents trying to reclaim their baby from foster parents. Much of the film, based on a true 1969 incident, centers on the pursuit of the couple by Texas state police. The production is deftly handled, but the chase gets tedious at times and wears thin by the end of the movie. Hawn and Atherton are superb, with fine support from Ben Johnson and Michael Sacks. **Director**—Steven Spielberg. (PG)

110 minutes

SULLIVAN'S TRAVELS (1941)

★★★★

Joel McCrea
Veronica Lake

McCrea is splendid in this charming satirical story about a disgruntled film director who goes out into the real world to learn about the life-styles of real people. The comic sequences prevail under the excellent screenwriting and directing by Preston Sturges, but the movie isn't without a message, and the lessons remain with you after the mirth fades away. Robert Warwick, Jimmy Conlin, Franklin Pangborn, Eric Blore, Margaret Hayes, and Porter Hall also star. *90 minutes b&w*

SUMMERDOG (1977)

 ★★

James Congdon
Elizabeth Eisenman

Just another run-of-the-mill shaggy-dog movie, which may be of interest to small fry, but will obviously put grown-ups to sleep. The predictable plot is about a playful mutt named Hobo, who's adopted by a family vacationing in the country. The acting is exaggerated, and the dialogue is corny. **Director**—John Clayton. (G) *90 minutes b&w*

SUMMER LOVERS (1982)

 ★

Daryl Hannah
Peter Gallagher
Valerie Quennessen

Dreary nonsense about a young college man and two young women involved in a ménage à trois on a sunny Greek island. It's hard to believe that Randal Kleiser, the director of *Grease*, is responsible for this exercise in tedium. The thin, half-baked plot meanders, the characters are shallow, and the acting is an embarrassment. A total washout. (R) *98 minutes*

SUMMER OF '42 (1971)

 ★★

Jennifer O'Neill
Gary Grimes

This story of young love is expertly produced and photographed, but the nostalgia approaches nausea at times. Herman Raucher's autobiographical screenplay also makes the mistake of putting the sexual attitudes and the emphasis on permissiveness of the late 1960s and 1970s into the 1940s. Grimes

MARILYN MONROE

Marilyn Monroe was born Norma Jean Baker or Mortenson in Los Angeles in 1926. She lived in several foster homes and an orphanage, and during her childhood she was subjected to neglect, humiliation, and even rape.

At 16, she married a small-town policeman, but the marriage ended in divorce. During World War II, while working in a defense plant, she was discovered by a photographer who asked her to pose for pinup pictures, which became popular among GIs. More modeling assignments followed,

and she was finally noticed by Hollywood studios who starred her in bit parts in poor movies in the late '40s and early '50s; she was usually cast as a dumb, bleached blonde.

In the mid-'50s, Monroe's roles became more significant, and she became a top box-office attraction as a Hollywood sex queen. In 1954, Monroe married baseball star Joe DiMaggio, a relationship that lasted less than a year. In 1956, she married playwright Arthur Miller, and she divorced him five years later, just prior to the completion of her last film, The Misfits (1961).

About a month after the opening of The Misfits *(the script was written by Arthur Miller), Monroe entered a mental hospital. In 1962, she died, apparently committing suicide with an overdose of drugs.*

Some of Monroe's other major films include The Asphalt Jungle (1950), All About Eve (1950), Don't Bother to Knock (1952), Niagara (1952), Gentlemen Prefer Blondes (1953), How to Marry a Millionaire (1953), The Seven-Year Itch (1955), Bus Stop (1956), *and* Some Like It Hot (1959).

plays a teenager of 15 who's infatuated with a 22-year-old war bride, played by O'Neill; both are superior to their material. When the subject isn't sex, the mood and tempo of the early '40s are superbly evoked. Jerry Houser, Oliver Conant, Christopher Norris, Katherine Allentuck, and Lou Frizell appear in supporting roles. **Director**—Robert Mulligan. (PG) **Academy Award Nominations**—Raucher, best story and screenplay (based on factual material or material not previously published); Robert Surtees, cinematography. *103 minutes*

A SUMMER PLACE (1959)

 ★★

Richard Egan
Dorothy McGuire
Sandra Dee
Troy Donahue

Novelist Sloan Wilson has an unerring instinct when it comes to portrayals of middle-class people and their value systems. This film version of his novel captures that aspect expertly, but the

script and plot don't measure up to the characterizations. Egan, McGuire, Dee, and Donahue appear to follow director Delmer Daves's directions exactly, in this story about adultery and young love at a summer resort in Maine. Arthur Kennedy, Beulah Bondi, and Constance Ford also star. *130 minutes*

SUMMER WISHES, WINTER DREAMS (1973)

 ★★★

Joanne Woodward
Martin Balsam
Sylvia Sidney

Woodward is captivating as a troubled housewife who's disturbed by the death of her mother, played by Sidney. Despite the kindness of Balsam, her understanding husband, Woodward lives in the past. But she finds new meaning in life when she accompanies her husband to sites where he served during World War II. The movie has its weaknesses, but the superior acting of this trio makes it a worth-

(Continued)

S
- The Sun Also Rises
- Sunburn
- Sunday, Bloody Sunday
- A Sunday in the Country
- Sunday Lovers
- The Sunday Woman
- The Sundowners

(Continued)

while viewing experience. Also with Dori Brenner, Win Forman, and Ron Rickards. **Director**—Gilbert Cates. (PG) **Academy Award Nominations**—Woodward, best actress; Sidney, best supporting actress. *93 minutes*

THE SUN ALSO RISES (1957)
★★

Tyrone Power
Ava Gardner
Errol Flynn

On screen, Ernest Hemingway's novel of the Lost Generation loses much of its punch; the characters seem to flutter, and the plot sputters. Some of the scenery—filmed in Mexico—is attractive, although the book dealt with adventures in Spain and Paris of the 1920s. Flynn is good and almost steals the show from the weaker acting efforts of Power and Gardner. Gregory Ratoff, Henry Daniell, Eddie Albert, Juliette Greco, Mel Ferrer, and Robert Evans are also in the cast. **Director**—Henry King. *129 minutes*

SUNBURN (1979)
 ★

Farrah Fawcett-Majors
Charles Grodin
Art Carney

Fawcett-Majors is lovely to look at and so is the lush Acapulco scenery, but that's all this silly comic mystery has going for it. Grodin and Carney work hard as oddball insurance investigators who crack a blackmail caper. Yet the film is mostly a setup for Farrah, who plays a model posing as Grodin's wife. All in all, it smacks of a limp TV pilot, with Farrah flashing her famous smile and repeating her *Charlie's Angels* bit. Also with Joan Collins, Alejandro Rey, and William Daniels. **Director**—Richard C. Sarafian. (PG) *94 minutes*

SUNDAY, BLOODY SUNDAY (1971)
 ★★★

Glenda Jackson
Peter Finch
Murray Head

Glenda Jackson is party to an emotional love triangle in Sunday, Bloody Sunday.

Jackson, Finch, and Head star in this story about a bisexual triangle, in which Finch and Jackson are both in love with Head. The prudish will object to the casual way the risqué subject is handled, but most of the movie is tastefully and superbly crafted. The acting of Jackson and Finch is excellent. Also with Tony Britton, Peggy Ashcroft, Maurice Denham, Harold Goldblatt, and Vivian Pickles. **Director**—John Schlesinger. (R) **Academy Award Nominations**—Schlesinger, best director; Finch, best actor; Jackson, best actress; Penelope Gilliatt, best story and screenplay (based on factual material or material not previously published). *110 minutes*

A SUNDAY IN THE COUNTRY (1984)
★★★

Elegant, thoughtful French film set during a summer day in 1912 when an elderly painter invites his children and grandchildren to his country home. The screenplay, based on a Pierre Bost novel, is filled with wise observations about family relations and the contrasts in outlook between the old artist and his offspring. Worthy performances from the entire cast, which includes Louis Ducreux, Sabine Azema, and Michal Aumont. In French with English titles. **Director**—Bertrand Tavernier. (No MPAA rating) *94 minutes*

SUNDAY LOVERS (1981)
(no stars)

Roger Moore
Gene Wilder

The amorous escapades of four middle-aged men are presented as four short films, produced in four separate countries, with four sets of stars. Moore, in the British segment, is miscast as a chauffeur who chases airline stewardesses. But the worst of the lot involves Wilder in America. He plays a mental patient who tries to solve his sexual problems with the help of Kathleen Quinlan. After four disappointing innings, there are no laughs, no decent acting, and lots of errors. **Director**—Edouard Molinara. (No MPAA rating) *125 minutes*

THE SUNDAY WOMAN (1976)
★★

Marcello Mastroianni
Jacqueline Bisset

A murder mystery set among the rich and bored of Turin, Italy. Mastroianni plays a police inspector on the trail of the killer of a vulgar architect. There are plenty of interesting suspects among the smart set, including the beautiful Bisset who plays the wife of a big-shot industrialist. The plot rambles on and provides no real excitement. Also with Jean-Louis Trintignant, Aldo Reggiani, and Pino Caruso. **Director**—Luigi Comencini. (R) *110 minutes*

THE SUNDOWNERS (1960)
★★★

Robert Mitchum
Deborah Kerr
Glynis Johns
Peter Ustinov

A splendid cast and excellent on-location photography in Australia brighten this tale of a 1920s sheepherding family. At times, the movie drags along and the production seems longer than it actually is, but the characterizations are superb, with especially good acting by Mitchum, Kerr, Johns, Ustinov, and Wylie Watson. Dina Merrill, Chips Rafferty, and Michael Anderson, Jr., perform well in supporting roles. Despite some faults, it's a film the entire family will enjoy. **Director**—Fred Zinnemann. **Academy Award Nominations**—best picture; Zinnemann, best director; Kerr, best actress; Johns, best supporting actress; Isobel

Deborah Kerr, Robert Mitchum, and Peter Ustinov in The Sundowners.

Lennart, best screenplay (based on material from another medium).
133 minutes

SUNRISE AT CAMPOBELLO (1960)

 ★★★

Ralph Bellamy
Greer Garson

Bellamy and Garson give very convincing performances as Mr. and Mrs. Franklin Delano Roosevelt in this biography about the early years of FDR's adult life, as he enters politics and confronts polio. This moving drama, however, was better as a Broadway play. Too much of the movie is static because of the less-than-successful transfer to the screen. Also with Hume Cronyn, Jean Hagen, Lyle Talbot, Tim Considine, and Ann Shoemaker. **Director**—Vincent J. Donehue. **Academy Award Nomination**—Garson, best actress.   *143 minutes*

SUNSET BOULEVARD (1950)

 ★★★★

Gloria Swanson
William Holden

An impoverished screenwriter, played by Holden, becomes the kept man of an aging movie queen, played by Swanson, in this memorable drama. The story is farfetched and has numerous flaws, but the acting is splendid. Just the cynical and acid commentary about Hollywood life-styles and morality would make the movie worthwhile. But there's much more, including superb photography and Billy Wilder's excellent direction. Erich Von Stroheim, Fred Clark, Nancy Olson, Buster Keaton, Hedda Hopper, Jack Webb, and Cecil B. De Mille star in supporting roles. **Academy Award**—Charles Brackett, Wilder, and D. M. Marsham, Jr., writing (story and screenplay). **Nominations**—best picture; Wilder, best director; Holden, best actor; Swanson, best actress; Von Stroheim, best supporting actor; Olson, best supporting actress; John F. Seitz, cinematography (black and white).   *110 minutes b&w*

THE SUNSHINE BOYS (1975)

 ★★★

Walter Matthau
George Burns

Matthau and Burns play two aging and feuding vaudeville partners who are reunited for a TV special after an 11-year separation. The lightweight comedy by Neil Simon is based on his Broadway play. Matthau and Burns are an effective comic combination, exuding warmth and charm as they bat their one-liners back and forth. It's an amusing and entertaining movie, yet the Simon touch lacks heft, and at times it's like watching a TV sitcom. Also with Richard Benjamin and Carol Arthur. **Director**—Herbert Ross. (PG) **Academy Award**—Burns, best supporting actor. **Nominations**—Matthau, best actor; Simon, best screenplay (adapted from another medium).   *111 minutes*

SUPERFLY (1972)

 ★★

Ron O'Neal
Carl Lee

O'Neal and Lee star in this vulgar tale glorifying Harlem drug traffic. It's about a drug dealer who vows to make one last big score before retiring. Admittedly, there's a lot of action in this well-made film, and there are comic moments, but there is excessive violence. Also with Julius W. Harris. **Director**—Gordon Parks, Jr. (R)
98 minutes

SUPERGIRL (1984)

 ★★

Faye Dunaway
Brenda Vaccaro
Helen Slater

She manages to fly but fails to soar. And whenever the characters open their mouths, the leaden banter nearly sinks this epic comic book adventure from the producers of the *Superman* movies. Slater is in the title role as the schoolgirl from inner space who tangles with two forces of evil (Dunaway and Vaccaro) over a magical source of power. Like the movie, the heroine is pretty to look at but lacks the easy charm found in Christopher Reeve high-flyers. (PG) **Director**—Jeannot Szwarc.   *105 minutes*

SUPERMAN (1978)

 ★★★

Christopher Reeve
Margot Kidder
Marlon Brando
Gene Hackman

That durable comic-book hero comes to the screen in this elaborate, $35-million production; it's great juvenile fun, and the special effects are super. Yet, the movie seems too extravagant for such mindless material. Reeve does yeoman's work as the Man of Steel who busily fights crime, saves airplanes, and courts Lois Lane (Kidder). Brando gets top billing—and top dollar—as Superman's father, but it seems he's on and off the screen faster than a speeding bullet. Also with Ned Beatty, Jackie Cooper, Glenn Ford, and Valerie Perrine. **Director**—Richard Donner. (PG)   *143 minutes*

SUPERMAN II (1981)

 ★★★★

Christopher Reeve
Margot Kidder
Gene Hackman

The Man of Steel, played by Reeve, is a super lover who takes Lois Lane to bed tastefully in this thrilling sequel that outshines the 1978 film. Lois is once again played by Kidder. The film brims with exquisite special effects, heroic
(Continued)

S
- Superman III
- Supervixens
- Support Your Local Gunfighter
- Support Your Local Sheriff
- Suppose They Gave a War and Nobody Came?
- The Survivors
- Susan Slept Here

(Continued)

splendor, and some surprising humanizing touches. This time, Earth is threatened by three power-crazed villains from the planet Krypton. But our hero triumphs over evil in a glorious, slam-bang battle amid Manhattan's skyscrapers. Also with Jackie Cooper, Valerie Perrine, and Susannah York. **Director**—Richard Lester. (PG)
127 minutes

SUPERMAN III (1983)

★★

Richard Pryor
Christopher Reeve

Christopher Reeve and Richard Pryor in Superman III.

Pryor, playing a bumbling computer programmer, adds some welcome comic touches to this third adventure of the Man of Steel. Otherwise, this is a routine glossy. Reeve is still Superman, this time battling a sinister conglomerate boss (Robert Vaughn) who wants to destroy the world's coffee crop. Annette O'Toole co-stars as Superman's new love interest while Lois Lane (Margot Kidder) takes a back seat. This time around, the comic-book adventure lacks the zip of its predecessors. **Director**—Richard Lester. (PG)
123 minutes

SUPERVIXENS (1975)

(no stars)

Director Russ Meyer once again comes up with a mixture of nudity, brutality, simulated sex, and cheap jokes. The film is sophomoric and idiotic through and through. (X)
106 minutes

SUPPORT YOUR LOCAL GUNFIGHTER (1971)

★★

James Garner

Garner fans might enjoy this weak and silly movie about a gambler who flees from a woman who wants to marry him. Many of the attempts at laughs are keyed to Garner's subsequent plight when he's mistaken for a professional gunfighter. The supporting cast includes Harry Morgan, Suzanne Pleshette, Joan Blondell, Jack Elam, and Chuck Connors, and they are all in step with the spirit of this enterprise. **Director**—Burt Kennedy. (G)
92 minutes

SUPPORT YOUR LOCAL SHERIFF (1969)
★★★

James Garner
Joan Hackett

In Support Your Local Sheriff, *James Garner kneels over the loser of a gunfight.*

In this amusing movie, spoofing many conventional westerns, Garner becomes sheriff of a town. He outwits the bad guys and romances Hackett. Garner has just the right comic touch for such a farce. And the performances of Hackett and Walter Brennan, as the chieftain of the bad guys, enhance the production. Jack Elam, Bruce Dern, Henry Jones, and Harry Morgan appear in supporting roles. **Director**—Burt Kennedy. (G)
92 minutes

SUPPOSE THEY GAVE A WAR AND NOBODY CAME? (1970)

★

Tony Curtis
Brian Keith
Ernest Borgnine
Ivan Dixon

This lackluster comedy revolves around the conflicts caused in a Southern town by the presence of an Army base. Curtis, Keith, Borgnine, and Dixon have all been better in other movies. Even a potentially good scene—when the soldiers arrive at a dance in a tank—falls flat. The supporting cast includes Tom Ewell, Don Ameche, Arthur O'Connell, and Suzanne Pleshette. **Director**—Hy Averback. (PG) **Alternate Title**—*War Games*.
114 minutes

THE SURVIVORS (1983)

★

Walter Matthau
Robin Williams

Matthau and Williams flounder about in this aimless social satire that takes pot shots at Reaganomics. The overloaded, rickety plot has fired executive Williams and dismissed gas station owner Matthau involved with a cockeyed paramilitary training organization after they encounter a desperate hit man (Jerry Reed). Williams digs into his role with desperation while Matthau appears constantly bored. **Director**—Michael Ritchie. (R)
102 minutes

SUSAN SLEPT HERE (1954)

★★

Dick Powell
Debbie Reynolds

Powell and Reynolds star in this comedy about a Hollywood scriptwriter who's doing a movie about juvenile delinquency. He's given custody of a problem child, and that development is supposed to be the foundation for a lot of laughs. Instead the production crumbles. Powell is the scriptwriter, and Reynolds is the delinquent. Also with Anne Francis, Horace MacMahon, Alvy Moore, and Glenda Farrell. **Director**—Frank Tashlin. *98 minutes*

- Swamp Thing
- The Swan
- The Swarm
- Swashbuckler
- Sweet Bird of Youth
- Sweet Rosie O'Grady
- Sweet Smell of Success

S

SWAMP THING (1982)

★★

Ray Wise
Adrienne Barbeau
Louis Jourdan

Dick Durock, as the Swamp Thing, rescues his lucky girl friend, Adrienne Barbeau.

The DC Comics horror adventure is translated to the screen, but the filmmakers, unfortunately, do not have the courage of their camp convictions and the story lacks the outrageous dialogue and absurd situations that it needs. The plot concerns a scientist who is changed into a walking vegetable and hides in the swamp, where he battles the bad guys and woos his girl friend. Not enough hokeyness going on to make *Return of the Swamp Thing* a desirable idea. **Director**—Wes Craven. (PG)   *90 minutes*

THE SWAN (1956)

★★

Grace Kelly
Alec Guinness
Louis Jourdan

Aside from the always welcome presence of Kelly, this film lacks any other mark of distinction—despite the fine acting of Guinness and Jourdan. The story is about the search by a prince for a wife and is based on the play by Ferenc Molnar. Guinness plays the prince. Guess who married a prince after this movie? Also with Agnes Moorehead, Estelle Winwood, Robert Coote, Leo G. Carroll, and Jessie Royce Landis. **Director**—Charles Vidor.   *112 minutes*

THE SWARM (1978)

★

Michael Caine
Katharine Ross

Zillions of African killer bees are on the rampage in this movie by director Irwin (*The Towering Inferno*) Allen. The enraged insects attack an Air Force ICBM base and a nearby town, but they can't measure up in scariness to man-eating sharks or overgrown gorillas. The movie plods on with a lot of dull dialogue, questionable credibility, and not much sting. An all-star cast, which seems to number as many players as there are bees on screen, also includes Richard Widmark, Henry Fonda, Olivia de Havilland, Fred MacMurray, Richard Chamberlain, Lee Grant, Ben Johnson, and José Ferrer. (PG)   *116 minutes*

SWASHBUCKLER (1976)

★

Robert Shaw
James Earl Jones

A lavish yet tacky pirate adventure photographed mostly around Puerto Vallarta, Mexico. Shaw and Jones are a pair of daring pirates bent on ridding Jamaica of a corrupt governor, played by Peter Boyle. The uneven film can't make up its mind whether it's straight action melodrama or burlesque; it's mostly tedious and hardly in the spirit of those colorful pirate adventures of 20 years ago. Now Errol Flynn—there was a swashbuckler! Also with Geneviève Bujold, Beau Bridges, and Geoffrey Holder. **Director**—James Goldstone. (PG)   *101 minutes*

SWEET BIRD OF YOUTH (1962)

★★★

Paul Newman
Geraldine Page
Ed Begley

Newman, Page, and Begley sparkle in this film version of Tennessee Williams's play about a Hollywood actor who returns to his hometown with an aging and neurotic film star. Newman is the actor, and Page is the aging glamor queen. Newman confronts the boss of the corrupt Southern town, and they renew an old feud. It's fortunate that this trio shines so brightly because much of the original Williams play has been emasculated for its screen appearance. Nonetheless, there are vivid characterizations, crisp dialogue, and memorable scenes. Also with Rip Torn, Madeleine Sherwood, and Shirley Knight. **Director**—Richard Brooks. **Academy Award**—Begley, best supporting actor. **Nominations**—Page, best actress; Knight, best supporting actress.   *120 minutes*

SWEET ROSIE O'GRADY (1943)

★★

Betty Grable
Adolphe Menjou

Menjou is suave, debonair, and charming in this enjoyable musical about a former burlesque star and a reporter's efforts to dig into her past. Grable, the burlesque star, is attractive and lovely to look at—no wonder she was the favorite sex symbol of thousands of GIs. Unfortunately, most of the movie's songs are second-rate, but that doesn't jar the pleasant tone of this enterprise. Robert Young, Alan Dinehart, Reginald Gardiner, Virginia Grey, and Phil Regan appear in supporting roles. **Director**—Irving Cummings.   *79 minutes*

SWEET SMELL OF SUCCESS (1957)

★★★

Burt Lancaster
Tony Curtis

The characterizations are stunning in this startling drama of the rough-and-tumble world of a New York-based newspaper columnist and his dealings with a vile press agent. Curtis is superb as the scheming PR man, while Lancaster is competent but less convincing as the vicious columnist. The splendid photography of James Wong Howe adds to the realistic quality of the movie. Also with Barbara Nichols, Emily Meyer, Martin Milner, Susan Harrison, and Sam Levene. **Director**—Alexander Mackendrick.   *96 minutes b&w*

S·T

- Swept Away...By an Unusual Destiny in the Blue Sea of August
- Swing Shift
- Swing Time
- The Swiss Family Robinson
- The Sword and the Sorcerer
- Table for Five
- Take a Hard Ride

SWEPT AWAY...BY AN UNUSUAL DESTINY IN THE BLUE SEA OF AUGUST (1975)

★★★

Giancarlo Giannini
Mariangela Melato

Melato plays a spoiled, arrogant, and wealthy capitalist. Giannini is a communist deckhand on the yacht she has chartered. They become shipwrecked on an island, and the tables are turned as he dominates her in this gripping, political film by director Lina Wertmuller about the battle of the classes and sexes. In Italian with English titles. (R)   *116 minutes*

SWING SHIFT (1984)

★★

Goldie Hawn
Kurt Russell

Hawn plays a riveter at an aircraft factory in this sweet, nostalgic comedy that looks at America's home front during World War II. The period details are sharply defined, but the sluggish plot bogs down in mushy melodramatics over Goldie's guilt-ridden love affair with a co-worker (Russell). Performances are all decent, yet the story could benefit from a livelier gait. Christine Lahti and Ed Harris also star. **Director**—Jonathan Demme. (PG)
112 minutes

SWING TIME (1936)

★★★★

Fred Astaire
Ginger Rogers
Victor Moore

In Swing Time, *Ginger Rogers forlornly sings of Fred Astaire, "It's a fine romance—with no kisses; I simmer and my friend fizzes."*

Mandatory viewing to chase away the blues and to see the screen's greatest dancing couple at their best. Astaire stars as a professional dancer and gambler, whose prospective father-in-law demands he raise $25,000 to win his daughter. But since the debonair hoofer would rather not marry her anyway, he does everything possible to avoid coming into money. The Oscar-winning "The Way You Look Tonight" and the often-shown "Bojangles in Harlem" number—in which Fred tap dances along with three huge silhouettes—top the fine Jerome Kern score, which also includes "A Fine Romance," "Pick Yourself Up," and "Never Gonna Dance." Betty Furness and Eric Blore co-star. **Director**—George Stevens.   *103 minutes b&w*

THE SWISS FAMILY ROBINSON (1960)

★★★

John Mills
Dorothy McGuire
James MacArthur

John Mills and Dorothy McGuire in The Swiss Family Robinson, *a children's classic.*

This Walt Disney version of the famed Johann Wyss children's classic is an almost total escape into a fantasy world—no small accomplishment when you think about the harsh realities of the real world. The movie shows how a family—shipwrecked en route to New Guinea—adjusts superbly to life on a desert island, as they build a paradise of their own and dispatch pirate invaders. Also with Sessue Hayakawa, Janet Munro, Tommy Kirk, Cecil Parker, and Kevin Corcoran. **Director**—Ken Annakin.
126 minutes

THE SWORD AND THE SORCERER (1982)

★★

Lee Horsley
Richard Lynch

Nonstop sword fighting, torture, and other shenanigans dominate this hectic action-adventure set in the Middle Ages. Some of the special effects are hair-raising, but the jumbled story abandons logic and the acting is strictly second-rate. Horsley heads the unfamiliar cast as an invincible warrior who takes revenge on a wicked conqueror (Lynch). A spectacular mix of nonsense and fast-paced carnage. **Director**—Albert Pyun. (R)   *100 minutes*

T

TABLE FOR FIVE (1983)

★

Jon Voight
Richard Crenna

It had to happen—a tearjerker for men. This strained and sentimental tale stars Voight as an immature, divorced father who struggles to reestablish relations with his three children by taking them on a luxurious ocean cruise. When they're in mid-voyage, the children's mother dies in a car crash, and father and stepfather (Crenna) embark on a fight for custody of the kids. It's enough to make any red-blooded male reach for his handkerchief. John Wayne, where are you? **Director**—Robert Lieberman. (PG)
122 minutes

TAKE A HARD RIDE (1975)

★★

Jim Brown
Jim Kelly
Lee Van Cleef
Fred Williamson

A familiar western period drama where the good guys, like Brown, are blacks, and the villains, like Van Cleef, are white. The story involves the transporting of $86,000 hundreds of miles from Texas to a family in Mexico. All sorts of plotters, ready to grab the

• Take Care of My Little Girl
• Take Me Out to the Ball Game
• Take the Money and Run
• Take This Job and Shove It
• The Taking of Pelham One Two Three
• A Tale of Two Cities

T

loot, pop out of the brush along the way. Also with Catherine Spaak, Dana Andrews, Barry Sullivan, and Harry Carey, Jr. **Director**—Anthony M. Dawson. (PG)   *109 minutes*

TAKE CARE OF MY LITTLE GIRL (1951)
★★

Jeanne Crain
Mitzi Gaynor
Dale Robertson

Crain, Gaynor, and Robertson star in this melodrama about university life and the dynamics and demerits of belonging to a campus sorority. Even viewers who recall their school days with fondness will probably find this movie basically routine. Other cast members include George Nader, Jean Peters, Jeffrey Hunter, and Helen Westcott. **Director**—Jean Negulesco.
93 minutes

TAKE ME OUT TO THE BALL GAME (1949)
★★★

Gene Kelly
Frank Sinatra
Esther Williams
Betty Garrett

Kelly, Sinatra, Williams, and Garrett star in this unpretentious, turn-of-the-century musical about a woman who owns a baseball team. The plot is weak and most of the songs are forgettable, but the stars put enough of their energy into the show to make it highly pleasing for those who don't approach it with great expectations. "The Hat My Father Wore on St. Patrick's Day" and "O'Brien to Ryan to Goldberg" are two of the better-known songs. Also with Richard Lane, Tom Dugan, Edward Arnold, and Jules Munshin. **Director**—Busby Berkeley.   *93 minutes*

TAKE THE MONEY AND RUN (1969)
 ★★★

Woody Allen

Allen is in top form as writer, director, and actor in this comedy about the life of an inept thief. Some of the jokes fail and not all of the sight gags work, but the uninhibited spoof of gangster films is exhilarating at times because the laughs come at such a rapid rate. Janet Margolin, Marcel Hillaire, Jacquelyn Hyde, Louise Lasser, Lonny Chapman, and Mark Gordon also appear, with Jackson Beck as the narrator in the documentary-style sequences. (PG)
85 minutes

TAKE THIS JOB AND SHOVE IT (1981)
★★

Robert Hays

Barbara Hershey thinks her boyfriend should Take This Job and Shove It.

Hays of *Airplane* fame stars as a young man on the way up the corporate ladder who joins brewery workers protesting the takeover of their local brewery. The title is interesting, but the film doesn't live up to its potential of effectively revealing the tensions between labor and management. The up-the-conglomerate-and-down-with-computers theme is occasionally amusing, but there's too much triteness in the uneven script, which seems to have been written by a clock watcher. **Director**—Gus Trikonis. (PG)   *100 minutes*

THE TAKING OF PELHAM ONE TWO THREE (1974)
 ★★

Walter Matthau
Robert Shaw

A great idea doesn't necessarily make a great or even a good movie. This story about four gangsters who hold the passengers of a New York City subway car hostage falters because the script is needlessly confusing and too much of the acting is uninspired. Yet there is enough suspense to keep viewers interested. Matthau, who plays a transit detective, and Shaw, as a ruthless gang leader, have their moments. Martin Balsam, James Broderick, Hector Elizondo, Tony Roberts, and Earl Hindman appear in supporting roles. **Director**—Joseph Sargent. (PG)   *104 minutes*

A TALE OF TWO CITIES (1935)
 ★★★★

Ronald Colman

A tremendous cast fortifies this film version of the classic Charles Dickens
(Continued)

Elizabeth Allan learns of the plot against her fiancé in A Tale of Two Cities.

T

- The Talk of the Town
- Tall in the Saddle
- The Tall Men
- The Tamarind Seed
- The Taming of the Shrew
- Tammy and the Bachelor
- Tank

(Continued)

tale of the French Revolution. Although the production has a lavish Hollywood aura, it's a faithful reproduction of Dickens's masterpiece. Colman stars as the British lawyer who aids victims of the Reign of Terror and sacrifices his life to save another man from the guillotine. Also with Edna May Oliver, Elizabeth Allan, Fritz Leiber, Basil Rathbone, Claude Gillingwater, H. B. Warner, and Donald Woods. **Director**—Jack Conway.   *121 minutes b&w*

THE TALK OF THE TOWN
(1942)
★★★★

Ronald Colman
Cary Grant
Jean Arthur

Colman, Grant, and Arthur star in this compelling tale of a woman in love with a suspected murderer and the attorney who defends him. This charming and intelligent comedy about civil liberties is a fine example of Hollywood at its best. Today, such a theme would be presented with a heavy dose of profanity and loads of violence. Other stars in the cast include Charles Dingle, Rex Ingram, Glenda Farrell, Edgar Buchanan, and Emma Dunn. **Director**—George Stevens. **Academy Award Nominations**—best picture; Sidney Harmon, writing (original story); Sidney Buchman and Irwin Shaw, writing (screenplay); Ted Tetzlaff, cinematography (black and white).

118 minutes b&w

TALL IN THE SADDLE (1944)
★★★

John Wayne
Ella Raines

Wayne plays a cowpoke who hates women. But then—true to form in such western adventures—a spinster and her young niece take over the ownership of the ranch where the Duke is foreman. Raines is the ranch owner. Despite these predictable twists and turns in the plot, this is an enjoyable film. Also with Ward Bond, Gabby Hayes, Elisabeth Risdon, Raymond Hatton, Russell Wade, Paul Fix, and Audrey Long. **Director**—Edwin L. Marin.   *87 minutes b&w*

THE TALL MEN (1955)
★★

Clark Gable
Jane Russell
Robert Ryan

Gable, Russell, and Ryan bolster the appeal of this standard western yarn, but it doesn't really have much to offer beyond some action scenes and Russell's profile. Gable and Ryan play two Texans who head to Montana after the Civil War in search of their fortunes and meet many hazards along the way— including Indians, of course. Also with Cameron Mitchell, Emile Meyer, Juan Garcia, Mae Marsh, and Harry Shannon. **Director**—Raoul Walsh.

122 minutes

THE TAMARIND SEED (1974)
★★

Julie Andrews
Omar Sharif

Andrews and Sharif star in this romance with an international backdrop—London, Paris, and Barbados— and an espionage theme. Andrews plays a British widow who falls in love with a Russian agent, played by Sharif. The plot substitutes confusion for suspense, but the stars shine often enough to keep the story interesting. The cast includes Anthony Quayle, Oscar Homolka, Daniel O'Herlihy, and Sylvia Sims. **Director**—Blake Edwards. (PG)   *123 minutes*

THE TAMING OF THE SHREW
(1967)
★★★

Richard Burton
Elizabeth Taylor

At times, William Shakespeare seems to take a back seat in this movie, but there are enough remnants of the Bard's brilliance to tame the most critical of viewers. In addition, Burton is superb as Petruchio, Taylor is good as Kate, the supporting cast is first-rate, and the color photography is exquisite. The supporting actors include Michael York, Cyril Cusack, Victor Spinetti, Michael Hordern, Vernon Dobtcheff, Natasha Pyne, and Alan Webb. **Director**—Franco Zeffirelli.   *126 minutes*

TAMMY AND THE BACHELOR
(1957)
★★

Debbie Reynolds
Leslie Nielsen

Reynolds, in the title role, nurses an injured pilot, played by Nielsen, back to health in this lightweight comedy-romance. She falls in love with him, of course, and the rest is sweetness and corn and everything nice. The performance of Reynolds is spirited, energetic, and contagious enough so that the whole cast gets into step and makes the best of average material. Also with Walter Brennan, Fay Wray, Mala Powers, Louise Beavers, Sidney Blackmer, and Mildred Natwick. **Director**—Joseph Pevney.   *89 minutes*

TANK (1984)
★★★

James Garner
Shirley Jones

James Garner springs his son C. Thomas Howell from prison in Tank.

Garner plays a rootin'-tootin' Army sergeant major who owns his own Sherman battle tank, which he uses to rescue his teenage son from the clutches of a redneck sheriff. The implausible story wavers from social commentary to yahoo farce. And the fact that a sergeant would own such an elaborate weapon, complete with ammunition, is farfetched. But Garner's performance and quiet, comic authority carry the film. Worth watching. **Director**—Marvin J. Chomsky. (PG)   *117 minutes*

• Taps
• Taras Bulba
• Tarzan of the Apes

• Tarzan, The Ape Man
• Task Force
• Tattoo
• Taxi Driver

T

TAPS (1981)

★★

**George C. Scott
Timothy Hutton**

George C. Scott heads a military academy in Taps.

An ambiguous and rather farfetched drama about military school cadets who take up arms to defend their academy and prevent it from being converted to a condominium development. Essentially, the film is a sentimental analogy of the attitude that led to involvement in Vietnam. The ponderous and predictable story stars Hutton as a gung ho and misguided cadet leader; Scott is delightful as the school's superintendent, but he fades away before the film is half over. Also with Ronny Cox, Tom Cruise, and Sean Penn. **Director**—Harold Becker. (PG) *130 minutes*

TARAS BULBA (1962)
★★

**Yul Brynner
Tony Curtis**

Action, violence, and superior photography prevail in this Nicolai Gogol tale of a 16th-century revolt in Poland. Brynner portrays Taras Bulba, the famed Cossack leader, and Curtis plays one of the Cossack's sons. They merely give the conventional performances such films require. Also with Sam Wanamaker, Guy Rolfe, Abraham Sofaer, Christine Kaufmann, and Vladimir Sokoloff. **Director**—J. Lee Thompson. *122 minutes*

TARZAN OF THE APES (1932)

★★★

**Johnny Weissmuller
Maureen O'Sullivan**

The most popular of all the "Tarzan" movies remains the best. An expedition searching for ivory treasure discovers instead the great man of the jungle, the vine-swinger, leopard-wrestler, and elephant's best friend, convincingly portrayed by Olympic swimmer Weissmuller. He makes off with Jane (O'Sullivan), and the two discover love, high above in the treetops. The film is full of now-classic bits that are great fun to rediscover— especially Tarzan's first appearance, and the Me Tarzan–You Jane scene. From the novel by Edgar Rice Burroughs. With Neil Hamilton and C. Aubrey Smith. **Director**—W. S. Van Dyke. *99 minutes b&w*

TARZAN, THE APE MAN (1981)

★

**Bo Derek
Miles O'Keeffe**

The lord of the jungle is dethroned and relegated to the role of a mere silent sex symbol in this labored and shabby remake, which looks more like a pinup calendar layout than a movie. Practically all the attention is on Jane, played by beautiful Bo who's frequently photographed in various stages of undress. Jane loses her way in the jungle, where she finds the magnificent ape man played by O'Keeffe, and the two monkey around together. Tarzan doesn't say a word, which is probably wise because everyone else is saddled with silly dialogue. **Director**—John Derek. (R) *111 minutes*

TASK FORCE (1949)

★★

**Gary Cooper
Walter Brennan
Jane Wyatt**

Cooper, Brennan, and Wyatt star in this story about the growth of naval aviation and the development of aircraft carriers. At times, the plot seems to be lost at sea, and when the film

does roll along, there's too much emphasis on Navy propaganda. But the acting is good, and there are some fine action sequences. Julie London, Jack Holt, Wayne Morris, Stanley Ridges, and Bruce Bennett appear in supporting roles. **Director**—Delmer Daves. *116 minutes b&w/color*

TATTOO (1981)

★

**Bruce Dern
Maud Adams**

Dern once again portrays a weird character; this time he's a tormented tattoo artist who kidnaps a glamorous model, played by Adams, and plies his needlework all over her beautiful body. The story, which borrows heavily from *The Collector*, starts with some promise, but turns sour and predictable about midway and eventually falls apart at the seams. With Adams in a state of undress so often as Dern's human canvas, the film eventually resembles a sleazy soft-core skin flick. **Director**—Bob Brooks. (R) *102 minutes*

TAXI DRIVER (1976)

★★★

**Robert De Niro
Jodie Foster**

(Continued)

Cybill Shepherd and Robert De Niro in Martin Scorsese's brutal Taxi Driver.

T
- Tea and Sympathy
- Teachers
- Teacher's Pet
- Tea for Two
- The Teahouse of the August Moon
- Telefon
- Tell Me a Riddle

(Continued)

Easily one of the 10 best American films of the '70s. Director Martin Scorsese gives a brutally disturbing account of a lonely and psychotic New York cabbie. The experience evokes mixed emotions; it's depressing, violent, and cynical—yet undeniably brilliant. Paul Schrader's screenplay is his finest so far, and there's a dazzling performance by De Niro as the quietly unhinged Travis Bickle, who stalks a presidential candidate but instead turns his sudden fury on the pimp of a young prostitute. Foster is impressive as a 12-year-old hustler, as is Harvey Keitel who plays her pimp. The film is haunting and unforgettable. Also with Cybill Shepherd, Peter Boyle, and Albert Brooks. (R) **Academy Award Nominations**—best picture; De Niro, best actor; Foster, best supporting actress. *113 minutes*

TEA AND SYMPATHY (1956)
★★★

Deborah Kerr
John Kerr

Deborah Kerr and John Kerr—they're not related—both give extremely sensitive performances in this movie about a troubled schoolboy's affair with a teacher's wife. This film version of Robert Anderson's successful Broadway play drags at times, but the superior acting and characterizations more than justify the pace of the production. Leif Erickson, Edward Andrews, Norma Crane, Dean Jones, and Darryl Hickman also star. **Director**—Vincente Minnelli. *122 minutes*

TEACHERS (1984)
★★★

Nick Nolte
JoBeth Williams
Judd Hirsch
Ralph Macchio

Hooray for dedicated teachers who are on the side of the kids and effective education, while rejecting bureaucratic nonsense and self-serving interests. Nolte plays such a high-minded high school teacher in this social-issues comedy that tackles the chaotic state of public education as *The Hospital* dealt with medicine. Give Nolte and

other good cast members high marks for fine acting. **Director**—Arthur Hiller. (R) *106 minutes*

TEACHER'S PET (1958)
★★★

Clark Gable
Doris Day
Gig Young

Gable, Day, and Young are in fine form and give this unpretentious and enjoyable comedy just the right emphasis. Gable plays a tough newspaper editor who enrolls in Day's journalism course. He tries to romance her, but must also deal with the intellectual and eccentric Young. The supporting cast includes Nick Adams, Mamie Van Doren, and Charles Lane. **Director**—George Seaton. **Academy Award Nominations**—Young, best supporting actor; Fay and Michael Kanin, best story and screenplay (written directly for the screen). *120 minutes b&w*

TEA FOR TWO (1950)
★★

Doris Day
Gordon MacRae

A congenial cast including Day, MacRae, Eve Arden, and Billy De Wolfe keep this musical, inspired by the play *No, No, Nanette*, perking right along. Although amusing and enjoyable, the whole production is lacking in substance; most of the activity centers on Day's decision to become interested in show business. Gene Nelson, Patrice Wymore, Bill Goodwin, and S. Z. Sakall, round out the cast. **Director**—David Butler. *97 minutes*

THE TEAHOUSE OF THE AUGUST MOON (1956)
★★★

Marlon Brando
Glenn Ford

Brando is miscast as a cunning native interpreter in this pleasing film version of John Patrick's successful Broadway play. Fortunately, Ford, who plays a U.S. Army captain in charge of the rehabilitation of an Okinawan village in 1944, has a keen comic touch and

carries the film to its enjoyable conclusion. Also with Machiko Kyo, Paul Ford, Henry Morgan, and Eddie Albert. **Director**—Daniel Mann. *123 minutes*

TELEFON (1977)
★★

Charles Bronson
Lee Remick

Charles Bronson plays a Russian KGB agent in Telefon.

Bronson and Remick play two Russian spies who pursue a Russian saboteur in the United States who's trying to trigger World War III. The plot, which is hard to take seriously, owes much to *The Manchurian Candidate*; it's based on Walter Wager's novel. Bronson maintains his usual stone face amid the numerous action sequences that fade away moments after they start. Locations range all over the globe—Moscow, Canada, and several cities in the United States. Also with Donald Pleasence, Tyne Daly, Patrick Magee, and Alan Badel. **Director**—Don Siegel. (PG) *102 minutes*

TELL ME A RIDDLE (1981)
★★★

Melvyn Douglas
Lila Kedrova

Douglas and Kedrova star in this dignified, low-key film about an elderly couple who reconcile their long, quarrelsome marriage. Douglas and Ked-

• Tell Me That You Love Me, Junie Moon
• Tell Them Willie Boy Is Here
• Tempest
• 10
• The Tenant
• The Ten Commandments

T

rova create heartwarming, memorable characterizations. The film is often lacking in dramatic momentum, but there are many moments of beauty and sensitivity. Based on Tillie Olsen's acclaimed 1961 novella. Lee Grant, in her first time out as director, handles the job in a straightforward manner. (PG) *90 minutes*

TELL ME THAT YOU LOVE ME, JUNIE MOON (1969)
★★★

**Liza Minnelli
Ken Howard
Robert Moore**

There are some superb and moving moments in this strange tragi-comedy about three handicapped people who decide to live together. The excellent acting of Minnelli (facially scarred), Howard (an epileptic), and Moore (a homosexual paraplegic) helps to carry the film over its rough spots. There are many flaws in this movie, but this is a rare case in which Hollywood must be commended for having the courage to tackle a difficult subject. The supporting cast includes James Coco, Fred Williamson, Kay Thompson, and Leonard Frey. **Director**—Otto Preminger. (PG) *113 minutes*

TELL THEM WILLIE BOY IS HERE (1969)
 ★★★

**Robert Redford
Robert Blake**

In Tell Them Willie Boy Is Here, *sheriff Robert Redford tracks down a murderer.*

Redford and Blake star in this tale about an Indian who flees after killing a man in self-defense. Unlike most western adventures, this movie, under the excellent writing and direction of Abraham Polonsky, also explores the cruel treatment of the American Indian by the white man. Redford is good as the sheriff who hunts down the killer. Blake, who plays the fugitive Indian, is close to perfect. Also with Susan Clark, Barry Sullivan, Katharine Ross, John Vernon, Charles McGraw, and Charles Aidman. (PG) *96 minutes*

TEMPEST (1982)
 ★★

**John Cassavetes
Gena Rowlands
Susan Sarandon
Vittorio Gassman**

Director Paul Mazursky (*An Unmarried Woman*) fashions a latter-day, middle-class comedy upon the superstructure of Shakespeare's magical play. The upshot is a movie that's simultaneously intelligent yet cumbersome and overblown. It has some good moments, but pretension prevails. Cassavetes has the central role; he's a successful New York architect who retreats to an isolated Greek island to sort out his midlife crises. Rowlands portrays his actress wife. (PG) *140 minutes*

10 (1979)
 ★★★

**Dudley Moore
Julie Andrews
Bo Derek**

Moore stars as a middle-aged Hollywood songwriter in this romantic comedy about the frustrating pursuit of happiness. Director Blake Edwards skillfully sets up a number of funny situations for Moore, who stumbles and bumbles after a vision of beauty and youth, played by Derek. There are some slow spots, but Moore manages to keep the comic momentum rolling along. Andrews, in a brief throwaway role, is Moore's long-standing girl friend. Also with Robert Webber, Sam Jones, Dee Wallace, Max Showalter, and Brian Dennehy. (R) *122 minutes*

THE TENANT (1976)
 ★★★

**Roman Polanski
Isabelle Adjani
Melvyn Douglas
Shelley Winters**

Polanski directs and stars in this horror tale about a mild-mannered young Pole who rents a Paris apartment and believes he's being persecuted by his neighboring tenants. Polanski delivers striking shock effects and an intense performance of a man creating his own torture. However, the film doesn't reach the same degree of suspense or polish as Polanski's *Rosemary's Baby* or *Chinatown*. Excellent support from Winters, Adjani, and Douglas. Also with Jo Van Fleet, Bernard Fresson, and Claude Dauphin. Poor English dubbing of French-speaking cast members. (R) *125 minutes*

THE TEN COMMANDMENTS (1956)
 ★★★

**Charlton Heston
Yul Brynner**

Yvonne DeCarlo plays Moses's mother in the epic The Ten Commandments.

This biblical extravaganza about the life of Moses and leading the Jews out of Egypt to the Promised Land has all the good and bad points of such pictures. On the plus side, there's a star-studded cast, lush photography, and

T
- Tender Mercies
- The Tender Trap
- Ten North Frederick
- Ten to Midnight
- Terminator
- Terms of Endearment

(Continued)

brilliant dramatic moments. However, the movie occasionally is monotonous because of a heavy-handed plot and trite dialogue. Heston, who plays Moses, and Brynner head the huge cast, with Anne Baxter, Edward G. Robinson, Yvonne De Carlo, Martha Scott, Vincent Price, John Carradine, Cedric Hardwicke, John Derek, and Nina Foch among the many supporting actors. **Director**—Cecil B. De Mille. (G) **Academy Award Nominations**—best picture; Loyal Griggs, cinematography (color). *219 minutes*

TENDER MERCIES (1983)

★★★★

Robert Duvall
Tess Harper

Hearty cheers to Australian director Bruce Beresford (*Breaker Morant*) for his outstanding American debut with this extraordinary small film that has a big heart of gold. The story concerns a has-been, drunken country singer (Duvall) who reclaims his self-respect when he marries a shy widow (Harper) who has a young son. Duvall's brilliant performance projects an honest grittiness. Harper is magnificent in her first screen role, and the supporting players are, without exception, near-perfect. It's a compassionate, dignified portrait of loneliness, hope, and the tender mercies that help people deal with their lives. (PG) **Academy Awards**—Duvall, best actor; Horton

Foote, best original screenplay. **Nominations**—best picture; Beresford, best director. *89 minutes*

THE TENDER TRAP (1955)

★★★

Frank Sinatra
Debbie Reynolds
David Wayne
Celeste Holm

Delightful acting performances by Sinatra, Reynolds, Wayne, and Holm vitalize this ordinary comedy and make it worth viewing. Sinatra plays a New York agent who has a way with gals until he eventually falls for the trap of marriage set by Reynolds. Lola Albright, Tom Helmore, and Carolyn Jones are fine in supporting roles. **Director**—Charles Walters.

111 minutes

TEN NORTH FREDERICK
(1958)

★★

Gary Cooper
Geraldine Fitzgerald

Cooper plays a wealthy man pushed by his domineering wife into involvement with national politics. His bid for a shot at the vice presidential nomination of his party never gets off the ground because of his family problems. Fitzgerald plays his wife. The movie doesn't reach its full potential

either, although the acting and characterizations are interesting. Based on John O'Hara's novel. Also with Diane Varsi, Suzy Parker, Tom Tully, Stuart Whitman, and Ray Stricklyn. **Director**—Philip Dunne. *102 minutes b&w*

TEN TO MIDNIGHT (1983)

★★

Charles Bronson
Lisa Eilbacher

Tight-lipped Bronson portrays a veteran homicide detective trailing a psychopath who murders young women. The action heats up when the killer turns his attention to the detective's lovely daughter (Eilbacher). The lively screenplay packs in an unusual amount of suspense and some clever plot twists. Ultimately, however, the film yields to sensational eye-for-an-eye moralizing about practices that allow a killer to shelter under a plea of insanity. **Director**—J. Lee Thompson. (R) *101 minutes*

TERMINATOR (1984)

★★

Arnold Schwarzenegger
Michael Biehn
Linda Hamilton

Muscle-man Schwarzenegger plays a computer-controlled zombie from a future century who arrives in Los Angeles to assassinate a young waitress. Grim-faced Arnold lumbers about blasting everything in sight with various weapons while his intended target keeps a few steps ahead of him. The film is adorned with excessive scenes of screeching car chases and flaming explosions. **Director**—James Cameron. (R) *105 minutes*

TERMS OF ENDEARMENT
(1983)

★★★

Shirley MacLaine
Debra Winger
Jack Nicholson

This soap-opera tearjerker explores the love-hate relationship between a neurotic mother (MacLaine) and her daughter (Winger). The plot meanders ·

Robert Duvall and Allan Hubbard in a tender scene from Tender Mercies.

• Terror in the Aisles
• Terror Train
• Tess
• Testament
• Tex
• The Texas Chainsaw Massacre

T

Shirley MacLaine and Debra Winger play a mother and daughter who finally come to terms with each other in Terms of Endearment.

through emotional problems, funny situations, and tragedy spanning a 30-year period. The film is blessed with some endearing, lifelike characters expertly portrayed by the top cast. Unsurprisingly, Nicholson, in a supporting role, steals scenes as a womanizing, over-the-hill astronaut. **Director**—James L. Brooks. (PG) **Academy Awards**—best picture; MacLaine, best actress; Nicholson, best supporting actor; Brooks, best director; Brooks, best screenplay adaptation. **Nomination**—Winger, best actress.

129 minutes

TERROR IN THE AISLES (1984)
★★

A haphazardly assembled compilation of scenes from such horror classics as *Psycho* and *Rosemary's Baby* to tasteless exploitation fare including *Halloween* and *Scanners*. Juxtaposition generally is off-kilter, which lessens the impact of many sequences. Shock and grisly terror are more in evidence than traditional horror. Narrated by Donald Pleasence and Nancy Allen. **Director**—Andrew Kuehn. (R)   *82 minutes*

TERROR TRAIN (1980)
★★

Jamie Lee Curtis
Ben Johnson

This is another bloody, formula horror film that trips in the tracks of such

shockers as *Halloween* and *The Fog*. The setting is an excursion train, filled with partying college students chugging through Canada. On board is a revenge-seeking psychotic, who assumes various disguises as he murders some of the students and the train crew. Curtis, a regular in this sort of film, plays the heroine in routine fashion. Also with Hart Bochner. **Director**—Roger Spottiswoode. (R)

97 minutes

TESS (1979)
★★★

Nastassja Kinski
Peter Firth
Leigh Lawson

Nastassja Kinski plays the title role in Tess, based on Thomas Hardy's novel.

Director Roman Polanski's fine screen adaptation of the classic Victorian novel by Thomas Hardy is physically beautiful. Lovely Kinski plays the exploited peasant girl who resorts to murder. Polanski remains faithful to the novel and the historic period, and there are lush settings and striking costumes. Firth and Lawson co-star. Also with John Colin. (R) **Academy Award Nominations**—best picture; Polanski, best director.   *180 minutes*

TESTAMENT (1983)
★★★

Jane Alexander
William Devane

What happens to a small American community after a nuclear bomb destroys a nearby city? This grim small film deals with this "unthinkable" situation with an amazing lack of sensationalism and still manages to pack

an emotional wallop, unlike the made-for-TV *The Day After*, which it somewhat resembles. Alexander stars as a stalwart housewife who witnesses the deterioration of her community and the gradual deaths of her children and neighbors from radiation sickness. Debuting director Lynne Littman handles this devastating subject with intelligence. (PG) **Academy Award Nomination**—Alexander, best actress.

90 minutes

TEX (1982)
★★★

Matt Dillon
Jim Metzler

Walt Disney studios breaks out of the familiar, rosy-cheeked style with this engaging and realistic story based on the S. E. Hinton novel. It's the tale of two adolescent brothers (Dillon and Metzler), growing up in rural Oklahoma without parental support, and it touches on such areas as sex, drugs, and violence. The character portrayals are accomplished with grace. Dillon as Tex and Metzler as the older brother give rich and expressive performances. **Director**—Tim Hunter. (PG)

103 minutes

THE TEXAS CHAINSAW MASSACRE (1974)
★★★

Marilyn Burns
Allen Danzinger

(Continued)

The Texas Chainsaw Massacre *adds a technological edge to the gore film genre.*

T
- Thank God, It's Friday
- That Certain Feeling
- That Championship Season
- That Darn Cat!
- That Forsyte Woman
- That Hamilton Woman

(Continued)

A brutal but fascinating horror outing that has attracted a cult following among midnight movie fans, critics, and such directors as Steven Spielberg. A family of brutes in rural Texas engages in grisly mayhem on innocent people. The tension is made almost unbearable with the frequent screams of the victims and the incessant buzzing of chainsaws. The screenplay supposedly is based on true facts about a Wisconsin maniac who preyed on tourists. **Director**—Tobe Hooper. (R)
87 minutes

THANK GOD, IT'S FRIDAY (1978)

 ★★

**Donna Summer
Valerie Landsburg
Terri Nunn**

Donna Summer and Ray Vitte in Thank God, It's Friday, *a contemporary comedy.*

Like the title, there's little originality in this adolescent film about an evening at a Los Angeles discotheque. The style smacks of *Saturday Night Fever;* the climax is built around a dance contest. There's no plot to speak of—just a series of breathless vignettes acted out by a cast of newcomers. More than 30 ultraloud pop songs, including "Last Dance," are featured for the delight of teenagers. Also with Chick Vennera, Ray Vitte, and Jeff Goldblum. (PG) **Director**—Robert Klane.   *90 minutes*

THAT CERTAIN FEELING (1956)

★

Bob Hope

Hope is able to deliver some funny lines, and there are some delightful

moments in this story about a syndicated comic-strip artist who hires a "ghost" to do his work, but most of the movie is dismal. When Hope must act—he portrays a troubled cartoonist—he falters, and the rest of the cast, which includes George Sanders, Pearl Bailey, Eva Marie Saint, and Al Capp, fails to come to his rescue. **Directors**—Norman Panama and Melvin Frank.
102 minutes

THAT CHAMPIONSHIP SEASON (1982)

 ★★

**Robert Mitchum
Stacy Keach
Paul Sorvino
Bruce Dern
Martin Sheen**

Judging by Jason Miller's screen version of his prize-winning Broadway play, the action should have stayed on the stage. This portrait of four middle-aged men, who reveal their failures and frustrations during a 25th reunion of their championship high school basketball team, is long on talk and short on drama. Some decent performances come through, however, and Mitchum is especially believable as the aging coach. **Director**—Miller. (R)
110 minutes

THAT DARN CAT! (1965)

★★

**Hayley Mills
Dean Jones**

William Demarest just has to scold That Darn Cat!

Most Walt Disney animal films are pretty much the same—only the animals seem to change. Fortunately, kids and adults can take comfort in this movie about a talented cat who leads an FBI agent, played by Jones, to the lair of the gangsters to rescue a kidnapped woman. The film maintains the standards of wholesomeness that parents have come to expect of Disney productions. The talented cast also includes Roddy McDowall, Ed Wynn, Dorothy Provine, and Elsa Lanchester. **Director**—Robert Stevenson.
116 minutes

THAT FORSYTE WOMAN (1949)

★★

**Greer Garson
Errol Flynn
Robert Young**

Garson, Flynn, and Young make a valiant bid to bring the film version of John Galsworthy's novel *A Man of Property* to the screen with style and vitality. Although they succeed, Galsworthy on film is a fairly dull achievement. Garson is excellent as a faithless woman who falls in love with the man her niece plans to marry. Flynn and Young are good, too, with competent supporting performances from Walter Pidgeon, Janet Leigh, Aubrey Mather, and Harry Davenport. **Director**—Compton Bennett.   *114 minutes*

THAT HAMILTON WOMAN (1941)

★★★

**Laurence Olivier
Vivien Leigh**

Olivier and Leigh sparkle in this costume drama, detailing the tragic romance of British naval hero Lord Nelson and Lady Emma Hamilton. The movie is too long, but many attractive scenes and excellent acting make the movie worthwhile. The cast also includes Gladys Cooper, Alan Mowbray, Sara Allgood, Henry Wilcoxon, Halliwell Hobbes, and Heather Angel. **Director**—Alexander Korda. **Academy Award Nomination**—Rudolph Maté, cinematography (black and white).
128 minutes b&w

• That's Dancing
• That's Entertainment, Part 2
• That's My Boy
• That Touch of Mink
• Theatre of Blood
• Them!
• There's a Girl in My Soup

T

THAT'S DANCING (1985)
★★★

A sparkling compilation of memorable movie dance scenes featuring the fancy footwork of such greats as Gene Kelly, Fred Astaire, Ginger Rogers, Ray Bolger, Cyd Charisse, Bill (Bojangles) Robinson, and Eleanor Powell. Latterday hoofers John Travolta and Michael Jackson also show their stuff. While competent, they pale in comparison with the old pros from the heyday of Hollywood musicals. Kelly, Bolger, Sammy Davis, Jr., Mikhail Baryshnikov, Liza Minnelli, and others handle the narration. **Director**—Jack Haley, Jr. (G)   *105 minutes*

THAT'S ENTERTAINMENT, PART 2 (1976)
★★★★

**Fred Astaire
Gene Kelly**

Fred Astaire and Gene Kelly host—and star in— That's Entertainment, Part 2.

This is another delightful stroll down Hollywood's memory lane, with more snippets from MGM's classic movies. The experience is like a visit with friends you haven't seen in 20 years. The well-constructed compilation of scenes are taken from more than 70 musicals, dramas, and comedy treasures from the MGM library. Some 100 top performers are featured. Old pros Kelly and Astaire narrate to bridge the footage. It's as good, if not better, than the 1974 *That's Entertainment*. It was, and still is, great entertainment. **Director**—Kelly. (G)   *133 minutes*

THAT'S MY BOY (1951)
★★

**Dean Martin
Jerry Lewis**

This early Martin and Lewis comedy has too much serious subject matter to ever be very funny. It's about a clumsy son pushed by his father into becoming a football player just like the old man. Lewis is the teenage son, and Eddie Mayehoff is his father. Martin is hired to coach Lewis. Fans of Martin and Lewis might find something of merit, but otherwise it has little value. Also with Marion Marshall, Polly Bergen, and John McIntire. **Director**—Hal Walker.   *98 minutes b&w*

THAT TOUCH OF MINK (1962)
★★★

**Cary Grant
Doris Day**

Grant is so suave and debonnair in this fluffy story about a wealthy businessman who romances an unemployed secretary that it doesn't matter that the plot is silly and the script is flimsy. Day plays the secretary. Grant is tops, and Day, Gig Young, John Astin, Audrey Meadows, and Dick Sargent are adequate for the task at hand. **Director**—Delbert Mann. **Academy Award Nomination**—Stanley Shapiro and Nate Monaster, best story and screenplay (written directly for the screen).   *99 minutes*

THEATRE OF BLOOD (1973)
★★★

**Vincent Price
Diana Rigg**

Price portrays a Shakespearean actor who gets even with eight critics who have panned his performances by killing them. Rigg plays his daughter. Price is fine as the demented thespian, and the fine supporting cast includes Rigg, Robert Morley, Ian Hendry, Harry Andrews, Robert Coote, Jack Hawkins, Diana Dors, Milo O'Shea, Denis Price, Eric Sykes, and Joan Hickson. **Director**—Douglas Hickox. (R)   *104 minutes*

THEM! (1954)
★★★

**Edmund Gwenn
James Whitmore**

The giant ants are so vivid in this science-fiction film you might want to avoid picnics for a while. The mutated ants, in the giant economy size thanks to A-bomb radiation, run amok in the southwestern part of the United States. The movie is well done, and some of the scenes are truly startling—especially the tense climax in the sewers of Los Angeles. Joan Weldon, Fess Parker, James Arness, and Onslow Stevens do their share in supporting roles with quality acting. **Director**—Gordon Douglas.   *94 minutes b&w*

THERE'S A GIRL IN MY SOUP (1970)
★★

**Peter Sellers
Goldie Hawn
Tony Britton**

Peter Sellers and Goldie Hawn star in the comedy, There's a Girl in My Soup.

Sellers, Hawn, and Britton shine in this well-paced movie version of a successful play by Terence Frisby, but the plot and laugh rate are as blah as cold broth. Sellers plays a television gourmet in search of fun, and Hawn becomes the disruptive force in his life. Diana Dors, Judy Campbell, Nicky Henson, and John Comer appear in supporting roles. **Director**—Roy Boulting. (R)   *96 minutes*

T

- There's No Business Like Show Business
- They All Laughed
- They Call Me Bruce
- They Died with Their Boots On
- They Drive by Night
- They Live by Night
- They Shoot Horses, Don't They?

THERE'S NO BUSINESS LIKE SHOW BUSINESS (1954)

★★

**Ethel Merman
Dan Dailey
Marilyn Monroe
Donald O'Connor**

Vibrant Irving Berlin music props up this weak musical about a family of vaudevillians and its struggles on and off stage. Merman and Dailey play the parents; O'Connor is one of their children and Monroe is O'Connor's girl friend. The rest of the cast includes Mitzi Gaynor, Hugh O'Brian, Frank McHugh, and Johnny Ray. Merman sings the title song with gusto, and other tunes include "Play a Simple Melody" and "Heat Wave." **Director**—Walter Lang. **Academy Award Nomination**—Lamar Trotti, writing (motion picture story). *117 minutes*

THEY ALL LAUGHED (1981)

★

**Audrey Hepburn
Ben Gazzara**

Ben Gazzara charms Audrey Hepburn out of her shades in They All Laughed.

Director-writer Peter Bogdanovich misfires with this meandering comedy starring Hepburn and Gazzara. Essentially, it's about some inept private detectives in New York City who are assigned to trail various good-looking women married to jealous husbands. Yet nothing of great interest happens in this overstuffed sex farce; it has a hodgepodge of forgettable characters chasing around Manhattan. The film does feature some beauties like the late *Playboy* bunny Dorothy Stratten. (PG) *116 minutes*

THEY CALL ME BRUCE (1983)

 ★★

**Johnny Yune
Margaux Hemingway
Ralph Mauro**

Korean comic Yune squeezes a few laughs from this breezy send-up of chop sockey and gangster films. He's likable in his film debut as a sort of Oriental Walter Mitty who pretends he has the prowess of kung fu champ Bruce Lee. Some of the gags are inspired, but many of the comic situations are clichéd. This is a lighthearted romp, easy to digest, and just as easy to forget. **Director**—Elliott Hong. (PG) *88 minutes*

THEY DIED WITH THEIR BOOTS ON (1941)

 ★★★

Errol Flynn

Hollywood gives General George Armstrong Custer's fight at the Little Big Horn the lavish treatment with loads of stars, but little attention to historical accuracy. Flynn is dashing and fine as the defeated general, with Olivia de Havilland, Arthur Kennedy, Anthony Quinn, Gene Lockhart, Sydney Greenstreet, Charles Grapewin, Hattie McDaniel, Stanley Ridges, and Walter Hampden in supporting roles. **Director**—Raoul Walsh. *139 minutes b&w*

THEY DRIVE BY NIGHT (1940)

 ★★★

**George Raft
Humphrey Bogart
Ann Sheridan
Ida Lupino**

The fine acting of Raft, Bogart, Sheridan, and Lupino and sparkling dialogue fuel this melodrama about honest drivers battling against corruption in the trucking industry. The story lags at times, but there's enough excitement to please fans of action films, and the quality performances will satisfy everyone else. Also with Alan Hale, Gale Page, George Tobias, and John Litel. **Director**—Raoul Walsh. *92 minutes b&w*

THEY LIVE BY NIGHT (1949)

 ★★★

**Farley Granger
Cathy O'Donnell
Howard Da Silva**

Tempers flare among outlaws on the run in They Live by Night.

Captivating melodrama about the plight of two young lovers tragically involved with criminals during the Great Depression. Director Nicholas Ray, in his debuting effort, handles the assignment with sensitivity and steers clear of clichés. Based on the novel "Thieves Like Us" and remade under this title in the '70s by Robert Altman. *95 minutes b&w*

THEY SHOOT HORSES, DON'T THEY? (1969)

 ★★★

**Gig Young
Jane Fonda
Michael Sarrazin
Susannah York**

This movie about a six-day marathon dance exquisitely captures the impoverished mood during the Great Depression. The production is well conceived and expertly staged, with good acting. Unfortunately, a superficial quality prevails at the serious moments, and the strange ending is unjustified by the events in the film. Young, Fonda, Sarrazin, York, and Red Buttons are superb and make the movie seem better than it really is. Also with Bruce Dern, Bonnie Bedelia, and Allyn Ann McLerie. **Director**—Sydney Pollack. (PG) **Academy Award**—Young, best supporting actor. **Nominations**—Pollack, best

• Thief
• The Thief of Baghdad
• Thief of Hearts

• The Thing
• Things Are Tough All Over
• The Thin Man
• The Third Man

T

director; Fonda, best actress; York, best supporting actress; James Poe and Robert E. Thompson, best screenplay (based on material from another medium). *123 minutes*

THIEF (1981)
⊛ ★★★

James Caan
Tuesday Weld

Caan stars as a free-lance safecracker who pursues the American dream with passion and daring. He's in top form with this gripping character study, which involves stark, streetwise realism yet manages to evoke sympathy. Director-writer Michael Mann is off to an impressive start with his first theatrical production; he demonstrates a talented style of suspense, technical detail, and sleek drama. (R) *126 minutes*

THE THIEF OF BAGHDAD (1940)
⊛ ★★★

Conrad Veidt
Sabu

This enchanting fairy tale is about a young thief, played by Sabu, who prevails over the forces of evil. Veidt plays an evil magician. The tale remains fresh for those who don't take the story too seriously. The excellent photography and the good acting of Sabu, Veidt, and Rex Ingram capture the quality of *Arabian Nights* on film. The cast also includes John Justin, June Duprez, Mary Morris, and Miles Malleson. **Directors**—Michael Powell, Ludwig Berger, and Tim Whelan. **Academy Award**—George Perinal, cinematography (color). *107 minutes*

THIEF OF HEARTS (1984)
★★

Steven Bauer
Barbara Williams

A cat burglar (Bauer) steals the secret diaries of a frustrated married woman (Williams). The contents describe her innermost sexual fantasies. Such privileged knowledge paves the way for seduction. While this setup has potential for suspense and steamy passion, the story winds up in a dead end. Part of the problem is the excessive use of glittery settings and the stars' understated, unappealing performances. **Director**—Douglas Day Stewart. (R) *100 minutes*

THE THING (1982)
⊛ ★★★

Kurt Russell

John Carpenter's moody remake of the 1951 B-movie classic concentrates on outrageous, stomach-turning special effects without ignoring character and story. The plot involves scientists in Antarctica who stumble on a buried spaceship that contains a strange, frozen organism. When the creature thaws out it runs amok, killing and impersonating every life form within reach. Makeup wiz and glopologist Rob Bottin deserves a lot of credit for the success of the film, but Carpenter also manages to add some depth to the fright with a sustained sense of isolation and alienation. (R) *108 minutes*

THINGS ARE TOUGH ALL OVER (1983)
⊛ ★★

Cheech Marin
Tommy Chong

Cheech and Chong take a break from their familiar dope routine here, but they've failed to provide much humor in its place. The laid-back twosome's adventure begins in a car wash and takes them to Las Vegas, where they connect with some wealthy Arabs. The boys play dual roles as themselves and as Middle Easterners. Director Thomas Avildsen handles the assignment with a steady hand but fails to contribute any freshness. Things are tough, indeed. (R) *90 minutes*

THE THIN MAN (1934)
★★★★

William Powell
Myrna Loy

Highly enjoyable and entertaining combination of sophisticated humor and mystery distilled from a Dashiell Hammett detective story. Powell and Loy are perfect in the roles of Nick and Nora Charles, the fun-loving, charming couple adept at handling the sleuthing chores. This initial caper concerned the murder of a screwball inventor. Its success led the way to the ever-popular series of Thin Man adventures that continued for more than 10 years. **Director**—W. S. Van Dyke. **Academy Award Nominations**—best picture; W. S. Van Dyke, best director; William Powell, best actor; Frances Goodrich and Albert Hackett, writing (adaptation). *100 minutes b&w*

THE THIRD MAN (1950)
⊛ ★★★★

Joseph Cotten
Trevor Howard
Orson Welles
Alida Valli

Alida Valli and Joseph Cotten search for The Third Man.

This is one of the best thrillers in the history of cinema. Graham Greene's story about vile black market operations in Vienna after World War II is still fresh because of Carol Reed's direction, excellent acting, and Anton Karas's haunting zither music. Cotten portrays an American who writes westerns. He's in search of Harry Lime, a mystery man of dubious morals played by Welles—and therein lies the fascinating tale. Howard and Valli are excellent in supporting roles. Also with Wilfrid Hyde-White, Bernard Lee, Paul Hoerbiger, and Siegfried Breuer. **Academy Award**—Robert Krasker, cinematography (black and white). **Nomination**—Reed, best director. *104 minutes b&w*

T
- The Thirty-Nine Steps
- Thirty Seconds over Tokyo
- This Gun for Hire
- This Is Elvis
- This Is Spinal Tap
- This Is the Army
- This Thing Called Love
- The Thomas Crown Affair

THE THIRTY-NINE STEPS
(1935)

 ★★★★

Robert Donat
Madeleine Carroll

This memorable story is the model for many subsequent spy yarns and one of the best movies director Alfred Hitchcock ever made. Donat stars as an innocent man who becomes involved in espionage. He must flee from England to Scotland before he is able to find the real villains and clear his name. Carroll plays a woman who believes Donat is the criminal. Godfrey Tearle, Wylie Watson, and Peggy Ashcroft also star in this comedy-thriller classic.   *81 minutes b&w*

THIRTY SECONDS OVER TOKYO (1944)

★★★

Van Johnson
Spencer Tracy

Johnson and Tracy star in this exciting World War II film about the first attack on the Japanese mainland by the U.S. Army Air Force. Tracy plays Col. James Doolittle. Screenwriter Dalton Trumbo has done a fine job of providing lots of action in an enterprise that, at times, becomes a semidocumentary. Robert Walker, Phyllis Thaxter, Robert Mitchum, Louis Jean Heydt, Paul Langton, Stephen McNally, and Scott McKay appear in supporting roles. **Director**—Mervyn Le Roy. **Academy Award Nomination**—Robert Surtees and Harold Rosson, cinematography (black and white).   *132 minutes b&w*

THIS GUN FOR HIRE
(1942)

 ★★★

Alan Ladd
Veronica Lake

Ladd and Lake rose to stardom in this film version of the Graham Greene novel *A Gun for Sale*, about a hired killer who seeks revenge after being double-crossed. Ladd plays the professional killer. Laird Cregar, Robert Preston, and Tully Marshall also star in this well-made production and con-

Alan Ladd wants Veronica Lake to know that she can get This Gun for Hire.

tribute to the stark realism the movie evokes. **Director**—Frank Tuttle.
81 minutes b&w

THIS IS ELVIS (1981)

 ★★

A blend of old newsreels, videotapes, and even home movies provides an absorbing sociological portrait of the rock 'n' roll hero and the era of this popular music. The fascinating documentary segments are effective in charting Elvis Presley's rise and fall. Unfortunately, the film is flawed with false and poorly recreated scenes using actors for Presley at various stages of his life. Still, the faithful can savor the real Elvis, including some candid, unforgettable material and 38 songs. **Directors**—Malcolm Leo and Andrew Solt. (PG)   *88 minutes*

THIS IS SPINAL TAP (1984)

 ★★

Michael McKean
Christopher Guest

An unusual lampoon of rock music constructed as a mock documentary of a fading British heavy metal band on tour in the United States. Rob Reiner is the film's director as well as the deadpan interviewer of the far-out musicians. The humor is droll indeed, but the off-the-wall dialogue often lapses into babble that eventually becomes

tiresome. McKean and Guest play the lead rockers with tongue-in-cheek playfulness. (R)   *82 minutes*

THIS IS THE ARMY (1943)

 ★★

George Murphy

Song-and-dance man Murphy gets top billing in this wartime musical about soldiers during World War II who stage a show with the songs of Irving Berlin. Some of the materal is dated now, and even at the time of its production much of it was mediocre, but there are still some entertaining moments. Among the many other performers are Ronald Reagan, Joan Leslie, Alan Hale, Irving Berlin, Joe Louis, Kate Smith, George Tobias, Una Merkel, and Rosemary de Camp. **Director**—Michael Curtiz.
121 minutes

THIS THING CALLED LOVE
(1941)

★★★

Rosalind Russell
Melvyn Douglas

Russell and Douglas star in this slightly saucy adult comedy about newlyweds who agree to test their marriage by not sleeping together for the first three months. Although the movie seems tame now and just mildly delightful, it was banned by the Legion of Decency on its release. Binnie Barnes and Lee J. Cobb also star, with Allyn Joslyn, Gloria Dickson, Don Bedoe, and Gloria Holden in supporting roles. **Director**—Alexander Hall.   *98 minutes b&w*

THE THOMAS CROWN
AFFAIR (1968)

 ★★

Steve McQueen
Faye Dunaway

McQueen stars as a debonair millionaire who engineers a bank robbery because he's bored. Dunaway plays a glamorous investigator for an insurance company who stalks the suave robber. Unfortunately, you'll soon get bored with this overly slick production, which lacks any substance aside,

• Thoroughly Modern Millie
• Those Lips, Those Eyes

• Those Magnificent Men in
  Their Flying Machines,
  Or How I Flew from
  London to Paris in 25

Hours and 11 Minutes
• A Thousand Clowns
• Thousands Cheer
• Three Coins in the Fountain

T

from Dunaway's pursuit of McQueen. Jack Weston, Biff McGuire, and Paul Burke also appear. **Director**—Norman Jewison. *102 minutes*

THOROUGHLY MODERN MILLIE (1967)

★★

Julie Andrews

Beatrice Lillie runs a respectable place in Thoroughly Modern Millie.

Andrews shines in this musical spoof about a young lady who comes to New York City in the 1920s, falls in love with her boss, and becomes modern in the process. But even her immense talent can't sustain the production beyond the first hour. Despite its faults, there are some fine songs and dancing, plus quality supporting performances by Carol Channing, Beatrice Lillie, and James Fox. The cast also includes Mary Tyler Moore, John Saxon, Anthony Dexter, and Jack Soo. **Director**—George Roy Hill. (G) **Academy Award Nomination**—Channing, best supporting actress. *138 minutes*

THOSE LIPS, THOSE EYES (1980)

★★★

Frank Langella

Langella stars as a charming second-rate actor who dreams of making it big on Broadway in this '50s backstage romance. But there's nothing second-rate about Langella's performance here as he exudes poise, confidence,

and pathos. It's his presence that makes the picture really click. Although somewhat limited in scope, this film is a shining tribute to those striving and hopeful thespians performing in summer stock and other byways of the theater. Also with Glynnis O'Connor and Thomas Hulce. **Director**—Michael Pressman. (R) *106 minutes*

THOSE MAGNIFICENT MEN IN THEIR FLYING MACHINES, OR HOW I FLEW FROM LONDON TO PARIS IN 25 HOURS AND 11 MINUTES (1965)

 ★★★

Stuart Whitman
Robert Morley
Sarah Miles
Terry-Thomas

This long, lavish production with its superb photography and many stars starts well, but instead of soaring until the end it sputters a bit and becomes a little boring. Yet a comedy-adventure about a 1910 airplane race from London to Paris, with some cunning characters vying for the prize, should not have such a problem. Whitman plays an American cowboy turned pilot, and Terry-Thomas portrays a devious rogue out to win at any cost. Red Skelton does a pleasant prologue to the film; he details the early history of aviation—one reason the movie starts so well. The large cast also includes Eric Sykes, Alberto Sordi, Gert Frobe, James Fox, Benny Hill, and Sam Wanamaker. **Director**—Ken Annakin. (G) **Academy Award Nomination**— Jack Davies and Annakin, best story and screenplay (written directly for the screen). *132 minutes*

A THOUSAND CLOWNS (1965)

 ★★★

Jason Robards, Jr.
Martin Balsam
Barry Gordon
Barbara Harris

The splendid acting of Robards and Balsam sustains this strange comedy about a nonconformist New Yorker (Robards) who has dropped out of society's rat race for a life of philo-

sophical introspection. The plot gets tangled when a social worker, played by Harris, pressures him to conform again for the sake of Gordon, who plays his teenage nephew. Balsam plays a wealthy and successful brother of Robards. Also with William Daniels and Gene Saks. **Director**—Fred Coe. **Academy Award**—Balsam, best supporting actor. **Nominations**—best picture; Herb Gardner, best screenplay (based on material from another medium). *118 minutes b&w*

THOUSANDS CHEER (1943)

★★★

Kathryn Grayson
Gene Kelly

Grayson and Kelly head an all-star cast in this World War II musical about an army base that stages a variety show. Although the plot is pretty flimsy, the entertainment is tops. The large cast of stars includes Red Skelton, Lena Horne, Mary Astor, Margaret O'Brien, Judy Garland, June Allyson, Mickey Rooney, Eleanor Powell, and Lionel Barrymore. **Director**—George Sidney. **Academy Award Nomination**—George Folsey, cinematography (color). *126 minutes*

THREE COINS IN THE FOUNTAIN (1954)

★★★

Clifton Webb
Dorothy McGuire
Louis Jourdan
Jean Peters

This comedy-romance, set in Rome, is about the search for love by three American secretaries—McGuire, Peters, and Maggie McNamara. It's a pleasant film, which never makes the mistake of taking itself too seriously. The superior acting of Webb and Jourdan adds to the production's competence; the splendid on-location photography in Rome is another plus. Also with Rossano Brazzi, Howard St. John, and Cathleen Nesbitt. **Director**—Jean Negulesco. **Academy Awards**—Milton Krasner, cinematography (color); Jule Styne and Sammy Cahn, best song ("Three Coins in the Fountain"). **Nomination**—best picture. *102 minutes*

 Movie is available in Beta and VHS videotape

T

• Three Days of the Condor
• The Three Faces of Eve
• Three Little Words

• The Three Musketeers
• Three Women
• Threshold

THREE DAYS OF THE CONDOR (1975)

 ★★★

**Robert Redford
Faye Dunaway**

Redford plays a tweedy bookworm researcher working for a CIA department. One day he finds all his co-workers mysteriously murdered. He flees for his life, pursued by several factions within the spy agency. Dunaway is the girl who hides him. The movie is both slick and exciting in an attempt to exploit the post-Watergate syndrome. Based on James Grady's novel *Six Days of the Condor.* Also with Cliff Robertson, Max Von Sydow, John Houseman, and Walter McGinn. **Director**—Sydney Pollack. (R)

117 minutes

THE THREE FACES OF EVE (1957)

★★★

**Joanne Woodward
Lee J. Cobb**

Woodward stars as a troubled woman with three different personalities in this well-made drama about schizophrenia. Cobb is excellent as a psychiatrist who tries to cure her so she can lead a normal life, but Alistair Cooke almost spoils the movie with his typically pompous narration. David Wayne, Edwin Jerome, Nancy Kulp, and Vince Edwards appear in supporting roles. **Director**—Nunnally Johnson. **Academy Award**—Woodward, best actress. *91 minutes b&w*

THREE LITTLE WORDS (1950)

★★★

**Fred Astaire
Red Skelton**

This musical about famed songwriters Bert Kalmar and Harry Ruby is nourished by lots of good dancing, snappy songs, and pretty girls. Astaire and Skelton play the tunesmiths with charm and vitality, but the thin plot doesn't help them. In addition, the lack of dance numbers for Astaire weakens the show. The pretty girls

In Three Little Words, *Fred Astaire and Red Skelton play songwriters Bert Kalmar and Harry Ruby.*

include Vera-Ellen, Arlene Dahl, Gale Robbins, Debbie Reynolds, and Gloria DeHaven. Also with Keenan Wynn and Phil Regan. **Director**—Richard Thorpe. *102 minutes*

THE THREE MUSKETEERS (1939)

★★★

**Don Ameche
The Ritz Brothers
Binnie Barnes**

There are at least four versions of Alexandre Dumas's classic adventure tale, and some cinema historians claim there might be as many as 10. This film with Ameche, the Ritz Brothers, Barnes, and Joseph Schildkraut in the key roles is certainly not the worst, and you might rate it tops if you can accept the idea of the Ritz Brothers as musketeers. The movie has vibrant music, and the original story remains intact with the proper dose of romance and chivalric tradition. Also with Lionel Atwill, Miles Mander, and John Carradine. **Director**—Allan Dwan. *73 minutes b&w*

THREE WOMEN (1977)

★★★★

**Sissy Spacek
Shelley Duvall
Janice Rule
Robert Fortier**

Director Robert Altman's daring and absorbing psychological excursion of soul and character will send you away with your imagination spinning. Duvall's memorable and striking performance as the lonely and ostracized thoroughly modern Millie Lammoreaux is the cornerstone of this examination of the quality of American life. Brilliant acting and characterizations from Spacek and Fortier add to the emotion and poetry. It's one of Altman's best films, and Duvall emerges as a major actress. Also with Ruth Nelson and John Cromwell. (PG)

125 minutes

THRESHOLD (1983)

★★★

**Donald Sutherland
Jeff Goldblum
Mare Winningham**

A straightforward account of doctors attempting the first self-contained artificial heart transplant. The story, perhaps, could use a bit of drama, but the documentary approach and the avoidance of mushy sentiment are appropriate to the subject matter. Sutherland is adequately confident and dignified as the pioneering cardiac surgeon. Some of the operating room scenes are startlingly realistic. **Director**—Richard Pearce. (PG)

106 minutes

- The Thrill of It All
- Thunderball
- Thunder Bay
- A Thunder of Drums
- Thunder Road
- THX 1138
- Ticket to Heaven
- The Tiger Makes Out

T

THE THRILL OF IT ALL (1963)
★★★

Doris Day
James Garner

Day brightens this farce about a doctor's wife who becomes a star in television commercials. And Garner is able as her doctor-husband. Carl Reiner wrote the script, and anyone who has ever been angered or just mildly annoyed by the junk on TV and by the idiocy of most commercials will appreciate the brilliance of Reiner's counterattack against the tube. Also with Arlene Francis, Zasu Pitts, Edward Andrews, Elliot Reid, and Reginald Owen. **Director**—Norman Jewison.
108 minutes

THUNDERBALL (1965)

★★★

Sean Connery
Adolfo Celi

Claudine Auger and Sean Connery on the look-out for SPECTRE in Thunderball.

Connery is in top form as James Bond, and Celi is equally good as the archvillain who almost matches secret agent 007 step for step in this fourth Bond yarn, about a SPECTRE plot to destroy the city of Miami if a huge ransom isn't paid. The plot is somewhat weak, but there are many slick gimmicks and the usual bevy of beautiful girls. The cast also includes Claudine Auger, Lois Maxwell, Luciana Paluzzi, and Bernard Lee. **Director**—Terence Young.
132 minutes

THUNDER BAY (1953)
★★★

James Stewart
Joanne Dru

Off-shore drilling for oil is taken for granted now, but it wasn't always a fact of life. In this action-packed film, Stewart stars as an engineer who's convinced oil can be pumped from the sea off the coast of Louisiana. The conflicts between oil prospectors and shrimp fisherman provide the tension and action in the movie. Marcia Henderson, Dan Duryea, Gilbert Roland, Jay C. Flippen, and Anthony Moreno also appear in supporting roles. **Director**—Anthony Mann.
102 minutes

A THUNDER OF DRUMS (1961)
★★

Richard Boone
George Hamilton

This western tale about a young new officer striving for acceptance from his superiors and fellow soldiers has been told many times before. And the story of the Apaches fighting the U.S. Cavalry is even more familiar. Fortunately, above-average performances by Boone, Hamilton, Charles Bronson, Slim Pickens, Richard Chamberlain, and Luana Patten keep the movie from being totally ordinary. **Director**—Joseph M. Newman. *97 minutes*

THUNDER ROAD (1958)
★★★

Robert Mitchum
Keely Smith

Mitchum and Smith star in this exciting story about bootleggers in Kentucky. Mitchum is close to brilliant at times, as he wisely understates his performance to accommodate the plot. Smith is good as a country girl who likes her natural man, played by Mitchum. The splendid car chases over winding back roads with a bluegrass music background are exciting. Gene Barry and Jacques Aubuchon also star. **Director**—Arthur Ripley.
92 minutes b&w

THX 1138 (1971)

★★★

Robert Duvall

This early sci-fi effort by director George Lucas (*Star Wars*) is surprisingly mature. The cold, eerie Orwellian setting is impressive, as is the cast, headed by Duvall. It's the 25th century and an autocratic regime presides over a population of robotlike humans. Someone is bound to rebel against such conditions. (PG) *88 minutes*

TICKET TO HEAVEN (1981)

★★★

Nick Mancuso

A hard-hitting docudrama about religious cults as experienced by a young Toronto schoolteacher, played by Mancuso. He joins such a group in California and is at last rescued by friends and family. The film vividly details the young man's transformation into a near-robot through powerful indoctrination methods, and it concludes with a gut-wrenching deprogramming session. Some scenes are rather heavy-going, and the young man's background is never fully understood. Yet the story is consistently engrossing. Also stars Saul Rubinek, Meg Foster, and R. H. Thompson. **Director**—R. L. Thomas. (PG)
109 minutes

THE TIGER MAKES OUT (1967)
★★

Eli Wallach
Anne Jackson

Wallach is excellent as a frustrated postman-turned-kidnapper, and Jackson is good as the suburban housewife Wallach holds captive; in fact, she seems to enjoy the experience. Charles Nelson Reilly, Elizabeth Wilson, Bob Dishy, Ruth White, and John Harkins give solid supporting performances, but quality acting can't rescue this weird endeavor. Dustin Hoffman made his film debut in this wacky and uneven comedy. Fortunately, he has appeared in much better movies since. **Director**—Arthur Hiller. *94 minutes*

 Movie is available in Beta and VHS videotape

★ **STAR PROFILE**

T
- Tight Little Island
- Tightrope
- Till the Clouds Roll By
- Till the End of Time
- Till We Meet Again
- Time After Time

TIGHT LITTLE ISLAND (1948)
★★★★

**Basil Radford
Joan Greenwood**

Fine actors keep the laughs coming in this droll British comedy about a ship with a cargo of whiskey that is wrecked off a Scottish island during World War II. The thirsty natives covet the cargo, of course, and humorous problems and situations are created as they confront the local customs agent. Radford and Greenwood star in this fast-paced delight, with Jean Cadell, Catherine Lacey, Bruce Seton, Wylie Watson, Gordon Jackson, A. E. Matthews, and Compton Mackenzie starring in supporting roles. **Director**— Alexander Mackendrick.

82 minutes b&w

TIGHTROPE (1984)
 ★★★

**Clint Eastwood
Geneviève Bujold
Dan Hedaya**

Eastwood once again steps into a tough-cop role, now tracking a relentless sex killer in New Orleans. And the result is a crackling, compelling police drama that concentrates on complex character traits. Best of all, Clint accomplishes his mission without resorting to Dirty Harry mayhem. Much of the movie's appeal focuses on Eastwood's fascination with the seamy side of life. **Director**—Richard Tuggle. (R) *114 minutes*

TILL THE CLOUDS ROLL BY
(1946)
 ★★

Robert Walker

The entertaining songs of Jerome Kern make this star-studded movie about the life of the composer bearable. Walker does a passable job playing Kern. June Allyson, Judy Garland, Van Johnson, Lena Horne, Tony Martin, Lucille Bremer, Kathryn Grayson, Frank Sinatra, Virginia O'Brien, Dinah Shore, Van Heflin, and Mary Nash are delightful in guest appearances, but too much of the movie is

GOLDIE HAWN

In the late '60s, the television series Laugh-In *introduced Goldie Hawn, whose irrepressible giggle, delightful malapropisms, and radiant physical presence captured the hearts of the public. However, with her first film,* Cactus Flower *(1969), Hawn showed that she possessed more than most of the other blonde favorites of the past; she walked off with an Academy Award as best supporting actress. In subsequent films, such as* The Sugarland Express *(1973), The* Girl From Petrovka *(1974), and* Shampoo *(1975), she extended her range beyond comedy.*

Born Jeanne Hawn in Washington, D.C., in 1945, Goldie is the daughter of Laura and Edward Rutledge Hawn, a descendent of Edward Rutledge of South Carolina, who was one of the signers of the Declaration of Independence. At the age of three, she began studying ballet and later took up tap and modern jazz dancing.

At the Texas Pavilion at New York World's Fair in 1964-65, she made her professional dancing debut in Can-Can. *She continued working in musical comedies in New York, as a dancer in Puerto Rico, as a choreographer in California, and as a dancer in a Las Vegas revue.*

After her Las Vegas stint, she returned to Los Angeles and danced on an Andy Griffith television special. She then received attention for a continuing role in a short-lived but critically well received TV series entitled Good Morning, World. *Her flair for comedy was evident to audiences, and she was then signed as a regular on* Laugh-In *(she mostly played a wisecracking go-go dancer).*

After her successful debut in Cactus Flower, *she appeared in* There's a Girl in My Soup *(1970) opposite Peter Sellers;* $ *(1971) with Warren Beatty; and* Butterflies Are Free *(1972). After several dramatic roles, she returned to comedy in* The Duchess and the Dirtwater Fox *(1976) opposite George Segal. Her more recent movies include* Foul Play *(1978),* Seems Like Old Times *(1980),* Private Benjamin *(1980),* Swing Shift *(1984), and* Protocol *(1984).*

overly sentimental drivel. **Director**— Richard Whorf. *137 minutes*

TILL THE END OF TIME (1946)
 ★★★

**Dorothy McGuire
Guy Madison
Robert Mitchum
Bill Williams**

This powerful drama about the romances and adjustment problems of three GIs returning to their hometown after service in World War II seems slightly dated now. Despite this, the excellent acting of McGuire, Madison, Williams, and Mitchum keeps the story fresh for contemporary viewers. Also with William Gargan, Jean Porter, and Tom Tully. **Director**—Edward Dmytryk. *105 minutes b&w*

TILL WE MEET AGAIN (1944)
★★

**Ray Milland
Barbara Britton**

Britton plays a French nun who helps Milland, an American pilot, elude the Nazis and return to the Allies in this World War II drama. The good intentions surpass the weak plot, and the acting is rather good. Also with Mona Freeman, Walter Slezak, Vladimir Sokoloff, Lucile Watson, and Konstantin Shayne. **Director**—Frank Borzage. *88 minutes b&w*

TIME AFTER TIME (1979)
 ★★

**Malcolm McDowell
David Warner**

• Time Bandits
• The Time of Their Lives
• The Time of Your Life

• Timerider
• Times Square
• A Time to Love and a Time to Die

T

Mary Steenburgen and Malcolm McDowell fall in love across the centuries in Time After Time.

H. G. Wells and Jack the Ripper travel via time machine to contemporary San Francisco, where the Ripper resumes his favorite pastime of carving up prostitutes. Wells's vision of a future Utopia is dashed when he realizes the Ripper's bloodthirsty behavior is small potatoes compared with violence wrought by modern technology. A clever idea, well executed by writer-director Nicholas Meyer. McDowell, as Wells, is enjoyable. Warner plays the Ripper. Also with Mary Steenburgen, Charles Cioffi, and Kent Williams. (PG)   *112 minutes*

TIME BANDITS (1981)
 ★★★

John Cleese
Sean Connery
Shelley Duvall
Ian Holm

Sean Connery as King Agamemnon enjoys the antics of the Time Bandits.

A lively fantasy, done in imaginative Monty Python comedy style. It mocks science-fiction history, and good-vs.-evil conflicts. An 11-year-old English lad, played by Craig Warnock, joins a band of dwarfs in a rollicking romp through time holes in space, where they meet such historical figures as Napoleon (Holm), Greek warrior Agamemnon (Connery), and Robin Hood (Cleese). The film has appeal to children of all ages, and it boasts a playful script, tasteful direction, and splendid special effects. Also with Katherine Helmond, Michael Palin, Ralph Richardson, Peter Vaughn, and David Warner. **Director**—Terry Gilliam. (PG)   *116 minutes*

THE TIME OF THEIR LIVES (1946)
★★★

Bud Abbott
Lou Costello
Marjorie Reynolds

This imaginative comedy about ghosts haunting a country estate is one of the best Abbott and Costello films. Costello and Reynolds play ghosts from Revolutionary times. They complicate life for Abbott and his friends. In this movie, Bud and Lou don't play as a team. Fine supporting performances by Binnie Barnes, Jess Barker, Jess Shelton, and Gale Sondergaard help to make this a pleasant viewing experience. **Director**—Charles Barton.
82 minutes b&w

THE TIME OF YOUR LIFE (1948)
★★★★

James Cagney
William Bendix

Super acting by Cagney and Bendix spark this film version of the prize-winning play by William Saroyan. Broderick Crawford, James Barton, Wayne Morris, Paul Draper, and Ward Bond also star in this whimsical story about a group of off-beat characters who discuss their lives and the nature of things as they sit and drink in a small saloon in San Francisco. Although there's little action, everything is well handled. **Director**—H. C. Potter.
109 minutes b&w

TIMERIDER (1983)
 (no stars)

Fred Ward
Belinda Bauer

An absurd concoction of contemporary motorcycle riding and horse opera. Ward is a hot-shot biker who, through the help of a time machine, finds himself and his motorcycle in Mexico in the year 1875. There he gets involved with various outlaws in shoot-'em-up confrontations. The characters are cardboard and the dialogue is nonstop nonsense. **Director**—William Dear. (PG)   *93 minutes*

TIMES SQUARE (1980)
★★

Trini Alvarado
Robin Johnson
Tim Curry

Alvarado plays a runaway teenager whose land of Oz is the glittering sleaze of New York City's 42nd Street. She teams up with a streetwise urchin, played by Johnson, and together they perform in a strip joint—without stripping, put on a punk rock concert, and engage in various pranks. Curry plays a disc jockey. The film, aimed at teenagers, has ample energy, but the story is hardly convincing. The production seems mostly a promotion for the sound track, which contains some 20 New Wave musical numbers. **Director**—Alan Moyle. (R)   *111 minutes*

A TIME TO LOVE AND A TIME TO DIE (1958)
★★★

John Gavin
Lilo Pulver

At the time of this movie's release, it was unique because it portrayed soldiers in Nazi Germany during World War II in a human light. Gavin stars as a German officer who falls in love with a woman during a furlough. She's played by Pulver. The acting in this film version of Erich Maria Remarque's novel is above average, and there are some good scenes in the early part of the movie before the plot and
(Continued)

T
- The Tin Drum
- Tin Pan Alley
- Titanic
- Tobacco Road
- To Be or Not To Be (1942)
- To Be or Not To Be (1983)
- Tobruk

(Continued) script weaken. The cast also includes Remarque, Keenan Wynn, and Jock Mahoney. **Director**—Douglas Sirk.

132 minutes

THE TIN DRUM
(1980)
★★★

Angela Winkler
Mario Adorf
Daniel Olbrychski
David Bennent

In The Tin Drum, *David Bennent is a boy who refuses to grow, as a protest to the world.*

Artistic, stirring, yet complex allegory based on the epic German novel by Günter Grass. Bennent, who was 12 when filming began, is extraordinary as a dwarf who refused—from the age of three—to grow anymore as a protest against the absurdities and obscenities of the adult world. Director Volker Schlondorff captures much of the anguish of the Nazi period with haunting pictorial splendor. Yet the film is as puzzling as it is moving. In German with English titles. (R) **Academy Award**—best foreign-language film.

142 minutes

TIN PAN ALLEY (1940)
★★★

Alice Faye
Betty Grable
John Payne
Jack Oakie

There isn't an original thought in this typical musical about two struggling songwriters during and after World War I, but the music and dancing are so delightful it doesn't matter that the story is trite. Inspired performances by Faye, Grable, Payne, and Oakie are the main reason the production sparkles. The cast also includes Elisha Cook, Jr., Esther Ralston, Allen Jen-

kins, Billy Gilbert, and John Loder. **Director**—Walter Lang.

95 minutes b&w

TITANIC (1953)
★★

Clifton Webb
Barbara Stanwyck
Robert Wagner

Good acting by Webb, Stanwyck, Wagner, Thelma Ritter, and Richard Basehart keep this production from sinking to the level of a mediocre documentary about the destruction of the famous ship in 1912. There are some good scenes involving personal dramas before the vessel's collision with the iceberg, but the movie should have been much better considering the ingredients. Also with Audrey Dalton, Brian Aherne, and Allyn Joslyn. **Director**—Jean Negulesco. **Academy Award**—Charles Brackett, Walter Reisch, and Richard Breen, writing (story and screenplay).

98 minutes b&w

TOBACCO ROAD (1941)
★★★

Charley Grapewin
Elizabeth Patterson

This film version of Erskine Caldwell's famed novel and play loses some of its punch in its translation to the screen, but some vivid scenes remain in this tragi-comedy about poor whites in Georgia being pushed off their land. Grapewin and Patterson star, with Dana Andrews, Marjorie Rambeau, Gene Tierney, William Tracy, Russell Simpson, and Grant Mitchell in supporting roles. **Director**—John Ford.

84 minutes b&w

TO BE OR NOT TO BE (1942)
★★★★

Jack Benny
Carole Lombard

This brilliant black comedy is about a group of actors in Poland who get involved in a plot to outwit the invading Nazis. At times, it seems to take on a life of its own under the skillful direction of Ernst Lubitsch. He gets consid-

Jack Benny parodies Nazis, war, romance, and Shakespeare in To Be or Not To Be.

erable help from the excellent acting of Benny, Lombard, Lionel Atwill, Sig Rumann, Tom Dugan, Robert Stack, Stanley Ridges, and Felix Bressart. At the time of its release, some critics thought this propaganda movie was in bad taste, but now it's obvious a difficult subject was handled in a superb manner. It was Lombard's last movie.

99 minutes b&w

TO BE OR NOT TO BE (1983)
★★★

Mel Brooks
Anne Bancroft

Brooks and Bancroft aren't bad in this remake of the 1942 Ernst Lubitsch classic comedy. Although not as droll as the original, Brooks and Bancroft keep the laughter flowing freely as they apply their own brand of farcical humor to the misadventures of a second-rate acting troupe in wartime Poland. But why should anyone try to remake a comedy that was already so nearly perfect? Tim Matheson, Charles Durning, and José Ferrer are good in supporting roles. **Director**—Alan Johnson. (PG) **Academy Award Nomination**—Durning, best supporting actor. *107 minutes*

TOBRUK (1967)
★★

Rock Hudson
George Peppard

Hudson and Peppard are well cast in this adventure tale about a small band of soldiers assigned to destroy German Field Marshal Erwin Rommel's fuel supply at Tobruk in North Africa during World War II. Nigel Green, Jack Watson, Liam Redmond, Guy Stockwell, Percy Herbert, and Leo Gordon appear in supporting roles. The acting is passable, and the production is well done, but there's nothing about this movie to distinguish it from dozens of others. **Director**—Arthur Hiller.

110 minutes

TO CATCH A THIEF (1955)

 ★★

Cary Grant
Grace Kelly

This story is about a jewel thief—retired on the French Riviera—who's suspected of returning to his trade. The movie has a lot of the charm associated with an Alfred Hitchcock production. Grant, who plays the reformed thief, and Kelly, as the woman in his life, account for much of the film's enchanting quality. The beautiful scenery is another small plus. Jessie Royce Landis, Charles Vanel, Brigitte Auber, and John Williams star in supporting roles. **Academy Award** —Robert Burks, cinematography (color). *97 minutes*

TO HAVE AND HAVE NOT (1945)

★★★★

Humphrey Bogart
Lauren Bacall

Humphrey Bogart and Lauren Bacall foil the Nazis in To Have and Have Not.

Gregory Peck breaks down a key witness in To Kill a Mockingbird.

Bogart and Bacall are marvelous in this story about a fishing boat captain who reluctantly gets involved in fighting the Nazis. Some of the brilliant dialogue has become muted because the movie has been seen so often and become an object of adoration by the Bogart cult. The movie is very loosely based on one of Ernest Hemingway's worst novels. In this case, Hollywood helped—rather than hindered—the great novelist. Supporting cast includes Marcel Dalio, Sheldon Leonard, Dan Seymour, Dolores Moran, and Hoagy Carmichael. It was Bacall's film debut. **Director**—Howard Hawks. *100 minutes b&w*

TO HELL AND BACK (1955)

★★

Audie Murphy

Murphy stars in this story based on his military career in World War II; he was the nation's most decorated soldier. Murphy is surprisingly good and doesn't overdo the heroics, although the temptation is always there. The battle sequences are superior to the weak story line. The above-average supporting performances of Susan Kohner, Marshall Thompson, Charles Drake, Paul Picerni, Jack Kelly, and David Janssen also fortify the film. **Director**—Jesse Hibbs. *106 minutes*

TO KILL A MOCKINGBIRD (1962)

 ★★★★

Gregory Peck

This movie is one of Hollywood's better efforts at filming a story dealing with racial problems in the United States. Peck stars as a lawyer in a small Southern town who defends a black man accused of rape. Peck gets top-notch acting support from Mary Badham, Philip Alford, John Megna, and Brock Peters. Screenwriter Horton Foote did an excellent job of translating Harper Lee's novel to the screen, and much of the atmosphere of the time and place remains intact. **Director**—Robert Mulligan. **Academy Awards**—Peck, best actor; Foote, best screenplay (based on material from another medium). **Nominations**—best picture; Mulligan, best director; Badham, best supporting actress; Russell Harlan, cinematography (black and white).

129 minutes b&w

TOKYO JOE (1949)

★

Humphrey Bogart

Bogart stars in this dull, slow melo-
(Continued)

T
- **Tom Horn**
- **Tom Jones**
- **Tommy**
- **Tom Sawyer**
- **Tony Rome**
- **Too Far To Go**
- **Tootsie**

(Continued)

drama about an ex-nightclub owner who returns to Tokyo after World War II and becomes involved in smuggling and blackmail to protect his ex-wife and child. There are occasional moments that are reminiscent of better Bogart films, but they are few and far between. Also with Sessue Hayakawa, Florence Marly, Alexander Knox, Jerome Courtland, and Lora Lee Michel. **Director**—Stuart Heisler.

88 minutes b&w

TOM HORN (1980)

★

Steve McQueen

In this film, McQueen comes off as a second-rate actor in what appears to be a second-rate horse opera. He plays a cowpoke with a license to kill. He's hired to eliminate cattle rustlers, and he does such a thorough job that his alarmed bosses frame him for murder. Just about everything is off base with the film—sloppy editing, uninspired direction, routine acting, and a lack of energy. Also with Richard Farnsworth and Linda Evans. **Director**—William Wiard. (R) *98 minutes*

TOM JONES (1963)

★★★★

Albert Finney

Finney is splendid as the impish, free-spirited hero of this 18th-century story, based on Henry Fielding's novel. At times, there's too much emphasis on the bawdy humor, as if the production was geared for *Playboy* keyholders. But there's so much exuberance, the joy of the story prevails, and the sexual high jinks and culinary exploits of Tom Jones are enjoyed. Finney gets royal acting support from Susannah York, Edith Evans, Diane Cilento, Joan Greenwood, Joyce Redman, Rachel Kempson, Wildfrid Lawson, and Hugh Griffith. **Director**—Tony Richardson. **Academy Awards**—best picture; Richardson, best director; John Osborne, best screenplay (based on material from another medium). **Nominations**—Finney, best actor; Griffith, best supporting actor; Cilento, Evans, Redman, best supporting actress.

131 minutes

TOMMY (1975)

★★★

Ann-Margret
Oliver Reed
Roger Daltrey

The rock musical Tommy *features Jack Nicholson.*

This celebrated rock opera sung by The Who is a clamorous, energetic film about a child who becomes deaf, mute, and blind, after seeing his father killed. He grows up to become pinball champion of the world and a messiah. The colorful cast also includes Elton John, Jack Nicholson, Eric Clapton, Keith Moon, and Tina Turner. **Director**—Ken Russell. (PG) **Academy Award Nomination**—Ann-Margret, best actress. *111 minutes*

TOM SAWYER (1973)

★★

Johnnie Whitaker
Jeff East
Jodie Foster

This musical version of the Mark Twain classic is too squeaky clean to have much appeal for adults, but kids might still find it enjoyable. Whitaker and East play Tom Sawyer and Huck Finn, respectively. Although they haven't captured the magic of the characters, Foster plays Becky Thatcher with the gusto Twain seems to have had in mind. Celeste Holm (Aunt Polly) and Warren Oates (Muff Potter) appear in supporting roles. Filmed on location in Missouri. **Director**—Don Taylor. (G) *102 minutes*

TONY ROME (1967)

★★★

Frank Sinatra

This detective tale is about Tony Rome, a Miami private eye who tries to solve a jewel robbery and the murder of a beautiful woman. In some ways, it's reminiscent of the better 1940s films of the genre, but Sinatra lacks the grace of the Bogey-type detective. Nonetheless, there's some appeal to the tough dialogue, and there's enough sex and action to please most fans. The cast also includes Simon Oakland, Sue Lyon, Jill St. John, Richard Conte, Lloyd Gough, Lloyd Bochner, Jeffrey Lynn, and Gena Rowlands. **Director**—Gordon Douglas. *110 minutes*

TOO FAR TO GO (1982)

★★

Michael Moriarty
Blythe Danner

John Updike's stories of a dissolving marriage are adapted for the screen with Danner and Moriarty as the estranged couple. This view of middle-class social problems is true to Updike's mannered style but the presentation, unfortunately, is patchy and remote. Moriarty's performance doesn't match up to Danner's. Originally shown as a TV feature. **Director**—Fielder Cook. (No MPAA rating) *100 minutes*

TOOTSIE (1982)

★★★★

Dustin Hoffman
Teri Garr
Jessica Lange
Dabney Coleman
Charles Durning

Dustin Hoffman in drag? Yes, indeed. And he's charming, funny, and touching as a desperate actor who masquerades as a middle-aged woman to win a role in a soap opera. His character is so extraordinary that he (she) becomes a media celebrity. He also becomes wiser for his experience as a woman. The engaging comedy is filled with delicious complications and original humor. An acting triumph for

• Topaz   • Top Secret
• Top Hat   • Tora! Tora! Tora!
• Topkapi   • Torn Curtain

T

Director Sydney Pollack with Dustin Hoffman in drag in Tootsie.

Hoffman. Lange is terrific as the girl who thinks Hoffman's a girl too. **Director**—Sydney Pollack. (PG) **Academy Award**—Lange, best supporting actress. **Nominations**—best picture; Hoffman, best actor; Garr, best supporting actress; Pollack, best director; Larry Gelbart, Murray Schisgal, and Don McGuire, best screenplay (written directly for the screen); Owen Roizman, cinematography.

116 minutes

TOPAZ (1969)

 ★★

Frederick Stafford
John Forsythe

This espionage adventure about a French intelligence agent who works with an American agent because of Russian involvement in Cuba lacks any sparkling performances and seldom seems like a film directed by Alfred Hitchcock. Stafford plays the French spy, and Forsythe is the U.S. agent. John Vernon, Michel Piccoli, Philippe Noiret, Karin Dor, Roscoe Lee Browne, and Dany Robin give competent supporting performances in this rather routine enterprise, based on the Leon Uris novel. (PG)

124 minutes

TOP HAT (1935)

★★★★

Fred Astaire
Ginger Rogers

Astaire and Rogers are magnificent in this musical, and the superficial as-

pects of the mistaken-identity plot don't hamper the brilliance of the production one bit, as Fred pursues the love of his life from England to Italy. The performances of Edward Everett Horton, Erik Rhodes, Helen Broderick, and Eric Blore add to this film's charm and vibrancy. Irving Berlin songs include "Top Hat, White Tie and Tails" and "Cheek to Cheek." It's topnotch. **Director**—Mark Sandrich. **Academy Award Nomination**—best picture. *107 minutes b&w*

One of the routines performed by Fred Astaire and Ginger Rogers in Top Hat.

TOPKAPI (1964)

★★★

Melina Mercouri
Maximilian Schell
Peter Ustinov
Robert Morley

At moments when this jewel theft caper starts to take itself too seriously, the comic skills of Ustinov and Morley come to the rescue. The movie, based on Eric Ambler's novel *The Light of Day*, is about an international gang after jewels in the Topkapi Museum in Istanbul. Some of the richness of the story can be traced to Ambler. For the rest, credit excellent acting by Ustinov, Morley, Mercouri, Schell, and Akim Tamiroff. **Director**—Jules Dassin. **Academy Award**—Ustinov, best supporting actor. *119 minutes*

TOP SECRET (1984)

★★★

Val Kilmer
Lucy Gutteridge
Jim Carter
Omar Sharif

Directors Jim Abrahams, David Zucker, and Jerry Zucker, the creators of *Airplane*, spoof World War II spy movies with an abundance of smart sight gags and funny dialogue. It doesn't fly as high as *Airplane*, but it's jolly fun all the same. Val Kilmer stars as an Elvis-style rock singer caught up in a dastardly plot to unite East and West Germany by force. (PG)

90 minutes

TORA! TORA! TORA! (1970)

★★

Martin Balsam
Jason Robards, Jr.
Joseph Cotten

At the time of its release, some jokesters quipped that this movie about the attack on Pearl Harbor cost more than the actual military operation; the cost of the movie was estimated at about $25 million. Aside from the expense, this is an above-average war movie, but many cheaper ones have been much better. The film is at its best when it documents—from both sides—historical events, such as mistakes by those in charge, and reproduces the horrors of the infamous attack. Also with James Whitmore, E. G. Marshall, Soh Yamamura, Edward Andrews, Leon Ames, and Takahiro Tamura. **Directors**—Richard Fleischer, Ray Kellogg, Toshio Masuda, and Kinji Fukasaku. (G) **Academy Award Nomination**—Charles F. Wheeler, Osami Furuya, Sinsaku Himeda, and Masamichi Satoh, cinematography. *144 minutes*

TORN CURTAIN (1966)

★★

Paul Newman
Julie Andrews

This was director Alfred Hitchcock's 50th film, but the story of an American science professor who becomes involved with espionage and missions in East Germany falls flat and isn't worthy of the master of suspense. Newman, who plays the professor, is competent in his role, and Andrews sparkles as his secretary and lover. Also with Lila Kedrova, Ludwig Donath, Wolfgang Kieling, Tamara Toumanova, and David Opatoshu.

128 minutes

T

- Torpedo Run
- Torrid Zone
- Tortilla Flat
- To Sir, With Love
- A Touch of Class
- Touch of Evil
- Tough Enough

TORPEDO RUN (1958)
★★★

**Glenn Ford
Ernest Borgnine**

In Torpedo Run, *Ernest Borgnine wishes he could crush those dirty Japs with his bare hands.*

Ford and Borgnine star in this well-made submarine adventure. Ford plays a sub commander who sinks a ship carrying members of his own family and must live with the knowledge. The action sequences are better than the story, but there's enough of interest to make it worthwhile viewing for fans of such movies. Dean Jones and Diane Brewster appear in supporting roles. **Director**—Joseph Pevney. *98 minutes*

TORRID ZONE (1940)
★★★

**James Cagney
Pat O'Brien
Ann Sheridan**

Cagney, O'Brien, and Sheridan are at their ripsnorting best in this period piece about action and romance on a banana plantation in Central America. Cagney and O'Brien are rivals for Sheridan's affections. Sharp dialogue hides some of the holes in the plot and helps the trio brighten the movie. Also with George Tobias, George Reeves, Helen Vinson, Jerome Cowan, and Andy Devine. **Director**—William Keighley. *88 minutes b&w*

TORTILLA FLAT (1942)
★★★

**Spencer Tracy
Hedy Lamarr
John Garfield
Frank Morgan**

This uneven film version of John Steinbeck's novel is too philosophical and slow-moving to be a great film, but outstanding performances by Tracy, Garfield, and Morgan make the movie worth viewing. The story concerns the joys and sorrows of a group of poor Mexicans in a California fishing community. The three stars get excellent support from Lamarr, Akim Tamiroff, Connie Gilchrist, Henry O'Neill, Sheldon Leonard, John Qualen, and Donald Meek. **Director**—Victor Fleming. **Academy Award Nomination**—Morgan, best supporting actor.
106 minutes b&w

TO SIR, WITH LOVE (1967)
 ★★★

Sidney Poitier

Poitier is charming as a West Indian schoolteacher who's assigned to instruct tough white pupils in London's rough East End. The story borders on mush at times, as Poitier copes with his students, but his acting and good performances by Judy Geeson, Suzy Kendall, Christian Roberts, Patricia Routledge, and Faith Brook prevent the movie from becoming sentimental trash. **Director**—James Clavell.
105 minutes

A TOUCH OF CLASS (1973)
 ★★★

**Glenda Jackson
George Segal**

Without the classy performances of Jackson and Segal, this production would seem more like a touch of trash. The story is about an American insurance broker, played by Segal, who has an affair with Jackson, a British dress designer. There isn't much more to this romantic comedy than that, and even with the keen acting of the twosome, the tale falters at times. Paul Sorvino and Hildegard Neil also sparkle in

Glenda Jackson and George Segal have A Touch of Class.

supporting roles. **Director**—Melvin Frank. (PG) **Academy Award**—Jackson, best actress. **Nominations**—best picture; Frank and Jack Rose, best story and screenplay (based on factual material not previously published).
105 minutes

TOUCH OF EVIL (1958)
★★★

**Orson Welles
Charlton Heston**

A cavalcade of odd characters heightens this strange melodrama by Orson Welles, who contributes his talents for writing, directing, and acting. In Mexico, newly married policeman Heston gets tangled up in a murder case. Events unfold somewhat slowly, yet Welles's skillful touch leaves its mark. Janet Leigh, Marlene Dietrich, and Mercedes McCambridge also are in the cast. *93 minutes b&w*

TOUGH ENOUGH (1983)
 ★

**Dennis Quaid
Warren Oates
Carlene Watkins
Stan Shaw**

Repetitive and unimaginative boxing bouts dominate this imitation of *Rocky*. The story is set in Texas and Detroit, and Quaid is not impressive as a country singer who turns to amateur prizefighting to meet the mortgage payments. The script is shot full of fight-film clichés, and it's obvious from the start that Quaid will dispose appropriately of his various ring opponents. **Director**—Richard Fleischer. (PG) *106 minutes*

• The Towering Inferno
• Tower of London (1939)
• Tower of London (1962)
• The Toy
• Toys in the Attic
• Trading Places

T

THE TOWERING INFERNO (1974)

★★

**Paul Newman
Steve McQueen
William Holden**

Steve McQueen is about to drop Ernie Orsatti from The Towering Inferno.

This tasteless production about a raging fire at the world's tallest building could be defended as a fire-prevention movie if it weren't so well done. The special effects are brilliant, and the all-star cast performs professionally. But alas, the point of the film seems to be about gruesome ways of dying in a fire. The all-star cast also includes Fred Astaire, Susan Blakely, O. J. Simpson, Robert Wagner, Richard Chamberlain, Robert Vaughn, and Jennifer Jones. **Directors**—John Guillermin and Irwin Allen. (PG) **Academy Award**—Fred Koenekamp and Joseph Biroc, cinematography. **Nomination**—best picture; Astaire, best supporting actor.
165 minutes

TOWER OF LONDON (1939)

★★

**Basil Rathbone
Boris Karloff**

Rathbone and Karloff—those horror movie regulars—are present and in fine form in this movie, which distorts British history to give this view to the return to the throne of an exiled king—apparently Richard III. Some of the scenes are quite good for those who

care about such things, and the acting is fine. Also with Nan Grey, Barbara O'Neill, Ian Hunter, Vincent Price, and Leo G. Carroll. **Director**—Rowland V. Lee. *92 minutes b&w*

TOWER OF LONDON (1962)

★

Vincent Price

There are no towering performances in this flat remake of the 1939 movie, about a wicked king trying to return to power. Price, who played the Duke of Clarence in the earlier film, does a nice job of portraying Richard III in this effort. But aside from Price and the vivid addition of ghostly visions, there's little to warrant the price of admission. The cast also includes Joan Freeman, Robert Brown, Michael Pate, Bruce Gordon, Sara Salby, and Justice Eatson. **Director**—Roger Corman. *79 minutes b&w*

THE TOY (1982)

★

**Richard Pryor
Jackie Gleason**

In The Toy, *Richard Pryor won't let Jackie Gleason call him "boy" no more.*

The talents of Pryor and Gleason are shamelessly thrown away here. This threadbare comedy is out of control all the way. Pryor plays an unemployed journalist so desperate that he takes a job as playmate to the bratty nine-year-old son of a heartless tycoon (Gleason). Countless poor-little-rich-kid clichés are dredged up and mixed in with stale slapstick routines. Predictably, Pryor becomes the surrogate father of the affection-starved youngster. **Director**—Richard Donner. (PG)
99 minutes

TOYS IN THE ATTIC (1963)

★

**Geraldine Page
Wendy Hiller
Dean Martin**

Lillian Hellman's stimulating and provocative play becomes as uninteresting as a dull soap opera in this film treatment. Page and Hiller star as two spinster sisters who must deal with their roguish brother when he brings home his childlike bride. Martin is miscast as the brother, but Gene Tierney, Larry Gates, Yvette Mimieux, and Nan Martin are superior to the material they have to work with. **Director**—George Roy Hill. *90 minutes b&w*

TRADING PLACES (1983)

★★★

**Eddie Murphy
Dan Aykroyd**

Eddie Murphy and Dan Aykroyd are bullish partners in Trading Places.

Murphy is a glib street hustler who switches roles with a prissy, stuffed-shirt commodities trader, Aykroyd. This sharp, screwball comedy is hilarious. Murphy demonstrates extraordinary comic talent and he runs away with many of the scenes. Ralph Bellamy, Don Ameche, Denholm Elliott, and Jamie Lee Curtis stand out in supporting roles. **Director**—John Landis. (R) *106 minutes*

T
- Trail of the Pink Panther
- The Train
- The Train Robbers
- Trapeze
- La Traviata
- Treasure Island
- Treasure of Matecumbe

TRAIL OF THE PINK PANTHER (1982)

★★

**Peter Sellers
David Niven**

Capucine comforts Peter Sellers in Trail of the Pink Panther.

This sixth adventure of bumbling French detective Clouseau (Sellers) is a letdown. A wisp of a plot presents the inscrutable inspector as he prepares to investigate yet another theft of the "Pink Panther" diamond. Most of the time all we get are snippets of earlier Panther films, assembled after Sellers's untimely death, as a tribute to Clouseau's career. **Director**—Blake Edwards. (PG)   *95 minutes*

THE TRAIN (1965)

★★★★

**Burt Lancaster
Paul Scofield
Michel Simon**

This story about the efforts of the French Resistance to prevent the Nazis from removing French art treasures by train in 1944 is basically a simple story. Under John Frankenheimer's deft direction, there isn't a wasted moment, as he creates supreme tension up to the conclusion in a railroad yard. Lancaster plays a railroad boss, Scofield is a German officer, and Simon is a train engineer. Also with Albert Remy, Wolfgang Preiss, Jeanne Moreau, and Suzanne Flon. **Academy Award Nomination**—Franklin Coen and Frank Davis, best story and screenplay (written directly for the screen).

113 minutes b&w

THE TRAIN ROBBERS (1973)

★

**John Wayne
Ann-Margret**

Wayne and Ann-Margret head the cast of this dismal western in which the Duke is enlisted to help a widow recover gold stolen by her late husband. Ann-Margret plays the widow. They should have gotten on the train and ridden off the set rather than tarnish their acting reputations with this worthless enterprise. There's some action, but not enough to interest fans of blazing guns and ambushes. Rod Taylor, Ben Johnson, Christopher George, Ricardo Montalban, and Bobby Vinton appear in supporting roles. **Director**—Burt Kennedy. (PG)   *92 minutes*

TRAPEZE (1956)

★★★

**Burt Lancaster
Tony Curtis
Gina Lollobrigida**

Burt Lancaster and Tony Curtis in Trapeze, *a movie about circus life.*

Lancaster, Curtis, and Lollobrigida star in this thoughtful, well-made circus movie that's long on atmosphere, but short on plot. Lancaster and Curtis portray old and young aerialists, respectively, while Lollobrigida supplies some charm and lots of curves. The cast also includes Katy Jurado, Sidney James, Albert Evans, Thomas Gomez, and John Puleo. **Director**—Carol Reed.   *105 minutes*

LA TRAVIATA (1983)

★★★

**Placido Domingo
Teresa Stratas**

Placido Domingo brings the sensitive Alfredo to life in the Verdi opera La Traviata.

One of the finest film productions of grand opera ever brought to America. The sumptuous spectacle is directed by Franco Zeffirelli (*Romeo and Juliet*) with emotional realism and attention to authenticity, although his sentimentalism is also ever-present. Noted opera stars Stratas and Domingo sing beautifully and bring new life to Verdi's tragic romance. A refreshing interpretation. (No MPAA rating)

112 minutes

TREASURE ISLAND (1950)

★★★

**Robert Newton
Bobby Driscoll**

Newton is splendid as Long John Silver, and Driscoll is competent as Jim Hawkins, in this Walt Disney version of the Robert Louis Stevenson tale, about the discovery of a pirate map that leads to a search for buried treasure. There's nothing really wrong with this movie, and kids are sure to enjoy it; but it could have been much better if there was more attention to the detail of the original story and fewer glossy theatrics. Basil Sydney, Denis O'Dea, Ralph Truman, Walter Fitzgerald, Finlay Currie, and Geoffrey Wilkinson appear in supporting roles. **Director**—Byron Haskin. (G)

96 minutes

TREASURE OF MATECUMBE (1976)

★★★

**Robert Foxworth
Joan Hackett
Peter Ustinov**

• Treasure of the Four Crowns
• The Treasure of the Sierra Madre

• A Tree Grows in Brooklyn
• Trenchcoat
• The Trials of Oscar Wilde
• Tribute

T

A formula Walt Disney action adventure: Two appealing youngsters search for a buried chest and outsmart a lot of unpleasant grownups along the way. Johnny Doran and Billy Attmore play the spunky lads. The film is a cut above some recent children-oriented movies, thanks to a sturdy plot and an excellent cast. There are sparkling performances by Hackett as a runaway bride-to-be and by Ustinov as a rotund medicine man. The film is a bit long, but it packs plenty of fun. **Director**—Vincent McEveety. (G)

117 minutes

TREASURE OF THE FOUR CROWNS (1983)

 (no stars)

Tony Anthony
Ana Obregon

A shabby 3-D adventure film with a creaky plot that treads heavily on the heels of *Raiders of the Lost Ark*. The acting is atrocious and the scenery poorly constructed. The 3-D effect serves only to emphasize the shoddiness of this trashy production. Hardly a treasure. It's more like fool's gold. **Director**—Fernando Baldi. (PG) *97 minutes*

THE TREASURE OF THE SIERRA MADRE (1948)

 ★★★★

Humphrey Bogart
Walter Huston
Tim Holt

This is one of those rare Hollywood movies that tells a vivid story and provides a message. The objective is reached because of the excellent direction and screenwriting of John Huston, the vitality of the original novel by the mysterious B. Traven, the intense and realistic mood created by the superb photography of Ted McCord, and the stunning acting. Bogart, Walter Huston, and Holt star as three prospectors who find gold and are then done in by greed. Barton MacLane, Bruce Bennett, and Alfonso Bedoya star in supporting roles. **Academy Awards**—John Huston, best director; Walter Huston, best supporting actor; John Huston, writing (screenplay). **Nomination**—best picture.

126 minutes b&w

A TREE GROWS IN BROOKLYN (1945)
★★★★

Peggy Ann Garner
James Dunn

Garner and Dunn star in this sensitive story about a troubled Irish family in Brooklyn tenements at the turn of the century. Dunn plays an alcoholic father, and Garner portrays a young lady trying to mature despite her dismal surroundings. Joan Blondell, Lloyd Nolan, Dorothy McGuire, James Gleason, Charles Halton, Ted Donaldson, Ruth Nelson, and John Alexander provide fine supporting performances in this excellently directed film. **Director**—Elia Kazan. **Academy Award**—Dunn, best supporting actor. **Special Academy Award**—Garner, outstanding child actress. **Nomination**—Frank Davis and Tess Slesinger, writing (screenplay). *128 minutes b&w*

TRENCHCOAT (1983)

 ★★

Margot Kidder
Robert Hays

In Trenchcoat, *David Suchet tries to extract a confession from Margot Kidder.*

Kidder plays a court stenographer turned mystery writer turned detective in this Disney-made spoof of gumshoe movies. While on vacation in Malta, where she's trying to write a detective story, she becomes tangled in a cocaine smuggling scheme and a murder. Kidder turns in a spunky performance, but the chain of events is predictable and labored. Hays co-stars as the object of Kidder's affections. **Director**—Michael Tuchner. (PG)

91 minutes

THE TRIALS OF OSCAR WILDE (1960)
★★

Peter Finch
James Mason
Nigel Patrick
John Fraser

Excellent acting performances by Finch, Mason, Patrick, and Fraser sustain this flat account of the eccentric playwright's libel trial and subsequent prosecution for sodomy. Finch's portrayal of Wilde is a full and vivid characterization, although some might claim it puts him in too favorable a light. Yvonne Mitchell, Lionel Jeffries, James Booth, Maxine Audley, and Emrys Jones appear in supporting roles. **Director**—Ken Hughes.

123 minutes

TRIBUTE (1980)

 ★★

Jack Lemmon
Robby Benson

Jack Lemmon and Robby Benson are a feuding father and son in Tribute.

Bernard Slade's play, about a strained relationship between father and son, doesn't transfer to the screen. This emotionally unrewarding film provides a *tour de force* role for Lemmon, who mugs away as the clownish father dying of cancer. But what is supposed to be drama is merely a string of self-pitying temper tantrums. Benson, as the priggish and obnoxious son, performs mechanically and unevenly. Also with Lee Remick. **Director**—Bob Clark. (PG) **Academy Award Nomination**—Lemmon, best actor.

123 minutes

T
- Tron
- The Trouble with Angels
- True Confessions
- True Grit
- The Tunnel of Love
- The Turning Point

TRON (1982)

★★

**Jeff Bridges
Bruce Boxleitner**

Bruce Boxleitner really gets into playing video games in Tron.

The Disney studio presents a mechanical, garish sci-fi adventure that takes place in the innards of a computerized video game. It's quite a departure from the endearing tales and high quality of yore. The computer-generated effects are certainly splashy, but the characters are neither credible nor interesting, and what passes for dialogue is mostly technical jargon. **Director—**Steven Lisberger. (PG)   *96 minutes*

THE TROUBLE WITH ANGELS (1966)

★★

**Rosalind Russell
Hayley Mills
June Harding**

Mills and Harding give enthusiastic performances in this mild comedy about the fun and pranks that occur at a convent school where Russell is the Mother Superior in charge. This is an inoffensive movie, but it's also almost totally unappealing. Mary Wickes, Margalo Gillmore, Binnie Barnes, Gypsy Rose Lee, and Marge Redmond appear in supporting roles. **Director—**Ida Lupino.   *112 minutes*

TRUE CONFESSIONS (1981)

★★★★

**Robert De Niro
Robert Duvall**

De Niro and Duvall brilliantly play two brothers—De Niro as a priest, Duvall as a police detective—brought into conflict over a prostitute's murder. The grisly crime leads to the core of this engrossing film, based on John Gregory Dunne's novel; it explores hypocrisy among high church officials. Acting at all levels is superb, and the 1940s settings are rich with atmosphere. It's a tough, intriguing film, masterfully directed by Ulu Grosbard. Also with Charles Durning, Ed Flanders, and Burgess Meredith. (R)   *110 minutes*

TRUE GRIT (1969)

★★★★

**John Wayne
Kim Darby**

Although Wayne turned in many top-drawer performances, this movie was a turning point in his career because he got wider recognition than praise from fans of westerns and war movies by winning an Academy Award. Wayne plays Rooster Cogburn, a one-eyed, tough old marshal, who responds to the plea of a young girl, played by Darby, who wants to avenge the slaying of her father. Dennis Hopper, Robert Duvall, Jeff Corey, Strother Martin, and Jeremy Slate provide polished supporting performances. The use of pop singer Glen Campbell is the movie's only major distraction. **Director—**Henry Hathaway. (G) **Academy Award—**Wayne, best actor.   *128 minutes*

Glen Campbell tries to remember his dinner manners in True Grit.

THE TUNNEL OF LOVE (1958)
★★

**Richard Widmark
Doris Day**

Widmark and Day provide winsome performances in this somewhat vulgar movie that lacks much winning material. They portray a couple coping with insensitive bureaucrats as they endeavor to adopt a baby. Some bright dialogue and solid performances by Gig Young, Gia Scala, Elizabeth Wilson, and Elizabeth Fraser enhance the movie. **Director—**Gene Kelly.   *98 minutes b&w*

THE TURNING POINT (1977)

★★

**Anne Bancroft
Shirley MacLaine**

Bancroft and MacLaine play old rivals who are reunited in this backstage ballet drama, and their roles seem extracted from daytime TV soap operas. In addition, the script is rather mechanical; only the dance scenes perk up portions of the film. The young Russian-born dancer Mikhail Baryshnikov steals a few scenes with his acting as well as his ballet performance. Also with Tom Skerritt, Martha Scott, and Leslie Browne. **Director—**Herbert Ross. (PG) **Academy Award Nominations—**best picture; Ross, best director; Bancroft, Mac Laine, best actress; Baryshnikov, best supporting

• Twelve Angry Men
• Twelve O'Clock High
• 20th Century
• 20,000 Leagues Under the Sea
• Twilight's Last Gleaming
• Twilight Time
• Twilight Zone: The Movie

T

Shirley MacLaine and Anne Brancroft have it out in The Turning Point.

actor; Browne, best supporting actress; Arthur Laurents, best original screenplay.   *119 minutes*

TWELVE ANGRY MEN
(1957)

  ★★★★

**Henry Fonda
Lee J. Cobb
E. G. Marshall
Jack Warden**

A better title might have been *One Angry Man* because Fonda plays a conscientious and moral juror at the trial of a teenager accused of killing his father, and he prevails on eleven other jurors not to rush to judgment. The premise of the movie that a lawyer would be careless in the defense of a client borders on the preposterous, but it does set the stage for a superb drama in which Fonda defends the youth. The sensational cast also includes Ed Begley, Martin Balsam, Jack Klugman, Edward Binns, Joseph Sweeney, Robert Webber, George Voskovec, and John Fiedler. **Director—** Sidney Lumet. **Academy Award Nominations**—best picture; Lumet, best director; Reginald Rose, best screenplay (based on material from another medium).   *95 minutes b&w*

TWELVE O'CLOCK HIGH
(1949)

  ★★★★

**Gregory Peck
Dean Jagger**

Peck and Jagger are at the top of their acting skills in this story about the stress of leading U.S. fliers into combat during World War II. Peck plays the commander of a bomber unit based in England. All of the characterizations are excellent and far superior to the two-dimensional portraits seen in most war films. Hugh Marlowe, Gary Merrill, Millard Mitchell, John Kellogg, Paul Stewart, and Robert Arthur are among the fine supporting actors. **Director**—Henry King. **Academy Award**—Jagger, best supporting actor. **Nominations**—best picture; Peck, best actor.   *132 minutes b&w*

20th CENTURY (1934)

  ★★★★

**John Barrymore
Carole Lombard**

The crack New York to Chicago passenger train of the title serves as part of the setting for this top-notch screwball comedy taken from the popular play by Ben Hecht and Charles MacArthur. The backstage story involves big-shot producer Barrymore who makes a star of novice actress Lombard. Plenty of delightful complications develop. Also with Roscoe Karns and Walter Connolly. **Director**—Howard Hawks.   *91 minutes b&w*

20,000 LEAGUES UNDER THE SEA (1954)

  ★★★

**Kirk Douglas
James Mason**

The universe of novelist Jules Verne springs to life in this exciting Walt Disney production of life aboard a futuristic submarine. Douglas, Peter Lorre, and Paul Lukas get aboard Captain Nemo's sub for scintillating adventures. Nemo is played by Mason. All involved perform admirably as befits this cosmic tale. Carleton Young, Ted

Undersea divers like what they find 20,000 Leagues Under the Sea.

De Corsia, and Robert J. Wilke appear in supporting roles. **Director**—Richard Fleischer. (G)   *122 minutes*

TWILIGHT'S LAST GLEAMING (1977)

  ★★★

**Burt Lancaster
Richard Widmark
Charles Durning**

This political suspense-thriller stars Lancaster as a disgruntled U.S. Air Force general who blackmails the government by threatening to unleash nuclear missiles on Russia. Director Robert Aldrich forcefully fashions ample suspense and taut confrontations through his use of split-screen sequences. Lancaster and other Hollywood elder statesmen, such as Melvyn Douglas, Joseph Cotten, and Widmark, move the action along energetically. Durning plays the President. The compelling screenplay stirs the conscience about the Vietnam War era, but there are many lapses of credibility. Also with Paul Winfield, Richard Jaeckel, Burt Young, and Roscoe Lee Browne. (R)   *146 minutes*

TWILIGHT TIME (1983)

★★

Karl Malden

This sentimental film set in a remote Yugoslavian village concerns the efforts of a grandfather and two children to manage their family farm and uphold traditional values. Malden is reliably sympathetic as the wise old man who cares for the kids while their parents are in Germany pursuing materialistic goals. But, alas, this well-intentioned film lacks dramatic drive, and the story unfolds too slowly. **Director**—Goram Paskaljevic. (PG)   *102 minutes*

TWILIGHT ZONE:
THE MOVIE (1983)

  ★★

**Vic Morrow
Scatman Crothers
John Lithgow
Dan Aykroyd**

(Continued)

T
- Two-Minute Warning
- Two of a Kind
- 2001: A Space Odyssey
- 2010

- Two Weeks in Another Town
- Two Years Before the Mast

Vic Morrow finds that something is terribly wrong; that's because he's just landed in the Twilight Zone: The Movie.

(Continued)
Rod Serling's spooky TV series inspired this segmented film, and the final product is only partially successful. John Landis directed the least satisfactory vignette, about a hostile bigot (Morrow, who was killed while this movie was being made) who gets his comeuppance. Steven Spielberg does somewhat better with a tale of old people who become young again. A zany family trapped in a nightmare is the subject of Joe Dante's portion. And George Miller (*The Road Warrior*) skillfully directs a story about a hysterical airline passenger (Lithgow). (PG)
102 minutes

TWO-MINUTE WARNING (1976)
★★

Charlton Heston
John Cassavetes

A sniper, perched above the scoreboard of the Los Angeles Coliseum, opens fire on fans watching a championship football game. This gory action sequence takes place during the last 15 minutes of the movie. The rest is filled with tedious slice-of-life vignettes about selected spectators, who are eventually killed or injured. It's much in the familiar disaster genre of *The Towering Inferno*, *The Hindenburg*, and so on. It also resembles a patchwork affair of TV dramas. The large cast also includes Martin Balsam, Beau Bridges, David Janssen, Jack Klugman, and Gena Rowlands. **Director**—Larry Peerce. (R) *115 minutes*

TWO OF A KIND (1983)
 ★

John Travolta
Olivia Newton-John

This ridiculous romantic comedy is a desperate excuse for bringing Travolta and Newton-John together again. He's a wacky inventor who resorts to robbing a bank to pay off some loan sharks. She's the flaky teller who makes goo-goo eyes at him during the heist. If they fall madly in love, they will please God and save the world. All they do is damage their acting careers and bore the audience into a stupor with this tacky mess. **Director**—John Herzfeld. (PG) *90 minutes*

2001: A SPACE ODYSSEY (1968)
 ★★★★

Keir Dullea
William Sylvester
Gary Lockwood

Keir Dullea sees the wonder of the universe in 2001: A Space Odyssey.

This production about a journey into another realm of thought and time is a one-of-a-kind masterpiece. There are so many special effects and visually stunning scenes that at times it seems that actors aren't necessary, but Dullea and Lockwood are fine as two astronauts traveling to Jupiter with a complex and disturbed computer called HAL. Despite superficial resemblances to other sci-fi films, director Stanley Kubrick has fashioned a deep and deeply moving meditation on the meaning of the universe like no other film before or since. Also with Danial Richter. (G) **Academy Award Nominations**—Kubrick, best director; Kubrick and Arthur C. Clarke, best story and screenplay (written directly for the screen). *140 minutes*

2010 (1984)
★★

Roy Scheider
John Lithgow
Bob Balaban

Dazzling special effects and fancy space hardware dominate this follow-up to Stanley Kubrick's *2001: A Space Odyssey*. Yet, there's no feeling of awe, mystery, or imagination as a joint American and Russian space crew try to find out what went wrong with the spacecraft *Discovery* lost in space some nine years before. This high-tech misfire winds down with many loose ends dangling and a lot of double talk about peace among the superpowers. **Director**—Peter Hyams. (PG) *157 minutes*

TWO WEEKS IN ANOTHER TOWN (1962)
★★

Kirk Douglas

Douglas stars in this solid melodrama as a former alcoholic trying to make a comeback in the film industry. The movie is based on Irwin Shaw's bestselling novel. Douglas does his best to capture the better aspects of the book, but he's only successful some of the time. Also with Edward G. Robinson, Cyd Charisse, Claire Trevor, George Hamilton, Constance Ford, Dalia Lavi, George Macready, and Rosanna Schiaffino. **Director**—Vincente Minnelli. *107 minutes*

TWO YEARS BEFORE THE MAST (1946)
★★

Alan Ladd
Brian Donlevy

When Richard Henry Dana's book *Two Years Before the Mast* was published, it caused a stir because it exposed the many sordid conditions under which sailors were forced to work during the 19th century. The film, however, doesn't attempt to be an exposé, and regrettably it fails to capture much of the book's excitement. Donlevy plays Dana, Ladd is a sailor, and Howard da Silva plays the role of an oppressive captain. Also with William Bendix

• Typhoon
• The Ugly American
• Unchained
• Uncommon Valor
• The Undefeated
• Undercovers Hero
• Undercurrent
• Under Fire

T·U

and Barry Fitzgerald. **Director**—John Farrow. *98 minutes b&w*

TYPHOON (1940)
★★

Dorothy Lamour

Beautiful Lamour does her thing with a sarong—although that wasn't the way such things were said at the time of the film's release—in this romantic tale. In the film, sailors discover her on an island and learn that she has been there since childhood; the story builds from there. Lynne Overman, J. Carrol Naish, Robert Preston, Frank Reicher, and Jack Carson handle the supporting roles. **Director**—Louis King. *70 minutes*

U

THE UGLY AMERICAN (1963)
★★

Marlon Brando

With a moustache Marlon Brando becomes The Ugly American.

By Hollywood standards, this movie was a sincere effort to deal with America's confrontation with communism in Southeast Asia. Unfortunately, the story bogs down. Brando never shines as the U.S. Ambassador who fumbles his assignment and causes new problems in an Asian country despite his good intentions. Eiji Okada, Arthur Hill, Sandra Church, Jocelyn Brando, and Pat Hingle appear in supporting roles. **Director**—George H. Englund. *120 minutes*

UNCHAINED (1955)
★★

Chester Morris
Elroy Hirsch

Life on a prison farm in California is presented in vivid, realistic terms in this very atypical film. Morris and Hirsch star in this movie, based on a true story about a warden administrator who runs a prison without bars. Also with Barbara Hale, Jerry Paris, Peggy Knudsen, and Johnny Johnston. **Director**—Hall Bartlett. *75 minutes b&w*

UNCOMMON VALOR (1983)
 ★★★

Gene Hackman

Hackman is a rough-tough Marine colonel who leads a gung-ho band of veterans through the Laotian jungles to rescue American troops listed as missing during the Vietnam War. The film is high on macho, shoot-'em-up action, rather well done by the technical crew although it tends to celebrate violence under the pretense of nobility. Hackman is excellent, as are Reb Brown and Randall Cobb in supporting roles. **Director**—Ted Kotcheff. (R) *105 minutes*

THE UNDEFEATED (1969)
★★

John Wayne
Rock Hudson

Once again, the Duke—John Wayne—plays a cowboy in The Undefeated.

Wayne plays an ex-Union colonel in the horse-trading business who confronts Hudson, a former Confederate colonel. They mend their past differences just in time to fight together against Mexican marauders in this mediocre Civil War-era western. Tony Aguilar, Lee Meriwether, Bruce Cabot, Roman Gabriel, Merlin Olsen, and Ben Johnson are ordinary in supporting roles. **Director**—Andrew V. McLaglen. (G) *119 minutes*

UNDERCOVERS HERO (1975)
★★

Peter Sellers

Sellers, who often played multiple roles, has six parts in this British sex farce, set in a Paris bordello during the Nazi occupation in World War II. The talented Sellers—who impersonates Hitler, a French general, a British intelligence agent, and so on—is amusing indeed. However, the story itself is lamebrained and incoherent. With Lila Kedrova, Curt Jurgens, and Beatrice Romand. **Director**—Roy Boulting. (R) *95 minutes*

UNDERCURRENT (1946)
★★

Katharine Hepburn
Robert Taylor
Robert Mitchum

Hepburn, Taylor, and Mitchum give solid performances in this movie about a woman who gradually discovers that her husband is an evil man. The story drags, however, and isn't very well told. Modern viewers might give it more of a feminist interpretation, although it won't make this seem a better movie. Also with Edmund Gwenn, Marjorie Main, Dan Tobin, and Jayne Meadows. **Director**—Vincente Minnelli. *116 minutes b&w*

UNDER FIRE (1983)
 ★★★

Nick Nolte
Gene Hackman
Joanna Cassidy

Tough, gripping, yet flawed historical
(Continued)

U
- Under Ten Flags
- Under the Rainbow
- Under the Volcano
- Under the Yum Yum Tree
- Unfaithfully Yours
- Unfinished Business
- The Unforgiven

In Under Fire, *Nick Nolte and Joanna Cassidy are journalists caught up in the Nicaraguan revolution of 1979.*

(Continued)

drama about events that toppled Nicaraguan dictator Anastasio Somoza. The action is seen through the eyes and camera of free-lance photographer Nolte who compromises his journalistic ethics by siding with the Sandinista rebels. The acting and pacing are first-rate, but the newsman's abrupt radicalization and the occasional Hollywood treatment of the revolution lessen the film's impact. **Director**—Roger Spottiswood. (R) *100 minutes*

UNDER TEN FLAGS (1960)
★★

Van Heflin

This story about a kindly captain of a German attack ship during World War II who keeps escaping the British is one of those rare war movies told from the enemy point of view. Despite the different perspective, it's still just an average war story. Heflin plays the German raider captain. Charles Laughton, Mylene Demongeot, and John Ericson appear in supporting roles. **Director**—Duilio Coletti and Silvio Narizzano. *92 minutes b&w*

UNDER THE RAINBOW (1981)
  ★

Chevy Chase
Carrie Fisher

Chase and Fisher star in this meandering, unworkable comedy, which mainly deals with the problems caused by the scores of midgets hired as Munchkins for the 1939 *Wizard of Oz* movie.

Carrie Fisher and Chevy Chase find trouble Under the Rainbow.

Involved with the various cornball incidents are Japanese and German spies, touring Japanese photographers, and a duke and duchess threatened with assassination. There seems to be a lot going on, but there's nothing here that produces any solid laughs. **Director**—Steve Rash. (PG) *98 minutes*

UNDER THE VOLCANO (1984)
  ★★

Albert Finney
Jacqueline Bisset

Malcom Lowry's difficult novel about an alcoholic British ex-diplomat residing in Mexico is no less beset with problems on the screen, even under the skillful direction of John Huston. Finney pours out his soul as the former consul drowning in booze. Bisset also is exceptional as his estranged wife. But such good performances don't lead to an entertaining movie. It's heavy going most of the way. (R) *112 minutes*

UNDER THE YUM YUM TREE (1963)
★

Jack Lemmon
Carol Lynley
Dean Jones

The comic talents of Lemmon are wasted in this tasteless tale about a lecherous landlord who has designs on a cute coed tenant, played by Lynley. She, in turn, is involved with her fiancé, played by Jones. If you get involved

in this silly, tedious story, don't say you haven't been warned. Paul Lynde, Robert Lansing, Imogene Coca, and Edie Adams appear in supporting roles. **Director**—David Swift.
110 minutes

UNFAITHFULLY YOURS (1984)
  ★★

Dudley Moore
Nastassja Kinksi

This reworking of the 1948 Preston Sturges black comedy unfolds laboriously at first, but a rip-roaring payoff makes the film worthwhile and sets the film on course. That's when Moore, as a jealous symphony conductor, tries to fulfill his fantasy of murdering his kittenish young wife (Kinski), whom he suspects is being unfaithful. Moore's bumbling attempts result in a torrent of laughter. Also with Armand Assante and Richard Libertini. **Director**—Howard Zieff. (PG) *97 minutes*

UNFINISHED BUSINESS (1941)
★★

Irene Dunne
Robert Montgomery

Dunne and Montgomery star in this romantic comedy about a small-town girl's search for love and adventure in the big city. This silly story has been told many times before, and this version lacks energy and forcefulness. Eugene Pallette, Preston Foster, Esther Dale, Dick Foran, Samuel S. Hinds, and June Clyde star in supporting roles. **Director**—Gregory La Cava.
95 minutes b&w

THE UNFORGIVEN (1960)
★★

Burt Lancaster
Audrey Hepburn

Lancaster and Hepburn star in this uneven western drama with loads of conflicting elements. Charles Bickford, Lillian Gish, Lancaster, and Hepburn are all fine actors, but only Bickford and Gish seem at home in a western setting; the other two seem miscast. John Huston is a fine director, and there are some vivid scenes, in-

PAUL NEWMAN

Paul Newman has been a major film star for more than two decades. Oscar-nominated for his riveting characterizations in Cat on a Hot Tin Roof *(1958),* The Hustler *(1961),* Hud *(1963),* Cool Hand Luke *(1967),* Absence of Malice *(1981), and* The Verdict *(1982), Newman has also starred in such successes as* Somebody Up There Likes Me *(1956),* The Long, Hot Summer *(1958),* The Young Philadelphians *(1959),* Sweet Bird of Youth *(1962),* Harper *(1966),* Winning *(1969),* The Towering Inferno *(1974), and* Slap Shot *(1977), as well as in two of the most popular films in movie history,* Butch Cassidy and the Sundance Kid *(1969) and* The Sting *(1973). He directed and starred in* Harry and Son *(1983).*

Born in 1925 and raised in Cleveland, the second son of a business executive, Newman entered Ohio's Kenyon College to major in economics, but left to serve three years in the Navy during World War II. After he returned to Kenyon, he became seriously interested in acting.

A season of summer stock followed his graduation in 1949, but the death of his father forced Newman back to Cleveland to manage the family business. After 18 months, he turned the business over to his brother and entered Yale Drama School. Later, he went to New York, where he was accepted into Lee Strasberg's Actors' Studio and played the role of Alan Seymour in the Broadway production of Picnic, *in which he met Joanne Woodward, his second wife. During the play's 14-month run, he was placed under contract by Warner Brothers studio.*

Disappointed in his film debut as a Greek slave in The Silver Chalice *(1954), Newman was released from his contract and returned to New York to appear in the Broadway hit,* The Desperate Hours.

Hollywood beckoned again, and after his first solid film hit in 1956—as Rocky Graziano in Somebody Up There Likes Me—*he was catapulted to stardom.*

nelia Otis Skinner, Dorothy Stickney, and Barbara Everest. **Director**—Lewis Allen. **Academy Award Nomination**—Charles Lang, cinematography (black and white).   *98 minutes b&w*

UNION STATION (1950)

William Holden
Barry Fitzgerald

Real locations and loads of action enliven this suspense film starring Holden and Fitzgerald. It's about the kidnapping of a blind girl, played by Allene Roberts. The title refers to the crowded train station that the kidnappers decide to use as the ransom collection point. Also with Lyle Bettger, Nancy Olson, Robert Preston, and Jan Sterling. **Director**—Rudolph Maté.
80 minutes b&w

AN UNMARRIED WOMAN (1978)

Jill Clayburgh

Jill Clayburgh and Alan Bates in the bittersweet satire An Unmarried Woman.

cluding the Indian attack climax. At other points in the film, it seems that Huston was absent and that a committee of directors took over for him. And so it goes in this story of racism. It's about a woman living with whites, who's suspected of being an Indian. Hepburn is the woman. You'll have to decide if the good parts are worth savoring.   *125 minutes*

UNHOLY PARTNERS (1941)
★★

Edward G. Robinson
Edward Arnold

Robinson and Arnold sparkle in this story about the editor of a scandal sheet who accepts financial aid from a gangster. Robinson plays the newspaperman, and Arnold is the gangster. This unlikely premise mars the movie, but does provide action and conflict when the editor decides to expose the hoodlum and his rackets. Laraine Day and Marsha Hunt also star, with Don Beddoe, Marcel Dalio, Walter Kingsford, William T. Orr, and Charles Dingle in supporting performances. **Director**—Mervyn Le Roy.
94 minutes b&w

THE UNINVITED (1944)
★★★★

Ray Milland
Ruth Hussey
Gail Russell

If you don't like to be scared out of your wits, you might find this movie ghastly. But fans of chillers will find it one of the best in cinema history. Milland, Hussey, and Russell play their parts superbly, in this story about a haunted house and evil spirits. Also with Donald Crisp, Alan Napier, Cor-

This bittersweet satire, concerning a woman's struggle to piece her life together after her husband walks out, has a lot going for it—sophistication, wit, sensitivity, polished dialogue, superb acting, and Clayburgh in the title role. Clayburgh gives a triumphant performance. Writer-director Paul Mazursky skillfully explores America's rootless affluent society in this uncompromising film. Also stars Alan Bates,
(Continued)

U
- The Unsinkable Molly Brown
- Untamed
- Until September
- Up in Smoke
- Up the Academy
- Up the Creek
- Up the Down Staircase

(Continued)

Michael Murphy, Lisa Lucas, Cliff Gorman, Pat Quinn, and Kelly Bishop. (R) **Academy Award Nominations**—best picture; Clayburgh, best actress; Mazursky, best original screenplay. *124 minutes*

THE UNSINKABLE MOLLY BROWN (1964)
★★★

Debbie Reynolds
Harve Presnell

Debbie Reynolds stomps it up as The Unsinkable Molly Brown.

Reynolds is delightful in this lively comedy-musical about a country girl who rises to social prominence and wealth in Denver. She plays the title role and gets able support from Presnell, who portrays her gold-prospecting husband. The production is well-staged, and the music of Meredith Wilson is above average although unsensational. Ed Begley, Martita Hunt, Jack Kruschen, and Hermione Baddeley also star. **Director**—Charles Walters. **Academy Award Nominations**—Reynolds, best actress; Daniel L. Fapp, cinematography (color). *128 minutes*

UNTAMED (1955)
★★

Tyrone Power
Susan Hayward

Power woos Hayward in this romantic adventure about a Boer journey through the hostile South African countryside and close encounters with Zulu warriors. The plot gets tedious at times and the romance too complicated, but solid acting will eventually tame the restless viewer. Rita Moreno, Agnes Moorehead, and Henry O'Neill are among the supporting actors. **Director**—Henry King. *110 minutes*

UNTIL SEPTEMBER (1984)
 ★★

Karen Allen
Thierry Lhermitte

Syrupy soap-opera romance about a bright-eyed girl from the Midwest (Allen), temporarily stranded in Paris, who falls in love with a French "Mr. Wonderful" (Lhermitte). Much of the story is devoted to drawn-out, conversational sparring between the lovers, who gradually reveal details of their backgrounds—he's married, she's divorced. The overwrought ending is all too predictable. **Director**—Richard Marquand. (R) *110 minutes*

UP IN SMOKE (1978)
 ★★

Cheech Marin
Tommy Chong

Cheech and Chong make their debut in this uneven comedy based on the rock and marijuana scene. The story is no more than a concoction of the boys' familiar routines of bathroom humor and slapstick sketches, and just about everyone on screen gets high on grass. For many in the audience, it could be a low. Also with Stacy Keach, Tom Skerritt, Edie Adams, and Strother Martin. **Director**—Lou Adler. (R) *86 minutes*

UP THE ACADEMY (1980)
★★

Ron Leibman
Wendell Brown
Tim Citera

This uneven comedy, presented by *Mad* magazine, lampoons the military, blacks, women, Arabs, and other vulnerable targets. The so-so screenplay concerns the misadventures of four students at the unlikely Sheldon R. Weinberg Military Academy. The students tangle with Major Liceman, the school's scowling disciplinarian played with relish by Leibman. When he's on the screen, the film perks up nicely; otherwise, it stumbles along with a "What, me worry?" attitude. **Director**—Robert Downey. (R) *96 minutes*

UP THE CREEK (1984)
 ★

Tim Matheson
Stephen Furst
Dan Monahan

Tim Matheson and Stephen Furst find that they are Up the Creek.

Sophomoric humor dominates this absurd comedy rendered in the tradition of *Animal House*. Matheson stars as a smart-aleck student who leads other misfits on a white-water rafting race in hope of bringing notoriety to their unsung, third-rate college. The kids also engage in the expected girl chasing and boozing. Worn-out, formula, slapstick gags, and amateurish acting eventually send this silly mess down the tubes. **Director**—Robert Butler (R) *99 minutes*

UP THE DOWN STAIRCASE (1967)
★★★

Sandy Dennis

Dennis is sensational as a beleaguered schoolteacher in the New York City school system who tries to overcome the negativism of administrators while solving the problems of her high

- Uptown Saturday Night
- Urban Cowboy
- Used Cars

- The Valachi Papers
- Valley Girl
- The Valley of Decision
- Valley of the Dolls

 U·V

Up the Down Staircase finds teacher Sandy Dennis battling student's problems and administrators.

school students. Although there are weak parts in which there is a shrill emphasis on comedy, it's still one of the best motion pictures about teaching. Also with Ellen O'Mara, Jean Stapleton, Patrick Bedford, Eileen Heckart, Ruth White, Roy Poole, and Sorrel Booke. **Director**—Robert Mulligan.

124 minutes

UPTOWN SATURDAY NIGHT
(1974)
 ★★★

Sidney Poitier
Bill Cosby

Poitier and Cosby star in this uninhibited comedy about their efforts to recover stolen money and a winning lottery ticket before their wives discover that the items are missing. The good-natured performances of this pair get pleasant support from Harry Belafonte, who does an imitation of Marlon Brando's *Godfather* role. The movie also stars Richard Pryor, Flip Wilson, Roscoe Lee Browne, Paula Kelly, and Rosalind Cash. The film, under Poitier's direction and Richard Wesley's script, never makes the mistake of taking itself too seriously. (PG)

104 minutes

URBAN COWBOY (1980)
 ★★

John Travolta

Travolta plays a refinery worker who spends his nights at a huge honky-tonk on the outskirts of Houston, where he acts out his macho cowboy fantasies. Travolta has grown from tough teenager to young man and he still exhibits some special screen magnetism. But this low-key and rather routine melodramatic love story is no equal to the flashy and energetic *Saturday Night Fever* or *Grease*, which starred Travolta at his best. Debra Winger and Scott Glenn give first-rate supporting performances. Also with Bonnie Raitt and the Charlie Daniels Band. **Director**—James Bridges. (PG) *135 minutes*

USED CARS
(1980)
 ★

Kurt Russell
Jack Warden

The idea is intriguing: a comedy about unscrupulous competition between neighboring used-car dealers. But in the hands of writer-director Robert Zemeckis, the film falls apart amid stale jokes, uneven direction, and crude dialogue. The film is mean-spirited, too; the sort that finds humor in someone dying from a heart attack. It's a rusty clunker of a movie that should be relegated to the junk heap. Also with Gerrit Graham. (R) *113 minutes*

V

THE VALACHI PAPERS
(1972)
★

Charles Bronson

Instead of drawing on the available factual information from the life of Mafia informer Joseph Valachi, director Terence Young mistakenly decided to make just another cliché-ridden gangster film. Bronson is competent as Valachi, the gangster who talked about his career in the mob, and Lino Ventura is good in the role of Vito Genovese, but the other performances are as mediocre as the rest of this violent movie. Also with Fred Valleca, Gerald S. O'Loughlin, Joseph Wiseman, and Walter Chiari. (R) *127 minutes*

VALLEY GIRL (1983)
 ★★★

Deborah Foreman
Nicolas Cage

An exceptional and funny teenage movie, smartly directed by Martha Coolidge. Foreman plays a giddy, pampered denizen of the sprawling San Fernando Valley. She agonizes over her precarious involvement with a Hollywood punker—a solid performance by Cage. The script is liberally salted with hip jargon. This film is far superior to the typical teen exploitation movie. Like totally....(R)

95 minutes

THE VALLEY OF DECISION
(1945)
★★

Greer Garson
Gregory Peck

Garson portrays a young woman who becomes a servant in the home of an industrialist and later marries his son, played by Peck. Garson and Peck are fine in this rags-to-riches tale set in Pittsburgh, and there are excellent supporting performances by Donald Crisp, Lionel Barrymore, Preston Foster, Gladys Cooper, and Marsha Hunt. The movie, however, never delivers much excitement. **Director**—Tay Garnett. **Academy Award Nomination**—Garson, best actress.

115 minutes b&w

VALLEY OF THE DOLLS (1967)
★

Barbara Parkins
Patty Duke
Sharon Tate

Three young women—Parkins, Duke, and Tate—decide on a career in show business in this trashy film version of Jacqueline Susann's pulp novel. They are lovely to behold, but their acting is terrible, and no one else in this sorry affair does much better. The old adage that there's no business like show business is pushed to its outer limits in this production; intelligent viewers have no business watching it. Also with Su-
(Continued)

V
- Vanishing Point
- The Velvet Touch
- Vera Cruz
- The Verdict (1946)
- The Verdict (1982)
- Vertigo
- Vice Squad

(Continued)
san Hayward, Paul Burke, Martin Milner, Charles Drake, and Lee Grant. **Director**—Mark Robson. (PG)
123 minutes

VANISHING POINT (1971)

★

**Barry Newman
Cleavon Little**

There are enough serious moments in this silly story about a long car chase from Colorado to California to make one wonder what director Richard C. Sarafian had in mind. Newman stars as the driver of the car, and Little plays a blind, black disc jockey who helps him avoid the police. Victoria Medlin, Dean Jagger, Bob Donner, and Paul Koslo appear in supporting roles. Fans of rock will appreciate the music. (PG)
107 minutes

THE VELVET TOUCH (1948)

★★

Rosalind Russell

Russell stars in this murder mystery as a stage actress who kills her producer. Her conscience prevails at about the same time the detective assigned to the case solves the crime. The cast also includes Leo Genn, Sydney Greenstreet, Frank McHugh, Claire Trevor, and Leon Ames. The theater scenes add to the film's appeal. **Director**—John Gage. *97 minutes b&w*

VERA CRUZ (1954)

★★★

**Gary Cooper
Burt Lancaster**

Cooper and Lancaster provide the energy and pace that keeps this western from being ordinary. They play adventurers who become involved in the plot to unseat Emperor Maximilian from power in Mexico. Cesar Romero, George Macready, Ernest Borgnine, Denise Darcel, Charles Bronson, and Sarita Montiel appear in supporting roles and don't detract from the enjoyment of the film. **Director**—Robert Aldrich. *94 minutes*

THE VERDICT (1946)

★★

**Sydney Greenstreet
Peter Lorre**

There are so many tricky twists and turns in this murder mystery that, at times, it seems that Greenstreet and Lorre don't even know what comes next. These veterans are excellent in this film about an ex-Scotland Yard inspector, played by Greenstreet, who continues to work on a strange case despite his forced retirement. Good acting, however, can't salvage an overly contrived detective yarn. The cast also includes Joan Lorring, Arthur Shields, George Coulouris, Paul Cavanagh, Rosalind Ivan, and Holmes Herbert. **Director**—Don Siegel. *86 minutes b&w*

THE VERDICT (1982)

★★★★

Paul Newman

Jack Warden primes Paul Newman for trial combat in The Verdict.

Paul Newman stars as a down-and-out lawyer who is presented with one final chance to regain his self-esteem: a lawsuit involving a Catholic hospital and a lot of behind-the-scenes political pressure. Newman is superb as he spins with compassion and obvious conviction into the courtroom maneuvers. Director Sidney Lumet is able to create tension and maintain a vigorous pace even though the action is limited to only a few locales. The impressive supporting cast includes Charlotte Rampling, Jack Warden, Milo O'Shea, and James Mason. Enjoyable and convincing (if you don't watch it with a real lawyer). (R) **Academy Award Nominations**—best picture; Newman, best actor; Mason, best supporting actor; Lumet, best director; David Mamet, best screenplay (adapted from another medium).
128 minutes

VERTIGO (1958)

★★★★

**James Stewart
Kim Novak**

Kim Novak makes James Stewart forget all about his Vertigo.

This Alfred Hitchcock thriller about a detective who's drawn into a complex plot because he fears heights is arguably the director's best film, and one of the most nearly perfect films ever made. Each piece of the puzzle is fascinating in its own right, and the whole is greater than all its parts. Though romance plays a part in many of his other films, you feel Hitchcock put his heart and soul into this one. The result is a haunting study with Stewart as the unraveling detective and Novak as the mystery woman who loves and betrays him. Barbara Bel Geddes, Henry Jones, and Tom Helmore help to make this a superb cinema experience. *120 minutes*

VICE SQUAD (1982)

★★

**Season Hubley
Gary Swanson**

This gripping police drama, set against the seedy underworld of night-

• Victor/Victoria   • Videodrome   • Vigilante
• Victory   • The View from Pompey's   • The Vikings
           Head   • Village of the Damned

V

time Los Angeles, is typical sensational fare designed to exploit mindless brutality. But there are some remarkable virtues among the grim torture and killing—an imaginative, fast-paced script and decent acting by a rather unknown cast. Hubley performs ably as a "good girl" prostitute who's threatened by a sadistic pimp, played by Wings Hauser. Swanson is convincing as a cynical vice squad cop. **Director**—Gary A. Sherman. (R)

94 minutes

VICTOR/VICTORIA (1982)
★★★

Julie Andrews
Robert Preston
James Garner
Lesley Ann Warren

Robert Preston and Julie Andrews are buddies in Victor/Victoria.

Blake Edwards's spicy, breezy farce stars Andrews as a down-and-out singer in Paris in 1934 who impersonates a man impersonating a woman. That's heady stuff for the once prim Julie, and although she can't really convince us that she's a man she entertains just the same. There are fine performances, too, by Preston as a gay nightclub entertainer and Garner as an American gangster. Warren steals several scenes as Garner's dumb blonde girl friend. (PG) **Academy Award Nominations**—Andrews, best actress; Preston, best supporting actor; Warren, best supporting actress; Edwards, best screenplay (based on material from another medium).

133 minutes

VICTORY (1981)
★★

Michael Caine
Sylvester Stallone

Allied POWs and a professional German soccer team vie for athletic victory in a jam-packed Paris stadium in this World War II escape drama. The banal screenplay smacks of *Hogan's Heroes*, and the sentimental attitudes about winning the game strain credibility. However, the film, directed by John Huston, comes to life when the players take the field with legendary soccer great Pelé going through his extraordinary maneuvers. (PG)

110 minutes

VIDEODROME (1983)
★★

James Woods
Deborah Harry

This complex shocker about futuristic TV revels in high-tech horror and lurid effects. Woods stars as an unconventional TV executive seeking the source of a sadistic video program that causes hallucinations and brain tumors. The frantic story begins well enough but soon heads toward exploitative sleaze and gore. Pop singer Harry co-stars as a bizarre radio talk-show guru. **Director**—David Cronenberg. (R)

88 minutes

THE VIEW FROM POMPEY'S HEAD (1955)
★★★

Richard Egan
Dana Wynter

Where does soap opera end and the fabric of great drama begin? This movie about a New York City-based lawyer who returns to his small southern hometown on business and falls in love again with an old girl friend touches on the eternal issues of love and a death quite artfully, although it does get slightly soapy at times. Egan plays the lawyer, and Wynter is his sweetheart. Sidney Blackmer, Marjorie Rambeau, and Cameron Mitchell are fine in supporting performances. **Director**—Philip Dunne. *97 minutes*

VIGILANTE (1983)
★

Robert Forster
Fred Williamson

Thugs stalk the streets of a big city preying at will on innocent citizens. The cops are inept, and the courts rule in favor of the criminals. Justice prevails only when the victims personally take their bloody revenge on the villains. This theme was exploited in the *Death Wish* films and here it's hyped up with even greater cynicism and violence. A low blow, indeed, for due process of law. **Director**—William Lustig. (R)   *Running time not available*

THE VIKINGS (1958)
★★

Kirk Douglas
Tony Curtis
Janet Leigh

If you've seen one Viking adventure, you've probably seen them all. This one, however, has a strong cast with Douglas, Curtis, and Leigh in starring roles and vivid on-location photography in Norway. Action fans should enjoy the battle sequences and the invasion of England by the Vikings. Also with Ernest Borgnine, Maxine Audley, and Frank Thring. **Director**—Richard Fleischer. *115 minutes*

VILLAGE OF THE DAMNED (1960)
★★★

George Sanders
Barbara Shelley

Barbara Shelley and George Sanders kiss in Village of the Damned.

This low-budget, well-made chiller proves beyond a doubt that good movies need not be costly. There isn't a wasted motion in this story about an English village terrorized by strange children. Sanders and Shelley star in

(Continued)

V

- The Violent Men
- The V.I.P.s
- Virginia City
- Visiting Hours
- Visit to a Small Planet
- Viva Las Vegas
- Viva Zapata!

(Continued)
the movie, based on John Wyndham's novel *The Midwich Cuckoos*. Also with Martin Stephens, Michael Gwynn, Laurence Naismith, John Phillips, and Richard Vernon. This one may rivet you to your seat. **Director**—Wolf Rilla.
78 minutes b&w

THE VIOLENT MEN (1955)
★★

Edward G. Robinson
Barbara Stanwyck

Robinson portrays a corrupt, crippled cattle baron in this western saga that shows some promise before falling flat. Stanwyck plays his wife. Robinson, Stanwyck, and Glenn Ford provide good performances, and Brian Keith, Basil Ruysdael, Dianne Foster, Richard Jaeckel, and May Wynn are fine in supporting roles. The action sequences highlight the movie. **Director**—Rudolph Maté.
96 minutes

THE V.I.P.s (1963)
★★★

Richard Burton
Elizabeth Taylor
Maggie Smith
Rod Taylor

Louis Jourdan says hey while Richard Burton tells Elizabeth Taylor what a tramp she is in The V.I.P.s.

Quality acting and an excellent script by famed British writer Terence Rattigan make this story about passengers stranded at a London airport because of fog excellent entertainment. Under less competent direction it would be a soap opera, but the characters and their adventures prove to be very believable. Margaret Rutherford is the star among stars, but Burton, Eliza-

beth Taylor, Smith, Rod Taylor, Louis Jourdan, Orson Welles, and Elsa Martinelli also shine. Many other famous actors make an appearance. **Director**—Anthony Asquith. **Academy Award**—Rutherford, best supporting actress.
119 minutes

VIRGINIA CITY (1940)
★★

Errol Flynn
Randolph Scott
Miriam Hopkins
Humphrey Bogart

Flynn, Scott, Hopkins, and Bogart star in this Civil War western about a plot to steal a gold shipment for the Confederate cause. There's an uneven quality to the movie, as if there were five or six directors instead of just Michael Curtiz. The movie was intended as a serious western, but the action sequences are the best part of the film—so much for creating movies by committee. Also with Frank McHugh, Alan Hale, Douglass Dumbrille, and Guinn Williams.
121 minutes b&w

VISITING HOURS (1982)
 ★★

Lee Grant
Michael Ironside

Grant stars as an opinionated television reporter who is being relentlessly pursued by a knife-wielding psychotic (Ironside). The madman is so determined to kill Grant that he pursues her into a hospital where she is recovering from his earlier assault. The cliché-rife suspense story has its tense moments, but the hackneyed plot is strictly déjà vu. There are occasional references to the slasher's troubles with his mother. Nothing new or astounding here. **Director**—Jean Claude Lord. (R)
103 minutes

VISIT TO A SMALL PLANET (1960)
★

Jerry Lewis

Believe it or not this silly Lewis film is based on an urbane, satirical Gore Vidal play, in which a being from outer space visits Earth to get an insight into

our strange habits. Lewis is the alien creature, and he plays the part for heavy-handed laughs as slapstick prevails. Joan Blackman, Earl Holliman, Fred Clark, Lee Patrick, Gale Gordon, John Williams, and Jerome Cowan appear in supporting roles and don't prevail. Even Vidal deserves better treatment than this. **Director**—Norman Taurog.
87 minutes b&w

VIVA LAS VEGAS (1964)
 ★★

Elvis Presley
Ann-Margret

Run-of-the-mill star vehicle for Elvis Presley who sings and races a sports car. The glitter of the gambling city plus some exciting racing scenes perk up the proceedings. Ann-Margret is excellent as a cabaret dancer who attracts Presley's attention. Cesare Danova and William Demarest are also in the cast. **Director**—George Sidney.
86 minutes

VIVA ZAPATA! (1952)
★★★★

Marlon Brando
Jean Peters
Anthony Quinn

Marlon Brando and Jean Peters in the provocative classic Viva Zapata!

Brando, Peters, and Quinn are splendid in this classic about a Mexican peasant who becomes the president of his country during the Mexican Revolution. Brando plays Emiliano Zapata, and Quinn plays his brother. John Steinbeck's script is provocative without being preachy, and under Elia Kazan's superb direction the agony as well as the glory of the revolution is clearly presented. Joseph Wiseman,

- Voices
- Von Ryan's Express
- Voyage of the Damned
- Voyage to the Bottom of the Sea
- Wabash Avenue
- The Wackiest Ship in the Army
- Waitress

V·W

Arnold Moss, Frank Silvera, Margo, and Mildred Dunnock are fine in supporting roles. **Academy Award**—Quinn, best supporting actor. **Nominations**—Brando, best actor; Steinbeck, writing (story and screenplay). *113 minutes b&w*

VOICES (1979)
★★

**Michael Ontkean
Amy Irving**

A lackluster boy-meets-girl story about a young musician who falls in love with an overprotected deaf woman. The film is cluttered with contrived subplots. Ontkean, as the struggling rock singer, seems stifled in his role. The only appeal is from Irving as the girl who realizes her dream to become a ballerina despite her handicap. It all takes place in Hoboken, New Jersey. Also with Alex Rocco, Barry Miller, and Viveca Lindfors. **Director**— Robert Markowitz. (PG)
107 minutes

VON RYAN'S EXPRESS (1965)
 ★★★★

**Frank Sinatra
Trevor Howard**

Frank Sinatra and Trevor Howard star in the war drama Von Ryan's Express.

This action yarn about a group of prisoners who escape from an Italian POW camp is made memorable when they take over a German freight train in their bid for freedom. Sinatra is splendidly cast as an American colonel, leading English prisoners in their escape. Howard plays an English officer outranked by Sinatra. There are fine performances, too, from Sergio Fantoni, Edward Mulhare, Raffaella

Carra, and Brad Dexter. **Director**—Mark Robson. *117 minutes*

VOYAGE OF THE DAMNED (1976)
 ★★★

**Faye Dunaway
Oskar Werner
Max Von Sydow
Orson Welles**

Faye Dunaway and Oskar Werner screw up and book passage on the Voyage of the Damned.

This compelling melodrama deals with a tragic World War II episode, when a shipload of Jews sailed from Germany to Cuba only to be returned to face death. The film plods through a parade of soap-opera-like vignettes, yet the historical subject matter is so vital and absorbing that the ponderous form can be forgiven. A huge all-star cast portrays the doomed passengers and the onshore characters. Such luminaries as Welles and José Ferrer are there for fleeting moments. Dunaway and Von Sydow are outstanding in more significant roles. Also with Malcolm McDowell, James Mason, and Lee Grant. **Director**—Stuart Rosenberg. (PG) **Academy Award Nomination**—Grant, best supporting actress; Steve Shagan and David Butler, best screenplay adaptation.
134 minutes

VOYAGE TO THE BOTTOM OF THE SEA (1961)
★★

**Walter Pidgeon
Robert Sterling
Joan Fontaine**

Excellent trick photography and entertaining action sequences make this science-fiction tale worthwhile for fans of such movies. The adventures

of the atomic submarine assigned to destroy a radiation belt that threatens the planet are superficial by and large, but the acting of Pidgeon, Sterling, Fontaine, Peter Lorre, Frankie Avalon, and Barbara Eden make the sub's mission seem more important than it really is. **Director**—Irwin Allen.
105 minutes

W

WABASH AVENUE (1950)
★★★

**Betty Grable
Victor Mature
Phil Harris**

Mature and Harris have designs on Grable in this musical set during the 1892 Chicago World's Fair. Grable sparkles as she sings, dances, and tries to decide which man she'll have in her life in this colorful production. The cast also includes Reginald Gardiner, Margaret Hamilton, James Barton, and Barry Kelley. **Director**—Henry Koster. *92 minutes*

THE WACKIEST SHIP IN THE ARMY (1960)
★★

**Jack Lemmon
Ricky Nelson**

This entertaining movie, starring Lemmon and Nelson, treads a thin line between comedy and serious drama. It involves a reconditioned sailing ship that an inexperienced crew plans to use to land an agent behind Japanese lines in the South Pacific during World War II. Also with John Lund, Chips Rafferty, Joby Baker, and Tom Tully. **Director**—Richard Murphy. *99 minutes*

WAITRESS (1982)
 ★

**Carol Drake
June Martin
Renata Majer**

Crude and corny slapstick abounds in this jumbled comedy about waitresses
(Continued)

W

- Wait 'til the Sun Shines, Nellie
- Wake Me When It's Over
- Wake of the Red Witch

- Walk a Crooked Mile
- Walk, Don't Run
- Walking My Baby Back Home

- Walking Tall
- Walking Tall—Part 2

(Continued)
who aspire to more glamorous careers. The stale humor involves numerous food fights and the dopey, rapid-fire dialogue is delivered mostly at a shout. The producers appear to be trying to capture the *Animal House* style. Not with this mess, they won't. **Director**—Samuel Weil. (R)   *87 minutes*

WAIT 'TIL THE SUN SHINES, NELLIE (1952)
★★★

David Wayne
Jean Peters

Wayne and Peters star in this wholesome story about a small-town barber, played by Wayne, in the early 1900s. The characterizations of all the cast members are on the mark, and Wayne is superb in his portrayal of a typical American's life. Hugh Marlowe, Warren Stevens, Albert Dekker, Helene Stanley, and Alan Hale, Jr., are among the supporting actors. **Director**—Henry King.   *108 minutes*

WAKE ME WHEN IT'S OVER (1960)
★★

Ernie Kovacs
Dick Shawn

Kovacs and Shawn try a bit too hard to be funny in this comedy about soldiers who establish a luxury hotel on a Pacific island, using U.S. Army supplies. The cast also includes Jack Warden, Margo Moore, Robert Emhardt, Nobu McCarthy, and Don Knotts. **Director**—Mervyn Le Roy.   *126 minutes*

WAKE OF THE RED WITCH (1948)
★★★

John Wayne
Luther Adler

Missing pearls, combative treasure-seekers, and an alluring woman yield a standard adventure film and some action scenes. Wayne and Adler play two treasure-seekers. The story gets confusing at times, as the men seek their fortune in the East Indies, but there are enough good sequences

Gig Young, Gail Russell, and John Wayne check out the area in Wake of the Red Witch.

to make the viewing worthwhile. Gail Russell, Gig Young, Dennis Hoey, Henry Daniell, and Paul Fix also appear in supporting roles. **Director**—Edward Ludwig.   *106 minutes b&w*

WALK A CROOKED MILE (1948)
★★

Louis Hayward
Dennis O'Keefe

Hayward and O'Keefe star in this conventional semidocumentary melodrama. British and FBI agents search for a spy who's giving U.S. atomic secrets to the Russians. The story, which has been told many times before and since, is rather routine. It seems as if standard sets are kept handy just for such movies. Also with Louise Allbritton, Onslow Stevens, and Raymond Burr. **Director**—Gordon Douglas.
91 minutes b&w

WALK, DON'T RUN (1966)
★★

Cary Grant
Samantha Eggar
Jim Hutton

Only the charm and comic acting skills of Grant salvage this witless farce about two men and a young woman who share an apartment in Tokyo during the 1964 Olympics. Instead of winning the girl, this time Grant is a matchmaker and helps Eggar and Hutton find love; the viewer will find boredom. After this film, Grant retired from movies. John Standing, Ted Hartley, and Miiko Taka appear in supporting roles. **Director**—Charles Walters.   *114 minutes*

WALKING MY BABY BACK HOME (1953)
★★

Donald O'Connor
Janet Leigh
Buddy Hackett

O'Connor, Leigh, and Hackett brighten this lightweight musical, but they can't restore the tarnished plot. The dancing of O'Connor and Leigh is pleasant to see, and the music is fairly entertaining although often secondrate. Hackett's brand of comedy is funny more often than not. Also with Lori Nelson, Scatman Crothers, John Hubbard, and Kathleen Lockhart. **Director**—Lloyd Bacon.   *95 minutes*

WALKING TALL (1973)
★★★

Joe Don Baker
Elizabeth Hartman

This highly successful but too violent movie vividly depicts the courageous stand of Tennessee sheriff Buford Pusser against mobsters. The movie might have been even better without the emphasis on blood and gore. The story of a hero, however, remains. Baker is believable in the role of Pusser, and Hartman portrays his wife, who's murdered by the local mob. Noah Beery, Jr., Gene Evans, and Felton Perry appear in supporting roles. **Director**—Phil Karlson. (R)
125 minutes

WALKING TALL—PART 2 (1975)
★★

Bo Svenson

A continuation of the legend of Buford Pusser, the big-stick-wielding Tennessee sheriff who was determined to rid his community of the bad guys. Svenson takes over for Joe Don Baker in the lead role of this watered-down expansion of the popular and financially successful original film. Shot on location in Tennessee. Also with Luke Askew, Richard Jaeckel, Noah Berry, Jr., and Robert DoQui. **Director**—Earl Bellamy. (PG)   *109 minutes*

• A Walk in the Sun
• Walk on the Wild Side
• Walk Proud
• Walk the Proud Land
• The Waltz of the Toreadors
• The Wanderers
• War and Peace

W

A WALK IN THE SUN (1946)

 ★★★★

**Dana Andrews
Richard Conte
Sterling Holloway
John Ireland**

In A Walk in the Sun, *Dana Andrews comes to the aid of a frightened Lloyd Bridges.*

Honest characterizations by fine actors amid realistic settings make this one of the finest war films in cinema history. Andrews, Conte, Holloway, and Ireland star in the story of an Army platoon of infantrymen in Italy who must attack a German-held farmhouse. The production avoids the superficiality of so many war movies by stressing the human element over battlefield action. Also with George Tyne, Herbert Rudley, Richard Benedict, Norman Lloyd, Lloyd Bridges, and Huntz Hall. **Director**—Lewis Milestone. *117 minutes b&w*

WALK ON THE WILD SIDE (1962)

★

**Jane Fonda
Capucine
Barbara Stanwyck
Laurence Harvey**

This self-conscious piece of trash misrepresents perversion for characterization. Stanwyck plays a lesbian madam of a brothel, Fonda and Capucine portray prostitutes, and Harvey is a troubled man in search of his lost love. None of them lifts this production beyond the potboiler level. The movie is based on one of Nelson Algren's better novels; unfortunately, the story was left behind, and just the

seamy elements were brought to the screen. Also with Anne Baxter and Richard Rust. **Director**—Edward Dmytryk. *114 minutes b&w*

WALK PROUD
(1979)

★★

**Robby Benson
Sarah Holcomb**

Soft-spoken, clean-cut Benson plays a tough Chicano youth in this gang movie that leans heavily on *West Side Story*. Despite heavy makeup and an all-too-obvious accent, Benson is unconvincing in this portrayal, which is far removed from his typical wholesome kid characters. The déjà vu plot focuses on Benson's conflict between his love of an Anglo girl, played by Holcomb, and his loyalty to his gang friends. Also with Henry Darrow, Domingo Ambriz, and Pepe Serna. **Director**—Robert Collins. (PG) *102 minutes*

WALK THE PROUD LAND
(1956)

★★

Audie Murphy

Murphy is in fine form in this sensitive western as an Indian agent attempting to bring peace between the Apaches and white settlers. Some of the dialogue is riddled with clichés, but there are enough good scenes to keep most viewers interested. Also with Anne Bancroft, Pat Crowley, Robert Warwick, Charles Drake, Tommy Rall, and Jay Silverheels. **Director**—Jesse Hibbs. *88 minutes*

THE WALTZ OF THE
TOREADORS (1962)

 ★★

Peter Sellers

The translation of Jean Anouilh's saucy comedy from stage to the screen is mishandled. However, Sellers, playing a lecherous retired general, does a fine job as he tries to keep his young mistress away from his son. The movie is interesting, although the vibrance of the play is missing. Also with Mar-

garet Leighton, Dany Robin, John Fraser, Prunella Scales, and Cyril Cusack. **Director**—John Guillermin. *105 minutes*

THE WANDERERS (1979)

 ★★

**Ken Wahl
John Friedrich
Karen Allen**

A disoriented gang movie about growing up absurd in the Bronx in the '60s. The film, based on the novel by Richard Price, is a chop-suey affair of blaring vignettes. The Wanderers are Italian youths who try to survive in the city jungle among the fearsome Irish Ducky Boys, the grotesque Fordham Baldies, and other adversaries. Although the movie is overbearing, the young novice cast is rather appealing. Also with Alan Rosenberg, Linda Manz, and Toni Kalem. **Director**—Philip Kaufman. (R) *113 minutes*

WAR AND PEACE (1956)

 ★★

**Audrey Hepburn
Henry Fonda
Mel Ferrer
Herbert Lom
John Mills**

A young soldier says goodbye before battle in War and Peace.

This film version of Leo Tolstoy's great novel about Russia during the time of Napoleon's invasion is presented like a

(Continued)

 Movie is available in Beta and VHS videotape

W

• War Games
• WarGames
• Warlock
• Warlords of Atlantis

• The Warriors
• The War Wagon
• The Watcher in the Woods

(Continued)

Cecil B. De Mille Bible epic—there's too much emphasis on sweeping battle scenes and other spectacles. Because of this misplaced focus, Tolstoy's brilliant characterizations are lost despite an excellent cast of actors that also includes Barry Jones, Oscar Homolka, Wilfrid Lawson, Vittorio Gassman, Anita Ekberg, Helmut Dantine, and Mai Britt. **Directors**—King Vidor and Mario Soldati. **Academy Award Nominations**—Vidor, best director; Jack Cardiff, cinematography (color).

208 minutes

WAR GAMES

See Suppose They Gave a War and Nobody Came

WARGAMES
(1983)

★★★★

Matthew Broderick
Ally Sheedy
Dabney Coleman

Matthew Broderick and Ally Sheedy are working on their grades in WarGames.

A timely, on-target black comedy about a high school computer whiz (Broderick) who accidentally accesses the military's air defense computer system and touches off a panic. It's an exciting movie that offers much food for thought about thermonuclear war as the ultimate no-win situation. John Badham directs briskly. (PG) **Academy Award Nominations**—Lawrence Lasker and Walter F. Parkes, best original screenplay; William A. Fraker, cinematography. *110 minutes*

WARLOCK (1959)

★★★

Henry Fonda
Richard Widmark
Anthony Quinn

Fonda, Widmark, and Quinn star in this story that has more characterization than the typical western. Fonda plays a gunfighter hired to bring law and order to a small western town. The movie focuses on his rise when he succeeds in removing the bad guys and his fall when his friend, played by Quinn, betrays him. Some might object to the overuse of symbolism and excessive number of subplots. Also with Dorothy Malone, Richard Arlen, and Regis Toomey. **Director**—Edward Dmytryk. *123 minutes*

WARLORDS OF ATLANTIS
(1978)

★

Doug McClure
Cyd Charisse

A group of explorers visit the lost continent of Atlantis, where they encounter all sorts of makeshift monster creatures that look like they were borrowed from Macy's Thanksgiving Day parade. The dialogue is just as shabby. This is merely another B-movie with little inspiration, as demonstrated by one predictable scene that has a giant octopus attacking the explorers' ship. Also with Pete Gilmore, Daniel Massey, and Shane Rimmer. **Director**—Kevin Connor. (PG) *96 minutes*

THE WARRIORS (1979)

★★

Michael Beck
Thomas Waites

Youth gangs roam New York City's streets and subways in this glossy film that looks like a contemporary *A Clockwork Orange*. The story focuses on one gang, which is falsely accused of murder. They spend the movie making a dash for their home turf in Coney Island while being chased by rival gangs and the cops. There's lots of headbashing along the way, but not much good acting by the cast of unknowns.

Walter Hill's direction, however, is slick and spectacular. Also with Dorsey Wright, Brian Tyler, and Deborah Van Valkenburgh. (R) *90 minutes*

THE WAR WAGON (1967)

★★★

John Wayne
Kirk Douglas

John Wayne and Kirk Douglas set out to rob The War Wagon.

Wayne and Douglas are at their best in this western about an ex-con, played by Wayne, bent on revenge. Wayne teams up with Douglas to rob an armored wagon filled with gold; he believes it rightfully belongs to him. The plot is weak, but the action and solid performances will keep your interest. The excellent cast also includes Howard Keel, Robert Walker, Keenan Wynn, Bruce Dern, Gene Evans, Bruce Cabot, and Joanna Barnes. **Director**—Burt Kennedy. *99 minutes*

THE WATCHER IN THE WOODS (1980)

★★

Bette Davis
Carroll Baker

Davis and Baker star in this flimsy and silly suspense movie from the Walt Disney studio. It's about an American family that rents an old house in England and becomes involved with a supernatural mystery. The film maintains tension, but it's chock full of contrived scare effects that strain credibility. Davis has a minor role as the crusty landlady of the strange house where her daughter mysteriously vanished 30 years ago. She's terrific despite the nonsensical material. Also, with Lynn-Holly Johnson, Kyle Richards, and David McCallum. **Director**—John Hough. (PG)   *100 minutes*

WATCH ON THE RHINE (1943)

 ★★★

Paul Lukas
Bette Davis

Bette Davis and Paul Lukas in Watch on the Rhine, *set during World War II.*

Parts of this film seem superficial now, and propaganda gets in the way of some dramatic situations, but the brilliant performances of Lukas and Davis still brighten the movie. Lukas portrays a German underground leader confronted by Nazis wherever he goes—even Washington, D.C. Davis plays his wife. The movie is based on Lillian Hellman's play, and the film script was written by Dashiell Hammett, her good friend of many years. The excellent cast also includes Lucile Watson, George Coulouris, Henry Daniell, Donald Woods, and Geraldine Fitzgerald. **Director**—Herman Shumlin. **Academy Award**—Lukas, best actor. **Nominations**—best picture; Watson, best supporting actress; Hammett, writing (screenplay).

114 minutes b&w

WATERLOO (1970)

★

Rod Steiger
Christopher Plummer

The title, of course, refers to one of the most famous military encounters in

history. Unfortunately, the movie treats this piece of history as just another historical-action flick, and the mediocre performances reflect the dreary plot. Plummer is competent as the victorious Wellington who defeats Napoleon, but Steiger, as the famed French leader, delivers a losing performance. Other good actors lost in the enterprise include Jack Hawkins, Virginia McKenna, Orson Welles, Ian Ogilvy, Michael Wilding, and Dan O'Herlihy. **Director**—Sergei Bondarchuk. (G)   *123 minutes*

WATERMELON MAN (1970)

★★

Godfrey Cambridge

Cambridge stars in this comedy about a bigoted white insurance salesman who wakes up one morning to discover he's suddenly black. Once the impact of the funny and preposterous premise subsides, the movie drags, and some of the inherent social satire is weakened. Also with Estelle Parsons, Howard Caine, Mantan Moreland, Kay Kimberly, and D'Urville Martin. **Director**—Melvin Van Peebles. (R)   *100 minutes*

WATERSHIP DOWN (1978)

 ★★

This is an animated fantasy about rabbits based on Richard Adams's bestselling novel. No, it doesn't star Bugs Bunny. This is a serious story, with the cottontails fleeing their burrow because of man's encroachment. In their painful search for a new home, the rabbits are attacked by dogs, snared, ravaged by hawks, and set upon by other rabbits. It's perhaps too gruesome and unrelenting for children and somewhat unsophisticated for most adults. Sir Ralph Richardson and Zero Mostel provide some of the voices. **Director**—Martin Rosen. (PG)

92 minutes

THE WAY WE WERE (1973)

 ★★★

Barbra Streisand
Robert Redford

Robert Redford and Barbra Streisand have a rocky but passionate relationship in The Way We Were.

The splendid performances of Streisand and Redford sustain this nostalgic journey from the 1930s to the 1950s, including the McCarthy era. Parts of the film are worthwhile, such as when Streisand and Redford fall in love. But some of the nostalgia turns to mush, and the movie isn't a particularly accurate portrayal of the period. Bradford Dillman, Lois Chiles, Murray Hamilton, Patrick O'Neal, and Viveca Lindfors are fine in supporting roles. **Director**—Sydney Pollack. (PG) **Academy Award Nominations**—Streisand, best actress; Harry Stradling, Jr., cinematography.   *118 minutes*

A WEDDING (1978)

★★★

Carol Burnett
Desi Arnaz, Jr.
Amy Stryker

Innovative director Robert Altman reveals a host of family emotions and crises during an extraordinary wedding day. The tart, energetic comedy is rich with Altman's gems of insight and satire about marriage, religion, and middle-class values. A first-rate cast includes many newcomers with the veterans; they all do a great job. Altman fans won't be disappointed. Also with Vittorio Gassman, Geraldine Chaplin, Mia Farrow, Paul Dooley, Lillian Gish, and Howard Duff. (PG)

125 minutes

W
- Weekend at the Waldorf
- We of the Never Never
- We're No Angels
- We're Not Married
- The Westerner
- Western Union
- West Side Story

WEEKEND AT THE WALDORF
(1945)
★★

**Ginger Rogers
Walter Pidgeon
Van Johnson
Lana Turner**

This pleasant entertainment is a weak sister of the famous *Grand Hotel*, with less competent actors in a New York setting. If you don't expect too much, the characters at New York's largest hotel are interesting enough. The cast also includes Keenan Wynn, Robert Benchley, Edward Arnold, and Phyllis Thaxter. **Director**—Robert Z. Leonard.
130 minutes b&w

WE OF THE NEVER NEVER
(1983)
★★

**Angela Punch McGregor
Arthur Dignam
Tony Barry**

Arthur Dignam pesters aborigine chieftain Donald Blitner in We of the Never Never.

From Australia, a visually magnificent film with a familiar plot reminiscent of many a western. McGregor stars as the city-reared bride who follows her cattleman husband to the outback. There she struggles to overcome the prejudices of both the aborigines and the white ranch hands. Director Igo Auzins concentrates on majestic scenery and period details at the expense of dramatic involvement. (G)
136 minutes

WE'RE NO ANGELS (1955)
 ★★★

**Humphrey Bogart
Peter Ustinov
Aldo Ray**

Bogart, Ustinov, and Ray are delightful in this lighthearted story about three escapees from Devil's Island who help a beleaguered shopkeeper prosper and outwit his foes. The production would have been better, however, if the Albert Husson play wasn't adapted to the screen so literally. Joan Bennett, Basil Rathbone, John Smith, and Leo G. Carroll star in supporting roles. **Director**—Michael Curtiz.
106 minutes

WE'RE NOT MARRIED (1952)
★★★

**Ginger Rogers
Fred Allen
Victor Moore
Paul Douglas**

The ingenious premise of this film—five married couples are advised that their marriages are not legal—provides the fodder for a fine comedy with a provocative message. Married viewers will find themselves asking: How would I react if I got such a notice? The film, written by famed screenwriter Nunnally Johnson, is presented in five sequences, with the Allen and Rogers scene surpassing the others. The all-star cast also includes Eddie Bracken, James Gleason, Jane Darwell, Eve Arden, Marilyn Monroe, David Wayne, Louis Calhern, Mitzi Gaynor, and Zsa Zsa Gabor. **Director**—Edmund Goulding.
85 minutes b&w

THE WESTERNER (1940)
★★★

**Gary Cooper
Walter Brennan**

Cooper and Brennan star in this tale about land disputes and the problems they caused in the Old West. And Brennan shines in the role of Judge Roy Bean. Also with Fred Stone, Dana Andrews, Chill Wills, Doris Davenport, Forrest Tucker, Tom Tyler, Charles Halton, and Lillian Bond. **Director**—William Wyler. **Academy Award**—Brennan, best supporting actor. **Nomination**—Stuart N. Lake, writing (original story). *98 minutes b&w*

WESTERN UNION (1941)
★★★

**Randolph Scott
Robert Young
Dean Jagger**

This intelligent western, based on the Zane Grey novel, pinpoints the problems involved in constructing the first coast-to-coast Western Union wire in 1861. Scott, Young, and Jagger give polished performances, with Virginia Gilmore, Barton MacLane, John Carradine, and Chill Wills in supporting roles. **Director**—Fritz Lang.
94 minutes

WEST SIDE STORY (1961)
 ★★★★

**Natalie Wood
Richard Beymer
Russ Tamblyn
Rita Moreno
George Chakiris**

Richard Beymer and Natalie Wood practice their nuptials in West Side Story.

This dynamite musical remains fresh and vibrant many years after its release. Wood and Beymer seem slightly miscast at times in this story about rival gangs in a New York ghetto, but Moreno, Chakiris, and Tamblyn are superb. The excellent on-location photography enhances the Romeo and Juliet theme, and the Leonard Bernstein-Stephen Sondheim music is icing on the cake. **Directors**—Robert Wise and Jerome Robbins. **Academy Awards**—best picture; Wise and Robbins, best director; Chakiris, best supporting,

- Westworld
- What Did You Do in the War, Daddy?
- What Ever Happened to Baby Jane?
- What Price Glory?
- What's New, Pussycat?
- What's Up Doc?
- The Wheeler Dealers

W

actor; Moreno, best supporting actress; Daniel L. Fapp, cinematography (color). **Nomination**—Ernest Lehman, best screenplay (based on material from another medium). *155 minutes*

WESTWORLD (1973)

 ★★★

**Yul Brynner
Richard Benjamin
James Brolin**

Brynner portrays a robot who runs amok at a futuristic vacation resort that offers fantasies in this engaging science-fiction film. Brynner is as competent as an actor can be playing a robot. Benjamin and Brolin are fine as 21st-century men whose fantasy about the Wild West becomes real when the robot starts to stalk them. Victoria Shaw, Norman Bartold, and Alan Oppenheimer appear in supporting roles. **Director**—Michael Crichton. (PG)
90 minutes

WHAT DID YOU DO IN THE WAR, DADDY? (1966)

★★

**James Coburn
Dick Shawn**

A competent cast is unable to brighten this inane comedy about a group of American soldiers who must convince the eccentric residents of an Italian town during World War II that it's time to give up. The weak comedy that does emerge is keyed to the terms of surrender that the Italians seek. Also with Harry Morgan, Aldo Ray, Sergio Fantoni, Giovanna Ralli, Leon Askin, and Carroll O'Connor. **Director**—Blake Edwards. *119 minutes*

WHAT EVER HAPPENED TO BABY JANE? (1962)

 ★★★

**Bette Davis
Joan Crawford
Victor Buono**

This grim and chilling black comedy about an ex-child movie star who tortures her crippled sister and eventually kills her is made interesting by the excellent acting of Davis, Crawford, and Buono. If the plot had been better

Bette Davis shows us What Ever Happened to Baby Jane?.

constructed and if the movie was cut by about 30 minutes—with improved editing—it could have been a gem. Also with Anna Lee and Marjorie Bennett. **Director**—Robert Aldrich. **Academy Award Nominations**—Davis, best actress; Buono, best supporting actor; Ernest Hall, cinematography (black and white). *132 minutes b&w*

WHAT PRICE GLORY? (1952)

★★

**James Cagney
Dan Dailey
Corinne Calvet**

Energetic performances by Cagney and Dailey brighten this remake of the silent film classic about two tough Marines in love with the same woman in France during World War I. Calvet is the woman they love. The original film was better because it made a brilliant antiwar statement, but this version has some good moments, too. The cast also includes James Gleason, William Demarest, Robert Wagner, and Marisa Pavan. **Director**—John Ford.
111 minutes

WHAT'S NEW, PUSSYCAT? (1965)

 ★

**Peter Sellers
Peter O'Toole
Woody Allen**

At some future time, film historians may point to this tasteless production as an example of what was considered comedy in the new morality days of the 1960s. Even at the time of its release, this story about an eccentric psychiatrist (Sellers) and a troubled fashion editor (O'Toole) who's obsessed with women, seemed weak. The cast includes Ursula Andress, Capucine, Romy Schneider, Louise Lasser, and Paula Prentiss, who are exploited here for their good looks. Allen was learning his craft at this point, but that's no reason why you should suffer. **Director**—Clive Donner.
108 minutes

WHAT'S UP DOC? (1972)

 ★★★

**Barbra Streisand
Ryan O'Neal**

Director Peter Bogdanovich fails to successfully capture the uninhibited quality of the better 1930s comedies, but he came close enough to make viewing this movie worthwhile. A vibrant performance by Streisand as a wacky coed who manages to disrupt the life-styles of a square musicologist (O'Neal) and his fiancée (Madeline Kahn) makes the director seem better than he really is. Kenneth Mars, Austin Pendleton, Sorrell Booke, Michael Murphy, and Mabel Albertson appear in supporting roles. (G)
94 minutes

THE WHEELER DEALERS (1963)

★★

**James Garner
Lee Remick**

Garner and Remick star in this comedy about a Texas oil millionaire who decides to have some fun on Wall Street with the stock market. There's nothing about the plot or the production that justify such solid performances by Remick, Jim Backus, Phil Harris, and Louis Nye so you should be grateful for unexpected pleasures. The cast also includes John Astin, Shelley Berman, and Chill Wills. **Director**—Arthur Hiller.
106 minutes

 Movie is available in Beta and VHS videotape

★ STAR PROFILE

W
• When a Stranger Calls
• When Time Ran Out
• When Worlds Collide

• When You Comin' Back,
  Red Ryder?
• Where Angels Go, Trouble
  Follows

WHEN A STRANGER CALLS
(1979)

 ★★

Carol Kane
Charles Durning

This suspense thriller gets off to a promising start—a babysitter, played by Kane, is alone in a dark house and receives threatening phone calls. But the film soon goes rapidly downhill. Even a psychopathic killer, played by Tony Beckley, needs some kind of psychology to give the story meaning. Instead, everything happens with little more than scary effects in mind. Durning plays a pursuing detective; it's a skimpy role in a meatless script. Also with Colleen Dewhurst, Rachel Roberts, and Ron O'Neal. **Director—** Fred Walton. (R) *97 minutes*

WHEN TIME RAN OUT
(1980)

★

Paul Newman
Jacqueline Bisset

Irwin Allen, who brought us *The Towering Inferno* and other disaster movies, takes one more crack at his favorite subject. This time, he unleashes an erupting volcano on a Hawaiian resort hotel in rather routine fashion. Newman and other well-known stars slog through a dull script. Most of the cast is killed off by the force of nature while a few make it to safety. Allen seems to have run out of fresh ideas. Also with William Holden, Red Buttons, Ernest Borgnine, and James Franciscus. **Director—**James Goldstone. (PG) *121 minutes*

WHEN WORLDS COLLIDE
(1951)

 ★★

Richard Derr
Barbara Rush

Vivid and spectacular effects make this science-fiction tale about the rush to build a spaceship worthwhile. The reason for the haste is that Earth is going to be destroyed by another planet, so every second counts. The plot is weak, and the dialogue is trite.

ROBERT MITCHUM

Robert Mitchum's first film role was as a bad guy in a Hopalong Cassidy western in 1940. He had small roles in a number of movies after that, but didn't catch the attention of audiences until 1944, when he appeared in the low-budget movie When Strangers Marry *and in a supporting role in* Thirty Seconds Over Tokyo.*

Born in Bridgeport, Connecticut, in 1917, Mitchum dropped out of school when he was 14 and worked as a deckhand on a salvage vessel. During the Depression, he worked his way across the country. His sister introduced him to the Long Beach Theater Guild, where he began as a stagehand and only later became an actor, performing in The Petrified Forest *and* Remember the Day. *He also wrote children's plays and comedy material, and organized a road tour for astrologist Carroll Richter.*

During the late '40s, better roles in Till the End of Time *(1946),* Undercurrent *(1946),* Crossfire *(1947),* Desire Me *(1947),* Out of the Past *(1947),* Rachel and the Stranger *(1948),* Blood on the Moon *(1948), and* The Red Pony *(1949) made him a box-office favorite.*

Some of Mitchum's other films include My Forbidden Past *(1951),* His Kind of Woman *(1951),* Angel Face *(1953),* River of No Return *(1954),* Track of the Cat *(1954),* Not as a Stranger *(1955),* Heaven Knows, Mr. Allison *(1957), and* Fire Down Below *(1957). Under Charles Laughton's direction, he starred in James Agee's* The Night of the Hunter *(1955), which became one of the first cult films.*

In more recent years, Mitchum starred in The Sundowners *(1960),* The Longest Day *(1960),* Ryan's Daughter *(1971),* Farewell, My Lovely *(1975),* The Last Tycoon *(1976),* The Amsterdam Kill *(1978), and* The Big Sleep *(1978). When he's not making a motion picture, Mitchum lives in northern California.*

Aside from the splendid photography, the movie is ordinary. Derr and Rush star, with Peter Hanson, John Hoyt, and Larry Keating in supporting roles. **Director—**Rudolph Maté. **Academy Award Nomination—**John F. Seitz and W. Howard Greene, cinematography (color). *80 minutes*

WHEN YOU COMIN' BACK, RED RYDER? (1979)

★★

Marjoe Gortner

Gortner stars as an enraged Vietnam veteran who terrorizes some nice folks in a sleepy New Mexico diner. There are some decent performances by Gortner, Peter Firth, and Stephanie Faracy. However, the story, which was taken from the 1973 stage production, loses much of its sizzle by dwelling too long on the various characters before the action in the diner begins. The finale has its taut moments, but the outcome leaves a bad aftertaste. Also with Hal Linden, Lee Grant, Candy Clark, and Pat Hingle. **Director—**Milton Katselas. (R) *118 minutes*

WHERE ANGELS GO, TROUBLE FOLLOWS (1968)

★★

Rosalind Russell
Stella Stevens

This overly cute and simplistic story of nuns in conflict and their pupils threatening to get out of control holds little interest. Russell plays a Mother Superior who's challenged by Stevens, a younger and more progressive nun in this sequel to *The Trouble With Angels*. The supporting cast of Binnie Barnes, Susan St. James, Milton Berle, Arthur Godfrey, William Lundigan, Van Johnson, Robert Taylor, Mary Wickes, and Barbara Hunter brighten the production, but only slightly. **Director—**James Neilson. *95 minutes*

- Where Eagles Dare
- Where's Charley?
- Where the Boys Are (1960)
- Where the Boys Are (1984)
- Where the Buffalo Roam
- Which Way Is Up?
- Whispering Smith
- White Cargo

WHERE EAGLES DARE (1969)
★★★

Richard Burton
Clint Eastwood

This good old-fashioned adventure story about a dangerous mission to rescue an American officer from an escape-proof German prison has lots of action and many tense moments. Burton and Eastwood star as the leaders of the rescue expedition, with Patrick Wymark, Michael Hordern, Robert Beatty, Mary Ure, Donald Houston, and Peter Barkworth in supporting roles. Director Brian G. Hutton has the good sense not to take the movie too seriously. Based on the novel by Alistair MacLean. (PG)
156 minutes

WHERE'S CHARLEY? (1952)
★★★

Ray Bolger

Bolger sparkles in this musical version of *Charley's Aunt*, the story of an Oxford student who impersonates his best friend's rich aunt to solve problems only to end up causing new complications. Bolger is at his best singing "Once in Love With Amy," but the other Frank Loesser songs are good, too. The cast also includes Robert Shackleton, Allyn McLerie, Horace Cooper, Mary Germaine, and Margaretta Scott. **Director**—David Butler.
95 minutes

WHERE THE BOYS ARE (1960)
 ★★

George Hamilton
Dolores Hart
Paula Prentiss
Jim Hutton

Hamilton, Hart, Prentiss, and Hutton star in this silly musical about college boys and girls on vacation in Fort Lauderdale, Florida. The movie never pretends to be anything other than what it is—a teenage beach movie. The cast also includes Yvette Mimieux, Connie Francis, Barbara Nichols, Chill Wills, and Frank Gorshin. **Director**— Henry Levin.
99 minutes

WHERE THE BOYS ARE (1984)
 ★

Lisa Hartman
Lorna Luft
Lynn-Holly Johnson

In the girls' grasp, that's Where the Boys Are '84.

Charmless rehash of the '60s film of the same name that looks at the spring frolic of college students on the sun-drenched beaches of Fort Lauderdale. This less-innocent version features four coeds on the make and involved in assorted silly escapades. The dumb plot is frequently side-tracked for leering scenes of briefly clad young women and men showing off on the sands and at parties. **Director**—Hy Averback. (R)
97 minutes

WHERE THE BUFFALO ROAM (1980)
 ★★

Bill Murray

Low comedy about the high jinks of outrageous gonzo journalist Hunter Thompson, who ruffled the establishment's feathers in the late '60s. Murray, playing the role of Thompson, generates a few laughs as he covers a marijuana trial, the Super Bowl, and the Presidential election. But it's mostly preposterous slapstick that wears thin as the movie wears on. **Director**—Art Linson. (R)
98 minutes

WHICH WAY IS UP? (1977)
 ★

Richard Pryor

Comic Pryor, generally successful in screen endeavors, takes a step backward in this crude adaptation of Lina Wertmuller's Italian comedy, *The Seduction of Mimi*. Pryor plays three roles, but primarily he portrays a poor fruit picker who becomes a farm labor union organizer. Most of the material is shallow, and much is ruined by unnecessary vulgar language. Also with Lonette McKee, Margaret Avery, and Dewayne Jessie. **Director**— Michael Schultz. (R)
91 minutes

WHISPERING SMITH (1948)
★★★

Alan Ladd
Robert Preston
Brenda Marshall

Brenda Marshall, Robert Preston, and Donald Crisp in Whispering Smith.

Ladd, Preston, and Marshall star in this western, which combines a well-developed story with sufficient action. It deals with a government detective, played by Ladd, who discovers that a friend is involved in a series of robberies. The cast also includes Donald Crisp, William Demarest, Frank Faylen, Fay Holden, and Murvyn Vye. **Director**—Leslie Fenton.
88 minutes

WHITE CARGO (1942)
★

Hedy Lamarr
Walter Pidgeon

Lamarr plays Tondelayo, a scheming native girl who entices British rubber planters, in this campy film that's so bad it's worth seeing just as a frame of reference so other inept movies can be judged. Pidgeon plays the planter who loves Lamarr most of all. Other actors who risked their reputations in this movie include Richard Carlson, Regi-
(Continued)

 Movie is available in Beta and VHS videotape

W

- White Christmas
- The White Cliffs of Dover
- White Heat
- White Line Fever
- Who Is Killing the Great Chefs of Europe?
- Who'll Stop the Rain

(Continued)

nald Owen, Frank Morgan, Bramwell Fletcher, and Richard Ainley. Good for laughs. **Director**—Richard Thorpe.

90 minutes b&w

WHITE CHRISTMAS (1954)
★★★

**Bing Crosby
Danny Kaye
Dean Jagger**

A star-studded cast brightens this musical package about two old Army friends—Crosby and Kaye—who aid Jagger, an ex-officer, at his winter resort. The limp plot is merely a device for Crosby, Kaye, Rosemary Clooney, Vera-Ellen, Grady Sutton, Sig Rumann, and Mary Wickes to perform. The Irving Berlin songs—including the title tune—enrich the production. **Director**—Michael Curtiz.

120 minutes

THE WHITE CLIFFS OF DOVER (1944)
★★

Irene Dunne

This patriotic tearjerker, about an American woman in Britain who loses her husband during World War I and her son in World War II, has many vivid scenes, although the production seems too melodramatic now. Dunne gives an intelligent, controlled performance as the wife and mother, and there are solid supporting appearances by Alan Marshal, C. Aubrey Smith, Frank Morgan, Roddy McDowall, Dame May Whitty, Van Johnson, and Peter Lawford. **Director**—Clarence Brown. **Academy Award Nomination**—George Folsey, cinematography (black and white).

126 minutes b&w

WHITE HEAT (1949)
★★★★

**James Cagney
Edmond O'Brien**

Cagney is in top form in this realistic story of a psychopathic gangster. The movie vividly depicts his violent lifestyle and also gets top grades for excel-

A prison breakout takes place in White Heat.

lent action sequences and lots of suspense. O'Brien plays the clever cop who infiltrates Cagney's gang and finally collars him. The excellent cast also includes Margaret Wycherly, Virginia Mayo, John Archer, and Steve Cochran. **Director**—Raoul Walsh. **Academy Award Nomination**—Virginia Kellogg, writing (motion picture story).

114 minutes b&w

WHITE LINE FEVER (1975)
★★★

**Jan-Michael Vincent
Kay Lenz**

Jan-Michael Vincent finds it hard to drive his rig handcuffed to the outside of the cab in White Line Fever.

This action drama focuses on the long-haul trucking business. The story is about a young veteran who returns home, purchases a diesel truck, and battles the corruption of the bigger interests who want him to smuggle contraband across state lines. Although the plot is loaded down with clichés, the huge, barreling trucks are a show in themselves, and one smash-'em-up scene is said to have cost $130,000. Vincent and Lenz do a good job of revving up the action along with

the big trucks. The title refers to the tiring, hypnotic effect of the highway's white center line on drivers during long trips. Also with Slim Pickens, L. Q. Jones, and Don Porter. **Director**—Jonathan Kaplan. (PG) *89 minutes*

WHO IS KILLING THE GREAT CHEFS OF EUROPE? (1978)
★★★

**George Segal
Jacqueline Bisset
Robert Morley**

By Jove, it's that rotund Englishman Morley—overflowing with bombast and eating his way to oblivion as publisher of a gourmet food magazine. Segal and Bisset get top billing in this mystery comedy, but the film belongs to Morley, who provides most of the laughs with his caustic dialogue. The story is set mostly in famous European hotels and elegant restaurants, with scrumptious shots of marvelous dishes. It's entertaining, funny, suspenseful, and mouth-watering too. Also with Jean-Pierre Cassel, Philippe Noiret, Jean Rochefort, and Madge Ryan. **Director**—Ted Kotcheff. (PG)

112 minutes

WHO'LL STOP THE RAIN (1978)
★★★

**Nick Nolte
Tuesday Weld**

This hard-hitting action drama about a couple on the lam is based on *Dog Soldiers*, Robert Stone's emotional

• Wholly Moses
• Who's Afraid of Virginia Woolf?
• Who's Been Sleeping in My Bed?
• Whose Life Is It Anyway?
• Who Was that Lady?
• Why Would I Lie?
• The Wicked Lady

novel involving the backwash of the Vietnam War. Nolte is terrific as an ex-Marine who smuggles heroin into the U.S., and then, in company with a friend's wife, is relentlessly pursued by three colorful but sadistic villains. The woman is played by Weld. The film, like the novel, maintains a sense of tension and reflects on the war's impact on America. Also with Michael Moriarty, Anthony Zerbe, Richard Masur, and Ray Sharkey. **Director—**Karel Reisz. (R)   *126 minutes*

WHOLLY MOSES (1980)

Dudley Moore

Moore stars in this sporadically funny Bible tale that seems to be inspired by *The Life of Brian*, but is nowhere as outrageous. Moore plays a shepherd who's somehow two steps behind Moses when a famous incident occurs. Moore works in some mildly comic routines, but the film is in dire need of at least a few side-splitting laughs. Dom De Luise, Madeline Kahn, John Houseman, and Richard Pryor contribute some nice cameo performances—especially Pryor as a formidable pharaoh. **Director—**Gary Weis. (PG)   *109 minutes*

WHO'S AFRAID OF VIRGINIA WOOLF? (1966)

Richard Burton
Elizabeth Taylor
George Segal
Sandy Dennis

The famous Edward Albee play successfully makes the translation to the motion picture screen. Burton and Taylor were seemingly born to play the troubled middle-aged couple who impose on the innocent younger couple (Segal and Dennis). The film is loud, vulgar, wrenching, and also sadly truthful about the pitfalls of married life and life in general. **Director—**Mike Nichols. **Academy Awards**—Taylor, best actress; Dennis, best supporting actress; Haskell Wexler, cinematography (black and white). **Nominations**—best picture; Nichols, best director; Burton, best actor; Segal, best supporting actor; Ernest Lehman,

best screenplay (based on material from another medium).
        129 minutes b&w

WHO'S BEEN SLEEPING IN MY BED? (1963)

★★

Dean Martin
Elizabeth Montgomery

In this inoffensive comedy, Martin plays a TV star who's being pushed to the altar by his fiancée because she's worried by the competition. Montgomery plays his fiancée. Some bright dialogue sparks this very ordinary story, and some solid supporting efforts by Carol Burnett, Louis Nye, Elizabeth Fraser, and Richard Conte also push it up from mediocrity. **Director—**Daniel Mann.   *103 minutes*

WHOSE LIFE IS IT ANYWAY? (1981)

★★★★

Richard Dreyfuss

It's a grim subject, indeed: A quadriplegic with no chance of recovery fights for his right to die with dignity. Yet this amazing film is handled with such warmth, wit, and humanity that it evolves into a captivating experience, ably transcending any morbidity. The performance by Dreyfuss as the gutsy paralyzed sculptor is spellbinding. And the touching drama moves with dynamic precision despite the confined hospital setting. There's masterful support from Janet Eilber, John Cassavetes, Christine Lahti, and Bob Balaban. **Director—**John Badham. (R)   *118 minutes*

WHO WAS THAT LADY? (1960)

★★

Tony Curtis
Dean Martin
Janet Leigh

Curtis and Martin star in this entertaining farce. They pretend to be FBI agents to fool Leigh, who plays Curtis's wife, but new problems arise when foreign spies become interested in their identities. Although the movie begins well, it weakens near the end.

Dean Martin gives Tony Curtis and Janet Leigh lessons on smooching in Who Was That Lady?.

The cast also includes James Whitmore, Larry Keating, John McIntire, and Barbara Nichols. **Director—**George Sidney.   *115 minutes b&w*

WHY WOULD I LIE? (1980)

★

Treat Williams

Williams is a colorful liar in this romantic comedy that's too contrived in the romance department and weaker yet as a comedy. Williams plays an obscure character, who works as a social worker, adopts a young boy, and locates the boy's mother with whom he falls in love. All the sentimental complications are incredible, and the story is strictly corn—almost tastelessly so. Why would we lie? Also with Lisa Eichhorn, Jocelyn Brando, and Gabriel Swann. **Director—**Larry Peerce. (PG)   *105 minutes*

THE WICKED LADY (1983)

★★

Faye Dunaway
John Gielgud

Dunaway plays a 17th-century noblewoman-turned-highway-robber in this frothy remake of the 1945 British costume drama. This version actually comes off as a send-up of the original, with various comic pokes conveyed rather awkwardly. Most of the budget seems lavished on elaborate costumes

(Continued)

W

• The Wilby Conspiracy
• The Wild Blue Yonder
• The Wild Bunch
• The Wild Geese

• The Wild Life
• The Wild One
• Willie & Phil

(Continued)
and period settings. Apparently the producers couldn't afford a script. The distinguished cast, which also includes Denholm Elliott and Alan Bates, is shamelessly wasted. **Director—** Michael Winner. (R)   *88 minutes*

THE WILBY CONSPIRACY
(1975)
★★★

**Michael Caine
Sidney Poitier**

Sidney Poitier struggles against white oppression as a South African activist in The Wilby Conspiracy.

Poitier plays a political activist on the lam from the police in Cape Town, South Africa. He's locked together with a white apolitical businessman, played by Caine, a situation reminiscent of *The Defiant Ones*. The film is amusing and suspenseful, set against the backdrop of South African racism. Filmed mostly in Kenya. Also with Nicol Williamson and Persis Khambatta. **Director—**Ralph Nelson. (PG)   *101 minutes*

THE WILD BLUE YONDER
(1952)
★★

**Wendell Corey
Vera Hruba Ralston
Forrest Tucker**

The real hero and star of this movie about World War II is the B-29 bomber, and there are some sterling scenes of this stalwart aircraft doing its thing in the Pacific. The plot also involves the friendships and rivalries of pilots Corey and Tucker and the woman in their life, played by Ralston. The cast of this ordinary flag-waving movie also includes Phil Harris, Ruth Donnelly, and Walter Brennan. **Director—** Allan Dwan.   *98 minutes b&w*

THE WILD BUNCH (1969)
★★★

**William Holden
Ernest Borgnine
Robert Ryan**

This so-called modern western has loads of explicit violence as a gang confronts the law as well as the Mexican Army in 1914 along the Texas-Mexico border. There are many symbolic flourishes and brilliantly filmed scenes, but only you can decide if the violence is justified in that larger cinematic context. Holden, Borgnine, and Ryan star, with Edmond O'Brien, Warren Oates, Ben Johnson, Jaime Sanchez, Strother Martin, and L. Q. Jones in supporting roles. **Director—** Sam Peckinpah. (R) **Academy Award Nomination**—Walon Green, Roy N. Sickner, and Peckinpah, best story and screenplay (based on material not previously published or produced).
     145 minutes

THE WILD GEESE (1978)
★★★

**Richard Burton
Roger Moore
Richard Harris**

Burton, Moore, and Harris lead a mercenary army to Africa to rescue a kidnapped African president. The story is somewhat routine, but it's filled with ripsnorting action and adventure for traditional escapist appeal. The high-calibre cast does an effective job of portraying some interesting characters and giving the audience a full dose of jungle fighting. Also with Hardy Kruger, Stewart Granger, Jack Watson, and Frank Finlay. **Director—** Andrew V. McLaglen. (R)
     132 minutes

THE WILD LIFE (1984)
★

**Christopher Penn
Ilan Mitchell-Smith
Jenny Wright**

A moronic adolescent romp, constructed without much form, which follows the style of *Fast Times at Ridgemont High*. The movie is populated with various slobs, meatheads, nerds, and jerks who engage in partying, girl chasing, and assorted reckless pranks. In its desperate attempt to be outrageous and funny, the film winds up as rather tame stuff. **Director—**Art Linson. (R)   *95 minutes*

THE WILD ONE (1954)
★★★★

**Marlon Brando
Lee Marvin**

In The Wild One, *Marlon Brando makes Mary Murphy an offer she can't refuse.*

Motorcycle technology has changed more than Brando's acting technique, but this realistic slice of life about a gang of cyclists raising hell in a small California town still packs a wallop. Brando plays the sleazy leader of the pack. Other fine performances by Marvin, Mary Murphy, Robert Keith, and Jay C. Flippen. **Director—**Laslo Benedek.   *79 minutes b&w*

WILLIE & PHIL (1980)
★★

**Michael Ontkean
Ray Sharkey
Margot Kidder**

• Will Success Spoil Rock Hunter?
• Wilson
• Winchester 73

• The Wind and the Lion
• The Window
• Windows
• Windwalker

W

Ray Sharkey and Michael Ontkean are Willie & Phil.

Ontkean, Sharkey, and Kidder are appealing Bohemian types who develop a deep friendship in this comic romance that satirizes life in the '70s. Paul Mazursky directs with the same skill he showed in *An Unmarried Woman*, but the weakness here is that neither the characters nor the story go beyond parody. Mazursky's people are charming stereotypes; the more serious their story becomes, the less believable they are. (R)   *116 minutes*

WILL SUCCESS SPOIL ROCK HUNTER? (1957)

★★

Jayne Mansfield
Tony Randall

Mansfield and Randall star in this unsuccessful comedy that attempts to poke fun at TV commercials and the wimpy moral attitude of the 1950s. The plot, about a press agent who gets involved in touting the world's greatest lover, is disjointed, and the movie never seems to get organized. The performances of the stars don't salvage the effort. And the acting of supporting actors Betsy Drake, Mickey Hargitay, Joan Blondell, John Williams, Henry Jones, and Groucho Marx doesn't spoil the film. **Director**— Frank Tashlin.   *95 minutes*

WILSON (1944)

★★★

Alexander Knox

This honest and accurate biography of a great American president stars Knox in the title role. It's a rare biography by Hollywood standards because it doesn't compromise the story of the

man to achieve short-term glory with a flashy motion picture. Wilson's noble philosophy as well as his faults are portrayed. The outstanding cast also includes Geraldine Fitzgerald, Charles Coburn, Cedric Hardwicke, Thomas Mitchell, Vincent Price, Francis X. Bushman, Mary Anderson, Ruth Nelson, Ruth Ford, and Eddie Foy, Jr. **Director**—Henry King. **Academy Awards** —Lamar Trotti, writing (original screenplay); Leon Shamroy, cinematography (color). **Nominations**— best picture; King, best director; Knox, best actor.   *154 minutes*

WINCHESTER 73 (1950)

★★★★

James Stewart
Shelley Winters

Stewart and Winters star in this marvelous western about Stewart's search for an old foe and a stolen rifle. Before Stewart finds his man and settles the score, there's plenty of action. The excellent cast also includes Dan Duryea, Rock Hudson, Tony Curtis, Steve Brodie, Stephen McNally, Millard Mitchell, and John McIntire. This movie was so well received after its release that it sparked a revival in western films. **Director**—Anthony Mann.
92 minutes b&w

THE WIND AND THE LION
(1975)

★★

Sean Connery
Candice Bergen

Candice Bergen faces a moment of truth in The Wind and the Lion.

Teddy Roosevelt sends the U.S. Marines to Morocco in 1904 to rescue an American widow and her children who are kidnapped by the last of the Barbary pirates. An elaborate but absurd adventure. Connery plays the head pirate, Bergen is the widow, and Brian Keith is Teddy. Also with John Huston, Geoffrey Lewis, and Steve Kanaly. **Director**—John Milius. (PG)
119 minutes

THE WINDOW (1949)

 ★★★

Bobby Driscoll

This compelling thriller about a slum kid who witnesses a murder, but can't convince his parents about what he saw, is deftly executed and excruciatingly tense as the boy and murderer parry. Driscoll is excellent in the role of a boy who is often caught telling tales. And there are fine supporting performances by Arthur Kennedy, Ruth Roman, Barbara Hale, and Paul Stewart. The photography of William Steiner sets the mood and tempo of the story. **Director**—Ted Tetzlaff.
73 minutes b&w

WINDOWS (1980)

★

Talia Shire
Elizabeth Ashley

A gloomy, would-be thriller about a young woman, played by Shire, who's harassed by a psychotic lesbian, played by Ashley. The shoddy screenplay quickly deteriorates into a stale rip-off of *Klute*. Low-key and overwrought performances misfire, resulting in unintentional humor. Gordon Willis, the noted cinematographer (*The Godfather; Manhattan*), debuts in this movie as director. He offers some stunning views of New York City, but everything else is ridiculous and irrelevant. Also with Joseph Cortese. (R)
96 minutes

WINDWALKER (1981)

 ★★

Trevor Howard

(Continued)

W
- Windy City
- The Winslow Boy
- Winter Kills
- Wise Blood
- With a Song in My Heart
- Without a Trace

Injuns in Windwalker, *a sensitive portrayal of the savages.*

(Continued)

Howard plays a dying Cheyenne warrior who relates the tragic adventures of his life, much of it dealing with feuding between his tribe and the neighboring Crows. With the exception of Howard, who's unconvincing in the title role, cast members are Indians who perform adequately. The sentimental story, however, never develops with sufficient clarity or impact. Even the various battles involving revengeful Indians and wild animals become tiresome and exceedingly violent for this sort of wilderness film. **Director**—Keith Merrill. In Crow and Cheyenne with English titles. (PG)   *108 minutes*

WINDY CITY (1984)
★★

**John Shea
Kate Capshaw
Josh Mostel**

An overly self-conscious, sentimental drama of friendships, unfulfilled ambitions, and lost romance among a group of young men residing in Chicago. The film aims to follow the path of *Diner* and *The Big Chill*, but the characters come off as rather banal and unspontaneous. As for the dialogue, it's mostly a lot of hot air. **Director**—Armyan Bernstein. (R)   *105 minutes*

THE WINSLOW BOY (1948)
 ### ★★★★

**Robert Donat
Cedric Hardwicke
Margaret Leighton
Frank Lawton**

The splendid acting of Donat, Hardwicke, Leighton, and Lawton make this real-life story a gem of a film. It's about an attorney, played by Donat, who defends a naval cadet falsely accused of stealing. Based on a play by Terence Rattigan, the production brilliantly conveys the mood of British society and that country's legal system. The excellent cast also includes Ernest Thesiger, Neil North, Jack Watling and Basil Radford. **Director**—Anthony Asquith.   *117 minutes b&w*

WINTER KILLS (1979)
 ### ★★

Jeff Bridges

Jeff Bridges and Belinda Bauer keep themselves busy indoors because Winter Kills.

Bridges plays the half-brother of an American president who was assassinated 19 years ago, and now he sets out to solve the crime at a breathless pace. Bridges chases after CIA operatives, organized crime figures, eccentric industrial tycoons, and a Jack Ruby character. The film, based on the Richard Condon novel, is only entertaining in spots. Mostly, it's confusing and makes little sense. John Huston, Anthony Perkins, Eli Wallach, and Sterling Hayden make the most of their supporting roles. Also with Richard Boone, Ralph Meeker, and Dorothy Malone. **Director**—William Richert. (R)   *96 minutes*

WISE BLOOD (1979)
★★★

Brad Dourif

Director John Huston's 33rd feature film is a puzzling, offbeat story about Bible Belt evangelism that starts off as a parody, but then shifts into a gruesome nightmare. The film was shot in Georgia, but the setting seems to be the private world of some very eccentric characters. Dourif, who played the stutterer in *One Flew Over the Cuckoo's Nest*, turns in an intense performance as a preacher who's also an atheist. Huston's direction carries impact. Also with Amy Wright and Harry Dean Stanton. (No MPAA rating)   *108 minutes*

WITH A SONG IN MY HEART (1952)
★★

Susan Hayward

Hayward gives a vivid portrayal of Jane Froman, a singer who struggles to return to show business after being seriously injured in an airplane crash. Although Hayward is convincing as the crippled singer, the songs are actually sung by Froman. Those who find the story too much like soap opera will be able to take some consolation from the music. David Wayne, Rory Calhoun, Thelma Ritter, Helen Westcott, Una Merkel, and Robert Wagner appear in supporting roles. **Director**—Walter Lang. **Academy Award Nominations**—Hayward, best actress; Ritter, best supporting actress.   *117 minutes*

WITHOUT A TRACE (1983)
 ### ★★★

**Kate Nelligan
Judd Hirsch**

Judd Hirsch and Kate Nelligan search for a missing child in Without a Trace.

Initially, this film smacks of made-for-TV fare: A six-year-old boy vanishes on his way to school, the police and the media descend on the frantic household, and the investigation bogs down in false leads. But it's a better movie than you'd expect. Director Stanley Jaffe skillfully builds suspense and comes up with some plausible details and a jolting ending. The melodrama is graced by top performances from Nelligan as the distraught, determined mother, and Hirsch as a sympathetic detective. (PG)   *121 minutes*

WITNESS FOR THE PROSECUTION (1957)

 ★★★★

**Charles Laughton
Tyrone Power
Marlene Dietrich**

Clever dialogue, brilliant acting by Laughton, and some devious twists and turns in the plot make this ordinary production, based on an Agatha Christie play, seem extraordinary more often than not. Dietrich plays the wife of Power, an alleged killer. Laughton is hired to defend him. Excellent acting by Power, Dietrich, Elsa Lanchester, Ian Wolfe, John Williams, and Henry Daniel enhance this suspenseful courtroom drama. Christie invariably pulls one trick too many, thus lessening any chance an intelligent viewer has to solve the crime, and this movie is no exception. **Director**—Billy Wilder. **Academy Award Nominations**—best picture; Wilder, best director; Laughton, best actor; Lanchester, best supporting actress.
114 minutes b&w

THE WIZ (1978)

 ★★★

**Diana Ross
Michael Jackson
Nipsey Russell
Ted Ross
Richard Pryor**

Somewhere over the Brooklyn Bridge, skies are blue. Here we find Dorothy (Diana Ross), the Scarecrow (Jackson), the Tin Man (Russell), and the Cowardly Lion (Ted Ross) following the Yellow Brick Road in search of miracles from the Wiz; he's played by Pryor and is ensconced in the World Trade Center. This extravagant film musical, a black version of *The Wizard of Oz* adapted from the smash Broadway production, offers dazzling beauty,

Diana Ross as a geriatic Dorothy in The Wiz.

rousing singing and dancing, and a touching contemporary recreation of the famous children's fantasy. It's a sure-fire hit, but it doesn't upstage the enduring Judy Garland version. Also with Mabel King and Theresa Merritt. **Director**—Sidney Lumet. (G) **Academy Award Nomination**—Oswald Morris, cinematography.
133 minutes

THE WIZARD OF OZ (1939)

 ★★★★

**Judy Garland
Frank Morgan
Ray Bolger
Jack Haley
Bert Lahr**

Judy Garland as the one true Dorothy in The Wizard of Oz.

This fantastic tale about a Kansas farm girl who's spirited off to the land of Oz still tingles with freshness. Garland as the girl is memorable, and such songs as "Over the Rainbow" are unforgettable. The charming cast of this classic also includes Margaret Hamilton, Clara Blandick, Charley Grapewin, and Billie Burke. For added measure, the superb songs of E. Y. Harburg and Harold Arlen blend beautifully with the photography of Harold Rosson. **Director**—Victor Fleming. (G) **Academy Awards**—Arlen and Harburg, best song ("Over the Rainbow"); Garland, special award for her performance as a screen juvenile. **Nomination**—best picture.
101 minutes b&w/color

WOLFEN (1981)

 ★★

Albert Finney

This is a stunning, nerve-jangling horror film with many attributes and, unfortunately, a muddled and preposterous conclusion that cancels out some of the thrills. Finney gives a classy performance as a shrewd New York City homicide detective who connects some brutal murders to a marauding pack of superwolves. Director Michael Wadleigh creates an extraordinary eerie atmosphere, but the film becomes bogged down with unclear rationalization about man's callousness toward nature. (R)   *114 minutes*

THE WOLF MAN (1941)

 ★★★

**Lon Chaney, Jr.
Claude Rains**

Chaney, Rains, Bela Lugosi, and Maria Ouspenskaya appear in this grim, intelligent, and well-made horror classic about Larry Talbot, an ordinary man who turns peculiar whenever there's a full moon. Chaney, of course, is the troubled man; Rains plays his father. The movie is eerie enough to make you think twice about going out for a walk at night. The outstanding cast of this engrossing film also includes Ralph Bellamy, Warren William, Patric Knowles, Evelyn Ankers, and Fay Helm. **Director**—George Waggner.
70 minutes b&w

W

- A Woman in Flames
- The Woman in Red
- The Woman in the Window
- Woman of the Year

- The Women
- Women in Love
- Wonder Man

A WOMAN IN FLAMES (1984)

 ★

Gudrum Landgrebe

Poor Eva (Landgrebe). She's a lousy conversationalist and can't cook. So she walks out on her bourgeois husband and sets up shop as a prostitute specializing in kinky sex. Then she's on to a series of mechanical encounters with masochistic men. At times, the film strives toward comedy, but the sordid mess leaves the viewer cold and bored. Mathieu Carriere co-stars. In German with English titles. **Director**—Robert van Ackeren. (No rating) *106 minutes*

THE WOMAN IN RED (1984)

 ★★★

Gene Wilder
Kelly Le Brock
Judith Ivy

Lightweight, déjà vu comedy about the misadventures of ·a philandering advertising manager. The film reworks the French comedy *Pardon Mon Affaire* and it owes much to *The Seven Year Itch* and *10*. Mop-haired Wilder, as the smitten middle-aged family man, makes it work with gentle charm. He awkwardly pursues a gorgeous model (Le Brock) while keeping his loving wife (Ivy) in the dark. Charles Grodin, Joseph Bologna, and Gilda Radner are in supporting roles. **Director**—Wilder. (PG–13) *87 minutes*

THE WOMAN IN THE WINDOW (1944)

★★★

Edward G. Robinson
Joan Bennett

Robinson and Bennett shine in this taut thriller about a professor, played by Robinson, who befriends a beautiful woman, played by Bennett, while his family is on vacation and then becomes involved in a murder case. The movie weakens slightly toward the end, but not enough to spoil a top-notch film. Raymond Massey, Dan Duryea, Arthur Loft, Bobby Blake, Edmund Breon, and Dorothy Peterson also star. **Director**—Fritz Lang. *99 minutes b&w*

WOMAN OF THE YEAR (1942)

 ★★★

Spencer Tracy
Katharine Hepburn

Tracy and Hepburn are charming in this story about a sportswriter and a famed political columnist, who seems to know about everything except sports. Tracy is the sports reporter, and Hepburn plays the political commentator. The acting and dialogue are tops, although the comedy falters at times, as the couple struggles to keep love free from the intrusion of world events. Fay Bainter, William Bendix, Reginald Owen, Roscoe Karns, Minor Watson, and Dan Tobin are in supporting roles. This was the first pairing of Tracy and Hepburn on the screen. **Director**—George Stevens. **Academy Award**—Michael Kanin and Ring Lardner, Jr., writing (original screenplay). *114 minutes b&w*

THE WOMEN (1939)

 ★★★

Norma Shearer
Joan Crawford
Rosalind Russell

This comedy-drama is well titled because it has a cast of more than 125 women. It seems tame now, but there are still enough sparks and barbs in the complex plot to please most viewers. The large cast also includes Paulette Goddard, Mary Boland, Margaret Dumont, Hedda Hopper, Ruth Hussey, and Marjorie Main. Anita Loos and Jane Murfin wrote the script for this film version of the Clare Boothe Luce play and had the wisdom to keep much of the original biting dialogue intact. The story—keyed to a socialite's divorce—gets muddled at times, however. **Director**—George Cukor. *132 minutes b&w/color*

WOMEN IN LOVE (1970)

 ★★★

Glenda Jackson
Jennie Linden
Alan Bates

Jackson, Linden, and Bates star in this

Glenda Jackson and Jennie Linden discuss how wonderful it is to be Women in Love.

film version of D. H. Lawrence's celebrated novel. Whereas Lawrence attempted to be honest and realistic, the movie in director Ken Russell's inept hands is too self-conscious and even ostentatious. However, the period sets of the Midlands of England during the 1920s, the excellent acting, and a provocative nude wrestling scene make the film worthwhile. Oliver Reed, Eleanor Bron, Alan Webb, and Michael Gough appear in supporting roles. (R) **Academy Award**—Jackson, best actress. **Nominations**—Russell, best director; Larry Kramer, best screenplay (based on material from another medium). *130 minutes*

WONDER MAN (1945)

★★★

Danny Kaye

Kaye is sensational in this story of twins. Kaye, of course, plays both of them—one a quiet studious type, the other a brash nightclub entertainer. The action and comic pace pick up when the entertainer is killed, and the bookish twin must replace him. Virginia Mayo, Vera-Ellen, S. Z. Sakall, Donald Woods, Ed Brophy, and Steve Cochran also appear in this colorful and delightful production. **Director**—H. Bruce Humberstone. **Academy Award**—John Fulton and A. W. Johns, special effects. *96 minutes*

- The World According to Garp
- The World of Henry Orient
- The World of Suzie Wong
- The World's Greatest Lover
- Written on the Wind
- The Wrong Arm of the Law
- Wrong Is Right

W

THE WORLD ACCORDING TO GARP (1982)

 ★★

Robin Williams
Mary Beth Hurt
Glenn Close
John Lithgow

John Irving's trendy novel unfortunately translates to the screen only with difficulty. The story of a gentle writer (Williams), overwhelmed by eccentric characters and bizarre events, comes off as disjointed and lacking in dramatic weight. The actors are impressive, but even their skill can't hide the fact that this is a shallow film. **Director**—George Roy Hill. (R) **Academy Award Nominations**—Lithgow, best supporting actor; Close, best supporting actress. *136 minutes*

THE WORLD OF HENRY ORIENT (1964)

 ★★★

Tippy Walker
Merri Spaeth
Peter Sellers

Walker and Spaeth play two rich New York teenagers who adore an eccentric pianist, played by Sellers, in this congenial yet sensitive comedy. The young duo just about steal the show from Sellers and the other veterans as they harass the pianist by following him around New York City. The teens idolize him because they believe love is missing in their own lives. The minor theme of misplaced love is touchingly portrayed. The cast also includes Paula Prentiss, Phyllis Thaxter, Angela Lansbury, and Tom Bosley. **Director**—George Roy Hill. *106 minutes*

THE WORLD OF SUZIE WONG (1960)

★

William Holden
Nancy Kwan

The world in the title is that of a prostitute in Hong Kong, but in this insensitive Hollywood treatment everything is presented merely as offbeat. Holden gives a wooden performance as an artist who falls in love with Suzie, played competently by Kwan. The phony plot and the pace of the story also mar the movie. Sylvia Syms, Michael Wilding, Laurence Naismith, and Jackie Chan appear in supporting roles. **Director**— Richard Quine. *129 minutes*

THE WORLD'S GREATEST LOVER (1978)

 ★

Gene Wilder

Wilder—director, star, writer—can't make the humor click in this frantic tale about a Milwaukee baker who longs to become a silent-screen star in the '20s. The silly gags produce too few laughs, and the pacing is choppy. Wilder, who studied at the Mel Brooks comedy school, doesn't come close to the level of the master. This movie is a far cry from the world's greatest comedy. Also with Dom DeLuise, Carol Kane, Fritz Feld, and Carl Ballentine. (PG) *89 minutes*

WRITTEN ON THE WIND (1956)

★★★

Lauren Bacall
Robert Stack
Dorothy Malone

Bacall, Stack, and Malone star in this trite melodrama about the many problems within a wealthy oil family. The movie, however, is stabilized by some fine acting. In any case, the movie is so well-paced that many of the faults diminish. The cast also includes Rock Hudson, Robert Keith, and Grant Williams. **Director**—Douglas Sirk. **Academy Award**—Malone, best supporting actress. **Nomination**—Stack, best supporting actor. *100 minutes*

Robert Stack strikes Dorothy Malone in Written On the Wind.

THE WRONG ARM OF THE LAW (1963)

★★★

Peter Sellers

This British comedy about gangsters who impersonate cops and take loot from robbers they capture keeps the laughs coming at a fast pace. Sellers plays the brain behind the unusual London mob and seems at home with the role. He gets excellent support from Lionel Jeffries, Bernard Cribbins, Bill Kerr, and Davy Kaye. **Director**— Cliff Owen. *92 minutes b&w*

WRONG IS RIGHT (1982)

 ★★

Sean Connery
Robert Conrad
George Grizzard

Writer-director Richard Brooks rehashes *Dr. Strangelove, Network,* and other satirical portraits of a mad, mad world in this frenzied black comedy. The result is often too confused to be truly effective. This unstable panorama is seen through the experiences of a cynical, globetrotting TV reporter (Connery) who comments on the lunacy of it all. Brooks's handling of the satire lacks originality or wit. (R) *117 minutes*

 Movie is available in Beta and VHS videotape

443

W·X·Y

- Wuthering Heights
- W.W. and the Dixie Dancekings
- Xanadu
- Yankee Doodle Dandy
- Yanks
- The Yearling

WUTHERING HEIGHTS (1939)
★★★★

**Laurence Olivier
Merle Oberon**

Laurence Olivier and Merle Oberon are torrid lovers in Wuthering Heights.

A first-rate cast transforms the classic Victorian novel by Emily Brontë into a fine motion picture. Olivier plays the strange Heathcliff, and Oberon is Cathy. David Niven, Flora Robson, Geraldine Fitzgerald, Donald Crisp, Miles Mander, and Leo G. Carroll also star. Under William Wyler's excellent direction, with the well-written script by Ben Hecht and Charles MacArthur, this great love story never falters. **Academy Award**—Gregg Toland, best cinematography (black and white). **Nominations**—best picture; Wyler, best director; Olivier, best actor; Fitzgerald, best supporting actress; Ben Hecht and Charles MacArthur, writing (screenplay). *104 minutes b&w*

W.W. AND THE DIXIE DANCEKINGS (1975)
★★

**Burt Reynolds
Art Carney**

A friendly hold-up man, played by Reynolds, gets involved with a third-rate country-and-western music group in the '50s and leads them on to Nashville for a crack at Grand Ol' Opry stardom. The movie has ample good humor and energy, but an empty script. Carney plays an amusing preacher-detective. Also with Conny Van Dyke, Jerry Reed, and Ned Beatty. **Director**—John Avildsen. (PG) *106 minutes*

X

XANADU (1980)

★★

**Olivia Newton-John
Michael Beck
Gene Kelly**

Newton-John plays a glowing, singing, rollerskating muse who inspires a young artist, played by Beck, to open a disco. So much for the absurd plot. The only thing worthwhile in this mediocre movie is some fine singing and dancing, primarily by Newton-John. The always-charming Kelly plays a former clarinetist who was once smitten by the same muse; he does a number or two—rather well— with Olivia. But why he came out of retirement for this gig is puzzling. **Director**—Robert Greenwald. (PG) *93 minutes*

Y

YANKEE DOODLE DANDY (1942)

★★★★

**James Cagney
Joan Leslie
Walter Huston**

James Cagney plays that Yankee Doodle Dandy, *George M. Cohan.*

Cagney, Leslie, and Huston star in this stunning musical about the life and times of George M. Cohan, the famed vaudevillian song-and-dance man. Cagney is superb as Cohan. Even the slightly heavy patriotism doesn't tarnish the effort. Also with Richard Whorf, George Tobias, Eddie Foy, Jr., and Frances Langford. **Director**—Michael Curtiz. **Academy Award**—Cagney, best actor. **Nominations**—best picture; Curtiz, best director; Huston, best supporting actor; Robert Buckner, writing (original story). *126 minutes b&w*

YANKS (1979)
★★

**Richard Gere
Vanessa Redgrave
William Devane**

This movie is a sentimental account about the effect American soldiers had on an English community during their brief stay during World War II. The film is rich in detail and beautifully photographed, but the script suffers from the blahs. The events are predictable and are rarely exciting. Gere, Redgrave, and Devane are the principal players involved in various romantic episodes among the GIs and the English girls. Also with Chick Vannera, Rachel Roberts, and Wendy Morgan. **Director**—John Schlesinger. (R) *139 minutes*

THE YEARLING (1946)
★★★★

**Gregory Peck
Jane Wyman
Claude Jarman, Jr.**

This sensitive story of a young farm boy, who's devoted to a pet fawn that his father must destroy, is one of the finest family films of all time. The characterizations are vivid, and the emotions are honest in this rare motion picture. Peck, Wyman, and Jarman star, with Chill Wills, Clem Bevans, June Lockhart, Forrest Tucker, and Henry Travers in supporting roles. **Director**—Clarence Brown. **Academy Awards**—Charles Rosher, Leonard Smith, and Arthur Arling, cinematography (color). **Nominations**—best picture; Brown, best director;

• The Year of Living Dangerously
• Yellowbeard
• The Yellow Cab Man
• Yentl
• Yes, Giorgio
• Yor
• You Can't Cheat an Honest Man

Y

Peck, best actor; Wyman, best actress.
134 minutes

THE YEAR OF LIVING DANGEROUSLY (1983)

★★★

**Mel Gibson
Sigourney Weaver
Linda Hunt**

Mel Gibson and Sigourney Weaver succumb to the Jakarta heat and each other's charms in The Year of Living Dangerously.

Stylish and atmospheric romantic adventure by Australian director Peter Weir (*Gallipoli*). It's set in Indonesia of 1965, and we view poverty and political turmoil through the eyes of an eager journalist (Gibson). He's aided by a provocative, pint-sized cameraman—an extraordinary performance from actress Hunt. Unfortunately, a love affair between Gibson and a mysterious British embassy assistant (Weaver) fails to ignite. Bogart and Bergman they're not. (PG) **Academy Award**—Hunt, best supporting actress.
114 minutes

YELLOWBEARD (1983)

★

**Graham Chapman
Marty Feldman**

A patchy send-up of pirate movies, with a large cast of zanies in pursuit of buried treasure. Chapman, of the Monty Python troupe, is in the title role as a foul, incorrigible buccaneer who wants to reclaim his booty. But none of the Python magic shines through. Many of the individual performances are amusing, but the entire movie doesn't have much wind in its sails. How sad for Feldman that his

last performance should be in so lame a film. Peter Boyle, Madeline Kahn, James Mason, and Cheech & Chong also are on board. Director Mel Damski seems to have trouble even matching his shots up, let alone displaying any style. (PG)   *101 minutes*

THE YELLOW CAB MAN (1950)

★★

Red Skelton

Skelton is in top comic form in this tale about an offbeat cab driver who invents unbreakable glass, picks up pretty girls, and has trouble with gangsters and shady businessmen. The production has its rough spots, however, and at times it seems that Skelton tries too hard to get laughs. Walter Slezak and Gloria De Haven also star, with James Gleason, and Jay C. Flippen in supporting roles. **Director**—Jack Donohue.   *84 minutes b&w*

YENTL (1983)

★★★

Barbra Streisand

In Yentl, *Mandy Patinkin tells Barbra Streisand that he still loves her—even if she is a girl.*

Streisand is star, director, producer, and co-author of this far-removed version of Isaac Bashevis Singer's fable set in the early 1900s. Barbra, in the title role, is a rabbi's daughter who masquerades as a boy to attend an all-male yeshiva (religious school). Although the charade becomes somewhat preposterous, the film is occasionally warm and engaging. Streisand sings with her usual style and gusto throughout. Also with Mandy Patinkin and Amy Irving. (PG) **Academy Award**

Nomination—Irving, best supporting actress.
134 minutes

YES, GIORGIO (1982)

★★

**Luciano Pavarotti
Kathryn Harrold**

Opera great Pavarotti fills the screen with beautiful music (and his ample frame) in this old-fashioned romantic comedy. This may be a treat for opera lovers, but all Pavarotti's charm and gusto cannot make up for the film's flimsy story. It's about the egotistical tenor's pursuit of a woman physician (Harrold) during an American tour. A rousing "yes" for the masterful arias and popular songs. A resolute "no" for the hokey, paper-thin screenplay. **Director**—Franklin Schaffner. (PG)
111 minutes

YOR (1983)

★

Reb Brown

A noisy, birdbrained caveman adventure with blond, muscle-bound Reb Brown as a battler of giant reptiles and grungy-looking enemy cave dwellers. When Reb isn't swinging a mean ax, he's spouting dumb dialogue such as: "Drink! The blood of your enemies makes you strong." Toward the film's end it appears that we may be witnessing the future rather than the past—hardly a comforting thought. Corinne Clery and John Steiner are in supporting roles. **Director**—Anthony Sawson. (PG)   *105 minutes*

YOU CAN'T CHEAT AN HONEST MAN (1939)

★★★

**W. C. Fields
Edgar Bergen**

If you had to spend the rest of your life in Philadelphia with just one Fields film, this wouldn't be the one to take. However, this slice of nonsense about beleaguered circus owner Larson E. Whipsnade, who must elude the law and deal with the likes of Bergen's pals Charlie McCarthy and Mortimer
(Continued)

 Movie is available in Beta and VHS videotape

Y
- You Light Up My Life
- You'll Never Get Rich
- Young at Heart
- Youngblood
- Young Doctors in Love
- Young Frankenstein
- The Young Lions
- Young Man with a Horn
- Young Mr. Lincoln

(Continued)

Snerd, is still a lot of fun. Fields, of course, plays the role of Whipsnade. The cast also includes Constance Moore, James Bush, Mary Forbes, Edward Brophy, Thurston Hall, and Charles Coleman. **Director**—George Marshall. *79 minutes b&w*

YOU LIGHT UP MY LIFE (1977)

 ★

Didi Conn
Joe Silver

This melodrama about a young girl's struggle to become a pop singer is supposed to be a warm and touching film, but it never comes off as intended. Former ad man Joseph Brooks, who produced, directed, and wrote the screenplay, overstuffed the plot with too much triteness and sentimentality. Conn in the lead role, however, manages to exude some appeal. And Silver, who plays the girl's father—a second-rate stand-up comedian—does rather well among a cast of mostly unknowns. Also with Michael Zaslow, Melanie Mayron, and Stephen Nathan. (PG) *90 minutes*

YOU'LL NEVER GET RICH
(1941)

 ★★★

Fred Astaire
Rita Hayworth

Astaire and Hayworth sparkle in this comedy musical. It's about a showman who's still able to put on his show and land the girl of his dreams even though he's drafted into the Army. The plot and story line are as limp as those in most musicals, but the dancing is fine, and the Cole Porter music is great. John Hubbard, Robert Benchley, Osa Massen, Frieda Inescort, and Guinn Williams appear in supporting roles. **Director**—Sidney Lanfield.

88 minutes b&w

YOUNG AT HEART (1954)

 ★★★

Doris Day
Frank Sinatra

Sinatra romances Day in this polished musical version of *Four Daughters*, a story about the problems of a musical family in a small town. The singing and acting of the stars are at a high level, with fine supporting performances by Ethel Barrymore, Gig Young, Robert Keith, Alan Hale, Jr., and Dorothy Malone. **Director**—Gordon Douglas. *117 minutes*

YOUNGBLOOD (1978)

★★

Lawrence Hilton-Jacobs

Jacobs stars in this typical youth gang and drugs melodrama set in a Los Angeles ghetto. The story overplays the hard realism of street life and neglects drama and entertainment value. Tight direction keeps the action moving, but basically the film is familiar stuff with the inevitable neighborhood rumble, fatherless family situations, and so on. Also with Ren Woods and Bryan O'Dell. **Director**—Noel Nosseck. (R) *90 minutes*

YOUNG DOCTORS IN LOVE
(1982)

 ★★

Michael McKean
Sean Young

The hit comedy *Airplane* inspired this send-up of TV soap operas, but the outcome is a hopeless case of silly nonsense. The slapdash plot, set in a big city hospital, offers a steady stream of dumb sight gags, toilet humor, and sick jokes. A few skits manage to be funny, but the bulk of the satire needs the help of a laugh track. Garry Marshall, of TV sitcom fame, directed with an unsure hand and an over-reliance on bad taste. (R) *96 minutes*

YOUNG FRANKENSTEIN
(1974)

 ★★★

Mel Brooks
Gene Wilder
Marty Feldman

Mel Brooks is at the helm of this zany send-up of monster movies. Brooks regulars Wilder, Feldman, Madeline Kahn, and Cloris Leachman have a ball with the material, which contains some delirious moments. Wilder is in the title role as the grandson of the venerable doctor who returns to Transylvania to stir up more mischief. The moody black and white photography, reminiscent of the original Boris Karloff outings, adds to the madcap fun. **Director**—Brooks. (PG)

108 minutes b&w

THE YOUNG LIONS (1958)

★★★

Marlon Brando
Montgomery Clift
Dean Martin

Brando, Clift, and Martin star in this World War II tale that comes close to becoming a great film. It falls short of greatness because the plot is too complex, the story development is uneven, and the movie is too long. The story deals with the fate of two Americans—Clift and Martin—and a German officer, played by Brando. The cast also includes Hope Lange, Maximilian Schell, Mai Britt, Barbara Rush, and Lee Van Cleef. **Director**—Edward Dmytryk. **Academy Award Nomination**—Joe MacDonald, cinematography (black and white).

167 minutes b&w

YOUNG MAN WITH A HORN
(1950)

★★★

Kirk Douglas
Lauren Bacall
Doris Day

Douglas shines as a troubled and compulsive trumpet player in this biography about the life of famed jazz musician Bix Beiderbecke. Bacall and Day portray the women in his life. Hoagy Carmichael, Juano Hernandez, Nestor Paiva, Mary Beth Hughes, and Jerome Cowan appear in supporting roles. **Director**—Michael Curtiz.

112 minutes b&w

YOUNG MR. LINCOLN (1939)

★★★★

Henry Fonda
Alice Brady

• The Young Philadelphians
• Young Tom Edison
• You Only Live Twice
• You're a Big Boy Now

• Yours, Mine and Ours
• You Were Never Lovelier
• Zapped
• Zelig

 Y·Z

Good movies about great people are infrequent, but Fonda succeeds admirably in the role of young Abraham Lincoln in this story about the early years of the 16th President of the United States. Under John Ford's excellent direction, the attention to period atmosphere, such as a log-splitting contest and a tug of war, enhances the quality of the movie. Brady gives Fonda good support. Donald Meek, Eddie Quillan, Spencer Charters, Marjorie Weaver, and Arleen Whelan also star in supporting roles. **Academy Award Nomination**—Lamar Trotti, writing (original story).

100 minutes b&w

THE YOUNG PHILADELPHIANS (1959)
 ★★

**Paul Newman
Barbara Rush**

Despite the "young" in the title, this story about a young but poor lawyer on the make in Philadelphia society has been told many times before—and much better at that. Newman plays the role of the lawyer; Rush is a society girl he's pursuing. Solid performances by Newman, Rush, Alexis Smith, Robert Vaughn, Otto Kruger, Brian Keith, and Diana Brewster buoy this conventional potboiler. **Director**—Vincent Sherman. **Academy Award Nominations**—Vaughn, best supporting actor; Harry Stradling, cinematography (black and white). *136 minutes b&w*

YOUNG TOM EDISON (1940)
★★★

Mickey Rooney

Rooney in the title role of Tom Edison has the good sense to cool his usual exuberance and to play this modest biography conventionally. The movie traces the brilliant inventor's early experiments and details the problems he faced. Although the story is less than complete—some facts are out of focus—it's the kind of motion picture young people should find inspiring. Parents should appreciate the solid performances of Rooney, Fay Bainter, George Bancroft, Victor Kilian, and Virginia Weidler. **Director**—Norman Taurog. *82 minutes b&w*

YOU ONLY LIVE TWICE (1967)
 ★★

Sean Connery

If it wasn't for the violence, the bizarre story developments, the extravagant sets, and the superb special effects, this fifth James Bond movie could be mistaken for a travel film—*Agent 007 in Japan* or some such title. The production will please Bond fans despite the weak plot that has Connery, as the dashing hero, facing the villains from SPECTRE. Those who are neutral—or unBonded—might find some solace in the excellent performance of Donald Pleasence as the head of the bad guys. The cast also includes Bernard Lee, Karin Dor, Charles Gray, Lois Maxwell, Tetsuro Tamba, Akiko Wakabayashi, and Mie Hama. **Director**—Lewis Gilbert. *117 minutes*

YOU'RE A BIG BOY NOW (1967)
 ★★★

**Peter Kastner
Elizabeth Hartman**

This far-out comedy marked the beginning of the career of director Francis Ford Coppola, who coaxed some fine acting from the cast. He also wrote the screenplay about a mama's boy (Kastner) who learns about life and love the hard way from nightclub dancer Hartman. The pace is lively and the characters interesting. Geraldine Page, Rip Torn, and Karen Black are in supporting roles. *96 minutes*

YOURS, MINE AND OURS (1968)
 ★★★

**Lucille Ball
Henry Fonda**

Ball and Fonda star in this well-made farce about a widow and widower—both with large families—who marry. The problems encountered when two large families live in the same house create the comic situations in this movie. At times, the problems are so obvious they fail to bring laughs, but there are enough good moments to make this film mildly entertaining.

Van Johnson and Tom Bosley appear in supporting roles. **Director**—Melville Shavelson. *111 minutes*

YOU WERE NEVER LOVELIER (1942)
 ★★★

**Fred Astaire
Rita Hayworth**

If the viewer can forgive the inept plot and silly dialogue, this musical with Jerome Kern/Johnny Mercer songs and Astaire's dancing will still be delightful entertainment. Adolphe Menjou plays a matchmaking father for his daughter, played by Hayworth. Astaire, of course, is the other part of the matchup. The rest of the cast includes Leslie Brooks, Larry Parks, Adele Mara, and Xavier Cugat and his orchestra. The songs include "I'm Old-Fashioned," "Dearly Beloved," and the title tune. **Director**—William A. Seiter. *97 minutes b&w*

Z

ZAPPED (1982)
 ★

**Scott Baio
Willie Aames
Felice Schachter
Scatman Crothers**

The telekinesis gimmick is recycled in this dopey, sophomoric teenage comedy starring Baio as a whiz kid who acquires the amazing power. Baio's super thought control permits him to move objects, fix the basketball game, and remove girls' clothing (to the delight of adolescent boys). The youngsters are portrayed as cute and clever; the adults come off as bumbling and absurd. **Director**—Robert J. Rosenthal. (R) *96 minutes*

ZELIG (1983)
 ★★★★

**Woody Allen
Mia Farrow**

Allen once again pokes fun at neurotic behavior. He plays a fictional character
(Continued)

(Continued)

with the power to miraculously assume the personality traits of others, including celebrities. The satirical film is a well-crafted curiosity, expertly blending old newsreel footage with near-perfect simulations that position Woody in the midst of historical situations. Allen's unique wit abounds, and the original period-style songs by Dick Hyman are hilarious. A unique technical and creative triumph from director-writer Allen and cinematographer Gordon Willis. (PG) **Academy Award Nomination**—Willis, cinematography.

84 minutes b&w/color

ZIEGFELD FOLLIES (1946)
★★

Fred Astaire
Lucille Ball
William Powell

A better title for this all-star musical would have been *Heavenly Follies* or *Ziegfeld Follies in Heaven*. It's the kind of show you shouldn't take too seriously, as Powell, playing Ziegfeld, narrates the affair from Heaven. The movie has some splendid production numbers and some mediocre ones, and there are so many stars that you're bound to find someone you like. Besides Astaire, Ball, and Powell, the cast includes Jimmy Durante, Fannie Brice, Lena Horne, Gene Kelly, Hume Cronyn, Judy Garland, Red Skelton, Lucille Bremer, Victor Moore, and Edward Arnold. **Director**—Vincente Minnelli.

110 minutes

ZIEGFELD GIRL (1941)
★★

James Stewart
Judy Garland
Hedy Lamarr
Lana Turner

Stewart, Garland, Lamarr, and Turner star in this musical about the problems and triumphs of a "typical" Ziegfeld girl. Musicals that don't attempt to tell a story with any degree of seriousness are usually tolerable, but this production starts to creak and groan—after a delightful beginning—when it delves too deeply into the lives of Ziegfeld girls. The rest of the cast includes Tony Martin, Jackie Cooper, Charles Win-

ninger, Al Shean, Dan Dailey, Eve Arden, and Edward Everett Horton. The movie is noted for Garland's renditions of "Minnie from Trinidad" and "I'm Always Chasing Rainbows," but a Busby Berkeley number called "You Stepped Out of a Dream" is the best in the show. **Director**—Robert Z. Leonard.

131 minutes b&w

ZOOT SUIT (1982)
★★★

Daniel Valdez
Edward James Olmos
Tyne Daly

This is a powerful and colorful musical drama that captures the Chicano spirit and presents a compelling social message about racial prejudice. This worthy screen version of Luis Valdez's play involves a group of Mexican-Americans in 1942 Los Angeles, who were sent to prison on trumped-up charges. Even though the drama falters some, the Chicano characters are memorable because of fine acting by a novice cast. **Director**—Valdez. (R) *103 minutes*

ZORBA THE GREEK (1964)
★★★

Anthony Quinn
Alan Bates
Lila Kedrova

The mood and atmosphere of Nikos Kazantzakis's great novel are captured in this visually beautiful production, but the soul of the book and the major character remain elusive on screen. Quinn makes a commendable effort as the congenial Greek peasant, and Bates is excellent as the English writer who befriends him on Crete. Kedrova and Irene Papas also deliver solid performances in supporting roles. **Director**—Michael Cacoyannis. **Academy Awards**—Kedrova, best supporting actress; Walter Lassally, cinematography (black and white). **Nominations**—best picture; Cacoyannis, best director; Quinn, best actor; Cacoyannis, best screenplay (based on material from another medium).

142 minutes b&w

ZORRO, THE GAY BLADE (1981)
★★

George Hamilton

Hamilton knocks himself out in this wild spoof about the legendary masked-man adventures, made famous by Douglas Fairbanks, Sr., and Tyrone Power. Hamilton hams it up with a mock Spanish accent as he plays the role of Don Diego Vega, a champion of "the poor pipples" of Los Angeles. He also takes a turn playing foppish twin brother Bunny Wigglesworth, a swashbuckler indeed. But the jokes comes across with a dull edge. Ron Leibman and Brenda Vaccaro costar. **Director**—Peter Medak. (PG)

93 minutes

Alan Bates and Anthony Quinn discuss a plan to get logs down a hill in Zorba the Greek.

Movie is available in Beta and VHS videotape